English & Continental Pottery & Porcelain

AN ILLUSTRATED PRICE GUIDE

1st Edition

by
Susan D. Bagdade
and
Allen D. Bagdade

Warman Publishing Co., Inc.
Willow Grove, PA 19090

ISBN: 0-911594-11-6
LC: 86-051232
Printed in the United States of America

10   9   8   7   6   5   4   3   2

Additional copies of this book may be obtained from your bookstore, antiques book-
seller, or directly from the publisher, Warman Publishing Co., P.O. Box 1112, Dept.
PP, Willow Grove, PA 19090. Enclose $18.95 plus $2.00 for postage and handling,
Pennsylvania residents please add $1.14 state sales tax.

TABLE OF CONTENTS

FOREWORD

For the past few years we have been writing "Answers On Antiques," a column that appears in The *Antique Trader Weekly*. We realized that many of the questions that we received related to English and Continental pottery and porcelain. Our readers wanted to know: What is it? When was it made? How much is it worth?

As we did our research, we realized how little information was available from American publishers about English and Continental pottery and porcelain. The books that did exist were published by European firms, most notably the Antique Collectors' Club in England. They were expensive, difficult to obtain, and focused on the European market. The English antiques price guides reflected foreign prices and did not contain helpful introductory material to a collecting category that is now the hallmark of the American antiques price guides.

A void existed, and we decided to fill it.

This book represents a true division of labor. Al was in charge of the sixteen thousand data entries and their prices. Susan wrote over two hundred histories of the companies and categories listed in the guide. Both weathered the numerous crises involved with writing one's first book on a brand new computer.

Everywhere we turned in gathering information for this book, whether it was to a member of the staff of a large auction house or to a small antiques shop owner, we found encouragement for our efforts. We also queried these individuals about what type of information they felt should be included. This book is not only a response to their needs but to their numerous requests as well.

We are proud of this book. However, we also recognize that there is room for improvement. Since we want to be responsive to our readers, we invite you to send your comments to Susan and Al Bagdade, c/o Warman Publishing Co.

When we started to work on this book, Harry L. Rinker, our editor, suggested that a book has a far longer gestation time than a child, involves more work, and is much harder to deliver. We wish we could say that he was wrong. But, alas, he was right. We only hope that the final product brings you as much joy as our two real children and this adopted child in book form does to us.

Susan and Al Bagdade
Northbrook, Illinois

ACKNOWLEDGEMENTS

Harry L. Rinker, Editor-In-Chief of Warman's, has guided us through every step of this book. Without his advice, prodding, encouragement, and red pen, this price guide would not have come to fruition.

Al's partner in dentistry, Burton Turek, must be thanked for taking on the lion's share of work at the office, and for his infinite patience while Al made innumerable phone calls, did research, and delved through auction catalogues.

Our children, David and Felicia, have been very understanding when we spent hour after hour attached to the computer.

A special debt of gratitude must go to Rich Kleinhardt for drawing the pottery and porcelain marks required for the manuscript.

This book would not have been possible without the cooperation of hundreds of antiques dealers who allowed us to gather information and photograph their wares at antiques shows and in their shops.

A special thank you goes to the auction houses in the United States, England, and the Continent, who provided subscriptions to their extensive catalogues and access to their photographs. The authors express grateful appreciation to auctioneers Leslie Hindman of Chicago and Terry Dunning of Elgin, Illinois, who allowed us to photograph auction properties. Victor Bernreuther of Christie's East in New York provided considerable assistance for our project.

Additional thanks to Randi Schwartz who allowed us to invade her private collection and antique shop to photograph items for the interior, cover, and color sections of this book.

Al's brother, Dr. Charles Bagdade, deserves a great deal of thanks for taking the photograph that appears on this cover.

INTRODUCTION

ORGANIZATION OF THE PRICE GUIDE

Listings: More than two hundred categories dealing with English and Continental pottery and porcelain are listed alphabetically in this price guide. Most categories refer to a single manufactory. A general category for each country includes smaller firms that are not dealt with individually.

Every effort has been made to make the price listings descriptive enough so that specific objects can be visualized by the reader. Emphasis has been placed on examples being sold in the marketplace today. Some harder to find objects were included to provide a full range in each category.

History: Every category has a capsule history that details the founding of the company, its principal owners, the nature of the wares, the patterns utilized, and general information available on the specific company. Notes about marks are included in the history or collecting hints.

References: Reference books are listed whenever possible to encourage the collector to learn more about the category. Books are only listed if there is a substantial section on the specific category being considered. Included in the listing are author, title, publisher, (if published by a small firm or individual, we have indicated "privately printed"), and date of publication or most recent edition.

Many of the books listed are available in public libraries or through inter-library loan. It is best to check with your local library system. Readers also may find antiques book dealers at antiques shows, flea markets, and advertising in trade papers and journals. Many book dealers provide mail order services.

Periodicals: In addition to publications of collectors' clubs, there are numerous general interest newspapers and magazines that devote much attention to pottery and porcelain. A sampling includes the following:

Antique Monthly, P.O. Drawer 2, Tuscaloosa, AL 35402
Antique Review, P.O. Box 538, Worthington, OH 43085
Antique Showcase, Amis Gibbs Publications, Ltd., Canfield, Ontario, Canada, N0A 1C0
Antique Trader Weekly, P.O. Box 1050, Dubuque, IA 52001
Antique Week-Tri-State Trader, P.O. Box 90, Knightstown, IN 46148
Antiques and Collecting Hobbies, 1006 S. Michigan Avenue, Chicago, IL 60605
Antiques and The Arts Weekly, 5 Church Hill Rd., Newtown, CT 06470
Antiques (The Magazine Antiques), 551 Fifth Avenue, New York, NY 10017
Collector News, Box 156, Grundy Center, IA 50638
Maine Antique Digest, P.O. Box 645, Waldboro, ME 04572
New York-Pennsylvania Collector, Fishers, NY 14453
Southern Antiques & Southeast Trader, P.O. Box 1550, Lake City, FL 32055
West Coast Peddler, P.O. Box 5134, Whittier, CA 90607

Museums: Museums where significant collections in the category are on display are listed. Many museums have large collections of pottery and/or porcelains, but did not provide a listing for inclusion in this book.

Collectors' Clubs: All collectors' clubs have been verified to be active. Addresses are listed for membership information. Some clubs have regional and local chapters. English clubs welcome American members.

Reproduction Alert: Where reproduction alerts are listed for a particular category, the collector should be extremely careful when purchasing examples. Some reproductions are unmarked; the newness of their appearance is often the best clue to discovering them.

Collecting Hints: This section calls attention to specific hints if they are applicable to a category. Clues also are given for spotting reproductions when known.

Additional Listings: When more than one category is covered by a specific listing, other listings are added to help the reader find additional information.

Marks: When pottery and porcelain wares are marked, we have included representative marks for that manufactory. However, to see the full range of marks used by a firm, one must consult one of the marks books listed in the bibliography.

Index: The alphabetical index is generally set up by makers. In some cases, the reader should look for type of ware, i.e., ABC Plates.

DERIVATION OF PRICES USED

The prices in this book were derived from a variety of sources. Antiques shows, antiques shops, and flea markets representing all parts of the country were important sources. The prices listed reflect what the collector would have to pay for an item, i.e., the retail price.

Auction houses in the United States, London, Geneva, and Amsterdam were a valuable source of prices, not only for the upper level pottery and porcelain examples, but also for many of the middle and lower range price levels. Prices realized are noted with an (A) at the end of the listing preceding the price to denote an auction price. This price represents the actual hammer price plus the buyer's premium where applicable.

Antiques magazines, trade papers, and journals were an additional source for what is available currently on the market. They also indicate what is being sold and what is sitting on the shelf.

Specialized price lists featuring collections of one specific type of ceramics were invaluable. These lists included all ranges of prices in a particular field.

Where conflicting prices occured for similar pieces, an additional source was sought which included consulting with specialists to confirm or reject a specific item's value.

It is unlikely that the collector will be able to match exactly a specific piece with listings in the price guide. Each category represents a range of prices and should be used as a guide rather than an absolute determination.

CONDITION

Condition plays an important role in determining the value of ceramics. Porcelain and pottery from the early periods, i.e., 16th to 18th century, and rare pieces are less affected price–wise by condition than the more recent ceramic examples. One would be less concerned about missing fingers on a figure by the Meissen modeler Kaendler than by the same damage found on a 19th or 20th century Dresden "lace" figure. Availability is the key word.

Middle and lower priced pieces that are damaged should not be overlooked completely. In some cases they may act as a "filler" piece for a collection until a better example becomes available. However, these damaged pieces should reflect a lower price than a fine example. The price should be directly proportional to the extent of the damage. As an example, tin-glazed earthenware often shows signs of wear along the rim. Glaze flakes in this area are to be expected. However, glaze flakes affecting the central design are less acceptable, even if they are smaller in diameter.

Outright chips also should be reflected by a lower price. Under-the-rim chips are more tolerable than those on the surface or at a margin. Major defects such as breaks, cracks, fades in the design, pieces missing (knobs, handles, covers, etc.) or heavy cuts in the glaze greatly diminish the value of a piece. Remember that an age crack is still a crack and should be treated as such. It is wiser to spend extra dollars to purchase the best example available.

Repaired examples should be evaluated critically. A reglued handle detracts considerably from the value of a piece. A professionally restored handle may be more acceptable to the collector. Casual examination of a piece may not show the location or extent of a repair.

Changes in the glaze, brilliance and texture, and slight variations in the decorative colors are often signs of a repair. By examining the inside of a hollow figure, a repaired fracture may be quite visible since inside cosmetics often were overlooked during inferior restorations. It behooves the buyer to examine a piece carefully under a strong light or blue light before purchasing the piece since repaired merchandise is difficult to return when discovered at a later time.

THE CARE AND FEEDING OF CERAMICS

Ceramics by nature are fragile and should be treated with the utmost care. Dirt and dust are natural enemies to all ceramics and should be removed whenever encountered. The natural impulse is to plunge the dirty object into a sinkful of hot, sudsy water and give it a good "once-over." This is the wrong procedure to follow. Care was undoubtedly used in selecting the piece of ceramics, and care should be used in the cleaning process.

Visual examination of the piece is the first step. Check for obvious repairs, hairline cracks, and crazing, as these factors require additional care when cleaning the piece. It is important to know what the piece is made of, as this also controls the method of cleaning. Unglazed ceramics are washed differently than glazed examples.

Set aside a work area that is uncluttered and near running water. A textured towel makes a good work surface and adds support for the piece. Remove loose dirt and dust with a soft brush, such as an artist's brush. Never use a stiff brush since this can disturb surface decorations. Proceed slowly and carefully, especially around projections and handles. A good portion of the grime can be removed in this manner. In addition, pieces with hairlines will less likely soak up dirt when the washing process starts.

A solution of mild soap in lukewarm water with ammonia (1 oz. of ammonia to 10 ozs. of water) is an ideal working solution. Enough soap should be added to bring forth suds. Cotton swabs or balls dipped into the solution and applied gently to the surface will loosen and remove years of grime. Stains, such as grease and unknown stains, should be approached with caution.

On vertical pieces such as figures, begin at the top and work towards the base. Constantly change the wash water as it tends to become dirty with use. Continually rinse away the soapy solution using clean water and cotton swabs. Never use abrasive materials such as scouring or soap pads or harsh detergents. Unglazed ceramics such as earthenware and bisque should be wiped with moist, soft swabs.

Though the diswasher is a handy device for commercial dishware, it is not a friend to early ceramics. Hot water and strong detergents can dissolve water soluble glue joints and remove surface decorations. Pieces with metal bases should not be immersed in water. This is true especially for ormolu.

Never use bleach. This material is harmful to certain types of decoration. In addition, bleach can cause a stain to spread rather dramatically.

Dry pieces with equal care using cotton swabs or linen towels. A hair dryer can be a handy tool for getting into hard to reach areas.

If stains are persistent, are of unknown origin, or if a glue joint separates, it is wise to consult a professional restorer.

Once the pieces are clean, storage is the next consideration. Certain precautions apply. All pieces must be dried thoroughly before storing. When stacking plates, always keep the same sizes and shapes together. Tissue or felt should separate each plate. Cups should be hung from plastic coated hooks or stored individually. Never stack cups or bowls since this tends to damage surface decorations.

Plate hangers serve a purpose, but should be used with discretion. Always use the proper size. Too large a hanger will not support a piece properly. Hangers that are too small put excessive pressure on a piece. Wrap the wire projections in plastic tubing. This helps protect the rim glaze.

For additional hints on the care of ceramics, consult one of the following books: Frieda Kay Fall, *Art Objects: Their Care and Preservation*, Museum Publications, 1967; Albert Jackson & David Day, *The Antiques Care & Repair Handbook*, Alfred A. Knopf, 1984; Judith Larney, *Restoring Ceramics*, Watson-Guptill Publications, 1975; V.P. Wright, *Pamper Your Possessions*, Barre Publishers, 1972.

STATE OF THE MARKET

With few exceptions, the ceramics market in 1986/87 was somewhat lethargic. Meissen, Worcester, Dutch Delft, and Italian Majolica examples made up most of the American and European auction catalogues. In general, pieces sold reached their pre-auction estimates, with a smattering rising above this level.

Eighteenth century works of note continued to show strength, whereas later examples from the same factories struggled somewhat. Superb or rare examples, some of which had not been brought to public attention for many years, realized top prices despite the presence of repairs or defects. The money certainly is in the marketplace, but it is being spent carefully on the best available wares.

A few choice examples include a Wedgwood and Bentley caneware hare's head stirrup cup that brought $26,000 against a pre-auction estimate of $6,000-$8,000, and an exquisite Meissen snuff box decorated with Venetian scenes that knocked down for $34,000. Examples from the popular Meissen "Swan Service" were offered in several auctions with a fine dish reaching $16,800. This set continues to show strength.

Figural Chelsea and Whieldon wares rarely come up for consideration, but the few pieces that crossed the block in 1986-87 did quite well. A melon-shaped Whieldon tureen was hammered down for a surprising $22,000.

Polychrome ground Worcester and Meissen continued to draw interest with examples reaching or exceeding pre-auction estimates. French soft paste held its own with colored ground examples doing very well. Finely decorated wares from the Sevres factory were solid, as witnessed by a hitherto unrecorded pair of Louis XVI "vases oeufs" selling for $255,000, whereas the less important pieces found lower interest from the bidding floor.

Several important collections came across the auction block. Twenty-three figures from the Meisen "Cris de Paris" series either doubled or tripled the estimates, with a superb example of a dated "peep-show" man topping the group at well over $20,000.

Highlights of the 1986/87 auction scene include Arman's Historic Staffordshire and a wonderful collection of tulip vases offered at Christie's East featuring Rockingham, Derby, and Spode examples which doubled or tripled the pre-auction estimates. Documentary pieces, when placed on the block, were bid eagerly to upper price levels.

Interest in the middle and lower range ceramics slackened off, with some previously "hot" categories dropping back significantly. Limoges, Schlegelmilch, Haviland, Flow Blue, and Gaudy Welsh, stalwarts of the middle range, settled into stable price brackets. Many examples that were removed from the market during the heyday of the speculator now are back with the dealers. Prime and scarce wares in these categories continue to do well, but the bloom appears to be off the more common material.

Staffordshire figures and Toby jugs, the backbone of the English market, are holding their own. While examples by Enoch and Ralph Wood and Obadiah Sherratt continue to climb, luster, creamware, saltglaze, and parian ware were quite soft.

While quantity is abundant, antique buyers tend to be more selective in buying better examples and passing up the more ordinary pieces. The sale of lesser patterns requires the right buyer at the right place and the best price. Consequently, many dealers are finding middle to lower range ceramics remaining on the shelves for longer periods of time. For example, many dealers carry floral R. S. Prussia, but few find the "hot" pieces such as "Admiral Byrd" or "Melon Eaters" which sell easily. Dealers are expanding their horizons by advertising in trade papers to reach a broader range of collectors.

All of these marketing trends are good news for the beginning collector who can venture into the marketplace as a competitive buyer and find stable prices and available examples. The intermediate collector can still find some bargains, but less material is available. The auction houses provide the main arena for the intermediate collector. Advanced collectors notice that top dollars are necessary to add quality wares to their prized possessions.

With more specialized books pertaining to one particular type of ceramics being published, such as recent books on Goss, Shelley, Heraldic Ware, etc, previously overlooked areas of collecting are coming to the forefront. Collectors are becoming knowledgeable and competitive buyers in these "new" areas.

Interior designers and speculators have played less important roles in the ceramics marketplace in 1986/87. In previous years, desirable styles and investment opportunities often dictated price and availability. The antiques market is back where it belongs, in the hands of collectors. This has brought a stabilizing influence to the world of pottery and porcelain.

The serious collector should consider a new publication appropriately titled "Ceramics." This bi-monthly journal, published by Art Focus of London, England, features several scholarly articles in each issue as well as an insight into upcoming American and European auctions. The photography is superb.

GLOSSARY

The following list is a collection of terms that the reader is likely to encounter in the text of this guide. These terms are in common use in the ceramics world.

Applied. Parts or ornaments attached to the body by means of liquid clay (slip). Also called sprigging.

Anthemion. A formal type of decoration in the shape of stylized honeysuckle flowers and leaves.

Bail Handle. Arched fixed or movable overhead handle.

Baluster Form. Bulbous center with narrow top and bottom usually with flared ends.

Bargeware. Earthenware of narrow proportions for use on canal boats and barges. These pieces were decorated with florals and luster. Larger pieces featured modeled teapots on the covers or handles.

Bat Printing. The transfer of a design by means of glue-like slabs. Most often used on glazed surfaces.

Bellarmine. Stoneware jug or bottle featuring bearded mask and coat of arms under neck.

Bell-Toy Pattern. Oriental pattern featuring child holding toy composed of stick with bells. Popular pattern at Worcester.

Bird of Sparrow Spout. Modeled spout in form of open bird beak. These were closely associated with examples fabricated in silver.

Blanc de Chine. French term referring to a translucent white or ivory porcelain covered in thick glaze. Produced by several English and French companies after Chinese originals.

Bleu Lapis. Streaked or veined bright blue ground color often found in combination with gold accents. Used at Vincennes.

Bleu Persan. Dark blue ground color used on Nevers faience often in conjunction with white or yellow ornamentation.

Blind Earl Pattern. Low relief design of rosebuds, leaves, and insects which covers entire surface. Designed for the blind Earl of Coventry in 1755. The pattern was used at Worcester and Chelsea.

Bocage. Modeled foliage, branches, and flowers which form arbor or canopy background for figures. A method of covering unfinished backs of figures.

Bonbonniere. French term for small covered sweetmeat container.

Cachepot. Ornamental container designed to hold utilitarian flowerpot.

Cartouche. A method of framing or outlining a design, usually with elaborate borders. (See Laub-und-Bandelwerk)

China. Term frequently used to refer collectively to pottery and porcelain, but correctly applies only to porcelain.

Chinoiserie. European decoration utilizing pseudo-Chinese figures, pagodas, and landscapes. Used extensively in early 18th century England and the Continent.

Crabstock. Modeled in form of branch of crab apple tree. Found on handles, spouts, and feet.

Dentil. Border treatment of small rectangular blocks giving appearance of teeth. Usually in gilt.

Diapering. Diamond or lozenge type pattern that is usually repetitive and connected.

Ecuelle. French term for small, covered shallow bowl with double parallel handles. Used for serving soup.

Engine-Turned. Machine–applied design that cuts into the surface of the clay.

Etched. Method of decoration using an acid–resistant covering in which the design is cut, exposed to hydrofluoric acid and pigment added to the etched recesses.

Famille Rose. Chinese-style design which incorporates opaque pink or rose-colored enamels.

Flambe. French term for red shaded glazes derived from reduced copper.

Fuddling Cup. Group of cups joined together internally and externally, usually with multiple handles.

Gadrooned. Continuous pattern of reeding or fluting used mainly as a border treatment. Inspired from silver examples.

Grisaille. French term for printing in gray shades on porcelain to give the effect of relief.

Hausmalerei. German term for ceramic decorators who literally worked at home. They purchased whiteware from factories such as Meissen and Vienna or finished partially decorated pieces.

Imari. Japanese style using designs based on native Japanese textiles. Colors of red and dark underglaze blue predominate.

Istoriato. Italian term for mythical, biblical, or genre historical scenes that were painted in polychromes on earthenwares. These paints often cover the entire surface of the object.

Kakiemon Style. Based on the Japanese decorations of the Kakiemon family. The main features include asymmetrical patterns of florals, birds, and Orientals in iron-red, yellow, and shades of blue utilizing large masses of white ground in the color scheme. Popular on 18th century Meissen, Chantilly, Chelsea, Bow, and Worcester.

Lambrequin. French term for a scalloped border pattern that consists of hanging drapery, lace and scrollwork, and leaves. This pattern reached its zenith at Rouen.

Laub-und-Bandelwerk. German term meaning leaf and strapwork. This elaborate type of design was used extensively in the cartouche borders at Meissen and Vienna.

Mon. Japanese inspired form representing circular stylized florals. Frequently incorporated in European interpretations of Oriental designs.

Ozier. German term which describes a molded or painted woven basket-type treatment. Many variations exist including continuous and interrupted patterns.

Posset Pot. Multi-handled pot with center spout designed to hold mixture of wine or ale and milk.

Potpourri Vase. Designed to hold liquid, flower petals, and herbs. Pierced shoulder or cover allows for the escape of the aromatic scents.

Prunus. Plum blossom-type decoration which is based on the Chinese symbol for spring.

Putto. Italian term referring to nude or semi-nude young boy. Frequently used as accessory decoration.

Quatrefoil. Shape or design divided in four equal lobes or sections.

Reserve. An area of a design without ground color designated to receive a decorative panel.

Silver Shape. Copies in porcelain and pottery of existing silver pieces. These usually were reserved for borders, spouts, and handles.

Transfer Printing. The transfer of a design from prepared copper plates by means of tissue paper. The design, once cut into the copper plates, was prepared with color. A thin sheet of tissue transfered the design to the dry ground of the piece prior to glazing.

Trembleuse. French term used to describe a well or vertical projections found on saucers that were devised to keep the accompanying cups from shifting on the saucers. They were designed specifically for those with unsteady hands.

Additional glossary terms can be found in the following books: Louise Ade Boger, *The Dictionary of World Pottery & Porcelain*, Scribners, 1971; George Savage & Harold Newman, *An Illustrated Dictionary of Ceramics*, Van Nostrand Reinhold Company, 1974.

ADDITIONAL NOTES ON MARKS

Bisque - see Heubach and Sevres for marks.

Creamware - see Leeds and Wedgwood for marks.

Crown and Royal Crown Derby - Year ciphers were incorporated in some marks.

Delft - see Bristol and Liverpool for additional marks.

Flow Blue - see Staffordshire General for additional marks.

Majolica - See Keller and Guerin, Minton, and Sarreguemines for additional marks.

Minton - Year ciphers were incorporated in some marks.

Mulberry China - see Flow Blue and Staffordshire General for marks.

Parian - see Copeland-Spode and Minton for marks.

Pate-Sur-Pate - see Minton and Sevres for marks.

Pearlware - see Clews, Davenport, Ridgway, Staffordshire General, Wedgwood, and Enoch and Ralph Wood for marks.

Piano Babies - See Heubach for marks.

Pitcher and Bowl Sets - see Staffordshire General for marks.

Pot Lids - see Pratt for marks.

Royal Worcester - Year ciphers were incorporated in some marks.

Samson - no identifiable marks recorded. Used marks simulating those of Chelsea, Meissen, and Sevres.

Sevres - Year ciphers were incorporated in some marks.

Tea Leaf Ironstone - see Ironstone marks.

Tiles - see Minton and Wedgwood for additional marks.

Toby Jugs - see Pratt and Enoch and Ralph Wood for marks.

Wedgwood - Year ciphers were included in some marks.

Willow Ware - see Staffordshire General for marks.

ABC & MAXIM WARE

Staffordshire, England and Continental 19th Century

Feeding Dish, 6¾" d, black printed alphabet border, multicolored decal of children and pieman, England, $60.00.

History: Nineteenth century English ABC plates from Staffordshire are not considered great works of art, but are quite collectible. They were made by many potteries, most of whom did not mark the plates with a factory mark.

ABC plates were designed to teach a child letters and numbers. In addition, knowledge of important people, places, or things also was transmitted via these plates at mealtimes.

ABC plates were made in forty-four different sizes, ranging from 4" to the large size of approximately 9". Usually the alphabet was on the rim of the plate, either applied (transferred) or embossed (raised). The center of the plate usually had a scene of a person, animal, or some type of design transferred onto it.

When the picture was transferred to the plate and fired, the basic color was added as well. When additional colors were used, the plate had to be fired one or more additional times depending on the number of the colors.

ABC plates also were made in braille for the blind child. These are quite rare today.

Benjamin Franklin's *Poor Richard's Almanac* was the source for many of the maxims and moral lessons used on maxim ware. Biblical passages and nursery rhymes also were used on these plates to present a message to the child.

Plates are most frequently encountered. But teapots, cups, bowls, and porringers also carried lessons for the young. Most of the maxims were illustrated with transfer printed pictures that helped make the lesson more palatable. Some were hand painted, but most were multicolored transfers. The same maxim or rhyme frequently was illustrated by various manufacturers, each using a slightly different drawing.

References: Mildred & Joseph P. Chalala, *A Collector's Guide to ABC Plates, Mugs & Things*, Pridemark Press, 1980.

Collecting Hints: Interest in ABC plates has increased dramatically in the past five to ten years. Make certain the transfers are in good to very good condition. Avoid pieces that are cracked or crazed.

Bowl, 6" d, printed alphabet border, scene of children and teeter-totter in center, Germany mark **45.00**

Creamer, printed alphabet with kittens and ladybug **40.00**

Feeding Dish, printed alphabet border Children and pieman, transfer in center, blue letters on border, 6¾" d, English **60.00**

"Our Baby" in center, green letters on border, German **36.00**

Two children feeding bear in chair in center, multicolored **25.00**

Mug

2", Franklin's maxim, black transfers, Staffordshire mark **90.00**

2⅜", "S" and "T" with designs, red transfer (A) **55.00**

2½"

Franklin's maxim, white body, black letters and scene of teacher and pupil **235.00**

"Little Bo Peep," alphabet, multicolored **45.00**

Sign language alphabet for deaf, black transfer (A) **55.00**

2⅝"

"Sobriety and Domestic Comfort," coat of arms and motto, blue transfer (A) **55.00**

"Speak not to deceive, listen not to betray," black transfer, polychrome enamels (A) **35.00**

2¾"

Alphabet, gold trim, German **25.00**

Franklin's maxim and scene of family at home, black transfer **65.00**

2⅞", "The Way to Wealth," black transfer, chips (A) **35.00**

3"

Franklin's maxim, scene of tree feller, black transfer, applied leaf handle **110.00**

"Shuttlecock" with alphabet, red transfer, Allerton **58.00**

"The Top Spinner" on front, "Going
To Market" on reverse, black transfers, Staffordshire **85.00**

Plate

5" d, raised alphabet border
"Animated Conundrum," answer
on reverse, blue rim, polychrome
transfer **50.00**
Man and boy fishing, blue, green,
red, and yellow transfer, unmarked **68.00**

5⅛" d, raised alphabet border
"Creditors Have Better Memories
Than Debtors...," black transfer
with enamels, unmarked (A) ... **55.00**
Franklin's maxim, multicolored
scene of boy in barnyard, unmarked (A) **30.00**
Shepherd, black transfer with
enamels, unmarked (A) **35.00**

5¼" d, raised alphabet border
Franklin's Proverbs around scene of
farmer plowing, green, yellow,
red, and black transfer, c1852,
"J. & G. Meakin" **87.50**
"I Ever Live Mans Unrelented
Foe...," girls playing with sticks
and hoops, dark brown transfer,
unmarked (A) **55.00**

5½" d, raised alphabet border
"Behold Him Rising...," multicolored transfer, imp "MEAKIN" . **60.00**
Franklin's maxim, "Three Removes
Are As Bad...," girl in wagon
with chairs, transfer, colored accents, imp "MEAKIN" **87.00**
Harvest Home, blue, red, green,
and yellow **58.00**

5⅝" d, Aesop's Fables - "The Wolf
and the Crane," printed alphabet
border, dark brown transfer, green
and red enamels, unmarked (A) .. **35.00**

5¾" d, Moral maxim, blue transfer,
"R. & J. Clews" **45.00**

6" d
Boy fishing, rhyme, raised alphabet
border, transfer **35.00**
Football game, raised alphabet border, multicolored transfer **75.00**
Franklin maxim center, raised grape
border **65.00**
"He That Hath a Trade Hath an
Estate," raised alphabet border,
green transfer, enamels, unmarked (A) **50.00**
"Intemperance Produces Starva-
tion," raised grapes and vines on
border, multicolored transfer,
green outlined rim, imp
"MEAKIN" **45.00**
Letter "S", raised alphabet border,
red transfer **68.00**
"The New Pony," raised alphabet
border, black transfer, enamels,
red rim, chipped back, un-
marked (A) **35.00**
Three children with kite, raised alphabet border, red, yellow,
brown, and green transfer, unmarked **85.00**
6⅛" d, kite flying scene, raised alphabet border, brown transfer, England **55.00**

6¼" d
Children with goose, hand signals
for deaf, pink transfer, "H. Aynsley, Longton, England" **125.00**
"Highland Dance," raised alphabet
border, transfer with green and
red highlights, unmarked **80.00**
"How Wars Start," gold alphabet
border, brown transfer of puppy
and kittens **35.00**
Organ grinder and children, raised
alphabet border, multicolored
transfer, c1890, "Malkin & Co."
.... **45.00**
Pair of dancing rabbits, raised alphabet border, inner border of
sign language, blue transfer **85.00**

**Plates, multicolored, raised alphabet borders, left, 6" d, scene of children with kite, $85.00;
center, 7" d, maxim, $75.00; right, 6¼" d, "Highland Dance" scene, $80.00.**

Pair of strolling rabbits, raised alphabet border, inner border of sign language, green transfer ... **85.00**

Seeing-eye dog, alphabet and braille, green center scene **24.00**

"The Young Artist," baby with palette, printed alphabet border, brown transfer, unmarked (A) .. **40.00**

White center, raised alphabet border with gold, "Germany" **30.00**

6½" d

Advertisement for "N. Currier, Lithographer," printed alphabet border, "Adams" (A) **65.00**

Franklin Maxim, "For Age & Want...," black transfer, green border **68.00**

"There Are No Gains Without Pain & Help Hands For I Have No Lands," raised alphabet border, center scene of two men at work, unmarked **135.00**

6¾" d

Hunter holding fox with two dogs, raised alphabet border, red transfer, unmarked **75.00**

"Little Strokes Fell Great Oaks," raised alphabet border, multicolored scene of man with axe on tree stump **75.00**

"Machinery Build," raised alphabet border, brown transfer **85.00**

Maxim, raised floral border with green band, black, green, and red transfer **75.00**

Sioux Indian Chief, raised alphabet border, transfer center, Stafford . **55.00**

6⅞" d, raised alphabet border, blue with raised sign language on inside border, unmarked **50.00**

7" d

"B is For Bobby's Breakfast," raised alphabet border, red transfer center of two children eating, cow looking through window, verse . **72.00**

"Baseball-Caught on the fly," raised alphabet border, black transfer, unmarked **75.00**

Child looking over fence, raised alphabet border, pink transfer, unmarked **52.00**

"Chinonca Watching The Departure Of The Cavalcade," raised alphabet border, unmarked **65.00**

"Constant Dropping Wears Away Stones, & Little Strokes Fell Great Oaks," raised alphabet border, multicolored transfer of boy felling tree, unmarked **75.00**

Dog cart with two children, blue printed alphabet border, "Staffordshire, England" **40.00**

"Experience Keeps A Dear School, etc," horse racing and school, multicolored and painted transfer, unmarked **45.00**

"Flowers That Never Fade. Generosity...," children, black transfer, emb rim, unmarked (A) **30.00**

Girl in barn tending cows and chickens, pink printed alphabet border **75.00**

Girl in large hat standing by gate, raised alphabet border, pink transfer, "Staffordshire, England" **75.00**

Girl with rabbits eating lettuce, raised alphabet border, multicolored, "Malkin & Co." **85.00**

"Going to Market," chromolithograph, printed alphabet border, unmarked **45.00**

Hunting dogs chasing deer, raised alphabet border, multicolored transfer, unmarked **86.00**

Men fighting on donkeys, raised alphabet border, transfer, unmarked **28.00**

Mother and child, raised alphabet border, multicolored transfer, unmarked **60.00**

Shepherd on fence, raised alphabet border, transfer and painted scene, imp "Malkin & Co., England" **65.00**

"The Guardian," dog watching over sleeping girl, raised alphabet border, multicolored transfer **110.00**

7⅛" d, hunter with dogs shooting birds, raised alphabet border, transfer, color highlights **62.00**

7¼" d

"Crusoe At Work," printed alphabet border, brown transfer, handcolored center of Robinson Crusoe, c1887 .... **75.00**

"Crusoe Rescues Friday," printed alphabet border, green, blue, and brown transfer, "B.P. Co." . **100.00**

Family in woods, October verse, raised alphabet border, brown transfer, unmarked **68.00**

Finch on limb, printed alphabet border, brown transfer with blue, green, and brown enamels, unmarked (A) **55.00**

George Washington, raised alphabet border, brown transfer, unmarked (A) **85.00**

"Hotel Brighton & Concourse," raised alphabet border, pink transfer **48.00**

"Hotel Brighton & Concourse," raised alphabet border, red,

brown, green, and blue transfer, unmarked 48.00

"Nations of the World-Greek," printed alphabet border, blue, red, and brown transfer, "B.P. Co." 95.00

"The Fishing Elephant," raised alphabet border, pink transfer, "Staffordshire, England" 85.00

7⅜" d, "Would you like it curled sir?", monkeys in barber shop, raised alphabet border, multicolored transfer, unmarked 85.00

7½" d

"American Sports," baseball game, raised alphabet border, magenta transfer, unmarked 75.00

"Canary, Bullfinch & Goldfinch," three birds, raised alphabet border, black and colored transfer, unmarked 45.00

"Chinonca Watching The Departure Of The Cavalcade," raised alphabet border, brown transfer, unmarked 68.00

Clock and calendar, printed alphabet border, red transfer (A) 37.50

Football game, raised alphabet border, brown transfer with hp highlights 85.00

Fox hunt scene with man and woman, raised alphabet border, magenta transfer, unmarked ... 45.00

Girl with cow, raised alphabet border, printed alphabet at inner border, unmarked 65.00

Horse racing, raised alphabet border, red transfer 45.00

"Iron Pier, West Brighton Beach," raised alphabet border, red, brown, blue, and green transfer, unmarked 54.00

Man sliding down hill, raised alphabet border, multicolored transfer 65.00

Pair of hunters on horses, raised alphabet border, brown transfer, unmarked 62.00

Teddy bears jumping from pier, printed alphabet border, brown transfer with red, tan, and green enamels, unmarked (A) 85.00

"The Candle Fish," raised alphabet border, brown transfer 64.00

Villagers at ferry dock scene, brown transfer with added colors, c1890, "Chas. Allerton" 35.00

8" d, raised alphabet border

Boy and two girls fishing, transfer, color accents 35.00

Bull charging two fisherman, brown and green transfer (A) ... 45.00

"Old Mother Hubbard" nursery rhymes 58.00

Zebra hunt scene, multicolored, unmarked 28.00

8½" d, two men watching deer on mountain, raised alphabet border, red, brown, green, and yellow transfer, c1890, unmarked 75.00

ADAMS

Burslem, Staffordshire, England
1770–Present

The Adams family established themselves in Burslem. The first potter was William Adams, but this name was used repeatedly throughout the Adams' history. Eventually there were Adams potteries in seven different locations. Most of the potteries, if they marked their works, simply used the name "Adams."

WILLIAM ADAMS

Brick House, Burslem and Cobridge, 1770–c1820

He produced blue-printed wares with chinoiserie patterns early in the 1780s. They were probably not marked. Two of his potteries were lent to other potters among whom were James and Ralph Clews in 1817.

WILLIAM ADAMS

Greengates, Tunstall, c1779–1805 (1809)

Blue-printed wares were made. They were the first pottery in Tunstall to do so. William died in 1805, but the works were continued by trustees. Benjamin, his son, took over in 1809.

WILLIAM ADAMS

Stoke-on-Trent, 1804–1819

Large quantities of blue and white transfer wares were made both for the home market and for export to America. In 1810, William, his son, joined the partnership and three other sons joined soon after. The company was then called "William Adams & Sons."

BENJAMIN ADAMS
Greengates, Tunstall, 1809–1820

Benjamin used the impressed mark "B. Adams." He continued making blue-printed wares.

WILLIAM ADAMS & SONS
Stoke-on-Trent, 1819–Present

William Adams died in 1829; and William, his eldest son, took over. In 1834, the Greenfield pottery was added to the firm. The Stoke factory was closed in 1863. The Greengates pottery was added to the group in 1858.

William Adams joined the Wedgwood Group in 1966.

ADAM'S ROSE
1820s–1830s

This pattern was named for its maker William Adams & Sons of Stoke-on-Trent. It consists of a border of large red roses with green leaf sprigs on a white ground.

G. Jones & Son, England, produced a variation known as "Late Adam's Rose." The colors are not as brilliant. The background is a "dirty" white.

References: A. W. Coysh, *Blue-Printed Earthenware 1800–1850.* David & Charles, 1972.

Biscuit Jar, "The Hunt," blue and white
  design, SP lid and handle **200.00**
Bowl
  7½", porridge, "Save Your Breath To

Condiment Jar, 5½" h, "Calyx Ware," pink bird, gray ground, (A) $20.00.

Cool Your Porridge," rooster in center, "Wm Adams & Sons" **30.00**
9" d, "Titian-Ware," bands of fruit and
  leaves in relief, ftd **45.00**
10" d
  "Cattle Scenery," ftd **195.00**
  "Old Rural Scenes," woman feed-
    ing farm animals, dark blue, iron-
    stone, "W Adams & Co." **45.00**
  "Portia Pleads With Shylock," red
    transfer, cream ground, orange
    transfer borders and foot, luster
    trim, 5" h **100.00**
11" l, vegetable, cov
  "Old English," rural scene, "W Ad-
    ams, England" **60.00**
  Rural scene, cobalt transfer **55.00**
Vegetable, cov, Mazara pattern, "Wm
  Adams & Son" **90.00**
Creamer and Sugar
  "Cries of London" **20.00**
  "Titian Ware", Royal Ivory pattern .. **20.00**
Cup and Saucer
  Adam's Rose, unmarked (A) **35.00**
  Transfer, "Dr Syntax setting out on his
    tour" on cup, "Pursued by a bull"
    on saucer **45.00**
  White patterned ironstone, emb
    wheat pattern **18.00**
Cup Plate, 4⅛" d, black transfer of man
  fishing, imp "ADAMS" (A) **25.00**
Dessert Service, 13½" w dbl handled
  tazza, four 11½" w dbl handled oval
  ftd dishes, four dbl handled 11" w sq
  dishes, four 10½" w leaf shaped
  dishes, twenty-four 9" plates, painted
  view of England, green borders, gilding, and shaped rims, "W Adams &
  Sons, Stoke Upon Trent" in brown,
  c1840, 37 pcs (A) **1,980.00**
Fruit Bowl, 10" d, "Cries of London-
  Turnips & Carrots Ho" **85.00**
Fruit Set, bowl, twelve 9" plates, "Italian
  Scenery," 13 pcs **775.00**
Ginger Jar, 6" h, multicolored fruit,
  cream ground **65.00**
Mug, 5" h, medium blue transfer of Oriental scene with flowers and birds,
  strap handle with emb floral terminals, "Wm Adams" (A) **80.00**
Plaque, 10¾" l, 8¾" h, pair of lions in
  relief, enameled in brown, orange,
  green, yellow, and blue, "William
  Adams, Stoke, Sept 19th, 1818" (A) **1,200.00**
Plate
  4¼" d, red transfer of garden urn, imp
    "ADAMS" (A) **12.50**
  6", dark blue transfer of Oriental
    domed bldg, imp "ADAMS" (A) .. **35.00**
  7½"
    Spatter, gaudy floral design, poly-
      chrome, "Wm Adams & Co" (A) **10.00**

Transfer of "Vassar College, Taylor Hall," blue 38.00

7¾", emb rim and feather edge highlighted in blue, imp "ADAMS" (A)   45.00

8"

Adam's Rose, vine border, imp "ADAMS" 225.00

"Cries of London-Sweet China Oranges" 42.00

8½"

Adam's Rose, rose center, design spatter border, imp "ADAMS" (A) 23.00

"Cries of London-Fresh Gathered...," octagonal 42.00

"Cries of London-Knives, Scissors & Razors to Grind," green, yellow, and black, octagonal 42.00

Plate, 7⅞" d, "Cries of London-Sweet China Oranges," multicolored, $20.00.

8⅝", Adam's Rose, rose center, blue spatter border, (A) 55.00

8¾", dark blue transfer of English country scene, imp "ADAMS" (A)   55.00

8⅞", dark blue transfer of cows in meadow (A) 50.00

9"

"Cries of London-Hot Spice Gingerbread, Smoking Hot" 40.00

Design spatter, apples in colors, "Wm Adams & Co, England," c1900 .... 40.00

9¼", Adam's Rose

Red, green, and black (A) 55.00

Vine border, imp "ADAMS" 145.00

9½", Adam's Rose 30.00

10"

"Cries of London-Old Chairs to Mend" 50.00

"Cries of London-Turnips & Carrots Ho" 50.00

Delphi pattern, blue 25.00

"Dr Syntax disputing his bill with the landlord," blue transfer 75.00

"Dr Syntax taking possession of his having," blue transfer 100.00

Jamestown Church Tower, pink transfer 12.00

Plymouth Rock, black transfer ... 18.00

Stone bridge scene, blue transfer, imp "ADAMS" (A) 80.00

10⅛", blue feather edge, imp "ADAMS" (A) 25.00

10½"

Adam's Rose

Deep center, unmarked 135.00

Unmarked 135.00

Audubon series, "Wild Turkey" .. 20.00

N. Currier print of "Home For Thanksgiving," gray border, red and yellow flowers, "Adams & crown" 10.00

Parliment Bldg, Victoria, blue transfer 22.00

10⅝", blue feather edge, imp "ADAMS" (A) 25.00

Platter

12⅝" l, dark blue transfer of sheep, horse, and rider, imp "ADAMS" (A)   155.00

15", blue and white pastoral scene, ironstone 150.00

15⅜", blue feather edge, imp "ADAMS" (A) 45.00

15½", blue feather edge, imp "ADAMS" (A) 55.00

17¾", blue feather edge, imp "ADAMS" (A) 55.00

18", "Calyx Ware" 75.00

20", "Falls of Niagara," pink transfer   350.00

Soup Plate

9" d, "Cattle Scenery," blue transfer, imp "ADAMS" 9.00

9½", "Caledonia" pattern, black transfer 36.00

10⅛", English country scene, dark blue transfer, imp "ADAMS" (A) .   55.00

10¼", Wells Cathedral, blue printed view (A) 25.00

Tea Service, teapot, creamer, cov sugar, six cups and saucers, "Titian Ware"   135.00

Teabowl and Saucer

Adam's Rose dec on saucer, blue spatter (A) 65.00

"Beehive" pattern, purple transfer .. 45.00

Blueberry and leaf sprig design, ftd cup, scalloped rim and sholder, smooth rimmed bowl, c1810 ....   48.00

Oriental scenery, dark blue transfer, imp "ADAMS" (A) 45.00

Teapot

8¼" h, garden scene with pagoda, dark blue transfer, imp "ADAMS" (A) 105.00

10¾" h, sprig pattern in colors, imp
"ADAMS" (A) **80.00**
Toddy Plate, 4½", blue feather edge,
imp "ADAMS" (A) **45.00**
Urn, cov, 14½" h, "Cries of London"
series, dog finials, pr **300.00**
Vase, 10" h, "Cries of London-Turnips
& Carrots Ho" **88.00**

AMPHORA

**Turn-Teplitz, Bohemia, now
Czechoslovakia
1892–to the present**

History: Riessner and Kessel started the Amphora
Porzellan Fabrik in 1892 for the manufacture of
earthenware and porcelain. This pottery was established at Turn-Teplitz, Bohemia. It produced
mostly porcelain figures and Art Nouveau styled
vases which were widely exported. Many of the
wares were hand decorated. They marked their
wares with a variety of stamps, some incorporating the name and location of the pottery with
a shield or a crown. Before WW II, Bohemia was
part of the Austro-Hungarian empire so that the
name "Austria" may have been used as part of
the mark. After WW II, the name "Czechoslovakia" may be part of the mark.

The Amphora Pottery Works was only one of
a number of firms that were located in Teplitz,
an active pottery center at the turn of the century.

**Planter, 9" w, cream and light green, imp
crown, "AMPHORA, AUSTRIA,"
$200.00.**

Basket
7" l, pink flower medallions and jewels, beige and brown ground, turquoise handle, mkd **68.00**
8¼" H-H, reserve of woman's portrait, buildings, and steeples on reverse, winged handles, blue and
red enamel leaves and cobalt trim,
"AMPHORA, MADE IN CZECHO-
SLOVAKIA" mk **170.00**
9" l, 7" h, multicolored, attached figural cupid, mkd **350.00**
12" h, multicolored painted bearded
man in Art Deco style, imp "AM-
PHORA" mk **165.00**
15" l, 11" h, two cherubs and multifloral dec, handled, mkd **595.00**
Two portrait medallions, cobalt glaze,
orange matte ground, jewelings
and vines on handle and wings,
green int., mkd **365.00**
Bowl, 6" l, 6½" h, figural, turkey in
brown and mauve, orange, white,
and green enameling **235.00**
Candleholder, 10" h, flower basket with
candleholder on top of handle, two
girls heads with flowing hair on each
side of handle, mkd **75.00**
Centerpiece
9" d, brown, green, and gold roses,
mottled ground, center bowl supported by four curved columns, circ
base, imp crown and "AMPHORA"
mks **175.00**
9½" d, Art Nouveau style design of
birds in flight, (A) **30.00**
13½" l, multicolored molded water-
lilies and applied blackberries **145.00**
28" d, multicolored jewels, gold reticulated ground, "crown, AM-
PHORA and AUSTRIA" mk **475.00**
Brown, gold, and green florals, yellow ground, four handles, "AM-
PHORA and crown" mks **175.00**
Cracker Jar, 8" h, raised green and lavender stylized flowers, cobalt and
light blue trim **75.00**
Figure
8" h, multicolored figure of girl selling
flowers, Art Deco style, mkd **79.00**
8¼" h, 11" l, stylized duck centerpiece, beige, purple, and green,
circ feathers outlined form, unmkd **600.00**
8½" h, 10" l, multicolored peasant girl
kneeling with basket at side, imp
"AMPHORA, AUSTRIA" mk **225.00**
14½" h, 10" l, porcelain, lion climbing down rocky ledge, mkd **345.00**
28" h, woman holding mirror, standing in bowl, gold star on forehead,
green glaze **950.00**

Jug, 6" h, Greek male figure on one side, red-brown tree bark ground, cobalt base, handle, and spout, "AMPHORA, MADE IN CZECHOSLOVAKIA" mk, c1920 .... **50.00**

Loving Cup, woman's portrait in reserve, incised royal blue body, three cobalt handles, "AMPHORA, MADE IN CZECHOSLOVAKIA" mk **155.00**

Mug
   3" h, multicolored, Arab on horseback, mkd **40.00**
   5¾" h, fox and bear design, mkd ... **95.00**

Rose Bowl, enameled Art Deco leaves and flowers, pebbly off-white ground, cobalt rim, mkd **70.00**

Vase
   2" h, hp, multicolored florals, mkd, c1920 .... **26.00**
   3¼" h, applied grapes and leaves, bark textured ground, dbl handles, mkd **85.00**
   5" h
      Yellow-orange flowers, brown ground, matte finish, four open loop squared off handles, green glaze, mkd **235.00**
   5¼" h, jeweled body, narrow neck, mkd **35.00**
   5½" h
      Art Deco style painted multicolored bird, imp "AMPHORA" mk ... **75.00**
      Art Deco style panels of incising with jewels, enamel accents, ovoid shape **60.00**
      Cobalt rim and base, colored oval and round stones, tan mottled ground, mkd **125.00**
   6½" h, applied pink roses, basketweave ground, four gold twig handles, mkd **65.00**
   6¾" h, 4⅛" d, emb enameled parrots, beige satin ground, cobalt top and base, sgd, "campana," Amphora mkd **165.00**
   7" h
      Applied grapes and leaves, bark surface, dbl handles, mkd **100.00**
      Art Deco style enameled long beak birds, trees, and water, open dbl handles, mkd, pr **275.00**
      Art Deco style enameled yellow roses, four handles, imp "AMPHORA" mk **98.00**
      Blue and red irid, large leaves and acorns, dbl handles **125.00**
      Enameled Indian, blue spatter ground, five spouts **275.00**
      Geometric and loop designs in red, blue, green, and gold, four small loop handles at neck, imp "AMPHORA" mk, pr **38.00**

Vase, 11" h, light pink roses, green shaded ground, chips on roses, imp crown, "AMPHORA," $300.00.

      Multicolored molded flowers, branches and leaves, cream ground, "AMPHORA, AUSTRIA #2228" mk **110.00**
      Purple and red gooseberries, biege ground, hollow handles, mkd .. **170.00**
      Relief of gold grapes and purple leaves, turquoise brick ground, four handles, mkd **375.00**
   7½" h
      Art Deco style birds and houses multicolored design, dbl handles **50.00**
      Art Nouveau style dragonfly design, jewels, dbl handles, mkd **350.00**
      Blown-out cobalt florals at top, pink-red and green leaves, mottled green and brown ground, irid glaze, leaf handle, imp crown mk **155.00**
      Floral design, mottled green and brown ground, four handles, imp crown mk **120.00**
      Shaded rose to bronze, four cut-out spoke-shaped gold bubbles with cobalt jewels in each, cobalt back wall, four cobalt jeweled handles, imp "IMPERIAL AMPHORA" mk **215.00**
   7¾" h
      Blown-out cobalt flowers at top, molded leaves, mottled brown and green body, leaf handles, imp crown and "AMPHORA" mks **80.00**
      Spider web, butterflies, fishnet and jewels, cobalt and irid green ... **250.00**
   8" h
      Applied flowerhead on neck, dbl wide wishbone handles, ftd, silver overlay **365.00**
      Art Nouveau style bizarre face near top, multicolored, mkd **48.00**
      Center portrait of blond girl with

jewels, pear shape, mkd "R. S.
& K." **450.00**
Figural roses, raised petals, blue
beading, four handles, mkd **65.00**
Pair of figural birds perched on rim,
multicolored, mkd **125.00**
8¼" h, bud, stylized florals in shades
of blue, bright alternating florals,
mkd **400.00**
9" h
Panels of ducks in flight, tall grass
and moon, textured green and
irid red surface **220.00**
Shaded green, pink, and yellow
flowers, gold trim, mkd **85.00**
9¼" h, Art Deco style, matte gray bkd
with shadow flowers, cobalt gloss
top band and trim, stylized glossy
raised flowers around center,
smaller band of flowers on lower
border, mkd **185.00**
9½" h, matte gladiator, maroon enameled dec, dbl handled with spout in
each handle, mkd **105.00**
10" h
Gold flowers, green ground, dbl
gold handles **175.00**
Gold irid Egyptian figures, copper
ground, mkd **650.00**
Light green floral design, dbl handles, mkd **110.00**
Relief of crowned queen with pink
and blue dress, brown stars and
blue dots, blue skies with turquoise stars, triangles, and dots,
"AMPHORA, AUSTRIA &
crown" mk **295.00**
10½" h
Art Deco style multicolored bird,
cross-hatched narrow neck, bulbous body, imp "AMPHORA"
mk **118.00**
Light blue and mauve florals with
gold trim, four open circles on
base, four handles with blue
enamel dots, "crown, AM-
PHORA & AUSTRIA" mk **450.00**
11", Art Deco design, dark green and
brown, inset jewels, elephant head
handles, mkd **300.00**
11½" h
Art Nouveau style leaf design and
gold buds at neck, green irid
glaze **235.00**
Purple irises with raised gold,
cream body, four gold handles,
mkd "R. S. K." **225.00**
Roses, dark blue ground, handled **68.00**
13½" h, multicolored scene of two
children pulling on doll, "IMPE-
RIAL AMPHORA" mk **425.00**

14" h
Multicolored long legged birds,
lozenge design at necks, matte
finish, small dbl loop handles,
imp "AMPHORA" mk, pr **118.00**
Plums, grapes, and applies, irid
green glaze, dbl handles **250.00**
Raised purple and green flowers,
green to steel gray mottled body,
four bands converging at peak
with graduated holes in bands,
four looped feet on wavy base,
mkd **245.00**
Wisteria design, multicolored, dbl
handles, imp "AMPHORA, AUS-
TRIA" mk **135.00**
14" h, 13" d, Art Deco sculptured
bird, stylized flowers in pink and
lavender, cobalt trim, Czech,
c1922 .... **165.00**
15½" h, reserve with agate swirled
stone blossoms and reserved neck
and rim, irid gold ground, ovoid
shape **410.00**
16" h
Stylized cosmos, cream ground,
gold leaf design top and bottom,
gold dbl handles, ftd, pr **275.00**
Two seated children on front,
grapes and leaves, shades of
brown and tan, mkd **280.00**
16¾" h, applied blackberries, emb
cream basketweave ground, green
rope top, bottom and dbl handles,
mkd **395.00**
21" h, purple grapes molded in relief
on sides, mkd **250.00**
Green with gold threads, blue jewels
and grapes around collar, sgd
"Molly," mkd **175.00**
Wall Pocket, 8½" h, Art Deco style,
brown and tan basketweave, mosaic
flower band **45.00**

ANGELICA KAUFFMANN

Switzerland
1741–1807

History: Marie Angelique Catherine Kauffmann
(1741–1807), a Swiss artist, worked primarily in
a neo-classical style. Many artists copied her
original paintings and used them on hand decorated porcelains during the 19th century.

Bowl
10½" d, two classical women in bottom, blue and gold trim, sgd **255.00**

Berry, center classical scene, multicolored, pink four sectioned scalloped border, sgd **95.00**
Box, covered
2" l, classic figures, multicolored, sgd **55.00**
Classic figures int. and on cov, multicolored **35.00**
Cake Set, cake plate, six serving plates, center classical scene, multicolored, turquoise and gold borders, sgd, 7 pcs **95.00**
Candy Dish, 6¼" d, scene of women and cherubs, multicolored, rococo gold border, unmarked **23.00**
Chocolate Pot, 11" h, classical scene on center panel, white ground, purple trim, gold finial, sgd "Angelica Kauffmann" **55.00**

Clock, 14¾" h, multicolored decal of classical scene, blue, red, and brown accents, cream ground, sgd, "Chelsea, England," $165.00.

Coffee Set, coffeepot, creamer, sugar, rainbow luster finish, emb florals, inserts of maidens and Cupid, gold trim, sgd and mkd Germany, 3 pcs **145.00**
Cup and Saucer, center medallion of classical scene, gold trim, sgd **38.00**
Dessert Plate, 8⅜" d, set of 12, each with different allegorical scene, black and gilt accented green borders, scalloped rims, sgd, "blue beehive," 12 pcs (A) **605.00**
Ewer, 8½" h, center band of classical scenes, multicolored, body in shades of green, gargoyle shape, sgd "Angelica Kauffmann," pr **125.00**
Humidor, classic women with cherubs, green ground, SP top with pipe, sgd **400.00**

Inkwell, 3½" h, classical scene, multicolored, gold trim, sgd **95.00**
Planter, 6½" d, 2½" h, seated female with Cupid at side, two women, multicolored, brown-white shaded ground, gold florals, "Victoria, Austria" **125.00**
Plaque, 12" sq, center scene of four women, dark red and gold, sgd **125.00**
Plate
6" d
Center classical scene, cobalt and gilt rim, sgd **34.00**
Classical setting with four full figures, multicolored, blue border, cream, Austria **25.00**
7" d, four full figures in pink and green, sgd **18.50**
8" d, center classical scene with two figures, multicolored, cobalt border with open work, sgd **55.00**
8½" d, center classical scene
Hp, green border with gold overlay, sgd, "blue beehive" **100.00**
Multicolored, dark green and gilt border, sgd, "blue beehive" ... **34.00**
Three women and cherub, blue and gold border, sgd "Kauffmann, Victoria, Austria" **85.00**
9" d, center classical scene
Multicolored, rows of cut outs along pink border, sgd **35.00**
Sleeping warrior and woman with flower garland behind, dark green open border, sgd **84.00**
Three full figures, dark green, maroon, cream and gold, pierced for hanging, Austria **75.00**
9¼" d, center classical scene of three full figured women, dark red, green, and gold, scalloped edge, sgd **25.00**
9½" d
Center classical scene, multicolored, cobalt and gilt reticulated border, sgd, "Victoria, Austria" **34.00**
Center Roman scene, multicolored, blue border, open double handles, sgd, R. S. Prussia red mk . **40.00**
9¾" d
Center portait of classic woman, dark green border with gold tracery, sgd, "Victoria, Austria" .. **43.00**
Center scene of shepherd and three draped maidens, narrow blue border, sgd **100.00**
10" d
Center classical scene of four figures, cobalt and gold border, sgd **95.00**
Center classical scene of two maidens and Cupid, green and cream border, small gold roses, sgd ... **85.00**

Scene of two maidens and baby, multicolored, maroon and gold border, sgd **50.00**

Scene of two women and cherub, cream ground, band of dark green and gold tracery, dbl open handles, "Victoria, Carlsbad" .. 10½" d **75.00**

Center classical scene of four maidens, maroon and gold border, sgd **50.00**

Center scene of four full figures, blue border, gold tracery, pierced for hanging, sgd **50.00**

Tea Set, teapot, creamer, sugar, classic portraits on sides, high luster finish, "Prov. Saxe," 3 pcs **95.00**

Tray, 16½" d, lg multicolored center portrait, sgd **175.00**

Urn
7" h, multicolored scene of Rinaldo and Almido, gold dbl handles, sgd **135.00**
12" h, two different classical scenes, multicolored, gold emb dbl handles, sgd, Royal Vienna **200.00**

Vase
8" h, classical scene, pale blue-green and gold, sgd, Royal Vienna **55.00**
8½" h, two classical scenes of women and ruins, pastels, sgd **55.00**
10½" h, classic portait center, white, blue, pink, wine, and green lusters, gold tracery, sgd "Angelica Kauffmann" **125.00**
12" h
Classical center medallion, cobalt ground, dbl handles, sgd **195.00**
Classical center scene, multicolored, shaded peach ground, gold dbl handles, sgd **80.00**
16" h, center multicolored portrait of woman, cobalt ground, dbl handles, sgd **145.00**

AUSTRIA

ᴬᵁˢᴛᴿᴵᴬ
1884-1909

16th Century–Present

History: Salzburg was the center of peasant pottery or pottery stove making during the 16th and 17th centuries. These wares were similar to those being made in Germany at the same time. Sometimes they were colored with tin enamels. Factories in Wels, Enns, and Steyr also made this type of pottery ware.

Peasant pottery, known as "Habaner ware" or Hafner ware, was decorated in an unsophisticated style with flowers, animals, and figures. These faience wares were made in Salzburg and Wels during the late 17th century. Most was used locally.

The only porcelain being produced in the early eighteenth century was made by a Vienna factory founded by Claudius I Du Paquier in 1718 with assistance from Meissen workers. This was the second factory in Europe to make hand paste porcelain. The factory was sold to the Austrian State in 1744.

Many of the later Austrian porcelain factories such as Schlaggenwald, Klosterle, Prague, Dallwitz, Pirkenhammer, and Elbogen are classified with Bohemia porcelain because of their location.

A number of porcelain factories originated in the nineteenth and twentieth centuries to make utilitarian and decorative porcelains. These included Brux, Frauenthal, Turn, Augarten, Wienerberger, Spitz, and Neumann.

In 1897 the Vienna Secession Movement provided a stimulus to Austrian ceramics. A group of young painters, sculptors, and architects desired to overthrow conservatism in the arts and design and revolutionize taste. Moser and Peche were designers of tableware and decorative porcelains associated with this movement.

In 1903 Moser and Peche founded the Wiener Werkstatte, an association of artisans, along with porcelain maker Joseph Bock. They made innovative designs in both shape and pattern.

Michael Powolny and Berthold Loffler founded the Wiener Keramik Studio in 1905 which produced advanced tablewares and figure designs in earthenware and porcelains. Products include black and white majolica, generally decorated with Cubist inspired geometrical patterns from designs by J. Hoffmann, D. Peche, and Powolny. Figures were modeled by Loffler and Powolny. Art Nouveau and Art Deco designs were utilized. The products of the Wiener Keramik Studio became the foundation for the international Modern Movement that developed after World War I.

References: George Ware, *German & Austrian Porcelain*. Lothar Woeller Press, 1951.

Museums: Osterreiches Museum fur Angewandtekunst, Vienna, Austria; Vienna Kunsthistoriches Museum, Vienna, Austria.

Bouillon Cup and Saucer, Napoleonic scenes in polychrome reserves outlined in gilt, green band borders, "VIENNA, AUSTRIA," set of 6 (A) **255.00**

Bowl, cover, and stand, 10" d, oval

panels of classical scenes in gilt surrounds, green ground, marked, c1890 (A) **1,100.00**

Butter Dish, cover, and insert, 7½" d, small yellow flowers, green vines, and gold trim, white ground, dbl handles, "VIENNA, AUSTRIA" **28.00**

Cabinet Cup, landscape reserve with two women, gilt decorated white ground, bird and acanthus motifs (A) **120.00**

Cabinet Cup and Saucer, portrait of period man, multicolored (A) **25.00**

Candelabras, 19½" h, leaf and flowered central socket with three branches, two draped women on pastel rose covered stumps, scalloped cylindrical bases, damaged, pr (A) **100.00**

Celery Tray, 12" l, pink roses, deeply scalloped gold rim **30.00**

Ceremonial Cup, 8" h, reserve painting of "Augustus" and "Cleopatra," floral gilding on irreg magenta ground (A) **75.00**

Cheese Dish, cov
　3" l, autumn leaves and flowers, cream ground, Vienna **52.00**
　Scattered multicolored florals, Vienna **48.00**

Chocolate Pot
　9¾" h, small pink roses with green leaves, gold bands and trim, white ground, "M Z Austria" **70.00**
　10" h, pink and white wild roses motif, pearlized ground, ovoid ribbed body, dbl handles and scalloped ft, molded dome cov, floral finial, "M Z Austria" (A) **90.00**
　12" h, large pink roses, emerald green and gold trim, "Imperial, Austria" **100.00**

Chocolate Set
　10" h pot, five cups and saucers, melon ribbed pot with acorns and leaves, cups and saucers with scalloped rims and bases, unmarked, 11 pcs **65.00**
　Pot, six cups and saucers, pink florals, white ground, marked, 13 pcs ... **75.00**

Coffee Service, 10" h coffeepot, milk jug, cov sugar, six coffee cans and saucers, rect reserves of rural landscapes, cobalt ground, gilt lattice and floral overlay (A) **935.00**

Cookie Jar, 6½" h, melon sectioned, pink roses, green leaves, gold trim, white ground, "M Z Austria" **88.00**

Creamer, 4½" h, figural, moose, marked **35.00**

Creamer and Sugar
　5" h creamer, 6" h sugar, small pink flowers, white ground **39.00**
　Painted roses, cream-white ground, "M Z Austria" **35.00**

Cruet, 9" h, hp, brown and yellow corn, gold handle and stopper, "VIENNA, AUSTRIA" **200.00**

Cup and Saucer
　Floral and gilt motif, royal blue accents, ftd (A) **50.00**
　Gilt banding, scalloped edge (A) ... **150.00**
　Landscape scene, multicolored, gilt foliates between gilt bands, tall, slender shape (A) **62.50**
　Musical instruments, multicolored (A) **50.00**
　Seashell cup, coral base and handle (A) **75.00**

Dessert Service, tea server, creamer, cov sugar, six plates, six cups and saucers, portrait medallions and gold tracery, cobalt ground, "blue beehive," 22 pcs (A) **170.00**

Dish
　7½" d, decal of child feeding chickens, fruit rim and sides, "M Z Austria" **30.00**
　8" d, thistles and small flowers on cream ground, "Imperial, Austria" **35.00**

Egg Caddy, porcelain, 12 cups, caddy with multicolored rooster, pink roses on cups, "Victoria, Austria" **55.00**

Ewer, 8½" h, hp, bouquets of flowers, dark to light cream shaded ground, open shell scalloped rims, gold dbl scroll handles, c1916, "red crown over shield" mks, pr **120.00**

Figure
　2" h, porcelain, mouse seated on haunches, preening self, white body, Vienna **70.00**
　5⅛" h, Cupid seated on green frog, c1900 (A) **42.00**
　6¾" h, 11" l, porcelain, gray and white polar bear, pink accents, "Made in Austria" **115.00**
　9⅜" h, porcelain, winged maiden wearing gilt jeweled costume, blue robes, arms outspread (A) **216.00**
　9¼" h, man mounted on horseback, multicolored, marked, pr (A) **110.00**
　9½" h, Aphrodite and Cupid, matte colors (A) **80.00**
　14½" h, girl leaning over open basket with hand extending into basket, cream ground, gold accents, "Ernst Wahliss, Austria" **375.00**
　19" h, porcelain, white stallion standing on hind legs, marked (A) **150.00**

Fish Set
　7 pcs, platter, six plates, six species of fish with florals, aqua and gold, ruffled edges **375.00**
　12 pcs, 16½" l, 11½" w tray, 9" l gravy boat and undertray, nine 8¾" l plates, multicolored fish and seaweed, blue ground, scalloped borders, "Made in Austria" **150.00**
　14 pcs, platter 20" l, twelve 8" d

plates, gravy boat, painted fish in water scenes, "Victoria, Austria" . **250.00**

15 pcs, sauceboat and undertray, 21" l, 9" w platter, twelve 8½" d plates, multicolored scenes of fish, blue shell and scroll borders, scalloped rims, "Victoria, Austria" **300.00**

Hair Receiver, small pink roses, pink and green accents, white ground, gold trim, "M Z Austria" **30.00**

Hatpin Holder, 4" h, cameo portrait, trumpet shaped, ruffled saucer base, unmarked **55.00**

Humidor

5½" l, 7¾" h, figural, Indian head, dark brown hair, head band and feathers, multicolored, "Royal Floretta Ware, Austria" **75.00**

6½" l, 7" h, figural, top hat, modeled animal on top, rat on rim, multicolored, "Floretta Ware, Austria" . **65.00**

Jug, 10¼" h, dark red leaves and flowers, mustard ground, $125.00.

Jug

8½" h, wide bulbous body, narrow neck, white int., red, green, cream, and gray elaborate body design, gold trim, "Alhambra" **135.00**

10" h, polychrome scene of traveling man, floral setting, upper and lower trellis banding, pear shape, initialed pewter lid, c1780, attrib to Gmunden **750.00**

Mint Dish, 4½" l, red roses and gold trim, beige ground, figural owl handle, "Bawo & Dotter, Austria" **15.00**

Nappy, 6" d, mother and child with bird cage in center, orchid border, gold trim, leaf shape, sgd "Maude Goodman, Victoria, Austria" **45.00**

Oyster Plate, 8" sq, cobalt, white and gold shell outlines, "Victoria, Austria" **28.00**

Perfume, 3" sq, pillow shape, 4 gold ball feet, turquoise ground, shaped cartouche with rose on white ground, turquoise and roses on stopper **125.00**

Pitcher, 4" h, multicolored, $35.00.

Pitcher

8⅜" h, maroon, cream, gray, and green geometrics, gold trim, "Alhambra" **135.00**

12½" h

Floral design, gilt trim, base and handle, "M Z Austria" (A) **100.00**

Roses, hp, pink and white flowers, green leaves, shaded green and pink ground, gold edge, tankard shape, green and pink handle .. **165.00**

Plaque, 12" d, young girl, blue dress, pink flowers in center, gold filigree on maroon border **135.00**

Plate

8" d, girl picking cherries, iris beaded rim, pierced for handing, "Victoria, Austria" **50.00**

8½" d Green grapes, hp, gold scalloped border, "R. Austria" **35.00**

9" d, porcelain, biblical scene, multicolored, unmarked (A) **45.00**

9¾" d, Napoleon with cavalry scene, multicolored, green and gold border, sgd "Foney" **250.00**

10" d, porcelain, hp, birds and flowers in center, green rim outlined in gilt (A) **35.00**

Platter, 16½" l, shaded pink roses, green leaves, "M Z Austria" **40.00**

Powder Dish, cov, 5¼" d, hp, small light blue roses on cov, gold trim, "VIENNA, AUSTRIA" **50.00**

Relish Dish, 7½" l, hp, red florals and green leaves, gold trim, "VIENNA, AUSTRIA" **15.00**

Ring Tree, hp, pink and green flowers, gold ring tree, "M Z Austria" **65.00**

Stamp Box, 3⅛" l, 1¼" w, ftd, hp, roses, gold trim, dbl compartments, "M Z Austria" 35.00

Syrup Pitcher, matching underplate, portrait center, "beehive & Austria" 90.00

Tea Set
 5 pcs, teapot, creamer, sugar, and tray, "Holly" pattern, "Imperial Austria" 175.00
 7 pcs, teapot, creamer, sugar, tray, cup and saucer, portrait panels and floral garlands, royal blue ground, gilt tracery (A) 55.00
 24 pcs, teapot, creamer, cov sugar, serving bowl, nine cups and saucers, cherry design, white ground, gold bands (A) 650.00

Teapot, 8¼" l, 4½" h, red and green geometric designs, gold scrolling, gold handle, spout and knob, "VIENNA, AUSTRIA" 60.00

Tray, 17" l, 15" w, portrait center, multicolored, raised gold tracery, cupids around edge 250.00

Vase
 5" h, lavender and purple pansies, buff ground, dbl handles, unmarked 18.00
 6" h
  Flowers on branch, hp, yellow, salmon, and chartreuse, fluted top and bottom, gold tracery ... 55.00
  Medallion, oval, bust of young woman, multicolored, ornate dbl handles 65.00
  Portrait of Victorian woman, multicolored, dbl handles 65.00
  Roses, large pink blossoms, buff ground, dbl handles 25.00
 6¼" h, hp, floral design, multicolored, shaded ground (A) 45.00
 7" h
  Flowers, cream, tan, and yellow . 15.00
  Woman holding bouquet, multicolored 32.00
 8¼" h, porcelain, allegorical scene of big bad wolf and sheep, multicolored (A) 20.00
 8¾" h, 5" d, portrait of woman, multicolored, "Victoria, Austria" 85.00
 9" h, shaded cream and pink pansies and daisies, brushed gold at top and bottom borders, dbl handles . 65.00
 9½" h
  Autumn flowers, tan and cream, dbl handles, "blue crown" 32.00
  Portrait of Victorian woman, gold trim, turquoise ground, sgd "LeBrun, Victoria, Austria" 135.00
 10½" h, sculptured design of Dutch children by seashore, flowers at

top, bent tree shaped dbl handles, green and gold, pedestaled 90.00
 11" h
  Art Deco style brown trees reflecting in water, yellow ground and pearlized glaze, cylindrical, "M Z Austria" 70.00
  Pottery, beige ground, brown, green, blue, and gilt florals, Vienna 40.00
 11½" h, polychrome florals, elongated necks, bulbous body, pr (A) 100.00
 11¾" h, pink, purple, and yellow flowers, blue ground 200.00
 12¾" h, full length painting of woman wearing thin gown, standing next to vase 250.00
 14" h, multicolored scene of grazing cattle, long loop dbl handles, pr . 150.00
 15" h
  Irises, large purple blossoms, purple ground, "VIENNA, AUSTRIA" 300.00
  Porcelain, transfers of classical scenes 100.00
 16" h, hp, multicolored chrysanthemums, gold trim, "M Z Austria" . 235.00

Wine Jug, painted scene of stag, mountains, and trees, gold handle, sgd, Vienna 90.00

BAVARIA

Bayreuth, Bavaria, now West Germany
c1713–1852

History: By the eighteenth century many factories were established in the Bavarian region. Bauscher at Weiden produced utility wares, some of which featured cobalt-blue ornamentation. J.N. Muller at Schonwald supplied painted and unpainted utility wares. Other factories operating in Bavaria included Schuman, Thomas, and Zeh, Scherzer and Company.

J. G. Knoller founded the Bayreuth factory in Bavaria and produced faience and brown glazed wares with silver, gilt, and engraved decorations. The finest work was done from 1728 until 1745. Bayreuth brown glazed wares were a lightly fired reddish earthenware covered with a manganese brown or red glaze. Yellow glazed wares were lighter in body and were covered with a buff or pale yellow glaze. About 1745 Frankel and Schrock took over and started to make porcelain. J.G. Pfeiffer acquired the firm, later selling it in 1767.

After 1728, the pottery and porcelain pieces were marked frequently. The mark consisted of the initials of the place and the owner, along with the painter's mark.

Museums: Sevres Museum, Sevres, France.

TIRSCHENREUTH

1838–Present
The Tirschenreuth Porcelain Factory was established in 1838 and made tablewares, utilitarian and decorative porcelains, figures, and coffee and tea sets. In 1927 the company was acquired by the Porcelain Factory Lorenz Hutschenreuther in Selb.

Additional Listings: Hutschenreuther.

Ashtray, combination match holder and ash receiver, hp cloverleaf dec, "Bavaria" **38.00**
Berry Set, 9" d bowl, four 5¼" d bowls, rose dec, white ground **28.00**
Bowl
  5" d, 8" l, cov, boy and girl picking grapes framed in gold, cobalt, raised rococo design, gold rim and scalloped edge, "Schumann Bavaria" **68.00**
  7" d, four feet, transfer of swans on lake, blue ground, gold scalloped rim, "X'd swords & JPVS" **45.00**

Celery Dish, 9¼" l, multicolored florals, "Schumann," $20.00.

7½" d
  Forest scene with hp pheasants, reticulated, sgd "FM" **100.00**
  Multicolored parrots in center, lavender pierced edge, octagonal . **35.00**
8½" d, 12½" l, overall floral painting,

reticulated sides, "Schumann, Bavaria" **45.00**
9" d
  Florals, pastels, reticulated sides .. **22.00**
  Roses, hp, white porcelain ground, scalloped top and bottom, "Mirmare, Bavaria" **36.00**
  Roses, pink and yellow flowers, white ground, "Bavaria" **16.00**
  Water lilies, white ground **15.00**
10½" d
  Fruits in center, multicolored, dark green rim **16.00**
  Roses, large pink flowers, green leaves, gold trimmed scalloped edge, "RXC Chrysanthemum, Bavaria" **60.00**
Bread Plate, 9" d, rose center, inscribed "Give Us This Day," open handles . **10.00**
Butter Dish, cov, ice holder center, pink roses, white ground, "H & C Bavaria" **30.00**
Cake Plate
10½" d, large rose in center, reticulated border, small roses, Schumann **20.00**
11" d
  Grape clusters, gold trim, open handles, sgd "Koch," "J. & C. Louise, Bavaria" **45.00**
  Iris blooms, molded pansies, fern leaves, gold trim, open dbl handles **50.00**
  Iris blooms and leaves in center, molded pansies, fern fronds on edge, gold trim, "RXC Pensee, Bavaria" **65.00**
Cake Set, large plate, four matching serving plates, hp yellow center, pink roses, blue border, "Bavaria" **45.00**
Candleholders, pr, 8½" h, irid blue, gold cut-out handles, "Royal Bavaria" ... **25.00**
Candy Dish
4½" sq, yellow roses, gold trim, pleated edges, set of 4 .... **32.00**
8½" l, large pink and yellow roses, shaded ground, gold finger handle, dated 1916 .... **32.00**
Celery Tray, 12" l, pink roses, green ground, dbl gold handles **35.00**
Charger
12" d, lilac sprays, sky background, unmarked **40.00**
12½" d, hp, red and yellow roses,

green leaves, shaded ground, "Z & S Bavaria" **45.00**

Chocolate Pot, 9¼" h, pink floral and chartreuse, gold trim, six sided base with molded leaves at intersections, reticulated handle and back rim **80.00**

Chocolate Set

7 pcs, pot, five cups, shaded dark pink at bottom to off-white at top, small florals at rims, scalloped base **75.00**

8 pcs, pot, four cups and saucers, small pink roses, large white daisies and green leaves, light green borders **150.00**

14 pcs, pot, six cups and saucers, pink, red, and white roses, shaded gray-blue to white ground, white leaf border **235.00**

21 pcs, pot, creamer, sugar, six plates, six cups and saucers, Ivy pattern, white ground **125.00**

Cracker Jar, 8½" d, 5" h, large pink roses and green stems, white ground, gold trim, "MV. ZS. & Co., Bavaria" **32.00**

Creamer and Sugar, purple and white pansies, "Meschendorf, Bavaria," $45.00.

Creamer

5" h, polychrome florals and maidens, gilt edge (A) **10.00**

Ring of blue pansies, gold fleur-de-lis rim, white ground **8.00**

Creamer and Sugar

Flowers, red and green, gold trim, cream ground, matte finish, "Meschendorf, Bavaria" **45.00**

Gold bands and handles, bow form, "H. & C Bavaria" **16.00**

Cup and Saucer

Greek key border, narrow black border outlined in gold, "H. & Co. Selb, Bavaria" **12.00**

Leaf design, light green, yellow, and pink, gold trim **38.00**

Cup and Saucer, bread and milk size, large pink roses, pink luster finish, "Bavaria" **35.00**

Cup and Saucer, demitasse, Dresden type flowers, multicolored, "Schumann, Bavaria" **15.00**

Cup, Saucer, and Plate Set, 7" d plate, orchids, white ground, gold trim, Tirschenreuth **30.00**

Decanter, 9" h, figural, grape cluster, natural colors (A) **10.00**

Dessert Set

7 pcs, cake plate, 9" d, six plates, 6" d, green grapes and shaded leaves, green-brown ground, "Charlotte, Bavaria" **52.00**

23 pcs, tray with dbl handles, 2 creamers, cov sugar, six plates, six cups and saucers, pink roses and green leaves, green lattice borders **135.00**

Dish

3" d, Dresden type flowers center, multicolored, reticulated border, "Schumann, Bavaria" **20.00**

5" d, roses, hp, light green ground, 3 gold feet **25.00**

9½" sq, white roses, light orange ground, pink rose and gold border, dbl handles **40.00**

12" l, bird of paradise center, reticulated edge, dbl handles **35.00**

14" d, roses, brown and cream ground, leaf shape, divided **45.00**

Dresser Box, yellow roses, white ground, hinged lift top, artist sgd ... **95.00**

Lamp, 7½" h, figural, clown, multicolored **35.00**

Match Holder, matching underplate, pinecone dec, upright form, artist sgd **15.00**

Mustard Jar, shell shape, irid finish, ftd, space for serving spoon, "Bavaria" . **35.00**

Pin Dish, 5" l, 3" w, floral design, white ground, gold trim, lattice edge, pierced handles **15.00**

Pitcher

3" h, Kewpie design, "Rosie O'Neill Wilson, Bavaria" **48.00**

6" h, two pheasants with foliage background, multicolored, white ground, marigold luster trim **35.00**

6½" h, two pheasants with foliage background, multicolored, white ground, marigold luster trim **35.00**

Plate

7" d

Classical scene of three women in garden, multicolored, reticulated border **17.50**

Grapes, hp, shaded brown to green, yellow ground, gold scalloped edge, sgd "A. Koch," marked "G. & C. Bavaria" **20.00**

7½" d

Floral garlands, multicolored, white scalloped center, gold trim, "Schumann, Bavaria" **15.00**

Flowers, small pink and blue blossoms, gold lines **3.00**

Flowers, yellow, pastel border ... **6.50**
8½" d
  Gold center, engraved gold border
  with pink roses **35.00**
  Gold swags, white center, rust border, cream trim, set of 6 ...... **45.00**
  Roses, hp, pink, "Sevres, Bavaria" **35.00**
  Roses, yellow flowers, white
  ground, "P. M. Bavaria" **24.00**
  Violets and large leaves, gold border **35.00**
8¾" d, floral center, gold and green
  borders, set of 12 (A) **150.00**
9" d, octagonal, bird of paradise on
  blossoming branch, multicolored,
  wide green border, gold trim **35.00**
9½" d, pink and yellow roses, rose
  and white ground, beaded trim, dbl
  handles, "Royal Bavarian China" . **20.00**
9¾" d, "Auf der Flucht," two maidens
  chased by Cupid, gilt floral motif
  on green border, sgd "Wagner,"
  c1910 (A) **330.00**
10" d
  Floral dec in gold, wide green border, set of 11 .... **80.00**
  Floral garlands, multicolored,
  white scalloped center, gold
  trim, "Schumann, Bavaria" **18.00**
  Floral reserve, gold borders, incised
  stylized motif, Schumann, set of
  12 (A) **160.00**
  Pears, two, green leaves, scalloped
  edge **45.00**
  Woman and child making wreath
  for man in armor, "Royal Bavaria" **80.00**
10" handle to handle, violets, white
  ground, gold handles, sgd "L. Leo-
  hard" **45.00**
10¼" d, multicolored bust of classical
  woman, green border with gold overlay, scalloped edge, "Schumann,
  Bavaria" **75.00**
10½" d, hp, grapes and leaves, gold
  trim, "Schumann, Bavaria" **18.00**
10¾" d, fruit basket reserve, polychrome, molded gilt and lime green
  border, c1900, set of 12 (A) **150.00**
11½" d, bust portraits of 18th C
  women in court clothes, dark blue
  borders, gold tracery, gold etched
  rims, c1920, "green S T W Bavaria,
  Germany, and crown", pr **160.00**
12" d
  Poppies, hp, orange flowers, light
  green ground, "J & C Bavaria" . **55.00**
  Roses, pink and yellow, around
  edge **65.00**
Salt and Pepper Shakers, silver overlay
  design, jade green ground, "Johann
  Haviland, Bavaria" **40.00**

Sugar Shaker, 4¼" h, hp, pink roses,
  pastel ground, Roman gold feet and
  top, artist sgd **40.00**
Tea and Coffee Service, teapot, coffeepot, five plates, 7" d, two cups and
  saucers, fluted bodies, "China Blau"
  pattern, blue and white Oriental florals, gold trimmed scalloped edges,
  "Seltmann, Weiden, Bavaria" **110.00**
Tea Service, teapot, creamer, cov sugar,
  four cups and saucers, multicolored
  florals, silver overlay **85.00**
Teapot, hp, yellow and pink roses,
  white ground, "Bavaria" **25.00**
Tray
  9" l, 4" w, roses and green leaves,
  pearlized ground, dbl open handles, "Schumann, Bavaria" **28.00**
  9½" l, azalea design, open handles . **14.00**
Vase
  5¾" h, hp
    Birds and flowers, multicolored,
    c1912 .... **25.00**
    Corn and leaves, hp, yellow and
    russet, orange luster dragon
    handle **40.00**
  6" h, hp, corn and leaves, dragon
  handle **55.00**
  6¾" h, hp, bird design, multicolored,
  cream ground (A) **45.00**
  8" h, 4¼" w, purple and green grapes
  and leaves, green ground, gold
  handles, flattened oval shape **75.00**
  8¼" h, irid blue, lacy openwork,
  flared rim, cylindrical **22.00**
  10" h, red poppies, green and red
  ground, gold trim, cylindrical, 4 ftd **95.00**
  14" h, large red roses and green
  leaves, shaded green ground, gold
  neck **150.00**
  16½" h, hp, poppies, cream-white
  ground (A) **140.00**
Vegetable Dish, cov, 8½" d, "Queen's
  Rose" pattern, Tirschenreuther **45.00**

1751-96

BELGIUM-GENERAL

1751–1891

History: Belgium's principal pottery and porcelain manufacturing center was Tournai. When
Francois J. Peterinck came from Lille to Tournai

in 1751, he took over a faience factory belonging to Carpentier. Empress Maria-Theresa gave him a grant to make porcelains. The early decorations were done in underglaze blue. Oriental patterns, mostly derived from Chantilly, and some Meissen-style decorations were used.

In 1763 Duvivier joined the factory as chief painter and added Sevres-style decorations, adopting the Louis XVI style in 1780. The principal background colors were bleu de roi and yellow. Figures and groups also were made in biscuit and glazed porcelain.

When Peterinck died in 1799, the factory experienced difficulties. Peterinck's descendents continued production until 1815 when the firm went bankrupt. Henri de Bellingnies reopened the factory in 1817 and managed it until 1850. Porcelains with a blue ground, similar to earlier styles, were made. The Boch brothers of Luxembourg purchased the factory in 1850. They made creamwares until 1891.

Francois Peterinck's son Charles established a second factory for stoneware production at Tournai that operated from 1800 to 1855.

Another smaller porcelain center in Belgium was in Brussels and its suburbs. Several factories operated on a small scale, mostly as decorating workshops utilizing in the Paris style of decoration.

Museums: Chateau Mariemont, Brussels, Belgium; Musee du Cinquantaine, Brussels, Belgium.

Bowl
    4¼" d, rose flowers, blue and green leaves at middle, "Manufacture Imperiale et Royal Made in Belgium"   **24.00**
    4½" d, 2⅜" h, design spatter, floral design, red and black, "Made in Belgium" (A) **20.00**
    10⅞" d, gaudy spatter, floral design, zig-zag rim, green, red, blue, and ochre, "Made in Belgium" **37.00**
    11" d
      Design spatter rim, red, green, and blue flowers **35.00**
      Floral spatter, green and red design, black with white flower trim ...   **38.00**
      Gaudy polychrome floral spatter design, zig-zag rim, "Made in Belgium" (A) **22.50**
Centerpiece, 11⅝" h, bisque, modeled as 2 seated ladies supporting bowl on head, Neo-classical costumes, rect tooled gilt base, applied griffins and fruit baskets, early 19th C, Brussels .   **300.00**
Cup and Saucer
    Painted exotic birds, landscape vignettes, gilt rims, c1770, Tournai (A) **530.00**

Rose painted bouquets of flowers, brown rims, c1775, Tournai (A) ..   **435.00**
Custard Cup, cov
    Painted flower bouquets and sprays, late 18th C, "blue X'd sword & star," Tournai (A) **95.00**
    Rose colored bouquets of flowers, spirally fluted bodies, dbl scroll handles, fruit finials, c1770, Tournai, set of 6 (A) **5,200.00**
Dish
    13½" d, pottery, painted polychrome flowers, c1700, Flemish **125.00**
    13¾" d, faience, painted bird on branch, stars and flowers, serrated panels, blue sponged ground, c1800, Brussels **250.00**
    14⅛" d, painted partridge in landscape, gilt border of pendant foliage, inscribed on reverse, late 18th C, "puce L. Crette a Brux." **150.00**
Ewer, 9½" h, majolica, dark red, blue, and brown Art Nouveau style designs, "Made in Belgium," pr **50.00**
Figure
    3¾" h, frog, crouching, black sponging, green body, ochre base, black line border, Brussels **400.00**
    4⅛" h, recumbent lion, sponged mang glaze, ochre feet and tail, oblong base, c1760, Brussels (A) ...   **385.00**
    5⅜" h, faience, seated cat, sponged in mang, black and green features, Brussels (A) **385.00**
    5⅞" h, white, birds perched on tree stump, rockwork base, Tournai, pr (A) **1,260.00**

Figure, 11⅜" h, faience, blue and white putto playing flute, flute missing, c1760, "Fabrique de la Montagne," $900.00.

6" h, faience, pug dogs, brown and black fur marks, puce ribbon, yellow bell collars, one with suckling puppy, rockwork mound base, c1765, Tournai, pr (A) 11,372.00

7⅞" h, gallant, standing with recumbent companion, multicolored period clothes, flowering tree stump, pierced rockwork green splashed base, applied flowers, c1780, Tournai 3,000.00

8¼" h, white, 2 men and woman before flowering tree, Cupid at feet, putto behind tree, rococo scroll base, man's hand missing, c1765, Tournai 800.00

16" h, faience, cockerels, striated mang glaze, sq base, c1750, Brussels, pr 3,500.00

Jug
7⅞" h, faience, dentil panels, inscribed "Litre" or "Bierre," dark blue ground, hinged pewter cov, early 19th C, Brussels, pr (A) 165.00

9" h, faience, printed crowned female on chair, figure in clouds with inscription, reserved on powder blue ground, late 18th C, Brussels 275.00

10⅝" h, painted figure and flowers in shaped panels, blue sponged ground, 19th C 65.00

Medallion, 4⅛" d, bisque, white and blue, royal portraits of Leopold I and Louise d' Orleans, 19th C, pr 80.00

Plate
6½" d, cream ground, magenta and yellow flowers with green leaves, "NIMY, Made in Belgium" 16.00

9" d
Painted center, birds in landscapes, spirally molded border, 3 blue floral sprays in gilt foliage and C-scroll cartouches, c1775, "blue X'd swords & star," Tournai, set of 3 (A) 950.00

Painted ribbon tied floral medallion, c1785, Tournai 85.00

Rose colored scene of figures with ships, basketweave border, flower sprays, spirally gadrooned, c1770, Tournai, pr (A) . 885.00

9¼" d
Blue painted flower bouquets, spirally gadrooned silver shape, c1760–70, Tournai, pr (A) 120.00

Painted flower sprays, spirally molded border, gilt rim, c1765, "gilt X'd swords & X," Tournai . 450.00

Rose painted figures in landscape, spiral ozier border, gilt rim, c1770, "gilt X'd swords & star" 300.00

9⅜" d, painted center, bunches of flowers, spirally gadrooned and gilt border, c1770, Tournai, pr (A) ... 570.00

9½" d, painted bouquets of flowers, spiral ozier rim, c1770, Tournai .. 325.00

9⅝" d
Painted center, 2 putti holding portrait medallion, spirally molded puce line border, yellow ozier molded rim, c1780, Tournai (A) 88.00

Puce pairs of birds in landscapes, serrated gilt scroll cartouches, rim scattered flowers, c1770, "gold anchor," Tournai 350.00

Sauce Tureen, 8⅛" l, melon shape, turquoise-green glaze, yellow stemmed handle, mang glazed green leaves base, c1750 (A) 660.00

Snuffbox, 4" w, ext. painted with figures in landscape vignettes, int. cov painted with woman bathing in pond and man watching in reeds, contemporary gold reeded mounts, c1770, Tournai 9,500.00

Soup Plate
9¼" d, blue painted flowering plants and branches, spirally molded borders, c1775, Tournai, set of 6 .... 465.00

9½" d, red open stylized flowers in center, smaller blue flowers and green leaves, red honeycomb rim, "Belgium" 25.00

10" d, design spatter, gaudy polychrome floral design, zig-zag border, "Made in Belgium (A)" 40.00

Tea Service, 3 teapots, milk jug, cov sugar, 5 large cups and saucers, 4 small cups and saucers, gilt and pierced rims, Brussels 135.00

Teabowl, 2½" h, brown transfer of country scene on yellow ext., brown transfer of goat int., "NIMY, Made in Belgium" 16.00

Tobacco Jar, 11⅞" h, raised blue horizontal ribs, brass cov, inscribed "Tabac de Virginie," c1800, Flemish . 250.00

Tray, 25⅛" l, gilt foliage band border . 80.00

Tureen, 16" l, faience, modeled as seated chicken, incised brown and yellow feathers, red wattle and comb, repaired, c1780, Brussels 1,500.00

Vase
3½" h, tan, white and green ground, incised swirls, glossy green drip .. 12.00

7" h, matte brown and green textured glaze, glossy green drip, melon shaped 15.00

8" h, two tone blue drip, blue-gray pebbly glaze, amphora shaped ... 24.00

8" d, 12" h, Art Deco, dark red and

Tureen, 12½" l, brown, yellow, and manganese incised feathers, c1775, Brussels, (A) $1,650.00.

gray, dbl handles, "Made in Belgium, Faience Rib, Thulin" **185.00**
12" h, molded with blue and yellow stylized flowers between vertical banding, buff ground, gourd shaped, c1925, "B. F. K. La Louriere Beligique D751, Catteau" ... **150.00**

BESWICK

MADE IN
ENGLAND

Staffordshire, England
Early 1890s–Present

History: James Wright Beswick and John, his son, acquired the Gold Street Works in Longton, Stoke-on-Trent in 1896. They made utilitarian and ornamental wares, but are best known for their series of figures of horses and domestic pets. All of their animals are created with utmost accuracy and attention to details. In 1918, the Beswicks added the Warwick China Works in Longton.

After James Beswick died in 1920, John took over the firm. In 1934, John was succeeded by John Ewart Beswick, his only son. John Ewart worked along with Gilbert Ingham Beswick. They expanded the firm and increased their reputation for excellent equestrian figures. The firm was called John Beswick Ltd. from 1936.

The firm continued to expand by acquiring the site of Williamson & Son's factory in 1945 and Thomas Lawrence's site in 1957. They were converted to a public company in 1957.

Since neither Ewart or Gilbert had a successor to take over, they sold the firm to Royal Doulton Tableware Ltd. in 1969. Their reputation for figures of animals continues to the present day.

Beswick's best known models of horses are part of the "Connoisseur Series." Though the "Connoisseur Series" was developed in the early 1970s, it incorporated figures that had been made many years before. Cats, dogs, farm animals, birds, wildlife, and figures identified with children's literature such as "Winnie the Pooh," "Alice in Wonderland," and the works of Beatrix Potter have been modeled by Beswick.

The Beswick name is stamped on most pieces, but the earliest examples are unmarked.

Basket, 10½" l, blown out palm trees, cobalt ground, gilt trim **58.00**
Children's Feeding Dish, 6½" d bowl, Disneyland dec **18.00**
Figure
  3" h, dog, black and brown tipped tail, black ears **13.00**
  3½" h, multicolored
    Dog, Spaniel **28.00**
    Panda **18.00**
  4" h, dog, Spaniel, black and white . **18.00**
  4½" h, Beatrix Potter "Pickles" **18.00**
  5" h
    Donkey, multicolored **45.00**
    Horse
      "Highland," multicolored **75.00**
      Seated, gray **45.00**
      With foal, on stand, multicolored **125.00**
    Owl, multicolored **15.00**
  5" h, 5½" l, Persian cat **20.00**

Figure, 7" h, "Scottish Highland Horse," tan, brown mane and tail, "Highland, Beswick England," $45.00.

5½" h
  Cat, seated, black and white neck and face, green eyes, pink nose **65.00**
  Welsh lady, multicolored **35.00**

5½" h, 7¾" l, dog, Collie, multicolored, "Lockinvar of Lady Park" underneath 48.00
6" h, 6" l, horse, standing, white and gray, Welsh "M" mark 36.00
6½" h, cat, green eyes 42.00
7" l, pig, white, piglets on back 20.00
8¼" h, Indian on horse, multicolored 80.00
8½" h, 10" l, Clydesdale horse, standing 48.00
Bird on sunflower, multicolored, #929 . . . . 36.00
Ducks, wings spread, pr 195.00
Mickey Mouse characters, set 95.00
Jug, 6½" h, "Scrooge" character, multicolored, #372 . . . . 35.00
Mug, 2¾" h, handleless, "Tony Weller," #673 . . . . 18.00
Pitcher
7½" h, figural, Robert Burns 35.00
7⅝" h, gold and green palm trees, gray ground 25.00
8" h, Shakespeare Series, Hamlet scene, multicolored, c1951 . . . . . . 135.00
Platter, Shakespeare Series, Romeo and Juliet, multicolored 95.00
Salt and Pepper Shakers, 3" h, "Mr. Micawber," by Betsy Trottera, c1930s . 85.00
Tea Set, teapot, creamer, and sugar, figural, Dickens characters, multicolored 70.00
Teapot, 5½" h, "Sairy Gamp" dec 135.00
Toby Jug, 3½" h, multicolored
"Mr. Micawber" 30.00
"Pickwick" 30.00
"Mr. Varden" 30.00
"Mrs. Varden" 30.00
"Tony Weller" 30.00

About one and one-half years after the company started, Grondahl died. The Bings hired top designers and decorators to continue fabricating utilitarian and art wares. In 1886 the firm first used underglaze painting. Previously, the firm manufactured pieces with "biscuit" or overglaze porcelain decorations.

In 1895 the first Christmas plate was issued. A seven inch blue and white plate utilizing the underglaze technique is made every year with the molds being destroyed after Christmas to prevent later restrikes. From 1910–1935 Easter plaques also were issued.

Several great artists were employed by the company such as J.F. Willusmen, Effie Hegermann-Lindercrone, Fanny Garde, Haus Tegner, Kai Nielsen, and Jean Gauguin. In 1914, stoneware was made for the first time. Soft paste porcelain began in 1925. In 1949 a new factory was built for producing dinnerwares.

Every piece of Bing and Grondahl work is signed with either the artist's name or initial. While today's collectors know Bing and Grondahl primarily for their figurals and annual Christmas plates, the company still produces a porcelain line.

References: Pat Owen, *The Story of Bing & Grondahl Christmas Plates*, Viking Import House, Inc., 1962.

Museums: The Bradford Museum, Niles, Illinois; Metropolitan Museum, New York.

Cup and Saucer, "Falling Leaves" pattern 18.00
Dish, 7" l, 6" w, blue-gray relief, crab at one end, sea plants in center, white ground, c1915 . . . . 48.00

BING AND GRONDAHL

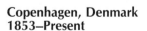

Copenhagen, Denmark
1853–Present

History: The Bing and Grondahl Porcelain Factory was established in Copenhagen in 1853 when Frederich Grondahl left the Royal Copenhagen Porcelain Manufactory due to an artistic disagreement and joined with M. H. and J. H. Bing. The Bing brothers provided the business expertise, while Grondahl was the artistic force.

Figure, 4½" l, blue, gray, and white, $68.00.

Figure
2" h, mouse
Gray, #1881 . . . . 30.00
White, #1728 . . . . 20.00
2½" h, polar bear, #2217 . . . . 45.00

3" h

Bulldog, #1676	**75.00**
Monkey, #1667	**30.00**
Penguin, standing, #1821	**60.00**

3¼" h, 4¼" l, young girl kneeling over

basket, holding white cat, #2249	**250.00**

3½" h, parakeet on stump

Blue, #2210	**75.00**
Green, #2341	**75.00**

3⅞" h, cockatoo, #2178	**35.00**
4" h, rabbit, seated, brown and white, #1596	**135.00**
4" h, 5" l, goat, standing with head down biting foreleg, #1700	**135.00**
4¼" h, bird, long pointed gray beak, blue and white body	**125.00**
4½" h, Cocker Spaniel, standing, tan and white	**55.00**
5" h, "Two Reading," multicolored (A)	**50.00**

5½" h

Macaw on stump, tan and blue, #2019	**125.00**
Polar bear, standing with head tilted upwards	**130.00**
Siamese cat	**65.00**

6" h

Little boy buttoning blue pants, #1759	**125.00**
Mother, seated, holding standing child and flowers, #2255	**145.00**

6" l, goat, white and tan, #1699 . . .	**65.00**
6½" h, 10" l, girl standing next to sheep, sgd "Locher," #2010	**275.00**
6⅝" h, young girl, blue dress, purse over shoulder, "B. & G., Made in Denmark" mark (A)	**60.00**
7" h, little boy and girl kissing (A) . .	**70.00**
7" h, 7½" l, Schnauzer, standing, black and white, #2091	**180.00**
7¼" h, nude girl, reclining, suckling baby, carp behind, incised "Kai Nielson, 1913" mark (A)	**78.00**
7¼" h, 15½" l, peacock	**375.00**

7½" h

Cat, #2256	**100.00**
Cat, seated, licking self, gray and white, #2251	**145.00**
Girl holding doll, polychrome (A)	**60.00**

8" h

Boy kissing girl in party dress	**125.00**
Young boy in short pants, wading, "B. & G., Denmark" mark (A) .	**25.00**

9" h, dancing boy and girl, #1845 .	**165.00**
9¼" h, girl with 3 geese, sgd "Axel Locher"	**225.00**
9½" h, "Farm Girl Feeding Chickens" (A)	**90.00**
Boy and girl kissing, shades of blue, white ground	**70.00**
Ice skater, #2351	**115.00**

Tray

5" sq, windmill and country scene, blue and beige	**30.00**
5" w, 7½" l, Copenhagen scene, blue and white	**45.00**
Sauce Tureen, attached tray, water lily, seahorse handles	**35.00**

Vase

3¾" h, black band of linked ovals, blue and mauve motifs on shoulder (A)	**48.00**
5" h, hp, lily-of-the-valley dec	**40.00**
8" h, seagull, gold trim	**75.00**

BISQUE

England/Continental
1750–Present

History: Bisque, or biscuit china, is white, marble-like, unglazed hard porcelain or earthenware that has been fired only once. The composition of the body and the firing temperature are most important to achieve the matte, porous surface of the figure. Since there is no glaze or decoration, the surface has to be completely free of imperfections. Razor-sharp modeling of details is made possible by the absence of glaze.

Bisque figures first were produced around 1751 at Vincennes and Sevres in France. They became very fashionable. Many French porcelain factories during the latter part of the 18th century added them to their product lines. Bisque figures also were made at Meissen in Germany.

Beginning in 1773 Derby was the principal manufacturer of bisque figures in England. Bisque figures in soft paste porcelain have a great smoothness to the touch and a warm soft tone.

About 1850 German factories produced bisque dolls. Delicacy of coloring and realism of features could be achieved with this material. In the late 1850s France also started producing bisque dolls. Both French and German factories manufactured bisque dolls in the image of children rather than ladies during the 1880s. They were called "bebes" even though they depicted girls from about eight to twelve years old.

Most bisque examples are unmarked.

Museums: Bayerisches National Museum, Munich, Germany; Victoria & Albert Museum, London, England.

CONTINENTAL

Bottle, 5½" h, figural, monk, brown robe, white apron with 4 bottles, hat stopper, "GERMANY" mark	**85.00**

Box, 4" l, turtle figure with woman's head resting on folded arms, Art Nouveau, int. shows body of woman, soft pastels, "GERMANY" mark **185.00**

Candelabra, 13" h, modeled classical dancing figures, 2 light, damaged, pr, late 19th C, France **200.00**

Clock Case, 10¾" h, white, modeled young girl, bird's nest on wall, clock fitted to wall opening, oval base, milled circ feet, early 19th C, France **300.00**

Dish, cov, 9" l, cov modeled as brown and white recumbent dog with bone, stein and beer keg, gold and white basketweave base, France **550.00**

Figure

2" h, angel, pastels, "GERMANY" mark **28.00**

3" l, bathing beauty with cap, Germany **70.00**

Figures, 14" h, light blue and white, France, unmarked, pr, $1,900.00.

3½" h

Black boy and girl, seated, boy with white shorts, pink sash, white bowler hat, girl holding pink bow on yellow bonnet, pr **175.00**

Boy and girl, standing on swings, pastels, Germany, pr **90.00**

Seated shelf figure, girl holding doll, brown dress, blue apron, hat, and shoes **60.00**

4" h

Discus thrower, white, Germany . **35.00**

Young girl, raised beaded dress . . **45.00**

4" h, 3¾" l, boy, sitting, black and tan oval bucket tub washing with sponge, multicolored, Germany . . **80.00**

4¼" h, black boy with watermelon, sitting on potty, multicolored **45.00**

4½" h

Black boy, sitting on tree stump, playing squeeze box, multicolored, Germany **115.00**

Comic man, top hat, multicolored, Germany **95.00**

5" h, wolf, standing, red jacket, blue pants, yellow shirt, and bow tie . . **45.00**

5½" h, monk in robe, holding basket and lantern, multicolored, Germany **35.00**

5½" l, child, crawling, white gown, green bows **75.00**

5½" h, 8" l, six ladies, orchid dresses, black hats and gloves, rect bases, "blue crown & X'd bars" mark . . . **110.00**

5¾" h, monkey, seated, holding upside down top hat, tan and white, blue dot bow tie, France **365.00**

6" h, busts of children wearing fur trimmed hats, pr **40.00**

6" l, shoe, pigs and shamrocks relief **115.00**

6½" h, Germany

Monk in robe, holding wine glass, multicolored **40.00**

Venus, pastels **35.00**

7" h

Cherubs at play, conforming gilt bases, pr (A) **100.00**

Wild boar, standing on hind legs, natural brown and black, "GERMANY" mark **170.00**

7½" h, woman in peasant dress, applied flower at neck, France **225.00**

7⅞" h, rect rockwork base, c1800, "incised interlaced L's" mark

Boy, holding bird beside basket of grapes **100.00**

Girl, holding corn beside basket of corn **100.00**

9⅞" h, huntsman and lady, multicolored, Germany, pr (A) **50.00**

10" h, child holding cat, wearing grandmother's clothes, multicolored, "Grandma" on base, Germany **85.00**

10" h, pr, France

Boy page and lady in waiting, pastel blue and gold **85.00**

Busts of young girl and boy, native costumes, small circ bases, pastels **750.00**

10¼" h, young woman riding goat, basket of fruit on knee, scroll base, applied florals, multicolored **80.00**

11" h

Lovers surrounding tree, gilt base, France **150.00**

Man and woman, seated on dark

brown wooden benches, period clothes, soft pastels, France, pr . **750.00**

12" h

Diana and cherub, modeled base, Sevres **175.00**

Girl with bonnet, deer and rabbits around her feet, gold, green, and beige, white ground, Germany . **295.00**

12" h, 13" l, man, woman, and child in boat, pastels, gold trim, Germany **395.00**

12¼" h, woman, seated, child in lap, another at side, basket and jug, octagonal base, late 19th C, France . **100.00**

12⅜" h, boy carrying bookbag, girl with music portfolio, lavender, green, and cream colors, Germany, pr **300.00**

12½" h, Pascal seated on chair, gazing at tablet, books, and papers on shaped base, c1783, Sevres, (A) **15,165.00**

13" h, busts of Louis XVI and Marie Antoinette, white, cobalt and gilt plinths, sgd "Letourneur," pr (A) .. **160.00**

13¼" h, bust of Marie Antoinette, bleu-du-roi waisted socle and pedestal, late 19th C, France (A) **115.00**

13½" h

Man and woman in peasant clothes, pastels, floral trim on pants and apron, wooden brooms, France, pr **395.00**

Man and woman in Victorian clothes, holding brown shell, Germany, pr **375.00**

Young lady, letter in one hand, other hand over heart, blonde hair, blue, pink, and rosebud gown, sgd "Bauer" **375.00**

13¾" h, "The Welsh" Tailor, white (A) **130.00**

14" h

Boy and girl, blue period clothes, France, pr **1,900.00**

Lovers, seated on bench, child (A) **125.00**

15" h, bust of woman, gilt blouse, rose and ribbon in hair, imp "A. Carrier," France **175.00**

16" h, busts of boy and girl on socle, bleu-du-roi glaze, edged in gilt, "C Tharaud, Limoges" marks, pr **525.00**

17½" h, man carrying basket of flowers, woman carrying 2 baskets, soft blue, lavender, green, pink, and yellow pastels, "green anchor" mark, France, pr **1,200.00**

18⅜" h, bust of Marie Antoinette, classic clothes, waisted socle, floral garlands, gilt bronze base, sgd "Tajou" (A) **275.00**

20¾" h, woman with Roman style

garb, man offering rose, polychromes, late 19th C, Germany, pr (A) **275.00**

22" h, lovers, strolling under umbrella, multicolored, Germany (A) **425.00**

22½" h, woman in full cape, taking off mask, man in full cape, multicolored, late 19th C, Germany, pr (A) **425.00**

22⅞" h, ladies holding basket of grapes or fan, brown and light blue, circ bases **150.00**

Naughty, 4" l, lady lying on stomach, head of a turtle, under shell, body of woman in underwear, Germany, unmarked **165.00**

Nodder

7¼" h, Oriental girl pulling cart, pink, yellow, and blue, France **150.00**

7½" h, standing figure of old woman, cloak and apron, green, cream ground, Germany **165.00**

Planter

6" l, 3" h, molded child on one end, molded pinecones and leaves on body, multicolored, unmarked ... **45.00**

8½" l, lady holding fishing net, multicolored, unmarked **150.00**

Plaque

4½" l, portrait profile bust of Louis XV, classical dress, curly hair, oval shape, c18th C, Germany, hairline crack **300.00**

6" l, boy and girl kissing, nude with drape on upper branch, applied flowers, gold outline, heart shape, crossed arrows mark and #'s **30.00**

14" w, 19" h, girl playing violin, purple dress, framed in flowers and leaves, Vienna, Austria **180.00**

Tobacco Jar, figural

Devil, smiling, strong red and black coloring, unmarked **110.00**

Negro smoking pipe, strong colors, "GERMANY" **65.00**

Vase

6" h, green with gold tree trunks and rocks, white figural Victorian boy and girl leaning on trunks, Germany, unmarked, pr **55.00**

8" h, 3" sq, Grecian woman relief holding flower basket and dove, masks, lyres, and horns, violet and green, white ground **35.00**

Water well shape, girl feeding rooster next to well, girl with wide brimmed hat, green and lavender pastel coloring, unmarked **100.00**

Whimsy, 3¼" l, figure of two frogs sitting in front of two eggs, multicolored, unmarked **75.00**

ENGLAND

Figure

2½" w, 4" h, two young girls in bonnets and aprons, holding flowers, multicolored, oval base, unmarked   **32.00**

4" h, seated child wearing pinafore, cobalt bonnet, unmarked   **90.00**

5" l, sleeping child, head resting on basket of fruit and flowers, white, rect base, c1800 (A)   **135.00**

5½" h

Babies, seated, one holding cup, other holding saucer, green and white dresses, pr   **150.00**

Boy standing beside ewer on rock (A)   **40.00**

Child holding cornucopia with fruit and sickle, rockwork base, 18th C   **275.00**

6¼" h, children sitting in chairs, green and white clothing, gold dot trim and gold shoes, green, tan, and gold chairs, unmarked, pr   **165.00**

6½" h, young man sitting in chair drinking tea, multicolored pastels and gold   **55.00**

7¾" h, young boy, clasped hands standing next to flower basket, rect base, c1775 (A)   **220.00**

7¾" and 8⅛" h, Swiss girl carrying bundle of sticks and basket of flowers, Swiss boy with satchel across shoulder, both wearing straw hats, white, circ mound bases, applied flowers, c1836–40, imp griffin and "ROCKINGHAM WORKS. BRAMELD," pr (A)   **550.00**

8⅜" l, 4¼" h, reclining cat, black spots, green eyes and pink bow on neck   **110.00**

8½" h, young girl holding apron, standing before tree trunk, rect base, c1775 (A)   **220.00**

8¾" h, Victorian girl, ball, multicolored, unmarked   **70.00**

9" h, twin girls, soft colored wash, unmarked   **225.00**

11" h

Boy, pastel and gold trimmed ruffled clothes, wreath on head, unmarked   **80.00**

Boy with dog, girl filling pitcher, country clothes, multicolored, English mark, pr   **500.00**

Modeled as children playing with dogs, goats, and sheep, Derby (A)   **175.00**

11½" h, boy and girl holding cats, pastel colors, unmarked   **250.00**

12½" h, lovers in garden, pastel colors and gilt (A)   **40.00**

12¾" h, cavalier, gold horn, peach, and gold dot colored clothes   **88.00**

13¾" h, girl carrying fish, dressed in blue, unmarked   **150.00**

14" h, boy with beret, holding basket, girl holding flowers, soft pastel blue on white, unmarked, pr   **500.00**

14⅝" h, boy, badminton racket, multicolored, unmarked   **250.00**

15" h, "Evening," seated god listening to maidens playing instruments, "Night," seated maiden with Psyche, white, sq plinths, molded foliate swags, c1870   **2,000.00**

15⅜" h, woman, blue dress and stole, fleshtones on face and bare feet, Robinson & Leadbeater   **325.00**

16" h, boy, Irish costume, shamrocks on coat   **100.00**

Flower Holder, 8¾" h, figural, winged Cupids holding six petal flower form, pierced top, pastel colors and gold, unmarked   **185.00**

Match Holders, 4¼" h, boy and girl next to baskets, white, pr   **60.00**

Trinket Box, 3" d, bust of Victorian woman on cov, emb lavender flowers, ftd, unmarked   **30.00**

BOCH FRERES KERAMIS

La Louviere, Belgium
1841–Present

History: The Boch Freres factory at La Louviere, called Keramis, was founded in 1841 by Victor and Eugene Boch and Baron J. G. Nothomb. Previously, the Boch brothers were associated with the Villeroy and Boch concern.

The designs of Alfred William Finch, an English artist, and Marcel Goupy, a French artist, were produced at the Keramis factory. Finch signed vases, dishes, jugs, and candlesticks featuring a rough, red earthenware body covered with slip and glazed in ochre, blue, bottle-green, or fawn along with incised linear decoration and dots of light colored glaze in the Art Nouveau style.

Marcel Goupy made earthenware services decorated in ochre and blue for the Keramis factory. His pieces usually were signed.

Tiles were made from the 1880s at a branch factory in France. The Keramis factory also produced earthenware and stoneware similar to Staffordshire wares. Imitations of Delft china were produced along with Rouen and Sevres copies.

Museum: Museum voor Sierkunst, Ghent, Belgium.

Bowl
11″ d, large yellow enamel leaves, green ribbon and circles, grainy brown ground, "Boch Freres, Belgium" **95.00**
11″ d, 2¼″ h, yellow and green leaves, sanded brown glaze int. ... **110.00**
Lamp, 18″ h, turquoise deer and fawn dec, blue and green enamels, ftd metal stand **175.00**
Plate, 10″ d, multicolored cartoon scene of "Les Sport of Fishing" ... **28.00**
Vase
6″ h, black, yellow, green vertical leaves, gray crackle ground **295.00**
7¼″ h, yellow band, open flowers around neck, black vertical stripes, white ground **85.00**
8″ h
Enameled flying birds, blue ground, turned lip, "KERAMIS, BELGIUM" **150.00**
Open white and red flowers, black vertical lines, yellow neck band **155.00**

9″ h, stylized seagulls over waves, cream ground **190.00**
11¼″ h, panels of florals in baskets, turquoise vertical bands, cream crackled ground, bottle shaped ... **425.00**
11¾″ h, vertical bands, red centered yellow stylized flowers, blue ground, cream crackled ground panels **465.00**
12″ h
Blue, yellow, and turquoise geometrics, ivory crackle ground, blue neck and base band **350.00**
Blue streak glaze, metal mounts, pr **325.00**
13″ h, basket of multicolored flowers, gilt brass mounts (A) **30.00**
15⅜″ h, white flowers and scrolls relief, black ground, pr (A) **260.00**

BOHEMIA-GENERAL

Germany
Late 1700s–Present

History: Franz Anton Haberditzel pioneered the Bohemian porcelain industry. In 1789, along with twenty-five partners, he established a fac-

Vases, left, 8¼″ h, blue, turquoise and yellow bands, ivory crackle ground, #D1174, $350.00; center, 11″ h, turquoise flowers with yellow centers, turquoise vertical lines, ivory crackle ground, "BOCH FRERES, KERAMIS, BELGIUM," $275.00; right, 13″ h, brown and earthtones, cream ground, $500.00.

tory in his native Rabensgrun near Schlaggenwald. Johann Gottlieb Sonntag of Rudolstadt was the technical director. When Haberditzel died in 1792, Sonntag carried on. The company disbanded in 1793 due to the unsatisfactory nature of the porcelain.

The first successful porcelain factory in Bohemia was started by Johann George Paulus and Georg Johann Reumann at Schlaggenwald. Production initially was limited to earthenware because their patent to produce porcelain was refused in 1793 as a means of protecting the porcelain production in Vienna. Louise Greiner acquired the firm in 1800, enticed workers to move from Meissen in 1808, and received a regional patent in 1812. After 1876 the firm became Haas and Czizek.

Johann Nikolas Weber established a porcelain factory at Klosterle in 1794. This firm was rented by Christian Noone in 1799 to distribute Volkstedt porcelain. In 1820 Count Thun assumed management of the factory. Karl Venier, as director, improved the quality of the porcelain and produced examples that were gilded richly. Important sets, such as the "Empire" set (1851) and the "Thun" service (1856), and fine figures were made during his tenure.

Christian Noone set up a new factory near Carlsbad. After Noone died in 1813, Anton Hladik took over. There was a succession of owners. The factory eventually was sold to Johann Schuldes.

Johann Wenzel, Karl Kunerle, Josef Longe, and Josef Hubel started a factory in Prague in 1795. At first stoneware was made. Later the plant became the largest porcelain factory in Bohemia. In 1800, the firm was called Hubel and Company. It was sold to J.E. Hubel in 1810 who took in his son in 1820. Many figures were made during the 1840s for the wealthy bourgeois of Prague.

Friedrich Hocke established the Pirkenhammer factory in 1803 near Carlsbad. He sold out to Johann Fischer and Christof Reichenbach in 1811. By 1830, this was a fine Bohemian porcelain factory. All kinds of subjects were used on their porcelains: views, flowers, mythological, antique, and allegorical themes. Lithophane bedside lamps, dessert dishes, vases, and figures were made.

Christian Fischer became managing director in 1831. Fischer bought out Reichenbach in 1846. From that date until 1853, Reichenbach was the sole proprietor. In 1853 Ludwig von Mieg, Reichenbach's son-in-law, entered the business. The name was changed to Fischer and Mieg from 1857 to 1918 and used after both Fischer and Mieg died. After 1875 the wares became less important artistically and more practical. In 1918, the firm operated at Branch Pirkenhammer by Opiag. The name eventually was changed to Epiag and existed until 1945.

By the mid-19th century, there were thirty new porcelain factories in Bohemia. Forty-three factories existed by the end of the century.

References: E. Poche, *Bohemian Porcelain*, Artia, 1954.

Museums: Industrial Art Museum, Prague, Czechoslovakia; Museum of Bohemian Porcelain in the State Castle, Klosterle, Czechoslovakia.

Basket
  7″ d, applied roses, 2 putti holding cornucopia, hexafoil shapes **105.00**
  7⅞″ d, applied flowers and pierced rim bowl, triangular scroll base, 3 applied putti playing musical instruments **50.00**
Cabaret Set, tray, coffeepot, milk jug, cov sugar, 4 cups and saucers, painted roses, ribbon borders **135.00**

Sweetmeat Dishes, 3″ h, pink florals, blue rims, Pirkenhammer, pr, (A) $40.00.

Cabinet Cup, 2¾″ h, painted castle on hill in landscape (A) **55.00**
Cabinet Cup and Saucer, turquoise ground, painted domestic scene, tooled gilt borders, "blue S," Schlaggenwald (A) **250.00**
Cabinet Cup and Stand
  Painted house in landscape panel, gilt ground, palmettes, "Souvenir d' Auerbach" (A) **45.00**
  Painted musicians and peasants panel reserve, dark red and gilt ground . **100.00**
Coffee Service, pot, 6¼″ h, cov milk jug, cov sugar box, 2 coffee cans and saucers, painted mythological figures in landscape with Cupid, sporting trophies cov, c1804–30 .... **575.00**
Cup and Saucer
  Gilt bird and leaves ftd cup, gilt butterflies saucer, gilt and scalloped rims, c1865, Pirkenhammer **50.00**
  Gilt broad leaf trailing vine, white ground, Elbogen (A) **110.00**

Two painted birds under draped cloth, green ground, gilt int., inscribed **130.00**

Figure, 5½" h, lady in regional costume standing by tree stump, sq base, gold edge **80.00**

Jug, 6⅛" h, painted goatherder panel, playing pipes to companion, dressed in "Costume di Triventi" reserve, dark red and gilt ground, script title **70.00**

Pipe, 5¾" l, painted panel, Eastern woman fetching water **60.00**

Plate, Pirkenhammer
7" d
Multicolored birds, insects, and flowers **25.00**
Multicolored hp florals **32.00**
8" d, floral design, gilt birds and insects **48.00**
9" d
Birds, butterflies, and bees, florals, ivory ground, gold trim **20.00**
Butterfly center, gilt florals **35.00**

Sugar, 5" h, attached underplate, brown body, cobalt bands, gold filagree overlay, Pirkenhammer **62.00**

Tea Service, 2 teapots, jug, cov sugar, 12 cups and saucers, Oriental figures, multicolored buildings and foliage and gilt, cov missing (A) **320.00**

Vase
10½" h, applied gold flowers, white ground, c1850, Pirkenhammer, pr **85.00**
19" h
Blue flowers, green leaves, cream ground, neck ring, ftd, Pirkenhammer **325.00**
Painted Renaissance portraits, heavy gold relief foliage, Pirkenhammer, pr **550.00**

1760 - 76

BOW

East End of London, England
c1741–1776

History: The Bow factory, one of the earliest English porcelain factories, was located in what is now the East End of London from c1741–1776. Mostly utilitarian wares that imitated the im-

ported Chinese porcelains were made; underglaze-blue designs also were made. Bow's porcelains were the soft paste variety, incorporating a high percentage of bone ash in the paste mixture.

In the 1760s and 1770s numerous decorative figures and animal models were made. The back usually had a square hole to hold a metal candle holder. Bow figures were press molded and thick walled.

Bow pieces of the 1760s are not marked with a true factory mark. They usually have the painter's mark or a reference number painted under the base. Later pieces often have an anchor and dagger mark painted in red enamel.

Bow porcelains found a willing audience in American buyers. Many pieces were exported. American clay also was utilized to manufacture some of the wares.

References: Elizabeth Adams & David Redstone, *Bow Porcelain*, Faber & Faber, 1981; Egan Mew, *Old Bow China*, Dodd, Mead & Co., 1909; H. Tait, British Museum Catalogue of the 1959 Bow Exhibition, Faber & Faber.

Basket, pr
6⅛" l, blue pagoda scene in center, floral and cell diaper border, basket molded ext., floral and loop handles, c1765–70 .... **550.00**
8" d, "Quail" pattern, 2 quail under flowering branch, repaired, c1760 (A) **175.00**

Beaker, 2¾" h, white, applied flowering branches, c1752 (A) **215.00**

Bowl, 8" d, blue paneled florals, white ground, c1753, $3,500.00.

Bowl
3½" d
Blue painted trailing vine, c1754 (A) **275.00**
Blue painted trailing vine, c1760 (A) **150.00**
"Golfer & Caddy" pattern, blue painted Chinese man and boy

under pine branch, wavy border, dbl ogee shaped, c1760 (A) ... **182.00**
4½" d, blue trailing vine, white ground, c1770 (A) **165.00**

Candlestick

7⅝" h, pr

Seated putto holding flowers supporting foliage nozzles, 4 ftd scroll molded base, multicolored enamel, c1762 (A) **455.00**

Seated woman holding mandolin, lamb at side, man playing bagpipe, dog at feet, candle socket, rococo scrolled and pierced, bases, bocage background, multicolored, repaired **350.00**

8⅜" h, figural putto wearing wreath and garland, carrying basket, multicolored bocage supporting blue and gold flower form nozzle, pierced scroll edged base, green and gold accents, c1760–65, "iron-red anchor and dagger," pr (A) **715.00**

8⅞" h, molded yellow finches perched on flowering branches, single stalk and petal nozzle, oval base with dog, multicolored, c1762, pr (A) **1,555.00**

9¾" h

Molded with bird in fruiting tree and bird in nest, tole peinte support candle nozzle, pierced oval base, applied flowers, multicolored, c1755 (A) **880.00**

Two birds perched on flowering branches, base with dog and sheep, tole peinte stalks candle nozzle, circ grass mtd base, c1755, pr (A) **1,045.00**

11½" h, modeled as 2 birds perched on flowering tree with nest and 3 young, pierced molded dog base, tole peinte branches with flower heads candle nozzle, multicolored, c1755 (A) **682.00**

Centerpiece, 2 piece, blue Grecian motif, reticulated border **110.00**

Coffee Cup and Saucer, white prunus molded ground, c1755 (A) **133.00**

Cream Jug

Blue flowers, branches, and rockwork, white ground, c1770 (A) ... **66.00**

Blue Oriental scene of buildings on islands, white ground, c1770 (A) . **66.00**

Cup and Saucer, 3 molded prunus branches, c1755 (A) **175.00**

Dish

7" d, seated Chinese lady with fan and incense burner painted center, fluted rim, radiating panels of emblems, flowers, and landscapes,

floral sprigs on reverse, c1758–60 (A) **555.00**

7½" d, shallow depressions in center, Chinese designs, powder blue, c1760, pr **1,500.00**

7⅝" d, famille rose phoenix in flight, another perched on shrubs, floral border, c1750–53 (A) **330.00**

8⅝" w, bunches of fruit painted center, molded and vine colored border, gilt line rim, c1768, "iron-red anchor and dagger," pr (A) **822.00**

8¾" d, reserved center roundel of Chinese man in boat, blue ground, fan shaped panels of river scenes and floral roundels rim, scalloped edge, c1758 (A) **275.00**

9½" l, pale blue ground, oval, circ, and fan reserves painted with Oriental water scenes, painted seaweed forms on reverse, octagonal, c1760, pr **1,500.00**

10¼" l, enameled bouquets of summer flowers on molded puce veined cabbage leaf, c1770 (A) .. **465.00**

12¼" w, iron-red, blue, green, and gilt Oriental style quail pattern and plants, band of iron-red scrolling foliage with gilt flower heads rim, c1755 (A) **880.00**

Egg Cup, 2½" h, two half panels of flowers, powder blue ground, c1760, "pseudo Oriental" mark (A) **842.00**

Figure

2½" h, seated cat, puce stripes, yellow eyes, oval flower painted base, c1756 (A) **1,210.00**

3¾" h, white figure of gentleman seated on rock, playing flute **95.00**

3⅞" h, seated child, blue and yellow scarf, puce vase balanced on knee (A) **145.00**

4¾" h, harlequin playing bagpipe, playing cards on trousers, Columbine in flowered apron playing hurdy-gurdy, white rockwork base, c1755, pr (A) **1,210.00**

5⅛" h, sphinx, brown fur marks, tasseled yellow saddlecloth, rococo scroll molded base, c1750 (A) ... **325.00**

5¼" h, white seated sportsman, gun on arm, tricorn hat, sq mound base, c1752 (A) **310.00**

5⅜" h, putto draped in flowers, basket of flowers, circ mound base, c1760 **100.00**

5⅝" h, "Tasting" man seated on barrel, dressed in rose-pink jacket and flowered breeches, bottle in left hand, goblet in right, c1755 .....**1,200.00**

5¾" h, multicolored "The Continents," America, Africa, Asia, and Europe on pierced plinths, bocage background, c1765, "red anchor and dagger," set of 4 . . . . **500.00**

5⅞", h, seated "Sight" holding looking glass, flowered dress, "Smell" in flowered dress with apron of flowers, green washed molded base, c1756, pr (A) **2,150.00**

6½" h

Cook holding plate of ham and chicken, multicolored period clothes, tree stump on circ flowered base, c1762 (A) **665.00**

"Father Time" seated on globe, holding hourglass and scythe, puce scroll base, applied flowers, c1755–60 . . . . **525.00**

Seated multicolored Cupid, basket of fruit, quiver, and flowering tree, 4 ftd scroll molded base, c1768 (A) **233.00**

6¾" h, white standing peddler leaning on stick, wares on back, sq base, c1755–56 (A) **985.00**

6⅞"

"New Dancer" boy, white coat, large multicolored flower branches, applied flowers base, "red anchor and dagger" (A) . . . **315.00**

White "La Bonne Aventure" old man stooping, reading palm of lady in flowers, irreg base, applied flower (A) **1,105.00**

7" h

Man playing flute, seated, woman playing mandolin, period clothes, bocage background, scroll molded and ftd base, c1765, "iron-red anchor," pr (A) **2,200.00**

Minerva wearing blue and gilt helmet, breastplate, and puce cloak, holding shield with mask, sq marbleized base, c1758, "blue cross and iron-red anchor" (A) **.1,100.00**

7¼" h, sailor, black tricorn, blue and yellow jacket, pink striped culottes, outstretched arms, 2 bales on scroll molded base, applied flowers and puce accents, c1760 (A) **3,160.00**

7½" h

Male and female dancers, multicolored period clothes, rococo scroll base, applied flowers, c1758–60 (A) **3,060.00**

Youth leaning on spade, offering bunch of flowers, companion holding basket of flowers in apron, multicolored, bocage base, c1765, "blue cross and dot," pr (A) **1,170.00**

7⅞" h, "Liberty" holding bird's nest, "Matrimony" before tree stumps,

flowered clothes, pierced scroll molded base, c1768, pr (A) **410.00**

8" h

Mercury leaning on casket and bales, holding bag of gold and caduceus, flowered scroll base, damaged, c1760 (A) **222.00**

2 children, multicolored Turkish costumes, bocage background, 4 ftd scrolled base, c1765, "blue crescent" (A) **935.00**

8¼" h

Cupid reaching for nesting bird, hound and quiver on scroll ftd base, bocage background, multicolored, c1765, "iron-red anchor and dagger," pr (A) **275.00**

Man and woman seated on flowering multicolored tree stumps, period clothes, man with bird on knee, woman with bird in cage, scroll molded ftd base, c1760, "iron-red anchor and dagger," pr (A) **1,045.00**

Owlet perched on branch, circ base, brown accents, white ground, c1760 (A) **4,320.00**

8⅝" h, 9" w, white glazed lion and lioness, oval mound base, c1753, pr (A) **12,210.00**

9" h

Boy in breeches and jacket next to multicolored basket, bocage background, pierced scroll ftd base, damaged, c1765, "blue M" (A **462.00**

Two birds perched on flowering trees with nest, molded dog, sheep, and applied florals pierced base, multicolored, c1755, pr (A) **880.00**

10" h, boy or girl dancing on high scroll base, native dress, flowering maybush behind, multicolored, c1765, pr (A) **765.00**

Jug, 3¼" h, famille rose enamels of peony from puce rock, c1750 (A) . . **875.00**

Mug

3½" h, painted famille rose colors, pink chrysanthemum and rockwork, green diaper border reserved with half flower heads, c1752 (A) **860.00**

4" h, Chinese pattern, powder blue decoration, c1760 . . . . **500.00**

Pickle Dish

3⅜" l, blue painted scattered flower sprays, feathered border, leaf shaped (A) **90.00**

4" w, painted flowers and grape, blue leaf shape, molded veins, serrated edge, c1760 (A) **140.00**

4¾" w, circ medallions of river scenes

and grapes, blue ground, serrated edge, leaf shaped, c1770 (A) **250.00**

Plate

6½" d, "Quail" pattern, 2 multicolored quails in center, Chinese style, rust border, c1760 .... **950.00**

6½" h, blue painted boy jumping next to seated lady on rockwork, ribboned emblems, diaper and demi-floret border, c1760 (A) **246.00**

7⅛" d, blue ground, center panel of Oriental island scene reserve, circ and fan shaped panels of landscapes and flowers border, octagonal, c1765, "pseudo Oriental" mark (A) **440.00**

7⅞" d, rose, yellow, and blue sprays of blossoms, shaded green leaves, insects, and sprigs, brown rim, octagonal, 1756–58 (A) **550.00**

8¼" d

Blue painted pierced rock, shrubs, and scrolling border, octagonal, c1750–55, pr (A) **100.00**

Blue painted rock, fence and flowers in garden, flower head border (A) **95.00**

8⅞" d

Painted Oriental sprays and sprigs in center, prunus molded rim, c1750–53 (A) **330.00**

White with applied prunus sprays on rims, c1752, pr (A) **435.00**

9" d

Famille rose rock, peonies, and bamboo, octagonal **80.00**

"Quail" pattern, painted pr of quail and flowering branches, iron-red wreath border, c1755–60 ..... **195.00**

9⅛" d

Oriental scene of pagoda and river, cobalt blue, pink, and green, c1761, rim chip **25.00**

Transfer and enameled mandarin figures in center and border, c1765–68, pr (A) **410.00**

9¼" d, painted center of blue boat in river, shaped panels of Oriental style florals and riverscapes border, c1755 (A) **242.00**

9⅜" d, blue and white centers of Oriental lady and boy, jumping by flowering trees, Oriental symbols, diapering, and flower heads border, 1765, pr (A) **415.00**

Salt, 3⅞" w, scallop shell shape, int. painted with grapes, blue ground, dashes on ext., 3 ftd, c1765 (A) **100.00**

Sauce Boat

3¾" h, leaf molded, blue grapes, painted grapes int., c1760 (A) **210.00**

5½" l, fluted sides, molded with foli-

age and painted famille rose and chrysanthemums, flat base (A) ... **265.00**

6⅞" w, painted flowers, molded scroll, foliage cartouches, insect on lip, tulip int., iron-red oval loop foot, c1770 (A) **400.00**

7" l, blue painted "Desirable Residence" pattern, ribboned scrolls int., paneled diaper rim, c1753 (A) **260.00**

7" w, blue painted bird on flowering tree, diaper border, dbl lipped and handled, c1750 (A) **580.00**

7⅜" l

Blue and white "Desirable Residence" pattern, fluted, scrolls and trellis diaper border int., c1760, "imp B" **180.00**

Puce, blue, green, and yellow florals, puce feathered rim, c1765 (A) **235.00**

7¾" l, molded floral cartouches, diamond pattern ground, blue painted sprays and diaper border, c1762 (A) **275.00**

7⅞" l, blue and white flowers, diaper border int., molded flowers ext., c1765 .... **100.00**

8¼" l, blue painted "Desirable Residence" pattern, house between rocks, trees, and poles, ribboned emblem and diaper border int., barbed rim, 3 paw feet, c1750–52 **600.00**

8⅝" l, blue painted "Desirable Residence" side pattern, Chinese scrolls and diaper border int., leaf shaped, c1752 (A) **275.00**

Spoon Tray, 6¾" w, famille rose colors with flying birds and chrysanthemums from rockwork enamels, brown rim, c1755 (A) **495.00**

Teabowl and Saucer, chrysanthemums and trailing blossoms, famille rose colors, hairline on rim, c1755, "iron-red 33" **300.00**

Vase

4¾" h, flower sprays in scroll molded cartouches, applied flowers at neck, spirally molded flared foot, turquoise and yellow, c1755 (A) .. **66.00**

7" h, spirally molded urn, 2 mask handles supporting orange trees, blue and puce, c1755, pr (A) **495.00**

7½" h, enamel painted bouquet and scattered sprays, c1760–65 (A) ... **520.00**

7¾" h, spirally molded campana shape, supporting trees, applied flowers, mask handles, puce, turquoise, and gilt, c1750, pr (A) ... **440.00**

9¾" h, cov, applied multicolored florals and foliage, blue and puce petals band, pierced body, mask handles with florals, domed floral

applied cov, finial missing, c1765
(A) **335.00**
Wine Taster, 3¼" h, blue painted stylized flower, cell border, circ, foliate
handle, damaged, c1760 (A) **86.00**

BRISTOL

1770-81

Bristol, England
c1749–1752, soft paste
c1770–1781, hard paste

History: Soft paste porcelain called "Lund's Bristol" was made in Bristol, c1749–52. Pieces show
a strong Chinese influence. There usually was no
factory mark. Hence, it is easily confused with
early Worcester porcelains. In 1752 the Worcester Porcelain Company, under Dr. John Wall,
purchased the Bristol soft paste factory and relocated it at Warmstry House in Worcester.

In 1770 a second porcelain factory at Bristol
was established by William Cookworthy. This
venture made hard paste porcelain, rather than
soft paste. Richard Champion continued the factory between 1774 and 1778. A group of Staffordshire potters bought Champion's patent for
hard paste porcelain and formed the New Hall
Company, closing the Bristol factory in 1781.

Bristol porcelains of the 1770–78 period are
rare. Tea services, dessert services, and dinner
wares were made with simple floral patterns.
Some gilding was used. Figures and vases were
decorated with florals too. The factory is best
known for its oval biscuit floral encrusted
plaques.

Much Bristol porcelain was unmarked. Sometimes a cross in blue was accompanied by a
painter's or gilder's mark. Copies of Dresden
crossed swords also were used on some Bristol
pieces.

References: F.S. Mackenna, *Cookworthy's Plymouth & Bristol Porcelains*, F. Lewis, 1947; F. Severne, *Chapmion's Bristol Porcelain*, F. Lewis,
1947; Dr. B. Watney, *English Blue & White Porcelain of the 18th Century*, Faber & Faber, rev.
ed, 1973.

Museums: Gardiner Museum of Ceramic Art, Toronto, Canada.

Collecting Hints: Fake Bristol porcelains ofter
bearing the cross mark with a date are in the
marketplace.

Barber Bowl, 10" d, blue painted center
scene of ships at sea, 2 bands of stylized flower heads and loops border,
c1740 (A) **1,295.00**
Basin, 13" d, Delft, painted blue, iron-
red and green scene of 2 cockerels
near shrubs in roundel surrounded by
insects, foliate border, c1725 (A) ... **400.00**
Basket, pierced lattice sides, painted
spray of flowers and sprigs int., blue
flowers and leaves ext., dbl branch
handles, c1770–72 (A) **640.00**
Bleeding Bowl, Delft, painted center
bowl of flowers, sponged rim, shell
handle, c1720 (A) **2,280.00**
Bowl, Delft
7⅞" d, mang and blue Oriental river
landscape ext., inscribed center,
formal border (A) **385.00**
8⅝" d, painted bird on branch int.,
radiating geometric borders, c1730
(A) **370.00**
9" d, inscribed "Success to the King
of Prussia," mang and blue continuous Oriental landscape ext.,
c1760 (A) **260.00**
10½" d, painted squirrel in fruiting
vine, cracked, c1730 A) **230.00**
10⅝" d, polychrome Oriental style
buildings ext., blue flowers and
trellis int., c1740 (A) **176.00**
11⅞" d, blue trees and terrace, green
and mang balloon, flowering plants
ext., c1740 (A) **182.00**
13¾" d, Documentary int., blue
painted center scene of farmer
ploughing, inscribed, panels of
birds and rockwork reserved on
diaper ground ext., c1735 (A) ...**11,500.00**
Butter Boat, 4½" l, molded fruit and
leaves, painted floral spray and puce
scrolls under spout, loop handle,
c1775 (A) **616.00**
Candlestick, 2¼" h, Delft, blue painted
scalloped border, conc rings on
knobbed stem, scrolling foliage at ft.
c1750 (A) **600.00**
Charger, Delft
13" d, blue, green, and yellow central
tulip with flower heads, conc cartouche, stylized flower heads border, blue sponged rim, c1730 (A) . **435.00**
13⅛" d, three tulips in polychrome,
blue and yellow cartouche, blue
dash border, c1700 (A) **435.00**
13¼" d, polychrome scene of Adam
and Eve, dash and roundel border,
c1740 .... **895.00**
Cream Jug, 3¾" h, painted green festoons, gilt rims, lobed, c1775 (A) ... **615.00**
Cup and Saucer
Central iron-red banded armorial, gilt

cable pattern, gilt dentil rim, c1775 (A) **103.00**

Green swags, gilt line border, c1820 (A) **200.00**

Painted scattered flowers and sprigs, blue ribbon band with gilt lines border, c1775 (A) **380.00**

Polychrome garlands, gilt rims, c1775 (A) **125.00**

Dish, Delft

11⅞" d, blue chrysanthemums, bamboo, and insect, pr (A) **300.00**

12¼" d, blue painted lovers in landscape, sponged trees (A) **175.00**

13⅛" d, iron-red and green pagoda and plants by river in cartouche, pagoda, flowers, and insects border, c1730 (A) **290.00**

13½" d, peacock perched on rock with fly, diaper and floral paneled border, mid 18th C (A) **87.00**

13¾" d, blue painted center scene of Oriental harpooning flying fish, fish and flower sprays border, c1760 (A) **460.00**

Dessert Dish, 10" l, painted swags, sprays, and sprigs, blue, lilac, and gilt "dbl ribbon" border, diamond shaped, c1775, pr (A) **615.00**

Figure

5½" h, Delft, blue tinted recumbent sheep and lamb, mang accents, green-wash rocky base, mid 18th C (A) **2,200.00**

6¾" h, Delft, lady's shoe, molded buckle blue trim, c1760 (A) **550.00**

10⅞" h, "Air" in robe standing on pink and yellow cloud base with putto's head, c1775 (A) **842.00**

Flower Brick, 5¾" w, Delft, blue painted Oriental man fishing under tree, pierced top, c1740 (A) **230.00**

Jar, Delft

5½" h

Blue, green, and iron-red birds, flanked by vases of flowers, whorls and stylized foliage bands, acron shape, dbl handles, c1740 (A) **930.00**

Blue, green, and iron-red groups of flowers, scroll borders, dbl twisted handles, c1730 (A) **500.00**

6¼" h, Green, red, and blue exotic birds in foliage, dbl twist handles, c1730 (A) **410.00**

Jug, 5" h, painted flower spray with insects and dragonfly, bearded mask spout, c1775 (A) **160.00**

Mug, 3" h, painted pendant bands of pink roses, gilt line borders, blue and gilt scalloped border bands, barrel shaped, c1775 (A) **585.00**

Plaque, 4⅞" d, applied white bisque

baskets of flowers, lilac ground, c1775, pr (A) **460.00**

Plate

8⅝" d, Delft, blue painted center scene of sailing ships in harbor, looped cartouche, c1740 (A) **1,650.00**

8¾" d

Delft, blue tasseled center panel, 4 leaf shaped border panels of Oriental fisherman, reserved on powdered mang ground, c1755, pr **450.00**

Delft, polychrome flowers growing from rockwork with fence, rim chipped, c1770 (A) **197.00**

Light cobalt dolphin in centers, precious objects on borders, damaged, mid 18th C, pr (A) **350.00**

Polychrome Oriental and pagoda in garden, pinecone and scroll borders, lobed rims, c1760, pr **250.00**

8⅞" d, Delft

Two cockerels in garden under pillar and foliage, blue and white, stylized foliage and rockwork border, c1750 (A) **96.00**

Yellow and blue cockerel between mang sponged trees, c1730 (A) **822.00**

Plates, 9" d, Delft, polychrome florals, c1750-70, pr, $1,200.00.

9" d, Delft

Blue, green, and mang clumps of stylized Oriental flowers, mid 18th C (A) **95.00**

Blue painted exotic bird in plants, shaped rim, c1750 (A) **88.00**

Blue, yellow, ochre, and mang Oriental and gazebo, fluted border, scrolls and pinecones, c1760 .. **112.00**

Manganese figure near gazebo in park, c1750 (A) **260.00**

Polychrome basket of flowers, stylized flowers and diaper panels rim, c1760, pr **195.00**

9¼" d, Delft, cobalt and mang "I.L. 1768," crackle border reserved with floral panels (A) **260.00**

9⅞" d, Delft, mang flowering and scrolling foliage, c1760 (A) **137.00**

11¾" d, Delft

Blue painted Oriental fisherman with pavilion, trellis band rim, c1760 (A) **145.00**

Center painted with figure in front of pagoda, yellow, mang, and blue, scalloped rim with pinecones, light blue ground, c1760 (A) **235.00**

12" d, Delft, painted mang, green, yellow, and blue chinoiserie landscape with pavilions, c1750–60 (A) **264.00**

12¼" d, Delft, blue figure in landscape scene, pinecone and scrolling foliage border, c1760 .... **100.00**

13¼" d, Delft, cobalt mimosa sprays from circle of mimosa, rim with trellis cartouches, c1740 (A) **88.00**

Posset Pot, cov. 9" H-H, Delft, blue painted birds on branches, band of whorl and blue lines, c1730 (A) **1,865.00**

Punch Bowl, Delft

10¼" d, multicolored continuous river landscape, flying bird on int., c1760 (A) **840.00**

10½" d, ext. blue painted with flowering plants, cross-hatched diaper border, c1740–60 (A) **220.00**

11¾" d, cobalt painted insects, birds and Oriental flowers on ext., precious objects on int. cracked, c1730 (A) **260.00**

Salt, 3¼" h, Delft, washed mang, iron-red and blue borders, stylized Budda symbol well, waisted body, flared neck and foot, c1730 (A) **800.00**

Sauce Boat, 7¼" l, molded rose sprays, border of molded foliage sprays with pink accents, sprig on int., foliate scroll handle, c1775 (A) **1,170.00**

Saucer

6¾" d, painted with trailing floral swags suspended from gilt rings and puce scroll pattern, gilt dentil border, c1775 .... **125.00**

Enamel star shaped foliage swags with gilt, c1770, pr (A) **115.00**

Spoon Tray, 5⅞" l, Delft, blue painted scrolling foliage, hatched lined border reserved with flower heads, fluted hex body, c1750 (A) **475.00**

Teabowl and Saucer, multicolored festoons, brown rims, c1775 (A) **125.00**

Teapot, 5½" h, painted flower sprays

and sprigs, spherical, loop handle, leaf molded spout, repaired handle, c1755 (A) **172.00**

Vase, Delft

5" h, blue painted "Crucifixion" on front, "The Flagellation" on reverse, sunburst on foot, urn shaped, scrolling strap handles, damaged, mid 18th C **650.00**

5¾" h, blue landscape with sponged trees, urn shaped, molded masks on sides, flared foot, rim chips, c1750 (A) **308.00**

7½" h, blue painted continuous scene of European figures in landscape with sponged trees, satyr's head handles (A) **248.00**

BRITISH ROYALTY COMMEMORATIVES

Staffordshire, England
1600s–Present

History: British commemorative china dates from the 1600s, although the early pieces were rather crude in form and design. When transfer printing was developed about 1780, the likeness of the king or queen was much improved.

With coronations or jubilee celebrations of England's royalty, a great number of souvenir wares appeared on the market to commemorate the occasions. This practice started in earnest with the coronation of Queen Victoria and has been in use ever since.

The bulk of these wares were manufactured in the Staffordshire district of England. Many small potters, finding a ready market for these souvenir products, produced them well in advance of any upcoming celebration. At times this was premature. The number of pieces prepared for the coronation of Edward VIII is an excellent example. With his abdication of the throne, the coronation ware quickly became abdication ware. Since large quantities were produced and sold previously, wares for this event that never happened are not scarce.

It was not long before the major houses such as Minton, Royal Doulton, Aynsley, and Wedgwood began producing commemorative wares. Plates, jugs, pitchers, and tea sets were the popular pieces.

Transfers and decals that often featured busts of the king or queen and the consort graced most pieces. Other royal symbols used on the pieces include: crowns, dragons, royal coats of arms, national flowers, swords, sceptres, dates, messages, and initials.

Some items were issued in limited quantities and are very desirable, but the bulk of materials prepared for coronation and jubilee celebrations were mass produced and are readily available.

References: Josephine Jackson, *Fired for Royalty*, Heaton Moor, 1977; John May, *Victoria Remembered, A Royal History 1817–1861*, London, 1983; John & Jennifer May, *Commemorative Pottery 1780–1900*, Heinemann, 1972; David Rogers, *Coronation Souvenirs & Commemoratives*, Latimer New Dimensions Ltd, 1975; Sussex Commemorative Ware Centre, *200 Commemoratives*, Metra Print Enterprises, 1979; Geoffrey Warren, *Royal Souvenirs*, Orbis, 1977; Audrey B. Zeder, *British Royal Commemoratives With Prices*, Wallace-Homestead, 1986.

Collectors Clubs: Commemorative Collectors Society, 25 Farndale Close, Long Eaton, United Kingdom, NG 10 3PA, $20.00 per year, *Journal of the Commemorative Collectors Society*; Royalty Collectors Association of North America, 30 East 60 Street, Suite 803, New York, NY 10022. Annual membership of $15.00 includes 3 issues of the newsletter, *Sceptre*.

Museums: Brighton Museum, Brighton, England; London Museum, Kensington Palace, London, England; Victoria & Albert Museum, London, England.

Collecting Hints: Some collectors specialize in just one monarch while others include several different ones. Another approach is to collect only pieces for special occasions, such as coronations, jubilees, marriages, investitures, births, or memorials. Others specialize in one specific form such as mugs, teapots, spoons, etc.

Since the marriage of Prince Charles in 1981 to Lady Diana Spencer and the birth of their two sons, a whole new area of collecting emphasis has begun.

Queen Elizabeth II
  Bell, 4½" h, Silver Jubilee, multicolored coat of arms, Kings and Queens of England on reverse, gold crown handle, "Aynsley" 25.00
  Bowl, 6" l, 4½" w, Coronation, multicolored decal of Elizabeth and flags, "Mid-Winter, Staffordshire, England, Semi-Porcelain" 20.00
  Cup, Silver Jubilee, gold lion handles, color decal of Royal Coach, gold trim, "Paragon" 65.00
  Cup and Saucer, Coronation
    Color portrait of Elizabeth 25.00
    Sepia portrait and colored decal, gold rim, commemoration inside cup rim, "Aynsley" 70.00
  Jug, Coronation
    4¾" h, black portrait of Elizabeth, flower sprigs, "Royal Worcester"   80.00

Raised design, "Royal Doulton" . .   100.00
Loving Cup, 11" h, Coronation, portraits of Elizabeth I and II, emb ships from Armada, flags and crests, "Royal Doulton" 500.00
Mug, Coronation
  4¼" h, Guyatt pattern of unicorn, black, gold trim, Queen's name in inside rim, "Wedgwood" . . .   135.00
  4½" h, pink, yellow, and black coat of arms by Eric Ravilious, "Wedgwood" 125.00
  Silhouette of Elizabeth, "Burleigh"   18.00
Pitcher, Coronation
  5½" h, white and brown, portrait of Queen Elizabeth and Coronation, June 2, 1953, unmarked . .   35.00
  6½" h
    Brown portrait of Elizabeth enclosed in colored flags, raised dec, Windsor on reverse, "Royal Doulton" 160.00
    Picture of Elizabeth on front, emb Windsor Castle on reverse, "Royal Doulton" 135.00
Plaques, 5" w, Coronation, light blue jasper, Elizabeth and Philip, creamware oval frames, oak leaf and acorn molding, pr, "Wedgwood" .   350.00
Plate, 10" d, Coronation, decal of coats of arms, "Castleton" 25.00
Tea Set, Coronation, teapot, creamer, and sugar, white cameos of Elizabeth and Philip in wreaths, blue jasper ground, "Wedgwood" 300.00
Teapot
  9" l, 4½" h, white cameo of Elizabeth on front, Philip on reverse in wreaths, blue jasper ground, imp "WEDGWOOD" 210.00
  9" l, 5¼" h, Coronation, sepia portrait, gold dec, blue ground, "Ringstone, Ltd" 70.00
  9" l, 5¼" h, Coronation, sepia portrait, colored and white dec, gold ground, "Sadler" 70.00
Charles, Prince of Wales, mug, 5" h, Investiture, gold inscriptions, dates, plumes, and laurel wreaths, black ground, "Wedgwood" 60.00
King George VI
  Baby Bowl, 6¼" d, Coronation, sepia portraits of George and Elizabeth, red and blue flags, unmarked 50.00
  Cup, 6" d, Coronation, multicolored dec, gold trim, brown lion handles, "Paragon" 125.00
  Plate, Coronation
    9" d, sepia portraits of George and Elizabeth, red and blue flags, beige band, "Shelley" 55.00

10" d, color portrait of George, gold
rim . . . . Coronation **28.00**
Scuttle Mug, Coronation, multico-
lored decal of George and Eliza-
beth, unmarked **35.00**

**Edward VIII, mug, Coronation, multico-
lored decal, dated May, 1939, Minton,
$25.00.**

King Edward VIII
Beaker
4" h, Coronation, sepia portrait, red
and blue flags, dates, and initials
on reverse, "Shelley" **45.00**
4⅛" h, Coronation, sepia portrait,
colored flags, national flowers,
and coat of arms, gold rim,
"Aynsley" **55.00**
4½" h, white cameo portrait, pink
ground **45.00**
Bowl, 7¼" d, Abdication, multico-
lored flags and crown around sepia
portrait of Edward, abdication date,
"Sovereign" **70.00**
Creamer and Sugar, Coronation, col-
ored flags around sepia portraits,
gold trim, "Kensington Ware" . . . **35.00**
Cup, Coronation, decal of Edward,
floral outline at top, dbl handles
outlined in gold, "Anchor China,
Bridgewood, England" **45.00**
Cup and Saucer, Coronation
Multicolored decal of Edward,
"Royal Albert" **45.00**
Sepia portait of Edward, red and
blue flags, crown, date, and ini-
tials on reverse, "Shelley" **50.00**
Mug
2⅞" h, Coronation, sepia portrait,
colored flags and crown **30.00**
3" h, 5" d, Coronation, multico-
lored coat of arms, brown lion
handles, gold trim, "Paragon" . **100.00**

3¼" h, Coronation, portrait of Edward, "Royal Arms, and St.
George, Burleigh Ware" **70.00**
3¾" h, Coronation, color portrait,
multiple flags and gold rim,
"Made in England" **20.00**
4" h, Coronation, portrait of Edward
in coronation robes **18.00**
4¼" h, Abdication, sepia portrait,
color dec, "The Uncrowned
King," accession and abdication
dates, unmarked, hairline **55.00**
Coronation, decal of Edward on
front, cream body, crest on reverse, "British Pottery Manufac-
tures Federation" **30.00**
Coronation, sepia decal of lion, un-
icorn, unmarked **35.00**
Plate, Coronation
6½" d, sepia portrait of Edward, red
and blue flags, commemoration
and flowers, octagonal, "Shel-
ley" **36.00**
8½" d, sepia portrait of Edward,
colored flags at top, cream at bottom, gold trim, sq, cut cornes,
"J. & G. Meakin" **30.00**
9" d
Color portrait, red and blue border, emb flowers, "J. Maddock
& Sons" **44.00**
Relief of bust of Edward **20.00**
10" d, blue and white bust of King,
detailed blue and white border,
"Copeland-Spode" **120.00**
Teapot, 7½" l, 5" h, Coronation,
beige portrait, colored dec and gold
trim **65.00**
King George V
Beaker, 4" h, Coronation, sepia portrait of George on front, Mary on
reverse, "Royal Doulton" **50.00**
Bowl, Coronation
4⅝" d, colored portraits of George
and Mary in ovals, flags, crown,
and commemoration on reverse,
gold trim, unmarked **38.00**
7⅝" d, multicolored portraits of
George and Mary, flags, flowers,
and "Long May They Reign,"
fluted edge **30.00**
Bust
4" h, Coronation, parian, George in
navy uniform, Mary, pr **120.00**
5½" h, Ascension, bisque bust,
multicolored and gold glazed
base, ascension dates on reverse,
"Arcadian" **75.00**
Cup and Saucer
Coronation, hp enameled portrait,
unmarked **65.00**
Jubilee, color portraits of George

and Mary, arms, flags, flowers, and world map, list of events of reign, "Alma Ware" **50.00**

Decanter, 10½" h, Coronation, emb King on cream flags, green ground, beige trim, "Copeland-Spode" ... **120.00**

Dish, 5" sq, Silver Jubilee, color portraits of George and Mary joined by Union Jack, silver trim, shell handles, "Shelley" **25.00**

Loving Cup, 10" h, Silver Jubilee, molded and multicolored busts of George and Mary with flags, reverse with St. George and Windsor Castle, c1935 (A) **335.00**

Mug, Coronation, black and white portraits of George and Mary, multicolored flags, arms, flowers, birth, marriage, and coronation dates .. **50.00**

Pitcher, 4" h, Coronation, photos of George, Mary, and Royal Crest ... **30.00**

Plate

5⅝" d, Silver Jubilee, sepia portraits of George and Mary, colored flags, crown, flowers, and "Empire on Which the Sun Never Sets," "Aynsley" **40.00**

7½" h, Coronation, colored portraits of George and Mary, open basket rim, unmarked **65.00**

8¾" d, Coronation, black portraits of George and Mary, multicolored flags, pink rose border, gold trim, "Cauldon Ltd" **40.00**

9" d, Coronation, colored portraits of George, Mary, Prince Edward, and Prime Ministers, gold trimmed scalloped edge, molded body, unmarked **112.00**

Stirrup Cup, 3½" h, Silver Jubilee, sepia portraits of George and Mary, colored dec, silver trim, dbl handles, "Paragon" **150.00**

Tea Tile, 10¼" d, Coronation, blue and white portraits of George and Mary **45.00**

Teapot, 8¼" l, 5" h, Silver Jubilee, sepia portraits of George and Mary, colored trim, "England" **45.00**

King Edward VII

Beaker, 3¾" h, Coronation

Multicolored portraits of Edward and Alexandra on front, Borough of Eastbourne on reverse, gold trim, "Foley China" **45.00**

Purple portraits of Edward and Alexandra, "Royal Doulton" **75.00**

Creamer, 4½" h, Coronation, multicolored decals of Edward and Alexandra **65.00**

Cup and Saucer

Coronation, multicolored portraits of Edward and Alexandra, gold trim, "Royal Doulton" **85.00**

Marriage, purple dec of Edward and Alexandra, "A. & C." **200.00**

Demitasse Cup and Saucer, Coronation, portraits of Edward and Alexandra, gold trim, four sided, "Royal Doulton" **78.00**

Jug, 8" h, Coronation, stoneware, brown and tan portraits of Edward and Alexandra, "Royal Doulton" . **165.00**

Milk Jug, 3¾" h, multicolored portraits of Edward and Alexandra, unmarked **50.00**

Marriage Jug, 8½" h, blue and white portraits of Edward and Alexandra, color accents, "J. & M. P. Bell & Co." **300.00**

Mug

2½" h, multicolored coat of arms, lithophane of Edward on bottom, unmarked **75.00**

3" h

Coronation, multicolored portraits of Edward and Alexandra, handle on reverse, unmarked **55.00**

Multicolored coat of arms, Edward on one, Alexandra on other, lithophane bases, pr .. **200.00**

Plaque, 10", Memorial, blue portrait, emb border, unmarked **100.00**

Plate

7" d, Coronation, multicolored design of coronation throne and House of Lords throne, "Aynsley" **55.00**

7⅜" d, Coronation, multicolored portraits of Edward and Alexan-

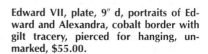

Edward VII, plate, 9" d, portraits of Edward and Alexandra, cobalt border with gilt tracery, pierced for hanging, unmarked, $55.00.

dra, coat of arms, gold trim, and border, unmarked **60.00**

8" d, Coronation, portraits of Edward and Alexandra and English crest in center, flowing blue border, unmarked **65.00**

10" d, Coronation, portraits of Edward and Alexandra, flow blue **75.00**

Scuttle Mug, 3¾" h, multicolored portraits of Edward and Alexandra, gold trim, unmarked **85.00**

Teapot, 9¾" l, 4" h, Coronation, multicolored dbl portraits of Edward and Alexandra on front, gold trim, unmarked, light crazing **125.00**

Tumbler, 4" h, Memorial, black portrait of Edward, inscription and dates, white ground, silver rim ... **65.00**

Queen Victoria

Beaker, Diamond Jubilee

3½" h, color coat of arms, gold trim, "Foley China" **50.00**

Tan and brown relief portraits, "Doulton-Lambeth" **125.00**

Bust

7¾" h, 1887 Jubilee, parian **165.00**

9" h, Jubilee, painted bisque **65.00**

Cup, 3½" h, Diamond Jubilee, black portrait of mature Victoria in wreath, "Doulton-Burslem" **100.00**

Cup, Saucer, and Dessert Plate, Diamond Jubilee, double portraits in blue, white ground, unmarked ... **100.00**

Figure

7½" h, parian, seated young Victoria, British Royal Crest on back of chair **325.00**

17" h, Jubilee, regal pose of Victoria, multicolored, gold trim, unmarked **300.00**

Flask, 8¼" h, saltglaze, molded on sides with portraits of Victoria, emblems on cushion **150.00**

Jug, Jubilee

5¼" h, cameos of young and old Victoria and credos, "Doulton-Lambeth" **200.00**

6" h, emb cream figure of seated Victoria, figures of Commonweath nations on tan, "Doulton-Lambeth" **225.00**

6½" h, beige and brown emb portraits of young and old Victoria, emb flags and banners, "Doulton-Lambeth" **175.00**

6", 7", 9" h, Diamond Jubilee, stoneware, molded portraits of young and old Queen, flowers and inscriptions, blue, green, and brown glazes, c1897, "Royal Doulton" (A) **555.00**

Mug

5" h, light brown portrait of Victoria, dates, white ground, c1887 **65.00**

5⅜" h, cream band, purple printed portraits of Victoria and Albert, copper luster ground **150.00**

7" h, puce transfer of Queen with rose, Duchess of Kent, florals, inscription, molded scroll handle, molded borders, c1837, "Read & Clementson" (A) **850.00**

Pitcher, Jubilee

6½" h, portraits of young and old Victoria, 1837–97, "Royal Doulton" **200.00**

7½" h, cobalt, olive, and brown glazes, cameos of young and old Victoria, "She Wrought Her People...," thistle and rose border, c1897, "Doulton-Lambeth" ... **150.00**

Plate, Diamond Jubilee

7" d, sepia portrait of Victoria and sporting scene, color dec, shaped gold rim, unmarked **65.00**

7", square, colored coat of arms, gold rim, "Foley China" **50.00**

9" d, blue and white portraits of young and old Victoria **70.00**

9⅜", black portrait of mature Victoria, framed in black line, gold trim, octagonal, unmarked ... **115.00**

9½" d, black portraits of Victoria and Prince of Wales, color accents, gold rim, octagonal, unmarked, light crazing **135.00**

10" d, portrait of Victoria, 1837–97, "Royal Worcester" **40.00**

10½" d, blue dec, bust of young Victoria, national flowers on border, "Royal Worcester" **90.00**

Teapot, 7" l, 5½" h, Jubilee, color coat of arms, gold trim on spout and handle, "Foley China" **100.00**

Tumbler, 4" h, Jubilee, circ portrait of Victoria, raised beads, white ground, "W & R Stoke on Trent, Carlton Ware" **65.00**

Edward V

Beaker, 3¾" h, Coronation, purple dec, ribbons and initials on reverse, "Royal Doulton" **65.00**

Cup and Saucer, Coronation, multicolored coat of arms, crown, lion, and unicorn, portraits of Edward and Alexandra, "Regent" **45.00**

William IV

Jug, 6⅝" d, purple printed half portraits of William and Adelaide, crown and union wreath (A) **165.00**

Mug

3½" h, printed portrait of King and "Reform," pink luster ground,

c1835, "Chetham & Robinson"
(A) **180.00**
5⅜" h, creamware, black portrait of
William on front, Adelaid on re-
verse (A) **140.00**

CAPODIMONTE N

Near Naples Italy
1743–1759
Buen Retiro, near Madrid, Spain
1760–1812

History: Capodimonte was a royal palace in Naples where a porcelain factory was established
in 1743. Charles III, the Bourbon King, and his
Queen, who had brought quantities of porcelain
from Meissen, were the founders. The factory
produced primarily soft paste porcelain in a
milky white color for the court.

Guiseppe Gricci was the chief modeler. His
specialties included religious subjects (madon-
nas, pietas, and holy water stoups,) snuff boxes,
and mythological figures. Gricci was in charge
when the factory created an entire room for the
king that featured porcelain panels in high relief
decorated in chinoiserie and which can be
viewed today at the Museo di Capodimonte in
Naples. Pieces usually were marked with the
armorial fleur-de-lis of the Bourbon family.

When Charles inherited the throne of Spain
and became king in 1759, he moved the factory
and workers to Madrid with him. Gricci, now
signing his works Jose Gricci also made the tran-
sition. The new factory, located on the palace
grounds was called Buen Retiro. They continued
to make soft paste porcelains similar to those
made at Capodimonte including elaborate tablewares, centerpieces, flowers, and figures. Sometimes the factory used the Bourbon fleur-de-lis
mark. An attempt to make hard paste porcelains
was made shortly before the factory closed.

When Ferdinand IV governed Italy in 1771, he
revived the royal factory. Styles were influenced
by a classical revival, inspired by the unearthed
treasures at Pompeii. Best known are the pieces
decorated with mythological reliefs.

After 1807 the factory declined and closed
several years later. In 1821 the molds and models
were sold to the Ginori factory at Doccia.

Museums: Metropolitan Museum of Art, New
York; Museo di Capodimonte, Naples, Italy;
Woodmere Art Museum, Philadelphia, PA.

Collecting Hints: Many factories in Hungary,
Germany, France, and Italy copied Capodimonte
examples. Many of the pieces on the market
today are of recent vintage.

Bowl, 5" d, raised cherubs, pastels, un-
marked (A) **30.00**
Box, cov
2" sq, relief of children at play, pastels, brass trim, blue "crowned N"
mark **100.00**
4½" l, cherubs and maidens, pastels,
unmarked (A) **25.00**
5" d, molded and painted cherubs and
roses, gilt collar on base, "crowned
N" **100.00**
5" l, 4" w, relief of children eating fruit
in garden, pastels, gilt, gold int.,
blue "crowned N" **225.00**
5½" d, 3" h, relief of angels playing
musical instruments, multicolored,
gilt bronze closure **135.00**
6½" d, raised cherubs design, lion fi-
nial, multicolored, round, blue
"crown" mark **75.00**
7" l, 5" h, scenes of cherubs at play
painting, sculpting, and viewing
world, oval, hinged cov, c1860 . . **600.00**
7¾" d, polychrome relief of allegorical scenes, brass fittings, "crowned
RE" (A) **240.00**

**Tea Service, teapot, milk jug, cov sugar
bowl, four cups and saucers, brown and
green, made in Germany, decorated in
Italy, blue "crowned N" marks,
$1,250.00.**

18" h, molded Bacchic panels on
sides and applied at corners, figural
knob, set in ebonized frame, late
19th C (A) **2,275.00**

Candelabra, 7½" h, figural, Chinese woman holding cornucopia of fruit and flowers, white, fluted nozzles, rococo base, c1755 ....**1,450.00**

Centerpiece Bowl, 20" l, 8" w, oval, mask of gargoyles form handles, cherubs in relief on sides, scalloped edge, unmarked **400.00**

Compote
    8" d, cov, relief of cherubs in landscape and scrollwork, pastels, figural cherub finial, unmarked **65.00**
    13" d, 6½" h, relief of cherubs and classical figures, shell shaped body, scroll base **115.00**

Cup, molded relief of single flowers, white, singular handle, c1750, Carlo III (A) **220.00**

Cup and Saucer
    Cherubs, various poses, multicolored, unmarked **60.00**
    Children playing in field, cherubs holding garlands, pastels, gold int **45.00**
    Classic figures in relief, unmarked .. **110.00**
    Multicolored cherubs on cup, rust colored dbl handles, raised florals on saucer, unmarked **75.00**
    Painted fruit arrangement in landscape, gilt lambrequin, colored flower borders, c1750, blue "fleur-de-lis" mark (A) **8,130.00**

Demitasse Cup and Saucer
    Maidens, dogs, trees, and mountains, pastels, branch handle, unmarked **65.00**
    Relief of ducks and herons in landscape, pastels, "crowned N" mark **68.00**
    Relief of "Phaeten Myth," pattern, gilt, branch handle, "crowned N" mark **50.00**

Glove Box, 10½" l, 5½" h, pastel colors, $500.00.

Demitasse Set, pot, tray, six ftd cups and saucers, raised allegorical scenes, gold and pastels **250.00**

Dessert Service, eight dinner plates, seven dessert plates, eight cups and saucers, painted coats of arms centers, relief figural borders, 19th C, Naples (A) **650.00**

Dish, 7" l, children in relief, triangular, unmarked **50.00**

Dresser Box, relief of cherubs and allegorical scene, pastels and gilt (A) ... **75.00**

Ewer, 14" h, semi-nude raised figures, pastels, unmarked **110.00**

Figure
    3½" h
        Five hunchback dwarf musicians and conductor, multicolored, c1860, set of 6 .... **275.00**
        Nude child, sitting on draped seat, holding gold trimmed book, "crowned N" mark **50.00**
    5" h, standing gypsy, holding tambourine, parrot on shoulder, unmarked **55.00**
    5½" h, Capitano Spavento, standing, sword at side, tree stump mound base, white, c1750, Carlo III, blue "fleur-de-lis" mark (A) **5,050.00**
    6" h
        General, wearing uniform, pastels **35.00**
        Man, playing trumpet, multicolored, blue "crowned N" mark **125.00**
        Man, playing tuba, multicolored, blue "crowned N" mark **125.00**
    7" h, 6" l, child standing between two seated children, pastels **250.00**
    7¼" h
        Huntsman, shouldered rifle, multicolored hunt clothes, tree stump mound base, c1745, Carlo III .**4,200.00**
        Couple dancing, period dress, mounted on scroll base, c1910, unmarked **175.00**
    7½" h, dancer, pastel colors, "crown and N" mark **115.00**
    8" h, Flamenco dancers, multicolored, blue "crown" mark, pr **125.00**
    8¼" h, "Carlo III" by Gricci, dressed in conventional clothes, wearing mask, dagger in belt, shaped rockwork base, white, c1750, unmarked **4,000.00**
    9" h, two horses, peasant family and children, oval base, "crowned N" mark (A) **100.00**
    9" h, 8" l, soldier, mounted on prancing horse, multicolored, blue "crowned N" mark **350.00**
    13" h, two cherubs, flower rope, multicolored, circ base **625.00**
    13" l, Roman warrior, classical scene, multicolored **225.00**
    20" h, woman, period clothes, large bonnet, circ base, blue "crowned N" mark **575.00**

Flagon, 11½" h, cov, overall relief, farm scene, putti seated on goat finial, metal thumbrest with grotesque, early 20th C, blue "crowned N" mark (A) **600.00**

Garniture Set, two rect, four 10½" l, 8½" h round troughs with draped urns, six oval ftd pedestals with pr of dancing nymphs, cream ground, gilt accents, blue "crowned N" mark, set of 12 (A) **1,100.00**

Plate, 10" d, multicolored bust of Dauphine de France, inscribed "M. ANT. ARCHES. D'AUTRICHE," blue "crowned N," $215.00.

Jewel Box
   3¾" l, 3" w, classic figures on cov, cupid scenes on each panel, cut corners, early 19th C, "crowned N" mark (A) **200.00**
   Relief scenes of cherubs at play, multicolored, dbl handles, four feet, dbl cherub finial **100.00**

Perfume Bottle, 3" h, cherubs in garden, pastels, blue "crown" mark **100.00**

Plaque, 9½" l, 6" h, relief of battle scene, pastels, gilt **150.00**

Plate
   10" d
      Allegorical scene, semi-nude bathers beside brook, flowered border, blue "crowned N" mark .. **100.00**
      Border of raised classical figures, multicolored, "crowned N" mark **200.00**
   12" d, florals, raised cherub borders, c1875, unmarked, set of 12 ....**2,800.00**

Snuff Box
   3¼" w, molded pattern of floral diaperwork, int. cov with painting of lady admiring portrait, cartouche shape, red-gold mounts, c1750 . .**2,000.00**
   3⅜" d, ext. molded with multicolored overlapping shells and coral, int.

cov painted with Middle Eastern figures at seaside, body int. gilded, reeded contemporary mounts, c1750, Carlo III (A) **8,850.00**

Tankard, 6" h, multicolored allegorical figures, gold wash int., figural handle (A) **110.00**

Tureen
   15" H-H, matching undertray, relief of classical women and cherubs with foliage, fruit and flowers in colors, "crown, N & Capo-Di-Monte, Italy" mark **240.00**
   8½" h, cov, tray, overall relief of classical scenes, Bacchus finial (A) ... **225.00**

Urn, 8" h, pastels and gilt, $150.00.

Urn
   7" h, champleve, dore bronze trim, c1890, unmarked **200.00**
   9½" h, relief painted allegorical scenes, angels and chariots, scroll handles, 19th C, Italy, pr (A) **100.00**
   13" h, cov, continuous relief of classical scene, dbl handles, acorn finial, domed cov, pr (A) **225.00**
   14" h, cov, raised figures on body, dolphin handles, c1870 ....**1,400.00**

Vase
   8" h, cherub decorations, multicolored, molded lion heads, pr **150.00**
   11" h, cherubs in various scenes, pastel colors, pedestal bases, unmarked, pr **125.00**

Wine Cup, 3¾" h, relief scene of satyrs accompanying Bacchus in vineyard, raised flowers on handle, c1860, "crowned N" mark **225.00**

AUSTRIA

CARLSBAD-GENERAL

Bohemia, now Czechoslovakia
1848–Present

History: Carlsbad and the vicinity surrounding it was the center of the Bohemian porcelain industry. Many factories used the name Carlsbad in their marks despite the fact that they were not located in the city itself. The factories manufactured household and decorative porcelains and gift items.

Opiag, Austrian Porcelain Industry AG, changed its name to Epiag after Bohemia was removed from the Austrian Empire at the end of WWI to become part of the newly created state of Czechoslovakia. Epiag was nationalized after WWII.

Ashtray, 5¼" d, multicolored scene,
   Dutch men and women strolling by
   waterfront 15.00
Bone Dish
   Blue and beige florals 8.00
   Pink floral design, set of 6 .... 38.00
Bowl, 16" l, 9" w, hp, purple and white
   flowers, gold trim, fluted edge 35.00
Butter Dish, 7½" d, cov, small pink
   flowers, green leaves, white ground,
   wavy gold lines 55.00
Cake Plate, 10" d, hp, scenic center,
   floral border, pierced dbl handles .. 30.00
Coffeepot, 9½" h, emb florals, gold trim 30.00
Cup and Saucer, brown leaves, gray
   flowers, raised yellow dots 10.00
Cuspidor, 5½" w, 6½" h, ladies size,
   small multicolored flowers on scalloped edge 200.00
Dinner Service
   Acid-etched, elves at play, light green
   ground, gilt borders, set of 62 pcs 335.00
   Sepia, wildflower design, gilt edged
   white ground, set of 109 pcs (A) . 200.00
Dish, 7¼" d, molded in shape of flower
   blossom, blue-purple irid glaze 85.00
Ewer, 13⅝" h, cov, pink blossoms in
   branches, matte cream ground, gilt
   accents, fluted neck, circ foot (A) ... 100.00
Fish Service, platter, sauceboat, eleven
   plates, multicolored fish in natural
   settings 175.00
Hair Receiver
   4" d, cobalt design, white ground,

emb basketweave at top, gold accents 30.00
Dark blue and gold borders, white
   ground, "Carlsbad, Austria" 28.00
Pitcher
   5¾" h, hp, ivory flower, pastel and
   gold ground 65.00
   7" h, two cherubs at fountain, pink
   and white ground, gold handle ... 25.00
   9" h, yellow flowers, enameled centers, brown branches, cream
   ground, gold scroll handle 75.00
Plaque
   7" w, 12" h, relief of nude woman,
   off-white 200.00
   13" d, scene of grazing buffalo, scalloped edge, "L. S. & S." 85.00

Plate, 6½" d, multicolored floral center, lilac border, gilt edge, $15.00.

Plate
   7" d
      Multicolored decal of farmhouse
      and meadow, shaped and
      molded border 32.50
      Multicolored man and lady, period
      clothes, pr 24.00
   7½" d, multicolored center portrait of
      young girl, pierced for hanging ... 30.00
   8" d, cherubs playing drum and vio-
      lin, rust border, gold overlay 20.00
   8½" d
      Pansy pattern, gold trim 12.00
      Pink and blue small flowers border,
      white ground, gold edge 5.00
      Roses and violets, gold trim 20.00
   10½" d, hp, multicolored florals,
      "Victoria, Carlsbad, Austria" 65.00
Plate, Oyster 8¾" d
   Lavender flowers, white ground, gold
   outlines 50.00

Molded oyster wells, white ground, gold trim, set of 6 .... **225.00**
Molded shells, central floral designs, green detail (A) **25.00**
Rose Bowl, raised gold, dark pink rose shaded green leaves, red "Carlsbad, Austria" **125.00**
Toothpick Holder, small multicolored flowers **40.00**
Tray, 11½" l, 7" w, hp, flowers and birds, emb border, butterfly shape .. **30.00**
Tureen, 12¼" l, cov, small dark red and yellow flowers, green leaves, white ground, cov slotted for ladle, dbl handles, c1895 .... **75.00**
Urn, 14½" h
Alternating panels of figures and flowers, sgd "Stahl," pr **150.00**
Large rose bouquet on front, shaded ivory ground, "Carlsbad, Austria" **145.00**
Vase, 8" h, multicolored florals, dbl gourded shape (A) **30.00**
Vegetable Bowl, 9" d, cov, roses, mint green leaves, fluted body **50.00**

CARLTON WARE

Stoke-on-Trent, Staffordshire, England
c1890–Present

History: Staffordshire porcelain and earthenware were produced at the Carlton Works, Stoke-on-Trent, by a firm that traded as Wiltshow and Robinson from about 1890 until 1957, after which it's name became Carlton Ware Ltd.

The background color most often used on the wares was black. Ornamental wares, including porcelain vases, with luster decorations in Oriental designs were made during the 1920s. Some pieces were decorated with bright enameled and gilt flowers in Art Deco designs.

Most products are marked with a circular printed mark with W & R/STOKE ON TRENT enclosing a swallow and topped by a crown.

Biscuit Jar
6" h, raised white figures of hunters and dogs, green ground **118.00**

6½" h
Mauve orchid, green and tan leaves, cream-pink ground, SP handle, rim and top **80.00**
Red roses, green foliage, beige satin ground, SP handle, rim and top **75.00**
7" h, lavender, pink and yellow petunias, green foliage, beige satin ground, SP handle, rim and top .. **75.00**
Bowl
10¾" d, enameled chinoiserie scene, dark blue ground, rolled edge **220.00**
11" d, enameled chinoiserie scene, blue accents **225.00**
13¼" l, 9" w, multicolored florals, gilt int. and ext., open dbl handles ... **110.00**
Box, 5¼" l, 4" w, "Rouge Royale," scene of duck flying over irises and foliage, pearlized int., rect shape, cov **120.00**
Cheese Dish, 9" l, multicolored florals, cream ground, slant cov, handle, c1890 .... **85.00**
Compote, 9" d, 4½" h, "Rouge Royale," scene of spider in web, dragonfly and butterfly near web over flora **155.00**
Creamer and Sugar, "Australian" design, #2115 .... **20.00**
Dish
9" d, "Blue Royale," multicolored, gilt exotic birds and trees, blue ground, raised wavy trim (A) **38.00**
14¼" d, "Rouge Royale," multicolored, gilt Oriental scenes, foliate borders reserved on shaded dark red ground (A) **48.00**
Jar, 5⅜" h, polychrome Oriental decor, orange-red trim, "Carlton Ware, England" (A) **20.00**
Jardiniere, 11" l, hp, parrots on cherry tree limbs, black ground, dark orange int., borders of cherries, vines and leaves **250.00**
Pin Dish, 4" d, lavender and dark pink flowers, pink blown-out body **18.00**
Pitcher
6" h, two anemones, light green ground **38.00**
6¼" h, multicolored florals, cream ground, pewter lid, c1890 .... **75.00**
6½" h
Multicolored florals, gilt, beige ground, pewter lid **85.00**
"Rouge Flambe," Oriental design, maroon ground **85.00**
Sugar Shaker, 4½" h, Art Deco multicolored emb tree design, cream ground, tree shape **45.00**
Sugar Sifter, 3½" h, multicolored fruit design **65.00**
Teapot, 5½" h, multicolored florals, cream ground, c1890 .... **85.00**
Tray, 12" l, multicolored dragonfly, flo-

Left, plate, 9″ d, gilt, cobalt ground, $55.00; center, compote, 5″ w, yellow and green, $25.00; right, bowl, 9″ H-H, brown tree, yellow-brown leaves and acorns, blue ground, blue script "Carlton Ware," $475.00.

rals and gold outlined spiderweb, black ground, gold rim **175.00**

Vase

5½″ h

Lavender, black and gold stylized trees, cobalt ground **100.00**

Multicolored, gilt exotic bird beside tree, pendant flowers, green and orange ground (A) **100.00**

6″ h, multicolored Oriental and pagoda design, blue ground **65.00**

6⅛″ h

Multicolored and gilt outlined exotic birds and foliage, mottled orange ground, pr (A) **84.00**

Multicolored leaves and florets, geometric green and brown mottled panels, gilt accents (A) **84.00**

7″ h, "Rouge Royale," irid int., helmet shape **80.00**

8½″ h, Oriental design on green ground, panels on bottom, pr **285.00**

8½″ h, 6″ d, maroon enameled Oriental motif, ornate band at neck . . **50.00**

10″ h, yellow luster, painted kingfisher **55.00**

10¼″ h, multicolored exotic bird, gilt willows and stylized flowers, tan and blue-streaked ground (A) **50.00**

10½″ h, chinoiserie scene medallions, black and flambe **250.00**

1775-90

CAUGHLEY

ROYAL SALOPIAN PORCELAIN MANUFACTORY

Shropshire, England
c1775–1799

History: Thomas Turner, who received his training at the Worcester porcelain factory, converted an existing pottery at Caughley in Shropshire in 1772 to make possible the manufacture of porcelain products. He developed a uniformly smooth, transparent glaze that lent itself well to the transfer printed decorations. Basic Caughley porcelain has a white soapstone body.

Blue and white ware with printed transfer decorations in a Chinese design was the chief item of manufacture. The "willow pattern," c1780, and the "Broseley dragon" were two of the most characteristic and popular Caughley patterns. Sometimes the Caughley blue and white china was painted in underglaze blue as well as transfer printed. The china often was enriched with bands of gilding.

Turner established a London warehouse called the "Salopian China Warehouse" in 1780 for the sale of Caughley chinaware. Tablewares, tea and coffee services, and other utilitarian items were the chief Caughley products. Few decorative pieces were made.

In 1870 Turner brought back several French china decorators leading to a greater variety in decoration. Turner sent some of his porcelain pieces to be gilded and enameled at the Chamberlain factory at Worcester. By 1796 hard paste porcelain was introduced.

The factory was taken over by John Rose of nearby Coalport in 1799 and continued to offer whiteware for decoration at London and Coalport until its closing in 1814.

References: G.A. Godden, *Caughley & Worcester Porcelains, 1775–1800*, Herbert Jenkins, 1969.

Museums: Clive House Museum, Strewbury, England; Metropolitan Museum of Art, New York; Victoria & Albert Museum, London.

Bowl

5″ d, transfer of cottage scene, Salopian, chipped (A) **120.00**

5½″ d, transfer of flowers and exotic birds, Salopian (A) **400.00**

Bowl, 6" d, 3" h, blue Oriental scenes, white ground, blue center floral group, c1770, $350.00.

5⅞" d, blue printed flowers and butterflies, blue "S" (A) **25.00**
6" d, transfer of cow scene, Salopian (A) **375.00**
6⅛" d, blue printed "Three Flowers" pattern **25.00**
7" d, blue floral transfer design (A) .. **85.00**
7¼" d, blue printed "Fence" pattern **80.00**
Butterboats, 3¾" l, blue printed "Fisherman" pattern, cell diaper borders, leaf shape, twig handles, pr (A) **165.00**
Coffee Cup and Saucer, blue and white transfer of fenced pattern and flowering plants, c1775 (A) **70.00**
Coffeepot
  6⅞" h, blue printed "Bell Toy" pattern **30.00**
  8⅞" h, gilt bands of berried foliage, fluted body **55.00**
  9½" h, multicolored scene of stags, woodland setting, Salopian (A) ...**1,000.00**
  10½" h, light brown transfer of rural scene, dome top and gooseneck spout, Salopian (A) **210.00**
Creamboat
  4½" l, blue painted bridge, two islands, reverse with windmill and two huts on island, herringbone int. rim, spiral molded, c1790 (A) **350.00**
  Blue and white printed flowering plants and buildings, c1775, pr (A) **250.00**
Creamer
  5¼" h, milkmaid and cow scene, Salopian (A) **180.00**
  5½" h, Sheepherder design, Salopian (A) **100.00**
  White stag pattern, polychrome, Salopian **385.00**
Cup and Saucer, Salopian
  Blue, cottage scene, chipped (A) ... **30.00**
  Circ landscapes, gilt foliage cartouches, flowerhead and foliage border, spiral molded, c1792 (A) . **80.00**

Cottage scene, trees and floral border (A) **175.00**
Cottage scene in circle (A) **180.00**
Oak leaves and floral design (A) **170.00**
Oriental pagoda scene, floral border (A) **140.00**
Oriental pagoda scene, three people (A) **160.00**
Reaping scene (A) **400.00**
White stag design, chipped (A) **70.00**
Cup Plate, 4½" d, shepherd scene, Salopian (A) **210.00**
Custard Cup, 3⅛" h, cov, blue printed buildings, Oriental riverscape (A) ... **25.00**
Dish
  3" w, blue and white Oriental style landscape, leaf shaped, c1790 (A) **100.00**
  6" l
    Blue florals and swags, lozenge shape, c1770, imp "Salopian" . **100.00**
    Blue florals, sprigs and swags, kidney shape, c1770, imp "Salopian" **100.00**
  8" d, Imari pattern of flowering shrubs, diapering and orange bands, cushion shape, c1785 (A) . **315.00**
  8⅞" sq, blue transfer of "Fisherman" pattern on int. and ext., lobed body, c1780-90, blue "S" (A) **120.00**
Egg Drainer, 3⅛" d, printed "Fisherman" pattern, crabstock handle, c1785, "S" **250.00**
Flask, 4⅞" h, blue transfer of "Birds in Branches" pattern, key fret borders (A) **470.00**
Gravy Creamer, Salopian
  5¼" h, Oriental design (A) **300.00**
  5½" h, deer design (A) **275.00**
Inkwell, blue and white printed Oriental figures on terrace, c1770 (A) **110.00**
Jug
  1½" h, blue painted Oriental scene of two buildings and fishing junks, bucket shape, sparrow beak spout, c1790 (A) **525.00**
  4" h, white tobacco leaf blank, blue Chinese design, Salopian, repaired spout chip **350.00**
  5" h, multicolored floral border, pattern #158, Caughley-Coalport (A) **15.00**
  5¾" h, blue transfer of "Pecking Parrot" pattern, int. cell diaper rim, mask form spout, c1790, blue "C" mark (A) **200.00**
  7¼" h, cabbage leaf molded, gilt entwined "JPM" in oval gilt and blue cartouche, swags of gilt and blue flowers from pink ribbons, mask spout, c1795 (A) **285.00**
Loving Cup, 8⅝" h, blue printed, two large flower sprays between blue band borders, dbl loop handles (A) . **150.00**

Miniature

Cup and Saucer, yellow bird design, Salopian (A) **115.00**

Tea and Coffee Service, blue and white painted Oriental river landscapes, Salopian, "blue crescent and S" marks, set of 29 pcs (A) .. **935.00**

Tea Service, teapot, jug, sugar, three coffee cups and saucers, teabowl, blue "Island" pattern **480.00**

Teabowl and Saucer

Blue "Fence" pattern, blue line borders, c1775, "blue crescent" marks, set of 4 (A) **175.00**

Blue painted sampans and island, loop and flowerhead border, c1785 (A) **185.00**

Mug

2¼" h, 2½" d, white stag design, Salopian (A) **300.00**

4⅛" h, blue transfer of "Bell Toy" pattern, c1780 (A) **200.00**

5½" h, sepia painted winged goddess holding tablet, blue and gold "C" in center, floral cornucopia, border of gilt scrolling foliage, star crack, c1795 (A) **485.00**

Mustard Jar, 4" h, blue printed "Fence" pattern, "C" (A) **40.00**

Night-Light Teapot, Salopian, 3 piecestand, pot and cov, multicolored pastoral scene with figural spout, lid repair (A) **3,900.00**

Pickle Dish

3⅜" l, blue "Fisherman" pattern (A) **90.00**

4⅜" w, blue printed "Fisherman" pattern, leaf shape, pr **80.00**

Plate

1¾" d, blue painted dwellings on is-

Plate, 8″ d, blue Oriental motif, white ground, gold inner and outer rim, Salopian, $185.00.

land, paneled border, blue "S" mark (A) **130.00**

6½" d

Blue painted floral sprigs, scalloped rim, blue "S" **20.00**

Transfer of vase of flowers, Salopian (A) **300.00**

7½" d, transfer of deer stag and floral border, Salopian (A) **350.00**

8" d

Printed "Pine Cone" pattern, scalloped edge, painted scroll and diapered border, fluted, c1780, "C" **235.00**

Transfer of fishermen and net, Salopian (A) **85.00**

Transfer of house, two fishermen and stream, Salopian (A) **140.00**

8⅝" d

Blue painted center, ruins in rustic landscapes, dark blue and gold borders, gilt palmettes, scrolls and loops, Salopian, pr (A) **250.00**

Blue painted cottages in landscapes, borders of gold scrolling athemion, blue rims, gilt interlaced loops, c1790, pr (A) **170.00**

Painted center, farm buildings and boat in foreground, dark blue and gold border, palmettes, scrolls and loops, imp "Salopian" **100.00**

Painted center, fishermen on bank, dark blue and gold borders, palmettes, scrolls and loops, imp "Salopian," pr **240.00**

9⅜" d, blue painted flowers and insects in center, ozier molded border **40.00**

10" d, multicolored florals, blue, dark red, and yellow, beaded border, Salopian (A) **600.00**

Punch Bowl, 10⅜" d, blue transfer of "Fisherman" pattern on int. and ext., cell diaper, scallop, dot into rim border, c1785 (A) **440.00**

Sauce Tureen, 5¾" w, blue painted, four landscape views in gilt dot cartouches, gilt dot borders, band of gilt medallions, lobed gilt rims, c1780, pr (A) **1,725.00**

Sauceboat, 8½" l, blue flowers, scrolls, and diapering, white ground, Oriental water scene on int., ribbed body, c1780 .... **650.00**

Saucer

4½" d, "Bell Toy," Chinese pattern, multicolored **90.00**

Black transfer of deer, polychrome enamels, Salopian **45.00**

Spoon Tray, 6" l, "Temple" pattern, gold trim, scalloped edge, c1780 .... **200.00**

Sugar Bowl
  5" h, cov, blue, yellow, and orange
    decor, yellow bird, Salopian (A) .. **325.00**
  Blue Oriental pavilions and sampans,
    fretwork border, c1785 (A) **220.00**
  Blue painted Oriental river scene,
    c1790 (A) **200.00**
Tankard
  5⅝" h, blue printed "Fisherman" pat-
    tern, handle with heart thumb rest
    and wavy band with commas,
    c1780, "S" **650.00**
  7" h, blue and white "Fisherman" pat-
    tern, c1780 .... **650.00**
Taster, 2½" d, blue printed "Fisherman"
    pattern, leaf handle (A) **85.00**
Tea and Coffee Service, teapot, stand,
    milk jug, cov sugar, slop basin, eight
    teacups, five teabowls, two coffee
    cups, ten saucers, gilt dot pattern,
    "HC" monogram, interlocking med-
    allion border, white ground, c1785
    (A) **365.00**
Tea Caddy
  4¾" h, blue printed "Fence" pattern,
    barrel shape **50.00**
  5¼" h, blue printed bouquets and but-
    terflies, c1770 (A) **65.00**
Teabowl and Saucer
  Blue and white Oriental design of
    woman in garden (A) **70.00**
  Blue painted Oriental water scene
    with island and fishing junks, blue
    "S" marks, set of 4 (A) **490.00**
  Blue printed fruit sprays, blue "S" .. **20.00**
  Blue printed "Pagoda" pattern, gilt
    rims **20.00**
  Iron-red, rose, and green swags of
    flowers and hops, pink and gold
    stripes, diaper borders, c1770, blue
    "S" marks **75.00**
Teapot
  3" h, blue painted Oriental water
    scene, loop handle, c1790 (A) ... **625.00**
  3¼" h, blue Oriental pavilion and
    sampans in fretwork border, c1785
    (A) **220.00**
  5" h, blue and white decor, flower
    finial, c1780 .... **675.00**
  5¼" h, blue printed fruit and flowers,
    white ground, ovoid, strap handle,
    flower finial, c1775 .... **675.00**
  5½" h, blue printed "Fisherman" pat-
    tern, gilt rims, mushroom finial .. **150.00**
  6¼" h, blue printed fruit sprays, floral
    sprays on cov (A) **150.00**
  Salopian
    Oriental scene (A) **200.00**
    White stag design, chipped (A) ... **30.00**
Teapot Stand, 5" sq, blue and white "Pa-
    goda" pattern, gilt trim, scalloped
    edge, c1780 .... **300.00**

Waste Bowl, 6⅜" d, brown transfer of
    Britannia, floral designs, poly-
    chromes, Salopian (A) **55.00**

CAULDON

Shelton, Hanely, England
1905–1962

History: This Staffordshire pottery, a direct de-
scendant of the Ridgway potteries, operated from
1905 to 1920 at Cauldon Place, Shelton, Hanely.
After John Ridgway dissolved his partnership with
William, his brother, in 1830, he operated the
Cauldon Place Works. A wide variety of china
and earthenware were made including utilitarian
and decorative pieces.

Ridgway sold to T.C. Brown-Westhead, Moore
& Company in 1855. Brown-Westhead, Moore
& Co. (1862–1904) became Cauldon Ltd. in
1905. From 1920 to 1962 the firm operated as
Cauldon Potteries, Ltd., at which time it became
known as Cauldon Bristol Potteries, Ltd. It was
eventually acquired by Pountney & Co. Ltd. of
Boston in 1962.

Box, 5" sq, cov, lime green, porcelain,
    gold trim **25.00**

**Vase, 7" h, "Highland Cattle," multico-
lored, sgd "Donald Birbeck," $250.00.**

Cup and Saucer, hp, different flower on each, set of 8 .... **125.00**
Dessert Service, two circ dishes, two oval dishes, twelve plates, gray, light yellow and gilt borders, floral panels **160.00**
Dinner Service
  17 pcs, six 10½" d plates, six 9¼" d plates, 15" l, 12" w platter, 13" l, 10½" w platter, gravy boat, cov tureen, flowing blue design of dragons and flower clusters, inner cell diaper border **325.00**
  106 pcs, green printed "Premier Rose" pattern, c1895 (A) **275.00**
Fish Set
  10 pcs, 21" l, 10" w platter, gravy boat, eight 8½" d plates, blue trout on platter, leaping salmon on plates, seashell and seaweed borders, imp "Cauldon" **600.00**
  14 pcs, twelve plates, sauceboat and undertray, hp, fish reserved in gilt, pink borders (A) **250.00**
Jar, 6" h, cov, hp, "Highland Cattle" scene, cream ground, sgd "D. Birbeck," c1905 .... **150.00**

black Swallowtail butterflies, white emb flower and leaf border **25.00**
9½" d, hp, large roses, gold and turquoise enamels, sgd "Hillman" .. **450.00**
9¾" d, black and white scene of Anne Hathaway's cottage **15.00**
10½" d
  Hp, pink flowers and green leaves, brown basketweave border, raised loop rims, set of 6 ...... **55.00**
  Multicolored portrait of bulldog, sgd "Pedersen," dated 1901 ... **70.00**
  Perry Centennial-1913 .... **30.00**
Platter, 13" l, 10" w, "Byzantium" design, cobalt transfer, "Cauldon, England" **75.00**
Sauce and Gravy Set, 7½" l gravy, blue and white flowers, gilt trim **75.00**
Tea Set, teapot, creamer, sugar, white ground, heavy gold trim **125.00**
Tray, 18" l, blue and white pastoral scene, castle, scalloped edge **135.00**
Vase, 7½" h, wide ruffled opening, floral medallions, gold tracings, mint green ground **100.00**

Plate, 8½" d, cobalt, rose, and rust, gold trim, $45.00.

Plate
  8¾" d, painted view of Newcastle Church, name on reverse, wide acid-etched gilt border, sgd "A. Winkle" (A) **100.00**
  9" d
    Depressed center, radiating gold center, gold border, c1890 .... **15.00**
    Multicolored "Thames Boat House," "Royal Cauldon" **45.00**
    Painted water birds, wide acid-etched gilt borders, sgd "S. Pope," pr (A) **180.00**
  9¼" d, multicolored Monarch and

CHANTILLY   **1725 - 1800**

Chantilly, France
1725–c1860

History: The Chantilly factory, established in 1725 in the Chantilly district of France, produced soft paste porcelain. The first manager of the works was Ciquaire Cirou who worked under the guidance and influence of the Prince de Conde. The factory's original purpose was to copy old designs rather than initiate new ones.

Conde's love for Japanese porcelain dictated that the first products assume the form and color of the classic Japanese porcelains. In order to achieve the strong colors of the Japanese palette, a milky glaze was developed to present a satisfactory surface for decoration.

In addition to the Japanese designs, many of the popular Meissen designs and decorations were imitated. The factory also made soft paste of old silver pieces. A lobulated body form characterized Chantilly porcelain of this period.

By the mid-18th century, the opaque glaze was replaced with a more transparent type. The decorative style now shifted to imitating the porcelains from the Sevres factory. This second glaze gave a softer look to the finished products.

"Chantilly Sprig," a sketchy type blue floral motif, appeared about this time. Table services, statuettes, writing paraphernalia, and boxes and jars for the ladies dressing table were the staple products of the factory.

About 1800 the factory ceased operation. Several other factories in the area picked up the production of the most popular Chantilly designs in hard paste porcelain. These pieces were characterized by a soft pastel coloring and dull surface finish, contrasting with the early products of the original factory. They are classified under the general heading of "Chantilly."

References: W.B. Honey, *French Porcelain of the 18th Century*, Faber & Faber, 1950; George Savage, *Seventeenth & Eighteenth Century*, Hamlyn Publishing Co., Ltd., 1969.

Museums: J. Paul Getty Museum, Malibu, California; Musee Conde, Chantilly, France; Musee des Arts Decoratifs, Paris, France; Victoria & Albert Museum, London, England.

Figure, 15″ l, gold accents, white ground, light blue tufted sleigh int., gold buttons, c1860, $1,400.00.

Basket, 8⅝″ d, pierced border of interlocking ovals, Kakiemon palette trailing flowers, chrysanthemums, and grasshopper, c1735 (A) **2,465.00**
Bourdalou, 7¼″ l, Kakiemon palette Oriental florals, dark brown rim, loop handle, c1735, iron-red "hunting horn" mark (A) **1,230.00**
Bowl, 5¼″ d, cov, painted multicolored flower sprays, rope twist dbl handles, branch finial, c1725 . . . . **550.00**
Cache Pot, 9″ d, Kakiemon palette and style, squirrel eating grapes on branches, seeded border, cylinder shape, dbl dragon handles, c1735 (A) **1,815.00**
Charger, 17″ d, center painted flowering tree, spiral molded, basketweave border, underglaze blue painted flower-

ing bushes, manganese rim, late 18th C **600.00**
Cheese Keeper, 7¼″ w, blue flower sprays, blue edged pierced floral motif, bow shape dbl handles, three ball feet, c1760 (A) **440.00**
Coffee Can and Saucer, panels of grotesques, marbled green "Chantilly" sprig borders, purple ground, early 19th C, iron-red "Chantilly" mark . . **85.00**
Cup and Saucer
  Blue floral sprigs, white ground, c1780 (A) **40.00**
  Kakiemon palette flowerheads and bundle of wheat, bucket shape, entwined branch handle, flower terminal, saucer with Ho-Ho bird on branches, c1740, iron-red "hunting horn" mark **1,000.00**
  Painted bouquets and sprays, fluted, bucket shape, scroll handle, chocolate rims, c1745, iron-red "hunting horn" mark (A) **550.00**
  Painted flower sprays in gilt scrolls reserved on blue trellis ground, gilt dots and rims, c1760, blue "hunting horn" mark (A) **770.00**
Custard Cups, cov, blue painted flower sprays, spirally fluted ground, c1760, blue "hunting horn" mark, pr (A) . . . **380.00**
Dinner Service, twelve 9½″ d plates, nine soup bowls, two oval dishes, blue carnations and insects, basketweave border, damaged, c1745, blue "hunting horn" mark (A) **770.00**
Dish
  8⅝″ sq, blue painted carnation and sprays, ozier borders, c1775, blue "hunting horn" mark, pr (A) **200.00**
  9¾″ d, Kakiemon palette, chrysanthemums, brown rim, quatrefoil shape, c1740 (A) **175.00**
  9¾″ l, painted flowers in each of four lobes, brown rim, c1760, red "hunting horn & G" marks (A) . . . **480.00**
Drug Jar, Cov, 6″ h, Kakiemon palette berried foliage cartouche, inscription, flower sprays on reverse and cov, c1735, iron-red "hunting horn" mark (A) **2,640.00**
Figure
  5½″ h, Chinese man, wearing painted coat with exotic birds and animals, outstretched arms, c1735 (A) . . .**15,400.00**
  6¼″ h, young man, period clothes, holding basket of fruit and apple, pastel colors, tree stump mound base, rococo scrolls, mid 18th C . **735.00**
  7⅞″ h, Chinese girl seated, turquoise Kakiemon decorated dress, multicolored base, flowering tree, c1730 (A) **12,635.00**

11" h, man and woman, period clothes, leaning on fluted columns, hp, pastel colors, gold trim, c1890, pr **1,400.00**

11¼" h, man and woman, period clothes, leaning on post, pastel colors, gold trim, matte finish, c1845, pr **1,200.00**

12½" h, man and woman, French classical costumes, hp, pale blue, c1880, pr **1,400.00**

Figure, 13¼" h, pastel matte colors, c1875, $1,000.00.

14" h, females seated, one with dog and bird, other with extended swan at her feet, soft pastel coloring, c1885, pr **1,400.00**

20" h, ladies, classical dress, pastel colors, gold trim, raised flowers incorporated into figures, hand detailed, c1885, pr **2,400.00**

Finger Bowl, 3⅛" d, painted Chinese boys playing games on terrace, flared octagonal rim, c1735 (A) **650.00**

Jardiniere

4½" h, Kakiemon palette, exotic birds, flowering plants, and bamboo, dbl branch handles, c1735, iron-red "hunting horn" mark (A) .**4,180.00**

5½" w, Kakiemon palette, painted chinoiserie figure on front, bouquet and insects on reverse, cylindrical, dbl dragon handles, c1730, iron-red "hunting horn" mark (A) **3,100.00**

Jug, 7½" h, cov, Kakiemon palette, flowering plants from rocks, insects, pear shape, cov with phoenix, silver mounts, c1735, iron-red "hunting horn" mark (A) **7,150.00**

Knife, Kakiemon palette, Chinese fig-

ures, flowering foliage, contemporary blades, c1735, set of 6 (A) **712.00**

Plate

9¼" d, painted floral bouquets, ozier border, ochre rim, c1740, blue "hunting horn" mark (A) **285.00**

9⅜" d, scattered flowers and insects, blue and enamels, basketwork border, c1740, blue "hunting horn" mark (A) **40.00**

9½" d, underglaze blue, painted flowering sprigs, scalloped blue rims, 18th C, set of 5 .... **350.00**

9⅝" d, hp flowers, chocolate rim, spiral molded, c1740, iron-red "hunting horn" mark (A) **285.00**

Platter, 13⅝" d, underglaze blue floral sprigs on rim and center, scalloped edge, late 18th C **300.00**

Pot-A-Creme, flower sprays, spiral molded ground, c1760, blue "hunting horn" mark (A) **150.00**

Sauce Tureen, Cov

6" l, Kakiemon palette, florals and insects, quatrefoil shape, flowerhead knobs, c1735, iron-red "hunting horn" mark, pr (A) **720.00**

6¼" d, Kakiemon palette, flowering chrysanthemums and insects, quatrefoil shaped, c1735, iron-red "hunting horn" mark **125.00**

8⅞" l, blue painted single flowers, blue rims, entwined branch handle on cov, ozier border, octafoil shape, c1750 (A) **465.00**

9" w, attached tray, blue floral sprigs, dbl scroll finial, ladle with pierced star, c1760, blue "hunting horn" mark (A) **420.00**

9¼" h, white modeled grouse, wings forming cov, bird finial, leaf form stand, pierced spoon with branch handle, c1735 (A) **2,640.00**

Stand, 9¼" w, molded foliage scrolls, green accents, painted flower sprays, brown rim, mid-18th C, blue "hunting horn" mark (A) **200.00**

Sugar, 4¾" h, painted flower sprays, brown rim, lemon branch finial on cov, c1745, iron-red "hunting horn" mark (A) **550.00**

Teabowl and Saucer

Kakiemon palette, squirrel on fence, fluted, c1730 (A) **1,540.00**

Kakiemon style, fan shape panels of flowers from dark blue rock, iron-red surrounds, white ground, c1735–40 (A) **425.00**

Vase, 7⅝" h, painted bouquets, molded fluted body, rococo scroll dbl handles with iron-red edged foliage, brown rim, c1740 .... **350.00**

1769-84

CHELSEA

London, England
c1745–1769

History: As early as 1745, soft paste porcelains were being manufactured at Chelsea in London, one of the most famous English porcelain factories. Nicholas Sprimont, originally a silversmith, was manager of the factory for most of its history. Chelsea porcelains were the most richly decorated of English 18th century ceramics. Pieces were ornate and made for the higher class market.

Various periods of Chelsea porcelain are classified according to the anchor-like mark. But before these were used, there was an incised triangle mark, c1745, and a painted mark of a trident piercing a crown.

From 1749 to 1752, a "raised-anchor" mark was used. This mark was relief molded on a small applied oval pad. Porcelains of this period have the tin-added glaze and mostly are decorated with Oriental motifs or simple, floral designs.

The "red-anchor" period (1752–56) has the anchor painted directly on the porcelain. Small light colored "moons" can be seen on these porcelains when held up to the light. Animal fables and botanical studies were characteristic of this period along with florals and Oriental motifs.

The Chelsea "gold-anchor" period dates between c1756 and 1769. Porcelains of this era were richly decorated and ornately gilted. The glazes tend to be thickly applied.

The anchor period dates are only approximations. More than half of all Chelsea porcelains had no mark at all.

William Duesbury of the Derby factory purchased the Chelsea factory in 1770. The wares of the 1770–1784 period are called "Chelsea-Derby." Because of the interaction of these two factories and the interchange of molds, clay, and workmen, it is difficult to distinguish between the Chelsea and Derby porcelains of this period. Further complications resulted when Duesbury used the Chelsea gold anchor mark on some Derby pieces. A "D" and anchor mark also was used, as was a crowned anchor mark. By 1784 the last of the Chelsea works were demolished and the molds and workers transferred to Derby.

References: John C. Austin, *Chelsea Porcelain at Williamsburg*, Colonial Williamsburg Foundation, 1977; John Bedford, *Chelsea & Derby China*, Walker & Co., 1967; Yvonne Hacken-

broch, *Chelsea and other English Porcelains, Pottery and Enamel in the Irwin Untermyer collection*, Harvard University Press, 1957; William King, *Chelsea Porcelain*, Benn Brothers, 1922; F. Severne Mackenna, *Chelsea Porcelain, The Triangle & Raised Anchor Wares*, F. Lewis, 1948; F. Severne Mackenna, *Chelsea Porcelain, The Red Anchor Wares*, F. Lewis, 1951; F. Severne Mackenna, *Chelsea Porcelain, The Gold Anchor Period*, F. Lewis, 1952.

Museums: Colonial Williamsburg Foundation, Williamsburg, Virginia; Gardiner Museum of Ceramic Art, Toronto, Canada; Henry E. Huntington Library & Art Gallery, San Marino, California, (gold anchor); Museum of Fine Arts, Boston, Mass.; Seattle Art Museum, Seattle, Wash.; Walters Art Gallery, Baltimore, Maryland.

REPRODUCTION ALERT: Samson made copies of Chelsea pieces, but these were generally marked as copies. Many forgeries and imitations are seen every year bearing red or gold anchors.

Dish, 12½″ l, Hans Sloane, multicolored, named on reverse, red anchor mark, $3,400.00.

Basket, 10″ l, tray, lidded, enameled lilies, roses, and Carpathian harebells, applied flowers and boughs (A) **225.00**
Beaker, 2⅝″ h, multicolored painted Oriental flower sprays, sprig int., c1750–52, octafoil shape, raised anchor mark (A) **1,430.00**
Bowl
  4″ h, butterfly and insect decor, leaf shape (A) **160.00**
  9″ d, cov, stand, modeled sunflower, seed center cov, green stem handle, c1755, brown anchor mark (A) .. .**6,325.00**
Bust, 5⅛″ h, William Augustus, Duke of Cumberland, white, c1751 (A) **3,370.00**
Cabinet Cup, 5″ h, tooled gilt rim, scrolls, three exotic birds, claret ground, ormolu foliate scroll base, c1760–69 (A) **880.00**

Candlesticks

7" h, "Finch," yellow and black birds, magenta trim, pale yellow supports with molded flowers, c1755, red anchor period, pr **5,500.00**

10" h, modeled with fox and stork with plate and vase, multicolored, bocage backgrounds, supporting nozzle, pierced scroll molded base, c1770, Chelsea-Derby, pr (A) **2,420.00**

Charger, 13¾" d, exotic birds on branches in center, gilt scroll, "Mazarine Blue" border, gilt dentil rim, c1760–65, gold anchor mark (A) . . . **360.00**

Coffee Cup and Saucer, painted bouquets and sprays, pinecone molded turquoise ground, gilding, c1765, gold anchor mark (A) **360.00**

Cream Jug, 3½" h, white baluster form, molded floral terminal, c1755 (A) . . **135.00**

Creamboat, 2½" h, dark turquoise enamel ground, gilt rim, lamprey handle, leaf molded base, c1770–75 (A) **470.00**

Cup, painted gentleman and lady, landscapes in rect panels reserved on blue ground, gilt dbl handles, c1770, gold anchor mark (A) **58.00**

Cup and Saucer

Multicolored floral decorations, octagonal shape, c1820, red anchor mark (A) **150.00**

Striped pink tulip and columbine, yellow ground, gilt rim, scroll and puce foliage handle, c1760, gold anchor mark (A) **325.00**

Painted sprays and sprigs, green stalk handle, blue flowered branches, brown rims, c1752–56, red anchor marks (A) **550.00**

Dish

7½" l

Multicolored insect pattern, brown stem handle, leaf shape, c1760, brown anchor mark **850.00**

Green, yellow edges, stem handle, leaf shape, c1755, red anchor mark **950.00**

8" d, multicolored florals, yellow butterfly, shallow depression, c1755, red anchor period **750.00**

8¼" d, painted flower bouquets, butterfly and leaves, molded overlapping petals on reverse, barbed rim brown edged, red anchor mark (A) **435.00**

8¼" w

Painted botanical specimen and onions, shell molded ground, brown line rim, silver shape, c1755, iron-red anchor mark (A) **1,430.00**

Painted scattered flowers, brown or

turquoise line rims, silver shape, c1755, pr (A) **550.00**

8½" l, leaf shape superimposed on basketweave edge, multicolored, c1755 (A) **330.00**

9" d, scattered flowers, stalk handles, peony mold, two overlapping leaves, gilt serrated rims, c1765, gold anchor mark, pr (A) **500.00**

9¼" d, painted urn suspending floral swags, border of gilt flowerheads, floral garlands and insects, green enamel flowers on reverse, gilt dentil rim, c1780, gilt interlaced anchor and D mark, "Chelsea-Derby" **225.00**

9¼" l, molded overlapping leaves, scattered multicolored insects, vine handle, c1760, brown anchor mark **850.00**

9½" l, multicolored flower sprays, shaped green rim, leaf shape, repair to handle, c1752, iron-red anchor mark (A) **880.00**

9⅝" l

Molded grapevines, painted florals and sprigs, brown shaped rim, leaf shape, c1755 (A) **600.00**

Painted center, wooded river landscape, silver shaped border with spray, shell thumbpieces edged in brown, c1752 (A) **3,400.00**

11" d

Painted bouquet and leaves, shaped raised brown line rim, c1755, iron-red anchor mark (A) **770.00**

Painted bouquet and flower sprays, fluted ground, lobed brown line rim, c1755, iron-red anchor mark (A) **880.00**

11" l, "Imari" pattern, scalloped rim divided in 12 panels, reserves of mons, reverse rim of blue peonies and buds, c1755, blue anchor mark **2,500.00**

11½" l, overlapping leaves, lime green edges, puce veins, c1760, iron-red anchor mark, pr (A) **1,870.00**

11" w, painted urn of draped flowers in border of lappets, stylized emblems, pink ground, gilt outline, c1770, gold anchor mark (A) **100.00**

12½" d, Kakiemon palette, "The Hob in the Well" pattern, chrysanthemums, flowerheads and foliage, lobed, repaired, c1752 (A) **260.00**

12½" l, painted bouquets and sprays, trellis pattern and flowerheads in molded borders, painted butterflies, insects, and sprays cartouches, brown line rim, octagonal, c1750, pr (A) **1,760.00**

13" l, multicolored center, floral sprays, insects and butterfly, brown edged, shell mold, oval shape, c1755, red anchor period **1,100.00**

13¼" w, painted bouquets and insects, borders with four shaped puce cartouches with painted river scenes, trellis pattern shaped molded, brown line rims, oval, c1755, iron-red anchor mark, pr (A) **3,100.00**

13⅜" d, painted center, lion attacking stag, horse, goat, sheep, and monkey on donkey, flower sprays and insects on border, brown edged shell mold, oval (A) **480.00**

Figure

2⅛" h, goat, painted, sepia patches, white rocky mound base, red anchor mark (A) **550.00**

4½" h, bird, seated on dbl branch, acorn, multicolored, gold anchor mark **125.00**

5" h

Cupid dressed as beggar, wearing black hat and eye patch, peg-leg, and crutch, circ base, gilt scrolls, c1756, red anchor mark (A) ... **585.00**

Man, basket of flowers, lady, hat in lap, multicolored, repairs, gold anchor mark, pr **325.00**

5⅜" h, "La Nourrice," nurse cradling infant in lap, seated on stool, white, rect floral applied base (A) **500.00**

5½" h, 4½" w, boy and girl seated, period clothes, shades of blue, white ground **200.00**

6⅜" h, "Spring" and "Summer," seated putti, flowered rockwork base, overturned basket at side, red anchor mark **1,200.00**

7½" h, man and woman, colonial clothes, multicolored, detailed, gold anchor mark **215.00**

7⅝" h, "Masquerader," youth carrying bird in cage, multicolored, tree stump and floral scroll molded base, c1759–63, gold anchor mark **1,200.00**

10¼" h, pilgrims, man holding flower and rod, dog on base, woman holding rod, period clothes, multicolored, applied gilt shells on clothes, bocage background, scroll molded base, c1765, gold anchor mark, pr (A) **1,540.00**

11" h, man and woman, period clothes, standing against tree trunks, lamb at feet, lady with tambourine, multicolored, applied flowers, gold anchor mark, pr **710.00**

Mug

5½" h

Painted floral bouquets and sprays,

brown line rim, baluster shape, c1752, red anchor mark (A) ...**1,000.00**

Painted flower sprays and sprigs, brown line rim, baluster-shape, c1752, red anchor mark (A) ...**1,480.00**

9½" h, full seated man, holding mug, rust coat, c1760, gold anchor mark **500.00**

Needle Case, 5⅜" h, modeled marble column, puce, pink, and gold, arrow pierced heart on capital, purple heart, inscription on base, gold mounts, c1765 (A) **365.00**

Perfume Flask, 5" l, modeled twisted tree, painted leaves and berries, iron-red inscribed ribbon on base, modeled colored plummage bird cov, c1760–65 (A) **1,430.00**

Plate

8" d, "Damask'd," paneled border, raised white flowers, painted Meissen style flowers, c1755, red anchor period, pr **1,600.00**

8¼" d

Center exotic birds, cornucopia shaped dark blue border, C-scroll and foliage in shaped gilt dentil rim, c1760, gold anchor mark (A) **975.00**

Painted bouquets and sprays, border with tulips, iron-red shaped rim, c1755, red anchor mark (A) **660.00**

8½" d

Bouquets and insects, multicolored, birds in scroll and foliage molded border, brown rim, c1755, iron-red anchor mark .. **550.00**

Exotic birds, foliage, and rockwork, shaped brown line rims, brown anchor mark, pr (A) **880.00**

"Hans Sloane," puce stem, fruit, and butterfly, c1752, red anchor mark (A) **500.00**

Painted bouquet and insects, molded scroll border enclosing

Plate, 9″ d, bowl, yellow, green, and magenta sunflower, c1755, red anchor mark, $14,500.00.

birds, brown rim, c1755, iron-red anchor mark (A) **385.00**

8⅝" d, painted fruit sprays and moths, brown and green scroll border, brown anchor mark **85.00**

8¾" d, painted centers, naturalistic flower sprays, two butterflies, floret diaper molded borders, brown rim, octagonal, red anchor mark, pr (A) **500.00**

8⅞" d

Center bouquets of flowers and fruits, shaped borders divided by molded C-scroll cartouches with insects, c1758, gold anchor mark, pr (A) **415.00**

Multicolored painted harbor scene, floral spray border, molded shield devices, silver shape, gilt edged, c1752 ....**6,000.00**

Multicolored river front scene, florals and insects, silver shape border, chocolate rim, c1752 (A) . **5,835.00**

9" d

Birds on floral garlands, shaped blue border, gilt flowers, shaped gilt dentil rim, c1760, gold anchor mark (A) **350.00**

Lavender thistles pattern, pr **45.00**

Multicolored fruit sprays, scroll and foliage molded borders, c1755–59, iron-red and gilt anchor marks, set of 6 (A) **1,760.00**

Painted bouquets and sprays, feather green and iron-red molded rims, c1755, iron-red anchor mark, pr (A) **770.00**

9⅛" d, molded flower sprays, center painted flowers, rims divided into eight compartments, four with molded and four with painted flowers, c1755, pr **1,600.00**

9¼" d

Center painted flower sprays, molded wreath, borders with four panels of painted birds divided by molded flower sprays, c1758, pr (A) **285.00**

"Hans Sloane," convoluted stem, three puce flowers, heart shaped leaves, insects, and caterpillar, brown rim, c1754, red anchor mark (A) **1,850.00**

9⅝" d

"Imari Brocade" pattern, multicolored underglaze, central chrysanthemums, radiating panels of diapering with seven mons, c1756 (A) **500.00**

Kakiemon style of bamboo and prunus, iron-red center rosette, c1775, red anchor mark **275.00**

12½" l, "Hans Sloane," painted plu-

mepoppy, two insects on rim, molded gallery edged in brown, octagonal, c1756, red anchor mark .**3,400.00**

Potpouri Vase, 11⅞" h, exotic birds, applied orange blossom cartouches, quatrefoil scroll molded feet, domed covs with turquoise and gilt accents, c1765, gold anchor mark, pr (A) ...**1,230.00**

Salt, 3" h, black crayfish, rockwork base, shells and coral, color accents, red anchor mark (A) **575.00**

Saucer, 4⅜" d, painted "Flaming Tortoise" pattern, Kakiemon style, green dragon center, border with tortoise, exotic birds, and blossoms, c1750–52 (A) **760.00**

Scent Bottle, 3¼" h, painted perched bird on front and back, applied floral vines to side, floral cluster stopper, gold mounted bottle and stopper necks, c1760 (A) **600.00**

Soup Plate

9¼" d

"Damask'd," alternating molded and painted florals, c1755 (A) .. **165.00**

"Hans Sloane," painted pink convolvulus, three red gooseberries, brown and turquoise feather molded rim, crack, red anchor mark (A) **430.00**

9⅝" d, large painted center florals, flowers and insects on border, chocolate line rim, c1753 (A) **125.00**

Stand, 6" h, painted floral spray and scattered sprigs, scalloped rim, red anchor mark (A) **275.00**

Sweetmeat Dish, modeled figures of seated Turk and companion holding shells on rockwork, multicolored, c1756, red anchor mark, pr (A) **3,370.00**

Teabowl, 2⅛" h, iron-red dragon and symbol on ext., flowerhead on int., c1750, octagonal, raised anchor mark (A) **1,100.00**

Teabowl and Saucer

Exotic birds in gilt trellis and flower cartouches between gilt dentil rims, blue ground, c1760, gold anchor mark (A) **625.00**

Painted oval medallions of portrait busts, light puce ground, foliage swags, blue borders, gilt, c1765, gold anchor mark **175.00**

Puce design of warriors, forest and castle setting, gilt rims, octagonal, c1752 ....**2,400.00**

Puce military scenes, birds, and flowers, bowl int. with butterfly and flower, octagonal, c1752, red anchor mark (A) **3,370.00**

"Queen Charlotte" pattern, iron-red, gold, and blue, spiral fluted **180.00**

Tureen, Cov

6¼" h, modeled artichokes, green and yellow, puce splashes, finch finials, c1755, red anchor mark, pr (A) **19,350.00**

18" l, modeled billing doves, puce, blue, gray, and manganese incised feathers, tree stump base, applied multicolored foliage and branches, cov repaired, c1755, iron-red anchor mark (A) **18,700.00**

Vase

6½" h, three birds in tree, C-scroll half cartouche, insects on reverse, gilt line rims, oviform, c1756 (A) **900.00**

8⅝" h, modeled, seated and standing boys holding fish forming vase, light green, yellow, and puce, shaped oval rockwork base, c1765, iron-red anchor mark (A) **1,100.00**

9" h

Painted chinoiserie scene, mother and child playing checkers, reverse with flower bouquet and sprays (A) **200.00**

Painted flower sprays, turquoise, puce, and gilt accents, scroll molded dbl handles, modeled flowering orange tree in center, c1760 .... **550.00**

10" h, ovoid, six sides, three panels with birds in shrubs, three "Mazarine Blue" panels, tooled gilding, butterflies, and insects, entwined scrolled dbl handles, c1760, dbl gold anchor mark, pr (A) **1,430.00**

13" h, cov, Duplessis form, floral encrusted (A) **150.00**

Wax Seal,¾" h, red molded squirrel, mounted on gilt metal ring, c1755 (A) **275.00**

CHILDREN'S WARE

English/German
Late 17th C – Present

History: Initially miniature English china dinnerware sets were made primarily to furnish miniature decorative rooms. By the late 19th century the emphasis shifted. Most of these dinnerware and tea sets now were made as children's playthings. They served a dual purpose, first as playthings and second as a means of teaching the social graces to children in families of means.

Children's dinnerware sets were made in two basic sizes. One size was used by children to entertain their friends. A smaller size was used when playing with dolls. Various designs were used on these sets, including historical scenes,

moral and educational phrases, botanical lessons, and art works of famous illustrators.

Children's feeding dishes, often divided into sections, were made during the late 19th and early 20th century, and used for children's meals. Many have a unit to hold hot water to keep the food warm during the meal. These dishes were designed with colorful animals, nursery rhymes, and children's activities to make mealtime fun for the child.

German children's dishes also were designed with rhymes, animals, children, and florals. Paints, decals, and lusters were used in abundance on these dishes. Among the leading German manufacturers was the R.S. Prussia factory of Schlegelmilch.

References: Doris Anderson Lechler, *Children's Glass Dishes, China, & Furniture*, Collector Books, 1983; Lorraine May Punchard, *Child's Play*, published by the author, 1982; Margaret & Kenn Whitmyer, *Children's Dishes*, Collector Books, 1984.

Chamber Pot, 8" d, 4¾" h, Oriental scene, blue transfer, white ground, unmarked, $165.00.

Biscuit Jar, 3½" h, pink transfer of birds, branches, and peacock, reeded handle, Staffordshire **95.00**

Bowl, 6" d, orchid luster, flowers, boy, girl, and lamb with crowned frog, black cow and winged nymph in flowers around sides, "GERMANY" . **30.00**

Cereal Set

3 pcs, pitcher, bowl, and plate, "Little Bo Peep" design and verse, German **75.00**

14 pcs, six 1⅞" h mugs, six 4¼" d cereal bowls, three handled cream and sugar, nursery rhymes and figures, holly and berry borders, blue Royal Bayreuth mark **700.00**

Coffeepot, white, pear shape, rococo handle and finial, German **42.00**

Coffee Set, 11 pcs, coffeepot, creamer, sugar, four cups and saucers, decals of German children on sides **135.00**

Creamer, "Banbury Cross" verse **37.50**

Cup and Saucer

Children playing with ball of twine, kitten, rabbit, and dog transfer, "GERMANY" **18.00**

Punch and Judy, brown transfer, Staffordshire **40.00**

Spatter, blue, handleless, glaze nick **65.00**

Dinner Service

18 pcs, pitcher, three oval scalloped platters, two cov dishes, and twelve plates, "Old Curiosity Shop" in blue, "Ridgway Humphrey Clock" **175.00**

32 pcs, cov soup tureen and undertray, two cov vegetables and undertrays, six soup bowls, twelve plates, open vegetable dish, five small plates, four platters, orange and brown floral motif, orange rims, white ground, English **300.00**

36 pcs, red and green painted stripes, white ground, Ridgway, c1850 ... **285.00**

Dish

4½" d, "Cries of London-Fine Black Cherries," multicolored, "Plex St. Pottery, Tunstall" **8.00**

7" d, scenes of Humpty Dumpty, multicolored, three sections, "Made in Czechslovakia" **6.00**

7½" d, scene of three children and monkey in center, animals on border, multicolored, "GERMANY" . **45.00**

Feeding Dish

5" d

Jack and Jill, rhyme, three feet, blue Royal Bayreuth mark **135.00**

Jack and the Beanstalk, rhyme, three feet, blue Royal Bayreuth mark **135.00**

7" d

Four children laundering, decal, German **45.00**

Girl in poppy field, decal, German **45.00**

Three girls in red dresses, decal, German **45.00**

Washington at Valley Forge, decal, semi-porcelain **32.00**

7½" d

Children on swing, decal, Bavaria **47.50**

Two children standing at fence, blue and white, "Royal Doulton" **65.00**

8" d

Girls at beach with boat, decal, divided, German **47.50**

Little boys with toys, decal, divided, German **45.00**

"Simple Simon Met a Pieman," multicolored, "Royal Schwartzburg, Germany" **65.00**

"Baby Bunting" in center, decal **20.00**

Cats, multicolored, decal **12.00**

"Changing the Guard," decal, England **50.00**

Old woman in shoe, rhyme, blue rim, decal **25.00**

Feeding Set

"Bunnykins" pattern, 3 pcs (bowl, cup, and plate), sgd "Barbara Vernon," Royal Doulton **75.00**

Child seated with dog and cat, pink transfer, 3 pcs (cup, plate, and saucer), Staffordshire **27.50**

Children at play, multicolored, 3 pcs (bowl, cup, and plate), "Shield & P.T." **42.50**

Farm animals, 3 pcs (bowl, cup, and plate), Spode **45.00**

Cup, 2½" h, black transfer, yellow handle, "Portland Pottery," $35.00.

Mug

1⅞" h, iron-red transfer of florals, "A Present For Eliza" in panel, pink luster borders, canary ground, c1825, Staffordshire (A) **465.00**

2" h, black transfer of seated girl and goat, inscribed "A Present For My Dear Girl," canary ground, c1825, Staffordshire (A) **55.00**

2⅛" h

Boy flying kite, inscribed "A Reward of Innocence," brown transfer, silver luster bands, canary ground, c1810, Staffordshire (A) **55.00**

Silver luster, resisted floral border, canary ground, c1820, Staffordshire (A) **55.00**

2¼" h, iron-red transfer of mother and child along with "A Present For My Dear Girl," pink luster bands, canary ground, Staffordshire (A) **475.00**

2⅜" h

"March," red transfer (A) **50.00**

Floral design, gaudy, red and green enamels, underglazed blue and luster **65.00**
2½" h
"The Actors," red transfer, Staffordshire **35.00**
Bird, resisted on silver luster oval, silver luster banding, canary ground, c1810–20, Staffordshire (A) **425.00**
"Cock Robin," brown transfer, purple luster rim, soft paste (A) **20.00**
"The Foxglove" and "Convolvulus," purple transfer **60.00**
"George" in floral and geometric cartouche, black transfer **65.00**
"Goldfinch," brown transfer, purple luster rim (A) **45.00**
House decoration, purple luster, soft paste (A) **12.00**
"Little Polly Finders," blue transfer   **15.00**
2⅝" h
"Billy Button," black transfer and polychrome, Staffordshire (A) . .   **30.00**
Florals, gaudy, underglaze blue and red, green and yellow enamels (A) **55.00**
Vine with white flowers resisted on green band, copper luster rims and handle, c1820, Staffordshire (A) **50.00**
2¾" h
Bears dressing up and "Getting Ready for a Walk," green transfer (A) **55.00**
Children on swing, green transfer, "Staffordshire, England" (A) . . .   **5.00**
"Darling" in gold, children's scene on white, "GERMANY" **12.00**
"Feeding the Chickens," pink transfer, Staffordshire (A) **35.00**
"V" and vulture, green transfer (A)   **35.00**
2⅞" h, "Pet Lamb," black transfer, polychrome enamels, Staffordshire (A)   **35.00**
3" h
Children and four line verse, black transfer **62.50**
"Come Away Pompey," blue and red transfer **45.00**
Family of mice, green transfer (A)   **35.00**
3½" h, seated cat and running zebra, black transfer and polychromes (A)   **85.00**
4⅝" h, child with bird, black transfer, dark red rim, imp "Wood" (A) . . .   **35.00**
Copper luster, blue band, int. rim with pink luster **45.00**
"Little Boy Blue" rhyme, English . . .   **45.00**
Nappy, children on sled, multicolored, Royal Bayreuth **70.00**
Pitcher, 4" h, "Blind Man's Bluff," decal   **15.00**
Plate
2¾" d, Franklin and kite, blue transfer   **85.00**

3½" d, children at play, transfer, rust border, imp "Wood" **75.00**
4" d, children playing in snow, multicolored, Royal Bayreuth **60.00**
5"
Octagonal, clown and elephant, German **40.00**
Square, circus and animals, decal, turned-up corners **45.00**
5½" d, school boys and "Birch Academy," green transfer, emb daisy rim with polychrome dots (A) **55.00**
5⅞"d, "Robinson Crusoe," blue transfer, emb rim with green stripes, octagonal (A) **35.00**
6" d
Boy and sailboat, blue and white, Villeroy and Boch, Saxony **65.00**
Sporting bears, multicolored, English **65.00**
6⅜" d, "A Reward for Diligence," dark brown transfer, emb polychrome enameled floral rim (A) . .   **40.00**
6½" d, "Uncle Tom's Cabin-Eva Wreathing Tom," dark red transfer, emb daisy rim with green stripe edge, octagonal, imp "C. W. P." (A)   **45.00**
7" d
"Boy Blue" in straw, Ridgway . . .   **10.00**
"Hey Diddle Diddle," multicolored, decal, "Hanley, England"   **32.00**
"Margery Daw," multicolored, decal **8.00**
Two girls with dolls, decal, "3 crowns Germany" **45.00**
7½" d
Cat and bird, "Oh! Beat Her…Wicked Puss," black transfer, emb polychrome enameled floral rim (A) **45.00**
"For a Good Child," light blue transfer, ironstone (A) **37.50**
7⅝" d, "Robinson Crusoe & Family Dining," black transfer and polychromes, emb daisy border (A) . . .   **35.00**
8¼" d, white center, color transfer of Dutch children at play on border, dated 12/25/16 . . . .   **38.00**
Potty, 8" d, 4¾" h, blue and white Oriental scene, handled **165.00**
Serving Set, 21 pcs, teapot, creamer, open sugar, six plates, six cups and saucers, "Old Curiosity Shop" pattern, "Ridgway" **250.00**
Sugar Bowl, "Water Hen" pattern, blue transfer, "Carson, England" **35.00**
Sugar Bowl, Cov, "Pet Goat," transfer, Staffordshire **25.00**
Tea and Coffee Set, 16 pcs, 4⅞" h coffeepot, four cups and saucers, 3½" h pitcher, 3⅛" h sugar bowl, 3¾" d waste bowl, 4" h teapot, 3¾" h tea

caddy, 12¾" h side handled coffeepot, 3⅛" d stand, pearlware, blue
feather edges, damage (A) **1,000.00**

Tea Service

7 pcs, teapot, creamer, sugar, two
cups and saucers, Punch and Judy
pattern, blue transfer, white
ground, c1900, "Staffordshire" ... **275.00**

7 pcs, teapot, creamer, sugar, two
cups and saucers, Victorian girl and
pets, blue transfer, white ground,
Staffordshire **120.00**

7 pcs, teapot, creamer, cov sugar, and
four cups, peafowl at fountain,
transfer, Staffordshire **135.00**

8 pcs, teapot, creamer, sugar, two
cups and saucers, 9½" l x 8½" w
tray, shaded green, gold trim **120.00**

11 pcs, teapot, creamer, sugar, four
cups and saucers, "Tiny Blue and
White" pattern, c1890–1910, German **125.00**

11 pcs, teapot, cov creamer, sugar,
four cups and saucers, wide gold
decorative band, white ground,
German **70.00**

11 pcs, teapot, creamer, sugar, four
teabowls and saucers, white ironstone **125.00**

12 pcs, teapot, creamer, cov sugar,
waste bowl, four cups and saucers,
girl and dog in doorway, florals,
and wheel design, blue transfer,
c1880s, blue English registry mark **175.00**

14 pcs, teapot, creamer, sugar, five
cups and six 4" d plates, spatterware, red band at edge, black
crosses and blue dots **275.00**

15 pcs, teapot, creamer, sugar, four
plates, four cups and saucers, pink
and white caladium leaves on
white ground, c1900, German ... **125.00**

15 pcs, teapot, creamer, sugar, six
cups and saucers, circus designs,
luster trim, "Bavaria" **125.00**

15 pcs, teapot, creamer, sugar, six
cups and saucers, Dutch children
and windmills, blue and white ... **150.00**

15 pcs, teapot, creamer, sugar, six
cups and saucers, nursery rhymes,
Bavaria **150.00**

15 pcs, teapot, creamer, sugar, six
cups and saucers, Old Mother Hubbard, blue transfer **250.00**

16 pcs, teapot, creamer, sugar, waste
bowl, four plates, four cups and
saucers, child and dog on white,
blue transfer, octagonal shape,
c1890, Staffordshire **185.00**

16 pcs, teapot, creamer, sugar, waste
bowl, four plates, four cups and

saucers, "Little Mae," red transfer,
c1890, Staffordshire **225.00**

16 pcs, teapot, creamer, sugar, waste
bowl, six cups and saucers,
"Chintz" pattern, blue, Ridgway . **300.00**

16 pcs, 5¼" h teapot, 4½" h sugar,
3½" h creamer, four 5½" d plates,
4" d, waste bowl, four cups and
saucers, white with red and blue
stick spatter, "Staffordshire, England," repairs (A) **90.00**

17 pcs, teapot, creamer, sugar, four
plates, five cups and saucers, kittens dressed as children, tan and
blue luster, raised designs, c1900,
German **225.00**

18 pcs, teapot, creamer, sugar, five
plates, five cups and saucers, children with farm animals, decal, German **215.00**

18 pcs, teapot, creamer, sugar, six
cups and saucers, waste bowl, two
servers, brown and white trellis design, Copeland **300.00**

21 pcs, teapot, creamer, sugar, six
plates, six cups and saucers, boy
and girl with animals, silhouette,
decal, German **125.00**

21 pcs, teapot, creamer, sugar, six
plates, six cups and saucers, children and toys, multicolored, decal,
c1900, German **225.00**

21 pcs, 4" h teapot, creamer, sugar,
six cups and saucers, and six serving pieces, leaves and buds, green
transfer, stoneware, English **150.00**

21 pcs, teapot, creamer, cov sugar,
six plates, six cups and saucers,
white, beaded edges, German ... **150.00**

23 pcs, "Blue Willow" pattern, Bavaria **175.00**

**Vegetable Tureen, cov, 8½" l, "This is the
Cow," multicolored decal on cov, "This
is the Cat" on base, white ground, England, $35.00.**

23 pcs, teapot, milk jug, sugar, five
 cups and saucers, trailing roses and
 gilt rims, c1830, Paris (A) **200.00**
Tea Set, 3 pcs, teapot, creamer, and
 sugar
 French man and woman, multicolored, Royal Bayreuth **450.00**
 "Turkey Boy" design **100.00**
Tea Set, part, creamer, sugar, teabowl
 and saucer, sprig design, Staffordshire **70.00**
Teabowl
 Mother and child sewing dolls
 clothes, blue transfer **22.00**
 "The Play Fellow," girl and cat in garden, blue transfer **22.00**
Teapot, "Capering Elves" design, pink
 luster, c1900 .... **70.00**
Tete-A-Tete Set, porcelain, teapot, cake
 plate, creamer, sugar, two cups and
 saucers, cobalt inserts of French period figures, French **165.00**

CHOISY-LE-ROI

Seine, France, 1804–Present

History: This French factory produced porcelain
and white earthenware at Choisy-le-Roi in Seine,
France from 1804. First, table services and toilet
sets that featured French views or classical scenes
printed in red or black were made here. Later,
relief decorative motifs were added.

The factory began making earthenware about
1830. Black transfer prints were used with occasional touches of color. After 1860 more relief
work was used, and some pieces were glazed
with brilliant colors. Other works included tiles
and *trompe l'oeil* pieces in the form of ducks,
pigs, and plates of asparagus or oysters.

Beginning in 1836 the factory traded as Hautin
and Boulanger. Marks incorporate Choisy, or Ch
le Roy, or HB & Cie. The factory still remains in
operation.

Dessert Stand, 8½" d, majolica, multicolored, dark brown ground **200.00**
Plate
 8" d
 Black transfer, "La Marguerite
 No.19," young woman seated
 with suitor in garden, flying bird
 border, "H. B. & Cie" **35.00**
 Multicolored scene of bullfight
 characters, Alicante crest, green
 berry border, gilt rim, "H. B. &
 Cie" **20.00**

**Plate, 7½" d, black transfer, blue border,
"Terre de Fer, H. B. & Cie," $25.00.**

8¼" d
 Brown printed, named views of
 France, yellow ground, shaped
 rims, green accents, c1830 .... **350.00**
 Majolica, girl with two goats in
 center, border of wild animals,
 green crackled glaze, brown
 band separating center from border, c1850, "H. B. & Cie" **70.00**
8½" d
 Black scenes, "Paul & Virginia,"
 yellow ground by Bernardin De
 St. Pierre, each plate numbered,
 c1815, "Choisy-Le-Roi," set of
 12 ....**3,900.00**
 Majolica, strutting peasant, pale
 blue glaze, c1860, "H. B. & Cie" **30.00**
 Majolica, swimming swan in cen-
 ter, turquoise crackled glaze,
 c1860, "H. B. & Cie" **48.00**
 Scene of young girl waving at ducks
 in flight **25.00**
 9" d, Black transfer, swimming series,
 boy and girl in swimming suits,
 green border, "H. B. & Cie" **22.00**

**Plate, 9" d, multicolored, "H. B. & Cie,"
$65.00.**

10½" d, Guinea hen, multicolors, extending to border, "H. Boulanger & Co." **10.00**

Tile, 6⅛" sq, polychrome underwater and hippos shooting fantasy, "H. Boulanger Cie, Choisy-Le-Roi," mantel set of 17 (A) **400.00**

WILKINSON LTD
ENGLAND

CLARICE CLIFF

Burslem, England
1925–1963

History: Clarice Cliff, 1899–1972, began her training at Stoke-on-Trent at age 13 when she joined the staff at A.J. Wilkinson, Ltd.'s Royal Staffordshire Pottery at Burslem. They acquired the adjoining Newport factory along with a huge supply of undecorated bowls and vases that were assigned to Clarice Cliff to decorate. She utilized vivid colors and eccentric Art Deco designs with chunky, angular shapes that contrasted sharply with the flowing lines of the earlier Art Nouveau period. Cliff became art director of A. J. Wilkinson, Ltd. in 1930.

Cliff's earthenwares were gay and colorful. Circles, squares, colored bands, diamonds, conical shapes, and simple landscapes were incorporated in the designs. Pattern names included: Applique, Bizarre, Fantasque, Gay Day, Latonia, Lodore, Ravel, and the most popular Crocus. These patterns were all mass–produced and achieved tremendous popularity in both England and America.

Shapes also had special names such as: Athens, Biarritz, Chelsea, Conical, Daffodil, Iris, Lotus, Lynton, Stamford, and Trieste. A customer could order the shape that he wanted decorated with the pattern of his choice. Many novelty pieces such as flower holders, vases, inkwells, candlesticks, cruet sets, bookends, umbrella stands, and even a ceramic telephone cover all were made in Clarice Cliff designs.

In 1965, Wilkinson was bought by Midwinter. Midwinter merged with J & G Meakin in 1968. In 1970 Meakin was absorbed by the Wedgwood Group.

References: Peter Wentworth-Shields & Kay Johnson, *Clarice Cliff*, L'Odeon, 1976.

Museums: Brighton Museum, Brighton, England.

Collecting Hints: Clarice Cliff used several different printed marks, each of which incorporated a facsimile of her signature and usually the name of the pattern. Unmarked pieces of Clarice Cliff china are rare. The large number of back stamps that were used leads to confusion in dating examples.

Basket, 12¾" d, 9¼" h, "Celtic Harvest," cream and gold, brightly painted fruit flowers **300.00**

Bone Dish, "Tonquin" pattern, brown transfer, "Royal Staffordshire, Clarice Cliff" **10.00**

Bowl
3½" d, "Gay Day" design **50.00**
7¼" d, "Inspiration," brown, yellow, orange, and blue flowers, trees and hills, mottle turquoise ground, three short feet, "Wilkinson, Ltd." **120.00**
7½" d, "Bizarre-Delicia," orange and yellow fruits on ext., cream int., dark brown running over lime green band **500.00**
8" sq, "Zigurat," swirling blue, turquoise, and pale blue, satin finish, stepped shape **900.00**
8¾" d, "Bizarre," orange banded top rim, orange and green striping on bottom, orange, green, and cream geometrics outlined in black **500.00**
9" d, "Fantasque-Canterbury Bells" . **125.00**

Candlesticks, 3½" h, "Fantasque," cream body, blue drip guards, orange flowers, green leaves on bases, outlined bottom edges, pr **500.00**

Coffeepot
7" h, "Bizarre," green flowers, orange leaves, cream to brown ground, shaded green **150.00**
7½" h, "Fantasque/Bizarre-Autumn," black trees, orange, blue, and green foliage, red meadows, cream body, red circled cov **750.00**

Cup and Saucer
10" d, "Bizarre Cruiseware," lady on deck of ship, fine line drawing, ships in background, ship on cup **225.00**
"Charlotte" pattern, brown **8.00**
"Tonquin" pattern, blue transfer ... **12.50**

Dinner Service, six 10" d plates, 9" d plates, 8" d plates, six 6½" d bowls, two cov 8" d bowls, 9" d bowl, 3 piece condiment set, six 4¾" d handled bowls and saucers, milk pitcher, 11½" l, 12½" l, 14½" l trays, three shaded brown concentric rings, outer green ring, cream ground **600.00**

Figure, 3½" h, Art Deco shoe, gray, gold, and brown leaves, cream ground **90.00**

Flower Frog, 3⅝" d, "Bizarre," mottled green and cream, pile of rocks **70.00**

Left, vase, 12½" h, blue and yellow birds, gray body, turquoise edge, puce shadow florals, $700.00; center, bisquit jar, 6¾" h, "Fantasque Melon," orange bands, yellow, red, and green fruits, brown accents, wicker handle, $700.00; right, jug, 11½" h, "Lotus," black, green, and orange geometrics outlined in black, cream ground, $3,400.00.

Gravy Boat and Tray, "Tonquin" pattern
Black transfer 25.00
Brown transfer 22.00
Inkwell, 3" h, stylized apples and leaves, green, yellow, orange, and puce (A) 75.00
Jardiniere, 7⅞" h, "Fantasque," band of stylized fruit, off-white, orange lower section (A) 540.00
Jug
5½" h, "Bizarre," royal blue, green, and lavender, cream ground, brown trim outlined 200.00
5¾" h, "Bizarre," orange, blue, green, and cream triangles, black trim outlined 175.00
6¾" h, blue trees and shrubs, tan accents, gray ring emb body 110.00
7½" h, "My Garden," bright red and brown dripping colors, floral handle 175.00
8⅝" h, 5½" d, Art Deco style emb pink and blue flowers, green leaves, light gray ground, tan branch handle 75.00
10¼" h, 6" d, "Celtic Harvest," cream and gold 165.00
12" h, "Bizarre/Lotus," multicolored geometrics, dbl handles 2,500.00
12½" h, "Bizarre/Lotus," orange, yellow, and brown banding and upper geometrics, single cream handle .2,700.00
Pitcher
4½" h, "Fantasque/Bizarre," black tree trunks, red foliage, cream body, green upper band, imp wave pattern on spout 350.00
5½" h, "Tonquin" pattern, brown transfer 25.00

6½" h, "Bizarre," trees, yellow and cream ground 350.00
7" h, "Pineapple" pattern 65.00
7¾" h
"Autumn Crocus" 450.00
"Fantasque," cream body, orange foot, single orange banded handle, black outlined blue and orange florals 375.00
11½" h, "Tonquin" pattern, brown transfer 14.00

Planter, 10" l, blue and green birds, gray ground, $175.00.

Plaque
6⅞" d, "Libra-Zodiac," red, yellow, blue, and black relief Libra motif, scales and stars, inscribed, cream ground, star shape, dated 1923, Wilkinson (A) 85.00
12⅝" d, white flowers, green centers, brown branches, green leaves, light gray ground, pierced for hanging . 150.00
18" d, "Cottage Garden," multicolored 1,900.00

Plate

6" d, "Tonquin" pattern, blue transfer   **5.00**
9½" d, "Rural Scenes" pattern, purple
  and white **10.00**
9¾" d, tan trees, aqua foliage, light
  gray ground, aqua edge **85.00**
10" d, large basket full of flowers,
  bright multicolors **22.00**

Platter, "Tonquin" pattern, brown transfer

11" l..........................   **30.00**
11½"l **35.00**

Sandwich Set, 11¾" l, 6" w platter, three
  5¾" d plates, "Fantasque," bright
  slashes of purple, orange, blue,
  cream, and brown, in brown center
  circle, octagonal **925.00**

Soup Plate, 10" d, "Charlotte" pattern,
  lavender **12.50**

Sugar

5½" h, relief of two multicolored
  clowns, white ground, finial of two
  clown heads, c1934 (A) **100.00**
"Chelsea" pattern, pink **12.50**

Tea Plate, 6" d, "Fantasque," bright orange dec, cream, blue, green, and
  brown, octagonal **45.00**

Tea Service, demitasse, teapot, creamer,
  sugar, six cups and saucers, orange
  poppies, green and black ground, orange body, orange and black trim
  banding **1,800.00**

Teapot, 5" h, Bizarre Ware, multicolored, $200.00.

Teapot

5" d, 5" h, "Gay Day," rust, orange,
  and purple flowers, green and blue
  foliage, yellow and green trim ...   **150.00**
6" h, "Celtic Harvest," multicolored   **215.00**

Toast Rack, 6¾" l, "Crocus," orange,
  purple, and blue crocuses, yellow
  and green trim **100.00**

Toby Jug, seated figure of Winston
  Churchill, "Clarice Cliff-Wilkinson"   **660.00**

Tray

10" l, 8½" w, stylized sunflower, multicolored **85.00**
11" l, "Sunburst," geometric pattern   **175.00**
12¾" l, 5¾" w, molded orange and
  yellow flowers at ends, gray ground   **65.00**

Vases

3" h, Art Deco stylized florals, pastels,
  triangular **50.00**
6" h, emb pink and blue flowers,
  green leaves, light gray ground,
  aqua shading at top **65.00**
6½" h
  "Bizarre-Delicia," oranges and
    lemons around neck, dripping
    variegated foliage, pedestal foot   **300.00**
  "Fantasque," stylized multicolored
    fruit and leaves, green and orange bands (A) **100.00**
6⅝" h, "Delicia," oranges and lemons, gray and green drippings **225.00**
7" h, 8¼" d, "Bizarre," raised concentric rings, orange top band, tree
  with orange, purple, green, and
  brown leaves hanging down, cream
  body **400.00**
7¼" h, emb orange, green and gold
  flowers, light gray ground, shaded
  green top **75.00**
8" h, 5¾" d, Art Deco stylized florals,
  heavy brown and tan tree branches
  around   base,   green   raised
  branches, small blue leaves, orange
  and yellow raised flowers, light
  gray ground, green inside top edge   **110.00**
8¼" h, 4" d, Art Deco stylized florals,
  raised tan, rust, green, and yellow
  florals and leaves, green splash inside top edge, light gray ground,
  tan branch handles **75.00**
8½" h, multicolored leaves and flowers, cream ground **325.00**
8¾" h, 4¾" d, Art Deco stylized florals, raised pink and blue flowers,
  green leaves, light gray ground,
  blue inside top edge, tan branch
  handle **85.00**
9¼" h, 5¼" d, Art Deco stylized florals, emb gray, green, and yellow
  leaves and branch, light green
  ground **85.00**
11⅝" h, "Bizarre," orange, black,
  rust, and mauve stylized flowers on
  green at neck, orange lower section, dbl handled, "Newport Pottery" (A) **480.00**
12" h, "Inspiration/Lotus," multicolored, single handle **7,000.00**

Vegetable Bowl, 9" d, "Charlotte" pattern, blue **18.00**

Wall Pocket, 5½" l, "Dolphin" design   **50.00**

CLEWS

Cobridge Works, Staffordshire, England
1818–1834

History: James and Ralph Clews were Staffordshire potters who operated the Cobridge Works from 1818 to 1834. They were known for the fine quality of their blue transfer-printed earthenwares, mostly made for the American market. American views used on their wares were taken from contemporary prints. In addition, designs were taken from books, e.g., the Clews series of Dr. Syntax and Don Quixote. Plates also were made from the comic pictures drawn by Sir David Wilkie. The company's English views consisted chiefly of castles, abbeys, and cathedrals.

References: N. Hudson Moore, *The Old China Book*, Charles E. Tuttle Co., second printing, 1980.

Museums: Cincinnati Art Museum, Cincinnati, Ohio; Metropolitan Museum of Art, New York.

Collecting Hints: The two most famous patterns by Clews are "Landing of Lafayette" and the "States." The "Landing of Lafayette" pattern contains an extremely large number of accessory pieces.

Plate, 6¾" d, "Christmas Eve," dark blue transfer, imp "Clews," $175.00.

Berry Bowl, girl, fruit basket, floral border, dark blue transfer **100.00**
Bowl
10½" d, "Escape of the Mouse," blue transfer, dbl handles, "Ralph Clews-Cobridge" **550.00**

12⅞" d, 5" h, classical ruins, medium blue transfer, imp "Clews" (A) ... **70.00**
Cup and Saucer, handleless, fruit, dark blue transfer, imp "Clews" (A) **75.00**
Dish, 5¾" d, still life pattern, dark blue transfer, imp "Clews & Stone China" **50.00**
Foot Bath, 20" H-H, pearlware, painted summer flowers on int. and ext., foliate and lobed handles, sepia accents, c1825, imp "J. & R. Clews" (A) **975.00**
Plate
4⅜" d, "The Letter of Introduction," dark blue transfer **300.00**
4½" d, "Christmas Eve," dark blue transfer **145.00**
7¼" d, "Dr Syntax Stargazing," blue transfer **75.00**
8" d
Dark blue and white florals, mottled light blue background **80.00**
"Dr Syntax Returning From His Tour," blue transfer **165.00**
8¾" d
"Dr Syntax Reading His Tour," dark blue transfer **225.00**
Emb rim, blue feather edge, imp "Clews" (A) **35.00**
"The Meeting of Sancho and Dapple," blue transfer, c1820 ..... **275.00**
9" d
"Christmas Eve," dark blue transfer, imp "Clews" (A) **155.00**
"The Valentine," dark blue transfer **200.00**
10" d
"Knighthood Conferred on Don Quixote," dark blue transfer ... **150.00**
"The Valentine," dark blue transfer, imp "Clews" (A) **125.00**
10⅛" d
"Dr Syntax Painting a Portrait," dark blue transfer, imp "Clews" (A) **150.00**
Fishing scene, cathedral in background, dark blue transfer, imp "Clews" (A) **100.00**
10¼" d
"Escape of the Mouse," Wilkie Series, dark blue transfer **185.00**
"Playing at Draughts," dark blue transfer, imp "Clews" (A) **120.00**
"The Valentine," dark blue transfer **185.00**
10½" d, "Dr Syntax Painting a Portrait," blue transfer, rim chip **85.00**
10¾" d, English hunting scene, dark blue transfer, imp "Clews" (A) ... **85.00**
Platter, 17" l, blue feather edge, imp "Clews" (A) **150.00**
Sauce Tureen, 9½" l, matching tray, "Dr Syntax Bound to a Tree" on bowl, "Dr Syntax Pursued by a Bull" on lid, and "Death of Punch" on tray, dark

blue transfers, hairlines, imp "Clews"
(A) **625.00**
Soup Plate
8⅝" d, fishing scene, cathedral in
background, dark blue transfer, imp
"Clews" (A) **85.00**
9⅞" d, "Dr Syntax Mistakes a Gentle-
man's House for an Inn," dark blue
transfer, imp "Clews" (A) **160.00**
Teabowl and Saucer
Birds, black transfer, imp "Clews" (A)   **20.00**
"Brush Strokes," blue transfer **225.00**
"Christmas Eve," dark blue transfer,
imp "Clews" (A) **170.00**
Floral design, dark blue transfer **135.00**
Toddy Cup, 4⅝" h, emb blue rim, imp
"Clews" (A) **12.50**

ENGLAND
COALPORT
A.D. 1750.

ENGLISH PORCELAIN
CO-ALPORT
1830 - 50

COALPORT

Severn Gorge, Shropshire, England
c1796–Present

History: After John Rose completed his apprenticeship at Caughley, he established a pottery at
Coalport in Shropshire in 1796. Rose expanded
his original factory with the purchase of Caughley
in 1799. His original soft paste formula eventually was superseded by bone china ware.

By 1822 molds, models, and some key per-
sonnel were acquired from the South Wales porcelain manufacturers at Swansea and Nantgarw
and incorporated into the Coalport factory. In
1820 John Rose won a Society of Arts medal for
his lead-free glaze.   The most characteristic type
of Coalport porcelains are the distinctive Rococo
style flower-encrusted decorative pieces called
"Coalbrookdale." "Indian Tree," first made in
1801, and "Hong Kong," made c1805 are two
tableware patterns that are still popular to this
day.

John Rose died in 1841. Production at Coalport continued under Thomas Rose, his son, W.F.
Rose, his nephew, and William Pugh. The influence of Sevres is reflected in the style and decoration of table and ornamental wares made during the mid-nineteenth century.

In 1885 the Bruff family took over. The Coalport firm was sold to Cauldon Potteries Ltd. in
Staffordshire in 1923 and moved to the Staffordshire area in 1926 along with many of the workers.

By 1936 both Coalport and Cauldon became
part of Crescent potteries at Stoke-on-Trent. In
1958 Coalport was acquired by Brain of Foley
China and preserved its separate identity. Many
traditional patterns and lines were revived. In
1967 Coalport became part of the Wedgwood
group. The Coalport name continues on a line of
modern china products.

References: G. Godden, *Coalport and Coal-
brookdale Porcelains*, Praeger, 1970; Compton
MacKenzie, *The House of Coalport, 1750–1950*,
Collins, 1951.

Museums: Cincinnati Museum of Art, Cincinnati,
Ohio; Coalport China Works Museum, Ironbridge Gorge Museum Trust, Shropshire, England.

Basket
7" l, applied pastel flowers on rim and
handle, turquoise ground, c1830
(A) **240.00**
9" h, applied flowers on rim ext., orange ground, int. with painted
sprays, gilt, oval shell form, handle
(A) **360.00**
10" w, 4½" h, center cobalt flowers,
ftd, c1830–40 .... **400.00**
Box, 4½" l, 3" w, "Blue Willow" pattern, egg shape **80.00**
Cake Plate, 10½" l, hp, sprays of summer flowers, gilt border, lozenge
shape, pr (A) **115.00**
Candlesticks, 4" h, Kingsware, black
"crown" mk, pr **30.00**
Card Tray, 7½" l, painted center multicolored spray, shell basket shape,
edged with sprays of modeled flowers, stalks form overhead handle, blue
"Coalport" mk (A) **180.00**
Compote, 9½" d, hp, birds in center,
dark pink and gold border, sgd "John
Randell," c1842, set of 3 .... **500.00**
Cup, 7" d, anniversary of Coronation of
Queen Elizabeth II, black silhouette

**Cup and Saucer, blue leaves, white
ground, gold trim, $25.00.**

with gold trim on front, Drury Lane theater in color and gold trim on reverse, dbl handled, mkd **85.00**

Cup and Saucer, multicolored floral medallions, tan ground, gilt trim, c1820, $50.00.

Cup and Saucer
"Harebell" pattern **25.00**
Multicolored landscape scenes (A) .. **35.00**
Paneled orange and iron-red border, gilt and black flowers, c1810 (A) . **80.00**
Small red flowered borders, swirl shape, c1883 .... **40.00**
Demitasse Cup and Saucer, pate-surpate roses, gold trim, pink ground .. **350.00**
Dessert Plate
8⅝" d, painted center, named views of "Tintern Abbey" and "Blea Tarn," dark blue scale ground, reserved panels of flowers, gilt scrollwork, sgd "J.H. Plant," pr (A) **360.00**
Reserved painted flowers, reserved and molded puce borders, gilt flowers, three panels with painted flowers, yellow foliage molded rims, c1840, set of 12 (A) **365.00**
Dessert Service
14 pcs, two cov cream tureens, fruit dish, eleven 8¾" d, plates, painted rustic views and landscapes, shaped rim, gilt foliage scrolls, yellow florets, blue ground c1840 (A) **285.00**
16 pcs, ten plates, two oval cake plates, two quatrefoil bonbon dishes, two cov sauce tureens, white ground with reserves of summer flowers in gilt and puce scroll work with green diapering (A) **1,300.00**
18 pcs, three shell shaped dishes, three 10¾" l lozenge shaped dishes, two sq dishes, ten 8" d plates, "Japan" pattern, peonies and Oriental flowers in fenced garden, "Brocade" border of floral and diaper panels, c1805 (A) **2,530.00**
26 pcs, three 9¼" w sq dishes, three 10" w shell shaped dishes, two cov

sugar and stands, eighteen 9½" d plates, painted bouquets and sprays, shaped blue borders, gilt foliage, c1825, Pattern #N210 (A) .**2,100.00**
28 pcs, painted fruit and flowers sprays, olive border molded with C-scrolls and sprays, gilding, c1820, "Coalport Imported Felspar Porcelain" (A) **6,050.00**
Dinner and Dessert Service, blue ground molded with flowers reserved on white, gilt scrolling, damage, c1820, set of 67 pcs (A) **3,520.00**
Dinner Service
31 pcs, Imari style, shaped panels of trees, gilt, and white foliage, iron-red ground, border of flowerheads, iron-red basketweave, c1810 (A) .**3,888.00**
38 pcs, two tazzas, three oval serving plates, three rect serving plates, thirty dessert plates, floral sprays reserved in cobalt border, molded gilt accented scalloped rim, c1860 ..**3,200.00**
80 pcs, apricot ground, sheaf of corn tied with ribbons and flower sprays, c1820 (A) **6,820.00**
110 pcs, seventy–four 10¼" d soup plates, thirty–six 10¼" d dinner plates, botanical centers, three gilt cartouches of florals on royal blue rim, light yellow and gilt foliage edge, c1840, purple "John Rose & Co, Colebrookdale, Shropshire" .**2,500.00**
Dish
8" w, cobalt border reserved with four panels of Kakiemon and palette flowers, kidney shape, c1820 (A) . **155.00**
10" l, multicolored florals, white ground, burgundy edge, oval shape, c1825 .... **100.00**
12¾" w, pierced basketweave border, gilt and flower sprays, painted bouquets and sprays, molded scroll and foliage rim, c1820, blue "X'd swords and dot" mk **275.00**
Ewer, 12¼" h, Renaissance style, Venus on two dolphins, white slip with green, blue ground, white and gilt scrolling, c1855, imp "CBD" mk (A) **585.00**
Figure, 7" h, "Judith Anne," plum dress, hat, muff, and shawl, blue necklace **85.00**
Flower Arrangement, 1½", multicolored molded flowers, "Coalbrookdale" .. **12.00**
Fruit Cooler, 13½" h, sprays of roses, morning glories, and tulips in cobalt bands, gilt, tapered cylindrical form, crenalated lid, early 19th C (A) **200.00**
Inkstand, 7½" l, modeled stag's head, cornucopia sander, baluster well, applied painted foliage, two quill holders, four scroll molded feet, c1840, "Coalbrookdale" (A) **530.00**

Jardiniere

4½", matching stand, river landscape on front, floral cluster on reverse, gilt ground panel, gilt scroll dbl handles **150.00**

5⅞" h, bronze and gold painted continuous scene, classical figures and dragon between formal borders (A) **200.00**

Jug, 8" h, painted sprays of hops, fruit, and flowers, gilt "RR," gilded scrollwork border (A) **300.00**

Letter Rack, 6¼" w, cobalt ground, reserves of painted florals, backplates reserved with songbirds, pierced gold and white leaves on sides, four gilt feet, c1820, pr (A) **900.00**

Miniature, tea service, quatrefoil teapot, milk jug, sugar, four cups and saucers, pink ground, green and white jeweling, gilt borders, c1891 (A) ... **825.00**

Pastille Burner, 7" h, bone china

Church, removable plinth, molded fruit on roof, gold outlined windows, "CD" mk **1,500.00**

Cottage, two open flowers on roof, c1835, "CD" mk **1,000.00**

Pitcher

4" h, Oriental florals, blue, orange, and green, gilt trim and handle, c1800 .... **150.00**

6" h, Oriental florals, blue and white, top and bottom blue bands **60.00**

Plate

8" d

Molded "Blind Earl" pattern, lobed gilt rims, set of 4 (A) **770.00**

Painted central floral bouquet, white ground, lavender border, gilt accent, set of 10 (A) **225.00**

8⅜" d, multicolored "Japan" pattern, vase of flowers on terrace, wide borders of floral panels, birds, insects, small gilt panels of iron-red florals, c1805, set of 8 (A) **1,320.00**

Plate, 8½" d, "Cigar" pattern, Imari palette, blue seashells on back, $185.00.

8½" d

Blue mountain scene, elaborate gold border, by Percy Simpson, c1907 .... **225.00**

Botanical hp scenes, green and gilt borders, set of 4 (A) **175.00**

Floral center, pink border, scalloped gilt rim, pr **165.00**

Gilt center, cobalt rims with gilt, four reserves on rims of birds and flowers, multicolored, c1820, pr **400.00**

Imari "Cigar" pattern, blue slashes on reverse, c1810 .... **185.00**

8⅝" d, center dragon, dbl floral panel border, multicolored, c1820 (A) .. **155.00**

9" d

Kingsware, Oriental flowers, rust, blue, and green, raised border design **25.00**

Pink roses, dark green garlands, gold rim **85.00**

Scene of "The Rugged Hills of Skye" by Percy Simpson, gilt border, c1907 .... **225.00**

White, gold trimmed wavy edge . **25.00**

9¼" d

Gilt center medallion, turquoise border reserved and painted in puce, children with trophies in gilt scroll cartouches, pierced with bands of foliage, gilt dentil rim, c1865 (A) **70.00**

Painted buildings in landscapes, shaped gilt outlines, borders with S-scroll bands, c1885, pr (A) ... **350.00**

Painted center scene, sailing boat on stormy sea approaching quay, formal gilt border, c1805–10 (A) **70.00**

9⅜" d, Imari style, trees, rocks, and fences, paneled six-lobed borders, set of 4 (A) **435.00**

9½" d

Floral center, six different flowers, blue, gilt trim, c1830, unmkd .. **125.00**

Landmark series, scenes of Windsor Castle and Kenilworth Castle, pale ruby border, gilt tracings, sgd "Percy Simpson," pr **335.00**

10" d

Floral bouquet center, hp pink rim with molded ribbon and twine decor, Thomas Dixon **175.00**

Scenic center, girl holding child, green and gold border, sgd "Hancock" **225.00**

Scenic center, girl, donkey, and child, wide red and gold border, sgd "Hancock" **225.00**

10¼" d, painted center, coronet, and interlaced initials, gilt line rim, set of 12 .... **375.00**

Platter, 14½" l, center pink roses, green

and yellow leaves, blue, red, and gold oeil-de-perdrix rim **150.00**

Potpourri Jar, 14¾" h, painted bouquets and applied flowerheads, foliage molded handle, pierced cov, cornucopia shape, four feet, "Coalbrookdale" (A) **350.00**

Sauce Tureen, 8" l, matching stands, iron-red and gold vine borders in gilt bands, gilt scroll handles and knobs, c1805–10, pr (A) **330.00**

Soup Plate, 9¼" d, "Japan" pattern, flowering plants and willow tree near terrace, borders of brocade panels, multicolored, c1820, set of 12 (A) . . **1,760.00**

Tea Container, 5½" h, top and bottom trim, green, four large enameled reserves around center and top, gilt touches **150.00**

Tea Set, teapot, creamer, cov sugar, oval tray, painted insects, white ground, cobalt band, "Coalbrookdale" **300.00**

Tray
6" l, cobalt, rust, and green florals, gold outlined pattern, oval **75.00**
8" l, hp, Chinese pattern, gilt trim, oval, c1830 . . . . **75.00**

Urn
8¼" h, blue and gilt decorations on white ground, pr **300.00**
11" h, cov, reserve of "Loch Achray," river, hills, and Roman ruins, cobalt and ivory ground, gold tracery . . . **285.00**

Vase
5⅛" h, named views of "Windermere" and "Loch Arne," oval gilt bands, light yellow cartouches, scrolls on blue ground, gilt angular handles and feet, c1910 (A) **415.00**
6" h, turquoise raised dots, gold ground, gold tracery, red enamel jewels, lion head handles **445.00**
6½" h, flowers on gold ground, flanked by two green bands, band of stylized flowers on lower section, c1805 (A) **116.00**
7¾" h, painted panels, lake scenes, spray of garden flowers, gilt borders, dark blue ground, spiral fluted bands on neck and foot, shield shape, looped garland handles, c1855, "Coalbrookdale," pr (A) . . **300.00**
9¼" h, cov, painted oval panels, lake scenes reserved on gilt ground, turquoise enamel studs, ram's mask handles, damage to handles, c1910 (A) **110.00**
10¼" h, painted continuous band of flowers on pink ground, bands of molded gilt foliage, fixed gilt ring and lion mask handles, pr (A) **336.00**
10½" h, cov, painted flower panel,

reserved on yellow cell-diaper ground, pink roses, garden flowers on shoulder, shield shape, dbl upright scroll handles, late 19th C, London-decorated (A) **300.00**
11" h, painted bouquet, in gilt mirror, blue ground, vase shaped cartouche, gilt scrolling, horned faun's mask handles, oviform, c1810 (A) **400.00**
20" h, cov, painted bouquets, molded and gilt cartouches, applied florals on foliate molded ground, turquoise and gold, elaborate scroll handles and foot, domed cov, pierced flame finial, c1835 (A) . . . **600.00**

Vegetable Dish, 9⅝" l, cov, blue, iron-red, salmon, and gilt central Oriental floral spray, border of floral and bird panels, gilt scroll knob, rect, c1810   **100.00**

1833 - 47

COPELAND
1850 - 67

ENGLAND
New Stone

COPELAND
1851-55

COPELAND-SPODE

London and Stoke-on-Trent, England
1833–Present
(see Spode for early history)

History: William Copeland died in 1826, and Josiah Spode II died in 1827. In 1833 William Taylor Copeland bought the Spode share in the London showroom and warehouse as well as the Spode Factory. Copeland took Thomas Garrett, a London colleague, as a partner and the firm was known as Copeland & Garrett from 1833 to 1847.

About 1842 Copeland's statuary porcelain body was developed and achieved success. Statuary porcelain, a major new art product, was sponsored by the new Art Unions. Many competitors adopted it, renaming it "Parian." Copeland statuettes, portrait busts, and other objects dominated the market until 1914. Production was halted after that date.

The name Spode was subordinated to that of Copeland after 1847, but the high standards of quality in all its products both in design and execution were maintained. The Spode Factory has held Royal Warrants from 1806 to the present time. The Spode Factory survived many difficult times, constantly striving to maintain its reputation as the producers of fine ceramic wares.

In 1966 the Copeland family sold the firm to the Carborundum Company Ltd., who injected much needed capital to help the firm compete with the other English pottery and porcelain companies. In 1970 the bicentenary year of the firm's establishment, the name of the company was changed back to Spode to honor the founder. In 1976 Spode joined with the Worcester Royal Porcelain Company to form Royal Worcester Spode.

Up to 1833 the name "Spode" refers to the period during which the two Josiahs controlled the company. From 1833 onwards "Spode" refers to the Spode Factory irrespective of ownership. From about 1842 to 1880 the name Spode seldom appears on its products. Remember all Copeland & Garrett and Copeland wares are Spode factory productions.

Copeland & Garrett 1833–1847
Copeland c1847–1970
Spode 1970–Present

References: see Spode.

Museums: see Spode.

Platter, 14¾" l, 11½" w, "Spode's Tower" pattern, blue transfer, "Copeland-Spode," $125.00.

Candlesticks, 13" h, dark red ground, female figures, "Copeland," pr	**400.00**
Charger, 14" d, "Shanghai" pattern	**45.00**
Coffeepot	
"Billingsley Rose" pattern	**40.00**
"Rosebud Chintz" pattern	**90.00**
Creamer	
4" h, "Spode's Tower" pattern, blue transfer	**48.00**
"Mayflower" pattern	**25.00**
"Maytime" pattern	**28.00**

Creamer and Sugar, hp, blue and rust Oriental design, c1857	**165.00**
Cup and Saucer	
"Buttercup" pattern	**20.00**
"Cowslip" pattern	**35.00**
"Cupid," gold, white ground	**30.00**
"Fairy Dell" pattern	**35.00**
"Fitzhugh" pattern, green	**35.00**
"Florence" pattern	**40.00**
Flower and border, green, white ground	**30.00**
Flower sprays, blue transfer, gilt rim, green "Spode Copeland China, England" mk, set of 8	**175.00**
Milkmaid, cows, and pasture, brown transfer, imp "Copeland"	**14.00**
"Rosalie" pattern	**32.00**
"Royal Jasmine" pattern	**22.00**
"Royal Windsor" pattern	**20.00**
"Trophies" pattern	**35.00**
Victorian views, hp, pink, jeweling, c1890	**200.00**
Vine design, green, white ground	**30.00**
Demitasse Cup and Saucer	
"Fleur-De-Lis" pattern, blue	**10.00**
"Italian" pattern, blue and white transfer scenes of animals, castles, and homes, "Copeland-Spode"	**22.00**
"Valencia" pattern	**20.00**
Dinner Service, "Bowpot" pattern, set of 76 pcs (A)	**230.00**
Figure	
6¼" g, kingfisher, multicolored	**75.00**
7¾" l, recumbent spaniel, brown and white, green cushion, gilt, c1833, "Copeland & Garrett" (A)	**1,540.00**
Gravy Boat, "Camellia" pattern, blue	**75.00**
Jam Jar, underplate, "Spode's Tower" pattern, blue transfer	**50.00**
Jug	
2" h, enameled multicolored jewels below lime green bands, gilt roundels and swags, strap handle, c1895 (A)	**150.00**
8¼" h, 6½" d, pottery, "Landing of Columbus," bright blue ground, raised ivory figures on front and bk, raised leaf trim at top, "Copeland, England"	**200.00**
Meat Dish, 22⅝" l, "King's" pattern, flowering tree and running floral border, lobed gadroon border, "Copeland & Garrett" (A)	**265.00**
Pitcher	
6½" h, white figures of classical women, blue ground, pewter lid	**75.00**
6¾" h, Churchill commemorative piece, designs on front and back	**150.00**
7½" h, diamond shape, wishbone handle, each panel on steel gray ground, green veined leaves, red and yellow thistle flower, panels	

Left, plate, 9″ d, black transfer, $25.00; center, vegetable bowl, cov, "Landscape" pattern in blue-gray transfer, c1891, $125.00; right, dessert service, eight 7¼″ d cake plates, eight cups and saucers, green griffins, white ground, c1840, $320.00.

separated by blue bands with red and white flowers, turquoise and gold accents, blue int. 300.00
8″ h, "Spode's Tower" pattern, blue transfer, "Copeland" 85.00
9″ h
    Raised figures of cherubs and goat, gray, c1833–37, "Copeland & Garrett" 150.00
    Hunting scene, blue and white ... 75.00
10¾″ h, "Spode's Tower" pattern, blue transfer 125.00
Plate
    5½″ d
        "Fleur-De-Lis" pattern in blue ... 12.00
        "Wickerdale" pattern 10.00
    6″ d, castle scene, hp, raised white floral border, gold trim 15.00
    7″ d, "Old Bow" pattern, multicolored 7.00
    7½″ d, "Mandarin" pattern, pink ... 10.00
    8″ d
        "Imari," blue, green, orange, and gold, scalloped edge, imp "Copeland" 185.00
        Center of Highland mountain and lake scene, cobalt scalloped, fluted border, inner jeweled ring, "Copeland-Spode" 135.00
    8¼″ d, "Florence" pattern 25.00
    9″ d
        Ovoid green borders, gilt dec, set of 12 (A) 60.00
        "Western Tanager," Audubon design 25.00
    9¼″ d, four polychrome reserves of pheasants, robin's egg blue ground, gilded scroll borders, two repaired, late 19th C, set of 11 (A) 250.00
    9⅜″ d, painted named view of "Leghorn," gilt linked scroll, hatched border, waved convex rim, c1845, green "Copeland & Garrett" mk (A) 100.00
    9½″ d, scattered polychrome florals, molded scrolled ground, late 19th C, set of 6 (A) 80.00

9¾″ d
    "Austen" pattern 18.00
    Bird design, magenta, gold border 40.00
    "Firenze" pattern 16.00
    "Fleur-De-Lis" pattern, blue 18.00
    "Golden Bracelet" pattern 25.00
10″ d
    "Christmas Tree" pattern, c1890 . 20.00
    "Mandarin" pattern, pink 20.00
    Painted centers, landscape views of England and Continent, gilt octagonal band cartouches, named on reverse, royal blue and gilt flowerhead borders, octagonal, c1880, set of 17 (A) 1,685.00
10½″ d
    "Royal Jasmine" pattern 10.00
    "Spode's Tower" pattern, blue transfer 35.00
11″ d, "Lion in Love" pattern, green transfer, "Copeland/Garrett" 100.00
12″ d, "Romany" pattern 38.00
14½″ d, blue and white portrait of Friar Tuck 50.00

Platter
    11″ l, 8½″ w, cobalt fuchsia blossoms and vines, gold accents and trim, scalloped shell border, dated 1887 35.00
    12″ l
        "Buttercup" pattern 42.00
        "Rosebud Chintz" pattern 48.00
    12½″ l, "Blue Camellia" pattern ... 75.00
    13″ d, "Wicker Lane" pattern, circ, "Copeland-Spode" 35.00
    13″ l, "Maytime" pattern 65.00
    15″ l, "Wickerdale" pattern 100.00
    16″ l, "Cowslip" pattern 100.00
    20″ l, 10″ w, cream colored earthenware, rust leaves, blue forms on black band border, gold trimmed dbl handles, c1847 .... 65.00

Punch Bowl
    10½″ d, blue peonies int. and ext., melon ribbing, luster border, ftd, dated 1883 .... 85.00

15½" d, "Spode's Tower" pattern, blue transfer **140.00**
Salt, white blossoms, cobalt trim, ftd .. **10.00**
Soup Plate
  9½" d, center of florals and leaves, lobulated border, multicolored florals **62.00**
  10¼" d, "Romney" pattern **15.00**
Tazza, 4⅞" h, majolica, modeled shell, supported by three dolphins, dished triangular base, imp "Copeland" (A) **160.00**
Tea Set
  "Auld Lang Syne" pattern, blue transfer, hexagonal teapot, creamer and sugar, gold boar finials, service for 12 .... **850.00**
  Pattern #5794, cov sugar, milk jug, slop bowl, nine cups and saucers, molded gilded panels of foliage scrolls and hatched design, white ground, c1840, "Copeland & Garrett" **100.00**

Teapot, 9½" h, cream cameos, dark green ground, c1890, $250.00.

Teapot and Tea Tile, overall floral and leaf decor, animal finial **135.00**
Tureen, 9½" d, matching ladle, cov, tray, grape leaf and floral pattern, black transfer **65.00**
Tureen, Sauce
  7" l, cov, Imari style decor, typical colors (A) **25.00**
  7¾" w, cov, matching stands, cell pattern with painted flowers, blue transfer, rect, dbl mask handles, artichoke finials, c1860, blue "Copeland-Spode," pr (A) **265.00**
Urn
  10" h, hp, floral center panels on pink ground, green on base and top, gold overlay, c1847, "Spode-Copeland, Stoke-on-Trent," pr **500.00**

17" h, 13" d, "Spode's Tower" pattern, blue transfer **700.00**
Vase
  2" h, turquoise jewels, marbleized panels, gilt scrolls, c1895 (A) **150.00**
  5" h, "Spode's Tower" pattern, blue transfer, ruffled edge **35.00**
  9" h, cov, iron-red, blue, gilt, and salmon flower sprays on shaped lappets, gilt scroll handles and finial, c1890 (A) **100.00**
  9½" h, cov, panels of flowers, blue and green ground, gilt borders, cylindrical, cov repaired, c1906, sgd "J. Worrall" (A) **100.00**
  10" h, majolica, presentation, Art Nouveau style, Bacchus faces on dbl handles, brown, beige, and blue colors, c1900, imp "Copeland," pr **1,200.00**

COW CREAMERS

Staffordshire, England
2nd half 18th C–mid 19th C
Delft, Holland
c1755

History: Cow creamers are cream jugs in the shape of a cow. There is an oval hole opening in the top of the back of the cow for filling the creamer. The spout is the mouth with the curved tail serving as a handle. Historically, most filling holes had lids. Today they frequently are missing.

Some cow creamers have a seated milkmaid alongside the creamer. The earliest earthenware cow creamers were made in Staffordshire during the second half of the eighteenth century.

English cow creamers were made in Whieldon ware, creamware, Prattware, and many others. Large size versions often are called cow milk jugs. Cow creamers in tin-glazed ware, c1755, were made at Delft, Holland.

Museums: City Museum and Art Gallery, Stoke-on-Trent, Hanley, England.

Blue and white, unmarked, $68.00.

COVERED

4¼" h, rust and white, gilt trim, hairline on hoof (A) **80.00**

4¾" h, black, gilt trim, head tilted, "Jackfield" (A) **65.00**

5" h, Sunderland-type splashed purple luster, mounted on rect base, repaired, c1820 .... **475.00**

5⅛" h, ochre and brown sponging, standing on flower shaped molded base, crumpled horns on bull, yellow horns, flowers and edge of base, lancet cov with floral knob, c1760, repaired **2,100.00**

5⅛" l, pearlware, late 18th, "Yorkshire"
Large brown spots, beside seated multicolored milkmaid, shaped flat green base edged in black **200.00**
Russet spots, black hoofs, mouth, and eyes, oval green molded base **200.00**
Spotted brown and russet, brown hoofs, horns, and eyes, green shaped rect base **150.00**

5½" h
Cream, buff, and brown clays, spotted dark glaze, tail, horns, pail, and milkmaid in red clay, cream base, replaced cov, c1760 .... **2,200.00**
Pale tan, rect wave topped cov, black and dark red on sponged oval base, c1810, attrib to Don Pottery, repaired **1,200.00**
Purple luster and iron-red patches, green mound base **650.00**

5⅝" l, spotted pink and iron-red, black horns, eyes, and hoofs, oval green base, c1820 .... **200.00**

5¾" l
Pearlware, iron-red and blue spots, enameled brown horns, black eyes and hoofs, rect green mound base, late 18th C, "Yorkshire" **150.00**
Purple luster and russet spots, purple horns, mottled brown and green oval base, c1820 .... **200.00**

5⅞" l
Puce sponging, black band, seated milkmaid, green sponged rect chamfered base, cov replaced (A) **200.00**
Purple luster spots, brown hoofs, eyes, and horns, mottled brown and green oval base, c1820 ..... **200.00**

6" l
Seated girl milking cow, black and white coloration, c1840 .... **650.00**
Tan and sepia spotting, seated milkmaid, irreg green base, c1700, Staffordshire (A) **730.00**

6⅛" l, manganese sponging, yellow splashes, washed green chamfered base, "Prattware" (A) **250.00**

6¼" l
Pink and gray sponging, seated milkmaid, shaped green sponged base, late 18th C, "Staffordshire" (A) ... **330.00**
Puce and black sponging, milkmaid in blue sponged dress, splashed green base (A) **450.00**
"Rockingham" type glaze(A) **10.00**

6½" l
Cream glaze, manganese, yellow, green, and gray splashes, tail forms handle, shaped base, c1760 (A) ..**1,600.00**
Pink luster, iron-red enamel and silver luster streaks, green oval mound base, c1825, "Staffordshire" (A) .. **415.00**
Pink splash luster, rect base, c1825, "Swansea," repair to tail and horns (A) **385.00**

6⅝" l
Sponged gray markings, waisted rect green base, c1800, "Staffordshire" (A) **550.00**
Black sponging, rect base, three green splashes, "Yorkshire" (A) **425.00**

6¾" l, iron-red and gray, stylized flowerheads, oblong grass mound base, late 18th C, "Staffordshire" (A) **330.00**

7" l
"Blue Willow" design on body, "Staffordshire" **185.00**
Iron-red sponged and pink luster spots, pink luster horns and cov, mottled green and brown oval mound base, c1825, "Swansea" (A) **415.00**
Modeled, standing, tail forming handle, seated milkmaid, gray sponging, oblong base, green accents, c1780, "Whieldon Ware" (A) **420.00**
Red and pink luster patches, green grassy base (A) **200.00**

7½" l, standing cows, seated milkmaids, mottled ochre and white glazes, covs missing, c1830, "Prestonpans", pr (A) **430.00**

7⅝" l, puce and black sponged patches, rect edged blue green base, c1830, "Scotland" (A) **285.00**

Cow with calf, semi-translucent brown glaze, creamware, mounted on fluted cream base, repaired, c1810 ......**2,000.00**
Ochre sponging, brown spots, ochre and blue foliage device, c1760 ....**1,200.00**
Sponged, gray-green and yellow, spotted in orange and blue, c1760 .....**1,000.00**

OPEN

5" h, white body, orange and blue dots, orange tail, and horns, blue hooves, "Czechoslovakia" **40.00**

Pink sponging on white, green base, repaired, c1830, imp "E. Brown," $600.00.

5¼" h, sponged rust spots, gilded horns
(A) **135.00**
5½" h
Bone china, white, shell scroll base,
dated 1883, "Copeland" (A) **50.00**
Pearlware, gray sponging, brown
spots on sides, black horns and
eyes, seated multicolored milkmaid, blue sponged octagonal
base, late 18th C, "Yorkshire" ... **250.00**
Pearlware, gray sponging, brown
spots on sides, black horns and
eyes, standing next to milkmaid,
flat green shaped base, late 18th C,
"Yorkshire" **250.00**
Recumbent cow, blue farm scene,
dated 1891, "Germany" **125.00**
6¼" l
Black, "Jackfield" (A) **10.00**
Black and brown patches, seated
milkmaid on green base, "Staffordshire" (A) **175.00**
Brown sponged, head turned, green
and ochre sponged stepped rect
base (A) **550.00**
Splashed ochre, yellow and gray
glaze, curled tail forms handle,
seated milkmaid, oblong base,
canted corners, c1765 (A) **825.00**
6½" l
Porcelain, recumbent, brown-red
colors (A) **50.00**
Red and black spots, green rect base,
molded feather border, "Staffordshire" (A) **300.00**
6⅝" l, red patches, head turned, fluted
oval base with green edge, "Staffordshire" (A) **175.00**
6¾" l, modeled, standing, tail forming
handle, seated milkmaid, sponged
blue and ochre, shaped oblong green
accented base, c1780, "Whieldon
Ware" (A) **425.00**
6¾" l, 4½" h, shades of brown, white
body, rect base **40.00**

7¼" l, recumbent, black and white,
"Bavaria" **75.00**
Black body, gold trim, oval base **85.00**
"Blue Willow" design, mid 19th C,
"Staffordshire" **175.00**

CREAMWARE

English/Continental
c1740–Present

History: Creamware (cream-colored earthenware) provides a fine form and thin body in addition to a clean and brilliant glaze. Creamware
made no pretense to imitate porcelain in color,
form, or decoration. Yet, it found a ready ac-
ceptance in the market place.

Creamware was made from the beginning of
the 18th C. The materials were identical to those
used to make salt glaze. The principal difference
is that creamware is fired at a lower temperature
and glazed with lead.

In 1740 Enoch Booth of Tunstall in Staffordshire invented a fluid glaze that provided a brilliant, transparent cream color. Thomas Whieldon
and Josiah Wedgwood both used this glaze. By
1760 enameled decoration was being added to
the creamware glaze. Derbyshire, Liverpool,
Yorkshire, and Swansea also produced creamware products.

Creamware was improved in 1768 by introducing china clay and china stone from Cornwall
into the body and glaze. This resulted in creamware that was paler in color, plus lighter and
more brilliant in the glaze.

Since there was much interchange and copying of ideas among a number of potteries, simi-
larities in both the body and glaze are found.
Hence, it is quite difficult to assign early creamware to a particular factory since most creamware was unmarked prior to that manufactured
by Wedgwood. Creamware was the main product in England between 1760 and 1820. It sup-
planted the manufacture of white salt glaze by
c1780. Creamware's prominence during these
years provided the death blow to tin-glazed earthenware in England and on the continent. From
c1760 English creamware was exported to nearly
every European country.

Many Staffordshire potters left England and established factories in France, thus threatening the
faience factories and undercutting the sale of porcelains. The European factories turned to the
manufacture of creamware in self defense.

References: Donald Towner, *Creamware*, Faber
& Faber, 1978.

Museums: Castle Museum, Norwich, England;
Cincinnati Art Museum, Cincinnati, Ohio; City
Museum & Art Gallery, Hanley, Stoke-on-Trent,

Ewer, 10½" h, ribbed, floral and leaf terminals, attributed to James and Charles Whitehead, c1785, pr, $3,000.00.

England; Victoria & Albert Museum, London, England.

Basket, 9" l, woven lattice, stand, rust enamel, gilt, imp "WEDGWOOD," repaired **200.00**
Bidet, mahogany covered case, c1830, "Wedgwood" **1,750.00**
Bowl
 8" d, dbl walled, molded, cov, stand, and pierced basketwork, domed cov, apple knob, 1780–85, "Neale & Co." (A) **370.00**
 9" h, cov, open work on cover with slot for ladle, flower finial, ftd, c1780 ....**1,000.00**
 13" d, matching 11⅛" l stand, pierced multilobes, scalloped band of roping, oval husks, crabstock handles ending in grapevine terminals, perforated center, c1780 ....**1,450.00**
Candlestick
 7½" h
 Fluted columns, sq fluted bases, molded flowers below drip pan, c1875, "Wedgwood," pr **2,250.00**
 Ribbed columns set, sq bases, c1785, "Wedgwood," pr **2,250.00**
 10⅝" h, form of caryatid, sloping base, canted corners, molded foliage supports fluted column, c1791, attrib to Lakin & Poole **750.00**
Charger, 13⅝" d, scalloped and emb rim (A) **65.00**
Condiment Caddy, 7¾" h, reticulated circ containers, rope handle (A) **55.00**
Condiment Set, 10¼" h, urn shaped centerpiece, handle and shaped foot, cylinder containers set in pierced cylinder cups (A) **150.00**

Cottage, 4¾" h, russet roof, yellow body, c1820, "Staffordshire" (A) ... **300.00**
Cup and Saucer
 Chocolate style, inverted bell shaped cups, ribbed dbl twist handles, floral and leaf terminals, c1780, pr .**1,350.00**
 Green printed daisy pattern, c1882, imp "WEDGWOOD" **60.00**
 Green printed chrysanthemum pattern, imp "WEDGWOOD" **60.00**
Dinner Service, lion-mask dbl handled oblong cov tureen with lion finial, 7" w cov sauce tureen and stand, six soup plates, thirteen dinner plates, fifteen side plates, twelve breakfast plates, blue transfer of bird feeding young, fruits, and flowers, c1840, imp "B & W." mark for Wood & Brownfield (A) **2,200.00**
Dish
 5¾" l, 5" w, reticulated rim (A) **50.00**
 7" l, leaf shape, molded multicolored vines, leaves, and berries, blue feathered edge, c1780 .... **475.00**
 7¾" d, shell molded, puce flower sprays and rims, c1765, "Wedgwood," pr (A) **770.00**
 8" d, green enamel crustacea, fluted, "Wedgwood" (A) **22.00**
 8¼" l, printed center, iron-red peafowl in landscape, buds and leaves, feather edges, pierced rims, oval, pr **575.00**
 9" d, center outlined by acanthus in relief, border of female masks and husks suspended from cherubs, scalloped edges, pierced rims, c1780, pr **1,125.00**
 9½" w, int. multicolored scene of family, young girl playing with cat, shaped ochre rim, oval, c1865, imp "WEDGWOOD" (A) **550.00**
 9¾" w, painted fruit, borders of green

Dessert Dish, 9½" d, c1780, pr, $1,125.00.

flowering branches, gilt rims, c1880, sgd "F. H. Cox," imp "WEDGWOOD," pr (A) **150.00**

10¼" w, 7¼" w, marbleized underglaze blue and white, "Wedgwood" **65.00**

10⅜" d, six compartments decorated with brown wheat ears, brown edged salmon band border, ftd, c1810, imp "WEDGWOOD" **65.00**

11¼" d, three nude putti in multicolored landscape, ochre rim, diamond shape, c1870, imp "WEDGWOOD" (A) **80.00**

13½" l, wide pink border painted with flowers and cornucopia, black band borders, rect, c1810, imp "WEDGWOOD" **65.00**

14" d, black transfer of rural scene, foliate scroll border, fruiting oak rim, 1780–90, "Staffordshire" (A) **300.00**

Egg Cups, 2¾" h, encircling design of hearts, leaves, and circles, pierced, c1790, pr **575.00**

Egg Drainer, 3½" l, pierced open work, tiny handle, c1790 .... **225.00**

Figure

3½" h, Yorkshire woman, basket, cream body, yellow-brown spots, c1770, unmarked **300.00**

3½" w, recumbent pony, brown and black glazes, grass base, c1780 (A) **2,200.00**

3⅝" h, bird on tree stump, spotted ochre and brown, c1780, "Staffordshire" (A) **300.00**

3⅞" h, recumbent dog, brown and tan patches, mound base, late 18th C, "England" **200.00**

4" l, Yorkshire sheep at rest, cream, rust and yellow-brown spots, c1770 .... **425.00**

5¼" h, Apollo, standing on rocks, pile of books, holding lyre, brown and tan accents, late 18th C, "England" (A) **150.00**

6½" l, mountain goat, standing, incised hair splashed in brown, c1790, "Staffordshire" (A) **770.00**

Fruit Basket, 10" l, oval form, 12 lobes, pierced sides, dbl twisted handles ending in briar terminals below and flower foliage above, mounted on stand, c1770 ....**1,450.00**

Fruit Stand, 10⅜" d, rect, chamfered, gray ivy vine on black edged yellow band border on rim edge and foot, c1810, "Staffordshire" **65.00**

Jug

4¾" h, applied trailing fruit vines, three paw feet, c1750, "England" (A) **215.00**

5¼" h, pear shape, entwined strap handle, flowerhead finial, c1800, imp "WEDGWOOD" (A) **300.00**

12" h, entwined floral monogram, border of trailing vines, c1800, imp "WEDGWOOD" **75.00**

12¼" h, helmet shape, green, iron-red, and brown band of fruiting vine, brown lines on handles and rim, c1900, imp "WEDGWOOD" (A) **150.00**

Knives, 8⅛" l, green and brown grapevines, painted handles, fluted edges, oval brown buttons, Sheffield blades, c1809, "Wedgwood," pr **375.00**

Miniature, green leaf design, red and brown stripes

Dish, 4¼" l, cov and tray (A) **40.00**

Plate, 2½" d (A) **36.00**

Platter, 5⅜" l, 4⅛" w (A) **36.00**

Soup Plate, 3" d (A) **36.00**

Tureen, 2½" l, cov and tray (A) **45.00**

Mug, polychrome design of woman, sponged trees, hinged pewter lid, Masonic compass and "1805" (A) **350.00**

Pickle Dishes, 5½" l, leaf shape, small hole in handles, c1780, pr **800.00**

Pitcher

3⅛" h, red transfer of "Ladies All, I Pray Make Free; & Tell Me How You Like Your Tea," dark red and green enamels, pink luster (A) **100.00**

4¼" h, John Peel, relief of horses and hounds, hound handle, "Wedgwood" **65.00**

4½" h, blue, green, brown, and tan florals, small (A) **15.00**

6" h, transfer of "Disraeli," c1881, imp "WEDGWOOD" **225.00**

8¼" h, floral design, c1807, "Staffordshire" (A) **130.00**

Plaque, 15" d, paintings of Hamlet and Ophelia, multicolored leaf and floral ground, c1879, imp "WEDGWOOD," pr (A) **1,650.00**

Plate

3" d, green leaf design, red and brown stripe (A) **36.00**

3¾" d, purple luster floral design, polychrome enamels (A) **50.00**

7¼" d, emb scalloped rim (A) **40.00**

8" d, strawberry decorations, reticulated borders, 1784–95, "Neale & Co," pr (A) **20.00**

8½" d

Chinoiserie designs of pagodas, etc, in blue, c1780, pr **475.00**

Enameled design of roses and strawberries in shell (A) **30.00**

Profile of William of Orange, multicolored motto, dbl vine border, shaped rim (A) **150.00**

8⅝" d, purple ruffled feathered edges, c1785, set of 11 (A) **770.00**

8¾" d, pink shell motif center, gilt foliage, brown net pattern ground, gilt rims, c1820, "Spode," set of 4 (A) **330.00**

8⅞" d, reticulated basketweave rim (A) **85.00**

9" d

Molded Tudor rose center, pierced rim, feathered edge, c1780, "Wedgwood" **450.00**

Reticulated rim (A) **55.00**

9¼" d

Brown sponging, green dots, emb feather rim (A) **60.00**

Painted center, three children in landscapes, named "Sluggishness, Disdain & Quarrelsome" on reverse, c1866, sgd "E. Lessore," imp "WEDGWOOD," set of 3 (A) **440.00**

9½" d, ribbon edge, gilt, imp "WEDGWOOD" **65.00**

9¾" d, blue painted Oriental, parasol and pavilions, feathered rim, molded drapery, c1775, "England" (A) **70.00**

9⅞" d, reticulated rim (A) **55.00**

10¼" d, hp, "Little Red Riding Hood," c1880, imp "WEDGWOOD" **185.00**

11¼" d, multicolored nymph and two putti, ochre rim, c1870, imp "WEDGWOOD" (A) **80.00**

Platter

9¼" l, molded basketweave, reticulated border, imp "WEDGWOOD" **72.00**

10" l, 8" w, "Melton" pattern, sepia transfer of setter and quails, "Wedgwood" **55.00**

12" l, hp, floral design, imp "WEDGWOOD" **125.00**

15½" l, blue feather edge (A) **50.00**

17" l, 13¼" w, emb border, octagonal (A) **55.00**

Quintals, 7⅞" h, blue painted florals on sides, green glazed ruffled rims on fingers, molded foliate feet, rect bases, c1780, "England," pr (A) **315.00**

Salt, 4½" l, boat shape, grooved rims, four flared feet, c1780 .... **500.00**

Sauce Tureen, 7" l, painted purple flowers, rect, chamfered corners, c1785, "England," star crack (A) **80.00**

Sauceboat, 6" l, swan shape, arched neck, molded green wings and beak, brown legs, c1775 ....**1,500.00**

Soup Ladle, 11" l, curved, flared handle, ribbing, c1790 .... **250.00**

Soup Plate, 9¾" d, emb scalloped rim (A) **25.00**

Spirit Flask, 3½" h, reserves of polychrome flower baskets, outlined in raised brown, red roses and green leaves at periphery, tapered neck, c1800 .... **600.00**

Sweetmeat Dish, 6⅝" d, reticulated edge, emb Greek key design, imp "WEDGWOOD" (A) **160.00**

Tankard, 3⅝" h, inverted bell shape, dbl twist handle, flower terminals, polychrome scene of Orientals and temples, ftd, c1770, repaired hairline .. **950.00**

Tazza, 12¼" w, young child and couple seated under tree, multicolored, entwined dbl snake handles, c1870, sgd "Emile Lessore," imp "WEDGWOOD" **750.00**

Teabowl and Saucer, gaudy floral design, red, blue, and green enamels, purple luster (A) **25.00**

Tea Service, 9" l, 8" h teapot, waste bowl, creamer, eight cups and saucers, red transfers, "Jack the Sailor," c1840, $475.00.

Teapot

7" h, blue pagodas and willow tree, entwined handle, flowerhead finial, cylindrical shape, c1770, "Staffordshire," repair to spout (A) **85.00**

7¼" h, multicolored transfer printed, plants, foliage, and insects, ochre handle, spout, and finial, c1870, imp "WEDGWOOD" (A) **55.00**

Tête-à-Tête Set, 8" h coffeepot, milk jug, sugar, two cups and saucers, multicolored flower sprays, iron-red rims, c1785, French **600.00**

Tray

8" l, emb leaf edges, blue rims, oval, pr (A) **220.00**

8¼" l, 9¾" w, reticulated rim, emb design, oval (A) **35.00**

8½" l, 9¾" w, reticulated borders, pr (A) **100.00**

Tumbler
    2⅜" h, polychrome enameled florals,
        purple luster (A) **40.00**
    2⅝" h, gaudy floral design, red and
        green enamels, purple luster rim (A)   **35.00**
Tureen
    6⅞" d, 8¾" h, reticulated lid, hair-
        lines on lid (A) **120.00**
    7" l, melon form, leaf shaped under-
        tray, melon knob finial, c1770 . . .**1,200.00**
    10" h, cov, painted cornflower sprigs,
        lower section and pierced cov with
        grooves accented in green, pome-
        granate finial, c1790, "Stafford-
        shire" (A) **420.00**
    10" l, 7⅝" h, molded and applied de-
        sign, rope twist handles (A) **150.00**
    13¼" l, 9½" h, emb design, rope twist
        handles (A) **270.00**
    16¼" l, cov, modeled, duck, brown
        bill and feet, multicolored body,
        19th C, body crack (A) **1,100.00**
Vase
    7" l, green garland and ribbon trim,
        c1780, "Neale & Co." **375.00**
    7¾" h, modeled, two green entwined
        dolphins supporting flowerheads,
        shell molded base, c1770, imp "Ra
        Wood Burslem" **1,200.00**
    8" h, molded foliage, ochre, three
        strap   handles,   c1870,   imp
        "WEDGWOOD" (A) **55.00**
    9" h, cov, applied drapery swags sus-
        pended from rings, band of key pat-
        tern, pierced cov, ball finial, late
        18th C (A) **110.00**
    13½" h, cov, multicolored, Holy Fam-
        ily, St John, Virgin and Child, front
        and reverse, modeled caryatid han-
        dles, bird finial, c1870, sgd "E. Les-
        sore," imp "WEDGWOOD" (A) . .   **770.00**
Wall Pockets, 13¼" h, figure of Hamlet
    on one, Ophelia on other, applied
    wings, petals, and flowers, brown and
    ochre touches, c1780, repairs to pet-
    als, pr **8,400.00**

CREIL
LM & CIE
MONTEREAU

CREIL

Seine-et-Marne and Oise, France
1784–1895

History: About 1784 the Englishman Bagnad in
association with M. de St. Cricq-Cazeaux established a factory for the manufacture of English–
style earthenware. These two founders united

with Montereau during the early 19th century,
forming a firm that continued until 1895.

    The Creil factory was the first French pottery
to use transfer printing on earthenware. Transfer
views of Paris, French chateaux, portraits of important people, English country houses, fables of
La Fontaine, or religious or allegorical subjects
in monochrome graced white or cream colored
ware. Porcelain never was made.

    Marks were either stamped in the paste or sten-
ciled. They included "Creil et Montereau" or
"LM & C."

**Plate, 8⅜" d, "Palais de la Chambre des
Deputes," black transfer, imp mark, (A)
$75.00.**

Basket, 11" l, open white basketweave
    design with gilt trim, mounted on
    stands, c1810, pr **1,400.00**
Bough Pots, 8¼" d, D-shape, band of
    circles around rims over classical de-
    tail, green glaze, early 19th C, pr (A)   **50.00**
Dish, 14" d, transfer, painted overlap-
    ping playing cards, blue cell ground,
    late 19th C, black "Creil et Monter-
    eau" mk (A) **825.00**
Pitcher
    6" h, figural, monk, brown robe, mul-
        ticolored facial features **100.00**
    8¼" h, black classic designs in ovals,
        white ground **650.00**
    8½" h, black classic scenes, white
        earthenware ground, c1840, re-
        stored **650.00**
    10" h, brown classic scenes in round
        and oval panels, cream ground,
        mkd **300.00**
Plate
    8" d, black transfer, "Chateau de
        Chiswick," white ground **50.00**
    8½" d
        Black transfer, "Liberty," foliate

border, canary ground, imp
"Creil" (A) **50.00**
Polychrome transfer, chinoiserie
scene (A) **10.00**
9" d, black transfer
"Flore," classical dress, grape bor-
der, cream ground, 18th C **50.00**
French song verses, yellow ground **150.00**
List of "Dont's" in French, yellow
ground **150.00**
Soup Plate, 8" d, black transfer, French
military scene, foliate border, canary
ground, imp "Creil" (A) **40.00**
Urn, 8" h, cov, black design, Apollo and
Clio on cov, underplate with black
floral design, canary ground, c1850 **950.00**

1878-90

CROWN AND ROYAL CROWN DERBY

Osmaston Road, Derby, England
1876–Present

History: Edward Phillips, formerly of the Royal Worcester Company, established the Royal Crown Derby Porcelain Company, on Osmaston Road in Derby in 1877. This new company had no connection with the original Derby works. By 1878 the new factory was producing earthenwares called "crown ware" in addition to porcelains.

The new Derby porcelain was richly decorated in the old "Japan" patterns featuring reds and blues along with rich gilding very much in the manner of the earlier Derby porcelains. Additionally, the new Derby company produced ornamental forms including figures and highly decorated vases and services.

1890 marked the beginning of the Royal Crown Derby period, when the company was appointed manufacturers of porcelain to Queen Victoria and "Royal Crown Derby" was added to the trademark.

Desire Leroy was the most distinguished artist employed by Royal Crown Derby. He trained at the Sevres factory, went to Minton in 1878, came to Royal Crown Derby in 1890, and stayed until his death in 1908. His most successful contribution was the use of white enamels painted over rich dark blue ground in the style of Limoges enamels. He exhibited a great versatility of de-

sign and remarkable use of colors. His lavish designs usually featured birds in landscape, fruits, flowers, and occasional figures. He also added gilt embellishments.

In 1904 toy shapes were produced that attracted the attention of miniature collectors. Figures were made in the late 1920s and early 1930s. During the post-war period, Arnold Mikelson modeled lifelike birds and animals.

In 1935 the Royal Crown Derby company purchased the small King Street works which had been established by some former Derby workers in 1848. This provided a link with the original Derby factory founded by William Duesbury in the mid 18th century.

References: F. Brayshaw Gilhespy, *Crown Derby Porcelain*, F. Lewis Ltd., 1951; F. Brayshaw Gilhespy & Dorothy M. Budd, *Royal Crown Derby China*, Charles Skilton Ltd., 1964; John Twitchett & Betty Bailey, *Royal Crown Derby*, Barrie & Jenkins, Ltd., 1976.

Museums: Cincinnati Art Museum, Cincinnati, Ohio; Gardiner Museum of Ceramic Art, Toronto, Canada; Royal Crown Derby Museum, Osmaston Road, Derby; Derby Museums & Art Gallery, The Strand, Derby; Victoria & Albert Museum, London, England.

Collecting Hints: Royal Crown Derby continues production to the present day as part of Royal Doulton Tablewares Ltd. From 1882 onwards, all Crown Derby can be dated. A year cypher appears under the trademark, the key for which can be found in Geoffrey A. Godden's *Victorian Porcelain*, Herbert Jenkins, 1961.

Bell, Pattern #6299, dark blue and
gold, faceted handle, dated 1907 ... **75.00**
Bone Dish, 9" l, overall floral clusters,

Vase, 10" h, cobalt, dark red, and gold Oriental design, pattern #6299, c1905, $250.00.

gold trim, "Royal Crown Derby," set
of 8 .... **75.00**

Bowl
6½" d, Pattern #2451, fluted body,
c1902 .... **200.00**
9" d, Imari pattern, gold trim, shell
shape, c1889 .... **100.00**
9½" d, birds and flowers, burnt orange, white ground, octagonal ... **125.00**
11" d, Imari pattern, multicolored,
"Royal Crown Derby" (A) **150.00**
12" d, Imari pattern, multicolored,
"Royal Crown Derby" (A) **150.00**

Box, cov
4" l, Imari pattern, underglaze blue,
orange transfer, gilt rim (A) **25.00**
4¾" l, Imari pattern, blue, iron-red,
green, and gilt, c1916 (A) **80.00**

Cake Plate, 9" d, four panels, Pattern
#2451, Oriental design, rust, cobalt,
and gold, c1892 .... **215.00**

Coffee Cup and Saucer, Imari pattern,
multicolored, c1921 .... **70.00**

Compote, 6½" d, 2½" h, Pattern #2451,
ftd, c1950 .... **250.00**

Creamer, 1½" h, florals, cobalt, orange,
and white, "Crown Derby" **118.00**

Creamer and Sugar, cov, Imari pattern,
Dublin shape, "Royal Crown Derby" **300.00**

Cup, 3⅞" h, molded bearded man,
crown, polychrome enamels, "Crown
Derby" (A) **80.00**

**Cup and Saucer, gray pattern, yellow
ground, gold rim, "Royal Crown Derby,"
$25.00.**

Cup and Saucer
"Blue Mikado" pattern, c1928 ..... **45.00**
"Cigar" pattern, Imari, pattern
#1128, multicolored, dated 1917
(A) **70.00**
Cobalt panels in border separated by
gold and white bands, four panels
in center, two panels in cobalt and
gold, others with open flowers in
rust, blue, and gold **90.00**

Imari pattern, multicolored, dated
1887, "Royal Crown Derby" **25.00**
Imari pattern, multicolored, pattern
#1128 .... **75.00**
Imari style chrysanthemums, dark
blue, red, and gold borders, "Royal
Crown Derby," set of five **100.00**
"Ives" pattern, blue and white,
"Royal Crown Derby" **32.50**
"Old Witches" pattern, Imari, pattern
#2451, dated 1921, set of 6 (A) .. **100.00**
"Royal Antoinette" pattern **48.40**

Demitasse Cup and Saucer
"Blue Ives" pattern, "Royal Crown
Derby" **30.00**
Birds of Paradise, trees, and foliage,
rust colors, dated 1901 .... **45.00**
"Cigar" pattern, cobalt, orange, and
gold, c1940 .... **65.00**
"Pembroke" pattern **35.00**
White ground, continous gold leaf
pattern, gold accents, set of six .. **50.00**

Dessert Service
18 pcs, six shaped dishes, twelve
plates, Imari pattern of flowering
peony and prunus, red, blue, and
gold, dated 1899 .... **265.00**
18 pcs, two compotes, two oval, two
heart shape dishes, twelve plates,
pink and yellow roses, light yellow
ground, sgd "C. Harris," dated
1899 (A) **720.00**

Dinner Service, Imari pattern, blue,
iron-red, green, and gilt foliate panels
and borders, "Royal Crown Derby,"
service for 8, matching candlesticks **600.00**

Dish
9⅞" d, Imari style panels of peonies
between dark blue bands, gilt diapering, "Royal Crown Derby," pr . **65.00**
11½" d, Imari pattern, underglaze,
gold trim, oval, ftd, c1887 ...... **65.00**

Ewer
7¼" h, tooled gilding, flower garlands
and scrolls, formal borders, canary
yellow ground, looped and mask
handle, c1895, pr (A) **370.00**
8½" h, cobalt iris design, gold leaves
and trim, gold twist handle, c1890 **175.00**
8½" h, 6" d, cobalt and light blue iris
design, gold florals, gilt, cream
ground, gilded twist bracket handle, c1890 .... **200.00**

Figure
6" h, mother and child, cradle in foreground, multicolored, c1887
"Royal Crown Derby" **975.00**
6½" l, swans, white, open, base,
c1876, "Royal Crown Derby," pr . **200.00**
9⅜" h, peacock, perched on vase of
flowers, applied florals on base,
dated 1905 .... **90.00**

10" h, falcon, rocky base, natural colors, dated 1959 (A) **100.00**

10¼" h, woodpecker, tree stump, natural colors, dated 1959 (A) **100.00**

10⅝ h, monk, tugging at bridle of mule, green oval base, "Crown Derby" **135.00**

Forks, blue and white Oriental scenes on handles, "Royal Crown Derby," set of six **65.00**

Fruit Stand, 11" h, painted rose flower spray, gilt swag border, green and gilt gadroon rim, raised foliage molded foot, c1912 (A) **160.00**

Lamp Base, 7¼" h, blue and white seascape, dated 1937 .... **125.00**

Milk Churn, cov, 2½" h, Imari style, pattern #6299, floral panels, blue loop handles, dated 1913 .... **80.00**

Pitcher

2¼" h, "Derby Posies" pattern, "Royal Crown Derby" **14.00**

6½", multicolored florals, outlined in gold, cobalt ground, dated 1881 . **125.00**

Plate

6" d, Imari pattern, multicolored, "Royal Crown Derby" **40.00**

8" d, Imari pattern, multicolored ... **28.00**

8¼" d, Imari pattern, multicolored, "Royal Crown Derby" **70.00**

8½" d

Blue flower and ivy leaf vine, gold accents, "Royal Crown Derby," set of eight **65.00**

Multicolored scene of pheasants and trees in center, gold accents, "Royal Crown Derby," set of eight **100.00**

Multifloral center, border of green sprays, scalloped gold edge, "Royal Crown Derby" **50.00**

8¾" d

Center scene of Tissington Spires, Dovedale, painted by E. Troswell, turquoise and gold encrusted jewel border, scalloped edge **200.00**

Painted pastel floral spray and foliage, shaped green border and gilt pendants, gadroon rim, sgd "A. Gregory," c1926 (A) **200.00**

Painted view of "Lathkill Dale" or "Monsal Dale," rims molded with vines, gilt line borders, sgd "W. E. J. Dean," "Royal Crown Derby," (A) **100.00**

8⅞" d, painted Japanese style pattern, stylized flowers and foliage, earthenware, "Crown Derby," set of twelve (A) **400.00**

9" d

Flower spray and foliage, painted,

shaped pink border, gardroon and gilt rim, sgd "A. Gregory," c1921 (A) **435.00**

Roses, red, pink, and yellow, apple-green border, gilt and foliage scrolls, molded rim, sgd "C. G.," c1902 (A) **435.00**

9¼" d, Imari pattern, vase and large flowers in center, cobalt border, butterflies, c1889 .... **150.00**

9½" d, painted bouquet of flowers, border with fruit, shaped oval gilt panels, pierced foliage rim, c1880, "Crown Derby" (A) **310.00**

10" d

Multicolored floral centers, aqua borders, raised gold grapes and vines, set of ten **650.00**

Stylized floral border, orange, cobalt, and gilt, "Royal Crown Derby" (A) **15.00**

10½" d, centers of sailing vessels, multicolored, "Taormina" and "Endymion," cream border, ship's rope gilt edge, sgd "W. E. J. Dean," "Royal Crown Derby," pr **335.00**

10⅝" d, printed woodland cottage, royal blue border, gilt stylized foliage, waved milled gilt rim, c1930 **132.00**

10¾" d, Imari pattern, "Royal Crown Derby" **100.00**

11" l, Imari pattern, red, cobalt, and gilt, "Crown Derby," (A) **110.00**

Pot, 3" d, Imari pattern, blue, iron-red, green, and gilt, c1914 (A) **80.00**

Shrimp Dish, 10" l, Imari pattern, molded edge **250.00**

Soup Plate, 10½" d, stylized floral border, orange, cobalt, and gilt, "Royal Crown Derby" (A) **15.00**

Sugar, cov

Crest of Ceylon, multicolored, white ground, gilt rim, "Royal Crown Derby," pr **40.00**

"Old Witches" pattern #2451, dated 1935 .... **30.00**

Sweetmeat Dish, 5" l, Oriental flowers, rust, cobalt, and gold, pattern #2451, c1931 .... **200.00**

Tea Service

Imari pattern, blue, iron-red, green, and gilt, c1915–29, set of 31 pcs (A) **620.00**

"Japan" pattern #1128, teapot, jug, basin, four plates, cups, and saucers, dated 1912 (A) **540.00**

"Kings" pattern, flowering trees in paneled scroll border, teapot, jug, cov sugar, six cups and saucers, dated 1887, "Crown Derby" (A) . **210.00**

Toby Jug, 4" h, copy of French Toby .. **75.00**

Toothpick Holder, Oriental design, set
of four small feet **100.00**
Tray, 18⅞" d, "Old Witches" pattern,
border with gilt dots on blue, octagonal, dbl handles, dated 1890 . . . . . **100.00**

**Vase, 10½" h, raised gold florals and geo-
metrics, magenta and cream ground,
"Royal Crown Derby," pr, $900.00.**

Vase
4" h, Oriental florals, peach and gold,
"Royal Crown Derby" **100.00**
4½" h, Imari pattern, multicolored . . **125.00**
5" h, Imari pattern, blue, iron-red,
green, and gilt, campana form,
c1917 (A) **80.00**
5⅜" h, cov, green ground, gilt reserve
jeweled panels, painted floral
sprays, four scroll feet, dated 1905 **120.00**
5¾" h, painted birds and branches,
yellow ground, mask and loop handles, c1885, "Crown Derby," pr (A) **135.00**
6" h, gilt birds, insects, and leaves,
blue ground, c1885 (A) **70.00**
6¾" h, enameled and gilt leaves and
grass clumps, cream ground,
c1884, "Crown Derby," pr (A) . . . **250.00**
7" h
Blue and white striped ground, reserved with gilt jeweled panel of
painted flowers, dbl scrolled
handles, dated 1904, sgd "Wil-
liam Mosley" **170.00**
Stylized floral panels, Imari colors,
geometric handles, "Crown
Derby," pr **130.00**
7¼" h, gilt flowers and bird, mottled
blue ground, c1889, "Crown
Derby," pr (A) **25.00**
7½" h, cov, center floral panel, dark
blue ground, gilt foliage and scrollwork, turquoise and white jewel-

ing, sgd "Desire Leroy," dated 1905
(A) **380.00**
8" h
Covered, Japanese stylized flowers,
blue and orange, gold trim,
cream ground, cobalt neck,
c1884 . . . . **280.00**
"Hawthorn" pattern, yellow
ground, dbl gourd shape, c1885,
"Crown Derby," pr (A) **300.00**
Oriental pattern, shades of brown,
gilt trim, "Royal Crown Derby" **100.00**
8¼" h, Imari style "Cigar" pattern
#1128, dated 1920, pr **130.00**
9" h, cov, enameled and gilt clover
and butterflies, yellow ground, gilt
bifurcated handles, c1900 (A) **450.00**
9¼" h, cov, reserved panels of painted
flowers, turquoise and dark blue
ground, dbl handles, dated 1898 . **265.00**
10⅜" h, gilt flowers and foliage, dark
blue ground, globular shape, trumpet neck, "Royal Crown Derby" (A) **150.00**
10½" h
Blue iris, cream ground, c1873
"Crown Derby" **285.00**
"Old Imari" pattern, swan neck,
"Royal Crown Derby" **125.00**
12" h, Imari pattern, blue, iron-red,
green, and gilt, gilt lion knob, faceted body, damaged, c1808, pr . . **110.00**
13¼" h, printed and painted sprays,
cream ground, apricot foot and rim,
three curved branch handles,
c1893, "Royal Crown Derby" (A) **425.00**

Vegetable Dish, cov, 10½" l, curved
shape, gilt trim, "Crown Derby" . . . **750.00**

Watering Can, 3" h, Imari pattern, blue,
iron-red, green, and gilt stylized flowers, florets, and scrolls, c1916 (A) . . **200.00**

STOKE ON TRENT
ENGLAND

CROWN DEVON

Stoke-on-Trent, England
1870–Present

History: S. Fielding and Co., Ltd. established a
pottery at Stoke-on-Trent, England in 1870. This
Staffordshire factory produced a wide variety of

products including majolica wares, terra cotta wares, and earthenwares for domestic use.

Their "majolica argenta" was a white body and glaze introduced in the early 1880s. The wares were decorated with high temperature colors and designs in relief. From 1913 lustre wares were sold under the trade name Crown Devon, including works done in the Art Deco style.

Marks used were an impressed "FIELDING" and "SF & CO" printed with the title of the pattern.

Mug, 4¾" h, John Peel, multicolored, cream ground, musical movement in base, $80.00.

Cheese Dish, Cov
   5" h, "Windsor" pattern, basket of pink flowers, pink and blue florals, gold trim, beige ground **80.00**
   7" l, "Spring" pattern, pink and blue flowers, green leaves, satin beige ground, "Crown Devon" **70.00**
Condiment Set, salt, pepper, cov mustard jar, 7" l, 4" w tray, pink and lavender fuchsias, gray ground, "Crown Devon" **50.00**
Demitasse Cup and Saucer, woodland scene, pheasants, gold int. and handle, "Crown Devon," set of 4 ...... **125.00**
Humidor, enameled gallions, blue luster finish, sgd "D. Cole" **115.00**
Jam Jar, 4½" h, raised pink and lavender fuchsias, green leaves, gray ground, "Crown Devon" **40.00**
Jug, 6½" d, 8¼" h, "John Peel," cream ground, emb John Peel, hunters, and horses, words to music on sides, fox handle, "Crown Devon" **200.00**
Pitcher
   5" h, cov, "Fairest Gems Lie Deepest" motto, multicolored **60.00**
   6½" to 8¼" h, pink and blue florals and swags, beige ground, "Crown Devon, Stoke-On-Trent," set of 3 . **150.00**

Sugar Shaker, florals, beige ground, "Crown Devon" **75.00**
Vase, 9¼" h, cov, pastel rose garlands, rose–filled hanging basket, orange-pink to ivory ground, leaf shape handles, gold finial and trim, "Crown Devon" **60.00**

C. TIELSCH GERMANY

Silesia, Germany; now Walbrzych, Poland
1845–1945

History: Beginning in 1845, the C. Tielsch and Company factory located at Altwasser made household, hotel, and decorative porcelain, along with coffee and tea sets. The C.M. Hutschenreuther Company in Hohenberg acquired most of the stock of Tielsch in 1918 and merged the factory with its own. Hutschenreuther continued using the C. Tielsch name until after WWII.

Berry Set, master bowl, six serving bowls, multicolored holly design ... **75.00**
Bowl
   9⅛" d, multicolored florals, gold trim **20.00**
   10½" d, multicolored flowers, gold border, eagle mark **60.00**
   12½" l, 9¼" w, man and woman in center, period clothes, irreg rose and yellow edge **110.00**
   13½" l, 9" w, pink, red, and yellow roses, green leaves, green ground, pierced dbl handles **70.00**
Cake Plate
   10" H-H, two cherubs in center, green border, scalloped gold rim, dbl open handles **65.00**
   10¼" d, large peacock feather in center, peacock feathers around outer edge, gold trim, cut-out handles .. **65.00**
   11" d, orchids, beige ground, brown trim, dbl handles, "C. Tielsch, Altwasser" **20.00**
Cake Set, master plate, 12" d, six plates, 6" d, yellow and red roses, "C. T. Altwasser, Silesia" **200.00**
Chocolate Set
   19 pcs, chocolate pot, eight cups and

saucers, tray, hp roses, brown
shaded ground, c1855 .... **450.00**
20 pcs, chocolate pot, nine cups and
saucers, large pink rose pattern,
brown and white ground **360.00**
Creamer, 3" h, white and pink roses,
yellow-brown shaded ground, gold
trim **15.00**
Creamer and Sugar
Small flowers, gold trim **45.00**
Yellow roses, light lilac ground **25.00**

**Cup and Saucer, multicolored florals,
cream ground, gold trim, $25.00.**

Demitasse Cup and Saucer, violets,
white ground, gold trim **20.00**
Dish
12" d, blue and yellow flowers, gold
trim, divided, scrolled center handle **50.00**
13½" l, painted multicolored florals,
ivory ground, dbl handles **150.00**
14" l, light yellow daises, green ferns,
divided, center twist handle **55.00**
Plate
8" d
Center hp fruit, border of alternating panels of leaf shape and gold
reticulated design **15.00**
Multicolored ring neck pheasants in
forest, floral borders, set of 6 .. **150.00**
Multicolored scene, lady and gentleman in garden, wide green
border **50.00**
8¼" d, purple, yellow, and green
grapes **25.00**
Ramekin and Underplate, pink floral
and leaf band, light lavender, gold reticulated rim, ribbed, set of 6 ...... **110.00**
Vase
7" h, multicolored peasant scene,
brown ground **65.00**
8½" h, peasant scene, warming hands
over coals, dark brown **80.00**
10" h, pastel pastoral scene, gold dbl
handles **200.00**

Made in
Czechoslovakia

CZECHOSLOVAKIA

1918–Present

History: In 1918 the Czechs and Slovaks became
free of Austro-Hungary domination and were
granted their own country, Czechoslovakia. Portions of the regions of Bavaria, Bohemia, Mora-
via, and Austrian Silesia made up the new country. Bohemia, now the metropolitan area of
Czechoslovakia, was the chief ceramic producing area in the Astro-Hungarian empire in the
19th century.

A variety of china wares were made by the
many Czechoslovakian factories, among which
are Amphora in Egyptian and Art Deco styles and
Erphila Art Pottery. Decorative items such as
flower holders and wall pockets in the form of
birds were produced. Creamers, salt and pep-
pers, and napkin rings were made in interesting
shapes. Kitchen or cereal sets and complete dinner sets, with pattern names such as Iris, Royette,
Royal Bohemia, Ivory Rose, etc., kept factory
production high.

The Karlsbad Porcelain Factory "Concordia"
Brothers Lew & Co. operated from c1919 until
1937. From 1939 until 1945 the factory was
operated by Winterling & Co. It was nationalized
in 1945 and merged with the former Count
Thun's Porcelain nationalized factory in Klosterle. Several other factories such as Meierhofen,
Alp, and Altrohlau merged with Epiag in Karlsbad
about 1939. This merged firm was nationalized
in 1945.

Between 1871 and 1940 B. Bloch & Company
made table, household, and decorative porcelain
and earthenware, some in the onion pattern. After 1920 the name was changed to the Eichwald
Porcelain and Stove Factory Bloch & Co., then
to the Eichwald Porcelain Stove and Tile factory
for the period from 1940 until 1945.

Most items are stamped "Made in Czechoslovakia" with an ink stamp.

References: Ruth A. Forsythe, *Made in Czechoslovakia*, Richardson Printing Corp., 1982.

Baby Dish, 9" d, multicolored decal,
two children and animals, rolled edge **25.00**
Basket, 4" l, 5½" h, Art Deco style design, red, white, blue, and green ... **50.00**
Biscuit Jar, 6½" h, relief white figures,
violet ground **50.00**

Tea Service, teapot, creamer, cov sugar bowl, six cups, multicolored classical scenes, caramel luster ground, gold handles, white spouts, $65.00.

Bowl, 9" sq, floral design, white ground, gold rim **25.00**
Box, 5" l, 3" w, lobster shape, red **20.00**
Butter Tub, cov, overall floral pattern, acorn finial, "Crown Imperial" **40.00**
Cake Set, cake plate, six serving plates, red grapes, green leaves, brown branches, blue-green ground, majolica **75.00**
Candlestick
   5½" h, matte purple, band of orange and red below nozzle, loop handle **16.00**
   6¼" h, multicolored butterflies, yellow-orange shaded ground, loop handle **12.00**
   9" h, hp, roses, brown, green, and gilt (A) **40.00**

Canister Set, pearl luster ground, gold letters, set of 5, $125.00.

Canister Set
   9 pcs, blue hummingbird design ... **225.00**
   10 pcs, roses, blue luster **250.00**
   15 pcs, 6 large, 6 small containers, oil, vinegar, and salt box, hp orange flowers, dark green ground . **200.00**
Cigarette Box
   4½" l, multicolored cigarettes and matches on cov, orange ground .. **12.00**

Black scene of woman, children, and dog, yellow ground, "Erphila" ... **35.00**
Console Set, bowl, 6" d, two candlesticks, black and white bands of florals, yellow ground **40.00**
Creamer
   4" h, white luster, figural cat, handle with black spots, "Made in Czechslovakia" **12.00**
   4½" h, multicolored figural Mexicans, pr **44.00**
   4¾" h, figural parrot **25.00**
Demitasse Cup and Saucer
   Multicolored scenic design, gold int. **20.00**
   Florals, white int., gold handle, "Victoria" **10.00**
Dinner Service, polychrome floral pattern, "Epiag, Czechoslovakia," set of 69 pcs (A) **310.00**
Figure
   5½" h, girl seated, Victorian clothes, holding fan, pink and cream, "Erphila, Czechslovakia" **18.00**
   7" w, 12" h, two businessmen, talking, multicolored, sgd "J. M." ... **200.00**
   14" h, Art Deco dancing girl, multicolored **415.00**
Humidor, 5" w, 8" h, figural, man's head, holding stein, shades of brown **175.00**
Lamp, 24" h, Dutch windmill scene, orange and red shades, cloth painted shade **235.00**
Miniature, tea set, teapot, creamer, sugar, panels outlined in red, pomegranate finials, "Victoria, Czechslovakia" **55.00**
Perfume Bottle, 5" h, painted flowers, gold accents, light green ground ... **40.00**
Pitcher
   6" h, multicolored figural cow **30.00**
   6½" h
      Orange, five narrow red and blue center stripes, luster finish **18.00**
      Painted woodgrained porcelain .. **30.00**
   8", cov, multicolored poppy design . **18.00**
   Blue, orange, and gold butterfly design, yellow ground **16.00**
Plate
   9" d, painted centers, multicolored romantic panels, set of 12 .... **100.00**
   9½" d, "Indian Tree" style pattern, "Czechoslovakia" **12.00**
   10¾" d
      Floral centers, heavy gold borders, set of 8 .... **128.00**
      Multicolored floral sprays, gold trim, "RM Czechoslovakia" ... **20.00**
   11" d, floral decor, gold-ivory ground, "RM Czechoslovakia" **21.00**
Relish Tray, 8" l, pink pearlized violets, silver trim **12.00**
Teapot, 4¼" h, pearl luster finish **20.00**

Toby Jug, 4" h, seated period gentleman, blue, rust, and yellow, "Made in Czechoslovakia" **40.00**

Urn, center classical scene, vining pattern on neck, base, and stem, scrolled and fluted, female heads and scroll form dbl handles, majolica, sgd "Echwold" **4,500.00**

Vase

8" h, floral design, gourd shape **85.00**

8½" d, head and shoulder view of maiden, scarf in orange, black, and gold, "Coronet, Czechoslovakia" . **65.00**

10" h, multicolored florals, pr **55.00**

Vegetable Bowl, 6" d, cov, pink roses, green leaves, white ground, blue filigree border **35.00**

Wall Pocket, multicolored figural owl . **30.00**

DAVENPORT
LONG PORT
STAFFORDSHIRE

1805-20   1870-1886

DAVENPORT

Longport, Staffordshire, England
1794–1887

History: John Davenport and family established the factory in 1794. Earthenware, ironstone, porcelains, cane ware, black basalt, and glass were made. Few of the early examples were marked. Porcelains were not manufactured until 1805–1810. The earliest Davenport porcelains were marked with the word "Longport" in red script.

About 1825 Davenport teawares and dessert services came under the influence of the Rococo revival. The shapes of pieces resembled the Coalport forms of this period. Landscape decorations were used frequently.

Porcelain painted plaques were decorated both at the factory and by independent artists about 1860–1880. Earthenware table services for use on ships became a specialty product. Colorful Japan patterns were produced in the Derby manner in the 1870s–1880s. These were a specialty of the Davenport factory. The firm ceased operation in 1887.

References: T.A. Lockett, *Davenport Pottery and Porcelain 1794–1887*, Charles E. Tuttle, Inc., 1972.

Museums: British Museum, London, England; Cincinnati Art Museum, Cincinnati, Ohio; Hanley Museum, Stoke-on-Trent, England; Liverpool Museum, Liverpool, England; Victoria & Albert Museum, London, England.

Basket and Stand

11½" H-H, "Muleteer" pattern, blue and white, c1820 .... **330.00**

11½" l, reticulated, underglazed blue transfer, Oriental temple scenes, 19th C, pr (A) **200.00**

Biscuit Barrel, 5" h, blue and rust, gold trim, SP top, c1870–86 .... **185.00**

Bough Pots, 4¾" w, purple painted church in wooded landscape, gilt line rims, D shape, fixed ring handles, c1810, imp "anchor and Davenport," pr (A) **575.00**

Bowl

11½" l, 6" h, Chinese-type scene, gilt edge, mounted on short pedestal, c1820 ....**1,450.00**

12" d, transfer, painted flower sprays, gilt scrolls **175.00**

Light blue ground, white cameo design, gold trim, early 19th C **80.00**

Breakfast Set, four shaped covered dishes, 21½" w egg stand with six cups, blue transfer, fishermen in river landscape, white ground, c1860, imp "anchor" and Davenport (A) **660.00**

Butter Tub, 7¼" d, attached stand, pattern #6060, Imari style, iron-red, blue, and gilt, imp "Davenport" (A) **40.00**

Children's Dinner Service, six plates, four graduated platters, four soups, two rect bowls, gravy boat, tureen, and underplate, "Erica" pattern, green transfers **450.00**

Coffee Service, coffeepot, cov milk jug, cov sugar, three cups and saucers, "Old Witches," pattern #2614 ..... **130.00**

Pitcher, 6" h, ironstone, blue and orange Oriental design, gilt trim, green handle, c1805, "W. Davenport & Co., Longport, Staff. Potteries," $165.00.

Compote, 8½" d, 2½" h, hp center scene, man fishing with cows near lake, turquoise and gold band, small raised flowers **85.00**

Creamer and Sugar, child size, light green pastoral scene, repaired **60.00**

Cup and Saucer, Imari pattern, iron-red, cobalt, and gold, c1820 .... **50.00**

Dessert Service
  9 pcs, oval fruit stand, eight plates, centers with different specimen flowers, gilt borders of interwoven ribbon bands, scrolls and flowers, c1860, "anchor and crown" (A) ..**1,025.00**
  10 pcs, two tazzas, eight 9¼" d plates, Imari pattern, central vase of flowers, blue, iron-red, and gilt, stylized flowers, scrolls, and panels, c1875 (A) **350.00**
  14 pcs, two triangular ftd dishes, twelve 9" d plates, "Japan" pattern, iron-red, blue, green, and gold field of flowering vines, four lappet panels, c1875, iron-red crowned "DAVENPORT LONGPORT STAFFORDSHIRE" (A) **1,210.00**
  20 pcs, twelve plates, two ftd shaped dishes, three dbl handled ftd dishes, dbl handled oval ftd dish, two cov sugars, painted flower sprays in scroll surrounds, gilt foliage borders, green ground, shaped rims, c1850, green "DAVENPORT LONGPORT" **750.00**
  27 pcs, center dish, four tazzas, four low stands, eighteen plates, painted named Irish and English views, shaped green borders, reserves of pink lappets and gilt scrolling, c1855, "blue anchor and ribbon cartouche" (A) **1,944.00**
  27 pcs, tall tazza, two low tazzas, four oval dishes, twenty plates, painted landscape vignettes, shaped borders, green and accents, damage, imp "anchor and wreath" **400.00**

Dinner Service, famille rose, table and Oriental flowers, set of 46 pcs (A) .. **960.00**

Dish
  4" d, Imari pattern, SP stand and handle, c1870 .... **135.00**
  8¼" d, blue printed "Chinoiserie Ruins" pattern, shell form, unmarked (A) **35.00**
  9⅝" w, painted "Convolvulus Major," matte green border, gilt edging, c1815, "crown and anchor" (A) .. **168.00**
  10" l, gray and green floral border, black trim, c1800, imp "anchor" mark (A) **45.00**

13¾" l, red botanical plant, orange ground, red and black border, imp "anchor" mark (A) **132.00**

Jug
  7" h, white smear glaze, molded fox hunt scene, brown glazed border, imp "anchor" mark **60.00**
  7⅞" h, "Hydra," Imari style panels of foliage, red mark **65.00**

Meat Dish, 18⅞" l, printed blue, two Oriental figures and pagodas **25.00**

Mug, child's size, transfer print, "Feeding the Rabbit" **90.00**

Mustard Pot, 3½" h, hp, turquoise and gilt florals and leaves, SP hinged lid, c1870–86 .... **58.00**

Pitcher
  4" h, Oriental design, gilt trim, faceted shape, c1820 .... **225.00**
  6¾" h, white clay body, emb hunt scenes, imp "DAVENPORT" (A) .. **65.00**
  7½" h, blue and white rural scenery **100.00**
  8½" h, "Winchester," purple luster and black **300.00**

Plate
  7⅛" d
    Creamware, basket molded borders and pierced rims, imp "Davenport" mark, set of 6 .... **85.00**
    "Legend on Montrose," "anchor" **40.00**
  7¼" d, purple transfer, couple in park, emb flower, butterfly, and bird border, enamels, "Davenport"(A) ... **35.00**
  7½" d, multicolored botanical centers, pierced trellis borders, imp "anchor," set of 3 (A) **400.00**
  7¾" d, blue transfer, Chinese fence with birds, red, green, and luster trim, c1860, "anchor" **48.00**
  7⅞" d, green leaf border **15.00**
  8" d, lavender, Grecian urns and florals on portico **25.00**
  8½" d, lavender scene of cattle at stream, spires in background **45.00**
  8⅝" d, sepia painted landscapes in centers, leaf molded borders, imp "anchor" marks, set of 5 .... **135.00**
  8⅞" d
    Painted centers, view of Lake Windermere, pierced scroll borders, pr (A) **100.00**
    Stone China, exotic pheasant and flowering tree, famille rose colors, gilt, set of 10 .... **75.00**
  9" d, blue feather edge, imp "anchor" mark (A) **25.00**
  9¼" d, "Chantilly" pattern, flow blue, c1844, imp "anchor" mark **65.00**
  9⅞" d, blue printed "Bisham Abbey" pattern **20.00**

10" d, floral center, white ground, tan
and gilt border, scalloped rim **175.00**
10⅛" d, underglaze blue, gaudy floral
design, polychrome enamels and
gilt, "Davenport Stone China" (A)   **85.00**
Platter
10½" l, 8¼" w, blue transfer, Chinese
fence with birds, red, green, and
luster trim, c1866, "anchor" **85.00**
12" l, light blue romantic transfer
scene, octagonal, "anchor" **65.00**
18" l, blue floral pattern, white
ground (A) **75.00**
18" l, 15" w, blue and white "Chinoiserie Bridgeless" design, c1810   **450.00**
19¼" l, painted insects, florals, and
sprigs, iron-red, ochre, and
salmon, ochre edged gadroon bor-
der, c1835 (A) **66.00**
20" l, blue floral pattern, white
ground (A) **75.00**
20½" l, centered roundel of steam-
ship, blue and gilt borders, 19th C   **175.00**
Punch Bowl, 14" d, int. with iron-red,
blue, and gilt chrysanthemums from
rockwork in iron-red trellis border,
rim with foliage on blue ground, ext.
painted with gilt seaweed on light
blue ground, bands of dark blue foliage, c1830, puce "Davenport, Manufacturers to Their Majesties, Long
Port Staffordshire" (A) **2,200.00**
Sauceboat, 3⅝" h, blue feather edge,
imp "Davenport" (A) **75.00**
Sauce Tureen, 7½" l, white, orange and
blue floral trim, gilt accents, covs slotted for ladles, dbl handles, c1815–30,
pr **650.00**
Soup Plate, 9¾" d, light blue transfer of
English country scene and ruined abbey, imp "Davenport" (A) **30.00**
Stand, 8⅞" d, painted exotic flowers,
gilt dentil rims, pr **32.00**
Tea Service, teapot, cov milk jug, cov
sugar, four cups and saucers, rect
18¼" l tray with shell handles, Imari
pattern, floral panels, leaf, and floret
motifs, blue, iron-red, green, and gilt,
c1870 (A) **765.00**
Vase
9" h, Imari pattern, wide base, narrow
neck, flared lip, c1870 ....   **135.00**
17¾" h, painted basket of flowers on
marble ledge, reverse with swan in
gilt cartouche, cornucopia, oviform, gilt bird's head handles,
c1820, pr (A) **1,220.00**
19" h, cov, Stone China, exotic birds
in trees, flowering plants, and
peonies in Imari colors, gilt, ovoid,
raised scrolled dbl handles, domed
covs, lion finials, pr (A) **3,120.00**

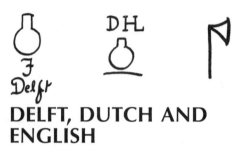

DELFT, DUTCH AND ENGLISH

Delft, Holland c1613–Present

Bristol, Lambeth, and Liverpool, England 1690–1790

DUTCH

History: Tin enamel ware was first manufactured
in Delft about 1613 as a result of Italian potters
immigrating to Holland and bringing the techniques with them. Prior to this the Dutch relied
heavily on the Dutch East India Company's importing Chinese porcelains to fulfill their china
needs.

When the imported supply was reduced,
through disruption of the trade routes, the local
Dutch pottery industry thrived. Idle breweries
were refitted as potteries. By the mid 1600s more
than thirty pottery manufacturers were operating
out of the defunct breweries making imitations
of Chinese and Japanese porcelains in blue and
white tin glazed wares. A transparent lead glaze
was added as a "flashing" or overglaze to make
the tin enamel copies closely resemble Chinese
porcelain.

Two types of blue and white wares were made.
The first type featured blue and white motifs in
the monochrome Chinese style. The blue and
white motifs of the second type included Dutch
subjects such as landscapes, windmills, sailing
ships, portraits, Bible stories, views of towns, and
other "series" plates. The prime period of production for both types of blue and white wares
was 1640–1740. Other towns in Holland also
produced blue and white in addition to Delft.
Few pieces are found with identifying maker's
marks.

After 1700 more polychrome wares were produced in tones of copper green, iron red, and
yellow. Japanese Imari wares were the source of
inspiration for the polychrome wares. In addition
to plates, tiles, vases, and other dishes, Delft
potters also specialized in novelties such as
shoes, cow milk jugs, violins, and small figures
especially of animals.

The decline of Dutch Delft was accelerated by
the introduction of Wedgwood's creamware in
the second half of the 18th century. In addition,
the works of Meissen and Sevres surpassed the
tin glazed wares from Delft. By the beginning of

the 19th century, the number of pottery manufacturers in Delft was reduced to three.

Today only one of the original producers of Delftwares remains in operation. De Porceleyne Fles began producing pottery in 1653. This firm was saved from bankruptcy in 1870 by Joost Thooft. To make the company competitive, Thooft made some changes in the manufacturing process, among which was importing white baking clay from England. Each piece is marked with the logo of De Porceleyne Fles, Joost Thooft's initials, and the initials of the decorator.

ENGLISH

History: Tin enamel pottery came to England from Antwerp in the Netherlands in the 16th century. At first the tin glazed earthenware was called "galley-ware." The name changed to Delftware in the mid-18th century because of its similarity to Dutch Delft products. English Delft production was centered in Bristol, Lambeth, and Liverpool after strong beginnings in London in the mid-17th century.

At Lambeth, apothecary wares, barber basins, and puzzle jugs were among the most popular forms produced. In Bristol, the glaze had a more bluish tone. Plates, bowls, and flower holders with a naive treatment predominated. Liverpool Delft with its harder body resembled Chinese porcelains more closely than that made elsewhere. By 1790 tin enamel glaze wares fell into decline in England due to the rise of Wedgwood's creamware.

References: John Bedford, *Delftware*, Walker & Co., 1966; Carolene Henriette De Jonge, *Delft Ceramics*, Praeger, 1970; H.P. Fourest, *Delftware*, Rizzoli, 1980; F.H. Garner & Michael Archer, *English Delftware*, Faber & Faber, 1972; Ivor Hume, *Early English Delftware from London and Virginia*, The Colonial Williamsburg Foundation, 1977; Diana Imber, *Collecting European Delft and Faience*, Praeger, 1968; Anthony Ray, *English Delftware Pottery in the Robert Hall Warren Collection*, Boston Book & Art Shop, 1968.

Museums: Ashmolean Museum, Oxford, England; Fitzwilliam Museum, Cambridge, England; Gemeente Museum, Arnhem, Holland; Gardiner Museum of Ceramic Art, Toronto, Canada; Hius Lambert van Meerten Museum, Delft, Holland; Musees Royaux d'Art et d'Historie, Brussels, Belgium; Prinsenhof Museum, Delft, Holland; Rijksmuseum, Amsterdam, Holland; Royal Factory "De Porceleyne Fles" Collection, Delft, Holland; Sheffield City Museum, Sheffield, England; Victoria & Albert Museum, London, England.

REPRODUCTION ALERT: The old Dutch wares have been copied as souvenirs and are quite popular with the foreign traveler. Be careful not to confuse these modern pieces with the older examples.

DUTCH

Drug Jar, 9½" h, blue floral and vine design, white ground, 18th C, Dutch, $1,275.00.

Asparagus Tureen, 7¼" l, modeled asparagus body and cov, manganese and blue tips, tied with yellow string, c1760 (A) 3,800.00
Barber Bowl, 12" l, two pheasants and peony in scrolled border, Imari colors, ext. of well with scrolled floral border, c1770, iron-red "PAK" mark (A) 1,000.00
Baskets, 10½" w, strawberry baskets, matching stands, blue and white Chinese designs, 18th C, pr 1,750.00
Bottle, 9" h, blue Oriental scene of child watching two ladies in garden, knobbed neck, c1765, black "GK & #6" mark 360.00
Bowl
  6" d, blue and white windmill and sailboat scene, "Delft, Holland" mark 24.00
  10" d, 5¾" h
    Polychrome floral and bird designs in white reserves, blue ground, "A. K." mark (A) 80.00
    Polychrome florals int. and ext., blue outer edge band, unmarkd (A) 75.00
  11⅞" d, polychrome scroll, floral edge cartouche of landscape, c1775 (A) 690.00
Butter Dishes
  4½" l, base molded as multicolored rockwork, recumbent goats in manganese and florals on cov, early 18th C, blue "L:P:K:" marks, pr (A) 2,200.00
  5¼" l, modeled as polychrome crested birds on nests, c1760, pr (A) 3,300.00

Butter Tub

4⅞" l, figures in multicolored Italian landscape scene, molded ribbing, cov with quay scene in iron-red scrollwork, c1740 (A) **1,320.00**

5" h, molded polychrome mermaid with plants on cov, scalloped bowl with molded vines, oval, c1758–64, blue "A/D/12 & #103" marks (A) **1,500.00**

5" l, molded polychrome hen, molded and painted base, oval, mid 18th C (A) **1,650.00**

5¼" l, blue scrolled florals on dot field, leaf shaped handle, dog finial, mid 18th C (A) **550.00**

5½" l, white ground, blue decor, octagon shape, dbl handles and cov, panels of birds and florals, alternating marbleized panels, flowerhead motif pierced handles, scroll finial, mid 18th C, "Lampetkan" **450.00**

Soup Bowl, 8¼" d, blue Oriental design, white ground, Dutch, $135.00.

Calendar Plate, 10" d, blue scenes representing various months, month name at top, blue "ax" marks, set of 9 (A) **5,500.00**

Charger

13" d, polychrome florals, gold, yellow, green, blue, and purple (A) . **225.00**

13¼" d, blue central design of florals and balustrade, white ground, late 18th C (A) **175.00**

13½" d

Blue and white center design of fox in bushes, stylized floral border, 18th C (A) **350.00**

Blue and white vase of flowers and foliage enclosed in drapery band, "De Drie Klokken" (A) **290.00**

Blue floral design, white ground, late 18th C, "P" (A) **250.00**

Polychrome floral design, blue, yellow, and green, cream ground, 18th C (A) **250.00**

Polychrome portraits of Princess Frederica of Prussia and William V of Orange, initials in orange vine, entwined yellow band borders, c1780–90, pr (A) **1,760.00**

13¾" d

Blue and white flowering tree in center, floral border, unmarked (A) **220.00**

Blue "Bird on Rock" pattern, heavy floral border with peonies, c1740–60, blue "ax & X" marks **500.00**

Blue center leaf cluster, wide border of stylized flowers and scrolls, c1770, blue "A/iVDB/22" mark (A) **200.00**

14" d, blue biblical center scene, iron-red, yellow, and blue cherub border, inscribed "Lucas," mid-18th C (A) **1,870.00**

14⅛" d, blue scene of three swans swimming before building, dentil border, floral reserves, mid 18th C, blue "slash" mark (A) **120.00**

15⅜" d, blue and white Oriental scene of two men in garden (A) .. **150.00**

15⅝" d, blue design of Oriental warrior in center, black outlines, panels of seated Orientals and flowers in border, star and lozenge pattern under rim, c1690 (A) **825.00**

16" d, blue and white basket, flowers in center **1,050.00**

24" d, tavern scene of three gentlemen at table, multicolored, floral and dot border, sgd and marked .. **750.00**

Cream Jug, 3½" h, white glaze, flattened body, loop handle (A) **35.00**

Cruet Set, two cov ewers and stand, painted continuous landscape, blue green fret, stand with scroll handle, mid 18th C, blue "LPK" mark **700.00**

Cuspidor, 3⅛" h, blue Chinese figures in fenced garden, birds, and flowers, brown rim, handled quatrefoil body, blue "CK 9" mark (A) **715.00**

Dish

11¾" d, blue building in border of stylized flowerheads and foliage, fluted, c1740, "B:P" mark, repaired (A) **88.00**

13½" d

Blue figure of "Plenty" among trees, c1750, repaired (A) **100.00**

Polychrome plants and tree on terrace, blue ground, stylized flowerheads border, c1750 (A) **100.00**

Polychrome vases of flowers, stylized flower sprays border, c1750, pr (A) **330.00**

13¾" d
Blue and white center vase of flowers, stylized flowerheads and sprays border, pie crust border, c1750, "3 bells" mark 250.00
Blue center design of tower in landscape, c1660, attrib to Rotterdam, hairline 3,000.00
14" d, blue scene of villa by waterfront, sponged trees, c1660, attrib to Rotterdam 1,000.00
15½" d, blue and white center chinoiserie figures on terrace, stylized Oriental flowers in border alternating with figures, c1720, unmarked 650.00

Drug Jar
6¼" h, rect cartouche, green, yellow, and blue, "Nuxmuscat" in manganese, c1760 (A) 110.00
8⅝" h, blue cartouche, inscription, c1725 (A) 440.00

Ewer, 7" h, cov, blue and white painted peacocks on rocks, flowering plants between bands of foliage, c1740, cracked (A) 170.00

Figure, 3⅝" l, polychrome
Baby in wicker cradle, iron-red and green flowered coverlet, mid 18th C (A) 825.00
Seated lion with paw on coin, decorated cut corner rect base, 18th C, "AK" mark (A) 150.00

Figure, 5" h, blue, white ground, c1700, marked "iHF," Dutch, $375.00.

Figure
3¾" l, blue and white rabbit with florals, blue oval base, late 18th C (A) 100.00
4¼" h, seated dog, manganese features (A) 100.00
4½" l, blue and white striped recumbent cats, green bases, c1755, blue "ax" marks, pr (A) 2,860.00
4¾" h
Polychrome, child seated in hex-

agonal marbleized high chair, floral quatrefoil reserves, mid 18th C (A) 770.00
Seated blue and white spotted hound, bells on collars, oval base, mid 18th C, pr (A) 550.00
5" l, blue and white windmill, Thuringia mark 15.00
5½" l, modeled pear, foliage, mid 18th C (A) 150.00
5¾" l, milking group, polychrome florals on white cows, seated facing milkmaid, ear missing, mid 18th C, pr (A) 1,100.00
6" h, polychrome equestrian group, figure removable from horse, rect inscribed base, c1790, blue "1. p. Kan" mark (A) 715.00
7" l, blue and white recumbent horses, facing right and left, flowered saddles, c1775, pr (A) 1,430.00
7¼" h, blue and white seated spaniels, c1740 (A) 2,640.00
7¾" w, cows standing, blue and white foliage and dots, facing right and left, oblong bases with scrolls, c1760, blue "PVB" marks, pr (A) . 2,200.00
8¼" h
Polychrome man on horse (A) 275.00
Prancing horses, facing right and left, dressed in saddles, applied florals, white ground, c1750, pr (A) 1,210.00
8½" l
Milking groups, facing right and left, seated milkmaid and milkman, white, gilt horns, mid 18th C, pr 800.00
Polychrome cow, rect base (A) ... 275.00
11¾" h, polychrome seated woman in floral dress holding black shawl forming handle, hole in head and shoe for spigot, c1760 (A) 550.00
13" h, polychrome man with bottle and goblet, period clothes, seated over barrel, dated 1783 (A) 2,640.00

Fish Drainer, 17" d, blue and white painted scattered fish, pierced surface, dbl handles, three small feet, c1700 (A) 900.00

Inkstand, 8" l, painted landscapes on sides, pierced front, oval portrait, relief of recumbent dog on top between wells, c1760 (A) 550.00

Jar
3⅝" h, cobalt Oriental design, lappet border, octagonal ribbed body, 18th C (A) 110.00
10" h, blue and white bird and floral design, cylindrical neck, lappet border (A) 200.00

Jar, cov, 16" h, blue fishing scene with sailboat, c1800, Dutch, $875.00.

Mug
  4¾" h, blue reserves of windmill and house, florals, white ground, "Delft, Holland" marks, pr **15.00**
  10" h, polychrome floral design, manganese sponging, unmarked (A) .. **130.00**
Pancake Plate, 8¾" d, blue insect on rockwork in star shaped panel, border with emblems in ovals, brown rim, c1740 (A) **100.00**
Pilgrim Bottle
  9" h, design of man in native costume walking in countryside, blue and white, molded handles, sgd and marked **450.00**
  9½" h, blue and white scenic, molded snake edges **600.00**
Plaque
  13¼" d, blue and white Rembrandt's portrait, "Royal Delft" mark **100.00**
  16" d, blue and white center open basket of flowers, tracery border, 18th C, unmarked **750.00**
  16½" d, flowing blue, portrait of young Dutch girl, pierced for hanging, "urn" mark **425.00**
  16½", 10¾" h, blue and white windmill and sheep in scenic setting (A) **90.00**
  16⅞" w, polychrome bird in cage recessed from painted drapery and figural scenes, mid 18th C (A) **1,210.00**
  21½" l, 15" h, blue and white cartouche of huntsman in landscape (A) **220.00**
  22½" l, blue and white castle and lake scene, lower portion with scrollwork on blue field, oval, 19th C, marked **950.00**
  23" l, blue and white village scene, marked **1,050.00**

Plate
  7" d, dark blue decor, concentric circles, petal center, and worm bands, 18th C **225.00**
  8¾" d, mango flower sprays, border of flowerheads and foliage, c 1740 (A) **76.00**
  8⅞" d
    Pale blue bianca sopra bianca border, dark blue Oriental design, unmarked (A) **230.00**
    Polychrome flower sprays, brown ground, 18th C (A) **250.00**
    Polychrome portrait of William V of Orange, poem dated 1788, floral borders, c1780–90, pr, repaired (A) **412.00**
  9" d
    Blue and white, center floral basket, five shaped floral reserves on rim (A) **110.00**
    Blue and white floral design, lambrequin borders, late 18th C, set of 6 .... **300.00**
    Polychrome of tree, flowers, and birds, mid 18th C **40.00**
  9⅛" d, blue "Peacock" pattern, white ground, yellow rims, c1720, blue "3 bells" marks, pr (A) **360.00**
  10" d
    Blue and white design commemorating 1928 Olympics **275.00**
    Blue Chinese pattern, unmarked .. **300.00**
    Blue chrysanthemum surrounded by florals and scrolling, set of 4 (A) **350.00**
  10⅛" d, iron-red hatchwork reserved with blue edged panels of floral sprays, 18th C (A) **250.00**
  12⅜" d, polychrome bowknotted floral spray in border of sprigs and butterflies, c1789 .... **200.00**
  13½" d, polychromes of William of Orange and Queen Mary, convex centers, fluted borders with tulips, scalloped edges, c1689, pr (A) ...**1,650.00**
  13¾" d, polychrome Oriental flowers and rockwork in paneled border, c1760 .... **300.00**
  14⅛" d, blue "Peacock" pattern, white ground, yellow edged rim, mid 18th C, blue "claw & #3" marks (A) **250.00**
Pot, cov
  7¼" d, blue paneled stylized Oriental flowers, dbl handles, mid 18th C (A) **440.00**
  9" d, blue open peony design, dgl handles, mid 18th C, hairline on handle (A) **440.00**
Potpourri Jar, 10½" h, blue floral design, four lobed body, blue dot branch han-

dles and finial, blue foliage on domed
foot, c1740, blue "A:H" mark (A) .. **500.00**
Puzzle Jug, 8" h, blue and white, three
panels of birds and flowers, head and
scroll border, three spout tubular rim,
pierced design above and below,
c1710, "De Drye Porceleyne
Flesschen" (A) **1,430.00**
Salt, 4⅜" h, blue and white painted
buildings and scattered flowers,
molded foliage borders, rococo form,
c1760 (A) **280.00**
Stein, blue and white center panel of
windmill surrounded by open florals,
pewter lid, Delft mark **250.00**
Tankard, 7½" h, blue Chinese figures in
garden, wavy line borders, dashes on
handle, early 18th C (A) **330.00**
Teapot
4¼" h, iron-red, blue, and gray-green
Oriental flowers, ribbed barrel
body, early 18th C **75.00**
5¼" h, blue birds and florals, dot
field, c1700–05, blue "PK" mark
(A) **715.00**
Tobacco Jar, 11¾" h, blue painted Indian smoking pipe seated by cargo,
two Dutch ships, metal cov, late 18th
C, blue "3 bells" mark (A) **1,430.00**
Tulipierre, 31" h, blue and white Oriental motif, c1765, unmarked **1,450.00**
Urn
15" h, cov, six panels of floral and
bird design, ribbed body, dog finial
(A) **100.00**
20" h, blue and white Dutch portrait
medallion and scenic panels,
mounted as lamp (A) **130.00**
Vase
6¼" h, manganese and blue, car-

Tulip Vase, 11" h, blue flower and vine design, white ground, five openings on shoulder, c1760, Dutch, $775.00.

touche of canal scene, manganese
trellis pattern ground, baluster
shape, bird finial, c1740 (A) **110.00**
6⅜" h, manganese Oriental design of
two men and pavilion in landscape,
c1793 ....**200.00**
7" h, blue painted exotic birds and
flowers, bands of scrollwork, octagonal bottle shape, pr (A) **240.00**
8" h, blue and white stylized flowers,
"DP Delft, Holland" mark **100.00**
11" h, Tulip, white ground, lower sections of birds and plants in blue,
upper sections with masks outlining
openings, 4 paw feet with molded
female heads, c1701, blue interlaced "APK" marks **1,700.00**
17½" h, blue and white florals, flared
rim, ribbed body and flared foot,
20th C, pr (A) **500.00**

ENGLISH

Argyle, 5⅜" h, blue painted ribbon-tied
bouquets on sides, Oriental floral and
lappet border, c1770, London (A) .. **260.00**
Bottle
6⅛" h, white glaze, pear shape, flaring neck, everted rim, c1720, Lambeth (A) **418.00**
9½" h, painted flowers in shaped foliate and pomegranate reserves,
powder blue ground, pear shape,
c1750, pr, hairline (A) **500.00**
Bowl
6½" d, polychrome flowering plants
and rockwork, c1760, Lambeth (A) **66.00**
8⅞" d, blue painted band of flowers
and foliage in line borders on ext.
(A) **50.00**
9" d, int. with blue peony spray, ext.
with powdered manganese ground,
late 18th C, Lambeth (A) **185.00**
13¾" d, blue rows of floral sprigs and
petal-shaped panels, c1780 (A) ... **200.00**
Charger
10½" d, polychrome scene of Adam
and Eve with serpent, blue dash
border, c1700, cracked (A) **1,465.00**
13⅜" d
Blue and yellow painted crowned
portrait of Charles II, "CR2," border of tulips, blue line rim, riveted, c1680, Brislington (A) ...**11,500.00**
Blue painted portrait of King William on rearing horse, "WR,"
yellow and manganese accents,
yellow line and blue dash rim,
c1690, Lambeth (A) **3,600.00**
13⅝" d, blue, green, and yellow tulips and carnations, rocky mound,
yellow line and blue dash border,

ochre glaze on reverse, c1690,
London (A) **575.00**
13¾" d
Blue, manganese, and yellow portrait of King William, "KW,"
looped curtain in border, c1690
(A) **2,660.00**
Blue painted standing Queen Anne,
"AR," yellow accents, blue dash
rim, c1705, Lambeth (A) **3,735.00**
Cobalt, manganese and green portrait of William III in armor,
"WR," green lead glazed re-
verse, c1700 (A) **2,048.00**
15¾" d, blue, yellow, and ochre portrait of William II in court robes,
borders of leaf motifs and dashes,
c1685–90, London (A).........**14,000.00**
Dish
7¾" d, cobalt lotus and foliage, rhom-
boidal leaves, c1730, Lambeth (A)   **30.00**
8¼" d, center and rim cobalt painted
with Oriental figures and rockwork,
lobed, late 17th C, London **250.00**
8½" d, painted half figures of King
William and Queen Mary in coronation robes, "WMR" in line border, octagonal, c1690, London, repaired A) **1,084.00**
8⅝" d, blue radiating geometric pattern, c1700, London (A) **320.00**

**Dish, 9" d, blue Oriental design, white
ground, c1760, $285.00.**

13⅜" d, multicolored "Ann Gomm"
pattern (A) **75.00**
13½" d, central flowerhead design,
four heart shaped panels, red, yellow, and blue Oriental foliage,
green washed ground **280.00**
13⅝" d, polychrome pagodas in landscape, c1740, Lambeth (A) ... **150.00**
13¾" d, blue painted bird and two
ducks in flight, foliage around cen-

tral raised boss, scroll and flower
panels border (A) **110.00**
Drug Jar
7" h
Blue and white cartouche, Latin beneath basket of fruit at spout,
bird's and angel's head, early
18th C, blue "WO" mark (A) .. **135.00**
Dark blue cherub and shell label,
Latin inscription, bluish glaze,
c1730–40, London (A) **150.00**
Dark blue "Song Bird" label, Latin
inscription, mid 18th C, London
(A) **515.00**
14⅛" h, polychrome, arms of "The
Worshipful Society of Apothecar-
ies," unicorn supports, rhinoceros,
and Apollo, elaborate scrolled pomegranates, tulips, and foliage,
c1656, London, restored (A).... **25,855.00**
Figure
3" h, seated spaniel, manganese accents, oblong base, c1780 (A) ... **200.00**
3½" h, portrait bust of man, wig and
robes, blue, white ground, c1710–
15, London **1,680.00**
4" h, lamb feeding at sheep, incised
fleece, oblong grass base, c1750,
repairs (A) **440.00**
6⅝" h, shoe, blue trailing sprays and
buckle, yellow heel, inscribed "E S
1759" in manganese on sole (A) **.1,700.00**
Flower Brick
4" l, blue flowering branches on sides,
tops pierced and painted with trelliswork, pr (A) **528.00**
5" l, blue landscape scenes and figures in boats, blue dot pattern,
pierced top, four ogee feet, c1750,
unmarked (A) **350.00**
6" h, dark blue panels of prunus
sprays and trelliswork, perforated
top, mid 18th C, Lambeth (A) **270.00**
6⅛" l, cobalt building on island in
river, sailing ships, top pierced with
large and small holes, c1760 (A) . **425.00**
Fuddling Cup, 5⅜" d, four pear shape
cups, intertwined handles, white
glaze, c1700, Lambeth (A) **1,760.00**
Jug, 4½" h, cov, blue bird on rock,
shrubs and insects, blue dash loop
handle, sparrow beak spout, early
18th C **560.00**
Marriage Dish, 13⅜" d, polychrome
house in landscape, "BIS and 1733"
in band of trellis diaper, floral border
(A) **250.00**
Meat Dish, 14¼" d, cobalt Oriental lady
fishing with man in gazebo, trellis and
diaper rim, c1760–70 (A) **293.00**
Ointment Pot
2¼" d, blue, "W. Singleton, Lambeth

Butts," 18th C (A) **150.00**
4¾" d, black painted chain motif be-
tween narrow bands, London (A) . **45.00**
Pancake Plate, 7⅞" d, blue mimosa
flowers in bottle vase, leaf and dash
borders (A) **36.00**
Plate
7½" d
Painted blue pagoda and garden in
central panels, compartments of
stylized flowers, pr **225.00**
Two blue triangular houses in cen-
tral panels, band of leaf scrolls,
borders of whorl diaper, pr **225.00**
7¾" d, blue verse in circ leaf car-
touche, c1752 (A) **338.00**
8½" d
Marriage, cobalt, cream ground,
florals and initials (A) **250.00**
"Merryman," blue, "Let him do all
what he kan" in cartouche of
crown, griffins, and cherub,
c1740, London (A) **730.00**
8⅝" d
Blue bunch of grapes and foliage
(A) **100.00**
Blue, yellow, and manganese
crowned half portraits of William
and Mary, "WMR," dbl line border, riveted, c1690–95, London
(A) **1,320.00**
8¾" d
Blue, red, green, and yellow stylized Oriental flowers in rock garden, rim with trailing flowers,
c1750, London (A) **120.00**
Polychrome parrot on branch in
rock garden, c1750–60, London,
pr (A) **200.00**
Red, blue, green, yellow, and man-
ganese "Ann Gomm" pattern,
London (A) **55.00**
8⅞" d
Blue painted buildings and pagodas
in river landscapes, c1750, set of
4 . . . . **375.00**
Iron-red and blue flowering plants,
c1740, Lambeth (A) **140.00**
Polychrome exotic birds on
branches, rockwork, borders of
flowering and fruiting branches,
c1760, Lambeth, pr (A) **132.00**
Sgraffito plant accented in yellow,
polychrome center of foliage and
pavilion, powdered manganese
base (A) **216.00**
9" d, blue
Flowerpot, sponged trees, and fo-
liage border, c1750 (A) **100.00**
Oriental style plants on terrace,
c1750 (A) **100.00**
Painted lotus and willow tree,

c1760, cracked (A) **50.00**
9¼" d
Blue painted stylized flowers and
foliage, brown rims, set of 3 (A) **45.00**
Cobalt, green, yellow, and red trailing Oriental flowers in rock garden, late 18th C, Lambeth (A) . . **50.00**
9½" d, blue painted chinoiserie riverside, mid 18th C, London (A) . . **60.00**
9¾" d, armorial, cobalt arms of
"Butchers' Company," inscribed
and dated 1724, foliate scroll rim,
London (A) **440.00**
10" d, polychrome bird and trailing
flowers, Chinese export style, mid
18th C, London (A) **265.00**
11⅞" d, blue, green, yellow, and
manganese scene of balloon flying
over houses and trees, foliage spray
and loops of cross and dot pattern
border, blue rim, c1785 (A) **1,865.00**
13" d, blue stylized flowering plants,
trellis pattern, white ground, c1740 **175.00**
13⅜" d, red, blue, and green large
flowers, scrolling foliage **240.00**
13½" d
Cobalt pavilion in riverside garden,
trellis band on rim, c1770 (A) . . **70.00**
Polychrome vase of flowers on low
table, mid 18th C (A) **300.00**
14" d
Cobalt and manganese chinoiserie
landscape, scrolling border,
c1750, London (A) **200.00**
Painted cobalt chinoiserie land-
scape with pavilion, cavetto with
band of trellis, rim with narrow
band of dots and squares,
c1740–60, London **200.00**
14¼" d, blue pagoda on hill, c1770
(A) **135.00**
Porringer
7½" w, trefoil, pierced handle, white
glaze, c1700 (A) **2,310.00**
8⅝" d, int. blue painted with mimosa
plants, blue dashes on ext., 2 loop
handles (A) **145.00**
Posset Pot
5⅜" h, blue painted grapes and foliage outlined in black, strap handle **150.00**
8¼" w, cov, blue painted Orientals in
rocky landscape, curved spout,
loop handles, manganese scrolls,
c1690, repairs (A) **100.00**
9" w, blue and white Chinese design,
brown trim, dbl handles, single
spout, c1760 . . . .**1,800.00**
Punch Bowl
8" d, blue inscription "A Health to the
Brave" on int., flowers and fenced
garden on ext., late 18th C, cracked
(A) **80.00**

13¾" d, ext. painted panels of flowers reserved on blue wash ground, c1720 (A) **235.00**

Salts, 3¼" h, dark blue Oriental flowers in trellis and floret borders, hexafoil shape, three feet, early 18th C, pr (A) **740.00**

Tankard, 8½" h, white glaze, raised rows of circ bumps, mid 16th C, London (A) **10,800.00**

Tea Caddy, 4⅞" h, blurred blue figure on front, cottage and trees on reverse, octagonal, c1750 .... **250.00**

Vase
  5⅜" h, blue painted bird and exotic insect in flowering plants, pear shape (A) **150.00**
  7¼" h, blue willow tree, peony, and bamboo, neck with feathered border, baluster shape (A) **200.00**

Wall Pockets, 7⅜" h, cornucopia shape, molded mask at top, trailing rose branch, blue accents, pr (A) **235.00**

GERMAN

Charger, 19¾" d, polychrome chinoiserie design (A) **225.00**

Ewer, 9" h, blue and white windmill and landscape scene **48.00**

Pitcher, 5" h, blue and white lighthouse scene **12.00**

Tray, 11" l, 8½" h, blue and white scene of boats and windmills, "Made in Germany" **42.00**

1872–1881   1882–1898   1898–1907

WILLIAM DE MORGAN

1889–1907

Chelsea, England 1872–1881

Merton Abbey, near Wimbledon, England 1882–1888

Sand's End Pottery, Fulham, England 1889–1907

History: William De Morgan, 1839–1917, was primarily a designer and decorator, not a potter. He purchased many tile blanks from commercial firms, e. g., Architectural Pottery Company, to decorate with his own designs. In 1872 De Morgan established a pottery in Chelsea to produce his own underglaze blue tiles while experimenting with other colors such as red luster. In the mid-1870s he used the Persian colors purple, blue, and green for decorating tiles and ornamental vases. William Morris, De Morgan's friend, influenced his design motifs in areas such as flowers, birds, fish, ships, or mythical beasts.

In 1882 De Morgan moved to Merton Abbey near Wimbledon. He still made tiles, but increased his output of jugs, bowls, and globular vases. In partnership with Halsey Ricardo, an architect, he moved to Sand's End Pottery at Fulham in 1888. Together they produced pottery, tiles, panels, and murals. De Morgan's pottery body was lightly fired, rather granular, and well suited to the ornamental nature and broad designs of his work. Vases were decorated in the "Isnik" style with the strong Persian colors. Although some pieces showed an Art Nouveau influence, De Morgan was associated with the Arts and Crafts Movement during the Sand's End Pottery period. The more important decorators to work for De Morgan were: Charles and Fred Passenger, James and John Hersey, and Joe Juster. Their initials usually appeared with the standard factory marks on their works.

De Morgan was the first English potter to rediscover the secrets of older luster decoration. Later lusters used by Pilkington (see Tiles) are related to De Morgan's successful experiments in the 19th century.

After 1892 De Morgan lived much of the time in Italy due to illness. In 1898 his partnership with Ricardo ended and the showroom closed. De Morgan reorganized and took into partnership the artists Charles and Fred Passenger and his kiln master, Frank Iles. The factory stopped making its own pots and bought biscuit wares from Carter and Co. of Poole. The factory closed in 1907. De Morgan gave permission to the Passengers to continue using his designs.

References: Julian Barnard, *Victorian Ceramic Tiles*, Mayflower Books, 1972; John Catleugh, *William DeMorgan Tiles*, Van Nostrand Reinhold Company, 1983; W. Gaunt & M.D.E. Clayton Stamm, *William De Morgan*, N.Y. Graphic Society, 1971.

Museums: Art Institute of Chicago, Chicago, Illinois; Battersea Old House, London, England; Castle Museum, Norwich, England; City Art Gallery, Birmingham, England; Fitzwilliam Museum, Cambridge, England; Leighton House, Kensington, England; William Morris Gallery, Waltham-

Dish, 12⅞" d, pink ground, ruby luster, "C. P. & W. DE. MORGAN & Co. FULHAM," (A) $1,210.00.

tow, England; Victoria & Albert Museum, London, England.

Bottle
  8½" h, three swimming swans with young, plants, icicle and squiggle neck, ruby and pink luster, c1895, "W. De. Morgan & Co. Fulham" (A) **715.00**
  9¼" h, "Persian," flowers on pink ground, ruby and pink luster, c1895, blue "W. De. Morgan & Co. Fulham" (A) **715.00**
  9¾" h, pinwheel design, scalework lower border, icicle band at neck, ruby and pink luster, c1888–97, imp tulip mark (A) **715.00**
  18" h, thistle headed, "Persian," large flowerheads and leaves below cobalt and turquoise border of tulips, black outlines, imp tulip mark (A) **2,530.00**
Bowl
  5⅝" d, silver luster and light blue eagle, tulips border, lapis lazuli ground, c1907–11 (A) **600.00**
  6⅜" d, flowerhead center, band of blossoms and leaves on border, vine and rings on ext., tan, blue, and iron-red, c1921–33 (A) **330.00**
  15½" d, int. with dragon, ext. with blue and green luster floral motifs, c1898–1907 (A) **475.00**
Charger, 12¾" d
  Falcon design, luster colors (A) **550.00**
  Peacock design, luster colors (A) ... **250.00**
Dish
  11¾" d, two coiled snakes around rock, flying birds in sun rays, ruby,

copper, and gold luster, mauve, orange, ochre, and olive enamels, c1907–11 (A) **1,430.00**
  12⅛" d, center stylized peony, stylized border lotus, ruby luster, pink and orange, c1907–11 (A) **825.00**
  14⅛" d
    Two eagles perched on crescent surrounded by vines beneath owl's head, reverse with arabesque border, scalework, and wavy lines, ruby luster, dark red enamels, c1898–1907 (A) **550.00**
    Vase with flowers extending to border, ruby luster, yellow and pink shading, c1898–1907, imp pinwheel mark (A) **1,100.00**
  14¼" d, two leaping antelopes, stylized country setting, ruby luster, dark red enamel, c1898–1907 (A) **1,320.00**
  14⅜" d, two eagles with beast between perched on branch, grotesque mask, and two fish, concentric rings, dots, and flowerheads on reverse, pink with ruby luster, buff ground, c1898–1907 (A) **440.00**
Ewer, 7⅝" h, three deer on foliage scroll field, amphora shape, neck and spout with triangles and squiggles, ruby luster, c1888–97 (A) **1,000.00**
Jug, 12⅞" h, birds, fish, and lizards in stylized foliage, pink with ruby luster, amphora style, dbl handles, c1888–97, imp tulip mark (A) **825.00**
Rice Dish
  8⅞" d, raised flowerhead center, concentric rings, stylized leaves on border, wide vine and ring design on reverse, pink with ruby luster (A) **220.00**
  12⅜" d, center wild beast in arabesque, dragon border, ruby luster, c1907–11, "C. P. & W. De. Morgan" (A) **935.00**
  16½" d, center peacock, leaf and peacock border, reverse with foliate and band border, ruby luster, dark red, drab-green, and cream, c1898–1907 (A) **1,000.00**
Tazza, 9⅝" d, center stylized bird, dragon border, lotus flowers on underside, palmettes and scrolling on foot, pink with ruby luster (A) **770.00**
Tile
  3" sq, relief of stork in flight, ruby luster, c1890, imp "De Morgan" (A) **125.00**
  6" sq, relief of two lions, ruby luster, c1900, imp "D. M." (A) **125.00**
  6⅛" sq
    "New Persian," stylized flowers and leaves, cobalt, green, tur-

quoise, and black, c1882, imp "W De Merton Abbey" (A) **50.00**

"Persian," bellflowers, chartreuse, green, and brown, c1890, imp "W. De Morgan & Co. Sand's End Pottery" (A) **40.00**

"Persian," carnations and stylized foliage, cobalt, turquoise, manganese, green, and black, c1900, imp "D. M. 98" (A) **40.00**

"Persian," flowers and foliage, light and dark green, c1900, imp "Wm De Morgan & Co-Sand's End Pottery-Fulham" (A) **36.00**

6¼" sq, raised design of fish, luster glaze (A) **55.00**

18" l, 6" w, "Persian," peacock perched on two lizards and brick wall, blue, green, turquoise, tan, brown, and iron-red, c1888, imp "W. De Morgan & Co. Sand's End Pottery," set of 3 (A) **1,870.00**

37¼" l, 10" w, "Persian," two peacocks and vase of flowers, cobalt, turquoise, green, and manganese, c1888, imp "Wm De Morgan & Co-Sand's End Pottery-Fulham," panel of four tiles (A) **1,320.00**

73" l, 9⅛" w, "Mongolian," Persian flowers and vines, cobalt, turquoise, green, lilac, manganese, and black, c1888, panel of eight tiles (A) **935.00**

Vase

4⅜" h, wild beasts and vines, triangle and squiggle lower border, ruby luster, c1888–97, imp tulip mark (A) **385.00**

12" h, "Persian," flowers, turquoise, green, white, and yellow, cobalt ground, manganese scalework at neck, dbl gourd shape, c1888, imp "W. De Morgan Sand's End Pottery," damaged (A) **770.00**

12⅛" h, "Persian," two birds on leaves, cobalt, turquoise, manganese, and yellow, loop handles and neck with stylized flowers, c1898 (A) **1,760.00**

13" h, floral motifs, blue, green, and burgundy glaze, ovoid, swollen cylindrical neck (A) **150.00**

13⅛" h, "Persian," swans swimming by trees, cobalt, green, and turquoise, chalice shape, loop handles, triple knopped flared standard, stylized tulips, c1898, "W De. Morgan. Fulham" (A) **1,870.00**

16¾" h, "Persian," two exotic birds, cobalt, turquoise, green, manganese, yellow, and black, two snakes on reverse, cats at neck, dbl

loop handles, c1888, "W De Morgan & Co. Sand's End Pottery" (A) **5,500.00**

18⅜" h, parade of lions between spiralling foliate arabesque borders, ruby luster, c1898 (A) **6,500.00**

21¼" h, "Persian," swimming fish, cobalt, turquoise, green, yellow, manganese, and gray, bottle shape, c1888, "W. De Morgan & Co Fulham" (A) **4,300.00**

DENMARK-GENERAL

1759–Present

History: Louis Fournier, a Frenchman, made soft paste porcelain in Denmark from 1759 to 1765. These wares had a yellow tone with a dull glaze and were decorated with flowers and cupids in the French style. The principal products were tableware.

Franz Muller made the first hard past porcelain in Denmark in 1773. From 1779 until his death, Muller managed the Royal Porcelain Manufactory in Copenhagen. Furstenberg and Meissen models were copied. Anton Carl Luplau, master modeler, came from Furstenberg to work in Denmark. His strawflower pattern in underglaze blue achieved tremendous popularity.

The Flora Danica Service was begun in 1790 and not completed until 1802. This was the first independent achievement of the Copenhagen porcelain factory. More than eighteen hundred pieces were painted with botanical decorations based on the flora of Denmark.

Neo-classical decorations were used on the majority of Copenhagen porcelains. Gustav Hetsch served as managing director of the Royal Porcelain Manufactory about 1815. During the 1830s many state services were designed for the royal residences. Denmark's national sculptor Berthel Thorwaldsen made numerous sculptures and reliefs during the 1840s. Copies of his works were made in biscuit porcelain and these statuettes sold extensively. Christian Hetsch continued his father's Neo-classical style at the Royal Porcelain Manufactory, but enhanced the pieces with colorful decorations, relief, and gilt. In 1863 the Flora Danica service was reissued with less pieces for the trousseau of a Danish princess.

Financial problems occured after 1850. By 1868 the factory was Royal in name only. It was privately owned. In 1882 the firm regained some prominence when it merged with the Faience

Alumina factory which had been established in Copenhagen in 1863. Philip Schou served as manager.

Arnold Krog became artistic director in 1885. He reinstituted the original strawflower ornamentation and designed new tableware shapes. Krog's revival of underglaze blue decoration utilizing the strawflower and other patterns started a prosperous period for Copenhagen. Animal sculptures were introduced by Carl Liisberg in 1888.

The Bing and Grondahl factory was the second factory established in Copenhagen. Starting in 1852 the sculptor Hermann Bissen produced biscuit statuettes and reliefs based on the same models as the Royal Porcelain Manufactory. Harold Bing became managing director in 1885. He appointed Pietro Krohn as artistic director in 1886. Krohn's greatest design was the "Heron Service" where the heron appeared on each piece.

Museums: Royal Porcelain Factory, Copenhagen, Denmark.

Dish, 11⅝" d, white glaze, two rows of
flutes, lobed rim, Delft **66.00**
Figure
  3½" h, seated nude woman, cream-
  white glaze (A) **22.00**
  5" h, seated "Harlequin Dane" dog,
  "Dahl Jensen" **95.00**
  5½" h, boy dressed as boxer with
  gloves, #1069, "Dahl Jensen" . . .   **140.00**

Figures, 9″ h, multicolored, crowned "DJ" mark, pr, (A) $220.00.

6" h
  Boy reading book, polychrome,
  crowned "DJ" mk (A) **70.00**
  Young girl with doll, polychrome,
  crowned "DJ" mk (A) **100.00**
6½" h, child with pipe, polychrome,
  crowned "DJ" mk (A) **80.00**

9" h
  Peasant woman with children,
  crowned "DJ" mk (A) **80.00**
  Seated peasant woman, poly-
  chrome, crowned "DJ" mk (A) .   **120.00**
  Seated peasant woman, holding

Shaker, 5½″ h, rust and green trim, cream ground, Faience Mfg Co., (A) $18.00.

  pipe, polychrome, crowned
  "DJ" mk (A) **100.00**
9½" h, dancing Balinese woman,
  multicolored, crowned "DJ" mk .   **285.00**
9½" l, 4½" h, ermine, standing on
  wood log, #112/Z, "D J Copen-
  hagen, Denmark" **100.00**
10" h
  Slave girl dancer, polychrome,
  crowned "DJ" mk (A) **120.00**
  Young woman holding bouquet of
  flowers, polychrome, crowned
  "DJ" mk (A) **100.00**
11" h, Dutch girl holding puppy, po-
  lychrome, crowned "DJ" mk (A) .   **70.00**
11½" h
  Seated boy, polychrome, crowned
  "DJ" mk (A) **90.00**
  Peasant girl with geese, crowned
  "DJ" mk (A) **150.00**
12½" h
  Dutch girl waving farewell,
  crowned "DJ" mk (A) **60.00**
  Slave girl with baby, polychrome,
  crowned "DJ" mk (A) **100.00**
Pitcher, 3" h, dark blue painted flowerhead on front, molded basketweave
border, dark blue, "Faience Mfg Al-
umina" **15.00**
Teabag Holder, dark blue flowerhead in
center, molded tab handles, "Faience
Mfg Alumina," set of 6 (A) **36.00**
Vase
  4" h, cream green mottled glaze (A)   **22.00**
  11½" h, dark gray glaze, molded geometric cross shapes, "Faience Mfg
  Alumina" **170.00**
  16" h, Art Deco style birds in flowers,

blue, green, and yellow, white ground, baluster shape, "Faience Mfg Alumina" **125.00**

1782- 1825   1820-40

DERBY

Derby, England
1755–Present

History: William Duesbury I opened the Derby works at the Nottingham Road factory in 1755. Tablewares and ornamental wares were produced. Chinoiserie designs, exotic bird paintings, and blue and white patterns were the favorite design motifs. Derby had no factory mark before Duesbury purchased the Chelsea factory.

In 1769 Duesbury acquired the Chelsea factory and transfered some of the extremely skilled craftsmen from Chelsea to Derby. 1770 witnessed the production of the first biscuit or unglazed porcelain and figure groups. Originally developed at the Sevres factory about 1752, biscuit figures were to make Derby famous.

In 1784, Duesbury closed the Chelsea works, moving the remainder of the craftsmen to Derby. He died in 1786, and William Duesbury II, his son, assumed control.

Between 1786 and 1797, under the guidance of Duesbury II, the Derby factory became a major British pottery. Great advances were made in body, glaze, potting, and decoration. A tremendous variety of lavishly decorated objects were made. Added to the popular floral patterns were landscapes, maritime subjects, and hunting scenes. Duesbury's group of painters and craftsmen were among the finest in England during the eighteenth century.

In 1795 Duesbury took Kean as his partner. Duesbury died in 1797. Kean continued to produce landscape and marine subjects, but the quality of the body and the glaze deteriorated. Robert Bloor leased the factory in 1811 and then took over completely. The shapes tended to be larger, utilizing flamboyant gilded decoration as a reflection of the current tastes. The Japan or Imari patterns with their rich colorings and lavish use of gold typified the period. Imari patterns that started about 1770 are still being produced. Many figures were also modeled during the Bloor period. Bloor experienced a long illness during which the factory declined. He died in 1846. In 1848 the factory was sold.

The Nottingham Road factory closed. Several of the potters and painters began manufacturing china at King Street, trading as Sampson Hancock until the eventual merger with Royal Crown Derby in 1935. Utilitarian wares were made with an emphasis on the popular Japan and Imari designs. This small factory is the a link to the claim of continuous china production in Derby.

References: F.A. Barrett & A.L. Thorpe, *Derby Porcelain 1750–1848*, Faber & Faber, 1971; H. Gilbert Bradley, ed, *Ceramics of Derbyshire, 1750–1975*, privately published, 1978; F.B. Gilhespy, *Derby Porcelain*, Spring Books, 1961; Dennis Rice, *Derby Porcelain - The Golden Years, 1750–1770*, Hippocrene Books, 1983; John Twitchett, *Derby Porcelain*, Barrie & Jenkins, no date.

Collectors' Club: Derby Porcelain International Society, Derby City Museum & Art Gallery, The Strand, Derby, DE1 1BS, England, newsletter, society journal. International membership: 20 pounds.

Museums: see Crown & Royal Crown Derby.

Bough Pot, 7" l, multicolored landscape scenes, gilt and green trim, gold lattice tops, pr, $1,150.00.

Basket
  9⅛" l, painted center butterflies, insects, and grapes, yellow and blue florettes at intersections, rope twist dbl handles, reticulated, c1760 (A) **825.00**
  9¾" l, 3", Imari design and palette, cobalt dragon on base, cavetto molded reticulated sides, twig handles, pr (A) **750.00**
Bowl
  9" d, five raised area designs around rim, hp floral, raised gold **50.00**
  11½" d, painted flowers in outlined ovals, gilt scrolls and foliage, blue ground, c1820 .... **350.00**
Bust, 11" h, Voltaire, polychrome, gilt trim, circ base, garland dec, porcelain, late 18th C **275.00**

Butter Tub, 4⅞" l, painted exotic birds on sides, moths and insects on ends, brown outlined rim, strawberry and leaf knob, octagonal, c1760 ...... **3,100.00**

Candlesticks, 11" h, multicolored, c1794–1824, pr, $750.00.

Candlestick
 6½" h, roses, morning glories, and asters, diapered gilt ground, 19th C, pr (A) **375.00**
 8¾" h, applied cockerels on base of one, hen and chicks on other, bocage background supporting nozzles, scroll molded bases, c1775, pr (A) **1,045.00**
 9½" h, Venus in robe, Cupid at side, Mars in helmet and cape holding war trophies, multicolored, each before tree trunk supporting nozzles, scroll molded bases, c1760, pr **600.00**
 9⅞" h, Mars, shield and banner on one, Venus with Cupid on other, scroll and foliage molded bases, tree stumps holding candle nozzles and wax pans, multicolored, c1758, pr, repaired (A) **600.00**
 10½" h, modeled girl, flowers in apron, bocage background supporting two branches with nozzles, pierced scroll molded base, c1765 (A) **350.00**
 11" h, molded cherubs hold candle holder, wrapped in flowers, gilt trim, c1765, pr **1,700.00**
Caudle Cup and Saucer, wide applegreen shaped borders, painted insects with fruit clusters, c1776, blue crowned "D" mark (A) **550.00**
Child's Cup and Saucer, "Japan" pattern, borders of diamond devices and

floral panels, green, gilt, blue, and iron-red, quatrefoil shape (A) **85.00**
Creamer and Sugar, painted sweet peas, tiger lilies, and flowers, multicolored, border of gilt stylized foliage, mask handles and rings on bowl, c1780 (A) **530.00**
Cup and Saucer
 Basket and scrolling motifs, polychrome (A) **40.00**
 Cup painted with "Near Breadsall Derbyshire" and saucer with "Near Derbyshire," salmon ground, gilt teardrop pattern ground, c1795–1805, iron-red crown, X'd batons and "D" marks (A) **170.00**
 Cup with "Matlock High Tor, Dobyshire," saucer with "Near Derby," multicolored reserves, royal blue ground, gilt foliage scrolls (A) **125.00**
 Green floral vines, intersecting rose lines and gilt, fluted, c1780 (A) .. **244.00**
 Imari palette of birds and flowering trees, c1790 (A) **145.00**
 "Japan" pattern, c1800 .... **75.00**
 Painted figures in landscapes between bands of pearls, dbl seahorse handles, four paw feet, c1810, iron-red crowned X'd batons mark, pr (A) . **220.00**
 Stylized motifs, polychrome and gilt (A) **50.00**
Dessert Dish
 9⅞" l, "King's" pattern, iron-red, gilt, and blue peony and florals, shell shape, c1825, iron-red crowned X'd batons and "D" marks, pr (A) **200.00**
 10¾" l, "King's" pattern, iron-red, gilt, and blue peony and florals, lozenge shape, c1825, iron-red crowned X'd batons and "D" marks, pr (A) **200.00**
Dessert Service, scattered flower sprays, multicolored, shaped gadroon borders, c1810, iron-red crowned X'd batons and "D" marks, set of 35 pcs (A) **1,540.00**
Dish
 8½" d, painted named views of "In Italy" and "In Wales," gilt stylized scrolling foliage borders, c1810, iron-red crown, X'd batons and "D" marks, Bloor-Derby, pr (A) .. **315.00**
 9⅛" d, "King's" pattern, iron-red, gilt, and blue peony and florals, scalloped edge, c1825, iron-red crowned X'd batons and "D" marks (A) **100.00**
 9¾" l, painted with different flowers on each dish, gilt edges, botanical inscription on verse, kidney shape, c1813–15, iron-red crowned X'd batons and "D" marks, set of 4 (A) **8,000.00**

9⅞" l, gold and blue foliate center medallion, vine and tendril border, shell shape, iron-red crowned X'd batons and "D" marks **165.00**

10" l, center florals, three sprigs, gilt sprigged blue borders, kidney shape, c1780, blue crowned "D" marks, pr (A) **300.00**

10" w, painted floral bouquet, gilt line rim, kidney shape, c1790 .... **240.00**

11⅞" d, Imari style, cell and whorl borders, gilt accents, oval, c1800, carmine crown, X'd batons and "D" marks (A) **200.00**

13¾" w, rose sprays, borders of stylized blue flowerheads, iron-red oeil-de-perdrix, three ovals with rose sprays, gilt shaped rim, c1840, pr (A) **530.00**

20" l, "King's" pattern, iron-red, gilt, and blue peony and florals, c1820, iron-red crowned X'd batons and "D" marks (A) **1,000.00**

Eel Basket, 8½ and 9½", vertical ribbing, pierced necks and shoulders, molded foliage dbl handles, bases modeled with two ducks and foliage, multicolored, gold anchors mark, set of 3 (A) **1,555.00**

Figure
2½" h

Pug dog, seated, black coat, gilt collar, mounted on scrolled green, turquoise, and gilt oval base, incised worker's mark ... **700.00**

Whippet dog, tan coat, brown and green oval base with tree stump and gilt line, hairline, c1820 ... **600.00**

3"½" h, red squirrel, seated, chewing nut, gilt collar, circ green mound base, c1825, Bloor-Derby (A) **585.00**

4" l, leopard, seated, salmon coat, purple spots, applied florals on mound base, c1760 (A) **660.00**

4⅜" h

Putto, standing before tree stump, holding flower garland, applied florals on pad base, c1760 (A) . **180.00**

Youth and companion, seated, straw and flowers in hair, multicolored, scroll molded bases, pr, repaired (A) **778.00**

4¾" h

Boy with hat filled with fruit, girl with basket of flowers, multicolored, seated on scroll molded rockwork bases, c1830, blue X'd sword marks, pr (A) **330.00**

Man with flute, woman with hurdy-gurdy, flowering clothes, circ scroll molded bases, c1775, pr (A) **260.00**

5⅜" h, seated ewe and ram, bocage backgrounds, c1780, pr (A) **200.00**

5½" h

Boy seated on upturned basket, flowered breeches and waistcoat, oval base, c1785 (A) **275.00**

Boy with spaniel, girl holding lamb, multicolored, circ bases, c1785, pr (A) **550.00**

Welsh tailor, seated on goat, basket carrying kittens, wife in same pose carrying two babies, multicolored, oval scroll molded bases with grass, c1835, Bloor-Derby marks, pr (A) **530.00**

5½" and 6⅛" l, boars, painted, black streaked brown ground, applied florals on oval mound base, c1775–60, pr (A) ...**1,100.00**

6" l, Cupid, reclining on rocky base, white bisque, 18th C **100.00**

6" to 6⅜" h, seated putti representing Four Seasons, multicolored, scroll molded bases, c1775, set of 4 (A) **525.00**

6⅝" h, shepherd and shepherdess, 18th C clothes, girl with apron full of flowers, boy with lamb under arm and coins, Bloor-Derby, pr (A) **100.00**

7" h

Dancing gallant and companion, white period clothes, edged in gilt, green tree stump on oval scrolled base, c1775 (A) **715.00**

Conductor, 12 figure monkey band, each playing instrument, multicolored, seated on sq base, c1830, Bloor-Derby marks (A) .**6,050.00**

7⅛" and 6½" h, Mansion House dwarfs, Stevenson and Hancock, advertising on hats, green circ mound bases, c1861–75, pr (A) ..**1,760.00**

7½" h, young girl, multicolored apron and skirt, carrying satchel, pierced scroll molded base, c1835, blue X'd swords mark **225.00**

7⅝" h, "Renaldo and Armida" and "Cephalus and Procris," multicolored, grass mound bases with tree and applied flowers, c1775–80, pr (A) **440.00**

8" h

Shepherd with fruit basket and dog, shepherdess with lamb, multicolored, scroll molded tree trunk bases, c1780, pr, repaired (A) .. **285.00**

Stags, recumbent position, oblong bases, brown and beige, c1790, repaired, pr (A) **660.00**

8¼" h, set of four continents of Africa, Asia, Europe, and America, multicolored, mounted on pierced scroll molded bases, names of continents, c1785, set of 4, repairs, (A) **2,000.00**

8⅝" h

"Europe" holding orb, "America" as Indian in headdress standing on crocodile, c1770, pr (A) **335.00**

"Liberty" with bird's nest and "Matrimony" with bird cage, flowered clothes, tree stumps on scroll molded circ bases, c1760, pr (A) **365.00**

Sportsman with gun, lady with dead bird, hounds at sides, pink and green, scroll molded bases, c1765, pr (A) **972.00**

9¼" h, St. Thomas, dressed in Roman clothes, circ molded base, c1760 (A) **300.00**

9⅝" h, shepherd with sheep, shepherdess with basket and apron of flowers, multicolored, tree stumps on scroll molded bases, c1820, Bloor-Derby (A) **625.00**

9¾" h, Juno, seated on chariot, wearing cloak, holding flower and ball, multicolored, peacock on back of chariot, c1765 (A) **715.00**

9⅞" h

Gallant with barrel and glass, companion with flask and apron of fruit and flowers, flowered clothes, tree stump pierced scroll molded bases with dog and sheep at feet, c1765, pr (A) **570.00**

Shepherd holding spirit barrel under arm with dog at side, shepherdess with flask and lamb at side, multicolored, scroll molded circ bases, applied tree stumps and flowers, c1770, pr, chips (A) **418.00**

10" h

"Music," biscuit group, c1790, unmarked **325.00**

Shakespeare leaning on column with stack of books, Milton holding scroll leaning on column, multicolored, c1800, iron-red crown, X'd batons and "D" marks, incised "309 and 207," pr **600.00**

11" h, Britannia, holding shield, multicolored, flag, globe, lion, and cannon on oval base, c1760–65 (A) **715.00**

11⅛" h, "Ranelagh," modeled dancers, period dress, mounted on scroll molded bases, c1760–65, pr (A) **935.00**

14⅜" h, James Quinn, dressed as Falstaff, shield and sword (missing), multicolored, tree stump scroll molded base, c1760 . . . . **180.00**

Inkwell, 6¼" l, "Japan" pattern, green, gilt, blue, and iron-red floral panels in border of diamond devices, crown and Bloor-Derby mark, cov and well missing (A) **40.00**

Mug

3½" h, "IS" monogram in floral cartouche, loop handle, gilding, c1780 (A) **168.00**

5⅛" h, gilt leaf border on rim, iron-red crowned X'd batons and "D" mark (A) **150.00**

Pastille Burner, 4⅛" d, cottage shape, sq white house, brickwork and applied vines, ochre thatched roof, green mound base, applied florals, c1825 (A) **330.00**

Pitcher, 8" h, molded leaf pattern, floral medallion and inscribed panel (A) . . **45.00**

Plaque, 11½" l, painted clusters of fruit, porcelain, c1830, pr (A) **1,980.00**

Plate

8" d

Central device and four scalloped floral panels, blue scale ground rim (A) **155.00**

Oriental motif, hand decorated, gold rim, c1825 . . . . **125.00**

8¼" d, exotic birds, shaped gadroon molded borders, stylized flowerheads, gilt line rim, c1770, pr (A) **500.00**

8⅝" d

Center painted "Moss Rose," lobed gilt line and berried foliage rim, c1790, blue crown, X'd batons and "D" mark (A) **1,000.00**

Named landscapes of "On the River Wye" and "Near Bakewell," circ gilt foliage cartouches, green bands edged in gilt, c1815, iron-red crown, X'd batons and "D" marks, Bloor-Derby, pr (A) **365.00**

Painted named views of "Stonebyers Seat of Daniel Verge Esqr" and "Bothwell Castle," gilt foliage borders with birds and beasts, c1815, iron-red crown, X'd batons and "D" marks, pr (A) **544.00**

8⅞" d, Imari pattern, two birds in flowering tree, c1820, iron-red crown, X'd batons and "D" mark, Bloor-Derby (A) **50.00**

9" d

Imari design, Oriental flowering plants, multicolored, shaped gilt rim, c1840, set of 12 (A) **880.00**

"Larkspur" pattern, blue, c1820 . . **50.00**

Modified "Cigar" pattern, three blue and gold panels, crown and X "D" mark **220.00**

Oriental design, hp, blue and rust, gilt edge and trim, c1825 . . . . . **125.00**

9⅛" d, dessert. "King's" pattern, iron-red, gilt, and blue peony and Oriental florals, c1825, iron-red crowned X'd batons and "D" marks, set of 15 (A) **715.00**

9¼" d

Painted named view "In Italy," gilt scrolling foliage and swans border, c1815, iron-red crown, X'd batons and "D" mark, Bloor-Derby **250.00**

Plate, 5½" d, blue and orange Oriental florals, gilt trim, c1770–82, $50.00.

Painted named views of "Near Bulls Crofs Enfield" and "Near Palmers Green Edmonton," gilt scrolling and foliage cartouches, lime-green borders, gilt edges, c1800, blue crown, X'd batons and "D" marks, pr **360.00**

Painted named "View in Lancashire," gilt scrolling foliage border, c1805, black crown, X'd batons and "D" marks **250.00**

9½" d, "Amaranthus" in center, multicolored, gilt edged yellow band border, brown crowned X'd batons and "D" mark **100.00**

9⅞" d, painted "Vue d'une Partie du Palais J. R. a Vien," octagonal cartouche, burnished gilt scrolls and foliage border, c1810, black crown, X'd batons and "D" mark (A) **500.00**

10" d, Imari pattern and palette, scroll and gold tracery, c1825 .... **190.00**

10⅛" d, "King's" pattern, iron-red, gilt, and blue peony and Oriental florals, foliate scroll handles, iron-red crowned X'd batons and "D" marks, set of 18 (A) **440.00**

10¼" d, painted garden flowers, blue borders, gilt scrolls and foliage, shaped rims, c1820, set of 18 (A) **935.00**

Platter, 13½" l, painted "Angouleme Sprig" pattern, gilt rim, c1820, iron-red crowned X'd batons and "D" marks **65.00**

Sauceboat, 7⅛" l, blue and white florals and bamboo scroll, cell diaper border, int. pavilion scene, fluted, c1770 **180.00**

Sauce Tureen, matching stand

6¾" l, "King's" pattern, iron-red, gilt, and blue peony and Oriental florals, diku c1825, iron-red crowned X'd batons and "D" marks, pr (A) **825.00**

7¼" l, "Japan" pattern, exotic birds on branches and florals, blue, gilt, and iron-red, gilt foliate scroll knobs, quatrefoil shape, c1815, iron-red crowned X'd batons and "D" marks, pr (A) **500.00**

Painted bunches of fruit between gilt line rims, dbl handles, cov, c1815, iron-red crowned X'd batons and "D" marks, Bloor-Derby (A) **450.00**

Soup Plate, 10⅛" d, "King's" pattern, iron-red, gilt, and blue peony and Oriental florals, c1825, iron-red crowned X'd batons and "D" marks, set of 14 (A) **440.00**

Soup Tureen, 14½" H-H, cornflower sprig design, blue, green, and gilt, white ground, gilt modeled lion heads on sides, c1810 ....**1,250.00**

Sugar, cov, 6" d, cobalt, gold, and cream Imari pattern, Bloor-Derby (A) **100.00**

Sweetmeat Dish, 6¼" h, six tiered shells on central rockwork, kingfisher on top, shells painted with insects, c1770, repairs (A) **1,870.00**

Tazza, 9" d, painted rose sprays, iron-red borders, blue oeil-de-perdrix, c1820, iron-red crowned X'd batons and "D" marks, pr **325.00**

Tea and Coffee Service, spoon tray, cov sugar, saucer dish, three coffee cups, four teabowls, five saucers, fluted, radiating blue and gold chain and dot pattern, c1780 (A) **250.00**

Tea Service

Teapot, milk jug, cov sugar, waste bowl, seven cups and saucers, "King's" pattern, iron-red, gilt, and blue peony and Oriental florals, c1825, iron-red crowned X'd batons and "D" marks (A) **660.00**

Teapot, stand, cov sugar, waste bowl, creamer, twelve tea cups, nine demitasse cups, eleven saucers, two cake plates, aubergine palmetted band highlighted in gilt, white ground (A) **550.00**

Teabowl and Saucer, spirally molded, blue and gilt radiating foliage, c1785,

puce crown X'd batons and "D"
marks, pr (A) **66.00**
Tureen, cov
   9½" d, modeled as pigeons seated on
     nests, applied feathers and grass on
     nests, multicolored, pr (A) **660.00**
   "King's" pattern, iron-red, blue, and
     gilt, four gilt lion's mask and paw
     feet, gilt lion's mask terminals for
     handles and finial, c1820, iron-red
     crowned X'd batons and "D" marks
     (A) **990.00**
Urn, 9" h, landscape scenes, dark blue
   body, gilt flowers, base, set on four
   feet, harp shaped handles, c1810,
   pr **1,500.00**
Vase
   5¾" h, painted birds, flower spray on
     reverse, applied floral wreaths on
     neck, c1758 (A) **180.00**
   24" h, painted floral body, diamond
     design at base, loop dbl handles,
     gilt trim, c1820–40, Bloor-Derby **.3,000.00**
Vegetable Dish, "Lilly" pattern, blue
   floral ground, gilt accents, pr (A) ... **90.00**

DERUTA

Near Perugia, Italy
Late 15th Century–Present

History: A large pottery industry was established
at Deruta near Perugia, Italy. Metallic luster decorations in a golden mother-of-pearl iridescence
and ruby colors were used on the polychrome
wares utilizing special firing techniques. Deruta
also was known for the excellence of its border
patterns usually encircling a central motif of a
bust or heraldic arms.

   At first, yellow colored pieces outlined in blue
were prominent at Deruta. Later wares included
olive green shades. Large dishes were made,
some with raised decorations.

   Today Deruta produces souvenir wares for
tourists.

Museums: Gardiner Museum of Ceramic Art, Toronto, Canada; Victoria & Albert Museum, London, England; Wallace Collection, London, England.

Bowl, 10¼" d, majolica, convex center
   painted with portrait of saint, blue,
   manganese, green, yellow, and light

**Dish, 16¼" d, majolica, cobalt, ochre,
green, and yellow, pierced for hanging,
c1550, $2,500.00.**

   blue, molded border, grotesques,
     early 17th C **500.00**
Charger, majolica
   12½" d
     Center bust of Dante, red and green
       flowered border, Holy mark ... **150.00**
     Large dragons and scroll design,
       red, blue, green, and yellow, pr **50.00**
   16¼" d, bust of woman, border of
     entwined strapwork and flower-
     heads, copper luster and cobalt,
     early 16th C **7,500.00**
Condiment Dish, 8¼" d, majolica, center painted with female saint, border
   with grotesques, three reservoirs,
   early 17th C **135.00**
Dish
   7⅞" d, gold luster and blue radiating
     peacock feather design, late 16th C **900.00**
   8⅜" d, letter "E" in center square,
     starburst border alternating with
     stylized florals, yellow and blue
     glaze, blue and white outer bands,
     early 16th C (A) **2,860.00**
   9¼" d, recessed center painted with
     concentric medallion and radiating
     flowers, blue, gold, and ruby luster,
     c1520, repaired (A) **455.00**
   14½" d, center with coat of arms, tur-
     quoise, ochre, and blue, spiral blue
     and ochre leaves on border, ochre
     and blue bands in well, c1500
     (A) **9,720.00**
   15" l, painted center of Cupid holding
     two garlands in landscape, four ra-
     diating panels of grotesque motifs,
     gilt metal frame, 17th C (A) **760.00**
   15¼" d, majolica, gold luster and co-
     balt radiating panels of leaf and
     scrollwork, mid 16th C **4,000.00**
Drug Jar, 8¼" h
   Green spout and armorial handle,
   ochre and blue oak leaves, contents

in Latin in ribbon, c1530, repaired
(A) **285.00**
Painted child saint wearing hair shirt
and saint dressed as monk with
crook flanking inscribed label, entwined foliage ground, dated 1640
under strap handle **675.00**
Figure, 5½" h, bust of young bearded
man, cobalt, ochre, and light green
accents, dated 1551 (A) **600.00**
Jar, 8½" h, majolica, polychrome oval
inscribed wreath under winged putto,
18th C, pr, damaged (A) **310.00**
Plaque
    12¼" w, 13" h, polychrome scene of
    Jesus in the stable at Bethlehem,
    angel with inscribed scroll, raised
    rim, overlapping petals, late 16th C
    (A) **1,200.00**
    12⅕" w, 19" h, majolica, Madonna
    and Child in arch of pillars and
    cherubs, cobalt, ochre, yellow, and
    green, inscription on base, mid
    16th C (A) **2,375.00**
Plate, 7¾" d, majolica, center bust of
Italian nobleman, borders of dragons,
gargoyles, and scrolling devices,
brown, blue, red, and green, black
"Deruta, Italy" marks, set of 6 ..... **75.00**

DOULTON AND ROYAL DOULTON

DOULTON OF LAMBETH

Lambeth, near London
1815–1956

History: In Lambeth, near London, John Doulton
founded the Doulton Lambeth Pottery in 1815.
Utilitarian salt glazed stonewares were the mainstay. When John Watts joined the firm, it became
known as Doulton and Watts (1820–1853).
Stoneware barrels, bottles, spirit flasks, and jugs
were produced in vast quantities.

Henry Doulton, John's second son, joined the
firm in 1835. His inventiveness led to the application of steam to drive the potter's wheel, plac-
ing Lambeth Pottery ten years ahead of the other
potteries. Architectural terra-cotta and garden ornaments were added to the catalog. Production
of stoneware drainpipes, conduits, and other
sanitary wares also began.

The Lambeth School of Art, under John
Sparkes' direction, became associated with the
Doulton wares. Through Sparkes, George Tins-
worth began working with Doulton in 1866.
Hannah and Arthur Barlow, students at the
school, joined Doulton in 1871. They made pots

with incised decorations worked directly into un-
coated clay. During the next twenty years, the
number of artists and designers grew; 250 artists
were at work by 1885. The monogram, initials,
or signature of the artist appeared on the piece;
often the assistants' initials appeared too. In 1887
Queen Victoria knighted Henry Doulton for his
achievements in the advancement of ceramic art.

Sir Henry died in 1897; Henry Louis Doulton
succeeded his father. In 1899 the family company became Doulton & Co., Ltd. During the
20th century, reductions took place in the production of artist signed pieces from Doulton Lambeth. By 1925 only 24 artists were employed.
Leslie Harradine did excellent stoneware figures
of Dickens' characters. He also modeled spirit
flasks of comtemporary politicians.

During the 1920s and 1930s, collectors' pieces
in simple shapes, subtle colors, and uncluttered
decorations were made. A large range of commemorative wares also were produced. Agnete
Hoy, working at Lambeth from 1951–1956,
achieved fame for her cat figures. She used salt
glaze techniques and developed a new transparent glaze. In 1956 production ceased at the
Doulton Lambeth pottery.

DOULTON OF BURSLEM

Staffordshire, England
1877–Present

History: In 1877 Henry Doulton acquired the
Nile Street pottery located in Burslem, Staffordshire, from Pinder, Bourne & Co. The name was
changed to Doulton & Co. in 1882. Beginning
in 1884 porcelains of the highest quality were
manufactured. Simple, inexpensive earthenware
tablewares also were made. A large group of
artists under the direction of John Slater assembled at the Burslem factory.

Doulton's china was exhibited at the Chicago
Columbian Exposition in 1893. Charles Noke,
who joined the company in 1889 and became
one of the most important workers at Burslem,
exhibited his vases. Many Noke figures portrayed
contemporary people as historical personages.
His early achievements included Holbein, Rembrandt, and Barbotine wares plus a popular range
of flasks, jugs, and other shapes in subdued
colors. Rouge Flambe was perhaps the most important ware introduced by Noke. He became
art director in 1914.

At the Burslem factory, a tremendous amount
of tablewares were produced. In addition to the
earthenwares, fine bone china ornamented in
gold and frequently exhibiting elaborate designs
also was manufactured. In 1901 King Edward VII
granted the Royal Warrant of appointment to
Doulton. From that point on they used the word
"ROYAL" to describe their products.

Royal Doulton Figures

Nearly all Royal Doulton figures are made at the Burslem factory. Three basic ingredients, china clay, Cornish stone, and calcined bone ash, are blended together with water to make a fine body able to withstand the high temperature firings needed to produce a superfine, yet strong translucent ceramic body. Figurine subjects include child studies, street sellers, and historical, literary, or legendary characters in large and miniatures sizes.

In 1913 Royal Doulton began marking each new figurine design with an "HN" number. Harry Nixon was the artist in charge of painting the figures. The "HN" numbers refer to him. "HN" numbers were chronological until 1949 after which blocks of numbers were assigned to each modeler. Over two thousand different figures have been produced. New designs are added each year. Older designs are discontinued. Currently there are approximately two hundred designs in production.

Character and Toby Jugs

Character jugs depict the head and shoulders; Toby Jugs feature the entire figure either standing or seated. Noke revived the old Staffordshire Toby tradition in the 20th century by modeling characters based on songs, literature, legends, and history. The first jugs were produced by Noke in 1934. Large jugs measure 5¼" to 7½", small jugs 3¼" to 4", miniatures 2¼" to 2½", and tinies 1¼" tall or less. The shape and design of the jug handle aids in establishing the age of a jug. For a brief period all seated Tobies were discontinued. Production of the seated Tobies began again in 1973.

Series Ware

Series Ware, created by Charles Noke, used a large number of standard blank shapes decorated with a selection of popular characters, events, and illustrators. A series ranged from two to three to as high as twenty scenes.

A variety of printing techniques were used on Series Ware. Transfer printing from engraved plates and lithography supplemented with hand coloring was one technique. The block printing and silk screening techniques produced denser, more colorful images. A photographic process captured famous views and characters.

Series Ware production was interrupted by WWII. However, a revival of decorative plate production led to the Collectors International plates during the 1970s, featuring plates for special holidays such as Valentine's Day and Christmas and designs by international artists.

Today, Doulton and Company is the largest manufacturer of ceramic products in the UK. Minton, Royal Crown Derby, Ridgeway, Royal Albert, Royal Adderley, Colclough, Paragon, John Beswick, and Webb Corbett are all part of the company.

References: Richard Dennis, *Doulton Character Jugs*, Malvern Press, 1976; Desmond Eyles & Richard Dennis, *Royal Doulton Figures Produced at Burslem*, Royal Doulton Tableware Ltd., 1978; Desmond Eyles, *The Doulton Burslem Wares*, Royal Doulton & Barrie Jenkins, 1980; Desmond Eyles, *The Doulton Lambeth Wares*, Hutchinson, 1975; Louise Irvine, *Royal Doulton Series Ware*, Vol. 1 & 2, Richard Dennis, 1980, 1984; Ralph & Terry Kovel, *The Kovels' Illustrated Price Guide to Royal Doulton*, Crown, 1980; Katherine Morrison McClinton, *Royal Doulton Figurines & Character Jugs*, Wallace-Homestead, 1978.

Gallery: Sir Henry Doulton Gallery, Doulton Fine China Nile Street Pottery, Burslem, England.

Collectors' Club: Royal Doulton International Collectors Club, P.O. Box 1815, Somerset, NJ 08873. Annual membership: $15 per year. London address: 5 Egmont House, 116 Shaftesbury Avenue, London W1V 7DJ, England.

1882 - 1902   1882 - 1902

BURSLEM

Biscuit Jar, hp, multicolored florals, overlaid gold leaves, cobalt ground, SP lid, "Doulton-Burslem" **200.00**
Box, cov, 3¼" sq, hp, flowers and beetles, matte finish, c1888 .... **135.00**
Chocolate Pot, 8¼" h, floral panel dec, pastel colors, peaked spout, loop handle, "Doulton-Burslem" **225.00**
Coffeepot, 6⅞" h, blue windmills, white ground **55.00**
Dessert Service, two heart shape dishes, two ftd sq dishes, two ftd oval dishes, eighteen 9" d plates, painted animals and insects teasing each other, shaped bronze and gilt rims, c1890 (A) **1,235.00**
Jug, 6½" h, painted pansies, cream ground, pink and gilt neck, sgd "S. Hall" (A) **120.00**
Pitcher
    6¼" h, mottled colors, bulbous, loop handle, narrow top, "Emily Perdington" **145.00**
    8" h, "May" pattern, blue and white **110.00**

Plate

7¾″ d, hp, center raised water lilies, fluted border of dark florals, gold trim, cloverleaf shape, c1872 .... **95.00**

9″ d, hp, fish design, scalloped edge, sgd "Joseph Hancock, Doulton-Burslem" **60.00**

Teapot, multicolored florals, beige ground, gilt trim, "Doulton-Burslem, England" **85.00**

Tray, 12½″ l, painted center, yellow and white roses, lattice pierced and foliate molded ivory rim, c1895 (A) **250.00**

Vase

4⅛″ h, white flowers and green leaves, gold scrolls and foot, beige satin ground, brown "Doulton-Burslem" mark **100.00**

6″ h, large blue flower on top, gold accents, gold and cobalt designs on lower section, gold and cobalt handle, "Doulton-Burslem" **125.00**

7½″ h, 7″ l, "Paisley" pattern int. and ext. rim, stylized florals, reserves on cobalt and gold on body, spitoon shape **150.00**

10″ h, painted dog in landscape, gilt oval surround, burgundy ground, c1895 (A) **135.00**

11″ h, yellow lilies, pink, rose, and brown band at top, cream ground, gold banding, #A3596 .... **150.00**

11¼″ h

Allegorical musicians and couple in landscape, beige and light green, acanthus leaves and swags in neck bands, "Luscian Ware" (A) **750.00**

Bust of Countess Grosvenor, painted panel on royal blue ground, gilt borders and flowers, mask handles on shoulders, sgd "S. N. Sutton," c1900 (A) **250.00**

LAMBETH

1880-1902

Biscuit Jar, 7″ h, Slater, flowers and leaves, snakeskin ground **150.00**

Bowl

4″ d, donkey frieze, silver rim, "Hannah Barlow" **140.00**

8⅞″ d, 4¼″ h, incised grazing cows and horses, blue and brown geometric borders, silver top band, dated 1885, sgd "Hannah Barlow" **650.00**

Box, cov, 5″ sq, Silicon Ware, flowing beige design, blue leaf border **125.00**

Dish, 15¼″ d, portrait of Venetian Doge, wearing blue skullcap and mauve coat, dated 1881 (A) **300.00**

Ewer

14½″ h, Canara Ware, clematis, gilt outline (A) **40.00**

18¾″ h, faience, painted daffodils and daisies, shaded yellow-green ground, #155 (A) **120.00**

Figure

3⅛″ h, stoneware, modeled as wicker bag, plane, saw, and tools, oval base (A) **155.00**

6⅞″ h, stoneware, modeled as monkey on tortoise, coach on back with three monkeys, orange glaze, blue base and coach roof, "Doulton-Lambeth" (A) **840.00**

Jam Jar, 4″ h, raised design of men and oxen plowing, tan ground, metal handle and cov, sgd "Hannah Barlow" . **665.00**

Jar, 6¾″ d, 7¼″ h, beaded design, imp "Lambeth-Doulton" (A) **80.00**

Jar, cov, 3¾″ h, Silicon Ware, white and blue smear design, sgd "A. Horton" **85.00**

Jug

3½″ h, brown and tan, applied scene of cherubs with musical instruments, "Doulton-Lambeth" **65.00**

5½″ h, tan body, olive trim, dbl emb Queen Victoria busts, c1897 ..... **200.00**

5¾″ h, raised hunt scene, tavern scenes at middle **100.00**

6″ h, red and gold figures, black ground, silver rim, three handles . **200.00**

6¼″ h, stoneware, applied portrait, classical medallions, inscribed (A) **40.00**

6½″ h, emb pink flowers, blue-gray leaves, blue ground, brown handle and rim **90.00**

7¼″ h, stoneware, medium brown, dark brown bands and mottos, raised cameo heads, applied handle, "Doulton-Lambeth" **175.00**

8½″ h, 6¼″ d, stoneware, leather like dark brown surface, emb motto "Fill What You Will and Drink What You Fill," SP trim top **150.00**

8¾″ h, incised lioness in foliage, cobalt accents, scroll handle, silver cov, c1875, "Hannah Barlow, Doulton-Burslem" (A) **385.00**

10½″ h, cov, stylized flowers and foliate panels, brown, green, and blue accents, buff ground, white florals, pewter cov, c1883, "Margaret Aitken" (A) **100.00**

16¼″ h, incised bands, raised gray and green geese, stippled buff ground, tapered, "Florance Barlow" (A) **650.00**

Left, vase, 5¾" h, blue flowers, raised yellow centers, enamel jewels, dark brown ground, "Doulton-Lambeth," $90.00; center, jug, 9" h, dark brown upper section, tan base, SP cov, "Doulton-Lambeth," $300.00; right, vase, 9" h, blue and brown incised design, "Hannah and Lucy Barlow," c1883, pr, $1,000.00.

"Highland Whiskey," Viking ship scene, "Doulton-Lambeth" **75.00**
Raised Dutch figures, demi size **45.00**
Lamp, oil, 19½" h, stoneware, incised stylized foliage and roundels, white beading, blue, green, and amber glaze, wrought iron support, dated 1883 (A) **250.00**
Loving Cup
  6" h, applied hunt and tavern scenes, two shades of tan, SP rim, "Lambeth-Doulton, England" (A) **75.00**
  6¼" h, stoneware, incised design of three cats stalking birds, three handles, dated 1876, "Hannah Barlow" (A) **315.00**
Match Holder, 4" d, stylized hearts, light blue and brown **70.00**
Pepper Pot, 5¼" h, stoneware, blue leaves, gray body, greenish bands, SP top, sgd "E. S." **70.00**
Pitcher
  5½" h, dark brown top, tan bottom, figural Neptune spout, c1870 .... **50.00**
  6½" h, overall fish scale pattern (A) . **130.00**
  7" h, simulated copper finish with riv-

Pitcher and Bowl, 6½" h pitcher, 17" l, 14" w bowl, steel blue transfer, ivory ground, gold edge, c1891, $310.00.

ets, bands, seams, and dents, SS rim, Silicon Patent, c1891–1912, "Doulton-Lambeth, England" **225.00**
  7½" h, light and dark brown, four framed with white lace gray-blue portraits of child, woman, veiled woman, and old man, white sayings and florals **125.00**
  7⅞" h, emb cream flowers, gold and aqua trim, dark green tapestry finish, SP top band, tan handle with aqua, "Lambeth & Doulton and Slater's Patent" **165.00**
  8½" h, overall open flowers, small flowers in lower panel, thin form, sq handle, "Doulton-Lambeth" .. **300.00**
  8⅝" h, tan, applied white foliage, gray and dark green motto "Good Measure...," "Lambeth-Doulton" (A) **65.00**
  9" h, cobalt top, dark brown ribbed bottom **75.00**
  9¼" h
    Black and tan goats in three oval panels, cobalt bands, tankard shape, c1880, "Hannah Barlow" **575.00**
    Stoneware, white cows grazing, tan ground, brown, and green glossy border, sgd "Hannah Barlow" . **750.00**
  11" h, relief of birds and blossoming trees, finely emb ground, "Hannah Barlow" (A) **120.00**
  11½" h, bulbous, floral design, textured black, gold, and cream, mottled straight gold neck, gold dragon handle, c1885, "Doulton & Slater" **385.00**
Plaque, 8" sq, terra cotta, "The Wheelwright Shop," modeled as boy carrying wood in shop, woman looking in window, child at door, "H. Doulton & Co" (A) **1,680.00**
Rum Keg, 12" h, rust and blue bands, multicolored florals and geometrics,

mounted on mahogany tripod base, c1880, "Doulton-Lambeth" **520.00**
Salt, 2" w, master, geometric and applied flower design, blue ground ... **55.00**
Spill Vase, 5¼" h, modeled as three mice playing instruments, mouse looking out window of house, oval blue and brown shaped base, titled "The Waits," George Tinsworth **2,250.00**
Sundial, 44⅞" h, stoneware, relief of bushes and stems, Zodiac signs form dial, inscribed, circ column support, imp "Doulton" (A) **475.00**
Teapot
  5¼" h, stoneware, tapestry, aqua and white flowers, beige and brown ground, gold trim, wide looping handle, "Doulton & Slater's Patent" **175.00**
  7½" h, 5" w, raised bird design, matte green and brown, "Florance Barlow" **800.00**
Tobacco Jar
  5½" h, geometric design, soft colors, putty ground, "Lambeth Doulton" (A) **20.00**
  6" h, incised black cows and geese, putty ground, blue and green edging, SP rim and handle, "Lambeth-Doulton" (A) **35.00**
Vase
  3⅜" h, 4" d, beige, blue, and green scrollwork, dated 1886, sgd "M. G. T." **135.00**
  3½" h, 4" d, stoneware, green and blue geometrics, beige ground, three small feet, c1886, sgd "MGT, Doulton-Lambeth" **125.00**
  3¾" h, faience, painted chrysanthemums, shaded blue ground, #696 (A) **55.00**
  4" h, flaring top, applied bands of classical dec (A) **35.00**
  6¾" h, stoneware, panels of imp leaves and applied beading and florets, satyr's face on neck, blue, green, and amber glaze, dated 1875 (A) **55.00**
  8" h, incised design
    Butterflies and fan, Silicon Ware . **250.00**
    Cat, swirl and scroll border, blue int., c1885, sgd "Hannah Barlow" **825.00**
    Stylized blue leaves and geometrics, brown stoneware, dbl gourd shape, c1884 .... **350.00**
  8⅞" h, faience, white anemones, shaded brown and yellow ground, onion shape, #724 (A) **100.00**
  9½" h, incised blue and rust deer, "Hannah Barlow, Doulton-Lambeth" **700.00**

10" h
  Brown top and bottom bands, small flowers, emb leaves, blue-gray ground, c1885, sgd "Florance Roberts" **175.00**
  Stoneware, applied stylized amber clematis blossoms and green branches on stippled ground, beaded borders, panels of pate-sur-pate blossoms, dark brown ground (A) **125.00**
  Tapestry, white and brown florals, rust buds, and gold trim, gold ground, aqua bands and feather dec on neck, aqua int., "Doulton-Lambeth, Slater's Patent" .. **250.00**
  10½" h, incised birds on branches, blue, brown, and tan, sgd "Florance Barlow" **875.00**
  11¼" h, faience, large gold chrysanthemums, tan and brown shaded ground, initialed "L. H." **225.00**
  12" h, incised
    Brown grazing horses and leaves, tan and steel blue, wide body, narrow neck, sgd "Hannah Barlow" **750.00**
    Reclining lion, cobalt trim, c1887, "Hannah and Florance Barlow" **850.00**
  12¾" h, 4½" d, incised black circus horses, tan ground, blue leaf border, "Hannah Barlow, Doulton-Lambeth" **650.00**
  13⅛" h, faience, painted scene of two girls, standing in garden by hedge and hollyhocks, wearing gowns (A) **325.00**
  14¼" h, faience
    Pink and white blossoms on center band, tan and green bands **150.00**
    Pink and white flowers, green leaves, green ground, green and tan trim, ftd, initialed "C. M. B. and A. C.," "Doulton-Lambeth" **165.00**
  15" h, 9" d, five incised grazing horses, Art Nouveau style apron top and base, blue and greens, sgd "Hannah Barlow" 1,575.00

ROYAL DOULTON

Biscuit Jar, 7" h, Dickensware, "Tony Weller," metal handle **400.00**
Bouillon Cup and Saucer, painted, three fauna reserves, blue and gilt ground, set of 12 (A) **375.00**

Bowl
  7½" d, Dickensware, "Dick Swiv-
    eller" **135.00**
  7¾" d
    Dickensware, three Dickens char-
      acters featured around outer rim
      and int. **150.00**
    "Under The Greenwood Tree" se-
      ries, Robin Hood and Friar Tuck **50.00**
  8" d
    Dickensware, "Sam Weller," sgd
      "Noke" **85.00**
    "Under The Greenwood Tree" se-
      ries, Robin meets Friar Tuck ... **100.00**
  8½" d, int. scene of two bearded men
    in top hats, flowers, and stone
    fence, octagonal, sgd "Noke" ... **140.00**
  8¾" sq, Dickensware, "Mr. Pick-
    wick" **85.00**
  9" d, Dickensware, "Sam Weller-Aus-
    tralian," octagonal **100.00**
Candlesticks, 8¾" h, "Bayeaux Tapes-
  try," pr **75.00**
Character Jug
  'Arriet
    Large, D6208 .... **160.00**
    Small, D6236, "A" mark **70.00**
    Tiny, D6256 .... **150.00**
  Anne Boleyn, large, D6644 .... **50.00**

**John Barleycorn, large jug, D 5327,
$125.00.**

Aramis, large, D6441 .... **50.00**
Auld Mac
  Small, D5824, "A" mark **30.00**
  Tiny, D6257 .... **250.00**
Baccus, large, D6499 .... **50.00**
Beefeater, small, D6233 .... **17.00**
Bootmaker, mini, D6586 .... **17.00**
Capt Henry Morgan, small, D6469 . **35.00**
Capt Hook
  Large, D6597 .... **275.00**
  Small, D6601 .... **275.00**
Cardinal
  Mini, D6129 .... **50.00**
  Small, D6033 .... **70.00**
Cavalier
  Large, D6114 .... **125.00**
  Small, D6173 .... **70.00**

Clown, large
  Red Hair, D5610 .... **3,500.00**
  White Hair, D6322 .... **850.00**
Dick Turpin
  Large, D5485 .... **150.00**
  Mini, D6128 .... **45.00**
  Mini, masked, D6542 .... **20.00**
  Small, D5618, "A" mark **70.00**
Don Quixote, large, D6455 .... **50.00**
Drake
  Large, D6115 .... **125.00**
  Small, D6174 .... **50.00**
Falstaff, small, D6385 .... **27.50**
Fat Boy
  Mini, D6139, "A" mark **50.00**
  Tiny, D6142 .... **110.00**
Fortune Teller
  Large, D6497 .... **425.00**
  Mini, D6523 .... **325.00**
  Small, D6503 .... **315.00**
Gardener, small, D6643 .... **40.00**
Gladiator
  Large, D6550 .... **455.00**
  Small, D6553 .... **335.00**
Granny
  Large, D5521 .... **50.00**
  Large, D5521, "A" mark **125.00**
  Small, D6384 .... **30.00**
Guardsman, small, D6575 .... **35.00**
Gulliver, small, D6563 .... **315.00**
Gunsmith, small, D6580 .... **35.00**
Izaak Walton, large, D6404 .... **85.00**
Jester, small, D5556 .... **120.00**
John Barleycorn, mini, D6041, "A"
  mark **45.00**
John Peel
  Large, D5612 .... **125.00**
  Mini, D6130, "A" mark **50.00**
  Small, D5731 .... **72.00**
  Tiny, D6259 .... **250.00**
King Cole
  Large, D6036 .... **235.00**
  Small, D6037 .... **120.00**
Long John Silver, large, D6335 ..... **50.00**
Lord Nelson, large, D6336 .... **240.00**
Lumberjack, large, D6610 .... **80.00**
Mad Hatter, mini, D6606 .... **25.00**
Mine Host
  Large, D6468 .... **60.00**
  Small, D6470 .... **38.00**
Monty, large, D6202 .... **50.00**
Mr. Micawber
  Mini, D6138 .... **55.00**
  Small, D5843 .... **90.00**
  Tiny, D5843 .... **85.00**
Mr. Pickwick
  Large, D6060, "A" mark **135.00**
  Mini, D6254 .... **55.00**
Neptune, Mini, D6555 .... **18.00**
Night Watchman, mini, D6583 .... **18.00**
Old Charley, tiny, D6144 .... **90.00**

Paddy
Large, D5753 .... **125.00**
Mini, D6042, "A" mark **35.00**
Tiny, D6145 .... **90.00**
Parson Brown
Large, D5486 .... **125.00**
Small, D5529, "A" mark **64.00**
Pied Piper
Large, D6403 .... **40.00**
Mini, D6514 .... **22.50**
Small, D6462 .... **27.50**
Poacher, large, D6429 .... **60.00**
Rip Van Winkle, large, D6438 ..... **50.00**
Robin Hood
Large, D6205 .... **150.00**
Small, feather handle, D6234 .... **60.00**
Sairy Gamp
Large, D5451 .... **50.00**
Tiny, D6146 .... **75.00**
Sam Weller
Mini, D6140 .... **52.50**
Tiny, D6147 .... **110.00**
Samuel Johnson, large, D6289 ..... **200.00**
Sgt Buz Fuz, small, D5838 .... **120.00**
Simon The Cellarer
Large, D5504 .... **150.00**
Small, D5614 .... **65.00**
Smuggler
Large, D6616 .... **80.00**
Small, D6619 .... **30.00**
St George, large, D6618 .... **150.00**
Tam O'Shanter, small, D6636 ..... **30.00**
The Falconer, mini, D6547 .... **18.00**
The Poacher, large, D6429 .... **50.00**
Toby Philpots
Large, D5736 .... **125.00**
Mini, D5737, "A" mark **35.00**
Small, D5737 .... **50.00**
Tony Weller
Large, D5531, "A" mark **125.00**
Mini, D6044, "A" mark **45.00**
Small, D5530, "A" mark **55.00**
Touchstone, large, D5613 .... **175.00**
Trapper, small, D6612 .... **38.00**
Ugly Duchess, large, D6599 .... **315.00**
Uncle Tom Cobbleigh, large, D6337 **350.00**
Viking
Large, D6496 .... **125.00**
Mini, D6526 .... **110.00**
Small, D6502 .... **75.00**

Coffee Service, 8½" h coffeepot, creamer, sugar, four cups and saucers,
"Carnival" pattern **125.00**

Creamer, Furness Bermuda Line, bird
and flower design **18.00**

Creamer and Sugar, cov, "Malvern" pattern **20.00**

Cup and Saucer
"Amulet" pattern **15.00**

"Beaumont" pattern **18.00**
"Bell Heather" pattern **20.00**
"Belmont" pattern **15.00**
"Berkeley" pattern **25.00**
"Campagna" pattern **12.00**
"Chalet" pattern **10.00**
"Clairmont" pattern **12.00**
"Delacourt" pattern, white and gold,
#H5006 .... **16.00**
Dickensware, "Fagin" on cup, "Mr.
Micawber" on saucer **68.00**
"Fairfield" pattern **8.00**
"Glamis Thistle" pattern **48.00**
"Grantham" pattern **12.00**
Kingsware, "Don Quixote" **70.00**
"Miramont" pattern **18.00**
"Norfolk" pattern, blue, octagonal . **18.00**
"Rondo" pattern **18.00**
"Under the Greenwood Tree" **65.00**
"Warwick" pattern **10.00**

Demitasse Cup and Saucer
Dickensware, "Fagin," sgd "Noke" . **65.00**
"Fairfax" pattern **18.00**
Flambe, landscape **75.00**

Dresser Set, tray and three sq boxes,
Dickensware, "Bill Sykes" and "Fat
Boy" **400.00**

Egg Cup, "Tintern" pattern **14.00**

Figure
A Courting, HN2004 .... **400.00**
A La Mode, HN2544 .... **150.00**
A Yeoman of the Guard, HN6888 (A) **560.00**
Airdale, HN1024, Cotsford Topsak . **120.00**
Alchemist, HN1282 ....**1,500.00**
Alsatian, HN1117 .... **100.00**
Angelica, HN2013 .... **600.00**
Autumn Breezes
Green, HN1913 .... **165.00**
Pink, HN1911 .... **155.00**
Babie, HN1697 .... **50.00**
Baby Bunting, HN2109 .... **350.00**
Bachelor, HN2319 .... **225.00**
Ballerina, HN2116 .... **265.00**
Balloon Seller, HN583 .... **500.00**
Bather, HN687 .... **450.00**
Bedtime, mkd (A) **30.00**
Belle O'Ball, HN1997 .... **170.00**
Bess, HN2002, red cape **215.00**
Blithe Morning, HN2065 .... **140.00**
Blossom, HN1667 .... **600.00**
Bonnie Lassie, HN1626 .... **210.00**
Bride, HN2166 .... **220.00**
Bridesmaid
HN2196 .... **80.00**
HN2874 .... **48.00**
Bridget, HN2070 .... **275.00**
Broken Lance, HN2041 .... **400.00**
Bull Pup, K2 .... **45.00**
Bulldog, HN1072 .... **85.00**

Butterfly
HN719 .... **700.00**
HN2379 .... **75.00**
Calumet, HN2068 .... **550.00**
Capt MacHeath, HN464 (A) **250.00**
Captain, HN2260 .... **250.00**
Cellist, HN2226 .... **300.00**
Chitarrone, HN2700 .... **400.00**
Christine, HN2792 .... **135.00**
Christmas Time, HN2110 .... **260.00**
Cissie, HN1809 (A) **25.00**
Clockmaker, HN2279 (A) **170.00**
Coachman, HN2282 .... **475.00**
Cobbler, HN1706 .... **225.00**
Country Lass, HN1991 .... **115.00**
Craftsman, HN2284 .... **400.00**
Cup of Tea, HN2322 .... **75.00**
Curly Knob, HN1627 .... **225.00**
Cymbals, HN2699 .... **600.00**
Dachshund
HN1129, Shrewd Saint, small **100.00**
HN1141 .... **75.00**
K17 .... **65.00**
Daffy Down Dilly, HN1712 .... **80.00**
Dainty May, HN1639 (A) **62.00**

Royal Doulton Figures, left, Autumn Breezes, HN 1954, $100.00; right, Gollywog, HN 2040, $250.00.

Darby, HN2024 .... **175.00**
Darling, HN1319 .... **125.00**
Dawn, HN1858 .... **825.00**
Delight, HN1772 .... **145.00**
Detective, HN2359 .... **100.00**
Diana, HN1980 .... **100.00**
Dimity, HN2169 .... **310.00**
Dinky Doo, HN1678 (A) **25.00**
Dorkas, HN1558 .... **180.00**
Drake, HN807 .... **45.00**
Dreamweaver, HN2283 .... **130.00**
Enchantment, HN2178 .... **95.00**
English Setter, HN1051, Maeaydd
Mustard **85.00**
Ermine Coat, HN1981 .... **320.00**

Estelle, HN1566 (A) **560.00**
Fair Lady, HN2193, green **80.00**
Falstaff, HN2054 .... **85.00**
Family Album, HN2321 .... **300.00**
Fat Boy, HN555 .... **350.00**
Fiona, HN2694 .... **120.00**
Flute, HN2493 .... **975.00**
Foaming Quart, HN2162 .... **75.00**
Forty Winks, HN1974 .... **225.00**
French Horn, HN2795 .... **650.00**
French Peasant, HN2075 .... **500.00**
Galadriec, HN2915 .... **16.50**
Gay Morning, HN2135 .... **200.00**
Geraldine, HN2344 .... **135.00**
Gollum, HN2913 .... **45.00**
Good King Wenceslas, 8¾" h, poly-
chrome enamel, mkd (A) **115.00**
Good Morning, HN2671 .... **125.00**
Goody Two Shoes, M80 .... **250.00**
Grace, HN2318 .... **115.00**
Granny's Heritage, HN1874 (A) **250.00**
Greta, HN1485 .... **200.00**
Gypsy Dance, HN2230 .... **250.00**
Harmony, HN2824 .... **90.00**
Heart To Heart, HN2276 .... **275.00**
Helen of Troy, "Les Femmes Fatales"
series **900.00**
Her Ladyship, HN1977 .... **300.00**
Hilary, HN2335 .... **150.00**
Honey, HN1963 .... **365.00**
Huntsman, HN2442 .... **130.00**
Hurdy Gurdy, HN2796 .... **650.00**
Invitation, HN2170 .... **125.00**
Irene
HN1621 .... **300.00**
HN1952, blue **700.00**
Irish Setter, HN1055 .... **80.00**
Jovial Monk, HN2144 .... **175.00**
June, HN1691 .... **335.00**
Kate Hardcastle, HN2028 (A) **280.00**
Katrina, HN2237 .... **260.00**
Lady April, HN1958 .... **310.00**
Lady Betty, HN1967 .... **350.00**
Lady Charmian, HN1949 .... **150.00**
Lambing Time, HN1890 .... **100.00**
Lavinia, HN1955 .... **85.00**
Leading Lady, HN2269 .... **130.00**
Legolas, HN2917 .... **16.50**
Lilac Time, HN2137 .... **225.00**
Lily, HN1798, pink **125.00**
Little Boy Blue, HN2062 .... **125.00**
Little Bridesmaid, HN1433 .... **155.00**
Long John Silver, HN2204 .... **450.00**
Loretta, HN2337 .... **110.00**
Lucy Lockett, HN524 (A) **250.00**
Lunchtime, HN2485 .... **140.00**
Lute, HN2431 .... **950.00**
Marguerite, HN1928 .... **300.00**
Marie, HN1370 .... **50.00**
Market Day, HN1191 .... **200.00**

Mary Jane, HN1990 .... **225.00**
Mary, Mary, HN2044 .... **110.00**
Masque, HN2554 (A) **55.00**
Master Sweep, HN2205 .... **425.00**
Maureen, HN1770, pink **260.00**
Medicant, HN1365 .... **265.00**
Meditation, HN2330 .... **135.00**
Melanie, HN2271 .... **115.00**
Memories, HN1855 .... **315.00**
Mephistopheles, HN775 .... **500.00**
Midenette, HN2090 .... **210.00**
Milkmaid, HNB2057, green **115.00**
Millicent, HN1714 .... **800.00**
Minuet, HN2019, white **260.00**
Miss Demure, HN1402 .... **170.00**
Miss Muffet, HN1936, red coat **150.00**
Monica, HN1467 .... **65.00**
Newsboy, HN2244 .... **375.00**
Nina, HN2347 .... **150.00**
Noelle, HN2179 .... **275.00**
Old Mother Hubbard, HN2314 .... **225.00**
Omar Khayyam, HN2247 .... **85.00**
Orange Lady, HN1953 .... **188.00**
Organ Grinder, HN2173 .... **575.00**
Owd William, HN2042 .... **200.00**
Paisley Shawl, HN1392, Style 1 .... **275.00**
Pan On A Rock, white glaze (A) **165.00**
Parisian, HN2445 .... **135.00**
Parson's Daughter, HN564 .... **400.00**
Past Glory, HN2484 .... **150.00**
Patchwork Quilt, HN1984 .... **325.00**
Pearly Boy, HN1547 .... **420.00**
Pearly Girl, HN2036 .... **185.00**
Pierrette, HN643 .... **625.00**
Polka, HN2156 .... **255.00**
Polly Peachum, HN550, "potted"
　mark **500.00**
Premier, HN2343 .... **120.00**
Professor, HN2281 .... **200.00**
Puppy in Basket, HN2586 .... **48.00**
Rabbit, K37 .... **35.00**
Repose, HN2272 .... **175.00**
River Hog, HN2663 .... **125.00**
Romance, HN2430 .... **135.00**
Romany Sue, HN1757 (A) **250.00**
Rose, HN1369 .... **40.00**
Roseanna, HN1921 .... **275.00**
Rough Haired Terrier, HN1014,
　"Crackley Starter" **60.00**
Sabbath Morn, HN1982 .... **200.00**
Santa Claus, HN2725 .... **125.00**
Sea Harvest, HN2257 .... **150.00**
Sealyham, K3 .... **35.00**
Sgt Buz Fuz, HN538 .... **200.00**
Shepherd, HN1975 .... **190.00**
Siesta, HN1305 (A) **2,220.00**
Sir Walter Raleigh, HN2015 .... **515.00**
Skater, HN2117 .... **265.00**
Sleepy Scholar, HN16 ....**2,200.00**
Sleepyhead, HN2114 .... **550.00**
Spring, HN2085 .... **288.00**

Spring Flowers, HN1807 .... **275.00**
Spring Morn, HN1922 .... **210.00**
St Bernard, K19 .... **55.00**
Stitch-In-Time, HN2352 .... **130.00**
Stop The Press, HN2683 .... **175.00**
Summer, HN2086 .... **288.00**
Suzette, HN1487, white **225.00**
Sweet & Twenty, HN1298, "potted,"
　dated 1929 .... **250.00**
Sweet Anne, M5 .... **225.00**
Sweeting, HN1935 .... **120.00**
Symphony, HN2287 .... **285.00**
Teanager, HN2203 .... **200.00**
Teatime, HN2253 .... **115.00**
The Balloon Man, HN1954 (A) **80.00**
The Cobbler, HN1705 .... **225.00**
The Corinthian, HN1973 .... **550.00**
The Drummer Boy, HN2679 .... **250.00**
The Dunce, HN310 (A) **2,125.00**
The Fiddler, HN2171 ....**1,100.00**
The Flounced Skirt, white, lavender
　and blue flowers **1,800.00**
The Huntsman, HN2492 .... **150.00**
The Jovial Monk, HN2144 .... **160.00**
The Lavender Woman, HN22 (A) ... **400.00**
The Mermaid, HN97 .... **600.00**
The Modern Piper, HN756 (A) **1,120.00**
The New Bonnet, HN1728 .... **550.00**
The Old Balloon Seller, HN1315 (A) **130.00**
The Orange Lady, HN1953 .... **250.00**
The Parson's Daughter, HN564 (A) . **160.00**
The Professor, HN2281 .... **135.00**
Tinkle Bell, HN1677 .... **55.00**
To Bed, HN1807 .... **100.00**
Top O' The Hill
　HN1834 .... **120.00**
　HN1849, green **170.00**
Town Crier, HN2119 .... **250.00**
Toymaker, HN 2250 .... **325.00**
Twilight, HN2256 .... **175.00**
Uncle Ned, HN2094 .... **300.00**
Uriah Heep, HN1892 .... **375.00**
Venetia, HN2722 .... **115.00**
Viola d Amore, HN2797 .... **650.00**
Virginia, HN1693 .... **450.00**
Vivienne, HN2073 .... **250.00**
Votes for Women, HN2815 .... **140.00**
Wardrobe Mistress, HN2145 ...... **350.00**
Wigmaker of Williamsburg, HN2239 **180.00**
Windflower, M79 .... **225.00**
Winter, HN2088 .... **288.00**

Figure, flambe finish
　Bulldog, English Union Jack on back **100.00**
　Cat, 4¾" **300.00**
　Owl **250.00**

Ginger Jar, 9¼" h, flambe, mottled red,
　blue, pink, mauve, and yellow (A) .. **165.00**

Hatpin Holder, Dickensware, Mr. Mi-
　cawber **87.50**

Jardiniere
8" d, "Shakespeare" series, Falstaff,
c1920 .... **165.00**
10" d, " Shakespeare" series, Ophelia
on one side, Hamlet on other **325.00**
Flambe, blue and white scene of
woman playing guitar (A) **210.00**
Jug
6⅜" h, "Egyptian Scenes" series,
Egyptian women, men, and child,
green, brown, and tan geometric
border, cream ground, c1920 .... **100.00**
7" h, 5½" d, "Special Highland Whiskey" **75.00**
7¼" h, Dickensware, "Mr. Pickwick,"
sq **150.00**
7½" h, 5½" d, Kingsware-Dewars,
Ben Johnson, emb, green, brown,
and gold **200.00**
9½" h, 7¼" d, Shakespeare series,
"Dogberry Watch," set of three .. **345.00**
10" h, "Dewars Perth Whiskey" and
"The Fair Maid of Perth," emb figures, two tone tan, "Royal Doulton" mark (A) **50.00**
10¾" h
Shakespeare series, molded, multicolored Shakespearian charac-
ters, c1933 (A) **500.00**
The Regency Coach, emb scene of
coach at inn, c1930 .... **475.00**
Loving Cup, 6⅛" h, applied glazed light
green and blue foliage design, tan
ground, "Royal Doulton" (A) **20.00**
Luncheon Service, "Merry Weather"
pattern, 28 pcs (A) **250.00**
Match Holder
3¼" h, Dickensware, "Sam Weller" **68.00**
3¾" d, emb hunt and tavern scene,
tan glaze, "Royal Doulton" (A) .. **15.00**
Mug
4¼" h, Dickensware, "Tony Weller" **135.00**
5" h, "Under The Greenwood Tree"
series **118.00**
5¾" h, Dickensware, "Tom Pinch" . **100.00**
Pitcher
2" h, flow blue, scenic, white ground **55.00**
2½" h, Dickensware, "Bill Sykes" .. **80.00**
5⅛" h, "Jackdaw of Rheims" series,
He Solemnly Cursed That Rascally
Thief **118.00**
6" h
"Arabian Nights" series, Ali Baba
With The Treasure, paneled design **250.00**
"Under The Greenwood Tree" series **140.00**
6" h, 5" d, Kingsware, "Watchman -
Enough is as good as a feast," white
letters **200.00**
6½" h, "Jesters" series, Many kiss the

child for the nurse's sake, sgd
"Noke" **250.00**
7" h
Green and tan Oriental scene,
flowers on handle and spout ... **70.00**
"Zunday Zmocks" series, man in
tall black hat, hot water type, cov **165.00**
7½" h, "Sketches From Teniers" series, tavern scene, multicolored .. **125.00**

**Pitcher, 7⅜" h, "Galleon," multicolored,
$75.00.**

8¼" h, black cats, "May we kiss...,"
amber ground **125.00**
8¾" h, Dickensware, "Barnaby
Rudge" **135.00**
Plate
6", flambe, landscape scene **45.00**
9¼" d
"Babes in Woods"
Girl with doll and frog, sitting on
log **200.00**
Three girls at edge of forest **200.00**
"Motor" series, "Itch Yer On Gu-
venor?" multicolored scene of
auto, gentleman and two seated
lads, "Royal Doulton" **165.00**
9½" d
"Provence" pattern **30.00**
Shakespeare, multicolored transfer
of Falstaff on one, Ophelia on
other, gold tracery border, pr .. **36.00**
9¾" d, "Tintern" pattern **14.00**
10" d
Flowers in center, blue border, gold
trim, sgd "E. Percy," pr **150.00**
Mosaic pattern, cobalt, yellow,
rose, and green accents **45.00**
"Motors" series, "Room For One" **165.00**
Portrait of Robert Burns **65.00**
"Shakespeare's Country" series,
Anne Hathaway's Cottage, co-

balt border, scalloped edge, sgd
"J Hughs" **225.00**
"The Gaffers" series **90.00**
"Under The Greenwood Tree" se-
ries **90.00**
10⅜" d, French and North Wales
scenes in center, indented outlined
borders, sgd "J. H. Plant," pr **400.00**
10½" d
Hunting dog, pastoral setting, pastel colors **65.00**
"Sketches From Teniers" series,
tavern scene **85.00**
13⅜" d, "Under The Greenwood
Tree" series, Robin Hood, Maid
Marion, and Friar Tuck under tree,
multicolored, cream ground **160.00**
Platter
12" d, "Grantham" pattern **14.00**
15" d, "Grantham" pattern **20.00**
16" l, "May" pattern **55.00**
Pot, 3½" h, stoneware, blueberries and
green leaves, brown glaze, crimped
edge, "Royal Doulton X5404,
F.J.E.G." **50.00**
Salt and Pepper Shakers, "Grantham"
pattern **6.00**
Tea and Coffee Service, coffeepot, teapot, creamer, sugar, twelve cups and
saucers, "Reynard the Fox" design . **950.00**
Tea Set, teapot, creamer, and sugar,
"Tintern" pattern **85.00**

**Plates, 9¾" d, multicolored florals, blue
and gold borders, gilt rims, set of 12,
$500.00.**

Teapot
6" l, 6" h, Dickensware, "Bill Sykes,"
rect **225.00**
8½" l, 4¾" h, "Under The Green-
wood Tree" series, seated Friar
Tuck and company **300.00**
Toby Jug
Cap'n Cuttle, small, D6266 .... **140.00**
Cliff Cornell
Large
Blue **225.00**

**Winston Churchill, large toby, D 6171,
$55.00.**

Tan **400.00**
Small, blue **280.00**
Falstaff
Large, D6062 .... **52.50**
Small, D6063 .... **25.00**
Happy John
Large, D6031 .... **55.00**
Small, D6070 .... **25.00**
Honest Measure, small, D6108 .... **25.00**
Huntsman, large, D6320 .... **55.00**
Jolly Toby, medium, D6109 .... **30.00**
Old Charley, large, D6030 .... **180.00**
Sairy Gamp, large, D6263, "A" mark **175.00**
Winston Churchill
Medium, D6172 .... **27.50**
Small, D6175 .... **24.50**
Tray, 6" l, 4" w, red flowers, blue
ground, #D6224 .... **75.00**
Vase
4" h
Dickensware
"Artful Dodger" **60.00**
"Sam Weller," sq, ftd **140.00**
Moonlight scene, blue shades,
c1922 .... **85.00**
4¼" h, flambe, black rural scene,
horse and plowman, daisies in fore-
ground (A) **20.00**
4½" h, "Egyptian Scenes" series,
Egyptian desert scene, green
ground **150.00**
4¾" h, Dickensware, "Barnaby
Rudge" **70.00**
5¼" h, "Babes in Woods" series
Girl with dog and frog on rock ... **285.00**
Young girls with dog, under tree,
gold dbl handles and trim **165.00**

5½" h
Dickensware, "Alfred Jingle," dbl
    handles **90.00**
"Harlech Castle," artist sgd **300.00**
"White Lodge," sgd "J. Price" ... **300.00**
5⅞" h, Dickensware, "Mr. Micaw-
    ber," dbl handles **80.00**
6" h
Dickensware, "Poor Joe," long oval
    loop handles **150.00**
Flambe
    English country scene, black ... **200.00**
    Shepherd and sheep, mountain **250.00**
7" h
Dickensware, "Sidney Carton" ... **135.00**
Flambe, landscape and deer, bullet
    shape, sgd "FM & OCK" **225.00**
"The Gaffers" series, sq **150.00**
7½" h, flambe, woodcut design **100.00**
8¼" h, "Babes in Woods"
Bonnet babies talking to pixies,
    flow blue, dbl handles **300.00**
Girl with basket, winter setting,
    gold trim, dbl handles **300.00**
8½" h
"Babes in Woods," scene of boy
    and girl, playing hide and seek,
    flow blue **275.00**
Continuous scene of sheep and
    lambs in meadow, c1910 ..... **250.00**
Dickensware, "Barnaby Rudge,"
    dbl handles **150.00**
8¾" h, 4⅜" d, "Coaching Days" se-
    ries, barrel shape **165.00**
9" h, "Babes in Woods," woman,
    walking in snow, bonnet, basket . **285.00**
9½" h, 3⅛" d, Dickensware, "Sgt Buz
    Fuz," dbl handles **165.00**
10" h, "Babes in Woods," scene of
    mother playing with young girl and
    horse, flow blue, dbl handles **365.00**
10¾", "Babes in Woods," three girls
    watching firefly in forest **300.00**
10⅞" h, 4" d, "Babes in Woods,"
    three children and dog at picnic,
    gold rim **325.00**
11¼" h, painted blue scene, fishergirl
    at shore and maiden playing guitar,
    c1913, pr (A) **500.00**
13" h, "Babes in Woods"
Mother and young child, dbl han-
    dles **375.00**
Young girl, carrying basket, wear-
    ing hood, dbl handles **375.00**
Vegetable Bowl, 10½" l
Blue transfer of classical scene, man
    playing horn, two women in gar-
    den, gold rim **38.00**
"Grantham" pattern **15.00**
"Hampshire" pattern, cov **24.00**

DRESDEN
1927

Dresden
1883-93

DRESDEN
1905

AR
1883

N
Dresden
MODERN MARK

DRESDEN

Germany
1694–Present

History: Two men, working for Augustus II Elector of Saxony, rediscovered the technique to
make hard paste porcelain of the Oriental type.
Count Tschimhaus, who began his research in
1694, was joined by Johann Bottger, an alchemist, in 1701. At first they produced a red stoneware. By 1709 Bottger was producing white
porcelain. Tschimhaus did not live to enjoy their
success, having died in 1708. The king established the Royal Saxon Porcelain Factory in Dresden in 1710 and then moved it to Meissen one
year later.

During the 18th century, Americans and English used the name "Dresden china" for the
porcelain ware produced at Meissen. This has
led to much confusion. Dresden, the capital of
Saxony, was better known in 18th century Europe
than the city of Meissen, fifteen miles away. In
addition, Meissen products were sold in Dresden. Hence, Dresden became a generic term for
all porcelains manufactured and decorated in the
city of Dresden and its surrounding environs,
including Meissen.

In the mid-19th century, about thirty factories
were operating in the city of Dresden producing
and decorating porcelains in the style of Meissen
wares. Marks were adopted which were similar
to the crossed swords of the original Meissen
factory. Many simply faked the Meissen mark.

Helena Wolfson and her successors imitated
AR Meissen porcelain between 1843 and approximately 1949. Her firm had a large staff of
painters trained to imitate the 18th century porcelain. Wolfson also purchased "white" china
blanks from the Meissen factory and had then
decorated by her own staff of painters and gild-

ers. After much litigation, Wolfson was forced to abandon the AR mark. About 1880 the firm adopted a mark using the word "Dresden" with the letter "D" surmounted by a crown.

Meyers and Son was the greatest rival of Wolfson in the production of imitation Meissen porcelains. They used the crossed swords with an "M" to mark their examples. Franziska Hirsch, another copyist, used a mark similar to that of Samson, the French potter, on her Meissen and Vienna imitations made between 1894 and 1930.

The porcelain factory of Carl Thieme of Potschappel produced Rococo imitations of Meissen pieces from 1872 until 1972, often marketing them as Meissen 18th century figures. They also produced household, table, and decorative porcelains, knickknacks, souvenirs, and gift articles, all decorated in the Meissen and Vienna styles.

A "Dresden style" came into being when four decorators, Richard Klemm, Donath and Co., Oswald Lorenz, and Adolph Hamann, all registered the same mark in 1883. The mark was a crown with "Dresden" underneath in blue. Later this group altered their marks. Eight other decorators then used the "Dresden" and the crown mark.

Donath and Co. produced porcelain in the Meissen and Vienna styles from 1872 until 1916. The company merged with Richard Klemm's decorating workshop for three years. In 1918 the firm became the Dresden Art Department of C.M. Hutschenreuther, continuing in that relationship until 1945. Adolph Hamann, another member of the "Dresden style" group, operated a porcelain decorating workshop from 1866 until 1949. It was acquired by Heinrich Gerstmann in 1933 and continued with its earlier name.

Franz Junkersdorf, A. Lamm, Henfel and Co., Anton Richter, Max Robra, Wilhelm Koch, and others had decorating workshops from the last quarter of the 19th century and extending into the 20th century. All of these firms imitated Meissen porcelains.

Museums: Bayerishes Nationalmuseum, Munich, West Germany; Kunstgewebemuseum, West Berlin, West Germany; Museum fur Kunst und Gewerbe, Hamburg, West Germany; Staatliche Porzellansammlung, Dresden, East Germany.

See: Hutschenreuther

Basket
  7½" l, 6¼" h, applied florals, leaves,
    two cherubs, multicolored, four
    flared feet **85.00**
  11½" l, 7⅜" h, basketweave, irregular
    pierced rim, applied flowers,
    leaves, and two winged cherubs,
    one with mandolin, other with
    sheet music, four scroll feet, re-
    paired **125.00**

Bowl
  9⅝" d, cov, stand, painted landscape
    vignettes with lovers, alternating
    black panels reserved with florals
    and gilt, quatrefoil shape, lemon fi-
    nial, c1880 blue "AR" mark (A) .. **415.00**
  Four groups of applied multicolored
    flowers, oblong, applied handles,
    unmarked **215.00**
Cache Pot, 5" d, 5" h, pink roses and
    florals, twisted twig handle, crown
    and "Dresden" mark **1,138.00**

Candelabras
  13½" h, hp, flowers, applied multi-
    colored flowers, c1875, pr **1,250.00**
  19¼" h, one with molded mother and
    son, other with father and daughter
    reading, applied blackberries and
    vines, circ bases molded with car-
    touches reserved with insects and
    birds, four lights, late 19th C, blue
    X'd swords mark, repaired, pr (A) **880.00**
Candelabrum
  6" h, 10" l, three arms, figural, cherub
    and deer, applied multicolored
    flowers, chips **500.00**
  37½" h, six lights supported by
    molded putto with quiver, standard
    with spiraling bands of turquoise,
    white ground, applied florals, three
    scrolling feet **1,500.00**
  75" h, seventeen scrolling branch
    arms with flower clusters, edged in
    turquoise, black and gilt checker-
    ing, standard painted with Arms of
    Count Bruhl, applied florals, wood
    painted base, late 19th C, repaired
    (A) **3,500.00**
Candlesticks, 9" h, applied leaves and
    florals, bases formed from modeled
    leaves, multicolored, pr (A) **250.00**
Centerpiece, 18¾" h, bowl with upright
    handles, turned column, quatrefoil
    base on lion feet, bowl and base with
    applied flowers and leaves, four full
    standing Cupids on base, pink and
    green matte glaze, drilled, late 19th
    C (A) **200.00**
Charger
  14½" d, scene of sailing ships in
    storm, border with gilt florals in
    puce, pink, purple, and iron-red
    panels, c1900 (A) **725.00**
  18¾" d, polychrome spider mum mo-
    tif, dark blue ground, gilt rim, early
    20th C, blue X'd swords mark (A) **275.00**
Chocolate Set, chocolate pot, creamer,
    cov sugar, six cups and saucers, ro-
    coco style, relief shell and scroll de-
    sign, dark brown and white glaze,
    gold accents, blue X'd swords mark **350.00**

Clock

11⅞" h, French clock mounted in sq
domed column, painting of couple
in landscape, ormolu flame finial,
molded putto, writing on tablet,
oval base, molded florals, c1880,
blue saber and star mark **450.00**

14" h, 8" w, white body, all over pink
applied flowers and leaves, cherub
on top holding garland, lady on
each side holding bird, c1870, unmarked **1,430.00**

23" h, molded figures of Four Seasons
at base, applied florals and scrolling, four feet (A) **2,000.00**

Clock Set, pair of two socket candelabra
with porcelain flowers, ormolu tendrils and small figure on scroll base,
French clock with ormolu foliate
spray, porcelain blossoms, 19th C (A) **250.00**

Coffeepot, 8" h, floral, gilded scroll motif (A) **20.00**

Compote

5" h, polychrome florals, gilt trim,
early 20th C (A) **16.00**

12" h

Cherubs, applied flowers, pastel
colors (A) **180.00**

Fully modeled children supporting
dishes, raised flowerheads, multicolored, pierced bowls, pr (A) **360.00**

12½" h, swan form, three open swans
on base, applied florals, raised
compote portion, open work bor-
der, c1890, unmarked **1,250.00**

13" h, group of children dancing
around blossoming tree, multicolored, (A) **450.00**

Cherub holding open weave basket,
applied flowers on base, stem, and
basket, c1900, Castle mark **275.00**

Console Set, two 8" h, 11" w, dbl armed
candelabras with seated putti, 13" w
basket, four standing putti support
basket, applied flowers and shells .. **675.00**

Cup, cov and stand, bouquets, brown
border reserved and molded with stylized ornaments, gilt laural wreath finial, c1900, blue "AR" mark (A) ... **80.00**

Cup and Saucer

Alternating floral and figural reserves,
multicolored (A) **15.00**

Architectural view, reserved on white,
gilt floral banded ground (A) **350.00**

Figures in harbor scene, gilt band cartouches, trefoil shape, c1900 (A) . **80.00**

Painted shepherds in landscape,
molded basketwork borders, late
19th C, blue X'd swords mark (A) **145.00**

Reserved and painted with coat of
arms, yellow ground, quatrefoil
shape, blue cross mark **60.00**

Reserves of figures alternating with
panels of flowers, yellow ground,
dbl handles **60.00**

Cutting Board, 10¾" l, "Blue Onion"
pattern, pierced for hanging, crown
and "D" mark **135.00**

Demitasse Cup and Saucer, flower bud
shape, gold int., gold tracery on saucer **22.00**

Desk Set, 13⅛" w, rect, two circ and
one rect covered recesses, encrusted
floral sprays, gilt rims, pierced sides,
damaged, c1900 .... **100.00**

Dish

5" l, polychrome florals, gilt trim,
oval, late 19th C (A) **16.00**

9½" sq, florals, gilt trim, scalloped
edge **35.00**

Figure

3½" h, girl, seated, lace dress **50.00**

4" h, boy and girl, period dress, carrying baskets of flowers, multicolored, pr **225.00**

4¼" h, boy seated on stump with basket of flowers at feet, girl seated on
rock, container of grapes, multicolored, late 19th C, pr (A) **150.00**

4½" h

Woman, lacy period dress, holding
fan, applied flowers, multicolored **42.00**

Young boy, holding basket, multicolored, c1800, unmarked (A) . **35.00**

5" h

Boy, seated in sled, girl standing by,
multicolored, gold trim **150.00**

Boy, seated in sled, hatchet and
firewood, multicolored (A) **112.50**

Young girl, wearing bonnet with
sprigs and flowers and feathers,
multicolored **185.00**

5¼" h

Boot, overall floral design, gold tracery, gold int. **50.00**

Two dancers and two musicians,
white ground, gold scrolled base,
unmarked **500.00**

5⅜" h, boy and girl, 18th C dress,
boy with flower garland, girl with
basket of flowers, blue X'd swords
mark, pr (A) **375.00**

5½" h

Dancer, seated on settee, multicolored, lace (A) **85.00**

Young lady, seated on chaise, multicolored, lace, lace damage (A) **50.00**

5¾" h, dwarfs, extended bellies, multicolored attire, pr (A) **325.00**

6" h, 11" l, pheasant, natural colors **225.00**

6½" h

Colonial lady, green lace dress,
flower basket, applied flowers,

multicolored, "D" under crown
and Germany mark **70.00**
Parrot sitting on tree stump, flower
dec, natural colors, unmarked,
pr **300.00**
Two parrots, perched on tree
stump, multicolored **335.00**
7" h
Colonial couple, dancing, multicolored, lace trim, "N" under
crown, #450A mark **130.00**
Young lady, bird cage on shoulder,
lamb at feet, multicolored (A) .. **115.00**
Young woman, 18th C dress, dove
in cage on shoulder, lamb at feet,
blue X'd swords mark (A) **225.00**
7¼" h, young lady, period clothes,
multicolored, lace (A) **65.00**
7½" h
Boy and girl, 18th C dress, supporting sweetmeat dish above
heads, multicolored, pierced
base, blue X'd swords mark (A) **325.00**
Farm girl, feeding chickens, multicolored, unmarked **125.00**
Woman, 18th C dress, holding
flowers, light green, pink, and
blue, unmarked **150.00**
Woman, seated at dressing table,
multicolored, lace (A) **120.00**

Figure, 8″ h, white with multicolored accents, $50.00.

8" h
"Camargo," young man and
woman dancing, multicolored,
lace (A) **25.00**
Colonial woman, lace dress, holding basket of flowers, multicolored, "D" under crown, Ger-
many mark **125.00**
Colonial woman, lace dress, para-

sol, applied flowers, "D" under
crown, Germany mark **115.00**

Figure, 12″ h, multicolored pastel colors, c1880, unmarked, $1,150.00.

Young lady, holding flower garland,
multicolored, lace (A) **50.00**
Young man and woman, courting,
multicolored, lace (A) **60.00**
8⅛" h, woman, winter period dress,
feathered muff, multicolored (A) .. **90.00**
8¾" h, family at picnic, man raising
glass of wine, foliated tree, c1885,
unmarked **850.00**
9" h, 14" l, man and woman, period
lace dress, playing piano and base
fiddle, multicolored **400.00**
9½" h
Woman, 18th C dress, holding dog
in arms, unmarked **750.00**
Young man with game birds,
woman with bird cage, multicolored, pr (A) **60.00**
10" h, two children standing, period
dress, arms around waists, pastel
colors, repaired **135.00**
10½" h, young lady, wearing bonnet,
multicolored, lace (A) **70.00**
10¾" h, man with basket of fruit and
dog at feet, woman with fruit in
apron, multicolored period dress,
blue X'd swords marks, pr (A) **500.00**
11" h, maiden, yellow cloth, blind-
folding Cupid, c1900 .... **175.00**
11½" h, 27½" l, pair of white porcelain peacocks, giltwood base, late
19th C, crown mark **425.00**
13" h, "Coldstream Guard," sword,
multicolored **250.00**
23" l, "Belle of the Ball," dancers,
seated women and musicians, outlined dance floor, multicolored,

green and gold base, finely modeled and painted, title, unmarked **2,200.00**

Ice Cream Set, 16" l tray, twelve plates, gilt design dividing surface into four alternating figural and floral sections, yellow ground (A) **250.00**

Inkstand, 14" l, gilt bronze, porcelain florals, lacquer base, two porcelain ink pots, Oriental figures on each side **500.00**

Jardiniere, 24" h, multicolored flowers, scroll handles, shell motifs, flower terminals, fitted with tree, variety of garden flowers, c1860 (A) **1,000.00**

Lamp, 14½" h, 7" d, brown base, three putti holding font, applied multicolored flowers, pink satin glass mushroom shade, unmarked **650.00**

Mirror, 35" h, top with painted court lady surrounded by molded putti, base with painted putti and wheat sheaves, scroll molding, sides with applied painted flowers between beaded borders, oval, late 19th C (A) **1,650.00**

Mirror Frame, 30" sq, applied florals, cherubs, pastel colors, pr (A) **500.00**

Mug

Hp, florals under drapery, blue and white diapering, "Klemm" **50.00**

Plaque, 8" l, 5⅞" h, painted scene of Leda bathing, swan in wooded setting **670.00**

Plate

8½" d, scene of woman in garden, two Cupids, raised gold **125.00**

9½" d

Center florals, basketweave border, scalloped edges, c1843, "AR-Helena Wolfsohn", set of 7 ....**1,900.00**

Man courting woman, formal clothes, cobalt border, reticulated gold, imp "Meissen and Helena Wolfsohn" **350.00**

9⅞" d, painted center scene, three men drinking in tavern, reserved on turquoise ground, pierced trellis border, painted floral panels (A) .. **135.00**

10½" d, multicolored florals, water scene, unmarked **16.00**

13" d, hunter and woman on horses, landscape, urns on iron-red border, shaped panels in green and puce, gilding, early 20th C, "AR" mark (A) **90.00**

Pots A Creme, cov, matching saucer, polychrome floral dec, gilt trim, pr (A) **32.00**

Ramekin, cov, matching underplate, garlands of flowers, gold trim **85.00**

Scent Bottle, 3⅜" h, modeled nymph, Cupid, and dog looking at clock, two doves modeled as stopper, c1900 (A) **155.00**

Servers, cov, 11" d, polychrome floral

dec, gilt, dbl handles, pear knobs, unmarked, pr (A) **225.00**

Tea Caddy, 5¼" h, two panels of boy and girl courting, two panels of multicolored flowers, gold tracery **130.00**

Tea Service, teapot with bronze swing handle, teapot on stand, coffeepot, milk jug, cov sugar, waste bowl, dish, twelve cups and saucers, applied white florettes ground, applied enameled fruit, flowers, and birds, late 19th C (A) **5,500.00**

Urn

10⅜" h, oval reserve of figures and horses, landscape, baluster form, upright curved handles, modeled goat heads on shoulders, tapered stem, sq base (A) **70.00**

12" h, oval portrait reserve, maroon ground, gilt rococo dec, sq ftd base, high dbl scroll handles, sgd "K Weingel," blue X'd swords mark (A) **130.00**

18½" h, cov, raised blue florette ground, modeled birds and flowerheads, multicolored, bird finials (A) **600.00**

Vase

4" h, applied florals, multicolored (A) **30.00**

7½" h, 5" d, multicolored floral dec, heavy gold accents, triple handle . **150.00**

9¾" h, cov, portrait of Marie Antoinette and Princess Lambelle, gilt borders, lattice, and florals, cream ground, metallic green border, c1900, sgd "Wagner," pr (A) **1,100.00**

10" h, oval portrait of dark haired woman, pink garland in hair, irid olive ground, gilt details, c1910 (A) **300.00**

10½" h, cov, applied cherubs and flowers, bright colors, flower and leaf finials, c1887, unmarked, pr .**1,200.00**

11" h, applied flowers, multicolored, c1889, unmarked, pr **1,200.00**

14½" h, cov

Figures in landscapes, turquoise panels, flower sprays, gilt foliage, domed covs, c1860, blue interlaced "AR" mark, pr (A) .. **800.00**

Lovers in landscape vignettes alternating with loose bouquets, yellow ground, small curled gilt handles, domed cov, berried finial, c1880, blue "AR" mark, pr (A) **500.00**

20⅞" h, painted panels of classical ladies, flowers on reserve, ogee shape, two putti and fruit sprays applied to each side, pr (A) **760.00**

24¼" h, cov, painted scenes of hunting parties, panels of florals on

sides, gilt scroll borders, cobalt
ground, late 19th C, pr (A) **2,475.00**
39" h, cov, stand, painted with view
of 18th C lovers, landscape, ap-
plied florals, Cupid, c1900 (A) . . .**2,475.00**
41½" h, cov, matching stand, painted
panels of lovers in garden setting,
border of applied flowers, molded
cherubs holding wreaths, domed
cov, crowned shield, Polish coat of
arms of Augustus the Strong,
flanked by cherubs, late 19th C,
Carl Thieme, pr (A) **6,385.00**
Wall Pocket, multicolored flowers, gold
trim, center cartouche of 18th C couple, yellow ground, scalloped edge,
unmarked **100.00**

ENGLAND-GENERAL

PORCELAIN
1700–Present

History: Before the 1740s porcelains available in
England were of Chinese or Japanese origin and
were imported by the British East India Company.
Many early English pottery manufacturers tried
to duplicate Oriental porcelains and the Continental porcelains of Meissen and Sevres, but
achieved only limited success.

The earliest English porcelains date about 1745
and were made at the Chelsea factory. This porcelain was the soft paste type. By the mid 18th
century production of soft paste porcelain was
well established at Bow and Chelsea. Other factories, including Bristol, Longton Hall, Derby,
Worcester, Liverpool, and Lowestoft soon followed. The English factories were private enterprises, not subsidized by royal families or
princely households as were those on the Continent.

Soft paste was fragile. Hot liquids could crack
it. Sometimes it collapsed or lost its shape in the
kiln. Efforts were mounted to find a material that
was more stable in the kiln and durable. The
Bow factory tried adding ash of calcined bones.
Bristol and Worcester incorporated a soapstone
paste to their mix to strengthen their porcelains.

Many credit William Cookworthy of Plymouth
with the rediscovery of the Chinese method of
hard paste porcelain manufacture in England
about 1768. The second Josiah Spode of Stoke
developed bone china by adding bone ash to the
ingredients of hard paste porcelain. This "bone"
china lead to the development of cream colored
earthenware. Based on the hard paste rediscovery and Spode's bone china, England became a
major supplier to the world wide market.

POTTERY
17th Century–Present

History: Early pottery wares in England included
stoneware, Delftware, slipware, and salt glaze
ware. Potters such as Thomas Toft, John Dwight,
and the Elers were among the principal manufacturers.

During the early 17th century, Staffordshire became the center of the pottery industry due to an
abundant supply of coal, availability of clays and
adequate transportation to the marketplace. Astbury, Whieldon, and the Woods experimented
with all forms of earthenwares from figure groups
with colored glazes to numerous types of vessels
and dishes. Earthenware production dominated
the first half of the eighteenth century.

As the newly perfected cream colored earthenwares introduced by Josiah Wedgwood in the
1760s came to the forefront, Staffordshire salt
glazed wares started to go out of fashion. Numerous Staffordshire makers such as the Turners,
Elijah Mayer, Palmer and Neale, Wilson of Hanley, Leeds, William Adams of Tunstall, and Josiah
Spode of Stoke copied Wedgwood's cream colored earthenwares. They also imitated Wedgwood's black basalt, jasper, and cane colored
stoneware. Spode introduced the manufacture of
blue printed earthenwares.

During the 1800s lusterwares became popular
with the Staffordshire potters. New techniques in
the early 19th century included overglaze transfer printing and ironstone china. Underglaze blue
printing was developed in the first half of the
19th century.

Figures, depicting all sorts of people and animals, were made during the 1800s by John Walton, Ralph Salt, and Obadiah Sherratt. During
the reign of Queen Victoria, earthenware cottage
mantelpiece figures were decorated in enamels
and some gilding. Underglaze blue was the most
important color used. Sampson Smith was the
principal manufacturer. Pot lids were another
19th century product with decorations in polychrome underglaze.

Other pottery firms making utilitarian and dec-
orative wares during the 19th century included
H. & R. Daniels, Miles Mason, W. Ridgway &
Co., Cauldon Place Works, John Davenport, Job
Meigh, Lakin & Poole, Mintons, and Doulton of
Lambeth.

Since the late 1800s the studio potter has become important in England. This movement is a
reaction against the emphasis on mass produced
pieces. The studio potter usually throws his own
wares with the glazing and decorating done either by himself or under his supervision. The first
of the studio potters were William de Morgan
and the Martin Brothers. Bernard Leach of the
St. Ives Pottery made stoneware influenced by
early Chinese and Japanese wares. The studio

potters use many traditional methods of manufacture such as tin glaze, salt glaze, slipware, agate ware, and sgraffito work.

Patent Office Registration Marks: From 1842 until 1883 many manufacturers' wares were marked with the "diamond mark" which was an indication that the design or form of the piece was registered with the British Patent Office and protected against piracy for three years. The mark could be applied by either printing, impressing, or applying a molded piece of clay. Pottery and porcelains were in Class IV. In the diamond the numbers or letters in each corner were keyed. A ceramic marks book is necessary to decipher the mark and discover the date the design was registered with the Patent Office. After 1884 the diamond mark was replaced by a registry number.

References: Cyril G.E. Bunt, *British Potters & Pottery Today*, F. Lewis Publishers, 1956; J.P. Cushion, *English China Collecting for Amateurs*, Frederick Muller, 1967.

Museums: British Museum, London, England; Cranbrook Academy of Art Museum, Bloomfield Hills, MI; Gardiner Museum of Ceramic Art, Toronto, Canada; Victoria & Albert Museum, London, England.

Collectors' Clubs: English Ceramic Society, Membership Secretary, 5 The Drive, Beckenham, Kent BR3 1EE, England. Membership: 19 pounds. *Transactions* published annually. Northern Ceramics Society, Membership Secretary, Bramdean Jacksons Lane, Hazel Grove, Cheshire, England. Membership $21.00. Newsletter four times a year, journal every other year.

Additional Listings: Adams, Beswick, Bisque, Bow, Bristol, Carlton Ware, Caughley, Cauldon, Chelsea, Clews, Coalport, Copeland-Spode, Creamware, Crown & Royal Crown Derby, Davenport, Delft, De Morgan, Derby, Doulton, Flow Blue, Ironstone, Jackfield, Leeds, Liverpool, Longton Hall, Lowestoft, Lustreware, Majolica, Martin Brothers, Mason, Meakin, Meigh, Minton, Mocha Ware, Moorcroft, Bernard Moore, Nantgarw, New Hall, Plymouth, Pot Lids, Pratt, Ridgway, Rockingham, Royal Worcester, Salt Glaze, Slipware, Spode, Staffordshire, Stoneware, Swansea, Wedgwood, Whieldon Ware, Willow Ware, Enoch Wood, Ralph Wood, Worcester.

Biscuit Jar
   6" h, Imari design, wicker handle, ironstone (A) **25.00**
   6½" h, four Dutch girls, multicolored middle section, SP top, handle, and rim **75.00**
   Pink and white blossoms, pale orange ground, advertising on bottom ... **35.00**

Bone Dish, Quail pattern, blue and white, pr **20.00**
Bottle, 10" h, emb busts of Queen Victoria and Duchess of Kent, tan glazed pottery (A) **25.00**
Bough Pot, 6⅞" w, oval cartouche with gilt scroll and seaweed, green dot ground, pierced cov, c1800, "Pinxton" (A) **575.00**
Bowl
   5¾" d, cov, orange and gold bands, stylized birds, flowers, and willow, dbl handles (A) **75.00**
   7¼" d, black basalt, classical figure groups frieze (A) **100.00**
   9" d
     Central flowerhead, ext. with floral sprays, late 18th C **150.00**
     Painted bands of flowers, gilt foliage borders, recumbent spaniel, scroll handles, porcelain, c1810 (A) **140.00**
   10¼" d, chinoiserie figures on terrace, famille rose palette, late 18th C **150.00**
   11" d, stylized painted florals, gray glazed ground, c1925, "Carter, Stabler & Adams, Poole, England" .. **35.00**
   11¾" d, blue floral int., gray ground, c1940, "Bernard Leach" **150.00**
Bust, 10" h, Wesley, c1790, Yorkshire, unmarked **900.00**
Cake Set, ftd 6¼" h cake plate, two 3¼" h compotes, twelve 11" d plates, center reserves of polychrome floral sprays, cobalt and gilt border with ten oval floral reserves, cream, and gilt scalloped rim, early 19th C (A) **425.00**
Card Tray, 8" l, central flower, dark red ground, porcelain **30.00**
Chamber Pot, pink roses and ribbons, green leaves, white ground, "Booths China, Silicon, England" **65.00**
Charger
   12" d, Imari, cobalt blue flowers, scrolls, Eng reg mark **145.00**
   13½" d, tin glazed Chinese blue and white design, 18th C (A) **200.00**
   13⅞" d, central chrysanthemum, border of blue and white flowering trees (A) **375.00**
Cheese Dish
   6¼" d, cov, molded Art Nouveau style florals, multicolored (A) **20.00**
   10" l, cobalt and gilt floral design (A) **50.00**
Compote, 8½" d, 4½" h, hp, rose and floral pattern, gold outlined scalloped foot and rim, "Devonshire" **32.00**
Cream Jug, spirally molded, blue painted buildings in landscape, c1760 (A) **50.00**

Creamer
 4" h, polychrome floral enamels, porcelain (A) **10.00**
 4⅛" h, floral band, enamels and gilt, porcelain (A) **20.00**
 4¼" h, vertical ribbing, basalt body, imp "J. Glass" (A) **45.00**
 4⅜" h, black and gold floral enamels, Oriental Export style, porcelain (A) **20.00**
 4½" h, black transfers of children and fawn, stag on reverse, purple luster trim, porcelain (A) **30.00**
 4¾" h, polychrome floral design (A) **10.00**
 5" h
  Red transfer, Oriental scene, polychrome, "H. & S." (A) **15.00**
  Small floral on sides, wavy line at rim, helmet shape, porcelain (A) **45.00**
Cup and Saucer
 Black transfer
  Country house, purple luster trim, porcelain (A) **30.00**
  South Sea Island scene, enamels (A) **20.00**
 Crest, gilt swags, and diamond pattern border, apricot ground, c1850 (A) **155.00**
 Green, red, and gilt floral motif (A) . **40.00**
 Magenta enameled florals, porcelain (A) **10.00**
 Magenta transfer of "Faith, Hope, and Charity," polychrome enamels, porcelain (A) **10.00**
 Oriental Floral Dec
  Multicolored, enamels, porcelain (A) **5.00**
  Polychrome, gilt, porcelain (A) ... **30.00**
  Red and blue enamels, porcelain (A) **10.00**
 Pink and purple floral swags, gaudy polychrome enamels (A) **35.00**
 Polychrome, floral design (A) **10.00**
 Purple Luster
  Resist, floral design, ochre stripe (A) **15.00**
  Strawberry design, red, and green enamels, porcelain (A) **40.00**
 Shaped genre reserves in gilt scrollwork, late 18th C (A) **165.00**
 Shell, seaweed, and floral design, polychrome enamels, porcelain (A) . **30.00**
Dessert Service
 15 pcs, two compotes, thirteen 9" d plates, ivy vine and gilt design (A) **22.50**
 18 pcs, two compotes on openwork bases, two pairs of dishes, eight plates, borders of flower panels, flowing blue scrolls, rococo scroll edge (A) **285.00**
 23 pcs, central bouquet of painted flowers, borders molded with fruiting vine and flowerheads, lavender and gilt, c1825 ....**1,850.00**

Figure
 2¼" h, cats, seated on pillows, multicolored, porcelain, "anchor" marks, pr (A) **75.00**
 7" h, dairyman and milkmaid, holding detached wooden pails, multicolored, green circ base, porcelain, pr **135.00**
 7" w, huntsman, gray horse, two hounds, stepped rect base, flat back, porcelain (A) **165.00**
Garden Seat
 15" h, hexagonal top, pierced base, overall blue chrysanthemums and gilt, porcelain (A) **325.00**
 18¾" h, octagonal, convex sides, black transfer band of light orange classic Greek figures, dark orange ground, porcelain (A) **200.00**
Honey Pot, 5⅛" h, painted beehives and bees in trees, "Wemyss" **140.00**
Inkwell, 2⅜" h, painted band of flowers, gilt borders, gilt top, flowers, and leaves, drum shape, porcelain (A) .. **75.00**
Invalid Feeder, 7¾" h, emb head of queen, and foliage, mottled tan and cream (A) **125.00**
Jardiniere
 8" h, red, yellow, and blue chrysanthemums, green foliage, c1900, "Wemyss" (A) **325.00**
 9" l, emb stylized Oriental leaves and flowers, turquoise glaze, faience, c1904, "Burmantofts Faience, Made In England" **75.00**
 13" l, black ext., white int., pottery, "Dartmouth, Devon" **200.00**
 33" h, cobalt, blue, and orange florals, white ground, molded scalloped rim, baluster base, late 19th C (A) **400.00**
Jardiniere Stand, 20" h, octagonal top, sides molded with portrait reserves, Gothic style blossoms, late 19th C (A) **190.00**
Jug
 6⅝" h
  Painted country house by river, bouquet divided by gilt "JSH," gilt loop pattern border with flowers and dots, gilt gadrooned rim, fluted oviform shape, porcelain, c1830 (A) **200.00**
  Upper part glazed in mottled olive green, buff ground, 16th C (A) . **36.00**
 9" h, molded acanthus leaves, gilt dentil rim, loop handle, c1830, porcelain (A) **30.00**
 9¼" h, 5¼" d, emb aqua leaves, dark red ground, gold branches, and berries, pottery **65.00**
Loving Cup, 5⅜" h, gold "Bell Hotel" in floral frame, reverse with "A Pledge

of better times" in frame, dbl handles, porcelain **125.00**

Mug
2¼" h, purple luster floral design, red, and green, porcelain (A) **30.00**
2½" h, child's, "Little Boy Blue" scene, rhyme, "England" **65.00**
4" h, painted mountain landscape, sq gilt cartouche, border of gilt and iron-red anthemion, gilt line rim, porcelain, c1800 (A) **170.00**

Oil Bottle, 5" h, Imari design, multicolored, English reg mark **40.00**

Pitcher
4⅝" h, yellow transfer of Chinese design, dark brown ground (A) **35.00**
6¼" h
   Emb tavern scene, light green pottery, "William, F. W. P. & Co" (A) **10.00**
   Yellow transfer of Chinese design, dark brown ground (A) **70.00**
6¾" h, multicolored floral design on sides, iron-red rim, early 19th C (A) **180.00**
6⅞" h, melon ribs and ivy, light green pottery (A) **20.00**
7⅜" h, emb grain design, cream colored pottery, pewter lid (A) **45.00**
7⅞" h, emb hunt scene, unglazed buff clay, brown glaze at top, imp "Turner" (A) **100.00**
8½" h
   Emb ivy design, light green pottery (A) **32.00**
   Floral motifs, turquoise, orange, and black, geometric shape, pottery, c1925, "Wadenheath" . . . **60.00**
8⅝" h, emb florals, green pottery, English reg mark (A) **10.00**

Pitcher, 6" h, puce and brown tulips, green leaves, white pebble ground, blue rim, $65.00.

9⅜" h, floral dec, green and gilt, white, magenta, and beige, vining handle, porcelain (A) **125.00**

Plaque
4½" d, mother with child in lap, high relief, basalt, "Mayer" **300.00**
10⅜" d, painted vase of roses, flowers, and fruits, gilt border, porcelain, (A) **200.00**
11" w, 13", painted scene of "Chillingham on Wye" and river passing through valley, multicolored, giltwood frames, pr (A) **300.00**
21" sq, painting of three pre-Raphaelite women, multicolored, porcelain,, sgd "Henry Ryland" **3,300.00**

Plate
7½" d, purple luster floral design, polychrome enamels, porcelain (A) . **10.00**
8" d, tin glazed blue and white floral design (A) **75.00**
8½" d
   Imari, blue pot of flowers, red, and green trees and grass on border **65.00**
   Imari, typical design and colors, set of 12 (A) **550.00**
8⅝" d
   Center hunting scene, gilt line circ cartouche, green ground, late 19th C, pr (A) **80.00**
   Painted "Rievaulx Abbey Yorkshire," gilt well, molded rim, gilt foliage, sgd "Doe & Rogers" . . . **95.00**
8¾" d, wide border of floral sprays, gold and pink, gold and cobalt rim, c1860 (A) **8.00**
9" d
   Blue transfer, Daffodil pattern **18.00**
   Center red and pink hp roses, green leaves, wide border, scalloped and ornate emb ozier, robin's egg blue band, "Simpsons," set of 12 **125.00**
   Painted floral sprays, multicolored, gadrooned rim, gilt accents, porcelain **35.00**
   Polychrome floral design, green rim, "T. Peace & Son, 23 Ludgate Hill, London" (A) **20.00**
   Tin glazed blue and white center medallion of flowers, border flowers, late 18th C (A) **100.00**
   Tin glazed center, mulberry flowers, late 18th C (A) **100.00**
9¼" d
   Scattered pink roses alternating with blue sprigs, lobed gold rim, "Pinxton" **125.00**
   Tin glazed blue and white central pagoda, cross border, late 18th C (A) **75.00**

9⅜" d, polychrome enameled roses, gilt trim, porcelain (A) **20.00**

9½" d, different multicolored landscape scenes, cobalt border, c1892, "Bodley," set of 12 ......**1,200.00**

10" d

"Blue Onion" pattern **15.00**

Imari, multicolored base of flowers, orange and cobalt scalloped border **80.00**

Transfer of Disraeli, earthenware, octagonal (A) **275.00**

Platter

6½" l, 4½" w, Imari, typical colors, English reg mark **160.00**

13" l, 10" w, black transfer, "Eglington Castle on the Clyde," dbl handle, four feet, c1820, "Belle Vue Pottery" **120.00**

Potpourri Basket, 4½" d, two gilt scroll panels, painted landscapes, reserved on claret ground, encrusted flowers and leaves on handle, rim, and cov **100.00**

Potpourri Bowl, two 7⅝" h bowls, one 9½" h, applied multicolored flowers on body, pierced cov, dbl twig handles, foliate molded feet, c1835, set of 3 (A) **935.00**

Sauce Tureen, 8" w, attached undertray, colored and printed bouquets, blue ground, matte blue bands, gilt, animal head finial, c1845, pr (A) **155.00**

Scent Bottle

3⅜" h, modeled as girl, flowered dress, playing hurdy–gurdy, circ mound base, c1751, "Girl in a Swing" period (A) **1,575.00**

3½" h, necks with bands of pink roses between white beads, gilt florals, matte blue ground, porcelain, c1820 (A) **235.00**

5½" h, cov, painted lovers, quatrefoil panels, gilt scroll and hatched quatrefoil cartouches, lavender-blue ground, scales, flat pear shape, flower finial, c1880, porcelain (A) **80.00**

Soup Plate

10¼" d, brown printed and multicolored painted flowering rockwork and peonies, "REAL STONE CHINA," set of 11 (A) **200.00**

10⅝" d, centers and borders painted with flower sprays, wavy rims, set of 3 (A) **85.00**

Sugar, 6⅞" w, cov, Imari style, panels of shrubs, blue cartouches, divided by iron-red trellis, iron-red ground, c1880, "Pinxton," (A) **430.00**

Sugarboat, 7" l, stylized black pattern, orange band, pattern #125, porcelain (A) **30.00**

Syrup Pitcher, 6⅜" h, emb flowers and vines, white, pottery, dated 1846 (A) **40.00**

Tea Service

6" h teapot, 4⅝" h creamer, 4½" h sugar, cobalt blue butterfly handles, sq shape, dark blue flowers and bird dec, porcelain **200.00**

6⅛" h teapot, 6½" h creamer, 6½" h sugar, 6¾" d waste bowl, six cups and saucers, Imari design, damaged, marked (A) **55.00**

10" w teapot and stand, dish, cream jug, cov sugar, waste bowl, five coffee cups, tea cups, saucers, gilt band of flowers, seeded ground, fluted bodies, c1840 (A) **600.00**

Teapot, four cups and saucers, Imari **300.00**

Teabowl and Saucer

Polychrome enamel floral design (A) **40.00**

Red and green enameled florals (A) . **35.00**

Sepia printed pastoral scene, gilt rims with foliage (A) **65.00**

Teapot

5⅞" h, hp, stylized tree in blue cartouche, reserved on coral ground, gilt and white plants, gilt line rims, ribbed tapered cone finial, c1800, "Pinxton" (A) **515.00**

9¼" h, basketweave, emb, basalt, "Widow Warburton" finial (A) ... **300.00**

11½" h, "Bargeware," applied naive colored florets and flowers around label, imp "To Mother From Luke, 1884," brown glazed ground, teapot knob, Derbyshire (A) **320.00**

Teapot Stand, 7⅛" d, black printed band of corn, gilt rim, "Pinxton" **35.00**

Tray

10¼" l, painted group of roses, rect, chamfered corners, "Wemyss" ... **50.00**

13" l, 5¾" w, multicolored Viking ship, outlined in gold, luster wares, luster ground, dbl handles, "Maling" **75.00**

Tureen, 8¼" l, stand, melon form, green, brown, and yellow glaze, leaf molded green glazed stand, branch handle, mid 18th C (A) **600.00**

Umbrella Stand, 24" h, Imari, orange, blue, and gold florals between moth and chrysanthemum border, late 19th C (A) **625.00**

Vase

3½" h, hp, orchid panels framed in deep green, "ENGLAND" **175.00**

4" h, Imari, floral dec, typical colors, modern mark (A) **10.00**

4⅞" h, painted basket of flowers and bouquets, gilt borders pierced with hearts and diamonds, porcelain, c1820, pr (A) **115.00**

5" h, famille rose style flowering chrysanthemum, pink ground, gilt rim, ovoid, porcelain, c1840 .... **70.00**

5⅛" h, famille rose style chrysanthemum, pink ground, gilt rim, porcelain, c1840, pr **70.00**

6⅝" h, reserved and painted, shells and seaweed, blue ground, gilt and white neck bands, white and gilt circ foot, c1830 (A) **100.00**

8" h, large white rose, applied flowers, white ground **40.00**

8¼" h
Blue enamel flower sprays, blue line rim, urn shape, fixed ring handles, pierced cov, c1800, "Pinxton" (A) **350.00**
Sprays of large red roses and foliage, turquoise neck border, ovoid, c1900, "Wemyss Ware" (A) **190.00**

8¾" h, large applied flowers and leaves, green and gilt scroll handles, pr (A) **35.00**

9¼" h, painted band of garden flowers, pink and magenta ground, rim and lower section with gilt scrolling foliage, molded white flowerheads, pierced gilt scroll handles, porcelain, c1815 (A) **100.00**

9⅝" h, gilt flowers and birds, ivory ground, putti form handles, four sq feet, pr **65.00**

9⅞" h
Applied flowers, multicolored accents, light yellow and white ground, pierced necks, handles with multicolored modeled parrots, pr **325.00**
Pink and gold stripes, campana shape, dbl handles ending in vine terminals, molded rococo foot, pierced cov, rose finial, porcelain **65.00**

10" h, molded scroll panels painted with landscape on front, flowers on reverse, reserved on green and gilt ground, pr (A) **140.00**

12¼" h, painted landscape panel, framed in gold, apple-green ground, porcelain, bottle shape .. **80.00**

24½" h, Imari, typical colors, late 19th C 1,500.00

36" h, Moorish type polychrome floral design, green, pink, and gilt, filigree finial, elongated neck, bulbous body, c1920 (A) **130.00**

Waste Bowl
6" d, polychrome floral designs, porcelain (A) **35.00**

9¾" d, floral designs, porcelain (A) . **15.00**

Whistle, 3½" l, bird shape, white porcelain (A) **12.50**

FAIRINGS AND TRINKET BOXES

Locket, Elbogen, Germany, now Czechoslovakia
c1860–1890

History: Fairings, common during the Victorian era, were small porcelain groups of gaily colored human and animal china figures designed to catch the eye with their humor and sentimentality. One figural, captioned "The last in bed to put out the light," shows a man and woman bumping heads as they jumped into bed while a lighted candle stands on a table nearby. "Five o'clock tea" features humanized cats at a tea party. Fairings were made to be given away as prizes or purchased at English fairs.

Although fairings were associated with England, they were actually made by Springer and Oppenheimer of Locket, Elbogen, Germany, now Czechoslovakia. Themes included courtship and marriage scenes, events in the lives of the people, war, politics and the law, children at work and play, and animals behaving like people. Most fairings had inscriptions written in English. Often the inscriptions were naive or intended to be risque.

Colors mainly were shades of pink and blue with the inscriptions in black. Early examples were usually 3½ to 4½" high with plain, undecorated bases. Gilt was used sparingly. After 1890 the colors became more garish.

Fairings are made of white heavy paste. Most have numbers incised or impressed beneath their bases, though the earliest and best examples have no numbers.

References: W.S. Bristowe, *Victorian China Fairings*, Taplinger Publishing Co., Inc., 1965.

Trinket Box, 4½" h, gilt trim, $120.00.

Fairing

2½" h, "Evening Exercise," pig on
chamber pot **60.00**
3" h, "Returning at 5 o'clock in the
Morning," woman spanking child   **65.00**
3¼" h
"Come Pussy Come" (A) **30.00**
"Go Away Mama, I Am Busy" . . .   **40.00**
"Oft in the Stilly Night" (A) **25.00**
"The Last in Bed Put Out the Light"
(A) **30.00**
3½" h, "The Night Before Christmas"   **45.00**
4" h
"Morning Prayer" (A) **25.00**
"Who Said Rats?," cat seated on
bed **110.00**
"God Bless Our Home" **50.00**

Trinket Box

1¾" h, dresser, mirror, drum and blue
horn on top, gold trim **75.00**
2⅛" h, piano, book, painting, and
flowers (A) **45.00**
2¼" h
Bottle and bowl, draped crest (A) .   **20.00**
Child looking in mirror with vase
(A) **25.00**
Dresser, mirror frame, cross, and
crown (A) **25.00**
Three boys sitting on brown log,
arms and legs folded **100.00**
2½" h
Boy, dog lying in lap (A) **55.00**
Boy, trumpet on lid **50.00**
Brown and white dog, seated on
green cushion, ball and horn . .   **100.00**
Goose preening back, damaged
base (A) **50.00**
2¾" h, fireplace, mirror, Madonna in
blue robe, gold crown, holding in-
fant Jesus **100.00**
3" h
Baby, hatching from egg on lid,
wings damaged (A) **30.00**
Dog, sitting on pile of "Punch"
books, wearing rose hat with
plume **200.00**
Girl, dog on lid **50.00**
Red fox, duck in mouth (A) **100.00**
3¼" h, girl, table and painting on top
of table (A) **50.00**
3½" h
Angel, sleeping child, blue, puce,
and white, gold trim **38.00**
Child at desk, mirror **70.00**
Dresser set, hand mirror, two per-
fumes and hair comb (A) **50.00**
Lamb, cross, deer head on base (A)   **60.00**
Piano, open music book, gold trim,
white ground **100.00**
Recumbent fox on lid, foliage,
landscape body **160.00**
Stove, china cupboard with dishes

on top, blue, gold trim, white
ground **100.00**
Teapot, coffeepot, two cups and
saucers on lid (A) **50.00**
3¾" h
Clock, pistol, and book, gilt and
enamels on lid (A) **20.00**
Dresser top, shelves, two pitchers,
cup, and saucer (A) **40.00**
4" h
Baby, lying on quilted coverlet,
white, gilt trim, green woven
base, unmarked **45.00**
Dressing table, mirror, two boxes,
candle on lid **65.00**
Fireplace, girl, mirror frame on lid   **75.00**
Fireplace, "Little Red Riding
Hood" and wolf **65.00**
Girl, dog jumping through hoop,
part of hoop missing (A) **20.00**
Girl, doll, trumpet on lid **75.00**
Wash stand, pitcher and bowl on
lid **75.00**
Wash stand, sword and bugle on
lid **75.00**
4¼" h
Girl, sitting on drum (A) **50.00**
Ship, mirror back, mirror missing
(A) **50.00**
4½" h
Child, seated on fireplace mantle,
looking in mirror, pots on man-
tle, multicolored accents **70.00**
Fruit, open picture frame back (A)   **50.00**
4¾" h, blond girl holding umbrella on
lid **65.00**
5" h
Dresser top, two bottles, damaged
(A) **30.00**
Fireplace, clown seated on drum
on lid **65.00**
7" h
Boy, seated in front of mirror, book,
long pipe **100.00**
Young girl in pram, multicolored,
Conta & Boehme **275.00**

FISCHER

Herend, Hungary
c1839–Present

History: Moritz Fischer established a porcelain
manufactory at Herend, Hungary, about 1839.
His factory was noted for the high quality of its
reproductions of Chinese porcelains and 18th
century European porcelains from Meissen, Vi-

enna, Capodimonte, and Sevres. Reticulated vases, ewers, and chimney ornaments also were made in very bright enamel colors, almost majolica–like in appearance. Oriental patterns such as famille rose, famille verte, and Imari decorations were imitated by Herend craftsmen. They employed no independent designers, only craftsmen.

When the Imperial Vienna factory closed in 1864, Fischer received the right to use the patterns and models selected by Emperor Franz Joseph for continued use. These old Vienna molds and patterns were marked with a beehive. Many wares were exported to the United States.

Fischer was raised to the nobility and used the name Farkashazi in 1865. Fischer was succeeded by his sons. The factory failed in 1874 and then underwent a series of changes in ownership.

New prosperity was achieved under Jeno Farkashazi, the grandson of Moritz. The factory was taken over by the state in 1948 and continues to produce hard paste porcelain dinnerware, vases, and figures similar to those of Meissen and Sevres.

Museums: Victoria & Albert Museum, London, England.

Ewer, 15½" h, hp, multicolored tavern scene, poppies on reverse, cobalt ground, gilt handle and spout, "J. Fischer-Budapest," $300.00.

Bowl, 5¼" d, spaghetti strand, braided rim, hp cherries in center 35.00
Box, cov, 6½" l, 3½" h, green chrysanthemums and butterflies, gold, white ground, chrysanthemum and leaf finial 100.00
Ewer
   7½" h, cherubs on front panel, cobalt, gold trim, gold handle 200.00
   9½" h, gold beads and roundels, blue and beige ground 200.00

10½" h, stylized design, dark orange, turquoise, and pink, cobalt handle, gold accents, ftd 150.00
13" h, floral design, multicolored (A) 80.00
16½" h, reticulated body and handle, oblong center medallion–type pattern, rose, green, and blue shades, gold accents 300.00
Figure
   4", shoe, multicolored 40.00
   13" h, Madame Deury, multicolored, sgd "Legeti" 600.00
Jug, 5¾" d, 9¾" h, Japanese style, multicolored chrysanthemums and leaves, fan shaped reserves with butterflies, mottled blue ground 200.00
Mug
   4⅛" h, "Eggshell," painted famille rose style, panels of Oriental figures in garden 80.00
   5½" h, multicolored peacock and floral design, blue "Fischer, Budapest" 100.00
Planter, 7½" l, open reticulated body, multicolored, gilt trim 325.00
Scent Bottle, 6" h, multicolored and reticulated, steeple stopper, "J. Fischer, Budapest" 100.00
Tea Service
   6 pcs, teapot, creamer, cov sugar, 8¾" d cake plate, cup and saucer, Kakiemon style radiating panels of stylized florals or scrolling florals on white or iron-red ground, 19th C, imp "HEREND" (A) 600.00
   16 pcs, teapot, creamer, cov sugar, six plates, cups, and saucers, tray with green branch handles, overall floral design, white ground, red floral finials, gilt outlined teapot spout, c1930 . . . . 750.00
Teapot, 3½" h, painted, multicolored flowers, bullet shape, grotesque spout 40.00
Vase
   3¾" h, heron and arabesques, cream and cobalt, unmarked 150.00
   4¾" h, blue, magenta, and tan mosaic leaf and floral design, cream ground, incised gold rim, bulbous body, narrow neck 185.00
   11" h, three open work panels on top, light blue ext., gold int., gourd shape 160.00
   13" h, "Chinese Bouquet," rose, cobalt, gold, and green enamels, pilgrim shape 165.00
   18⅞" h, painted on each side with Near Eastern hunters in landscapes, raised gilt borders, pilgrim shape, c1900, imp "Fischer/Budapest," pr (A) 935.00

STOKE POTTERY
GRIMWADES

COLONIAL POTTERY
& W C°
STOKE ENGLAND

THOMAS FURNIVAL
& SONS

ALLERTONS

ENGLAND

FLOW BLUE

**Staffordshire, England
Early Victorian 1835–1850s
Mid Victorian 1860s–1870s
Late Victorian 1880s, 1890s, and the
early 1900s**

History: "Flow" or "Flowing" Blue was developed for commercial consumption in the 1820s by Josiah Wedgwood. Flow Blue was marketed in many countries including France, Germany, Holland, and the U.S. The peak production period was from the mid-1800s to the early 1900s.

The Flow Blue process occurs when a transfer printed design, originally in cobalt oxide, receives volatizing agents such as lime of chloride or ammonia causing the pattern to "bleed" during the glaze firing stage. The cobalt when first applied is brown in color and changes to a deep blue during the firing. The degree of flowing varies considerably with some designs barely discernable while others show a slight hazing of the pattern.

The earliest patterns were Oriental in style, named in most cases by the manufacturer. These names often were incorporated with the maker's mark. Scenics and florals were popular during the Victorian period; some Art Nouveau designs were also produced. Most designs were applied by transfers. In some cases, hand painted designs were done.

Though some of the designs were registered, it is not unusual to find the same name used by two different companies for two entirely different designs. Manufacturers also had a habit of changing design names. Over 1,500 patterns were manufactured during the peak years of Flow Blue production.

Early Flow Blue is characterized by a dense coloration. Later pieces had a softer look to them. By the mid-Victorian era, colors as well as gold embellishments were added to enhance the designs.

Many early examples were made of stoneware, but porcelain and semi-porcelain also served as bodies for the Flow Blue patterns. By the latter half of the 19th century, semi-porcelain was the material of choice. The designs of this period usually were sharper and cleaner. The body design was more elaborate.

Back stamps usually provide the pattern name and initials or name of the maker. Often the location of the factory is included. Transfer marks outnumber all other types. Marks with a pattern name date after 1810.

References: Sylvia Dugger Blake, *Flow Blue*, Wallace-Homestead, 1971; Mary Gaston, *The Collector's Encyclopedia of Flow Blue China*, Collector Books, 1983; Veneita Mason, *Popular Patterns of Flow Blue China with Prices*, Wallace-Homestead, 1982; Petra Williams, *Flow Blue China, An Aid to Identifications*, Fountain House East, 1971; Petra Williams, *Flow Blue China II*, Fountain House East, 1973; Petra Williams, *Flow Blue China & Mulberry Ware*, Fountain House East, rev. ed., 1981.

Museums: Margaret Woodbury Strong Museum, Rochester, NY.

REPRODUCTION ALERT: New Flow Blue has been manufactured by Blakeney Pottery Limited in Stoke-on-Trent since 1968. Objects are termed "Victorian Reproductions" and are made with large blue roses in many forms. Evidence shows that some of these items have been sold as old.

Collecting Hints: The center for collecting Flow Blue is in the United States. Even though the vast majority of Flow Blue was made in England, the English do not attach much antique value to Flow Blue since it was mass produced, transfer decorated, and inexpensive. Since most was exported to the U.S. during the 19th century, it is not prevalent in the English market.

Miniatures and children's dishes are scarce in Flow Blue because not many examples were made. Art or decorative items are harder to find than ordinary table and utilitarian wares.

"Abbey" pattern
Bowl
    7" sq, "George Jones & Son" **50.00**
    8" d, ftd, "George Jones & Son" . **150.00**
    13" d, "George Jones & Son" **175.00**
Cake Plate
    9½" d, "George Jones & Son" ... **48.00**
    10¼" d, "George Jones & Son" ... **40.00**
Chocolate Pot, 6" h, "George Jones &
    Son" **85.00**
Creamer, "George Jones & Son" ... **30.00**

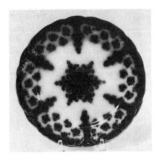

Left, plate, 7″ d, "Elsa," marked "W. & E. Corn," $45.00; center, plate, 10″ d, "Sabroan," unmarked, $85.00; right, sugar bowl, 8″ h, "Tonquin," $195.00.

Cup and Saucer, "George Jones & Son" 40.00
Fruit Bowl, 9⅜″ d, "George Jones & Son" 180.00
Jam Jar, cov, 4½″ h, "George Jones & Son" 75.00
Plate
  7″ d, "George Jones & Son" 20.00
  7⅜″ d, "George Jones & Son" ... 18.00
  8¼″ d, "George Jones & Son" ... 10.00
  10¼″ d, "George Jones & Son" .. 40.00
Teapot, "George Jones & Son" 70.00
Trivet, 5″ sq, "George Jones & Son" 45.00
"Alaska" pattern
  Bowl, 10″ d, "W. H. Grindley" 50.00
  Egg Cups, "W. H. Grindley", set of 6 180.00
  Gravy Boat, "W. H. Grindley" 65.00
  Plate, 9″ d, "W. H. Grindley" 40.00
  Platter
    12″ l, "W. H. Grindley" 60.00
    16″ l, "W. H. Grindley" 125.00
"Albany" pattern
  Gravy Boat, "W. H. Grindley" 60.00
  Plate
    8″ d, "W. H. Grindley" 35.00
    9″ d
      "Johnson Bros" 47.00
      "W. H. Grindley" 48.00
    10⅛″ d, "Johnson Bros" 45.00
  Platter, 12″ l, "W. H. Grindley" 55.00
  Soup Plate, 10″ d, "Johnson Bros" .. 45.00
"Amoy" pattern
  Plate
    7¼″ d, "Davenport" 65.00
    8¼″ d, "Davenport" 75.00
    9½″ d, imp "anchor" mark 85.00
    10½″ d, "Davenport" 95.00
"Andorra" pattern
  Gravy Boat, "Johnson Bros" 75.00
  Platter, 11″ l, 7″ w, "Johnson Bros" . 45.00
"Anemone" pattern
  Plate
    10¼″ d, "Bishop & Stonier" 55.00
    10½″ d, "Bates & Bennet" 45.00
"Arabesque" pattern, plate, 9½″ d, "Mayer" 52.00

"Arcadia" pattern, plate, 10″ d, "Arthur Wilkinson" 35.00
"Argyle" pattern
  Bone Dish, "Ford & Sons" 28.00
  Gravy Boat, undertray, "W. H. Grindley" 75.00
  Plate
    9¾″ d, gold trim, "W. H. Grindley" 46.00
    10″ d, "W. H. Grindley" 45.00
  Platter
    15″ l, 10½″ w, gold trim, "W. H. Grindley" 100.00
    17″ l, 11″ w, "W. H. Grindley" .. 130.00
    17″ l, 12″ w, "W. H. Grindley" .. 50.00
  Sauce Tureen, cov, tray, matching ladle, "Ford & Son" 175.00
  Vegetable Bowl, cov, "W. H. Grindley" 175.00
  Vegetable Tureen
    11″ l, "W. H. Grindley" 90.00
    Covered, "Ford & Son" 165.00
  Waste Bowl, "W. H. Grindley" 45.00
"Ashburton" pattern
  Creamer and Sugar, "W. H. Grindley" 175.00
  Gravy Boat, "W. H. Grindley" 68.00
  Plate
    8″ d, "W. H. Grindley" 35.00
    9″ d, "W. H. Grindley" 38.00
  Tureen, cov, "W. H. Grindley" 200.00
"Asiatic Pheasants" pattern, plate, 9″ d, "John Meir & Son" 40.00
"Astoria" pattern
  Cup and Saucer, unmarked 50.00
  Shaving Mug, "Pitcairns" 80.00
"Athens" pattern
  Plate, 7″ d, "Grimmades Bros" 35.00
  Soap Dish, "W. Adams & Co" 115.00
"Atlanta" pattern
  Butter Pat, "New Wharf Pottery" ... 18.00
  Plate, 8″ d, "New Wharf Pottery" .. 28.00
"Baltic" pattern,
  Bowl, 12″ d, "W. H. Grindley" 100.00
  Plate, 10″ d, "W. H. Grindley" 40.00
  Platter, 16″ l, 12″ w, "W. H. Grindley" 135.00
"Barinet" pattern, platter, 16½″ l, "Sam-

uel Hancock & Sons, Made in England'' **200.00**
"Beauties of China" pattern, plate, 9½" d, "M. V. & Co." **65.00**
"Beauty Roses" pattern, creamer and sugar, "W. H. Grindley" **70.00**
"Belmont" pattern, plate, 7½" d, "J. H. Weatherby & Sons" **22.00**
"Bentick" pattern, plate, 8½" d, "Cauldon" **45.00**
"Bisley" pattern, plate, 10" d, "W. H. Grindley" **30.00**
"Blue Rose" pattern
  Cup and Saucer, "W. H. Grindley" . **35.00**
  Plate, 7" d, "W. H. Grindley" **18.00**
"Brunswick" pattern
  Cup and Saucer, "Wood & Son" ... **40.00**
  Plate, 9" d, "N. W. P." **45.00**
"Burleigh" pattern, plate, 9½" d, "Burgess & Leigh" **30.00**
"Cabul" pattern, handleless cup and saucer, "T. Edwards" **85.00**
"Cambridge" pattern, plate, 8¾" d, "Alfred Meakin" **55.00**
"Candia" pattern, vegetable bowl, 11½" l, "Cauldon" **85.00**
"Canton" pattern, cup and saucer, unmarked **115.00**
"Carlton" pattern,
  Gravy Boat, "Samuel Alcock" **150.00**
  Plate, 9½" d, "Samuel Alcock" **60.00**
"Cashmere" pattern
  Creamer, "F. M. & Co." **200.00**
  Platter, 17" l, "F. M. & Co." **350.00**
"Cavendish" pattern
  Jug, 6⅝" h, octagonal, "Keeling & Co" **88.00**
  Vase, 11" h, "Keeling & Co" **150.00**
"Cecil" pattern, bown, 9" d, "Till & Son" **25.00**
"Celtic" pattern
  Bone dish, "W. H. Grindley" **45.00**
  Cup and Saucer **75.00**
  Gravy Boat, "W. H. Grindley" **42.00**
  Platter, 19" l, "W. H. Grindley" **135.00**
"Chantrey" pattern, soup bowl, 10" d, "B. W. M. & Co" **75.00**
"Chapoo" pattern
  Plate
    4½" d, "J. Wedgwood" **55.00**
    6½" d, "J. Wedgwood" **60.00**
    8¼" d, "J. Wedgwood" **80.00**
    9¼" d, "J. Wedgwood" **85.00**
    10" d, "J. Wedgwood" **95.00**
  Soup Plate, 10½" d, "J. Wedgwood" **110.00**
  Teabowl and Saucer, "J. Wedgwood" **130.00**
"Chatsworth" pattern, tureen, cov, 12" l, "K. & Co. Late Meyers" **50.00**
"Chein-Si" pattern
  Plate
    6½" d, unmarked **125.00**

7½" d, "Maddock" **65.00**
8½" d, "J. Meir" **75.00**
9" d, "I. M." **80.00**
9½" d, "Maddock" **110.00**
"Cheswick" pattern
  Cup and Saucer, "Ridgway" **45.00**
  Gravy Boat, "Ridgway" **75.00**
"Chinese" pattern
  Platter, 10½" l, imp "WEDGWOOD" **20.00**
  Tray, 14½" d, "Dimmock" **225.00**
"Ching" pattern, plate, 9" d, "Davenport anchor" mark **80.00**
"Chusan" pattern
  Cup and Saucer, handleless, "Clementson" **64.00**
  Plate, 7¼" d, "Clementson" **65.00**
"Claremont" pattern
  Cup and Saucer, "Johnson Bros" ... **40.00**
  Platter
    11" l, 7" w, "Johnson Bros" **40.00**
    18½" l, "Johnson Bros" **50.00**
"Clarence" pattern, plate, 6" d, "W. H. Grindley" **25.00**
"Clarissa" pattern
  Bone Dish, "Johnson Bros" **45.00**
  Butter Pat **15.00**
"Clifton" pattern, plate, 9½" d, "W. H. Grindley" **40.00**
"Coburg" pattern
  Plate
    7" d, "J. E." **40.00**
    10" d, "J. Edwards" **65.00**
    10½" d, "John Edwards" **65.00**
  Platter, 16" l, 12" w, "John Edwards" **160.00**
"Colonial" pattern, plate, 9" d, "J. & G. Meakin" **30.00**
"Conway" pattern
  Bowl
    8" d, "N. W. P." **60.00**
    9" d, "N. W. P." **45.00**
  Plate
    9" d, "N. W. P." **32.00**
    10" d, "N. W. P." **50.00**
  Platter
    10" l, "N. W. P." **85.00**
    10½" l, 7¾" w, "N. W. P." **85.00**
  Vegetable Bowl, 9", "New Wharf Pottery" **60.00**
"Countess" pattern, plate, 8" d, "W. H. Grindley" **32.0**
"Crumlin" pattern
  Gravy Boat and Undertray, "Myott, Son & Co" **100.00**
  Plate, 10" d, "Myott" **45.00**
"Dahlia" pattern
  Plate
    6¾" d, "Upper Hanley" **10.00**
    8½" d, "Upper Hanley" **65.00**
"Dainty" pattern
  Cake Plate, 10½" d, shaped dbl handles, "John Maddock & Son" **85.00**

Vegetable Tureen, cov, "John Maddock & Son" **200.00**
"Daisy" pattern
Cake Stand, pedestal, "Burgess & Leigh" **200.00**
Creamer and Sugar, "Burgess & Leigh" **190.00**
Cup and Saucer, "Burgess & Leigh" **42.00**
Plate
9" d, "Burgess & Leigh" **30.00**
10" d, "B & L" **75.00**
Vegetable Bowl, 10" d, "Burgess & Leigh" **45.00**
"Davenport" pattern, cake plate, ftd, "Longport" **75.00**
"Del Monte" pattern, plate, 9" d, "Johnson Bros" **30.00**
"Delft" pattern
Bone Dish, "The Brownfield Guild Pottery Society, Ltd," set of 8 .... **110.00**
Creamer, "Harcourt" **70.00**
Ladle, 10" l, "The Brownfield Guild Pottery Society, Ltd," **65.00**
Plate, 10" d, "Minton" **38.00**
Platter, 13½" l, 10¼" w, "Minton" . **75.00**
"Devon" pattern
Bone Dish, "Alfred Meakin" **45.00**
Plate, 7½" d, "Alfred Meakin" **20.00**
Platter, 10" l, 7½" w, "W. H. Grindley" **48.00**
Vegetable Bowl, cov, "Ford & Sons" **110.00**
"Diana" pattern
Dish, 8" l, 5" w, "J. & G. Meakin" . **20.00**
Gravy Boat, "J. & G. Meakin" **40.00**
Platter, 16" l, 12½" w, "J. & G. Meakin" **48.00**
"Dover" pattern, plate, 5⅞" d, "Ford & Sons" **20.00**
"Dresden" pattern, butter pat, "Johnson Bros" **12.50**
"Duchess" pattern
Bowl, 9½" d, scalloped edge, "D. B. & C." **60.00**
Gravy Boat and Undertray, "W. H. Grindley" **100.00**
Plate, 10" d, "W. H. Grindley" **28.00**
"Dudley" pattern, platter, 12" l
"Ford & Sons" **55.00**
"Myott, Son & Co" **55.00**
"Dundee"
Bone Dish, "Ridgway" **25.00**
Demitasse Cup and Saucer, "Ridgway" **65.00**
"Ebor" pattern, sauce dish, "Ridgway" **15.00**
"Eclipse" pattern, platter, 14" l, "Johnson Bros" **100.00**
"Egerton" pattern, tureen, cov, 8" h, "Royal Doulton" **75.00**
"Fairy Villas" pattern
Bowl
7¾" d, "W. Adams & Co." **45.00**
10" d, "W. Adams & Co." **80.00**

10⅛" d, "W. Adams & Co." **60.00**
Plate
7" d, "W. Adams & Co." **45.00**
8½" d, "W. Adams & Co." **48.00**
8¾" d, "W. Adams & Co." **70.00**
10" d, "W. Adams & Co." **45.00**
10½" d, "W. Adams & Co." **50.00**
"Fairy Villas II" pattern, plate, 8¾" d, "W. Adams & Co." **45.00**
"Florence" pattern, gravy boat and undertray, "Wood & Sons" **100.00**
"Florentine" pattern, platter, 13" l, "Bourne & Leigh" **55.00**
"Florida" pattern, bowl, 9" d, "Johnson Bros" **50.00**
"Formosa" pattern, soup plate, 9½" d, "T. J. & J. Mayer" **75.00**
"France" pattern, soup plate, 10¼" d, "Brown-Westhead, Moore & Co" .. **45.00**
"Geisha" pattern
Cup and Saucer, "Upper Hanley Potteries, Ltd" **38.00**
Plate
5" d, paneled daffodil border **40.00**
9" d, "Upper Hanley Potteries, Ltd" **40.00**
"Geneva" pattern, cheese dish, "Royal Doulton" **140.00**
"Georgia" pattern, plate
7" d, "Johnson Bros" **32.00**
10" d, "Johnson Bros" **55.00**
"Gironde" pattern
Bone Dish, "W. H. Grindley" **30.00**
Platter
15" l, "W. H. Grindley" **100.00**
19" l, 13½" w, "W. H. Grindley" **150.00**
"Gladys" pattern, cup and saucer, "N. W. P." **45.00**
"Glenwood" pattern, platter, 10½" l, 7½" w, "Johnson Bros" **28.00**
"Gothic" pattern, soup plate, 10½" d, "Furnival" **100.00**
"Grosvenor" pattern, cake plate, 10" d, "Myott & Son" **45.00**
"Haddon" pattern
Cup and Saucer, "W. H. Grindley" . **45.00**
Plate, 9" d, "W. H. Grindley" **45.00**
Platter, 14" l, "W. H. Grindley" **135.00**
"Harvard" pattern, platter, 14" l, "Alfred Meakin" **75.00**
"Hindustan" pattern
Plate
8½" d, "John Maddock" **65.00**
9½" d, "John Maddock" **80.00**
Platter, 13½" l, "John Maddock" ... **85.00**
"Holland" pattern
Plate
8⅞" d, "Johnson Bros" **35.00**
10" d, "Johnson Bros" **40.00**
Sugar, "Johnson Bros" **125.00**
"Hong Kong" pattern
Bowl, 7" d, "Charles Meigh" **48.00**
Plate, 10" d, "Charles Meigh" **80.00**

Relish Dish, "Charles Meigh" **125.00**
"Indian" pattern
Cake plate, "F. & R. Pratt" **175.00**
Plate
  8" d, "F. & R. Pratt" **45.00**
  9" d, "F. & R. Pratt" **60.00**
Sauce Tureen and Tray, "F. & R. Pratt" **150.00**
"Indian Jar" pattern
Plate
  6" d, "J. & J. F." **30.00**
  7" d, "J. & J. F." **22.00**
  9" d, "J. & J. F." **95.00**
  10½" d, "J. & J. F." **75.00**
Platter, 10¾" d, "J. & J. F." **150.00**
Sauce Dish, 5" d, "J. & J. F." **20.00**
Teabowl and Saucer, "Pratt" **110.00**
"Iris" pattern
Gravy Boat, "W. H. Grindley" **15.00**
Plate, 10" d, "Royal Pottery" **20.00**
"Italia" pattern, cup and saucer, "W. & E. Corn" **60.00**
"Ivanhoe" pattern
Butter Pat, "Wedgwood" **27.00**
Plate, 10" d, "Wedgwood, Etruria, England" **75.00**
"Ivy" pattern
Bowl, 10" d
  "Myott, Son & Co" **50.00**
  Unmarked **50.00**
"Japan" pattern, bowl, 10½" d, "J. & G. Meakin" **400.00**
"Jenny Lind" pattern, bow, 8" d, "Arthur J. Wilkinson" **32.00**
"Jewel" pattern
Cup and saucer, "Johnson Bros" ... **45.00**
Platter, 14" l, "Johnson Bros" **85.00**
"Josephine" pattern, vegetable bowl, cov, 10¾" d, ftd, "Ridgway" **160.00**
"Kaolin" pattern
Plate, 9½" d, "P. W. & Co" **65.00**
Platter, 13" l, 10¼" w, "P. W. & Co." **165.00**
"Kelvin" pattern
Bowl, 7" d, "Alfred Meakin" **48.00**
Plate, 9½" d, "Alfred Meakin" **40.00**
"Kenworth" pattern, relish tray, 8" l, "Johnson Bros" **50.00**
"Kirkee" pattern
Creamer, "Meir, Ironstone" **120.00**
Plate, 9½" d **95.00**
Platter, 15½" l, 12" w, "John Meir & Son" **200.00**
"Kyber" pattern
Plate
  6" d, "W. Adams & Co" **25.00**
  8¾" d, "W. Adams & Co" **26.00**
  9" d, "W. Adams & Co" **75.00**
  10" d, "W. Adams & Co" **60.00**
Platter
  10" l, "W. Adams & Co" **125.00**
  17" l, "W. Adams & Co" **300.00**

Tureen, cov, 10" l, dbl handles, "W. Adams & Co" **275.00**
Vegetable Bowl, cov, 10½" l, dbl handles **165.00**
Waste Bowl, "W. Adams & Co" **65.00**
"Ladas" pattern, platter, 14" l, 10¾" w, "Ridgway" **80.00**
"Lancaster" pattern
Plate, 9" d
  "Bishop & Stonier" **35.00**
  "N. W. P." **35.00**
  "W. & E. Corn" **35.00**
Saucer **18.00**
Platter, 14" l, "N. W. P." **90.00**
"Le Pavot" pattern, platter
  8¾" l, 4¾" w, "W. H. Grindley" ... **28.00**
  12½" l, "W. H. Grindley" **60.00**
"Leicester" pattern
Plate, 7¾" d, "S. H. & Sons" **42.00**
Platter, 17" l, "S. H. & Sons" (A) ... **100.00**
"Lily" pattern, vase, 9" h, "Adderley" **125.00**
"Linda" pattern
Butter Pat, "John Maddock & Sons, Ltd" **22.00**
Creamer, "John Maddock & Sons, Ltd" **55.00**
Cup and Saucer, "John Maddock & Sons, Ltd" **30.00**
Gravy Boat, "John Maddock & Sons, Ltd" **35.00**
Plate
  8" d, "John Maddock & Sons, Ltd" **20.00**
  9" d, "John Maddock & Sons, Ltd" **38.00**
Platter
  11½" l, "John Maddock & Sons, Ltd" **60.00**
  12½" l, "John Maddock & Sons, Ltd" **62.00**
  15" l, "John Maddock & Sons, Ltd" **65.00**
  17" l, "John Maddock & Sons, Ltd" **80.00**
  19" l, "John Maddock & Sons, Ltd" **90.00**
"Lobeilia" pattern, pitcher, 8¼" h, octagonal, "Phillips, Longport" **175.00**
"Loncarne" pattern, plate, 10" d, "Gibson & Sons" **12.00**
"Lonsdale" pattern
Plate, 8¾" d, "Ridgways-semi-porcelain" **45.00**
Platter, 15" l **80.00**
"Lorne" pattern
Bacon Platter, 10" l, "W. H. Grindley" **75.00**
Plate, 10" d
  "N. W. P." **60.00**
  "W. H. Grindley" **20.00**
"Lorraine" pattern, sauce tureen, cov, "Wood & Sons" **65.00**
"Lotus" pattern, bowl, 10½" d, "C. & H., Tunstall" **160.00**
"Lusitania" pattern, bowl, 8" d, "Wood & Sons" **60.00**

"Madras" pattern
Cake Plate, 10" d, "Doulton-Burslem" **45.00**
Gravy Boat, "Doulton-Burslem" **55.00**
Pitcher
7" h, "Doulton-Burslem" **120.00**
8½" h, "Doulton-Burslem" **125.00**
Plate
7" d, "N. W. P." **35.00**
9" d, "Doulton-Burslem" **35.00**
Platter
15¼" l, 12½" w, "Doulton-Bur-
slem" **175.00**
16" l, "Doulton-Burslem" **135.00**
Soup Bowl, 9" d, "N. W. P." **40.00**
Tureen, cov, tray, and matching ladle,
"Doulton-Burslem" **675.00**
Vegetable Bowl, 10" d, 7½" w,
"Doulton-Burslem" **45.00**
"Malta" pattern
Plate, 9½" d, "W. A. A. & Co" **20.00**
Soup Plate, 9½", "W. A. A. & Co" . **22.00**
"Mandarin" pattern, plate, 10" d,
"Poultney" **65.00**
"Manhattan" pattern, plate, 7½" d,
"Henry Alcock" **38.00**
"Manilla" pattern
Plate
7" d, "P. W. & Co. Stoneware" .. **48.00**
9" d, "P. W. & Co" **75.00**
10" d, "P. W. & Co" **60.00**
10½" d, 12 sided, ironstone, "P. W.
& Co" **75.00**
Relish Dish, "Podmore, Walker &
Co" **100.00**
"Marechal Niel" pattern
Butter Pat, "W. H. Grindley" **18.00**
Plate, 10" d, "W. H. Grindley" **55.00**
Platter, 16" l, "W. H. Grindley" **68.00**
Sugar, "W. H. Grindley" **95.00**
"Marguerite" pattern, sugar, "W. H.
Grindley" **95.00**
"Marie" pattern
Plate, 8¾" d, "W. H. Grindley" **25.00**
Platter, 16" l, "W. H. Grindley" **95.00**
"Martha" pattern, platter, 16½" l, 12"
w, "Bridgett & Bates" **50.00**
"Massina" pattern, plate, 10" d, "Caul-
don" **48.00**
"Meissen" pattern
Bowl, 5" d, "Libertas, Prussia" **18.00**
Butter Dish, cov, "Maddock" **155.00**
"Melbourne" pattern
Bowl, 9" d, "W. H. Grindley" **55.00**
Creamer, "W. H. Grindley" **85.00**
Gravy Boat and Undertray, "W. H.
Grindley" **125.00**
Plate
6¾" d, "W. H. Grindley" **15.00**
7½" d, "W. H. Grindley" **16.00**
7¾" d, "W. H. Grindley" **22.50**

8¾" d, "W. H. Grindley" **25.00**
Platter
10" l, "W. H. Grindley" **55.00**
11" l, "W. H. Grindley" **80.00**
12" l, "W. H. Grindley" **70.00**
14½" l, "W. H. Grindley" **110.00**
16" l, "W. H. Grindley" **95.00**
Sugar, "W. H. Grindley" **95.00**
Tureen, cov, 8" d, "W. H. Grindley" **125.00**
Vegetable Bowl
9" l, "W. H. Grindley" **60.00**
10" l, "W. H. Grindley" **70.00**
Waste Bowl, "W. H. Grindley" **75.00**
"Melrose" pattern
Plate
9" d, "Doulton" **35.00**
9½" d, "Doulton" **20.00**
10¼" d, "Doulton" **40.00**
Platter
11" l, "Doulton" **50.00**
16" l, "Doulton" **75.00**
18" l, "Doulton" **100.00**
Sauce Tureen, cov, and tray, "Doulton" **100.00**
"Messina" pattern, plate
8" d, "Cauldon" **32.00**
10" d, "Cauldon" **48.00**
"Mikado" pattern, vegetable tureen,
cov, "W. & E. Corn" **125.00**
"Milford" pattern, vegetable bowl, cov,
and tray, 10¾" l, "Burgess & Leigh" **145.00**
"Mongolia" pattern, milk pitcher,
"Johnson Bros" **75.00**
"Montana" pattern, milk pitcher, "John-
son Bros" **150.00**
"Nankin" pattern, miniature cup and
saucer, "Ironstone-Ashworth" **140.00**
"Navy" pattern, cup and saucer,
"Thom. Till & Sons" **50.00**
"Nelson" pattern
Bowl, 10" d, paisley border, "Upper
Hanley Pottery" **35.00**
Plate, 9" d, "N. W. P." **40.00**
"Ning Po" pattern, platter, 15¾" l, 12"
w, "R. H. & Co." **185.00**
"Non Pariel" pattern
Bone Dish, "Burgess & Leigh" **8.00**
Cake Plate, closed handles, "Burgess
& Leigh" **50.00**
Creamer and Sugar, "Burgess &
Leigh" **95.00**
Cup and Saucer, "Burgess & Leigh" **50.00**
Plate
8½" d, "Burgess & Leigh" **28.00**
8¾" d, "Burgess & Leigh" **45.00**
10" d, "B & L" **40.00**
10" d, "N. W. P." **48.00**
Platter
10" l, 8" w, "B & L" **65.00**
13" l, 11" w, "Burgess & Leigh" .. **130.00**
Waste Bowl, "Burgess & Leigh" **60.00**

"Normandy" pattern
Bowl
  8" d, "W. H. Grindley" **45.00**
  9" d, "W. H. Grindley" **55.00**
  10" d, "W. H. Grindley" **55.00**
Cup and Saucer, "W. H. Grindley" . **45.00**
Gravy Boat, "W. H. Grindley" **75.00**
Plate
  7" d, "W. H. Grindley" **20.00**
  8" d, "W. H. Grindley" **25.00**
  10" d, "W. H. Grindley" **35.00**
Platter
  14" l, 10" w, "W. H. Grindley" .. **70.00**
  14½" l, 10½" w, "Johnson Bros" . **125.00**
  16" l, 12" w, "W. H. Grindley" .. **90.00**
Soup Bowl, 8" d, "W. H. Grindley" **35.00**
Sugar, "Johnson Bros" **125.00**
Vegetable Bowl, cov, "W. H. Grind-
  ley" **90.00**
"Olympia" pattern, bowl, 9" d, "W. H.
  Grindley" **30.00**
"Oregon" pattern
Cup and Saucer, "T. Mayer" **85.00**
Pitcher, 13" h, water, "T. Mayer" ... **400.00**
Plate, 9⅝" d, T. J. & J. Mayer" **90.00**
Platter
  13½" l, "T. J. & J. Mayer" **225.00**
  18" l, 14" w, T. J. & J. Mayer" ... **200.00**
Sauce Tureen, cov, rose knob, "T. J.
  & J. Mayer" **300.00**
Tea Set, teapot, creamer, cov sugar,
  "T. J. & J. Mayer" **900.00**
Teabowl, 6" d, "T. J. & J. Mayer" .. **50.00**
Teabowl and Saucer, "T. Mayer" ... **85.00**
"Oriental" pattern
Bowl
  8" d, "Regout, Maastricht" **45.00**
  10" d, "N. W. P." **45.00**
Compote, 10" l, 5½" w, dbl handles,
  "Ridgways" **225.00**
Plate
  9" d, "Regout, Maastricht" **35.00**
  10" d, "J. Kent" **35.00**
Relish Tray, "Ridgways" **58.00**
"Ormonde" pattern, cup and saucer,
  "Alfred Meakin" **24.00**
"Osborne" pattern
Butter Pat, "T. R. & Co.," set of 9 .. **18.00**
Egg Cup, "Ridgways" **85.00**
Plate, 7" d, "W. H. Grindley" **18.00**
"Oxford" pattern, candy dish, 12" l,
  fluted and scalloped, "Johnson Bros" **200.00**
"Pansy" pattern
Bowl, 10" d, unmarked **45.00**
Plate, 10" d, unmarked **45.00**
"Paris" pattern
Bowl, 9" d, "N. W. P." **35.00**
Plate
  4½" d, "Johnson Bros" **4.00**
  9" d, "N. W. P." **35.00**
"Peach" pattern
Bone Dish, "Johnson Bros" **45.00**

Plate, 9" d, "Johnson Bros" **17.50**
Sugar, 6" h, loop handles, "Johnson
  Bros" **45.00**
"Peach Royal" pattern, plate, 10" d,
  "Johnson Bros" **50.00**
"Pekin" pattern
Cup and Saucer, "Ford & Sons" **45.00**
Dish, 4" d, "Dimmock" **14.00**
Gravy Boat and Undertray, "W. & B.-
  Pearl White" **75.00**
Plate
  7¾" d, "Wilkinson" **30.00**
  10" d, dark blue, orange and green,
    gold edge, "Albert & Jones" ... **35.00**
  10¼" d, "Albert Jones" **75.00**
"Peking" pattern, platter, 13½" l, un-
  marked **100.00**
"Pelew" pattern
Plate
  8½" d, "E. Challinor" **75.00**
  9" d, "E. Challinor" **95.00**
Platter, 10¾" l, "E. Challinor" **185.00**
Sauce Dish, "E. C.-Ironstone" **38.00**
Soup Plate, 10½" d, "E. Challinor" . **110.00**
Teabowl and Saucer, "E. Challinor" **100.00**
"Penang" pattern, plate, 7" d, "Ridg-
  way" **35.00**
"Persian" pattern
Bone Dish, "Johnson Bros" **40.00**
Bowl, 9½" l, 7" w, dbl handles,
  "Johnson Bros" **100.00**
Plate, 9", "Johnson Bros" **25.00**
"Plymouth" pattern, cup and saucer,
  "N. W. P." **135.00**
"Poppy" pattern
Cup and Saucer
  "N. W. P." **45.00**
  "Wedgwood" **45.00**
Platter, 18" l, "W. H. Grindley" **125.00**
"Progress" pattern
Plate
  9" d, "W. H. Grindley" **30.00**
  10" d, "W. H. Grindley" **58.00**
"Queen" pattern, chamber pot, 9" d,
  "T. Rathbone" **100.00**
"Regent" pattern
Gravy Boat, 8" l, "Johnson Bros" ... **45.00**
Platter, 12" l, 9½" w, "Johnson Bros" **65.00**
Soup Plate, 10¼" d, "George Jones &
  Son" **10.00**
"Rhine" pattern
Plate, 10" d, "Dimmock" **75.00**
Vegetable Bowl, 9" l, 6½" w, "T. D.
  Kaolinware" **100.00**
"Rhone" pattern, platter, 20" l, 15" w,
  unmarked **270.00**
"Richmond" pattern, platter, 16" l,
  11½" w, "Alfred Meakin" **125.00**
"Rock" pattern, platter, 14" l, 10" w, "E.
  Challinor" **125.00**
"Rose" pattern
Creamer, "W. H. Grindley" **100.00**

Plate
 7" d, "W. H. Grindley" **12.00**
 8" d, "Ridgways" **38.00**
 9" d, "W. H. Grindley" **20.00**
Platter, 16" l **100.00**
"Roseville" pattern, plate
 7" d, "Maddock" **25.00**
 9" d, "Maddock" **40.00**
"Roslin" pattern, plate, 8" d, "Thom.
Rathbone" **42.00**

**Mug, 8" H-H, 5" h, "Singa," marked
"C.E.& M," $125.00.**

"Sabraon" pattern, gravy boat, unmarked **185.00**
"Scinde" pattern
 Butter Dish, "T. Walker" **225.00**
 Chamber Pot, cov, "T. Walker" **300.00**
 Plate
  7¼" d, "J. & G. Alcock" **70.00**
  7¾" d, "J. & G. Alcock" **50.00**
  8¼" d, "J. & G. Alcock" **75.00**
  8½" d, "J. & G. Alcock" **55.00**
  9" d, "T. Walker" **75.00**
  10½" d, "J. & G. Alcock" **75.00**
 Platter
  11" l, "J. & G. Alcock" **225.00**
  15½" l, "T. Walker" **275.00**
  16" l, "J. & G. Alcock" **400.00**
  18¼" l, "J. & G. Alcock" **200.00**
 Sauce Dish, 5" d, "T. Walker" **40.00**
 Soup Plate, 10½" d, "J. & G. Alcock" **90.00**
 Sugar, 7½" h, "J. & G. Alcock" **285.00**
 Teabowl and Saucer, "J. & G. Al-
 cock" **110.00**
"Seville" pattern, gravy boat, "Wood &
Sons" **45.00**
"Shanghai" pattern
 Plate, 10" d
  "W. & T. Adams" **35.00**
  "W. H. Grindley" **50.00**
 Platter
  15½" l, 12" w, "Furnival" **125.00**
  20" l, 16" w, "W. H. Grindley" .. **200.00**
"Shapoo" pattern
 Cup and Saucer, "T. & R. Boote" .. **120.00**
 Plate
  7½" d, "T. & R. Boote" **60.00**

 9" d, "T. & R. Boote" **85.00**
 10¼" d, "T. & R. Boote" **95.00**
Platter, 12½" l, 9½" w, "T. & R.
 Boote" **225.00**
Soup Plate, 9½" d, "T. & R. Boote" **110.00**
Toothbrush Box, cov, "T. H." **185.00**
"Shell" pattern
 Bowl, 11½" d, "W. & C" **425.00**
 Sauceboat and Tray, 5¾" h **545.00**
"Sobraon" pattern
 Gravy Boat **175.00**
 Plate, 8" d, unmarked **50.00**
"Somerset" pattern, cup and saucer,
 "W. H. Grindley" **40.00**
"Spinach" pattern
 Bowl
  8" d, "P. Regout, Maastricht" **40.00**
  10" d, "P. Regout, Maastricht" ... **45.00**
 Cup and Saucer
  "Libertas" imp mark **95.00**
  "P. Regout, Maastricht" **55.00**
 Plate, 8" d, "Libertas-Prussia" **40.00**
 Waste Bowl, "P. Regout, Maastricht" **35.00**
"Splendid" pattern
 Bowl, 9" d, "Societe Ceramique,
 Maastricht" **40.00**
 Plate, 9" d, "Maastricht" **40.00**
"St. Louis" pattern, bone dish, "Johnson
Bros" **45.00**
"Syndenham" pattern, plate, 10" d,
 "Morley" **45.00**

**Teabowl and Saucer, "Temple," marked
"P. W. & Co.," $115.00.**

"Temple" pattern, plate, 9⅞" d, "British
Anchor Pottery Co., Ltd" **100.00**
"The Blue Danube" pattern, plate, 10"
d, "Johnson Bros" **35.00**
"The Hofburg" pattern
 Butter Pat, "W. H. Grindley" **16.00**
 Pitcher, 6" h, "W. H. Grindley" **55.00**
"The Holland" pattern
 Gravy Boat, "Alfred Meakin" **95.00**
 Plate, 10" d, "Alfred Meakin" **45.00**
 Vegetable Bowl, cov, "Alfred
 Meakin" **125.00**
"The Imperial" pattern, platter
 12" l, 9" w, "W. H. Grindley" **65.00**
 16½" l, 12" w, "W. H. Grindley" .. **135.00**

"The Marquis" pattern, plate, 8" d ... **15.00**
"The Temple" pattern, plate, 8¾" d, "P.
W. & Co" **85.00**
"Togo" pattern
 Bowl
  9" d, "Colonial Pottery" **35.00**
  10" d, "F. Winkle" **35.00**
 Charger, 12" d, "F. Winkle" **125.00**
 Compote, cov, and undertray, "Hol-
  linshead & Kirkham" **375.00**
 Plate
  6¾" d, "F. Winkle" **15.00**
  8" d, "F. Winkle" **18.00**
  9" d, "Stone, England" **38.00**
  10" d, "F. Winkle & Co" **35.00**
 Platter, 16" l, 12" w, "Colonial Pottery, England" **95.00**
 Tureen and tray, 12" l, "F. Winkle" . **300.00**
"Tokio" pattern, plate, 10" d, "Johnson
 Bros" **58.00**
"Tonquin" pattern
 Plate
  4½" d, "J. Heath" **55.00**
  8½" d, "J. Heath" **75.00**
  8½" d, "W. Adams & Co" **45.00**
  9" d, "J. Heath" **55.00**
  9" d, "W. Adams & Co" **60.00**
  9½" d, "J. Heath" **65.00**
 Platter
  17" l, 13" w, "J. Heath" **345.00**
  17" l, 13½" w, "W. Adams & Co" **175.00**
 Teabowl and Saucer, "J. Heath" ... **95.00**
"Touraine" pattern
 Bone Dish, "Henry Alcock & Co" .. **35.00**
 Creamer and Sugar, "Henry Alcock &
  Co" **250.00**
 Cup and Saucer
  "Henry Alcock & Co" **38.00**
  "Stanley Pottery Co" **55.00**
 Gravy Boat and Undertray, "Henry
  Alcock" **150.00**
 Plate
  6½" d, "Henry Alcock" **15.00**
  7½" d, "Henry Alcock" **25.00**
  7¾" d, "Henry Alcock" **38.00**
  8½" d, "Henry Alcock" **50.00**
  8¾" d, "Henry Alcock" **35.00**
  9" d, "Henry Alcock" **40.00**
 Platter
  10" d, "Henry Alcock" **75.00**
  10½" l, "Stanley Pottery Co" **95.00**
  12½" l, "Stanley Pottery Co" **110.00**
  15" l, "Stanley Pottery Co" **145.00**
 Sauce Dish, "Stanley Pottery Co" .. **15.00**
 Vegetable Dish
  9" d, cov, "Stanley Pottery Co" .. **200.00**
  10" d, "Stanley Pottery Co" **85.00**
 Vegetable Tureen, cov, 12" H-H,
  "Henry Alcock," repaired handle . **100.00**
"Tower" pattern, 6" d cup and 8½" saucer, "R. M. & Co" **125.00**

"Trent" pattern
 Bowl
  6" d, "Wood & Sons" **30.00**
  7" d, "N. W. P." **30.00**
 Vegetable Tureen, 11" l, "Ford &
  Sons" **175.00**
"Troy" pattern, vegetable bowl, cov,
 "C. M." **325.00**
"Tulips" pattern, pitcher, 7½" h, un-
 marked **95.00**
"Turkey" pattern, 10½" d, "Copeland" **80.00**
Unknown Patterns
 Ladle, 6" l, unmarked **100.00**
 Plate, 10" d, peacock, gold border,
  "Canton, England" **55.00**
 Tureen, cov, and undertray, Art Nou-
  veau fruit design, unmarked **125.00**
"Valencia" pattern, bowl, 9¼" d, "S.
 Hancock" **65.00**
"Venice" pattern
 Butter Pat, "Johnson Bros" **16.00**
 Gravy Boat
  "Johnson Bros" **65.00**
  "Upper Hanley Potteries, Ltd" ... **65.00**
 Tureen, cov, "Grimwade Bros" **55.00**
"Vermont" pattern
 Butter Pat, "Burgess & Leigh", set of
  8 .... **38.00**
 Creamer, "Burgess & Leigh" **55.00**
 Demitasse Cup and Saucer, "Burgess
  & Leigh" **65.00**
 Pitcher, "Burgess & Leigh" **45.00**
 Platter, 12" l, "Burgess & Leigh" ... **75.00**
 Teapot, 8" h, "Burgess & Leigh" ... **210.00**
 Vegetable Bowl
  10" l, 6" w, "Burgess & Leigh" ... **30.00**
  11½" l, cov, "Burgess & Leigh" .. **125.00**
"Verona" pattern
 Bowl, 9" d, "Alfred Meakin, Ltd" .. **20.00**
 Butter Pat, "Alfred Meakin, Ltd" ... **16.00**
 Gravy Boat and Undertray, "Ford &
  Sons" **95.00**
 Plate
  8" d, "Wood & Sons" **58.00**
  10" d, "Ford & Sons" **45.00**
 Platter, 17" l
  "Ford & Sons" **150.00**
  "Ridgway" **150.00**
 Sauce Tureen, 8" l, Ridgway **150.00**
 Sauce Tureen, Tray, "Ford & Sons" . **150.00**
"Victoria" pattern
 Bowl, 10" d, "Wood & Sons" **75.00**
 Vegetable Bowl, 10" d
  "W. H. Grindley" **65.00**
  "Wood & Sons" **45.00**
"Virginia" pattern, plate, 9¾" d, "John
 Maddock & Sons" **35.00**
"Waldorf" pattern
 Bowl, 9" d, "N. W. P." **60.00**
 Cup and Saucer, "N. W. P." **55.00**
 Plate
  9" d, "N. W. P." **35.00**

10" d, "New Wharf Pottery" 50.00
10" d, "Wood & Sons" 55.00
Platter, 10½" l, 8" w, "N. W. P." ... 50.00
Soup Bowl, 9" d, "New Wharf Pottery" 50.00
Waste Bowl, "N. W. P." 40.00
"Washington Vase" pattern
Relish Dish 38.00
Waste Bowl 95.00
"Watteau" pattern
Bowl, 9½" d, "N. W. P." 55.00
Butter Pat, "N. W. P." 15.00
Jug, 8" w, 7" h, "Doulton-Burslem" . 125.00
Pitcher
5¼" h, "Doulton-Burslem" 100.00
10" h, "Doulton-Burslem" 185.00
Plate
7½" d, "Staffordshire, England" .. 27.00
10" d, unmarked 50.00
10¼" d, "Doulton-Burslem" 62.00
10½" d, "Doulton" 80.00
Platter, 16" l, 12" w, "N. W. P." 185.00
Soup Bowl, 9½" d, "Staffordshire, England" 35.00
Vegetable Bowl, cov, 10½" l, "Ashworth" 35.00
"Waverly" pattern, platter, 10¾" l, 8" w, "W. H. Grindley" 50.00
"Whampoa" pattern, plate, 10¼" d, "Swansea" 100.00
"Wild Rose" pattern, plate, 10½" d, "George Jones & Son" 45.00
"Willow" pattern, bowl
6¾" d, "Doulton & Co, Burslem" .. 95.00
7" d, unmarked 80.00
7¼" d, unmarked 80.00
8" d, "Doulton-Burslem" 75.00
8¼" d, "Minton" 70.00
9" d, scalloped rim, "MINTON" ... 80.00
"Woodland" pattern, plate, 9" d, "Wood & Sons" 15.00
"Yeddo" pattern, plate, 9" d 28.00

FRANCE-GENERAL

ROUEN
1673–1696

Louis Poterat, a faience maker, was granted a patent to make the earliest French soft paste porcelain at Rouen in 1673. The decorations were dark blue in the style of faience ware with lambrequins and gadroons. Relief work appeared on the body of pieces such as salt cellars, mustard pots, and vases. Poterat died in 1696.

LILLE
1711–1817

Barthelemy Dorenz and Pierre Pelissier estab-lished a soft paste porcelain factory in Lille in 1711. Pieces were decorated with Chinese designs. Leperre Ducot began manufacturing hard paste porcelains in 1784. The French Dauphin became a patron of the factory in 1786. The dolphin was chosen as the factory's mark.

STRASBOURG
1721–1781

Charles Hannong, who started a porcelain factory in Strasbourg in 1721, manufactured clay pipes and stoves that were decorated in relief and glazed. For a short time he was a partner with Johann Wachenfeld who came from Meissen. Together they made faience and porcelain wares. In 1724 a second factory was established in Haguenau.

Hannong transfered the factories to his sons, Paul Antoine and Balthasar, in 1732. Between 1745 and 1750 hard paste porcelains were produced that were decorated in red and pale gold. Adam Lowenfinck arrived from Hochst in 1750 and became co-director of the porcelain factory. He brought the Rococo style and introduced flower painting to Strasbourg.

By 1753 Paul Hannong assumed control of both factories. When Louis XV of France ordered him to dismantle his porcelain factory and demolish his kilns, Paul Hannong went to Frankenthal. As a result, early Strasbourg ware and Frankenthal ware resemble each other.

By 1766 Joseph-Adam, Hannong's son, tried to reestablish a hard paste porcelain factory in Strasbourg. Opposition by the authorities forced its closure in 1781.

SCEAUX
1748–1795

Under the patronage of Duchess de Marne, the architect de Bay established a porcelain factory that was managed by Jacques Chapelle. The firm's soft paste porcelains were decorated with exotic birds, flowers, and cupids in the fashion of the Louis XVI period. The factory closed in 1795.

NIDERVILLER
1754–1827

Baron Beyerle established a faience factory in 1754. Porcelains were produced by 1765. When opposition arose from the Sevres potters, Beyerle took Count de Custine into partnership in 1770 because of his influence at the French Court. On Custine's death, the factory was sold to Claude-Francois Lanfrey and continued until 1827. Tea sets, tablewares, and services were made and decorated in the manner of Sevres.

PARIS AREA

The majority of French hard paste porcelains available in today's market were made at numerous small factories in the Paris area. Production of porcelain began in the early eighteenth century.

Museums: Frick Collection, New York, NY; Louvre, Paris, France; Musee des Arts Decoratifs, Paris, France; Musee des Beaux-Arts et de la Ceramique, Rouen, France; Musee National de Sevres, Sevres, France; Victoria & Albert Museum, London, England.

Additional Listings: Chantilly, Choisy-le-Roi, Creil, Faience, Limoges, Malicorne, Mannecy, Old Paris and Paris, Quimper, Saint Cloud, Sevres, Vincennes.

Egg Cups, 3½" h, blue florals, white ground, "Made in France," pr, (A) $30.00.

Animal Dish, cov, hen, 8¾" h, painted bisque top, gray basketweave base, unmarked 550.00
Basket, 7¼" d, pierced, painted oval reserves, puce, blue, and light green flowers, int. flower spray, loop ribbon entwined handles, c1785, blue interlaced "C and 349", Niderville (A) .. 175.00
Bookends, 6¾" h, molded stylized turkeys, crackled cream and silver glaze, pr 150.00
Bottle, 6⅛" h, portraits of Louis XIV and Mme de Lamballe, names on bases, gilt line and red enamel beaded cartouches, dark blue ground, enameled jeweled ornaments, turquoise bead borders, sq, matching stoppers, c1880, pr, (A) 2,600.00
Bowl
  6" d, Chinese decor, multicolored, white ground, Luneville, pr 25.00
  7" d, porcelain, reticulated, floral and gilt decor, ftd, Niderville (A) 25.00
  9" h, hp, garden scenes, multicolored, fitted with gilt metal mounts, pr (A) 415.00

14½" d, porcelain, boat shape, supported by two kneeling angels, resting on plinth with paw feet, 19th C (A) 250.00
21" l, bleu-du-roi glaze, gilt bronze pierced rim, scroll molded handles, pierced base, late 19th C (A) 825.00
Box
  1⅝" l, porcelain, pink and blue enamel, "C" on lid, egg shape, (A) 20.00
  2⅜" d, 1½" h, porcelain, pink roses, ivory ground, gold trim, "L" and "France" mark 30.00
  3¼" w, molded basketwork ext., green painted buildings and landscape on int. cov, cartouche shape, silver gilt mounts, c1775 .... 375.00
  4⅝" h, gilt trim and gilded brass trim, drum shape, "France," (A) 30.00
  4⅞" d, cov reserved with 5 putti before winter campfire in winter landscape, gilt line and berried cartouche, royal blue ground, c1900 .... 120.00
  9" h, porcelain, figural, seated Oriental man, yellow, rust, and red .. 85.00
  10" l, int. scene of royal blue ground reserved with men and women dancing, gilt eagle and scroll cartouche, box with panels of rustic cottages, gilt metal mounts, c1880 (A) 830.00
Butter Tub, 8¼" h, matching stand, panels of painted birds reserved on green ground 120.00
Bust
  6" h, terra cotta, child crying, newspaper hat, fly on nose, "G D Paris" mark 80.00
  13½" h, terra cotta, Art Nouveau style, young girl, corsage of daisies on bodice, light green patina, sgd "E. Drouot" (A) 25.00
Cabinet Cup and Saucer
  Painted panel of building by river reserved on green ground 50.00
  Portraits of Napoleon and Josephine, gilt rect cartouches reserved on claret ground, sgd "Garnier", c1900, pr (A) 155.00
Cachepot, 9¾" h, front panels of shepherd lovers, three side panels of multicolored florals, narrow bleu-du-roi borders, gilding, gilt bronze mounts, four scroll feet, late 19th C, blue interlaced "L's," pr, (A) 1,980.00
Center Bowl, 18" w, center panel of reclining woman, Cupid offering dove, reverse with temple and river scene, gilt borders, reserved on bleu-du-roi ground, roses on int., gilt bronze mounts, sgd "C Rochette", late 19th C (A) 1,650.00

Centerpiece, 17½" h, pierced compote and cov, supported by standard, modeled leaves and figures of children, stepped base, underglaze blue motifs and gilding, blue interlaced "L's" (A) **220.00**

Chamberstick, 3" h, rose design, open trellis edge **75.00**

Charger, 21¼" d, pottery, incised vase of carnations and pomegranates, initials, "1724," scroll and foliage border, iron-red and green, yellow ground, pie crust rim, Colmar **1,400.00**

Coffee Can, oval panels of painted Orientals, gilt trellis ground, late 19th C, gilt interlaced "L's" (A) **80.00**

Coffee Can and Saucer
  Porcelain, famille rose style coat of arms and flowers, set of 4 .... **75.00**
  Painted bird panels reserved on turquoise ground **60.00**

Cup
  Light blue ground reserved and painted, bands of flowers, gold entwined dbl handles, cov with flower bud finial, stand, late 19th C (A) **100.00**
  Multicolor French landscape scene (A) **90.00**
  Relief enamel florals and dots, dark blue ground, (A) **450.00**

Cup and Saucer
  Entwined florals below turquoise border, reserved and gilt, entwined dbl branch handles, cov with gilt berried finial, c1900 (A) **130.00**
  Exotic birds in berried cartouches, pink and trellis ground, dbl handles, cov with gilt spire finial, c1900 (A) **110.00**
  Floral and gilt motif, (A) **25.00**
  Multicolored fruit, florals, gilded scrolls, gilt int. band, (A) **90.00**
  Nymph and Cupid in woodland, flowers and trophies on saucer, gilt cartouches, blue ground, gilt and jeweled, trellis and flowerheads, c1880, blue interlaced "L's" mark (A) **390.00**
  Porcelain, painted red, yellow, blue, and green floral sprays, gilt scalloped rims, 18th C, blue "X'd L's and horn" mark **125.00**
  Three small portraits in court clothes, portrait of Louis XVI inside bowl, saucer, small circ portraits, blue, dark rose, and gold, "N and crown" **90.00**

Dish
  6⅞" d, center reserved, Cupids in clouds in gilt floral cartouche on royal blue ground, gilt dentil rim,

cushion shape, c1880, blue interlaced "L's" mark (A) **100.00**
  16⅞" l, center scene of youths and maidens dancing in wooded setting, green ground, gilt line well, band of entwined berried foliage, late 19th C (A) **235.00**

Figure
  3⅞" h, porcelain, lilac dbl turret castle, gilt accents, applied white foliage borders **70.00**
  6¾" h, porcelain, street vendor, multicolored, blue "X'd arrows" mark (A) **30.00**
  7½" h, shepherd playing fiddle, shepherdess, sheep, multicolored **65.00**
  7¾" h, Apollo playing lyre, Polyhymnia playing lute, seated on rock, white, mid 18th C (A) **225.00**
  7⅞" h, seated nude Diana, bow, doves, and torch, rockwork base, c1770, imp "H/F" mark, Strasbourg (A) **1,120.00**
  9⅜" h, boy holding dove, girl with fruit in apron, sq base, turquoise glaze, gold accents, pr **210.00**
  10⅝" h, Neptune and Amphitrite, seated on dolphins, gilt scale pattern, turquoise glaze, oval turquoise and dark blue banded and jeweled base, c1900, blue interlaced "L's," pr (A) **220.00**
  11" h, terra cotta, colonial girl, fan, incised details **135.00**
  12" h, porcelain, polychrome figures of Napoleonic military figures, pr (A) **70.00**
  17¾" h, boy, sheaf of corn and lamb at side, girl, sheaf of corn and flowers in apron, goat at side, multicolored, circ bases, c1860, pr(A) **500.00**

Game Dish, cov, 9" l, vert ribbing, quail head finial, brown ground **120.00**

Inkstand
  5¼" l, figural, book, dbl wells, black matte covs, painted multicolored bird and florals, gold edged pages, "Aladin, France" **75.00**
  7⅛" l, reserved, wide pink band and berried foliage, royal blue ground, pink and gilt lines, quatrefoil shape, gilt metal mounts and finial, late 19th C, blue interlaced "L's" mark (A) **105.00**

Knife Handle, 3¾" l, porcelain, painted figures in landscape, multicolored, 18th C **175.00**

Luncheon Set, twelve plates, cups, saucers, and bread plates, milk pitcher, nappy and bonbon dish, hp violets, pearlized finish (A) **150.00**

Mug, 4⅜" h, reserve of gallant kneeling

before companion in garden scene, white, ruby, and turquoise jeweled, gilt oval cartouche, turquoise ground, gilt and jewels on reverse, gilt dentil border, c1880 (A) **470.00**

Patch Box, 2¼" l, 1¾" w, porcelain, pink roses and blue forget-me-nots, roses on int., gold trim and gold floral clasp **135.00**

Pedestals, 41¼" h, continuous bisque frieze of dancing maidens, instruments and men drinking, bleu-du-roi, white palmette bands and gilding borders, gilt bronze mounts, pr (A) ...**22,550.00**

Plaque

5⅛" l, painted view of figures in front of church **115.00**

8¼" l, 6¾" h, lithophane of "Le Seaux Du Parc De Versailles" **140.00**

11¾" w, 15½" h, earthenware, couple seated on stone bench in garden, gate, sgd "Crommer," late 19th C (A) **495.00**

12½" l, 8⅝" h, painted Eastern scene of woman lying on balcony, two attendant slaves, sgd "Lucien Levy," late 19th C (A) **715.00**

14¾" d, porcelain, multicolored, sgd "Gleize"

"Young Maiden Playing Flute" (A)   **90.00**

"Young Maiden Playing Pipes" (A) **110.00**

16" d, porcelain, center scene of Napoleon on battlefield, multicolored, gilt roundels, maroon border **300.00**

17¼" w, 25½" h, maiden, musician, and page offering crown, sgd "J Pascault" (A) **7,150.00**

18" d, pottery, center painted "Liberty", border of playing cards, French allegorical named figures, multicolored,green ground, dated 1795, firing crack (A) **10,450.00**

22" d, porcelain, "Children," multicolored, sgd "J Pascault" (A) **400.00**

Porcelain, raised design of woman and Cupid being pulled by butterflies, sgd "L'Homme," 18th C **2,500.00**

Portrait of woman in period dress, wreath of flowers in hair and dove in lap, other portrait with dove carrying letter around neck, gilt bronze molded, beaded frames, ribbon tied crests, 19th C, pr (A) **1,650.00**

Plate

6½ d, sepia transfer of golfers, "Les Sports," Montereau mark **12.00**

8" d, multicolored transfer of girl and officer, "Daughter of the Regiment," Montereau **35.00**

8⅜" d

Painted coat of arms, silver and gold in center, black border, stylized florals and scrolls in gilt, late 19th C, "CHS Pillivuyt and Cie" **50.00**

Porcelain, central sunburst rimmed, names of fifteen states in oval chain links around rim, green enamel and gilt, enameled snake on rim (A) **75.00**

Youth and companion in landscape, border with flowers in gilt foliage cartouches, reserved on turquoise ground, late 19th C .. **50.00**

8½" d, two center figures, green and gold border **30.00**

8¾" d, center and border printed in florals and geometrics, flow blue style, "Luneville, France" **50.00**

Plate, 8" d, black transfer, white ground, $125.00.

9" d

Black transfer, "Le Bolero-Seville," costumed dancers, yellow and green open basketweave border, "Lebeuf Millet and Co" **45.00**

"Two Quail" pattern, painted in Kakiemon style, octagonal **40.00**

9¼" d, center painted with Italian castle scene, border with ivy, light brown ground **65.00**

9⅜" d, center portrait of Mademoiselle Montpensier in gilt and ruby jeweled cartouche, inner floral and ribbon in gilt and turquoise, royal blue border with jewels and gilt, waved gilt dentil border, c1880, blue interlaced "L's" mark (A) **195.00**

9½" d, portrait, multicolored

Louis XV, gilt tracery border, sgd "Debrie" (A) **70.00**

Louis XVI, floral garland and gilt tracery border, sgd "Debrie" (A) **70.00**

Madame de Lavalliere, wide green border, gilt garland and ribbons, sgd "Bihet" (A) **30.00**

Madame Elizabeth, floral garland and gilt tracery boarder, sgd "Debrie" (A) **60.00**

13½" d, Art Nouveau style, painted girl's head in gold circle, enamel accents, irid ground and border, c1900 (A) **170.00**

8" d, ironstone, polychrome decor of "Les Gastronomiques de la Sante," "Gien" mark, set of 8 (A) **45.00**

8⅝" d, polychrome decor, operatic composers, scenes from works, set of 7 (A) **160.00**

9⅜" d

Center painted court ladies in shaped cartouches of drapery with gilt rope, yellow ground, five blue fleur-de-lis with gilt, gilt rims, sgd "Rochette", c1900, set of 6 (A) **350.00**

Center equestrians and tents, gilt lined wells, royal blue borders reserved and painted with tents in landscapes in gilt scroll cartouches, lobed gilt rims, c1900, pr (A) **250.00**

9½" d

Different scenes of cherubs and cupids at various activities, gilt tracery borders, marked, set of 10 (A) **100.00**

Maiden churning butter, boy and dog and maiden with child in basket on back, blue celeste borders, gilt latticework and fleur-de-lis, sgd "Dupoigny", 19th C, pr (A) **525.00**

9⅞" d, center painted multicolored floral sprays, blue borders edged in gilt, set of 10 .... **150.00**

10"d

Center painted baskets of flowers, molded cherubs with arrows by urns and foliage swag rims, c1814, blue "crowned N" mark, set of 12 (A) **800.00**

Painted court portraits, named on reverse, blue borders with gilt foliage, shaped rims, mid 19th C, blue interlaced "L's" mark, set of 12 (A) **715.00**

Punch Bowl, 11⅜" d, famille rose style, ext. painted with florals and spiral husks on trellis ground, int. with scattered sprigs **65.00**

Scent Bottle

3¾" h, modeled as flowering tree with two boys, girl, and dog, multicolored **50.00**

6⅛" h, panels of shepherdess and goat herder reserved on blue ground, sq with chamfered corners (A) **85.00**

Snuff Box, 3⅛" d, painted panels of putti in landscapes, scroll molded dark blue ground, sgd "Millot" **125.00**

Soup Tureen, 11½" d, cov, porcelain, painted bunches of flowers and sprays, gilt rims and finial, c1785, blue interlaced "C's" mark, Niderville (A) **365.00**

Tray, 18¾" d, center panel with named portrait of Louis XIV surrounded by named court ladies, reserved on dark red ground **135.00**

Tureen, 15⅜" d, cov, matching stand with sun ray center, porcelain, painted bouquets, bull's mask handles with suspended loose gilt rings, c1790, Niderville (A) **650.00**

Urn

14½" h, porcelain, polychrome floral and figural reserves, gilt accents, maroon and blue ground, pierced rim, handles and ftd base, 19th C (A) **75.00**

31" h, cov, continuous scenes of lovers on embankment and by cottage between bleu-du-roi borders, shoulders with swirling flutes and gilding, sgd "E Collot," c1910, blue interlaced "L's" mark, pr (A) **4,620.00**

Vase

7½"h, cobalt flowers with yellow centers, blue-green ground, dark red-orange, large leaves with yellow edges on mottled tan, tapered neck, sgd "Page, Paris" **110.00**

7¾" h, dark cobalt flowers, orange and yellow leaves, mottled ground, "France" **75.00**

10½" h, poppies, green ground, luster glaze **195.00**

11⅜" h, painted, maiden playing instrument with Cupid, gilt bronze neck, base enriched with champleve mounts, sgd "A Collot", c1900, pr **550.00**

11½" h, modeled as cornucopia from gilt foliage, painted flower sprays in gilt scroll surrounds reserved on light blue ground, oblong scroll pedestal, c1840, blue "MA" mark **150.00**

12" h, multicolored floral sprays, turquoise ground, gilt floral handles, pr **120.00**

13⅝" h, porcelain, polychrome figure groups in 18th C landscape, hp over transfers on cream ground, gilt rims and pierced borders, dbl handles, pr (A) **350.00**

14" h, pottery, floral relief decor, gold and glossy red accents on brown

glaze, narrow neck and bulbous body, early 20th C, Luneville (A) . **200.00**
14¾" h, portrait panels of young girl and troubadour in gilt framework, landscapes on reverse, royal blue ground, pr (A) **400.00**
15" h, cov, figures in river scene, yellow ground, gilt scroll and female masks, ram's head on lower portions, flared feet with gadrooning, pomegranate finials, sgd "Leber", c1860, blue interlaced "L's" mark, pr (A) **605.00**
17" h, Grecian figures between borders of green stylized leaves, key fret border on foot **65.00**
18" h, famille verte landscape panel, blue ground, brass base, c1850 .. **125.00**
18⅝" h, landscape with young woman and Cupid in oval reserve, maroon and gold accents, baluster urn shape, dbl snake handles with acanthus leaf details, pr (A) **400.00**
20¾" h, earthenware, neo-Egyptian design, anthemion on base, neck and shoulder and stylized leaves in red and gilt on black ground, reverse with cameos of Pharohs and winged scarabs, painted by Pinon Heuze, c1920, pr **2,400.00**
21⅝" h, polychrome figural scene in rect reserves, cerese ground with daises, baluster shape with scroll, leaf dbl handles, late 19th C, pr (A) **350.00**
24½" h, cov
Scene of lovers in garden with putti, riverscape on reverse, musical trophies on cov and flared foot, rams head ormolu handles, c1860, sgd "Naudon," blue interlaced "L's" mark, (A) **550.00**
Transfer and painted scene, shepherd and three maidens, flock on river bank, molded scroll borders and gilding, bleu-du-roi ground (A) **300.00**
39" h, cov, continuous scene of Napoleon at Rivoli battlefield, bleu-du-roi borders with gilding, crowned "N" on cov, gilt bronze mounts, sgd "Debarle," late 19th C (A) **5,500.00**
Vegetable Dish, 9⅞" sq, figures in landscapes, gilt and puce rims, domed covs, sq finials, c1860, pr **130.00**
Water Fountain
10" h, pottery, body with applied medallion of two figures playing instruments, lion's mask with spigot, dbl rope twist handles, translucent green glaze, dated 1654 (A) **240.00**
10¼" h, pottery, oval with molded

fruit branch suspended from rim above spigot, dbl loop handles, rope twist divider, translucent green glaze, 17th C (A) **155.00**

FRANKENTHAL

Palatinate, Germany, 65 miles north of Strasbourg, France
1755–1799

History: Paul Hannong established the Frankenthal hard paste porcelain factory in 1755 with the consent and patronage of the Prince Elector Karl Theodor of Palatinate. Previously Hannong worked at Strasbourg, France.

Dinner services and accessory pieces were marketed along with biscuit and decorated figures, some of which were excellent artisticly. The Rococo style dominated and was similar to that appearing on Vincennes-Sevres pieces.

A very white hard paste body was produced which featured a very bright and hard glaze.

Frankenthal decorators used a full range of colors along with the Vienna style of raised gilt work. Classical and natural themes proved the most popular.

Despite high quality pieces, the company suffered from financial difficulties. In 1762 Karl Theodor purchased the factory and personally supervised its operation. Luck and Melchior, modelers, fashioned figural pieces of note. Nevertheless, the company failed in 1799. Nymphenburg acquired the Frankenthal molds to reproduce the old forms. The Nymphenburg factory used the blue lion mark and "CT" with a crown on their pieces made from Frankenthal molds.

Frankenthal's forty-four years of production was the shortest production period experienced by a major German porcelain manufacturer. However, Frankenthal's high quality and variety of products produced during this brief period were enough to rank it among the greatest of the German factories.

References: George Ware, *German & Austrian Porcelain*, Crown, Inc., 1963.

Museums: Bayerisches Nationalmuseum, Munich, W. Germany; Museum fur Kunst und Gewerbe, Hamburg, W. Germany; Schlossmuseum, Berlin, Germany.

Cup and Saucer
Chinese figures, multicolored, one figure holding staff, three exotic

Teapot, 6¼" h, multicolored harbor scene, dark brown surround, powdered lilac ground, c1770, blue crowned "CT" mark, (A) $4,265.00.

birds, other figure with birdcage in landscape vignette, gilt rococo scrolls, puce trailing flowers, rims with gilt tassles, c1765, blue crowned interlaced "CT" mark . . .2,200.00

Chinese figures on terraces, one with parasol, other with long tailed animal, gilt and cisele, border of insects with gilt dentil rims, c1772, blue crowned interlaced "CT" mark 2,200.00

Landscape imitations of etchings with inscriptions, simulated wood grounds, c1780, blue crowned "CT" mark (A) 400.00

Multicolored florals and brown rims, c1770, blue crowned "CT" mark (A) 200.00

Painted and gilt trailing flowers and foliage on seeded gilt ground divided by panels of gilt and green foliage, c1775, blue crowned interlaced "CT" mark (A) 600.00

Panels of houses in wooded landscapes, puce, rococo gilt C-scroll cartouches, puce scattered sprays, gilt husk and dot borders, c1765, blue crowned "CT" mark (A) 820.00

Sheep in landscape scene, multicolored, gilt scroll support, rims with gilt foliage, c1765, blue crowned interlaced "CT" mark 750.00

Dish
11⅞" d, painted nuts, fruit and flowers, pierced border, blue and gold lines, c1786, blue crowned "CT" mark (A) 495.00

14" l, bouquets of flowers with scattered multicolored flower sprays, basketweave molded border, shaped gold rim, c1775, blue crowned interlaced "CT" mark . . . 350.00

Figure
4⅜" h, girl, seated, playing lute, iron-red skirt, yellow bodice and puce striped petticoat, puce and gold rococo base, c1759–62 (A) 570.00

4½" h, three men and two women in various activities, mounted on circ tree trunk bases with gilt scrolls, modeled by Luck, blue crowned interlaced "CT" mark, set of 5 . . . . .4,200.00

4⅝" h, Autumn, modeled as standing girl, grapes in hand and apron, iron-red, puce, and gold striped clothes, grasswork base, c1755–56, imp "PH" mark, (A) 1,425.00

4⅞" h, Erato, modeled as seated nymph, blue and gilt flowered cloth holding lyre, purple and gilt plinth, scroll molded base, c1755–60, blue crowned "CT" mark (A) 515.00

5" h
Multicolored girl holding bird, boy with yellow flower leaning on tan sheep, mottled green and brown mound base with yellow scrolls, c1778, blue crowned "CT" mark (A) 880.00

Oriental boy, actor's mask, pointed yellow and white hat, white jacket and trousers trimmed in iron-red, yellow boots, seated on tree trunk base, gilt accents, modeled by Luck, c1776, blue crowned interlaced "CT" mark .3,000.00

Sheepshearer, seated youth with sheep over lap, shears, multicolored, scroll edged base, c1760, blue "lion rampant" mark (A) . . 500.00

Dish, 11" l, 10" w, puce flowers, red and green accents, cream ground, gilt rim, c1770, crowned "CT" mark, $1,700.00.

5¼" h, boy playing cymbals, white coat with blue trim, puce breeches, girl, white dress trimmed in puce and yellow, both in dancing pose, sq scroll-molded bases, gilding,

modeled by Lanz, c1770, blue crowned interlaced "CT" mark, pr repaired **1,300.00**
5½" h

Young woman holding bowl, wearing scarf and apron, multicolored, green mound base, c1775, blue crowned "CT" mark (A) . . **715.00**

Pyramus, modeled as young man standing over armor, cloth around waist, stabbing self with sword, c1770, sword missing, (A) **470.00**

5¾" h, boy carrying bagpipe leaning on tree stump, white jacket, black striped trousers, iron-red waistcoat, grasswork base, c1755–56, imp "PH" mark (A) **620.00**

6" h, white, figure of young woman holding tray, foliage and scroll molded base, c1775, blue crowned "CT" mark (A) **285.00**

6¼" h, man aiming gun, woman with gun at side, dressed in hunting clothes, white and gold rococo scroll bases, c1759–62, pr (A) . . .**3,560.00**

6¾" h, two seated Chinese lovers embracing and drinking wine beside loving cup, gold and white, blue crowned "CT" mark, (A) **1,650.00**

7⅜" h, "Discord in Marriage," irate woman, raised hand over seated cowering man, period dress, multicolored, moss encrusted base, scrollwork, c1766, blue crowned "CT" mark **990.00**

7⅝" h, Summer, modeled as three putti in various activities, wine fountain, rococo base, puce and gilt C-scrolls, c1756–59, blue "lion rampant" and imp "PH" mark (A) **380.00**

7¾" h, two figures of putti on gilt scroll-molded plinths, one holding instrument in front of tree stump, pr **250.00**
8⅝" h

"Liberty," man with bird in hat, "Matrimony," woman with birdcage, multicolored, gold scroll bases, modeled by Luck, c1760, "lion rampant and JAH and blue crowned CT and B" mark, pr (A) **3,590.00**

Young girl dancing, ribbon trimmed white period dress, blue dentil edging, gilt bows, scroll mound base, c1756–59 (A) **1,590.00**

10" h, multicolored knight, modern mark **165.00**

Plate
9" d

Bouquets and floral sprays, multicolored, shaped chocolate bor-

ders, c1786, blue crowned interlaced "CT" mark, pr **350.00**

Urns in oval panels, floral and ribbon garlands, banded borders tied with gilt ribbons, c1785, blue crowned "CT" mark, pr (A) **365.00**

9¼" d, two exotic birds in center, lobed ozier rim, blue crowned "CT and AB" mark (A) **500.00**

Sauceboat, 8⅜" l, int. painted, birds in landscape scene, gilt foliate handles and rim, c1770–80, blue crowned "CT" mark (A) **770.00**

Saucer, figure seated by urn in landscape, c1770, blue crowned interlaced "CT" mark **115.00**

Soup Plate, 9⅛" d, flowering plants and rocks, Kakiemon palette, iron-red edged ozier-molded border, blue "lion rampant" mark (A) **70.00**

Teapot, 5¾" w, bouquets, multicolored, strap handle with puce accents, birds head spout with traces of puce, c1770, blue crowned interlaced "CT" mark **320.00**

1740-60

FRENCH FAIENCE

Nevers, c1632–1800
Rouen, 1647–c1800
Moustiers, 1670–1800
Marseilles, 1677–c1800
Strasbourg, 1721–1780

History: Faience, a porous pottery, is lightly fired earthenware that is painted and then covered with an opaque stanniferous glaze. Tiny particles of tin oxide suspended in the glaze provide the characteristic white, opaque nature of the pottery.

Italian potters migrated to France in the 1600s, first to Nevers, and later to Rouen, Moustiers, Marseilles, and other pottery centers. In Nevers the potters transformed the Italian majolica tradition into something distinctively French. The Nevers potters developed a Chinese style employing Oriental subjects and the Chinese blue and white color scheme. They also added a richly intertwining border pattern of leaves and flowers. Nevers was the leader during the 17th century.

In the third-quarter of the 17th Century, four main schools—Rouen, Moustiers, Marseilles, and Strasbourg—developed. Rouen faience was characterized by "decor rayonnant," a richly intricate pattern of stylized leaves and florals which adorned the outer border, cascading in swags around a central flower burst that was adapted from the delicate lace and iron work of the mid-18th century Rococo patterns. Polychrome chonoiserie styles also were introduced.

Moustiers derived its early system of decoration from Nevers. The pioneer was Pierre Clerissy (1679–1739). The Chinese influence is in evidence in pattern design, form, and the blue and white palatte. The use of "grotesques," fantastic human or animal figures in scenes of wild vegetation, added excitement to the pieces.

In 1677 Joseph Clerissy came from Nevers to Marseilles. The Marseilles potters used border patterns that were heavier than at Moustiers. Landscape panels, acanthus leaves, or birds with foliage followed the Nevers style.

Strasbourg faience was influenced by the Rococo motifs from Rouen. In 1748–1749 a group of artists, who had worked at Meissen, arrived in Strasbourg from Hochst. They applied enamel painting techniques, giving the wares a more German than French appearance.

Before the French Revolution, faience factories were thriving. After the revolution and the treaty of commerce between England and France, English potters flooded the market with their industrial pottery that was cheaper to make, lighter in weight, easier to transport, and less liable to chip or crack under heat. This pottery appealed to both wholesale dealers and the public. The French factories experienced great difficulties competing. Many factories closed. By 1850 the French pottery industry was practically extinct.

References: Diana Imber, *Collecting European Delft and Faience*, Frederick A. Praeger, 1968; Arthur Lane, *French Faience*, Faber and Faber, 1970.

Museums: Musee Ceramique, Rouen, France; Musee des Arts Decoratifs, Paris, France; Victoria and Albert Museum, London, England.

REPRODUCTION ALERT: Collectors of French faience should be very wary of imitations being made in large quantities in modern day Paris. Genuine French faience is rare and only is offered for sale when a famous collection is dispersed.

Bird Cage, 18" h, blue and white coloration, "France" **1,250.00**
Bourdalou, 9" l, puce, green-blue, and purple flower sprays, scroll handle

Bell, 8¼" h, multicolored, "Bayeux," $85.00.

with puce accents, c1750, attrib to Strasbourg 110.00
Bowl
  8" w, cov, painted floral garlands, entwined handles, blue accents, branch finial, blue dot rims, c1770, Sceaux (A) 715.00
  10" d, painted bouquets of flowers, late 18th C, rim chips 75.00
  10½" d, blue floral and scroll design, white ground, mid 18th C 150.00
  11" d, 3" h, floral design, yellow, blue, green, and purple (A) 75.00
Butter Tub, 9½" w, multicolored floral sprays, oval shape, fixed stand, dbl handles, c1760, Strasbourg 240.00
Candlesticks, 8" h, painted flowers, sprays and butterflies, brown rims on nozzles, octagonal, wide bases, c1770, Strasbourg, pr (A) 6,380.00
Chamberstick, 8" h, overall floral design in blues, greens and rust, large blue and green loop handle, Rouen 85.00
Cistern, 13⅞" h, multicolored florals on upper section, fluted lower section with brown and iron-red mask, baluster form, late 18th C (A) 150.00
Coffee Can and Saucer, painted coat of arms, lion, eagle, and crown, gilt floral sprays on border, gilt dentil rims, c1775, Marseilles (A) 825.00
Compote, 9" h, peasant woman with distaff, floral and cross-hatched border, scalloped edge, banded center, sgd "Roscoff," Mont St Michel mark 150.00
Cruet Stand
  8½" h, lobed body with bands of scrolls and foliage divided by two masks, top with four openings with net pattern panels, three paw feet, blue coloring on white body, late 18th C 80.00

10½" l, modeled as ship, pierced gallery, bow and stern form scroll handles, puce accents, turquoise base simulating waves, two fitted glass stoppered bottles, four circ openings, c1750, blue "iH" mark, Strasbourg (A) **1,650.00**

Cup and Saucer, dark green painting of women in landscape panels, gilt rims with foliage and flowerheads, c1760, Marseilles (A) **336.00**

Dish

5" l, cov, polychrome flowering plants from cornucopia, int. divided into three sections, oval, flowerhead finial, c1750, Rouen (A) **1,650.00**

7¼" w, polychrome chinoiserie figures on terrace, border of plants and rockwork, octagonal, c1730, Rouen (A) **990.00**

7½" l, painted garden flower sprays, chocolate rim, quatrefoil shape, c1750, Strasbourg (A) **910.00**

8¾" d, blue and white flowerheads in center in chain, raised border with band of foliage and scrolls, blue ground, everted pie crust rim on three knob and ball feet, c1735, Lille (A) **355.00**

10½" d, scattered flowers with manganese rims, c1760, Strasbourg, pr(A) **520.00**

11¼" l, center painted bouquets, molded border with green and manganese, c1765, Meillonas (A) **1,540.00**

12" d, bouquets of multicolored flowers, hexafoil shape, shaped rim, c1730, blue "PH" mark, Strasbourg (A) **235.00**

12⅛" d, manganese bird, butterfly, and flowers, molded rim, c1755, Luneville (A) **415.00**

13¼" d, center painted basket of flowers on ledge, border with band of stylized flowerheads, scrolls, and foliage, blue ground, octagonal, raised rim, c1725, blue "iH" mark, Strasbourg (A) **3,520.00**

13⅜" d, man on galloping horse in center, floral vine border, multicolored, late 18th C (A) **175.00**

14⅛" l, painted Oriental figures in landscapes and scattered florals, shaped ovals, c1780, pr **100.00**

14¾" d, three bouquets of painted flowers, molded border, c1750, blue "PH" mark, Strasbourg (A) .. **285.00**

18" d, dark blue glaze with white spotting, late 18th C, Nevers, repaired (A) **300.00**

Drug Jar, 8½" h, cobalt Latin inscription in floral wreath, inverted baluster shape, early 18th C, Nevers (A) **200.00**

Ecuelle

7½" d, matching stand, multicolored cornflowers and roses, branch handles end in fruiting terminals, gilt rims, c1780, St. Clement **200.00**

10½" d, cov, polychrome bouquets of flowers, blue line borders, dbl handled, c1750, Moustiers **360.00**

Ewer, 15" h, Renaissance Revival period, shell form, polychrome bust and lizard decoration, overall vine and trailing leaf decor, late 19th C **170.00**

Figure

4¼' h, "Autumn" and "Winter" as children in cloaks, multicolored, grass mound bases, c1770, Sceaux, pr **750.00**

5½" l

Shoe, polychrome flowers and tied ribbon, c1730, Nevers (A) **330.00**

Shoe, portrait of woman and foliage, multicolored, dated 1745, Sinceny (A) **220.00**

6½" h, "Spring" and "Winter" as children on rockwork base, applied flowers, white glaze, c1750, Sceaux **750.00**

7" h

Begger boy with arms tucked under jacket, sq grass mound base, unglazed c1755, (A) **420.00**

Boy in jacket, breeches, and cap, arms tucked under jacket, multicolored, grass mound base, c1775, St Clement (A) **165.00**

7¼" h, Magician, young girl carrying magic box, dog inside, holding magic wand, multicolored, grass mound base, c1775, St Clement (A) **275.00**

7½" l, recumbent cows, facing right and left, manganese splashes, oblong bases, c1780, Lille, pr (A) ...**1,430.00**

8" h, huntsman, blowing horn, multicolored hunt clothes, tree stump mound base, c1750, Strasbourg . **4,500.00**

8¼" h, 2 boys and girl, playing instruments, peasant clothes, multicolored, tall scroll-molded base, c1770, Sceaux **750.00**

8¼" h, 8½" h, boy in tricorn hat and period clothes next to game board on pedestal, girl, weeping, holding losing hand, peasant dress, multicolored, early 19th C, pr **600.00**

18½" l, 14" h, polychrome recumbent lion, oblong white and green sponged base 18th C, Luneville (A) **2,200.00**

Flask

5½" h, chinoiserie figures in landscapes, yellow, manganese, and white on sides, opaque blue ground, c1755, St Omer (A) **2,310.00**

8½" h, painted sportsmen in landscapes in ribbon cartouche, dbl loop handles, flared foot and garlic formed neck with accents, c1700, Nevers (A) **310.00**

Inkstand

4⅝" l, pentray, inkwell, and ponce pot, blue ferns, white ground, 18th C (A) **120.00**

9½" l, pentray, two covered wells, and ponce pots, gold griffins, white ground, pale blue dolphin finials in covers, set on four blue feet, "Gien" **285.00**

Inkwell, 5″ l, 3″ h, multicolored Oriental florals, yellow ground, "Aladin, France," $75.00.

Inkwell

3¾" l, hp pastoral scene, florals, "Nidervilles, France" **250.00**

6"l, single, blue, green, yellow, and rust florals, white ground, scalloped edge, "Rouen, France" **135.00**

Jar, 11" h, cov, polychrome continuous scene of Oriental figures and dragons, cylindrical, screw cover, spike finial, c1760, Rouen (A) **3,300.00**

Jardiniere

3¾" h, white birds, insects and florals, blue ground, dbl rope twist handles, 18th C, attributed to Nevers **150.00**

7¼" w, painted Cupid and lady, spindle on side, rope twist dbl handles, blue accents, c1670, Nevers (A) . .**1,650.00**

Jug

5" h, peasant man, native costume, multicolored, Rouen **75.00**

9" h, polychrome ribbon-tied bouquet and sprays, ribbed body, molded strap handle, 18th C, Strasbourg (A) **140.00**

Knife Rest, floral decor, pale blue ground, Rouen **20.00**

Milk Jug, 5" h, "Bleu Persian" design, white pavilion and Oriental shrubs and rocks, blue ground, rope twist handle, c1660–80, Nevers (A) **605.00**

Pitcher

5" h, man in peasant costume on front, soft colors, Rouen **45.00**

7" h, large crimson rose, blue floral sprays tied with red ribbon, ribbed body, molded strap handle, 18th C, Strasbourg (A) **100.00**

Plaque, 12½" w, 15¾" h, Emperor Augustus on horse, blue, ochre, and yellow, Latin inscription, c1625, Nevers (A) **4,400.00**

Plate

8" d

Hp red and blue flowers, green leaves, red dash border, scalloped edge, late 18th C **175.00**

Multicolored rooster **20.00**

8½" d, center section of French chateau, multicolored, blue and yellow outline of border, scalloped edge, c1800, Nevers "A. Montagnon" **120.00**

8¾" d

Folk style floral decor, bright colors, 19th C, set of 4 (A) **45.00**

Polychrome leaf and floral decor, mid 19th C, pr **110.00**

9" d

Blue, green, and pink floral sprays, white ground, c1800, attributed to Tourniere, set of 6 . . . . **450.00**

Painted masonic emblems, Hebrew and Latin inscription, foliage and flowerhead border, shaped rim, c1765, Nevers (A) **550.00**

Painted putto in clouds, foliage and flowerhead border, shaped rim, c1765, Nevers (A) **550.00**

9½" d

Center figures and river landscape, multicolored, border with lambrequin, shaped rim, c1700, Moustiers (A) **2,200.00**

Painted flowers and insects in center, pierced basketweave border, puce and light yellow accents, c1765, Sceaux (A) **2,420.00**

Painted insects, bouquets and flower sprays, pierced border, green and puce foliage and puce line rim, c1770, black "VP", Marseilles (A) **440.00**

9⅝" d

Painted Chinese man holding fan in rockwork vignette, butterflies and insects on border, puce rim, c1780, Luneville (A) **220.00**

Painted large spray of flowers, two small sprays, brown rims, c1780, blue"IH", Strasbourg, pr (A) . . . **300.00**

Painted scattered garden flowers, shaped chocolate rim, c1750, Strasbourg **480.00**

9¾" d
Painted floral sprays and insects, shaped brown line rims, c1770, Marseilles, set of 3 (A) **1,045.00**

Painted floral sprays, insects, and shells, shaped rim, gilt foliage, c1770, Marseilles (A) **440.00**

Painted carnation in center, shaped rim, three flower sprays, c1770, Sceaux (A) **880.00**

Plate, 9¾" d, blue, red, and green florals, blue "Rouen" mark, $175.00.

9⅞" d
Bouquet of flowers and sprays, puce rim, hexafoil shape, c1780, Luneville **160.00**

Green and manganese birds and flowering plants, shaped borders, c1760, Moustiers, pr (A) **260.00**

10¼" d, green and ochre figures in landscape, flowered border, shaped rim, c1740, Moustiers (A) **845.00**

10½" d, hp floral decoration, basket-weave border (A) **40.00**

12⅜" d, polychrome outdoor country scene of men smoking at table, woman behind fence, shaped hexagon rim, "Fait Parmoy Gilot 1773" (A) **60.00**

Platter, 12½" l, 9" w, blue phoenix in center, indented rim outlined in blue with blue border of Oriental flowers, mid 18th C, Moustier **750.00**

Potpourri Jar, 10½" w, cov, center harbor scene in molded floral garland, scroll handles, suspended garlands, three scroll feet, pierced cover with flowering finial, c1750, Moustiers . .**1,400.00**

Puzzle Jug, 6" h, blue and ochre single flower, pierced neck, 18th C **100.00**

Salt
3¼" d, cov, blue and white bird, stripes on cover, stylized foliage on foot, c1700, Rouen (A) **310.00**

7¼" h, figures of period ladies holding oval dishes on scrollwork stands, multicolored, late 18th C, pr (A) . **350.00**

8½" h, master, dbl, figure of peasant woman, white ground trimmed in green and blue flowers, salts trimmed in rust, "1792" on front, Mont St Michel **265.00**

Sauce Tureen, 9" l, attached base, molded scrolls, multicolored flowers, scroll knob, c1770, Luneville **500.00**

Saucer, painted flower sprays, brown rim, mid 18th C, blue "PH" (A) **75.00**

Snuff Box, 3" l, molded basketwork, white glaze, gilt metal mounted, mid 18th C, "Pont Aux Choux" (A) **715.00**

Spice Box, 5¼" w, cov, iron-red and blue floral baskets and shells, blue ground, center with three trellis panels, trefoil lappet shape, three stump feet and flowerhead finial, c1730, Rouen (A) **2,860.00**

Spirit Flask, 7⅞" h, molded mask and dolphin in mottled manganese, green, and ochre glazes, 18th C (A) **90.00**

Stand, 15½" l, blue lambrequin with flowerheads and scrolls, white ground, multiple stump feet, c1760, Tavernes **550.00**

Sugar, cov, bouquets of flowers, yellow ground, lemon finial, c1770, Moustiers (A) **65.00**

Tankard, 7¾" h, dark blue ground, white spots, c1680–1700, Nevers (A) **415.00**

Tazza, 11¼" d, center basket of flowers, yellow, ochre, and blue, border of heavy scrolling foliage with putti, raised rim, trellis, and florals, raised foot, band of florals, octagonal, 18th C, Rouen (A) **1,210.00**

Teapot
7" w, painted flowers, branch handle and foliage terminals, flowerhead finial, globular, c1750, Strasbourg (A) **2,200.00**

9¾" w, painted center of chinoiserie figures in river landscape, green border with insects, c1765, St Clement, repaired (A) **1,540.00**

Tureen, Covered
8¼" l, modeled walking partridges, facing right and left, puce and brown incised feathers, oval grass mound bases, foliage stalks, c1748, Strasbourg, pr (A) **18,700.00**

11" h, pale blue decor and red dots, white ground, early 19th C, Nevers **225.00**

12¾" w, modeled as cabbage, yellow and blue-green, c1760, Sceaux (A) **2,530.00**

15¼" l, figural, nesting hen in purple wash, three chicks and eggs modeled on base, early 19th C **1,450.00**

Vase

6⅝" h, "Bleu Persian" design, dentil and dot border, (A) **715.00**

7½" h, blue painted bands of Berlainesque scrolls, foliage, and tassels, late 17th C, Rouen, damaged (A) . **935.00**

8" h, floral and scroll design, dark blue and gold-yellow, red accents, wide bulbous body ends in flared top, narrow base on four feet, two small handles, c1920, "Rouen and #'s", pr **150.00**

16" h, "Persian," blue ground, overall white splashes, bottle shape, c1660 (A) **6,600.00**

18⅛" l, cov, shaped panels with Orientals, multicolored dogs and birds, outlined in chocolate, blue ground, oval baluster shape, pearl finials on domed covers, pr **720.00**

Wall Jardiniere, 7" h, yellow, green, manganese, and blue fruit bouquet, two birds under tassels, 19th C, Moustiers (A) **110.00**

services and various utilitarian and decorative wares were competitive with those produced by other 18th century factories.

The period of 1770 to 1790 was the golden age at the Furstenberg factory. Materials improved considerably, additional enamel colors were utilized, and gilding was employed in the border patterns. After 1775 Neo-classical influences appeared.

During the French occupation, Brunswick was part of the Kingdom of Westphalia ruled by Napoleon's brother, Jerome Bonaparte. The factory became the Royal Porcelain Manufactory from 1807 to 1813. After Napoleon's defeat, Brunswick regained its independence. In 1813 the former name was restored. The factory continued to produce tablewares, decorative porcelains, figures, and coffee and tea sets.

In 1859 Furstenberg was leased by the Brunswick government. Private ownership took over again in 1876. The company was reorganized as a joint stock company and named Furstenberg Porcelain Factory AG. Today, the factory still manufactures a great variety of vases, tablewares, and other porcelains.

References: George A. Ware, *German & Austrian Porcelain*, Crown, Inc., 1963.

Museums: Museum fur Kunst und Gewerbe, Hamburg, Germany; National Museum, Stockholm, Sweden; Victoria and Albert Museum, London, England.

1753 - 70   1922-58

FURSTENBERG

Brunswick, Germany, now West Germany
1747–1859 Royal-State
1859–Present-Private

History: The Furstenberg factory was founded in 1747 in the castle of Karl I, Duke of Brunswick, primarily to satisfy his vanity. Six years passed before porcelain was produced in 1753. The technique came from artists who left Hochst. By 1770 the porcelain paste closely approximated that made at Meissen.

Many figures were modeled, but the amount of production was not great. The figures imitated figural molds and decorations produced at Meissen and Berlin. English styles—Bow, Wedgwood, Chelsea, and Sevres—also were copied. After 1760, Frankenthal vases became famous. China

Coffee Service, 9½" h coffeepot, cream jug, cov sugar bowl, five cake plates, cups and saucers, pink florals, white ground, blue "F" mark, $165.00.

Bonbonniere, 3½" h, painted, figures in landscape vignettes, oviform, contemporary silver gilt mounts, c1770, (A) **570.00**

Candlestick, 10¼" h, "Kiss," shepherd and shepherdess embracing between two trees supporting rococo candle nozzles, dog on base (A) **785.00**

Cup and Saucer

Brown ivy wreaths, white ground, early 19th C, blue "F 19" mark .. **85.00**

Painted bouquet and scattered flowers, c1775, blue "F" mark **115.00**

Painted purple putti in clouds, gilt dashed C-scroll and trellis borders, c1765, blue "F" mark (A) **490.00**

Sepia portrait of Martin Luther in oval, gilt rims, c1775, blue "F" mark (A) **285.00**

Cups, Covered, and Saucers, painted silhouettes of lady or gentleman on light pink ground in gilt medallions, scattered florals, monogram and electoral hat on saucers, c1790, blue script "F" marks, pr (A) **3,695.00**

Custard Cups, cov, painted flower sprays, ribbons and swags, borders with gadroons, fruit finial, c1775, blue "F" marks, set of 3 (A) **425.00**

Figure

3½" h, miner, seated, hammering rock, black coat, yellow breeches, and green hat, splashes in blue, green, and yellow, rococo scroll base, c1757 (A) **5,200.00**

5" h

Mezzatin, standing, touching nose, manganese breeches, jacket, cap, and cloak, tree stump scroll base, c1759–62 (A) **490.00**

Miner, standing, holding hammer before rock, black and red hat, lilac blouse, green breeches, and black apron, c1773, blue "F" mark (A) **5,200.00**

6¾" h, Russian lemonade seller, holding jug in one hand, glass in other, pink and mauve clothes, c1775, blue "F" mark (A) **810.00**

6⅞" h, Zeus, nude, holding thunderbolt, eagle at side, lilac cloak, c1760 (A) **855.00**

9½" h, Pan modeled as seated nude bearded man playing flute, multicolored, flower-applied base, c1774, blue "F" mark (A) **1,960.00**

10⅜" h, Cossack riding horse, rockwork ground, shaped oval scroll-molded base, white, blue "F" mark (A) **300.00**

19¼" h, Frederick the Great, mounted on horse, rect base with crown monogram and martial trophies, white, 19th C, blue script "F" mark, (A) **120.00**

Medallions, 3⅛" d, painted silhouette busts of Prussian Royal Family, molded gilt borders, named on reverse, c1786, blue script "F" marks, set of 6 (A) **4,930.00**

Plaque

3" h, bisque, portrait bust of Selchow, glazed border, inscription on reverse, c1782 (A) **85.00**

6¼" l, 4¾", each painted with pastoral scenes in landscape vignettes, gilt frame surrounds, pierced scroll and foliage angles, rect, c1765, blue script "F" mark, set of 5 (A) **29,100.00**

7⅞" l, 5⅞" h, painting of shepherds and flock in river landscape, ruined buildings, molded gilt rococo frame, c1770, blue "F" mark (A) **.8,980.00**

Plate

8¼" d, painted bouquet in spirally molded border, four sprays, c1770, blue "F" mark (A) **150.00**

9" d, pear, apple and grape center, multicolored, imp gold leaf edge, marked **75.00**

9⅛" d, painted landscape centers, spirally-fluted rims, borders of flowers and puce scrolls, c1760, view identification on reverse, blue "F" mark, pr (A) **880.00**

9½" d, centers with turkey and fowl in meadow, and cockerel, hen, and chick by fence, borders with molded scale and foliate scroll panels, birds in branches, shaped gilt dentil rims, c1770, blue "F" mark, pr (A) **1,115.00**

10" d, fruit center, gold leaf border, inlaid effect, marked **55.00**

Scent Bottle, 4⅜" l, painted flowers in C-scroll molded cartouches, contemporary gilt mounts, c1770 (A) **385.00**

Scent Flask

4¾" h, painted floral bouquets in molded gilt C-scroll cartouches and basketwork, pink ground, contemporary gold mounts, c1775 (A) ... **525.00**

5⅞" h, molded rococo cartouches, multicolored gallants, and ladies, gilt metal neck and stopper, c1770 (A) **715.00**

Snuff Box

3⅛" w, base painted, putti in landscape in molded C-scroll and foliage cartouches, cov with horseman, engraved foliage on silver mounts (A) **1,296.00**

3½" w, molded Bacchanalian figures and animals in vines, cov with portrait bust of youth in molded scroll, int. of cov with Bacchanalian figures and goat in landscape, gilt metal mounts, c1775 (A) **375.00**

Solitaire Set, 3⅜" h teapot, 4⅜" h wooden handled coffee pot, tea

caddy, cup and saucer, "CW" formed
from painted florals, puce and gray
coronet, gilt scrolled rims, c1775,
blue "F" mark (A) **1,760.00**
Vase
13⅛" h, multicolored figures in landscape, leaf molded handles,
painted by Hartmann, c1780, blue
"F and AD" mark (A) **770.00**
14⅜" h, cov, multicolored German
flowers, gilded cartouche and scroll
handles, pierced covs, (one replaced,) c1770, blue "F" mark, pr
(A) **990.00**
15" h, cov, painted mountainous
landscapes on sides, fluted lower
section, gilt laurel band on shoulder, sq base, dbl handles, c1780
(A) **1,045.00**

Museums: Bowes Museum, Barnard Castle, Dur-
ham, England; Musee des Arts et Metiers, Paris,
France.

Collecting Hints: Galle faience now is prevalent
in the American antiques market. Cat, parrot,
and dog figures are seen in various colors and
sizes. Sets of plates, three sectioned dishes, tureens, wall vases, and inkwells are eagerly
sought. Large candlesticks with figures of lions
are among the most expensive pieces.

**Figure, 9¼" h, pottery, black glaze,
$700.00.**

GALLE

**Nancy, France
1874–1904**

History: Emile Galle, a leading designer and
manufacturer of art glass, first made faience in
Nancy, France, in 1874. Later he experimented
with both stoneware and porcelain. Galle's decorations included heraldic motifs and scenes that
resembled Delft ware. A series of souvenir dishes
was made to commemorate the Franco-Prussian
War.

Glazes used were flowing and opaque in nature. Sometimes several colors were mixed together. Most of the forms were simple in design.

Victor Prouve, an artist friend of Galle, provided designs for figures of bulldogs and cats.
The most popular figures were painted yellow
with blue hearts and circles, black and white
with pale indigo blue, or beige with pink and
green decorations of naturalistic flowers. Green
glass eyes were used. Prouve's designs were used
for candlesticks of heraldic lions and grotesque
and fantastic ducks, fox, owls, swans, and par-
akeets. Plant designs of dandelions, chrysanthemums, and orchids were used in Art Nouveau
style decorations that duplicated Galle's work on
glass.

All of Galle's ceramics were marked with the
impressed initials E.G., Em. Galle Faiencerie de
Nancy, or some version of his signature.

Basket, 9" h, "Ancient Coins" design,
multicolored **550.00**
Bowl, 9½" w, 5¼" h, blue coastal scene
in molded cartouche, molded wavy
rim, gilt trim, repaired **225.00**
Box, cov, multicolored design on pottery body, fleur-de-lis shape **350.00**
Centerpiece, 14" l, painted harbor
scene, lotus pond on reverse, cream
ground, dragonfly on int. and ends,
gilt accents, c1880 (A) **520.00**
Cup and Undertray, overall cornflower
design, oblong, circ black mark **85.00**
Ewer, 8" h, painted scene of man on
barrel and couple fishing, multicolored **575.00**
Figure
13¼" h, dog seated on haunches,
mustard glazed body, black glass
eyes, dark brown coat, and light
blue collar **850.00**
15½" l, 7" h, faience, ducks, blue,
white, and rust-orange, pr **900.00**
19" h, cat, seated, blue inverted
hearts and circles on orange-yellow
ground **850.00**
Planter, 13½" l, dark gray-green ground,
harbor scene in tan and brown

shades, gold accents, canoe shape, four small feet, "Emile Galle" **1,275.00**
Plate, 9" d, intertwined initials in center, white body with blue decor, pierced border, "Galle, France" **90.00**
Teapot, enameled flowers on each side, shaded beige, rust, and blue ground, gold accents, bird's head spout, lion's head on edge **850.00**

Vase, Posey, 12½" h, molded hydrangia design, multicolored, "E. Galle, Nancy, France," $1,250.00.

Vase
  6" h
    Pink and green dots, white flowers on lavender ground **475.00**
    Front panel with two figures, reverse with bird in cage, gold, blue, and red **350.00**
  11" h, raised white flowers and gray trailing leaves, brown glazed ground, raised points on rim, dbl rect handles, "E Galle, France" ..**1,250.00**
Wall Pocket, 14" h, faience, painted blue and brown butterflies and bows, gold and black accents, fan shape .. **450.00**
Watch Holder, 10" h, painted country scenes, leaves, branches, and insects **600.00**

GAME PLATES AND SETS

English/Continental c1870–1915

History: Game plates and sets, usually including a large platter, serving plates, and a sauce or gravy boat, were popular between 1870 and 1915 both in England and on the Continent. They were specially decorated plates used to serve game and fish. Subjects utilized by the makers included all types of game birds, e. g., quail, snipe, pheasants, mallards, etc., and fish. Among the principal French manufacturers were Haviland and firms in Limoges. Makers in England included Crescent and Sons, Mason, Royal Doulton, Wedgwood, and Royal Worcester. Factories in Bavaria, Villeroy and Boch in Germany, and Royal Vienna in Austria also made game plates and sets.

Charger, 12" d, game bird in woodland setting, pink and yellow roses, connecting garlands, scalloped rim, Bavaria **75.00**
Plaque
  9¾" d, quail on one, partridge on other, multicolored, pierced for hanging, "B and H," pr **90.00**
  11½" d, game bird, shades of brown, green, and cream, gold rococo border, Bavaria **235.00**
  13½" d, pair of snipe in forest setting, gold rococo border, sgd "Du Bois," "L. S. and S. Limoges" **250.00**
Plate
  6" d, pheasants in meadow, cobalt and gilt border, sgd "Stinton," Royal Worcester **195.00**
  8" d, mallards, swimming, multicolored, sgd "Beck" **20.00**
  8¼" d, pheasants, house and tower landscape, multicolored, R S Germany **55.00**

Plate, 8¾" d, multicolored snipes, magenta border with gold overlay, sgd "Birbeck," "Crescent & Sons, England," $35.00.

9" d
  Bird in woods in center, four smaller scenes of ducks in fall

colored setting, gold scrolling, "P M Bavaria" **50.00**

Duck in pond, brown and yellow shades, sgd "A. Porter" **60.00**

Ducks, browns and yellows, natural setting **100.00**

Forest bird in center, dark blue coloration, tracery border, sgd "R. J.," "Royal Worcester" **190.00**

Game Birds, each decor with different game bird, gilt borders, yellow ground, gilt vert lines, scalloped edges, bone china, sgd "J. Birbeck," England, set of 12, (A) **275.00**

Game Birds, each decor with different game birds, natural settings, light yellow ground, formal borders, titled on reverse, sgd "J. H. Plant," Royal Doulton, set of 6 .... **700.00**

Game Birds, each painted with different game bird, shaped and gilt rims, "Copeland, made for Tiffany and Co," set of 6 (A) **175.00**

Pheasant in center, multicolored, green border, gold trim, "Petrus Regout, Maastricht, Holland" .. **10.00**

"The Red Grouse", multicolored, Mason **40.00**

Woodcock in center, multicolored, green border and gold trim, "Petrus Regout, Maastricht, Holland" **10.00**

9⅛" d, game birds, each decor with different game bird, landscape setting, cream ground, border with six panels of florals and gilt trellis and diapering, sgd "T Wilson," c1913, Royal Doulton, set of 12 (A) **1,760.00**

9¼" d

Flying prairie chicken, multicolored, sgd "R. K. Beck" **70.00**

Forest bird in rust, yellow, brown, and green, multicolored ground, lone tree, sgd "Max," "Coronet, Limoges" **125.00**

Game birds, each hp with different game bird, natural setting, scalloped and gold rims, Haviland and Co, set of 8 .... **350.00**

Game birds, each with different game birds, landscapes extending to gilt shaped rims, sgd "J. Birbeck," Royal Doulton, set of 11 (A) **475.00**

Pair of birds in soft natural setting, buildings, flowers, and leaves, gold rococo rim, "B. H., Limoges" **50.00**

Snipes in woodland setting in central medallion, green rim, stenciled gilt design **145.00**

9½"

Fish, different fish species in centers, multicolored, species named on reverse, sgd "C. Hart," Royal Doulton, set of 12 .....**1,500.00**

Game birds in natural settings, cobalt borders, shaped rims and wide etched gilt borders, sgd "Muville" and "Dubois," Limoges, set of 22 (A) **825.00**

Grouse in center, five medallions of birds and insects, shaded brown to tan, border shaded green, "Z. S. and Co.Bavaria" **45.00**

Grouse on one, partridge on other, earthtones of gray, tan, brown, and lt orange, sgd "J. Mongars," Limoges, pr **150.00**

Pair of pheasants, multicolored, "Coronet, Limoges" **35.00**

Pheasant in center of one, snipe in other, cobalt borders, gold filigree, sgd "Charles Hart," Royal Doulton, pr **400.00**

Pheasant in flight, multicolored, gold rococo border, "Coronet, Limoges" **50.00**

Pheasant in wooded setting, multicolored, scalloped border, Bavaria **45.00**

9¾" d, game birds, each painted with different game bird in natural setting, cream and light green ground, gilt accents, Minton, set of 10 ... **600.00**

10" d

Canadian geese, transfers, pink and gold borders, Royal Vienna, pr . **65.00**

Deer and doe, multicolored, gold scalloped edge, pierced for hanging, sgd "Pradet," "Coronet, Limoges" **90.00**

Elk, multicolored, dark brown to amber scalloped border, Limoges **20.00**

Geese in flight, multicolored, pearlized finish, Hutschenreuther .. **60.00**

Two grouse in water scene, "Imperial Crown China" **45.00**

10⅛" d, large quail, pastel meadow setting, gold scalloped border, sgd "L. Coudert," "Coronet, Limoges" **175.00**

10¼" d

Pair of pheasants in meadow in center, green border, gold lace, scalloped edge, "Schumann, Bavaria" **75.00**

Pheasant on one, quail on other, multicolored, dull gold borders, scalloped edges, sgd "Max," Limoges, pr **250.00**

10¾" d, center of game birds in brown, yellow, and gray, green and yellow background, scalloped edge, pierced for hanging, sgd "L. Coudert," Limoges **135.00**

11½" d

Quail and duck medallions, multicolored, "P. M. Bavaria" **30.00**

Pheasant on branch, yellow, orange, and blue, mountain and lake setting, gold rococo border, pierced for hanging, sgd "Felix," "Limoges, F. Dartigeas, France" paper label **225.00**

12" d

Duck in flight with iris, hp, multicolored, "Limoges Flambeau" . **80.00**

Ram and two ewes in glade, sgd "R. K. Beck" **95.00**

Spaniel and flying pheasant forest setting, hp, multicolored, Limoges **175.00**

Two ducks swimming, landscape setting, irreg gold edge, Limoges **165.00**

Two snipes standing by water, landscape setting, irreg gold edge, Limoges **165.00**

12¼" d, pair of grouse in flight, multicolored, gold rococo border, pierced for hanging, sgd "Rogin", Limoges **250.00**

13" d

Scottish grouse on fir tree branch, landscape setting, transfer print, gold border, dbl handles, Limoges, Haviland blank **235.00**

Two deer in natural wooded setting, blue and green **295.00**

13¼" d, flying and grounded pheasant on one, flying and grounded snipe on other, gold rococo borders, pierced for hanging, Limoges, pr **600.00**

Platter

12" l, scene of three birds in flight, "Coronet, Limoges" **110.00**

21" l, 14⅛" w, multicolored male and female pheasant in meadow, gold scalloped edge, dbl gold twist handles, sgd "Duc," Limoges **450.00**

Platter Sets

9¼" d plates, set of eleven, cov sauceboat and undertray, each painted with different game bird, brown arabesque borders, c1890, Royal Worcester (A) **350.00**

13" d charger, twelve 9" d plates, charger with two quail in sunset landscape, plates with different game birds, gold rococo edges, Limoges **650.00**

14" l, 8" w platter, twelve 5½" d plates, small birds and florals, white ground, gold trim, "GDM Limoges" **350.00**

16" l platter, seven 8½" d plates, game birds in flight, multicolored, Limoges **300.00**

16" l, 10" w platter, four 10" d plates, two partridges in field, multicolored, gold borders, Limoges **280.00**

16¼" l platter, eight 8½" d plates, hp grouse in flight, wavy edges, Limoges **285.00**

16½" l, 12" w platter, pheasants in natural setting, four 8½" d plates, ducks in natural settings, green shaded borders, emb beaded rims, Victoria, Austria **135.00**

18" l platter, ten 9" d plates, quails and pheasants in fields, multicolored, c1892, sgd "Muville," Limoges **550.00**

18" l platter, twelve 9" d plates, hp game birds in centers, openwork edges, gold trim, "BWM and Co, England" **575.00**

18" l platter, six 9½" d plates, two game birds, dark brown ground, pink dogwoods, gold borders, Limoges **600.00**

18½" l platters, two 8½" l platters, twelve 7½" sq plates, printed and painted with different game birds in natural settings, cobalt borders accented with gilt, bronze, and silver branches, "CFH/GDM, Haviland, Limoges" (A) **880.00**

19" l, 13" w platter, eight 8" d plates, deer in meadow, borders of wild animals, emb scrollwork rims, imp "J. S. and fleur-de-lis" mark, Germany **160.00**

19½" l platter with pair of game birds, six 9⅝" d plates, three bird designs, hp gold scrolled borders, c1900, Haviland, France (A) **300.00**

23½" l platter, twelve 9" d plates, fish decor, different fish on each plate, chrome yellow border, gold trim, "Limoges, France" **400.00**

Tray

14" l, two pheasants, brown border and gold, rect, sgd "R. H. Beck" . **50.00**

14" l, 7" w, multicolored pheasant, oval beaded medallions, open dbl handles, "R S Prussia" red mark . **525.00**

Turkey Set, 20½" l platter with scene of two wild turkeys, twelve 10" d plates, six hp different designs, artist sgd, "Limoges, France" **600.00**

ГАРДНЕРZ

GARDNER

Verbiki, near Moscow, Russia
1766–1891

History: Francis Gardner founded his factory in 1766. He brought experienced European potters and decorators to Russia, where utilitarian wares, artistic objects, and articles for sale at fairs comprised the production.

Floral motifs and pastoral scenes were favored. Many dinner sets were made on commission. The Gardner family controlled the factory until 1891 when it was acquired by the Kuznetsov family.

Collecting Hints: The initial "G" or name "Gardner" was used as the mark.

References: Marvin Ross, *Russian Porcelains*, University of Oklahoma Press, 1918.

Museums: Hermitage, Leningrad, Russia.

Figure, 8¼″ h, peasant woman, brown coat, purple skirt, green scarf, porcelain, (A) $770.00.

Figure
    4½″ h, porcelain, young peasant woman picking mushrooms, multicolored, 19th C (A) **410.00**
    5¼″ h, porcelain
      Balalaika player, striped pants, white tunic, 19th C **275.00**
      Old peasant woman, seated on bench holding spindle and thread, multicolored, 19th C (A) **415.00**
    5½″ h, painted standing peasant man

holding hat in hands on grassy knoll, 19th C **400.00**
5¾″ h, porcelain, boy wearing white apron and kerchief pushing wheelbarrow, multicolored, mid 19th C (A) **880.00**
6⅜″ h, porcelain, boy gardener wearing purple jacket, carrying plant, early 19th C (A) **1,210.00**
6½″ h, porcelain, Samoyed wearing fur tunic, bow and arrow in one hand, animal in other, multicolored, c1840, (A) **825.00**
6¾″ h, bisque, Russian male, seated, playing concertina, dressed in boots, cape and cap, multicolored, sq base **500.00**
7⅜″ h, porcelain, peasant woman, long blue dress, purple kerchief, carrying basket on shoulder, 19th C (A) **715.00**
8¾″ h, porcelain, young woman, tunic and skirt, wreath of flowers in hair, multicolored, 19th C (A) **550.00**
9⅛″ h, porcelain, classical maiden holding cornucopia in arms, multicolored, marbleized base, 19th C **400.00**
9½″ h
    Bisque, drunken man, bottle in hand, woman with child in back, multicolored, oval green base, brown rim **550.00**
    Porcelain, three drunken men, one playing accordian, multicolored tunics, 19th C (A) **1,430.00**

Plates, 9¾″ d, Star of Order of St. Andrew, multicolored, gilded rims, pr, (A) $4,125.00.

11″ l, sprawled bear, multicolored, late 19th C (A) **415.00**
11⅛″ h, porcelain, peasant woman carrying small boy on shoulder, unpainted, late 19th C **275.00**
11¾″ h, porcelain, peasant man carrying small girl on shoulder, unpainted, late 19th C **275.00**
12″ h, father holding child on shoulders, doe on base **1,200.00**

Tazza, 4½" h, fluted top, painted with flowers in center, borders of gilded scrolls, supported by figural seated Chinese man, mid 19th C (A) **470.00**

Teapot
4½" d, 5¼" h
  White medallion, multicolored florals, rose ground, white knob and handle **125.00**
  Round panels, hp flowers on sides, blue ground, white handle, gold trim **145.00**

GAUDY DUTCH

Staffordshire, England
c1810–1830

History: Staffordshire pottery with a gaudy Dutch motif was made for the American trade and experienced wide popularity from c1810–1830. White earthenwares, mostly plates and teawares, were made by a number of Staffordshire potters among whom were Riley and Wood. Painted patterns include: Butterfly, Grape, King's Rose, Oyster, Single Rose, Strawflower, Urn, War Bonnet, etc. Dominate colors are cobalt blue, bright yellow, green, red, and pink.

Reference: Eleanor J. Fox and Edward G. Fox, *Gaudy Dutch*, privately printed, 1970, out of print. Sam Laidacker, *Anglo-American China Part I*, Keystone Specialties, 1954, out of print; Earl F. Robacker, *Pennsylvania Dutch Stuff*, University of Pennsylvania Press, 1944, out of print.

Museums: Philadelphia Museum of Art, Philadelphia, PA; Reading Art Museum, Reading, PA.

REPRODUCTION ALERT: Cup plates, bearing the impressed mark "CYBRIS," have been reproduced and are collectible in their own right. The Henry Ford Museum has issued pieces in the Single Rose pattern, although they are of porcelain and not soft paste.

Creamer
  "Double Rose" pattern, unmarked .. **400.00**
  "Warbonnet" pattern, chipped (A) .. **55.00**
Cup and Saucer
  "Carnation" pattern (A) **250.00**
  "Grape" pattern (A) **130.00**
  "Oyster" pattern, unmarked (A) **65.00**
  "Single Rose" pattern
    Cup with handle (A) **180.00**
    Handleless **350.00**
    Three blue panels, three floral panels, c1815 .... **95.00**
Dinner Service, plate, seven small plates, four soup bowls, two side plates, two teabowls, floral design, c1830, imp "Riley" **3,600.00**

Plate, 7" d, "Single Rose" pattern, blue rim, $300.00.

Gravy Creamer, "Double Rose" pattern (A) **300.00**
Plate
  6¾" d, "Single Rose" pattern (A) ... **100.00**
  6⅞" d, "Single Rose" pattern, unmarked (A) **45.00**
  7" d
    "Grape" pattern, unmarked (A) .. **225.00**
    "Warbonnet" pattern **575.00**
  7¼" d
    "Double Rose" pattern, unmarked (A) **150.00**
    "Single Rose" pattern, unmarked (A) **100.00**
  7½" d, "Single Rose" pattern, unmarked (A) **125.00**
  8" d
    "Grape" pattern, unmarked **250.00**
    "Single Rose" pattern, unmarked . **350.00**
  8¼" d, "Carnation" pattern, unmarked (A) **160.00**
  8½" d
    "Carnation" pattern, unmarked .. **450.00**
    "Grape" pattern, unmarked **400.00**
    "Oyster" pattern, unmarked **675.00**
  9¾" d
    "Carnation" pattern, unmarked .. **450.00**
    "Grape" pattern, unmarked (A) .. **220.00**
Sugar, cov, "Single Rose" pattern, unmarked **675.00**
Teabowl and Saucer
  "Carnation" pattern, unmarked .. **500.00**
  "Double Rose" pattern, unmarked .. **400.00**
  "Dove" pattern, unmarked (A) **75.00**
  "Oyster" pattern, unmarked **400.00**
  "Sunflower" pattern, unmarked **775.00**
  "Warbonnet" pattern, unmarked ... **475.00**
Teapot, 6½" h, "Warbonnet" pattern, unmarked, repaired, (A) **225.00**
Toddy Plate, 5½" d
  "Urn" pattern, unmarked (A) **220.00**
  "Warbonnet" pattern, repaired (A) .. **325.00**
Waste Bowl, "Dove" pattern, unmarked **575.00**

GAUDY IRONSTONE

Staffordshire, England
1850–1865

History: Gaudy Ironstone was produced in the Staffordshire district between 1850 and 1865. Edward Walley's "wagon wheel" was a popular Gaudy Ironstone design similar to the design of Gaudy Welsh. Walley, who worked at Villa Pottery in Cobridge, utilized bright colors and floral designs to give a country or folk character to his pieces.

Collecting Hints: While some of the examples used the same colorations as Gaudy Welsh, other pieces used varying shades of red, pink, and orange with light blue and black accents. Some designs utilized copper luster, while others did not. The flow blue technique also was used on some Gaudy Ironstone pieces.

Bowl
    5¾" d, urn of flowers, design in blue,
      red, and green enamels and luster
      (A) **15.00**
    9⅞" d, 5½" h, floral design in blue,
      red, and green enamels and luster,
      ftd (A) **110.00**
Butter Dish, 3¼" h, leaf design in blue,
    red, blue, and luster border bands,
    octagonal (A) **85.00**
Coffeepot, 10⅜" h, copper luster swirl
    design (A) **115.00**
Creamer
    5" h, "Morning Glory" pattern, blue
      with luster (A) **45.00**
    5½" h, floral design in blue, red, and
      green enamels and luster (A) **40.00**
    5⅞" h, blue floral design, blue
      enamel (A) **15.00**
Cup and Saucer
    Floral and vine design
      Black, red and green enamels and
        luster, handleless (A) **10.00**
      Blue, brown, green, ochre, and
        black enamels, handleless (A) .. **10.00**
      Blue, green, ochre, and orange
        enamels and luster, handleless
        (A) **15.00**
    Floral design
      Blue, purple luster, red enamels,
        handleless, (A) **45.00**
      Blue, purple luster, red, green, and
        yellow enamels, handleless (A) . **55.00**
      Blue, red and green enamels and
        luster, handleless (A) **35.00**
      Blue, red enamel and luster, han-
        dleless (A) **20.00**
    Floral design with strawberries, blue
      and red, green and yellow enamels,
      handleless (A) **40.00**

Leaf and berry design, English registry
    mark (A) **55.00**
Leaf design in blue and red, luster and
    blue border bands, handleless (A) **30.00**
"Morning Glory" pattern, blue with
    luster, handleless (A) **5.00**
Seaweed design in blue, red, green,
    and luster, handleless (A) **30.00**
"Strawberry" pattern in blue, green
    and red enamels and luster, handle-
    less (A) **50.00**
Urn of flowers design in blue, red,
    green, and luster (A) **10.00**
"Wheel" pattern, blue, luster and red
    enamels (A) **35.00**
Dish
    5" l, "Morning Glory" pattern in blue,
      luster, shell shape (A) **40.00**
    7½" l, "Strawberry" pattern in blue,
      red, and green enamels (A) **40.00**
    8⅝" d, "Morning Glory" pattern in
      blue, luster and enameled red and
      green strawberries (A) **40.00**
    8⅝" l, "Morning Glory" pattern in
      blue, luster, octagonal (A) **35.00**
Hot Water Jug, Cov, 12" h, blue and
    orange florals, gold accents, fluted
    sides, "James Dixon and Sons" mark **155.00**
Miniature Teabowl and Saucer, "Morn-
    ing Glory" pattern, blue with luster
    (A) **40.00**
Mug
    2⅞" h, blue stripes, luster and wavy
      red lines (A) **25.00**
    3⅜" h, "Morning Glory" design, blue
      and copper luster (A) **20.00**
Pitcher
    5¾" h, multicolored florals, octago-
      nal, sea serpent handle, unmarked **125.00**
    6¼" h, red, blue, and green streaks,
      luster, unmarked (A) **50.00**
    8" h
      Floral design in blue, red and green
        enamels (A) **150.00**
      Seaweed design in blue, red, green,
        and luster (A) **125.00**
      9⅝" h, floral and vine design, blue
        and brown, green, ochre, and
        black enamels (A) **150.00**
Plate
    7" d, urn design, multicolored, un-
      marked **10.00**
    7½" d, "Morning Glory" pattern, blue
      with luster, red and green enamel
      strawberry (A) **30.00**
    8" d, "Strawberry" pattern, cobalt
      leaves, 12 sided, unmarked **75.00**
    8⅛" d
      "Berry" pattern, blue, copper,
        ochre, and orange, imp "Pearl
        White" (A) **15.00**
      "Morning Glory" pattern, blue,

green, black, and red enamels
(A) **40.00**
8¼" d
Floral design in blue, red and green
enamels and luster (A) **25.00**
Floral design in blue, red and yellow enamels (A) **35.00**
8⅜" d, floral and vine design in blue,
orange, yellow, and green enamels
and luster (A) **20.00**

**Plate, 8½" d, blue, rust, green, and luster,
$90.00.**

8½" d
"Berry" pattern, blue, purple and
copper luster, yellow and orange
enamels, imp "Paris White Ironstone" (A) **15.00**
Floral and foliage design in blue,
red and green enamels and lus-
ter, 10 sided (A) **35.00**
Floral and vine design in black, red
and green enamels and luster (A) **25.00**
Floral design in blue, red and green
enamels and luster (A) **40.00**
Floral design in blue, red, green,
and yellow enamels and luster,
imp "Pearl White" (A) **25.00**
Leaf and berry design, underglaze
blue, red and yellow enamels
with luster, imp "B. Walley" (A) **35.00**
Seaweed design in blue, red and
green enamels and luster (A) ... **30.00**
8⅝" d, "Morning Glory" pattern,
blue, green enamel (A) **35.00**
8¾" d
Floral design and strawberries in
blue, red and yellow-green
enamels and luster (A) **35.00**
Floral and vine design in blue, red
and green enamels and luster (A) **35.00**
"Morning Glory" pattern, blue with
luster (A) **20.00**
8⅞" d, rose design, red, green, blue,
and black, unmarked (A) **50.00**

9⅛" d, "Morning Glory" pattern, dark
blue with luster (A) **45.00**
9¼" d, floral design in blue, red and
green enamels and luster, imp
"Real Ironstone" (A) **5.00**
9⅜" d, "Morning Glory" pattern,
blue, green enamel (A) **65.00**
9½" d
Floral design in blue, red enamel
and luster (A) **25.00**
Leaf design in blue, red, blue, and
luster border bands (A) **10.00**
9⅝" d
Floral and leaf design, three large
flowers in blue, red and green
enamels and luster, 10 sided (A) **90.00**
Floral design in blue, red and green
enamels and luster (A) **20.00**
"Strawberry" pattern, blue, red,
pink, and green enamels, purple
luster **35.00**
9⅞" d, floral and vine design in blue,
red and green enamels and luster
(A) **35.00**
Platter
11" l
"Berry" pattern, blue, copper luster, ochre, and orange, imp "E.
Walley, Niagara Shape," (A) ... **65.00**
"Strawberry" pattern, blue, red and
green enamels, octagonal, imp
"Elsmore Forster and Co" (A) **45.00**
14¼" l, "Berry" pattern, blue, copper
luster, ochre and orange (A) **65.00**
14½" l, "Morning Glory" pattern,
blue and copper luster, unmarked
(A) **135.00**
Sauce Tureen, 7" h, leaf design in blue,
red, blue, and luster border bands,
octagonal (A) **155.00**
Sugar Bowl, Cov
4⅞" h, urn of flowers design, blue,
red, green and luster, emb lion
head handles (A) **35.00**
6⅞" h, "Morning Glory" pattern, blue
with luster (A) **40.00**
7¾" h, floral design in blue, red and
green enamels and luster (A) **20.00**
Tea Set, teapot, creamer, sugar bowl,
"Morning Glory" pattern, blue with
luster (A) **350.00**
Teabowl and Saucer
Floral design, red, blue, green and
black, unmarked (A) **50.00**
Floral design in blue, red and green
enamels, purple luster (A) **90.00**
Morning glory and strawberry design
in blue, red, green and luster (A) . **35.00**
Teapot
8¼" h, floral design in blue, red and
green enamels and luster (A) **65.00**
9¾" h, "Morning Glory" pattern,

blue, red, green, and black, unmarked (A) **25.00**
Toddy Plate
4⅜" d, "Morning Glory" pattern, blue
with luster (A) **20.00**
5" d, "Sleeping Eye" design **225.00**
Tureen, 8" h, seaweed design in blue,
red and green enamels and luster,
grape knob, octagonal (A) **30.00**
Tureen and Tray, 13" l, leaf design in
blue, red, blue, and luster border
bands, emb fruit, foliage handles (A) **95.00**
Waste Bowl
5¼" d, "Berry" pattern, blue, copper
luster, ochre and orange (A) **45.00**
5⅝" d, urn of flowers design, multicolored, unmarked (A) **65.00**
6½" d, 3⅛" h, floral design, red, blue,
green, and black, unmarked (A) .. **35.00**

GAUDY WELSH

England, Wales
1820–1860

History: Gaudy Welsh, manufactured between 1820 and 1860, was produced for the working class people in England and Wales. It traces its decorative motifs to Japanese Imari. Gaudy Welsh is identified by its colors of underglaze cobalt blue (often in panels), rust (burnt orange), and copper luster on a white ground, plus its decoration which most often is floral, although trees, birds, or geometric forms are sometimes used. The body can be earthenware, creamware, ironstone, or bone china.

Swansea and Llanelly were the two areas in Wales where the Gaudy Welsh motif began. At least four firms in Newcastle and two Sunderland firms copied the design to their wares. However, it was the Staffordshire potteries at Stoke-on-Trent that produced the greatest amount of Gaudy Welsh.

Collecting Hints: Grape leaves, panels, cartouches, fences, and flower petals appear repeatedly in Gaudy Welsh designs and reflect the Oriental influence. Many patterns have names indicative of the design, e. g., "Tulip," "Sun Flower," "Grape," and "Oyster," while other names are more fanciful and bear little resemblance to the decorative motif. True Gaudy Welsh has the cobalt portion of the design under the glaze and the additional enamel colors including the lusters over the glaze. In addition to the bold colorations of cobalt, orange, and luster decorations, pieces can be found with shades of green and yellow highlights added. As many as 300 designs have been identified.

Tea cups and saucers were made more than

any other forms. Most Gaudy Welsh designs are painted on the inside of the cups. Tea sets, jugs, bowls, and miniatures were produced in smaller quantities.

Much of the Gaudy Welsh is unmarked. Design and techniques allow some pieces to be traced to specific companies.

References: Howard Y. Williams, *Gaudy Welsh China*, Wallace-Homestead, 1978.

Museums: Royal Institution of South Wales, Swansea, Wales; St. Fagen's Welsh Folk Museum, near Cardiff, Wales; Welsh National Museum, Cardiff, Wales.

REPRODUCTION ALERT: Gaudy Welsh has been reproduced during this century by several Staffordshire potteries. The most prolific was Charles Allerton & Sons (1859–1942) who specialized in jugs in the "oyster" pattern. The orange-red pigment, often streaked and uneven, is the sign of a reproduction.

Cake Set, teapot, 10" d cake plate, ten
7" d plates, waste bowl, ten cups and
saucers, "Tulip" pattern, c1820–40,
unmarked **1,300.00**
Child's Tea Set, teapot, creamer, cov
sugar bowl, slop bowl, four cups and
saucers, "Wagon Wheel" pattern ... **400.00**
Condiment Set, 5¼" w, porcelain, "Tu-
lip" pattern, "ENGLAND" mark **85.00**
Creamer
3½" h, "Oyster" pattern, unmarked **45.00**
4" h, "Grape" pattern, Allerton (A) . **35.00**
Creamer and Sugar
"Grape and Lily" pattern, c1840, un-
marked **165.00**
"Morning Glory" pattern, unmarked **170.00**
Cup and Saucer
"Cosmos" pattern, unmarked **45.00**
"Morning Glory" pattern, unmarked **50.00**
"Onion" pattern, unmarked **25.00**
"Tulip" pattern, unmarked **20.00**
"Urn I" pattern, unmarked **45.00**
Cup Plate, 4¼" d, "Geranium" pattern,
12 sided **40.00**
Dinner Service, "Tulip" pattern, set of
117 pieces (A) **585.00**
Jug
1⅞" h, "Tulip" pattern, unmarked (A) **45.00**
4½" h, "Oyster" pattern, unmarked **70.00**
Mug
3" h, "Wagon Wheel" pattern (A) .. **40.00**
3⅞" h, "Grape" pattern, Allerton (A) **40.00**
Mustard Jar, 3" h, "Tulip" pattern **40.00**
Pitcher
3¼" h, "Oyster" pattern, unmarked **55.00**
5½" h, "Oyster" pattern, unmarked **75.00**
5⅝" h, "Pagoda" pattern, unmarked
(A) **15.00**

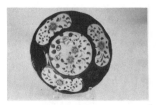  

Left, dish, 5½" d, "Floret" pattern, $20.00; center, cup and saucer, "Columbine" pattern, $35.00; right, tea set, "Tulip" pattern: 8½" h teapot, 5½" h cream jug, 8" h cov sugar bowl, $265.00.

Plate
6" d
 "Oyster" pattern, unmarked 20.00
 "Tulip" pattern, unmarked 25.00
 7½" d, "Wagon Wheel" pattern, unmarked 35.00
 8" d, "Morning Glory" pattern, unmarked 65.00
 8¼" d, "Columbine" pattern, three
  panels of open pink flowers, dark
  blue ground, unmarked 30.00
 9" d, "Tulip" pattern, unmarked ...   65.00
 10½" d, "Strawberry" pattern, unmarked 75.00
Serving Dish, 9" H-H, "Tulip" pattern,
 unmarked 40.00
Tea Cup and Saucer, "Oyster" pattern,
 unmarked 35.00
Tea Service
 Teapot, creamer, sugar bowl, six cups
  and saucers, "Morning Glory" pattern 750.00
 Teapot, creamer, cov sugar bowl, four
  cups and saucers, "Cambrain
  Rose" pattern 850.00
 Teabowl and Saucer, "Feather" pattern,
  unmarked 55.00
 Teapot, 7¼" h, "Tulip" pattern, white
  ribbed ground, unmarked 145.00
Waste Bowl, 5½" d, "Tulip" pattern, unmarked (A) 20.00

GERMAN FACTORIES-MAJOR

History: Many small, but highly important factories were established in the German provinces during the last half of the 18th century. Some were started by princes, but the majority were private commercial enterprises.

ANSBACH
Hesse, 1758–1860

Under the patronage of Hohenzollern Margrave Alexander of Brandenburg and with the help of workers from Meissen, this porcelain factory was established in 1758 in connection with an old faience works. In 1762 the firm moved to a hunting castle at Bruckberg. Fine pieces were made during the Rococo period, c1775. The factory was sold to private interests in 1807 and continued to make a variety of wares until 1860.

Wares imitated those made at Berlin, Meissen, and Nymphenburg. Exotic groups and figures, white and painted decorative and utilitarian wares, especially coffeepots, souvenir plates, monogrammed cups and saucers, and silhouette medallions were made. The principal mark in the c1760 to 1785 period was an "A" of varying sizes and shapes.

FULDA
Hesse, 1765–1790

This factory was established for the Prince-Bishop of Fulda in 1765. The predominant decorative style was from the late Rococo period. The products resembled those manufactured at Frankenthal. The main subjects of the figures were shepherds, children, ladies, cavaliers, and comedians positioned on Rococo trellises. The factory mark in underglaze blue was a double "F" with or without a crown. A few pieces were marked with a cross.

KASSEL
Hesse, 1766–1788

Friedrich II founded the factory. It made attractive tablewares with underglaze blue decoration and some simple figures. The mark was a lion or "HC" in underglaze blue.

THURINGIAN FACTORIES
From 1757

Nine hard paste porcelain factories were established in the Thuringian region. The three main ones were Gotha, Kloster Veilsdorf, and Volkstedt-Rudolstat. (see Volkstedt)

BAYREUTH
Bavaria, West Germany,
1899–1920

Sigmund Paul Meyer's factory produced utilitarian and hotel porcelains. The firm changed its name to First Bayreuth Porcelain Factory in 1920, continuing to make ovenproof pots and coffee machines.

GOTHA
1757–1782

Wilhemn von Rotberg established this factory in 1757. His cream colored paste had a translucent glaze. Products included coffee sets, tea sets, and decorative porcelain figures. At first, the Rococo style was predominant. Later the Louis XVI and Neo-classical styles were used. Underglaze blue marks were first an "R" and then "R-g" and "G." The factory survived until 1782.

KLOSTER VEILSDORF
1760–Present

The factory was established in 1760 under the patronage of Friedrich Wilhelm Eugen. Tablewares and decorative porcelains, coffee sets, tea sets, and figures were made. The typical decorations were large freely painted purple, red, and yellow flowers evolving from thread-like stems. The underglaze blue monogram "CV" was used, occasionally supplemented with a coat of arms. After 1799, the mark became a three leaf clover.

LIMBACH
1772–Present

Gotthelf Greiner established this factory in 1772. Porcelains were decorated primarily in blue and purple tones. Figures were rustic subjects and small town people. The marks "LB" or crossed "L"s were applied on the glaze in red, purple, or black. About 1787 an underglaze blue clover leaf mark was used. Later clover leaf marks were purple, black, or red.

Greiner and his five sons acquired other factories such as Grossbreitenbach in 1782 and Kloster Veilsdorf in 1791. From 1797 to 1850 G. Greiner's Sons made utilitarian and decorative porcelains and figures.

WALLENDORF
1764–1833

Johann W. Hammann established this factory in 1764. The first products had Rococo style decoration. Later dinner services were made in formal styles. Pastoral and street scenes in monotones of purple, brown, black, and gray tones featured figures of rural characters. The factory's mark were underglaze blue was "W"'s. In 1833 the factory was sold to Hutschenreuther, Kampfe, and Heubach.

References: George W. Ware, *German & Austrian Porcelain*, Crown, Inc., 1963.

Museums: Bayeriches Nationalmuseum, Munich, West Germany; Gardiner Museum of Ceramic Art, Toronto, Canada; Museum fur Kunst und Gewerbe, Hamburg, Germany; Schloss Museum, Berlin, Germany; Victoria & Albert Museum, London, England.

ANSBACH

Cup and Saucer
   Multicolored game bird on cup, rooster on saucer, brown rims, c1770–80 (A) **340.00**
   Painted interlaced floral "MGT", floral garland, entwined handles, c1765, blue "A" mark (A) **440.00**
Plate, 9" d, molded cartouches painted with swags of flowers, borders with puce line, trailing foliage, gilt dentil rims, c1775, blue "A" mark, pr (A) . **875.00**
Saucer, painted, scattered flower sprays, c1770, blue "A" mark **115.00**
Soup Plate, 10" d, bouquet of painted flowers in center, molded and gilt paneled border, green ground and painted flowers and trellis, blue "A" mark (A) **1,170.00**
Tankard
   9½" h, faience, multicolored stork in marsh, framed in columns, scrolling trellis and shells with sprigs, pewter lid and foot, c1772 (A) .. **4,435.00**
   11" h, blue, yellow, green, and black stylized flowers, scrolling foliate medallion, sponged manganese ground, leaftip borders, pewter lid, mid 18th C **700.00**

BAYREUTH

Birnenkrug, 10½" h, floral spray, manganese, green, yellow, and blue, pewter foot rim, hinged cov, ball thumbpiece, c1800 .... **750.00**
Canister, 6⅛" h, blue and white baskets of fruit and florals, yellow and gold accents, hexagon, c1730 (A) **885.00**

Chocolate Cup and Saucer, brown glazed redware, gilt chrysanthemums and ferns, formal borders, cov with dbl handles, c1735 (A) 250.00

Coffeepot, 7⅞" h, brown glazed redware, gilt Chinese figures on terrace, quatrefoil laub-und-bandelwerk cartouches, gilt zig-zag spout, borders of chrysanthemums, c1730 (A) 7,775.00

Dish, 8⅝" d, faience, center painted with two birds on basket of fruit in blue foliate, scrollwork border, pie crust rim 275.00

Enghalskrug, 13½" h, spirally molded, urn of flowers in oval cartouche, scrolling foliage and flowering plants, blue and white colors, pewter foot and lid, ball thumbpiece, c1745 . . .3,200.00

Figure. 9⅝" h, Autumn and Spring modeled as putti, green and manganese. sq mound bases, c1765, manganese "BP" mark, pr 800.00

Plate
8¾" d, blue painted center, coat of arms under crown, strapwork scroll, foliage border, c1735 . . . . . 300.00
9⅝" d, painted multicolored flower sprays, brown rim, hexafoil shape, c1761–67 . . . . 300.00

Tankard
6⅝" h, brown glazed red ground, silver mirror monogram, laub-und-bandelwerk and glitterwerk cartouche, baskets of fruit, flowers on sides, c1735 (A) 415.00
7¼" h, red body, gilded rococo motif, hinged pewter cov, c1745 (A) 1,040.00
9¼" h, black glazed brown stoneware, cylindrical, hinged contemporary silver gilt cov, c1720 (A) . .1,770.00
9⅜" h, faience, multicolored eagle on branch, two sponged trees, blue band borders, pewter foot and cov (A) 500.00

Tea Caddy, 4⅜" h
Brown glazed redware, gilt design of lady kneeling at altar, man with package on head on each side, c1730 (A) 4,925.00
Brown glazed red ground, silver Oriental dec, silver cov, c1730–40 (A) 1,870.00

Teabowl and Saucer
Brown glaze, gilt scroll borders, mid 18th C (A) 300.00
Brown glazed redware, gilt figures, dogs and altars, c1730, pr (A) 390.00

Waste Bowl, 6½" d, brown glazed redware, gilt design of jester leading leopard, sultan on ext., crowned man and attendant with parasol on int., c1730 (A) .2,335.00

CASSEL

Figure, 5⅛" h, putto, wrapped in purple cloak, holding crab in hand, c1770, blue "HC" mark 1,650.00

FRANKFORT

Dish
8½" d, faience, blue painted Oriental figures in landscape, scalloped rim   80.00
8⅞" d, faience, blue and yellow painted panels of Oriental seated in garden 135.00
16" d, blue painted Chinese style figures in landscape, white ground, paneled border, figures divided by foliage, early 18th C (A) 535.00

Jug, 7½" h
Chinese figures in river landscape, multicolored, neck with stylized lotus, loop handle with dots, pear shape, c1720 (A) 500.00
Faience, painted purple-cobalt, Oriental style figures in landscape, stylized tulips on tapered neck, late 17th C (A) 210.00

Plate
13⅜" d, faience, dark blue painted seated Oriental figure, border with alternating panels of Oriental figures, stylized florals 80.00
15½" d, blue and white Chinese figures in landscape, paneled border divided by flower sprays, early 18th C (A) 390.00

Vase
5⅛" h, faience, blue painted seated Chinese figure in landscape (A) . . 100.00
11⅝" h, blue painted Oriental figures in landscape, stylized motif and leaves on trumpet neck (A) 175.00
18¾" h, blue Oriental figures in continuous landscape outlined in manganese, lapid shape floral borders, c1740 (A) 965.00

FULDA

Cup and Saucer
Painted portrait busts, oval panels surrounded by pink, gilt band with laurel swags, gilt rims, c1785, blue crowned "FF" mark 1,000.00
Painted sailboat, classic buildings and ruins, brown rims, c1770, blue crowned "FF" mark 200.00

Figure
5¾" h
Young girl in winter clothes, hands in muff, circ grass mound base,

puce scrolls, c1770, blue "cross" mark (A) **6,600.00**
Woman carrying basket of buttons and buckles, button card in hand, multicolored jacket and apron, c1781, blue crowned "FF" mark (A) **10,400.00**
Plate, 8½" d, faience, blue, white and manganese flower in vase, border of stylized foliage, c1740–50 (A) **475.00**
Saucer, painted central urn, butterflies and insects, blue crowned "FF" mark **115.00**
Tea Service, part, cov jug, cov sugar bowl, teacup, four saucers, painted bouquets and scattered flowers, c1775, crowned "FF" mark (A) . . . **2,780.00**
Tray, 12¾" l, figures in boat beside Italian ruins, border with four landscape vignettes in C-scroll cartouches, basketweave border, gilt rim, oval, c1780 (A) **4,040.00**

GERA

Figure, 5⅛" h, goddess draped in pink, three cherubs heads in clouds, c1780, blue "G" mark (A) **235.00**

GOTHA

Coffee Can and Saucer, painted portrait of young girl in oval cartouche, mid 19th C, saucer chipped (A) **80.00**

HANAU

Dish
10¼" d, center with blue painted Oriental figure amongst rocks, lobed rim, mid 18th C (A) **80.00**
12½" d, faience, turquoise heron flying over shrubs and rockwork, border with floral panels reserved on trellis and lambrequins, octagonal, c1740–50 (A) **1,600.00**
13⅞" d, center painted with Chinese figures in landscape, border with stylized flowers and foliage, mid 18th C (A) **200.00**
14" d, blue and white design of two birds perched on tree in landscape, fluted body, c1720 . . . . **375.00**
Jug, 10⅛" h, scene of town buildings, blue, yellow, and manganese, pewter cov, mid 18th C **850.00**
Vase, 19" h, faience, painted with shaped panels of Oriental buildings and trees divided by scrolling foliage, c1750, pr (A) **825.00**

KASSEL

Sugar Bowl, 3⅝" h, Italian landscape scene, brown, green, blue, and iron-red, rosebud knob, c1770–80, blue "rampant lion" mark (A) **2,090.00**

KLOSTER VEILSDORF

Coffeepot, 7⅞" h, each side with vignettes of three Chinese figures, green trellis borders, c1770, blue "CV" mark (A) **1,420.00**
Figure
3" h, Pantalone, actor's costume, holding candlestick, multicolored, splashed brown base, c1768 (A) . . **2,135.00**
3½" h, fish seller, seated on tub, basket of fish at feet, multicolored, c1769, damaged (A) **660.00**
3⅝" h, Scaramouche, actor's costume, playing mandolin, multicolored, splashed brown base, c1768 (A) **3,320.00**
4" h, old peasant, seated on tub, child in arms, multicolored, c1770 (A) . **665.00**
4⅛" h, seated sportsman, gun on lap, multicolored hunting clothes, tree trunk in background, c1772 (A) . . **1,660.00**
4¾" h, crouching leopard, brown and black marks, brown mound base, c1775 (A) **875.00**
5⅜" w, shepherd playing flute, leaning on tree trunk, companion seated on rock, iron-red flowered jacket and skirt, c1768 (A) **2,275.00**
5¾" h
Female playing hurdy-gurdy, dressed in beggar's clothes, multicolored, c1766 (A) **1,090.00**
Sportswoman holding musket, black hat, multicolored jacket and dress, c1755–66, incised "V" mark **2,100.00**
7½" h, blacksmith, pink headband and loin-cloth, holding hammer, multicolored, anvil on sq base, c1766 (A) **80.00**
8" h, Turk, multicolored, holding guitar and kerchief, striped turban, rococo molded base, c1775 (A) . . . **1,350.00**
8½" h, leopard attacking mule, natural colors, shaped rococo scroll base, c1775, damaged **2,000.00**
Needle Case, 5½" l, top modeled as head of woman in pink checked shawl and gilt bow, body painted with girl in landscape, contemporary gold mounts, c1770 (A) **1,750.00**
Plate, 10" d, painted bouquets in foliage garland borders from puce ribbons, c1775, blue interlaced "CV" mark (A) **265.00**

Scent Bottle, 4" h, modeled as Hungarian, pack resting on rock, yellow and brown clothes, silver mount, c1765–66 (A) **660.00**

Tea Caddy, 3¾" h, painted scattered flower sprays, finial missing (A) **585.00**

LIMBACH

Candlesticks, 5" h, painted exotic birds on branches, insects and florals, hexagon, c1775, blue "X'd L's and star" mark, pr (A) **935.00**

Chocolate Pot, 4⅜" h, blue painted "Immortelle" pattern, reeded body, wooden handle, blue "leaf" mark (A)   **35.00**

Figure, 4¾" h, young man, kneeling, fixing skate on companion, scroll molded base, c1780 (A) **1,300.00**

NUREMBERG

Ewer, 8⅜" h, blue reserve of Francis of Assisi greeting birds, dotted field, pewter foot and hinged cov, c1750, blue "K" mark (A) **1,870.00**

Tankard, 5½" h, blue painted basket of fruit, oval leaf frame, light blue glaze, pewter lid, mid 18th C (A) **640.00**

RAUNSTEIN

Figure, 6" h, nude Venus seated on rock, holding iron-red drapery over head, Cupid at side, c1775, green "R" mark, repaired (A) **235.00**

Tea and Coffee Service, "Wallendorf," brown cornucopia, multicolored flowers, gilt husk swag borders, c1780, blue "W" marks, (A) $1,930.00.

WALLENDORF

Coffeepot
9⅝" h, painted shepherd boy playing

dbl flute, dog dancing at feet, pear shape, duck's head spout, imp "W" mark **165.00**

Rose colored bouquets of flowers, c1770, blue script "W" mark **260.00**

Cup and Saucer, puce painted buildings on fluted ground, gold husk border, blue "W" mark **60.00**

Figure
3⅛" h, woman, powdered wig, period clothes, multicolored, grasswork base, c1775–85 (A) **700.00**
6" h, St. Paul, holding sword, iron-red cloak, named on base in rococo cartouche, c1775–85 (A) **865.00**
13" h, white, Adam and Eve holding forbidden fruit standing before tree stump, molded bases with fruit, c1775, blue "W" mark, pr **525.00**

Milk Jug, rose colored bouquets of flowers, c1770, blue script "W" mark .. **245.00**

WURZBURG

Cup and Saucer, molded rococo foliage scrolls, panels of puce landscapes of houses and figures, c1770 (A) **4,300.00**

Figure
5" h, white, standing Pantalone, right hand holding beard, left hand in cloak, sq base, c1775–80 (A) **7,585.00**
6" h, gardeners, man holding flower basket, pedestal with vase in background, woman holding hoe, pedestal with basket in background, multicolored scroll bases, c1770, each with hand missing, pr (A) ..**18,000.00**

GERMANY-GENERAL

POTTERY
15th Century to Present

History: Some of the earliest forms of German decorative pottery were made by the Hafner or stove-makers. The stove tiles of the 15th century were covered with a green lead glaze. Later 16th century stoves contained tiles of yellow, brown, and white clays or with tin-glaze over red clay bodies. Hafner wares also include large vessels or jugs made in Nuremberg.

In 1712 Marx and Hemman first made tin-glazed earthenwares. They continued in a series of partnerships until 1840. Most of the wares were decorated in blue with Baroque style scrolls, foliage, or strapwork. Subjects encompassed landscapes, heraldic shields, and biblical or mythological scenes.

Hamburg faience falls in the period of the second quarter of the 17th century. Pear shaped jugs decorated with a coat-of-arms in a blue motif were best known.

The most prolific center of German faience was at Hanau, near Frankfort-am-Main, from 1661 until 1806. The wares imitated Delft ware. Many Chinese forms were copied. At first only blue decoration was used. By the early 18th century wares were decorated with landscapes and biblical scenes in a variety of colors. Naturalistic flowers in enamel colors dominated the mid-18th century wares.

Ansbach, Bayreuth, Cassel, Erfurt, Frankfort-am-Main, Proskau, and Schrezheim were other areas where faience factories were established.

PORCELAIN
16th Century to Present

History: In Germany there were many small principalities which competed with each other in establishing porcelain factories. Each developed an individual style. There was no royal monopoly in Germany as there was in France since there was no unified Germany.

In addition to the major German factories of Berlin, Frankenthal, Furstenberg, Hochst, Ludwigsburg, and Meissen, at least twenty minor manufactories were established in the German provinces during the last half of the 18th century. Some of these include Ansbach, Fulda, Gera, Gotha, Grossbreitenbach, Gutenbrunn, Ilmenau, Kassel, Kelsterbach, Kloster Veilsdorf, Limbach, Ottweiler, Rauenstein, Volkstedt, and Wallendorf.

Though some of these factories were established by princes, most were formulated as private commercial enterprises to make wares that could be sold competitively. For the most part, these wares copied works of the major German factories, such as Frankenthal and Meissen, etc. The majority of the minor factories were able to continue operation despite changes in ownership, economic disruptions, and competition from larger firms, especially those established in the 19th and 20th centuries that were close to the source of raw materials.

Independent painters developed soon after the establishment of the Meissen factory about 1720. Porcelains painted by these independent decorators in their homes or studios are known as Hausmalerei. The painters are designated as Hausmaler. Hausmalers were experienced painters of faience and other ceramics. The large porcelain factories feared their competition. Hausmalers obtained Meissen and Veinna blanks and painted them as they wished. Ignaz Bottengruber of Breslau was the best known of the independent decorators. Hausmalers were active for about forty years during the mid-18th century.

A smaller group of factories were in operation during the last half of the 18th century. These included Baden-Baden, Blankenhain, Eisenberg, Ellwangen, Hanau, Hoxter, Schney, and Tettau. Only Tettau still operates today.

Germany was in the forefront of the hard paste porcelain industry. Many new factories, making high quality utilitarian and decorative porcelains, were established during the 19th and 20th centuries. Most of these 19th and 20th century factories, approximately two hundred of them, are concentrated near the source of porcelain's raw materials, i. e., the central and eastern regions of Germany, (mainly North Bavaria, Thuringia, Saxony, and Silesia). Among the dominant factories are Sitzendorf, Rosenthal, Schumann, Hutschenreuther, and Heinrich. Factories located at Altwasser, Passau, Plaue, Potschappel, Rudolstadt, and Selb concentrate on the production of utilitarian and decorative porcelains.

References: William B. Honey, *German Porcelain*, Faber & Faber, 1947.

Museums: Arts & Crafts Museum, Prague, Czechoslovakia, Bayerishes Nationalmuseum, Munich, West Germany; Kunstgewerbemuseum, West Berlin, West Germany; Metropolitan Museum of Art, New York, NY; Museum fur Kunst und Gewerbe, Hamburg, West Germany.

Additional Listings: Bavaria, Bohemia, Carlsbad, C.T. Germany, Dresden, Frankenthal, Furstenberg, Heubach, Hochst, Hutschenreuther, KPM, Ludwigsburg, Major German Factories, Meissen, Nymphenburg, Rosenthal, Royal Bayreuth, Royal Dux, Rudolstadt, Schlegelmilch, Sitzendorf, Volkstedt.

Ale Set, pitcher and four mugs, emb figural king on keg, multicolored **100.00**
Basket, 6½" l, 5" h, applied rose sprays, white ground, raised rococo design, swirl handle, ftd **25.00**
Berry Set, master bowl and four serving bowls, molded and scalloped edges and floral decorations, raised flower on underside (A) **65.00**
Bowl
  5¼" d, "Blue Onion" design, "Meissen" in oval mark **10.00**
  10" d
    Large light yellow roses, lilacs, and green leaves, fluted edge **45.00**
    Pink and white roses on pearl luster ground, gold scalloped edge, "GERMANY" **45.00**
  20" h, matching stand, two molded figures applied to stem, period dress, multicolored applied florals on bowl and stem, molded base with four small feet and gilt accents, c1920, "C. G. Shierholz and Sons, Thuringia" mark **750.00**
Cabinet Cup and Saucer, multicolored Architectural scene (A) **150.00**

Landscape scene (A) 250.00
Nautical scene (A) 40.00
Candle Snuffer, 2" h, figural, lady, orange and yellow 35.00
Candlestick, 13" h, figural, couple in garden, multicolored (A) 80.00
Centerpiece, 9" d, 6⅝" h, porcelain gnomes on each side of open bag, gnomes in coral and yellow, bag in green, "GERMANY" 175.00
Chamberstick, 3" d, emb floral sprig, irid orange ground, "GERMANY" .. 10.00
Charger, 13" d, bird on gray-blue flower in center, coral flowers on border, c1930, "Rouenstein, Germany" 150.00
Chocolate Pot
  4½" h, white porcelain body, purple flowers and gold trim, relief of ferns and flowers, unmarked 55.00
  9½" h, pink and white roses, green tints, ribbed body and bead trim, "GERMANY" 50.00
  9¾" h
    Center medallion of lady, dark hair, green floral dress, holding flowers and flowers in hair, white ground, turquoise and gold trim, unmarked 95.00
    Pink and white roses on lavender and white ground, satin finish, gold trim, unmarked 90.00
Chocolate Set, chocolate pot, five cups and saucers
  Large pink, yellow, and white roses with green foliage, gold trim, "Germany" in circle mark 200.00
  Roses and stylized florals, pearlized cream and green ground 125.00
Coffeepot, 11½" h, figural
  Old woman holding umbrella, handbag and creamer, applied ribbon handle, pastel colors 325.00
  Old woman with removable head and vegetable pouring spout, multicolored 375.00
Creamer, figural
  4½" h, seated green alligator, red collar and int., "GERMANY" 30.00
  4½" h, 5" l, black dachshund head, orange int., "M. W. Co., Germany" 35.00
Creamer and Sugar, poppies, luster ground, unmarked 20.00
Cup and Saucer
  "Aesop" in gilt banded reserve on light blue ground (A) 350.00
  Floral and gilt decoration (A) 40.00
  German inscription, multicolored (A) 50.00
  Round scenic reserves against gold squiggle line ground, late 18th C (A) 165.00
Cup, cov, and Saucer, architectural scene accented with foliate gilding (A) 350.00

Cuspidor, 7¾" d, 4½" h, large red roses, white ground, flared neck 80.00
Demitasse Cup and Saucer, pink and yellow anemones, swirled body, gold scalloped rim 25.00
Demitasse Set, demitasse pot and five cups, porcelain, Art Deco style, blue luster and gold trim, "A. S. Germany" 110.00
Dessert Set, tea server, sugar bowl, cake tray, seven plates, seven cups and saucers, gold encrusted design with light green borders (A) 420.00
Dish
  4" l, 2⅝" h, cov, porcelain, blue and gilt, white reserves of polychrome flowers, reticulated cov, unmarked (A) 45.00
  15⅜" l, faience, multicolored bouquets of small flowers, white ground, shaped chocolate rim, c1760 .... 700.00
Dresser Box, 9½" h, figural, standing Art Deco woman, blue dress and peaked hat 165.00
Figure, porcelain
  3" h, boot, multicolored flowers, "Elfinware, Germany" 15.00
  3⅛" h, sleeping Cupid with pink wings, blue scarf on orange pillow, blue "X'd swords" mark 100.00
  3¼" h, 4½" l, sleeping cat, white and brown-gray, blue collar 55.00
  4" h, bird seated on branch, white, pr 100.00
  4½" h, shepherd boy carrying lamb, white, "Royal Berlin" 45.00
  5" h
    Art Nouveau style nude woman emerging from open water lily, multicolored, unmarked 115.00
    Cupid, picking flowers, blue wings, multicolored 100.00
  5⅜" h, monkey, playing bagpipe, tricorn hat and waistcoat on tree stump base, multicolored, c1770 (A) 260.00
  6" h
    Cellist, multicolored, "Carl Thieme" 175.00
    Circus elephant (A) 35.00
  6⅝" h, woman playing lute, multicolored (A) 65.00
  7" h
    Equestrian figure of military officer, multicolored, crowned "S" mark (A) 15.00
    Young man holding pug dog, multicolored, unmarked (A) 100.00
  7½" h, porcelain, seated woman holding fan, unmarked (A) 100.00
  7½" h, 5½" w, white colonial man and woman, gold trim, blue "N and crown" mark 90.00

8" h
Art Deco style, nude riding gazelle
(A) **70.00**
Group of children picking fruit (A) **110.00**
8½" h, 11" l, Russian wolfhounds,
one standing other lying down on
oval base, white with brown ac-
cents, drilled as lamp base **130.00**
8¾" h
Girl confronting Cupid, multicolored, unmarked (A) **40.00**
Man in floral coat holding goat and
flute, late 19th C, damaged **50.00**
Woman holding tea service, multicolored, unmarked (A) **40.00**
9" h
Man and woman dancing, multicolored unmarked (A) **40.00**
Napoleon, polychrome (A) **25.00**
Ney, military uniform, polychrome
(A) **25.00**
Soldier, period uniform, multicolored, sq base (A) **35.00**
9" l, 6½" h, basset hound, seated on
haunches, multicolored **45.00**
9¼" h, gallant holding flower, multicolored, unmarked (A) **150.00**
10½" h, cockatoos, polychrome, pr
(A) **120.00**
11" l, 6½" w, standing retriever, gray
and white, yellow collar, "GER-
MANY" **50.00**
11⅞" h, girl offering fruit to gallant,
both seated on tree trunk, mound
base with applied plants and raised
gilt scrolling, repaired (A) **85.00**
13" h, young gentleman serenading
lover under garden trellis (A) **190.00**
14" h, parrot on tree perch, yellow
bird, blue, black, and red accents,
late 19th C, unmarked (A) **185.00**
Frogs, dressed in 18th C costumes,
playing instruments, set of 10 .... **150.00**
Fish Set, 15" l platter, six 7½" d plates,
multicolored scenes of fish and sea
plants **85.00**
Fruit Bowl
Apples in center, deep colors, sgd "A.
Koch" **70.00**
Grapes in center, deep colors, sgd "A.
Koch" **70.00**
Hair Receiver, pink roses, blue shaded
ground **20.00**
Ink Bottles, Ma and Pa Carter, multico-
lored, heads form stoppers, "GER-
MANY," pr **50.00**
Inkwell
3½" d, 4¾" h, seated figural buddha,
multicolored **65.00**
3¾" w, 3" h, emb roses, green
ground, "Elfinware, Germany" ... **35.00**
5⅞" d, 3½" h, attached scalloped

plate, flying bird and leaves, blue
and cream ground, unmarked **80.00**
Jug
9" h, faience, shepherd and flock in
flowering foliage, yellow, green,
blue, and manganese, bands of zig-
zag and trellis pattern panels, flared
neck with narrow opening, c1760,
attributed to Habaner **550.00**
10⅞" h, cov, spirally molded, painted
in manganese, bird and mask
heads, baluster shape, foliage handle, shell shape cov, c1760 (A) ... **455.00**
Lobster Set, 14" d master dish, twelve
7¼" d dishes, green with red raised
lobster, c1902, "GERMANY" **175.00**
Match Holder, porcelain, lobster and
frog dec, "GERMANY" **60.00**
Mug
2½" h, polychrome floral design, German inscription, dtd 1826 (A) **10.00**
Floral pattern and irid luster finish,
applied flowers, c1890, unmarked **40.00**
Nodders, 8½" h, seated Oriental man
and woman with fans, multicolored,
pr **495.00**
Oyster Plate
8" d, small yellow flowers and scrolling foliage, irreg pink borders, gold
trim, set of six **150.00**
9¼" d, white oyster wells, cross-
hatched   background,   "GER-
MANY" **90.00**
Pitcher, 6½" h, floral design, "J. S. Germany" **25.00**
Place Card Markers, 1½" d, porcelain,
pink and white roses, green stems, set
of ten **55.00**
Plaque
4⅛" w, 6" h, "The Last Supper," gilt
and plush frame, c1900 (A) **170.00**
5" w, 7½" h, bust length portrait of
Madonna and Child **150.00**
5½" w, 8¾" h, porcelain, painting of
black haired woman in period costume holding jug, unmarked (A) .. **650.00**
5⅝" w, 8⅝"h, "Antigone" holding
urn in black drape, dark landscape,
late 19th C (A) **500.00**
7⅝" h, Magdalene reading Bible, blue
and white robes, c1880 (A) **415.00**
10¾" d
Emb head of boy on one, girl on
other, multicolored, gray and
blue, gilt trim borders, pr **550.00**
Pottery, high relief busts of boy and
girl in native German costumes,
busts extend to edge of plaques,
gray and blue etched borders,
gold edges, gold satin centers,
pierced for hanging, unmarked,
pr **550.00**

13" w, 16½" h, faience, blue, manganese, and black scene of Christ at table with saints, Latin inscription, yellow molded self-frame, black vines, c1724 (A) **500.00**

13¼" d, terra cotta, raised design of man and woman in wine cellar, Musterschutz **225.00**

13½" d, raised figures of maiden with pitcher and cavalier with drink, dark colors, pierced for hanging, Musterschutz **175.00**

Plate

6¼" d, "Blue Onion" design, "arrow and Meissen" mark **5.00**

7"d, Victorian children, multicolored, pr **30.00**

Vase, 11¼" h, blue birds, brown branches, raised gold and enamel dots, white ground, gold dbl handles, $60.00.

8" d

Gold center, blue and pink flowers, green leaves, green open edge . **35.00**

Grapes, multicolored, sgd "A. Koch" **30.00**

Hp, floral center, green and gold rim, "U. S. Zone, Germany" .. **15.00**

Hp, pink poppy **15.00**

Hp, violets, wide gold border, "LHS Germany" **35.00**

Large pink roses, blue ground **50.00**

Queen Victoria in center, moss green with flowers **40.00**

Water lilies, pink and green **20.00**

8½" d

"Blue Onion" design, "Meissen" in oval mark **20.00**

Snowflake design, blue and white **15.00**

8⅞" d, man and companion in landscape, pierced border with pink

linked circles and blue flowerheads, c1880, blue "X'd swords and star" mark **85.00**

9" d

Pink roses and buds outlined in white, gray, purple, yellow, and green shaded ground **25.00**

Porcelain, painted Hebrew inscriptions, unmarked (A) **45.00**

9½" d

"Blue Onion" design, imp "Meissen" and blue "arrow" mark .. **25.00**

Polychrome floral centers, shaped rims, raised white foliate and scroll motifs, green "crown" and "X'd hammer" mark, set of eleven (A) **75.00**

Red poppies and white daisies, shaded green ground, gold scrolled rim, "Royal Munich" .. **45.00**

9¾" d

Cupid and lovers in center, pastel floral border, tapestry finish, "GERMANY" (A) **205.00**

"Sommerblume", blond lady with basket of flowers, Art Nouveau style gilt, brown border, sgd "Wagner," c1910 (A) **330.00**

10" d

Green grapes and red chrysanthemums, gold accents, artist sgd, "GERMANY" **55.00**

Tavern scene, multicolored, gold overlay, pierced for hanging, Swartzburg **35.00**

10¾" d

Porcelain, portraits of "Spring" and "Boating," multicolored, ornate gilt borders, pr(A) **140.00**

Venus reclining on white drapery, Cupid crowning her, landscape, off-white border, gilt panels reserving blue and white jewels, c1910 (A) **500.00**

Platter, 12" d, pink fan design, lily of the valley, blue flowers and green leaves **50.00**

Powder Box, cov, vertical ribs on body, cov with figure of kneeling woman clutching breast, multicolored, c1920, Hertwig and Co **200.00**

Powder Jar, 9" h, figural of woman, hand extended holding flowers, green and yellow gown, unmarked **45.00**

Salt, figural, wheelbarrow, "Elfinware" **45.00**

Serving Dish, 11¾" l, polychrome floral dec, wide gilt border, dbl handles, imp "beehive" mark (A) **55.00**

Snuff Box, 3" w, ext., equestrian military scenes, int., portrait of man in cloak, gilt metal mounts, 19th C (A) **260.00**

Soup Plate, 9¼" d, "Blue Onion" design, "Meissen" in oval mark 35.00

Tankard, 7½" h, brown stoneware, two bands of circ grooves, pewter cov with medallion, cylindrical shape, 16th C, attributed to Annaberg 300.00

Tea Caddy, porcelain, "Blue Onion" design, silver cov (A) 45.00

Tea Tile, large pink roses, "3 crowns" mark 35.00

Teapot
    4⅜" d, 5¾" h, basket of pink roses, cream ground, gold spout, handle and trim, unmarked 55.00
    7½" h, figural seated black and white Scottie dog, pink bow, ribbon handle 30.00
    8¼" h, figural dachshund, multicolored 50.00

Tobacco Jar, majolica, small size, smiling monk with cigarette, pink and blue colors 95.00

Toothpick Holder, 2½" h, scenic, tapestry finish, ftd, "GERMANY" 45.00

Tray
    10¾" l, 9¼" w, porcelain, center portrait of "Koniginluise Von Preusson," dark and light blue and gilt, reserves of cherubs in corners (A) . 35.00
    11⅞" l, 7⅝" w, sq center portrait of ladies and cherubs in garden scene, panels of red and green, gold sprays, irreg cream and gold spray border 110.00

Tureen, Cov
    12½" w, painted bouquets, gilt line rims, female mask handles, gilt ball finials, 20th C, pr (A) 340.00
    12½" l, 12", gilt floral bands on white, bud finial on twisted top, ftd base, c1900 (A) 75.00

Urn, 11" l, 9" h, faience, gold edged flowers and leaves, central statuary, oblong, pr 750.00

Vase
    4½" h, sailboat in river scene, tapestry finish, flared top 55.00
    6" h, portrait of three ladies, tapestry finish 165.00
    6½" h, scenic, tapestry finish, "GERMANY" 65.00
    8⅝" h bust of young woman, gold accents on matte black ground, baluster shape, unmarked (A) 45.00
    12½" h, marbled clay bodies with relief of grapes and vines, baluster shape, unmarked, pr 750.00
    13" h, blue and white panels of Chinese figures in landscapes on lower octagon section separated by bands of scrolling foliage, c1700, damaged (A) 450.00

GINORI

Doccia, near Florence, Italy
1737 to Present

History: In 1737 the Ginori family established a factory to manufacture porcelain and earthenware at a villa in Doccia, a few miles from Florence. Marquis Carlo Ginori, the founder, operated the factory until 1757. Carlo Ginori's management is known as the "first period."

Stencil decorated dark blue plates, teapots, coffeepots, and cups were the earliest wares. Ginori produced many examples of snuff boxes, extremely popular in the 18th century, in a variety of shapes and decorations. Sculptures and large reliefs depicting mythological or religious subjects also were made.

In 1757 Lorenzo, his son, took over. This is the "second period." Lorenzo introduced an imitation Sevres blue ground, and strong use of colors. He continued making figurals in the Rococo style.

Anton Maria Fanciullacci served as director from 1791–1805, the "third period," changing the designs to reflect the Empire style. In 1792 the manufacture of creamware helped subsidize the production of porcelain.

Doccia was the only Italian pottery that survived and prospered during the 19th century. It remained in the control of the Ginori family. Around 1821 the Doccia factory acquired Capodimonte molds from the Naples factory and continued production. Ginori used the Old Naples mark on these examples.

Lorenzo Ginori II took charge in 1848. The firm started to make lithophanes, majolica, and egg-shell porcelains. A large number of pieces were decorated with urban scenes enclosed within a shield shaped reserve on a white ground in the classical style. The crowned "N" mark was used on some of the wares. Industrial ceramics for the electrical industry also were manufactured on a large scale.

In 1896 the firm incorporated with Societa Ceramica Richard in Milan to become Societa Ceramica Richard-Ginori. The Art Nouveau style was introduced. In addition to modern forms and decorations, some traditional motifs such as cockerels, narrative reliefs, and tulip motifs continued to be used.

Collecting Hints: Early Ginori porcelains were frequently not marked. During the Third Period, the "F" or "PF" incised marks appears. In the 19th century, "G", "Ginori", or a "N" crowned and impressed was used. The present mark is "Richard-Ginori" with a crown.

References: Arthur Lane, *Italian Porcelain*, Faber & Faber, 1954; Francesco Stazzi, *Italian Porcelain*, G.P. Putman's Sons, 1964.

Museums: Doccia Museum at Sesto Fiorentino, Florence, Italy; Fitzwilliam Museum, Cambridge, England; Metropolitan Museum of Art, New York; Victoria & Albert Museum, London, England.

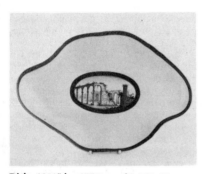

Dish, 12⅝" l, c1775, pr, $1,000.00.

Beaker, scattered flower sprays, late 18th C (A) **90.00**
Beaker and Saucer, Chinese figures, puce, iron-red, luster, and gold laub-und-bandelwerk cartouches, quatrefoil borders, dbl handles, c1775, pr (A) **2,155.00**
Bowl
  6⅛" d, cov, white, relief of classic figures in landscape, dbl ogee shape **140.00**
  6⅝" d, cov, painted multicolored interlaced floral garlands, three paw feet, scale molded finial **275.00**
Charger, 15¾" d, Imari, cobalt, iron-red, and gold prunus and peonies, trellis diaper and floral border, c1755–65 (A) **300.00**
Chocolate Cup and Saucer, white, cup with relief of classic figures, saucer with festoons, blue "crowned N" mark **120.00**
Cup and Saucer
  Multicolored enameled flower sprays, pr **50.00**
  Red and gilt painted fighting cockerels near tree, late 18th C **500.00**
Custard Cups, cov, gold crowned "E", anthemion and trellis borders, c1790 "iron-red or gold star" mark, set of 6 (A) **475.00**
Dinner Service, polychrome enameled floral designs, gold trim, "Richard Ginori, Italy," set of 58 (A) **675.00**

Ecuelle, 4½" h, cov, painted, multicolored flowers, molded fluted ground, applied flower finial **165.00**
Figure
  2¾" h, male dwarf, black hat and coat, purple suit, gilt ruffles, sq stepped base, c1760 . . . . **470.00**
  3⅛" h, female dwarf, apron and cap holding dog, multicolored, sq stepped base, c1750 . . . . **1,225.00**
  5" h, Spring, molded as girl, apron of flowers, multicolored, sq rockwork base (A) **700.00**
  6⅛" h, harvesters, modeled as man holding sheaf of corn standing over recumbent woman, seated boy at foot of tree, blue, red, puce, and white peasant clothes **1,350.00**
  7¼" h, Diana and Endymion, goddess rising from clouds, companion sleeping, spotted dog, multicolored, rockwork base, c1770 . . . . **1,000.00**
  7½" h, pastoral group of peasant woman with basket, seated shepherd, and child, rockwork and tree trunk base, c1785, repaired **570.00**
Knife Handles, 3⅜" l, molded zig-zag band, painted "Flying Dog" pattern, pr **100.00**
Plate
  6½" d, "Souvenir of Mt Vesuvius," multicolored, Italian inscription, gold trim **15.00**
  7½" d, floral centers, one with pink ground, other with blue ground, gold rims, pr **45.00**
  8½" d, large daisy, center, multicolored, sgd "Fedi" **30.00**
  9" d, Tulipano, painted, multicolored, gilt, shaped rim, c1770 (A) **155.00**
  9⅜" d, painted floral sprays, wavy puce rims, "red star" mark, Doccia, set of 6 (A) **280.00**
  9½" d, painted central floral spray and sprigs, ozier molded rims, set of 6 . . . . **245.00**
Platter, 16" d, "Egyptian" pattern **65.00**
Sauce Tureen, 7½" l, molded mythological figures, puce sprigs, cov with scroll edged cartouches, dog knob, c1760, cracked (A) **300.00**
Saucer, Tulipano, multicolored, gilt (A) **90.00**
Snuff Box, 3" d, white, top and base molded with spider webs, basketwork sides **135.00**
Soup Plate, 9⅜" d, enamel and gilt Tulipano, shaped rim, c1770–80, imp "M" mark **200.00**
Urn, 11¼" h, green leaves, yellow ground, campana shape, c1900, pr, damaged (A) **200.00**

Vase
    5" h, 7½" l, green, purple, and orange
    exotic florals, gilt rim **40.00**
    5½" h, multicolored landscape motif,
    two mask handles (A) **20.00**
    7" h, floral design, green, orange, and
    purple, sgd "G Faine" **155.00**

GOEBEL

Rodental (formerly Coburg), Bavaria, West Germany
1871 to Present

History: In 1871 Franz and William Goebel, father and son, applied for a permit to manufacture porcelain in the village of Oeslau near the city of Coburg. When Duke Ernst II of Saxe-Coburg intervened, the permit finally was granted in 1879. The firm, F. D. & W. Goebel Porcelain Works, began manufacturing dinner services, milk pitchers, beer steins, and egg cups.

When Franz died in 1909, William expanded the porcelain dinnerware and figurine business into an export-oriented concern. Max-Louis, William's son, took over in 1912 when William died. Max-Louis introduced many new porcelain figurine designs and added a ceramic figurine line as well. Frieda, wife of Max-Louis, Franz, son of Frieda and Max-Louis, and Dr. Eugene Stocke, Frieda's brother, assumed control when Max-Louis died in 1929.   Franz Goebel first saw Sister Maria Innocentia Hummel's sketches in 1934. In March 1935 the first "M. I. Hummel" figure was made. These were an immediate success, especially in America.

During WWII the Goebel works concentrated on the manufacture of dinnerware for the domestic market. A few figurines were made. When the United States Military Government of Germany lifted the wartime embargo and gave permission for production and exportation of "M. I. Hummel" figurines and other objects in 1946, a rapid recovery by the firm followed.

When Franz died in 1969, the management of the company transferred to Wilhelm, his son, and Ulrich Stocke, Eugene's son. They continued expansion of the company and acquisition of other factories. In 1971 the company was renamed Rodental.

Today the Goebel factories manufacture high quality porcelain dinnerware for the home and export markets. In addition to the popular Hummel series, they manufacture figurine series that include Disney characters, birds, animals, and

Friar Tuck monks. A collectors plate series also is made.

References: Eric Ehrmann, *Hummel,* Portfolio Press Corp., 1976; John F. Hotchkiss, *Hummel Art II,* Wallace Homestead, 1981; Thomas E. Hudgeons, III, ed., *The Official Price Guide to Hummel Figurines and Plates,*House of Collectibles, 1980; Carl F. Luckey, *Hummel Figurines and Plates,* 5th Edition, Books Americana, 1984.

Collectors' Clubs: Goebel Collectors' Club, 105 White Plains Road, Tarrytown, NY 10591. Membership: $17.50. *Insight,* quarterly newspaper; "Hummel" Collectors Club, P. O. Box 257, Yardley, PA 19067. Membership: $20.00. Quarterly newsletter on M. I. Hummel Figures. The "Hummel" Collectors Club is not affiliated with W. Goebel Porzellanfabrik.

Museum: Goebel Museum, Tarrytown, NY.

Honey Pot, 5" h, yellow ground, $30.00.

Ashtray
    Art Deco, Scottie dog, repaired,
    #RT116 . . . . **30.00**
    Devil **22.50**
    Elephant **22.50**
Bank, boy blowing horn, multicolored,
    "crown & 29/0" mark **65.00**
Child's Feeding Dish, yellow, eight
    molded chicks around sides, tin screw
    cap, imp mark **15.00**
Cigarette Set, box with four ashtrays, figural, black cat, dated 1929, 5 pcs . **45.00**
Condiment Set, figural, Friar Tuck, 5 pcs **45.00**
Cookie Jar, cardinal, red robe **125.00**
Creamer, figural
    2½", Friar Tuck, multicolored, "Goebel bee & V Germany" **20.00**
    3½", pheasant, "full bee" **20.00**
    Cow, bell on neck, multicolored . . . **17.00**
Cruets, oil and vinegar, figural, Friar
    Tuck, pr **25.00**
Decanter, 10" h, figural, Friar Tuck,
    brown robe **25.00**
Dresser Box, 5¼" d, black base, yellow
    and white trim, orange top, multicolored soldier with umbrella finial **118.00**
Fairy Lamp, figural, dog, glass eyes,
    crown mark **75.00**

Figure
   4⅜", young girl, Russian wolfhound
      at side **28.00**
   4½", Art Deco style white rabbit, gold
      and black **24.00**
   6", white swan, red beak **16.00**
   8½"
      Hawk, natural colors, bisque finish
      (A) **100.00**
      Young girl playing cello **138.00**
   10", Art Deco style flamenco woman
      dancer, multicolored **150.00**
   10½", bust of Madonna, white,
      crown mark **85.00**
   11", Madonna and child, pastels ... **95.00**
   14", Madonna, white glaze **25.00**
   16½", Passing the Peace Pipe, white
      matte finish (A) **70.00**
   Boy and goose, "W. Goebel & #194"
      mark **100.00**
   Friar Tuck, brown robe **45.00**
   European goldfinch, multicolored .. **25.00**
   Trouble Shooter **35.00**
Jug, Mrs. Gamp, "full bee" mark **39.00**
Liquor Set, bottle and six tots, blue flow-
   ers, orange trim, "full bee & crown"
   marks **40.00**
Mug
   5" h, figural, Friar Tuck, multicolored,
      "Goebel bee & V Germany" mark **39.00**
   Figural, Friar Tuck, multicolored, four
      handles **20.00**
   Relief of parading elephants, orange
      and white **60.00**
Night Light, figural, dog, light missing,
   "crown" mark **60.00**
Pin Tray, Art Deco girl, multicolored .. **75.00**
Pincushion Doll, 5" h, woman holding
   fan, #1202/3 .... **180.00**
Pitcher, figural, Friar Tuck, brown robe
   3" h **30.00**
   5" h **45.00**
Plaque
   5" sq, modeled angel, multicolored,
      HUL-718B **38.00**
   7" w, 10" h, white relief of girl carry-
      ing water jugs, light green jasper
      ground, crown mark **295.00**
   White cameo of girl with jars and fish-
      erman, blue jasper ground **225.00**
Salt and Pepper Shakers, pr, figural
   Egg Head **28.00**
   Rooster and hen, black, red, and
      white, 3" h **45.00**
Sugar, cov, figural, Friar Tuck, brown
   rose **10.00**
Toby Jug, 5" h, Mrs. Gamp, multicol-
   ored, full bee mark **35.00**
Toothpick Holder, figural, orange rabbit
   seated beside pussy willow branch,
   "full bee & V" marks **45.00**
Wall Pocket, figural, umbrella **35.00**

GOLDSCHEIDER

Vienna, Austria
1885 to Present

History: Friedrich Goldscheider founded the
Goldscheider Porcelain and Majolica Factory in
1885. Goldscheider's family owned a factory in
Pilsen, Czechoslovakia, along with decorating
shops in Vienna and Carlsbad. Decorative earthenwares and porcelains, faience, terra cotta,
and figures were made.

Regina Goldscheider and Alois Goldscheider,
her brother-in-law, ran the firm from 1897 until
1918. They made figures along with sculptured
vases in the Art Nouveau style. Regina's sons,
Walter and Marcel, took control in 1920 and
adopted styles prevailing in Vienna during the
1920s.

The factories experienced several name
changes both before and after World War I and
II. Following Hitler's invasion of Austria, the family left and settled in Trenton, New Jersey, in the
early 1940s. They established a factory in Trenton and made art objects and tablewares.

After World War II, Marcel Goldscheider established a pottery in Staffordshire, England, to
manufacture bone china figures and earthenware. The company's mark was a stamp of Marcel's signature.

Figure
   4¾" h, Art Deco style, orange terrier
      dog **45.00**
   7", brown bust of woman, turquoise
      curls **350.00**
   7½", Art Deco style chorus girl, plum
      dancing skirt with flowers **300.00**

**Dish, cov, 11" h, multicolored, c1925,
"Goldscheider, Wein," $400.00.**

8", busts of Orientals, multicolored,
pr **35.00**
9¼", brown bust of woman, turquoise
curls, Vienna, Austria mark **450.00**
11", wolfhound, sgd "Genugnam" . **180.00**
13"
Gypsy woman, plum and jonquil
dress, flower garlands, imp
"Lindner Austria" mark **850.00**
Peasant woman, dark red and yellow dress, festooned with flowers, Austria **75.00**
14⅛", Negro gentleman seated on
rock, wearing top hat and green
suit, holding cane (A) **325.00**
14¼", Negro gentleman seated on
rock, holding top hat and cane,
wearing brown suit (A) **325.00**
16⅜", bust of maiden, brown curly
hair and gilded helmet, gilt bodice,
socle base, gilt patinated terra
cotta, c1900 (A) **330.00**
22", Bacchanalian woman dancing
with leopard, natural glaze colors,
gray oval base **500.00**
25⅝", Rebecca standing by stone wall
with jug, circ named base, patin-
ated terra cotta, c1900 (A) **465.00**
39¾ and 43⅜" h, Middle Eastern
tribesman in turbans and robes
shaded in gold leaf, terra cotta,
shaped bases, pr **500.00**
Plate, mermaid pattern, multicolored,
unmarked **150.00**
Wall Mask
9⅝" h, girl's face, green eyes, orange
lips, orange hair swept to side (A) **180.00**
11", curly haired girl, orange lips,
holding green mask in hand (A) .. **312.00**
12", girl with golden hair, orange lips,
wearing turquoise scarf (A) **96.00**
13½", girl with green curly hair, red
lips, black mask covering part of
face (A) **360.00**

W.H. CROSS

GOSS AND CRESTED WARE

Stoke-On-Trent, England
1858 to 1930

History: William Henry Goss founded the Goss
China Company in 1858 at Stoke-on-Trent. Goss
began producing a fine grade parian which was

used for figural groups, busts of famous people
both past and present, pierced baskets, and a
variety of other items. Terra cotta tobacco jars
and wine vases decorated with transfers also
were produced. Goss developed a method of
imbedding colored glass into the parian body to
make "jewelled" vases, patenting the technique
in 1872. Fine tea services appeared in his catalog
by 1880.

In 1883 Adolphus, William's son, joined the
firm. William's aggressiveness helped launch the
company into new and profitable fields. It was
William who introduced crested china.

Victorian England had increased leisure time
and great accessability to the seacoast and resort
areas. These vacation sites were perfect for the
introduction of inexpensive souvenir items.
Adolphus, much to the chagrin of William, produced and marketed the now famous white
glazed souvenir pieces complete with enameled
decorations and coats of arms of various towns
and resorts. The technique was simple. A paper
transfer was applied to the glazed body, and the
colors hand painted in the design. These heraldic
souvenirs were an instant success. Shops were
established in the resort areas to sell Goss crested
china. Other factories quickly imitated the Goss
crested ware.

In 1893 Goss China began producing miniature full color buildings, duplicating every detail
of the original buildings from which they were
modeled. Expansion was necessary to meet the
demands for the Goss products. Victor and Hunt-
ley, Adolphus' sons, became partners in 1900.
Goss china even published its own journal,
"Goss Records," to promote its products.

The company suffered during the Great
Depression. Its assets were sold to Cauldon Potteries in 1929. Cauldon began the manufacture
of figurines of young girls similar to the Royal
Doulton figurines. Coalport China Co. purchased
the rights to Goss in 1945; Ridgway and Adderly
took control in 1954. The company currently is
part of the Royal Doulton organization.

Other manufacturers of crested ware in Eng-
land were: Arcadian, Carlton China, Grafton
China, Savoy China, Shelley, and Willow Art.
Gemma in Germany also made crested wares.

References: Sandy Andrews, *Crested China*,
Milestone Publications, 1980; Sandy Andrews &
Nicholas Pine, *1985 Price Guide to Crested
China*, Milestone Publications, 1985; John Ma-
gee, *Goss for Collectors - The Literature*, Mile-
stone Publications; Nicholas Pine, *Goss China:
Arms, Decorations & Their Values*, Milestone
Publications, 1982, revised ed.; Nicholas Pine,
The Price Guide To Goss China, Milestone Pub-
lications, 1984.

Collectors' Clubs: Goss Collectors Club, The
Secretary, 3 Carr Hall Gardens, Barrowford, Nelson, Lancashire B89 6PU, England. Membership

7 pounds. Monthly newsletter; The Crested Circle, 42 Douglas Road, Tolworth Surbiton, Surrey KT6 7SA, England. Membership: 7 pounds. Bimonthly magazine, and *Crested Circle Annual Magazine*. This circle covers the products of W. H. Goss, Arcadian, Carlton, Grafton, Shelley, and Savoy factories and commemoratives from the different factories.

Collecting Hints: Early Goss pieces tend to be heavier and less perfectly rounded than later pieces, gilding tends to come off easily if rubbed, and a heavy mold line is often apparent. By 1890-1900 the molding technique was improved, resulting in a thinner, more precise mold. Gilding also was of better quality and did not rub off easily. Greater color and more precision was used in the application of the coats of arms transfers.

Aberdeen Bronze Pot, crest-Cardinal Woolsey, Goss	19.00
Abergavenny Jar, crest-Basingstoke, Goss	15.00
Antwerp Oolen Pot	
Crests-Dorothy Vernon/Duke of Devonshire/Buxton, Goss	26.00
Crests-England/Scarborough/Yorkshire, Goss	26.00
Crests-Inverness/Sir William Wallace/Arms for Burns, Goss	26.00
Bath Roman Ewer, crest-Ambleside, Goss	12.00
Bideford Mortar, crest-Folkstone, Goss	45.00
Bristol Puzzle Cider Cup, crests-St George/Wm The Conqueror/Andover/Hamshire, Goss	58.00
Caerleon Lamp	
Crest-Arms for Burns, Goss	24.00
Crest-Bath Abbey, Goss	28.00
Canary Covered Jarra, crest-Sandgate, Goss	28.00
Canary Earthen Jar, crest-Kirkwall, Goss	22.00
Canary Jarra, crest-Bergen, Goss	24.00
Candlestick	
2⅛" h, City of Carlisle	7.50
3¼" h	
Bournemouth	7.50
Worcester	7.00
Carlisle Salt Pot	
Crest-Belfast, Goss	12.00
Crest-Huddersfield, Goss	12.00
Crest-Leicestershire, Goss	12.00
Carnarvon Ewer, crest-See of Wells, Goss	20.00
Channel Isle Lobster Trap, crest-Luton, Goss	35.00
Cheese Dish, mini	
Crest-North Berwick, Goss	48.00
Crest-St Leonards, Goss	48.00
Crest-The Island & Royal Manor Of Portland, Goss	50.00

Chester Roman Vase, crest-Cork, Goss	15.00
Chester Roman Vase, large, crest-See of Lichfield, Goss	38.00
Coffee Can Cup and Saucer, crest-Lyndhurst, Goss	25.00
Colchester Famous Vase	
Crest-Hornsey, Goss	14.00
Crest-Manor of Bramber, Goss	12.00
Crest-Walton-on-Naze, Goss	14.00
Cone Extinguisher, crest-Warminster, Goss	18.00
Coronation Cup, 3½" h, Edward VII and Queen Alexandra, colored coat of arms, miniature handles, "W. H. Goss" mark	72.00
Cottage	
2¼" h, Manx Cottage, printed goshawk mark (A)	75.00
2½" h	
Cat & Fiddle Inn, Buxton, printed goshawk mark (A)	110.00
Old Thatched Cottage, Poole, printed goshawk mark (A)	290.00
2¾" h	
Ellen Terry's Farmhouse, Tenderden, printed goshawk mark (A)	215.00
First & Last Post Office in England, printed goshawk mark (A)	75.00
The Priest's House, Prestbury, Cheshire, printed goshawk mark	650.00
3½" h, Portman Lodge, Bournemouth, printed goshawk mark (A)	220.00
3¾" h	
Dove Cottage, Grasmere, printed goshawk mark (A)	175.00
Thomas Hardy's Birthplace, printed goshawk mark (A)	290.00
4" h, Rt. Hon. D. Lloyd George's Early Home, printed goshawk mark (A)	110.00
5¾" h, First and Last House in England with Annex, printed goshawk mark (A)	290.00
Small, Ann Hathaway, Goss	135.00
Cream Jug	
Big Lipped	
Crest-Barnstable, Goss	18.00
Crest-Beaumaris, Goss	22.00
Ribbed, crest-Manor of Bramber, Goss	32.00
Taper-medium, crest-Windsor, Goss	20.00
Taper-small, crest-Lynton, Goss	20.00
Cup and Saucer	
Bag	
Crest-Bournemouth, Goss	32.00
Crest-Suffolk, Goss	32.00
Tapered, crest-See of London, Goss	18.00
Dart Sack Bottle, crest-Floreat Etona, Goss	18.00
Devon Oak Pitcher, crest-Warwick, Goss	12.00
Dorchester Jug, crest-Fowey, Goss	12.00

Dover Stone Vessel, crest-Tonbridge
Wells, Goss **25.00**
Eddystone Lighthouse
Crest-Shoreham, Goss **42.00**
Crest-Truro, Goss **80.00**
Eddystone Spanish Jug, crest-City of
London, Goss **12.00**
Egyptian Mocha Cup
Crest-Barmouth, Goss **12.00**
Crest-Tonbridge, Goss **15.00**
Ewer, crest-School of Musketry, Hythe,
Goss **18.00**

**Figure, 8″ h, "Birth of Venus," turquoise
trim, $325.00.**

Figure
5″ h, bust of Sir Walter Scott, Goss . **45.00**
8″
Bust of Charles Dickens, Goss ... **90.00**
Bust of Greek woman, Goss **75.00**
Bust of Lord Byron, Goss **45.00**
15¼″, bust of Disraeli, circ socle, par-
ian, Goss (A) 1,047.00
Bust of Shakespeare, polychrome,
Goss **65.00**
Peggy, mini size, Goss **100.00**
Fountains Abbey Cup
Crest-Ramsgate/Kent, Goss, large ... **30.00**
Crest-Sheringham, Goss **14.00**
Glastonbury Jack
Crest-Floreat Hova, Goss **15.00**
Crest-Gloucester Ancient, Goss **12.00**
Crest-Selby, Goss **8.00**
Glastonbury Salt Cellar, crest-Crediton,
Goss **42.00**
Glastonbury Vase, crest-Tonbridge
Wells, Goss **12.00**
Gloucester Jug, crest-Battersea, Goss .. **12.00**
Goodwin Sands Carafe
Crest-Hastings, Goss **12.00**
Crest-Royal Arms of Scotland, Goss . **14.00**
Hamworthy Lamp, crest-Folkstone,
Goss **35.00**
Hernebay Ewer, crest-See of York, Goss **14.00**
Highland Cuash, crest-See of Lincoln,
Goss **24.00**

Hornsea Roman Vase, crest-Richmond,
Goss **18.00**
Horsham Mediaeval Jug
Crest-Brighton, Goss **12.00**
Crest-Devizes, Goss **12.00**
Hythe Cromwellian Mortar, crest-Hun-
stanton/St Edmonds, Goss **22.00**
Hythe Crypt Skull, Souvenir of Hythe-
yellow, Goss **95.00**
Ilkley Roman Ewer, crest-Richmond
(Surrey), Goss **10.00**
Irish Mather, crest-Glasgow, Goss **22.00**
Irish Wooden Noggin
Crest-Bromsgrove, Goss **22.00**
Crest-Hitchin, Goss **20.00**
Crest-Oakham, Goss **22.00**
Itford British Urn, crest-Great Yar-
mouth, Goss **20.00**
Japan Ewer, crest-See of Exeter, Goss .. **28.00**
Kendal Jug, crest-Ashford (railroad en-
gine), Goss **18.00**
Kettering Urn, crest-Quebec, Goss **14.00**
Lanlawren Celtic Urn, crest-Nurnberg,
Goss **14.00**
Lewes Roman Vase, crest-Ramsgate,
Goss **8.50**
Lichfield Jug
Crest-Eastbourne, Goss **12.00**
Crest-York, Goss **12.00**
Lincoln Jack
Crest-Boulogne-Sur-Mer, Goss **15.00**
Crest-Rickmansworth, Goss **17.00**
Lloyd George's Home, with annex, Goss **250.00**
Lobster Trap, crest-Channel Isles, Goss **35.00**
Looe Ewer, crest-Falmouth, Goss **12.00**
Loving Cup, three handles, crest-Henry
of Navarre/Ramsgate/Kent, Goss **26.00**
Low Melon Cup and Saucer, small
Crest-Farnham, Goss **18.00**
Crest-Faversham, Goss **18.00**
Crest-Margate, Goss **18.00**
Melon Cream Jug, small, crest-City of
Leicester, Goss **17.00**
Mug, 1½″ h, slogan transfer, "Seeke Out
The Good In Every Man...," sgd
"Adolphus Goss" **25.00**
Mug, mini, 1 handle
Crest-Battersea, Goss **12.00**
Crest-Deal, Goss **12.00**
Newberry Leather Bottle
Crest-Com Southern Hampshire, Goss **14.00**
Crest-Southend-On-Sea, Goss **12.00**
Crest-West Dereham Abbey, Goss .. **12.00**
Crest-Woodhall Spa, Goss **14.00**
Newcastle Roman Jug
Crest-Abergele, Goss **13.00**
Crest-New Zealand, Goss **14.00**
Night Light, Manx Cottage, Goss **195.00**
Norwich Urn
Crest-Bishop Auckland, Goss **13.00**
Crest-Ealing, Goss **13.00**

Crest-Greece, Goss	15.00
Crest-Nurnberg, Goss	14.00
Crest-Southampton, Goss	13.00
Crest-Wolverhampton, Goss	15.00
Ostend Bottle, crest-Egham, Goss	18.00
Ostend Tobacco Jar, crest-Paddington, Goss	13.00

Ostend Vase

Crest-Cirencester Abbey, Goss	13.00
Crest-Preston, Goss	13.00

Painswick Roman Pot

Crest-St Annes-On-Sea, Goss	12.00
Crest-Walton-On-Naze, Goss	12.00

Penmaenmawr Urn

Crest-Bishops Stortford, Goss	12.00
Crest-Las Planches Montreaux, Goss	13.00
Crest-Seal of Leominster, Goss	13.00
Pin Tray, crest-Darlington, sq, gilt tassels in corners, Goss	10.00

Pitcher, 2¼" h, crest, Stoke-Upon-Trent, "F. Robinson, Victoria, porcelain," $15.00.

Pitcher, 1¾" h, crest on front, bottom reads "Model of Oak Pitcher Peculiar to Devon," Goss	5.00

Plate

Bag, 5" d, crest-Hastings, Goss	18.00

Melon

4⅛" d, crest-Sussex, Goss	15.00

6" d

Crest-Flintshire, Goss	18.00
Crest-Newquay, Goss	18.00
Rim, 7" d, crest-Callander, Goss	18.00

Portland Vase

Crest-Bodian, Goss	14.00
Crest-Great Yarmouth,, Goss	12.00
Reading Vase, crest-Skegness, Goss	12.00
Scarborough Jug, crest-Somerset, Goss	15.00
Shakespeare's Jug, crest-Shakespeare's Arms, Goss	42.00
Skull, "Alas poor Yorick," Goss	65.00
Southampton Pipkin, crest-Filey, Goss	12.00
Southwold Jar, crest-Glasgow, Goss	15.00

Staffordshire, Tyg-1 Handle

Crest-Ancient Port of Minehead, Goss	14.00
Crest-Earl of Cromartie, Goss	14.00
Crest-Hertfordshire, Goss	14.00
Crest-Interlaken, Goss	14.00

Staffordshire, Tyg-2 Handles

Crest-Brighton, Goss	15.00
Crest-Christchurch, Goss	15.00
Crest-Norfolk, Goss	15.00
Crest-Portsmouth, Goss	15.00
Crest-Richmond, Surrey, Goss	15.00

Swindon Vase

Crest-Broadstairs, Goss	16.00
Crest-Swindon (railroad engine), Goss	45.00
Crest-Walton-On-Naze, Goss	13.00
Crest-Waterlooville, Goss	13.00

Swiss Vinegar Bottle

Crest-Eastbourne, Goss	24.00
Crest-St Columb Minor, Goss	27.00
Trinket Tray, 9⅜" l, crest-Keswick, Goss	55.00
Tesco Old Brazier, crest-Clacton-On-Sea, Goss	38.00
Tumbler, Mini, crest-See of Worcester, Goss	12.00

Vase

4¾" h, white ground, "Fishguard" decal in scroll, gold line trim, "Model of Kang Hi Vase Presented to George V" on bottom, Shelley mark 5.00

Bag

Crest-Maidenhead, Goss	20.00
Crest-St Peters, Goss	20.00
Crest-Weymouth & Melcombe Regis, Goss	7.50

Ball, crinkle top

Crest-Cambridge University, Goss	18.00
Crest-City of Wells, Goss	14.00
Crest-Hastings, Goss	14.00
Ball, small, crest-Sandwich, Goss	15.00
Cylinder, 3 ftd, crest-Wiesbaden, Goss	12.00
Taper, small, crest-Japan, Goss	18.00

Taper, wide

Crest-Lewes, Goss	18.00
Crest-Manor of Shrewton, Goss	18.00

Walmer Roman Vase

Crest-Harrogate, Goss	14.00
Crest-Kingston-On-Hall, Goss	12.00
Crest-Yorkshire, Goss	14.00

Wareham Roman Bottle

Crest-Hoylake & West Kirby, Goss	12.00
Crest-St Osyth Priory, Goss	14.00
Welsh Milk Can, medium, crest-Wrexham, Goss	22.00
Weymouth Roman Vase, crest-Marblethorp, Goss	16.00
Windsor Urn, crest-H M Queen Victoria, Goss	15.00
York Roman Ewer, crest-Morecombe, Goss	14.00

MADE IN

Zuid HolLaND

GOUDA

Gouda, Holland
17th Century to Present

History: Gouda and the surrounding areas of Holland have been producing Dutch pottery wares since the 17th century. Orginally Delft-type tin glazed earthenwares were manufactured along with the clay smokers' pipes.

When the production of the clay pipes declined, the pottery makers started producing art pottery wares with brightly colored decorations. These designs were influenced by the Art Nouveau and Art Deco movements. Stylized florals, birds, and geometrics were the favorite motifs, all executed in bold, clear colors. Some Gouda pieces have a "cloisonne" appearance.

Other pottery workshops in the Gouda region include: Arnhem, Plazuid, Regina, Schoonhoven, and Zenith. Utilitarian wares, vases, miniatures, and large outdoor garden ornaments also were included in the product line.

REPRODUCTION ALERT. With the recent renewal of interest in Art Nouveau and Art Deco examples, reproductions of earlier Gouda pieces now are on the market. These are difficult to distinguish from the originals.

Clock, 12" h, matte earthtones, "Ali Gouda, Holland," $650.00.

Ashtray
  4" d, 1½" h, multicolored floral and scroll int., green banding, "Anive Royal" mark **52.00**
  4⅛" d, green and cobalt, multicolored int., "Anne Royal" mark **38.00**

  4¼" d, blue-green matte finish, wide cobalt rim, house mark **48.00**
Basket
  7½" w, brown, tan, and orange design, wicker handle, "Sepia, Zenith Gouda" mark **145.00**
  7½" l, 5½" h, stylized decor int. and ext., blue and dark red handle, "Plazuid" mark **80.00**
  8" l, frog design, rope twist handle, "Regina" mark **120.00**
Bottle, figural, "Bols" man and woman, pr **90.00**
Bowl
  9½" d, brown and tan earthtones, c1860, sgd "Kawi" **125.00**
  18¼" d, 5" h, peacock design, multicolored **300.00**
Candlestick
  4½" h, orange, blue, and green geometrics, "Iottea" mark **70.00**
  13" h, vine, flower and dot design, multicolored, "Karta Rood, Diamond & house" marks, pr **410.00**
  14½" h, earth color florals on base and drip pan, matte finish, large loop handle, house mark **145.00**
Candy Dish, black matte finish body with rope twist handle, multicolored stylized flowers on int. **62.00**
Chamberstick
  3" h, gold and white panels, colored flowers, matte black ground with gold accents **75.00**
  5⅜" h, blue and green flowers, gold panels and satin black and gold, Art Deco style, house mark **70.00**
  Earthtones and brown handle, matte finish **65.00**
Clock, 17" h, Art Nouveau style, flowing wisteria and tendrils, cream ground, painted face, "Zuid, Holland" **600.00**
Compote
  6¼" h, 5⅜" d, Art Nouveau design, multicolored, house mark, pr **135.00**
  6½" h, dark orange and green, cobalt and black designs, "Trudy & house" marks **60.00**
Cup and Saucer, windmill scene, multicolored, "Royal Gouda" **50.00**
Dish, Covered, 6" d, 4" h, green and bronze Art Nouveau style pattern, green matte ground **110.00**
Dish, Serving, 7¼" d, multicolored floral pattern, wide handle, "Anjar & house," mark **85.00**
Dresser Jar, attached tray, green, black, orange, and gold Deco design, matte finish, silver lid, "Collier, Holland & house" mark **60.00**

Ewer

4¾" h, multicolored geometric slashes, matte finish **65.00**

6¼" h, "Dora" pattern, multicolored **30.00**

6½" h, Art Deco, cobalt, rust, and yellow, #2960, "Metz Royal Zuid Holland" mark **115.00**

9¾" h, Art Nouveau style, multicolored flowers and leaves, dark green ground, high glaze, house mark .. **450.00**

Figure, 10½" l, shoe, brown and tan earthtones, matte finish **145.00**

Flower Holder, blue, turquoise, and gold design, brass top, "Gouda, Holland & house" mark **85.00**

Food Warmer, matte yellow color, "Plazuid house" mark **22.00**

Inkstand, 7⅞" w, painted stylized foliage in green, amber, blue, and dark red, brown ground, "Regina 103 CH W. B. Gouda Holland" mark (A) **75.00**

Inkwell, 9" w, brown and black earthtones **185.00**

Jardiniere, 13" d, green and brown stylized peacock feather design, "Fredij Gouda" mark (A) **140.00**

Jug and Tray, 11" h jug, 13" l x 10" w tray, Art Deco multicolored design, black matte ground, sgd "Emanuel" **275.00**

Lantern, 9½" h, green and brown matte finish, repaired, $300.00.

Lamp, 11½" h, abstract floral design, multicolored, "Ivora Gouda" mark . **120.00**

Pipe, 5½" l, figural, man with turban and mustache, "Goede Waagen's PIJP" mark **12.50**

Pitcher

2½" h, red dots, turquoise, black matte ground, gold trim, "Z Waro" **22.00**

2⅝" h, black and gold peacock eyes, red and blue ground, house mark **30.00**

3½" h, multicolored dots, black ground **20.00**

5" h, gold slashes, matte black ground **55.00**

5½" h

Dark multicolored florals and geometrics, matte finish, house mark **65.00**

Maroon, gold, and blue flowers, mottled gray ground, green int., "Areo. Royal Gouda" mark **35.00**

7" h, black slashes, purple glaze ... **75.00**

Serving Set, double handled 6⅝" d dish, twelve side dishes, dark colored painted flowerheads and foliage, "Zenith, Gouda" marks, 13 pcs (A) **35.00**

Tea Caddy, 4" sq, Art Deco style, multicolored, high gloss, unmarked **60.00**

Tobacco Jar, 6½" h, melon ribbed, dark matte finish **130.00**

Vase

3" h

Florals, crackle ground, high gloss, "Zuid Holland & house" mark, pr **125.00**

Multicolored florals, matte finish . **30.00**

4½", windmill scene, farmer and wheelbarrow, "Zenith, Gouda" mark **85.00**

4¾", rust, blue, and yellow sunflowers, "Hava Plazuid, Holland" mark **85.00**

5¼" h, 6" H-H, cobalt and multicolored bands, black matte ground, "Blareth" mark **48.00**

5½", multicolored florals, cobalt bands, black matte glaze, double handles, "Blareth & house" mark **55.00**

5½" h, 5¾" d, multicolored stylized florals, black double handles and lower section, "Blareth & house" mark **60.00**

5¾", Art Nouveau style, multicolored matte finish **95.00**

6"

Art Deco design, black, gold, and blue shades **100.00**

Open burnt orange flower center, earthtone ground, "Waalwijk & house" mark **165.00**

6¼", multicolored earthtones, matte finish, "Kapel & house" mark **125.00**

6½"

Blue, rust, and white matte design, green borders, "Lapac" mark .. **85.00**

Earthtone floral decor, two ear handles, "Royal Gouda" mark **58.00**

Earthtone geometric design, matte finish, "Habea & house" mark . **195.00**

6½" h, 7" d, rust and blue daisies, tan ground, "Janerio" mark **75.00**

7¾", windmill and canal scene, multicolored, brown top and bottom bands, sgd "N. Oudes," "Z Holland Gouda #68/412" mark **125.00**

8⅛"

Art Deco design, blue, black,

Urn, cov, 8" h, earthtones, blue trim, "Zoma Royal Zuid, Holland," $55.00.

brown, red, gold, and green, matte finish, bulbous body, house mark **88.00**
Art Deco design, royal blue, black, gold, red, green, and brown, matte finish, house mark **85.00**
8¼"
Art Deco design, mauve, green, and lavender flowers on shaded green ground, glossy finish, ewer shape, house mark **110.00**
Art Deco style lavender flowers, mauve and green ground, luster finish, ewer shape, house mark **110.00**
8¾", slashes and geometrics, earthtones, high glaze, bottle shape, pinched waist **325.00**
10½", multicolored florals, high glaze, dbl handles, "Zuid, Holland" mark **125.00**
11", yellow and blue dec, matte finish, "Royal Pottery House of Zuid" mark, pr **125.00**
26⅛", green, rust, purple, and crimson exotic flowers, foliage, and cobwebs, dark blue ground, "Gouda, Holland" mark (A) **445.00**
Water Pipe, Delft style cameo of dancing people, "Godenewaagen, Holland" **145.00**

H&Cº

L

HAVILAND

Limoges, France
1842 to Present

CFH

GDM

FRANCE

History: David and Daniel Haviland, two brothers, had a china import business in New York.

When traveling to France in search of china, David decided to remain in Limoges, the leading center for the manufacture of pottery. By 1842 David and his family were firmly established in Limoges. David supervised the purchasing, designing, and decorating of stock for export from several Limoges companies. In 1865 he acquired a factory in Limoges to produce porcelains directly. Instead of sending whiteware to Paris to be decorated, David established studios at his own factory. He hired and trained local decorators.

In 1852 Charles Field Haviland was sent by Robert Barclay Haviland, his father, to learn the business from Uncle David. Charles Field married into the Alluaud family who owned the Casseaux works. When Charles Field took over, the mark used on the whiteware was "CFH."

Charles Edward and Theodore, sons of David Haviland, entered the firm in 1864. By 1878 the Haviland factory was the largest in the Limousin District. When David died in 1879, the firm passed into the hands of his two sons. A difference of opinion in 1891 led to the liquidation of the old firm. Charles Edward produced china under the "Haviland et Cie" name. After Charles died in 1922, his firm lost its significance and went out of business in 1931. Theodore started his own factory, "La Porcelaine Theodore Haviland," that produced china until 1952.

In 1875 Charles and Theodore Haviland founded a faience studio in Paris that was headed by Bracquemond, the famous engraver. This Auteuil Studio gathered together the greatest artists and decorators of the period. The entire French china production at the end of the 19th century was influenced by this studio's output.

William David, son of Theodore, took over in 1919. William David's three sons, Theodore II, Harold, and Frederick, eventually became involved. Members of the Haviland family, all direct descendants of the founder David Haviland, always have directed the French firm in Limoges. Each has chosen to retain their U.S. citizenship.

Marks: Until 1870 only one back mark was used for the "H & Co." or the Haviland & Co. After that time, two back marks were used - one for the factory where a piece was made and the other for the factory in which the piece was decorated. Department stores, hotels, railroads, and restaurants that placed special orders received individual marks.

All the whiteware marks are under the glaze. The decoration back marks are over the glaze. Various colorings used in the back marks designate different periods in the Haviland factory production. Pattern names often appear on many older sets between the whiteware and decorating marks.

References: Jean d'Albis & Celeste Romanet, *La Porcelain de Limoges*, Editions Sous le Vent, 1980; Mary Frank Gaston, *Haviland Collectables & Objects of Art*, Collector Books, 1984; Mary Frank Gaston, *The Collector's Encyclopedia of Limoges Porcelain*, Collector Books, 1980; G.T. Jacobson, *Haviland China: Volume One & Volume Two*, Wallace-Homestead, 1979; Arlene Schleiger, *Two Hundred Patterns of Haviland China, Books I-V*, published privately, Omaha; Harriet Young, *Grandmother's Haviland*, Wallace-Homestead, 1970.

Collecting Hints: The term "blank" refers to the whiteware piece before any pattern decoration has been applied. A blank can be a simple, all white finished glazed piece. Blanks can be smooth or have embossed edges and designs in the whiteware itself. Decorations and gold trims were applied later.

One must know both the blank number and the pattern number to make an exact match of a Haviland piece. The width and placings of the gold trims also exhibited tremendous variety and must be checked carefully.

Haviland matching services use Arlene Schleiger's reference books to identify patterns. Xerox a plate on both sides and indicate colors of the patterns when sending a sample to a matching service.

Monsieur Jean 'Albis, Haviland & Company historian, believes that more than 20,000 patterns were created and produced by artists of the company. Many old patterns have been discontinued, but Haviland Limoges porcelain dinnerware still is being made and sold in department and specialty stores.

In addition to the popular floral pattern tablewares, collectors of Haviland also should be alert for the art objects and richly decorated and unique non-tableware items that the company also manufactured.

Bouillon Cup, "Symphony" pattern, dbl handles	10.00
Bowl	
6¼" d, "Belfort" pattern, "T. Haviland"	5.00
9" d, cov, red-brown leaves, white ground, dbl gold handles	30.00
Cake Plate, 13½" d, center rose, green leaves, forget-me-nots, pink line edge, "Haviland and Co"	60.00
Chocolate Pot	
8¾" h, blue floral, gilt decor, "Haviland and Co, Limoges"	100.00
10½" h, sprays of pink roses, melon shape, scalloped top and base, gold handle and finial	135.00
Coffeepot, groups of small pink flowers, white ground, gold accents, "T. Haviland"	30.00

Cup and Saucer	
"Annette" pattern, "Theodore Haviland"	30.00
"Moss Rose" pattern	25.00
Violets pattern, lavender int., ftd, "Haviland, France"	35.00
Violets and leaves, hp, green ground, gold trim, "H and Co"	30.00
Demitasse Cup and Saucer	
Green and gold geometric designs, white ground, "C. F. Haviland," set of 4	50.00
"Holly" pattern, "T. Haviland"	40.00
Pink shaded morning glories, green leaves, "T. Haviland," set of 12	235.00
Rose decor int. and ext., gold band, beaded edges and handle	30.00
Dish, 8½" d, pink florals, gold handles, hexagon	40.00
Dresser Tray, 10½" l, pink overall roses, gold trim	40.00
Fish Set, 21" l platter, twelve 9" d plates, multicolored fish, red and purple coral	600.00
Hatpin Holder, rosebud top, hp purple flowers, gold trim	40.00
Jam Jar, 5½" d, 7" h, blue flower design, gold trim, dbl handles, "GDM"	90.00
Oyster Plate	
7½" d	
Small pink flowers, brushed gold edge, "Theodore Haviland"	25.00
Violets, gold trim, five molded wells, "CFH/GDM" mark	45.00
8¼" d, small flowers, white ground, gold trim	60.00

Gravy Boat, 8" l, matching undertray, small pink and blue floral, red "Theodore Haviland, Limoges France" mark, $42.00.

8⅝" d, five molded wells, salmon pink, dark green, and brown trim	55.00
8¾" d	
Bright yellow, gold separations, brown trim, "Haviland and Co"	45.00
Gold florals, green leaves, white ground, "Haviland and Co"	45.00

Six molded wells, yellow and brown trim **50.00**

Pin Tray, 5" l, center three red roses, gilt edge, "T. Haviland" **25.00**

Pitcher

5½" h, gold and black rim, white ground, "T. Haviland" **20.00**

6" d, 8½" h, hp pink flowers, pink and green ground, gold handles, "Haviland, France" **110.00**

Plate

6¼" d, "Lancaster" pattern, "Theodore Haviland" **10.00**

7", hp scene of bluebirds on pond with irises, "C. F. H.," sq **65.00**

7¼" d, "Drop Rose" pattern, "Haviland, France" mark **20.00**

7½"

Bud design, multicolored, gold trim, "C. F. Haviland," sq **25.00**

Dessert, "La France" pattern, "T. Haviland Limoges, France," set of 6 .... **30.00**

Different floral center, multicolored, wide blue band, "Haviland and Co, France," set of 6 ...... **40.00**

7¾" d, snowflake center, band of light green and gold on border, "Theodore Haviland" **15.00**

8" d

"Ransom" pattern **10.00**

"The Baroness" pattern, floral swags, blue bows, scalloped rim **10.00**

9" d

Center roses and gold medallions, int. bands covered with gold designs, blue center bands separated by pink and gold roses, set of 8 .... **160.00**

Peasant girl carrying basket of fruit, hp gold border **50.00**

Small pink roses, "T. Haviland" .. **10.00**

9¼" d, "Annette" pattern, "Theodore Haviland" **30.00**

9½" d

Cream center, wide emb gold border **25.00**

"Rani" pattern, "T. Haviland, France" **20.00**

9¾" d, "Stafford" pattern, "T. Haviland" **10.00**

10" d

Blue chrysanthemums, "Haviland and Co, Limoges" **20.00**

Pink center, harbor scenes, gold rims, border scenes, 12-sided, sgd, "Theodore Haviland," pr .. **155.00**

11" d, multicolored portrait of bearded man, sgd "MEB, H and Co" **30.00**

12½" d, chop, white roses, light geen, yellow, and pink centers, gold edge **45.00**

12¾" d, purple grapes and green leaves, pink and blue ground **95.00**

12⅞" d, purple and green grapes, green leaves, pastel ground, gold trim, Ranson blank, "Haviland and Co" **95.00**

13" d, chop, "Symphony" pattern .. **35.00**

Oyster Plate

7½" d

Small pink flowers, brushed gold edge, "Theodore Haviland" ... **25.00**

Violets, gold trim, five molded wells, "CFH/GDM" mark **45.00**

8¼" d, small flowers, white ground, gold trim **60.00**

8⅝" d, five molded wells, salmon pink, dark green, and brown trim **55.00**

8¾" d

Bright yellow, gold separations, brown trim, "Haviland and Co" **45.00**

Gold florals, green leaves, white ground, "Haviland and Co" ... **45.00**

Six molded wells, yellow and brown trim **50.00**

Marine figural, molded oyster pockets, "H and Co" **45.00**

Platter

11½" l, 8¼" w, "Autumn Leaf" pattern **65.00**

13¾" l, floral center, scrolled border with flowers, imp "T. H." **45.00**

15" l, 9½" w, three large pink flowers, green leaves, gold trim, pink satin ground, scalloped edge with dbl open handles **90.00**

20" l, small pink flowers, green leaves **75.00**

20½" l, 14½" w, variegated pink poppies, green leaves, scrolling blue and pink border, gold, dated 1897, "T. Haviland" **75.00**

Ramekin and Underplate

Green floral borders, gold brushed edges, hp, "CFH/GDM," set of 6 . **55.00**

Pink roses, green leaves, gold trim, "C. F. H.," set of 6 .... **125.00**

Shaving Mug, rose garlands, "G. D. Haviland" **35.00**

Soup Tureen

11" l, "Bretagne" pattern, light blue and green flowers, green leaves, white ground, pink accents, ribbon handles and finial, "Haviland and Co, Limoges" **90.00**

14" l, "Wild Rose" pattern, hp, "Charles Field Haviland" **125.00**

Tea Set, teapot, creamer, and sugar bowl

Butterflies on one side, lavender flowers on other, center gold band, handles, and rims, "H and Co, L. France" **225.00**

Raised gold beading, scalloped bases, "Theodore Haviland" **250.00**
Teapot
8" h, small blue flowers, gold trim . . **75.00**
Green luster ground, black handles . **80.00**
Tray
13" l, 11" w, blue violets, pink roses, white ground, diamond shape, "C. F. H." **35.00**
16½" l, 8" w, sprays of small lavender flowers, scalloped edge, "Theo Haviland, Limoges, France" **75.00**
Vase
10½" h, brown, crackle ground, gilt rim, three handles and band, tapered cylinder form, "Haviland and Co, Limoges" **90.00**
11½" h, yellow roses, brown, blue, and green ground, ovoid, three handles, sgd "J. Towner," dated 1910 . . . . **600.00**
13" h, 9" d, applied fruit and leaves, blue ground, "H and Co over L" .**1,025.00**
Vegetable Bowl
"Drop Rose" pattern, gold trimmed scalloped edge, ftd, "Haviland, France" **90.00**
9" l, small pink flowers int. and ext., gold trim, "Haviland and Co" . . . **50.00**

HEUBACH

Thuringia, East Germany
1840s to Present

History: Christoph and Philip Heubach founded the Heubach factory to manufacture decorative and household porcelains, figures, dolls heads, and dolls. Their doll heads, animal figures, and piano babies are their most famous products. There is no connection between this factory and the Ernst Heubach factory in Koppelsdorf.

After World War II, the company was nationalized and experienced several name changes. The present company name is VEB United Decorative Porcelainworks Lichte.

Figure
3" h, dog, seated, white and brown markings, wearing muzzle, mounted on base, bisque **85.00**
4" h
Baby, standing, wearing only shoes and socks **250.00**

Figure, 11½" h, pastel colors, white ground, imp rising sun mark, $325.00.

Boy, seated, hand over eye, wearing brown shoes and white socks, white basket as side, sq "Heubach" mark **95.00**
Dog, Beagle, brown and white coloring, "sunburst" mark **110.00**
4" h, 3" l, puppy, brown and white, sitting on green wooden planks . . **85.00**
4" h, 4⅛" l, dove, white, pink beak, bisque **75.00**
4" h, 8" l, dog, Great Dane, recumbent, front paws crossed **110.00**
4½" h
Bust of boy and girl, hands on cheeks, pink, aqua, and white, pr **325.00**
Dog, shaggy, white, pr, "sunburst" mark **125.00**
Dutch girl, seated, white bonnet, orange-red skirt, green top, bisque, imp **70.00**
4¾" h, Dutch boy and girl, seated, orange, green, and white clothing, bisque, pr **175.00**
5" h
Bulldog, standing, black and white coloring **110.00**
Rabbit, sitting, pink eyes **100.00**
5" h, 10" l, dog, Setter, standing, long hair, gray and white, mounted on green grass base **115.00**
5½" h, baby, sitting in nightcap and gown, bisque **135.00**
6" h
Dutch boy and girl, standing in front of large egg, imp **135.00**
Peasant girl, seated, head tilted, green, orange, and white dress . **78.00**
6⅜" h, peasant boy, blue shirt, tan pants and shoes, standing in front of sq vase **110.00**
6½" h, duck, white, colored bill and feet **250.00**

7" h

Dutch boy and girl, seated, green, orange, and gray, bisque, pr, imp 225.00

"Mrs Bardell," from Pickwick Papers, multicolored 85.00

7" h, 5" l, puppy, seated, long ears, imp "Heubach" 285.00

7¼" h, bisque

Dutch boy and girl, standing back to back, red, green, white, and gray 195.00

"The Fat Boy," from Pickwick Papers, multicolored, imp 125.00

7½" h

Dutch boy and girl, facing each other, kissing, hands at sides, blue and white 265.00

Dutch boy and girl, standing back to back, orange, green, and white, unmarked 165.00

"The Marchioness," from Old Curiosity Shop, multicolored 85.00

7¾" h

Boy and girl, seated, bubble pipes, multicolored, green bench 325.00

Oriental girl with umbrella, multicolored 75.00

8" h, man, standing, blue and white period dress 50.00

8½" h

Boy and girl, seated, native red and green costumes, pr, "sunburst" mark 385.00

Young girl, peasant dress, holding peanut basket 200.00

Young girl, sitting, large blue ruffled bonnet, white pleated skirt with aqua dots, bisque 245.00

9" h, bisque

Peasant girl, leaning over basket, green, orange, and white, imp . 225.00

Woman, brown glazed classical tunic, green "Heubach" 60.00

9¼" h, boy, beachsuit, sandpail, shaded pastel and gold 150.00

9½"

Baby, sitting up, touching toes, white gown, blue trim 375.00

Boy, sitting on stool, fez, glasses, and cigar, lavender and purple, bisque 165.00

Boy, standing and holding rabbit, pastel colors, bisque 145.00

Dutch girl, holding bucket, lavender, peach, and green, bisque . 175.00

Monkey, sitting, top hat in lap, tan and white body, white formal collar, blue dot bow tie 425.00

Negro girl, white dress, blue and pink fringed shawl over shoulders, pink and white fan in right hand 950.00

Woman, wearing classical draped gown, band in hair, glossy glaze 165.00

10" h

Baby, sitting, legs crossed, arms raised, white gown, pink trim .. 400.00

Boy and girl, bowing, dark blue and pink floral native costumes, pr 650.00

Boy and girl, fancy country clothes, peach colors, pr, "sunburst" mark 300.00

Boy, green suit, pockets turned out, flesh tones 175.00

Figure, 10½" h, blue-green skirt and gray top, green mark, $285.00.

11¼" h, woman, standing behind ship's wheel, bisque, imp "Heubach" 285.00

11½" h

Boy and girl, dressed in farm clothes, gleaners tools, pr 175.00

Dancing girl, blonde, turquoise sanded dress, white ruffles, gold trimmed pasted base, bisque, imp 245.00

12½" h, boy, blonde, moon face, pink knickers, blouse and ruffled collar, blue bow, kite in hand 135.00

12¾" h, young boy, clown costume, red peaked hat, c1900 .... 500.00

13" h

Boy, sailor suit and cap, girl, bonnet and Victorian dress, blue and white, orange and yellow bases, pr 400.00

Girl with parrot, blue skirt, pink vest 300.00

Young girl, lilac dress and bonnet, c1900 .... 500.00

13½" h, boy and girl, winter clothes, multicolored, three snowballs, girl with muff, pr 325.00

14" h, baby, standing in front of chair, chip on toe **450.00**
15" h, woman, dressed in court clothes, pastel colors, intaglio eyes, pr, imp **300.00**
16½" h, dancing girl, holding skirt, tambourine on base, multicolored **550.00**
Miniature, vase, portrait piece **30.00**
Vase
4" h, Dutch girl in pink, emb figure, "sunburst" mark **22.00**
6" h, overshot, hp rural scene **75.00**
7" h, overall rose decoration, multi-colored **45.00**
9½" h
Flowers, pink and lavender, pebble gold at top, dark blue border accents **195.00**
Portrait of sea captain smoking pipe, shades of brown **95.00**
10" h, mermaid protruding from top **350.00**

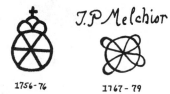

1756-76   1767-79

HOCHST

Hesse, West Germany
1746 to 1796

History: Though in existence for a short time, the porcelain factory at Hochst produced a high quality product. Johann Goltz and Johann Clarus, his son-in-law, founded the porcelain factory together with Adam Friedrich von Lowenfinck, a decorator, who came from Meissen. The group did not work well together and soon split up. By 1750 Johann Benchgraff from Vienna joined Glotz and Clarus to produce porcelains.

After Benchgraff left in 1753, Goltz had financial difficulties. The Prince-Elector, Friedrich Carl von Ostern, from Mainz, took over. Johann and Ferdinand Maass were appointed managers of the factory, now known as the Prince-Electoral Privileged Porcelain Factory, from 1756 to 1776. Tablewares, decorative porcelains, coffee and tea sets, and figures were made. Oriental, Rococo, and Neo-classical decorative themes were used. Piercing and fretwork were common design elements.

Hochst porcelain is probably best known for the figurals that were modeled under the supervision of Johann Melchior. These painted and biscuit figures showed a high degree of artistic ability. Religious and pastoral groups, figures of children, and mythological characters were modeled with special attention to detail. Pinks and light rose tones were most prominently used by Melchior on his figures of children.

The new Prince-Elector, Breidbach-Burresheim, converted the company into a joint stock company in 1776. The factory was renamed to Prince-Electoral Fayence Manufactory. With the departure of Melchior to the Frankenthal factory in 1779, a gradual decline in quality occurred, although attempts at modeling continued. The factory ceased operations in 1796.

References: George Ware, *German & Austrian Porcelain*, Crown, Inc., 1963.

Museums: Metropolitan Museum of Art, New York, NY; Museum fur Kunsthandwerk, Frankfurt, Germany; Schlossmuseum, Berlin, Germany; Seattle Art Museum, Seattle, WA.

REPRODUCTION ALERT: Following the closing of the Hochst factory, many of the molds were sold in 1840 to the Muller factory at Damm near Aschaffenburg. Muller produced many of the more popular items including the figures. The Hochst mark was used, but these new copies lacked the subtle coloration of the earlier Hochst originals.

The Fasold & Stauch Company of Bock-Wallendorf and Dressel, Kister & Co. of Volkstedt employed a mark which often is confused with Hochst. The quality of their products differs significantly from the high quality of the Hochst material.

Basket
4¼" l, int. painted with trailing flowers, puce diaper borders, pierced sides, center handle, c1755, puce "wheel" mark (A) **670.00**

Coffeepot, 11⅝" h, multicolored garden flowers, gilt line rim, c1765, blue crowned wheel mark, (A) $2,780.00.

10¼" w, painted bouquets of flowers, dbl handles, puce and gilt trim, c1755 (A) **180.00**

Beaker and Saucer, saucer painted with black bust in oval, suspended by puce ribbon, foliage and garlands below, gilt rim, c1780, puce "wheel" mark **420.00**

Bowl, 5⅛" d, reserved bands of husks, gilt-edged blue border, c1790, blue "wheel" mark (A) **200.00**

Bouillon Cup, Cov and Stand, painted pink and green flower sprays, borders of interlaced circles, entwined handle and fruit finial, c1775, blue "wheel" mark (A) **990.00**

Candlestick, 10" h, modeled as rustic couple embracing, arm holding sconces, multicolored, sheep and dog on mound base, gilt scrolls, c1753, purple "wheel" mark, sconce and center sheep missing (A) **2,090.00**

Chocolate Pot, 6⅝" h, quatrefoil cartouche, harbor scene, yellow ground, metal fittings on cov, c1755, gilt "wheel" mark (A) **1,570.00**

Coffee Cup and Saucer, paintings of peasants, multicolored, branch handle with green accents, gilt rim, c1755, gilt "wheel" mark **1,700.00**

Coffeepot

7" h, painted figures in river landscape, pear shape, spout and dbl scroll handles, puce with flowerheads, gilt flowerhead finial, c1770, blue "wheel" mark (A) ... **385.00**

Puce painted mountains and river scene by castle ruins with insects, pear shape, dbl scroll handle, scroll molded spout, puce trim, c1765, brown crowned "wheel" mark ... **900.00**

Cup and Saucer

Cup with brown doe, saucer with spaniel by river, brown rims, c1770, blue "wheel" mark (A) ... **550.00**

Painting of figures by river scene and classical ruins, puce cup with scroll handle and gilt rims, c1755, iron-red "wheel" mark **450.00**

Peasant figures in landscape vignettes, bright colors, branch handles with gilt, c1755, gilt "wheel" mark, pr, repaired **2,800.00**

Portrait roundels, puce, gilt foliage wreath tied with colored ribbons, gilt rims, c1775, blue "wheel," incised "IN" mark **320.00**

Silhoutte of gentleman in wreath of forget-me-nots, saucer well, purple and gilt medallion, c1775–80, blue "wheel" mark (A) **400.00**

Silhoutte portrait bust of lady in for-

get-me-not border of cup, gilt interlaced "CF," same border on saucer, c1775, blue "wheel" mark (A) ... **465.00**

Custard Cup, 3" h, body with multicolored trailing flowers, rims with shaped panels enclosing trellis pattern, panels outlined in yellow, branch handle, green accents, cov with rose finial, c1760, puce "wheel" mark **220.00**

Figure

2⅝" h, youth standing, hand on hip and sack over shoulder in jacket and skirt, tree stump mound base, c1765, blue "wheel" mark (A) ... **630.00**

4½" h, Hercules seated on lion skin, draped in puce, cloak on oval rockwork base, right arm holding bearded chin, c1755–60, iron-red "wheel" mark **1,000.00**

5" h

Boy dressed as Charlatan, black tricorn hat, flowing pink jacket, gilt scrolls, green breeches, iron-red cloak, flask in right hand, circ scroll-molded base, puce and gilt, c1755, iron-red "wheel" mark **815.00**

5½" h, young boy resting on tree stump, young girl in dancing pose, native dress, multicolored, c1770, blue "wheel" mark, pr (A) **910.00**

5¾" h, Venus and Juno, modeled as putti, seated on cloud, scrolls with puce, blue accents, Venus with dove, c1760, imp "wheels" mark, pr (A) **1,320.00**

5⅞" h, Cupid sharpening arrow on grindstone, two putti, quiver and bow, grass rockwork base, multicolored, gilt, blue "wheel" mark (A) **360.00**

6" h, "Taste," nymph standing against tree trunk holding grapes, seated monkey holding fruit, circ scroll-molded base, c1755, iron-red "wheel" mark, repaired (A) **275.00**

6½" h

"The Tongue Seller," black beret, white jacket with green trim, brown breeches, dagger at waist, salmon cape, tongue in outstretched right hand, yellow basket of tongues on left arm, shaped oval tree trunk base, blue and iron-red molded flowerheads, c1753, green "wheel," "IZ" mark (A)...............**15,400.00**

Dr Balanzon, black snood, iron-red trimmed black jacket and pants, standing on circ tree stump base, applied multicolored flower-heads and foliage, c1752, black "AL" and incised "Bl" mark, repairs......................**11,000.00**

6⅝" h, Autumn, young man squeezing grapes into cup, multicolored costume, grasswork base, c1770, blue "wheel" mark (A) 810.00

7" h
Boy and girl in Turkish costumes, multicolored, mounted on grass base, modeled by Melchior, c1775, blue "wheel" and impressed "MS" mark **1,400.00**

Male and female dancers, puce, flowered gilt-edged period clothes, yellow ribbons, tree stump mound bases, puce and gilt scrolls, c1755, iron-red "wheel" mark, pr (A) **11,375.00**

7" h, 7⅝" h, children dressed as Sultan or Sultana, each holding mask, pastel colors, grasswork bases, contemporary rococo ormolu bases, modeled by Melchior, c1770, pr (A) **16,430.00**

7½" h, Grape Harvesters, man in green jacket and black breeches pruning vine, woman in flowered blouse, black skirt, and straw hat holding basket of grapes, watering can and grapes at feet, tree trunk bases, c1750–53, pr, restored (A) .**1,380.00**

8⅝" h, modeled as woman seated on box, child in lap, cat on base, blue "wheel" mark (A) 360.00

11¼" h, man and woman in flowered period clothes playing hurdy–gurdy, child asleep on box, rock and grass mound base, c1770, blue "wheel" mark **3,750.00**

Game Basket, 4½" w, pierced, central divider, painted flower sprays on six shaped and two round game chips, c1760, gilt "wheel" mark (A) **1,210.00**

Hot Water Jug, 7¼" h, cov, black oval medallion, painted with yellow birds on branches, scattered floral sprays, gilt rims, basketweave C-handle, late 18th C, blue "wheel" mark (A) 300.00

Oil Pot, 5½" h, 6¾" d, cov with stand, molded gadroon and scrolls, painted florals, c1750–55, green "wheel" mark (A) 440.00

Plate
9½" d, molded florals and painted flower bouquets, gilt rim, octafoil shape, c1765, blue crowned "wheel" mark (A) 285.00

10" d, multicolored Venus on shell, angel in sq panel, draped by ribbon and foliage garland, incribed "Venus," border in puce, scale outlined with gilt scrolls, and flower sprays, shaped gilt rim, c1780, blue "wheel" mark **1,800.00**

10¼" d, painted scattered flower sprays, shaped ozier border, gilt rim, c1765, puce "wheel" mark (A) 285.00

Punch Bowl, 14" d, rose painting of drinkers at inn, reverse of Dutch canal scene, inscribed in gold, scattered insects and flowers, gilt line rim, c1755, gilt "wheel" mark **1,300.00**

Saucer, painted flower sprays, c1765, blue "wheel" mark (A) 60.00

Slop Bowl, 6⅞" d, rose painted rural landscape, shaped green banded rims, int. with sprays and insects, c1765, blue "wheel" and incised "NI" mark (A) 530.00

Soup Tureen, 14⅛" l, multicolored painted riverscape, vignettes on sides, molded leak handles tied with pink ribbons, modeled finial in form of parsnips, peas, garlic, and cauliflower, painted leaves extending on cov, gilt rim, c1765, blue crowned "wheel" mark **4,300.00**

Tea Caddy
Rose painted putti supporting foliage entwined ribbon, gilt "EM," gilt ribbon and floral sprays on shoulder, c1765 (A) 160.00

Scene of monkeys painting portrait, multicolored, lower portion molded, gilt lappets, silver cov, c1770, blue "wheel" mark **1,200.00**

Teabowl and Saucer
Cup painted with putto drinking from glass, saucer with standing putto, gilt borders, puce "wheel" mark (A) 300.00

German flowers, multicolored, brown edged rims, puce "wheel" mark (A) 70.00

Puce and gilt painted Chinoiserie figures seated in landscapes on rococo wave scroll supports, c1755, iron-red "wheel" and incised "NI" mark, pr (A) **1,390.00**

Rose painted flower sprays, gilt rims, c1765 (A) 135.00

Teapot, 4¾" h, purple figures and landscape on one side, church in landscape on other, insects and flowers, dbl scroll handle, animal head spout with bearded mask, cov with pine cone finial and polychrome flowers, c1765, purple "wheel" mark **1,000.00**

Tureen and Stand, 15" l, painted sprays of garden flowers and insects, blue and yellow branch handles, cov with green bud and foliage finial, c1750 .**1,440.00**

HOLLAND-GENERAL

PORCELAIN
1757 to 1819

Porcelain by Dutch manufacturers is not as well known as the country's Delftware. Dutch porcelain factories at Weesp, Oude Loosdrecht, Amstel, and The Hague produced some wares, although production was limited and frequently imitated styles from other areas.

Hard paste porcelain was made at the Weesp factory near Amsterdam beginning in 1757. The factory was sold to Count Diepenbroick in 1762. The factory used French and German styles for inspiration, e.g., white porcelains decorated with flowers and other motifs in relief. Perforated baskets were made along with rococo relief decorated wares featuring landscapes in cartouches or adorned with birds or flowers. The factory did not prosper and was sold in 1771. The mark used by Weesp was a copy of the Meissen crossed swords in underglaze blue with the addition of three dots between the points of the blades and on either side.

De Moll bought the factory, and the company moved to Oud Loosdrecht between Utrecht and Amsterdam. The wares exhibited more Dutch characteristics; landscapes were especially popular. The mark used at Loosdrecht was "M.O.L." either incised or in underglaze blue, black, or colored enamels.

The company moved again in 1784 to Ouder-Amstel and was taken over by Frederick Daeuber. The wares now imitated the Empire style wares from Sevres.

In 1800 the factory belonged to the firm George Dommer and Co. It was moved to Nieuwer-Amstel in 1809 and was closed in 1819. Sometimes the "M.O.L." mark was used with the word Amstel. Other wares were marked "Amstel" in black.

Lynker, a German, established a porcelain factory in 1775 at The Hague. It produced hard paste porcelain similar to Meissen. The pieces were decorated with landscapes, seascapes, and birds. The factory also decorated china from other sources. It closed in 1786. The Hague mark was the stork from the city arms in blue underglaze. When other blanks from other firms were decorated, the mark was painted on the glaze.

POTTERY

The earliest pottery in Holland was made before 1609, long before Holland became an independent nation state. Tin glazed wares of the early sixteenth century that were made in Antwerp, Haarlem, Rotterdam, and Amsterdam were similar to Italian wares known as majolica.

Mid 16th century dishes made in Antwerp utilized the "blue-dash" around the edges that was later a design element found on 17th century English wares. Drug jars and spouted drug pots painted in high temperature blue tones similar to Italian wares were quite popular in the Netherlands.

With the founding of the Dutch East India Company in 1609, trade flourished with both China and Japan. As the Dutch potters became familiar with Far Eastern porcelains, they imitated the Oriental designs on the earthenware. By the early 17th century, Delftware had developed.

When English salt glazed stonewares and cream colored earthenwares were imported from England in large quantities about the 1760s, Dutch potteries experienced a decline. Customers prefered the English goods over the tin glazed wares made in Holland.

Museums: Gemeente Museum, The Hague, Holland.

Additional Listings: Delft, Gouda, Maastricht, Rozenburg.

Bowl
    3⅛" h, children playing games in landscape in rose, gilt rim, c1770, Amstel **200.00**
    8⅞" d, blue and white birds and flowering plants, rockwork, cell pattern, foliage border, manganese rim, c1760, Arnhem (A) **180.00**
Clock, 18" w, circ clock house supported by two loop handles, painted flowers and foliage, brown, green, and lilac, blue ground, c1905, Amsterdam (A) **315.00**
Coffeepot, 7⅞" h, painted oval medallion of insects on parchment, green tied ribbon, c1775, Loosdrecht (A) . **225.00**
Cup and Saucer
    Figures in landscape, puce, gilt rims, c1775, blue "MOL" marks (A) ... **200.00**
    Painted landscapes, light rose, gilt C-scroll rims, c1780, blue "stork" marks, set of 3 (A) **170.00**
    Painted lovers in landscape, gilt scroll borders, c1775, blue "stork" marks, The Hague **275.00**
Dish
    9⅜" d, majolica, blue, white, and manganese, inscribed centers, 18th C, pr (A) **120.00**
    9⅞" d, blue and white panels of symmetrical flowers, mid 18th C (A) . **165.00**
    10¼" d, majolica, octagon center painted with blue aquatic plants, molded border, alternating scallop shells and stylized faces, mid 17th C **400.00**

10⅜" d, majolica, center painted with pomegranates, foliage in ochre, blue and green, pie crust rim, raised knobs, c1620 (A) **1,100.00**

11⅜" d, majolica, blue and white inscribed sentences, foliage surrounds, late 18th C, pr (A) **330.00**

11⅞" d

Blue and manganese bird on rock between sponged trees, hexagon border designs, late 17th C (A) . **180.00**

Blue, manganese, and yellow tulip and Cupid in centers, fluted, 17th C, pr (A) **400.00**

12½" d, majolica, center scene of Madonna and Child, four border panels of birds and foliage, painted in orange, blue, yellow, and manganese, early 17th C **95.00**

12¾" d, blue painted coat-of-arm coronet, above "1666" date, Eastern Holland (A) **1,135.00**

13½" sq, majolica, purple, yellow, and ochre, radiating petals and conc rings, overlapping crescent border, early 17th C (A) **610.00**

14⅛" l, yellow painted stylized chrysanthemums, green and blue panels, pink ground, rim with four strap handles, "Holland Utrecht 605K" mark (A) **155.00**

17½" l, painted cornflowers, multicolored, c1775, blue script mark, Amstel (A) **45.00**

18¾" d, painted trailing roses and cornflowers, multicolored, shaped gilt rim, c1775, blue script mark, Amstel (A) **50.00**

Ewer, 14½" h, brown, yellow, and ochre flowers and foliage, pink ground, high loop handle, trumpet neck, "Holland Utrecht 621" mark (A) **175.00**

Figure, 6¼" l, modeled shoes, manganese and white, painted grapes on toes, c1770, Rotterdam, pr (A) **355.00**

Holy Water Font, child's head in bisque, glazed porcelain **25.00**

Inkstand, 6" w, fitted sander, covered well, stepped body, blue and white sailing ships in river landscape, stylized scrolling foliage, 18th C, Maakum (A) **120.00**

Jug, 7⅜' h, gray poppies, polychrome abstract ground, Purmerende (A) . . . **220.00**

Pitcher

6¾" h, cov, porcelain, blue floral sprays, gilt accents, ribbed cov, pinched spout, dbl C-scroll handle, late 18th C, "MOL" mark **350.00**

7" h, Dutch children, windmills, multicolored **135.00**

Plate

9" d, majolica, blue "I. F." in center, stylized tulips, scalloped rim, 17th C (A) **350.00**

9½" d, central figure, inscription and trophies, scalloped edges, mid 18th C, unmarked, pr **130.00**

9¾" d, central biblical scenes, inscriptions, scalloped borders, mid 18th C, unmarked, pr **130.00**

9⅞" d, painted cornflowers, multicolored, shaped rims, early 19th C, Loosdrecht, set of 7 (A) **140.00**

10" d, black and pink "Liberty," two books in green circle surrounded by scrollwork and flowers, molded wavy rim, four black inscriptions . **135.00**

12⅜" d, small multicolored landscapes in centers, four scroll-molded border cartouches, c1765, blue "X'd swords and three dot" marks, Weesp, pr (A) **440.00**

Puzzle Jug, 6½" h, blue and ochre painted tulip, neck pierced with flowerheads, single spout **110.00**

Vase, 10¼" h, brown peacocks, turquoise feathers, mauve and green striped base, dark green ground, restored lip, "PURMERENDE, HOLLAND," $1,500.00.

Sauceboat and Stand, painted trailing roses and cornflowers, multicolored, scroll handle, c1785, blue script mark, Amstel (A) **15.00**

Saucer, painted putto on cloud scroll, blue "stork" mark, The Hague (A) . . **85.00**

Tazza, 10" d, majolica, multicolored, radiating panels of stylized flowers around central spray, ochre dash, blue dot yellow borders, 17th C, cracked **775.00**

Tea Service, part, teapot, cov milk jug, sugar bowl, ten cups and twelve saucers, painted wasps, scrolling foliage, multicolored, Arnhem (A) 100.00

Teabowl and Saucer
  Multicolored peasants in landscape, floral sprays, puce rims, c1765, blue "X'd swords and dot" marks, Weesp 400.00
  Painted hen in landscape on bowl, cockerel on saucer, pink ground, c1765, Weesp (A) 275.00

Vase
  5½" h, mottled green textured glaze, "Made in Holland" mark (A) 10.00
  6⅛" h, Art Deco style, orange and black glaze, Mobach (A) 20.00
  6⅝" h, molded, coiling serpent, gray and brown streaked glaze, cone shape, three feet, Distal (A) 20.00
  8" h, blue and white gourd shape (A)   35.00
  11" h, painted carp, waterscrolls and seaweed, flared pinched neck, thin dbl handles extended to top, Purmerende (A) 590.00
  12¼" h, Prussian blue glaze, flared neck, molded dbl loop handles, "De Kat Bergen op Zoom" mark (A)   65.00
  12½" h, cov, green birds and lizards, brown-green waves, cream ground, dated 1942, Piet Wiegman (A) . . . 110.00
  14" h, painted polychrome stylized cockerel on abstract ground, dbl handles, sgd "C J Lan," Purmerende (A) 440.00

HUNGARY-GENERAL

Holitsch
1743 to 1827

History: The Holitsch pottery factory was established in 1743 by Francis of Lorraine, consort of the Empress Maria Theresa. Decorative motifs followed the popular Strasbourg style. Tureens were made in the form of birds. Most of the painting favored a Hungarian peasant pottery style. When the firm started to produce English style earthenwares in 1786, they used workers from the Vienna factory. It continued in operation with State support until 1827.

Collecting Hints: The early faience wares were marked with the "HF" monogram for "Holitscher Fabrik." Later creamwares bear the full name "HOLICS" or "HOLITSCH."

References: Tivadar Artner, *Modern Hungarian Ceramics*, Art Foundation Publishing House,

1974; Gyorgy Domanovszky, *Hungarian Pottery*, Corvina Press, 1968.

Additional Listings: Fischer, Zsolnay.

Dish, 13⅜" l, multicolored, yellow ground, c1760, manganese "H" mark, Holitsch, $3,000.00.

Asparagus Box, 8⅝" l, faience molded brown, yellow, and green spears, red berry, entwined stem knob, restored, black "HH" mark (A) **1,870.00**

Box, 6½" l, cov, faience, leaf shaped dish, applied flowerheads, branch handle, modeled lemon box, yellow glaze, c1760 (A) **1,430.00**

Figure, 4¾" h, faience, man crushing grapes with foot, seated companion holding grapes, multicolored, c1760, Holitsch, repairs **1,500.00**

Jug, 9⅞" h, faience, multicolored enameled saint between large flower sprigs, inscribed, pear shape, strap handle, dated 1803 (A) 395.00

Teapot, 5¾" h, polychrome birds and butterflies, gilt trim, "Hungary" mark (A) 125.00

Tray, 15⅛" l, painted, classical landscape, scattered flower sprays, c1760–70, black "HG" mark, cracked 650.00

HUTSCHENREUTHER

Hohenberg, Bavaria, West Germany
1814 to Present

History: Carl Magnus Hutschenreuther established a German porcelain factory, Hutschenreuther A.G., at Hohenberg, Bavaria, in 1814. When Carl Magnus died in 1845, he was succeeded by Johanna, his widow, and Christian and Lorenz, his sons. Lorenz was not satisfied simply to carry on the family business. He was bought out by his partners and established his own porcelain factory in Selb. The Lorenz Hutschenreuther and Carl Magnus Hutschenreuther porcelain factories co-existed as two totally independent businesses. When Lorenz Hutschenreuther died in 1856, Viktor and Eugen, his sons, took over his company.

The Lorenz family enlarged their firm through acquisitions and the creation of new factories during the first part of the 20th century. In 1906 they acquired the porcelain factory Jaeger, Werner & Co. in Selb. In 1917 Lorenz Hutschenreuther bought the Paul Muller Porcelain Factory in Selb. In 1927 they purchased the Tirschenreuth Porcelain Factory and Bauscher Brothers Porcelain Factory in Weiden. The following year the Konigszelt Porcelain Factory was added.

Both branches of the Hutschenreuthers were noted for the high quality of their tablewares and figures. In 1969 all branches of the Magnus and Lorenz firm were united under the group name Hutschenreuther AG.

A merger with Porzellanfabrik Kahla AG of Schoenwald in 1972 brought the Arzberg and Schonwald brands of porcelain along with two earthenware factories into the Hutschenreuther group of enterprises. The company is still in business today producing limited edition plates, figures, dinnerware, and other china. Distribution companies have been established in France, the United States, Canada, Scandinavia, Belgium, and Italy.

Bowl, 8½" d, center of man and
  woman, period clothes, band of royal
  blue and gold filigree, border of
  panels of figures in period clothes,
  "Hutschenreuther lion" mark **120.00**
Coffeepot, "Apart" pattern, marked ... **30.00**
Cup and Saucer
  Demitasse, "Apart" pattern, white,
    marked **15.00**
  Dutch-African Ship Lines, black map
    of Africa, "D. A.L." marked **15.00**
  Lavender flowers, gilt trim, sgd
    "Clarke," marked **35.00**
Dish
  9" d, "Blue Onion" pattern, pierced
    borders, pedestals, marked, pr (A) **30.00**
  10⅝" d, "Blue Onion" pattern,
    fluted, metal swing handle (A) ... **15.00**
Figure
  2" l, butterfly on branch, multicolored, marked (A) **45.00**
  2½" h
    Bird feeding baby bird, brown,
      marked (A) **45.00**

Three birds on branch, multicolored, marked (A) **45.00**
3½" l, dog, shaded body, blue eyes,
  marked **80.00**
4½" h, Blanc de Chine figure, "Three
  Frolicking Cherubs," sgd "K. Tutter," marked (A) **50.00**
5¼" h, deer feeding, fawn colored,
  artist sgd, marked **125.00**
5½" h
  Canary on tree stump, bright
    colors, sgd "Granet" **135.00**
  Young woman skating, balanced on
    one skate, marked **155.00**
6" h, Mephistopheles, sword and scissors, marked **130.00**
6" l, 9½" h, "The Traveling Musicians," donkey with pyramid of animals **235.00**
6½" h, cardinal on branch, berries
  and leaves, marked **40.00**
8" h, Blanc de Chine figure, "Girl
  with Fawn," sgd "K. Tutter,"
  marked (A) **50.00**
8" l, 6" h, bird feeding two baby birds,
  brown, white branch, marked **75.00**
8½" h
  Great Reed Warbler, multicolored,
    sgd "K. Tutter" **110.00**
  Standing dachshund, smooth hair,
    tan and brown, marked **145.00**
9" h
  "Fairy Riding Stag," mulitcolored,
    sgd "C. Werner," marked (A) .. **170.00**
  Two Deco style dancing girls,
    white, sgd "C. Werner," marked **140.00**
9" w, 11" h, seated nude woman, sgd
  "C. Werner," marked **300.00**
9¼" h, ballerina and male dancer,
  kissing while in ballet pose, marked **260.00**
10¼" h, Polar bear, upright walking
  position, marked **200.00**
10⅜" h, woman, arms extended,
  head tilted, flowing hair, sgd "C.
  Werner," marked **225.00**
10½" h, girl with ball, crouched position, flowing hair, pastel colors,
  sgd "K. Tutter," marked **245.00**
13" h, seated young girl on tree
  stump, holding gold ball, multicolored tunic and skirt (A) **200.00**
"Bremen Town Musicians," marked **110.00**
Dbl robins, sgd Tutter, marked **100.00**
Peacock grouping, marked **250.00**
Reclining donkey, marked, No 2421/
  2F **55.00**
Seagull in flight, marked **250.00**
White figure, kneeling lady, Art Deco
  style, sgd, marked **225.00**
Kettle and Stand, 13⅜" h, "Blue Onion"
  pattern, SP oval handle, burner in
  stand (A) **60.00**

Plaque
   4" w, 6" h
      Painting of Hansel and Gretel, sgd
         "Wagner," marked **635.00**
      Portrait of peasant woman holding
         sheaf of wheat, marked **235.00**
      "Ruth," multicolored, sgd "Wag-
         ner," "HR" in circle, marked .. **750.00**
      5" l, painting of Daphne, gilt frame,
         oval sgd "Wagner," marked **950.00**
Plate
   6" d, portraits of George and Martha
      Washington, marked, pr **75.00**
   7¾" d, "Apart" pattern, marked **5.00**
   8½" d, "Jaffrey" pattern, set of 8 ... **45.00**
   9" d, "Autumn Leaf" pattern, marked,
      set of·12 .... **95.00**
   9¾" d, painted centers, "Countess
      Grey and Children" and "Lady
      Smythe and Children," cobalt bor-
      ders, gilt and silver floral motifs,
      sgd "Wagner," late 19th C, pr (A) **1,650.00**
   10" d
      Multicolored pears, wide gold rim,
         marked **45.00**
      Scene of woman in cart, pulled by
         four cherubs, marked **115.00**
   12" d, decal of indian, hp accents,
      blue shading, gold border, marked **45.00**
Platter, 15" l, multicolored florals,
   cream ground **15.00**
Teapot, "Blue Onion" pattern **55.00**
Tray, 9" d, multicolored florals, light
   blue ground, gold trim, marked **35.00**

IMPERIAL ST. PETERSBURG

St. Petersburg, now Leningrad, Russia
1744 to Present

History: Initially the Imperial St. Petersburg porcelain factory enjoyed only limited success.
Catherine the Great was associated with the factory by 1762. Her imperial patronage helped
insure success.

Most of the wares were basically French in
form, but often were painted with Russian views.
When Jean-Dominique Rachette became head of
the modeling workshop in 1779, he increased
the sculpture output by making porcelain statues,
groups in bisque, and portrait busts.

Enormous dinner services were made for the
Tsar's palace and the nobility of the court, e.g.,
the "Arabesque Service" of 973 pieces in 1784

and the "Cabinet Service" of 800 pieces. The
War of 1812 disrupted production at the factory
somewhat. Portraits of heroes and military motifs
appeared on the porcelains during and immediately following the war.

Reorganization took place in 1901. The Art
Nouveau style was utilized. About 1907 soft
paste porcelains were developed. A series of figures entitled "Peoples of Russia" was designed
by P. Kamensky and issued beginning in 1907.
The factory's work continued after World War I
and during the Civil War. The revolution inspired
designs for porcelains reflecting industrialization
of the country.

The factory was renamed Lomonosov Factory
in 1925 in honor of M. Lomonosov, the Russian
scientist. Production continues today.

Marks changed many times. Until 1917 the
cypher of the reigning monarch was used.

References: R. Hare, *The Art & Artists of Russia*,
Methuen & Co., 1965; L. Nikiforova, compiler,
Russian Porcelain in the Hermitage Collection,
Aurora Art Publishers, 1973; Marvin Ross, *Rus-
sian Porcelains*, University of Oklahoma Press,
1968.

Museums: Hermitage, Leningrad, Russia; Russian Museum, Leningrad, Russia.

Box, cov, 4½" l, 4½" h, green and magenta, dark green leaves, brown handle,
$4,500.00.

Cup and Saucer, overall trailing flowers,
   cup with crowned dbl eagle and
   "NA", gilt int. **135.00**
Dish, cov, 6" l, 6" h, cov, royal crown
   in gilt, each side with iron-red trim,
   white ground, gold finial, c1860,
   marked **1,600.00**
Figure, 2¾" h, porcelain, egg with
   gilded monogram of Alexandra Feo-
   dorovna, c1900 (A) **500.00**
Plate
   7¼" d, multicolored flower sprays
      and foliage, blue shellwork bor-
      ders, gilded rims, dated 1901, set
      of 12 (A) **550.00**
   8¾" d, centers painted with orange

flowerhead, gilt stellar motif, multicolored Russian Imperial Eagle, green ground, inscribed, green, blue, and black scroll borders, gilt ground, c1825–55, pr (A) **1,870.00**

9⅛" d, center painted with Star of the Order of St. Vladimir, sash and Badge of Order border, waved gilt rim, c1894–1917 (A) **715.00**

9¼" d
Black Russian Imperial Eagle holding anchor, gilded borders, c1894–1917 (A) **45.00**

Center painted with wounded soldier walking horse, battle in background, gilded borders with Russian Imperial Eagle, French inscription on reverse, dated 1836 (A) **1,100.00**

Plate, 9½" d, multicolored, gilt accents, $75.00.

9⅜" d
Center painted with view of military encampment, gilded borders with Russian Imperial Eagle, trophy and inscribed medallion, French inscription on reverse, dated 1833 (A) **2,200.00**

Center painted with Star of the Order of St. Alexander Nevsky, border with sash and badge of order, waved gilt rim, c1894–1917 (A) **935.00**

Center painted with two soldiers near building, borders with gilded Russian Imperial Eagle and trophies, French inscription on reverse, dated 1836 (A) **2,200.00**

Center with roundel, green, blue, and orange, black ground, surround painted with stylized trees, edge with painted rubies and sapphires, gold ground, c1825–55 (A) **480.00**

9½" d
Center scene of officer, two soldiers in landscape, border of gilded military trophies and dbl headed eagles, French inscription on reverse, c1825–55 (A) **600.00**

Painted mounted officer, gilded border with four Imperial Eagles and trophies, French inscription on reverse, c1825–55 (A) **1,980.00**

Puce portraits of Catherine II and Anna Petrovna, basketweave borders with painted flowers, c1762–96 (A) **440.00**

9⅝" d
Center with stylized gilt flowerhead, iron-red, blue and green strapwork border, four roundels with Imperial Eagle, c1825–55 (A) **470.00**

Center with painted mermaid, Chinese red ground, inner border with seraphim, light yellow ground, outer border with three roundels of classical figures, c1881–94 (A) **1,760.00**

9¾" d, painted center of five horsemen and soldiers in landscape, gilded borders with ribbon tied branches, lilac ground, black Imperial Eagle reserved at top, inscribed on reverse, 1855–81 (A) . .**1,650.00**

Tazza, 15" h, three tiered, gilt painted with band of green sqs, front molded with foliage and burnished gilt, c1825–55 . . . . **125.00**

Vase, 14½" h, applied black grapes and leaves, painted panels of birds, gilt dbl handles, Nicholas I mark **240.00**

INDIAN TREE

English
Mid 1800s to Present

History: Indian Tree is a popular dinnerware pattern that was made by English potters, e. g., Burgess & Leigh, Coalport, John Maddock & Sons, S. Hancock & Sons, and Soho Pottery from the middle of the 1800s until the present. The main theme is an Oriental landscape with a gnarled brown branch of a pink blossomed tree. The remainder of the landscape features exotic flowers and foliage in green, pink, blue, and orange on a white ground.

Bowl
5½" d, "John Maddock and Sons, Ltd" **10.00**

8½ d, 4" h, fluted, Coalport **65.00**

**Demitasse Cups and Saucers, "Coalport,"
set of 6, $30.00.**

10½" d, imp "MINTON"	60.00
11" l, 8½" w, ftd, imp "MINTON" .	45.00
Butter Pat, "John Maddock and Sons, Ltd"	15.00
Cereal Bowl, "Johnson Bros"	10.00
Charger, 13" d, fluted, Coalport	75.00
Compote, 8½" d, brown and luster design, imp "Copeland"	45.00
Cream Soups and Saucers, Coalport, c1900, set of 6	125.00
Creamer	
3" h, "John Maddock and Sons, Ltd	15.00
"Alfred Meakin, England"	5.00
Creamer and Sugar	25.00
Cup and Saucer	
Fluted, Coalport	25.00
Gold key border, octagon, c1890, Coalport	40.00
"Johnson Bros"	10.00
Demitasse Cup and Saucer	
"Copeland-Spode"	20.00
"John Maddock Sons, Ltd," set of 8	25.00
Dish	
6" l, 5" w, fluted, Coalport	20.00
8" l, 6½" w, fluted, Coalport	25.00
9" l, "Wedgwood and Co"	20.00
Egg Cup, 4" h, "John Maddock and Sons, Ltd"	25.00
Gravy Boat	
7" l, "W. A. and Co"	50.00
Cov, "Brownsfield and Sons"	30.00
Hancock	20.00
"Johnson Bros"	10.00
Pitcher, 5½" h, Coalport	35.00
Plate	
3½" d, "Copeland-Spode," pr	20.00
6" d, fluted, Coalport	15.00
6¾" d, "John Maddock and Sons, Ltd"	10.00
7½" d, Lamberton	10.00
8" d	
Cauldon	10.00
"John Maddock and Sons, Ltd	10.00
"Johnson Bros," octagon	10.00
"M. Z. Czechoslovakia"	20.00
"MINTON," imp mark	15.00
9" d	
Ashworth Bros	20.00

"Burgess and Leigh"	15.00
Coalport, fluted	25.00
Hancock	10.00
9¼" d, "Johnson Bros"	10.00
9½" d, "John Maddock and Sons, Ltd"	15.00
9¾" d, "John Maddock and Sons, England"	15.00
10" d	
"Alfred Meakin, England"	5.00
Hancock	15.00
"Johnson Bros"	20.00
10¼" d, fluted, Coalport	30.00
10½" d, Hancock	15.00
Platter	
11" l, "John Maddock and Sons, England"	10.00
11½" l, Hancock	30.00
12½" l, "John Maddock and Sons, Ltd"	15.00
13½" l, Burgess and Leigh, c1895 . .	45.00
15" l, "John Maddock and Sons, Ltd"	20.00
16" l, 12" w, "Myott, Son and Co, England"	55.00
16½" l, "John Maddock and Sons, Ltd"	25.00
19"l, "John Maddock and Sons, Ltd"	85.00

**Plate, 10¼" d, "Copeland-Spode,"
$25.00.**

Sauce Tureen, "MINTON"	40.00
Sauce Tureen and Tray, "MINTON" . .	50.00
Saucer, Hancock	5.00
Soup Bowl	
7" d, fluted, Coalport	15.00
7½" d, "Myott, Staffordshire"	10.00
8" d, "John Maddock and Sons, Ltd"	15.00
10" d, "Johnson Bros"	10.00
Soup Plate, 7½" d, Hancock	15.00
Tea Caddy, 7" h, "Johnson Bros"	65.00
Tea Tile, Coalport	35.00
Teabowl and Saucer, Coalport, c1900, set of 12	165.00
Teapot, Burgess and Leigh	55.00
Tureen, cov, 13½" l, ironstone, gilt finial and handles, England (A)	150.00

Vegetable Bowl
    8½" w, "Johnson Bros" **20.00**
    9" H-H, cov, green, Coalport **150.00**
    10" d, "Johnson Bros" **10.00**

FIRST MARK 1863-90

Second Mark
1891-1926

THIRD MARK
1926-46

IRISH BELLEEK

County Fermanagh, Ireland
1857 to Present

History: Pottery production using native clay deposits began in 1857 in Belleek in County Fermanagh, Ireland. Although David McBurney and Robert Armstrong, the founders, started with earthenwares, they soon produced Belleek parian china, a fine porcelain. William Bromley brought some workers from the Goss factory at Stoke-on-Trent when he moved to Belleek about 1860.

Native marine motifs, such as seashells, corals, marine plants and animals, seahorses, and dolphins were the subjects of early Belleek pieces. The Irish shamrock also was a favorite subject. Many of these motifs continue in production. From its beginning, the factory produced both utilitarian and decorative wares.

Belleek porcelain is extremely thin and light with a creamy ivory surface and iridescent luster. Probably its most distinctive quality is its delicate cream or pastel tone with a pearl like luster. All pieces are hand crafted.

William Henshall's introduction of basketwork and flowers in 1865 gave Belleek porcelains a world wide audience. Each basket is woven out of fine rods of clay, not cast; each leaf and flower is made by hand. These intricate and highly decorative pieces are most sought after by collectors.

Irish Belleek parian china still is hand crafted, just as it was when he made over one hundred years ago. Each piece is made by one craftsman from start to finish; there is no assembly line technique.

References: Richard K. Degenhardt, *Belleek*, Portfolio Press, 1978; Walter Rigdon, *Illustrated Collectors' Handbook*, Willkins Creative Printing, 1978.

Museums: National Museum, Dublin, Ireland; Ulster Museum, Belfast, Ireland.

Collectors' Club: The Belleek Collectors' Society, P.O. Box 675, Pine Brook, N.J. 07058. Membership: $20.00. "The Belleek Collector" is the quarterly newsletter.

Collecting Hints: Belleek pieces are marked with the Belleek backstamp consisting of an Irish Wolfhound, a Harp, a Round Tower, and Sprigs of Shamrock. This first mark was used from 1863 to 1890. The marks were either printed or impressed into the china. Early marks are usually black, but can also be red, blue, green, or brown.

With the second mark, 1891 to 1926, "Co. Fermanagh, Ireland" was added along with a ribbon. The third mark was used from 1926 to 1946; the fourth mark in green from 1946 to 1955; the fifth mark in green from 1955 to 1965; and, the sixth mark in green from 1965 to the present.

Specialty shops and department stores usually carry contemporary Belleek wares. These are good sources for comparing the new examples with the older ones. In the modern pieces, the paste has a creamy white appearance and the high, brilliant glaze has a yellowish color tone. Modern pieces usualy have more color used in the design than their older counterparts. Christmas collector plates were started in 1970.

Basket
    4½" l, four strand, heart shape, "Belleek Co, Fermanagh, Ireland" **165.00**
    5¼" d, four strand, pink applied roses and green leaves, blue trim, 2nd black mark **1,190.00**
    6" d, purse style, pearl finish, 2nd black mark **450.00**
    6" l, applied floral sprays, dbl handled, lst black mark **140.00**
    6½" d, two strand, flat rod, rope edge **1,000.00**
    8" d, three strand, flowers, buds, and branches, c1870, "Belleek Co, Fermanagh" **2,875.00**
    9" d, three strand, "Sydenham" pattern, flower encrusted **1,890.00**
    9½" d, three strand, "Hexagon" pattern, dbl rodded edging **1,250.00**
    12" d, 3 strand, "Sydenham Lily," luster finish **2,150.00**
    "Henshaw" pattern, open handles . .**1,800.00**
    Three strand, shamrock shape, florals at indentations **450.00**
    Three strand, small size, "Shamrock" pattern **450.00**
Biscuit Jar
    8" h
        "Shell" pattern, green trim, 2nd black mark **1,190.00**

Shells and coral, green trim, 2nd
  black mark **1,050.00**
Bowl
  3½" l, 2" w, "Shamrock" pattern, 2nd
    black mark **45.00**
  9" d, lily pad center, molded leaf
    base, 1st black mark **1,925.00**
Box
  Heart shape, cov, green trim, 2nd
    black mark **220.00**
  "Mask" pattern, cov, rectangular, 3rd
    black mark **45.00**
Cake Plate
  9¼" d, four strand, hexagon shape,
    pearl finish **750.00**
  10½" d, three strand basketweave de-
    sign **890.00**
  "Neptune" pattern,
    Green trim, 2nd black mark **135.00**
    Pink trim, 2nd black mark **165.00**
Candlestick, 7" h, "Thorn" pattern, 2nd
  black mark **200.00**
Centerpiece, 12½" h, pinched base
  opening to flared mouth, pink trim,
  2nd black mark **1,850.00**
Chamberstick, 8" h, figural, boy on dol-
  phin, pearl and biscuit, 1st black
  mark **890.00**
Compote
  7½" h, tri-dolphin base, pearl luster,
    pink, green, and lavender trim, 1st
    black mark **1,250.00**
  9½" h, "Prince of Wales" design, tri-
    horse base with open shells, large
    open shell forms bowl, 1st black
    mark **2,250.00**
  10" d, "Greek" pattern, gilded, 2nd
    black mark **750.00**
Condiment Set, 6½" d, open salt, cov
  mustard, pepper and stand, green
  "Harp Shamrock" pattern, 2nd black
  mark **500.00**
Cream Jug, 4½" h, "Mask" pattern,
  looping handle, 1st black mark **290.00**
Creamer
  "Celtic" pattern, red, gilt trim, ftd,
    3rd black mark **190.00**
  "Nautilus" design, 1st black mark . . **275.00**
  Swan shape, white body, 2nd black
    mark **70.00**
Creamer and Sugar
  "Limpet" pattern, gold handles and
    edge, 3rd black mark **150.00**
  "Lotus" pattern, 3rd black mark **85.00**
  "Mask" pattern, 3rd black mark **110.00**
  "Thistle" pattern, gilded, 2nd black
    mark **350.00**
Cup and Saucer
  Farmer size, "Tridacna" pattern,
    green trim, 2nd black mark **95.00**
  "Grasses" pattern, 1st black mark . . **185.00**

"Grasses" pattern, large size, 1st
  black mark **225.00**
"Limpet" pattern, gold handles and
  edge, 3rd black mark **75.00**
"Mask" pattern, 3rd black mark **65.00**
"Shamrock" pattern, harp handle,
  3rd black mark **100.00**
"Thorn" pattern, multicolored, 1st
  black mark **490.00**
"Tridacna" pattern, 2nd black mark **60.00**
Tulip shape cup, saucer and matching
  tea plate, green tinted, gold trim,
  2nd black mark **225.00**
Dejeuner Set
  17" d tray, "Hexagon" pattern, green
    trim, 2nd black mark, 6 pcs **2,400.00**
  "Neptune" pattern, pink trim, 2nd
    black mark, 6 pcs **2,250.00**
  Teapot, creamer, sugar bowl, two
    cups and saucers, and tray, " Nep-
    tune" pattern, pink trim, 1st black
    mark **1,900.00**
Demitasse Cup and Saucer
  "Limpet" pattern, 3rd black mark . . **60.00**
  "Shamrock" pattern, 3rd black mark **70.00**
Demitasse Set, "Limpet" pattern, 3rd
  black mark **550.00**
Dessert Plate, shell shape, white glaze,
  2nd black mark **125.00**
Dessert Set, cake tray, four cups and
  saucers, "Shell" pattern, green mark
  (A) **80.00**
Echinus, 7¾" h, "Tri-Mermaid Globe,"
  pearl finish, 1st black mark **890.00**
Egg Cup, basketweave, pink trim, 1st
  black mark **150.00**
Egg Server, 5½" h, egg cup holder, six
  egg cups, 1st black mark **850.00**
Figure
  2⅞" h, seated pig, 2nd black mark . **375.00**
  5¼" h, Leprechaun sitting on mush-
    rooms, yellow luster trim, 2nd
    black mark **495.00**
  5½" h, "Dolphin Shell" supported by
    two arms, brightly colored, 1st
    black mark **16,500.00**
  5¾" l, 4¾" h, swan, open top, 1st
    black mark **195.00**
  6" l, 4¾" h, swan at rest, 2nd black
    mark **145.00**
  7" h
    "Cherub Cornucopia" mounted on
      back of cherub, round base, 1st
      black mark **1,850.00**
    "Dragon Shell," 1st black mark . .**1,250.00**
  7½" h, whippet, round base, 1st black
    mark **1,650.00**
  8½" h, shell on coral, bright glaze,
    2nd black mark **490.00**
  9½" h, "Imperial" shell, green trim,
    ftd, 2nd black mark **1,650.00**
  11" h, "Bust of Joy," 1st black mark **2,900.00**

11½" h, bust of Lord James Butler, glazed circ socle, c1863–91 (A) .. **740.00**

14" h, "Affection," mounted on round base, 1st black mark **1,800.00**

Greyhound, 3rd black mark **640.00**

Spaniel on pillow, 3rd green mark .. **100.00**

Flasks, 6" h, relief of flowers and Star of David, center panel of gilt initials, reverse with blue printed Belleek factory mark, pr (A) **865.00**

Flower Bowl, 3" h, raised decorations, dbl handled, 2nd black mark **345.00**

Flower Holder

8" d, "Acanthus Leaf" design, 1st black mark **1,450.00**

"Prince of Wales" design, pearl and biscuit finish, c1869 ....**2,500.00**

Flower Pot

3⅝" h, applied roses, leaves and shamrocks, scalloped edge, 3rd black mark **195.00**

11" d, "Rathmore" design, two birds with heavy flower decor, 2nd black mark **1,850.00**

Foot Bath, 22" d, dbl handled, imp bands, 1st black mark **890.00**

Holy Water Fountain

11" l, angel design, 2nd black mark **1,150.00**

Sacred Heart style, 2nd black mark . **70.00**

Honey Pot, 6" h, "Shamrock" pattern, ftd stand, ribbed body with spoon hole in cov, 2nd black mark **535.00**

Jam Jar, 3⅝" h, "Shamrock" pattern, barrel shape, 3rd black mark **75.00**

Jam Pot, ribbon design, 1st black mark **265.00**

Jardiniere

9" l, applied roses, daisies and chrysanthemums, coral handles, 2nd black mark **1,100.00**

10½" h, applied flowers, ftd, 2nd black mark **1,750.00**

11" h, "Rathmore" pattern, 2nd black mark **1,250.00**

Jug

6" h, "Lily" patern, pink trim, 2nd black mark **365.00**

7" l, "Snail" pattern, 1st black mark **575.00**

Harp handled, pearl finish, 1st black mark **475.00**

Large swan figural, 2nd black mark . **190.00**

Mirror Frame, 6½" h, raised flowers, 1st black mark **1,800.00**

Nightlight, 8" h, lighthouse shape, 1st black mark **700.00**

Paperweight, recumbent whippet, 1st black mark **1,450.00**

Pitcher

3½" d, 5½" h, harp handled, 1st black mark **250.00**

6¼" h

"Shamrock" design on basketweave, 6th green mark (A) **40.00**

Shell texture, coral handle, 6th green mark (A) **45.00**

Pitcher and Bowl

Earthenware, brown floral design, 1st black mark **575.00**

"Thistle" pattern, 1st black mark ... **975.00**

Planter, 8½" l, series of shells in rect form, pink coloration, 1st black mark **350.00**

Plate

5¾" d, "Celtic" pattern, 3rd black mark **75.00**

6½" d, "Limpet" pattern, gold edge, 3rd black mark **40.00**

8" d, "Shamrock" pattern, 2nd black mark **40.00**

9½" d, "Greek" pattern, blue and gilt trim, 2nd black mark **350.00**

"Grasses" pattern, 1st black mark .. **185.00**

Root Center, 2¾" h, brown and green branch, large open water lily in pink, luster finish, 2nd black mark **325.00**

Salt Dip

"Limpet" design, coral legs, 2nd black mark **95.00**

"Limpet" pattern, coral legs, 2nd black mark **95.00**

Salt Stand, 4" h, figure of seahorse, turquoise, shell trimmed in pink and gold, 1st black mark **550.00**

Soup Bowl, 10¼" d, earthenware, green, orange, and brown floral border, 1st black mark, imp harp and crown mark **75.00**

Spill Vase, small size, "Lily" pattern, 2nd black mark **125.00**

Spirit Flask, 11¾" h, earthenware, panel edged with scrolls, inscribed "Rum" reserved on pink ground, black edged hoops, barrel shape, c1863–91 (A) . **740.00**

Spoon Rest, 4" l, boat shape, 1st black mark **275.00**

Table Center, 12½" h, trumpet shape, pink trim, 2nd black mark **1,750.00**

Tazza, 5½" h, tri-dolphin shell style, turquoise dolphins, pearl finish on shell and base, 1st black mark **1,650.00**

Tea Set

Teapot, creamer, sugar bowl, two cups and saucers and tray, "Hexagon" pattern, green trim, 2nd black mark **1,650.00**

Teapot, creamer, sugar bowl, two cups and saucers, cone design, green trim, 2nd black mark **695.00**

Teapot, creamer, sugar bowl, two cups and saucers, "Low Lily" pattern, green trim, 2nd black mark . **975.00**

Teapot, creamer, sugar bowl, two cups and saucers and tray, pearl "Tridacna" pattern, 2nd black mark **1,450.00**

Teapot, creamer, sugar bowl, two

cups and saucers and tray, pink "Tridacna" pattern, 1st black mark **1,550.00**

Tea Urn, 9½" l, 6½" h, "Dragon" design on four paw feet, brown and purple luster with gilding, 1st black mark ..**3,800.00**

Teacup, saucer, and teaplate, "Tridacna" pattern, pink trim, 2nd black mark **125.00**

Teapot
    4½" h, "Grasses" pattern, 1st black mark **435.00**
    4⅞" d, 4" h, "Erne" design, 2nd black mark **225.00**
    5" h, "Neptune" pattern, pink trim, 1st black mark **295.00**
    6" d, 5½" h, green shamrocks, basketweave ground, brown handle, 2nd black mark **225.00**
    "Blarney" pattern, 2nd black mark . **450.00**
    "Neptune" pattern, 2nd black mark **425.00**
    "Shamrock" pattern, green trim, 2nd black mark **195.00**
    "Shell" patten, bright colors, 1st black mark **1,250.00**
    "Tridacna" pattern, green trim, 2nd black mark **175.00**

Tray
    11" l, "Limpet" design, 2nd green mark **60.00**
    14" w, "Hawthorne Spider" pattern, silver and pearl, 1st black mark ..**1,050.00**
    14½" sq, "Thorn" pattern, dark orange webbing, imp 1st mark and regular mark **1,250.00**
    15" d, hexagon shape, green trim, 2nd black mark **950.00**
    17¼" d, "Harp Shamrock" pattern, 2nd black mark **980.00**

Tulip Vase, 9" h, purple luster, 1st black mark **1,100.00**

Vase
    4" h, "Cleary" pattern, 1st black mark **290.00**
    4¼" h, "Frog" design, 2nd black mark **1,190.00**
    5" h
        Ten joined balls, orange trim, 1st black mark **1,550.00**
        Seahorse trumpet shape, dark brown horse, 1st black mark .. **590.00**
    5½" h, frog design, 1st black mark . **575.00**
    5¾" h, applied pink flowers and blue forget-me-nots, green and pink leaves, chips, 3rd black mark **195.00**
    6" h, applied spray of roses and foliage, 3rd black mark **135.00**
    6½" h, ear of corn shape, 1st black mark **195.00**
    7" h
        "Amphora" pattern, classic design with gilding, 1st black mark ... **750.00**

"Honeysuckle" pattern, mounted on base, pink int., 1st black mark **950.00**
7½" h, "Fish" design, 1st black mark **625.00**
8" h, tan "Lily" design with gilding, 2nd black mark **975.00**
9" h
    Figural of girl with basket, 1st black mark **950.00**
    "Princess" design, 3rd black mark **950.00**

Vase, 9¼" h, "Princess," 2nd black mark, $425.00.

9½" h
    "Aberdeen" design, applied and lustered rose buds, daisies, carnations, and leaves, 2nd black mark **525.00**
    "Princess" design, open dbl handles, 1st black mark **1,650.00**
11" h, "Marine Center" design, 1st black mark **2,000.00**
11½" h, upright cornucopia form, green and gilt trim, 2nd black mark **1,250.00**
12" h, dbl handled, trumpet shape neck, painted pink and gilt trim, 2nd black mark **1,250.00**
13" h
    "Hoof" tripod, 1st black mark ... **695.00**
    "Nile" pattern, 2nd black mark .. **550.00**
16" h, "Triple Fish," multicolor, 1st black mark **2,450.00**
"Horse Trumpet" shape, pearl finish, rect base, 2nd black mark **390.00**
Miniature, tan "Celtic" design with gilding, 1st black mark **225.00**

Wall Pocket
    9" h, "Swan" design with gilding, 1st black mark **1,450.00**
    9" l, dbl swan design with gilding, 1st black mark **1,650.00**

Water Kettle, "Grasses" pattern, 1st black mark **950.00**

ROYAL   PREMIUM
SEMI PORCELAIN
T. & R. BOOTE.
ENGLAND.

WEDGWOOD & CO
ENGLAND

IRONSTONE, WHITE & PATTERNED

Staffordshire, England
Early 1840s to c1891

History: White ironstone in Gothic shapes was first produced from Staffordshire in the early 1840s. Gothic shapes already had been used by Staffordshire potters for cobalt and mulberry transfer wares. Roses, lilies, and human profiles comprised the finials or the trim under the handles.

The firm of James Edwards of Burslem made a tremendous variety of designs in white ironstone. T.J. & J. Mayer designed "Prize Puritan" and "Prize Bloom." "Adam's Scallop," "Line Trim," and "Scalloped Decagons" by J. Wedgwood and Davenport all used scallops in the pottery design. "Fluted Pearl" by J. Wedgwood and "Fig" by J. Wedgwood and Davenport are among the most collectible patterns.

William Adams, John Alcock, E. Challinor & Co., Davenport, C. Meigh & Son, and J. Wedgwood were some of the firms making white ironstone in the 1840s and 50s. Thomas and Richard Boote's "Octagon Shape" in 1851 was the forerunner of the famous "Sydenham Shape" from 1853. Many potters proceeded to copy these popular shapes.

"President" by James Edwards and "Columbia," made by six different companies, were registered in 1855. The potters of "Columbia" used the same borders on the plates and platters, but used varied finials and foliage decorations. "Dallas," "Mississippi," and "Baltic Shapes" also were registered in that year. Numerous other shapes appeared from the Staffordshire Potteries during the 1850s.

Collecting Hints: Many white ironstone patterns used corn, oats, and wheat in the design such as "Corn and Oats" manufactured by J. Wedgwood and Davenport from 1863, "Wheat & Black-

berry" by J. & G. Meakin from 1865, "Prairie Shape" from 1862, and "Ceres" by Elsmore and Forster from 1859.

During the 1860s gardens and woods inspired the designers of white ironstone. Patterns such as "Sharon Arch," "Hanging Arch," "Winding Vine," and "White Oak and Acorn" are just a few that developed. Flowers also influenced the Staffordshire potters during the 60s in such patterns as "Morning Glory" by Elsmore & Forster, "Moss Rose" by J. & G. Meakin, "Bordered Fuchsia" by A. Shaw, and "The Hyacinth" by J. Wedgwood.

Ribbed patterns also were popular as in Meakin's "Ribbed Raspberry with Bloom" and Pankhurst's "Ribbed Chain" during the 1860s. A classical revival was seen in "Athens Shape" by Podmore Walker & Co. and "Athenia" by J.T. Close.

Rectangular shapes became popular during the 1870s and 1880s. After 1891 ironstone diminished as the demand for porcelains increased.

References: Jean Wetherbee, *A Look at White Ironstone*, Wallace-Homestead, 1980; Jean Wetherbee, *A Second Look at White Ironstone*, Wallace-Homestead, 1984.

PATTERNED

Basin, 12" d, brown transfer of Japanese
  design on int. (A) **65.00**
Bowl
  10" sq, "Japan" pattern in under-
    glazed blue, iron-red and gilt,
    fenced garden scene, c1815, blue
    crown and "Ironstone Warrented
    #3" mark (A) **440.00**
  11" d
    Black leaf pattern, white ground,
      twelve sided, unmarked **195.00**
    "Botanic Garden" pattern, poly-
      chrome, England (A) **75.00**
    "Excelsior" pattern, floral center,
      blue-green border, "G. Wollis-
      croft" and reg mark **45.00**
  12" d, blue feather edge, unmarked
    (A) **45.00**
Chamberpot, 8" d, "Grecian Border"
  pattern, unmarked (A) **60.00**
Coffee Set, 8¾" h pot, 6½" h creamer,
  7" h sugar, pink moss roses, gold trim,
  c1872, "Vodrey and Bros, Dublin" . **175.00**
Compote, 10½" d, 5⅞" h, brown trans-
  fer of squirrel in tree, enamels, un-
  marked (A) **40.00**
Cup and Saucer, blue leaves, red and
  green enameled berries, "Tunstall,
  England" (A) **20.00**
Cup Plate, 4⅛" d, "Madlle Jenny Lind,"
  purple transfer, blue edge stripes, sgd
  "J. T. Close" (A) **85.00**

Dinner Service,
Multicolored Oriental fenced garden,
set of 72 pcs (A) **5,150.00**
Thirty dinner plates, twelve luncheon
plates, ten soup plates, three platters, oblong vegetable dish and
three cov vegetable dishes, centers
with Oriental style vase, branches
and two birds, borders of alternating chrysanthemums and lotus
flowers with sunflowers between,
English (A) **4,500.00**
Dish, 10" l, Oriental garden, flower
sprays, blue, iron-red, and salmon
with gilding, yellow rims, molded
blue rose sprig handles, shell shape,
c1820, pr **115.00**
Jug, 9" h, black transfer, domestic animals and birds flanked by two
clowns, "J M and 1859" on front, Elsmore and Forster (A) **610.00**
Pitcher
5¾" h, figural "Portia," multicolored,
"Burleigh Ironstone, Staffordshire,
England" **55.00**
7½" h, molded and lustered leafy
branch design, floral bouquets,
"Livesley, Powell and Co" (A) ... **50.00**
12" h, blue and white florals, gold
accents, England **200.00**
Plate
7" d, "Zamara" pattern, pink, multicolored, "F M and Co" **25.00**
7¾" d, "Persian Rose" pattern, dark
pink transfer, "Baker and Co" **10.00**
8"d
"Cleopatra" pattern, purple, multicolored, "F M and Co" **20.00**
Florals, blue and rust, c1870, "Ashworth" **165.00**
"L'aviation Droleries," black transfer, center of comic scenes depicting history of aviation, blue
rims, "France," set of 4 .... **140.00**
8⅛" d, Japanese transfer design, multicolored, Moorew and Co, set of
12 (A) **160.00**

8¼" d, printed and painted flowering
tree, birch and Orinetal figures at
table, "IMPROVED IRONSTONE
CHINA," set of 7 (A) **295.00**
8⅜" d, "Syndenham" pattern, dark
blue transfer, "Clementson and
Son-Ironstone" **30.00**
8½" d
Cobalt ground, multicolored
enamel accents, unmarked **35.00**
Strawberry, blue and gold trim,
c1850, unmarked **125.00**
8¾" d
Blue transfer of eagle, shield and "E
Pluribus Unum" banner, blue
stick spatter border, "R Hammer-
sley" (A) **35.00**
"Canella" pattern, brown, multicolored, "E Challinor" **30.00**
9¼" d
"Grecian Vases" pattern, floral reserve centers, brown drapery
rims, England, set of 15 (A) **225.00**
"Lozere" pattern, blue transfer,
castles on border, scalloped
edge, "Challinor-Ironstone" ... **25.00**
9½" d
"California" pattern, blue, multicolored, "F M and Co" **30.00**
"Etruscan" pattern, lavender, mulitcolored, "Woolscroft" **45.00**
9¾" d, Oriental style flowering plants,
iron-red, blue, green, and gilt,
band of iron-red trellis borders,
c1840, England, set of 18 (A) **2,100.00**
10" d
"Aurora" pattern, black, multicolored, "W C" **30.00**
Blue and white Art Nouveau designs, "Trent, Semi-Porcelain,
England," set of 6 (A) **110.00**
"Lily pattern, sepia, multicolor,"
"W C" **20.00**
Multicolored bird in tree, "Opaque
Granite China" (A) **10.00**
10¼" d, enameled multicolored floral
designs, set of 6 (A) **75.00**

Left, tureen, 8¾" l, 6" h, "Japanica" pattern, rust, blue, and gold, c1840, $150.00; center, pitcher, 7½" h, hp English wild flowers, copper luster oak leaves, $155.00; right, sauce tureen, 8" l, 7" h, Oriental florals, green, yellow, and orange, gilt trim, c1800s, "Ironstone China," $325.00.

10¾" d, woman and child with bunch of grapes, blue and white, three urns of flowers on border, c1850, "Clementson" **75.00**

10⅞" d, blue feather edge (A) **15.00**

Platter

10½", leaves and berries, white ground, "Edward Bros" **110.00**

12¼" l, blue feather edge, octagonal, unmarked (A) **35.00**

13½" l, "Japan" pattern, underglazed blue, iron-red and gilt, Oriental flowers, panels of birds, c1815 (A) **660.00**

14¼" l, blue feather edge, octagonal, imp "Best Goods" (A) **35.00**

14½" l, blue feather edge, octagonal, unmarked (A) **75.00**

15¼" l, "Japan" pattern, underglaze colors of Oriental flowers and fruits, octagonal, c1825, blue crown and "Ironstone Warrented #3" mark (A) **440.00**

16¾" l, 13" w, orange and pink flowers, "Adams, Tunstall" **100.00**

17" l, black transfer of Oriental scene, red and green enamels, "Ashworth Bros Hanley" (A) **55.00**

17⅜" l, black transfer of flowering trees and birds, polychrome enamels, imp "Ashworth" (A) **65.00**

Potpourri Vase, 8¼" h, matching lid and pierced cov, painted trailing chrysanthemum and sprays, apple-green ground, yellow and gilt dbl handles and finials, c1830 (A) **145.00**

Punch Bowl

10½" d, brown transfer of morning glories, blue, red, and green, blue sponged rim and gilt (A) **55.00**

14½" d, black transfer of cherubs and flowering vines, polychrome enamels, ftd, unmarked (A) **175.00**

Punch Set, 11⅞" d, 6½"h bowl, twelve cups, polychrome "Farmers Arms" transfers, "B and L, England" (A) ... **150.00**

Puzzle Jug, 8½" h, multicolored florals, gray trim, "Elsmore and Foster" **135.00**

Shaker, 4¼" h, figural leprechaun, pastel enamels and gilt, unmarked (A) . **10.00**

Soup Bowl, 10½" d, "Wreath" pattern, twelve panels, ftd, c1845, "Thos Furnival-Real Ironstone" **50.00**

Stand, 14⅝" d, center with crest motto, multicolored florals, gilt scrolls on dark blue border, "Morley and Ashworth" (A) **40.00**

Tea Kettle, 3½" h, printed and colored panels of Oriental flowers, green ground (A) **40.00**

Teabowl and Saucer, "Etruscan" pattern, lavender, multicolored, "Woolscroft" **50.00**

Toothbrush Holder, blue flowers, white ground, unmarked **15.00**

Tray, 11" l, 8½" w, Oriental scene, polychrome **275.00**

Tureen, 11" d, 9¼", cov, red transfer of florals and bamboo, reserves of rope bridge, huts and river scenes, "Turner and Son" (A) **85.00**

Vase, 9⅜" h, blue ground, gilt bouquets, satyr's mask handles, gilt front and rim, c1835 (A) **120.00**

WHITE

Bone Dish, pleated rims, set of 6 ..... **35.00**

Bowl

8¼" sq, "Spring," "W. H. Grindley" **25.00**

9½" d, 6" h, cov, "Lily of the Valley," unmarked **195.00**

10" d, "Alfred Meakin" **20.00**

Butter Dish, cov, 6¾" d, "Trent Shape," "Imperial Ironstone China, John Alcock," drain **60.00**

Butter Pats, emb scrolled rims, set of 6 **35.00**

Cake Plate

9½" d, "Lily Pod," ftd, c1860, "J W Pankhurst and Co" **200.00**

10½" d, 4¼" h, "Grenade Shape," three clusters of three berries and leaves, pedestal base, imp "T and R Boote" **65.00**

10½" l, 8½" h, dbl handled, basketweave, "Opaque Stone China, Anthony Shaw and Son, England" mark **35.00**

12" l, 8⅞" h, "Cable and Ring," reticulated handles, "Anthony Shaw and Son, England" **10.00**

Chamber Pot

8" d, "Gothic," "C Meigh and Son" mark, cov **90.00**

Ribbon knob, cov, Meakin **30.00**

"Thistle," "Anthony Shaw" mark ... **40.00**

"Wheat," emb, cov, Adams **45.00**

Coffee Service, 11" h pot, 6½" h creamer, 7¾" h, sugar, six 8¹¹⁄₁₆" d plates, six handleless cups and saucers, "Ceres Shape," copper luster trim, "Elsmore and Forster" **595.00**

Compote, 10⅝" d, 7⅞" h, scalloped rim and base, "T and R Boots and Co" (A) **80.00**

Creamer

4⅛" h, child's size, "Prairie Shape," imp "Clementson" **45.00**

4½" h, "Gothic," unmarked **35.00**

5¼" h, "Fuchsia," unmarked **30.00**

5½" h, "Wheat and Clover," 12-sided, black "Ford, Challinor and Co" **90.00**

6" h, rect, basketweave, "Opaque

Stone China, Anthony Stone and
Son, England" **30.00**
7" h, "Grenade Shape" flower, bud at
throat, imp "T and R Boote" **55.00**
Cuspidor, 5½" d, relief masked spout
and handle, unmarked **35.00**
Dessert Set, 4¹¹⁄₁₆"d, child's size, cup,
saucer, and plate, "Lily Shape," imp
"Burgess, Burslem, Lily Shape" **60.00**
Dish
4¼" d, "Wheat," "J and G Meakin" **15.00**
9¼" l, 5⅜" w, "Hill Shape," imp
"J Clementson, Hanley" **15.00**
11" l, 9" w, cov, ftd, ribbed with fruit
and foliage finial on dome lid,
"Pankhurst Stone China" (A) **30.00**
Food Mold
6⅛" l, 4⅝" w, "Cauliflower," imp
"John Alcock" **50.00**
6⅝" l, 5⅞" w, "Rose," unmarked ... **50.00**
7⅛" l, 5½" w, "Poinsetta," unmarked **50.00**
7⅛" l, 6" w, "Fish," unmarked **40.00**
7¾" l, 5⅞" w, "Leaf," "G Jones and
Sons" **60.00**
Gravy Boat
5" h, "Ceres Shape," unmarked **50.00**
Relief of elephant head and trunk on
spout, "Henry Alcock and Co" .. **35.00**
Ladle, 12½" l, unmarked (A) **35.00**
Milk Pitcher, 8¼" h, "Gothic Shape,"
copper luster band at front and lip,
"Livesley, Powell and Co" **60.00**
Pitcher
8½"h, "Corn and Oats," "J Wedgwood" **70.00**
9¾" h, "Full Ribbed," "J W Pankhurst, Hanley" **80.00**
Plate
6½" d, "Gothic Shape," 12-sided,
"Imperial Ironstone China, H.John
Alcock" **10.00**
8½" d, "Columbia Shape," "Jas Edwards and Sons" **25.00**
9" d, octagonal, unmarked **30.00**
9½" d
"Acorn," 10-sided, imp "J Wedgwood" **30.00**

"Sydenham Shape," imp "T and R
Boote" **15.00**
9¾" d, "Wheat," imp "Ironstone
China, J and G Meakin" **20.00**
9⅞" d
"Baltic Shape," imp "G Wollis-
croft" mark **20.00**
Copper luster scalloped rim, "Elsmore and Forster," unknown pattern **20.00**
10" d
"Bordered Hyacinth," imp "W B
and Co" **20.00**
Octagon, unmarked **30.00**
"Prairie Flowers," "Ironstone
China, Powell and Bishop" **20.00**
11¾" l, 10¼" w, "Give Us This Day
Our Daily Bread," unmarked **40.00**
Platter
13½" l, 10⅝" w, "Prairie Shape," imp
"Prairie Shape, J Clementson, Han-
ley" **20.00**
14" l, "Spring," "W H Grindley" ... **30.00**
14½" l, 10¼" w, "Lily of the Valley,"
"Alfred Meakin" **40.00**
16½" l, 11½" w
"Alfred Meakin" **165.00**
Oval, "T and R Booth" **15.00**
20⅜" l, 15⅜" w, "Wheat," imp "J and
G Meakin" **50.00**
Punch Bowl, 8¾" d, 5⅞", "Sydenham
Shape," unmarked **60.00**
Relish Dish, 9¼" l, "Cameo," c1848, "J
Wedgwood" **45.00**
Sauce Dish
5⅜" d, round, imp "T and R Boote" **15.00**
6" d, cov, undertray, 6⅞" l, ladle, "Sy-
denham Shape," unmarked **115.00**
6" l, 9" l, 5⅞" w undertray, ladle, cov,
"Baltic Shape," imp "T Hulme" .. **120.00**
6⅛" l, cov, "Wheat," "Turner, God-
dard and Co" **80.00**
6⅜" l, undertray, ladle, "Columbia
Shape," pod finial, emb pod and
leaf design, imp "W Challinor and
Co" **135.00**
Cov, undertray, ladle, "Ribbed

**Left, vegetable tureen, "Fuschia" pattern, 13" H-H, 8½" w, 5" h, "Meakin Bros. & Co.,"
$75.00; center, jug, 5½" h, "Alfred Meakin," $20.00; right, tureen, 14" l, 9" w, 10½" h,
"John Maddock & Son - Royal Semi Porcelain" marks, $115.00.**

Chain," "J W Pankhurst, Stone
China, Hanley" 120.00
Sauce Tureen, 7½" h, cov, undertray
and ladle, "Octagon Shape," un-
marked 95.00
Shaving Mug
  3¼" h, basketweave, "Opaque Stone
  China, Anthony Shaw and Son,
  England" 25.00
  3⅞" d, "Potomac Shape," unmarked 70.00
Soup Bowl, 9¾" d, "Lily of the Valley,"
"James Edwards and Sons" 30.00
Sugar, 6½" h, "Corn and Oats," "J
Wedgwood" 55.00
7" h
  "Hyacinth," unmarked 35.00
  "St. Louis Shape," imp "J Edwards,
  Fenton, St. Louis Shape" 55.00
7½" h
  "Ceres Shape," imp "Elsmore and
  Forster, Tunstall" mark 125.00
  "Wheat and Clover," cov, black
  "Turner and Tomkinson" 55.00
  "Corn," cov, "J Wedgwood" 50.00

Tea Set, 9½" h teapot, 5¼" h creamer,
7½" h, sugar, "Dbl Sydenham," copper luster trim, "Livesley, Powell and
Co" 200.00
Teabowl, "Trent Shape," unmarked ... 15.00
Teabowl and Saucer, "Huron Shape,"
imp "Huron Shape, Adams" 25.00
Teapot
  8½" h, "Cable and Ring," "J and G
  Meakin" 60.00
  8⅞" h, "Forget-Me-Not," "Wood,
  Rathbone and Co, Cobridge, Staf-
  fordshire" 80.00
9" h
  "Gothic," "T J and J Mayer's Im-
  proved Ironstone China" 140.00
  "St Louis Shape," imp "J Edwards,
  Fenton, St Louis Shape" 100.00
9¼" h
  "Lily of the Valley," "Stone China,
  Anthony Shaw, Burslem" 110.00
  "Niagra Shape," imp "Paris White,
  Ironstone China, Walley" mark 110.00
  9⅜" h, octagonal, unmarked 75.00
9½" h
  "Hyacinth," imp "J Wedgwood and
  Co, Stone Granite" 85.00
  "Lily of the Valley," imp "Edwards
  and Son, Dalehall" 75.00
  "Wheat and Clover," black "Turner
  and Tomkinson" 100.00
Toddy Cup
  2⅝" d, 3¾" h, "Sydenham Shape,"
  unmarked 25.00
  2¾" d, 3½" h, unmarked 10.00
  2¾" d, 3⅝" h, scrolled border, unmarked 25.00

2¾" d, 4⅛" h, "Little Palm," unmarked 15.00
3⅛" d, 3⅜" h, "Trumpet Vine," unmarked 20.00
Toothbrush Holder
  5" h, basketweave, "Opaque Stone
  China, Anthony Shaw and Son,
  England" 30.00
  5½" h, matching underplate, 4⅞" d,
  "Wheat and Clover," black "Turner
  and Tomkinson" 60.00
  5¾" h, "Ironstone China, Thomas
  Hughes," no pattern 30.00
Tureen, cov, dbl handled, pedestal foot,
floral finial, "J Wedgwood" 75.00
Vegetable Dish
  6⅜" d, cov, "Gothic Cameo," octagonal, copper luster trim, "E Walley" 75.00
  6½" h, cov, "Fuchsia," "J and G
  Meakin" 45.00
  7" h, cov, "Atlantic Shape," artichoke
  finial, "T and R Boote" 85.00
  8¾" l, 6⅛" h, cov, "Star Flower,"
  "Stone China, J W Pankhurst, Hanley" 75.00
  9⅝" l, "Wheat and Blackberry,"
  "Ironstone China, J and G Meakin" 80.00
  10⅛" l, "Berlin Swirl," apple finial,
  "Berlin Ironstone, Mayer and El-
  liot" 115.00
  12⅛" l, "Fig," "J Wedgwood" 90.00
Vegetable Tureen, 11½" l, 7½", "Alfred
Meakin" 165.00
Wash Pitcher, 12½" h, "Ceres Shape,"
imp "Elsmore and Forster" 115.00
Water Pitcher, 11" h, "Sharon Arch,"
imp "Ironstone China, J Wedgwood" 110.00

ITALY-GENERAL

VENICE
1727–1812

    Hard paste porcelain was made by Francesco
and Guiseppe Vezzi in Venice with pieces
brought from Meissen between 1720 and 1727.
The products resembled the early Meissen and
Vienna wares. Teawares were the most popular
form. The oldest pieces have black and gold
coloring. Later Venetian red was used. Porcelains
were marked with various forms of the word
Venice: VENEZIA, VEN, or Va in either gold,
underglaze blue, or red.
    After the Vezzi factory closed, a new factory
was established by Friedrich Hewelke in 1758.
His china was marked with the letter "V." The
factory failed in 1763 during the Seven Years
War.
    A more successful factory to manufacture hard
paste porcelain was established by Geminiano

Cozzi from 1764 until 1812. Both utilitarian and ornamental wares were made and exported throughout Europe. Cozzi's wares featured pouring spouts on coffeepots molded with leaf decorations. Figures from the Italian Comedy were made along with colored and white tea sets, services, and vases. Pieces were marked with an anchor in red, blue, or gold.

LE NOVE
1750–Late 19th Century

Pasquale Antonibon established a porcelain factory in Le Nove in 1750. He took Francisco Parolini as a partner in 1781. The painter Giovanni Marconi was the factory's most prolific decorator. He signed several Meissen–type examples of harbor scenes and rural romances. The factory was leased to Baroni in 1802, reverted to the Antonibon family in 1825, and continued to produce until the late 19th century. Its principal production was tablewares. Special pieces included fish shaped tureens. The Sevres influence was strong. The mark used was a comet or a star in red, blue, or gold.

NAPLES
1771–1807

King Ferdinand IV, son of Charles IV, established the Royal Naples Factory in Naples in 1771 to manufacture porcelain and fill the gap left by the transfer of Capodimonte to Buen Retiro in Spain in 1759. Neo-classical wares were made along with the rococo styles formerly used by the Capodimonte workers. Domenico Venuti became director from 1779 until 1807. Filipo Tagliolini modeled figures of people from Naples in the fashions of the day. The factory was taken over by the French in 1807 and then closed in 1834.

The marks used were "FRF" under a crown until 1787 and then a crowned "N" impressed or painted in underglaze blue.

VINOVO
1776–1840

Gian Brodel from Turin and Marchese Birago of Vische, assisted by Peter Hannong, established a hard paste porcelain factory in Vinovo in 1776. It went bankrupt after a few years. Dr. Victor Gioanotti and Tamietti, a modeler, reopened the factory in 1780. They made mythological figures in colored and white porcelain, services with rococo decorations, vases with rural landscapes, groups and statuettes in the Capodimonte style, and busts of famous people in biscuit ware. The

factory remained in operation until 1815 when Gioanotti died.

Giovanni Lamello, after working there as a sculptor from 1798, bought the factory in 1815. The factory marks imitated those of Sevres and the Meissen swords. The marks were either impressed or painted in underglaze blue or in red, gray, or black on the glaze.

MAJOLICA OR FAIENCE
1400–Present

The earliest majolica was produced by potteries located near Florence at Orvieto, Faenza, Siena, and Arezzo and used manganese purple and copper green decoration on pieces made for everyday use. These wares were inspired by earlier Spanish examples. Early in the 15th century, a cobalt blue was introduced from the Middle East. About 1450 new colors of yellow, turquoise, and orange appeared.

The rise of Faenza coincided with the brilliant colors used in the istoriato or pictorial style of Urbino. The entire surface of the piece was covered with historical, classical, mythological, or biblical scenes. Subjects included heraldic lions, birds, portraits, and foliage designs. Large drug jars with strap handles were made. Grotesques and arabesques were introduced in the 16th century. Faenza wares were at their finest from about 1480 until 1520.

Pictorials in the istoriato style were done at Castel Durante and Urbino. Venetian majolica exhibited an Oriental influence due to trade with the East. Large globular jars were a favorite shape.

Savona in Liguria made majolica in the 17th and 18th centuries. A wide variety of wares were made including teawares and figures. Castelli, near Naples, made majolica in the 17th and 18th centuries, reviving the Istooriato style.

During the 17th and 18th centuries, many factories produced majolica wares. Eventually they turned to the production of lead glazed earthenwares in the English style. Manufacturing of tin enamel wares still continues in Italy. Some of the production is directed toward making souvenirs for tourists.

"Maiolica," the Italian spelling, is frequently seen in references to these Italian wares.

CANTAGALLI
1878–1901

Cantagalli, an Italian potter, opened his faience factory in Florence in 1878 and used the crowing cock as its mark. The firm traded as Figli di Giuseppe Cantagalli. This factory manufactured imitations of early Italian majolica, similar to pieces from Urbino, Faenza, Gubbio, Deruta, and at the Della Robbia workshop. The factory also imitated tin glazed earthenwares in the Isnik and Persian styles. Art Nouveau style is found in vases decorated with elongated plant motifs. Vases and dishes designed by William De Morgan were manufactured. Among its original products were decorative tablewares.

References: A. Lane, *Italian Porcelain*, Faber & Faber, 1954; B. Rackham, *Italian Maiolica*, Faber & Faber, 2nd Edition, 1963; John Scott-Taggart, *Italian Majolica*, Hamlyn Publishing Group, Ltd., 1972.

Museums: Bargello Museum, Florence, Italy; Birmingham Museum of Art, Birmingham, Alabama; British Museum, London, England; Gardiner Museum of Ceramic Art, Toronto, Canada; Musee National de Ceramique, Sevres, France; Museo Civico, Turin, Italy; National Museum of Wales, Cardiff, Wales; Seattle Art Museum, Seattle, WA; Victoria & Albert Museum, London, England; Wadsworth Atheneum, Hartford, CT.

Additional Listings: Capodimonte, Deruta, Ginori.

Urn, cov, 37″ h, faience, multicolored, (A) $200.00.

Barber Bowl, 13″ l, pale blue Cupid in center, white ground, "Savona" mark **2,500.00**
Basin, 15″ d, center painted with scene of St. Luke writing Gospel, multicolored kneeling angel, grotesques sides, masks and pendants ext., c1750–80, Urbino, repaired base (A) **3,700.00**
Basket, 7⅞″ d, majolica, polychrome flowering plants and rocks, sides pierced with trellis, blue and red trim (A) **200.00**
Beaker and Saucer, majolica, painted river god and Bacchanalian figures holding grapes, c1530, Castelli (A) . **650.00**

Bonbon Dish, 14″ h, pottery, shell form supported by blackamoors, pr (A) .. **50.00**
Bottle, 20″ h, majolica, painted figures in landscape, township on reverse, grotesque masks applied on sides, 20th C (A) **130.00**
Bowl, 12½″ d, majolica, battle between Darius and Alexander, multicolored, four putti and scrolling foliage borders, painted by Carlo Grue, c1715, Castelli (A) **2,850.00**
Box, 4″ d, 2¾″ h, cov, white terra cotta, modeled Art Nouveau style, woman's head on cov, relief poppies and scrolls on body, "Impruinita Terra Cotta" mark **45.00**
Charger, 19¾″ d, mythological center scene, surrounded by cherubs, armor and musical instruments in yellow, blue, green, and brown, unmarked (A) **145.00**
Coffeepot
  10″ h, shepherds in landscape, multicolored, pear shape, foliage molded spout, strap handle, c1780, Naples Ferdinand IV, repaired (A) . **880.00**
  11⅞″ h, painted bird on flowering branch, vases and flying birds, fluted baluster form, domed cov, scroll handle, c1750, Faenze (A) . **715.00**
Cup and Saucer, sepia painted cherubs and animals, ochre ground rect panel, band of gilt foliage, c1785, Le Nove **100.00**
Custard Cup, Cov
  Painted flowers, late 18th C, red "anchor" mark, Cozzi (A) **475.00**
  Vertical lines in iron-red, blue, and gold, peach finials, c1770, red "anchor" mark, Cozzi, set of 6 (A) ..**1,660.00**
Dish
  5⅞″ d, majolica, Istoriato, painted Cupids in landscape, bows, arrows and shield, c1575, Venice, pr (A) **1,170.00**
  8¼″ d, Istoriato, scene of two putti and Venus, ochre, yellow, blue, green, and black, fluted rim, cobalt gadroons on reverse, ftd, 16th C, Urbino (A) **400.00**
  9″ d, faience, blue, green, and ochre bird under palm tree, foliage border, c1775 (A) **100.00**
  9¾″ d, sgraffiato design of fleurs-de-lis, shaped panel, scrolling foliage, green-brown glazes, c1600, Bologna, repaired (A) **145.00**
  9⅞″ d
    Incised seated dog, coat of arms and poplar trees, yellow and green, zig-zag border, c1500, Bologna **2,000.00**
    Sgraffiato bust of woman in center,

zig-zag border, foliage between, brown, ochre, and green, 16th C **800.00**

10" d, ochre, blue and green painted fruit and flowers, light blue ground, reverse with band of leaves, c1550, Venice **1,050.00**

10⅜" d, majolica, painted battle between Hercules and Centaurs in landscape, c1530, Urbino, repaired (A) **2,330.00**

11¼" d, majolica, central figure of Cupid in circ panel, grotesques and foliage in green, blue, ochre, and manganese, fluted 17th C (A) **415.00**

11½" d, Istoriato, scene of warrior before castled city, ochre, yellow, blue, green, white, and black, 16th C, Urbino, repaired (A) **1,200.00**

12¼" d, stylized flower in center, four radiating striped leaves, ochre, green, manganese, and blue, mid 17th C, Montelupo **250.00**

12½" d, majolica, blue, green, manganese, and ochre scene from Old Testament, early 17th C, Urbino .**1,000.00**

Dish, 13¾" l, blue and white aqueduct in center, trellis and foliage border, c1735, Rossetti, (A) $3,240.00.

14¾" l, enameled sprigs of summer flowers, gilt rims, c1800, Le Nove, pr (A) **465.00**

15" w, painted flower sprays, multicolored, fluted, c1775, black "PH" mark, Le Nove (A) **1,040.00**

15⅜" d, blue and manganese center buildings and radiating flowers, bands of gadroons, mid 17th C, Savona (A) **580.00**

16½" l, center with stylized flower, blue and manganese flower border, dated 1712, Savona, cracked (A) . **145.00**

Drug Jar
6½" h, manganese inscription around waisted middle, blue lambrequins

on shoulder and lower section, 18th C, Savona (A) **120.00**

7¼" h, blue with gadroons and Latin inscription in manganese, strap handle with lappets, mid 17th C, Savona (A) **75.00**

7⅝" h, blue bands of hares and birds, manganese inscription, late 18th C, Savona (A) **180.00**

9¼" h, painted portrait medallions of Turk and monk in blue, green, and ochre, ivory ground, cylindrical, early 17th C, Venice, pr **2,000.00**

9¾" h, blue bands of scrolling foliage, white ground, "Aq.Fl.Nymph" in manganese, c1720, Savona **380.00**

Ewer, 12½" h, cov, bodies with foliage, yellow, blue, manganese, and green, scroll handles, bird's head spouts, swag covs, 18th C, Sicilian, pr (A) .. **280.00**

Figure
5½" h, putti on neoclassical plinths, molded drapery, medallions and foliage rockwork bases, multicolored, c1780, Le Nove, damaged, pr **1,200.00**

6¼" h, peasant woman holding rose and basket, multicolored, marked (A) **90.00**

6½" h, seated cobbler with shoe, wife holding pitcher and tumbler, multicolored, mid 19th C, pr (A) **50.00**

7" h, adoring shepherd, green, blue, and yellow polychromes, early 16th C, Tuscan **210.00**

8" h, porcelain, man and woman musicians, multicolored, lace, pr (A) **140.00**

8¼" h, porcelain, family with children holding music sheets, multicolored (A) **35.00**

8½" h, 18th C man on white prancing horse, late 19th C (A) **100.00**

8⅝" h, porcelain, boy and girl, peasant clothes, multicolored, named under green washed bases, c1800, Savona, pr (A) **8,750.00**

8¾" h, seated couple, period clothes, lamb on rect base (A) **90.00**

9" h, standing French Hussar, Naples **85.00**

10¼" h, Pan seated on tree trunk, applied vine, four putti and goat, rect base **135.00**

10½" h, terra cotta bust of Satyr, black block base, 19th C (A) **25.00**

11⅞" h, seated woman, circ base with child in lap, multicolored, "Lenci-Made in Italy, Torino, IV-XII" (A) **360.00**

13⅛" h, Winter modeled as bearded man holding fur-lined cape around body, splashed yellow, brown, and

green tree stump base, dated 1779
on base (A) 2,480.00
14" h, porcelain, "Battling Stallions,"
multicolored, matte finish, mounted
on wood base (A) 80.00
18¾" h, terra cotta bust of woman,
peasant garb, early 20th C (A) ... 200.00
23½" h, porcelain, polychrome lady
and gentleman, 18th C period
clothes, pr (A) 400.00

Holy Water Fountain
13¾" h, polychrome molded angels,
St Francis receiving Stigmata, late
17th C, Southern Italy (A) 220.00
14⅛" h, painted Madonna between
rope-twist pillars and arched cor-
nice, cherubs, 18th C (A) 415.00

Jar
5⅛" h
Blue and ochre coat of arms, band
of birds, contents named in Latin,
c1700 (A) 170.00
Blue and white Latin inscriptions
above coat of arms, scrolling foliage, dated 1708 on reverse, pr
(A) 545.00
6⅝" h, green and ochre stylized
branch scrolls outlined in manganese, blue ground (A) 150.00
8⅝" h, blue Latin inscription between
animals and foliage, c1660, Savona
(A) 260.00
9¼" h, majolica, painted clerical
busts, reserved on floral motif
ground, early 17th C 1,500.00
10½" h, majolica, painted helmeted
warrior, reverse with kneeling saint,
scrolling floral motifs, late 16th C,
Venice 1,500.00
11" h, ochre and green flowering
plants, blue ground, early 18th C,
Caltagirone (A) 180.00

Jug
7⅝" h, blue, yellow, manganese, and
light green foliage, scrolling motifs,
early 15th C 225.00
7⅞" h, molded Garibaldi on horse,
color accents (A) 80.00
8¼" h, majolica, mask spout painted
in blue, yellow, and manganese,
17th C (A) 80.00
12¼" h, majolica, painted scrolling
foliage, inscribed medallion, 18th
C (A) 95.00
29⅜" h, green, yellow, and ochre
overlapping peacock feather, blue
ground, scratched scrolls, pear
shape, twist handle, c1480 (A) ... 945.00

Knife Handles, painted flower sprays between puce molded scrolls, fitted
blades, 19th C, Le Nove (A) 90.00

Mold, 12" d, glazed heart shape, unmarked (A) **45.00**
Oyster Plate, 8¾" d, molded shells, lavender accents, unmarked (A) **25.00**
Pharmacy Bottle, 9⅝" h, Latin inscription, ribbon cartouche, figures in
landscape, blue and white, c1700 (A) **780.00**

Pitcher
6¼" h, multicolored harbor scene,
merchants, entwined strap handle,
early 19th C, Le Nove (A) **720.00**
7" d, 12½" h, pottery, hp purple
grapes, green leaves **55.00**
7" h, Art Deco style sea life, multicolored **20.00**

Plaque
7½" l, 9½" h, majolica, manganese,
blue, green, and ochre scene, sack-
ing of a town, equestrian groups,
Baroque giltwood, shell form
frame, late 17th C 3,000.00
10¼" l, 7½" h, painted figures, extensive landscape, lake and Italian
ruins, early 18th C (A) 1,135.00
11⅛" l, 8⅝" h, majolica, painted al-
legory of America, blue, green, and
ochre, early 18th C, Castelli,
chipped 2,400.00
11⅜" l, 8" h, painted Virgin in clouds,
cherubs, yellow ground (A) **390.00**
18¾" d, raised rim centering cherubs,
blue, yellow, and green garlands
and coat of arms, cream ground,
unmarked (A) **325.00**

Plate, 7½" d, tin-glazed bird and florals,
multicolored, black "Italy" mark, $40.00.

Plate
9" d
Istoriato, scene of two rearing
horses before men and seated
women, blue, green, yellow,
ochre, and white, 16th C, Urbino, cracked (A) 1,250.00
Painted putto fighting wild boar in

landscape, yellow rim, early 18th C, blue "R.B. Savona" mark (A) **985.00**
9¼" d
Blue painted tiger creeping through bamboo and prunus, scattered flowers, enamel accents, gilt rim, c1775, iron-red "anchor," Venice **350.00**
Blue and white figure on rock, flowering plants, c1760, Savona **360.00**
9⅜" d
Embracing putti and garden statuary, rococo scrolled cartouches, diaper and floral borders, c1760, Turin, pr (A) **1,950.00**
Majolica, center painted with lady and man hunting with crossbow in landscape, putti border, hares and scrolling foliage, c1720, Castelli (A) **4,930.00**
Painted manganese, green, and yellow, panels of figures and buildings, manganese wash, Savona (A) **100.00**
Painted putti in gardens, rococo scrolled cartouches, diaper and floral borders, c1760, Turin, pr (A) **1,170.00**
9½" d, faience, iron-red and blue peonies in center, sprays around rim, c1760, blue "M.C." and iron-red "M" marks (A) **110.00**
12⅜" l, multicolored Oriental scenes of two swimming ducks under bridge, gilt chain, floral borders, c1770–75, red "anchor" mark, Cozzi-Venice, pr (A) **990.00**
Platter, 13¼" l, pink and puce rose sprigs, green foliage, bud borders, scalloped edges, oval, c1780–90, Le Nove, pr (A) **880.00**
Ponce Pot, 2¾" h, majolica, polychrome chinoiserie landscape, mid 18th C (A) **55.00**
Potpourri Vase, 17" h, applied draped figures with white slip and gilt, blue ground, gilt floral swags and ribbon, lion's masks handles, pierced cov, late 19th C, Naples **275.00**
Sauceboat, 8" l, majolica, blue painted, flower sprays outlined in manganese, dbl loop handles, blue "Da; Marcelina Galle G. O. S." mark (A) **95.00**
Saucer, pierced gallery painted with two sprays of colored flowers, c1760, iron-red "V" mark (A) **820.00**
Spirit Barrel, 6⅝" w, molded tap and ribbing in manganese, blue, and ochre with foliage, 18th C, Southern Italy (A) **100.00**

Spirit Flask, 8¼" h, yellow, iron-red and blue birds, scrolling foliage, grayish ground, oviform with pewter screw cov, late 17th C (A) **200.00**
Tazza
7⅞" d, painted woman's head in circ foliage garland, mid 17th C, Southern Italy (A) **240.00**
11" d, blue and white horseman in landscape, c1700, blue "crown and arrow" mark, Savona (A) **210.00**
Teabowl
3" d, multicolored flower stems, iron-red sprig on int., line border rim, c1723–27, Vezzi-Venice (A) **1,870.00**
Chinoiserie figures playing instruments in landscape, late 18th C, Cozzi (A) **90.00**
Painted insects, foliage, figures, 18th C, Savona, pr (A) **90.00**
Porcelain, gilt and iron-red Oriental figures, quatrefoil panels, c1730, Vezzi (A) **165.00**
Teabowl and Saucer
Chinoiserie figures, one with horn in landscape, multicolored, gilt, iron-red panels of Oriental landscapes, reserved on blue ground, c1770, iron-red "anchor" marks, Cozzi (A)**1,100.00**
Green enamel stylized lappets and gilt foliage, gilt rims, c1770, iron-red "anchor" mark, Cozzi (A) **220.00**
Iron-red and gilt pagodas on islands, birds in flight, gilt rims, c1765, iron-red "anchor" mark, Venice .. **400.00**
Painted gilt insects, white ground, c1770, Cozzi (A) **40.00**
Tray, 18½" l, lead glazed earthenware, blue and white classical scene of fruit offering, scalloped edge, 18th C, attrib to Savona **475.00**
Tureen
10⅝" d, cov, modeled pumpkin, green and yellow splashes, 18th C **650.00**
11¼" l, cov, modeled faience duck, multicolored, pierced eyes, late 18th C (A) **825.00**
Urn
13½" h, 10" w, majolica, four panels of lizards in vines, diapering and geometrics in olive and dark green, brown and brown-red on cream, green griffin dbl handles, pedestal, 19th C **350.00**
28" h, tin glazed foliate ground, applied masks, loop handles, late 19th C (A) **150.00**
Vase
9" h, majolica, polychrome leaf and floral design, circ waisted form, 18th C **40.00**

13½" h, cov, manganese, blue and green painted flowers and insects, fluted ground, flower finials, dbl handles and ftd, c1775, pr (A) ...**1,460.00**

15½" h, vert panels of stylized flowers alternating with panels of palmettes, quatrefoils, two seated lion handles, ruby luster, bottle shape, long thin neck, c1890–1900, green "rooster" mark, Cantigalli (A) 110.00

18" h, faience, polychrome floral design, white ground, "M. C. P. Piediluc, Italy" (A) 25.00

24⅜" h, majolica, blue, green, yellow, and manganese bands of foliage, ribbed baluster shape, entwined snake dbl handles, early 18th C (A) 570.00

Wall Pocket, 8" h, blue classic scene, white ground, Savona 250.00

Wall Sconce, 12" h, pottery, modeled as cherub holding orb, Satyr mask below (A) 90.00

Wet Drug Jar, 8⅞" h, ochre and green, black ribbon cartouche, floral ground, green strap handle, 17th C (A) 520.00

JACKFIELD

Staffordshire and Shropshire, England 2nd half 18th Century

History: Jackfield was a generic term used for black glazed earthenware made during the second half of the 18th century. The red clay body was covered with a blackish glossy slip that was ornamented with scrollwork and relief flowers, oil gilding, and unfired painting. Jackfield was named after the Shropshire Pottery center.

From c1750–1775 the Jackfield factory was managed by Maurice Thursfield. John Rose of Coalport assumed control of the firm about 1780. Staffordshire potters such as Astbury and Whieldon also produced Jackfield wares.

References: R.G. Cooper, *English Slipware Dishes*, 1650–1850, Tiranti, 1968; The Jackfield Decorative Tile Industry, pamphlet (12 pages), published by Ironbridge Gorge Museum Trust, England, 1978.

Museums: British Museum, London, England.

Brandy Pot, 4¼" h, cov, relief of vines, bird finial, mid18th C 300.00

Coffee Cup, 3" h, gilt dec centering figure, c1760–80 .... 300.00

Coffeepot
9" h, molded flowering branches, three paw feet, bird finial, c1765 . 350.00

Teapot, 5¼" h, c1760, Whieldon-type, $500.00.

10¼" h, pear shape, three paw feet, silver chain attachments, c1765 .. 850.00

12" h, pear shape, silver rims, finials, chain attachments, c1765, pr **1,000.00**

Comforters, 12½" h, black figural dogs, c1880–90, pr 345.00

Condiment Dish, 4" w, heart shape, black glaze, c1790 .... 400.00

Figure, 12" h, spaniels, black glaze, unmarked, pr 350.00

Jug
5½" h, pear shape, peak spout, c1765 150.00
6⅛" h, pear shape, scroll handle, unmarked 50.00
8½" h, pear shape, peak spout, c1765 165.00
11" h, gilt horse and hounds in landscape, gilt scroll and foliage surround, "I and A" and "True Blue," c1760 .... **1,000.00**

Loving Cups, dbl loop handles, c1765, pr 400.00

Milk Jug, 5" h
Black glaze, c1770 .... 250.00
Raised leaves, gilt, three legs, c1760 400.00
Silver shape, black glaze, c1760 ... 400.00

Mug, reeded loop handle, c1765 ..... 250.00

Mustard Pot, barrel shape, loop handle 150.00

Sauceboat, 7¼" w, silver shape, c1765, pr 650.00

Tea and Coffee Service, teapot, coffeepots on three paw feet, cov milk jug, cov tea caddy, cream jug, two cups and saucers, applied flowering foliage, gilt accents, c1765 ....**1,500.00**

Tea Service, teapot, chocolate pot, cov sugar bowl, waste bowl, teabowl and saucer, black glaze, c1765 ....**1,200.00**

Teabowl and Saucer, black glaze, gilt accents, c1750 .... 350.00

Teapot
4¾" h, round bulbous shape, C-handle, chain on finial, c1750 ...... 200.00
5½" h, three paw feet, reeded strap handle, c1765 .... 250.00
Raised leaf design, black glaze 65.00

JASPER WARE

Staffordshire, England
Continental
1774 to Present

History: About 1774 Josiah Wedgwood perfected a hard, unglazed stoneware whose body was capable of being stained throughout its substance with metallic oxides. Shades of blue, lavender, sage, olive green, lilac, yellow, and black could be used. With jasper dip, color was applied only on the surface.

Many firms, in addition to Wedgwood, produced jasper wares. Adams made jasper from the early 1800s into the 20th century. Adams blue jasper is distinguished from that of Wedgwood because it has a faint violet shade. Initially Adams modeled many of the designs for his jasper ware. In 1785 he employed Joseph Mongenot from Switzerland as a modeler. Together they designed the bas-reliefs and border decorations that were applied in white jasper to the colored bodies of vases, urns, tea and coffeepots, plaques, medallions, and candelabra drums. Most of the Adams jasper is marked.

Another producer of jasper ware was Spode. Other Staffordshire manufacturers produced marked jasper ware. Unfortunately, many examples do not include a maker's mark. Several continental potters, e.g., Heubach also manufactured jasper ware.

Museums: British Museum, London, England; Memorial Hall Museum, Philadelphia, PA; Museum of Fine Arts, Boston, MA; Victoria & Albert Museum, London, England.

Additional Listing: Wedgwood jasper ware pieces are found in the Wedgwood listing.

Biscuit Barrel
   Relief of hunt scene, blue ground, SP bale and lid, Adams **175.00**
   White cameos of hunting scenes, blue ground, silvered handle, rim and top, Adams **120.00**
Biscuit Jar, white cameos of classic women, lavender ground, SP base and top, unmarked **65.00**
Bottle, 6½" h, raised white cameos of lady, gentleman, cherubs, and "Prosit," green ground, Germany ... **65.00**
Box
   3½" l, 2" w, white Cupid cameo, green ground, unmarked **40.00**
   6" d, cov, white cameos of cherubs and lovebirds on cov, scrolling, gray-green ground, ftd, unmarked **175.00**
Cheese Dome, 11" h, white cameos of cherubs, various pursuits, foliate bor-

der, blue ground, acorn finial, unmarked **490.00**
Coffeepot
   8½" h, white cameos of dancing maidens, dark blue ground, "Copeland-Spode" **85.00**
   10½" h, white cameos of hunt scene, dark blue ground, "Copeland-Spode" mark **135.00**
Cream Jug, 2½" h, white cameos of putti, border of interlaced circles, blue ground, engine-turned base, England **65.00**
Creamer
   2½" h, white Kewpies, blue ground, sgd "O'Neill" **225.00**
   White Kewpies, blue ground, unmarked **185.00**
Creamer and Sugar, white cameos of busts of Clowes and Bourne, blue ground, Adams **55.00**
Dish
   4½" d, white cameo of Indian with hatchet and shield, green ground, wheat border, Heubach **60.00**
   9⅞" d, cov, applied white cameos of cherubs and acorns, blue ground, Stilton **80.00**
Ewer, 8½" h, three white classical cameos of music and drama, framed leaf border, dark blue ground **135.00**
Flask, tri-color, green, white, and blue, design of toasting couple, "Prosit" in raised letters, imp "crown and wreath, Germany" mark **135.00**
Flower Pot, 3" h, Cupid and winged goddess playing mandolin on front, dancing on reverse, green ground .. **40.00**
Humidor, 6" d, 5½" h, white cameo busts of Washington and Franklin in wreaths, green ground, Germany ... **135.00**
Jar, 3½" h, white classical cameos, blue ground, SP lid and handle, "Adams Tunstall, England" (A) **110.00**
Jardiniere, 6¼" l, white cameos of florals, green ground **55.00**
Jewelry Box, 4" l, white cameos of Cupid and Venus holding hands, unmarked **20.00**
Jug
   6" d, 9" h, white cameos of leaf and hanging berry florals, blue ground, pewter lid, imp "E. I. RIDGWAY" **135.00**
   7" h, white cameos of Seasons, arcaded panels, shallow flutes on lower section, blue ground, silver rim, late 18th C, Adams (A) **135.00**
Lamp, boudoir type, white classic figures, lilac ground, "GERMANY" mark, pr **65.00**
Mirror and Brush Set, white cameos of

ladies and cherubs, green ground, ornate brass handle and frames **110.00**
Pitcher
4½" h, white cameos of two women, flowing gowns, grapes and leaves, blue ground, unmarked **55.00**
5" h, white cameos of cherubs in roses, green ground, unmarked .. **125.00**
6" h
White cameos of drinking scene, blue ground, grape and vine handle **75.00**
White classic figures, blue ground, Germany **80.00**
7½" h, white cameo of football game, blue ground, Copeland-Spode ... **75.00**

Plaque, 7" d, white cameos, green ground, "Germany," $90.00.

Plaque
3" w, 8¼" h, white cameo of goddess and cherub, green ground, Germany **110.00**
4" w, 3" h, white cameos of prancing horses with riders, acanthus leaves, brown ground, "crown and star" mark **45.00**
5¾" w, 3⅞" h, white cameos of seated classic woman holding urn of fire, cut and incised design, light blue ground, unmarked **95.00**
6" d, white cameo of cherub whispering to stork, green, Germany .. **40.00**
6" sq, white cameos of boy with net, girl with jug, green ground, "GERMANY" **40.00**
7½" w, 5" h, three cameo cherubs dancing, green ground, Germany . **110.00**
10½" w, 6½" h, white cameo design of woman picking flowers from tree and carrying basket, pink ground, framed **265.00**
Powder Jar, Art Nouveau style, woman with jewels and luster, pink ground, "crown and star" mark **25.00**

Roundels, 6¼" d, white classic figures, sage green dipped ground, late 19th C.·(A) **160.00**
Teapot, 8½" h, white cameos of hunt scene, blue ground, Copeland-Spode **120.00**
Tumbler, 4" h, white classic cameos, brown ground **65.00**
Vase
4" h
Small white flowers, green ground, small holes near top **20.00**
White cameos of man with spade, woman under tree, blue ground **25.00**
White cameos of Cupid, Pan on sides, blue ground, "crown and star" mark **55.00**
5" h
White cameo of bust of Art Nouveau style woman, mauve ground, green scrolling rim, three feet, triangular **165.00**
White cameo of bust of woman playing lyre, green ground, rect **45.00**
7" h, white cameo of classic woman with flowing hair, carrying torch, light green ground **50.00**
9" h, white cameos of man and woman standing by column, brown ground, oval **100.00**
Wall Pocket, 7½" h, white cameos of Grecian lady, florals and bow, green ground **30.00**

JOHNSON BROS
ENGLAND

JOHNSON BROTHERS

Staffordshire, England
1883 to Present

History: Henry, Robert, Alfred, and Fred, the four Johnson brothers, founded a pottery in 1883 in Staffordshire, England. Although begun on a small scale, it soon expanded. Its principal success was derived from earthenware tablewares that were quite successful in both England and the United States.

By 1914 the Johnson Brothers had five factories scattered throughout Hanley, Tunstall, and Burslem. Some popular patterns include "Granite" made for the overseas market, "Green & Golden

Dawn," and "Rose." Johnson Brothers' wares originally were white ironstone. It was replaced by a lighter weight ware known for its uncommon lightness and finish.

Johnson Brothers became part of the Wedgwood Group in 1968.

Butter Pats
"Baroda" pattern, set of 6 .... 35.00
"Florentine" pattern, green, set of 5 30.00
Cake Plate, "Historic America" pattern, pink 25.00
Cereal Bowl, 6" d, "Rose Chintz" pattern 5.00
Compote, 8" sq, 4½" h, pink flowers, brown foliage, pedestal, "Johnson Bros Late Pankhurst Royal Ironstone" mark 65.00
Creamer
"English Chippendale" pattern
Blue 10.00
Pink 10.00
"Fruit Sampler" pattern 10.00
"Harvest Time" pattern 15.00
"Lemon Tree" pattern 10.00
"Old Mill" pattern, brown 10.00
"Sheraton" pattern 10.00
Creamer and Sugar
"Old British Castles" pattern, pink .. 30.00
"Strawberry Fair" pattern 20.00
Cup and Saucer
"Coaching Scenes" pattern, blue ... 10.00
"Devonshire" pattern, pink 10.00
"English Chippendale" pattern, pink 10.00
"Friendly Village" pattern 10.00
"Historic America" pattern
Blue 10.00
Brown 10.00
"Horton" pattern, octagon 10.00
"Indigo" pattern 10.00
"Lemon Tree" pattern 10.00
"Mill Stream" pattern, pink 10.00
"Old English Countryside" pattern, brown 10.00
"Rose Chintz" pattern 10.00
"Sheraton" pattern 10.00
"Staffordshire Bouquet" pattern 10.00
"Strawberry Fair" pattern 10.00

Demitasse Cup and Saucer, gold banding and trim, set of 8 .... 55.00
Egg Cup, "Friendly Village" pattern ... 10.00
Gravy Boat and Stand, "Lemon Tree" pattern 20.00
Plate
4½" d, "Fruit Sampler" pattern 5.00
5" d, "Mill Stream" pattern, pink ... 5.00
6" d
"Devon Sprays" pattern 5.00
"Coaching Scenes" pattern, blue . 5.00
"Rose Chintz" pattern 5.00
6" sq
"Friendly Village" pattern 10.00
"Indigo" pattern 5.00
"Pastorale" pattern, pink 5.00
"Sheraton" pattern 10.00
"Winchester" pattern 10.00
6½" d, "English Chippendale" pattern, blue 10.00
7" d, "Turin" pattern 10.00
8" d, "Regis" pattern 15.00
9" d, portrait of "Lord Roberts," multicolored uniform, "Johnson Bros, England" 35.00
9¼" d
"Arbor" pattern 10.00
"Coaching Scenes" pattern, blue . 10.00
"Devonshire" pattern, pink 10.00
"Dorchester" pattern 10.00
"English Chippendale" pattern
Blue 10.00
Pink 10.00
"Friendly Village" pattern 10.00
"Garden Bouquet" pattern 10.00
"Greydawn" pattern 10.00
"Historic America" pattern, blue . 10.00
"Indigo" pattern 10.00
"Mill Stream" pattern, pink 10.00
"Old English Countryside" pattern, brown 10.00
"Sheraton" pattern 10.00
9½" d
"Pastorale" pattern, pink 10.00
"Staffordshire Bouquet" pattern .. 5.00
"Strawberry Fair" pattern 10.00
9¾" d
"Horton" pattern, octagon 10.00

Left, vegetable bowl, 9½" l, "Old English" pattern, gray and green, $15.00; center, cup and saucer, "Old Britain Castles" pattern, red transfers, $15.00; right, chamber pot, 8¾" w, pink base with lime green accents, gold trim, $45.00.

"Old British Castles" pattern

Brown	**10.00**
Pink	**10.00**

10" d

"Harvest Time" pattern	**10.00**
"Raleigh" pattern	**10.00**
"Regis" pattern	**10.00**
"Rose Chintz" pattern	**10.00**
11¼" d, "Historic America" pattern, blue	**15.00**

Platter

12" l

"English Chippendale" pattern, blue	**20.00**
"Indigo" pattern	**20.00**
"Mill Stream" pattern, pink	**20.00**
"Old English Countryside" pattern, brown	**15.00**
"Old Mill" pattern, brown	**15.00**
"Sheraton" pattern	**20.00**
"Strawberry Fair" pattern	**20.00**

12½" l

"Devonshire" pattern, pink	**20.00**
"Fruit Sampler" pattern	**15.00**
"Greydawn" pattern	**20.00**

14" l

"Friendly Village" pattern	**25.00**
"Old English Countryside" pattern, brown	**25.00**
"Regis" pattern	**10.00**
15½" l, "Lemon Tree" pattern	**30.00**
16" l, "Sheraton" pattern	**35.00**
17½" l, "Wild Turkey" pattern	**50.00**
20½" l, "Friendly Village" pattern	**65.00**

Soup Bowl, 7" d

"Pastorale" pattern, pink	**10.00**
"Sheraton" pattern	**10.00**
"Winchester" pattern	**10.00**
Soup Plate, 7" d, "Old British Castles" pattern, pink	**10.00**

Vegetable Bowl

9" d, "Indigo" pattern	**15.00**
"Greydawn" pattern, oval	**15.00**

KELLER AND GUERIN

Luneville, France
1778 to Present

History: Keller and Guerin bought the old faience factory of Jacques Chambrette from Gabriel,

his son, and Charles Loyal, his son-in-law, in 1778. The factory made blue decorated faience similar to that of Nevers and rose and green faience that imitated old Strasbourg motifs.

Schneider was the most celebrated of the potters that worked at Keller and Guerin. The company commissioned designs from sculptors Ernest Bussiere and E. Lachenal among others. Biscuit porcelain figures, especially of large animals, were a specialty.

The company switched from faience to English style earthenware at the end of the 19th century. Majolica and transfer printed wares entered the product line. The company is still in operation.

Plate, 8¼" d, majolica, raised red raspberries, green leaves, gray ground, imp leaves, $55.00.

Bowl

5¾" d, 3" h, "Violettes" pattern, c1891	**30.00**
6" d, 3¼" h, "Luneville Eglantine" pattern, c1891, marked	**30.00**
Cup and Saucer, "Luneville Eglantine" pattern, c1891, marked	**30.00**
Dish, 7" l, lobster handle, divided, marked	**25.00**

Plate

8" d, center design of open florals, red and green, open, pierced border outlined in red, raised white weave inner border, marked	**45.00**
8¾" d, painted purple plums in center, pierced for hanging, sgd "Obert," "K and G Luneville Depose France" mark	**55.00**
Tray, 8" l, "Marine Ware-Dans La Marine," rose transfer border of sailors, "K and G, demi-porcelain, Luneville" mark	**20.00**
Vase, 7¾" h, stoneware, blue crystalline glaze, c1920, imp "Guerin" mark (A)	**25.00**

ENGLISH POTTERY

Figure, 10½"h, Staffordshire, c1815, $875

Cow Creamer, 7½"l, Portobello, early 1800s, $775

Hen on Nest, 7"l, 7"h, bisque, Staffordshire, $575

Teabowl & Saucer, 3"h, Sewell, c1804, $450

Basket & Stand, 8½"l, one of a pair, unmkd, $875/pr

Pitcher, 7½"h, Sunderland, Mariner's design, early 1800s, $375

PLATE 1

Basket, 10½"H-H, Minton, early 19th C,
A-$400

Tureen, Sauce, 7½"H-H, 5½"h, one of a pair,
Worcester, c1820, $650/pr

Tureen, cov, 10"d, 6½"h, Davenport,
c1840, $450

Plate, 10"l, 8"w, Derby, c1770, $265

Compote, 15"h, Spode, "Spode Copelands China
England" mk, A-$110

Urns, 7½", 5½"h, Spode, c1820, $1250

PLATE 2

WEDGWOOD

Bowl, Krator, Rosso, Antico, 11"H-H, 6"h, c1820, $1100

Portland Vase, stoneware, 11"h, c1830, $2500

Compote, Drabware, Queensware, 12"H-H, 5½"h, c1840, $400

Vase, Basalt, 19½"h, "Pegasus," c1800, $7500

Vase, Fairyland Luster, 12"h, Daisy Malkig Jones, c1925, $3500

Urn, Diceware, cov, 9"h, "Dancing Hours," c1900, $2250

PLATE 3

Vase, 9¼"h, Dutch Delft, c1750–95, $575

Jardinaire, 16½"H-H, Nevers, $750

Plate, 9"d, Old Paris, Schoelcher, "Vue de L'ecole Militaire," c1810, $450

Planter, 7"h, Capodimonte, "blue crown & N" mk, $165

Vase, 9¼"h, Nevers, c1860, $250

Bowl, 13"d, 7½"h, Spain, 18th c, $1275

PLATE 4

EUROPEAN—GENERAL

Centerpiece, 19"h, Royal Dux, raised pink triangle mk, $450

Chocolate Pot, 10¼"h, Dresden, "crown over Dresden" mk, A-$200

Urn, cov, 15"h, Royal Vienna, "blue beehive" mk, A-$225

Pitcher, 3½"h, Royal Bayreuth, Rose Tapestry, blue mk, $225

Figure, 12½"h, Bing & Grondahl, mkd, $590

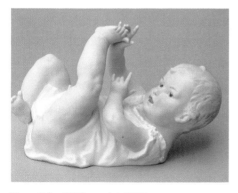

Piano Baby, 7½"l, unmkd, $250

Cup & Saucer, oversized, Meissen, blue X'd swords mk, $195

PLATE 5

MAJOLICA

Urn, 11½"h, Copeland, early
1870s, $850.

Tea Set, Wedgwood, c1875, $675.

Plate, Artichoke, 9½"d,
Luneville, c1900, $225.

Wine Jug, 12"h, Italy,
c1920, $350

Vases-pr, 6¼"h, Napoleon &
Josephine, Germany, c1900,
$150

Platter, 14"l, England, c1875–80, $750

Platter, 13"l, England, c1880, $550.

PLATE 6

QUIMPER

Wall Pocket, 10¼"h, "Henriot
Quimper, France 82" mk,
$375.

Platter, 17¼"l, 13½"w, "Porquier-Beau Quimper" mk,
$895.

Crepe Dish, 3¼"h, 8¼"l, 5½"w, applied bows on
sides, pierced for hanging, "blk HB" mk, $985

Inkstand, 12¼"l, 10¾"w, "HR Quimper" on
front, $900

Oyster Plate, 9¼"d, 2½"h, ftd, "HR
Quimper" mk, $550

Figure, 7½"h, artist sgd, "Henriot
Quimper" mk, $400

PLATE 7

R. S. PRUSSIA

Tray, 13"H-H, mkd, A-$375

Cracker Jar, 9"H-H, mkd, A-$400

Cream & Sugar, mkd, A-$100

Vase, 7¾"h, mkd, A-$410

Vase, 10"h, unmkd, A-$110

Bowl, 10"d, unmkd, A-$325

PLATE 8

KPM

KPM   1835-44   1870-PRESENT

KING'S PORCELAIN MANUFACTORY (KPM)

Berlin, West Germany
1763 to Present

History: The King's Porcelain Manufactory (KPM) was purchased and controlled by Frederick the Great. He ran the factory according to his own ideas and was responsible for its successes and failures, even though he employed Johann Grieninger as director.

The early porcelains were characterized by a dense, clear glaze over a fine white body. Many of the more talented German painters were employed by Frederick, resulting in products that competed with the highly successful Meissen factory.

The 18th century at KPM was characterized by technically superior figures in the glazed and biscuit state that showed a critical attention to details. However, the mainstay of the company was a line of popular, fine tablewares and ornamental pieces. Large quantities of tablewares were decorated with detailed florals and period and pastoral paintings. These early pieces showed a discriminating use of gilding, often used to highlight rather than to decorate. The later periods saw an increase in the use of gilding to the point of excessiveness. After the death of Frederick the Great in 1786, the factory continued to produce dinner services and other utilitarian and decorative porcelains.

The King's Porcelain Manufactory was also known for the fine miniature plaques in porcelain which featured copies of popular paintings of the period. KPM, along with other major European houses, kept up with the times and changing styles, adopting the Rococo, Neoclassical, and Empire styles as each became fashionable. KPM was among the first to produce lithophanes. During the 19th century, the emphasis shifted to simple, clean designs.

From its beginnings, KPM was under the control of the Prussian monarchy. With the abdication of William II, the last of the kings, in 1918, KPM became the property of the Prussian state. It was renamed the States Porcelain Manufactory Berlin. Severe damage from bombings during World War II resulted in the factory being moved

to Selb where it leased the porcelain factory of Paul Muller.

After WWII the factory in Berlin was reconstructed. Since the two factories were in separate occupation zones, both branches remained legally separated until 1949. When the Federal Republic of Germany was established in 1949, the factory in Berlin became the property of the City of Berlin (West Property.) The branch in Selb returned to Berlin in 1957. Products from Selb have a "S" beneath the scepter.

References: Winfred Baer, *Berlin Porcelain,* Smithsonian Institution Press, 1980; George W. Ware, *German & Austrian Porcelain,* Crown, Inc., 1963.

Bowl, 12" l, floral design, oval, dbl handles, "KPM" **60.00**
Cabinet Cup
    3½" h, painted named view of "Salzbrunn," waisted shape, curved strap handle (A) **160.00**
    5⅜" h, painted named view of ruins, sheep and figures, oblong octagon gilt cartouche, reverse with stylized foliage, gilt scroll acanthus, leaf handle, three paw feet, c1845, blue "scepter, eagle, and KPM" mark (A) **140.00**
    Gilt bands and foliage (A) **150.00**
Cabinet Cup and Stand, painted views of "Die Domkirche Zu Berlin," and "Strasse unter den Linden mit Zeughaus," rect cartouches, green ground, gilt handles, laurel wreath finials, c1880, blue "scepter" mark, pr **1,295.00**
Cake Plate
    10" d, portrait of Queen Louise, violet sprays, maroon and gold trim **85.00**
    10½" d, dark purple iris in center, pierced edge, blue floral motif (A) **115.00**
Candlestick, 5⅞" h, painted panels of lovers, blue scale ground, hexagon, blue "scepter" mark, pr (A) **325.00**
Chocolate Set, pot with wooden handle, milk jug, cov sugar bowl, and 11⅞" d tray, puce flower sprays, c1780, blue "scepter" mark, hairlines (A) . . **490.00**
Clock
    10¼" h, arched rococo style design, floral decoration, Waterbury movement, "KPM" (A) **90.00**
    36¾" h, stylized pediment supported by molded classical figures, head of maiden on top, scroll molded base, two putti, late 19th C, iron-red "KPM" and orb, blue "scepter" marks (A) **4,400.00**
Coffee Can and Saucer, can with oval panels of silhouettes of lady and gentleman, yellow ground, saucer with

flowers in panels, c1780, blue "scepter" mark, pr (A) **195.00**
Coffeepot
9" h, puce sprays of garden flowers, pear shape, bud finial, branch handle, c1780, blue "scepter" mark . **300.00**
10" h, orange and blue flowers, white ground **35.00**
Cream Jug, 4½" h, multicolored scenes of playful cherubs and florals, c1870, "orb and scepter" mark **290.00**
Creamer and Sugar, powder blue band at top, middle band of blue forget-me-nots, ivory ground, diamond shape, gold handles, marked **100.00**
Cup, cov portrait of young woman, cobalt ground, gilt overlay **350.00**
Cup and Saucer
Cov, cup painted with medallion of maiden and putti supporting silhouette of nobleman, pink ground, saucer with putti holding foliate "H" and crown, laurel borders (A) **2,460.00**
Cup painted with silhouette of gentleman in gilt oval, gilt vermicule iron-red ground, saucer with gilt and rose entwined "G", c1800, blue "scepter" mark (A) **360.00**
German inscription, three leaf clover (A) **40.00**
Gilt designs, magenta ground, late 19th C, iron-red "KPM" mark (A) **110.00**
Heraldic crest, multicolored (A) **50.00**
Hp forget-me-nots, blue and pink ground **35.00**
Landscape scene, multicolored (A) .. **225.00**
Oak leaf border above cross, crowned and dated in gilt foliate wreath, royal blue ground (A) **75.00**
Painted calvary scene, reserved on white and gilt banded ground, ftd (A) **100.00**
Painted en grisaille of figures in landscape, gilt dentil rims, entwined gilt garland around scene, tea size c1775, blue "scepter" mark **480.00**
Painted landscape scene (A) **100.00**
Silhouette of gentleman, primrose ground, apple-green borders, gilt swags, gilt "FR" on saucer, c1800, blue "scepter" mark (A) **185.00**
White angelic figure on handle, ending in mask, royal blue ground (A) **100.00**
Dinner Service, Art Deco style, turquoise and pink jewels, gilt and iron-red ground, sea green borders, molded swags and gilding, c1880, blue "scepter" and red "orb and KPM" marks, set of 89 pcs, service pcs (A) **7,920.00**
Dish
9½" w, painted birds on branch, bur-

gundy border, gilt drapery, leaf shape, c1860, blue "scepter" and red "orb and KPM" mark (A) **180.00**
11⅞" d, "Blue Onion" pattern, c1771, blue "scepter" mark (A) .. **290.00**
9½" l, 12" w, green and lilac florals, divided with handle, marked **120.00**
Figure
5" l, 4¼" h, Diane sitting with reclining deer, Art Deco style **225.00**
5¼" h, warrior with eagle helmet, face-molded shield, multicolored, late 19th C, iron-red "KPM and orb," blue "scepter" marks (A) ... **140.00**
6" h, angel with Horn of Plenty, multicolored, c1850, ... **750.00**

Figure, 7" h, turquoise shawl with red flowers, purple skirt, c1913, $585.00.

8" h
Seated woman with peacock, natural colors, lavender and coral accents **395.00**
Standing bird with incised brown body, circ grass mound base, water weeds, c1780, blue "scepter" mark (A) **1,430.00**
8½" h
Venus seated on shell holding apple, pr of putti, Cupid holding flaming torch, hunter and dog, scroll molded base, multicolored, late 19th C, iron-red "KPM and orb," blue "scepter" marks (A) **525.00**
Young couple with flower basket and garland, girl holding empty bird cage, rock molded circ base, blue "scepter," iron-red "orb" marks (A) **400.00**

9¾" h, female seated on column, wearing bear cape and holding scepter, soft multicolors, c1832 . .**1,200.00**

10½" h

Ceres with cornucopia and fruit, putto with spade and farm tools at feet, late 19th C, iron-red "KPM and orb," blue "scepter" marks (A) **140.00**

Parrot, multicolored, ormolu base, c1876 .... **500.00**

6¼", 6⅝" h, male violinist, bagpiper, female vocalist, hurdy-gurdy player, period clothes with lace, sq base, scrolling, iron-red "KPM and orb," blue "scepter" marks, set of 4 .... **700.00**

6½" h, gallant and companion, dancing pose, wearing pastel period clothes carrying garlands, c1780–90, blue "scepter" mark, pr, repairs (A) **500.00**

12" h, man with hound, woman with deer, multicolored, c1850, pr **1,600.00**

Small boy with grapes and goblet .. **140.00**

Gravy Boat and Undertray, white body, dbl handles, red "KPM" mark **25.00**

Inkwell, 9¼" h, molded figure in Eastern costume beside molded vase inkwell, circ base, quatrefoil tray, iron-red and gilt berries, c1840, blue "scepter" mark (A) **350.00**

Lithophane

5¾" w, 7½" , scene of castle on hill before river, cobalt leaded frame, sgd "Rheinstein," late 19th C (A) . **100.00**

9½" h, woman overlooking balcony, mounted in frame, ... **200.00**

Milk Jug, 6⅛" h, painted scattered flowers and insects, ozier molded border, blue "scepter," iron-red "KPM" mark **50.00**

Plaque

5" w, 7" h, portrait of young girl with red hair, framed **1,500.00**

6" w, 7½" h, young girl in brown smock reading book, late 19th C, imp "KPM and scepter" mark (A) .**1,045.00**

6¼" l, portrait of young girl, mounted in brass frame, marked **850.00**

6¼" w, 9⅜" h, gypsy girl in shawl with coins on forehead, leaning on red cushion, sgd "Tenner," imp "KPM and scepter" mark (A) **825.00**

6⅜" w, 9⅜" h, Ruth standing in field holding wheat bundle, late 19th C, imp "KPM and scepter" mark (A) .**1,100.00**

6½" w, 9" h, painted angel holding girl in arms, moonlit landscape, oval, late 19th C, imp "scepter, KPM" mark (A) **825.00**

6½" w, 9⅜" h, musician playing mandolin in claret vest, leaning on stone wall, sgd "E. Wolff," late 19th C, imp "KPM and scepter" mark (A) **610.00**

6¾" h, bust of woman, flowing chestnut hair, red dress, "Reveuse and KPM" mark (A) **525.00**

7" l, Madonna, multicolored, "KPM and scepter" mark **225.00**

7" l, 11" h, "The 16th Madonna" by Raphael, multicolored, sgd "Wagner" **1,200.00**

8" w, 7" h, old man reading to child, mother and son in bkd, c1900, imp "dbl-headed eagle" mark (A) **550.00**

8" w, 10" h, young girl in gray hat and dress, periwinkles on collar, late 19th C, imp "KPM and scepter" mark **550.00**

8⅝" w, 11" h, painted St. Jerome seated at desk, lion at side, imp "KPM and scepter" mark **575.00**

8⅞" h, old man in chains, jug and bread on table, c1880, imp "scepter and KPM" mark (A) **210.0**

8⅞" w, 11⅛" h, embracing lovers in boat in seascape, late 19th C, imp "KPM and scepter" mark (A) **1,760.00**

10½" h, "Solitude" gazing downward with claret robe, late 19th C, sgd "Schinzel," imp "KPM and scepter" mark **1,100.00**

11¼" l, 8½" h, painted nymph, arms around recumbent lion, arrow in hand, c1860 (A) **3,300.00**

12" w, 14½" h, seamstress seated by window, woman holding chicken, sgd "P v slingelant," imp "KPM" (A) **2,500.00**

12¾" w, 14¼" h, Art Deco style, painted mountain scene, c1908 (A) **1,430.00**

13⅜" w, 15½" h, lady sewing, Flemish costume, baby in cradle, int. scene, c1860, imp "scepter and KPM" mark (A) **3,300.00**

13½" h, bust of Princess Lambelle, plumed hat and period dress, sgd "Wagner," late 19th C, imp "KPM and scepter" mark (A) **1,045.00**

13⅝" w, 15¾" h, painted int. of woman playing spinet, man holding music, boy watching, 17th C clothes, imp "KPM and scepter" mark (A) **7,150.00**

16¼" w, 21½" h, lady and cavalier, multicolored, sgd "E M Bertz," c1842 ....**2,750.00**

20¼" w, 25½" h, maidens in mountainous landscape, multicolored, imp "KPM and scepter" mark ...**3,500.00**

21¼" w, 17⅛" h, "Death of Philip of Spain," king in armor, priest and

courtiers, sgd "C Meinelt," imp
"KPM and scepter" mark (A) **4,400.00**
Two lightly draped female water car-
riers, multicolored (A) **6,240.00**
Plate
  6" d, blue leaves, gold accents **40.00**
  8¼" d, butterfly, dragonfly, and bird
    in center, gilt scalloped border,
    light blue inner edge, mono-
    grammed "S" **95.00**
  8½" l, multicolored florals in center,
    gilt trim, leaf shape, c1870, "orb
    and scepter" mark **190.00**
  8¾" d, scattered polychrome florals,
    gilded molded borders, early 20th
    C, set of 4 (A) **75.00**
  9⅜" d, center painted with bouquets
    and insects, pierced basketwork
    borders, green and brown rims,
    gilt, c1780, blue "scepter" mark,
    set of 12 (A) **3,285.00**
  9⅝" d, painted center of bouquets
    and sprays, border pierced with fo-
    liage, blue florets at junction,
    "scepter, orb, and KPM" mark, set
    of 3 (A) **315.00**
Platter, 17¾" l, 12½" w, center with
  man playing horn, woman holding
  open birdcage, multicolored, gilt lattice and scrollwork, open gold rect
  handles, pink ribbons, blue "scepter"
  mark **495.00**
Portrait, 8½" l, 6¼" w, young peasant
  girl, mounted in frame, marked . . .**2,250.00**
Relish Tray, 10" l, gilt and enamel decorations, marked **100.00**
Scent Bottle
  4⅜" h, painted figure and flower
    sprays, scroll-molded outline, ac-
    cents, c1880, blue "scepter, KPM"
    mark (A) **150.00**
  Molded scrolls, iron-red Cupid on
    clouds, gilt metal C-scroll stopper,
    blue "scepter," red "orb and KPM"
    mark (A) **140.00**
Smoking Set, ashtray, cov match con-
  tainer, cigarette holder, chamberstick
  and tray, Attic black and red figure,
  orange ground, set (A) **125.00**
Snuff Box
  3⅛" l, painted fruit, molded C-scroll
    flower sprays, foliage cartouches,
    int. of cov with bowl of flowers and
    birds, c1765, blue "scepter" mark
    (A) **2,640.00**
  3¾" w, painted Oriental vignettes,
    molded rococo-scrolled sections,
    gilt metal mounts, late 18th C, blue
    "scepter" mark (A) **170.00**
Tea Caddy, 5⅞" h, painted galloping
  horseman and peasants in landscape,

gilt borders, rect, c1775, blue "scep-
  ter" mark (A) **765.00**
Tea Set, demitasse, teapot, creamer, cov
  sugar, cup and saucer, and tray,
  shaded pink ground, gold scroll ov-
  erlay, blue "scepter" mark **350.00**
Teapot
  4" h, painted with two river land-
    scapes, yellow ground, basket-
    molded borders, c1770–80, blue
    "scepter" mark, repaired (A) **800.00**
  9⅞" w, painted bouquets and insects,
    ozier molded borders, blue "scep-
    ter," iron-red "KPM" mark **50.00**
Teapot and Sugar Bowl, 5½" h, teapot,
  4¾" h, sugar bowl, iron-red design of
  peasants, landscape scene, gilt trellis
  outlined with scrolls, turquoise foliage, flowerhead finials, c1775, blue
  "scepter" mark (A) **850.00**
Tête-A-Tête Set, coffee jug, cov milk
  jug, cov sugar bowl, two cups and
  saucers, 16⅝" l, tray, each painted
  with two views of Berlin, robin's egg
  blue ground, gilt, late 19th C, iron-
  red "KPM and orb," blue "scepter"
  mark (A) **5,500.00**
Tray
  8" l, gilt and enamel floral design (A) **100.00**
  12" l, 6" w, multicolored florals, green
    "scepter" mark **65.00**
  14½" l, painted stag and hinds in
    landscape, insects on border, gilt
    rim, shell molded dbl handles,
    c1775, blue "scepter" mark (A) . . **660.00**
Tureen
  10" d, cov, painted exotic birds and
    insects, cherub finial, 19th C, blue
    "scepter" mark (A) **350.00**
  11¼" d, cov, painted vignettes of vil-
    lagers dining, scattered bouquets
    and spray between, molded border,
    gilt rim, kneeling putto finial,
    c1880, blue "scepter" mark (A) . . **750.00**
Vase
  5⅞" h, painted putti on sides, holding
    shields enclosing lions, dbl han-
    dled, four lion's mask, scroll feet,
    c1885 (A) **175.00**
  7¼" h, hp flowered vine on white
    body, marked **20.00**
  9" h, cov, painted panels of period
    lovers in garden, reserved on green
    ground, emb gilt husk festoons,
    raised sq bases, blue "scepter"
    mark, pr (A) **360.00**
  10" h, floral motif on pierced bodies,
    satyr hand handles, rose finials,
    19th C, blue "scepter" mark, pr (A) **200.00**
  18⅛" h, commemorative-inscribed to
    Carl Werner, reverse with painted

view of opera house and background, neck and dbl handles, gilt and burnished gold, sq base with donors' names, dated 1844, "scepter, orb, and KPM" marks (A) **3,960.00**

Vase, 8½", hp multicolored florals, celery green ground, $185.00.

18½" h, cov, blue ground, painted flowers in gilt reserves, shaped panels on shoulder and flared front, molded foliage on cov and front, loop handles with foliage terminals, c1860, blue "scepter and KPM" mark (A) **1,100.00**
25¼" h, cov, two panels of lovers in landscape scene, white ground, applied blue ribbon, rams head handles, pierced cov with floral knob, late 19th C, blue "scepter" mark, cov damaged **650.00**
26½" h, cov red lacquered body, chinoiserie figures in boats, divided by panels of flowering plants, shoulder with applied flowerheads, cockerel finial on cov with painted trailing flowers, baluster shape, c1720, blue "pseudo seal" mark (A) **750.00**

KING'S ROSE AND QUEEN'S ROSE

Staffordshire, England
c1820 to 1830

History: The King's Rose pattern, decorated on a soft paste body, is related closely to Gaudy Dutch in form as well as in the colors used in decoration. A large orange or red cabbage rose with green, yellow, and pink leaves surrounding it as accents forms the center of the design. Many plates also featured relief motifs.

The Queen's Rose pattern has a pink rose as the center with the accent colors in more delicate tones.

Cup and Saucer
  Handleless, scalloped rims, vine borders (A) **320.00**
  Pink broken borders (A) **55.00**
  Vine borders (A) **90.00**
Plate
  5½" d, pink border, unmarked **120.00**
  7" d, c1810 . . . . **150.00**
  7¼" d, "Oyster" pattern, pink border (A) **50.00**
  8" d, pink border (A) **70.00**
  8¼" d
    Brick red enameled rose, pink border, unmarked (A) **85.00**
    Brick red rose, sectional border, unmarked (A) **75.00**
  8⅜" d
    Brick red enameled rose, pink border, unmarked (A) **75.00**
    Pink rose, vine border, unmarked (A) **65.00**
  9⅞" d, pink rose, vine border, unmarked (A) **35.00**
Soup Plate, 7" d, pink border (A) **55.00**
Tea Service, teapot, four teabowls and saucers, imp "WOOD" mark **450.00**
Teabowl and Saucer
  Pink rose, vine borders, chips (A) . . . **45.00**
  Vine borders (A) **85.00**
  Vine borders, ribbed body, scalloped rim **240.00**

Plate, 6½" d, pink border, $40.00.

LEEDS

Yorkshire, England
c1757 to 1878

HARTLEY GREENS & CO.
LEEDS POTTERY

History: The original Leeds factory was located in Yorkshire and was founded by John and Joshua Green about 1757. Among its products were salt glaze, basalt, and stoneware, plus a very fine pearlware using a bluish glaze similar to that of Wedgwood. Figures, transfer wares, lusters, and mottled wares, similar to Whieldon's, also were produced.

Probably the most recognized Leeds product was yellow glazed creamware, first produced about 1760. This creamware was characterized by its soft yellow-cream color and the extensive use of perforations and open work, especially evident in the border treatments.

All types of utilitarian and decorative items were made in creamware from the simplest plate to elaborate, multisectioned fruit coolers and figural groups. The basic body often was augmented with painted and printed designs. Floral and fruit finials were a Leeds trademark.

The Green brothers had several different partners in their enterprises; shortly after forming the company, it traded as Humble, Greens & Co. Financial difficulties beset the Yorkshire pottery. After several additional owners and attempts at resurrection, the company failed and closed its doors in 1878. Only a small amount of Leeds wares bear factory marks.

References: Heather Lawrence, *Yorkshire Pots and Potteries*, David & Charles, 1947; Donald Towner, *The Leeds Pottery*, Cory, Adams & MacCay, 1963.

Museums: Everson Museum of Art, Syracuse, NY; Fitzwilliam Museum, Cambridge, England; Museum of Fine Arts, Boston, MA.

Asparagus Dishes, 5½", scrolled acanthus form, c1780, pr (A) **100.00**
Basket
  8½" h, creamware, twisted inter-
twined handles, ribbon base with open work on top half **2,900.00**
  9½" h, creamware, open lattice work design, applied grapes and vines, ring handles, early 18th C, pr **275.00**
Basket and Stand, creamware, basket 10⅜" l, stand 11⅛" l, molded basket-work centers, elongated pierced loop borders outlined in iron-red, plum and green highlights, oval, marked "Leeds Pottery" **950.00**
Basket on Stand, 8½" d, creamware, magenta intertwined handles, rust trim on edge, c1790 . . . . **950.00**
Bough Pot, 9" l, cov, "D" shaped body, three molded arched panels, silver resisted bird and prey in center panel, florals on side panels, iron-red enamel highlights, three knob feet, c1810-15 (A) **350.00**
Bowl, cov, 4¾" h, quatrefoil shape, emb base and reticulated lid, flower finial, imp "Leeds Pottery" (A) **160.00**
Cake Plate, 9" d, 4⅜" h, ftd, reticulated edge, imp "Leeds Pottery" (A) **65.00**
Candlestick, 9" h, silver luster, fluted columns, rams' heads below nozzles, sq bases with beadwork and gadrooning, c1900, imp "Leeds Pottery," pr (A) **250.00**
Charger
  12¼" d, blue feathered edge, unmarked (A) **200.00**
  15⅝" d, urn of flowers in five colors, blue feather edge (A) **400.00**
Compote 10" l, creamware, oval form, pierced decoration, scalloped edge, early 19th C **150.00**
Creamer
  4" h, cream ground, cobalt leaves, applied handle, c1810 . . . . **40.00**
  5½" h, floral design, multicolored, spout repaired (A) **300.00**
Creamer and Sugar, child's size, blue and yellow-ochre floral band, pearl finish, marked **285.00**

Left, plate, 9" d, c1820, $140.00; center, bowl, 4½" d, 3" h, blue florals and rim, $75.00; right, plate, 9½" d, multicolored mayfly in center, black outlined rim with blue fleur-de-lis, red flowerheads, c1800, $135.00.

Cup and Saucer, mustard-yellow strawberries, handleless (A) **210.00**
Cup Plate, 3¾" d, gaudy blue and white
floral design, unmarked (A) **235.00**
Dish
6¼" d, flower border, serrated edge,
imp "Leeds Pottery"(A) **25.00**
8" d, creamware, blue and white Oriental style building, three feet,
shell-molded, imp "Leeds Pottery"
(A) **130.00**
11 l, 8¾" w, enameled eagle and
shield in five colors, blue feather
edge (A) **400.00**
Figure, Horse, standing, Pearlware
Blue and yellow muzzle, tan body
with brown tail and mane, oblong
base with splashed green, blue and
ochre, 16" h, c1795 (A) **6,100.00**
Black sponging, black mane, tail, and
muzzle, green checkered saddlecloth, sponged green, black and
blue oblong base, 16" h, c1800,
repairs (A) **13,200.00**
Fruit Cooler, 12" h, creamware, circ
shape with domed lid and floral finial,
baluster form pedestal, late 18th C . **160.00**
Jug
5" h, creamware, landscape dec, baluster form, braided handle, floral
finial on lid, late 18thC **90.00**
6½" h, silver resisted stylized floral
and foliage design, baluster shape,
c1810 (A) **200.00**
6⅝" h, silver luster resisted with songbird, insect, and flowers, "JT" under spout, c1812-15 (A) **310.00**
7½" h, purple-pink luster resisted with
grapes, vines, and lozenges, inscribed "I. Ingle" under spout,
c1810-15 (A) **475.00**
7¾" h, purple pink lustered ground
resisted with blue and iron-red
grapes and leaves, olive green handle, c1810-15 (A) **500.00**
8" h, silver luster with Prussian double
eagle and sailboats, c1810 (A) ... **225.00**
Mug, 3½" h, resisted bird on branch and
flowers, silver luster ground, c1815
(A) **100.00**
Plate
7½" d, strawberry type decoration in
five colors, blue feather edge (A) . **300.00**
7⅝" d, black enameled "Mary Lees
Jackson" in center, silver resisted
grapevine border, c1810 (A) **195.00**
8⅜" d, multicolored floral design,
green feather edge, unmarked (A) **125.00**
8½" d, Gaudy blue
Floral design, blue feather edges, pr
(A) **320.00**

Blue and white floral design, blue
feather edge (A) **325.00**
9¼" d, saltglaze, gentleman playing
horn and lady playing lute in polychrome, scroll, basket and fretwork on rim touched with turquoise, yellow, and blue, painted
by Robinson & Rhodes **1,800.00**
9½" d, creamware
Octagonal, green draped vines in
border, single open flower in
brown and yellow in center,
c1800, unmarked **135.00**
Round, beaded and fluted bowls,
stylized foliate sprig pierced borders, c1790, pr **100.00**
9⅞" d, blue and white floral design,
blue feather edge (A) **100.00**
Platter
16" l, gaudy blue and white floral design, blue feather edge, unmarked
(A) **250.00**
18½" d, blue floral design, white
body, circular shape, strainer, late
18th C **350.00**
Puzzle Jug
6¾" h, silver luster pierced bodies,
tubes with three nozzles at necks,
c1915, pr (A) **250.00**
7" h, creamware, pierced petal pattern at neck, C-form handle, c1740 **400.00**
12" h, silver luster resisted with vines,
pierced body with multicolored
pinwheels, trumpet neck, loop han-
dle, wide foot, repaired, c1810 (A) **195.00**
Tea Service, teapot 7½" h, tea caddy,
two teabowls and saucers, green and
black vases of flowers, iron-red
ground, c1760 (A) **775.00**
Teapot, creamware, blue oriental
theme, floral bud finial, c1790 ..... **600.00**
Toddy Plate, 5½" d, multicolored peafowl in tree, green feather edge, unmarked (A) **265.00**
Tureen, 9" d, creamware, circular
shape, domed lid with flower finial,
early 19th C **150.00**
Vase
5" h, pink luster ground, reserved with
brown transfer butterflies, resisted
with multicolored enamel florals,
c1810-15, pr (A) **675.00**
6¼" h, yellowware body, purple-pink
luster reserved with stylized flowers
and leaves, c1810-15, pr (A) **715.00**
7⅜" h, flowerheads and foliage resisted on silver luster ground, sq
bases, c1810-15, pr (A) **200.00**
7½" h, pink luster ground resisted
with vines, iron-red rim and outlined sq base, c1810-15 (A) **100.00**

J. Granger & Cie

LIMOGES

Limousin region of France
c1770 to Present

History: Limoges first hard paste porcelain dates from about 1770 and is attributed to the company of Massie, Grellet, and Fourneira. Permission was granted to make porcelain by the Council of the Court. The company came under the patronage of Comte d'Artois, brother-in-law of King Louis XVI, in 1777. Since the company was financed and supported by the court, the products were marked with the initials "C.D."

Due to financial and technical problems, the company was sold to the King in 1784. He used the factory as a branch of Sevres. Whitewares were made at Limoges and sent to Sevres for decoration.

Grellet served as manager from 1784 until 1788. J. Francoise Alluaud followed as manager and remained until 1794. About 1794 the factory was sold to Joubert, Cacate, and Joly, three of the workers.

At the end of the French Revolution, circa 1796, the progress of porcelain making continued at Limoges with the addition of many new factories. Alluaud, Baignol, and Monnerie were among those establishing their own factories during the 1790s.

Additional factories developed between 1800 and 1830, among which were two factories begun in 1825 at Saint-Leonard, the Recollet factory, which continued in production until 1963, and the Pont de Noblat factory, still in production. These factories responded to the growing demands of a large export market for Limoges porcelains, with America as the largest customer. The mid to late nineteenth century was the golden age for Limoges porcelain.

David Haviland also established himself in Limoges during the 1850s. Many of the other factories imitated his techniques. Limoges porcelain is usually more bold than Haviland.

With the tremendous amount of porcelain produced, the market could not absorb all the wares. After World War I and the economic crisis of the 1920s and 1930s, many older companies were forced out of business. There was some revitalization after World War II. Today Limoges still is the center of hard paste porcelain production in France.

A wide range of objects were made with vivid decoration of florals, fruit, figural, and scenic themes that were embellished with gold. Decorative pieces included vases, large plaques, trays, tankards, mugs, bowls, plates, paintings, and jardinieres.

Smaller accessory pieces such as dresser sets, trinket boxes, cache pots, candle holders, baskets, and inkwells added variety. In addition, a whole range of dinnerware sets, compotes, coffee, tea, and chocolate sets, and fish and game services bore the Limoges mark.

Early Limoges porcelain whiteware blanks were sent to Paris for decoration over the glaze. Decoration under the glaze did not begin in Limoges until the late 1800s. Transfer decoration was used mostly on tablewares. Hand painting usually appeared on accessory art pieces and decorative porcelain pieces. Mixed decoration, where the transfer outline was filled in or trimmed with hand painting, was used primarily on tablewares. The decoration is found in both over and under the glaze styles.

Floral decor is most prominent on Limoges porcelain. Fruit themes of berries, cherries, and grapes are next. Oyster, fish, and game sets contain birds and marine life subjects. Figurals of either allegorical subjects or portraits were also used, but in a more limited context.

Most of the Limoges colors are deep and vivid. The lavish gold embellishments have a rich patina.

References: Mary Frank Gaston, *The Collector's Encyclopedia of Limoges Porcelain*, Collector Books, 1980.

Museums: Limoges Museum, Limoges, France; Musee National Adrien Dubouche, Limoges, France; Sevres Museum, Sevres, France.

Additional Listing: Haviland.

Collecting Hints: Limoges porcelains are still in production. Marks aid the collector in determining the age of a piece of Limoges.

The quality of the craftsmanship and decoration on the older pieces are superior to the new examples. Less gold decoration is used on newer pieces

The newer marks usually are found over the glaze. Many pieces have factory whiteware marks in addition to marks to indicate whether the piece was decorated at the factory or at another decorating studio.

Asparagus Set, platter with insert, gravy boat with underplate and six plates, 7" d, asparagus design in mauve tones, "L. D. & C." **450.00**

Basket, 4½" l, 3½" h, small violets on mint green ground, "T & V, Limoges" **95.00**

Berry Set, bowl 9½" d and 3" h on three scroll feet, eight serving bowls, purple berries on ext., white blossoms on int., sgd "L. Moore," "T & V, Limoges" **240.00**

Biscuit Barrel, 7" h, ivory colored ground with peacock feathers, bamboo motif handle, "T & V, Limoges" **125.00**

Bowl
   6¾" d, 3" h, pastel floral center design, blue scroll trim, three feet, sgd "T. Burroughs" **45.00**
   7¾" d, 3⅛" h, daisies on yellow-white ground **65.00**
   8¾" d, large pink, purple, and yellow asters and leaves on dark green to cream ground, gold rim and feet, "Guerin, Limoges" **70.00**
   10" d, light pink wild roses and blue leaves on int. and ext., irreg gold edge **45.00**
   10" d, 7½" h, hp pink and white flowers, gold scalloped top and pedestal base edge **65.00**
   Blood–red enamel surface, late 1800's, sgd "Fauvre" **750.00**

Box
   5" d, pale blue ground, Cupid leaning on branch of blue flowers and green leaves, gold trim, round shape **90.00**
   8" d, 4½" h, dome cov with two girls in classic dress in landscape, gilt tracery, turquoise body with gilt, "A. K. France" **350.00**

Butter Dish, cov, 7½" d
   Gold thistle, green leaves, cream vellum ground **65.00**
   White, gold trim **35.00**

Butter Pat, white, gold band **5.00**

Cache Pot
   12½" h, fox chasing rabbit in forest setting, sgd "A. Heidrich," "Guerin" **375.00**
   12¾" h, one fox hunt scene, other with lion stalking deer in landscape scene, gold bun feet and handles, oval shape, sgd "A. Heidrich," marked "W. G. & Co.," pr **1,650.00**

Cake Set, cake plate and eight cups and saucers, plate with open reticulated border, overall gold finish on all pieces, c1900 .... **325.00**

Candy Dish, blue floral design, three feet **30.00**

Charger
   12½" d
      Horse and dog multicolored center, gold scrolled edge, sgd "Baumy," marked "Limoges-France" **395.00**
      Nude woman center portrait, gold rococo border, pierced for hanging, sgd "Dubois" **155.00**
   13¼" d, portrait center of girl in costume, lavender and blue colors, molded edge, sgd "R. Comby" .. **225.00**
   13½" d, Indian girl portrait in center, brown, green, and blue, scrolled gold, border, ruffled edge, sgd "Dubois," marked "Limoges-France" . **450.00**
   15¾" d, multicolored "Virgin of the Donors" by Van Dyke, gilded scrolled rim, c1900 (A) **275.00**
   16" d, scene of deer at sunrise in forest **200.00**

Chocolate Pot, peach blossoms on branches, gold trim, floral finial **125.00**

Chocolate Set, tray 19½ x 15½", pot 10½" h, six cups and saucers, pink roses and white florals, green leaves, white ground, poppies and scrolls in relief with gold trim, scalloped footings, dated 1906, marked "J. P. L. wreath" **445.00**

Cider Set, pot and four cups, hp cherries, green ground **180.00**

Cookie Jar, 7½" h, cream to pale brown body, gold decoration with three blue and gilt flower sprays on upper portion and cov **80.00**

Cracker Jar
   8" h, 7½" d underplate, hp pink and white flowers, off white ground, raised scrolls, gold figural scroll handle, dated 1894, "GDM/CFH" **200.00**
   Cream ground, vines, blue and pink flowers, gold stippling, finial of three bamboo sprigs joined to-

Demitasse Cup and Saucer, yellow and white florals, gold trim and handle, $30.00.

gether in gold, c1890, "T & V, Lim-
oges" **125.00**
Pink ground, and large pink and white
flowers, green leaves, gold trim,
twig finial, "T & V, Limoges" **75.00**
Creamer and Sugar
Gold Ferns, pale blue ground, c1888,
"T & V, Limoges" **35.00**
Handled basket shaker 4" l x 5" h,
creamer with hp purple flowers and
raised gold scrolls, scalloped
edges, "T & V, Limoges" **125.00**
Cup and Saucer
Gold band, white ground, "Guerin,
Limoges" **15.00**
Rose and forget-me-not garlands, pink
and yellow, gold scrolling and gold
monogram on int., c1895, "J. P. L.
Limoges" **40.00**
Roses, dark pink and white, gold trim,
"T & V, Limoges" **15.00**
Demitasse Cup and Saucer
Couple, period, seated, gold enamel
and trim, blown-out base **40.00**
Flowers, small pink, gold trim Elite,
Limoges **15.00**
Game birds in flight, multicolored .. **15.00**
Dessert Plate, 8½" d, polychrome center
floral spray, royal blue and gold floral
rims, shaped edges, late 19th C, set
of 6 (A) **150.00**
Dinner Service, "Saint-Saens" pattern,
blue on white foliate motifs, molded
basketweave borders, set of 88 (A) .. **400.00**
Dish
10½" d, yellow roses, pale blue
ground, scalloped edge, gold figural floral handle, oval **40.00**
12", sq, applied gold flowers, pink
shaded border, three sections, center handle **135.00**
Dresser Set
Hair receiver, pin tray, hatpin holder,
ring holder, and dresser tray, violets, blue ground, white beading,
"GDA, Limoges" **165.00**
Hatpin holder, powder jar, heart
shape pin tray, tray 10 x 8½", gol-
denrod, light blue ground, gold
borders **200.00**
Dresser Tray
10" l, cream center, blue flower
bunches on border, gold trim **25.00**
11½" l, geometric Art Deco design,
gold and black, cream ground,
"GDA Limoges" **35.00**
12" l, pink roses, yellow centers,
brown and green leaves **75.00**
Egg Cup, floral dec
2½", multicolored florals, "Limoges,
France" (A) **10.00**

Blue florals, light green ground, gold
trim **40.00**
Pink florals, gold enamel, light blue
ground **40.00**
Fish Set, oval platter and plates
Eleven 8¼" plates, platter 23½" l,
sauce, and underplate, reserve of
fish in water, floral and gilt trimmed
borders (A) **150.00**
Twelve plates, multicolored fish
scenes **575.00**
Twelve 8½" plates, platter 24" l, tray
10½ x 6½", hp fish in shells and
seaweed, pastel tones, gold bor-
ders, double gold handles **1,025.00**
Twelve 9¼" plates, sauce, platter
22½" l, scene of two fish in water,
olive tones, gilt scroll borders, sgd
"Brunet" (A) **300.00**
Fish Platter, 20¾" l, pink and white poppies, light blue ground, pink and blue
scrolled border, gold rococo edge,
dated 1897, "Theodore Haviland" . **125.00**
Hair Receiver, small blue flowers and
butterflies, off-white ground, gold
trim, "J. P. Limoges" **65.00**
Ice Cream Set, tray 15¾ x 10", twelve
7" d plates, daisies, yellow-white
ground **155.00**
Liquor Set, decanter, 9" h, four cordials
2¾" h, red and orange poppies, light
blue to white ground, gold handles
and rims, "Kittle & Klingenberg" ... **70.00**
Mug
5" h, monk scene, multicolored, "J.
P. L." **35.00**
5¼" h, monk reading fashion pages,
red ground, "Pouyat" **80.00**
5½" h, rust, gold band and fruit, sgd
"G. Moser" **35.00**
6" h, brown and white terrior, brown
to yellow ground, "Guerin" **85.00**
Oyster Plate, 8½" d, pink roses, green
leaves, and blue ribbons, white
ground, scalloped rim **50.00**
Painting on Porcelain, 11 x 14¼", black
curly haired woman in profile, hands
folded across chest, c1900 (A) **500.00**
Pancake Dish, cov, pink poppies and
blue cornflowers, gold trim, bow handle, "CFH/GDA" **60.00**
Plaque, 10½ x 11", multicolored scene
of Napoleon in battle, scalloped
edge, gold border **375.00**
Plate
6" d
Cherubs in colors with gold trim,
scalloped edge **30.00**
White, lacy gold borders, "T & V,
Limoges," set of 6 .... **25.00**
6⅜" d, blue borders, gold rims, "Vig-
naud, Limoges," set of 6 .... **25.00**

6½" d, holly berries and leaves, white centers, gold trim, scalloped edges, "T & V," set of 6 .... **150.00**

7" d, multicolored center of man and woman in period clothes, gold and maroon border, sgd "Fragonard" on front **15.00**

7¼" d, hp roses with raised uneven gold edge **20.00**

7½" d

Floral design, gold scalloped edge, "A. K. Limoges" **10.00**

Friar Tuck designs, one eating, and one drinking from stein, multicolored, pr **15.00**

8" d, fish scene, fern, gray-green scalloped edge **50.00**

8½" d

Raised gold shaggy chrysanthemums, leaves around border, "T & V, Limoges" **45.00**

Yellow roses all over, scalloped border, "Old Abbey" **45.00**

Yellow rose medallions, pink roses, blue border **10.00**

8¾" d, green ground, lilies of the valley, gold edge, "Coronet, Limoges" **35.00**

8⅞" d, pale green ground, lavender water lily, green leaves, "Old Abbey" **25.00**

9" d, two large fish, water lilies and grasses, gold rococo border, sgd "T. Golse" **70.00**

9½" d, hp peaches in center, scalloped edge **30.00**

9⅝" d, painted scene of bearded composer, cobalt border, three panels of flowers, gold musical notes, sgd "Fehl" **200.00**

9¾" d

Dbl gold borders, copper rings, "C. Ahrenfeldt, Limoges," set of 12 **225.00**

Gilt and pink floral border, "C. Ahrenfeldt," set of 12 .... **185.00**

Portrait of cavalier, multicolored, gold rococo border, "Coronet, Limoges" **45.00**

10" d

Different species of orchid in center, multicolored, species name on reverse in black, heavy gold trimmed borders, artist sgd, "Limoges," set of 12 ....**1,500.00**

Man playing guitar, multicolored, "Coronet, Limoges" **100.00**

Roses in basket, hp, multicolored, "Martin, Limoges" **35.00**

Two large baskets of roses, multicolored, wreaths, "Martin, Limoges" **30.00**

10½" d, wide scroll, urn molded gold band (A) **10.00**

11" d

Geometric design of four wild animals, head of child in center, "This is the Hour of Pride & Power" on border, brown and gray on cream ground, "Wm Guerin & Co., Limoges, France" **50.00**

Polychrome floral wreath centers, cobalt and gilt borders, scalloped rims, set of 12 (A) **450.00**

Scenes of children at lake, painted to ruffled edge, sq shapes, sgd "F. Villetelle," pr **950.00**

Oyster Plate, 10½" d, multicolored florals, white ground, gold trim, "G. D. & Co.," $70.00.

11⅛" d

Center scene of period man on horse, woman in garden, yellow border, sq scalloped edge, pierced for hanging, unmarked . **75.00**

Winter scene, woman with basket walking across snowy landscape, windmill and trees, irreg edges, pr **250.00**

12" d

Grapes, peaches, and strawberries with jug, scalloped gold border, pierced for hanging, sgd "C. Fernand" **200.00**

Two multicolored hummingbirds, gold rococo edge **140.00**

12½" d

Peaches, grapes, and flowers, purple, gold, and green ground, gold rococo border, pierced for hanging, sgd "Golse," "green crown & L.R.L., Limoges" **225.00**

Strawberries, blossoms, and leaves, multicolored pastel ground, scalloped rim, "J. P. L." **65.00**

13½" d

Pink and rose flowers, pastel ground, gold wavy edge, pierced for hanging **250.00**

Pink roses, pastel ground, irreg border outlined in gold, pierced for hanging 250.00

13¾" d, scenes of lovers in garden, gold scalloped borders, pierced for hanging, pr 550.00

14⅛" d, scene of cottage by pond, winter and summer, heavy gold scalloped borders, pierced for hanging, pr, unmarked 500.00

Platter

15" l, "The Narbonne" design 40.00

16¾" l, 10¾" w, small pink flowers in center and border, scalloped rim, "Elite" 30.00

Punch Bowl

14" d, hp, clusters of grapes int. and ext., wavy border, gold foot 650.00

14½" d, clusters of grapes and leaves int and ext., four gold feet 950.00

Ramekins and Underplates, hp

Green floral borders, gold brushed edges, "CFH/GDM," set of 6 .... 65.00

Small roses, gold rims, "T & V, Limoges," set of 12 .... 185.00

Ring Tree, multicolored blossoms, white ground, "T & V, Limoges" 40.00

Tankard

10" h, large pink and red roses, tinted ground, green dragon handle, scalloped gold rim, "Pouyat, Limoges" 210.00

11" h, hp

Currents and foliage design, dated 1908, "J P Limoges" 130.00

Purple grapes design, "T & V, Limoges" 215.00

13" h, red cherries, purple ground, "D. & C., France" 225.00

13½" h, hp portrait of cavalier, sgd "Baumy," "B. & H. Limoges" 450.00

14" h, silver leaves and grapes, pink accents, black ground, c1909 .... 190.00

15" h, multicolored floral dec, "J. P. L. Limoges" 215.00

15½" h, grape clusters, pastel ground, serpent handle, "J. P. L., Limoges" 150.00

16" h, three color grapes, emb gold grape leaves along base, grapevine and leaf entwined gold handle, "T & V, Limoges" 265.00

Tankard Set, 14" h, four matching cups, grapes, gold and green ground 300.00

Tea Set, teapot, creamer, and sugar, dogwood pattern, gold wishbone handles, "J. P. L." 180.00

Teapot, large pink, yellow, and white chrysanthemums, white ground, gold trim 50.00

Tray

8" l, violets, white ground 25.00

12" d, magenta, pink, and yellow roses, rust, black and yellow

ground, gold dragons on edge, scalloped rim, sgd "Rousset," "T & V, Limoges" 150.00

12" l, 9½" w, yellow, lilac and light brown pansies, dark brown ground shading to yellow and light green, scalloped rim, oval 35.00

16" H-H, hp, grape and leaf design, scrolls along border, open center . 450.00

18" l, 12" w, roses and leaves, pink and white ground, Art Nouveau style, dbl handles, dated 1896, "T & V, Limoges" 60.00

Vase

10¼" h, hp, scene of woman with cherubs, gold lip, base, and dbl handles, c1905 .... 135.00

11" h, hp, dogwood and bluebell flowers, gold trim, ewer shape ... 100.00

11" h, 12½" w, cameos of flowers, beige ground, gold argyl dbl handles 250.00

12½" h, floral dec, green and gold border, dbl handles 235.00

13" h, multicolored florals, green and gold base, twisted dbl handles ... 225.00

15½" h

Blue and red hp flowers, green ground, c1895, "Wm Guerin" . 500.00

Lavender wisteria, gold trim and handles, "T & V, Limoges" 320.00

Red hp poppies, green leaves, wide gold border, sgd "Graham," "T & V, Limoges" 250.00

Vegetable Bowl, cov, 8" d, pink roses, green leaves on white, gold double handles and knob 35.00

Vegetable Dish

8" d, cov, roses, gold handles and knob, "W. G. & Co., Limoges, France" 40.00

12½ x 9", white ground, flowers, gold on ext., white drain, "T & V, Limoges" 85.00

LIVERPOOL

City and port of Liverpool, England c1754 to 1840

History: During the 18th century, a group of potteries in Liverpool were producing mostly tin-glazed Delft-type wares and some porcelains.

Utilitarian wares usually were made without distinguishing factory marks. Among the Liverpool potteries were:

Richard Chaffers & Co., c1754–65, made soapstone-type porcelain. Chaffers' blue and white and enameled pieces featured Oriental designs.

Samuel Gilbody, c1754–61, took over his father's earthenware pottery and switched production to enameled porcelains.

William Ball, c1755–69, used a soapstone body with a glossy glaze that gave a wet appearance to his Chinese designs in underglaze blue.

Willaim Reid & Co., c1755–61, also used underglaze blue Oriental motifs on an almost opaque body.

Philip Christian & Co., c1765–76, took over Chaffers' factory and made soapstone-type porcelains, mostly with underglaze blue designs.

Pennington & Part, c1770–99, produced lesser quality wares decorated with underglaze blue prints. Their enameled pieces exhibited simple decorations.

Thomas Wolfe & Co., c1795–1800, made hard paste porcelains.

The **Herculaneum-Liverpool factory at Liverpool**, c1796–1840, was established by Samuel Worthington. Most of the workers were brought from the Staffordshire Potteries. At first only earthenwares and stonewares were made. "Herculaneum Pottery" was the name of the factory. Some pieces were marked with an impressed "Herculaneum." About 1800 porcelains were introduced. Some Empire-style vases were manufactured, but the principal production focused on teawares. Extremely large jugs were a specialty.

References: Dr. Knowles Boney, *Liverpool Porcelain of the 18th Century and its Makers*, B.T. Batsford, 1957; H. Boswell Lancaster, *Liverpool and Her Potters*, W.B. James & Co., 1936; Alan Smith, *The Illustrated Guide to Liverpool Herculaneum Pottery 1796–1840*, Barrie & Jenkins, 1970; B. Watney, *English Blue and White Porcelain of the 18th Century*, Faber & Faber, 1936.

Museums: City of Liverpool Museum, Liverpool, England; Potsdam Public Museum, Potsdam, N.Y.

Basket, emb flowers, basketweave ground, open lattice rim, "Herculaneum Pottery" **185.00**
Bowl
  6½" d, blue painted ext., Oriental buildings and large boulders, c1760 .... **200.00**
  7½" d
    Painted famille rose enamel, Chinese style flowers, c1775 (A) **150.00**
    Transfer, blue, two vignettes of

three Indians with axes, swords, and ships, separated by two Orientals holding birds, washed loop border int., c1775, Christian (A) **170.00**
9⅜" d, pearlware, blue dragon chasing flaming pearls, c1770 (A) **125.00**
9⅝" d
  Panels of multicolored fruit and flowers reserved on dark blue and gilt ground, sliced fruit and flowers int., Pennington (A) **145.00**
  Transfer blue figures near ruins and river, ext. with flower sprays and bouquets, cracked, c1785, Pennington **100.00**
12" d, Delft, bird on foliage in blue on ext. flowers in band of stylized flowerheads int., yellow rim, c1740, unmarked (A) **245.00**
Coffeepot, 10" h, famille rose enamels of flower sprays, cell diaper borders, c1775, Christian (A) **200.00**
Cream Jug
  3⅛" h, blue painted seated Oriental near fence and shrubs, int. with diaper rim border, blue tinted glaze, pear shape, sparrow beak spout, c1770 (A) **210.00**
  4" h, painted flower sprays and sprigs, sparrow beak spout with tongue, c1770, Pennington (A) **440.00**
  4¾" l, molded scalework reserved with cartouches of blue painted "Cannonball" pattern, c1775, Christian (A) **160.00**
  5¼" h, painted polychrome sprigs, sparrow beak spout, c1775 (A) ... **150.00**
Creamboat
  4" h, "Dolphin Ewer," dark blue floral sprays, handle restored (A) **45.00**
  4¾" h, painted blue and iron-red Oriental scenes in molded scroll borders, c1765 (A) **45.00**
  5½" l, molded arcaded, enameled exotic birds and foliage, c1775–80, Christian (A) **365.00**
Cup, incised flowers, painted flowering branch, c1780, Pennington (A) **50.00**
Cup & Saucer
  Floral sprays in scalloped band border, c1770, Christian **180.00**
  Imari butterflies and branches with indented rim, c1760, Wm Ball (A) . **500.00**
Dish
  11" l
    Blue printed water scene of fisherman, nets and lighthouse, imp "Herculaneum 10" **70.00**
    Multicolored printed "French Scenery" pattern, imp "Liver Bird," Herculaneum **20.00**

Dish, 5" w, blue and white, three spur feet, c1765, $450.00.

11¾", famille rose exotic bird on rock, florals and trees, rect, clipped corners, Pennington (A) **615.00**

11⅞" d, Delft, blue painted center scene of "The Taking of Portobello," border of suspended leaves and grapes, ochre rim, reverse with pennants, c1741 (A) **1,725.00**

13" d, Delft, blue Oriental scene of pagodas on islands, stylized floral border, brown rim, c1765, unmarked (A) **550.00**

13½" d, Delft, iron-red, green, and blue birds, insects, pagoda, and flowering plants, c1740, riveted (A) **185.00**

13⅝" d, Delft, polychrome bird on rockwork, plants on terrace, c1740 (A) **160.00**

Figure, 10" h, female, floral robe belted with Zodiac signs, holding sickle and wheat, fruit on base, multicolored, c1773, Champion (A) **500.00**

Flower Pots, 4¾" h, matching stands, painted band of garden flowers on yellow ground between bands of gilt foliage, gilt line rims and beast mask handles, Herculaneum, pr (A) **860.00**

Jug

5¾" h

Black transfer of "Telling Fortune in Coffee Grounds," country dancers on reverse (A) **125.00**

Cov, painted floral sprigs, dark blue, crow's foot border, pear shape, sparrow beak spout, Pennington, pr (A) **100.00**

7" h, "Bidston Hill," creamware, printed, painted view of Bidston Hill, list of flags, black transfer of "Thoughts of Matrimony" on reverse, c1793 (A) **660.00**

7¼" h, creamware

Black bat printed portrait of Nelson, putti, and map of Battle of Nile,

Neptune and inscription on reverse (A) **370.00**

Black transfer of soldier slaying lion, inscribed banner, American ship on reverse, enameled accents, strap handle, c1800 .... **700.00**

8½" h, creamware, black transfer of allegorical inscribed emblem, ship on reverse, strap handle, c1800 .. **500.00**

9" h, black transfer of Britannia viewing plans of Washington, Great Seal, and frigate (A) **350.00**

10" h, black transfer, enamels of "Jack Spritsail Coming on Shore," ship on reverse, "Apollo the God of Music" under spout, unmarked (A) **200.00**

11¾" h, black transfer of Washington's tomb surrounded by symbols of sainthood, encircled by thirteen states, ship, and flag on reverse, eagle under spout, polychrome accents, unmarked (A) **350.00**

Meat Dish, 20⅞" d, earthenware, blue printed panels of Oriental landscapes, florals and cell diaper ground, imp "Herculaneum 3" **95.00**

Milk Jug

4½" h, blue transfer of cow herd and shepherd, c1775 .... **100.00**

5" h, painted floral wreath and insects, iron-red, gilt, and blue, c1775 .... **100.00**

Miniature Teabowl and Saucer, blue painted birds over wooded island, c1762 (A) **830.00**

Mug, 2⅜" h, famille rose flowering branches, int. with two butterflies, yellow border, c1762 (A) **600.00**

Pitcher

4" h, black transfer commemorating Gen Lafayette (A) **350.00**

8" h, black transfer of "Commodore Bainbridge" and "Victory achieved," cracked, unmarked (A) **600.00**

Plate

8" d, painted blue flowering plants from rockwork on terrace, blue trellis bands on rims, c1770, pr (A) .. **265.00**

8⅝" d

Delft, cobalt painted and penciled scene of two Orientals in garden, cavetto, trellis, and florals, border of three flower sprays, inscription on reverse (A) **350.00**

Earthenware white, painted dog roses on puce ground on rim, Herculaneum **20.00**

8¾" d

Delft, painted cockerels in garden, c1760 (A) **100.00**

Delft, polychrome Oriental style flowers, inscribed on reverse, re-

paired and riveted. c1752, pr (A) **370.00**
8⁷⁄₈" d
Delft, blue painted coat of arms,
c1750 (A) **365.00**
Delft, polychrome basket of flowers, c1760 (A) **120.00**
9" d
Delft, cobalt boy chasing butterfly
in garden, c1750 (A) **90.00**
Delft, polychrome bouquet and
sprays in barbedwire border,
chipped, c1760-70 (A) **60.00**
9¼" d
Delft, cobalt jardiniere, Oriental
flowers, c1750 (A) **65.00**
Delft, cobalt peony and artimesia
in jardiniere, rim with precious
objects and florals, mid 18th c
(A) **100.00**
9½" d, Delft, enamel painted,
"Chinese Export" famille rose style,
garden and birds in tree, basket of
flowers, diaper inner border,
shaped rim, c1760-70 (A) **660.00**
10" d, blue printed farm animals in
landscape, imp "crown," Herculaneum **35.00**
10⅛" d, Delft, blue painted and penciled scene of rural lovers, dog near
brick wall, Chinese style border of
trellis scroll panels, mid 18th c, pr **550.00**
11" d, Delft, cobalt vase of flowers
and scattered flowers from pierced
rockwork, cell diaper cavetto, insects and flowers on rim, c1750 (A) **50.00**
12"d, Delft, blue painted Oriental
style river landscape, flower spray
border, c1750 (A) **90.00**
Sauceboat
3½" w, shell-molded sides, multicolored flower sprays, iron-red int.
rim, fish tail handle, c1760 (A) ... **275.00**
5¾" l, shell-molded, blue and white
flower sprays, dolphin handle,
c1775 (A) **150.00**
6" l, blue painted, molded ribbed
ground, foliate scrolls enclosing vignettes of Oriental style gardens, int.
stylized flowers, c1770, Christian
(A) **265.00**
7" l, blue painted Oriental garden
scenes in molded foliate scrolls,
lobed body, gadrooned foot,
c1775-80 .... **275.00**
7½" l, blue and white floral sprigs
reserved in rococo cartouches, basketweave ground, hair crack,
c1760 .... **180.00**
7¾" l, molded foliate scrolls and flowers, enameled Oriental style birds,
gilt and red border, int. stylized
flowers, damaged, c1770 .... **225.00**

Soup Plate
8" d, blue painted Oriental riverscape, two figures on bridge, pavilions and trees, diaper borders, octagonal (A) **470.00**
9⅞" d, black transfer of coat of arms,
"Let Wisdom Unite Us," black
enameled rim, unmarked (A) **80.00**
Tea Caddy, 5½" h, creamware, printed
black tea party, shepherd and flock on
sides, knob finial, c1765 .... **175.00**

**Teabowl and Saucer, multicolored,
c1768–75, Pennington, $675.00.**

Teabowl and Saucer
Black transfer, enamel of the "The
Shepherd," "The Tea Party" and
"La Cascade," c1765-70 (A) **185.00**
Blue and white scene of Oriental
woman seated on rock holding
flowers to jumping boy, saucer repaired, c1762 (A) **235.00**
Painted floral spray in thin, red line
border, Christian (A) **100.00**
Printed and painted Oriental scene,
Herculaneum **20.00**
Underglaze blue "Liver Bird" pattern
bird perched on flowering branch,
diaper border, Christian (A) **115.00**
Teapot
5" h, "Japan" pattern, enameled and
gilt man on diaper, panels of peony
and prunus, c1770 (A) **800.00**
5⅛"h, printed flowers and insects in
painted loop border, Pennington . **70.00**
6⅛" h, painted famille rose rockwork,
flowers, and birds, Christian (A) .. **60.00**
6¼" h, painted floral bouquets under
iron-red dbl line scroll pattern rim,
c1770 (A) **260.00**
6⅜" h, painted, Chinese man holding
flower, another seated with pipe,
red loop and dot border, Pennington (A) **180.00**
6½" h
Painted, multicolored, Chinese

couple and child near table on sides, iron-red scallop and dot borders, c1770-75, Christian (A) **500.00**
Polychrome bouquets of flowers, c1760-70 (A) **470.00**
7" h, famille rose palette of Orientals on terrace in molded scroll, flower cartouches, pleated ground painted with Oriental flowers, iron-red scrolls and flowerheads, body riveted, c1770 .... **125.00**
10¼" h, blue transfer of "Fisherman" pattern, rims with cell diaper, scallop and dot borders, c1780, Pennington (A) **170.00**

Vase
6⅛" h, painted bouquets, scattered flowers, c1765, Philip Christian's Factory (A) **245.00**
14½" h, Delft, painted Oriental chrysanthemums and magnolia branches, rockwork, butterfly on reverse, c1750 (A) **1,870.00**

Wall Pocket
7¾" l, cornucopia form, flower-molded flaired top, crackled ground, ribbing and flowers accented in shades of blue, white ground, c1760, unmarked **750.00**
8½" l, Delft, polychrome bird on branch with shell and flower motif at rim, c1760, unmarked **200.00**

Waste Bowl, 4¾" d, blue, iron-red, and gilt Oriental style flowering plants, and fencing (A) **65.00**

LLADRO

HAND MADE IN SPAIN

LLADRO

Almacera, Spain
1951 to Present

History: The Lladro brothers, Juan, Jose, and Vicente, started their small studio in 1951 in Almacera, Spain, They built their own kiln and began making small flowers for decorative lamps. All three brothers shaped the porcelains. Only Juan and Jose decorated them, Vicente supervised the firing.

As their business expanded, they formed Lladro Porcelanas in 1958 and produced their first porcelain figurine of a ballet dancer. Their distinctive style emphasizes the elongated look in porcelain sculpture. The figurines are hand painted in a variety of pastel colors.

Salvador Furio is one of the most senior and prolific sculptors at Lladro. His "Clown with Concertina" was the first figurine he designed for Lladro. Furio has become the Lladro sculptor specializing in particular thematic subjects such as historic characters, figures of literature, and personalities in public life.

Today the Lladro complex is located in Valencia, Spain and is known as "Porcelain City."

Musuems: Lladro Museum, New York, N.Y.

Collectors' Club: Lladro Collectors Society, P.O. Box 1122, 43 West 57th Street, New York, N.Y. 10101-1122. *Expressions* magazine. Membership: $25.00.

Figure, 4½" l, natural pastel colors, $105.00.

Figure
3½" l, reclining angel (A) **45.00**
5" h, girl, basket of vegetables (A) .. **90.00**
6" h,
    Angel, standing **40.00**
    Boy, and lamb **60.00**
    Pekingese dog **75.00**
6½" h, girl holding basket of oranges (A) **45.00**
7¼" h, two gray birds, long tails ... **60.00**
7½" h
    Little boy, puppy (A) **120.00**
    Girl smelling flowers (A) **200.00**
8" h, girl and boy on teeter totter, repaired (A) **30.00**
8½" h
    Girl, pups, multicolored (A) **120.00**
    Nativity figure, bisque finish (A) .. **10.00**
9" h, farm girl, ducks (A) **100.00**
9½" h
    Girl, kittens (A) **60.00**
    Two children, multicolored (A) ... **45.00**
10" h
    Boy, seated, dressed as harlequin holding cat, bisque finish (A) .. **140.00**
    Cobbler at work (A) **65.00**
    Girl, goats (A) **70.00**
10½" h, shepherd boy, "Lladro, Handmade in Spain" (A) **65.00**

11" h, "The Golfer" (A) 100.00
11½" h, "Geisha Girl," (A) 80.00
12" h
  Female tennis player 100.00
  Hamlet, and Yorick's skull 250.00
  Maiden, arm full of wheat (A) 25.00
  Mother and child (A) 195.00
12½" h, seated woman holding book
  in polychrome (A) 150.00
13½" h
  Ballerina 155.00
  "The Doctor" 95.00
16" h
  "Desnudo," bisque finish, #4511 100.00
  Hamlet, multicolored 600.00
17" h, Othello & Desdemona (A) ... 360.00
18½"h, 18" l, group, lady emerging
  from sedan chair, attendant standing by, limited edition, sgd "J.
  Ruiz" (A) 925.00
20" h, Bali dancers 190.00

LONGTON HALL   1749-55

Staffordshire Potteries, England
c1750 to 1760

History: Longton Hall existed for the ten year period between 1750 and 1760. There were several different partnerships during the factory's short production period.

Longton Hall porcelains featured an underglaze blue design in the Oriental style. Some pieces exhibited a streaky blue glaze. Most wares were thickly potted and finished in a crude fashion. Some leaf shaped tablewares were produced.

Most Longton Hall soft paste porcelain was unmarked. Although production was brief, the amount of production was large. Many examples survived to attract the attention of today's collector.

References: B. Watney, *Longton Hall Porcelain*, Faber & Faber, 1957.

Museums: Walters Art Gallery, Baltimore, Maryland.

Bowl 4½" d, painted flowering shrubs
  from rockwork in green, yellow, and
  puce, c1755 .... 350.00
Box, 4¾" w, cov, molded mauve grapes
  and green vine leaves, leaf finial,
  c1755 (A) 11,500.00

Candlestick
  8¼" h, Spring, modeled as boy emp-
  tying basket of flowers into girl's
  apron, dog at base, Autumn, modeled as old man and girl filling baskets with grapes, goat at feet, multicolored, rococo bases with
  scrolling stems, c1756, pr (A) ...2,587.00
  11¾" h, modeled Ceres wearing flowered robe holding corn, putto at
  side, foliage molded nozzle, scrolling support, c1753-54 .... 390.00
Coffee Cup
  Molded, painted overlapping yellow
  and pink striped tulip petals, green
  twig handle, cracked, c1755 ..... 145.00
  Painted, blue, Oriental figure with
  large vase holding trailing flowering
  branch, reverse with flower spray,
  split twig handle, c1755 .... 450.00
Cup and Saucer, painted flying exotic
  birds over river island, fluted, cracks,
  c1755 (A) 790.00
Dish
  6⅝" d, molded peony shape, pink
  and yellow, molded leaves, stem
  handles, c1753, pr (A) 4,147.00
  8" d, molded peony flowerhead in
  center, pierced leaf molded border,
  puce, green, and yellow, c1755
  (A) 2,200.00
  8½" d, painted center of insects and
  butterflies, molded ivy leaf border,
  green edging, c1755 (A) 1,100.00
  8¾" w
    Molded strawberry leaves, green
    edges, centers painted with bou-
    quets and insects, c1755, pr
    (A) 1,760.00
    Painted flower sprays, border
    molded with pansies and foliage,
    green puce and yellow accents,
    leaf-shaped, branch handle, re-
    paired, c1755 .... 700.00
  9½" w, molded overlapping leaves,
  puce veins, stalk handle, c1755 .. 750.00
  10⅞" l, center painted, bouquet of
  roses and flowers, leaf-shaped, serrated rim edged in green and yellow, stalk handle 550.00
Figure
  4¼" h, 4¾" w, gardener, watering
  potted plant, shovel at side, companion with basket of flowers, pink
  skirt, white apron, rococo scrolled
  bases, repairs, c1755-60, pr (A) .. 887.00
  5" h, seated abbess or novice, reading
  "Of Absolution" or "Of Purgatory,"
  multicolored, pr (A) 835.00
  5½" h, Hercules, wrestling lion, multicolored, rococo scroll base,
  c1755 (A) 678.00

5⅞" h, two putti and goat, holding basket of grapes, puce and green accented scroll base, c1755 (A) .. **460.00**

6⅝" h, market woman, holding white apron and bundle under arm, multicolored circ pad base, c1755 ... **420.00**

6¾" h, Ceres, holding corn, corn wreath in hair, putto clinging to side, scrolling base, color accents, c1753-55 (A) **495.00**

Figures, 5" h, puce-lined black veils, gilt trim, c1755, pr, (A) $835.00.

7" h, woman, puce jacket, yellow hat and bodice, checkered skirt, rect base, scrollwork, puce accents ... **165.00**

Soup Plate, 9" d, center painted, exotic birds in landscape, molded strawberry branches and foliage border, green, puce, and iron-red accents, c1755 .... **900.00**

Sauceboat, 8¼" l, ext. molded as overlapping cabbage leaves, puce and green accents, int. painted windmill in puce landscape, branch handle, hairline, c1755 .... **600.00**

Teabowl and Saucer, painted Chinese style peony and fence pattern (A) ... **200.00**

Tureen, cov

4½" h, modeled melon shape, raised veins in yellow and green, triangular foliage molded foot, molded stem finial, c1755, "puce W" (A)**12,100.00**

5¼" h, modeled cauliflower, green accents, c1755 .... **650.00**

9" l, modeled lettuce, overlapping leaves, green accents, cauliflower finial, damaged, c1755 ....**3,500.00**

Vases, cov, 5½" h, scroll molded bodies, painted flowers, applied colored flowers, covs molded as bunches of colored garden flowers, chips, c1755, pr **500.00**

LONGWY

LONGWY

Lorraine, France
1798 to Present

History: A French faience factory, known for its enameled pottery which resembled cloisonne, was established in 1798 at Lorraine. Utilitarian wares were made in addition to the enameled pieces.

About 1875 Emaux de Longwy introduced wares that were decorated with Persian inspired motifs. His designs were first outlined with black printed manganese resist and filled in with brightly colored glazes, especially the turquoise color for which the pieces are most famous. The company achieved its greatest fame for pieces with Art Deco motifs featuring bold colors and geometric designs.

Marks used on Longwy examples incorporate "LONGWY" either impressed or painted under the glaze.

Bowl

3¾" d, multicolored large florals, Prussian blue ground, light blue ext. **30.00**

4⅞" d, multicolored enamel florals, blue ground, octagonal **55.00**

5½" d, multicolored florals, dark red and blue ground **55.00**

5⅝" d, five petaled flowers, burgundy ground, Prussian blue ext. **60.00**

7½" d, large yellow flowers, small multicolored flowers, blue ground, dark blue rim, ftd, narrow band of flowers **265.00**

12" l, brown standing crane in center, blue enameled ground, paper label **145.00**

Box, cov, 5" w, enamel pink flowers, royal blue ground, dbl ogee shape .. **300.00**

Compote 10" h, multicolored enamels, blue ground, ftd **300.00**

Cup and Saucer

Bluebird in flight, bird with butterfly, floral branches, white ground, floral banding, cobalt trim **40.00**

Hummingbird in flight, band of flowers on borders, blue "Longwy" .. **90.00**

Dish 4½" sq, brown enameled fox in center, turquoise radiating lines to corners **40.00**

Egg Cup, 3" h, floral design, blue raised accents **55.00**

Figure, 6¼" l, 2⅞" h, Dutch shoe, pink and white flowers, blue ground, pink lining, pierced for hanging **135.00**

Left, vase, 4″ h, multicolored florals, blue ground, $55.00; center, jar, cov, 5½″ h, white flowers with red centers, cream ground, $175.00; right, vase, 7½″ h, white flowers with red centers, dark blue ground, $275.00.

Lamp
  11″ h, multicolored florals, white center medallion, small flowers extending to larger flowers at top and bottom **500.00**
  20″ h, multicolored Oriental floral design, dark red ground, cylindrical shape, sq black base, wired for two lights **135.00**
Oil Lamps, 20″ h, enameled white flowers, blue ground, electrified, pr **950.00**
Shaker, multicolored flowers, white ground, blue-green border, orig top, imp mark **50.00**
Teapot
  5¼″ h, white enamel flowers, brown branches, blue ground, blue handle **265.00**
  Floral design, cobalt spout and handle **275.00**
Tile
  8″ sq, coat of arms, pink, blue, and yellow geometrics, ftd **125.00**
  8⅛″ sq, center scene of enameled butterfly, floral branch, cream ground, florals on edges, scrolls on light blue ground **95.00**
Trivet, 8″ sq, stylized Art Deco design of woman, flowers, and trees, enamel colors **150.00**
Vase
  4″ h, incised enamel geometric design, gold, blue, and black eggshell ground, narrow base, wide mouth **95.00**
  4⅝″ h, multicolored florals, deep purple ground, cobalt int. band, imp mark, pr **125.00**
  6½″ h, portrait of bird on flowering branch and florals, blue ground, cylindrical **160.00**
  6½″ h, 3″ d, white reserve of winged bird, pink apple blossom branch, florals, light blue ground, cylindrical, imp mark **195.00**
  7¼″ h
    Florals, blue ground, yellow border with blue florals, cylindrical ... **165.00**
    Multicolored florals, blue ground . **155.00**

  7½″ h
    Blue panels, flowers and marbled pattern, rings around top **145.00**
    Yellow and pink flowers, royal blue ground, cylindrical, pr **550.00**
  10¼″ h, enameled florals, yellow ground, baluster shape **200.00**

/ 3 5
7 9 /3
XX ⟨

LOWESTOFT

Bell Lane, Lowestoft, England
c1757 to 1799

History: Soft paste porcelains were made in Lowestoft beginning about 1757 and ending in 1799. The principal production was utilitarian wares for the local community. Until 1770 all the designs used blue and white Oriental motifs. Sales were direct from the factory.

Later, formal floral patterns were introduced. During the 1770s blue-printed designs, copied from Worcester and Caughley, were produced. Lowestoft's enameled wares of the 1780s resembled the Chinese export figure and flower painted wares imported by the English East India Company. Rarer examples of Lowestoft have naturalistic flower painting and English views.

References: G. A. Godden, *The Illustrated Guide to Lowestoft Porcelain,* Herbert Jenkins, 1969; W. W. R. Spelman, *Lowestoft China,* Jarrold & Sons, 1905.

Museums: Castle Museum, Norwich, England; Christchurch Mansion, Ipswich, England; Fitzwilliam Museum, Cambridge, England; Museum of Fine Arts, Boston, Mass.; Victoria & Albert Museum, London, England.

Cup, 2½" h, multicolored florals and dot border, $40.00.

Basket, 9½" w, blue "Pine Cone" pattern, pierced sides, applied flower-heads, c1780 (A) **100.00**

Bowl
4⅜" d, turquoise swags and pink flowers ext., ochre line rim, c1785 (A) **135.00**
6½" d, blue and white waterfowl and florals, c1758 (A) **2,880.00**
6⅞" d, blue painted "Immortelle" pattern, stylized floral sprays, fine ribbing, c1775, "blue X'd swords" (A) **185.00**
8¼" d, blue painted bird on flowering branch and trellis fence, bird on reverse, c1764 (A) **130.00**

Coffeepot
5½" h, blue transfer seated Chinese man and lady trading mats, S-shaped spout, printed vase of flowers, scrolling handle, c1755 (A) .. **555.00**
9" h, blue painted Chinese man fishing in continuous river scene, trellis diaper borders on rims, c1770-75 (A) **880.00**

Cream Jug
3½" h, blue painted trailing peony design, c1768 (A) **215.00**
3⅜" h
Blue transfer, "The Good Cross Chapel" pattern in cartouches, c1775 (A) **430.00**
Famille rose enamels, two Orientals near fence, iron-red diaper and half flowerhead border, c1775 (A) **200.00**
3½" h
Blue painted pagoda on fenced river island, c1780 (A) **215.00**
Blue painted shrubs in fenced garden, c1780 (A) **215.00**
3¾" h, blue painted Oriental style flowers in garden, border of rings

on rim, sparrow beak spout, c1780 (A) **110.00**
4⅛" w, blue painted trailing branches, leaf molded lower section, c1780 (A) **145.00**
4½" h, blue Chinese figures, c1785 . **425.00**

Creamboat
4⅜" w, blue painted figures in garden, triple-arched cartouches, trailing flowers int., c1765 (A) **180.00**
4½" l, molded figures and shrubs in arcade cartouches, c1780 (A) **145.00**

Cup and Saucer
Blue "Mansfield" pattern, ribbed handle, c1775, "blue crescent" (A) .. **90.00**
Gilt "EL" and lion rampant, gilt swags, black flowerheads, gilt dentil rims, c1785 (A) **1,080.00**

Dish, 10½" d, blue and white scene of pagoda on island and landscape, white flowerheads and oval dots, blue border, cracked and riveted, c1775 (A) **415.00**

Feeding Cup
3⅛" h, blue transfer, butterfly and flowering branches, flared bucket shape, c1775 (A) **400.00**
7" w, blue flowers and butterflies, white ground, star crack, c1765 (A) **165.00**

Jug
3" h, painted floral spray and sprigs, sparrow beak lip (A) **100.00**
5⅛" blue painted pagoda, trees, and rocks, sailing boat and islands on reverse, scroll border on int., pear shape, sparrow beak lip (A) **700.00**
8" h, blue painted trailing branches and insects, molded leaves border, seeded ground, c1765 (A) **100.00**
8⅛" h, blue painted Chinese man and pagodas, river landscapes, molded floral cartouches, rim, handle, and spout with floral borders, c1765-70 (A) **360.00**
8½" h, blue and white painted Chinese and pagodas, landscape, molded floral cartouches, floral borders, c1765-70 .... **650.00**

Patty Pan
3½" d, blue painted butterfly and trailing flowers, c1765 (A) **260.00**
4⅛" d, blue painted insect in center, trailing flowers on border, trailing flowers, ext., c1768, "blue crescent" (A) **230.00**

Pickle Dish
3½" l, blue painted fruiting vine and berry border, leaf shape (A) **175.00**
4" l, blue painted fruiting vine, serrated blue border, leaf shape, c1765 .... **200.00**
4¼" l, dark blue fruiting vine, berry

Pickle Dish, blue and white, c1775, $400.00.

border, underside molded, veining, leaf shape, stalk handle, c1765-70 (A) **90.00**

4½" l, blue and white Oriental style flowering plants, shell molded (A) **106.00**

Plate, 8⅞" d, blue painted Oriental figure with parasol flanked by large vases of flowers, diaper border reserved with flowerheads and river scenes, c1765 (A) **285.00**

Sauce Tureen, cov, 7¼" d, blue painted flowering branches and insects, floral borders, ribbed bodies, c1760-65 (A) **1,830.00**

Saucer, blue printed scene of pagoda and man crossing bridge (A) **50.00**

Sugar, blue painted plants and butterfly, flowerhead finial, c1760, "blue crescent" (A) **150.00**

Tea Caddy

3⅜" h, blue painted bouquet, insect, scroll and flowerhead border, trailing branches on shoulder, octagonal, c1765 (A) **575.00**

4" h, blue painted trailing peony, rect, c1775, "blue crescent" (A) **240.00**

Tea Service, Part

Teabowl, cup and saucer, Imari-type design, carmine, blue, green, and iron-red, attrib to Redgrave, 3 pcs **475.00**

Teapot, milk jug, tea caddy, slop basin, eight teabowls and saucers, "Robert Brown" pattern, blue wavy scale bands divided by flowering plants, c1770-75, "blue crescent," 20 pcs (A) **1,440.00**

Teabowl, blue printed "Good Cross Chapel" pattern in cartouches (A) .. **50.00**

Teabowl and Saucer,

Blue painted "House" pattern, c1780 (A) **95.00**

Blue printed "Doll's House" pattern **25.00**

Painted floral sprays and sprigs, green rims **35.00**

Red, green, blue and pink rock, fence and chrysanthemum in garden (A) **260.00**

Teapot

3¼" h, blue painted pagodas on river island, loop and dot border c1765 (A) **1,075.00**

5⅜" h, famille rose floral sprays and sprigs, iron-red line, loop and dot border, button finial (A) **235.00**

5½" h, multicolored Oriental figures by pavilion, iron-red scalloped rim border, c1780-85 (A) **470.00**

6⅛" h, painted Orientals at table, divided by iron-red scrolling foliage, famille rose colors, base crack, lid repaired, c1775 (A) **270.00**

Vase

5" h, blue Chinese landscape scene, white ground, c1765 .... **575.00**

5½" h, painted mandarin figures in garden, iron-red borders, baluster shape, c1785-90 (A) **2,195.00**

5¾" h, blue printed flowering branches and insects, scroll border, c1763, (A) **935.00**

MODERN MARK   1756-1824

LUDWIGSBURG

Wurttemberg, Germany, now West Germany
1758 to 1824

History: Karl Eugen, Duke of Wurttemberg, founded a hard paste porcelain manufactory in 1758 at Ludwigsburg, twelve miles north of Stuttgart. A faience factory was established two years later. Joseph Jacob Ringler directed the porcelain factory from 1759 to 1799. Initially, copies of Meissen wares were made.

The peak period of production was between 1758 and 1776. Utilitarian wares decorated with birds and ornamental wares, e.q., candlesticks, were produced. Riedel, the major designer and modeler during this period, crafted mythological and classical figures. Berger, another sculptor, made small figural groups comprised of peasants, work and ballet groups. These figures did not match the quality of the figurines from Meissen, Nymphenburg, or Frankenthal.

Initially the Ludwigsburg shapes and decoration were in the Rococo style. The factory changed its forms and designs as tastes changed.

Rococo gave way to Neoclassical followed by Empire. Ludwigsburg porcelain started to decline after 1770. The enterprise never really was profitable or highly successful. Duke Karl Eugen died in 1793. Production deteriorated even more after his death. The factory struggled on for thirty more years, closing in 1824. During the 19th century, the Ludwigsburg molds were sold to Edward Kick, at Amberg in Bavaria, who reissued a number of the pieces.

References: George W. Ware, *German and Austrian Porcelain,* Crown Publishers, Inc., 1963.

Museums: Cincinnati Art Museum, Cincinnati, Ohio; Museum fur Kunst und Gewerbe, Hamburg, Germany; Shlossmuseum, Berlin, Germany; Wurttembergishes Landesmuseum, Stuttgart, Germany.

Bowl 6¾" d, Columbine in harlequin dress on front, playing lute on reverse in landscape vignettes, dark brown rim, c1759-63, "blue crowned interlaced C's" (A) **950.00**
Candlesticks, 2⅝" h, painted birds and insects, gilt edged puce trellis borders, fluted nozzles, molded and gilt cartouches, "blue crowned interlaced C's," pr (A) **3,110.00**
Coffeepot
    7" h, puce and gilt flowering plants, scroll and rams head mask, foliage scroll handle, three scroll feet, c1765, "blue interlaced C's" (A) . **220.00**
    9" h, painted flower bouquets, scroll spout and handle, domed cov, fruit finial, repaired, c1770, "blue crowned interlaced C's" (A) **135.00**
Cup and Saucer
    Painted birds on branches with insects, rim band of puce flowerheads, gilt scrolls, c1765, "blue crowned interlaced C's" (A) **550.00**
    Two birds on branch with insects, gilt edged puce trellis borders, gilt rococo scroll handle, c1765, "blue crowned interlaced C's" (A) **400.00**
Dishes, 9⅜" d, painted flower bouquets in ozier borders, red rims, c1775, "blue crowned interlaced C's," pr (A) **125.00**
Figure
    3⅞" h, youth, puce and lime-green hunter's tunic, tree stump, rifle missing, c1765 (A) **480.00**
    4¾" h, young man, blouse, cap and skirt before pile of wood, multicolored, mound base, gilt scrolls, c1765, "blue crowned interlaced C's" (A) **800.00**
    5" h, peasant woodsman, smoking pipe and holding club, multicol-

ored, c1765, "blue crowned interlaced C's" (A) **1,080.00**
5⅛" h, butcher, young man with ham on shoulder, tree stump, multicolored, c1768, "crowned interlaced C's" (A) **1,100.00**
5½"
    Mars, modeled as nude warrior leaning on shield, gray armor, rockwork base, c1765, "blue crowned interlaced C's" (A) ... **570.00**
    Man or woman in fur-lined clothes carrying muffs, gilt scroll grasswork bases, c1765-66, "blue crowned interlaced C's," pr (A) **2,000.00**
5¾" h, waiters, modeled as girl in flowered skirt carrying coffee tray, man in flowered jacket carrying tray with wine jug, pillars with vessels on bases, c1758, "blue interlaced C's," pr (A) **3,080.00**

Figure, 9½" h, gray gown, blue crowned interlaced "C's," $200.00.

6¼" h
    Hunter holding dead stag and gun, classic hunting clothes, multicolored, c1770, "blue crowned interlaced C's" (A) **1,170.00**
    Seated shepherd, flute, dog and satchel on base, multicolored, damaged, c1765, "blue crowned interlaced C's" (A) **1,040.00**
6¾" h, running boar attacked by three hounds wearing black and gold collars, rocky mound base, repairs, c1765, "blue interlaced C's" (A) .**1,260.00**
9" h
    Nude Juno in clouds with peacock and Jupiter opening door in rocks releasing three youths, c1760 ..**1,220.00**

Two putti, one with wine cup, other with wine press, white body, mauve robe under one, yellow drape on other, oval base, gold, green grass, c1800 ......**1,650.00**
9½" h, recumbent river god and goddess resting on overturned flowing urns, iron-red and floral cloths, grass mound, restored, c1775, pr (A) **510.00**
Plate, 9¼" d, shaped ozier molded rim, painted flowers, c1763, "blue crowned interlaced L's" **150.00**
Potpourri vases, 11", painted landscape panels, molded gold and blue enamel scrolls, dolphin head handles, pierced covs, Cupid finials, c1770, "blue interlaced C's," pr (A) **1,895.00**
Sauceboat, 9¼" w, painted bouquets and sprays, shaped rim, molded basketwork, dbl scroll handles, c1765, "blue interlaced C's" **275.00**
Snuff Box, 3¼" w, painted scattered flowers, molded basketweave ground, int. of cov with basket on ledge, gilt metal mounts, c1770 (A) . **935.00**
Tea Caddy
4½" h, painted exotic birds and trailing flowers, Kakiemon colors, rect, c1765 (A) **515.00**
5⅛" h, painted birds nesting in Indian flowers, c1770, "blue AR" (A) ... **710.00**
Teapot 5¾" h, painted birds and insects landscape scene, puce trellis border and gilt edges, globular, domed cov, apple finial, c1765, "blue crowned interlaced C's" (A) **520.00**

LUSTER

England
19th Century to Present

History: The exact beginning of luster decoration on British pottery cannot be dated accurately. The first pieces date from the first quarter of the 19th century and the luster process still is used today.

Luster decoration is achieved by applying thin metallic films to earthenware or china bodies. Gold luster comes from gold oxide, copper luster from copper oxide, silver luster from platinum, and pink or purple luster from "purple of cassuis."

All over lustering imitated metallic wares made in gold, silver, or copper. Luster decorations also were used on rims, details, and decorative highlights.

The "resist" process involved keeping parts of the object white through temporarily resisting

them with wax or paper cut-outs so that when the luster solution was applied to the object it would not affect the resisted portions. Reserved panels could be left plain, painted, or transfer printed. Stenciling also was used. Overglaze enamels could be added to the lustered ground.

Sunderland or "Splash luster," a mottled type of pink luster used on a white body, was very popular. The splash effect came from spraying an oil on the wet luster that had just been applied to the white ware. The oil expanded in the kiln to form bubbles and splashes. Manufacturers who used this technique were Southwick, Dixon & Austin, and Ball's. A large portion of Sunderland luster was produced at Newcastle-upon-Tyne.

Jugs, mugs, tea, and tablewares were among the most popular luster forms. An enormous variety of jugs were made, some featuring mottled pink with verses and others silver or other colors. Inscriptions on luster ware varied greatly. Events, landmarks in history, and popular sentiments, were commemorated. Plaques had either mottos or verses, sailing ships, or landscapes within painted frames.

Staffordshire and other potteries that made a wide variety of luster ware types include: Spode, Wedgwood, Lakin & Poole, Ralph & Enoch Wood, Davenport, New Hall, and Minton.

References: John Bedford, *Old English Lustre Ware*, Walker & Co., 1965; W. Bosanko, *Collecting Old Lustre Ware*, George H. Doran Co., 1916; Jeanette R. Hodgon, *Collecting Old English Lustre*, Southworth-Anthoensen Press, 1937; W.D. John & W. Baker, *Old English Lustre Pottery*, Ceramic Book Co., 1951; J.T. Shaw, *The Potteries of Sunderland & District*, Sunderland Library, 1961.

Museums: Art Institute of Chicago, Chicago, Illinois; Cincinnati Museum of Art, Cincinnati, Ohio; City Museum & Art Gallery, Stoke-on-Trent, Hanley, England; Cleveland Museum of Art, Cleveland, Ohio; Laing Art Gallery, 7 Museum, Newcastle, England; Potsdam Public Museum, Potsdam, N.Y.; Sunderland Museum, Sunderland, England

REPRODUCTION ALERT: Portmeirion Potteries Ltd., a Stoke-on-Trent firm, produces jugs which are reproductions of older luster types in museums and private collections. These new pieces have the maker's mark and are not intended to confuse the collector. Sometimes the mark is removed, and these reproductions are offered as old pieces.

COPPER

Barber Bowl, 11½" d, cut out at front, molded soap dish, lustered body, c1827, Staffordshire (A) **260.00**

Beaker 3" h, wide blue band, copper
luster foliage, cream berries (A) **10.00**
Bowl
6" d, 5" h, tan band, luster flowers,
luster ground, dbl handles, ftd ...   **135.00**
7" d, beaded, luster ground (A) **50.00**
Candlestick
4½" h, lustered figure of griffin, nozzle on back, oval base, c1815, Staffordshire (A) **250.00**
8⅜" h, lustered figural sphinx, acanthus molded nozzles, shell form
bobeche, oval bases, c1815, Staffordshire, pr (A) **880.00**
Cream Jug
2½" h
Resisted copper dots, pink luster
band, lustered body, c1825, Staffordshire (A) **20.00**
Wide white pebbled band, lustered
body, c1825 (A) **20.00**
Creamer
3½" h
Polychrome floral design, luster
ground, (A) **25.00**
Reserves on sides of Oriental
scenes, enamel accents, cobalt
ground, pink and copper luster
trim **145.00**
5¼" h, blue middle band, luster
ground **40.00**
Cup
2¾" orange and blue bands **30.00**
2⅞" multicolored textured middle
band, luster ground, pink int. rim   **45.00**
4¾" h, modeled head of Bacchus,
polychrome enamels and luster,
frog on int. (A) **105.00**
Cup and Bowl, enameled leaves and
flowers, luster, trim shaped rims and
handle, imp "Wood" **100.00**
Cup and Saucer
Leaf and berry pattern, luster ground   **30.00**
Sunflower decoration (A) **35.00**
Flower Pot, matching stand
4⅝" h wide blue center bands, lustered floral vines, lions, and ring
handles, lustered rim and int.,
c1825, Staffordshire, pr (A) **300.00**
Molded pink and luster flower sprays
on blue ground, lion's mask and
ring handles, 19th C, pr (A) **150.00**
Fruit Stand, 9⅝" l, brown outlined gilt
classical warriors, luster ground, palmette borders, c1815, England (A) ..   **2,000.00**
Furniture Support, 4¼, Bust of Duke of
Wellington, c1830, Staffordshire (A)   **230.00**
Goblet
4⅛" h, white band, polychrome and
luster florals, luster ground (A) ...   **55.00**
4½" h
Flowering vines resisted on pink

luster bands, luster int. and ext.,
c1820, Staffordshire, pr (A) **110.00**
Wide cream band, pink luster
sprigs, luster ground, ftd **75.00**
4⅞" h, purple transfers of "Faith" and
"Hope," stem repaired, c1820 (A)   **20.00**
5" h, canary yellow band, reserves of
mother and child, luster ground,
c1825 ....   **135.00**
7¼" h, overall luster, cylinder shape,
mid-19th C (A) **45.00**

Holy Water Font, 7⅛" h, lustered
molded crucifix over open shell ba-
sin, c1820 (A) **55.00**
Jug
3¾" h, brown transfers of Queen Caroline and verse in ribbons between
pink luster bands, c1820, Staffordshire (A) **40.00**
4⅜" h, blue border, luster ground (A)   **10.00**
4⅝" h, wide blue band, pink lustered
relief of cow, hound, fruit, and
flower basket, luster ground, c1820
(A) **50.00**
5¼" h
Enameled relief of flowers, tan
ground, luster rim, handle, and
spout, c1820, Staffordshire (A) .   **35.00**
Lustered relief of vertical acanthus
leaves, grapevines, beaded borders, blue ground, c1825, Staffordshire (A) **170.00**
5⅜" h, white relief of classical figures
in goat–drawn chariot, luster
ground, banded pink luster, rim,
handle, and spout, c1820, Staffordshire (A) **80.00**
5½" h
Black print of "General Jackson,
The Hero of New Orleans," wide
blue band, c1820, Staffordshire
(A) **1,310.00**
Blue relief florals below grape cluster rim, lustered handle and
lion's head spout, octagonal,
c1840, Staffordshire (A) **30.00**
Molded, enameled boy and dog in
oval panel, reserved on wide
green band, lustered rim, handle,
and spout, c1830, Staffordshire
(A) **55.00**
Multicolored hp florals, luster
ground, pear shape, vertical ribbing, foliate scroll handle and
spout, c1840, Staffordshire (A) .   **80.00**
5¾" h
Pink enamel and copper luster,
three rose sprigs, mustard
ground, lustered rim, handle,
and spout, c1840, Staffordshire
(A) **35.00**

Pink luster center, band, multicolored leaves (A) **10.00**

6½" h, transfer and enamel of "Charity," luster ground, (A) **110.00**

6¾" h

Enameled stylized flowers reserved on purple-edged pink luster band, c1820, Stafforshire (A) ... **35.00**

Wide pink luster band resisted with blue and white vines, lustered baluster body, 1825, Staffordshire (A) **30.00**

7" h, brown transfer and enameled pastoral scene in panel on wide yellow band, c1830, Staffordshire (A) **55.00**

7¼" h, wide blue band, relief of enameled flower clusters and rose, satyr mask spout, lustered body, c1820, Staffordshire (A) **50.00**

7½" h

Molded red and black scenes from "Punch," luster ground, c1820, Staffordshire (A) **145.00**

Molded satyr mask wearing grape wreath, multicolored, molded monkey handle, wide luster borders, c1815, Staffordshire (A) .. **300.00**

7⅞" h, 6⅛" d, blue Highland dancers, scrolls molded on sides, luster ground, set of three (A) **65.00**

Jug

8" h, transfers, on sides, of pilgrim and children with baskets, painted accents in ovals, yellow ground, c1840, Staffordshire, pr (A) **265.00**

9" h, puce transfer of "Charity," accents in octagonal panel, luster ground, scroll rim, handle, and spout, pink luster bands, c1810, Staffordshire **225.00**

Loving Cup, 4¾" h, two scroll handles, ftd, c1835, Staffordshire (A) **55.00**

Milk Jug 6" h, lustered relief of cow, hound, and flowered baskets, blue ground, spout repaired, c1835, Staffordshire (A) **20.00**

Mug

2½" h, luster beading at top, inner tan band, black and blue outer stripes **40.00**

2¾" h

Blue center band, luster ground (A) **10.00**

Pink center band, white burst bubbles, luster ground **55.00**

2⅞" h, turquoise bands, tan center band, int. rim pink band **45.00**

3" h

Blue and green bands, luster body **40.00**

Blue and tan stripes, narrow middle (A) **25.00**

Blue narrow band, luster ground . **35.00**

Blue wide leaf and berry band, luster ground **40.00**

Pink wide center band, luster ground **35.00**

3⅛" h

Black transfer and enameled florals and fruit clusters, c1820 (A) ... **70.00**

Purple transfer and enameled figure of "Hope," anchor, c1820, Staffordshire (A) **70.00**

Copper Luster, pitcher, 5" h, multicolored enameled circus scene, c1840s, $155.00.

3¼" h

Enameled relief of putti riding goat with four children, blue ground, lustered rim and int., c1830, Staffordshire (A) **90.00**

Flowering vine, white resisted wide pink luster band, pink splash luster int., c1820, Staffordshire (A) **50.00**

3⅜" h, blue band and floral design, luster ground (A) **10.00**

3½" h

Blue and green bands, luster ground **40.00**

Pink luster house on hill, octagonal panel, luster ground, c1815, Staffordshire, (A) **70.00**

3⅝" h, ribbed base, white band, polychrome and luster florals (A) ... **50.00**

3⅞" h, white relief of three groups of classical figures between pink luster bands, c1820, Staffordshire (A) ... **70.00**

5" h, 5" d, hp florals, frog in base, two climbing out, luster ground **250.00**

5⅜" h, amber band, multicolored pastoral scenes, pink luster int., border, perforated divider, dbl handles (A) **60.00**

Dark blue middle band, raised multicolored children **65.00**

Mustard Pot, cov, 2⅝" h, blue blossoms

on orange band, lustered rims and handles, c1830, Staffordshire (A) ...   **50.00**

Pitcher

3"h

Blue schematic design, luster ground **20.00**

Molded feather bands, luster ground **30.00**

Raised textured band, luster ground   **30.00**

3½" h, blue band, raised figures ...   **35.00**

3¾" h, tan center band with luster leaves, luster ground **75.00**

Copper Luster, pitcher, 7½" h, multicolored enamels, c1820–30, $435.00.

4" h

Green and yellow bands, luster ground **35.00**

Pink and white band, luster ground, floral dec (A) **65.00**

Pink luster "Schoolhouse," luster ground, chip on spout **40.00**

Yellow band, luster floral dec (A) .   **65.00**

4½" h, black transfer of "Hunt and Liberty," luster ext. band, pink int. band **185.00**

5" h

Enamel floral band, pink luster, ribbed body **75.00**

Irid center band and design **95.00**

5⅛" h, luster body, mask spout, Sunderland luster trim (A) **45.00**

5½" h

Blue band, luster ground **35.00**

Multicolored floral oval medallions on sides, luster ground **75.00**

Multicolored floral oval medallions, cream gound, luster body   **85.00**

Putty band, purple luster foliage, luster ground (A) **30.00**

Yellow transfer of swan and deer, beaded dec at top, c1830-40 ..   **155.00**

5¾" h

Cream band, raised multicolored florals, luster ground (A) **35.00**

Yellow bands, purple luster florals, luster ground (A) **30.00**

Yellow band, three white reserves, rust transfers of woman and child

playing badminton, yellow, blue, and green enamels (A) **60.00**

6" h

Blue and yellow bands, luster ground **45.00**

White band, floral dec, luster ground (A) **85.00**

6¼" h, royal blue center band, enameled flowers, luster ground **85.00**

6½" h, yellow dbl band, luster dec, luster ground (A) **110.00**

7" h

Enameled floral design, "Allertons, Longton, England" **85.00**

Yellow center band, luster ground   **65.00**

Yellow floral dec band, luster ground **80.00**

7¼" h, cream band, purple luster florals (A) **55.00**

7½" h, relief of dancers, blue trim ..   **85.00**

Quill Holder, 4⅝" l, lustered molded porcupine, six rows of holes, c1830 (A) **235.00**

Salt, 3" d, center blue band, luster ground (A) **15.00**

Shaker, overall luster (A) **50.00**

Shaving Mug, 4" h, blue, diagonal luster stripes, pink inner rim **55.00**

Tankard, 7¾" h, lustered tapered cylindrical body, loop handle, c1840 (A)   **125.00**

Tea Kettle, 8⅛" h, lustered lobed body, turned overhead handle, c1840 (A) .   **150.00**

Teabowl, 3" h, blue, luster leaf design, pink inner rim **45.00**

Teapot

6¼" h, blue band stylized resisted vines, lustered baluster form, phoenix handle, c1830, Staffordshire (A)   **20.00**

8½" h, molded gadroon bands, hp multicolored florals, luster ground, c1820, Staffordshire (A) **85.00**

9⅝" h, faceted sides, hp multicolored florals, luster ground, knob repaired, c1820, Staffordshire (A) ..   **85.00**

Blue band, luster ground, figural bird handle **95.00**

Toby Jug, 4½" h, seated gentleman, cobalt jacket **125.00**

Tumbler 4" h, blue floral band, luster ground (A) **10.00**

Vase

5¾" h, brown printed, and enameled badminton scene, brown-edged panel, yellow ground, lustered, rim and int., baluster shape, c1820 (A)   **90.00**

6½" h, puce transfers of clock face and Oriental figures in garden, enamel accents, lustered scroll handles and body, c1840, Llanelly (A) **190.00**

Waste Bowl, blue band, figure in relief, luster ground, ftd **40.00**

Wig Stand, 8½" h, spherical, lion on top, imp "Bailey & Batkin Sale Patentees," c1814 (A) **260.00**

PINK

Bowl
  5¼" w, 3" h, luster geometrics, border band **80.00**
  5½" d, "Victoria & Albert at the Well" **85.00**
  6" d, "Two Story House" pattern ... **60.00**
  7½" d, "House" pattern, target center, luster border **85.00**
Candlesticks
  5" h, ring turned shafts, dished circular nozzles, splashed luster, c1810, Staffordshire, pr (A) **360.00**
  7" h, ring turned cylindrical shaft, dished nozzle, circ base, splashed luster, c1810 (A) **130.00**

Pink Luster, creamer, 5" l, magenta transfers, luster border, $20.00.

Creamer, 2½" h, black scenic transfer, luster trim **45.00**
Cup, child's, girl and cat at old stove . **20.00**
Cup and Bowl
  Luster panels florals between enameled sprig flowers **75.00**
  Luster plaid, floral reserves and enameled sprigs, fluted body **75.00**
Cup and Saucer
  Black bat print, Princess Charlotte, dbl luster bands, c1817 .... **125.00**
  Luster floral design **15.00**
  Luster geometrics and border bands . **40.00**
  Pink and purple luster, polychrome florals (A) **35.00**
  "Two Story House" pattern **40.00**
  Victoria and Albert in country setting, luster trim **125.00**
  Victorian Royal Family, luster trim .. **140.00**
Dessert Service, creamer, sugar, four plates, four cups and saucers, luster and gold trim, 14 pcs **125.00**

Dish
  5½" d
    "Church" pattern **40.00**
    Pink transfer scene, mother and child on Empire couch **20.00**
  6½" l, pink and green lustered florals, heart shape, open handles, "Old Castle, Made in England" **20.00**
  9⅜" d, pink and purple luster, cottage in landscape, scroll molded ends, c1815 (A) **125.00**
Figure
  6⅜" h, mother carrying child, basket, and cauldron, multicolored, black spotted luster bodice, green mound base, iron-red edge (A) **80.00**
  25⅛" h, allegorical "Peace," right hand holding dove, lustered tiara and mantle, multicolored, green mound base, splash luster, c1801-18 (A) **715.00**
Flower Pots, 3⅝" h, tapered cylinders, splash luster rolled edges, c1810, pr (A) **65.00**
Goblet, 5⅛" h, tapered cylindrical shape, splash luster, c1820 (A) **80.00**
Jug
  4⅜" h, black transfers of Decator & Commodore Bainbridge, luster rim, c1820, Staffordshire (A) **330.00**
  4½" h
    Black transfer and enamels of boxers Spring & Langan, slogans, orange border base, pink and copper luster rim, c1825 (A) **825.00**
    Lustered and enameled vine below lustered lozenge border, lustered handle edge, c1810, Staffordshire (A) **90.00**
  5" h
    Creamware, bat printed sepia, titled portraits of "George Rex IV" wearing robes and crown, luster borders, c1821 (A) **590.00**
    Lustered bird on shrub, buff ground, lustered border of acorns and leaves, c1810-15 (A) **250.00**
    Lustered four floral medallions reserved on ribbed luster, buff ground, molded floral neck border, c1820, Staffordshire (A) ... **75.00**
    Lustered relief of griffons and urn, foliate scrollwork, blue ground, molded floral border, luster band, c1830, Staffordshire (A) . **80.00**
  5⅛" h, lustered and enameled green and black, molded leaves and bellflowers, molded floral border, lustered rim, handle, and spout, c1820, Staffordshire (A) **100.00**
  5¼" h, molded floral neck border,

splash luster, shield shape, c1820, Staffordshire (A) **80.00**

5⅜" h, black transfers of tributes to King George and William III of Orange, enamels, luster bordered, rim, and handle, c1815, England, (A) **115.00**

6" h

Molded eagle and floral luster sprig, buff ground, molded luster vine neck border, c1820, Staffordshire (A) **75.00**

Molded panels, trailing hop plants, turquoise and luster accents, c1820, Staffordshire **175.00**

6⅜" h, lustered and painted molded tavern scene, scalework borders, c1820, Staffordshire (A) **110.00**

6⅞" h, molded lustered stag, doe, and fawn, buff ground, molded palmette border, c1820, Staffordshire (A) **120.00**

7¼" h, four lustered stylized houses, lustered and green flower roundels, fluted border, molded caryatid handle, c1820, Staffordshire (A) **100.00**

7½" h, pink and purple luster molded hunter, horse, and dogs attacking stag, basketweave molded base, leaf molded purple luster handle and spout, c1820 (A) **440.00**

9⅜" h

Black transfers, enamels of ploughing scene, motto, farm tools, and animals, lustered vine roundels, inscribed and dated, lustered bands, c1814, Staffordshire (A) .**1,980.00**

Black transfers of Iron Bridge and verse on sides in floral wreaths, splashed luster borders, c1830 (A) **115.00**

Loving Cup 5⅛" h, U shape, S scroll handles, splash luster, c1820 (A) ... **80.00**

Mug

2" h, "House" pattern, pink and purple luster (A) **15.00**

2¼" h, "House" pattern, cream ground **35.00**

2½" h, landscape scene **60.00**

3¼" h, mottled luster ground, reserve of "E. Forsyth Scotchhouse 1836," black enamel, green and black crossed bows and boughs, c1836, Staffordshire (A) **220.00**

3⅜" h

Black transfers of figures near castle, buff ground, luster border bands, c1815, Staffordshire, pr (A) **220.00**

Lustered ground floral resist border and bands, engine-turned basketwork, c1825 (A) **165.00**

3⅝" h, horizontal luster bands, stylized lustered sprigs in ovals at upper borders, c1815, Staffordshire, pr (A) **220.00**

4¼" h, Oriental transfer, polychrome, luster ground (A) **20.00**

Pancake Dish, 8½" d, luster bands, gold ferns, perforated lid, dbl handles ... **50.00**

Planter and Tray, 5½" h, black transfer of castle scene, luster bands, animal head ring handles **195.00**

Plaque, 9½" l, 8¼" h, luster border, inscribed

"Prepare to Meet Thy God" (A) **190.00**

"Thou God, See'st Me" (A) **190.00**

Plate

6¾" d, luster floral and leaf design . **10.00**

7¼" d, scroll and flower pattern **70.00**

7½" d, freehand enamel design of lg bird in tree, luster trim **85.00**

7⅞" d, molded leaves, basketwork ground, luster accents, c1817, pr (A) **110.00**

8" d, transfer of mother and child in garden, luster border **25.00**

8¾" d, pearlware, splash luster fish, iron-red, blue, and green stylized flowers, iron-red sponged border, c1820, Staffordshire (A) **80.00**

Tea Service

Demitasse, teapot, creamer, cov sugar, six cups and saucers, six cake plates, luster trim on fluted bodies **95.00**

Teapot, creamer, sugar, waste bowl, eight cups and saucers, "School House" pattern **450.00**

Teabowl and Saucer, enameled "Red Plume," green leaf trim luster trim .. **100.00**

Tie Backs, 3⅝" d, luster house and tree pattern, scalloped edges **75.00**

Vase

5⅜" to 6½" h, painted yellowware bodies, lustered roses between light blue bands, scalloped rims, circ bases edged in luster, campana shape, center vase with pierced cov, c1815, set of three (A) **770.00**

6⅝" h, blue glazed, lustered relief of putti and classical figures at play, campana shape, palmette design on circ ft (A) **100.00**

SILVER

Bowl, 4⅞" d, molded vertical ribbing, copper int., c1820, Staffordshire (A) **25.00**

Candlesticks, 4" h, cylindrical shafts, circ bases, c1810-15, pr (A) **360.00**

Coffeepot, 10½" h, shield shape, vertical ribbing, luster ext., c1815, Staffordshire (A) **100.00**

Cup and Saucer
　Demitasse, flared rims, ftd bases, gold
　　lined int., luster ext., set of four .. **35.00**
　Transfer of church, "Gruss Aus Wed-
　　bem," luster rims and handle, Ger-
　　man **15.00**

Silver Luster, demitasse cup and saucer, resist partridges and florals, $30.00.

Egg Stand, 7⅛" d, fluted column, edge,
　and loop handle, quatrefoil ft, six
　goblet cups, c1810, Staffordshire (A) **660.00**
Figure
　6¾" h, Vulcan in cap and tunic, ham-
　　mer, arrows, helmet, and quiver, sq
　　base, c1815-20, Staffordshire (A) . **415.00**
　7⅝" h, "Wings," naked girl, arms
　　spread behind, black circ base,
　　Royal Crown Derby **140.00**
　13⅞" h, Venus holding two doves,
　　dolphin on sq base, c1815-20, Staf-
　　fordshire (A) **520.00**
Furniture Supports, 4⅛" modeled lions
　heads and paws, c1815-25, pr (A) .. **600.00**
Goblets
　4" h, resisted floral vine borders,
　　c1810, Staffordshire, pr (A) **165.00**
　4½" h, resisted with wheatears and
　　tendrils, c1810, Staffordshire, pr (A) **165.00**
　5¼" h, ring turned stems, copper
　　ints., c1820, Staffordshire, set of
　　four (A) **100.00**
Jug
　3⅞" h, vertical ribbing and gadroon-
　　ing, ext. luster, scroll handle,
　　c1820, Staffordshire (A) **100.00**
　4" h, olive drabware body, black
　　transfers of couples with children
　　on sides in silver roundels, luster
　　eagle on front and "1819," luster
　　outlines rim and handle (A) **770.00**
　4⅜" shield shape resist, blue ground,
　　painted flowers, c1820 .... **260.00**

4½" h
　Molded brown satyr head on front,
　　luster body, foliate resist (A) ... **385.00**
　Overall luster ground, 19th C, Staf-
　　fordshire **65.00**
　Resisted stylized foliage band, 19th
　　C, Staffordshire **65.00**
4⅝" h, black transfer of robin, enamel
　accents in resisted roundel, luster
　ground, c1815, Staffordshire (A) .. **715.00**
4¾" h
　Black transfer of boxers Molineux
　　& Cribbs in luster roundel, luster
　　banded borders, foliate handle,
　　c1810-15 (A) **825.00**
　Black transfer of Sir Frances Burdett
　　in luster roundel on one side,
　　commemorative black transfer
　　on other, luster band borders,
　　c1810-15 (A) **330.00**
4⅞" h, molded purple grapes, black
　and green leaves on sides, lustered
　rim, handle, and base, c1820 (A) . **410.00**
5" h, farm scenes in luster roundels,
　lustered floral sprays and rim band,
　dated 1804 (A) **180.00**
5¼" h
　Grapevines in yellow, turquoise
　　and iron-red enamels, resisted on
　　luster ground, c1815, Stafford-
　　shire (A) **500.00**
　"Harlequin" pattern, pineapple
　　molded, checkered luster,
　　c1802-08, imp "Harley" (A) ... **250.00**
　Pineapple molded, iron-red and
　　luster strawberry sprays, lustered
　　rim and handle, c1810 (A) **250.00**
5½" h
　Blue transfers of birds, resisted
　　ground, c1815 (A) **770.00**
　Painted strawberries and luster
　　leaves, lozenge-quilted body,
　　19th C **100.00**
6¼" h, brown transfers of "Hope" &
　"Charity" on sides in luster roun-
　dels, luster bands at rims and han-
　dle, c1810-15 (A) **140.00**
7⅜" h, lower portion with black trans-
　fer and enamels of motto, and farm
　workers, animals, and family, up-
　per portion with luster resisted
　grapevines, c1812 (A) **415.00**
Mug
　3⅜" h, black transfer of "Friends of
　　Liberty," luster banded rims and
　　handle, c1810 (A) **330.00**
　4⅛" h, scroll handle, copper int.,
　　c1820, Staffordshire (A) **25.00**
Pitcher
　1½" h, overall luster, white int. **10.00**
　7" h, transfer views of harbor, luster
　　rim, Staffordshire (A) **20.00**

Plate

    7⅛" d, orange glazed earthenware, lustered American eagle (A) **195.00**

    8¼" d, lustered grape vine motif, striped edges, Johnson Bros, set of four **85.00**

Quintals, 7⅝" h, molded flowerheads on sides, five scalloped edged nozzles, vertical ribbing, stepped rect bases, c1815, Staffordshire, pr (A) . . **220.00**

Shaker

    3⅝" h, horizontal ribbing (A) **35.00**

    4⅞" h, lustered figure of period man (A) **50.00**

Tea set, teapot, creamer, and sugar, wide luster band, brown ground with ivory classical figures, "Gibson's, England" **275.00**

Teapot, 6⅛" h, blue glazed ground, molded putto on one side holding bird, boy and dog on other in luster roundels, luster foliage, c1820 . . . . . **260.00**

Watch Stand, 8" h, rococo scrolls, pheasant and small bird at aperture, ribbed scroll edged base, c1825, Staffordshire (A) **520.00**

SUNDERLAND

Bowl

    9" d, printed and painted, verse, agricultural tools, and clipper ship, luster border, imp "Moore & Co." (A) **30.00**

    9¼" d, printed view of bridge over River Wear, gardener's arms, luster border (A) **30.00**

    11" d, black printed nautical scenes and verse, pirate and two sailors, luster border, imp "London" **60.00**

Cup and Saucer

    Lustered rims **30.00**

    "Moses in the Bullrushes," lustered leaves at border, wishbone handle **55.00**

Figure

    8¾" h, bust of Shakespeare, multicolored, splash luster pedestal base, c1815-20 (A) **605.00**

    8¼" to 9" h, four allegorical figures of "Four Seasons," multicolored, lustered costumes, sq splash luster bases, c1820-26, imp "Dixon, Auston & Co.," set of four (A) **1,320.00**

Jug

    7¼" h, creamware, black transfer of farmer's arms and sailor's farewell, inscription "God Speed the Plough," yellow and iron-red accents, lustered neck and foot, c1830 (A) **500.00**

    7¾" h

    Black printed bridge of Sunderland and sailing ship, iron-red, yellow, and green accents, lustered neck and foot, c1840 (A) **200.00**

    Black transfer of sailing ships named William IV and verses, iron-red, yellow, and green accents, lustered neck and foot, c1840 (A) **200.00**

    8¼" h, transfer and painted ship with nautical verse, inscribed, luster borders, c1845 (A) **380.00**

    8⅜" h, brown transfers and enamels of Iron Bridge and political satire, luster ovals and border, c1825 (A) **440.00**

    8½" h

    Black transfer and enamel of Cast Iron Bridge and clipper ship Northumberland, luster bands & squiggles, c1815 (A) **600.00**

    Black transfer and polychrome of "Success to all Sailors" and "A West View of the Iron Bridge at Sunderland," lustered neck (A) . **375.00**

    9" h, two rhyming nautical poems, ship, sailor, and girl on rocks, splotchy pink ground, mid-19th C **200.00**

Sunderland Luster, left, pitcher, 4" h, black motto in luster roundel, luster border, $155.00; center, plaque, 8½" w, 8" h, black transfers, luster border with copper luster shaped edge, c1830, imp "Dixon," $300.00; right, jug, 8" h, black transfer of mariner's scene, verse and Masonic symbols, "Dixon, Austin & Co.," $575.00.

9⅛" h, black transfers and enamel accents of couple with sayings, oval reserves on each side outlined in iron-red and green, lustered ground, dated 1838 (A) **330.00**

9¼" h

Black transfers and enamels of sailors, mariner's compass, Sailors Tear verse, and Cast Iron Bridge under spout, luster border and dashes (A) **220.00**

Mug

2¾" h, black printed scene of "Autumn" **40.00**

Printed and colored view of bridge with verse, "Moore & Co." **25.00**

Pitcher

5¾" h, black transfer of Iron Bridge, luster trim (A) **40.00**

7⅛" h, black transfer of Masonic designs with polychromes (A) **200.00**

Plaque, pierced for hanging

6⅛" l, 6⅜" w, modeled multicolored masks, of bearded and shaved men, splash luster halos, c1820, pr (A) . **385.00**

6⅝" d, black transfers of "Prepare to Meet Thy God," splash lustered frames edged in copper luster, c1840, imp "G. C. & Co.," pr (A) **80.00**

8½" l, black transfer of ship "May Peace & Plenty," pink and copper luster border **145.00**

8⅝" l, black transfer of "Prepare to Meet Thy God" in oval formed by trumpeting angels and florals, splash lustered foliate molded border edged in copper luster, imp "Dixon Co." (A) **40.00**

9½" l, black transfer of gothic landscape, enamels and luster, foliate molded luster frame, c1820 (A) .. **40.00**

Plate

7⅜" d, lustered rim (A) **10.00**

8⅝" d, black transfer of Cast Iron Bridge, sgd "Moore & Co." luster border, c1825, sgd and imp "Moore & Co." (A) **100.00**

Salt, 3"d, 2"h, lustered body, ftd (A) ... **65.00**

Tea Service, part, teapot, creamer, six cups and saucers, panels and small flowers, pink borders, copper luster trim **350.00**

Teabowl and Saucer, puce transfer, enameled putti at play, luster floral border, imp "Dawson" (A) ········ **70.00**

Watch Stand 11⅜', modeled splash luster tall case clock, flanked by multicolored figures of "Autumn" and "Summer" in pink luster costumes, splash luster rect base, c1820-26, imp "Dixon, Austin & Co." (A) **715.00**

Petrus Regout & C°
MAASTRICHT

MAASTRICHT

Maastricht, Holland
1836 to Present

History: Petrus Regout founded a glass and crystal works in 1834 in Maastricht, Holland. In 1836 he expanded his operation to include the De Sphinx Pottery that had a work force recruited from England. It was Regout's desire to introduce the manufacture of ironstone, a ware that had greatly reduced the market for Delftware.

From 1836 to 1870 Petrus Regout manufactured dinnerware in the style of English ironstone decorated with transfer printed patterns with scenic or romantic themes. Pattern names were back stamped in English for wares exported to English and American markets. Patterns included: "Amazone," "Mythology," "Pleasure Party," "Plough," "Ruth & Boaz," "Wild Rose," and "Willow." Until about 1870 Regout's decorations had been printed only in one color, either blue, black, violet, or red. If a second color was desired the piece was first decorated with a printed black transfer and the second color then hand applied. In 1870 lithographic decalcomania made possible multicolor printing on china. Brightly colored dinnerware became the rage until the end of the century.

When Regout died in 1878, his sons reorganized the company. They adopted the Sphinx trademark. During the 20th century, tastes became more conservative. In 1902 the company ended dinnerware production. Today the firm is called "N.V. Konmklijke Sphinx." Since 1974, it has been part of the British conglomerate Reed International.

Other potteries in Maastricht during the 1840s and 1850s included N. A. Bosch, W. N. Clermont and Ch. Chainage, and G. Lambert & Cie who merged with Sphinx in 1958.

Collecting Hints: Early Regout pottery always had a heavily crazed glaze. After the 1870s, the glaze was free of crazing. The tan luster did not wear well. The quality of the printing varied with the different transfers.

Pieces usually have a printed back stamp. Most dinnerware was marked with a pattern name. The company also made blanks for others to decorate. The phrase "Royal Sphinx" was authorized in 1959 and used on decorative tiles.

Berry Bowl, 4½" d, "Abbey" pattern, dark blue transfer, "Petrus Regout" . **10.00**

Bowl
- 4¾" d, gaudy design blue spatter, green, yellow, and red flowers (A) **20.00**
- 7½" d, "Timor" pattern **30.00**
- 8"d, Oriental pattern, blue and orange **20.00**
- 8¼" d, gaudy floral spatter, blue, green, and yellow, "Maastricht" (A) **25.00**
- 8¾" d, gaudy floral spatter, polychrome, "Maastricht" (A) **25.00**
- 9¼" d, gaudy floral spatter, polychrome, "Maastricht" **15.00**
- 10" d, "Timor" pattern **50.00**

Plate, 9⅛" d, design spatter flowers, green leaves, blue border, $65.00.

Cake Plate 12" d, orange and blue flowers, "Societe Ceramic Maastricht, Made in Holland" **60.00**
Charger, 15¾" d, blue Dutch scene of farm, windmill, and men in boat, scalloped rim, pierced for hanging, sgd "Sonneville" **75.00**
Compote, 8¼" d, 4½" h, "Pajong" pattern, Oriental scene, gold border, "Petrus Regout & Co." **55.00**
Cup and Saucer
- "Abbey" pattern, blue transfer **15.00**
- Gaudy floral spatter, polychrome, "Maastricht" (A) **35.00**
- Oriental pattern, dark red transfer . . **30.00**
- "Pekin" pattern, "Petrus Regout sphinx" **15.00**
Hot Plate, "Blue Onion" design **45.00**
Mug 3" h, gaudy floral spatter, polychrome, "Maastricht" (A) **65.00**
Pitcher, 4½" h, "Timor" pattern **65.00**

Plaque
- 10" d, portrait of Franklin Roosevelt, green wreath **30.00**
- Decal of clusters of pears, shaded rust borders **25.00**
Plate
- 5⅞" d, gaudy floral spatter, polychrome, "Maastricht" (A) **10.00**
- 6" d, "Pompeii" pattern **45.00**
- 6½" d, gaudy design spatter, polychrome floral border (A) **10.00**
- 6¾" d, blue design spatter, gaudy yellow and green flowers (A) **10.00**
- 7½" d
  - "Castillo" pattern, blue transfer, "Petrous Regout" **5.00**
  - "Pajong" pattern **55.00**
- 8" d, "Abbey" pattern, luster trim . . **10.00**
- 8½" d
  - Gaudy design spatter, floral design in red, blue, green, ochre, and lavender **20.00**
  - Oriental design, blue, green and orange accents, "Petrus Regout" . **20.00**
- 8¾" d, gaudy design spatter, floral design in red, blue, green, and yellow-ochre **15.00**
- 8⅞" d, gaudy blue and white floral designs, set of six (A) **90.00**
- 9" d
  - Blue and white gaudy spatter, floral design, "Maastricht" (A) **25.00**
  - Blue design spatter, gaudy yellow and green flowers (A) **10.00**
  - Gaudy spatter, floral design in blue, green, and ochre **25.00**
  - Multicolored fruit center, "Petrus Regout" **10.00**
  - "Paysage" pattern, blue transfer . . **30.00**
  - Rabbit vignette in folk style flowering vine borders, set of ten (A) **300.00**
  - "Superior" pattern, light blue transfer, "Petrus Regout" **35.00**
- 9¼" d, gaudy, floral rim, polychrome, "Maastricht" (A) **10.00**
- 12" d, central scenes of birds and flowers, borders with florals, scalloped rims, Royal Sphinx marks, set of five (A) **50.00**
- 22" d, floral design spatter, multicolored **30.00**
Porringer, 3½" d, "Pompeii" design, "Petrous Regout" **65.00**
Soup Plate
- 9" d, "Regout's Flower" pattern **70.00**
- 10" d, "Abbey" pattern, purple transfer **10.00**
Tray, 12" d, gaudy floral design, polychrome (A) **40.00**
Waste Bowl, 4⅜" d, gaudy floral spatter, polychrome, "Maastricht" (A) **10.00**

1874-1924

1890 - 1939

MAJOLICA

English and Continental
1850 to Present

History: During a visit to Rouen in 1849, Herbert Minton saw flower pots with a green glaze. When he returned to England, Minton instructed Leon Arnoux, his firm's art director, to copy these wares. Arnoux introduced English Majolica, an opaque tin-glazed earthenware, in 1850. The name Majolica originally came from the Spanish island of Majorca. Its popularity in England remained strong through the second half of the 19th century.

Minton's early majolica wares closely imitated Palissy ware, a pottery made by Bernard Palissy at Saintes, France, between 1542 and 1562 and later in a workshop on the grounds of the Palais des Tuileries in Paris.

Palissy ware was characterized by relief figures and ornaments that were covered with colored glazes, mainly yellow, blue, and gray highlighted with brown and manganese. Palissy is known for naturalistic designs of leaves, lizards, snakes, insects, shells, and other natural objects in high relief on plates and dishes. He also made vases, ewers, and basins. The reverse of his wares was covered with a mottled glaze in brown, blue, and manganese. Palissy developed the applique technique which consisted of making plaster casts resembling the natural objects separate from the main body and applying these later.

Early Minton majolica wares were modeled by the French sculptors Emile Jeannest, Albert Carrier-Belluse, and Hugues Protat. Protat made the models from which the wares were cast. Leading artists from the Victorian period who decorated the wares included Thomas Allen, Thomas Kirkby, and Edouard Rischgitz.

Early majolica wares by Minton also attempted to emulate Italian majolica, basic earthenware, that was coated with an opaque white glaze or covering slip. English majolica meant earthenwares that were decorated with deep semi-transparent lead glazes. Typical Victorian majolica examples included large garden ornaments such as seats and jardinieres plus many types of plates and dishes for utilitarian and decorative use.

Daniel Sutherland and Sons of Longton established a pottery in 1863 to manufacture the ma-

jolica wares. A tremendous variety of articles were made. Other manufacturers include: Brown/Westhead, W. Brownfield and Company of Cobridge, Holdcraft, George Jones and Sons, Moore and Company, and Wedgwood. George Jones, who was employed by Minton until he established his own Trent Pottery in Stoke in 1861, made lidded vases, ornamental bowls, candelabras, and wall plaques, along with more ordinary everyday majolica wares.

Wedgwood's majolica took the form of molded leaves and vegetables that were decorated with a translucent green glaze. Other Wedgwood majolica wares were covered with colored glazes on a white body that was molded with high quality relief ornamentation. Vases, umbrella stands, wall brackets, candlesticks, compotes, plates, and a variety of dishes were made.

Majolica wares were made on the Continent by Sarregumines in France, by Villeroy and Boch and Zell in Germany, and by companies in Austria, Bavaria, and Italy. Nineteenth century majolica is different from the earlier Italian majolica wares.

References: Alan-Caiger Smith, *Tin-Glaze Pottery in Europe & the Islamic World,* Faber & Faber, 1973.

Museums: Cleveland Museum of Art, Cleveland, Ohio; City Museum and Art Gallery, Stoke-on-Trent, England; J Paul Getty Museum, Malibu, California; Victoria & Albert Museum, London, England.

MAJOLICA-CONTINENTAL

Ashtray, 7" l, leaf shape, green, yellow, and orange, Italy	**30.00**
Asparagus Server, 10" l, molded asparagus spears, green ends, white stalks, ftd, France	**135.00**
Bowl	
11" d, yellow daisies, green leaves, turquoise ground, dbl handles, Germany	**80.00**
11" d, 5¼" h, large pink and yellow flowers, green leaves and branches, light green stippled ground	**95.00**
Cache Pot, 9" d, 8½" h, royal blue, brown, turquoise, and white design, dbl handles extend from rim to base, set on four small feet	**590.00**
Cake Plate, 10½" d, peaches, blue basketweave ground, dbl handles, Germany	**45.00**
Cake Set	
Master plate, 11"d, four serving plates, large grape leaves and tendrils, yellow dimpled ground, "Zell, Germany"	**85.00**
Master plate, 11¼" d, six plates, 7¾"	

Continental, left, figure, 5" h, red skull cap, lilac shirt, $55.00; center, planter, 11½" l, turquoise and brown, cream ground, $275.00; right, tobacco jar, 9" h, blue, green, and tan on yellow, $300.00.

d, raised light green and pink edged leaves and branches, cream ground, "GERMANY" **95.00**

Candlestick, 7½" h, figural, seated monkey, gray top hat forms candle holder, brown body, France **400.00**

Chargers, 14" d, pink and lavender tulips, white daisies, dark green ground, imp "Steidlzairn", pr **175.00**

Compote
9" h, molded yellow scroll detail, black glossy glaze, late 19th C (A) **60.00**
9¼" h, relief of tree, beetle and bench, dark yellow and green, cobalt sun, France **175.00**

Creamer and Sugar, Art Nouveau style lily pads and blossoms, turquoise, green, and yellow, Austria **130.00**

Ewer
12" h, relief Roman scene, blue int. **75.00**
19" h, middle band of cherubs and trees, mask head below spout, vertical gadroons on neck, pastel colors, ftd, "W. S. & S." **850.00**

Figure, 17½" h, boy feeding dog, shaded green circ base, c1870 ..... **300.00**

Hair Receiver, pink and green raised flowers **45.00**

Humidor, 6" d, 7" h, portrait of man smoking pipe, green basketweave ground, figural pipe on lid, Germany **70.00**

Jug 8½" h, hunter and dog in one oval panel, elk in other, raised trees between, twisted limb handle, Bavaria **95.00**

Oyster Plate 8½" d
Five open shells, crimped edges, dark red shading to blue, Italy, set of eight **225.00**
Six open shells, six painted, green, brown, and yellow, scalloped rims, Italy, set of eight **45.00**

Pitcher
4⅜" h, basketweave, pewter top (A) **25.00**
5½" h, molded branches, pink flowers, beige ground **40.00**
6" h, brown and green leaves, tur-

quoise ground, brown branch handle, pink int., octagonal **60.00**
6½" h, palm tree, tree bark textured surface, pale pink lining **25.00**
7½" h
Purple flowers, green and gold ground, rose int., France **145.00**
Roses, olive ground, magenta int., mustard handle, tankard shape . **110.00**
11" h, figural, rooster, multicolored, "St. Clement, France" **95.00**
12½" h, figural, parrot, multicolored, "St., Clement, France" **95.00**

Plaque
9¼" d, relief of chalet scene, multicolored, pierced for hanging, "Zell, Germany" **55.00**
17½" d, putti bust, blue ground, round gadrooned frame, late 19th C, Italy (A) **100.00**

Plate
6½" d
Two birds, grapes, and leaves, light blue ground, fancy scroll rim, "Zell, Germany" **30.00**
Young man, plumed hat, turquoise ground, brown border **45.00**
7" d, turquoise ground
Cherries and butterflies, Germany **35.00**
Yellow daisies and butterflies, Germany **35.00**
9" d, strawberries, flowers, and leaves, turquoise ground, geometric rim, "Zell, Germany" **45.00**
11" d
Raised dandelion, turquoise ground, Germany **25.00**
Shaggy dog center, multicolored . **55.00**
12" d, basket of fruit, polychrome, mangenta and yellow loop border, buff body, 18th C (A) **360.00**
12" l, 9" w, leaf shape, standing modeled multicolored squirrel **130.00**

Platter
11" l, cherries and butterflies, turquoise ground, Germany **65.00**

12¼" l, begonia, tree-bark ground, Bavaria **95.00**
14" l, 11" w, rope and begonia, basketweave ground **125.00**
Tobacco Jar, 8⅝" h, modeled as huntsman, watching fox, rifle, multicolored, Germany **100.00**
Tray
7" d, leaf shape, green and blue, gray and tan molded snail, France **145.00**
12" d, banana leaf shape, multicolored **145.00**

Continental, vase, 12¼" h, turquoise, tan, brown, and cream, turquoise int., "W. S. & S., Austria," $125.00.

Vase
8" h, Art Nouveau style, irises on front, France **80.00**
12½" h, poppies and leaves, shell and scroll dbl handles, lattice neck, France **70.00**
16" h, Corner, applied soft colored flowers and leaves, attached hanging basket, imp "Made in Italy" .. **195.00**
21½" h, mythological figural scenes, dbl griffin handles, ftd base, pr (A) **525.00**

ENGLAND

Biscuit Jar, 7½" h, green and brown mottled ext., robin's egg blue int., SP lid, sphinx finial, center band, and foot, imp "WEDGWOOD" **245.00**
Bottle, 10¼" h, molded primroses and daffodils, yellow ground, globular shape, stopper, English reg mark (A) **110.00**
Bowl
6" d, green emb cabbage leaves, imp "WEDGWOOD" **35.00**

10½" d, 6" h, multicolored scene, raspberries, border, ftd, English reg mark **135.00**
10¾" d, multicolored bird and fan pattern, ftd, "Wardle, England" .. **135.00**
Bowl, Cov and Underplate, brown and blue shades, green accents, seated goat finial, imp "MINTON" **550.00**
Centerpiece, 8" h, blue and lilac bowl set on branches, fox chasing rabbit around oak tree base, c1870, "P. O. D. R." George Jones mark (A) **5,120.00**
Cheese Dish, Cov
8½" d, domed cov, water lily knob, raised water lily design, foliate ground, tray with foliate center, brown leaf tip edge (A) **375.00**
12¾" d, molded fence, flowers, foliage, and grasses, turquoise ground, mottled green and brown glazed underside, imp "George Jones" (A) **920.00**
Compote
5" h, 9" d, green chestnut leaf, "George Jones" **100.00**
8½" h, green landscape design, figures in center, brown basketweave border, English reg mark **120.00**
Creamer
4" h, pink flowers, yellow and blue ground, English reg mark **30.00**
5"h, 3½"l, green emb grapes and leaves, imp "WEDGWOOD" **45.00**
Creamer and Sugar, blackberry pattern, turquoise ground, lavender int., English reg mark **75.00**
Cup and Saucer, multicolored bird and fan design, Shorter & Boulton **125.00**
Dessert Service, tall compote, low compote, twelve plates, overlapping leaves, tinted ground, English reg marks (A) **210.00**
Dish
8½" l, modeled as row boat with rudder, royal blue, brown, turquoise, and ochre, c1880, A. J. Holdcroft **130.00**
11" l, leaf shape, dbl handles, ftd, green glaze, c1840, English reg mark **225.00**
Ewer
11½" h, applied multicolored straps, turquoise ground, English reg mark **75.00**
16¾" h, "Sacred to Bacchus," seated satyr around neck, "Sacred to Neptune," seated, triton and dolphin, cobalt ground, raised leaf and beading, sq bases, c1868, imp "WEDGWOOD," pr (A) **990.00**
Flower Pot, 6" h, raised birds and flowers, turquoise ground, English reg mark **30.00**
Game Dish, 9" d, brown and green, liner, imp "WEDGWOOD" **585.00**

Goblet, 10" h, entwined sea creatures and sirens, multicolored, English reg mark **135.00**

Jardiniere

13¼" d, molded diaper and flower panels, brown, lilac, and green, four feet, c1880, English reg mark (A) **320.00**

16½" d, modeled peacock, flowering branches, multicolored, elephant mask, fixed ring handles, c1875, Joseph Holdcroft (A) **1,285.00**

Jug

3½" h, shell and fan pattern, brown and green shades, imp "WEDGWOOD" **125.00**

7½" h, raised turquoise ovals, blue and green ground, tan bands between ovals, motto circling vase, c1865, imp "WEDGWOOD" mark **190.00**

Match Box 4⅛" l, relief of acorns and leaves, lilac int., oval, striker on base, "George Jones" **65.00**

Match Pot, 4¾" h, splashed green, brown, and yellow, imp "WEDGWOOD" (A) **45.00**

Milk Pitcher, 8½" h, Grant portraits, American flag and eagle, English reg mark **225.00**

Oyster Plate

14¼" d, aqua and lavender indentations, green sea life around center, beige ground, shell feet **175.00**

Brown center, green and blue oyster depressions, imp "MINTON" **175.00**

Pedestal, 30" h, modeled dolphin, water from open mouth, rock, shell, and floral base, tail supporting mottled circ top, multicolored, c1880, "George Jones" (A) **9,510.00**

Pitcher

3½" h, seaweed and shell design, multicolored, English reg mark ... **100.00**

5¼" h, bent tree trunk shape, caramel ground, pink int., "Wardle, England" **40.00**

5½" h

Commemorative busts, Edward and Alexandra, horseshoe design, imp "WEDGWOOD" **225.00**

Multicolored bird and fan design, imp "WEDGWOOD" **325.00**

6" h, fish on waves pattern, "Shorter, England" **110.00**

6½" h, turquoise and green wheat, pink ground, yellow border, "George Jones" **85.00**

6¾" h, large leaf and flower sprays on each side, irregular cream ground, blue int., imp "WEDGWOOD" .. **95.00**

7" h, blue and yellow raised roses and daisies, English reg mark **75.00**

7" h, 7" d, green leaves on base, top, and handle, pink center, "Wardle, England" **75.00**

7¼" h, green and yellow lily pads .. **65.00**

7½" h, Wood Rose, cream, tree bark mold, imp "WEDGWOOD" **60.00**

7¾" h, white relief Japanese iris, dark brown tree bark ground, green strap handle and foliage, blue int., English reg mark **115.00**

8"

Raised grape design, multicolored, English reg mark **195.00**

Strawberries, white flowers, and green leaves, cobalt ground, tree trunk handle **75.00**

8½" h, blackberries, basketweave ground, English reg mark **85.00**

16" h, white stork, green rushes, yellow flowers, cobalt ground, figural fish pouring spout **260.00**

Planter, 6" h, shell and seaweed design, English reg mark **80.00**

Plate

6½", seashell shape, molded ribbing, green body, brown and yellow tones, imp "WEDGWOOD" **85.00**

7" d

Bamboo sprays in three sections, raised insects, pink and yellow flowers, imp "WEDGWOOD" . **120.00**

Vines, blossoms, and berries, multicolored, cream ground, imp "WEDGWOOD" **60.00**

7½" d, berries, basketweave ground, multicolored, "Banks & Thornley" **35.00**

7¾" d, fern and bamboo pattern, English reg mark **75.00**

8"d

Leaf pattern, shaped border, green glaze, imp "WEDGWOOD" ... **45.00**

English, plate, 8" d, green and brown splashed center, raised floral border with yellow centers, imp "WEDGWOOD," $135.00.

Raspberries, cream basketweave ground **40.00**
Shell shape, green and brown, c1868, imp "WEDGWOOD" .. **95.00**
8½" d
Fern and bow pattern, multicolored, "Banks & Thornley" **50.00**
Grape, leaf, fruit, and flower, multicolored, imp "WEDGWOOD" **65.00**
8¾" d, splashed green, yellow and magenta, pierced key pattern border, c1880, imp "WEDGWOOD," set of four (A) **155.00**
9" d
Lily pad design, "George Jones" . **135.00**
Raised pink flowers, yellow ground, imp "WEDGWOOD" . **50.00**
9½" d, yellow-brown and white flowers, foliage border **45.00**
Platter
10½" l, two molded brown baskets, yellow flowers and leaves, light green ground, lavender border, English reg mark **60.00**
12" d, multicolored leaves and grapes, c1883, imp "WEDGWOOD" **65.00**
Salad Bowl, 8" d, matching servers, shell form with designs of coral and seashells, aqua int., imp "WEDGWOOD" **465.00**
Salad set, 9½" d, scroll like multicolored ext., four sq feet, silver mounted rim and serving pieces, imp "WEDGWOOD" mark **375.00**
Salmon Dish, Cov, 19" l, brown basketweave molded base, lilac int., modeled fish in ferns on cov, c1880, "George Jones" (A) .... **.3,655.00**
Salt, Master, 6" l, figural, boy with cart, brown and tan, pink shell cart int., English reg mark **175.00**
Serving Set, platter, 16" l, ten plates, 6½" d, strawberries and flowers trim, tan ribbed ground, bow ribbons form handles for tray, imp "WEDGWOOD" **600.00**
Shaving Mug, daisy design, divided lavender int., English reg mark **150.00**
Teapot
4½" h, bird and fan design, Wardle & Co. **105.00**
Bamboo pattern, English reg mark .. **135.00**
Tobacco Humidor, 9" h, house shape, blue and green, yellow ground, ivy vine handle, tree trunk opening for pipe, wheat sheaf for matches **295.00**
Tray, 14" l, 11½" w, bird in flight, multicolored florals, basketweave ground, green bamboo border, imp "WEDGWOOD" **350.00**
Umbrella Stand, 32¾" h, modeled

heron standing by bullrushes, rocky base, green, brown, blue, and yellow glazes, damaged, A. J. Holdcroft (A) **950.00**
Vase
6" h, raised daisies, earth colored ground, dbl handles, pr **95.00**
12" h, raised florals, green ground, large ring handle, English reg mark **75.00**

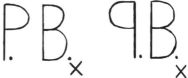

MALICORNE

West of Paris, France
Last Quarter 19th Century

History: Pouplard established his Malicorne factory in the Sarthe region west of Paris during the last quarter of the 19th century. He was making fine quality reproductions of the typical Quimper patterns, especially those of the Porquier-Beau factory.

To add to the confusion, Pouplard used the "P" from his own name and the "B" from his wife's name Beatrix to form a "PB" mark of his own. Though the design differed from the "PB" mark of Porquier-Beau because the letters were separated and followed by a small "x," Porquier-Beau still brought suit against Pouplard. When the suit was settled in 1897, Malicorne was ordered to cease production and forced to destroy all of his remaining pottery molds.

References: Sandra V. Bondhus, *Quimper Pottery: A French Folk Art Faience,* privately published, 1981.

Museums: Sevres Museum, Sevres, France.

Bowl, 13" d, decor riche pattern, green sponged border, "P.B.X." **600.00**
Cheese Dish, 8" l, blue and cream, "P.B.X." **225.00**
Jug, 7¾" h, crest, crown over white fleur-de-lis and blue shield, crossed olive branches **275.00**
Knife Rest, 3" l, multicolored
Peasant man and florals, "St. Lunaire" **80.00**
Peasant man, c1840 .... **60.00**
Mug, 2½" h, multicolored peasant woman, "P.B.X." **175.00**

Oyster Plate, 11" d, peasant scene in
  center, floral border, "P.B.X." **225.00**
Pitcher, 3" h, multicolored floral design   **60.00**

Plate, 8½" d, multicolored peasant woman, gray-pink crazed ground, "P. B. X.," $125.00.

Plate
  6½" d, frontal view of peasant
    woman, crest of Brittany on border,
    scalloped edge outlined in blue,
    "entwined CM" **245.00**
  8"d, two female peasants in field, de-
    cor riche borders, "P.B.X." **350.00**
  9" d, center frontal view of peasant
    couple, orange-yellow band bor-
    der, crest of Brittany and alternating
    fleur-de-lis **250.00**
  10" d, male or female peasant in field,
    multicolored, pr **400.00**
Platter
  12" l, peasant man holding umbrella,
    soft colors, mid-19th C **155.00**
  16" l, 11" w, Breton family at outdoor
    shrine, green on green single stroke
    floral border, "P.B.X." **575.00**
Porringer, 7" H-H, peasant woman holding knitting needles in center, red
  dash and green tab handles, "P.B.X."   **20.00**
Snuff Bottle, 3" l, multicolored peasant
  woman, figural bagpipe shape body,
  "Portieux" **275.00**
Vase 5" h, peasant woman and Rouen
  style border **135.00**
Wall Pocket
  5" h, peasant man harvesting pota-
    toes, multicolored, "P.B.X." **195.00**
  8½" h, Breton man and woman by
    farmyard wooden gate, bowknotted
    bag shape **375.00**
  12" l, peasant woman on front, "Le
    Croisic" below, gray glaze, mid-
    19th C, "P.B.X." **175.00**

MARTIN BROTHERS

Fulham, England
1873 to 1877

London and Southall, England
1877 to 1914

History: Robert, Walter, Edwin, and Charles
Martin, the first of the English "studio potters,"
were four brothers who produced salt glaze stoneware called "Martinware." The Martin tradition
evolved around ornately engraved, incised, or
carved designs on salt glazed ware. Glazes usually were mottled with colors including gray,
brown, blue, and yellow in muted tones.

Robert initially worked for the Fulham Pottery
of C. J. C. Barley. He and his three brothers
established their own workshop in 1873 at Po-
mona House in Fulham. They fired their wares
in the kiln at Fulham Pottery. When that kiln was
no longer available, they leased a kiln at Shepherd's Bush.

Robert, known as Wallace, was the sculptor
and director of the Martin team. He received his
training at the Lambeth School of Art. He was an
experienced stone carver and modeler of figures.
Wallace modeled grotesques, now eagerly
sought by collectors, for over thirty years. Grotesque birds were called "Walley birds" after
their maker.

Walter was in charge of throwing the large
vases, mixing the clays, and the firing process.
Edwin decorated the vases and other objects with
naturalistic forms of decoration. Often he used
incised or relief designs of fish, florals, and birds.
Charles handled the business aspects of the concern.

In 1877 the brothers founded a pottery in
Southall and built their own kiln. They opened
a shop in London the next year. The Southall
Pottery declined in 1910 with the death of
Charles Martin. When Walter died in 1912, pro-
duction ceased.

References: C. B. Beard, *Catalogue of the Martinware in the Collection of F. J. Nettleford,* privately published, 1936; Malcolm Haslam, *The
Martin Brothers Potters,* Richard Denis, Hugh

Wakefield, *Victorian Porcelain,* Herbert Jenkins, 1962.

Museums: Victoria & Albert Museum, London, England.

Collecting Hints: All pieces of Martinware are signed with their name, the place of production, and numerals and letters signifying the month and year. The information was incised into the soft clay before firing.

Between 1873 and 1883 the pottery was incised "R. W. Martin" followed by "Fulham" if fired at the Fulham Pottery, "London" if fired at Shepherd's Bush, and "Southall" if made at their own works. From 1879 when the shop was operating, the words "and London" were added to "Southall." From 1883 the full mark was "R. W. Martin & Bros. London & Southall."

Vase, 9¾" h, incised cobalt bird, floral, and leaf design, beige ground, $750.00.

Figure, 6⅞" h, stoneware, multicolored bird, wings tucked behind back, circ ebonized base, dated 1910, "Martin Bros., London & Southall" (A) **1,560.00**
Flask, 17" h, stoneware, "Water Baby," modeled as sleeping nude child, streaked blue and green reeds, entwined leaf handle, inscribed, titled, dated 1880, "R.W. Martin, London & Southall" (A) **3,360.00**
Inkwell, 2¼" h, incised blue, green, and brown waterfall, bridge and cottage, pyramidal, dated 1881, "Martin, London" **50.00**
Jardiniere, 9¼" h, dark brown lilies, blue stamens, hatched ground, mottled amber glaze, "R.W. Martin, London & Southall" (A) **90.00**
Jug
  3½" h, stoneware, dark brown and

blue primroses, mottled ground, dated 1886 (A) **25.00**
5" h, relief dbl faced **450.00**
9¼" h, brown foliate scrolls, blue lined ground, angular handle, dated 1879 (A) **35.00**
10¼" h, incised dark green pointed leaves, mottled tan-gray ground, loop handle, "Martin Bros., London & Southall" (A) **130.00**
10⅜" h, stoneware, incised and painted brown, black and white fish in aquatic foliage, gray ground, loop handle, wide foot, flared neck, dated 1887, "R.W. Martin & Bros., London & Southall" (A) ... **360.00**
Pitcher, 5" h, blue foliage, monogram . **90.00**
Teapot, 5⅞" h, dark blue fan shape plants, light blue florets, mottled brown ground, blue spout and handle, dated 1879, "R.W. Martin, London & Southall" (A) **145.00**
Vase
  2⅛" h, grotesque fish and jellyfish, light gray-blue ground, dated 1909, "Martin Bros., London & Southall" (A) **130.00**
  6" h, red-brown flambe streaked, squash shape **150.00**
  6⅛" h, stoneware, "Gourd," five vertical relief ribs, green glazed vertical grooves, horizontal incised design, brown body, dated 1905, "Martin Bros., London & Southall" (A) **460.00**
  7¼" h, stoneware, brown, blue, and white bullrushes and insects, medium brown ground, flattened pear shape, "Martin Bros., London & Southall" (A) **85.00**
  7½" h, stoneware, white relief pods, long stems, light brown body, dated 1907, "Martin Bros., London & Southall" (A) **480.00**
  7⅞" h, stoneware, brown, green, and blue incised long-billed birds and foliage, beige ground, dated 1897, "Martin Bros., London & Southall" (A) **530.00**
  9¼" h, stoneware, four molded faces sharing eyes, brown tones, sq ovoid shape, cylindrical neck, dated 1884, "Martin Bros., London & Southall" (A) **4,320.00**
  17⅛" h, dark brown leaves, green veins, light brown and olive ground, dbl handles (A) **160.00**
Wall Bracket, 5⅛" h, flat top, muted green-brown flowers, blue leaves in relief, "R.W. Martin & 1876" (A) ... **70.00**

MASON

Lane Delph, Staffordshire, England
c1804 to 1848

History: Although ironstone is the most familiar product associated with Mason's name, Miles Mason actually began his business career as an importer of china wares, specializing in matching pieces for incomplete sets. After studying the manufacturing methods at Worcester and Derby, Mason joined with Thomas Wolfe in Liverpool in 1780 to manufacture Chinese-style porcelain tablewares.

After the dissolution of the Wolfe-Mason partnership in 1804, Mason started a second concern at Lane Delph in Fenton, Staffordshire. The Fenton factory was devoted to the manufacture of quality blue and white transferware. Within a short time the factory was relocated at Minerva Works and expanded to incorporate the Bagnell factory. The new factory was known as the Fenton Stone Works.

Charles and George, Miles' sons, eventually became the managers. In 1813 they patented the ironstone formula and manufacturing technique. They were not the first to produce this hard and durable earthenware, but they certainly were the most successful. Mason's Patent Ironstone China became dominant in the market. Ironstone, designed to meet the middle class needs for utilitarian, durable china tablewares, was produced at Fenton from 1813 to 1848.

The first designs were Oriental in nature. The most common method of applying the design was by transfer. Areas were highlighted with touches of enamel. Hand painting and gilding of the ironstone blanks was not uncommon, especially in floral and scenic patterns. Every conceivable form was fashioned in ironstone, from common tableware to fireplace mantels.

Economic difficulties beset the works in 1848. Charles was forced to sell the family business to Francis Morley. Morley, in partnership with Ashworth from 1849 to 1862, acquired the Mason designs and molds. Ashworth reissues of Mason's original shapes and decorative patterns are hard

to distinguish from those produced at the Fenton works.

For over one hundred years, Ashworth and Brothers, Ltd, have been selling vast quantities of their Mason's type ware with the traditional Oriental-styled patterns. In 1968 the firm took the new name "Mason's Ironstone China, Ltd." The old mark was reinstituted.

References: Geoffrey A. Godden, *Godden's Guide to Mason's China & Ironstone Wares,* Antique Collectors Club, Ltd., 1980; Geoffrey A. Godden, *The Illustrated Guide to Mason's Patent Ironstone China,* Barrie & Jenkins, 1971; Reginald Haggar & Elizabeth Adams, *Mason Porcelain and Ironstone 1796-1853,* Faber & Faber, 1977; R.G. Haggar, *The Masons of Lane Delph,* Lund Humphries, 1952.

Collectors' Club: Masons Collectors Club, Secretary, 27 Roe Lane, Newcastle, Staffordshire ST5 3PH, England. Membership: 10 pounds. Bimonthly newsletter.

Museums: City Museum & Art Gallery, Hanley, Stoke-on-Trent, England; Potsdam Public Museum, Potsdam, N.Y.; Victoria & Albert Museum, London, England.

Collecting Hints: Don't overlook the Ashworth reissue pieces. They qualify as true antiques.

Bottle, 8" h, enamel dots forming flowers, cobalt ground, "MASON'S PATENT IRONSTONE" **60.00**
Bowl
  7⅞" d, ironstone
    Imari style vases of flowers, utensils and border, trailing flower sprays, iron-red, blue, green, and turquoise, c1830 (A) **120.00**
    Imari style vase of flowers on table, scrolling sprays, red, black, and gold, c1830 (A) **120.00**
  9½" w, 4" h, Chinese design, rust, blue, and white, pedestaled, fluted edge, c1812-25, imp "Mason" . . . **295.00**
  8⅝" d, cov, ironstone, Imari style vase, tree, and foliage, octagonal, lion finial, snake handles **125.00**
Chamberpot, 9" d, 6" h, ironstone, multicolored Oriental floral motif, green snake handle **125.00**
Coffee Can and Saucer, trailing flowers edged in gilt, orange ground, c1810 (A) **80.00**
Creamer, 4" h, Oriental style design, multicolored, "MASON'S PATENT IRONSTONE" **75.00**
Cup and Saucer, "Vista" pattern, blue and white **10.00**
Dessert Service, ironstone
  Rect center dish, two rect dishes, two leaf shape dishes, six plates, enam-

eled, gilt exotic birds and butterflies, gilt foliage, blue ground, c1825, 11 pcs **275.00**

Two cov sauce tureens and stands, rect centerpiece, two oval dishes, twelve plates, painted gold birds, flowers, and insects, blue ground, 21 pcs **480.00**

Dinner Service, Imari style red, blue, and gold, two exotic birds by fence, foliage, "MASON'S PATENT IRONSTONE", set of 108 pieces (A) **10,200.00**

Dish

7⅞" d, blue transfer, three Oriental figures near garden pavilion, enamels, borders, mons, alternating scrolls, and florals, c1810, set of six (A) **100.00**

8" l, bone china, black bat printed landscape scene in manner of Spode's pattern #557, curved shape, c1810 .... **65.00**

11⅞" d, ironstone, multicolored, Japan style pattern, wavy rim **60.00**

11" w, painted famille rose, vases of peonies, birds, and utensils, borders, whorl pattern lappets reserved with flowerheads, leaf shape, c1830, black printed "MASON'S PATENT IRONSTONE," pr (A) **100.00**

Footbath, 18" l, ironstone, Japan style, vases of peonies and chrysanthemums, oval, grotesque handles **400.00**

Gravy Boat, 2¾" h, ironstone, printed, painted, Oriental figures in landscape **25.00**

Jam Jar, cov, "Chartreuse" pattern, green and gold, white ground **35.00**

Jardiniere, 16½" h, painted iron-red, blue, and gilt panels of chrysanthemums, blue ground, alternating panels of stylized flowers, lappet border, c1820 (A) **2,445.00**

Jug

5½" h, 4½" d, "Blue Willow" pattern, octagon, "MASON'S PATENT IRONSTONE" **95.00**

7" h, blue and white, melon ribbed . **60.00**

7½" h, ironstone, "Hydra," blue printed birds and peonies **45.00**

7⅞" h, painted cottages and castle ruins in landscapes, gilt border, solid and hatched triangles **200.00**

8⅝" h, ironstone

Molded stag and boar chased by hounds, modeled oak tree handle, white (A) **105.00**

Mountainous river scenes and flowers, hexagon **65.00**

9" h, ironstone, Japan style vases and flowers, grotesque handle (A) **155.00**

9⅞" h, ironstone, dark blue and red Oriental landscapes, yellow neck flowers, green ground, hexagon, printed mark **135.00**

13⅜" h, ironstone, multicolored peonies and formal borders, lobed body, scroll handle **135.00**

Loving Cups, 6⅝" h, ironstone, painted flying birds, flowers and rustic table, dbl handles, green accents, pr **825.00**

Meat Dish, 14½" l, ironstone, painted Japan style water lily and flowers, chamfered corners (A) **200.00**

Pitcher

4" h, black bat printed landscape scene, c1810 .... **45.00**

5" h, ironstone

Iron-red and blue Oriental design, green snake handle, c1840, imp "Mason" **125.00**

Rust Oriental design, imp "Mason" **95.00**

5½" h

"Blue Willow" pattern, octagon, Mason's Ironstone **95.00**

Left, jug, 5½" h, multicolored florals, dark blue ground, gilt trim, green serpent handle, "Fenton Stone Works," $175.00; center, bowl, 9" d, "Blue Willow" pattern, $50.00; right, sauce tureen, 8" h, blue, orange, and green Oriental florals, white and gilt base, c1815, $575.00.

Ironstone, multicolored Oriental figures and florals, snake handle **120.00**

Ironstone, multicolored Oriental floral motif, cobalt snake handle **125.00**

6" h, ironstone

Blue pastoral scene, white ground, c1840's **50.00**

Multicolored Oriental floral motif, green snake handle **120.00**

Raised flowers and birds, gray-green ground, "MASON'S PATENT IRONSTONE" **65.00**

6¼" h, "Regency" pattern, "MASON'S PATENT IRONSTONE" ... **50.00**

6½" h

"Blue Willow" pattern, snake handle, ironstone **120.00**

"Vista" pattern, pink, cream ground, octagon **45.00**

7½" h, blue and white Oriental florals, "MASON'S PATENT IRONSTONE" **100.00**

Plate

8" d, ironstone, "Manchu" pattern in colors **10.00**

9" d, ironstone

Bird in flowering tree, blue transfer, polychrome enamel and gilt, pr (A) **70.00**

Green and red Oriental scene **65.00**

Multicolored Oriental design, two center sqs of Oriental scenes ... **45.00**

9¼" d

Center scroll cartouche of Oriental figures, black whorl ground reserved, panels of utensils, lobed rim, c1835, "MASON'S PATENT IRONSTONE CHINA" (A) **50.00**

Sepia transfer, jardiniere of flowers, gilt rim, c1845 .... **60.00**

10" d, ironstone, famille rose, "Tobacco Leaf" pattern, lobed rim (A) **170.00**

10¼" d, Imari pattern, vivid colors, Mason's Ironstone **125.00**

10⅜" d, "Japan" pattern, Oriental fenced garden, iron-red, blue, and salmon, diaper borders, floral sprays, c1815, imp "PATENTED IRONSTONE CHINA," set of six . **336.00**

10¾" d, "Vista" pattern, "MASON'S PATENT IRONSTONE" **10.00**

Platter, Ironstone

9⅝" l, multicolored Oriental terrace scene, c1825 (A) **110.00**

22" l, blue and white Oriental design, floral border, "Mason's Ptd. & Importers" **175.00**

Potpourri Vase, 11⅞" h, ironstone, painted, gilt Imari style rocks and peonies, gilt dbl handles, dragon finial on pierced cov (A) **785.00**

Sauce Tureen, 7½" d, matching stands,

ironstone, printed, painted multicolored flower vases, bands of flowers, dark blue and white ground, pr **265.00**

Serving Dish, "Vista" pattern, castle scene, blue leaf border, tri-corner, dragon at each point **20.00**

Serving Set, ironstone, hexagon ftd dish, 11⅜" d, five plates, painted Japan style flowers & foliage **160.00**

Soap Dish, Cov, 5" l, ironstone, Oriental motif, pierced drain, sea serpent handle, c1840 .... **145.00**

Soup Plates, 9¾" d, sepia printed, painted florals and butterflies, orange luster edged scalloped rim, c1820, pr **110.00**

Spill Vases, 3¾" h, ironstone, fence and flowering rockwork, Imari colors, cylindrical, imp "PATENTED IRONSTONE CHINA," pr (A) **94.00**

Tea Service

Broad band, gilt scrolling vine leaves, white ground, set of 32 pcs **180.00**

Gilt vines, puce leaves, iron-red grapes, five replaced saucers, pattern #308, set of twenty six pieces (A) **625.00**

Teacup and Saucer, black bat printed classic figures in gold band, "Bute" shape **125.00**

Tureen, undertray, and matching ladle, "Fruit Basket" design **385.00**

Vase

6½" h, reserves of chrysanthemums, Japan colors, cobalt ground, pr (A) **275.00**

6¾" h, 6" d, printed and painted Oriental style panels, mon and scrolls, dragon handles, c1830, set of three (A) **175.00**

7½" h, gilt butterflies and insects, dark blue ground, bottle shape, pr **70.00**

9⅞" h, cov, ironstone, green dragons and serpents, black ground, dolphin handles **55.00**

10" h, ironstone, multicolored birds and flowers, Oriental style, cylindrical, c1820 .... **250.00**

11⅝" h, ironstone, enameled and gilt, butterflies and flower sprays, blue ground, gilt loop handles with flower terminals, gilt rims, c1825, pr **275.00**

12½" h, cov, ironstone, panels of Oriental figures and trees, orange ground, gilt scales, on blue ground, octagon, "MASON'S IRONSTONE, ENGLAND" **100.00**

14½" h, ironstone, gold and white dragons, sea creatures, apple-green ground, cylindrical, octagonal necks, pierced flattened handles, pr **275.00**

19½" h, ironstone, gilt insects, Oriental flowers, light blue rockwork,

cobalt ground, dragon handles, gilt figural knob, hairline on base, c1820 (A) 550.00
27⅛" h, cov, ironstone, Imari style, panels of flowering plants, blue, red, orange, and gold, neck and foot with blue enameled dragons and white dots, hexagon dbl bellied shape, molded dragon handles (A)**1,020.00**
28" h, birds, cobalt ground, ewer top, dbl gold handles with two Cupids, "MASON'S PATENT IRONSTONE"**6,500.00**
39" h, cov, recessed panels, Oriental florals and pheasants, multicolored, cobalt ground, Oriental river scenes on sides, molded dragon handles, seated Chinaman knobs, restored, c1840-50, pr (A) **1,980.00**
Vegetable Bowl
8½" d, "Manchu" pattern 10.00
10¼" l, Imari pattern, cobalt, dark red, and gold, "MASON'S PATENT IRONSTONE" 65.00

Vase, 9½" h, multicolored portrait, blue, purple, and green irid ground, "Clement Massier," $325.00.

C. M
Golfe·Jurn·
(9.M)
1845-1917

MASSIER

Golfe-Juan, France
1881 to 1917

History: Clement Massier, who started work in 1881 in Golfe-Juan, France, was an artist and potter who produced earthenware with metallic luster decoration. He used plant motifs and other nature themes on shapes that were Art Nouveau in style.

Massier's wares usually are marked with an incised "Massier" or have his initial or the location of the pottery.

Candleholder, turquoise, brown drip glaze, loop handle, "C. Massier" . . . 135.00
Ewer
3" h, pink, copper, and green irid swirls, "C. M." 200.00
14" h, gold thistle, bronze metallic luster, "CM Golfe-Juan" 275.00
Jardiniere, 44" h, three Art Nouveau modeled women, gowns tapering to twisted standard painted with poppies, peach to rust glaze (A) 950.00
Jug, 12" h, Persian design, multicolored, heavy gold ground, "Clement Massier, Golfe-Juan" 350.00
Knife Rest, hp florals, triangular shape, Jerome Massier 45.00
Tile, 6" sq, flowers, beige ground 110.00

Toothpick Holder, irid green finish . . . 125.00
Vase
2¾" h, irid bees design 135.00
3½" h, red and gold glazes, "C. M. G. J." 100.00
4¼" h, bud, maroon luster finish, geometric overlay 235.00
4¾" h, irid purple and blue finish, pinched base, metal floral mounting, "C. Massier Golfe-Juan" 400.00
8¼" h, green luster flowers and leaves on stems, green, blue, orange, and gold luster ground, modeled snake loop handles, "J. Massier fils Vallauris" (A) 240.00

MEAKIN

Hanley, England
Alfred Meakin, 1873 to Present

History: Alfred Meakin was a Staffordshire potter who made a wide range of earthenware and ironstone china at his Royal Albert Works in Tunstall starting in 1873. Beginning in 1877 the firm traded as Alfred Meakin Ltd., a name it still uses today.

The earthenware is marked with a crown and "AlFRED MEAKIN/ENGLAND."

J. & G. Meakin, 1845 to Present

History: James Meakin established a pottery in Longton in 1845 and transferred it to Hanley in 1848. When he retired in 1852, James and George, his sons, succeeded him. The firm traded as J. & G. Meakin.

The Meakins built the Eagle Works in 1859 and enlarged it in 1868. Later there were branches of the factory at Cobridge and Burslem. Both earthenware and granite ware were produced. The wares were decorated in the style of French porcelain and made for export to the American market. Meakin also produced romantic Staffordshire and flow blue decorated pieces.

J. & G. Meakin joined the Wedgwood Group in 1970.

References: Bernard Hollowood, *The Story of J. and G. Meakin,* Bemrose Publicity Co., Ltd, 1951.

Vegetable Bowl, 9¾" H-H, "Riverdale" pattern, purple transfer, $15.00.

Bone Dish
"Greenville" pattern, blue floral design **25.00**
"Kenwood" pattern, blue-gray florals **10.00**
Bowl, 6¾" d, "Simple Simon" design . **10.00**
Butter Pats, hp florals, multicolored, set of six **35.00**
Cup and Saucer, "Blue Nordic" pattern **5.00**
Demitasse Cup and Saucer, "Ashbourne" pattern **15.00**
Pitcher, 6" d, 8" h, morning glories and vines, scroll handle **20.00**
Plate
8" d
Dickensware, "Tony Weller," multicolored, sq **35.00**
Hp country scene, brown and tan church, green and yellow accents, "Alfred Meakin" **10.00**

9" d, "Brier" pattern **25.00**
9¾" d
"Dresden Hopfen" pattern, green transfer, "Alfred Meakin" **25.00**
"Persian" pattern, brown transfer, ironstone **10.00**
10½" d, "Ardsley" pattern **10.00**
Platter
14" l, black palm trees and blue flowers, gold border, "J. & G. Meakin" **25.00**
16" l, 12½" w, "Blue Willow" pattern **95.00**
Soup Plate, 8" d, "Fair Winds" pattern **10.00**
Vegetable Tureen, 11½" l, "Rosalind" pattern, brown transfer, ironstone ... **165.00**

MEIGH

Staffordshire, England
c1805–1834 Job Meigh
1835–1901 Charles Meigh

History: Job Meigh operated the Old Hall Pottery at Hanley in the Staffordshire District beginning around 1805 and ending in 1834. Charles, his son, joined the firm and operated the pottery under his own name between 1835 and 1849. The factory produced earthenwares and stonewares.

Charles Meigh was famous for his firm's white stoneware jugs with relief decorations. The decorations were part of the mold from which the pieces were cast. During the 1840s, jugs with Gothic details were made. The "Minister" jug of 1842 was the most famous. Classical jugs featuring designs of sporting events and drinking scenes were produced during the 1840s and 50s.

For two years, 1850 and 1851, the firm operated as Charles Meigh, Son & Pankhurst. For the next eleven years, 1851 to 1861, the company was known as Charles Meigh & Sons.

Museums: Potsdam Public Museum, Potsdam, N.Y.

Bowl, 9⅜" sq, red, blue, and gilt flowers and trees, stone china, Hicks & Meigh **110.00**

Compote, 7¼" h, multicolored stylized flowers and foliage, pierced border, "printed Royal Arms" mark, Hicks, Meigh & Johnson **95.00**

Dessert Service

Center ftd dish, two sq dishes, oval dish, three shell shape dishes, fourteen plates, "Amherst Japan" pattern, blue and red, stone china (A) **675.00**

Compote, two sq dishes, four oval dishes, fourteen plates, "Amherst Japan" pattern **300.00**

Dinner Service

8 pcs, six plates, 9¾" d, two soup plates, 9" d, red rose, green, yellow, and blue accents, Oriental design, c1822, "Hicks & Meigh-Stone China" **475.00**

17 pcs, five meat dishes, vegetable dish, six dinner plates, five dessert plates, Oriental pattern, famille rose colors **195.00**

37 pcs, multicolored stylized flowers, ironstone **200.00**

Dish

19¼" l, painted fence, willow tree, and peony design, four border floral groups, ironstone, Hicks & Meigh **210.00**

Painted lotus and peony design, rect, ironstone, Hicks & Meigh (A) **70.00**

Footbath, 22⅞" l, "Chinese Scenery" pattern, blue transfer, bombe sides, "Hicks, Meigh & Johnson" (A) **520.00**

Jar, cov, 6½" h, "Japan" pattern, rust, blue, and gold, stone china, ftd, open finial, c1822, "Hicks, Meigh & Johnson" **175.00**

Jug, 6¾" h, "Minister," gothic style figural, tracery relief motif, stoneware, dated 1842 (A) **100.00**

Loving Cup, 6⅞" h, raised white figures of Bacchus and women, grapes and vines, blue ground, parian, c1840 .. **300.00**

Pitcher

9" h

Raised figures in classical clothes, parian, c1857 (A) **90.00**

Raised Julius Caesar design, caramel color, "Nov 1st 1839 Published by C. Meigh, Hanley, Julius Caesar" **400.00**

10½" h, Apostle, 8-sided, salt glaze, "Mar.17th,1842 Charles Meigh, Hanley" **235.00**

12" h, white relief of Bacchus and cherubs, blue ground, modeled crane handle, parian, pewter lid . **285.00**

Light brown body, grape clusters and leaves dec around upper section,

male figures on lower section, large sq twist form handle, c1844, "Charles Meigh" **325.00**

Pitcher, 12" h, salt glaze, c1844, $535.00.

Plate

8⅝" d, "Melting Snow" border, Hicks & Meigh **20.00**

9⅝" d, blue printed birds, florals design, ironstone, Hicks & Meigh (A) **15.00**

10¼" d, center painted, view of Windsor castle in landscape setting, matte tan border, gilt leaves, ironstone, printed "Ironstone," imp "Opaque Porcelain" **190.00**

Platter

19" l, 15" w, "Italy" pattern, dark blue transfer, c1860, "Charles Meigh & Sons" **65.00**

19½" l, "Priory" pattern, flowers, blue transfer, c1830, Hicks, Meigh & Johnson (A) **85.00**

Sauce Tureen, Cov, and Stand

Multicolored baskets of flowers,"Royal Arms" **25.00**

Red, blue, and gilt flowers and trees, stone china, Hicks & Meigh **115.00**

Sugar Bowl and Stand, printed and painted, famille rose colors Oriental style flowering plants, stone china, gilt accented molded rims, handles and finials, c1860, Hicks & Meigh, pr (A) **420.00**

Tea Set, teapot, jug, cov sugar bowl, "Apostle," white smear glaze stoneware (A) **55.00**

Vegetable Tureen, Cov, multicolored baskets of flowers, rect, "Royal Arms" **30.00**

Royal Dresden China
1938 - Present

1727

1736

1732

MEISSEN

Saxony, German Democratic Republic
1710 to Present

History: The history of Meissen porcelain design falls into distinct periods which were determined by the director of the company and the kings who appointed and controlled them. Located in the Saxon district of Germany, the Meissen factory, or Royal Saxon Porcelain Manufactory, was founded in 1710 by Frederich August I and first directed by Johann Boettger. It was Boettger who developed the first truly white porcelain in Europe. His white porcelain was exceptionally plastic and could be molded into a variety of applied decorations. Silver shapes were most popular.

After 1720 Meissen porcelain was decorated with fine enamel painting, even surpassing some of the Chinese porcelains. During this period, most of the Meissen tablewares were of relatively simple form which provided ample backgrounds for the beautiful painted decorations. The original crossed swords factory mark was adopted in 1723.

When Johann Horoldt was manager during the last ten years of the reign of Augustus the Strong (1694–1733), the porcelain was a brilliant pure white. Horoldt did pseudo-Chinese scenes in scrollwork of red, gold, and luster plus other adaptations of Chinese, Japanese, and other Oriental wares and motifs. Johann Kirchner (1727–1733) made life size figures of animals and birds for Augustus the Strong's Japanese Palace.

When Joachim Kaendler, a modeler, came to Meissen in 1731, he began producing figures, especially the Crinoline figures and groups. About 1738 Kaendler created numerous miniature figures used for lavish banquet decorations for the court of Dresden. He designed the world famous swan set for Count von Bruhl. Kaendler also introduced tablewares with low relief borders in the style of silver.

The Rococo influence occurred after 1740. The famous onion pattern appeared about that time. The factory was severely damaged during the Seven Years' War (1756–1763) and was occupied by the victorious Prussians.

Following a major reorganization, the master modeler Michel Victor Acier came to Meissen in 1764 and became the dominating influence. He moved the factory into the Neo-classical period with emphasis on mythological figures. Pictorial decoration was copied from Sevres. Under the directorship of Marcolini (1774–1813) the style shifted to that of Louis XVI. The Marcolini Period ended with the cessation of the Napoleonic Wars in 1814.

The factory experienced a decline in production under the management of Von Oppel from 1814 to 1833. The wares during this phase often imitated other successful European concerns.

The period from 1833 to 1870 is called the "Kuhn Period," after a director of the factory. The company's fortunes improved, both technically and economically. A revival of production of the great pieces from one hundred years earlier was carried out. Many figures were copied in the Rococo style, which was the popular taste of the times. Sales of the china wares continued to increase.

The "New Period" at Meissen started in 1870 when Kuhn died and Raithel became director. Exports of china to America increased during this time. Utilitarian wares in blue underglaze grew in popularity. Improvements continued to be made in the china production process.

From 1895 to 1901 the factory was managed by Brunnemann. A conflict developed between the supporters of old and new ideas of china manufactory. Between 1901 and 1910 there was increasing success artistically and financially, culminating with the two–hundredth anniversary Jubilee year of 1910. Many reforms were carried out. New buildings were constructed for furnaces and studios. A new drawing school was established at the factory.

Following World War II the factory was reorganized. Today it operates as the State's Porcelain Manufactory in East Germany. New models are made as closely as possible to the old shapes. Ornamentation also tends to follow the old models. In addition, some new forms are made. The Meissen factory also manufactures various commemorative wares for coronations, Christmas plaques, and Easter plaques.

References: Dr. K. Berling, Editor, *Meissen China, An Illustrated History*, Dover, 1972, Yvonne Hackenbroch, *Meissen & Other Conti-*

nental Porcelain Faience & Enamel in the Irwin Untermyeer Collection, Harvard University Press, 1956; W.B. Honey, Dresden China: An Introduction to the Study of Meissen Porcelain, Dresden House, 1946; Otto Walcha, Meissen Porcelain, G.P. Putman's Sons, 1981.

Museums: Cincinnati Art Museum, Cincinnati, OH; Cummer Gallery of Art, Jacksonville, FL; Dresden Museum of Art & History, Dresden, Germany; Gardiner Museum of Ceramic Art, Toronto, Canada; Metropolitan Museum of Art, New York, NY; National Museum of American History, Smithsonian Institution, Washington, D.C.; Schlossmuseum, Berlin, Germany; Woodmere Art Museum, Philadelphia, PA.

Collecting Hints: Collectors must distinguish between the productions from the greatest period 1710–1756 and later works. During the 19th century, Meissen reproduced some of its 18th century molds in addition to making new ones.

Numerous Dresden factories also reproduced Meissen wares and figures, some copying the original marks. One should be aware of Helena Wolfsohn's decorating shop in Dresden, who used the Augustus Rex (AR) monogram which had not been used by Meissen after 1730, but was applied by Wolfshon to reproductions of much later works. About 1833 the Royal Porcelain Manufactory in Meissen obtained a court decision against Wolfsohn ordering her to cease and desist using the AR mark.

Helena Wolfsohn operated the decorating shop, but probably did not produce her own porcelain. However, most of her AR pieces have the AR mark underglaze. Since this mark was applied before glazing and final firing, Helena Wolfsohn must have ordered the white porcelain blanks with the AR mark from some porcelain factory. The manufacturer is not known. Wolfsohn sold many thousands of pieces with the "AR" mark.

The Meissen factory itself used the "AR" mark in 1873 as a trademark and still uses it on special pieces. Therefore, every "AR" marked piece must be studied very carefully.

Beaker
  5½" h, white body, flared top, molded gilt branches, gilded female high relief masks, stepped foot rim, band of gilt scrolls at flared rim, attributed to Boettger, c1720, repaired (A) **1,500.00**
  Hunting scene, Bandelwerk cartouches, gilt int., dbl gilt handles, painted at Augsburg, c1720 (A) . . **500.00**
Beaker and Saucer, multicolored beaker, painted merchants and figures in harbor scene, trembleuse saucer, vignettes of figures in harbor, c1765, "blue X'd swords & dots" (A) **950.00**

Bell, 5⅛" h, body painted, two tiers of twenty nine Chinese figures, animals, birds, flowers and fruit, gilt scale, puce drape at stem junction, baluster handle, lake panels and gilt, c1730, "blue X'd swords" (A) **35,920.00**
Bottle
  2½" h, "Yellow Tiger" pattern, Kakiemon palette, c1730, "blue X'd swords & puce K.H.C." (A) **1,760.00**
  7½" h, white body, exotic birds on branch in bright colors, multicolored Indian style flowers, narrow neck ending in band of iron-red flowers, c1730, "blue AR" (A) . . .**9,500.00**
Bowl
  4½" d, multicolored florals, white ground, gilding, scalloped edge, "blue X'd swords" **135.00**
  6¾" d
    Multicolored scene of insects, ducks, butterflies, and Guinea fowl on rocks, reeds and flowers, int. design of butterflies and insects, gilt rim, c1750, "blue X'd swords" (A) **1,300.00**
    Polychrome sprays of summer flowers, late 18th C (A) **200.00**
  9" d, reticulated sides, four flower medallions, c1892, imp "Meissen" **40.00**
  9⅝" sq, 4⅜" h, "Blue Onion", "blue X'd swords" (A) **15.00**
  9¾" l, oval shape, florals on int. and ext., gold rim and scalloped border, c1874, "blue X'd swords" **75.00**
  10" d, ext. painted in continuous river scene, figures, and buildings, lower portion shows band of gilt trellis, enclosing quatrefoil puce cartouches, int. with band of scrolls and foliage in gilt enclosing cartouches with figures and landscape, shaped and paneled, c1740, "blue X'd swords" (A) **2,500.00**
  11" d
    Floral center, heavy gold encrustation, "blue X'd swords" **210.00**
    Gold ivy leaves on border, white ground, "blue X'd swords" **135.00**
  12" d, fruit in center, white ground, gold trim, "blue X'd swords" **175.00**
  12½" l, reticulated cartouche form, gilding, c1860 . . . . **300.00**
  Bowl, cov, and stand, reserved cartouches of European port scenes, Bandelwerk, white ground, inverted pyriform, "blue X'd swords & dot" (A) **800.00**
Candelabra, 28¾" h, white figural swans, brown, black, and salmon beaks, modeled by Kaendler, mounted in Louis XVI gilt ormolu can-

delabra, four feet, c1770-80, pr (A).......................... **148,500.00**

Candlesticks

9⅝" h, "Blue Onion," shaped, reeded ground, c1765, "blue X'd swords & dots" (A) **1,685.00**

12" h, figurals of nymph and putto holding sheaves of corn, scroll molded bases supporting branch and candleholder, turquoise, green, and puce, repaired, c1755, "blue X'd swords" (A) **600.00**

Center Dish, 14½" d, shepherd in turquoise hat and breeches with gold trimmed white coat, shepherdess, Indian floral white dress holding wreath, molded palm tree supporting oval pierced basket, lamb and dog applied to base, c1750, "blue X'd swords" (A) **1,400.00**

Charger, 11" d, four cobalt and raised gold panels, "blue X'd swords" **250.00**

Chocolate Cup and Saucer

Dragon on cup, phoenix, dragons, Chinese ribbons, and symbols on saucer, iron-red and gilt, dbl handles, 1735, "blue X'd swords" (A) **1,100.00**

Painted, mountain landscape and ruins, reverse with figures in night scene by campfire, iron-red, puce, and gilt Laub and Bandelwerk cartouches, painted Indian flowers on underside of saucer, "blue X'd swords," set of two (A) **1,000.00**

Coffee Cup and Saucer, multicolored European and Turkish soldiers on mountain battle scene, black outlined gilt Laub and Bandelwerk cartouches, rims with gilt scrolls and foliage, repaired, c1740, "blue X'd swords & gilder's," pr (A) **4,000.00**

Compote

8" h, reticulated bowl and foot, floral garlands, gold trim, "blue X'd swords" **250.00**

9" d, "Blue Onion," reticulated border, ftd **150.00**

Cream Jar, Cov, 4½" h, Chinese figures on terrace, florals, cov with exotic bird on rockwork, blue and white, set on three paw feet, c1730, "blue X'd swords" (A) **1,300.00**

Cream Jug

4½" h, painted scene of winter landscape, figures by castle, reverse of merchants in harbor scene, paintings in Laub & Bandelwerk cartouches, gilded strap handle, spout and cone finial, pear shape, c1728, "blue X'd swords with gilder's & former's" marks (A) **5,000.00**

Multicolored figures by monuments, river landscape, rim with gilt scrolls, three scroll feet, branch handle, c1765, "blue X'd swords & dot" (A) **350.00**

Cup, yellow tiger wrapped around bamboo and Indian florals, reverse with florals, dbl handles modeled as bird's heads, yellow beaks, c1730, "blue X'd swords" (A) **550.00**

Cup and Saucer

Cup with continuous river scene, figures, and building, saucer with multicolored scene of lady offering snuff to man, shallow ribbing, gilt scroll and foliage rims, c1750, "blue X'd swords" **850.00**

Flying phoenix among flowers, border of iron-red scrolls and foliage enclosing puce dot panels, quatrefoil shape, saucer cracked, c1735, "blue X'd swords" (A) **750.00**

Large rose, scalloped gold edge, "blue X'd swords" **30.00**

Multicolored bouquets and scattered flowers, gilt rims, lg size, c1755, "blue X'd swords" (A) **320.00**

Multicolored flowers, white ground, August Rex mark **95.00**

Multicolored Indian flowering plants and phoenix, chocolate rims, quatrefoil shape, c1735, "blue X'd swords (A) **140.00**

Multicolored small bouquets in medallions, turquoise jewels **100.00**

Scenic panels of men and horses, alternating cobalt panels and gold florals, "blue X'd swords" **145.00**

Cup and Underplate, polychrome reserve harbor scene, turquoise ground, dbl handles, "blue X'd swords" (A) . **275.00**

Demitasse Cup and Saucer, rosebud border with ribbed sides **15.00**

Dessert Plates, 9" d, center cherub pair, classical band relief, 20th C, set of six (A) **375.00**

Dessert Set, cups, saucers, dessert plates, fighting cock center, dragon borders, each set in different colors, "blue X'd swords," service for six .. **650.00**

Dish

4½" w, borders of scrollwork, figures, birds, and animals, mythological black and gilt subject in center, branch handle terminating at flower spray, leaf shape, Preissler, c1720 (A) **200.00**

7" d, Chinese figures on terrace and pavilion, shaped quatrefoil cartouche, painted in gold, c1725 (A) **320.00**

9¼" d, multicolored scene of peasant figures dancing in landscape, four

border flower sprays, c1745, "blue
X'd swords" (A) **2,200.00**
10" l, Watteau-type figures in land-
scape, green and flesh enamels,
German border florals, branch handle, formed floral terminus, leaf
shape, c1745, "blue X'd swords"
(A) **1,300.00**
11" d, "Hob in Well" pattern, Kakie-
mon palette, everted rim, band of
foliage outlined in brown, c1725,
"blue enameled X'd swords" (A) .**3,500.00**
Ecuelle, Cov, 6¼" w, bouquets and floral sprays in basketwork molded border, spirally molded multicolored
painted ground, puce accents with
scroll dbl handles, flowering foliage
terminals, flowerhead finial, c1755,
"blue X'd swords" (A) **160.00**
Egg Cup, "Blue Onion" **20.00**

Figures, left, 9" h, pastel colors, $1,000.00; right, 12½" h, multicolored, blue "X'd swords," $1,600.00.

Figure
2" h, pug, standing position, blue
collar, gold bells, "blue X'd
swords" **250.00**
2¼" h, mother eagle, wings spread
over three fledglings, multicolored,
"blue X'd swords" (A) **225.00**
2½" h, mouse, seated position, tail
curved over back, "blue X'd
swords" **185.00**
3¾" h
Boy and girl, garlands of flowers,
c1890 . . . . **880.00**
Finch, green, yellow, and white,
cobalt, repairs, c1800 (A) **75.00**
4" l, English bulldog, natural coloring,
"blue X'd swords" **225.00**
4⅜" h, man in pink coat holding
scroll, woman with mandolin multicolored, c1800, "blue X'd
swords," pr (A) **70.00**

5" h, "Columbine," by Kaendler, pink
hat, white bodice, painted multicolor Indian flowers skirt, figure
playing hurdy-gurdy, seated on circ
rockwork base, applied foliage,
c1755 (A) **2,200.00**
5" l, hound dog, lying position, white
body **165.00**
5¼" h, "Trumpeter," multicolored,
19th C **450.00**
5½" h
"Harlequin," by Kaendler, pointed
hat, white gilt etched jacket, yellow and pink breeches, figure
playing bagpipe while seated on
circ rock base, applied flowerheads and foliage, repaired,
c1755, "blue X'd swords" **1,300.00**
Musician in flowered jacket, yellow
hat, waistcoat, flowered breeches playing flute, dancer in yellow hat, puce bodice, flowering
skirt, holding mask in left hand,
figures mounted on scroll
molded gilt tree trunk bases,
c1750, "blue X'd swords," pr (A) **950.00**
Spaniel, seated position, white,
black markings, "blue X'd
swords" **250.00**
"Spring" from set of Four Seasons,
nymph wearing yellow lined
puce cloak, painted Indian flowers, figure with basket of flowers
in right hand, bouquet in left,
hen on nest at her feet, mounted
on scroll molded circ base,
c1745, "blue X'd swords" (A) . .**1,200.00**
Swan figures, one with spread
wings, other with young birds,
beaks and faces in iron-red and
black, circ bases, molded turquoise and green reeds, c1745,
"blue X'd swords and puce tri-
angle," pr **1,700.00**
5¾" h
Angel, barefoot playing French
horn, repaired, 19th C **175.00**
Young girl carrying basket of flow-
ers, yellow bodice, flowered yellow apron over light lavender
skirt, figure mounted on scroll
molded base, applied flowerheads and foliage, repaired,
c1750, "blue X'd swords" **400.00**
Venus, nude, flowing hair, standing
on shell (A) **150.00**
6" h
Cupid, quiver of arrows standing at
attention, c1880 . . . . **600.00**
"Oyster Setter," woman holding
shell, cov tray on head, multicolored, "blue X'd swords **550.00**

6¼" h

Cupid holding heart, round base (A) **100.00**

"Pulchinella," by Kaendler, dancing pose, pointed yellow hat, puce rosette, jacket diamond, iron-red, yellow, and green, playing cards on right sleeve, hooked nose and face, natural flesh tones, white slapstick in hand, circ stump base, c1745, "blue X'd swords" (A) **26,000.00**

6½" h, putti, one in puce lined yellow cloak with flowers seated by birdcage, other feeding grapes to panther while holding entwined staff, both figures seated on scroll molded oval bases, foliage, mounted on ormolu scroll and foliage bases, c1750 (A) **2,000.00**

6¾" h, 7⅜", chinoiserie musicians, man with mandolin, woman with keyboard instrument, 19th C, pr (A) **500.00**

7¼" h

Cupid, bellows, round base (A) . . **110.00**

Cupid, sewing heart, round base (A) **145.00**

"Hanswurst," by Kaendler, right arm raised holding sausage, left hand holding slapstick, gray plumed hat, blue rosette, yellow jacket, playing cards gilt etched, puce and black trousers, figure leaning against tree trunk, shaped circ base, damaged, c1740, imp "43" (A) **28,000.00**

7¾" h

Cupid, on tree stump, foot in trap, pedestal base, "blue X'd swords" (A) **225.00**

Lady holding painted Indian florals ochre skirt in left hand, pink bodice, flower spray in right hand, circ scroll molded base, applied flowers, modeled by Kaendler, repaired, c1755, "blue X'd swords" **400.00**

"Shepherd Lovers," male in lilac jacket, Indian flowers, puce breeches and flowers in hat, flowers in hand, female in puce bodice, yellow shirt, Indian flowers, apron filled molded flowers, lamb at side, both seated on rockwork base, c1765, "blue X'd swords & dot" (A) **1,500.00**

8" h, "Bouquetieres," by Kaendler, male figure holding pierced basket on knee, flowers in left hand, green hat, white jacket, multicolored Indian flowers, white breeches and yellow shoes, seated female figure,

basket on knee, lavender head scarf and skirt, pink bodice, yellow apron, Indian flowers, pr (A) **2,100.00**

8¼" h, Cupid, quiver, round base (A) **110.00**

9¼" h, "Four Seasons," each figure in pose representing highlights of the season, multicolored, applied foliage, rococo scroll molded bases, gilt, minor repairs, c1755, "blue X'd swords," set of 4 (A) . . **4,000.00**

9½" h

Couple, man entreats distraught woman, 18th C dress, two Cupids at feet, multicolored, damaged, "blue X'd swords" (A) . . . **450.00**

Grouping of three cherubs dressed as musicians, soft multicolors, c1850 . . . .**1,800.00**

Venus and Cupid, nude Venus holding Cupid by ribbon, putto seated on circ rockwork base, applied foliage, c1760, "blue X'd swords & painter's" **550.00**

9¾" h, "Broken Bridge" model, gallant male and female companion, rococo green and puce costumes, oval rockwork base, Cupid and putti holding flower sprays, repaired, c1775, "blue X'd swords & star" (A) **650.00**

11¼" h, "Golden Orioles," by Kaendler, incised yellow and black feather markings, one with beak open and outstretched wings, perched on tree stumps, puce, yellow, turquoise, and green applied foliage and cherries, scroll molded ormolu bases, repaired, c1740, "blue X'd swords," pr (A) **30,000.00**

12½" h, "Malabar," by Meyer, figure playing mandolin, dressed in fur lined puce cloak, flowered yellow skirt, scroll molded circ base, gilding, c1750, "blue X'd swords" . . .**1,100.00**

12¾" h, woman and two men, 18th C costumes, multicolored, woman leaning on pillar fragment, one man with arm around woman's waist, other kneeling (A) **400.00**

16" l, "Elaborate Animal Group," multicolored, sgd "Otto Pilz," c1908 . . . .**2,500.00**

18½" h, women, flowing gowns, holding bunches of flowers, hp, soft colors, c1850, pr (A) **2,600.00**

21¼" h, magpies, black, white and olive-green feathers, perched on tree stumps, applied foliage modeled by Kaendler, c1738-40 (A) .**23,300.00**

Parrots mounted on perches, painted, blue, puce, iron-red, green and yellow, yellow eyes and brown beaks, flared bases, scroll bands of iron-red and gilt, restored, c1730, pr (A)**2,800.00**

Fruit Cooler, 9" w, porcelain, three pcs, recessed cov, gilt handle, deep bowl within a circ tapered body, gilt handles, florals and gilt, white ground, 18th C (A) **650.00**

Inkwell, single, rose pattern, "blue X'd swords" **125.00**

Jug, 8" h, red stoneware, cut and polished, diamond and band surface, loop handle, pear shape, silver mounted foot, hinged lid, scroll thumbrest, attributed to Boettger, repaired, c1715 (A)..................... **22,000.00**

Milk Jug
5¼" h, multicolored, European and Turkish merchants in harbor scene, pear shape, scroll handle, shell thumbpiece, foliage molded spout, cone finial, gilt accents, age crack, c1738, "blue X'd swords & gilder's mark" (A) **1,500.00**
6¼" h, puce painting, Watteau-type figures alternating with vertical bands of gray outlined in gilding, pear shape, foliage molded spout, gilded scroll handle, cov and neck rim with bands of basketwork, flowerhead finial, repair to handle, c1740, "blue X'd swords" (A) **800.00**
Multicolored, figures and buildings in river scene, gilt, scroll, and foliage surround central figures, black outlines, pear shape, angular handle, scroll molded spout, age crack, c1745, "blue X'd swords & gilder's marks" (A) **1,000.00**

Mocha Set, tray 11½" l, six cups, quatrefoil shape, scroll handles, tray, branch shape dbl handles ending in molded flowers, scenes of classic figures, comedy characters, interspersed multicolored German florals, c1745, "blue X'd swords" (A) **5,000.00**

Monkey Band, monkeys, band outfits, instruments, blue, yellow, and purple, white bases trimmed in gold, set of eight **3,800.00**

Nut Dish, female figure, semi-reclined position, holding open bowl, period dress, pastel colors, c1780, (A) **750.00**

Pitcher, 5" h, floral bouquets, insects, basketweave border, set on three feet, "blue X'd swords" **100.00**

Plaque, 6⅛" l, 4½" h, painted stag, three does, wooded setting, molded gold rococo frame border, c1755, "blue X'd swords" (A) **1,350.00**

Plate
6½" d, Dresden-style flowers, multicolored **20.00**

8" d
"Blue Onion," reticulated border. "blue X'd swords" **50.00**
Central bouquet, floral medallions, butterflies, and bees, lace border, "blue X'd swords," set of ten .. **600.00**
Indian flowers, multicolored, gilt accents, blue lambrequin border, gilded and scalloped edge, blue and iron-red flowering branches on reverse, c1730, "blue X'd swords & dot" (A) **1,500.00**
8¼" d, center medallion, florals, gilt trim, four panels of painted florals on solid ground, alternating land and seascapes **175.00**
8¾" d
Center fighting phoenix pair, dragons, Chinese symbols, and ribbons on border, iron-red and gilt, c1734, Caduceus **1,000.00**
Raised insects and birds on border, gold trim **60.00**
9" d
Lobed gilt rims, squirrel pattern on lower portion, Kakiemon palette, c1738, "blue X'd swords," pr (A) **2,800.00**
Molded white center, two swans and crane flying above cranes in rushes, shaped, gilded rim, coat of arms at top, florals in fluted border of red, yellow, and green leaves, from Swan service modeled by Kaendler & Eberlein, c1737-41, "blue X'd swords" (A)**11,000.00**
Multicolored scene, four horses in landscape, scroll and foliage border, flowerheads, silver accents, c1780, "blue X'd swords & star" (A) **500.00**
"Schmetterling" pattern, butterfly in border of scattered flower sprays, Kakiemon palette, shaped chocolate rim, c1735, "blue X'd swords" (A) **550.00**
9¼" d,
"Blue Onion," "blue X'd swords" **100.00**
Center bird design, open pierced border, "blue X'd swords" **50.00**
Single rose with rosebud, "blue X'd swords under glaze" **40.00**
9½" d
Center of birds on branches, multicolored insect border, gilt rims, c1780, "blue X'd swords & star" **420.00**
Engraved retriever dog center, molded spiral panels enclosing flowerheads and engraved insects border, sgd "Busch," c1735, "blue X'd swords" **6,500.00**
Leaf and berry center, white and gilt

relief leaf ground, "blue X'd swords" **175.00**

Multicolored bouquets, floral sprays, ozier borders, chocolate rims, c1745, "blue X'd swords" (A) **320.00**

Multicolored bouquets, scattered floral sprays, molded basketwork border, shaped rim, age crack, c1755, "blue X'd swords" **75.00**

Multicolored butterfly pattern, shaped chocolate rim, c1765, "blue X'd swords & dot" **200.00**

Multicolored floral sprays, molded basketwork ground, pierced and gilded borders, chip repair, c1755, "blue X'd swords" **300.00**

Painted scene of Leeuwaerden, gilt ochre scroll and foliage cartouche, flower sprays border, three molded gilt cartouches, blue and gilt dentil rim, c1763, "blue X'd swords & dot" **3,200.00**

Polychrome tulips, peonies, and roses, small insects on rim, "blue X'd swords" (A) **50.00**

Red dragon pattern, gilt rim, c1755, "blue X'd swords" **200.00**

10" d, scattered flowers and insects, Kakiemon colors, shaped rim brown outline, c1740, "blue X'd swords" (A) **360.00**

10¼" d, bird perched on poppy plant, multicolored, basketwork molded border, insects, shaped gilt rim, c1745, "blue X'd swords" (A) **950.00**

11½" d, floral center, raised gold leaf design, white ground, "blue X'd swords" **135.00**

11⅞" d, "Blue Onion," c1780, "blue X'd swords & dot," pr (A) **700.00**

Rose Box, 5¼" d, molded overlapping puce petals, rosebud and branch finial, green accents, circ shape, c1755, imp "W" (A) **350.00**

Saucer, animals, landscape scene, butterfly, and birds, Kakiemon palette, shaped molded rim, shell motifs, gilt accents, c1741, "blue X'd swords" (A) **1,100.00**

Scent Bottle

3¼" h, flowering plants and insects, Kakiemon palette, silver stopper and chain, c1730, "#6 & W" (A) **650.00**

Molded as lady's leg, high-heeled shoe, puce florals, gilt metal hinged cov, "blue X'd swords" (A) **140.00**

Soup Plate

9¼" d, "Blue Onion", gilt edge, "blue X'd swords" (A) **15.00**

9¾" d, polychrome florals and in-

sects, paneled lattice borders, shaped gilt rims, set of six (A) **325.00**

Spoon Rest, "Blue Onion," "blue X'd swords" **65.00**

Sugar Basin, Cov, 4½" l, purple toned sailing ships, gilt outlines, two oval panels of ships in gilt scrolls, foliate cartouches on cov, painted Indian flowers between, octagonal shape, c1723, "blue K.P.F." (A) **7,000.00**

Sugar Bowl, Cov, 3¾" l, puce scenes after Rugenda's battle scenes, shaped quatrefoil cartouches reserved on sea green gound, molded flowering branch finial, c1740, "blue X'd swords" (A) **1,700.00**

Sugar Box, Cov, 4¾" l, painting Turks and merchants in extensive harbor scene, iron-red, puce and gilt cartouches, oval shape, domed cov, seated gilt dog finial, painted by Herold, c1728, "blue X'd swords" (A) . **7,000.00**

Sugar Caster, 7⅝" h, modeled by Kaendler as pair of Chinese embracing lovers, girl in iron-red cap and Laub & Bandelwerk coat, boy in blue gadrooned cap, pink and gilt screw covs, yellow lining, "blue X'd swords," pr (A) **29,185.00**

Sweetmeat Dish, 7½" h, seated Chinese figure, holding shell molded dish, circ base, "blue X'd swords" (A) **550.00**

Tankard

Chrysanthemums erupting from rockwork on terrace, interspersed flower sprays, blue and white, cylindrical shape, pewter lid, scrolled thumbpiece, c1735, "blue X'd swords" **2,000.00**

Three gilt and puce flowering branches, top bands of scrolls, bottom borders, gilt trellis and foliage, cylindrical shape, strap handle, silver cov, scroll thumbpiece, inset medallion, initials, dated "1725," "blue X'd swords" (A) **4,000.00**

Tea and Coffee Set, globular teapot, bird's head spout, flowered finial, pear shape coffee pot, cov milk jug, sugar bowl, four coffee cups, two teacups, trembleuse saucers, bouquets of German florals, quatrefoil cartouches, turquoise ground, damaged, c1755, "blue X'd swords & painter's marks" (A) **3,000.00**

Tea Caddy

3¾" h, painted scene, Turks and merchants in harbor, iron-red, puce and gilt cartouches, narrow sides painted with sportsmen and river scene, shoulders painted with rose outlined landscape and figures, gilt cov, c1735, "blue X'd swords, gilder's & former's marks" (A) **8,500.00**

4" h

Chinese figures, pagodas, and flowering branches painted in silver and gilt, octagonal baluster shape, dec at Augsburg, c1725, unmkd (A) **7,500.00**

Multicolored figures, boats in river, and mountain landscape scene, shoulders with Indian florals, powdered light lavender ground, rect, c1740, "iron-red" mk (A) . **800.00**

5" h, fantasy animals, shaped panels, purple ground, flowers and insects on shoulder and cov, Kakiemon palette, rect, flowerhead finial, c1735, "blue X'd swords" (A) **1,500.00**

Tea Set, teapot, creamer, two cups and saucers, and tray, elaborate raised gold decor, white ground, "blue X'd swords" **350.00**

Teabowl

Chinese figures, animals on terraces, flowering plants, iron-red and gilt Laub & Bandelwerk cartouches, c1725, gilder's mark **550.00**

Gilt scene of hare hunt, birds in branches, white body painted in Saxony, c1725, base crack (A) ... **1,150.00**

Teabowl and Saucer

Chinese figures on terraces, iron-red and gilt Laub & Bandelwerk cartouches, Boettger luster and gilt rims, c1730, unmkd **500.00**

Tray, 15" sq, multicolored floral center, cream ground, gold trim, $395.00.

Flowering plants divided by brocade pattern panels, luster ground, gilding, hatch pattern, stylized flowerheads, int. bowl band of scrolling

flowers on iron-red ground, c1735, "blue X'd swords and former's" marks (A) **2,000.00**

Gilt burnished flower sprays, sea green gound, c1740, "blue X'd swords" (A) **800.00**

Oval gilt cartouches around painted harbor scenes and multicolored Indian flowers, white ground, iron-red flower sprays inside bowls, gilded rims, c1723, gilder's mark, pr (A) **7,000.00**

Quail pattern, flowering prunus, Kakiemon colors, cinqefoil saucer, brown rims, c1800, "blue X'd swords & star," pr **550.00**

Rustic landscape, puce colored figures, shaped cartouches, puce flowering plants, birds & insects, yellow ground, gilt rims, c1735, "blue X'd swords" (A) **2,200.00**

Teabowl with flowers, Kakiemon colors, saucer with bird perched on branch among flowering plants, yellow ground lobed quatrefoil shape, c1735, "blue X'd swords" (A) **950.00**

Teacup and Saucer

European and Turkish soldiers on horseback landscapes, shaped Laub & Bandelwerk cartouches, multicolored scattered floral sprays, c1740, "blue X'd swords" (A) **1,000.00**

Figures in harbor scene, shaped quatrefoil cartouches, outlined in gilt and brown, yellow ground reserves of figures in boats in iron-red dbl rings int., gilt scrolls and trellis rims, gold shaped handles, quatrefoil shape, c1736, "blue X'd swords" (A) **3,200.00**

Teapot

5¾" h, merchants in harbor scene, reverse of figures in river scene, shaped iron-red and gilt quatrefoil Laub & Bandelwerk cartouches, Indian florals between, curved mast spout, handle ending in foliage terminals, domed cov, c1730, "blue X'd swords & gilder's" marks (A) . **4,000.00**

6½" h, men-of-war in battle scene, reverse of merchants at dockside, both scenes in gilt scroll, foliage, and net pattern, painted Indian flowers between, gilt mask at base of spout, white ground, c1723, "blue K.P.M." (A) **3,200.00**

7" h, Kakiemon palette, Indian flowers, arched panels outlined in gilt, shoulder with gilt flowerheads, scroll ground, quatrefoil baluster

shape, angular handle, faceted spout, c1735, "blue X'd swords & former's" marks (A) **2,800.00**
Teapot Stand, 6¼" l, Chinese figure holding fan and parasols by table, gilt scroll and foliage pedestal, multicolored, puce cartouches, iron-red enclosing design, Kakiemon palette flower sprays rim and underside oval, c1735, "blue X'd swords" (A) **1,600.00**
Tête-À-Tête set, miniature size, pear shape coffeepot, teapot, two coffee cups and saucers, two tea cups and saucers, circ sugar bowl, rect tray, 10½" l, painted multicolored bouquets and scattered flower sprays, gilt rims, c1800, "blue X'd swords & star" (A) **2,200.00**
Tureen, Cov, 14" d, clusters of fruits and flowers, ozier molded cartouches, cauliflowers and asparagus scroll handles, putto finial holding cornucopia, repaired, c1775, "blue X'd swords" (A) **750.00**
Urns
13" h, cov, applied multicolored flowers, applied florals on cov, scenic centers, female heads form handles, three sq feet, c1860, pr, (A) .**1,400.00**
16" h, gilt socle, yellow ground, spiraling snake form handle, c1880 . **680.00**
Vase
3" h, multicolored floral design, shell molded baluster shape, dolphin handles iron-red and brown trim, c1745, "brown K.P.C." (A) **300.00**
3¼" h, gold laurel wreath through two rams heads, flowers, and insects, "blue X'd swords" **65.00**
11" h, puce and gold design, intertwined snake handles, 19th C (A) . **150.00**
16¾" h, cov, center painting of Venus in chariot, reverse of putti, multicolored, scroll supports, figures carrying baskets of flowers, applied branch handles, flowering and fruiting terminals, dbl gourd shape, pierced dome cov, painted and molded scroll base, c1745, "blue X'd swords" (A) **1,800.00**

MENNECY

Villeroy, Ile de France
1734 to 1806

History: In 1734 Louis-Francois de Neufville, Duc de Villeroy, under the direction of Francois

Barbin, established a soft paste porcelain factory in Paris. The factory was moved to Mennecy in 1748 and to Bourg-la-Reine in 1773. Production was continued by Joseph Jullien and his descendants until 1806.

The porcelain was covered with a "wet-looking" brilliant glaze that absorbed the enamel decoration. Chinese designs were used. Styles used at Vincennes and Sevres soon were copied. Since gilding was forbidden by Louis XV, rose pink or bright blue enamel was used for edging.

Cylinder shapes were used at Mennecy for cups and covered boxes in a variety of sizes. Teapots, custard cups, and shell-shaped sugar basins were popular. Mennecy also produced attractive but impractical porcelain handles for cutlery.

References: Hubert Landais, *French Porcelain*, G. P. Putnam's Sons, 1961.

Museums: J. Paul Getty Museum, Malibu, California; Victoria & Albert Museum, London, England.

Figures, 9" h, sultan and sultana, c1740, incised "D.V." pr, (A) $4,725.00.

Bodkin Case, 4⅜" l, modeled as female leg, pink and yellow ribbon stocking tie, blue shoe, pink heel, painted sprays on cov (A) **550.00**
Bonbonnier
3¼" h, recumbent monkey, eating fruit, scattered florals painted on base, metal mount, c1750 .... **525.00**
3½" l, shoe shape, painted pastel flowers, contemporary silver mounted rims, c1740-50 .... **700.00**
Molded Turk's head multicolored, floral spray int. **135.00**

Coffee Cup and Saucer, painted bouquets and sprigs, incised "D.V." **20.00**

Cream, Jug, 3¾" h, painted bouquets and sprays, scroll handle, pink foliage, c1740, incised "D.V." **575.00**

Cup and Saucer

Painted bouquets and sprays, 1740, incised "D.V." (A) **165.00**

Painted exotic birds in landscapes, loop handle, puce rims, c1740, incised "D.V." (A) **275.00**

Cup and Stand, painted bouquets, scroll handle, puce, c1750 incised "D.V." **375.00**

Custard Cups, Cov, painted flower sprays, c1753, incised "D.V.," pr (A) **300.00**

Figure

3¾" h, Chinoiserie figure, painted Kakiemon palette coat, carrying satchel over shoulder, green grass mound base, c1740, incised "D.V." (A) **4,180.00**

5⅛" h, man playing violin, woman playing lute, bisque, tree stump bases, c1750, incised "D.V.," pr . **200.00**

5½" h, boy, Oriental costume, white glaze, shaped circ base, c1735 (A)**1,000.00**

5¾" h, figure, seated on rock, book on knee, quill, white glaze, oval rockwork base, c1750 .... **950.00**

6¼" h, young woman, arms raised, wearing cloak, apron, and skirt, swan at side, multicolored, c1740, incised "D.V." **400.00**

6⅞" h, dancing peasant girl, flowered apron, peasant boy, holding wheat sheaf, multicolored, tapered floral painted plinths, c1740, pr **2,400.00**

7" h

Two children, period clothes, one holding basket of figs, flowered rockwork base, multicolored, c1735 (A) **770.00**

Faun, animal legs holding club and scroll, white glaze, tree trunk base, c1750, incised "D.V." (A) **715.00**

11½" h, goddess "France," shield, recumbent horse, white, rockwork base, c1745 (A) **2,850.00**

Jar, Cov

3½" h, painted bouquets and sprays, blue line rims, cylindrical, flowering finial, c1745 .... **275.00**

4" h, painted bouquets and sprays, pink rims, cylindrical, rose spray finial, c1740 incised "D.V." (A) ... **245.00**

Jardinieres, 4¾" h, painted bouquets, sq, ormolu mounted four dbl scroll feet, c1750, incised "D.V.," pr (A) ..**1,050.00**

Jug, 4½" h, molded, sprays of prunus, white, contemporary silver mounts, c1740, incised "D.V." (A) **1,770.00**

Knife Handle, 3¼" l

Chinoiserie figures, buildings, landscape, multicolored, silver collar, steel blade, c1740 .... **325.00**

Painted pagodas and figures, c1740, set of four (A) **200.00**

Perfume Bottle, Cov, 6¾" h, vase, pierced at shoulder, multicolored flowers, body supported on rockwork, tree stump base, applied flowers, cov replaced, mid-18th C. (A) .. **660.00**

Pots A Creme, 2½" h, multicolored bouquets and scattered flowers, fruit finials blue stems, c1750, incised "D.V.," pr **320.00**

Sauce Tureen and Stand, painted bouquets, sprays in shaped gilt cartouche, blue celeste ground, fruiting finial, c1760, incised "D.V. g." (A) **720.00**

Snuff Box

1½" l, modeled as swan, head on back, molded flowers, contemporary silver gilt mounts, c1740 (A) . **765.00**

1⅞" w, modeled as recumbent horse, head on back, floral edge, multicolored, contemporary silver gilt mounts, c1740 .... **980.00**

2" w, modeled as sitting hen, two chicks, color accented plumage, contemporary silver mounts, c1756-62 (A) **1,400.00**

2¾" l, flower sprays and insects, Kakiemon palette, dbl covs, silver mounts, c1735 (A) **1,450.00**

3" l, molded flowerheads, white, contemporary silver mounts, c1750 (A) **230.00,**

Modeled as recumbent cat, suckling kittens on grass, multicolored, int. with flower spray, contemporary silver mounts, c1756–62 (A) **1,950.00**

Vase

4⅝" h, and 4¾" h, white, modeled figures of wild animals, animal skin draped urns, rockwork bases, damaged, mid-18th C, pr (A) **1,000.00**

4¾" h, painted bouquets and sprays, campana shape, flaring spirally molded feet, sq pedestals, c1745, pr **575.00**

7⅞" h, molded, flutes, spirally molded circ feet, filled with soft paste porcelain flowers, c1740, incised "D.V.," pr (A) **350.00**

11⅛" h, body encrusted with rows of raised petals, fourteen softpaste flowers on green stems, mid-18th C (A) **360.00**

MINTON

Stoke-on-Trent, Hanley, England
1793 to Present

History: Thomas Minton established his pottery in 1793 in Stoke-on-Trent. During the early years, he concentrated on blue transfer printed earthenwares, cream colored earthware, and plain bone china. By 1810 production expanded to include stoneware, Egyptian black, and printed and painted bone china. A tremendous number of shapes, styles, and decorations with printed, enameled, or gilted designs were manufactured. Many nineteenth century Minton patterns resembled those of Spode, Miles Mason, New Hall and Pinxton, the company's principal rivals. Most pieces were unmarked.

Between 1816 and 1824 production at the Minton factory was concentrated on earthenwares and cream colored wares. Bone china production resumed in 1824. A large selection of figures and ornamental wares augmented the tradional tableware line.

Much of Minton's success can be attributed to the decorations applied by the staff of painters. French porcelain artists and ex-Derby decorators were employed by Minton. By the late 1830s Minton had achieved a quality of modeling and decoration on bone china that was unequalled in Europe.

In 1836 Herbert took complete charge when his father died. Herbert Minton, Thomas' son, gradually changed the factory from a small scale producer into one of the greatest Victorian potteries in Europe. By 1858 Minton's employed over 1500 people utilizing new technologies and decorative styles. Encaustic floor tiles and Parian porcelain were developed under Herbert's jurisdiction.

Leon Arnoux became art director at Minton's in 1849. He encouraged many French artists to move to Stoke-on-Trent and introduced a revival of the Renaissance styles. Arnoux also developed a series of colored glazes for a "majolica" line.

Colin Minton Campbell took control in 1858. The acid gold process was developed, allowing rich gold decorations in bas–relief. Louis Marc Solon came to Minton from Sevres in 1870 and brought with him the technique of pate-sur-pate decoration. Pate-sur-pate became a major con-

tribution by Minton to the 19th century English ceramics heritage. After Campbell's death in 1885, Minton continued to be the leading English pottery manufacturer of the 19th century.

In 1968 Minton became a member of the Royal Doulton Tableware Group. Minton china still is being produced today. The company retains its reputation for high quality, hand painted, and gilted tablewares.

References: G. A. Godden, *Minton Pottery & Porcelain of the First Period. 1793–1850*, Herbert Jenkins, Ltd., 1968; G. A. Godden, *Victorian Porcelain*, Herbert Jenkins, 1961.

Museums: Minton Museum, London Road, Stoke-on-Trent, England.

Bouillon Cup and Saucer, pink and blue flowers, green leaves	**20.00**
Bowl, 7½" d, lily pad form, frog on one side, dark green glaze, dated 1873 (A)	**70.00**
Box, Cov, 2" d, 1½" h, hp, enamel florals, gold trim, heart shape	**35.00**
Cabaret Set, tray 15½" sq, teapot, creamer, sugar, two cups and saucers, "Willow" pattern, rust and gold, c1880	**325.00**
Condiment Set, salt, pepper, and cov jelly jar, "Haldon Hall" pattern	**30.00**
Cup and Saucer	
"Ancestral" pattern	**25.00**
"Marlow" pattern	**30.00**
Victorian pink design, pure gold trim c1902	**85.00**
Demitasse Cup and Saucer	
Birds of Paradise, turquoise band . . .	**30.00**
Lavender flowers, gold tooled bands, sgd "R. Wise," "MINTON, ENG-LAND"	**95.00**
"Salt Lake" pattern	**35.00**
Dessert Plates, 9¼" d	
Butterflies and flowers in gilded beaded edges, c1890, set of 5 (A)	**190.00**
Center view, "Old Weir Bridge, C Killarney," waved border, turquoise and gilt roundels, gilt lined ground, gilt dentril rim, c1860 (A)	**40.00**
Dessert Service, Part, two oval dishes, two circ dishes, seven plates, painted figures, landscapes, borders of blue and gilt oeil-de-perdrix, gilt rims, c1860 (A)	**350.00**

Dish

8" l, leaf shape, majolica, blue tit perched on oak branch, dated 1868, imp "MINTON" (A) **200.00**

9⅛" l, "Amherst Japan" pattern, bowl of flowers, garden, pavilion in distance, blue transfers, enamels, yellow band borders, brown rims, earthenware, crescent shape, c1883, imp "MINTON" set of 12 (A) **200.00**

10⅛" l, "Amherst Japan" pattern, bowl of flowers, garden, and pavilion in distance, blue transfer, enamels, c1845 (A) **30.00**

10⅜" d, floral spray, gilt cartouche, ochre ground, exotic birds, molded border cartouches, shell shape, c1845, pr (A) **80.00**

11¼" w, flower spray, gilt cartouche, ochre ground, exotic birds, c1845 (A) **40.00**

Egg Cup, "Ming Tree" pattern **30.00**

Figure

6" h, seated cat, turquoise, faience, 19th C **400.00**

8½" h, facing parrots, blue bodies, green touches on heads, yellow beaks, turquoise bases, raised "Minton," pr **90.00**

9", 9¾" h, children kneeling, bible, parian, imp "MINTON," pr (A) .. **150.00**

10¼" h, boy and girl, leaning on wicker baskets, rustic costumes, grapes on bases, majolica, dated 1866, imp "MINTON," pr (A) ... **720.00**

10¾" h, male and female blackamoors, jardinieres on heads, molded satyrs and masks on bases, multicolored, majolica, repairs, pr (A) **59,150.00**

16" h

Bust of Evangeline, multicolored, majolica **600.00**

"Di Medici Venus," parian, dated 1851, repaired **250.00**

19" l, two men leaning on grapevines, carrying wicker basket on metal rods, majolica, oval base, grapevines, c1863, imp "MINTON" (A) **2,860.00**

Garden Seat, Majolica

18¼" h, tan, brown, and green crouched monkey, rattan mat, holding fruit, tasseled cushion on head, c1870 (A) **5,000.00**

20⅝" h, relief florals and rosettes, streaky green glaze, hexagon, c1896, imp "MINTON" (A) **440.00**

Inkwell, 9½" l, "Double Dahlia," applied clusters of multicolored flowers, leaf shaped base, applied dahlias on well covs, c1840 (A) **250.00**

Jardiniere

5" h, florals, gold trim, white body, c1880, pr **425.00**

7" h, molded wooden planks, white vines, lilac int., majolica, matching stands, pr (A) **420.00**

Applied putti linked by laurel leaf pendants, lion's heads, acorn, and oak leaves at neck, majolica, dated 1868, imp "MINTON" **700.00**

Jug, 10" h, dark blue ground, raised yellow flowers, yellow mask under spout, gray handles, majolica, pewter lid, dated 1867 .... **175.00**

Mug, "Genevese" pattern, dark blue .. **55.00**

Oyster Plate

9" d, majolica, six shell recesses, central well, green and brown, turquoise shell glaze, borders of molded shells and seaweed, c1873, imp "MINTON," set of 12.........................**1,200.00**

Majolica

Green marbleized finish **100.00**

Light green shell and seaweed design, imp "MINTON" **175.00**

Mottled cream, shell and seaweed design, imp "MINTON" **180.00**

Pilgrim Flasks, 10" h, painted pug and cockatoo, gilt surround, turquoise ground, applied dbl handles, sgd "H. Mitchell," c1869, imp "MINTON," pr (A) **440.00**

Pitcher, 11½" h, "Arabic" design, $300.00.

Pitcher

7⅜" h, cream body, mask spout, pewter lid (A) **65.00**

7¾" h, molded cream hunters and dog, white grapes at top, c1840 .. **140.00**

Plate

6⅛" d, cobalt borders, etched gold
outer rims, set of 12 . . . .   **240.00**
6¾" d, floral emb heavy gold borders,
dated 1890, set of 12 . . . .   **100.00**
8" d
"Florentine" pattern **10.00**
Pink rose buds, blue enamel ac-
cents, wide gold borders, set
of 6 . . . .   **210.00**
8½" d
Pink, green and yellow flowers,
cream ground, enamel accents .   **15.00**
Specimen flowers, blue ground, radiating gilt brick pattern, blue
borders with flowers in gilt foli-
age cartouches, c1815, pr (A) . .   **245.00**
8⅞" d, art pottery, butterflies in flight,
natural colors, putty gray ground,
pr (A) **45.00**
9" d
"Amherst Japan" pattern, bowl of
flowers, distant garden, and pavilion scene, blue transfer, enam-
els, c1830, set of 8 (A) **225.00**
Dutch scene, blue and white, scal-
loped edge, dated 1917, sq **50.00**
Gold branches, hp green enamel
flowers, set of 12 . . . .   **225.00**
"Lorraine" pattern, multicolored
flowers sprays, swirled ribbed
border, gold trim, set of 12 . . . .   **120.00**
Portrait panels, multicolored, gilt
tracery, reticulated border (A) . .   **70.00**
Red roses and flowers, wide bor-
ders, set of 12 . . . .   **235.00**
9⅛" d, gold and silver enameled flo-
rals, red ground, "Gilman Colla-
more Co. New York" and Minton
marks, pr (A) **100.00**
9⅜" d, enameled exotic birds, tur-
quoise ground, gilt band rim, black
zig zags, c1875, set of 6 (A) **1,750.00**
9½" d
Center of putti, various scenes, gilt
and turquoise key band, pink
ground, gilt foliage and dots, late
19th C, set of 12 (A) **770.00**
Painted English scenes, named on
reverse, blue borders, gilt bands
and flowers, c1881, set of 8 . . .   **600.00**
9¾" d
"Fair Winds" pattern, brown **5.00**
"Marlow" pattern **30.00**
10" d
"Gold Ancestral" pattern, #S595 .   **5.00**
Maiden scattering flowers, blue and
brown outlined, blue ground,
wide white border, white glaze,
dated 1878 (A) **55.00**
"Ming Tree" pattern **20.00**
Painted centers, children at differ-

ent activities, named on reverse,
turquoise borders, gilt scrolls,
c1875, imp "MINTON," set of
18 (A) **3,300.00**
10¼" d, white centers, light yellow
borders, gilt rims, set of 11 (A) . . .   **150.00**
10½" polychrome floral swags, pink,
blue, green, and yellow, "MIN-
TON, ENGLAND" (A) **10.00**
Platter
12" d, "Gold Ancestral" design,
#S595 . . . .   **50.00**
12" l, 8" w, border of raised storks in
flight, bamboo rim, c1890, imp
"MINTON" **60.00**

**Sauceboats, 7" h, pastels, majolica, imp
"MINTON," pr, $1,200.00.**

Ring Tree, 3" h, pastel flowers on top,
gold edge and knob, "MINTON, ENG-
LAND" **40.00**
Sauceboat, 8" l, cov. undertray, white
body, black leaves, purple edge trim,
gold edge handle, late 19th C, "Min-
ton crown" **100.00**
Soup Plate
10" d, "Medway Decor" pattern, blue   **10.00**
10¼" d
"Infanta" pattern **15.00**
"Meadow" pattern **20.00**
10⅜" d, printed and painted famille
rose style, Orientals, molded floral
band border, ironstone, c1825 (A)   **50.00**
Tazza
7" d, young boy and girl, seated on
each side, white **150.00**
9½" d, 3" h, hp red rose, yellow and
white buds, blue-green ground,
c1877 . . . .   **75.00**
Tea Service, multicolored, painted gar-
den flowers, gilt ground, c1820, set
of 57 pcs (A) **6,600.00**
Tea Set, teapot, creamer, and sugar, stip-
pled ground, raised vines and leaves,
squirrel finials, c1869 . . . .   **160.00**
Teapot
5½" h, multicolored encrusted flow-

ers, branch finial, gilt scale, four ft
base, c1835 (A) **235.00**
8" l, figural crouching cockerel, head
forming spout, tail feathers forming
handle, leaf finial, multicolored,
majolica, c1872 (A) **2,700.00**
Teapot and Underplate, teapot, 4" h,
plate 4⅞" d, dog head, multicolored
white ground, sgd "Dean," dated
1891 and 1902 .... **165.00**
Tray
12" l, "Dresden Card Trays," center
views, "Llamgollen Castle" and
"Kirkstall Abbey," pink feathered
rims, four applied floral sprays,
c1820, pr (A) **485.00**
12" l, 9" w, large hp red roses, off-
white ground **100.00**
Urns, Cov, 16½" h, oval reserves of
country scenes, turquoise ground,
pierced dbl handles, sq bases, c1840,
pr **2,400.00**
Vase
4" h, emb flowers, #5 .... **125.00**
4½" h, multicolored, enameled, ribbon-tied garlands, light blue
ground, circ gilt edged ft, c1862-
71, imp "MINTON" **150.00**
4¾" h, encrusted, sprays of lilies,
ochre spreading feet, gilt rim,
c1850 (A) **170.00**
8" h, turquoise rosebuds reserves, gilt
jewels and swags **175.00**
9¼" h, painted garden flowers, gilt
ram's mask handles, sq black
bases, c1815, pr (A) **715.00**
10" h, cov, painted continuous landscape, radiating gilt and white borders, silver luster feet, urn shape,
gilt scroll handles, c1810, pr (A) . **400.00**
14½" h, four reserves of stag and
hunter, blue celeste ground, gilt
loop and pierced handles, sq gilt
and white bases, pomegranate finials, c1869, pr (A) **3,250.00**
17" h, cov, painted exotic birds reserve, floral bouquet on reverse,
apple-green ground, foliage festoons on necks, domed covs, pineapple finials, pr **1,200.00**
24⅜" h, painted classical figures in
porticos, panels, bathing maidens,
stylized foliate scroll and arabesque
borders, faience, ovoid, trumpet
necks, domed feet, dated 1877,
imp "MINTON", pr (A) **530.00**
Vegetable Bowl, "Ming Tree" pattern,
oval **40.00**
Vegetable Tureen, 12½" l, cov, undertray, underglaze blue florals, gilt, orange-red rims, ironstone (A) **100.00**

MOCHA WARE
Staffordshire, England
1760–1939

History: Inexpensive utilitarian wares with tree-like, feather, moss, and worm designs, known as "Mocha" wares were made during the 19th century. The name came from the mocha stone or moss agate which the design resembled.

William Adams made the first examples at his Cobridge factory in 1799. Since these wares were mainly used in public houses, jugs, tankards, coffeepots, porringers, and butter dishes were the principal shapes that were manufactured.

Basically the decorative portion of a piece consisted of a broad band of colored slip, usually blue, gray, or coffee colored in tone, upon which was the design itself. To achieve the "tree" design, mocha ware potters utilized a mixture called "tea" that was put into the slip while still damp, thus causing the color to spread out into tree-like fronds that contrasted with the white earthenware beneath. On some examples, black rings were added.

Mocha ware exhibited a large variety of patterns. Arboration was made with an acidic solution, forming patterns such as Tree, Shrub, Fern, Seaweed, and Landscape. Cat's Eye and Worm patterns evolved from the use of a three-chambered slip bottle. Marbled and splotched pieces were made by using a blow pipe.

When the background was green, brown, cream, or orange the designs usually were brown or black. Ale mugs, chamber pots, jugs, pitchers, and shrimp and nut measures are the forms most frequently found with mocha decoration.

It is rare to find a piece with a maker's mark. Among the known manufacturers of Mocha ware are Edge and Malkin in Burslem between 1871 and 1890, and T. G. Green & Co. in Derbyshire from 1864 to 1939. Additional mocha ware makers include Adams of Tunstall, Cork and Edge of Burslem, Broadhurst of Fenton, Tams of Longton, MacIntyre of Cobridge, Pinder and Bourne of Burslem, Green of Church Gresley, and Maling of New Castle-on-Tyne.

Museums: City Museum and Art Gallery, Stoke-on-Trent, England.

Bowl
4½" d, rust brown bands, seaweed,
translucent green **345.00**
4⅝" d, grayish band, dark brown
stripes, emb rim (A) **100.00**
4¾" d, 2⅞" h, cream band, black
striped, emb green rim, cracked
(A) **85.00**
5½" d, emb stripes, dots, and dashes,
white, green, brown, light blue,
and tan stripes (A) **235.00**

6⅛" d, marbleized, seaweed design, blue, white, brown, and green, brown rim (A) **425.00**

6½" d, blue and white bands, black wavy lines, emb green rim, (A) ... **200.00**

7¼" d, 3½" h, orange-tan band, dark brown seaweed design, emb yellow-green rim (A) **275.00**

7½" d, 3⅞" h, black band, blue and white stripes, blue, white, and ochre earthworm and circle designs (A) **230.00**

Chamber Pot, cov, looping multicolored swirls center band, single handle ... **225.00**

Compote, 5"d, 3½" h, blue, black, white, and brown marbleized design (A) **100.00**

Creamer

3¾" h, orange, brown, and white cat's eye, green, white brown and tan stripes (A) **450.00**

3⅞" h, blue stripes, white, and gray-blue (A) **75.00**

Cup Plate, 3½" d, light yellow, black seaweed design (A) **375.00**

Jug

4¾" h, wide center mocha band, black sponged trees, blue and black bands **65.00**

4⅞" h, wide center mocha band, sponged trees, blue and black bands **65.00**

5⅛" h, wide center mocha band, black sponged trees, blue and black bands **65.00**

5¼" h, center band of mocha, black seaweed, blue outer bands, raised "Royal 1 Pt." mark **175.00**

Milk Pitcher, center band, two lower bands, seaweed pattern, loop handle **550.00**

Mug

2½" h, black stripe, seaweed design, white ground (A) **215.00**

2⅝" h

Black stripe and seaweed design, emb green rim, cream ground (A) **190.00**

Light and dark brown bands and dashes, white ground, emb leaf handle (A) **235.00**

2¾" h, white band with blue seaweed, brown stripes, yellow ground (A) **95.00**

2⅞" h, orange band, brown seaweed and stripe, leaf handle (A) **175.00**

3⅛" h, brown and white band, black stripes and seaweed design, emb leaf handle (A) **225.00**

3¼" h, tan band, black seaweed design **165.00**

3½" h,

Beige band, brown stripes and seaweed (A) **225.00**

Orange, green, dark brown, and white emb stripes, emb leaf handle (A) **275.00**

3⅝" h

Orange, black seaweed design, blue rim (A) **525.00**

Dark brown bands and dashes, emb green, white ground, leaf handle (A) **185.00**

3¾" h, wide, mocha band, black sponged trees, black and blue bands **60.00**

4⅝" h, dark brown and white stripes, dark brown band filled with rows of cream, white, and blue cat's eyes, cream ground, emb light green rim, (A) **400.00**

4¾" h

Blue and gray bands, black stripes and seaweed design, white ground, applied and imp crown, "Imperial" (A) **200.00**

Blue and yellow ochre bands, black

Left, pitcher, 6¾" h, dark brown seaweed on rust band, cream handle and spout, $800.00; center, bowl, 6¼" d, brown, cream, and orange earthworm on tan ground, raised green border, c1790–1820, $600.00; right, pitcher, 6¾" h, tan center band, four black rings, light blue top band, black seaweed, "E. R. & crown" on front, $200.00.

stripes and cat's eyes, emb leaf handle (A) **575.00**

4⅞" h, emb black and white design (A) **135.00**

5" h

Blue, black, amd dark teal bands, sponged tree design, mocha ground (A) **185.00**

Brown, tan, green, and white stripes (A) **180.00**

Gray and blue bands, black stripes and seaweed, white ironstone (A)   **55.00**

5⅝" h, emb green bands, dark brown stripes, dashes, and zig-zags (A) . . **335.00**

5¾" h, white, dark brown, and blue stripes, dark brown seaweed design, light orange ground, emb borders (A) **525.00**

6" h

Grayish-green band, dark brown stripes and seaweed design (A) . **325.00**

White and gray band, blue stripes, black seaweed design, applied emb crown, "Imperial" (A) **130.00**

6⅜" h, brown, white, and blue dots, brown and white band borders, buff ground, c1835, England (A) . **160.00**

6⅜" h, 4⅛" d brown center band, black seaweed design, blue top band **90.00**

6½" h, wide blue band, black sponged trees, blue and black bands **65.00**

Mustard Pot, 3⅛" h, brown marbleized design, SP fittings (A) **75.00**

Pepperpot, 4½" h

Blue bands, mocha ground (A) **85.00**

Green, blue, and black bands, mocha ground (A) **125.00**

Pitcher

3¼" h, black spots, white zig-zag stripes, brown ground (A) **225.00**

5⅛" h, blue and white, black stripes (A) **40.00**

5⅜" h, cream band, orange-tan and dark brown stripes, brown, white, light blue and tan balloon design, white ground, emb leaf handle (A) **675.00**

5½" h, gray, white, and blue bands, black seaweed design **85.00**

5¾" h

Emb dashes and dots, white, green, gray, orange-tan, and dark brown stripes (A) **550.00**

Orange-tan bands, blue and emb green stripes, black seaweed design, barrel shape (A) **450.00**

6" h, blue, tan, and dark brown, white band, white slip designs (A)   **300.00**

6⅛" h

Dark brown band, white slip wavy line and dots, blue and white

stripes, green emb band at shoulder, cat's eyes on cream colored neck, cracked (A) **335.00**

Light blue and cream bands, dark brown stripes and earthworm design, emb leaf handle (A) **325.00**

6⅞" h, black transfer bands, blue, white, and yellow stripes, emb leaf handle (A) **300.00**

7" h

Brown stripes, brown and white balloon design, yellow ware, hairlines (A) **275.00**

Dark brown band, white designs, blue, orange, and brown stripes, emb leaf handle (A) **350.00**

Light blue band, dark brown stripes, brown, green, amd white earthworm design (A) **210.00**

7⅛" h, gray and blue bands, black stripes, white ground, emb leaf handle, hairline on base (A) **40.00**

7¼" h, wide tan band, dark brown seaweed design, blue, white, and emb green stripes, leaf handle, repaired (A) **350.00**

7⅜" h, brown and blue stripes, white squiggles, blue, brown, and white earthworm design, yellow ware (A) **400.00**

7½" h, white, orange, green, and dark brown emb stripes, emb leaf handle (A) **500.00**

7¾" h, dark brown and gray bands, black, white, and green emb stripes, yellow, white, and blue earthworm design, emb leaf handle (A) **450.00**

8⅝" h, gray bands, black stripes, blue, white, and brown earthworm design, spout cracked (A) **210.00**

Porringer, 4¼" d, 2¾" h, brown stripes, brown, black, and white balloon dec, dark tan ground (A) **600.00**

Salt

3" d, blue bands, gray-green stripes, white ground (A) **40.00**

3¼" d, blue, white, and black stripes (A) **20.00**

3¾" d, blue band, black and white stripes, brown, white, and black earthworm dec (A) **200.00**

Shaker

3¼" h, emb brown, orange, and green checkerboard design, white ground (A) **425.00**

4" h

Cream band, orange stripes, black seaweed design (A) **275.00**

Orange and black, circle design (A) **225.00**

Orange band, brown stripes and seaweed design, white ground (A) **250.00**

4⅛" h, narrow blue, black and white
horizontal stripes (A) **150.00**
4¼" h
Black and white wavy lines, blue
domed top (A) **175.00**
Blue and black, ochre and white
cat's eye design, (A) **300.00**
Blue band, orange and green
stripes, black seaweed design,
white ground (A) **225.00**
Orange and brown stripes, white
ground (A) **150.00**
4⅜" h, brown stripe, yellow ochre
bands, white ground, dark brown
domed top (A) **135.00**
4½" h
Black and green bands, sienna,
twigs, c1820 .... **225.00**
Blue and white bands, brown vertical stripes (A) **110.00**
Blue band, orange-tan, white, and
black stripes, white, tan, and
black cat's eye (A) **600.00**
4⅝" h
Blue bands, black, white, and emb
blue stripes, brown, white, and
black earthworm and cat's eye
design (A) **450.00**
Dark brown, white slip wavy lines,
blue dome top (A) **55.00**
Medium blue and white, ochre
wavy lines, dark blue dome top
(A) **200.00**
4¾" h
Blue and white, black stripes (A) . **100.00**
Wide blue, black, and white horizontal stripes (A) **125.00**
5" h, blue and white, black stripe (A) **45.00**
5½" h, blue and white, black geo-
metric band (A) **115.00**
Teabowl and Saucer, black seaweed design, tan ground (A) **425.00**
Tumbler, 3¾" h, marbleized brown,
white, and black design, yellow accents, blue and white cross hatched
border (A) **350.00**
Waste Bowl
4¾" d, white, beige band, black
stripes, edge chip (A) **10.00**
5⅞" d, light and dark blue stripes,
white ground, chips on ft (A) **10.00**
6½" d, dark brown and light blue
stripes, white ground, blue and
brown earthworm design (A) **160.00**
7" d, blue band, cat's eye, black
stripes (A) **45.00**
7⅛" d, gray band, black stripes, light
blue and black earthworm and cat's
eye design, ochre accents, white
ground (A) **225.00**
7⅜" d, gray and green bands, dark

brown stripes, tan, brown, and
white earthworm design (A) **175.00**
7½" d, tan band, black stripes and
seaweed design, emb green trim,
white ground (A) **75.00**
7⅝" d, tan bands, black stripes and
seaweed design, white ground,
chips on base (A) **100.00**

MOORCROFT

Burslem, Staffordshire
1897 to 1945

History: William Moorcroft was first employed
as a potter by James Macintyre & Co., Ltd. of
Burslem in 1897. Moorcroft's early works included vases, bowls, and biscuit jars that were
decorated in blue, red, and gold plant forms
called Aurelian ware.

Moorcroft also made Florian ware in a wide
variety of shapes and types of decorations. Florian ware featured poppies, violets, or cornflowers applied in relief or portrayed in slip trail outlines. It was marketed under various trade names
such as: Claremont, a toadstool design; Hazeldene, a landscape with trees; Honesty; Pansy;
Pomegrante; and, Flamminian, luster wares.
The principal markets were in London, New
York, Paris, and San Francisco. The signature
"W. Moorcroft" appeared on each piece along
with the standard Macintyre printed mark.

In 1913 Moorcroft built his own small factory,
the Washington Works, at Burslem, employing
potters and decorators with whom he had
worked at James Macintyre & Co. Moorcroft continued the floral styles, but now used simplier
and bolder designs. Dark colored exotic flowers
adorned many pieces. Landscapes were done in
the trailed outline technique. Monochrome luster
glazes were produced until the 1920s, followed
by flambe glazes in the decade that followed.
The flambe or transmutation glazes provided the
most interest for Moorcroft.

W. Moorcroft was appointed potter to Queen
Mary in 1928. The impressed phrase "Potter to
H.M. The Queen" was added to his mark. During the 1930s fruits, fish, birds, and boats joined
the traditional decorative motifs. Matte glazes
found favor. When Moorcraft died in 1945, Walter, his eldest son, continued the Moorcroft company.

References: A. W. Coysh, *British Art Pottery,*
1870–1940, Charles E. Tuttle, 1976; Richard
Dennis, *William & Walter Moorcroft, 1897–*
1973, an exhibition catalog, 1973.

Museums: Everson Museum of Art, Syracuse, N.Y.

Biscuit Box, 4½" h, "Eventide" design, dbl handles **900.00**
Biscuit Jar, 6½" h, maroon, blue, yellow-brown, and green pomegranates, berries, and leaves, dbl handles, sgd "W. Moorcroft," imp "Moorcroft, Burslem" (A) **115.00**
Bowl
  3¼" d, multi-hued orchid on int., blue-green ext., sgd & mkd **65.00**
  4" d, enameled orchid, indigo blue ground, paper label **70.00**
  6" d, coral hibiscus, green ground . . **35.00**
  8" d, "Grape Leaves" design **70.00**
  9" d
    "Red Flambe Orchid," multicolored orchids, red-orange ground **600.00**
    "Wisteria" design **75.00**
  9" l, 4½" h, "Moonlight" design, light blue trees, dark blue ground, pewter foot **875.00**
  10" d
    Orchids and white flowers **125.00**
    Red and yellow hibiscus, green ground, green "W.M." **125.00**
  11" d, "Poppies" design, ftd **150.00**
Cigarette Box, 4½" l, floral design on lid, light green ground, c1930, script mark **125.00**
Box, Cov, 6" d
  Pomegranate" design, blue shades **335.00**
  Three pansies, blue ground **225.00**
Butter Pat, floral design **25.00**
Candlesticks, 3¼" h, pink flower, dark olive green ground, pr **40.00**
Compote 7" d, 3½" h, pink flowers, green ground **85.00**
Creamer and Sugar, large open flowers, cobalt-green ground **130.00**
Cup and Saucer
  Blue, gilding, blue ground, hexagon shape, "Moorcroft-Macintyre" . . . **210.00**
  Red and ochre poppies, mottled blue ground, imp mark **225.00**
  "Vine" design, blue and gray grapes and vines, blue-gray ground **150.00**
Dessert Set, cup, saucer and plate, large pansy, cobalt ground, c1916 . . . . **75.00**
Dish
  4½" d, "Amaryllis" pattern, "Queen" mark **65.00**
  Pansies, green ground, two tiered . . **350.00**
Ginger Jar, 8" h, red and yellow pomegranate, cobalt ground **100.00**
Ink Pot, 2⅛" h, "Hazeldene," stylized trees and hills, "Moonlit Blue" pal-

atte, bell shape, plated rim, brass cov and brush, imp "Moorcroft" (A) **150.00**
Inkwell, green "Flamminian" glaze, "Made for Liberty & Co." **400.00**
Jam Jar
  3½" h
    Leaves and berries design, imp "Wm Moorcroft, Potter to H.M. Queen, Made in England" **125.00**
    "Moonlight" design, SP spoon, lid, and handle **500.00**
  3¾" h, oranges and grapes, dark ground, Tudric pewter cov, ... **200.00**
Jar, Cov, 6½" h, cobalt and green design **125.00**
Lamp
  15" h, multicolored leaves and berries, green ground, script mark . . . **400.00**
  27" h, multicolored flowers, cobalt ground, "Wm Moorcroft, Made in England" **450.00**
Lamp Base, 10" h, pomegranates and grapes, muted colors, cobalt ground . **165.00**
Pitcher, 5" h, pink and mauve orchids, cobalt ground **165.00**
Plate, 8¾" d, Queen Elizabeth Jubilee, mauve crown, yellow thistles, "E-R" at top, green ground, limited edition **250.00**
Tazza
  5½" d, 7" h, pomegranates and grapes, blue ground, Tudric pewter stand, "Moorcroft" signature **135.00**
  8½" d, 6" h, pomegranates and grapes, blue ground, Tudric pewter base, sgd and numbered, orig paper label **150.00**
Tea Set, teapot, creamer, and sugar, large pink flowers, cobalt ground, c1930 . . . . **225.00**
Teapot, 8" h, orchids, multicolored . . . **185.00**
Tray, 4½" l, coral hibiscus light green ground **30.00**
Urn, 8½" h, "Hazeldene" design, blue tree scene around top, green int. . . . **875.00**
Vase
  2⅛" h, floral relief, cobalt ground . . **55.00**
  2⅝" h
    Maroon, amber, and blue pomegranates, berries and leaves (A) **35.00**
    Maroon, amber, blue, and green anemones, imp "Moorcroft, England" (A) **55.00**
  3" h
    "Flambe Columbine" design **65.00**
    "Macintyre," lappet panels on shoulder, blue anemones on olive green, yellow anemones on white at base, sgd "W. Moorcroft" (A) **160.00**
    Pomegranates, multicolored **50.00**
  3⅛" h, olive green and dark blue vine leaves and grapes, shaded blue-

Vases, left, 4″ h, lilac pansy, dark blue ground, script mark, $110.00; center, 6½″ h, "Spanish" pattern, dark colors, $600.00; right, 8½″ h, "Moonlight" blue, $750.00.

green ground, globular, cylindrical neck, imp "Moorcroft-Made in England" (A) 60.00

3⅜″ h, stylized trees and hills, "Moonlit Blue" palette, globular, sgd "W.M.," imp "Moorcroft" (A) 200.00

3½″ h, maroon, light brown, and white cornflowers, green ground, dbl handled, "W. Moorcroft, XI-1913" (A) 240.00

4″ h
Bunches of flowers on upper section, white lower section, green neck 250.00
"Mushroom" design, "Made for Liberty & Co." 275.00

4⅛″ "Pomegranate" 110.00

4¼″ h, "Florian," dark and light blue stylized flowers outlined with white tube-lining, light blue ground, globular, SP cov (A) 150.00

4½″ h
Coral hibiscus, light green ground   35.00
Pink flowers, cobalt ground 65.00

5″ d, 5½″ h, orange, red, and purple cornflower, mottled green ground, c1913, green script "W. Moorcroft" 635.00

5″ h
Florals, cobalt ground, bulbous ..   70.00
Multicolored florals, shaded blue ground 125.00
Open flower, blue ground 110.00
Rust anemones, medium blue ground 65.00
Turquoise long narrow neck, shades of blue with yellow, blue and yellow florals on bulbous base, blue lipped opening 400.00

5¼″ h, plums and lemons, cobalt ground, Tudric pewter, flared top . 130.00

5½″ h, pomegranates, cobalt ground,

flared top, Tudric pewter base, sgd "Tudric, Moorcroft" 130.00

6″ h
Bright red flowers, blue centers, dark blue ground, narrow neck, bulbous middle 225.00
Large pink flowers, cobalt ground   75.00
Large purple and pink flowers, cobalt ground 75.00

6⅛″ h, blue, red, and yellow flowers, green stems, blue ground in elliptical panels, divided by pale green bands, sgd "W.M.," imp "Moorcroft Made in England" (A) 230.00

7¼″ h, "Florian," pink roses, blue florals, green ribbons and garlands, white ground, dbl handles 300.00

7½″ h, red hibiscus, cobalt ground, script mark 165.00

8″ h
"Aurelian," Nouveau design, gold, cobalt and orange, cream ground, "Moorcroft-Macintyre" 300.00
Pansy dec blue ground, c1920 (A)   80.00
Pomegranates, dark blue ground . 100.00

8¾″ h, "Burslem," dark blue, multicolored floral insert on white panel, narrow base and wide top 500.00

9″ d, dark blue flowers and stems, light blue ground, "Macintyre-Burslem" 325.00

9¼″ h, mauve pomegranate, cobalt ground, flared top 525.00

9½″ h, "Hazeldene," stylized trees and hills, "Eventide" palette, sgd "W. Moorcroft," imp "Moorcroft" (A) 265.00

9¾″ h, "Florian," blue poppy design, white ground, long slender neck . 350.00

10″ h, "Wisteria" design 140.00

10½" h
"Florian," multiple shades of blue,
raised design, bottle shape **700.00**
Red poppy, green leaves, cobalt
ground, stick shape **175.00**
11¼" h, "Florian," shades of blue,
dark blue long florals, lighter blue
panels on neck section, flared
mouth **850.00**
11⅝" h, "Flambe," red, rust, green,
blue vines and grapes, shaded red
glaze (A) **315.00**
12½" h, "Anemones" design, c1930 **375.00**

1853-1935

BERNARD MOORE

Stoke-on-Trent, Staffordshire, England
1870 to 1915

History: Bernard and Samuel Moore assumed control of their father's porcelain factory at St. Mary's Works, Longton in Staffordshire in 1870. They traded as the "Moore Brothers."

Bernard, a ceramic chemist, was very interested in fine glaze effects, especially those from the Far East. He ended his partnership with his brother in 1905 and established his own firm in Stoke-on-Trent. Bernard Joseph, Bernard's son, joined his father's new firm. Many experiments with glazes were undertaken. Used on simple porcelain or earthenware forms, Bernard produced great examples with flambe, turquoise, and sang de boeuf glazes, as well as a variety of styles.

The firm employed artists to paint highly decorative pieces with designs that included flowers, flying birds, and other motifs. Among these artists were John Adams, Hilda Beardmore, Dora Mary Billington, George Allen Buttle, Gertrude Jackson, Hilda Lindop, Annie Oliver, Reginald R. Tomlinson, and Edward R. Wilkes. Most of the artists signed their works.

Works were signed "BM" or "BERNARD MOORE." World War I caused the closing of Moore's factory in 1915.

References: A.W. Coysh, *British Art Pottery, 1870–1940,* Charles E. Tuttle Co., 1976.

Museums: Victoria & Albert Museum, London, England.

Bowl, 11" d, flambe and white motto
design **100.00**
Candlestick
2½" h, figural, monkey wearing turtle

shell, holding nut, crouched under
mushroom, iron-red and gilt, cream
ground, imp "Moore, B." (A) **75.00**
8½" h, figural, putti riding dolphins,
bobeche, lily form, gilt accents,
imp, (A) **200.00**
Figure, flambe
3½" h, ape, glass eyes, seated holding
foot, sgd "BM" (A) **80.00**
5⅜" h, demon, long ears, webbed
feet and tail, seated circ base, sgd
"BM" (A) **80.00**
Ginger Jar 7" h, flambe **175.00**
Vase
2½" h, dark flambe, baluster **50.00**
3½" h, blue, "Dragon" pattern,
c1905 .... **100.00**
4½" h, flambe, Oriental dragon design **200.00**
6¾" h, marbled, high glazed finish . **145.00**
9" h, flambe, "Gu" design **200.00**
9½" h, muted gold luster, bird flying,
branches of prunus, dark blue
ground, onion shape, sgd "Bernard
Moore" (A) **70.00**

MULBERRY WARE

Staffordshire, England
1835 to 1855

History: Mulberry ware was made by many of the same Staffordshire potters that produced Flow Blue. In fact, many patterns with identical design and name are found on both types of wares. The bulk of the Mulberry ware production occurred during the early Victorian period, i.e., 1835–1855.

The mulberry color was achieved by a chemical combination of red, brown, gray, and purple dyes. Mulberry refered to the color of berries from the English black mulberry trees. Some Mulberry patterns on earthenware or ironstone were "flown," producing a soft, hazy effect. Most were presented with a sharp, clear design.

Mulberry ware was a response to the public's need for something new and different. Its popularity did not last. Few pieces were made after 1855.

References: Petra Williams, *Flow Blue China & Mulberry Ware, Similarity and Value Guide,* Fountain House East, rev. ed., 1981.

Collecting Hints: Previously, Mulberry prices always had been priced higher than Flow Blue examples. However, in the past few years, there has been a reversal. Mulberry ware now sells for about one-third less than the prevailing price for a comparable Flow Blue piece.

Plate, 10¼" d, "Bochara," marked "J. & E.," $45.00.

"Abbey"
Platter, 12½" l, 9½" w **100.00**
Soap dish, cov, "L. P. & Co." **100.00**
"Alhambra" Plate, 10" d, unmarked .. **35.00**
"Alleghany" Basin 13¾" d, "Thomas
Goodfellow" **100.00**
"Athens"
Cup and saucer, "Charles Meigh" .. **35.00**
Platter, 13½" l, "W. Adams & Sons" **150.00**
Teabowl, "Wm Adams & Sons" **50.00**
"Avon"
Cup and saucer, unmarked **45.00**
Plate, 8½" d **30.00**
Teabowl and saucer **55.00**
Waste bowl, 5½" w, unmarked **55.00**
"Balmoral" Mug, 6¼" h, "W. A. & S." **40.00**
"Bochara"
Platter, 14" l, "J.& E." **100.00**
Sauce dish, cov **120.00**
Sauce tureen, cov **120.00**
Teabowl and saucer **65.00**
"Calcutta" Plate, 9¾" d, "E. Challinor" **30.00**
"Chusan"
Plate, 10½" d, "Thomas Fell" **35.00**
Platter, 15" l, 11½" w **100.00**
"Cologne"
Pitcher, 13" h, "J. Alcock" **200.00**
Wash Bowl type, "Samuel Alcock" . **175.00**
"Corea"
Creamer, "Clemenston" **40.00**
Dish, 5" d, "J. Clemenston" **30.00**
Plate
9¾" d, 12-sided **25.00**
10" d **50.00**
Platter, 15¾" l, 12⅛" w, octagonal . **120.00**
Sugar, cov, "J. Clementson" **85.00**
Water pitcher **275.00**
"Corean"
Creamer, "P. W. & Co." **100.00**
Cup Plate, 3¾" d, "P. W. & Co." ... **50.00**
Plate
7¾" d, "Podmore, Walker & Co." **30.00**
8¾" d, "P. W. & Co." **40.00**

9½" d, "P. W. & Co." **50.00**
9¾" d, "P. W. & Co." **45.00**
Platter
12½" l, "Podmore, Walker & Co." **40.00**
15¾" l, "P. W. & Co." **55.00**
18" l **275.00**
Teabowl and saucer, "Podmore,
Walker & Co." **20.00**
Waste bowl, 5½" w, "P. W. & Co." . **65.00**
"Cyprus"
Plate
7" d, "Davenport" **30.00**
9" d, "Davenport" **35.00**
9¼" d, "Davenport" **45.00**
10½" d **45.00**
Platter, 13¾" l, 10½" w **100.00**
Teapot, 10½" h, "Davenport-Iron-
stone" **150.00**
"Eastern Scenery" Plate, 9" d, "Enoch
Wood & Sons" **35.00**
"Flora" Platter, 14" l, "Hulme &
Boothe" **110.00**
"Genoa" Plate, 7½" d, "Davenport" . **35.00**
"Jeddo" Creamer, "W. Adams & Sons" **55.00**
Cup, Plate, 3¾" d **40.00**
Plate 9½" d **50.00**
Sugar, "Wm Adams & Sons" **85.00**
Teabowl and saucer, "W. Adams &
Co." **45.00**
"Kyber"
Plate, 10" d **55.00**
Teabowl and saucer, "Meir" **65.00**
"Loretta" Plate, 9¼" d **45.00**
"Marble"
Creamer **65.00**
Pitcher, 12½" **100.00**
Soap dish, cov **60.00**
"Milan" Relish Dish, 6-sided **40.00**
"Ning Po"
Cup and saucer **40.00**
Plate
7½" d **15.00**
9½" d **20.00**
10½" d **25.00**
Teabowl and saucer **55.00**
Vegetable bowl, 9½" l **50.00**
"Pelew" Plate
8½" d, "E. Challinor & Co." **30.00**
9" d, "E. Challinor & Co." **20.00**
9¾" d, "E. Challinor & Co." **20.00**
10" d, "E. Challinor & Co." **55.00**
10½" d, "Edward Challinor & Co." . **55.00**
"Peru" Tea Service, teapot, creamer,
sugar, seven dessert plates, nine cups
and saucers, "Holdcroft & Co." **800.00**
"Peruvian"
Plate, 9¾" d, "J. Wedgwood" **45.00**
Platter, 16" l, "J. Wedgwood" **125.00**
Soup Tureen, cov, 8-sided **650.00**
Teapot, "J. Wedgwood" **200.00**
"Rhone Scenery"
Plate, 9¾" d **45.00**

Teapot, "T. J. & J. Mayer" **185.00**
"Rose"
 Plate
  8½" d, "T. Walker" **20.00**
  9½" d, "Edward Challinor & Co.,
   Tunstall" **40.00**
  Vegetable Bowl, 10" d, "E. Challinor
   & Co." **65.00**
 "Scinde," soup plate, 10½" d, "T.
  Walker" **35.00**
"Shell"
 Cup and saucer **40.00**
 Teapot, 9" h **200.00**
"Simla" Plate, 8" d **22.00**
"Susa" Sauce tureen, cov, undertray,
 "C. M. & S." **200.00**
"Tavoy"
 Creamer, "T. Walker" **100.00**
 Plate, 6¾" d, "T. Walker" **30.00**
"Temple"
 Bowl, 10" d **200.00**
 Cup and Saucer, "P. W. & Co." **40.00**
 Plate
  8" d, "P. W. & CO." **30.00**
  9" d **35.00**
  9¾" d **20.00**
  10" d, "P. W. & C0. .... **25.00**
 Vegetable Bowl
  7½" l, 5" w **50.00**
  12" l, 10" w **125.00**
"Tonquin" Plate, 9¼" d, "Heath" **40.00**

Teabowl and saucer, "Samuel Alcock" **40.00**
Tureen, cov, undertray and ladle, 8¼"
 l, 8½", c1857, "J. Alcock" **150.00**
Vegetable bowl, 8½" l, "Samuel Alcock" **70.00**
"Washington Vase"
 Plate
  7" d **40.00**
  8" d, "P. W. & CO." **30.00**
  8½" d, "P. W. & Co." **30.00**
  8¾" d, "Podmore, Walker & Co." **30.00**
  8⅞" d, "P. W. & Co." **40.00**
  9" d, "P. W. & Co." **35.00**
  9¾" d **50.00**
 Platter
  13½" l, "P. W. & Co." **65.00**
  15¾" l, 12¼" w, "P. W. & Co." .. **135.00**
 Sauce dish, 5½" d, "P. W. & Co." .. **20.00**

MUSTACHE CUPS

English, Continental
1830 to Present

History: The mustache cup is a Victorian inno-
vation that owes its origin to Harvey Adams, a
Stoke-on-Trent potter who introduced the design
in 1830. It is a drinking cup used for imbibing
tea or coffee, featuring a raised lip guard attached
to the rim of the cup to keep the mustache and
beard from touching the liquid. Originally called
"Napoleons and Saucers" after the small beards
popular at the time, mustache cups reached the
peak of their popularity in the 1890s when wearing a mustache was the rage.

Mustache cups were first sold singly. Some had
matching saucers, most stood alone. As their
popularity increased, they were included in dinnerware sets. Gift sets that included a cup with
a mustache rim for the gentleman and an identical rimless cup for madam were common. Right
and left-handed cups were produced. Left-
handed examples are scarce. Although originat-
ing in England, the manufacture of mustache
cups quickly spread to other areas including
France, Germany, and Austria.

**Teapot, 10" l, 9" h, "Vincennes," marked
"John Alcock," $200.00**

"Vincennes"
 Plate
  7" d, "Samuel Alcock" **30.00**
  7½" d, "Samuel Alcock" **55.00**
  9¼" d **30.00**
  9½"d **30.00**
  10½" d, "Samuel Alcock" **45.00**
 Platter
  10½" l, 8" w **50.00**
  15½" l, 12" w, "Samuel Alcock" . **125.00**

Many different media were used for the body including earthenware, porcelain, and bone china. Free hand painting by artists along with transfer printing and other decorative techniques were used. Heavy raised and burnished decorations and rich gilding proved popular. These are the most frequently encountered pieces today. Some mustache cups employed several techniques in order to catch the fancy of the buyer.

Many of the major houses produced mustache cups and marked their products accordingly. Crown Derby, Wedgwood, Meissen, and Limoges all provided cups for the mustached gentleman. However, many of the examples found in today's market are unmarked.

The size of mustache cups ranges from demitasse to quart. The eight ounce size is most commonly found.

References: Dorothy Hammond, *Mustache Cups,* Wallace-Homestead, 1972; Thelma Schull, *Victorian Antiques,* Tuttle, 1963.

REPRODUCTION ALERT. Reproduced matching left-handed and right-handed mustache cups have found their way to antique shops. Since matched sets are very rare, collectors should be careful to make sure the matched set is old, not a reproduction.

Collecting Hints: Sayings and mottos are fairly common but do not add significantly to the value of the piece. Advanced collectors seek out Majolica, Imari, Rose Medallion, Sunderland, Luster, and Belleek cups.

Note: All listings are for right handed cups unless indicated otherwise.

CUP

Band of applied florals, "For A Gift" in gold	**100.00**
Blue top, raised flowers, gold leaf, swirl base	**30.00**
Black transfers of stylized gentleman, cream ground, orange rim and handle band	**100.00**
Multicolored sponge dec, Colonial couple in medallion, ftd	**125.00**
Festooned flowers, gold, white ground	**25.00**
Floral design, c1880, Limoges mark	**50.00**
Floral design, white ground, "GERMANY"	**35.00**
Green and yellow raised flowers (A)	**15.00**
Gold leaf rim, white ground, branch handle	**20.00**
Irish Belleek	
Basketweave, green trim, 2nd black mark	**425.00**
Gilt trim, ring handle, 1st black mark	**200.00**
Ivy leaves, gold, white swirl base, small guard for petite mustaches	**30.00**
Large rose bouquets, green tinted and	

white ground, green handle, Germany	**25.00**
"Merry Christmas" in script, floral ground	**50.00**
Molded gold and floral, "BROTHER," dark green ground	**50.00**
Multicolored scene, couple in winter setting, gold ribbon on rim, tied in bow on side	**85.00**
Multicolored tapestry, "Present" on front, raised gold floral border, red "MADE IN GERMANY"	**55.00**
Orange and blue butterfly on poppies, brown leaves (A)	**5.00**
Orange flowers, white ground, "Germany"	**40.00**
Pears and leaves, gold trim, light green gound, "GERMANY" (A)	**5.00**
Pink, gold and white raised design, "GERMANY"	**35.00**
Pink, gold tassels, Germany (A)	**10.00**
Pink, yellow, and white flowers, red and gold top border, gold and white lower section, "RICHMOND Z. S. & Co. BAVARIA" (A)	**10.00**
Pink and brown birds on branch, gold and blue flowers (A)	**5.00**
Pink and yellow asters, white ground, gilt accents, "Germany"	**30.00**
Pink forget-me-nots, green leaves, white ground	**15.00**
Purple raised flowers near top, roses, dark green ground (A)	**40.00**
Roses, flowers, leaves, and gold trim around top and handle, "R. S. Prussia" (A)	**40.00**
Scene of hunter in woods, three running deer, raised enamels (A)	**15.00**
Small blue flowers and green leaves, smaller design repeated on int., white scalloped base	**30.00**
Sponge design, medallion, ftd	**70.00**
"Think of Me," pink luster, Germany	**35.00**
Transfer of yellow and pink chrysanthemums, shades white to pink ground, Bavaria	**30.00**
Winter scene, birds flying over stream and woods, light green ground (A)	**20.00**
Young woman, lilacs in hair, smelling lilacs, flowers on reverse, gold trim (A)	**25.00**

CUP AND SAUCER

"A Present," multicolored floral pattern, Germany	**50.00**
Blue flowers on upper pink band, yellow fluted lower section, bronze handle & protector, "GERMANY"	**35.00**
"Christmas 1884" on front, "Germany"	**50.00**

Coral flowers, cobalt trim **50.00**
Blue bamboo and birds, wide blue geo-
metric border, white ground, Coalport **85.00**
Dogwood blossoms, red "R. S. Prussia" **60.00**
Floral design, gilt trim **65.00**
"Forget-Me-Not" inscribed in gold,
blue, orange, and rust flower, white
ground, plain saucer **30.00**

Cup and Saucer, purple and gilt florals, $30.00.

Gold bunches of grapes, white ground,
leaf entwined handles, pr **125.00**
Gold leaf medallions, fluted sides, scalloped base, white saucer **20.00**
Multicolored bird and fan design, ma-
jolica **225.00**
Multicolored florals, gold trim, light
green ground, Germany **25.00**
Multicolored flowers, gold trim, tan
ground, Germany **25.00**
Oval portrait of young girl, cobalt
ground **60.00**
Owl, tree, branch with green leaves,
and pink flowers, hp **40.00**
Peach and blue flowers, emb florals on
cut-out edge of saucer, "Eglantine,
Germany" **35.00**
Pink forget-me-nots, brown inscription,
white ground, farmer size, pr **250.00**
Pink roses, green leaves, lime green
ground **30.00**
Pink roses, swirled ribbing, green shad-
ing **30.00**
Pink roses, violets, gold trim **20.00**
Pink roses, white ground, Haviland ... **25.00**
"Present" inscribed in gold, large raised
purple and amber flowers, plain sau-
cer **35.00**
Shaded pink and green roses, Germany **30.00**
Small pink roses, white ground, Austria **65.00**
"Think of Me," multicolored violets,
daisies, and house design, Germany **65.00**
White scalloped roses **15.00**
Vertical flutes, green leaves and forget-
me-nots, white ground fluted saucer,
left–handed **125.00**

DEMITASSE

Gold band, raised geometric pattern
medallions, turquoise dots, green
dashes, white ground, covd guard .. **225.00**

NANT GARW
C. W.

NANTGARW

Glamorgan, Wales
1813 and c1817–1820

History: William Billingsley and Samuel Walker
started Welsh Nantgarw porcelains in 1813. The
cost of operations soon depleted their available
funds and production ceased. The pottery started
again about 1817 and survived until 1820. Most
pieces from this second period have the company
mark.

Nantgarw porcelains were soft, translucent,
and usually rather simple in decoration. Many
blanks were sold to London decorators. These
pieces frequently were more ornate in decoration.

Marked pieces have the impressed mark
"Nant-Garw," usually over the initials "CW"
(China Works). Sometimes the hyphen was omit-
ted.

References: W. D. John, *Nantgarw Porcelain,*
Ceramic Book Co., 1948. Supplement 1956; W.
P. John, *William Billingsley 1758–1828,* Ceramic
Book Co., 1968; E. Morton Nance, *The Pottery
& Porcelain of Swansea & Nantgarw,* Batsford,
1942.

Museums: Glynn Vivian Museum & Art Gallery,
Swansea, Wales.

Breakfast Cup & Saucer, painted bouquet of garden flowers in dark blue
border, reserved panels of flowers,
molded and gilt foliate scroll borders,
c1813–22 .... **350.00**
Cup and Saucer, C-scroll molded rim,
gilt-edged reserved flower panels, turquoise ground, kidney shape gilt handle, saucer painted with spray of florals, c1817–22, London decorated . **110.00**
Dessert Service, ftd center dish, two
cushion-shape dishes, three oval
dishes, twenty-one plates, painted
spray of pink roses and insects,

Plate, 9¼" d, multicolored center, blue and gilt border, c1820, London decorated, (A) $585.00.

molded borders with pink roses, gilt dentil rims, damage, c1820, imp "Nant Garw C. W." (A) 2,875.00
Dish
9⅜" sq, central bouquet, C-scroll molded rim, reserved flowers and fruit sprays, gilt dentil border, c1817–22, London decorated (A) . 530.00
9⅝" d, bouquet and bands of pink roses, gilt molded flower wreath, C-scroll border, c1820, imp "Nant-garw C. W." (A) 600.00
11¾" l
Center floral spray and scattered sprays, C-scroll molded borders, blue and gilt dentil rim, c1817, London decorated 250.00
Center rose spray, stylized multi-colored and gilt sprigs and dots border, London decorated (A) .. 225.00
Scattered sprays, C-scroll molded border, blue and gilt dentil rim, c1817, London decorated 250.00
Plate
8¼" d
Center floral spray, gilt foliate scrolls, diapering, stippling, and flowering plants border, c1820, London decorated (A) 335.00
Center floral spray and filberts, C-scroll molded rim with fruit sprigs, London decorated (A) ... 370.00
Center pink rose and delphinium, borders with three large flower sprays, imp "Nant-Garw C. W.," pr 200.00
Scattered bouquets, gilt dentil rim, c1820, imp "Nant-Garw C. W." 100.00
8⅜" d
Central floral spray, four large sprays, gilt dentil rim, c1817, London decorated 150.00
Pink rose sprigs, green leaves, trail-

ing berried branches, gilt line border and rim, c1817–22 .... 330.00
8½" d
Central bouquet in flower wreath, C-scroll molded border reserved birds and bouquet of fruit and flowers, gilt dentil rim, c1820, imp "Nantgarw C. W." (A) 430.00
Central bouquet of flowers, four sprays in gilt shell and rococo-scroll border, c1813–22 (A) 370.00
Central bouquet of flowers, neo-rococo borders, bouquets in C-scroll cartouches and trellis, c1813–22, pr 670.00
Center children on swing beside river, c1820, London decorated (A) 100.00
Floral sprays and insects, molded C-scroll border, gilt, c1813–22, imp "Nantgarw C. W." 550.00
8⅝" d
Bouquets and scattered flowers, green dot border molded with gilt wreaths and C-scrolls, c1820, imp "Nantgarw C. W." 325.00
Butterflies, bouquets, and sprigs, molded floral cartouches on borders, gilt dentil rims, c1813–22, London decorated, pr (A) 640.00
Scattered sprigs and fruit, gilt shaped border, c1820, imp "Nant-Garw C. W." (A) 350.00
8¾" d, center floral spray and filberts, C-scroll molded rim with fruit sprigs, c1817–22, London decorated 420.00
9⅜" d, center bouquet of garden flowers, border with swags of coral drapery, oval reserved panels of birds, landscapes, and fruit, edged in gilt scrolling foliage, c1820, imp "Nant-Garw C. W." (A) 1,870.00
9½" d, rose and chrysanthemum, border with ribbon-tied rose wreaths and swags of fruit, wavy gilt dentil rim, c1813–22, imp "Nantgarw C. W." (A) 675.00
9¾" d, flower sprays, molded C-scrolls rim, blue and gilt line borders, c1817, London decorated (A) 150.00
Tea and Coffee Service, teapot, stand, cov dbl handled sugar bowl, slop basin, milk jug, two plates, seven teacups, eight coffee cups, eight saucers, pink roses, green foliage, gilt moss, gilt line rims, c1820, imp "Nant-Garw C. W." (A) 5,500.00
Trio, teacup, coffee cup, and saucer
Multicolored sprays of flowers, gilt foliate scrolls, trelliswork, c1817, London decorated (A) 525.00

Gilt, multicolored pansies and pink roses, heart shape handles, c1817–22 (A) **150.00**

NEW HALL

Staffordshire Potteries, England c1781 to 1835

History: A group of partners purchased Champion's patent to make translucent porcelains. In 1781 they established the New Hall China Manufactory at Hanley in Staffordshire to make hard paste porcelains based upon the patent. Tea and dessert sets, along with blue and white wares showing Chinese influences, were characteristic products at New Hall. Gold was used in both simple and elaborate designs. Many early pieces only had elegant gilt borders.

Fidelle Duvivier, who had been employed at Worcester and Derby, worked at New Hall from 1781 to 1790. He did figure and landscape compositions and flower subjects on presentation jugs. Early New Hall teapots were globular in form. Pieces made during the hard paste period were not marked. Pattern numbers were used instead.

About 1812–14 bone china that was lighter and whiter was introduced at New Hall. The pieces were marked "New Hall" in a double lined circle along with a pattern number. Work declined after about 1820. The factory was put up for auction in 1831. Various firms using the original site continued the name until 1836.

References: David Holgate, *New Hall & Its Imitators,* Faber & Faber, 1971; G. E. Stringer, *New Hall Porcelain,* Art Trade Press, 1949.

Museums: City Museum & Art Gallery, Stoke-on-Trent, Hanley, England; Victoria & Albert Museum, London, England.

Creamer and Sugar, multicolored, puce rims, $225.00.

Bowl
2⅜" d, painted floral sprigs, Pattern #366 .... **25.00**
6¼" d, printed and colored reserved panels of mother and child, dark blue ground, gilt vines, Pattern #1277 (A) **100.00**
Coffee Can, "Window" pattern **20.00**
Coffee Can and Saucers, black bat printed landscapes, gilt lines, pr **20.00**
Coffee Cups, painted birds, bright plumage and rocks, foliage suspended vignettes with misty ground, c1781-85, pr (A) **1,325.00**
Creamer
2⅞" h, polychrome enameled florals, handle glued, (A) **10.00**
Urn crest design, c1810 .... **45.00**
Cup and Saucer
Multicolored berry border, c1800 .. **15.00**
Transfer and painted figures in roundels, blue ground, c1825, "Newhall in dbl ring" (A) **150.00**
Dessert Service, two oval dishes, eight plates, bat printed and colored named views, lavender-blue borders, light blue ground, c1815 (A) **420.00**
Dish, 8½" d, painted floral design **10.00**
Hot Water Jug, Oriental pattern, pewter lid and spout cov, c1812, mkd **235.00**
Jug, 5⅜" h, printed and colored "Butterfly" pattern, Oriental figures, trees, and fence, oval shape, long lip, Pattern #421 (A) **85.00**
Milk Jug, Oriental figures on terrace, multicolored, lobed body, c1790 (A) **130.00**
Plate, 8½" d, fruit, blue and gilt basket, light blue border, raised white birds, gilt trim, c1815, Pattern #1627, mkd **250.00**
Pot, 9" h, polychrome enameled florals, spout repaired (A) **55.00**
Punch Bowl, 10" d, puce and magenta enameled flowers, green leaves on ext., center bouquet of puce flowers, gold band on ft, c1780 .... **220.00**
Sugar Bowl
4" h, polychrome floral design (A) .. **20.00**
Multicolored bands of flowering foliage, puce rims, c1790 .... **140.00**
Tea and Coffee Service
17 pcs, waste bowl, four teacups, coffee cups, eight saucers, multicolored all over flowerheads, gilt, dark orange ground, c1820 (A) **420.00**
35 pcs, cream jug, two saucer dishes, twelve teacups and saucers, eight coffee cans, painted elephant near palace, blue, orange, red, green, and gilt, Pattern #876 (A) **1,175.00**
55 pcs, two teapots, stand, two cov sugar bowls, two milk jugs, coffeepot, waste bowl, twelve coffee

cans, fourteen teacups, twenty saucers, gilt flowering scrolling foliage,
blue ground, c1805, Pattern
#566 . . . .**1,800.00**

Tea Stand
Pattern #125, mkd (A) **30.00**
Pattern #471, mkd (A) **30.00**

Teabowl and Saucer
Bands of gilt foliage on blue borders,
spirally-molded, c1820 (A) **45.00**
Polychrome floral design (A) **20.00**

Teapot
4¾" h, polychrome, Chinese figures
near fence in garden, silver shape,
four florette feet, Pattern #20 . . . .   **550.00**
5½" h, polychrome enameled florals,
staple repair (A) **75.00**
5⅝" h, painted flower spray, red rib-
bon, floral, and puce leaf border,
silver shape, Pattern #195 (A) . . .   **45.00**
6¼" h
Multicolored floral sprays, silver
shape, Pattern #450 . . . .   **30.00**
Painted, Pattern #1435, rect shape
(A) **20.00**
6½" h, printed, painted "Window"
pattern #425 (A) **130.00**
7" h, painted famille rose palette, two
Orientals in fenced garden, flower
and parasol, blue flowerhead and
loop border, restored, c1785 (A) .   **230.00**
8¼" h, multicolored, Orientals in
landscape, vase finial, c1790 . . . .   **140.00**

**Cup, 2¾" h, brown and mauve leaf bor-
der, gold rim, c1800, $65.00.**

Teapot and Stand
5½" h, scattered floral sprigs, gold
rims, silver shape, leaf-molded
spout, four emb florette feet, arti-
choke finial **135.00**
7¼" h, painted floral sprays and
sprigs, dbl ogee shape, Pattern
#298 . . . .   **210.00**
Teapot Stand, 7⅞" d, painted Imari style
in colors, Pattern #446 . . . .   **35.00**
Tray, 8" l, pink flowers white ground,
green tracery border, oval, c1770 . .   **250.00**

Waste Bowl
6" d, multicolored basket of flowers
(A) **130.00**
Painted blue and gilt acorns and oak
leaves, c1820 (A) **50.00**

MODERN MARK

NYMPHENBURG

Near Munich, Bavaria, West Germany
1747 to Present

History: The Nymphenburg Porcelain Factory,
located in Neudeck ob den Au, near Munich,
was founded in 1747 by the Bavarian Elector. As
production increased, the factory was moved to
the grounds of Nymphenburg Palace in Munich.

As with many German porcelain firms, Meissen pieces strongly influenced the types of wares
produced at Nymphenburg. By 1765, under the
guidance of the Elector, Nymphenburg became
the most renown hard paste factory in Europe.
Shortly thereafter, a series of wars and economic
reversals created a decline in the popularity of
the porcelain. By 1770 the Nymphenburg factory
was hard pressed for markets in which to sell its
products.

During the early years at Nymphenburg, production was devoted to table services, accessory
pieces, and household wares that were painted
in a Rococo style featuring birds, fruits, flowers,
and the popular pastoral scenes. However, it was
the modeling of Franz Bustelli, the Swiss craftsman who worked at Nymphenburg from 1754–
1763, that contributed the most to the success of
the company. Bustelli's figures were modeled in
a light, graceful Rococo style and found a ready
market with the gentry.

The Nymphenburg pottery was transferred to
the control of the Elector of Palatinate who also
owned the Frankenthal factory, a competitor of
Nymphenburg. With more emphasis placed on
the Frankenthal pottery, Nymphenburg experienced a period of neglect and subsequent decline. When the Frankenthal Factory closed in
1799, many of the workers and artisans were
moved to Nymphenburg to revitilize the ailing
concern.

Melchoir, who achieved fame at Hochst and Frankenthal, was chief modeler at Nymphenburg between 1797 and 1822. He produced many biscuit portraits and busts.

When Melchoir died in 1822, Friedrich Gartner was appointed artistic director. He preferred to produce vases in a variety of decorative motifs. Gartner showed little interest in producing tableware. As a result, the factory declined economically. Royal commissions for Ludwig 1 (1825–1848) did result in the manufacture of several outstanding state services.

When Eugen Neureuther assumed control as director in 1848, the factory's finances were poor. Ludwig I abdicated in favor of Maximilian II, his son. Maximilian II had almost no interest in the pottery factory. Economies were taken. Popular wares such as paperweights, toothbrush racks, and cigar holders were made to attract working capital. Tablewares regained favor but the factory still lost money. In desperation the factory switched to industrial porcelains.

In 1862 the Royal Manufactory was leased to a private concern. The new managers produced art porcelain and reissued some of the earlier Rococo figures. The pottery again became profitable.

Albert Keller from Sevres and Louis Levallois, a student from Sevres, developed an Art Nouveau line for Nymphenburg based on the underglazed painting of figures. When Theodor Karner, a sculptor, came to Nymphenburg, he introduced a number of successful animal sculptures that were modeled after the animals and birds in Bavaria and the Munich Zoo. Animal motifs also were used on modern tablewares. Other tablewares were produced in the Art Nouveau style that encompassed linear decorations, stylized designs, and angular handles.

The popularity of the Neoclassical, Empire, and Biedermeyer movements that swept across Europe during the late 19th century did achieve the same success at Nymphenburg. In 1887, the Baum family from Bohemia gained control of the company. They still guide its fortunes today. Recently the company reproduced a number of pure white figures from its old models. The company still has not regained the position of prominence it enjoyed in the past.

References: S. Ducret, *German Porcelain & Faience,* Universe Books, 1962; George W. Ware, *German & Austrian Porcelain,* Crown Publishers, Inc., 1963.

Museums: Bayerisches Nationalmuseum, Munich, West Germany; Gardiner Museum of Ceramic Art, Toronto, Canada; Metropolitan Museum of Art, N.Y.; Schlossmuseum, Berlin, Germany.

Cabinet Cup and Saucer, relief busts of
    Prince Joseph and Princess Caroline

of Bavaria, matte blue ground, gilt oval, snake handles, rims, and foliage, monogramed gilt centers in saucers, c1800, imp "shield & A.C.," pr (A) **1,100.00**
Casket, Cov, 6⅛" w, white molded as scallop shell, shell handle and feet, copper-gilt mount c1775 (A) **2,025.00**
Coffeepot, 6½" h, blue and iron-red dancer on front, multicolored landscape, puce monument on reverse, c1765, imp "shield" mark (A) **500.00**
Cream Jug, 4¾" h, painted birds on branches and insects, suspended floral garlands on neck, pear shape, c1765, imp "shield" mark (A) **305.00**
Cup and Saucer
    Molded relief, painted flower sprays, c1765-70 .... **300.00**
    Painted buildings, mountainous landscape, gilt scroll cartouche, rims with suspended foliage swags, c1765, imp "shield" mark (A) ... **300.00**
    Painted large bouquet and scattered sprays, brown rims, c1765, imp "shield" mark (A) **200.00**
    Stippled mauve panels of putti in clouds, gilt rococo frames, enameled floral ground, gilt dentril rim, c1770-75 imp "shield" mark **500.00**
Demitasse Set, coffeepot, creamer, sugar, four cups and saucers, tray, silver geometric design, blue ground .. **275.00**
Dessert Service, three low compotes, two tall compotes, eight plates, painted center flowers, pierced scroll-molded turquoise, white, and gold rims **535.00**
Dish
    8⅝" w, painted center, figures and ruins in riverscape, gilt foliage and cell pattern border, shaped rim, c1770, imp "shield" mark **530.00**
    9⅝" painted puce and green landscape, flower sprigs, lobed rim edged in gilt, sq, imp "shield" mark **475.00**
Figure
    2⅛" h, recumbent hound, scratching ear, yellow-brown glaze, gray and black muzzle, green washed oval base, pink luster trim, imp "shield and crescent" mark **400.00**
    3¾" h, Autumn, modeled as seated putto, pink and yellow hat, holding bunches of grapes, sq gilt line base, c1760 (A) **700.00**
    4⅜" h, young satyr, seated on tree stump, holding grapes, natural color accents, modeled by Bustelli, c1755-60 .... **330.00**
    5½" h, Winter, modeled as bust of old bearded man, wearing fur trimmed

hat, blue drapery and muff, circ base, imp Bavarian shield in molded rococo cartouche, modeled by Bustelli, c1760 .... **550.00**

Figure, 5½", tan bird on light green perch, modern mark, $120.00.

5⅝" h, Minerva, standing, coat of mail, holding spear and shield, molded head of Medusa, sq base, c1765-70, imp "shield" mark **800.00**
6" h
  Andromeda, holding flowers to bosom, puce, blue, and gilt striped drape, baluster pedestal, puce and ochre marbleized, c1763 ....**1,500.00**
  Flamingo, outstretched wings, cream **150.00**
7" w, two hounds attacking boar, brown shades, hourglass shape base, multicolored applied foliage, c1765 (A) **1,800.00**
7⅛" h, shepherdess, seated on rock, peasant clothes, holding lamb in lap, multicolored, c1770-75 .....**1,100.00**
7⅝" h, ostrich-type bird, natural colors, dbl tree trunk support, shaped plinth, c1765 ....**4,000.00**
Young woman, dressed in crinolines, white **65.00**
Jugs, Cov, painted figures, imitations of engravings nailed to simulated wood panels, vase finials, domed covs, c1780, imp "shield" mark, pr **675.00**
Plaque, 15⅜" l, 10⅝" h, painted scene, Judith holding sword, wearing embroidered robe, imp "shield" mark .**1,300.00**
Plate
  7" d, nut dec, green and gold, green ground **50.00**
  7⅝" d, painted flower spray, pierced scroll molded borders, set of 10 (A) **110.00**

10" d, painted, figures in landscape, floral scroll cartouche, shaped rim, suspended green and gilt foliage garlands, c1763-67, "blue hexagram" mark (A) **500.00**
Salts 3½" w, painted, landscapes and florals, multicolored, four rococo scroll feet, c1762, imp "shield" mark, pr **900.00**
Sauceboat, 8" w, int. en grisaille of landscape, blue ribbon and gilt florals, ext. molded with band of puce dots at rim, lower portion molded with florals in blue and gilt, dbl strap handles, floral terminals, c1775, imp "shield" mark (A) **150.00**
Snuff Box
  3½" l, sepia landscapes reserved in molded rococo foliate scrolled borders, hinged cov, c1763-67 ...... **300.00**
  3⅝" l, white, relief medallion of bust of Maximilian III on cov, molded garlands and ribbon twist borders on sides, gilt metal mounts, c1765-70, imp "shield" mark **1,000.00**
Soup Plate, 9⅞" d, painted center, landscape and river, green and purple, gilt rococo scroll frame, shaped border, green and gilt vines, gilt edge, c1760-65, imp "shield" mark (A) **750.00**
Tea Caddy, 5¾" h, painted, figures carrying bundles in landscape vignettes, gilt C-scrolls on shoulder, domed cov, c1763-67, "blue hexagram" and imp "shield" mark (A) **800.00**
Teacup and Saucer, mythological subjects supported by scroll and shell motifs, rims with stylized lappets in gilt enclosing net pattern panels, c1765, imp "shield" mark (A) **1,600.00**
Teapot
  4¾" h, brown striated body, reserves of painted river landscapes, serpent spout, S-scroll handle, imp "shield" mark (A) **440.00**
  4⅞" h, puce painted river scene, gilt scrollwork, reverse with rural landscape, dragon spout, Meissen cov, imp "shield" mark **350.00**
  5⅛" h, painted bouquets of flowers on body, dbl scroll handle, fruit finial and flower sprigs on cov, c1765, imp "shield" mark **330.00**
Tray, 13" H-H, tulip in center, violets on shaped and ribbed border, puce trimmed open handles, c1870 ..... **200.00**
Vases, 3" h, painted, single figures seated in landscape with instruments, gilt scroll handles and shoulders, blue bands, c1765, imp "shield" mark, pr **325.00**

Clairon

OLD IVORY

**Silesia, Germany
Late 1800s**

History: Old Ivory dinnerware was made during the late 1800s in the pottery factories in Silesia, Germany. It derives its name from the background color of the china.

Marked pieces usually have a pattern number stamped on the bottom. The mark also may include a crown and "Silesia."

Basket, 8½" l, serving, #200 pattern ..	**65.00**
Berry Bowl	
9¾" d, #28 pattern, "Ohme, Silesia"	**68.00**
10" d, #11 pattern, "Clarion"	**65.00**
Berry Set	
5 pcs, master bowl, 9½" d, four serving bowls, Eglantine pattern	**135.00**
6 pcs, master bowl, five serving bowls, #VII pattern	**135.00**
7 pcs, master bowl, six serving bowls, #16 pattern	**175.00**
7 pcs, master bowl, six serving bowls, #84 pattern, "Ohme, Silesia" ...	**225.00**
9 pcs, master bowl, six serving bowls, creamer, and sugar, Killarney Rose pattern	**275.00**
Biscuit Jar, #XL pattern	**150.00**
Bouillon Cup and Saucer, Thistle pattern, "Germany"	**24.00**
Bowl	
6" d, #84 pattern, tab handle, "Silesia"	**55.00**
6½" d	
#28 pattern, set of six	**130.00**
#84 pattern	**20.00**
#16 pattern	**35.00**
6½" l x 4½" w, #XVI pattern	**40.00**
9" d, #16 pattern	**95.00**
9½" d	
#16 pattern, "Silesia"	**55.00**
#82 pattern, "Silesia"	**75.00**
#84 pattern	**60.00**
#XI pattern	**25.00**
10" d	
#16 pattern, "Silesia"	**55.00**
#XI pattern, "Clarion"	**75.00**
10½" d	
#84 pattern	**65.00**
#XI pattern	**35.00**

Cake Plate	
10" d	
#16 pattern, "Clarion, Silesia" ...	**45.00**
#73 pattern, pierced handles	**70.00**
#122 pattern, "Ohme, Silesia" ..	**90.00**
10½" d, #11 pattern, "Silesia"	**85.00**
11" d, #16 pattern, pierced handles	**135.00**
#84 pattern	**100.00**

Cake Plate, 11" H-H, #X, "Clarion, Germany," $70.00.

Cake Set	
VII pattern, cake plate, six serving plates	**200.00**
#X pattern, cake plate, five 6" d serving plates	**165.00**
Celery Tray	
8½" l, #90 pattern	**70.00**
11¾" l, #11 pattern, "Clairon"	**60.00**
Charger	
12¾" d, #11 pattern	**55.00**
13" d, #15 pattern	**135.00**
Chocolate Pot, #15 pattern, "Clairon"	**135.00**
Cookie Jar	
7" d, 5½" h, #84 pattern, "Silesia" .	**375.00**
#12 pattern, "Clairon," chipped lid	**250.00**
Cracker Jar, #XI pattern	**225.00**
Creamer	
4" h, #16 pattern, "Old Ivory, Clairon, Silesia"	**55.00**
5" h, pears dec, "Old Ivory, Germany"	**60.00**
Thistle pattern	**40.00**
#VIII pattern, "Germany"	**40.00**
#XVI pattern, "Clairon, Silesia"	**40.00**
Creamer, Sugar	
#15 pattern	**95.00**
#16 pattern	**155.00**
#28 pattern "Silesia"	**125.00**
#39 pattern	**75.00**
#84 pattern, "Ohme, Silesia"	**100.00**
#XI pattern	**75.00**
Cup and Saucer	
Thistle pattern	**40.00**
#15 pattern, "Silesia"	**45.00**
#16 pattern	**20.00**

#22 pattern, Holly 45.00
#75 pattern 40.00
#166 pattern, "crown and Silesia" . 25.00
#200 pattern, large 40.00
#202 pattern 30.00
#VII pattern 45.00
Mustard Pot, Cov, #84 pattern 80.00
Nappy
  #15 pattern 50.00
  #16 pattern 75.00
  #VII pattern 50.00
Pickle Dish
  6½" l, #16 pattern 25.00
  7¾" d, #84 pattern 80.00
  8½" l, #XI pattern 25.00
Plate
  6" d
    #84 pattern 40.00
    #200 pattern 15.00
  6¼" d
    #16 pattern, "Silesia" 20.00
    #84 pattern, "Silesia" 20.00
    #200 pattern, "Silesia" 15.00
    #XI pattern 15.00
  6½" d, #75 pattern 30.00
  6¾" d, #16 pattern, "Silesia" 20.00
  7" d, #16 pattern 25.00
  7½" d
    #12 pattern, "Clairon" 25.00
    #16 pattern, "Ohme, Silesia" ... 25.00
    #XI pattern 20.00
  7¾" d
    #11 pattern, "Clairon, Silesia" ... 25.00
    #16 pattern 30.00
    #28 pattern, "Ohme, Silesia" ... 25.00
    #75 pattern, "Ohme, Silesia" ... 25.00
    #82 pattern, dbl "Silesia" mark .. 55.00
    #84 pattern 60.00
    #XI pattern 18.00
  8" d
    Thistle pattern, "Germany" 15.00
    #62 pattern, Holly, "Old Ivory, Si-
      lesia" 75.00
    #84 pattern 50.00
  8½" d
    Large beige roses and clover bor-
      der, "fleur-de-lis" 30.00
    #16 pattern 40.00
    #XI pattern, Silesia 30.00
  9¼" d, #28 pattern 130.00
  9¾" d, #28 pattern 140.00
  10¾" d, #XI pattern, open handles . 40.00
  12" d, #84 pattern 80.00
Platter
  11" l, #16 pattern 50.00
  11½" l, #22 pattern, Holly 100.00
  11½" l, 8" w, #16 pattern 60.00
  13½" l, #84 pattern 150.00
Relish Dish
  6¾" l, #XI pattern 15.00
  8¼" l, #202 pattern 45.00

Relish Tray, 6¼" l, #84 pattern, "Silesia" 55.00
Salt and Pepper Shakers
  #15 pattern 95.00
  #16 pattern 75.00
  #84 pattern 110.00
Salt Shaker, #75 pattern, "Silesia" ... 40.00
Sugar Bowl, cov, La Touraine pattern,
  "Striegan" 35.00
Teapot, La Touraine pattern, "Striegan" 100.00
Toothpick
  #16 pattern, barrel shape, "Silesia" 200.00
  #84 pattern 100.00
Tray
  8½" l, 5" w
    #16 pattern, "Silesia" 55.00
    #200 pattern, single handle 70.00
  11½" l, #XI pattern 50.00
  11½" l, 5½" w, #75 pattern, "Silesia" 85.00
  11½" l, 7½" w, #84 pattern 110.00
  12" l, 7" w, #84 pattern, "Silesia" .. 150.00
Vegetable Bowl
  #VII pattern 30.00
  10" l, 6" w, #84 pattern 55.00
Waste Bowl
  5¼" d, #84 pattern 75.00
  #16 pattern 110.00

NAST a PARIS   H. DECK

J.P

1830-62

OLD PARIS AND PARIS

Paris, France
18th and 19th Centuries

OLD PARIS

History: Old Paris refers to porcelains made in the 18th and 19th centuries by various French factories located in and around Paris. Shapes were usually classical in design, decorations were elegant, and gilding was popular. Although some examples were marked, many were not.

PARIS

History: Most of the early porcelain factories of France were located in and around Paris. Without marks it is difficult to differentiate between the various factories because their shapes and designs were similar. Strewn flower sprigs, especially the cornflower, and lots of gilding were favorite decorative motifs.

Fabrique du Conte d'Artois was founded by Pierre-Antoine Hannong in 1773. Hannong's polychrome flower painting was similar in style to that of Sevres. Coal was used to fire the ovens since the woods around Paris had been depleted by earlier porcelain manufacture. In 1787, Hannong was granted the rights to make figures in biscuit, paint in color, and use gilding. Production ended about 1828. Hannong used the letter "H" as his mark.

Fabrique de la Courtille was founded by Jean-Baptiste Locre de Roissy, a potter from Leipzig, in 1773. He imitated German porcelains, including those of Meissen. Large vases were a specialty. The factory was taken over by Pouyat of Limoges about 1800. No exact date is known for its closing.

The factory mark was a pair of crossed torches that closely resembled the Meissen crossed swords.

Fabrique de la rue de Reuilly was established by Jean-Joseph Lassia of Strasbourg about 1775. He used an "L" mark. Lassia's porcelains often had ground and gilding. Production ceased in 1784. Henri-Florentin Chanou had a factory nearby from 1779 to 1785. His mark was a "CH."

Fabrique de Clignancourt was founded by Pierre Deruelle in 1771. Porcelains rivalling Sevres were made. The decorative motifs included polychrome flowersprays and landscapes along with gilding. Some figures were also made.

The first mark was a windmill, a tribute to the windmills of Montmartre located nearby. A later mark was "LSX," a monogram for Louis XVIII.

Fabrique de la Reine was organized by Andre-Marie Leboeuf about 1778 under the protection of Marie-Antoinette. Products were called "porcelaine de la Reine." The decorations included small sprigs of cornflowers, daisies, and roses, bird paintings, and some gilding. The factory was sold by Guy in 1797.

Fabrique Duc d'Angouleme was established by Dihl in 1780. Guerhard became his partner in 1786. The firm's main pattern was called "Angouleme Sprig," strewn cornflowers. The pattern was copied by many other factories. Biscuit figures were made. Dihl introduced the painting of portraits on porcelain. The favored decorative motif were designs in the Empire style. The factory was transferred to Fabrique rue du Temple in 1796.

Marks include "GA," "Dihl," "Guerhard and Dihl," or "Rue de Bondy".

Fabrique de la Popincourt, founded by Lemaire, was bought by Johann Nast in 1782. He moved it to Popincourt in 1784. Biscuit porcelains, biscuit clock cases, and Wedgwood imitations were made. The factory's were "Nast a Paris" or "N."

Fabrique du Duc d'Orleans was started by Louis de Villers and Augustin de Montarcy in 1784. Its mark was a monogram "MJ." In 1786 the factory changed hands. The mark became "LP." A single rose decoration appears on some pieces.

Factory of the "Prince de Galles," the "Prince of Wales" factory, was established in 1789 by the Englishman Christopher Potter. He was the first in Paris to use the transfer printing method. The factory changed hands several times. The first mark was "Potter Paris," then "EB" for E. Blancheron, the manager in 1792, and finally "PB."

Fabrique de Petit rue Saint Gilles was started by Francois-Maurice Honore in partnership with Dagoty about 1785. They made vases in the style of Wedgwood. The names "Honore and Dagoty" were used in the marks.

Fabrique du Jacob Petit was established by Jacob Petit Fontainebleau in 1834. Much of Petit's porcelain was inspired by eighteenth century French and German examples. His animal tureens and figurals all looked to the past for inspirations; he used English shapes for his tea services. Many pieces contained relief ornamentation in the form of flowers, jewels, and fruit. The factory closed in 1866.

References: George Savage, *Seventeenth & Eighteenth Century French Porcelain*, Spring Books, 1969.

Museums: Musee National Adrien-Dubouche, Limoges, France; Musee National de Ceramique, Sevres, France; Victoria & Albert Museum, London, England.

Beakers
3½" h, painted scattered bouquets,

Toilet Bottle, 4" h, hp, multicolored birds and butterflies on cobalt and cream panels, jeweled, dated 1838, Paris, $200.00.

berried cartouches, oval laurel medallions, reserved shaped gilt line panels, light pink ground, blue and gilt oeil-de-perdrix, c1840, Paris, pr (A) **85.00**

4⅞" h, painted continuous landscape and buildings, cracked, Paris (A) . **40.00**

Bough Pot, 10⅜" d, painted bouquets, puce laurel bands, gilt, D shape, pierced cov, c1820, Rue Thiroux (A) **340.00**

Cabinet Cup and Saucer
Garden flowers in rect panels, sponged ground, gilt leaves, Paris (A) **165.00**
Landscape and figures, and gilt anthemion, c1800, Halley **165.00**
Palmettes, gilt ground, Paris (A) **350.00**
Riverscape, horseman, and beggar, tooled gilt bands, scrolls and birds, blue ground, c1810, Paris (A) **200.00**

Cake Plate, 10½" d, floral center, dark pink border, gold trim, scalloped edge, c1840, Old Paris **65.00**

Candlesticks, 11¼" h, applied ram's head handles, oval plaques with court ladies, turquoise ground, nozzles, pans and flaring feet, molded foliage wreaths, white jeweling, c1840, Paris, pr (A) **770.00**

Clock, 15¼" h, white biscuit figure of soldier leaning on brick wall which forms clock case, oblong ormolu and biscuit base with putti, inscribed "Vaillant a Paris," c 1820, repaired head **1,500.00**

Coffee Can, painted two putti supporting flaming heart by altar, inscribed "Amour," billing doves on sides, Paris **100.00**

Coffee Can and Saucer, painted continuous scene, four putti representing four Seasons, divided by gilt bands, gilt line rims, c1800, blue X'd arrows marks (A) **475.00**

Coffee Pot, landscape scenes reserves, beaded bands, gilded ground, (A) .. **400.00**

Coffee Service
18 pcs, coffeepot with bird's head spout, milk jug, sugar, slop basin, seven coffee cans and saucers, painted cartouches mythological figures of Seasons, Months, Days, and Elements, light yellow ground, gilt trim, c1825, Legros D'Anisy, (A) **2,600.00**
26 pcs, coffee, teapot, creamer, cov sugar, waste bowl, ten cups and saucers, polychrome reserves of peasants in landscape, light blue ground, gilt rims and borders, Old Paris (A) **875.00**
31 pcs, coffeepot, cov milk jug,

cream jug, cov sugar, slop bowl, twelve cups and saucers, Empire style, painted bands of multicolored garden flowers reserved on gilt vermicule ground, bud finials, bird's head spouts and foliage handles, (A) **620.00**

Compote, 11½" h, reticulated open design, gilt base, white int., gilt ext., early 19th C, Old Paris **750.00**

Cup and Saucer
Black and gilt pendant foliage enclosing gilt insects, gilt rims, c1820, blue X'd torches marks (A) **100.00**
Enameled stylized florals, gilt, Paris (A) **50.00**
Female portrait reserve, white and gilt scroll ground, Old Paris (A) **125.00**
Figural landscape scene reserve, purple and foliate gilt ground, Old Paris (A) **100.00**
Flower panel reserve, apricot ground, Dagoty (A) **30.00**
Gilt and puce accents, coral branch handle, mid-19th C, Paris, (A) **50.00**
Gilt motif, Old Paris (A) **75.00**
Landscape reserve, multicolored, beaded band, gilded ground, Paris, set of three (A) **1,185.00**
Landscape scene reserve, white and gilt banded ground, Old Paris (A) . **175.00**
Pictorial and floral scenes, multicolored (A) **125.00**
Painted int., scene of figures playing flute, burnished gilt border, saucer painted billing doves in oval, gilt ground, Paris **150.00**
Scenic landscape, multicolored, Old Paris (A) **75.00**
Sepia painted Venus and Cupid, playing cards in panel, Dagoty (A) ... **30.00**
Strawberries, multicolored, Old Paris (A) **100.00**

Dessert Plate, 9" d. cobalt and gilt diamond border, center insect and animals, light ground, "Parte Fieres a Paun" on reverse (A) **150.00**

Dessert Service
13 pcs, 9" d compote, twelve 8" d, plates, floral centers, green borders, gilt trim, Old Paris **650.00**
26 pcs, teapot, creamer, cov sugar, serving bowl, ten cups, eleven saucers, gilt bands, cherry motifs, white ground, Old Paris **650.00**

Dessert Stands, 9" d, multicolored floral centers, cream-yellow border, gilt trim, mounted on pedestals, c1830, Old Paris, pr **450.00**

Dish
10⅜" d, gilt and puce accents, coral

branch handle, shell shape, mid-19th C, Paris (A) **50.00**

17³/₈" d, painted cornflowers, multi-colored, 19th C, Paris (A) **20.00**

Dish, Cov, 12" l, panels of flowers, cream-yellow border, gilt trim, gold finial, dbl handles, c1830, Old Paris **850.00**

Dresser Bottle, 6" h, blue and white panels, delicate gilt florals, late 19th C, Old Paris, pr **100.00**

Entree, Dish, Cov, floral and gilt decor, Old Paris (A) **70.00**

Ewer and Basin

8⅝" h, ewer, 11⅞" d basin, single tulip pattern beneath bands of arabesque and gilt swags, gilt rims, contemporary hinged mounts, Rue Thiroux, c1780 (A) **1,050.00**

10" h, ewer 13" l, basin gold banding, white ground, Paris (A) **300.00**

Painted and gilt foliage scrolls, cornucopia, ewer on sq ft, loop handle from grotesque mask, oblong basin with canted corners, c1780, iron-red "Manufacturer de Mor. le Duc d'Agouleme a Paris" (A) **1,650.00**

Figure

6" h, 7" l, monkey bandsman, playing symbols, riding poodle, Old Paris **225.00**

8¼" h, 8⅝" h, boy, holding hat with nest inside, girl with two birds at feet, multicolored, pierced base, Jacob Petit, pr **175.00**

Garniture Set, clock stand, 12⅝" h, pr campana vases and veilleuse, painted reserved flowersprays in roundels, on blue ground, early 19th C, iron-red "FR" (A) **600.00**

Inkstand

5⅛" h, modeled, sea creature before arched pavilion, brown and gray, gilt base, late 19th C, Paris (A) ... **40.00**

11¼" l, four panels of shipping scenes and florals, apple-green ground, two cov wells, ponce pot, swan finials, gilt winged paw feet (A) ... **300.00**

8¼" w, painted multicolored flowers and gilt, fitted sander and inkwell, c1800 (A) **110.00**

Jardinieres, 8" h, hp, birds, nest full of eggs, floral accents, pink borders, gilt trim, dbl handles, unmkd, pr **675.00**

Patch box, 2½" l, emb gold, white ground, Old Paris **35.00**

Plate

9" d

Green and blue cornflowers, gilt rims, c1800, set of 11 (A) **550.00**

Painted center seashells and seaweed, gilt lined well, border seaweed, gilt, c1830, Paris (A) **90.00**

Scenes of England and France by Marie Wildmann, gilt scrolled foliage borders, lion crest, sgd, dated 1820, set of 6 (A) **1,100.00**

9⅛" d, gilt berry vine roundels, flowers, lilac borders, gray grasses, reserved yellow petal panels, gray leaves, c1810, iron-red "Nast a Paris," set of 18 (A) **300.00**

9¼" d

Center basket of flowers, marble ledges, ochre ground, gilt line and borders, c1830, Paris, pr (A) **220.00**

Center scene of "Val-de-Grace," blue ground, gilt overlapping foliage rim, c1820, Darte **200.00**

Painted center figures in harbor scene, dark blue border, gilt, "Vanson 21 et 22 Palais Royal" (A) **200.00**

Painted center scene of peasants, winter setting, shades of gray, gilt Egyptian motifs on border, Paris (A) **70.00**

Stipple printed, painted portrait of Napolean, ermine robes and crown, Paris (A) **115.00**

9⅜" d

Center scene of greyhound, dead rabbit, figures on horses, gilt border, diamond and leaf design, c1830, Paris **130.00**

Painted center basket of flowers, floral swag cartouches, puce ribbon, lobed gilt dentil rims, c1800, blue X'd arrows, pr (A) . **250.00**

Portrait busts of named kings, pink, blue, or green ground, c1867, iron-red "CH. Pillvuit & Cie, Paris," set of 4 .... **350.00**

Pot-De-Creme Set, six cups and saucers, 9⅜" d stand, blue and green cornflowers, gilt borders, late 18th C, iron-red "Manuf. de M. le Duc D'Angouleme a Paris" (A) **770.00**

Sauce Tureen, stand, bouquets joined by blue lines, blue and gilt line rims, quatrefoil shape, branch handle on cov, Paris (A) **100.00**

Soup Plate

Blue and green cornflowers, gilt rims, c1800, set of 7 .... **400.00**

Gilt floral swags tied with ribbon borders, gilt band with florals, gold dot outer borders, early 19th C, Paris, set of 12 .... **600.00**

Soup Tureen, Cov, 14½" w, painted bouquets, scattered flowers, scroll handles, floral terminals, gilt dentil rim, artichoke finial, c1840, Paris (A) **180.00**

Sugar, Cov 7⅞" h, gilt reserves, birds,

trees, and vases, iron-red ground, gilt lion's mask handles and paw feet, domed cov, spire finial, Paris (A) ... **100.00**

Tea and Coffee Set, teapot, coffeepot, milk jug, sugar bowl, Empire style, painted exotic birds, multicolored, bird's head spouts, mask handles, 19th C, Paris **120.00**

Tea Service,

Floral insert panels, multicolored, blue and gold trim, molded handles, service for 6 .... **650.00**

Teapot, cov sugar, creamer, waste bowl, twelve cups and saucers, fourteen plates, spaced blue and gold floral sprigs, paneled sides, c1840, Paris (A) **175.00**

Teapot, sugar, two cake plates, five cups, eight saucers, brown painted landscape views, gilt handles, spout, and rims, c1800, Paris (A) . **600.00**

Teabowl and Saucer, pink floral design, white ground **175.00**

Tobacco Jar, 7⅞" h, faience, blue ribboned wreath, "Tabac/de/Paris," white glaze, late 18th C, Paris (A) .. **60.00**

Tray, 13⅛" sq, center bouquets in cartouche, blue border, gilt flowers, c1840, Paris (A) **120.00**

Tureen, Cov, 7⅞" h, modeled yellow cabbage, gilt, bouquet on int., blue "JP" (A) **300.00**

Urn, 18" h, multicolored scenes in molded gilt cartouches, cobalt ground, gilt floral handles with white centers, pr, $875.00.

Urn

11" h, reserved front and back naval scenes, white ground, oblong gilt bases, Paris, pr (A) **275.00**

14½" h, cov, painted hunting scenes, tooled gilt borders, molded acan-

thus and palmette scrolled dbl handles, sq plinth bases, pr (A) **1,000.00**

17⅝" h continuous painted 18th C landscape scenes on upper sections between gilt bands, blue ground, gilded neoclassic designs, shield shape, c1800, pr (A) **6,875.00**

23½" h, reserves of allegorical polychrome scenes of winter and spring, gilt ground, mounted as lamps, Old Paris, pr (A) **650.00**

Vase

5½" h, enameled bunches of tulips and poppies, burnished gilt flared rim and base, gilt three mask and wing feet, disk base, c1815, Paris, pr **335.00**

8¾" h, center panel of French woman watching sea, binoculars, coral, and gold bands top and bottom, pink ground, ftd, Old Paris **90.00**

9" h, painted bouquets, shaped cartouches, turquoise ground, molded gilt foliage branches, four scroll feet, lappet shape bases, c1850, Paris, pr (A) **250.00**

9¼" h, florals, light blue ground, pink accents, gold handles, Old Paris, pr **150.00**

9⅜" h, painted, two panels of figures, country costumes, reverse river landscape, gilt ground, baluster shape, dbl scroll handles, sq base, late 19th C (A) **50.00**

10¼" h, painted figure and landscape panels, Empire style, gilt ground, mask handles, sq bases, c1850, Paris, pr (A) **270.00**

10⅝" h, painted, gilt fountains, applied and molded flower sprays, shaped pierced rims, c1860, Paris, pr (A) **135.00**

10¾" h, dark maroon bouquet, light green ground, four large gilded leaves at base, open maroon bud . **100.00**

13" h

Floral medallion, light green ground, gilt accents, baluster shape, c1900, Old Paris (A) ... **150.00**

Reserved upper portions, painted classical portraits, apple-green ground, lower portions with molded leaves, gilt egg and dart borders, sq bases, four gilt paw feet, c1830, pr (A) **630.00**

13½" h, large roses, buds, and leaves, gold trim, Old Paris, pr **500.00**

13¾" h

Portrait scenes of wedding or christening, 18th C clothes, dark pink, white, and gold florals, gold frames, black and gold open dbl handles, Old Paris, pr **350.00**

13⅞", clock, gilt roundels of war trophies and musical putti, matte green ground, dbl gold ram's head and scroll handles, trumpet neck, ormolu frame clock front, c1820 (A) **2,750.00**

14" h, hp, gold overlay, applied flowers on sides, blue centers, c1865, pr **195.00**

14⅛" h, reserves of painted bouquets, dbl handles and necks, molded florals, fixed rect bases, mid-19th C, Paris, pr (A) **550.00**

15⅜" h, panels of maidens, period clothes, etched gilt borders, rose pompadour ground, late 19th C, Paris, pr (A) **385.00**

18" h, painted scenes of Napoleon in campaigns on front, cottages on reverse in gilt borders, campana shape gilt neck, rim, base, and dbl handles, late 19th C, Paris, pr ...**1,100.00**

23¼" h, cov, applied flower blooms, fruit, and vegetables, gilt vine branches, Paris (A) **730.00**

PARIAN

England/Continental
Early 1840s to 20th Century

History: Parian has a slightly translucent, natural creamy-white body fired to a matte finish. It was introduced in the early 1840s and remained popular during the entire Victorian era. Parian's strong resemblance to marble appealed to the Victorians since it suggested elegance, opulence, and wealth.

The best parian examples were characterized by the delicacy of the ware's texture. Its excellent molding versatility made it suitable for figures, utilitarian wares, and even floral jewelry pieces.

Among the many firms that have made parian china from the 1840s to the present time is Copeland. Pieces often were marked with an impressed "Copeland." After 1862 Minton impressed its parian with the name of the company and occasionally added the impressed year mark.

Parian also was manufactured by Belleek in Ireland and Coalport, Goss, Robinson and Leadbeater, Wedgwood, and Royal Worcester in England. Gustavsburg and Rorstrand in Sweden carried parian wares as part of their line. Most leading firms marked their parian wares. Smaller firms were less likely to do so.

References: G. A. Godden, *Victorian Porcelain*, Herbert Jenkins, 1961; C. & D. Shinn, *The Illus-*

trated *Guide to Victorian Parian China*, Barrie & Jenkins, 1971.

Museums: Victoria & Albert Museum, London, England.

Box, figural child on barrel (A) **25.00**

Bust
3½" h, cherub (A) **55.0**
5½" h
  Classical woman, late 19th C, England (A) **45.00**
  John Andrews, late 19th C, England (A) **45.00**
9" h
  "Asleep" and "Awaken," angels, sq plinths, gold verses, "Copeland," pr (A) **130.00**
  French statesmen, Limoges, pr (A) **360.00**
10½" h, Grecian woman, laurel wreath **60.00**
10¾" h, woman, lace headdress, roses draped over shoulder **155.00**
11" h, Juno **115.00**
11¾" h, Ophelia, wearing ivy leaves, ears of corn in hair, waisted circ socle, 1870, "Copeland" (A) **135.00**
12½" and 11¾" h, Prince of Wales, wearing cloak, Princess Alexandra, wearing fur–edged robe, waisted circ socle, c1863, "Copeland"(A) **400.00**
12¾" h, Princess Alexandra, wearing gown, bows, and lace, waisted circ socle, c1863, "Minton" (C) **265.00**
13" h, Couple, period clothes, circ base, c1869, pr **530.00**
14¼" h, Handel, wearing tasseled cap, waisted circ socle, c1857, imp "A.J. Ridgway Bates & Co." (A) .. **370.00**
14½" h, "The Veiled Bride," maiden, veil fastened with flower garland, waisted circ socle, c1861, "Copeland" (A) **1,000.00**
21¼" h, Prince Albert, sash, c1860 (A) **445.00**

Figure
5¾" h, kneeling nude woman, octagonal base, c1900, Germany **85.00**
6¾" h, peasant girl, England (A) **45.00**
7" h
  Match Making, pr of owls seated on branch, rect base, dated 1871, Eng reg mark **265.00**
  Seated woman, legs tucked under, drape tied around waist, skull at side **90.00**
7½" l, warrior, horse in colonnade setting, Germany **65.00**
7¾" h, 7¼" l, chubby nude child, lying on back, head on tasseled pillow, wearing lady's slipper **100.00**
8" h
  Nude boy, leaning against tree,

stroking bird, c1865-78, sgd "J. T. B." **135.00**

Pr of owls on branch, mounted on base, c1871 .... **150.00**

8¼" h, young girl, kneeling on tasseled cushion, playing Irish harp . **75.00**

9" h

Venus and Cupid, oval base, c1870, "Minton" (A) **185.00**

Woman, standing, holding flame, winged Cupid over left arm, flowers in hair, pillar at side, sq ftd base **150.00**

9½" h

Boy, period clothes, crouching, bone in hand, dog at side **75.00**

Man, seated on rock, holding birds over head, hunting dog seated at side **135.00**

9⅝" h, boy kneeling, butterfly on nose, rect base, England (A) **50.00**

10" h

Lincoln, standing (A) **75.00**

"Spring", c1850 .... **125.00**

Washington, standing (A) **75.00**

10⅜" h, Duke of Wellington seated, legs tucked under body, rect base, "Copeland" **45.00**

10½" h, 16" l, "Can't You Talk?" kneeling child facing dog, c1870, sgd "R. J. Morris," England **750.00**

10⅝" h, girl, seated, leaning on tree stump, dog at feet, England (A) ... **80.00**

11½" h, "The Net Mender," woman, fishing net over arm **150.00**

11⅞" h, sporting, recumbent, gun and dead game, "Copeland" (A) . **140.00**

12" h, "Narcissus," naked god, seated on draped rock, c1846, "Copeland" (A) **300.00**

12¼" h

"Evangeline," young woman wearing dress, seated on mound, one arm on headstone, c1860, "Kerr & Binns" (A) **350.00**

"The Good Samaritan," samaritan in robes, helping fallen man to feet, cane on base, c1860 (A) .. **115.00**

13" h, "Ruth," oval base **175.00**

13½" h, man, cloak and beret **115.00**

13⅞" h, Hamlet, seated, head in hands, ruined column, rect base, England **70.00**

14" h

Victorian woman, seated, "Art Union of Great Britain" (A) **60.00**

Woman, draped, hairline on base **55.00**

14¼" h, "The Greek Slave," modeled as naked woman, standing next to

draped pedestal, c1870, "Minton" (A) **200.00**

15¼" h, girl, peasant clothes, holding violin bow, tinted, sgd "R. J. Morris" **110.00**

15⅜" h, Venus, standing, holding apple and robe, color accents to head and robe, England (A) **110.00**

15¾" h, "Miranda," seated on rocky base, shells, c1864, "Minton" ... **250.00**

16¼" h, "Mercy," winged female, sheathing sword, hiding club, c1855, "John Rose & Co" **600.00**

16¾" h and 18⅛" h, "Bristomartis Unveiling Amoret-The Faerie Queen," and "Vision of the Red Crosse Knight-The Faerie Queen," "Jos. Pitts SC London, 1851," pr .**2,500.00**

17⅜" h, lady, period dress, circ base, "B & B", England (A) **40.00**

17¾" h, girl standing by seashore, holding up skirt, color tones, England (A) **85.00**

18½" h, "The Sleep of Sorrow and the Dream of Joy," sleeping maiden, lying on mound base, draped maiden rising above, c1875, "Copeland" (A) **2,000.00**

19" h, "Sunshine," Woman carrying flowers, sgd "R. J. Morris" (A) ... **60.00**

20½" h, "Prodigal's Return," father and son embracing, oval base, dated 1850, sgd "W. Theed," "Copeland" (A) **235.00**

21¾" h, "Beatrice," modeled as maiden wearing robe, star in hair, titled base, c1865, "Copeland" .. **200.00**

23" h, "Daphne," modeled as maiden rising from foliage, one arm raised to flowing hair, titled circ base, c1860, "Copeland" (A) **425.00**

25¼" h, "Chastity," modeled as maiden wearing dress, diadem in hair, carrying lilies, titled base, c1865, "Copeland" (A) **250.00**

29¾" h, Venus, nude goddess, Cupid on dolphin on base, late 19th C, "Robinson & Leadbeater" (A) **700.00**

Jug

5⅝" h, "Naomi & Her Daughters-in-Law," white, lavender ground, dated 1847 .... **230.00**

6⅝" h, white and green molded flowers and grass, blue ground, "Samuel Alcock Patent Parian" (A) **20.00**

7" h, crests of Scotland, England, Wales, Ireland, "Wm Brownfield, Cobridge, England" **400.00**

7½" h

Raised figure of boy climbing tree with bird's nest, reverse of boy

Parian, left, vase, 7" h, blue ring, $175.00; center, pitcher, 8½" h, relief of "Battle of Plassey" in lilac, c1857, $385.00; right, figure, 13½" h, imp "Copeland," $300.00.

sitting in tree holding nest, branch handle, c1850, "Mayer's, Longport" 200.00

Raised water lilies and leaves white, lavender ground, branch handle, c1850 .... 150.00

9½" h

   Man, woman on sides in relief, mask face on front 150.00

Raised classical figures, lavender, white ground, bearded mask on handle, pewter top, "James Dixon & Sons" 150.00

Loving Cup, 6⅞" h, white relief figures of Bacchus and women, grapes and vines, blue ground, c1840, "Meigh & Fine Arts Medal Award" 300.00

Nodder, 3¾" h, seated clown, retractible tongue, multicolored, c1860 .. 300.00

Pitcher

  2¼" h, raised grapes and leaves, c1880 .... 35.00

  4½" h, white relief of florals, leaves, vine handle 55.00

  5¼" h, white Napoleonic battle scene, lavender ground 135.00

  5½" h

    "Naomi," lilac figures, white ground, "Alcock" 85.00

    Raised overall wheat design 50.00

  6" h, raised lily of the valley dec, leaves 100.00

  6½" h, white relief of people and trees, brown ground, "Mayers, Dale Hall Pottery, Longport" 75.00

  7" h, Arabian scenes in relief, twig handle 175.00

  8" h

    Blue and white, scenes of Chicago burning around top, three medallions around middle of Indians, capital, lady, eagle, smaller cameos of Mrs O'Leary's cow,

sgd "Frank Burley," "Copeland Late Spode" 350.00

White raised classical figures, lavender ground, mask handle, c1830-59, "Alcock" 120.00

9" h, emb "Canterbury Bells," "Copeland" (A) 30.00

Planter, 14½" l, 10½" w, goat head decor (A) 35.00

Plaque, 13" d, modeled full figures of three Cupids, self-framed, pierced for hanging, imp "Enoret, Bing & Grondahl" 160.00

Spill Vase, relief of children in woods, sage green, "T. J. Mayer" 85.00

Vase

  4½" h, raised Bacchanalian design, everted rim (A) 60.00

  5½" h, bust of Grecian woman, laurel leaf crown on sides 35.00

  6" h

    Modeled cherub, raised florals, "blue crown" 30.00

    Relief of birds in swing, flowers and leaves 50.00

  6⅝" h, relief of children and baskets, pr (A) 25.00

  7½" h, grape and leaves on sides, pr 70.00

  9" h, white relief grape clusters, floral medallion, blue ground 50.00

  10" h, white monkeys and trees, blue ground, applied grapes on sides, pr ... 250.00

  11¼" h, applied grapes, fluted necks, scroll handles, pr (A) 100.00

  17¾" h, molded arabesques, "Endless Knot" motifs, leaf shape reserves, pierced slab dbl handles, c1855-60, pr (A) 445.00

Wall Brackets, 7½" h, shelf supported by winged cherub's head, foliate scrolls, garlands of fruit and flowers, gilt accents, c1860, "Copeland," pr (A) 445.00

PATE-SUR-PATE (PASTE ON PASTE)

Austria, England, France, Germany c1860 to 1900s

History: During the early 1860s, several Sevres potteries attempted to copy the Chinese technique of pate-sur-pate. In pate-sur-pate the design exhibits a cameo-like decorative motif achieved by using tinted parian as the background and adding layers of white parian slip which then are carved into the design before the firing. When fired, the layers of white parian slip become semi-translucent and vitrified. The dark ground shows through the thinner parts.

Marc Louis Solon, who trained at Sevres, brought the Victorian pate-sur-pate process to England in 1870 when he began employment at Minton. At first he depicted tall, thin classical female figures in diaphanous drapery. Later he expanded his repertoire to include children and cupids. Each creation was unique and signed.

Solon enjoyed a great reputation for his pate-sur-pate pieces. Since the painstaking pate-sur-pate technique was exceptionally slow and the market demand was great, Solon trained a series of apprentices while at Minton, the most talented of whom were A. Birks and L. Birks. Solon worked at Minton until 1904. After retirement, he worked free–lance until he died in 1913.

Not all pate-sur-pate examples were made at Minton. Royal Worcester, Grainger-Worcester, the Crescent Potteries of George Jones, and several other firms manufactured pate-sur-pate pieces. F. Schenk produced many examples for Crescent Pottery at Stoke. These pieces were inferior and repetitive when compared to those made at Minton and Worcester.

Meissen, Berlin, and Vienna on the Continent were also known for the production of pate-sur-pate. Pieces from these factories lacked the finesse of Solon's works and tended to be heavy and Germanic in style.

References: G. A. Godden, *Victorian Porcelain*, Herbert Jenkins, 1961.

Museums: National Collection of Fine Arts, Smithsonian Institution, Washington D.C.; Victoria & Albert Museum, London, England.

Collecting Hints: Collectors should be aware that some George Jones wares are being sold as Minton products in today's marketplace.

Bowl,
9" d, four panels, putti at various activities, musical instruments, brown ground, green band cartouches, ivory ground and gilt with panels of

Box, cov, 5½" d, white slip design, blue ground, blue, white, and gold rings, c1890, "Limoges," $200.00.

ornaments, pierced rim, four scroll feet, sgd "HH", c1884, Minton (A) **1,685.00**
22" d, polychrome slip portraits of classical maidens, trophies, and flowering motifs, sgd "J. Gely," dated 1864, Sevres **3,500.00**
Box 3¾" d, relief of cherubs pulling chariot, cobalt ground, gold trim, ftd, Limoges **120.00**
Box, Cov
3½" white cherubs, girl's head on cov, green ground, France **120.00**
4" w, 4½" l, white slip design, two cherubs on clouds, instrument, dark blue ground, Limoges **200.00**
5" sq, mythical lovers, dark blue ground, Limoges **160.00**
Cabinet Cup, 3" h, white slip design, Cupid fisherman seated at stream, olive-green oval panel, neoclassical motifs of light blue band, pink int., gilt accents, c1910, Minton (A) **135.00**
Cup and Saucer, white slip design, classical maidens, Cupids in landscapes, blue-gray panels, smaller panels of white slip flowerheads and foliage, gilt accents, sgd "A. Birks," dated 1931 imp "MINTONS," "TIFFANY & CO, NEW YORK, MADE IN ENGLAND," set of 12 (A) **1,430.00**
Dish, 9¾" d, white slip scene, two putti, dolphin, light green ground, polychrome, pate-sur-pate floral spray, C-scroll and gilt diaper borders, late 19th C, Meissen **300.00**
Jar, Cov, 5¼" d, white slip bust, woman on cov, dark blue ground, sgd "C. Tharaud," Limoges **250.00**
Plaque, white slip design
2½" w, 5" h, goddess presenting lantern to cherub, black ground, framed, sgd "M.L.S.," pr **1,650.00**
4⅜" w, 7" h, nymph rising from waves, cobalt ground, framed, c1900, Limoges **275.00**

6" h, Cupid cutting flaming heart with sword, rust ground, sgd "M. L. Solon," dated 1902, Minton (A) **1,100.00**

6¾" w, 10¾" h, lightly dressed couple in night scene, blue ground, Limoges **225.00**

9⅞" w, 6⅝" w, putti fishing or reclining in fruit and flowers, black ground, framed, pr **340.00**

Plate

6¼" d, white slip scenes, castles, scalloped rims, gold band, creamy ivory glaze, set of 8 .... **300.00**

10" d, birds in nest on florals, dark olive ground, gold trim, ring handles, George Jones **430.00**

10¼" d, borders with slip design of nymphs, cherubs, and plants, blue ground, flowerheads and foliage in gilt scroll surrounds on ivory ground, sgd "A. Birks," c1913, Minton, set of 12 (A) **1,980.00**

11" d, three oval reserves of Psyche and Cupid, various poses, raised gold trellis work, sgd "A. Birks," Minton **400.00**

11⅛" d, three gray-blue panels, slip designs of classical maidens and Cupids in love scenes, elaborate gilt motifs, sgd "A. Birks," c1916, imp "MINTONS, crowned globe, ENGLAND," set of 12 (A) **3,520.00**

Urns, 12" h, white slip design of bust of Grecian maiden on front, flowers, and butterflies on reverse, light blue-green ground, gilt handles and bases, pr **1,450.00**

Vase

3½" h, white slip florals, dark brown ground, narrow neck **225.00**

5¾" h

Center, white slip medallion of Pandora, dbl handles, sgd **180.00**

White slip design of young woman, dark blue ground, Germany ... **200.00**

6½" h, white slip design, angel chasing stork, light green ground, dark green cattails on base, sgd "Walter," Rosenthal **250.00**

7¾" h, 7" w, white slip design, lightly clad females, green ground, George Jones **550.00**

8⅝" h, polychrome slip design of Japanese butterflies, beetles, wasps and flowers on dark green ground, dbl scroll handles, dated 1869, Minton, pr (A) **220.00**

9¼" h, white slip design, bust of Minerva, dark brown ground, reverse with oil lamp, gilt cartouches, cream ground, sgd "A. Birks," Minton **225.00**

9⅜" h, white and green slip decorated trailing clematis, light blue ground divided by dark blue bands, dated 1879, Doulton-Lambeth, pr (A) .. **110.00**

9½" h, medallion of Diana, green ground, amphora shape, "Schultz-Marke" **575.00**

10" h, white slip design, flowers and leaves, light green ground **240.00**

12¼" h, white slip design, pointsettias, dark blue-green ground, gilt rim, gilt acanthus leaf and scroll mounts, "Royal China Works, Worcester, England" (A) **700.00**

14" h, panels of white cherubs on brown ground, panels of scrolls on sides, gilt diapering on cream ovoid body, gilt wreath and ribbon handles, c1901, Minton (A) **1,000.00**

15¾" h, white slip design of classical maidens, men, newborn Cupids, arcades of swinging Cupids, dark blue ground, necks, and bases, blue, green, and brown, pate-sur-pate floral motifs, gilt accents, c1884, sgd "L. Solon," Minton, pr (A) **14,300.00**

16¾" h, continuous scene of dancing nymphs with cymbals on blue ground, yellow and green painted foliage on shoulder, rosettes and scale pattern, dbl handles, sgd "L. Solon," c1890, gilt crowned Minton **6,000.00**

22" h, white slip designs of Cupids and maidens in panels, green ground, separated by columns, multicolored devices on necks and bases, dated 1880, sgd "L. Solon," Minton, pr **7,500.00**

22½" h

Japanese style white slip design of flying cranes over reeds, gilt floral and scroll gray ground, silver and gilt prunus branch handles, c1874, Minton, pr (A) **3,750.00**

White slip design of classical maidens with Cupids around column, dark blue ground, neoclassical gilt neck, base, and handles, sgd "L. Solon," c1904, Minton (A) .**5,000.00**

23½" h, alternating panels of white slip designs of muses or Cupids at various pursuits, olive-green or dark brown ground, polychrome pate-sur-pate palmettes and foliates on necks, shoulders, and bases, gilt accents, pedestal mounts, sgd, c1880, "L. Solon," pr (A)......**12,100.00**

25⅜" h, white slip design of Cupid as judge, court of maidens, reverse with Cupids and trophies, olive-green ground, polychrome pate-sur-pate flowerheads and laurels on shoulder and base, gilt and silver mask handles, rim and base, dated 1877, sgd "L. Solon," Minton **7,500.00**

30½" h, white slip of Cupid and Psyche on floral swing, reverse with Cupid on tightrope, gilt shell motifs, teal-blue ground, applied handles, duck head terminals gilt bronze mounted, dated 1876, Sevres (A) **5,500.00**

27" h, cov, white slip, continuous design of Cupids at various pursuits, oval panels with trophies on neck, light green ground, gilt accents . . .**2,500.00**

Wall Pocket, 9" h, white slip of classic woman and Cupid with harp, olive green ground, George Jones **585.00**

PEARLWARE

English
c1780 to c1865

History: Pearlware, a variation of white creamware body, has a slightly bluish tint due to the addition of a small quantity of cobalt to the glaze. Pearlware is closer in general appearance and whiteness to porcelain than creamware. Wedgwood first made pearlware about 1779.

Pearlware was made mostly in tablewares. Among the leading Staffordshire manufacturers were Herculaneum, Phillips Longport, Davenport, Clews, T. Mayer, Enoch Wood, Rogers, and Stubbs. Potteries at Leeds and Swansea also produced pearlware.

Polychrome floral decorations on pearlware became popular about 1800 and continued for approximately twenty years. These designs, usually in yellow, green, orange, or on silver luster resist, were most commonly found on pitchers and jugs. Mocha decoration also was used on pearlware bodies.

Vast quantities of pearlware were shipped to the United States between 1790 and 1830. Some firms, such as Enoch Wood, produced pearlware specifically for the American market. Shell edge plates were decorated with the American eagle and shield in polychrome; other plates depicted prints of American ships with polychrome flags. Later blue transfer prints of American landmarks were applied to pitchers, plates, and chamber pots.

Museums: Victoria & Albert Museum, London, England.

Bank, 5⅞" h, cottage shape, four black edged ochre windows, two doors, steep blue roof with chimney, black

and ochre dot base, c1840, Yorkshire (A) **330.00**

Basket, 9" w, sepia scattered bouquets and sprays, gilt line rims, pierced sided, dbl handles, c1820, Spode (A) **220.00**

Bowl, 7⅞" d, sepia printed Chinese figures and temples, red, blue, and green accents **35.00**

Bust

5½" h, weeping philosopher, puce shawl, ochre accents on shirt, waisted circ socle, c1800 (A) **150.00**

8¼" h, young boy, multicolored, rect plinth molded with urns and swags, stepped base, c1800, Staffordshire (A) **75.00**

8½" h, Admiral Duncan, multicolored, uniform, sash, waisted rect socle, naval trophies, c1800 (A) . .**1,330.00**

8⅞" h, Admiral, multicolored, uniform, sash, shaped waisted rect socle, orange and yellow accents, c1800, Staffordshire (A) **200.00**

Candlesticks

10½" h, molded foliage, ribbon, ram's heads, gilt and blue accents, imp "WEDGWOOD," pr (A) **200.00**

11⅝" h, vase surrounded by acanthus leaves, base with classical motif in blue, baluster shape, c1790 . . . . . **600.00**

Children's Dinner Set, blue printed "Monastery Hill" pattern, Hackwood, set of 48 pcs (A) **220.00**

Children's Tea Service, teapot, cov sugar, slop bowl, three cups and saucers, green, ochre, blue, and brown basket of flowers and sprigs, c1790, England (A) **260.00**

Coffeepot

9⅝" h, marbled, multicolored pattern of slip pieces under glaze, pear shape, leaf molded spout, seated dog finial (A) **135.00**

Coffeepot, 10½" h, blue Oriental design, c1780–1800, Staffordshire, $950.00.

10¼" h, yellow and green painted Oriental houses and trees, terra cotta ground, blue slip borders (A) **470.00**

10½" h, painted flowers and sprigs, paneled border, loop handle, late 18th C (A) **125.00**

10⅝" h, painted Orientals in landscape, trees, and flower pots, tall domed cov with swags and husk pattern rim, damaged, c1790, Staffordshire (A) **200.00**

Cruet Stand

7½" h, circ, vertical sides pierced with strapwork and florals, outlined in blue, mushroom finial, c1800, imp "WEDGWOOD & W" (A) ... **350.00**

8" d, circ pierced stand, openings outlined with blue enamel scrolls, three bottles, salt and pepper shakers, painted titles, c1800 (A) **750.00**

Dinner and Dessert Service, Imari style peonies and chrysanthemum sprays, blue, red, and gold, imp "WEDGWOOD," set of 136 pcs (A) **2,600.00**

Dinner Service

Blue transfer, three Oriental figures, pagoda, and zebra, wide floral borders, Greek key bands, imp "Rogers," set of 75 pcs (A) **4,100.00**

Multicolored botanical plant, brown line rims, sq dish, oval stand, six plates, 8 pcs (A) **820.00**

Dish

9½" d, blue printed baskets of flowers, lozenge shape, c1815, pr (A) **145.00**

11" l, Tellina Radiata shell shape, pink scalloped border shading to cream center, mid 19th C, imp "WEDGWOOD" **125.00**

14" d, blue florals center (A) **70.00**

Drainer 9⅞" l, black printed, two classical ladies, foliate and scroll border, Staffordshire **45.00**

Figure

4¾" h, Cupid astride lion, blue and red flowering green tree, green mound base, c1820, pr (A) **600.00**

5" h, classic maidens, multicolored, sq bases, c1810, Staffordshire, pr (A) **165.00**

5⅜" h, tan gothic castle, flanked by rocky embankments, green mound base, applied florals, molded curved road leading to castle (A) . **770.00**

6¾" h, Ceres, holding fruit, wearing lilac, green, and yellow robe, sq base, Neale & Co (A) **155.00**

7⅛" h, "Old Age," modeled as woman with basket, and man with crutches, multicolored, c1815, Staffordshire, pr (A) **375.00**

11¼" h, seated Elijah, wearing turban, feeding blackbirds, seated Widow of Zarephath, boy at side, barrel, and jug, bocage background, multicolored, c1825, pr (A) **385.00**

16½" h, standing horse, mottled green and yellow rect base, tree stump, applied moss, and serpents, c1820, Staffordshire (A) **1,150.00**

Foot Bath

17¾" w, blue transfer, "The Tower of London" pattern, dbl handled, c1840, "WEDGWOOD" (A) **1,210.00**

20" H-H, painted flowers and foliage, int. and ext., sepia accents, horizontal bands, c1825, "J. & R. Clews" **335.00**

Jug

5" h, satyr shape, multicolored enamels, pink luster **300.00**

7" h, cottage shape, multicolored, c1825, Staffordshire (A) **200.00**

7½" h, blue transfer, figures on stone bridge, castle ruins, c1820, Staffordshire (A) **100.00**

8½" h, blue transfer, "Willow" pattern, scroll and diaper border, c1800 (A) **110.00**

Meat Dish, 18½" l, brown printed, underglaze painted elephant carrying howdah, chinoiserie landscape, border with landscape vignettes (A) **210.00**

Money Box, 3½" h, sprays of roses, red, green, and black, "E. Wood" on front, flared foot, c1810 .... **800.00**

Mug

3⅞" h, blue transfer, "View of La Guillotine," England (A) **65.00**

4¼" h, painted sprays and flowers, "R. L. 1798," England (A) **190.00**

5¾" h, extensive blue printed Oriental landscape, England (A) **50.00**

6" h, continuous blue transfer, execution of Louis XVI, inscriptions, c1800 .... **500.00**

Pastille Burner

4½" h

Timbered cottage, two chimneys, tan thatched roof, steps to front door, hexagon Staffordshire (A) . **415.00**

Tudor cottage, brown thatched roof, pierced by two chimneys, green mound base, applied florals, molded curved road leading to cottage (A) **770.00**

4⅝" h, timbered cottage, tan thatched roof, two chimneys, four dormer windows, raised on grassy mound, four bun feet (A) **415.00**

Pipe 10" l, intertwined snakes form stem, tan, blue, and brown trim, c1790 ....**1,500.00**

Plaque

8¼" h, molded, Hercules supporting world, blue lion skin, yellow ground, self molded black frame, c1810, Staffordshire (A) **175.00**

9¼" d

Bacchanalian figure, blue ground, gilding, imp "WEDGWOOD" (A) **100.00**

Youth, playing mandolin, brown ground, gilding, imp "WEDG-WOOD" (A) **100.00**

9½" h, molded, painted scene of Prometheus chained to rock, eagle tearing at body, reverse inscribed, dated 1793 .... **160.00**

Plate

5" d, center blue and white flowers, intertwined line borders, c1795, imp "WEDGWOOD", set of 6 ... **575.00**

6⅜" d, "Queen's Rose" pattern, multicolored, imp "Davenport" (A) **30.00**

7⅝" d, green feather edge, imp "WEDGWOOD" (A) **35.00**

9⅜" d, blue printed "Leeds Independent Order of the Ark," animals entering Noah's ark (A) **360.00**

9⅝" d, central coat of arms in flower and foliage cartouche, rim and well with scattered sprays and urns, gilt waved fauille-de-choux rim, c1815, Swansea (A) **180.00**

9¾" d, black printed, farmyard and animals, rope twist and foliage band borders, shaped rims, acorns and oak leaves, c1765, imp "WEDGWOOD," pr (A) **415.00**

11¼" d, blue feather edge, reticulated insert, blue floral design on rim, imp "WEDGWOOD" (A) **575.00**

Platter

11" l, hp floral design, imp "WEDG-WOOD" **150.00**

20¾" l, blue feather edge, small blue florals, imp "WEDGWOOD" (A) . **350.00**

Potpourri Jar, 16½" h, blue and rust Oriental design, apple green ground, orange and white loop handles, pierced outer lid, imp "WEDGWOOD" **1,800.00**

Punch Bowl, 14" d, ext. with blue transfer of chinoiserie landscape, int. with "By Pipe & Pot, we banish fear, Sorrow, drown & kill Care," ochre, late 18th C, England (A) **150.00**

Sauceboat, 6½" l, molded shell edge, green accents **85.00**

Sifter 4½" d, green and ochre flower sprays, dark brown ground, Staffordshire **45.00**

Soup Plate,

8¼" d, ochre, brown, and yellow gar-

den pavilion, green molded border, c1810, Davenport (A) **265.00**

9⅞" d, "Willow" pattern, blue transfer, set of 4 .... **30.00**

10" d, green feather edge, imp "WEDGWOOD" (A) **35.00**

Stands, 9¼" w, molded, overlapping vine leaves, rust, green, and pink accents, late 18th C, "WEDGWOOD" pr **125.00**

Tea Caddy, 4⅛" h, bands of blue and white slip, rouletted rim, inlaid checkered band, engine-turned, cylindrical (A) **50.00**

Teabowl and Saucer

Blue printed, Britannia, Liberty, and Peace **15.00**

Blue transfer, railroad views, imp "WEDGWOOD," pr (A) **315.00**

Teapot

3½" h, blue painted borders, globular, large lip, (A) **60.00**

4⅜" h, sgraffito lines, brown marble band **80.00**

5½" h, molded vertical ribs, blue festoons and swags from shoulder, entwined reed handle, floral terminal, cylindrical, c1780 (A) **270.00**

6¾" h, molded borders, diamond sectioned, swan knob, c1805, "A. T. Harley" (A) **60.00**

Tray, 10⅛" l, 8⅞" w, rust and blue florals, gilt, emb rim, open handles (A) **20.00**

Vase

6⅞" h, blue printed Oriental scene, waisted cylindrical shape (A) **20.00**

13½" w, continuous band of painted and gilt foliage, pierced cov, brown lines, c1815, imp "WEDG-WOOD" **375.00**

Watch Stand

10¾" h, tall case clock, circ flower face, flanked by American Indian, king, and queen, multicolored, scalloped green base, c1790 ....**1,750.00**

11" h, Indian prince and princess on each side, acorn finial on false clock portion, blue border, florals, c1790 ....**1,750.00**

PIANO BABIES

England and Germany
19th Century

History: Piano babies, primarily in bisque, ranged in size from two to twelve inches long. They were popular additions to Victorian parlors, usually found on the top of a piano.

Piano babies were produced in a variety of poses from crawling, sitting, lying on their stomachs, to lying on their backs playing with their toes. Some babies were dressed; some were nude.

The most popular manufacturer was Heubach Brothers of Germany. Other identified makers included Hertwig and Company and Royal Doulton.

Figure, 8″ h, "Heubach," $485.00.

2½″ h
Blond child, lying on back, holding knee, c1910, "Hertwig & Co." ... **200.00**
Blond girl, lying on side, legs tucked up, light blue dress, c1910, "Hertwig & Co." **200.00**
Child, lying on stomach, holding doll, large curls, c1900 .... **100.00**
3″ h, sitting girl, light blue dress, large curls, c1900 .... **100.00**
3″ l, little boy, hands holding head, "Heubach" **75.00**
3½″ l
Black child, crawling, "Germany" .. **90.00**
Child, lying on back, white nightie, molded bonnet, "Heubach" **175.00**
4″ l, baby, lying back, touching toes, "Heubach" **100.00**
4½″ h
Child, wearing floppy hat, holding pot lid **100.00**
Seated child, feet and hands crossed, "Heubach" **75.00**
4½″ l, baby, arms upraised, crossed legs, white nightie, pink trim, enamel beading **65.00**
4¾″ h, seated baby, nude, head cocked, intaglio eyes, imp "Heubach" **150.00**
5¼″ l
Baby, semi-reclining, legs crossed, white nightie, blue ruffle, pink bow, "Germany" **65.00**

Rip Van Winkle, lying on stomach, blue pajamas, Royal Doulton **20.00**
5½″ l, baby, lying on back, foot on knee, blue and white **75.00**
5¾″ l, baby reclining on stomach, pink and white striped nightie **50.00**
6″ l
Baby, lying on stomach, blue dress, "Germany" **85.00**
Seated child, feet and hands crossed, "Heubach" **75.00**
6¼″ l, child, lying on stomach, holding dog, blue nightie, gold beading **150.00**
6½″ l, 7¼″ h, seated child, holding shoe in air **250.00**
6¾″ h, seated child, holding ruffled bonnet, white gown, pink bows **250.00**
7″ l
Baby, crawling, right leg up, imp "Heubach sunburst mark" **125.00**
Baby, reclining, fingers and toes extended, lace dress, Germany **225.00**
Baby, seated, holding watch to ear, multicolored nightie, Germany ... **150.00**
Child, crawling, right foot up, white and blue gown, imp "Heubach sunburst" mark **225.00**
7″ l, 8½″ h, seated baby, green ribbon through gown, imp "Heubach sunburst" mark **275.00**
7¼″ l, 6½″ h, seated child, holding rattle **225.00**

Figure, 5½″ l, white gown, blue trim, imp "Heubach" rising sun mark, $100.00.

8½″ l
Child, lying on stomach, pillow, and dog, blue flowered nightie **250.00**
Child, seated, feeding cat, colored gown, Germany **175.00**
Little boy, holding watch and chain, white clothes, blue trim, "Heubach" **225.00**
9″ h, child, sitting, cat eating from child's bowl **200.00**
9″ l
Baby, lying, rattle, dog climbing over her **200.00**

Baby, lying on side, wearing feathered cap, blue and white gown **200.00**

Baby, lying on stomach, thumb raised, white gown **325.00**

9½" l, child, lying on back, holding fruit, blue and white nightie, pink hat, "G. H." **300.00**

10" h, baby, sitting, jeweled moth on skirt, "GERMANY" **225.00**

10½" l, blond girl, butterfly on bottom of dress, bow at top **400.00**

11" h, child, seated in high chair, puppy in lap, cereal bowl and spoon **250.00**

11" l, baby, lying on stomach, detailed facial features, imp, #, "GERMANY" **300.00**

PITCHER AND BOWL SETS

English/Continental
19th and Early 20th Centuries

History: Pitcher and bowl sets or washstand china were popular during the 19th and early 20th centuries. A typical set consisted of a pitcher (ewer) and basin, soap dish, sponge dish, toothbrush tray, and slop pail. Additional specialized pieces, e.g., hair receivers and comb box, also were available. Wash sets allowed an individual to complete the washing up procedure in the privacy of the bedroom. The availability of piped water put an end to the Victorian and Edwardian jug and basin sets.

The list of manufacturers of washstand china was large. Principal English manufacturers included Minton, Wedgwood, George Jones, Doulton, Clarice Cliff, and Ridgway. Many Continental companies also made washstand china.

Collecting Hints: Not every set has the same number of pieces. Many sets featured only the pitcher and bowl.

Two Piece, pitcher and bowl

1½" h pitcher, 2" d bowl, multicolored small flowers, gold trim, "GERMANY" **45.00**

2¾" h pitcher, 1½" d bowl, Sunbonnet Babies, washing, blue "Royal Bayreuth" **300.00**

5" h pitcher, Chinese man and boy on pitcher, bowl with floral center, man and boy on ext., bone china, c1822-30, "Hilditch & Son, Lane End, Staffordshire" **225.00**

8" h pitcher, 11½" d bowl, blue and white sponging (A) **110.00**

8" h pitcher, 14¼" d, bowl, transfer, blue and green flowers, gold trim, Belgium **40.00**

9½" h pitcher, 12½" d bowl, scenic transfer, blue and white, "Copeland, England" **220.00**

10½" h pitcher, 14½" d bowl, medallions of roses, turquoise ground, England **185.00**

10½" h pitcher, 15" d bowl, "Fabulous Birds" pattern, c1890, "York, England" **350.00**

10½" h pitcher, 16⅜" d bowl, "Corinth" pattern, flow blue, Bishop & Stonier **265.00**

10½" h pitcher, 16½" d bowl, octagonal, "Lilacs," pattern, blue and lavender lilacs, green and black leaves, dark blue and gold edge, "Royal Doulton" **250.00**

11" h, pitcher, 13⅜" d bowl, peafowl in red, blue, green, and black, blue spatter borders, repaired pitcher, imp "Adams" (A) **400.00**

11" h pitcher, 13¾" d bowl, blue spatter (A) **230.00**

11" h pitcher, 15½" d bowl, brown transfer, "Lake Scenery" pattern, "J. F. Wileman" **165.00**

Left, 10″ h pitcher, 15½″ d bowl, cream, black, yellow, and rose floral band, cream ground, "Crescent Ivory, George Jones & Sons," $165.00; right, 10½″ h pitcher, 14″ d bowl, ironstone, orange, green, and black Oriental scene, scale ground, c1830, "Mason," $975.00.

11½" h pitcher, 16" d bowl, flow blue floral design, "England" **400.00**

12" h pitcher, 14" d bowl, white ironstone, blue band outlined in black, "H. Burgess, Burslem" **135.00**

12" h pitcher, 16" d bowl, blue and white underglazed sponging (A) .. **325.00**

12" h pitcher, 17½" d bowl, "Pagoda" pattern, red, green, and gray flowers, pagoda scene, "Losol Ware, Keeling & Co. Ltd, Made in England" **225.00**

12½" h pitcher, 16" d bowl, "Sylvia" pattern, flow blue **325.00**

13" h pitcher, 13½" d bowl, "Shanghai" pattern, flow blue **1,600.00**

15" h pitcher, 16½" d bowl, "Trellis" pattern, roses, cream ground, light green border, gold edges, "F. Winkle & Co. Whieldon Ware" **350.00**

Unknown sizes

"Abbey" pattern, flow blue, "George Jones" **300.00**

Cobalt splashes, c1873, "Brown-Westhead, Moore & Co." **225.00**

Multicolored jug and bowl, Oriental reds and blues, outlined in gold, ironstone, c1840, "Mason's Ironstone" **600.00**

"Panama" pattern, mulberry transfers, "Edward Challinor & Co." **175.00**

Pink roses, turquoise ground, "Stoke-on-Trent" **185.00**

Transfer, green stylized floral motif, cream ground, imp "WEDGWOOD" (A) **200.00**

Three Piece

12¼" h pitcher, 7½" d bowl, 8½" d chamber pot, blue and white windmill scenes, "Empire Ware, England" **225.00**

15" h pitcher, 17" d bowl, cov toothbrush holder, blue windmill and sailing scene, white ground, "E. J. Co., Stoke-on-Trent, Empire Ware" **125.00**

Pitcher, bowl, chamber pot, cherry blossom design, green ground, c1880, "Ridgway" **175.00**

Pitcher, two 16½" d bowls, painted branch of flowering peony, shaded gilt ground, dark blue border, gilt prunus and mon, c1890, "Doulton-Burslem" (A) **200.00**

Four Piece

7¾" h pitcher, bowl, beaker, cov soap dish, red, green, and blue stylized flowers, black outlines, yellow, blue, and red banding, "Clarice Cliff" (A) **1,120.00**

12" h pitcher, 16¼" d bowl, snake handle, 5" d cov soap dish, insert, toothbrush holder, blue dragon de-

sign, "MASON'S PATENT IRONSTONE" **185.00**

Five Piece

10" h pitcher, 14" d bowl, sm pitcher, tumbler, cov soap dish, overall brown leaf and branch design, ivory ground, gold accents, "Doulton-Burslem" **600.00**

10½" h pitcher, 15" d bowl, 9½" d chamber pot, cup, cov soap dish, hp "Bizarre Honeyglaze" pattern, orange and honey yellow, sweeps of orange, yellow, and blue vertical geometrics, chamber pot with orange, yellow, and black banding, single handled, "Clarice Cliff" . .**4,800.00**

Pitcher, bowl, cov jar, waste bowl, white semi-porcelain, band of purple and white flowers at middle, yellow border top and bottom, gold trim, c1890's, "Ridgway" **400.00**

Six Piece

9" h pitcher, 15" d bowl, 7" h sm pitcher, mug, vase, cov soap dish, "Versailles" pattern, red transfer, "F. Winkle & Co." **200.00**

Pitcher, bowl, cov chamber pot, cov slop jar, cov soap dish, toothbrush holder, polychrome rhododendron, cream ground, c1870, "Brown-Westhead Moore & Co." (A) **200.00**

Pitcher, bowl, chamber pot, soap dish, shaving mug, waste bowl, blue flowers, white ground, gold trim, "Doulton-Burslem, England" **700.00**

Seven Piece, large and small pitchers, washbowl, cov chamber pot, shaving mug, cov soap dish, toothbrush holder, rose decoration, gilt trim, "England" (A) **175.00**

PLYMOUTH

2 1768-70

Devon, England, 1768–1770
Bristol, England, 1771–1781

History: William Cooksworthy made hard paste type porcelain at Plymouth for only two years, 1768–70. In 1771, he moved to Bristol.

Pieces from the Plymouth pottery have an Oriental influence. Some under-the-glaze blue designs are enhanced with over-the-glaze enamels. Figurines and animal and bird groups also were made.

Although most Plymouth porcelain was unmarked, some pieces bear the mark for tin. Copies of Plymouth porcelains bearing the tin mark and fake inscriptions such as "Plymouth Manufacturing" are found on the market.

References: F. Severne MacKenna, *Cookworthy's Plymouth & Bristol Porcelain*, F. Lewis, 1947; B. Watney, *English Blue & White Porcelain*, Faber & Faber, rev. ed., 1973.

Museums: City Museum & Art Gallery, Stoke-on-Trent, England; Gardiner Museum of Ceramic Art, Toronto, Canada.

Figures, 12¼-13½" h, Continents, gray-green glaze, c1770, set of 4, (A) $4,435.00.

Cream Jug, 3½" h, painted bouquets and sprays, iron-red loop and line rim, c1768, Wm. Cookworthy **250.00**
Creamboat, 4⅛" h, scroll edged puce outlined panels on sides, painted cockerel and peacock in landscapes, molded rococo shape, spur handle (A) **270.00**
Figure
    5½" h, allegorical figures of Four Seasons as putti, multicolored, rococo scroll bases, repairs, c1770 (A) ...**1,000.00**
    7½" h, two putti and goat, seated by flowering tree stump, yellow, iron-red, and blue flowers, scroll molded base, c1770 (A) **235.00**
Mug, 6½" h, blue painted Oriental landscape with pavilion, formal border rim, bell shape, c1769 .... **450.00**
Sauceboat
    5½" l, molded rococo form, painted birds on sides, c1770 .... **800.00**
    6⅛" l, molded rococo cartouches on sides, painted "India Flowers," russet rim, hexagon shape, c1769-70 (A) **825.00**

PORTRAIT WARE

English/Continental
Mid 19th C to 1900

History: Plates, vases, and other pieces with portraits and busts on them were popular during the mid-19th century. Male subjects included important historical figures, such as Napoleon, Louis XVI, and James Garfield. However, most portraits featured beautiful women, ranging from the French Empress Josephine to unknown Victorian ladies.

Many English and Continental firms made portrait ware. Makers include Royal Vienna, Limoges, Schumann, and MZ Austria. Most examples were hand painted and often bore an artist's signature. Transfer prints supplemented the hand painted pieces.

Biscuit Jar, multicolored bust of woman on bowl and lid, dark green, gold, and burgundy ground, "Bavaria" ... **125.00**
Bowl, 5½" d, head and shoulder view of woman, brown hair, pink rim, "Victoria, Austria" **25.00**
Butter Pat, head and shoulder view of woman, long blond hair, plumed hat **30.00**
Creamer, 5½" h, head and shoulder view of woman, facing sideways, gold tracery, orange ground, "Austria" **65.00**
Cup and Saucer
    Bust of woman, multicolored, blue ground, gold tracery **20.00**
    Portrait, pink and maroon on int. of cup, flowers, gold tracery **40.00**
Plaque
    11¾" d, bust of woman, dark hair, dark red ground, raised gold accents, "Royal Vienna" **230.00**
    12" d, lady, blue dress, holding lilacs, gold beading, roses in border, "Germany" **100.00**
Plate
    6½" d, bust of woman, purple fan, large hat, scalloped rim, hp, "wreath & crown" **65.00**
    8" d
    Bust of woman, long brown hair, white scalloped edge **35.00**

Plate, 8½" d, multicolored bust of Napoleon, gold scalloped rim, "J. P. L., France," $150.00.

Bust of young woman, white ground, gold tracery **20.00**

Woman, plume in hat, green and white ground, pr **40.00**

8½" d

Bust of young woman, flowers and jewels, brown hair, maroon, blue, and ivory border, "GERMANY" **50.00**

Portrait of Duchesse de Bourqoqno, black rim, panels, gold tracery, "Pouyat, Limoges" **55.00**

Victorian woman in center, gold border, raised beading, "Limoges" **125.00**

9" d

Bust of young woman, wide plumed hat, fur collar, dark blue and gilt border, "Royal Munich" **175.00**

Woman playing lyre, multicolored, "Royal Munich" **125.00**

9½" d

Head and shoulder view of young woman, brown hair, purple dress, flowers, dark green border, olive green and gold inner border, Schumann **55.00**

Head and shoulder view of woman, white hair, large hat with plumes, white border, gold trim **35.00**

Victorian woman, forget-me-nots on border, gold, scalloped edge **70.00**

Woman, long blond hair, pink roses on border, gold trim, pierced for hanging, sgd "Constance," "M. Z. Austria" **55.00**

9⅝" d, bust of James Garfield in rect, gilt scrolling, maroon and blue border, c1880, blue "beehive" mark **125.00**

9¾" d

Bust of young woman, multicolored, blue ground, gold trim ... **100.00**

Center, bust of woman, green hat and plume, green border with medallions of six women, mauve ground, gold scalloped edge, "Blenheim" **100.00**

Head and shoulder view of young woman, flowing hair, gold band, tracery, green border, blue "beehive" mark **135.00**

10" d

Blond woman on one, brunette on other sgd "Constance," "AUSTRIA" **110.00**

Full figures of two young women, multicolored, gold tracery, scalloped rim, pierced for hanging, "Austria" **50.00**

Head and shoulder view of woman veiled in roses, wide gold border, hp, "Austria" **100.00**

Three maidens in center, multicolored, early 10th C, "beehive" mark **80.00**

Woman embracing child, dark green, gold rim, multicolored transfer **65.00**

10½" d

Full figures of three young women, multicolored, gold accents, "Royal Schwarzburg, Germany" **100.00**

Head and shoulder view of woman, purple hat and flowers, scalloped green and white border **15.00**

11½" d

Busts of man and woman, Gainsborough-type, wide dark blue borders, etched gold trim, "Bavaria," pr **150.00**

Head and shoulder view of young woman, dark pink border, pierced for hanging, "Victoria, Austria" **60.00**

11¾" d, maiden, long brown hair, blue border **45.00**

Powder Jar, head and shoulder view of woman, dark green ground, gold tracery **125.00**

Soup Plate, 8½" d, head and shoulder view of woman, yellow and white, gold edge **30.00**

Sweetmeat Jar, portrait of woman on each side, light blue ground, gold tracery **125.00**

Toothpick Holder, head and shoulder view of woman, dark blue ground, "GERMANY" **25.00**

Vase

3½" h, bud, portrait of young woman, multicolored, hp, "Heubach" **45.00**

5½" h, bust of young woman, dark blue ground, gold trim, three legs **80.00**

7" h, portrait of young woman, black hair, gold earrings, dark brown ground, "Germany" **85.00**

10" h, three-quarter view of woman, white dress, holding flowers, dark blue ground, gold handles and base **80.00**

10¾" h, center portrait of woman and peacock, multicolored, long slender handles, "Germany" **190.00**

PORTUGAL– GENERAL

**Ilhavo, Portugal
1824 to Present**

History: Jose Ferreira Pinto Basto established a factory to make porcelain at Vista Alegre in 1824.

Soft paste porcelains and earthenwares, based on English models, were made until 1832. Anselmo Ferreira, a modeler from Lisbon, and Joseph Scorder from Germany helped develop the factory. In the early 1830s the ingredients to manufacture hard paste porcelains were found in the region.

Vista Alegre's golden period began in 1835 when Victor Chartier-Rousseau, a French artist, arrived. He remained until his death in 1852. During his tenure, an improved hard paste porcelain became the standard product. Sevres forms replaced the earlier English–influenced pieces. Classical, Gothic, and Rococo Revival influences can be found among Vista Alegre's products. Gustave Fortier served as artistic director from 1851 to 1856 and from 1861 to 1869. French influences continued. The factory prospered.

During the late Victorian period, when the Portuguese Joaquim de Oliverra (1870–1881) was head painter, the factory experienced financial difficulties. These continued under head painters da Roche Freire (1881—1889) and Jose de Magalhaes (1889–1921). De Magalhaes was responsible for ornamental plates with high relief decorations that featured vibrant themes and Art Nouveau characteristics.

In 1924 the factory was reorganized and emphasis was placed on the production of classical patterns. Some contemporary designs were introduced.

The factory is still controlled by the descendants of the original owner Jose Basto. The "VA" mark in blue has been maintained. A laurel wreath and crown symbolizing the royal patent of 1826 were added, but later abandoned.

Museums: Vista Alegre Museum, Ilhavo, Portugal.

Bud Vase, 3½" h, brown flowerheads, cobalt stems, tan ground, "ALELUIA FABRICADO PORTUGAL," $375.00.

Barber Bowl, 13¾" l, painted cobalt
    bouquet of flowers, chain swags rim,
    late 18th C (A) **200.00**
Charger, 15⅜" d, tin-glazed polychrome
    floral design, "Made in Portugal" (A) **50.00**

Dish, 3½" l, shell form, yellow, gold
    rims, "VA Portugal," pr **30.00**
Drug Jar, 8½" h, blue armorial design,
    white ground, inscribed "RL Monsto
    Matallanh," c1680 .... **950.00**
Figure, 5¾" h, Four Seasons, multicolored, bisque **100.00**
Jardiniere, 11⅝" l, multicolored florals
    in ovals on sides, white ground, gold
    trim, shaped rim and foot, "VA Portugal" **450.00**
Jug, 12½" h, green molded lizard-form,
    dressed as praying monk, brown
    robe, mouth with green frog, early
    20th C , incised "J.A.C." **300.00**
Plaque, 35" l, 24" h, blue court scene,
    white ground, scalloped edge, mid
    19th C (A) **1,000.00**
Plate, 8" d, figural cabbage leaf, natural
    colors, majolica **15.00**
Pot-A-Creme, 3⅜" h, gold band dec,
    white ground, "PORTUGAL" set of
    six (A) **10.00**

POT LIDS

Staffordshire, England
c1840 to 1900

History: Pot lids are defined as under the glaze, chromatic, transfer printed Staffordshire pot covers. The pots were containers designed to hold food stuffs, delicacies, and cosmetics, such as potted meats, relishes, fish paste, sauces, rouge, lip salve, hair pomades for women, and bear's grease for men. First sold about 1840, they reached their popularity in the Victorian era. They were priced according to size. There were five basic sizes ranging from the smallest (under 1¾" diameter) to the largest (5½ to 8½" diameter).

The finest pot lids were made between 1850 and 1870. Production continued to the end of the 19th century. Although at least eight firms made pot lids, Pratt & Company was the major manufacturer.

In 1836 George Baxter patented his process to make an oil color printing from a number of plates and blocks. Ten years later the process was applied to ceramics. Pratt's 1847 "Grace Before Meals" was the first full chromatic transfer printed under the glaze on a pot lid. T. J. & J. Mayer followed suit in 1851. Chromatic transfer printing first involved painting a watercolor. Next a key plate was engraved. Prints from the key plate were then transferred to three other plates that held the three prime colors.

Pratt's master artist-engraver was Jesse Austin. His key plate color was brown. From 1852 to 1869 Austin engraved plates that portrayed portraits of royalty and famous people on pot lids. Between 1864 and 1873 eleven different views of London on pot lids were made. In addition to his own original watercolors, Austin also reproduced in miniature forms the paintings of famous artists.

Early Pratt lids frequently were flat topped. Shapes varied. The glaze had a bluish tint, especially before 1870. In the 1870s the glaze was more gray-blue in tone. The glaze also featured fine crazing. Forty-seven pot lids had the line and dot border design. Large Pratt pot lids made before 1863 show three stilt marks on the underside. Pratt's chief competitor from 1856–1862 was Cauldon Place Pottery.

References: A. Ball, *The Price Guide to Pot-Lids & Other Underglaze Multi-colored Prints on Ware,* 2nd ed., Antique Collectors' Club, Ltd., 1980; H. G. Clarke, *The Pictorial Pot Lid Book,* Courier Press, 1960; Ronald Dale, *The Price Guide to Black & White Pot Lids,* Antique Collectors' Club, 1978; Cyril Williams-Wood, *Staffordshire Pot Lids & Their Potters,* Faber & Faber, 1972.

Museums: County Museum, Truro, England; Fitzwilliam Museum, Cambridge, England. (Collection seen by appointment only.)

Collecting Hints: Full color lids are the most popular among collectors. Pot lids with broad gold bands that were either produced for display at trade exhibits or showrooms or as souvenirs for families and friends of the master potter are most prized.

Lid and Jar, 4¼″ d, "Strathfieldsay," multicolored transfer, $100.00.

Lid
3″ d
"Areca Nut Tooth Paste," white ironstone, label, England **20.00**
"Artic Expedition," multicolored transfer, rim chip, "T. J. & J. Mayer" (A) **320.00**
"Bears at School," multicolored transfer (A) **90.00**
"Lady Brushing Hair," multicolored transfer (A) **220.00**

"Lady, Boy & Goats," multicolored transfer **30.00**
"The Fisher Boy," multicolored transfer **30.00**
3½″ d
"Anchovy Paste," white ironstone, black label, England **15.00**
"R. B. Ede & Co., London, Shaving Cream," black transfer of man shaving (A) **35.00**
3¾″ d, "Dublin Industrial Exhibition," multicolored transfer (A) **50.00**
4″ d
"Albert Memorial," multicolored transfer (A) **25.00**
"Anne Hathaway's Cottage," multicolored transfer (A) **20.00**
"Deer Drinking," multicolored transfer (A) **25.00**
"Dr. Johnson," multicolored transfer **125.00**
"French Street Scene," multicolored transfer (A) **25.00**
"Garibaldi," multicolored transfer **100.00**
"Hauling in the Trawl," multicolored transfer, framed **30.00**
"I See You My Boy," multicolored transfer (A) **25.00**
"Peace," multicolored transfer (A) **50.00**
"Philadelphia Exhibition, 1876," multicolored transfer (A) **50.00**
4⅛″ d
Man and donkey begging, multicolored transfer **65.00**
"Persuasion," multicolored transfer **145.00**
"The Skaters," multicolored transfer **95.00**
"The Village Wedding," multicolored transfer, framed **120.00**
4¼″ d
"Hauling in the Trawl," multicolored transfer (A) **45.00**
"The Village Wedding," multicolored transfer, Pratt (A) **45.00**
"Transplanting Rice," multicolored transfer **125.00**
4½″ d
"Bloater Paste," white ironstone, black label, "England" **10.00**
"I See You My Boy," multicolored transfer (A) **20.00**
"May Day Dancers at the Swan Inn," multicolored transfer (A) .. **20.00**
"No By Heaven I Exclaimed..." on edge, multicolored transfer **175.00**
4⅝″ d, "The Ning Po River," multicolored transfer, F. & R. Pratt & Co. (A) **20.00**
5½″ l, "Peace," multicolored transfer, rect, lobed corners (A) **25.00**
6¼″ d, portrait of Edward VIII, multicolored, "Belgium" **25.00**

7¾" d, "Cries of London-Sweet Oranges," multicolored transfer (A) . **45.00**
Lid and Jar
4" d
"HRH The Prince of Wales Visiting The Tomb of Washington," multicolored transfer **175.00**
Woman with lamb, multicolored transfer, "William Wood" **135.00**
4⅛" d, "Embarking For The East," multicolored transfer, Pratt **80.00**
4¾" d, Old man courting woman, multicolored transfer (A) **55.00**

FENTON

PRATT WARE

Staffordshire, Shropshire, and other English pottery centers c1785 to 1840
Scotland 1750 to 1840

History: Pratt ware is relief decorated, high temperature fired, under–the–glaze, cream colored earthenware and pearlware that was made between 1785 and 1840. William Pratt headed a family of potters who worked at Lane Delph and Fenton. William was the first of six generations of Pratts to make Pratt ware. Felix, John, and Richard, William's sons, managed the pottery after their father's death in 1799.

Jugs with relief molded designs of sporting and bucolic scenes or commemorative subjects featuring naval or military heroes or royal figures were the most popular forms. Tea caddies, plaques, flasks, teapots, dishes, mugs, cow creamers, busts, and other forms also were produced.

The body usually was white or a pale cream color. The glaze consisted of lead oxide tinged with blue. The wares were decorated with relief designs pressed from intaglio molds. Colors used for the decorations included: yellow, orange, green, blue, brown, black, and mulberry. The under–the–glaze color technique that protected the colors under a transparent glaze retained the brilliance of the pieces.

The majority of Pratt's jugs were unmarked. Other potters that imitated the wares from Pratt's factory included Wedgwood, Leeds, E. Bourne, T. Hawley, and R. M. Astbury. Under–the–glaze colored figures of animal groups, Toby jugs, tall case clock money boxes, and watch stands appeared. Classical scenes were featured in relief decoration under the glaze on jugs. A number of

relief decorations on Pratt ware duplicated the intaglio patterns found on jasper ware.

The Scottish East Coast Potteries made Pratt ware style jugs and other forms from the mid-1700s until 1840. Some pieces contained motifs with a distinctive Scottish flavor.

References: John & Griselda Lewis, *Pratt Ware 1780–1840*, Antique Collectors' Club Ltd., 1984.

Museums: Fitzwilliam Museum, Cambridge, England; Potsdam Public Museum, Potsdam, N.Y.; Royal Scottish Museum, Edinburgh, Scotland; Victoria & Albert Museum, London, England.

Bowl
7" d, painted stylized flowerheads, multicolored (A) **130.00**
8" d, classical colored transfer, matte black ground **40.00**
9⅞" d, 3½" h, dark brown int., green transfer of "Dr. Syntax Drawing After Nature," polychrome enamel colors (A) **100.00**
Box, 4" d, Cov, "The Wolf & the Lamb," multicolored transfer (A) **65.00**
Bust 11½" h, Napoleon, dark orange and blue uniform, dark yellow tapered socle, brown line **475.00**
Compote
9½" d, 6¼" h, "The Spanish Dancers," multicolored, gold figural border **245.00**
12½" h, Highland music subject ... **400.00**
Cup and Saucer, scene of Queen Victoria's children in open carriage drawn by goat, Windsor Castle in background, multicolored, blue-green leaf borders, yellow luster rims **150.00**
Figure
4½" h, Roger Giles, crouching on sq base, breeches lowered, hat pierced forming pepper pot, multicolored (A) **180.00**
4⅞" h, standing girl, ochre robe and crown, holding cornucopia, green base **95.00**
5" h
recumbent lamb and ewe, grass mound, ochre, brown, and green, c1790 (A) **765.00**
Standing lady, long yellow dress, blue cloak, shaped green bordered base **55.00**
6⅛" h, standing race horses, blue, green, and yellow, brown reins and tails, yellow checked saddle-clothes, green washed chamfered bases, pr **2,050.00**
8½" h, and 8⅞" h, four seasons, modeled as maidens rocky mounds, sq bases, c1780-90, set of four (A) . **2,970.00**

9" h, St. George, slaying the dragon, two women at side, multicolored, c1780 ....**2,750.00**

9¼" h, soldier, brown and blue jacket, plumed helmet, holding rifle, green tree stump, tapered circ base, molded key pattern **450.00**

10¼" h, reclining woman, blue dress, orange cloak, yellow draperies, green washed rocky base **165.00**

11⅜" h, boy and girl on each side of grandfather clock, classical figures and foliage, multicolored, Yorkshire watch with pink and black face (A) **435.00**

Flask, 7¾" h, color printed with "The Late Duke of Wellington," reverse "Rt. Hon. Sir Robt. Peel," multicolored print, reserved on malachite ground, gilt borders, c1865 (A) **400.00**

Jar
4" h
Hounds with boar scene, blue ... **15.00**
Portrait of Shakespeare, blue **15.00**
4¾" h, relief of gentleman with mug, white and blue, raised trim, c1820 **340.00**
5" h, huntsmen and hounds, molded, colored (A) **175.00**
7¾" h, molded oval panels of peacocks in landscapes, blue, brown, green, and ochre, lower section with vertical leaves, band of foliage on rim, c1790 .... **600.00**
8½" h, cooper beside barrel, reverse with armorial and "The Coopers Arms," painted, inscribed "Joseph Chrimes, 1802" under lip **475.00**

Jug, 8" h, polychrome, cream ground, c1800, $575.00.

Mug
3⅛" h, brown and yellow checkered painted border inscribed "A Trifle shows Respect" **30.00**

3½" h, transfer of figures, ruins in landscape, reverse with horses in riverscape, shaped panels reserved on pink ground, c1840, "Pratt 123 Fenton" **70.00**

Mush Cup, pastoral scenes, multicolored **55.00**

Mustard Jar, dark blue hunt scene, tan ground **55.00**

Pipe
4½" h, modeled as seated woman on wicker stool, cat in lap, mask form pipe bowl, dbl snake form stem, c1810 (A) **115.00**
5⅝" h, modeled as seated man on wicker stool, "Jolly Pickman" incised on hat, holding glass, smoking spotted pipe, S-curved stem, molded leaf, c1810 (A) **115.00**
11¾" l, stem of irregular loops, three outer loops, ochre, blue, and green, bowl with two painted figures of boys, c1790 (A) **1,000.00**

Pitcher
5½" h, figures of Juno, Minerva, Petroclus, and horses **100.00**
7" h, relief of classic figures, multicolored **75.00**

Plaque
5¾" d, relief of bird perched on cherry branch with insect, brown, ochre, and green, c1775 .... **350.00**
7¾" d, scene of cottage, old woman reading to children, 1834, sgd "T. Webster" (A) **85.00**
8½" d, scene of "The Bully" and "The Truant," multicolored, late 19th C, pr (A) **160.00**
11" l, relief of two reclining lions, yellow ochre, brown, and green, blue border, oval, pierced for hanging, c1800 (A) **570.00**
12⅛" l, relief of two brown recumbent lions, brown, ochre, and blue striped plateau, molded self-frame, blue and ochre borders, pierced for hanging, c1790-1820 (A) **715.00**

Plate
5½" d, fishing scene, multicolored, rust border, gold trim **85.00**
7" d, market scene, multicolored, orchid colored border, gold trimmed edge **65.00**
9" d
"Hadden Hall," brown classic figures in border **100.00**
Wellington's castle, multicolored . **60.00**

Sauceboat, 6½" l, modeled as fox head, ochre open mouth spout, modeled swan handle, oval reed molded base, green accents, c1770 .... **450.00**

Tea Caddy
  4½" h, molded relief figures in wigs
    and costumes, green, ochre and
    manganese accents, blue and ochre
    sprigs on ground **150.00**
  4¾" h
  Relief bust of King George III, pol-
    ychrome **175.00**
  Relief figure of George Washington,
    polychrome **175.00**
  6½" h, modeled grotesque man and
    servant on one side, grotesque
    woman and servant on reverse,
    blue, ochre, green, and brown ac-
    cents, c1780 (A) **110.00**
Teapot Stand, 7½" d, "Lend a Bite,"
  multicolored transfer, turquoise border, gold rim, geometrics **75.00**
Watchstand, 8½" h, longcase clock,
  face, man, and woman on each side,
  dog at feet, rect base, painted and
  sponged colors, c1810 (A) **1,600.00**

PORQUIER-BEAU

QUIMPER

Quimper, Brittany, France
1600s to Present

History: Quimper faience derives its name from
the town in Brittany, in the northwest corner of
France, where the potteries were located. Three
of the major 17th and 18th century centers of
French faience strongly influenced the early
Quimper potters: Nevers, Rouen, and Moustiers.
  Jean Baptiste Bousquet settled in Quimper in
1685 and started producing functional faience
wares using Moustiers—inspired patterns. Pierre,

his son, took over in 1708. In 1731 Pierre included Pierre Bellevaux, his son-in-law, in the
business. He introduced the Chinese-inspired
blue and white color scheme, the Oriental subject matter, the intertwining border pattern of
leaves and flowers, and the use of the rooster as
a central theme.
  From Rouen, Pierre Clement Caussy brought
to Quimper many important features such as
"decor rayonnant," an intricate pattern of stylized leaves and florals on the outer border and
lacy designs that resembled wrought iron trellises. By 1739 Pierre Clement Caussy had joined
with Bousquet. He became the manager of the
faiencerie and expanded the works.
  Francois Eloury opened a rival factory in 1776
and in 1778 Guillaume Dumaine opened a second rival factory. Thus, there were three rival
faience factories operating in Quimper producing
similar wares by 1780.
  Through marriage, Antoine de la Hubaudiere
became the manager of the Caussy factory in
1782. The factory's name became the Grande
Maison.
  After the beginning of the 19th century, the
essential Breton characteristics began to appear
on the pottery - the use of primary colors, concentric banding in blue and yellow for border
trims, and single stroke brushing to create a flower
or leaf. Toward the end of the 19th century,
scenes of everyday Breton peasants became popular decortive motifs. Artists such as Rene Quil-
livic joined Grande Maison in 1920 and produced figures.
  Concurrently, the Eloury factory passed to
Charles Porquier and later to Adolphe Porquier.
In 1872 Alfred Beau, a master artist, joined the
firm and produced Breton scenes and figures.
  In 1884 Jules Henriot took over the Dumaine
factory. He added the Porquier factory to his
holdings in 1904. Mathurin Meheut joined the
Henriot factory in 1925 and introduced patterns
influenced by the Art Deco and Art Nouveau
stylistic trends. Other noted artists at Henriot
were Sevellec, Maillard, and Nicot. During the
1920s the "HB" company introduced the Odetta
line that utilized a stoneware body·and decorations of the Art Deco period.
  The Henriot factory merged with the Grande
Maison HB in 1968, each retaining its individual
characteristics and marks. Production ceased in
the early 1980s. An American couple recently
purchased the plant and renewed the production
of Quimper.
  Quimper pottery was made in a tremendous
number of shapes and forms among which were
utilitarian pieces, all types of figures and decorative articles, and in fact, just about everything
imaginable.

References: Sandra V. Bondhus, *Quimper Pottery: A French Folk Art Faience,* published pri-

vately, 1981; Millicent Mali, *Quimper Faience,* Airon, Inc., 1979; Marjatta Taburet, *La Faience de Quimper,* Editions Sous le Vent, 1979, (French Text).

Museums: Musee de Faiences de Quimper, Quimper France; Victoria & Albert Museum, London, England; Villa Viscaya, Maimi, Florida.

REPRODUCTION ALERT: A line of pottery called "museum quality" has appeared on the market. These pieces feature a brownish wash over a crazed glaze surface. The marks are generally in brown as opposed to the blue or black factory marks of the earlier period. Originally these reproductions had paper labels, but the labels are removed easily. The reproductions sometimes are sold as old peices.

The Blue Ridge Pottery and several Japanese firms have produced wares with peasant designs similar to those of Quimper. These are easily recognizable.

Peasant pottery similar in style and feel to Quimper has been produced by the Malicorne factory, near Paris. These pieces carry a Malicorne "PBx" mark. Examples have appeared on the market with the "x" removed and sold as genuine Quimper.

Modern Quimper pottery is still made and marketed in major department stores, such as Neiman-Marcus and Marshall Fields, and in china specialty shops.

Collecting Hints: Most Quimper available to the collector comes from the late 1800s to the mid-1920s. Since so much was produced, the collector should focus on pieces that are in very good or better condition. Missing covers to sugar bowls, teapots, inkwells, etc., greatly reduce the value of these pieces and should be avoided. Small flakes in the glaze are inherent in the nature of the pottery, and, for the most part, do not detract from their desirablilty.

Pieces from the Odetta period (c1920) are less desirable because of the emphasis on Art Deco designs rather than the country motif associated with the more traditional Quimper pottery.

Marks: The "HR" and "HR Quimper" marks are found on Henriot pieces prior to 1922. The "HenRiot Quimper" mark was used after 1922. The "HB" mark covers a long span of time. The addition of numbers or dots and dashes refers to inventory numbers and are found on later pieces. Most marks are in blue or black. Consignment pieces for department stores such as Macy's and Carson Pirie Scott carry the store mark along with the factory mark. These consignment pieces are somewhat less desirable in the eyes of the collector.

Newsletter: Quimper Faience, Inc., 141 Water Street, Stonington, CT 06378. Subscription: $3.00. Semi-annual.

Asparagus Plate, 9", molded asparagus center, male and female peasant above, rect, shaped corners, c1880, "HB," pr 1,100.00
Basket, 6¼" h, seated peasant, basket, decor riche border, "HB Quimper" . 150.00
Bookends, two young girls, rust and orange, "Ravallec-Mazet, Henriot Quimper," pr 300.00
Bowl
    4" d, cov, female peasant on cov, flowers on base, white ground, dbl handles, "HB Quimper" 150.00
    4¾" sq, peasant man, florals in center, spatter edge 35.00
    7" l, 4½" w, peasant man, ruffled border, pedestal base, blue sponged handles 45.00
    7½" d, peasant man, florals, multicolored, ruffled edge, "Henriot Quimper, France" 175.00
Box
  Cov
    3½" d, man playing bagpipe, "HR Quimper" 135.00
    5" d, seated male peasant playing flute, decor riche border, "HB Quimper" 235.00
  Open, 5" l, 3½" w, bust of peasant man, wide hat, black and tan, stoneware, "Odetta" 235.00
Butter Pat, 3" d, multicolored geometric design, "Henriot Quimper, France" . 45.00
Chamberstick
  Peasant woman, florals, leaf shape, "HR" 200.00
  Peasant man, flowers, blue and red, clover shape, "Henriot Quimper, France" 100.00
Cheese Dish, 9" l, peasant man, pipe . 400.00
Cigarette Holder, 7½" h, figural, pig, yellow, green spots 250.00
Coffeepot, 8" h, peasant man, florals, "Henriot Quimper, France" (A) 50.00
Compote, 10" w, 5½" h, multicolored florals, scalloped edge, footed, "Henriot Quimper, France" 150.00
Creamer
  4" h, peasant woman, blue and yellow, crimped spout, "Henriot Quimper, France" 65.00
  Small pink flowers, brown trim, white ground, "HB Quimper F424, D.289, L & M" 65.00
Creamer and Sugar, peasant woman, flowers, pink ground, green spatter handles, hexagonal shape, "Henriot Quimper, France" 80.00
Cruet, 6" h, oil and vinegar, joined at necks, male on one, female on other, blue and red floral decor, "Henriot Quimper, France" 125.00

Cup 4¼" d, blue and rust florals, octagonal, "HR Quimper" **35.00**
Cup and Saucer
  Peasant man, florals, green ground . **15.00**
  Peasant, man on one side, woman on other, yellow ground, "HB Quimper" **45.00**
  Red, blue, and green florals, gray-white ground **85.00**
Desk, 13" l, two sections, bagpipe shape, ribbon trim, bow handle, "Henriot Quimper, France" **475.00**
Dish
  3¾" l, dark brown bust of peasant woman, brown and beige ground, "HB Quimper" **85.00**
  4" l, red and blue florals, four rope handles, "AP" **400.00**
  7½" l, female peasant, florals, shell shape, "HB Quimper" **80.00**
  12¼" l, male peasant, pipe, crest in center, dbl compartments, blue sponged handle and reverse, decor riche border **1,200.00**
Door Pushers, man on one, woman on other, tan ground, blue and red florals, "HB Quimper," pr **150.00**
Egg Cup, 4½" h
  Peasant man, red and blue dashes, yellow ground, "Henriot Quimper, France" **35.00**
  Peasant woman, florals, grayish ground, ribbed center, "HB Quimper France" **60.00**
Egg Set, 8" d, flower handle stand on three feet, six egg cups, multicolored florals, "Lion-Sur-Mer Normandie" . **275.00**
Figure
  3¼" h, St. Anne, soft multicolors, title, sq base, "Henriot Quimper, France" **65.00**
  4" h, peasant woman, kneeling before chicken and egg basket, multicolored, "Henriot Quimper, France" **125.00**
  8" h
  Girl, seated, blue and violet dress, c1925, "HB Quimper" **225.00**
  Young girl, yellow dress, red and blue dots, sgd "B. Savigny," "HB Quimper" **550.00**
  13" h
  Dancing couple, native dress, blue, cream, and black, sgd "R. Micheau-Vernez" **200.00**
  St. Jean, holding book and lamb, multicolored, "HB Quimper" .. **325.00**
  13½" h, Deco style dancing peasant couple, dark blue costumes, light blue and white trim, "Kopoll AP Seizennou" on front, "R. Micheau-Vernez, Henriot Quimper" (A) ... **180.00**
Ginger Jar, 11" h, multicolored florals, bird finial, "HR" **275.00**
Inkstand
  4" w, seated peasant woman, basket, molded scroll front projections, dbl covd wells, "Henriot Quimper" .. **225.00**
  7" w, peasant man, horn, dbl wells, pen tray, "Henriot Quimper" **210.00**
Inkwell
  4" l, star shape, yellow ground, multicolored florals, "Henriot Quimper, France" **140.00**
  4" l, 3" h, figural, pig, yellow ground, green spots, brown ears, and snout, "HB Quimper" **85.00**
Figural
  Breton hat, blue, yellow, and green, seated peasant woman, "Henriot Quimper" **175.00**
  Star shape, seated peasant woman holding basket, blue, yellow, and rust florals, blue "Henriot Quimper, France" **75.00**

Left, mug, 6" h, multicolored, white ground, "Henriot Quimper, France," $110.00; center, vase, 9½" h, multicolored, white ground, "HR Quimper" on front, $225.00; right, jardiniere, 9" l, 6" h, red, blue, and yellow, "HB Quimper, France," $175.00.

Knife Rest, 3½" l
  Peasant woman, florals, multicolored, "AP" **100.00**
  Peasants, male on one, female on other, red, blue, and green florals, and trim, pr **65.00**
Lamp, 8½" h, modeled lady holding umbrella, green dress, yellow apron, green base, sgd "Porson," "HB Quimper, France" **400.00**
Letter Rack, 8" l, four vertical compartments, peasant decor, "HB Quimper" **325.00**
Menu Holder
  3" h, fan shape, blue fleur-de-lis design, "HB Quimper" **185.00**
  3½" h, figural, fleur-de-lis, female peasant, "HR" **185.00**
  7" h, man on front with basket, grayish ground, "Lisieux" on front, "Porquier-Beau, Normandie" **300.00**
Mug, 2½" h, peasant woman, florals, "HR" **120.00**
Mustard Jar, 3" d, multicolored florals, notched ends, "Henriot Quimper, France" **50.00**
Pin Tray, 6" l, multicolored flowers and ribbons, white ground, "HB Quimper" **75.00**
Pipe, 6" l, bowl with peasant woman holding spindle, stem with and blue S-link and brush strokes, "HR Qumiper" **375.00**
Pitcher
  2½" h, figural, peasant woman, dark colors **65.00**
  5" h, peasant woman, cobalt trim, sponged handle **65.00**
  7½" h, peasant woman, florals, crimped spout, "Henriot Quimper" **185.00**
  9½" h, portrait of peasant woman, "HB Quimper, Odetta" (A) **35.00**
Planter, 16" h, Hanging, Quimper coat of arms, peasant scene, multicolored, made for corner, "Porquier-Beau" .. **775.00**
Plaque, 2½" w, 9¾" h, seated peasant woman, florals, "Porquier-Beau" ... **850.00**
Plate
  4" d
    Center peasant woman, lobed rim, red, yellow, and blue, "HB Quimper, France" **30.00**
    Center peasant woman, multicolored, blue and yellow banded border, "HB Quimper" **20.00**
  6" d, center daisy-like flowers, multicolored, blue sponged border, "Henriot Quimper" **20.00**
  6½" d, floral sprigs, blue border, pale gray ground, club shape **100.00**
  6¾" d, portraits of male and female peasant, sunbursts, "Henriot

Quimper, France," pr **160.00**
  7½" d, male peasant and female peasant, "St. Anne" inscribed beneath, "HR," pr **300.00**
  8" d
    Black bust of Brittany woman, Art Deco style, beige ground, "Odetta" **275.00**
    Cobalt rooster, rust and green florals, yellow ground, "HB Quimper, France" **70.00**
  9¾" d
    Center of Brittany characters, multicolored, French titles, yellow borders, green leaves, irreg scalloped edges, green "Q," set of 4 .... **200.00**
    Peasant woman, florals, blue and yellow border banding, "Henriot Quimper, France" **100.00**
    Relief portraits of male and female peasants, "Henriot Quimper, France," pr **200.00**
Platter
  9" l, peasant woman, florals, scalloped edge, "Henriot Quimper, France" **40.00**
  14½" l, center peasant man, yellow ground, "HB Quimper" **150.00**
Porringer, 7" w, peasant woman, blue and red florals and dashes, "HB Quimper, France" **130.00**
Quintal
  3¾" h, peasant woman, seated, white ground, "Henriot Quimper, France" **110.00**
  6" h
    Peasant man, flowers and leaves, "HB Quimper" **100.00**
    Peasant woman, egg basket, "Henriot Quimper, France" **100.00**
  6½" h, rooster and flowers, multicolored, white ground, "HB Quimper" **150.00**
Salt, two swans, center ring, blue sponged ext., peasant and floral int., "Henriot Quimper, France" **50.00**
Salt, Dbl, 3½" h, figural, cat, multicolored, sponged, "HB Quimper" **150.00**
Sardine Box, undertray, peasant man, florals, "Henriot Quimper" **300.00**
Sauceboat, 7½" l, 4" h, florals, yellow ground, center handle, "Henriot Quimper" **80.00**
Shaving Bowl, 12" l, blue rooster, white ground, "HB Quimper" **375.00**
Snuff Bottle, 3" h, multicolored cock on front, peasant woman on reverse, "HR" **350.00**
Soup Plate, 8½" d, multicolored floral center, ribbed blue edge **200.00**

Tea Service, teapot, creamer, sugar, four cups and saucers, peasant man and woman, blue and red florals, green ground, "Henriot Quimper" **900.00**

Trivet, 9" sq, florals, white ground, ftd **135.00**

Tureen, Cov, 16" h, peasant man on base, woman on cover, "HR Quimper" **500.00**

Urns, 13½" h, sunburst, swirl, and floral designs, "Henriot Quimper, France," pr **575.00**

Vase

2½" h, seated peasant man playing pipe, florals, multicolored, "Henriot Quimper, France" **100.00**

3" h, 5" d, emb peasant man and woman, pastel colors, sgd "Sevellec" **150.00**

3½" h, portrait of peasant woman, sunburst, dbl handles, "Henriot Quimper, France" **65.00**

5" h, peasant woman, sunburst, multicolored, "Henriot Quimper, France" **100.00**

8" h

Peasant woman, typical colors, corset shape, "HR Quimper" .. **300.00**

Peasant man, florals, white ground,"HB Quimper" **65.00**

10" h, seated woman holding distaff, molded ribbons and shells, bagpipe shape, molded pipe forms handle, c1900, "HB Quimper" **500.00**

10½" h, brown, tan, and cream portraits of male and female peasants, looping dbl handles, pr **300.00**

12" h, man playing horn on one, woman with cup on other, florals on reverse, fleur-de-lis shape, c1930, "HB Quimper," pr **650.00**

12" h, seated peasant woman, basket, open florals on back, bulbous body, narrow neck, "Henriot Quimper, France" **350.00**

15" h, multicolored native flowers, ewer shape, "Henriot Quimper" . **65.00**

Vegetable Bowl, 9" l, Cov, peasant woman, florals on yellow ground, "Henriot Quimper, France" **150.00**

Vegetable Dish, 8½" d, lime green and magenta radiating center star, ext. blue band, "HB Quimper, France" . **75.00**

Wall Pocket

4½" h, male and female peasants, blue and red florals, "Henriot Quimper, France," pr **150.00**

7" h, figural, bagpipe, female peasant, "Henriot Quimper" **110.00**

7¾" l, male and female peasant, floral designs, "HR," pr **365.00**

RIDGWAY

Shelton, Staffordshire, England
c1808 to 1855

History: Job Ridgway trained at the Swansea and Leeds potteries. In 1808 he took John and William, his two sons, into partnership at his Cauldon Place Works at Shelton. At first the company only made pottery. Later porcelains were added to supplement the earthenware line.

The early porcelain pieces usually were unmarked. A few pieces done before Job Ridgway's death in 1813 are impressed "Ridgway & Sons." After 1813 the two brothers separated. John retained the Cauldon Place factory and made porcelains. William produced earthenwares at the Bell Works.

John Ridgway specialized in the production of fine porcelain tablewares, mostly tea and dessert services. He was appointed potter to Queen Victoria. Very few ornamental pieces were made. Most pieces remained unmarked. Hence, his wares often are attributed to other factories by scholars and collectors.

William Ridgway expanded the scope of his operation until he eventually owned six factories at Hanley and Shelton. Their principal production was utilitarian earthenwares, with a tinted bluish-mauve body. The earthenware products that were made between 1830 and 1845 had no mark, only a painted pattern number.

After 1856 there were a series of different partnerships with varying names. By 1862 the porcelain division of Cauldon was carried on by Coalport China Ltd.

The Ridgways used a distinctive system of pattern numbering, which is explained in G. Godden's *British Porcelain*.

References: G. A. Godden, *The Illustrated Guide to Ridgway Porcelains*, Barrie & Jenkins, 1972.

Museums: Cincinnati Art Museum, Cincinnati, Ohio; Potsdam Public Museum, Potsdam, N.Y.

Basin, 14″ d, "Palestine Ware," transfer printed (A) **100.00**

Bone Dish, yellow and orange vases .. **15.00**

Bowl

9½″ d, "Dog Rose" pattern, flowing blue, round scalloped edge, c1905 **60.00**

10″ d, "Coaching Days-Eloped," silver rim **65.00**

12″ H-H, "Indus" pattern, brown and orange, "Ridgway" **35.00**

12¾″ d, painted, flower sprays in gilt scroll and foliage surrounds enclosing mushroom colored border, c1840 .... **175.00**

Box

5¼″ l, 3¾″ w, "Coaching Days-A Breakdown Taking on the Mails," black transfer, caramel ground ... **65.00**

5½″ l, 4¼″ w, "Coaching Days," black transfer, caramel ground ... **110.00**

Cheese Dish

9″ d, "Desby" pattern, Imari colors (A) **50.00**

12¾″ l, Cov, "Lahore," floral pattern, orange, cobalt, gold, and peach, cobalt handle **135.00**

Coffee Cup and Saucer, painted floral sprigs **25.00**

Compote 13½″ w, printed and painted specimen flower, turquoise, light yellow and gilt foliage molded border, c1810, pattern #3510 (A) **150.00**

Cup and Saucer

Gold flower sprays, yellow and gilt borders, "Old English" shape, pattern #2/1150, set of 6 (A) **85.00**

Green transfer, children at play, c1830's **85.00**

Light gray band, white ground, florals and gold trim, footed cup, c1837, "John Ridgway" **50.00**

Dessert Service

12 pcs, eight 9¼″ d plates, four dishes, central spray of multicolored flowers, light green borders with shaped gilt rims, c1840, "John Ridgway" (A) **440.00**

21 pcs, footed compote, four leaf shape dishes, oval dish, rect dish, fourteen plates, green, puce, black, and white enameled florals, light blue ground, c1840 .... **950.00**

23 pcs, two cov tureens, undertrays, twelve sq handled dishes, four diamond shape dishes, oval dish, painted center scenes of castles in landscapes, blue ground borders, gilt flowers, c1820-25 (A) **1,600.00**

Dinner Service

27 pcs, cov soup tureen, meat dish, twelve dinner plates and soup plates, pattern #5853, printed and

painted flower sprays, white ground, "Royal Arms" mark **150.00**

44 pcs, Stone China, painted blue, enameled, and gilt Oriental garden with sprays (A) **925.00**

105 pcs, pattern #1542, painted scattered florals and butterflies, magenta borders outlined with scrolls, shaped rims, molded flowerheads, c1830 (A) **9,350.00**

Dish

10¼″ d, Oriental scenes, blue ground, pr **50.00**

11″ sq, blue molded flowers and scrollwork, dbl handles, pr (A) ... **20.00**

Jug

4½″ d, 5″ h, "Coaching Days," black transfer, caramel ground, bulbous shape **50.00**

5″ h, soft paste, white griffins and cherubs, brown body, mask spout **150.00**

Meat Dish, 21¼″ l, Stone China, blue printed Oriental foliage, vases, and fence pattern **25.00**

Mug

4″ h, "Coaching Days," black transfer, caramel ground **30.00**

5″ h, "Coaching Days," rust colors, copper trim **60.00**

Pitcher

4½″ h, "Coaching Days," black transfer, caramel ground **65.00**

6″ h, tavern scene, mustard, c1835 . **65.00**

6½″ h, raised lions, antelopes, and other animals, hound handle, dated Oct 1, 1835, "W. Ridgway & Sons, Henley, England" **125.00**

8¾″ h, molded, light gray, jousting knights, dated Sept. 1, 1840 ..... **150.00**

10″ h, salt glaze, raised scenes of Burns' poems, "Ridgway & Company, the design published Oct 1, 1835" (A) **225.00**

12¼″ h, "Coaching Days," black transfer, caramel ground, tankard shape **150.00**

Plate

6¾″ d, "Coaching Days-Racing the Mail," light green **15.00**

7½″ d, "Columbian Star" pattern, gray transfer, imp "John Ridgway" (A) **25.00**

8″ d

"Angel Rose" pattern **10.00**

Earthenware, pattern #580, painted overall fruit and foliage, white ground, brown wavy rims, set of 9 .... **200.00**

10¼″ d, "Indus" pattern, black transfer, "Ridgway, Sparks & Ridgway" **25.00**

10½″ d, "London Cries," muffin man, sgd "A. J. Wilkerson" **15.00**

Left, tile, 6⅛" d, "Coaching Days - The Broken Trace," black transfer, caramel ground, silver luster rim, $70.00; center, dinner service, serving tray, 11½" l, 9½" w, four double handled servers, fourteen 9" d plates, multicolored florals, pale blue ground, dark blue and gilt handles, c1840, $2,850.00; right, pitcher, 7½" h, blue Oriental scene, c1814–30, "John & William Ridgway," $125.00.

12½" d, "Tyrolean" pattern **75.00**

Platter

10⅜" l, three birds over Oriental garden, four multicolored floral
sprays, orange luster edged rim, octagonal, c1825, green "Royal Arms
& Stone China" mark (A) **65.00**

13" l, "Oriental" pattern, blue transfer **55.00**

14" l, "Lynton" pattern **35.00**

15" l, country scene, red transfer,
"Ridgway" (A) **50.00**

19" l, 15¾" w, "Boston & Bunkers
Hill," blue transfer, c1844, "Wm
Ridgway, Hanley" **165.00**

20½" l, "Chinese Garden" pattern,
blue, green, and rose, c1830 . . . . **500.00**

Sauceboat, 6¾" l, matching stand,
blue, red, green, and gilt Oriental
style flowers and paneled borders,
c1835, "John Ridgway, Imperial Iron-
stone China" (A) **175.00**

Soup Plate

9" d, "Marmora" pattern, brown
transfer, "W. R. & Co." **25.00**

10" d

Blue and white florals, floral border, scalloped edge, c1830, un-
marked **30.00**

"Occidental" pattern, dark blue
transfer **80.00**

10¼" d

Central coat of arms, claret, blue
borders, gilt scrollwork and radiating lines, scalloped rims, pr **105.00**

Central coat of arms, claret ground,
blue strapwork and gilt scrolls
border, c1850, pr (A) **225.00**

Soup Tureen

13½" l, "Indus" pattern, black transfer, "Ridgway, Sparks & Ridgway" **135.00**

12¾" w, cov, Stone china, florals and
butterflies in panels, blue transfer,
enamels, scroll handles, floral
knob, orange luster rim, c1825-30,
"JWR" **500.00**

Ironstone, matching stand, Japan pattern, stylized flowers and foliage,
"Royal Arms" **60.00**

Stand 7⅞" d, dark blue and gold flowers
(A) **15.00**

Tea and Coffee Service

32 pcs, pattern #2/1005, teapot, milk
jug, cov sugar bowl, waste bowl,
two bread and butter plates, eight
teacups, coffee cups, and saucers,
light blue and iron-red flowers in
shaped blue borders, gilt foliage,
c1825 . . . . **700.00**

32 pcs, pattern #2/1056, painted Japan style, gilt foliage and vase on
rockwork, "A. J. & W. Ridgway"
(A) **565.00**

52 pcs, pattern #4038, teapot and
stand, milk jug, cov sugar bowl,
waste bowl, two dishes, fifteen teacups, coffee cups, and saucers, Japan style, flowering rockwork, yel-
low, blue and gilt borders **275.00**

Teapot, 4¾" h, molded formal and
fluted borders, mid 19th C (A) **30.00**

Tray, 12½" d, Pickwick Series, "Mr.
Pickwick at the Election," black transfer, caramel ground, silver scalloped
edge **100.00**

Vase

6" h, porcelain, painted garden flowers in gilt octagonal cartouches reserved on blue ground, apricot
band on lower sections, gilt foliage,
gilt serpent handles, campana
shape, c1820, pr (A) **500.00**

9⅞" h, scroll panel printed with Oriental emblems reserved on green
ground, dbl handles **60.00**

10" h, narrow neck, gold bands, open
blue iris on bottom portion **75.00**

Vegetable Bowl

9½" d, "Oriental" pattern **40.00**

11" l, "Indus" pattern, black transfer,
"Ridgway, Sparks & Ridgway" . . . **45.00**

Rockingham Works Brameld

ROCKINGHAM

Swinton, South Yorkshire, England
Pottery 1745 to 1842
Porcelain 1826 to 1842

History: The Rockingham factory was located on the estate of Earl Fitzwilliam, Marquis of Rockingham, near Swinton in Yorkshire. The first pottery was manufactured in 1745. The factory continued production under various owners who concentrated on brown and yellow wares, blue and white dinner, tea and coffee services, and white earthenwares. In 1806 John and William Brameld took over the business and used the name "Brameld Co." They made pottery from 1806 to 1842.

Brown ware is the best known variety of Rockingham pottery. Its common forms include teapots, coffeepots, jugs, and cadogans (a pot from which liquid will not spill). The thickly applied glaze was intense and vivid purple brown when fired. The interior of pieces was often left white. Sometimes the brown exterior was decorated with gilding, enamel colors, or classical figures in relief. During the 19th century many companies copied the "Rockingham" glaze of a rich brown stained with manganese and iron.

The Bramelds introduced porcelain porduction in 1826. Rockingham bone china porcelain has a glaze somewhat prone to fine crazing. During the next sixteen years, until 1842, many ornamental wares and some utilitarian wares were made. Rockingham tea and coffee services with both simple and ornate decoration remained a mainstay of production. The company also manufactured animal groups featuring dogs, cats, squirrels, rabbits, hares, deer, or sheep. Vases, ewers, baskets, scent bottles, candlesticks, desk pieces, trays and pieces for the dressing table constituted the principal ornamental forms.

The red griffin mark was used from 1826 to 1830 and the puce griffin mark from 1831 to 1842.

References: Alwyn Cox & Angela Cox, *Rockingham Pottery & Porcelain 1745–1842*, Faber & Faber, 1983; Arthur A. Eaglestone & Terence A. Lockett, *The Rockingham Pottery*, David & Charles, 1973, rev. ed.; D. G. Rice, *Ornamental Rockingham Porcelain*, Adam, 1965; D. G. Rice, *Rockingham Pottery and Porcelain*, Barrie & Jenkins, 1971.

Museums: City Museum, Weston Park, Sheffield, England; Clifton Park Museum, Rotherham, England; Rotherham Museum, Rotherham; Victoria & Albert Museum, London; Yorkshire Museum, York.

REPRODUCTION ALERT: Rockingham brown glaze was copied extensively throughout the 19th century by many factories.

Figure, 4″ h, puce and green florals, iron-red and gold trim, (A) $100.00.

Bottles, 16¾″ h, applied green vines, large and small pastel blossoms, painted birds and vines, drilled and fitted as lamps, c1825, pr (A) **1,320.00**

Bust, white bisque, circ socle
  7″ h
    Duke of York, wearing tunic, and embroidered collar, c1826-30 (A) **215.00**
    William IV, wearing tunic, c1830 (A) **400.00**
  10¼″ h, William Wordsworth, c1828 (A) **350.00**

Candlesticks, 10¼″ h, "Pillar," baluster stems, molded leaves, scrollwork, gilt accents, applied multicolored florals, puce "griffin" and "Rockingham Works, Brameld," marks, pr **675.00**

Coffee Can and Saucer, cup reserved with octagonal panel of painted fruit on white marble table, reverse with fruiting cherry branch, white ground, gold banded borders, red "griffin" and "Rockingham Works, Brameld" **275.00**

Cream Jug, 3¾″ h, neo-rococo style, blue, yellow, gold, pattern #835 (A) **85.00**

Cup and Saucer
  Blue bands, gilt border, saucer with painted flower, scalloped edges, pattern #665 (A) **35.00**
  Cup with wide matte blue and gold border, painted primrose on saucer, "Etruscan" shape, red "griffin" mark **35.00**

Figure
  4″ h, shepherdess, feeding lamb from

bowl, foliage filled hat at feet, imp
"Rockingham Works Brameld" (A) **315.00**
7¾" h, griffins, outstretched gilt lined
wings, perched on rockwork base
applied moss on shaped sq bases,
c1830, pr (A) **130.00**
Honey Pot, 3⅞" h, cov, attached stand,
blue printed bands, "Blackberry" pattern, gilt edge **135.00**
Muffin Dish, 9¼" d, cov, painted landscape vignette, gilt oak branch bor-
der, gilt line rims, c1826 (A) **532.00**
Pastille Burner
6" h, "Toll House," octagonal shape,
flower encrusted, 1820 .... **350.00**
6½" h, cottage, outlined in applied
flowers, c1830 .... **350.00**
Plate
8¼" d, rose designs, apple-green borders, c1820, pr (A) **90.00**
8⅞" d, painted, named views of
"Swinton Church From the West"
and "Woodnook, Wentworth Park,
Yorkshire," gilt oak branch borders,
gilt rims, c1820, pr (A) **2,425.00**
9" d, painted "Scotch Thistle and
Pheasant's Eye," molded anthemion
and gadrooned border, c1835,
puce "griffin" mark (A) **350.00**
9⅜" d, painted and printed lilies and
morning glory, shaped molded border, gilt band, c1830, iron-red
"griffin," "Rockingham, Works
Brameld" **75.00**
Pot, 5¾" h, peach shape, raised berries,
leaves, and flowers, brown glaze, imp
"Brameld" **55.00**
Scent Bottle, 5⅜" h, multicolored encrusted flowers, puce "griffin" mark **325.00**
Scent Sprinkler, 4⅜" h, coffeepot shape,
modeled flowers, lilac ground, dbl
twisted lug handle (A) **320.00**
Tea and Coffee Service
35 pcs, 7" h, teapot, milk jug, cov
sugar bowl, two cake plates, plate,
nine teacups, six coffee cups, ten
saucers, blue borders edged with
gilt foliate scrolls and sprays,
c1830-40 (A) **715.00**
20 pcs, teapot, milk jug, slop bowl,
five teabowls, coffee cups, and saucers, molded primroses, painted
flowers on int., c1826-30 (A) **800.00**
Tea Service, teapot, stand, jug, cov
sugar bowl, waste bowl, two cake
plates, five teacups, two saucers, dark
blue bands, gilt foliage, molded basketweave ground, twig finials, pattern
#779 .... **475.00**
Teapot
7½" h, gray and gilt foliage and straw-

berries, 3-spur handle, coronet finial, pattern #1224 (A) **140.00**
7⅝" h, neo-rococo style, gray and gilt
berried foliage, flower finial, spur
handle, pattern #1451 .... **75.00**
Vase
4" h, molded open tulips on bases,
applied leaves and buds, c1820, pr
(A) **515.00**
4⅛" h, rect gilt edged panel, painted
flower sprays reserved on blue
ground **75.00**
4¾" h, painted landscape, white
ground, cylindrical, overhanging
lip **100.00**
6" h, molded open tulip, puce outlines, molded applied leaves and
moss on base, c1820 (A) **260.00**

RORSTRAND

Near Stockholm, Sweden
1726 to Present

History: Rorstrand, established in 1726 near
Stockholm, is the oldest porcelain factory in Sweden. Although formed for the production of tin-
glazed earthenware, porcelain was the ultimate
aim of the founder. A succession of German managers directed the production during the early
years. The company made little impact on the
ceramic world.

When Anders Fahlstrom became manager in
1740, the company began to flourish. Elias Ing-
man assumed control in 1753. The company
immediately undertook to imitate the successful
Sevres and Meissen wares. The company continued to prosper. Rorstrand absorbed the rival Marieberg factory in 1782.

Bengt Jeijer became manager in 1798. In the
early 1800s the fortunes of Rorstrand were altered by two major events - the introduction and
popularity of Wedgwood's creamware and the
ban on the exportation of English clay. Rorstrand
tottered on the brink of bankruptcy. Eventually
the clay ban was relaxed and workers from Stoke-
on-Trent were imported. Rorstrand's products
now had a finer clay body and strong English
influence.

In the mid-1870s a limited company was
formed. Production flourished due to the infusion
of the fresh ideas of talented Scandinavian artists
employed at the factory. Between 1895 and 1914

Rorstrand's art director and designer was Alf Wallander. He produced a wide range of tablewares and decorative pieces in the Art Nouveau style using delicate, sculptural modeling of figures and flowers, often in deep relief. Tonal qualities included delicate greens, pinks, and violets on a grayish off-white background. Wallander also used pale flower decorations contrasted with black grounds.

Following World War II, the entire factory was moved to the port city of Gothenburg, its present location.

The company has used the mark of three crowns of Marieberg with "RORSTRAND" since 1884.

Bud Vase, 4¾" h, black rings on sea-green ground, sea-green int., $875.00.

Beaker, 4½" h, sculptured pink and gray flowers, gray leaves **275.00**
Ewer, 20" h, molded coat of arms, majolica glazes, discoid shape **100.00**
Farmer Cup, 5¾" h, multicolored man and woman, native costumes, white ground **75.00**
Figure, 8" h, dwarf, kneeling, horn of plenty on back, ivory coloring **135.00**
Goblet, 15¾" h, cov, Renaissance style, multicolored glazes, putti finials, dated 1872, pr (A) **70.00**
Tankard, 7" h, multicolored peasant scene in oval medallion, white ground **65.00**
Urn, 24" h, cov, majolica, turquoise fish scale ground, mauve accents, masks on front and back, gargoyle handles, gilt outline **300.00**
Vase
  7" h, carved dragonflies, bodies forming handles, blue and pink, white ground, sgd "M. A." **650.00**
  8⅝" h, raised stringrays, tails forming handles, waves at base, muted blue, pink, and green glaze, off-white ground (A) **100.00**
  9" h, Art Nouveau style, pierced and raised design **250.00**
  9¾" h, poppy molded (A) **115.00**

ROSENTHAL

Selb, Bavaria, West Germany
1879 to Present

History: The Rosenthal factory was located in Selb, Bavaria. Philip Rosenthal started initially by purchasing whiteware from Selb's other potter, Lorenz Heutschenreuther, decorating it, and selling it from house to house. Rosenthal established his own factory in 1879.

The factory flourished, providing quality figurals and tableware that were decorated tastefully. Simplicity of designs and high quality workmanship made Rosenthal a household word.

Several additional factories were constructed and production rose steadily. Designers of dinnerwares included Theodor Karner, Karl Himmelstoss, Ferdinand Liebermann, Philip Rosenthal, and Walter Gropius. "Darmstadt," "Donatello," and "Isolde" originally were produced in plain white between 1904 and 1910. Later heart-shaped motifs in the Art Nouveau manner were added to "Darmstadt." "Donatello" was decorated with underglaze pate-sur-pate, painted cherries, or a geometric pattern.

Figures made during the 1920s and 1930s were shaped and decorated in the Art Deco style. Many were signed by the artists. Following World War II, most of Rosenthal's assets were destroyed or outmoded. Sources for raw materials, mainly from the Eastern bloc countries, were terminated.

Philip Rosenthal II assumed control, formed Rosenthal Porzellan AG, and began the restoration of the works. Many of the older designs, except for "Maria Weiss," "Moss Rose," "Sans Souci," and "Pompadour" were abandoned in favor of fresh ideas originated by designers familiar with the modern tastes, among whom were Tapio Wirkkala from Finland, Jean Cocteau from France, and Bela Bechem from Germany.

The U.S. market was the major goal. Raymond Loewy was hired to design medium priced dinnerware for the American market. Under Philip's supervision, Rosenthal regained its prestigious position and flourishes today.

Bowl
  5¼" d, black basalt, emb floral design, (A) **20.00**

9" d
Hp clusters of cherries on green
ext., gold trim, dbl handles, artist
sgd 85.00
Red and yellow floral center, red
plumed border, reticulated rim
cartouches, three feet 35.00
13" l, 8¾" w, scrolled body, Delft type
design, "Delft-Savoy-Germany" .. 150.00
Cake Plate
10" d, portrait of Mercury, violet
ground, gold trim 50.00
11" d, center light and dark blue bust
of Rembrandt 55.00
Charger, 15" d, blue and white Dutch
scene 155.00
Coffee Set, coffeepot, creamer, cov
sugar bowl, "Classic Rose" pattern . 125.00
Cream Soup and Saucer, "Empire Blue
Wreath" pattern 30.00
Cup and Saucer
"Antoinette" pattern 10.00
"Empress Flower" design, relief de-
sign 25.00
Red berries and leaves 15.00
Demitasse Cup and Saucer
Medallion portrait 45.00
"Moss Rose" pattern 20.00
Egg Cup, white glaze finish 15.00

Figure, 8½" h, $125.00.

Figure
1½" l, 2¾" h, moth on pine cone .. 30.00
2½" l
Butterfly, peacock eyes on wings,
multicolored (A) 60.00
Lizard, natural colors 40.00
Turtle, swimming position, natural
colors 45.00
3¼" l, Art Deco style, snail on base,
multicolored, sgd "Caasmann" ... 150.00
5" h, seated clown and woman, period clothes (A) 50.00
5¼" h, young girl kissing baby chick 90.00

5¼" l, reclining cat, yellow eyes, sgd
"Heidenreich" 150.00
6" h, dancer, enameled brocade skirt,
gold luster 225.00
6" l, Pouter pigeon 100.00
6" l, 4" h, bulldog, black and white
spots 100.00
6½" h, child holding flowers, spotted
fawn standing in front, sgd "Lote" 225.00
7" h
Blackamoors, multicolored, sgd
"H. Meisel," pr 275.00
Dachshund, standing on hind
legs, natural colors 150.00
8" h, street musician, dog (A) 40.00
8" l, 6" h, pointer, black and white . 125.00
8¼" h, harem dancer, arms extended,
irid skirt 325.00
8½" h, princess, bending over frog,
natural colors 235.00
8½" l, 9" h, poodle, standing, white,
green collar, #1163 .... 235.00
9" l, 5½" h, springer spaniel, bird in
mouth, brown marks, white ground 135.00
10 ⅝" h, kissing couple, modeled as
nude woman seated on draped
plinth, man standing behind, sgd
"Richard Aigner Munchen,"
c1920, "Rosenthal Selb Bavaria"
(A) 520.00
11⅝" l, "Pierrot," reclining, white
costume, multicolored accents,
c1920, sgd "C. Holzer Defanti,"
"Rosenthal Selb Bavaria" (A) 625.00
18 ⅞" h, nude girl, riding striding ostrich, gray and flesh tones, white,
c1902, sgd "Ferd. Liebermann,"
"Rosenthal Selb Bavaria" (A) 2,100.00
Owl, natural colors, shaped stepped
base, "Rosenthal Kunst-Abteilung"
(A) 210.00
Nubian, playing mandolin, white ... 150.00
Fruit Bowl, 12" d, ivory poppies, orange
ground, scalloped rim, footed 100.00
Gravy Boat and Tray, "Aida" pattern,
gold laced, c1920 .... 30.00
Hatpin Holder, 5½" h, figural, stylized
bust 30.00
Lamp, 14" h, shaded pink to mauve,
matching parchment shade, "Rosen-
thal-Selb, Bavaria" 50.00
Mug, 4¾" h, hp red cherries, leaves,
and vines, shaded green ground 65.00
Plate
4" d, white glaze finish, sterling silver
rim 10.00
5¾" d, hp, pink flowers, bold rim,
pierced for hanging 15.00
9" d, "Versailles" pattern 25.00
10" d
Bust of young woman, multicolored, cobalt rim with gold tracery 100.00

"Empress Flower" design 25.00
Portrait of young woman, long, curly hair, dark green to pale yellow ground, gold tracery, "Malmaison-Bavaria" 70.00
10 ¾" d, white with wide tooled gold border, c1920 .... 100.00
11" d
  Center flowered urns, ornate teal blue scrollwork, gold banding, set of 8 .... 150.00
  "Ivory" pattern-gold florals 35.00
Platter
  11¾" l, pink roses, blue and gold border 25.00
  15¼" l, "Winifred" pattern, blue and white long stemmed flowers 20.00
  18" l, 13" w, two fish and snails in center, cream ground, gold trim .. 50.00
Serving Dish, 12" d, hp, multicolored, blackberries and blossoms, shaped edge, molded open handle 100.00
Soup Plate, 9¾" d, "Louis XIV" pattern, white 25.00
Tea Service, "Magic Flute" pattern, white ground, broad gold border, figures in relief, set of 27 .... 425.00
Urn, 10½", cov
  Center bust of woman, native dress, dbl vert handles 185.00
  Portrait of woman in garden, multicolored 240.00
Vase
  3" h, seashell style, white satin finish, free form 35.00
  4½" h, bud, white porcelain, slender stalks and leaf bases, pr (A) 10.00
  8" h, blue and white Dutch scene .. 80.00
  9½" h, multicolored floral design, tulip shape, dbl handles, sgd "Walter" 150.00

ROYAL AUSTRIA

Altrohlau, Bohemia, now Czechoslovakia
1889 to Present

History: In 1899 Oscar Gutherz joined with Edgar Gutherz, the former manager of the New York and Rudolstadt Pottery, to manufacture household, table, and decorative porcelains, mainly for export to the United States. The mark used was "O & EG" and "Royal Austria" until 1918.

The Austrian Porcelain Industry combine acquired the factory, named it Opiag, Branch Altrohlau, and operated it from 1918 until 1920. Between 1920 and 1945 the factory was called Epaig, Branch Altrohlau. It produced household and decorative porcelains, gift articles, and souvenir items. After World War II the company was nationalized.

Sherbet, 3" h, blue florals, gold trim, irid int., $12.00.

Bowl, 5" d, pine cone dec, sgd "Dodd" 30.00
Box, 3" d, 1½" h, cov, white glaze ... 25.00
Butter Pat, small blue flowers, white ground, set of 4 .... 15.00
Cake Plate, 10" d, overall multicolored floral pattern, gold edge 25.00
Cracker Jar, 9" h, "American Beauty" pattern, "O. & E. G., Royal Austria" 115.00
Creamer, green, gold trim 20.00
Creamer and Sugar
  Small pink roses, gold trim, hairline on rim 10.00
  Yellow flowers, light green ground, gold handles and trim 85.00
Dresser Set, cov oval box, band shaped ring tree, candlestick, 16" l scalloped edge tray, pink and rose florals, cream center, turquoise border 200.00
Game Set, platter, six plates, game birds in natural settings, multicolored 150.00
Plate
  7" d, branch of dogwood blossoms, cream ground, gold rim, "O. & E. G., Royal Austria" 15.00
  8¾" d, overall red and pink roses, green foliage, shaped gold rim, green "O. & E. G., Royal Austria" 35.00
  9" d, hp, oak leaves and acorns, gold trim 30.00
  10" d
    "Blue Onion" design 25.00
    Pink roses, gold border 15.00
Salt and Pepper Shakers, hp, roses, gold trim 20.00

ROYAL BAYREUTH

Tettau, Bavaria
1794 to Present

History: Wilheim Greiner and Johann Schmidt established a porcelain factory at Tettau in 1794. They also maintained an association with the Volkstedt and Kloster Veilsdorf factories in Thuringia. The factory survived numerous wars, financial difficulties, and many changes in ownership until a great fire in 1897 destroyed most of the molds and early records. A more modern factory was built and operated until World War I.

The company operated under the name Porcelain Factory Tettau from 1902 until 1957. In 1957 the company adopted the name, Royally Priviledged Porcelain Factory Tettau GMBH, which it still uses today.

Animal and floral forms along with other unusual figural shapes were made at Tettau between 1885 and World War I. Designs included fruits, vegetables, lobsters, tomatoes, and people. Shapes ranged from ashtrays to vegetable dishes. Individuals often bought them as souvenir and novelty items because of their inexpensive cost. Much of the production was exported.

Today the firm produces dinnerware and limited edition collectibles. The name, "Royal Bayreuth," is used in the United States to identify the company's products.

ROSE TAPESTRY

Rose tapestry, similar in texture to needlepoint tapestry and called "matte finish" china, was made in the late 19th century. Rose tapestry has a rough effect that feels like woven cloth. It was made by wrapping the article in coarse cloth and then firing. The cloth was consumed in the firing, and the tapestry effect remained.

Decoration was added over the glaze. It varied from floral to scenic to portrait. The floral motifs included "rose tapestry," the most popular and prevelant design. The roses shaded from a pale pink to deeper red colors.

Occasionally pale yellow or white roses were combined with the pink or red roses. Rose tapestry also can be found in an apricot and deep orange-gold shade. The rarest rose tapestry is "sterling silver." The roses are deep gray to a pale silver gray shaded into white.

The background of rose tapestry is off-white or has a grayish or greenish tinge. Pale green leaves and small, faintly tinted flowers complete the decoration.

Floral, scenic, and portrait tapestries were made in plates, pitchers, cups and saucers, vases, pin boxes, trays, bells, and many other shapes.

SUNBONNET BABIES

Molly and Mae, the Sunbonnet Babies, were created by Bertha L. Corbett, an American artist, in the early 1900s. Corbett had no confidence in her ability to draw faces so she hid them under the large bonnets. The Sunbonnet Babies were drawn to develop good character traits and teach children their daily chores, e.g., washing, ironing, sweeping, dusting, mending, baking, fishing, and going to church.

Variations identified as Beach Babies and Snow Babies also were made.

References: Joan & Marvin Raines, *A Guide to Royal Bayreuth Figurals,* privately printed, 1973; Joan & Marvin Raines, *A Guide to Royal Bayreuth Figurals,* Book 2, privately printed, 1977; Virginia & George Salley, *Royal Bayreuth China* privately printed, 1969.

BABIES

Beach Babies

Cake Plate, 9½" d, girl with dog	**150.00**
Creamer, 3" h	**65.00**
Planter, 3" h, ...	**100.00**
Vase, 3½" h, blue mark	**55.00**

Sand Babies

Creamer, blue mark	**75.00**
Inkwell, black mark	**400.00**
Vase, 3⅝" h, three handles, blue mark	**90.00**

Snow Babies

Creamer and Sugar, blue mark	**185.00**
Hair Receiver, 3½" h, three legs, blue mark	**135.00**
Mug, blue mark	**75.00**
Plate 8" d, sledding, blue mark	**110.00**

Sunbonnet Babies

Bell, washing and hanging, unmarked	**325.00**
Bowl, cereal, sweeping, blue mark ...	**150.00**
Box	
2½" l, 2" w, cleaning, blue mark ...	**175.00**
Cov, sweeping	**190.00**
Cake Plate, 10½" d, washing and hanging clothes, blue mark	**225.00**
Cake Set, 7 pcs	**650.00**
Candlestick, cleaning, hooded	**325.00**

Plate, 6½" d, Sunbonnet Babies, ironing, blue mark, $60.00.

Candy Dish
    5¼" l, sweeping, marked (A) **100.00**
    9½" l, fishing, scalloped rim, dbl han-
       dles, footed, blue mark **200.00**
Creamer
    2¾" h, washing windows and floors,
       blue mark **150.00**
    3¼" h, ironing, blue mark **155.00**
    4" h, hanging clothes, marked **135.00**
    5¼" h, ironing, marked (A) **100.00**
Creamer and Sugar **200.00**
Cup and Saucer, sweeping **165.00**
Ewer, 3⅜" h, gold handle **250.00**
Feeding Dish, 7½" d
    Fishing, blue mark **165.00**
    Scrubbing and washing, blue mark . **250.00**
Flower Cup, 3½" d, washing and hang-
    ing clothes, blue mark **200.00**
Milk Pitcher, washing and ironing **210.00**
Mug 3¼" h
    Ironing, blue mark **150.00**
    Sweeping **110.00**
Mush Set, cleaning and hanging, 3 pcs **310.00**
Nappy
    Sweeping **150.00**
    Washing and hanging **150.00**
Pitcher
    3¼" h, ironing, blue mark **110.00**
    3¾" h, sweeping, blue mark **185.00**
    4" h
       Fishing, blue mark **165.00**
       Washing and ironing, blue mark . **210.00**
Pitcher, 4½" h
    Scrubbing and washing windows,
       blue mark **210.00**
    Sewing, pinched spout, marked **175.00**
    Sweeping, blue mark **200.00**
Plate
    4½" d, sewing, clover leaf shape . . . **125.00**
    6" d, cleaning, marked **125.00**
    6¼" d, washing and hanging, blue
       mark **40.00**
    7½" d, Sewing **150.00**

Washing and hanging clothes, blue
    mark **135.00**
Rose Bowl, 3" h, washing and ironing,
    blue mark **190.00**
Salt and Pepper Shakers
    Sewing, blue mark **190.00**
    Washing and hanging clothes, blue
       mark **190.00**
Tea Tile, cleaning **120.00**

GENERAL

Ashtray
    Devil head, red **110.00**
    Equestrian scene, multicolored, blue
       mark **50.00**
    Two men, Tyrolean costumes, blue
       mark **65.00**
Basket, scene of man with donkey,
    multicolored, blue mark **175.00**
Berry Bowl, figural, grapes, lustered
    purple, unmarked **150.00**
Bowl
    7¾" d, 2½" h, poppy form, matching
       ladle, marked (A) **100.00**
    9½" d, two large cows and trees,
       shaded green ground **85.00**
    10¼" d, yellow and green blown-out
       flowers, white ground, center pink,
       white, and green florals, lavender
       and green ground, gold trim, blue
       mark **200.00**
    11" d, yellow and white roses, purple
       luster, pansy blown-out mold **225.00**
Box, Cov
    2½" w, narrow chain of pink and
       white flowers around upper sec-
       tion, gold border on lid, blue mark **70.00**
    3¾" w, fisherman in boat, multicol-
       ored, blue mark **50.00**
    Pink and white flowers, outlined in
       gold, blue mark **50.00**
Butter Dish, 2" h, "Candlemas" girl on
    cov, marked **50.00**
Cake Plate, poppy pearlized lavender
    and green shading, open handles,
    blue mark **200.00**
Candleholder, 3½" h, Devil & Cards . . **265.00**
Candlestick
    3" h, figural, elk, pr **200.00**
    4" h, "Little Bo Peep," marked **100.00**
    6" h, Britanny girls, multicolored
       marked **125.00**
Candy Dish, Devil & Cards **250.00**
Celery Tray, 12½" l, overall rose design,
    blue mark **110.00**
Chamberstick, 5" d
    Black and white wading birds, yellow
       ground, marked **140.00**
    "Jack & Jill," blue mark **75.00**
Chocolate Set
    Chocolate pot, four cups and saucers,

General, left, pitcher, 5″ h, multicolored fishing scene, green luster borders, gold handle, blue mark, $60.00; center, creamer and sugar, purple, blue marks, $250.00; right, candlestick, 6½″ h, gray, $600.00.

barnyard scenes, multicolored, marked 550.00

Chocolate pot, four cups, scene of boy and three donkeys, multicolored, wishbone handles, marked . 275.00

Cookie Jar, 7″ h, figural, poppy, bud handle on cov, dbl loop side handles, marked (A) 60.00

Creamer

Bell Ringer, blue mark 190.00
Butterfly design, multicolored, marked (A) 80.00
Forest scene, brown, green, and orange, pinched spout, blue mark .. 75.00
Girl with pitcher, red, marked 300.00
Multicolored scene, monkey and girl with jug, marked 225.00
St. Bernard, multicolored, unmarked 110.00

Figural

Apple, multicolored, marked 55.00
Bird of Paradise, multicolored, marked 175.00
Bull, black 150.00
Bull, brown, tan, and gray 165.00
Bull, red, blue mark 165.00
Cat, black, marked 115.00
Cat, green with brown accents, white cat handles, marked 170.00
Lobster, red, unmarked 50.00
Maple leaf, multicolored, blue mark 65.00
Moose head, brown shades, marked 65.00
Pig, multicolored, blue mark 250.00
Santa Claus 485.00
Seal, multicolored, blue mark 165.00
Strawberry, gold twist handle and daisy, unmarked 90.00

4″ h

Farmer and chickens, multicolored, blue mark 65.00
Devil & Cards, blue mark 155.00

4½″ h, cavalier, red, yellow, and brown tavern scene, sgd "Dixon," blue mark 85.00
4¾″ h, figural, crow, black, marked 90.00
6″ h, figural goat head, orange jacket, green pants and shoes, marked ... 75.00

Creamer and Sugar

Corinthian, black, marked 85.00
Devil & Cards, green mark 325.00

Figural

Poppies, white, lustered finish, open style mark 150.00
"Jack & the Beanstalk" and "Little Miss Muffet," blue mark 85.00

Cup and Saucer

Pear shape, leaves, blue mark 45.00
Poppy and leaf shape, marked (A) .. 40.00
Rose pink and yellow flowers, blue mark 225.00
White classic figures, black ground, green mark 45.00
Demitasse, Devil & Cards, marked ... 160.00
shape, loop handle, marked 15.00
5½″ d, pansy design, ring handle, blue mark 70.00
5¾″ l, 3⅜″ w, fishing scene, multicolored, rolled edge, handle 55.00
13½″ l, 5½″ w, oak leaf shape, pearlized finish, blue mark 100.00
"Little Bo Peep," maple leaf shape, blue mark 115.00

Dish, cov, pastoral scene, multicolored, marked 50.00
Dresser Tray, Devil & Cards 475.00

Ewer

4″ h, two hounds in water, stag in woods, shades of brown, green int., blue mark 60.00
4⅝″ h, roses, lavender, turquoise, and yellow shaded ground, gold trim, blue mark 45.00
6½″ h, swimming swan scene, multicolored, marked 85.00

Ferner, roses, lustered finish, four handles and feet, marked **125.00**

Figure

3½" h, baby goat on rocks, blue and white, #4760 .... **90.00**

Oxford-style shoe, tan, eyelets outlined, unmarked **85.00**

Hair Receiver

4" h, boy with donkey design, blue mark **145.00**

4½" h, lady with ducks, light yellow ground, marked **100.00**

Hp sheep scene, blue mark **60.00**

Hatpin Holder

5" h, figural, penguin, multicolored . **300.00**

Oyster and pearl, blue mark **260.00**

Humidor, Devil & Cards **550.00**

Jug, 8½" h, tusk shape, ice spout, heavy gold vines, leaves, and berries, ivory figural stag horn handle, c1885, green mark **185.00**

Loving Cup, 3¾" h, Corinthian, three handles, marked **55.00**

Match Holder

Devil & Cards **350.00**

Red clown **240.00**

Mustard Jar, cov, figural, lobster, handle, unmarked **50.00**

Milk Pitcher

Corinthian, marked **115.00**

Devil & Cards, 2nd issue **200.00**

Figural, lobster in red, marked **75.00**

Monkey, green, blue mark **435.00**

Nappy

4¼" d, cabbage leaf, handle, blue mark **35.00**

"Jack & Jill," verse on reverse, green and pink, heart shape, emb loop handle, marked **60.00**

Pin Tray, boy and donkey scene, multicolored, blue mark **60.00**

Pitcher

5½" h

Devil & Cards, marked **550.00**

Figural

Conch shell, red coral handle, unmarked **60.00**

Crocodile, blue jewel eyes **265.00**

Fish, multicolored, blue mark .. **200.00**

6" h

Cavalier, green tavern scene, sgd "Dixon," blue mark **125.00**

Scene of farmer and turkeys in mountains, blue mark **150.00**

6½" h, figural, cabbage, green and orange, marked **225.00**

6¾" h, rose design, gold trim, marked **85.00**

7" h

Devil & Cards (A) **300.00**

Musicians, multicolored, blue mark **160.00**

7¾" h, Devil & Cards, blue mark ... **370.00**

8" h, Corinthian, white figures, black ground, orange-pink throat, blue mark **130.00**

9" h, man, two horses in front of house, rust, green, and cream shades, flattened shape, marked .. **350.00**

Plate

5" d, dog and horses scene, multicolored, marked **60.00**

7½" d, yellow roses, light green ground, pierced rim, gold trim, marked **40.00**

8" d, Devil & Cards, octagonal **300.00**

10" d, lime green band edged in gold, white ground, marked (A) **10.00**

10½" d, boy sitting on log with three donkeys, green and brown, open dbl handles, blue mark **150.00**

Relish Dish, 7½" d, poinsettia design, marked **125.00**

Salt, Dutch scene, dbl with entwined handles, blue mark **150.00**

Sauce Dish, figural, grapes, yellow, marked **50.00**

Sugar Bowl

Devil & Cards **175.00**

Figural

Lobster, red, matching tray, marked **70.00**

Peasant women, house and clouds in background, banded blue sky, blue mark **50.00**

Poppy, red, marked **85.00**

Rose, yellow and pink, blue mark **175.00**

Tankard

5½" h, farmer, country setting, blue mark **125.00**

8" h, Arab and two horses, multicolored, blue mark **150.00**

Teapot

3½" h, rooster and hen design, multicolored, marked (A) **80.00**

7½" l, shell form **200.00**

Tray, 10" l, scene of cows in meadow in colors, blue mark **80.00**

Vase

3" h, hunting scene, multicolored, dbl handles, blue mark **50.00**

4½" h, Gibson girls busts on top, green ground, blue mark **80.00**

5" h, "The Hunt" scene, multicolored, dbl handles, marked **100.00**

5½" h, mountain goats scene, multicolored **100.00**

6" h, multicolored portrait of young girl, long black hair, large hat, ruffled dress, blue mark **150.00**

7" h, cows scene, wide center band, marked **250.00**

8½" h, Cavalier Musicians, multicolored, marked **125.00**

9" h, scene of castle, maidens swimming, multicolored, blue mark ... **80.00**

Wall Pocket
9½" h, foliate hanger, pointed pendant, marked (A) **150.00**
Figural, grapes, lustered purple color,
blue mark **250.00**
Water Pitcher, Devil & Cards, green
mark **380.00**

ROSE TAPESTRY

Ashtray, 5½" sq, three color flowers .. **165.00**
Basket, Rose
6½" l, 3¾" h, pink flowers, blue mark **300.00**
6¾" d, blue mark **325.00**
8" l, 4" w, marked **185.00**
Box
2¼" sq, pink flowers, blue mark ... **175.00**
3" d **165.00**
Cake Plate
10¼" d, three color flower, open dbl
handles, marked **425.00**
10½" d, pink flowers, marked **195.00**
Creamer
4½" h, gilt handle and edge, blue
mark **325.00**
4¾" h, marked **225.00**
Three color flowers, blue mark **115.00**

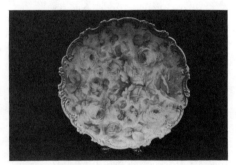

**Plate, 9½" d, three color roses, blue
mark, $180.00.**

Dish
5" d, three color flowers, clover
shape, handle, blue mark **130.00**
5½" d, yellow rose center, pink rose
border, leaf shape, marked **135.00**
10" l, gilt trim pierced handles, blue
mark **400.00**
Figure, shoe, blue mark **270.00**
Hair Receiver
Red and yellow roses, marked **200.00**
Two columns of roses, gold feet,
marked **200.00**
Yellow and pink flowers, three gold
feet, blue mark **175.00**
Picture Frame, 8" h, rect, oval opening,
blue mark **275.00**

Pitcher
3¾" h, three color flowers, marked . **95.00**
4" h, gilt rim, marked (A) **100.00**
Planter
2¾" h, dbl handles, blue mark **165.00**
3¼" d, 2¾" h, three color flowers,
liner, fluted rim, dbl gold handles,
blue mark **185.00**
Plate
5¾" d, marked **200.00**
7½" d, blue mark **175.00**
9½" d, gold border, blue mark **325.00**
Powder Box, three color flowers, ftd,
green mark **170.00**
Powder Jar, 4½" d, three gold feet, blue
mark **210.00**
Salt and Pepper Shakers
Blue mark **650.00**
Three color flowers **325.00**
Toothpick, dbl handles, marked **275.00**
Tray
10" l, 7½" w, blue mark **300.00**
11½" l, 8½" w, marked **375.00**
Vase
3¾" h, three color flowers, dbl gold
handles, blue mark **185.00**
5" h, rose, green mark **180.00**
Wall Pocket, 9" h, three color flowers . **425.00**

ROYAL BONN

Bonn, West Germany
1836 to 1931

History: Franz Anton Mehlem founded a factory
in the Rhineland in 1836 to produce household,
decorative, technical, and sanitary earthenware
and porcelain. Between 1887 and 1903 the factory reproduced Hochst figures in both porcelain
and earthenware using the original molds from
the defunct Prince-Electoral Mayence Manufactory in Hochst. Villeroy and Boch from Mettlach
bought the factory in 1921 and closed it in 1931.

Royal was added to the mark in 1890. After
that, products were marketed under the name
"Royal Bonn."

Biscuit Jar
6½" h, lavender, yellow, and rose
flowers, shaded blue ground, sq, SP
top, rim, and handle **85.00**

Pink and lavender flowers, green leaves, raised gold trim, beige ground, matte finish, SP top, rim, and handle **100.00**

Multicolored florals, matte finish, tapered body, SP top, rim, and shaped handle, button finial **85.00**

Bone Dish

"Apple Blossom" pattern, set of 4 .. **40.00**

"Wildrose" pattern, blue and white . **15.00**

Bowl

6" d, dessert, pink and yellow flowers, white ground, scalloped edge **10.00**

7" d, multicolored, chrysanthemum design, blue ground, pedestal base **45.00**

16" d, 8½" h, large hp florals, gold trim, large dbl handles, c1884 ... **475.00**

Cake Plate, 10¼" H-H, dark blue transfer, $20.00.

Cheese Dish

9½" l, pink roses, green leaves, gold trim, beige ground, c1870 .... **85.00**

10" l, painted multicolored bird design, cream ground, wedge shape, branch handle (A) **30.00**

Floral decor, slant front and cov **30.00**

Clock, 17½" h, floral transfers, polychrome enameling, pink and gilt trim, enameled floral face, French movement, "F. A. Mehlem, Germany" mark (A) **175.00**

Ewer

12" h

Multicolored hp parrot in tree **85.00**

Pink, yellow, and blue flowers, cream ground, gold trim **175.00**

14" h, Persian style, multicolored, marked **200.00**

Mug, 3⅛" h, ironstone, brown transfer of shepherd and flock, "Royal Bonn, Germany" (A) **10.00**

Plate

8½" d

Center portrait, Mme Le Brum and child, shades of green, scalloped edge **25.00**

Center red rose, green ground, "Franz Mehlem" **20.00**

Chrysanthemums, hp, outlined in gold, sq, pr **70.00**

9" d

Center of roses and violets, green and gold emb border, scalloped rim **35.00**

Gold outlined multicolored flowers, marked **55.00**

Urn

8½" h, cov, center portrait of woman, feathered hat, gilt trim, dbl handles **250.00**

32" h, hp center medallion of "Cries of London," maroon-red ground, gold trim on handles and finial, c1880 ....**1,900.00**

Vase

4" h, pink and yellow flowers, green ground, long tapered neck **85.00**

6" h, portrait center of young woman, framed in gold, dark red ground, sgd "Bouck" **200.00**

6½" h, rooster, hens, and chicks, green ground, sgd "Sticher" **165.00**

7½" d, pastel florals, gilt tracery, cream ground, gilt collar and side ring handles **225.00**

7½" h, portrait bust of young woman, green ground, gold neck, small dbl loop handles **450.00**

8" h

Bust of peasant girl on front, landscape on reverse, apple-green ground, gilt trim **100.00**

Pink and white orchids, green ground, blue bands, heavy gold trim, pr **225.00**

Tulips, green ground **100.00**

9½" h

Portrait of young woman with shawl on front, reverse with mountain scene, raised floral and gold tracery scalloped rim **575.00**

Woman, white gown and veil, crimped top, narrow body, wide base, artist sgd **550.00**

11" h

Floral decor, dbl gold handles, imp mark **325.00**

Orchids design, gold trim, scalloped edge, dbl handles, crown mark **150.00**

Pink, white, and purple chrysanthemums, cream and green ground, ftd **75.00**

Two peasant women seated in meadow, four twisted handles . **600.00**

11¼" h, floral tapestry pattern, multicolored **400.00**

13" h, multicolored design of maiden **550.00**

14" h
  Purple and yellow flowers, cream
    ground, dbl handles **120.00**
  Red and white roses, shaded
    ground, gold handles with rings   **35.00**
  15½" h, center portrait of Art Nou-
    veau style woman, multicolored,
    sgd "Muller" **800.00**
  16" h, center portrait of peasant girl,
    blue, pink, and gold, dbl handles   **800.00**
  28" h, overall painted roses, modeled
    foot, sgd "B. Gussgen" (A) **235.00**

ROYAL COPENHAGEN

Copenhagen, Denmark
c1760 to Present

History: During the 1760s the Danish royal family was interested in discovering the Chinese se-
cret for white hard paste porcelain. Louis Fournier, a French ceramist, came to Denmark to
conduct experiments in hopes of uncovering the
porcelain formula.

In 1772 Franz Muller, a Danish pharmacist and
chemist, produced the first genuine hard paste
porcelain. Muller, with the Queen's support,
founded the Danish Porcelain Factory in Copenhagen in 1775. By 1779 financial difficulties
forced him to relinquish his hold to the Danish
crown. The Dowager Queen Julianne Marie was
the chief patron. Under her influence, the Copenhagen trade mark of three wavy lines was
established. Each wave represented a waterway
from Kattegat to the Baltic.

Royal Copenhagen's Flora Danica, decorated
with the native plants of Denmark, is a famous
18th century service begun in 1789. A total of
1602 pieces were painted. All botanical illustrations were done free hand; all perforations and
edges were cut by hand. The service still remains
in the possession of the Danish crown.

Royal Copenhagen's most famous pattern,
Blue Fluted, was created in 1780. It is of Chinese
origin and has three edge forms, smooth edge,
closed lace edge, and perforated lace edge. It
was copied by many other factories.

Although the quality of the porcelain kept im-
proving during the early 19th century, and there
was strong popular approval for the company's
figures, vases, and accessory pieces in all pottery
and porcelain compositions, the factory was not
a financial asset for the crown. A. Falch, a private

owner, purchased the factory in 1867. A condition of purchase was his right to continue to use
the term "Royal" in the monogram. Philip Schou
purchased the works from Falch in 1882 and
moved to the present location at Smalzgade. Arnold Krog, who was appointed Art Director in
1885, was responsible for revitalizing Royal Copenhagen. The under-the-glaze painting technique was perfected under his control. Muller's
early creations were reproduced as the "Julianne
Marie Porcelain" line.

Dinner services, under-the-glaze painted figures, and vases were among the principal forms
being made at Royal Copenhagen when Dalgas
took over in 1902. The first Christmas plate was
made in 1908. As at the Bing and Grondahl
factory, the molds were destroyed each year after
the holiday season to prevent restrikes, in hopes
of preserving the value of each plate for collectors. During Dalgas' tenure, there also were experiments with stonewares and the renaissance
of the overglaze painting tecniques.

References: Pat Owen, *The Story of Royal Copenhagen Christmas Plates,* Viking Import
House, Inc., 1961.

Museums: The Bradford Museum, Niles, Illinois.

Collecting Hints: Royal Copenhagen dinnerware
sets are eagerly sought by collectors because of
their high quality. The blue and white limited
edition plates remain popular with collectors.

Bowl, 9" d, open lace, blue fluting ...   **75.00**
Butter Pat, "Symphony" pattern, set
  of 6 ....   **20.00**
Cheese Dish, 9" d, starburst motif, magenta, blue, and turquoise, faience
  body, wooden base, #418/2986 ...   **65.00**
Compote, 10"d, 6" h, hp peaches, gray,
  gold trim, crackleware **45.00**
Coolers, 9¼" h, liners, painted fruit and
  flower sprays, dbl branch handles, foliage terminals, molded gilt rims, liner
  with gilt dentil rims, cov with loop
  finials and green accents, c1775, blue
  "wave" mark, pr (A) **2,680.00**
Chocolate Cup and Saucer, "Flora Danica," blue "wave" and green printed
  mark, set of 12 (A) **1,870.00**
Cup and Saucer, "Blue Fluted" pattern,
  "Open Lace" borders, set of 12 (A) .   **120.00**
Demitasse Cup and Saucer, blue florals,
  white ground, fluted body **45.00**
Dinner Service
  "Blue Fluted" pattern, "Open Lace"
    borders, set of 75 pcs (A) **1,870.00**
  Centers painted with rustic scenes,
    gilt cartouches, molded borders
    painted with yellow band reserving
    four panels of violets, late 19th C,
    blue "wave" mark, set of 39 pcs
    (A) **990.00**

Cup and Saucer, blue and white, $45.00.

Figure

1¼" h, frog on rock, #507 .... **25.00**
2" h, mermaid baby, #2313 .... **35.00**
3" h, blue jay, tan, blue, and white . **20.00**
3" w, duck, spread wings **30.00**
3½" h
    Pug dog seated on haunches,
    #3169 .... **115.00**
    White baby rabbit, seated, #4705 **110.00**
4⅜" w, seated peasant girl in native
    costume holding floral garland,
    #12421, blue "crowned waves" . **85.00**
4½" h, mermaid girl, #3321 .... **60.00**
6" h
    Dutch girl seated, knitting, #1314 **185.00**
    "Goat Herder" (A) **130.00**
    Goose standing, another racing
    past, oval ground with water lil-
    ies, (A) **170.00**
    Little boy with umbrella, pointed
    hat and long coat, #1145 ..... **135.00**
6" h, 6" l, lady feeding cow **250.00**
6¼" h
    Boy trying to pull halter on calf (A) **100.00**
    Woman giving pail of milk to cow
    (A) **100.00**
    Young girls with dolls, sgd "C.
    Thomsen," pr **185.00**
6½" h
    Boy with ball, #3542 .... **100.00**
    Dog, seated, blue and white **150.00**
6½" l, swan, natural colors, #755 .. **110.00**
6⅝" h, nude female figure, legs
    tucked under body, white finish .. **250.00**
7" h, boy on goat (A) **70.00**
9½" h, girl with goose (A) **100.00**
12½" l, tiger, reclining position, soft
    coloring **500.00**
20" h, knight and maiden, multicol-
    ored, modeled by Holger Christen-
    sen **700.00**
Boy and sow, #848 .... **130.00**
Cobbler, #2228 .... **135.00**
Diana and deer, crackleware, #1531 **225.00**
Merlin, standing, white clothes, gold
    stars, blue robe, black edging **500.00**

Ostrich egg, natural colors, faience . **65.00**
Seagull, black head, #1468 .... **55.00**
Two old ladies, wearing native cos-
    tumes, one with basket over arm,
    blue gowns, steel gray tops, one
    with striped apron, other with
    checked apron **500.00**
Young girl, cradling doll, #1938 ... **115.00**
Jar, 10½" h, cov, "The Fight" scene,
    celadon type glaze **185.00**
Medallion, 4" h, parian, relief bust of
    Hans Christian Andersen **40.00**
Pitcher, 4" h, floral pattern, #10/7538 **50.00**
Plaque
    3¼" d, "Langelinie," blue and white
    scene of maiden and harbor **15.00**
    5½" d, bisque, relief of classic figures,
    sgd "Eneret," pr **110.00**

Vase, 8¼" h, green and black, gold accents, crackle ground, blue three wave mark, $350.00.

Plate
    7" d, blue and white "For Konge Og
    For Land-1848-98" **75.00**
    10" d
        Jubilee, silhouettes of king and
        queen, "26 April 1898-1923" .. **30.00**
        Painted partridge, multicolored,
        green and gilt border, gilt dentil
        rim, sgd "Larsen" **45.00**
        Wildflowers hp, gold trim (A) **12.00**
    10 ¾" d, "Flora Danica," pierced gilt
    borders, shaped serrated rims, blue
    "wave" and green printed marks,
    set of 12 (A) **4,180.00**
    11¾" d, service, "Flora Danica" pat-
    tern, reticulated borders, "Royal
    Copenhagen" and blue "wave"
    marks, set of 12 (A)............**10,175.00**
Soup Plate, 9¾" d, polychrome floral
    design, basketweave border, shaped
    gilt edge, set of 6 (A) **175.00**
Sugar
    4½" h, "Lace" pattern, #1/605 .... **50.00**

6¼" w, "Flora Danica," pink scale panels, branch finial, flowerhead terminals, blue "wave" and green printed mark (A) **350.00**
Tea Set, Teapot, Creamer, and Sugar
Blue fluted design **375.00**
Flowers, beige ground, #910/1870 . **225.00**
Teacup and Saucer, splashed blue flowers, white ground **15.00**
Tray
8½" w, "Flora Danica," pink scale border, gilt serrated rim, blue "wave" and green printed mark (A) **300.00**
11" l, 8" w, hp, beach scene of docked boat and boathouse, sgd "Harold Henriksen" **120.00**
Trencher Salt, vertical fluted sides, small blue floral basket design, blue "wave" mark **125.00**
Tureen, 12" w, cov, "Flora Danica," dbl branch handles, foliage terminals, blue "wave" and green printed mark (A) **1,870.00**
Vase
4" d, 3½" h, turquoise crackle glaze, gold trim **35.00**
5" h, bud, white flowers, multicolored mulberries **48.00**
7½" h, painting of carp on body of vase, c1930, marked **125.00**
12" h, 7½" d, goldfish and ship decor, crackled ground **345.00**
13½" h, horse chestnut blossoms, light blue ground, wide cylindrical shape, sgd (A) **230.00**

ROYAL DUX

Dux, Bohemia (now Duchow, Czechoslovakia)
1860 to Present

History: In 1860 E. Eichler established the Duxer Porcelain Manufactory in Dux, Bohemia. The factory was noted for its portrait busts and lavishly decorated vases. Much of the production was exported to America. After the turn of the century, the Art Nouveau style was used for large porcelain figures and vases.

Shortly after the conclusion of World War II, the factory was nationalized. The newly formed company produced household, decorative, and table porcelains, plus coffee and tea sets.

Figure, 14" l, 10½" h, brown and gray, "Royal Dux" and raised pink triangle mark, $135.00.

Bowl, 13½" l, 7" w, figure of woman holding flower on side, lavender, green, and gold, ovoid shape **660.00**
Dish, shell shape, reclining woman on int., earthtone colors, pink "triangle" mark **275.00**
Figure
3½" h, fawn, gold trim **65.00**
4" h
Bear with guitar **85.00**
Fawn, Art Deco style, white, gold trim, "MADE IN CZECHOSLOVAKIA" **55.00**
Monkey with horn **85.00**
4¾" h, young girl at well, green and tan, satin finish, pink "triangle" mark **100.00**
6" h, peasant girl, hands folded at waist, matte green, pale pink peasant clothes, pink "triangle" mark . **200.00**
7" h, young girl, gold sailor's suit, c1915 .... **125.00**
8" h
Greek potter, seated, multicolored, c1900 .... **215.00**
Woman with pottery, multicolored **575.00**
9" d, 16¼" h, mother with two children, beige and green, satin finish, burnished gold, pink "triangle" mark **695.00**
9" h
Lady, holding rose, blue and white dress **70.00**
Woman, Art Deco style, blue satin gown, green hat, flesh tones, wide spread base, pink "triangle" mark **275.00**
9" l, 9" h, two boys pulling two lambs, multicolored, pink "triangle" mark **175.00**
10" h
Boy with basket of fish, satin colors, pink "triangle" mark **200.00**
Lady, holding dress to one side, Art Deco glossy colors, raised pink "triangle" mark **275.00**

10" l, 14" h, boy and donkey, ivory, gold, bronze, and lavender, satin finish **325.00**

12¼" h, bowl with youth and water sprite, ivory, black and gold highlights, sgd "Hampel," imp "Royal Dux" (A) **225.00**

13" h, boy playing flute, sack over shoulder, lamb and tree on base, girl feeding goat, ivory and gold colors, pink "triangle," "Royal Dux & circle E" marks, pr **1,200.00**

13" l, donkey and cart, matte colors **135.00**

13½" h, African Crested crane, gray and cream, pink "triangle" mark . **165.00**

14" h
Bust, woman, green scarf, open pink vest, green bodice, scrolled gold base, matte finish (A) **350.00**
Classical lady, Cupid on shoulder, c1900 .... **390.00**

15" h, Art Nouveau style woman, filling lamp, companion with hourglass, multicolored, pr **900.00**

15" l, 11½" h, two stallions, one on hind legs, natural colors, pink "triangle" mark **125.00**

15" l, 12½" h, man and woman, period dress, seated at table set with tea service, poodle dogs under chairs, blue, gold, and pink coloring, marked **1,100.00**

15¼" h, nude female leaning on vine covered rock, stream and rocks on base (A) **350.00**

17" h
Man and woman, Napoleonic dress, "R. D. Boh" in pink "triangle" mark, pr **895.00**
Man holding mane of rearing horse, marked **750.00**

18" l, horse and rider, jumping fence, matte colors, pink "triangle" mark **650.00**

18" l, 9" h, Irish setter with bird, multicolored, pink "triangle" mark **125.00**

19½" h, 16½" l, hunter on horse, horn, three running dogs, multicolored, marked **850.00**

20" h, woman carrying jug, bowl in hand, beige and green gown, satin finish, burnished gold **595.00**

21" l, stalking tiger **75.00**

24" h, boy and girl at the well, pink "triangle" mark, pr **1,450.00**

31½" h, lady and gentleman, wearing elaborate hats and costumes, mound bases, applied flowers, pink "triangle" mark, pr (A) **530.00**

Jar, 9" h, molded Art Nouveau woman's face, multicolored, marked **400.00**

Lamp, 9" h, Art Deco style lady spread-

ing edges of cobalt blue gown, flesh tones, mounted on brass base **400.00**

Mantle Set, 12½" d dbl-handled bowl, pair 12½" h vases, applied pink roses, yellow and green ground **145.00**

Planter, 10" l, 7" w, figure of boy in boat with fish, multicolored **285.00**

Vase
5" h, applied flowers and fruit, shaded rose ground, dbl handles **85.00**
7¼" h, muted orange flowers, green leaves, cream ground, circ black mark **55.00**
7½" h, Oriental figures, green and pink outfits, satin finish, rect, raised pink "triangle" mark, pr **275.00**
8" h
Flowers and cherries, orange and green, pr **85.00**
Two large protruding roses and leaves, multicolored, matte finish **65.00**
9" h, green swirl, blown-out woman's face, flowing hair which forms handles, pink "triangle" mark **225.00**

Vase, 14" h, beige, green, and red matte finish, cream ground, "acorn & E," pink triangle mark, $385.00.

10" h, Art Nouveau style applied flowers, matte colors, dbl handles **115.00**

14" h
Heavy floral relief, multicolored, c1900 .... **165.00**
Heavy relief of leaves and open work, soft earth colors, c1900 . **200.00**

14¾" h, Art Deco style figure of woman draped over vase, cream, bronze, and gold, pink "triangle" mark **395.00**

15" h, applied orange poppies, green ground **100.00**

17" h
   Art Nouveau scene of "Sirens on
     Waves," multicolored, pr **695.00**
   Figure of peasant girl in front of
     tree-shaped vase, beige, green,
     and gold matte colors, pink "tri-
     angle" mark **425.00**
18" h, modeled Art Nouveau style
   woman, flowing gown and scarf,
   pastel colors, matte finish, pink
   "triangle" mark **400.00**

ROYAL VIENNA

Vienna, Austria
1864 to Present

History: After the Imperial Porcelain Factory
closed in 1864, some of the artists and workers
established their own small shops. They produced the same forms and followed the same
decorative motifs that they used at the Imperial
Porcelain Factory. The quality of the pieces varied from shop to shop. Some were overdeco-
rated; some cheaply done. Many of the pieces
imitating the earlier Vienna porcelains were
marked with the beehive mark.

The Vienna Porclain Factory Augarten, that
was established in 1922, considers itself the successor to the Imperial and Royal Porcelain Manufactory of Vienna which closed in 1864. This
factory still makes decorative porcelain and figures.

A company started by Josef de Cente in 1793
as a tile and stove factory made copies of the
porcelain and figures from the Imperial Vienna
factory after it closed in 1864. De Cente bought
many of the original molds and used them. His
reproductions always were marked with "de
Cente," mostly impressed in the base. In 1902
the Alexandria Porcelain works in Turn-Teplitz
bought the molds from the de Cente factory.

Bowl
   4½" d, cov, flower spray in gilt car-
     touches, pierced cov, rose bud fi-
     nial, c1900, blue "beehive" mark
     (A) **50.00**
   5" d, portrait of woman with Cupid,
     maroon panels, pink and gold int.,
     gold sq handles, bronze dore trim,
     c1860, "beehive" mark **525.00**
   8" d, bust of woman in center, rose
     and gold border with purple and
     white irises, green and white flow-
     ers background, ftd **145.00**

Box, 6¾" d, cov, painted scene of garden party on cov, royal blue ground,
   gilt foliage on int., sgd "Feier," blue
   "beehive" mark (A) **460.00**
Cabinet Cup and Saucer, oval panel of
   "Ariadne," maiden and weeping
   Cupid watching ships, multicolored,
   sgd "Reimer," late 19th C, blue "beehive" mark **200.00**

**Figure, 9½" l, 9" h, multicolored, c1880,
$750.00.**

Charger
   13⅜" d, center scene of maiden and
     companion being crowned,
     paneled ground, gilding, octago-
     nal, c1900, blue "shield" mark (A) **660.00**
   16¼" d, "Rape of the Daughters of
     Leucippus," multicolored, reserved
     on etched gilt ground, blue enamel
     accents, late 19th C, blue "bee-
     hive" mark (A) **2,310.00**
   20⅛" d, center scene of "Return of
     Columbus," multicolored, dark
     claret border, gilt, late 19th C, blue
     "beehive" mark **2,500.00**
Chocolate Set, tray, cup, saucer, creamer and sugar, each piece dec with bust
   of woman in medallion, maroon border, gold overlay **130.00**
Cup and Saucer
   Large portrait of young woman,
     multicolored, blue jeweling **300.00**
   Panel with en graillee portrait, burnt
     orange ground, gilt garlands, blue
     "beehive" mark (A) **25.00**
Dish
   10" w, rust, gray, and gold flowers and
     leaves, center in form of triangle
     with maroon and gold swirls, ma-
     roon ground triangular, indented
     corners, blue "beehive" mark **325.00**
   11¼" d, center scene of "Der Grazien
     Rache," gilt design border, light
     blue, mauve, apricot, and claret
     ground, c1900, blue "beehive"
     mark (A) **285.00**

14½" l, center scene of nymphs making sacrifice to Cupid, lavender border with green vines, gilding, late 19th C, blue "shield" mark (A)   **880.00**

Ewer
6⅞" h, painted reserve of two maidens in landscape, claret ground, gilt foliage, scroll handle, c1900, blue "beehive mark" (A) **48.00**
15½" h, painted continuous scene of Hector and military, reserved on gilt ground, enameled panels, sgd "Bauer," late 19th C, blue "beehive" mark (A) **1,760.00**

Figure
4½" l, wolf, rooster in mouth, white, blue "beehive" mark **50.00**
7" h, young boy, period dress, enameled colors, imp "beehive" mark .   **285.00**
16½" h, "Ulysses leaving Penelope," multicolored, blue "beehive" mark, damaged (A) **100.00**
35" h, 34⅝" h, lady with fan and metal shepherds hook, man with tricorn hat under arm, 18th C clothes, scroll bases, late 19th C, blue "beehive" mark, repaired, pr (A) **3,300.00**

Jardiniere, 12½" d, transfer printed, two classical maidens in oval panel, cobalt ground, gilding, multicolored paneled borders, late 19th C, blue "shield" mark (A) **330.00**

Plaque, 12" sq, scene of woman with basket seated on bench with Cupid, entitled "Ein Traum," sgd "Ullmar," "beehive" and "Robert Pilz, Vienna" mark **975.00**

Plate
6½" d, center portraits of Juno and Galaia with cherubs, green, gold rims, blue "beehive" mark, pr . . .   **80.00**
6¾" d, center portrait of young woman, gold jeweled border, sgd "Wagner" **450.00**
8¼" d, classic figures in flowing cloaks, gold ground, cobalt border, gold tracery **250.00**
8½" d
Bust of woman, long brown hair, maroon and white drape, maroon and gilt border, blue "beehive" mark **80.00**
Center scene of woman in classical setting, paneled border, c1895, blue "beehive" mark **100.00**
9½" d
Bust of woman in center, five medallions of busts, dark green and gold border **100.00**
Center panel of Cupid and woman, classical dress, holding flowers,

small panels in border, heavy gold trim, "beehive" mark **375.00**
Center musical Muse design, heavy gold sectioned border **65.00**
Center panels of peasants at work and play, cobalt and gold borders, "beehive" mark, pr **200.00**
Center portrait of seated woman with Cupid, gilt and colored border, blue "beehive" mark **350.00**
Portrait of Madame LeBrun, multicolored, irid brown border with claret and gilt detail, sgd "Wagner," late 19th C (A) **470.00**
Princess Louise, pink and gilt bands, cobalt, light blue, gilt, claret, and pink paneled border, late 19th C, blue "beehive" mark (A) **180.00**
"Mrs Robinson," dog, 18th C clothes, gilt Nouveau style design on brown border, sgd "Wagner," c1910, blue "beehive" mark (A) **330.00**
10" d
Center of "A Little Captive," multicolored, magenta and gilt border, blue "beehive" mark . .   **250.00**
Center medallions of nude women in ocean and seated on bench, jeweled, heavy gilt borders, pr .**1,850.00**
Center scene of Madonna and Christ, gilt scrolling border, pink, green puce and light yellow ground, c1900, sgd "Wagner," blue "beehive" mark (A) **120.00**
Center scene of Napoleon with army, multicolored, royal blue and gold border, sgd "Meissonier" **75.00**
Sunburst gold frame, candle girl and whispering girl, underglaze blue "beehive" mark **650.00**
10½" d, center medallion of two women gazing into fire, royal blue border, pierced for hanging **125.00**
12" d, head and shoulder view of woman, long brown hair, white low cut dress, maroon ground, gold scalloped edge **85.00**
Platter, portraits in medallions, c1850, "beehive" mark **750.00**
Tête-Á-Tête Set, coffeepot, cov milk jug, cov sugar bowl, two cups and saucers, 14½" l pierced tray, multicolored panels of allegorical subjects reserved on paneled purple, puce, white, green, blue, and claret ground, gilt, late 19th C (A) **1,100.00**
Tray
10¼" d, "Rinaldo und Armida," reserved on gold ground, border of

diamond panels with herons, light blue ground, claret rim, c1900, sgd "Forster," black "beehive" mark (A) **180.00**

11" H-H, center scene of Cupid and Psyche on river bank, reserved on blue ground, lobed border of pink and yellow panels, claret and gilt accents, lozenge shape, c1900, blue "shield" mark (A) **600.00**

12" d, center scene of "Die Sohne," rect gilt cartouche, claret border with gilt foliage, reserves of gilt vases on light blue, pink, gilt rim, c1880, sgd "Schone," blue "beehive" mark (A) **450.00**

15" d, male and female center medallion, maroon and gold border . **175.00**

Urn

5½" h, center band of allegorical scene, maroon ground, gold overlay, c1880, sgd "K. Weh" **325.00**

8¾" h, cov, scene of Paris and Helen, maroon ground, gold trim, figures around body, tripod base, sgd "Riemer," blue "beehive" mark **400.00**

13" h, cov, man and woman in classic garden setting, Cupid on reverse, multicolored, sgd "Wagner" **550.00**

35" h, portrait bust of young woman in medallion, dark maroon ground, heavy gold embellishments, sgd "Rosley & Liele" on base, "beehive" mark **2,500.00**

Vase

4⅞" h, portrait of young girl in center medallion, dark green irid ground, gold accents, marked **750.00**

5" h, portrait medallion, maroon ground, gold overlay, sgd "Erblicht" **450.00**

5¼" h, cherubs, cobalt ground, reticulated top **300.00**

5½" h, scene of two lovers and Cupid, sgd "Boucher" **100.00**

6¼" h, portrait of classical lady, cobalt ground, narrow neck, ruffled, flared top, sgd **500.00**

9" h, scenic motif in shades of maroon and gold, pierced dome **450.00**

11½" h

Center portrait of young girl, four feet, dbl handles **750.00**

Reserve of young woman whispering to putto in gilt foliate surround, light green ground, hp, dbl gourd shape, blue "beehive," "RC crowned & X'd swords" marks (A) **225.00**

12" h, cov

Multicolored scene of girl with stringed instrument, gold trim, four feet, dbl handles **750.00**

Printed and painted scene of three maidens, one with lyre, blue "beehive" mark **250.00**

12¾" h, cov and stand, panel of Rinaldo and Armida, warrior watching over hedge, putto on reverse, cobalt ground, c1910 .... **275.00**

15½" h, portrait center luster ground, raised gold, florals on stem, rolled rim, sgd "Wagner" **875.00**

20¼" h, cov, matching stand, large panels of courting couples, 18th C clothes, yellow panels with painted flowers, borders of white bands with gilt, late 19th C, blue "beehive" marks, pr (A) **550.00**

23½" h, Ruth on front, Princess Louise on reverse in gilt borders, reserved on light yellow ground, claret borders, gilt, molded as lamp (A) **935.00**

46½" h, cov and stand, continuous scene of Lohengrin and Elsa on shore near castle, cobalt borders with gilt, base reserved with two panels of maidens, sgd "F. Holzl," late 19th C (A) **3,080.00**

67" h, cov, painted continuous scenes of "Ein Baccanel," necks and flaring feet with two panels of mythological figures, circ pedestal bases painted with continuous mythological scenes, cobalt ground with gilding, late 19th C, blue "beehive" mark, pr (A)........... **121,000.00**

ROYAL WORCESTER

Worcester, England
1862 to Present

(See Worcester for early history)

History: In 1862 Worcester Royal Porcelain Company Ltd. was formed by Kerr and Binns. Limoges-style enameled porcelains, figures, and many dessert services were manufactured. Vases and other ornamental pieces were painted with figure subjects. Among the factory's popular wares was Ivory porcelain, a glazed parian ware.

During the 1870s, magnificent porcelains in the Japanese style were produced. Many were modeled by James Hadley, one of the finest ceramic modelers. Hadley left royal Worcester in 1875 to freelance, but almost all his work was bought by Worcester.

In 1889 Thomas Grainger's factory was bought by the Worcester Royal Porcelain Company. Grainger had started his own factory in 1801 at St. Martin's Gate. After having several different partners, George, his son, eventually took over.

James Hadley started his factory in 1896 to produce ornamental art pottery. It was located near Royal Worcester's main factory. By 1905 the Hadley firm was absorbed by the Royal Worcester Company. Binns retired in 1897 and Dyson Perrins took over.

Royal Worcester continues to make ordinary bone china patterns in the 20th century. Colored floral borders or blue and white transfer prints in the "Willow Pattern," "Royal Lily," and "Broseley Dragon" are most popular. Ornamental wares with a parian body are part of the product line.

During the 1920s and 1930s, the company maintained its fine quality wares in a depressed world market with some degree of success. Around 1924 luster wares were introduced, inspired by Wedgwood's dragon and fairyland lusters. In 1928 an electrical decorating tunnel kiln was installed, causing a great improvement in firing decorated wares and raising the standards of china production.

World War II restrictions forced china manufacturers to cut back on their production. Rich ornamental and decorated wares came to an end.

Worcester carried on production of some wares, especially the Doughty Birds for the United States market as part of the war effort involved with lend-lease. Dorothy Doughty's bird figures were absolutely correct in size and color as was the foliage on which they were modeled. Other figures also were produced during the war years including dogs by Doris Linder, Gwendoline Parnell's "London Cries," Miss Pinder-Davis's "Watteau" figures, and Eva Soper's series of small birds and children in wartime Britain.

After World War II things began to return to normal. A great number of young painters apprenticed to Royal Worcester. In 1948 Doris Linder modeled the first limited edition, an equestrian model featuring Princess Elizabeth on Tommy. It has become the most sought after of Worcester's equestrian models.

In 1950 the biscuit kilns were replaced by gas-fired tunnel kilns which produced even finer quality ware. The founding of the Dyson Perrins Museum at Worcester in 1951 marked the bicentenary of the Worcester Porcelain Company.

During the 1960s Doris Lindner's equestrian models achieved great success. In addition to limited edition figures Worcester produced tea, dinner and oven-to-table wares using both old traditional patterns as well as new ones. Demands for Royal Worcester porcelain continuously increased. A new factory opened in 1970. Much of the current porcelain decoration still is done by hand. Hard porcelain ornamental wares are part of the product line. Royal Worcester commemorative pieces include mugs, jugs, and trays.

References: Geoffrey A. Godden, *Victorian Porcelain*, Herbert Jenkins, 1961; Stanley W. Fisher, *Worcester Porcelain*, Ward Lock & Co. Ltd., 1968; Henry Sandon, *Royal Worcester Porcelain*, Barrie & Jenkins, 1973.

Museums: Dyson Perrins Museum, Worcester, England.

REPRODUCTION ALERT. Both Austria and Rudolstadt made copies of Royal Worcester wares.

Basket
    3½" h, light body, gold trim, green
      mark **120.00**
    Woven pattern, white body, gold
      edge, c1884, raised mark **325.00**
Biscuit Jar
    6" h, cov, underplate, flowers, beige
      ground **325.00**
    9" h, cov, floral design, gold handles,
      base, and finial, c1890 ....**1,150.00**
Bowl
    5¾" d, florals, ivory ground, matte
      ext. finish, glazed int., wide gold
      bands at rim and base, scalloped
      edge, c1890 .... **110.00**
    9" d
      Emb grape leaves, beige satin fin-
      ish, gold trimmed open work at
      top, c1896 .... **325.00**
      Overlapping tan and green leaves **400.00**
Box, cov, "Cottage Loaf" shape, sterling
    fittings, c1900 .... **125.00**
Caddy, 4" h, gilded leaf and floral dec-
    orations, ivory ground, green mark . **95.00**
Candle Snuffer
    3¾" l, "Nun" design **65.00**
    Mr and Mrs Caudle, c1889, pr **350.00**
Candlesticks
    10½" h, four ram's heads on each
      stick, light to dark blue coloring,
      c1893, pr **300.00**
    12" h, emb and twisted design on
      stems, sq bases, pr **330.00**
Chocolate Pot
    9" h, hp yellow thistles, purple mark **65.00**
    13" h, four paneled, hp flowers, matte
      ground, four ftd, dated 1888 ..... **600.00**
Cologne Bottle, 3¾" h, lavender, rust,
    yellow and green pansy-type flowers

and leaves, round form, SP cap, dated
1887 .... **220.00**
Cup and Saucer, heart shape, beige satin
finish, bow on handle, gold trim,
c1896, ... **125.00**
Demitasse Cup and Saucer
  Brown leaf design, c1882 .... **30.00**
  Floral decor, gold tracery **45.00**
Dinner Service, twelve dinner plates,
soups, luncheon plates, dessert
plates, cups and saucers, sauce
dishes, and ten butter pats, white
ground, three cov servers, gravy boat,
two open vegetables, cov tureen and
tray, and nest of three platters, blue
floral calico pattern, serving pieces
with gilt elephant handles (A) **500.00**
Dish
  7½" l, pink daisies, gold outlined bor-
    der, leaf shape **25.00**
  Beige and ivory, gold touches, leaf
    shape, one side rolled over, scal-
    loped and crimped, c1908 ...... **60.00**
Egg Coddle Cup, three birds dec **15.00**
Egg Server, 7" d, basket form, loop handle, set of six egg cups set in basket,
tan and cream **335.00**

**Left, vase, 11″ h, bronze birds, white
ground, c1872, $2,400.00; right, figure,
12″ h, "Water Carrier," cream and gold,
(A) $80.00.**

Ewer
  3½" h, florals, beige ground, applied
    gold fluted handles, flat backs, pr   **240.00**
  6½" h, flowers, white ground, gold
    trim, horn handle **180.00**
  7" h, flower, white ground, bulbous
    body, narrow neck, applied bird
    handle **220.00**
  8" h, flowers, beige ground, four
    lobed shape, gold applied thorn
    handle, c1896 .... **275.00**
  12" h
    Brown butterflies, flowers, and
      leaves outlined in gold, cream

ground, salamander handle,
c1880 .... **375.00**
Center medallion of grouse, beige
ground, reticulated top **825.00**
15½" h, gold and white daisy sprays,
turquoise body, cream shoulder,
handle, and base, scrolled acanthus leaf handle, bas relief acanthus
leaf and florals on shoulder, base,
and rim (A) **650.00**
17" h, seventeen emb figures of lions,
cherubs, dolphins, satyr, and lady's
face, beige ground, gilt trim,
c1894 ....**1,400.00**
17½" h, flowers and butterfly, cream
ground **750.00**
Fairy Lamps, 17" h, figures of water car-
riers, gilding, lights by Clarke Crick-
lite, Ltd., pr **1,980.00**
Figure
  2¼" h, Bullfinch, seated on rock, flo-
    ral spray, multicolored **60.00**
  3" h, bluebird on floral and fruit base **60.00**
  3" l, 1½" h, porcelain frog, white,
    c1891 .... **200.00**
  3¾" h, "Two Babies," blond baby,
    black and white dog **225.00**
  4¾" h, rabbit, basket on back, satin
    finish, c1911, #2514 .... **450.00**
  5" h, child leaning against large white
    dog, arms wrapped around tur-
    quoise candleholder, gold trim, tur-
    quoise base, c1876 .... **375.00**
  6" h
    "Only Me," young blond girl curl-
      ing bare feet **225.00**
    "The Scotsman," beige, green, tan,
      and gold, enamel accents, satin
      finish, c1903 .... **425.00**
  6½" h, "The First Cuckoo," girl wear-
    ing pink dress holding flowers in
    folds of skirt, sgd "F. G. Doughty" **220.00**
  6¾" h
    "Kate Greenaway" girl, off-white
      glossy finish, added flesh tones,
      c1882 .... **450.00**
    "John Bull," beige, green, tan, and
      gold body, enamel accents, satin
      finish, c1903 .... **425.00**
  8" h, seated Peter Pan with bird **170.00**
  9" h
    "Joy" and "Sorrow," satin finish,
      dated 1896, pr **900.00**
    "Kate Greenaway" boy with bas-
      ket, satin cream and beige finish,
      dated 1893 .... **550.00**
    "Kate Greenaway" girl with tam-
      bourine by tree trunk, dated
      1884, sgd "Hadley" **420.00**
  11⅛" h, young girl with cymbals,
    beige dress, beige satin finish, gold
    trimmed base, c1907 .... **600.00**

15" h, boy with instrument, Egyptian outfit, girl with tambourine, purple mark, pr **975.00**

18" h, women holding baskets on heads, draped figures, mounted on bases, tan coloring, gilded, pr ...**1,050.00**

Pitcher
4¼" h, multicolored florals, gold trim, beige satin finish, c1899 .... **175.00**

4¾" h, florals, beige satin finish, gold trim, c1903 .... **165.00**

6½" h, floral sprays, light ground, bands at top and bottom, elephant handle, #418 .... **275.00**

7½" h, gold vine and leaves, yellow ground, dolphin handle, dated 1885, marked **300.00**

10" h, florals, cream ground, stag horn handle **185.00**

Plate
9¼" d
Adam's style floral design, gold accents **10.00**

Luncheon, chrysanthemum prunus and floral sprays, gilt accents, cream ground, set of six (A) ... **50.00**

10" d
Commemorative design of Dr. Wall in center, oblong border inserts of factories and cathedrals, blue, white ground, c1890 .... **175.00**

Floral center, tapestry border **50.00**

Multicolored wildflower center, etched light green border, purple mark **65.00**

10⅜" d, wide pink, green, and gold scrolled borders, four round reserves with florals, set of twelve (A) **475.00**

10½" d, "Rosemary" pattern **25.00**

Ring Tree, maroon and yellow florals, beige satin finish, gold trim, c1912 . **100.00**

Rosebowl, 3" h, flowers, beige ground, four lobed shape, pr **190.00**

Sugar Shaker, 7½" h, molded figure of young girl with hat with holes in crown, beige satin finish, #1103 ... **450.00**

Teapot
3¼" d, 4" h, hp "Kingfisher," white ground, gold trim, sgd "W. Powell" **145.00**

5" h, pastel floral sprays, gold leaves, purple mark **265.00**

Blue leaves and gold trim, white ground, oblong, c1886 .... **50.00**

Tureen, 14½" l, 8" h, cov, ladle, brown ivy design, brown and gold elephant head handles, crow's feet finial, dated 1880 .... **250.00**

Urn
12" h, hp bird, white ground, reticulated handle and top **965.00**

15¼" h, cov, hp rose decor, flying fish shape handles, c1910, sgd "W. E. Jarman" **1,300.00**

Vase
3¼" h, butterflies on front and back, gilt foliage, dbl handles, c1883, green mark **95.00**

3½" h, raised gold leaf pattern, cream ground, c1875 .... **165.00**

6½" h
Floral, off-white ground, applied small circ handles **200.00**

Floral sprays, matte finish, stick style, c1886 .... **125.00**

6¾" h, nautilus shape, yellow to peach shading, gilt (A) **150.00**

7⅛" h, 6¼" l, multicolored florals, satin beige ground, cornucopia form on scroll base, footed, dated 1898 .... **335.00**

8¾" h, blue flowers, tan leaves outlined in gold, satin cream ground, ewer shape, dragon twist handle, c1887 .... **435.00**

9¼" h, pink, maroon, and yellow flowers, beige satin ground, gold trim, footed fluted tops, shape #1938, c1902, pr **600.00**

10" h, spiral shape with each spiral showing different floral bouquet, white ground, pink highlights **635.00**

10½" h, fern decor in relief, bamboo shape, bamboo handle **75.00**

Left, soup bowl, cov, 6" d, pink leaf and berry design, cream ground, gold handles and knob, $150.00; center, urn, 4½" h, ivory, brown scroll feet, $300.00; right, fruit bowl, 11" l, multicolored florals, tan ground, gold elephant heads, $750.00.

12" h, wisteria and green leaves outlined in gold, raised work on neck
and base **265.00**
13" h
  Flying and perched birds on gold
  background with setting sun,
  ivory body, pedestaled, flared
  stick reticulated neck, dated
  1885 .... **500.00**
  Gold leaves and flowers, ivory
  ground, masks at collars, animals
  on handles, narrow necks,
  c1880, pr **700.00**

ROZENBURG

The Hague, Holland
1884 to 1914

History: W. van Gudenberg established an earthenware and porcelain factory at The Hague in
1885. T. Colenbrander was the art director until
1880.

Rozenburg is best known for a line of exceptionally thin earthenware that was made during
the late 19th and early 20th century in the Art
Nouveau style. The delicate, translucent body
had over–the–glaze decorations of flowers, foliage, and birds derived from the design of Japanese batik-printed fabrics from the Dutch East
Indies, now Indonesia. Mauve, yellow ochre,
orange, and shades of green were some of the
vivid enamel colors used on the white ground.
The decoration on later examples was stiffer and
had less delicate colors. Shapes featured elongated handles and spouts contrasted with the
curved and flat surfaces of the body.

S. Juriaan Kok became director of the company
from 1895 to 1913. He was responsible for a
series of extraordinary Art Nouveau shapes. J.
Schellink was employed as a painter who decorated his works with stylized flowers in brick-red,
black, purple, green, and yellow on a bottle-
green ground. He also used sea horses and
spiked leaves in his motifs. Schellink painted in
a series of tense, nervous, spots and lines with
subtle color combinations. The egg-shell thin
porcelain that Schellink used was unique to Rozenburg. M. N. Engelen, the firm's chemist, developed it. Production stopped with the beginning of World War I.

Pieces were marked "Rozenburg/den Haag"
with a stork that was copied from the mark of
the 18th century porcelain factory at The Hague,
and a crown.

Beaker and Saucer, "Eggshell,"
multicolored bird on branch, mauve
flowers, shaped diaper borders,
c1914 (A) **180.00**
Cup and Saucer
  "Eggshell," multicolored bird on
  branch, mauve flowers, shaped
  diaper borders, c1914 (A) **180.00**
  "Eggshell," painted scrolling purple
  and green flowers, dated 1907,
  eight cups, nine saucers, cracks (A)**1,450.00**
  "Eggshell," hp stippled blue pansies,
  octagonal, dated 1904, "Rozenburg Den Haag," set of 5, damage
  (A) **550.00**
Dish, pottery
  8⅞" d, painted central flowerhead
  and foliage, leaves and flowers border, concentric rings and trefoil on
  reverse, c1910 (A) **125.00**
  10⅝" d, painted star pattern of stylized foliage, dark blue ground, lappets and foliage border, dated 1913
  (A) **140.00**
  11" d, painted peacocks, one perched
  on vase, other in yellow medallion,
  band of flames border, dated 1893,
  "Rozenburg Den Haag" (A) **180.00**
  12½" d, painted raven perched
  among scrolling foliage, dated
  1905 (A) **885.00**
Ewer, 12" h, Art Nouveau style, four
panels of flowers, muted brown
tones, "Rozenburg Den Haag" **950.00**

**Vase, 16½" h, yellow-orange flowers,
blue ground, "Rozenburg Den Hagg &
Stork," $1,800.00.**

Inkstand, 7⅞" d, pottery, green, yellow,
and amber iris and foliage, black
ground, flower shape, single well,
"Rozenburg Den Haag" (A) **40.00**
Jar, 3⅜" h, cov, pottery, hp abstract de-

sign, yellow and blue, cream ground, dated 1886, pr (A) **120.00**

Plate, 7⅞" d
"Eggshell," multicolored bird on green branch, two large purple chrysanthemums, mauve diaper border, octagonal, c1914 (A) **720.00**
"Eggshell," painted exotic bird perched on scrolling foliage, octagonal, dated 1900, "Rozenburg Den Haag" (A) **1,035.00**

Saucer, 4⅜" d, "Eggshell," purple flower, light green leaves, mauve diaper border, white ground, c1909 ... **145.00**

Tile, 6" sq, hp windmill scene, dated 1902 .... **110.00**

Vase
3¾" h, "Eggshell," Art Deco style, rust, green, and yellow, "Rozenburg Den Haag, Holland" **575.00**
6¾" h, swirl design, dark multicolors, dbl handles **400.00**
7" h, jungle-type pattern, bright colors **325.00**
7½" h, pottery, painted stylized flowers and leaves, dark colors, baluster shape, flared foot, dated 1896, "stork" mark (A) **150.00**
8¼" h, four panels, butterfly and florals, earth tone and dark red colors, slender middle, bulbous top **350.00**
9⅞" h, pottery, green crackle glaze, underglaze floral sprays in oval panels, dated 1894, "Rozenburg Den Haag," pr (A) **275.00**
10⅜" h, pottery, green crackle glaze, underglaze abstract design in blue, brown, and green, cylindrical shape, flared rims, dated 1893, "Rozenburg Den Haag," pr (A) ... **370.00**

RUDOLSTADT

Thuringia, Germany (DDR)
1720 to Present

History: Macheleid, with the patronage of Johann Friedrich von Schwartzbrug-Rudolstadt, established a Rudolstadt factory about 1720. During the factory's peak period, 1767–1797, the firm was leased to Noone. The arrangement lasted until 1800. Rococo style tablewares and large vases were made. After 1800 the firm was

sold to the Greiners. A series of partnerships followed.

Ernst Bohne Sons made decorative porcelain, coffee and tea sets, and figures between 1854 and 1920. Many products were similar to R. S. Prussia pieces. After 1920 the factory became a branch of Heubach Brothers.

Lewis Straus and Sons in New York were co-owners of the New York-Rudolstadt Pottery between 1882 and 1918. This firm received the right to use the Royal Rudolstadt designation. The firm produced household, table, and decorative porcelains and served as importers for the U.S. market.

The Rudolstadt-Volkstedt Porcelain Factory was nationlized in 1960.

Bowl
6¼" d, 5" h, yellow and lavender flowers, rust leaves, cream ground **120.00**
8⅜" d, hp poppies, cream ground, ftd **65.00**
9" d, 3" h, large hp flowers, white ground, gold scalloped border, "R. W." and shield mark **55.00**
10" d, pink, green, and white flowers, gold band **75.00**
10⅜" d, six figures, playing golf, period clothes, multicolored, Swartzburg **225.00**
12" l, 6" h, porcelain, tropical bird in relief with carved birds, bees and flowers, tan, light blue, and green, irreg edge, c1890 .... **725.00**

Bust, young lady in gown, multicolored **550.00**

Celery Tray, 10" l, hp large pink and white flowers, white ground **40.00**

Centerpiece, Pegasus and dolphin carrying shell chariot **250.00**

Chocolate Set, pot, four cups and saucers, roses and ferns, gold trim ... **100.00**

Condiment Set, creamer, sugar, toothpick, salt and pepper shakers, and tray, "Bluebird" pattern **100.00**

Creamer
5½" h, multicolored florals, cream ground **25.00**
Feathered gold over drape pattern, gold handle **45.00**
Kewpie design **65.00**

Creamer and Sugar
Apple blossoms, hp multicolored, artist sgd **60.00**
Pansies, cream ground **75.00**

Cup and Saucer
"Happifats" design **30.00**
Kewpies, eight action, multicolored, sgd "Rose O'Neill Wilson" **95.00**
Pastel flowers, gold trim **30.00**
Yellow and green roses **30.00**

Cup, Cov, and Stand
Molded multicolored classical scene, entwined branch dbl handles and

putto finial, gilt dentil rim, c1900
(A) **100.00**
Painted, man, woman, and two peasants in continuous landscape, gilt
dot and line border, dbl handles,
c1900 (A) **170.00**
Dish
8¼" l, open red flowers in center, tan
matte ground, leaf shape, ftd **40.00**
10" l, multicolored angels in center,
gray luster border **10.00**
10½" w, hp flowers, satin ivory
ground, gilt accents, shell shape . **70.00**

**Figures, 12½" h, polychrome, bisque fin-
ish, pr, (A) $850.00.**

Dresser Set, hair receiver, cov powder
jar, open handled tray, pastel roses,
white ground **60.00**
Ewer
5" h, flowers, pastel colors, c1890 .. **25.00**
9" h, molded mauve flowers, ivory-
pink ground, melon ribbed neck,
gold accents **75.00**
11¾" h, hp bird, butterfly, ferns, and
grasses, ivory ground, gold trim,
green serpentine spout, brown handle **150.00**
15" h, textured and enameled gold
leaves and flowers, white ground,
c1882 .... **200.00**
Figure, 3" l, lady's shoe, open design . **65.00**
Hair Receiver, 4¼" d, yellow roses,
green leaves, light yellow ground,
gold trim, "Prussia" over crown mark **55.00**
Hatpin Holder
5" h, ribbed body (A) **60.00**
Poppies, green and white ground, sgd
"Hahn" **50.00**
Inkwell, 6" l, 3½" h, attached tray,
multicolored flowers, cream ground **60.00**
Lamp, 20½" h, purple and pink clovers,
cream ground, emb top and base,
gold handles, urn shape **100.00**
Mug, 3¾" h, Kewpies, decals, sgd
"O'Neill" **125.00**

Pin Tray, 5" l, multicolored clover design **25.00**
Pitcher
5" d, 8" h, gray and gold bird, pink
leaves, cream ground **75.00**
5½" h
Floral design, cream ground, gold
trim **35.00**
Multicolored flowers, ivory ground **40.00**
9½" h, multicolored florals, gilt trim,
long thin neck, raised "Royal Rudolstadt" mark **165.00**
Plate
7⅜" d, Kewpies, eight multicolored
action, sgd "Rose O'Neill Wilson" **125.00**
7½" d, Kewpies, multicolored **110.00**
7¾" d, hp daisies, gold trim **10.00**
8" d
Kewpies, nine multicolored action,
sgd "Rose O'Neill Wilson" **135.00**
Lilies in center, sgd "Kahn," pr .. **45.00**
Open red poppies, green foliage
around outer edge, gold rim ... **40.00**
10½" d, blue transfer of old mill scene **85.00**
Serving Dish, 9" d, Art Deco style design, orange, yellow, black, and lime,
pedestaled **35.00**
Sugar Bowl, 6" h, multicolored flowers,
cream ground, gold dbl handles and
trim, blue mark **45.00**
Syrup, hp pink roses, burnished gold
handle and trim **40.00**
Tea Set, teapot, creamer, sugar bowl,
pink and purple pansies, heavy gold
trim **100.00**
Tray
7" d, pink Kewpies, green jasper
ground, cloverleaf shape, sgd
"Rosie O'Neill" **275.00**
12" l, day lilies pattern, cut dbl handles **70.00**
Urn, Cov
6½" h, hp flowers, cream ground,
gold trim, dbl handles **55.00**
7½" h, large multicolored florals, devil's head handles, gold trim, tan
matte finish **225.00**
10" h, mythological scene of Hector
and Andro crowning maiden, co-
balt ground, dbl gold handles **125.00**
Vase
4½" h, large clusters of pink and blue
flowers outlined in gold, beige
ground, amphora shape **75.00**
5¾" h, figural peacock, open wings,
multicolored **55.00**
8½" h, "Melitta at the Well," dark red
ground, dbl handles, sgd "Wagner" **400.00**
9½" h, porcelain, Satsuma style design, c1890 .... **325.00**
10½" h, 7" d, multicolored flowers,

yellow and beige ground, dbl handles **100.00**
Vase, Bud, gold dbl scroll handles, narrow neck with gold trim, pierced outer work, beige tones, c1884 .... **100.00**

ВРАТЬЕВЪ
Корниловыхъ

RUSSIA—GENERAL

Early 1800s to Present

History: The Kuznetsov family established a factory to manufacture porcelain and faience at Novocharitonowka in 1810. Their sons, trading as the Brothers Kuznetsov, managed the factory until the 1870s. They also operated other factories in Russia.

These factories produced powder boxes, vases, and toilet sets in blue and pink porcelain that were often enameled and gilded. Figures in biscuit porcelain were painted with regional costumes and other decorative motifs. Products from these Russian factories were exported to other European countries, the Far East, and India.

In 1891 the firm acquired the Francis Gardner factory near Moscow. Marks usually incorporated "Ms. Kuznetsov" along with the place of manufacture.

Native Russian porcelains developed during the 1800s due to the high duty on imported porcelains. The Kornilow Brothers established a factory to manufacture utilitarian wares in St. Petersburg in 1835.

The Yusupov Factory near Moscow operated from 1814 to 1831. White porcelain blanks for decoration were purchased from Sevres, Limoges, and Popov. Articles made at the factory were used as gifts for the members of the Tsar's family or for the friends and relatives of the Yusopovs.

The Popov Factory, established in 1806 at Gorbunovo, made dinner services, tea sets, and porcelain figures for an urban middle-class clientele. Popov's figures of Russian craftsmen, peasants, and tradesmen, are eagerly sought by collectors. The factory closed in 1872.

References: Marvin Ross, *Russian Porcelains,* University of Oklahoma Press, 1968.

Museums: Hermitage, Leningrad, Russia.

Bowl, 6½" d, blue flowers with yellow centers, dark rose-pink ground, "Moscow," $65.00.

Bowl
  6⅞" d, procelain, cobalt ext. mottled at molded lip, rubbed to white foot, late 19th C, Kuznetsov **75.00**
  8" d, bird and floral design, red, black, and gold, scalloped edge (A) **85.00**
  10½" d, radiating cobalt wavy lines, pink enameled sprigs, green grapes, gilt leaf sprigs, two center concentric rings, Kuznetsov, pr ... **750.00**
Box, Cov, 6¼" l, modeled as ram, black and white Kuznetsov (A) **25.00**
Breakfast Set, 6⅛" h, teapot, cov creamer, cov sugar, and rect cut-corner tray, military scenes, mustard ground, gold borders, reverse with farm birds in lavender, rosebud finials, domed covs (A) **2,600.00**
Ceremonial Cup, cov, shaped like samovar, "Kuznetsov" mark **200.00**
Coffee Can and Saucer, painted protrait of courtier in military uniform, cafe-au-lait ground, gilt star panels with musical instruments, c1800 (A) **240.00**
Coffeepot, 8" h, painted florals and leaves, white ground, molded lion head spout, coxcomb scrolled handle, early 19th C **135.00**
Cup and Saucer
  Dessert size, porcelain, white gilt, c1893, "Kornilow Bros" mark ... **60.00**
  Floral bouquet reserved on royal blue ground (A) **25.00**
  Green and red enameled Russian inscription in relief (A) **200.00**
  Iron-red and cobalt enameled Persian lion and rising sun reserved on vine ground, late 19th C (A) **125.00**
  Painted geometric designs, late 19th C, Kornilow Bros **75.00**
  Small blue flowers, white ground, "Made in U.S.S.R." mark **20.00**

Dessert Service, 9" h teapot, coffeepot, milk jug, waste bowl, stand, seven teacups, eight saucers, eight cake plates, trailing blue and green leafed rosevine, pink flowers, gilt accents (A) ... **440.00**

Dinner Service, multicolored folk decorations, gilt trim, set of 35 pcs (A) . **125.00**

Dish

7" l, porcelain, bird shape, blue and pink trim, gold beak, mid 19th C, pr **700.00**

9¾" l, central imperial crest in continuous landscape, molded Celtic interlaced design borders, canoe shape, late 19th C, Kornilow Bros **400.00**

Dish, cov, shaped as dove, "Kuznetsov" mark **200.00**

Figure

3" h, girl, cat, flowing blue **20.00**

5¾" h, porcelain, peasant, dancing, carrying hat in hand, polka-dot tunic, striped pants, 19th C, Popov . **275.00**

6" h, porcelain, Asiatic queen, seated on camel with palm, multicolored, mid 19th C, Popov (A) **880.00**

7⅝" h, porcelain, dancing girl, holding kerchief, pink dress, blue hat, mid 19th C, Kornilow Bros **675.00**

8½" h, porcelain, seated young girl, peasant clothes, large vase of flowers at side, multicolored, mid 19th C, Kornilow Bros (A) 1,**210.00**

8⅝" h, peasant woman, standing, holding fish wrapped in newspaper, child seated at feet, dated 1922, "hammer and sickle" mark **120.00**

9" h, porcelain, bearded pedlar leaning on tree stump carrying stick, long purple coat, basket, and knapsack, 19th C, Popov (A) **600.00**

10" d, 5½" h, porcelain, egg, pink floral spray, green leaves, blue ground **300.00**

Plate

8¾" d, central medallion of painted florals, four oval medallions with florals on border, cobalt ground, gilt tracery, early 19th C, Kornilow Bros **135.00**

9¼" d, purple grapes, white ground (A) **45.00**

9¾" d

Central design of gold armorial, blue and gilt edged border, shaped rim (A) **35.00**

Porcelain, center design of one warrior standing by stone marker, other seated on horse, scalloped edge, blue, green, red, white and gold enamel border, "Kuznetsov" mark **400.00**

Platter, 12½" l, 6" w, polychrome fish design, Kuznetsov **150.00**

Tea Service

Seven pcs, teapot, five 7" d plates, white ground, maroon, gold trim, "Made in U.S.S.R." **40.00**

Thirty pcs, 5½" h, teapot, cov creamer, dbl handled cov sugar, twelve cups and saucers, gilt flowers, cobalt ground, Kuznetsov (A) **825.00**

Teacup, porcelain, blue and green geometric design, gold trim, "Kornilow Bros" **45.00**

Teapot, 6¼" h, floral swags, cream ground, gilt neck, handle, spout, and cov, 19th C **175.00**

Vase

10⅞" h, porcelain, painted garden scene with groups of figures and ruins in gilt border reserved on lapis ground, reverse with gilt vase of fruit and flowers, acanthus-molded handles, female masks, early 19th C, Popov (A) **825.00**

40" h, black and gold drapery panels commemorating Revolution, c1927 **400.00**

SALT GLAZED STONEWARE

Staffordshire, England
1671 through the 19th C
Rhineland, Germany
1500s to Present

History: Stoneware is pottery that is fired at such high oven temperature that the body has vitrified and become impervious to liquids. A salt glaze is achieved by throwing salt into the high temperature oven causing the salt to volatilize. The sodium in the salt combines with the alumina and silica in the clay to form a thin vitreous coating on the surface of the stoneware. The glaze layer is also impervious and has minute pitting.

ENGLISH

In the late 17th century potters in north Staffordshire around Stoke-on-Trent began experimenting in hopes of producing a purely English style of salt glazed stoneware. John Dwight is credited with discovering the technique. In 1671 he was granted a patent for the manufacturing of salt glazed stoneware.

Six villages comprised "The Potteries" in Staffordshire. The greatest concentration of potters was in Burslem. Their salt glazed stoneware pieces were thin, lightweight, and made to compete with porcelain. A brown salt glaze stoneware was developed in the second half of the 18th century and used for beer jugs, tankards, flasks, and industrial wares.

With the advent of mold making and slip casting, more complicated shapes could be made. A wide range of utilitarian and decorative articles were produced. Few pieces contained factory marks.

The Burslem families of Wedgwood and Wood manufactured salt glaze stoneware beginning in the late 17th century. They trained a succession of master potters.

Enameled stoneware was introduced in the Staffordshire potteries about 1750. Enameled wares required a second firing, at a considerably lower temperature than the salt glaze oven, to "fix" the color to the pot. European and Oriental porcelain decorative motifs were enameled on salt glaze pieces. Transfer printing also was done on white salt glazed stoneware.

The first salt glazed figures were animals. These were not marked and rarely dated. Most salt glazed figures were made by pressing slabs of moist clay into a two-piece mold and then uniting the halves using a slip.

Groups of figures required the process of press-molding combined with hand modeling. A wide variety of salt glaze bird and animal figures were made between 1725 and 1755. Usually the figures were ornamental, but cow creamers and beer baiting jugs were useful exceptions.

GERMAN

Salt glazed wares were being manufactured in Germany by the early 16th century to fill the demand for drinking vessels for taverns. These brown salt glaze wares were also exported to England for more than two hundred years.

References: J. F. Blacker, *The ABC of English Salt-Glaze Stoneware from Dwight to Doulton*, Stanley Paul & Co., 1922; Arnold R. Mountford, *The Illustrated Guide to Staffordshire Salt-Glazed Stoneware*, Barrie & Jenkins, 1971; Louis T. Stanley, *Collecting Staffordshire Pottery*, Doubleday & Co., 1963.

Museums: American Antiquarian Society, Worcester, Mass.; City Museum, Stoke-on-Trent, England; British Museum, London, England; Colonial Williamsburg, Williamsburg, Virginia; Fitzwilliam Museum, Cambridge, England; Museum of Art, Rhode Island School of Design, Providence, Rhode Island; Nelson Gallery. Kins Museum, Kansas City, Missouri.

German: Kunstgewerbemuseum, Cologne, Germany; Metropolitan Museum of Art, New York; Rheinisches Landesmuseum, Bonn, Germany.

GERMAN

Condiment Dish, 6" l, molded, three melon cups resting on scalloped triform tray, crabstock handle with leaves **2,200.00**

Jelly Mold
3" d, form of thirteen pointed stepped star **450.00**
3¼" d, pleated bell shape, c1750 .. **425.00**

Jug
5¾" h, hand coiled oviform, spreading foot, 15th C, Sieburg **335.00**
6¾" h, rose-pink diapering on spout, green diapering with rose pink scrolls and florals around rim, multicolored florals on body, pear shape, strap handle and "kick," c1760 ....**1,100.00**
8" h, figures drinking at table between wheat borders in opaque colors (A) **100.00**
9" h, applied stylized rose medallion on front, brown mottled glaze, early 17th C, Germany (A) **180.00**

Mug
4⅜" h, incised and applied stylized flowers, gray globular body, reeded neck, Germany **100.00**
4¾" h, three rosettes imp on neck, loop handle, mid 17th C, Germany (A) **135.00**

Pitcher
5" h, raised scene of hunters, horses, hounds, and stag, twisted serpent handle wrapping around body, head forming spout **125.00**
8" h, tavern scene in relief, berry and vine border, gray body, vine handle **115.00**
11" h, relief of hunt scene, rustic subjects and gentleman, mid 19th C . **65.00**

Spirit Flask, 4" d, imp, exotic birds in molded compartments, c1760 ..... **500.00**

Sweetmeat Tray, 4⅞" l, triangular shape, ftd, c1750 .... **450.00**

Tankard, 11⅜" h, central band, three strap handles on shoulder, grooved foot, light brown and olive-gray glaze, Sieburg **225.00**

Teapot
3½" h, tan, dark green and white raised florals and beading **80.00**
4½" h, body molded with shells, anthemion, and scrollwork outlined in cobalt, faceted spout and loop handle, tripot feet molded with shells and claws, c1740 ....**1,900.00**

Tray, 12¾" l, rococo rim molded with panels of diapering, shells, and scrollwork, hexagon, c1750 .... **950.00**

ENGLISH

Baskets, 8¾" l, diamond reticulated mold, four petaled florets at junctions of scrolled handles, mounted on 10" l stand, c1760, pr 2,500.00

Bowl

7¼" d, painted scene of lady and man in farm setting, castle on reverse, diapering and reserved florals on int. rim, c1760 .... 2,050.00

8" d, painted famille rose style branches and rockwork, int. with chrysanthemum, diaper, and flowerhead border, c1755, Staffordshire (A) 200.00

9" d, polychrome enamels of bouquets and sprays, c1760-70, Staffordshire (A) 295.00

Creamer, 4½" h, emb flowers and eagles, blue striping, "Castleford" (A) . 50.00

Cup, 2⅞" h, molded, four shields of diapering, slip-cast, octagonal shape, ftd, ribbed handle with "kick," c1750 500.00

Dish

4½" w, molded int. with chinoiserie figures in landscape, chinoiserie figure, bird, and plants border, oval, c1765, Staffordshire (A) 880.00

8¼" d, center molded with geometrics and scrollwork, ozier molded rim, pierced cavetto 130.00

9⅜" l, leaf shape, emb songbird on fruit and leaf, veined ground, Thomas Wedgwood (A) 625.00

11⅞" d, white molded scroll panels of diaper and basketwork, pierced rim 85.00

14⅛" l, press-molded, patterned panels of basketwork, pierced rim with small cartouches of dots and diaperwork, c1760, Staffordshire (A) 70.00

Figure

3⅞" h, Kitty Clive, wide crinoline dress, grass mound base, c1760, Staffordshire (A) 715.00

4" l, press-molded fish, c1750, "Thomas & John Wedgwood" ... 350.00

5¾" h, seated monkey, paws under chin wearing collar, dark brown dots, ears, and eyes, c1750, Staffordshire (A) 2,261.00

6¾" l, recumbent lamb and ewe, grass mound base, c1750, Staffordshire 175.00

Jug

4" h, pierced and incised florals below "Nott. 1703," ribbed neck, rope twist handle, brown glaze, Nottingham (A) 3,950.00

6¾" h, white raised cherubs and boy

with animals, dark gray ground, white scroll designs on neck, octagonal 120.00

7¼" h, relief of British officers in combat, pear shape (A) 45.00

7¼" h, 4¼" d, three emb soldiers and large bird, gray, "E. Ridgway & Abington, Hanley" 120.00

7⅞" h, 3¾" d, "Argyle" design, blue and gray, Dudson 75.00

9½" h, relief of gentleman, hunter, hounds, and children, floral border, brown and beige glaze, c1834, imp "W.P. Scutts," (A) 100.00

10¼" h, cov, modeled as seated bear, chain in muzzle, dog between paws, clay chip fur, c1740, Staffordshire (A) 2,635.00

10½" h, multiple emb deer, gray-green, c1860, "D. Hughes & Co." 135.00

Jug and Bowl, 7¼" h jug, 6½" d bowl, painted chinoiserie figures in garden, iron-red diaper border, c1750-60, damaged (A) 440.00

Mug, 5⅞" h, molded profile of George III, initials "GR" forming flowerhead, neck with blue accented incised lines, c1760, Staffordshire 130.00

Pitcher, 5½" h, white, "Minton," $75.00.

Pitcher

4" h, off-white body, molded berry design, mid 19th C, Staffordshire . 60.00

4¼" h, raised "Good Samaritan" scene, violet accents 135.00

4½" h, Ichabod Crane motif, tan body, hand formed in handle, c1835 .... 80.00

8½" h, raised scene of Julius Caesar and flotilla of ships, tan, sq handle with intertwined ivy, c1839, "Charles Meigh" 250.00

9¾" h, continuous relief scene of "The Gypsy," tan body, glazed int., c1842, "Jones & Walley" 175.00

9⅞" h

Raised leaves and grain, white;

rope handle, "W. B. Cobridge, Bern" (A) **80.00**

Relief of American eagle and shield, Washington on reverse, dark brown, c1820 .... **400.00**

10" h, emb beehive, flowers and bees, white, imp "Dudson" (A) .. **185.00**

10½" h, Apostle in high relief, unmarked **265.00**

Plate

8⅜" d, molded relief scrolled reserves and geometric pattern, shaped and pierced border (A) **60.00**

9" d, border molded with portrait bust of King of Prussia, inscribed, divided by panels of trophies, eagle, c1765, Staffordshire (A) **600.00**

Sauceboat

3⅜" h, molded diaper panels, oval foot (A) **120.00**

4½" l, scratch blue design of flowers and foliage, scalloped rim, strap handle, c1750 .... **600.00**

5⅜" l, sides molded with rococo panel containing pineapple and leaves in basket, basketwork ground, ovoid, notched scroll handle, Cockpit Hill (A) **180.00**

6⅝" d, body molded with naked imp in grapevines outlined in cobalt, scalloped rim, grooved strap handle, four mask and claw feet, c1750 **800.00**

7⅞" l

Molded overlapping green leaves, painted flower sprays in pink line cartouches, c1760, Staffordshire **670.00**

Molded shells, scrolling foliage and branches, blue accents, two snails and cherub's head under spout, three mask and paw feet, c1750, Staffordshire (A) **1,300.00**

Spoon Tray, 6⅝" l, molded center of two

birds and scrolling flowers, lozenge shape, c1750 (A) **900.00**

Tankard, 5¼" h, painted scene of peasant girl in classical ruins, bell shape, flowers and scallops at rim, loop handle, c1760 ....**1,800.00**

Tea Caddy, molded diaperwork cartouches on sides outlined with scrolls on borders of trellis pattern panels, c1755, Staffordshire (A) **465.00**

Teapot

2½" h, line-turned body design, globular, dbl notched loop handle, faceted spout, c1740 ....**1,500.00**

3⅜" h, blue stylized florals, three paw feet, c1750-60, damaged (A) **310.00**

3½" h

Enameled Oriental blossoms and diapering, globular, crabstock handle and spout, c1760 ......**1,650.00**

Painted bird and peony, three paw feet, loop handle, restored, c1750, Staffordshire (A) **110.00**

Painted flower sprays and rock work, green and puce diaper border, crabstock handle, spout, and finial, c1755, repairs (A) **200.00**

3¾" h

Enameled famille rose colors of two Orientals seated in garden, cov with vignette of building, crabstock spout and handle, c1750-60, Staffordshire (A) **585.00**

Line and dot pattern, globular, faceted spout and acorn finial, c1740 ....**1,350.00**

4½" h

Molded as three story house, tiled roof, facade molded with rampant lion, fleur-de-lis and man in doorway, serpent spout, c1745 .**1,750.00**

One side shows castle and other

Left, pitcher, 7" h, tan, English registry mark, $100.00; center, shaker, 5½" h, cream, $165.00; right, jug, 8½" h, cream portrait of Robert Burns, beige ground, $475.00.

ruins with swans, globular, crabstock handle, spout, and knob
tinted in blue, carmine, yellow,
and turquoise, c1770 ....**2,700.00**
Polychrome Orientals in outdoor
scene, globular, crabstock handle and spout, sealed hairline,
c1760 ....**2,400.00**
5½" h
   Greek key and figure 8's molded
body, diamond shape, serpent
molded spout and handle at corners, stepped foot, Chinese lion
finial, c1750 ....**1,500.00**
   Pectin shell molded body, molded
naked boy and branch on spout,
cov with molded shells, c1745,
attrib to Thomas & John Wedgwood **1,550.00**
6¾" h, molded scrolling vine, cobalt
accents, heart shape, "bird's beak"
spout, c1745, Staffordshire (A) ... **800.00**
7" h, relief of birds flying with bamboo, white, cane handle, sq shape **135.00**
Spoon Tray, 6⅝" l, molded center of two
birds and scrolling flowers, lozenge
shape, c1750 (A) **900.00**
Tureen, 11¾" H-H, molded basket-
work, scroll-edged cartouches of diaper pattern, three claw feet, lion's
mask terminals, foliate scroll handles,
c1730, Staffordshire (A) **500.00**
Wall Pocket
   9½" l, cornucopia shape, molded
face of "Plenty," c1760, Staffordshire **875.00**
   10" l, cornucopia shape, relief center
portrait of Flora holding cornucopia
in scroll molded cartouche, pierced
scroll and shell rim, c1760, Staffordshire (A) **550.00**
Whistle, 3¾" h, press-molded, form of
woman wearing wide hooped skirt,
pleated cape, whistle attached to
back of skirt, c1725 .... **950.00**

SAMSON

**Paris, France
1845 to 1964**

History: Samson made reproductions and copies
of porcelains from famous manufacturers in hard
paste porcelains. Some of the items they copied
were originally only made in soft paste.

Edme Samson bought the Tinet factory in Paris.
Until 1873 he decorated porcelains produced by
other factories. Pieces he decorated had over the
glaze marks, often duplicating the mark of the
original factory.

Emile, his son, was the first in the family to
make reproductions of decorative porcelains and
figurals of the famous factories in England and
the Continent. He started in 1873. The reproductions also contained a copy of the original
mark under the glaze. Sometimes a small Samson
mark was added over the glaze.

The Samsons owned over 20,000 originals
of Meissen, Sevres, Chelsea, Capodimonte,
Chinese, and Japanese porcelains. They made
molds from these originals to produce their copies. Frankenthal, Ludwigsburg, Furstenburg, Vienna, Derby, Bow, Worcester, Chantilly, Tour-
nay, Vincennes, Mennecy, and Copenhagen
pieces also were copied, as were the tin glazed
earthenwares of Rouen, Sinceny, and Marseilles.

The company was operated by the Samson
family until 1964 when C. G. Richarchere took
over.

From about 1845 to 1905 the original marks
were imitated on the pieces they copied. The
company registered some trademarks after 1900
and used them underglaze after about 1905.

REPRODUCTION ALERT: Overglaze marks are
removed easily. There is evidence that a large
number of Samson marks have been removed so
that the pieces would appear to be from the
original manufacturers.

Candlesticks, 8¼" h, pastel colors, "gold
anchor" marks, pr, $500.00.

Box, cov
   3½" w, cov molded with profile portrait in laurel cartouche, molded
martial trophies, painted int. battle
scene, silver mounts, late 19th C
(A) **115.00**
   6¼" w, famille rose pattern, iron-red
whorl ground, cartouche shape,
hinged cov, c1860, iron-red "leaf"
mark (A) **130.00**

12¼" w, painted bouquets, floral "MA," gilt C-scrolls and trellis, bombe shape, gilt metal mounts, c1900, iron-red "Crowned A" mark (A) **350.00**

Candelabra, 9" h, five lights, applied foliage, leaf molded bobeches, pierced basket with flowers on top, scroll and shell molded bases, maid pouring water, pierced standards, late 19th C, blue "X'd swords & S," pr (A) **1,430.00**

Cup, cov, and stand, painted panels of exotic birds and insects in gilt scroll and mirror cartouches reserved on blue scale ground, trembleuse shape, berry finial, gilt dentil rims, c1890, blue "Sq Seal" marks (A) **155.00**

Dish, 16" d, ext. painted with two coats of arms, coronet in gilt scroll and winged cartouche, iron-red ground, beaded ormolu mount on rim, ormolu curled handles, foliage feet, late 19th C **425.00**

Figure

4" h, mother listening to little boy's prayers, white and gold **75.00**

5⅛" h, nymph, holding mask, puce cloak, sq pedestal, gilding, mid 19th C blue "X'd line" mark, (A) . **125.00**

6¼" h, gentleman, French court clothes, multicolored, late 19th C **85.00**

7" h, swans in Meissen style, pr **400.00**

7⅝" h, man playing bagpipe, woman with stringed instrument, both seated on tree stumps on scroll bases, pr **125.00**

7⅞" h, youth, feathered hat with flower, seated on tree stump, dog at side, floral encrusted base, ormolu mounted, late 19th C, blue "cross" mark **210.00**

8⅝" w, white rhinoceros, flesh tones, yellow horn, c1880, blue "cross" mark (A) **715.00**

8⅞" h, Neptune, dolphin on shell, scroll base, multicolored (A) **100.00**

9" h, boy seated on floral tree stump, pierced basket at side **200.00**

10¾" h, set of four continents, Asia, America, Africa, and Europe, tall scroll-molded bases, modeled after Bow, mid 19th C, gilt "A.B." marks (A) **715.00**

19¼" h, Venus in chariot in clouds, maidens and Cupids attending, swans with garlands on base, late 19th C, blue "X'd swords" mark .**1,500.00**

20½" h, bearded man in green cloak, knife in hand, before flaming altar, kneeling figure holding bowl, Diana in clouds, scrolls embracing nymph, oval grasswork base with

foliage border and gilt, c1880, blue "cross" mark, damaged (A) **2,500.00**

Hen on Nest, 7" l, florals, gilt trim, white ground **425.00**

Inkstand, 9" l, Royal Worcester style, florals and raised blue and gilt border, two cov ink pots **275.00**

Jar, 6¼" h, cov, painted armorial crown, shield, and chinoiserie floral and fruit sprays, blue, iron-red, black, and gold, devil's mask handles, late 19th C, pr (A) **350.00**

Jug, 11⅞" h, cabbage leaf shape, mask, blue scale ground reserved and painted with exotic birds in cartouches, late 19th C, blue "Sq seal" mark (A) **220.00**

Plate

9⅜" d, painted farmyard animals and exotic birds in landscapes, borders with insects and butterflies, shaped gilt foliage rims, blue "X'd swords" marks, set of 12 (A) **400.00**

9⅞" d, painted armorials, pink scale ground reserved with panels of flowers, late 19th C, pseudo Chinese marks, set of 6 (A) **310.00**

Potpourri Bowls

9⅞" h, bouquets on ledges in gilt line circ cartouches reserved on royal blue ground, gilt shell and foliage between, three gilt mask handles, three scroll feet above triangular bases, gilt pomegranate finials, late 19th C, pr (A) **970.00**

22" h, puce painted dancing figures and bouquets, ozier-molded border, pierced gilt metal rim, applied lion's mask and ring handles, seated putto finial, c1880, blue "cross & S" marks (A) **1,710.00**

Sauceboats

6" l, pink and gold Oriental designs with armorials, late 19th C, pr (A) **60.00**

7¾" l, matching tray, enameled florals and eagle with shield, late 19th C (A) **55.00**

Snuff Box, 3⅛" d, painted Watteau-type lovers and flowers in yellow scale border edged with gold scrolls **135.00**

Tea Caddy

4½" h, figures in landscape, iron-red, puce, pink and gilt scrolled cartouches, rect, c1880, blue "cross" mark **90.00**

5" h, flower panels, turquoise ground, rect (A) **60.00**

Vase

5⅜" h, painted exotic birds, Worcester style, dbl gourd shape, pr (A) . **60.00**

6" h, cov, Kakiemon palette of trailing peonies and floral band, cov with

fruit finial, c1880, iron-red "hunting horn & X'd S" marks **175.00**
6½" h, emb ladies' heads, white
ground, multicolored flowers, applied handles, c1840, pr **250.00**
7" h, cov, painted figures at quayside,
puce, gilt and iron-red laub-und-
bandelwerk cartouches, ormolu
branch handles, circ ormolu foot,
late 19th C (A) **290.00**
12¾" h, cov, painted exotic birds in
sunken panels, turquoise ground,
gilt insects, birds, and sprays, scroll
handles, shell motif terminals, mid
19th C, gold "anchor" mark (A) .. **175.00**
Vegetable Tureen, 8" l, 9½" w, polychrome and gilt flowers, eagles, and
shield, Oriental Export style (A) **120.00**

SARREGUEMINES

Lorraine, France
c1770 to Present

History: The Sarreguemines faience factory, one
of the most important manufacturers of French
faience, was established in Lorraine about 1770
by M. Fabray and Paul Utzscheider.

During the 19th century pottery and stoneware
in the English style were manufactured. Transfer
decorations were used frequently. Imitations of
Wedgwood's cream colored earthenware, black
basalt, cane, cameos, wall tiles, agate, and marbled wares were made in addition to biscuit figures and groups. Mocha ware also was manufactured.

Modern production includes faience and porcelain wares.

Museums: Sevres Museum, Sevres, France.

Basket, cov, 8½" l, majolica, ochre
ground, domed fruit lid **25.00**
Box, 6" d, multicolored, children in Kate
Greenaway-type clothes **60.00**
Butter Dish, Cov, 7½" d, majolica,
molded red strawberries, green and
yellow leaves, three berry knob, imp
"SARREGUEMINES, FRANCE" **115.00**
Compote
8½" d, 5" h, yellow, blue and pink
flower sprigs, ivory ground, ftd ... **48.00**
9½" d, majolica, series of five different raised fruits, natural colors ... **65.00**

Creamer, row of ducks and frogs, flower
border **45.00**
Dish, 10½" d, majolica, beige, tan, and
salmon coloring, shell shape, imp
"SARREGUEMINES" **110.00**
Figure, 8⅝" h, majolica, figure of vint-
ner beside barrel holding bottle and
glass, brown, green, and yellow oval
base, imp "SARREGUEMINES" **100.00**
Jug
5¼" h, majolica, character of man,
rosy cheeks, beige and brown colors, blue int. **65.00**
7½" h, majolica character of "The
Scotsman," red hair, blue and red
hat, grinning face **75.00**

**Pitcher, 8" h, white, imp "SARREGUEM-
INES," $125.00.**

Pitcher
7½" h, majolica, figural face, bushy
eyebrows, collar **85.00**
8¼" h, majolica, relief of rooster and
chicks, hawk overhead, green
glaze, blue int **50.00**
8½" h, majolica, figural, face,
multicolored **100.00**
Plate
6" d, "Yeddo" pattern, black transfer **45.00**
7" d, black transfer of man, pack on
back, woman and child in garden,
"Octobre," woven border, blue
line rim **10.00**
7½" d
Majolica, light green apples, gold
ground, imp "SARREGUEM-
INES," set of 10 .... **185.00**
Majolica, raised cherries and
leaves, beige ground, small scalloped edge **30.00**
Multicolored French comic scene **20.00**
7¾" d
Ironstone, black transfers of scenes
from Napoleon's life, green
transfer rims with banners, eagles

and "N," "Digoin & Sarreguem-
ines," set of 12 (A) **150.00**
Majolica, raised pomegranate design, natural colors **25.00**
8" d
Black transfers of Napoleonic
scenes, set of 6 .... **165.00**
Cobalt ground, wide lacy etched
gold centers and borders, set of
6 .... **100.00**
Majolica, scene of three running
rabbits, green glaze, verse on
border **35.00**
8½" d
Boy and girl in doorway, multicolored **35.00**
Two large green ferns in centers,
pink lattice work with white basketwork borders, set of 6 ...... **30.00**
9" d, molded beadwork, pierced and
beaded zig-zag border, pink luster,
c1820, imp "SARREGUEMINES"
(A) **50.00**
9½" d, "Cluny" pattern, cobalt and
gold trim **25.00**
12" d, majolica, raised strawberries,
grapes, and plums **85.00**
13½" d, multicolored country scene,
"Obernai, Digoin & Sarreguemines" mark (A) **10.00**
Potpourri Vase, 8⅝" h, shield shape,
molded satyr's mask handles, eight
holes in shoulder, splashed pink luster, c1820, imp "SARREGUEMINES,"
cov missing, (A) **90.00**
Vase, 9" h, "Sang de Boef," high gloss,
imp "SARREGUEMINES" **125.00**
Wall Shelf, 17" h, figural Norse god,
cobalt, green, and brown **850.00**

SCHAFER AND VATER

Thuringia, Germany (DDR)
1890 to 1962

History: The Schafer and Vater Porcelain Factory
was established in 1890 at Rudolstadt, Thuringia.
The factory produced many decorative pieces,
figures, dolls, and novelty wares in hard paste
porcelain. They also were decorators of white
ware blanks.

Records of the company ceased in 1962.

Basket, 6" l, white blown-out roses,
green jasper ground **65.00**
Bottle
5" h, figural Indian head in colors,
unmarked **70.00**
Figural, Santa Claus with bottle, doll,
and tree branch, blue, curved neck
handle **90.00**

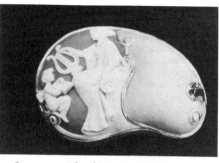

**Box, cov, 6" l, white cameo, light green
jasper ground, blue jewel on pink jasper
ground, imp mark, $100.00.**

Box
4¼" l, 3½" w, bisque, dog emerging
from doghouse, cat waiting on roof,
multicolored **85.00**
5" l
"Egyptian" series, girls, one reclining on cov and sides, pink
ground **115.00**
White cameo of nymph and Cupid,
blue ground, oval **55.00**
Chamberstick, female faces in relief .. **55.00**
Clock, 7" h, lady playing two lutes,
green and white coloring **85.00**
Creamer
3½" h
Figural, blue and white bear's
head, overcoat and muff **50.00**
Maiden, jug and keys **100.00**
3¾" h, blue cow in dress, #6517 .. **100.00**
4" h, figural blue and white kneeling
witch **50.00**
5" h, figural, goat, blue **45.00**
5½" h
Goose in bonnet and shawl, #6452 **125.00**
Seated goat, boutonnieres **110.00**
Figure
5¼" h
Boy holding flask, blue **85.00**
Dog, seated, light blue, red bow,
black base, placard on neck "I
am a Gay Dog" **100.00**
8½" h, multicolored violinist, matte
finish, unmarked **100.00**
Comical bust of sailor, blue suit, wide
open mouth, inscribed "H. M.
Breezy" on hat **65.00**

"Why Be Unhappy? I'm Ensured,"
dog with bandages, multicolored . **135.00**
Woman sitting on fence rail, nodding
head, multicolored **95.00**
Flask, figure of seated man in top hat
and tails, woman in lap, "What else
you want?," brown glaze **85.00**
Hair Receiver
  3½" l, pink jeweled jasper, triangular   **50.00**
  Raised woman's face on front, jew-
  eling on body, triangular **90.00**
Hatpin Holder
  Art Nouveau style ladies' heads, lav-
  ender jasper ground, gold trim . . . **95.00**
  "Egyptian" series **135.00**
  Figural, seated Geisha with fan **140.00**
  White cameo heads, pink jasper
  ground, blue trim **95.00**
  Woman's portrait, pink, green and
  gold, blue ground **135.00**
Match Holder
  3¼" h, two monkeys sitting back to
  back on tray, inscribed "Scratch My
  Back" **110.00**
  4½" h, black couple dancing, holder
  on back, multicolored **225.00**
Pitcher
  4" h, figural
    Devil, multicolored **100.00**
    Female clown kneeling, cape and
    fan, multicolored **50.00**
    Woman with fan, blue and white,
    marked **70.00**
  5" h, white cameos of cherubs and
  garlands, green jasper ground,
  ram's head spout **55.00**
Plaque, 4" w and 6" w, white classic
cameos, blue ground, pr **65.00**
Salt and Pepper Shakers, smiling pear
and apple, multicolored **90.00**
Teapot, single cup size, smiling apple,
multicolored **120.00**
Tray, 5" l, 4" w, emb pink cameos of
girls' heads **30.00**
Urn, 6" h, white Grecian lady in ship,
dark green ground **110.00**
Vase, 4⅛" h, "I'm So Discouraged," boy
facing wall **130.00**

SCHLEGELMILCH PORCELAINS

History: The manufacturing of R. S. Prussia hard
paste porcelains began when Erdmann Schlegelmilch founded his porcelain factory at Suhl, Thuringia in 1861. Reinhold Schlegelmilch, Erdmann's brother, established his porcelain factory
at Tillowitz, Upper Silesia in 1869. These two
factories marked the beginning of private ownership of porcelain factories in that region.

The founding of these factories coincided with
the time when porcelain items were experiencing
a big demand, especially in the United States
and Canada. The peak exporting years were from
the mid-1870s until the early 1900s. The brothers
were able to supply large quantities of porcelains
by utilizing new industrial production methodology and the availability of cheap labor.

R. S. PRUSSIA

Erdmann Schlegelmilch
Suhl, Thuringia, 1861 to 1920
Reinhold Schlegelmilch
Tillowitz, Upper Silesia
1869 to 1956

Both Erdmann and Reinhold used the "RSP"
mark. The famous "Red Mark" first appeared in
the late 1870s and was used until the beginning
of World War I. Decorative objects and tablewares were back stamped with the trademark
featuring the initials "R. S." inside a wreath, a
star above, and the word "Prussia" below.

There was a tremendous quantity of items produced with the "RSP" trademark. In addition to
art objects, dresser sets, a large variety of tablewares (including complete dinner sets), and
cake, chocolate, tea and coffee sets were all
manufactured.

An endless number of "RSP" molds were
made. Identical shapes were decorated differently; the same shape was made in a variety of
sizes. Many molds produced pieces in the Rococo
style, including ornately fashioned scrollwork
and flowers as part of the design of the blank.
Some blanks were exported to the United States
for the home decorating market.

Most "RSP" marked porcelains were decorated by transfer or a combination of transfer and
enameling or hand applied gilt. Decorations
were applied over the glaze. A few pieces were
hand painted.

Decoration themes on "RSP" porcelains included: animals, birds, figural, floral, portrait,
and scenics. Many pieces incorporated more
than one theme. Floral themes were the most
common; animal and fruit themes were the
scarcest.

Background colors were part of the decorating
scheme and not the finish or the glaze. These

colors were applied over the glaze by the transfer method to highlight the central theme.

A variety of finishes such as glossy, iridescent, luster, matte, pearl, satin, etc., were used to complete an "RSP" piece. Gilt trim often was utilized on borders, bases, handles, feet, or to outline a particular design.

The Suhl factory stopped producing R. S. Prussia marked porcelains in 1920, unable to recover from the effects of World War I. The Tillowitz factory was located in a region where political boundaries kept changing. It finally came under the Polish socialist government control in 1956.

E. S. GERMANY

Suhl, Thuringia, c1900 to c1925

Erdmann's factory at Suhl was associated with the E. S. marks. Some of the marks incorporated "Prov. Saxe," "1861," or "Suhl" in the mark.

The style and decoration of the porcelains were different in shape and decor from the "RSP" examples. Changes reflected fashions of the times. The porcelains had the elegant, flowing lines of the Art Nouveau period rather than the convoluted rococo shape between 1895 and 1905. A great number of "ES" pieces were totally hand painted. After 1905 the porcelain decoration returned to more classical and mythological themes and to simpler forms. Many of the transfers were in the style of Angelica Kauffmann.

R. S. GERMANY

Tillowitz, Upper Silesia

The forms and decorations of "R. S. Germany" were molded more simply, had more subtle decorations, and reflected the Art Deco period.

Reinhold concentrated on tablewares. Many examples were hand painted. Reinhold used a mark similar to the "RSP" mark at his Upper Silesia factory, except that "Germany" was in-

cluded instead of "Prussia." The mark was usually under the glaze as opposed to the overglaze "RSP" mark. A number of large American department stores had special patterns created just for their use. Many of the porcelain blanks used for home decorating contain the "RSG" mark. Some exported blanks were decorated professionally by Pickard, a decorating studio for china in Illinois.

R. S. POLAND

Poland, 1945 to 1956

R. S. Poland pieces have predominately classical decorations or simple designs rather than the ornate or rococo decorations and designs of "RSP" porcelains. Art objects, such as vases and jardinieres, dominated production over common tablewares. After World War II, little export business was done. R. S. Poland examples are quite rare.

Reinhold Schlegelmilch's factory came under control of the socialist government in Poland in 1956.

References: Mary Frank Gaston, *The Collectors Encyclopedia of R. S. Prussia & Other R. S. & E. S. Porcelains*, Collector Books, 1982; George W. Terrell, Jr., *Collecting R. S. Prussia, Identification and Values*, Books America, 1982; Clifford S. Schlegelmilch, *Handbook of Erdmann and Reinhold Schlegelmilch, Prussia-Germany & Oscar Schlegelmilch, Germany*, privately printed, 3rd edition, 1973.

REPRODUCTION ALERT: Since the 1960s, R. S. Prussia collecting has grown rapidly. "RSP" pieces are being reproduced. There is a fake RSP red mark in the form of a decal which can be applied, glazed, and fired onto a piece of porcelain. This mark has an overall new appearance when compared to the old mark.

Japanese porcelain imports try to imitate "RSP" porcelains in type, decor, and mold. There are marked and unmarked examples. Most pieces initially have a paper "Made in Japan" label, but it is removed easily. The Lefton China Company manufactures reproductions.

There are many ways to spot the reproductions. The reproductions and Japanese imports are fairly thick. The scallops, scrolls, and lattice are clumsy rather than delicate. Often the decoration is too bright. The background colors are not subtle, and the transfers are applied poorly. The gold trim lacks patina. These porcelains are sold in gift shops and flea markets.

Collecting Hints: Not all "RSP" is marked. Examples usually can be identified by studying the mold and the decor of an unmarked piece to see if it matches a known mold or design.

R. S. PRUSSIA

Berry Set
    6 pcs, 10" d, master bowl, 5" d five bowls, green leaves in different shades, pale greenish-white ground   **200.00**
    7 pcs, 10" d master bowl, six serving bowls, large open flowers, green, gold, blue, and white ground, red mark **350.00**
Biscuit Jar
    6" h, roses, cream and green ground, red mark **225.00**
    Pearlized lilies of the valley design, shells form rim and feet, red mark **150.00**
Bowl
    5½" d, lily design, cream and yellow ground, unmarked **40.00**
    6¼" d, lavender and white lilacs, blue and yellow shading, light lavender ground, scalloped rim, red mark . **185.00**
    6¼" d, 2½" h, four large lilies of the valley, trailing stems on int., pink, yellow, and white ruffled rim, 4-ftd, "R. S. Tillowitz, Silesia" mark ... **40.00**
    7" d, "Mill" scene, brown shades, 3-ftd, marked (A) **275.00**
    8½" d, gold flowers and gold chain tracery, yellow and blue iris design, green fronds, white ground, ruffled scallops alternating with indented U-forms, red mark **140.00**
    10" d
        "Countess Flora" portrait, Tiffany finish border with cherubs, unmarked **1,200.00**
        Florals, scalloped shell mold, red mark **150.00**
        Florals, white ground, 30 jewels, red mark **375.00**

Sprays of pink roses, green leaves, scalloped and beaded petal molded rim **85.00**
10¼" d
    Floral decor, blown-out rim, red bark **185.00**
    White puffed cosmos, white and yellow florals, buds, stems, and leaves, gold edge rim, white ground, red mark **180.00**
10½" d
    Center portrait of angels, light and dark skinned women, green ground, sgd "Boucher," "St. Kilian" mark **175.00**
    Iris mold, "Winter" season design, satin finish, red mark **950.00**
    Multicolored divided florals **190.00**
    Pink roses and snowballs, green and cream tinted ground, red mark **200.00**
11" d
    Blown-out leaf and grape rim, floral dec, unmarked **125.00**
    Icicle mold, "Old Man in Mountain" design, red mark **850.00**
    Mold #96, pink roses, red mark . **200.00**
    Swans and bluebirds overhead, molded flower rim, red mark .. **475.00**
13" l, 8½" w, multicolored flowers, red border, opal jewels, red mark **250.00**

Cake Plate
    10" d, laurel chain and hanging basket design, red mark **165.00**
    10½" d
        Irid jewels, large flowers, extensive gold trim, marked **340.00**
        Red roses, white flowers, gold trim, cream and green ground, open handles, unmarked **185.00**
    10¾" d, pears, grapes, and plums design, red mark **225.00**
    11¼" d, swans, gazebo scene, multicolored, open dbl handles, marked **545.00**
    11½" d
        Floral design, open handles, red mark **140.00**

R. S. Prussia, left, demitasse cup and saucer, white, camelia, gilt trim, red and green mark, $60.00; center, box, cov, 5" l, 1½" h, multicolored florals, white ground, sgd, $350.00; right, chocolate set, "Laurel Chain" pattern, $1,600.00.

Poppies, green leaves, green and gold shades ground, red mark .. **185.00**

12" H-H, pink and red tea roses, leaves, shades green ground, red mark **115.00**

Celery Tray

12" l, icicle mold, swan on lake, blue and cream, red mark **435.00**

12¼" l, satin snowballs, scalloped mold, pierced handles, unmarked **150.00**

Chocolate Pot

9" h, roses and snowballs design, 6 molded drape feet, floral finial, red mark **350.00**

10¼" h, point and clover mold, pink roses, red hydrangeas, outlined in gold, red mark **400.00**

10½" h, white floral motif, magenta and light yellow ground, domed cov, pierced finial, blown-out top, scrolled base, marked (A) **175.00**

Chocolate Set

Blue medallions, florals, gold trim, red mark **650.00**

Pink roses, white blossoms, pearlized yellow and green ground, scalloped rims, gold trim, Pot, four cups and saucers, red marks **375.00**

Roses, pale yellow ground, cups with rose blown-out tops, red mark ... **850.00**

"6 Flowers" design, ftd pot, six ftd cups and saucers, red mark (A) ...**2,150.00**

Compote

7" sq, white roses, red holly berries, pearlized green ground, ftd, red mark **150.00**

7" w, 4" h, center lilies, white, purple, blue pods, green leaves, scalloped edge, beige ground, satin finish, red mark **350.00**

Cracker Jar

8½" h, white clematis, cobalt ground, gold trimmed handles and finial, red mark (A) **1,980.00**

Blue ground, leaf handles and finial, red mark **250.00**

Dbl portrait of Mmes. Lebrun and Recamier, soft green and gold ground, floral border and finial, unmarked **700.00**

Creamer

4" h

Bluebirds, lavender and yellow flowers, gold trim, scalloped rim, ftd, unmarked **100.00**

Pheasant and pine tree design, marked **250.00**

Green and yellow flowers, green ground, melon shape, marked ... **75.00**

Creamer and Sugar

Chickens on creamer, turkeys on sugar, "Wheellock" mark **300.00**

Floral dec, gilt accents, red marks .. **65.00**

Icicle mold, three swans on lake, light blue and tan, red marks **700.00**

Light and dark blue and pink flowers, scalloped, gold stenciling, 4 ftd, red marks **200.00**

Mold #576, castle scene, multicolored, red marks **550.00**

Peach and pink roses, gold rope rims, red marks **185.00**

"Snowbird" pattern, marked (A) **500.00**

Cup and Saucer

Blown-out upper body, pink roses, gray shading, red marks **115.00**

Pink roses, green ground, unmarked **70.00**

Yellow roses design, red marks **55.00**

Demitasse Cup and Saucer

"Melon Eaters" panels, jewels, ftd, red marks, pr (A) **900.00**

Purple blossoms, light green and orange shading, blown-out upper portion, red marks **100.00**

Dish

7¼" l, pink flowers, multicolored leaves, shell form white emb scrolls and verticals, red mark **150.00**

12" d, bun, center roses, green and blue shading, irreg gold edge, open dbl handles, unmarked **135.00**

Dresser Tray

11" l, "Summer" season design, iris border, red mark **750.00**

12" l

Large pink and white roses, satin finish, fluted rim, pierced dbl handles, red mark **135.00**

Point and clover mold, yellow roses, turquoise and gold border, red mark **240.00**

Gravy Boat, "Melon Eaters" design, dbl handles (A) **475.00**

Hair Receiver

Clusters of rose asters, gold trim, white ground, applied light green bow, diamond shape, red mark .. **150.00**

Pink and red roses, light chartreuse ground, red mark **175.00**

Pink roses, white ground, green border, 4-ftd, red mark **65.00**

Hatpin Holder

"Admiral Perry-Midst Ice and Snow" design, red mark (A) **800.00**

Pink flowers and daisies reflecting in water, octagonal, marked **115.00**

Humidor, 5¼" w, 6" h, rose and chrysanthemum pattern, gray-blue ground, octagonal red mark **650.00**

Ice Cream Set, 11" d master bowl, 6" d five bowls, icicle mold, "Snowbird" design, red marks **4,000.00**

Muffineer, 4¾" h, pink and yellow roses, ruffled gold edge, turquoise

skirt, vertical ribs at base, flared top,
red mark 135.00

Mustard Jar
Floral bottom, white ground, jewels,
floral finial, red mark 165.00
"Snowbird" pattern, marked (A) 300.00

Pitcher, 10½" h, water, three colored
roses, cream and dark green ground,
blown-out leaves and gold cherries at
base, red mark 750.00

Planter, 7½" l, 3½" w, pink florals, green
leaves, jeweled, ftd, red mark 400.00

Plate
7½" d
Pink pansies, green ground, scalloped edge 65.00
Small pink roses, green leaves,
cream ground, red mark 50.00
8¼" d, multicolored castle scene, red
mark 695.00
8½" d
Black and white turkey, red mark . 550.00
Carnation mold, gold carnation,
red and pink roses, marked 140.00
Hp pink and white flowers, green
ground, raised gold scrolled
edge, red mark 135.00
Multicolored puffed florals and
pods, border of eight scallops
outlined by gold tracery and separated by emb fleur-de-lis, red
mark 125.00
Plume mold, lilac and pink flowers,
aqua to white ground, gold trim,
raised white emb leaves, scalloped edge, red mark 100.00
9" d
"Melon Eaters" design, marked (A) 825.00
"Spring" season design, keyhole,
red mark 900.00
White roses, green ground, "R. S.
Suhl" mark 85.00
"Winter" scene, satin finish,
blown-out iris, red mark 750.00
11" d
G-medallion mold, pink poppies,
small daisies, green and orange
shaded ground, red mark 165.00
Pink and white carnations, light
green ground, emb shell border,
red mark 215.00

Powder Box, cov, pink and yellow irises, gold outlining, open dbl handles, red "Reinhold Schlegelmilch,
Tillowitz,Germ" mark 65.00

Sugar
Multicolored dogwoods, upper sides
blown-out with pie crust edge, gold
trim cov, red mark 85.00

Syrup Pitcher and Tray, point and clover

mold, pink and white roses, ivory
ground, leaf finial, red mark 225.00

Talcum Shaker, 5" h, mold #539, rose
dec, red mark 225.00

Tankard
10½" h, ball and leaf mold base, large
open flowers, red mark 575.00
10¾" h, two swans, green fir tree,
white ground, marked, repaired .. 350.00
11½" h, acorn mold, mill scene,
shades of brown and tan, red mkd 1,700.00
14½" h, pink and yellow roses, eight
ball feet 625.00

Tea Set, teapot, creamer, sugar bowl
Dogwood blossoms, green ground,
gold trim, squat blown-out shape,
melon ribbing, red marks 335.00
"Melon Eaters" design, marked (A) .1,800.00

Tray
11½" d, roses in center, blown-out
roses on border, gold, unmarked . 135.00
12" l, 7½" w, pink and white roses,
satin finish, scalloped rim, pierced
dbl handles, marked 145.00
12¼" l, 6¼" w, swan scene, satin finish, red mark 270.00
12¾" l, 9" w, rose decor, open dbl
handles, red mark 150.00
14" l, 7" w, pheasants in forest scene,
beaded medallions, open dbl handles, red mark 525.00

Vase
2½" h, multicolored peacock, unmarked 200.00
4" h, "Hummingbird" design, unmarked 500.00
6" h, pink florals, green luster ground,
two small jewels, red mark 100.00
7" h, "Melon Eaters" design, jewels,
loving cup shape, red mark 900.00
8" h
"Dice Throwers," dark green, lavender, and yellow, opal jewels,
ftd, unmarked 550.00
Multicolored scene of four pheasants, Suhl mark 265.00
8½" h, "Melon Eaters" design, jewels, loving cup shape, red mark ..1,200.00
9½" h
"Melon Eaters" design, marked .. 475.00
White lilies, light green ground, dbl
handles, red mark 275.00
11" h, roses dec, loving cup shape,
red mark 400.00

E. S. GERMANY

Bowl
9½" d
Art Nouveau style portrait of

woman, lavender dress, luster green ground, gold border and trim, "E. S. Prov. Saxe" mark .. **265.00**

Bust of woman, flower garland in hair, green marbled ground, dark red rim, "Royal Saxe" mark ... **185.00**

12½" l, 8" w, pink, lavender, and white flowers in center, blown-out flowers on rim, rose shading, gold rim, "Prov. Saxe" mark **100.00**

Chocolate Pot, shaded pink peonies, raised enamel accents, "Prov. Saxe" mark **80.00**

Dish, 8" l, rust flowers, yellow, and lilac accents, orange and cream ground, leaf shape, "Prov. Saxe" mark **20.00**

Dresser Tray, 10½" l, long stemmed pink and peach tulips, "Prov. Saxe" mark **50.00**

Jar, 7½" d, portrait of woman with rose, irid ground, "Prov. Saxe" mark **155.00**

Pin Tray, 7" l, pink, white and yellow chrysanthemums on light yellow ground, border with large dark pink grape leaves outlined in gold, raised grape clusters, open dbl handles, "Royal Saxe" mark **50.00**

Plate

6½" d, center scene of three classical ladies and cherubs, gold outlined green and rose inner bands, "Prov. Saxe" mark **40.00**

8½" d

Multicolored portrait of Sitting Bull, "Royal Saxe" mark **125.00**

Orange poppies, heavy gold rim, "Prov. Saxe" mark **45.00**

9½" d

Center portrait of woman wearing bustle dress, multicolored, 6 blown-out floral sections on border, gilt rococo rim, "Royal Saxe" mark **140.00**

Scene of two women under tree with cherub, dark red band, gold tracery, garland of flowers, "Prov. Saxe" mark **110.00**

10" d

Center scene of lady and cherub, turquoise inner border, gold tracery, "Royal Saxe" mark **55.00**

Multicolored portrait of "Friedrich Wilhelm II Der Grosse Kurfurst," ivory ground, light blue irid border, gold tracery, "Royal Saxe" mark **75.00**

11" d, heavy raised multicolored floral border, dbl handles, "Royal Saxe, Germany" mark **175.00**

Powder Jar, painted geese, cobalt ground, ftd, "Prov. Saxe" mark **120.00**

Rose Jar, Cov, portrait of lady with rose, irid ground, "Prov. Saxe" mark **120.00**

Sugar, cov, large pink primroses, yellow ground, light blue bands at rim and lid, blown-out lower portion, "Prov. Saxe" mark **40.00**

Tea Strainer, floral decor, shape #491, "E. S. Prov. Saxe" mark **100.00**

Toothpick Holder, multicolored Indian chief, raised scrolls **100.00**

Vase

3½" h, white open flowers on neck, green leaves on base, raised gold tracery, Aladdin lamp shape, "Prox. Saxe" mark **110.00**

6" h

Center portrait of lady with doves, raised turquoise beading, gold ground, dbl gold handles **200.00**

Classic portrait, multicolored, apple-green ground, gold handles and trim, "Prov. Saxe" mark ... **75.00**

6½" h

Goddess with doves, multicolored, marked **250.00**

Portrait of Oriental girl, maroon ground, gold trim, dbl handles, "Prov. Saxe" mark **275.00**

8" h, center portrait of woman and Cupid in gold medallion, burgundy ground, "Royal Saxe" mark **165.00**

8½" h, butterflies and palm trees, matte white, marked **75.00**

9¼" h, center portrait of woman

Purple and cobalt, gold edging and medallion outline, heavy gold dbl handles, "Prov. Saxe" mark **225.00**

White gown, gold, and medallions, irid purple and white ground, cobalt trim, gold dbl handles, "Prov. Saxe" mark **275.00**

9½" h, painting of lady holding flaming heart, gold trim, three handles, "Prov. Saxe" mark **140.00**

10" h, center medallion of semi-nude lady with angel, green marbled ground, maroon rim, gold scroll dbl handles, "Prov. Saxe" mark **250.00**

11¼" h, center portrait, turquoise jeweling, irid ground, "Royal Saxe" mark **235.00**

11½" h, Art Deco style lady, red and aqua jeweling, gold beading, gold dbl handles, marked **450.00**

12" h, blue, pink, and purple iris design, multicolored ground, gold rim, dbl gold handles, "Prov. Saxe" mark **80.00**

13½" h, portrait of lady and peacock, front and reverse, lady and doves below portraits, gold dbl handles

and beading, "Prov. Saxe, Suhl"
mark **750.00**

R. S. GERMANY

Basket
4¼" l, 3" h, three yellow roses on
each side, pink shading, scalloped
rim and handle, steeple mark **50.00**
Hp pheasant scene, satin finish, blue
mark **160.00**
Berry Bowl, 5" d, irreg border, emb line,
six-sided scooped form, iris type flowers with flame centers, off-white
ground, apple-green accents **10.00**
Berry Set, master bowl, three serving
bowls, large lavender flowers, yellow-brown ground, ... **50.00**
Bone Dish, overall cherub decor,
multicolored, blue mark **25.00**
Bowl
6½" d, orange-red roses, black outlined leaves, gold band, 3 handles,
marked **65.00**
7¾" l, pink and white water lilies,
green ground, oval shape, dbl handles **65.00**
9" d, morning glories, pastels, scalloped edge **50.00**
10" d
Orange and yellow tiger lilies center, gray, blue, and lime green
ground, gold outlined scalloped
edge **75.00**
Orange florals, fluted, green mark **65.00**
10¼" l, four clusters of pink, orange,
and white roses, tan to white
shaded ground, gold tracery bor-
der, oval shape, open dbl handles **70.00**
12½" l, 8½" w, center cluster of pink
and yellow roses, small pink and
white flowers on inner edge, stippled floral edge, large yellow
leaves, steeple mark **150.00**

R. S. Germany, cake plate, 10" H-H, pink
roses, green and cream ground, green
mark, $40.00.

Bread Plate, center multicolored flowers, blue and white irises, gold outlined petals and rim, steeple mark .. **125.00**
Cake Plate, 10" H-H, three large orange
poppies, buds, and leaves, green
mark **70.00**
Cake Set
9⅝" d master plate, four 6¼" d plates,
long stemmed jonquils, shaded
gray, white, and yellow-brown
ground **85.00**
Candy Dish, 7" sq, orange roses, gray-
green ground, scalloped rim, ... **30.00**
Celery Tray
10" l, lavender flowers, light green
ground, ... **40.00**
10½" l, white and pink roses, pink
ground, gold tracings, blue mark . **60.00**
Chocolate Pot, 6" h, white rose, green
tints, gold trim, green mark **75.00**
Chocolate Set
10" h, pot, five cups and saucers,
large roses, green-yellow ground,
green leaf border, gold trim, green
mark **340.00**
Pot, six cups and saucers, hp grapes
and leaves in gold outlined, blue
and red marks **450.00**
Creamer, cov, apricot roses, gold **60.00**
Creamer and Sugar
Irid green bases, spattered yellow upper sections, black handles and
rims, steeple mark **40.00**
Pink roses, green tint, gold trim, green
marks **100.00**
Cup and Saucer
Dogwood blossoms, light brown
shading **40.00**
Tulips, hp, shaded ground **45.00**
Demitasse Cup and Saucer, open white
lilies, gold trim **35.00**
Dish
4¾" l, mint green border, violets on
int., leaf shape, open handles,
green mark **20.00**
8" l, large aqua-white snowballs,
green leaves, gold flowers, pearl
moss tones, yellow accents, basket
shape, figure-8 form handles **45.00**
Dresser Tray, 10¼" l, multicolored florals, blue to white ground, gold ruffled border, emb scoops **80.00**
Hair Receiver
Open flowers, pale green ground ... **40.00**
Roses, raised gold leaves, green mark **60.00**
Hatpin Holder
Art Deco style, shades of blue and
yellow **40.00**
Blue floral design **40.00**
Orange poppy pattern, green mark . **50.00**
Pink and white roses, green ground,
blue mark **70.00**

Inkwell, 3" d, 2¾" h, pink roses, white ground **75.00**

Match Holder
2¼" d, pink roses, shaded brown ground, molded ridges on bottom, barrel shape, steeple mark **100.00**
Figural, pipe on tray **35.00**

Miniature, creamer and sugar, pink iris, tan and brown ground **40.00**

Nappy, large groups of white hydrangeas, light green shaded ground, gold trim, triangular handle, blue mark . . **35.00**

Nut Set, large bowl, four smaller bowls, open white poppies, light green ground **100.00**

Pin Tray, 8" l, orange and white poppies, gray ground, open dbl handles, blue mark **35.00**

Pitcher
3¾" h, pastel roses, cream ground, gold knob and handle, scalloped rim **65.00**
9½" h, large white flowers, smaller pink flowers, profuse green stems and pods, apple-green, gold tracery at top, beige and gold on bottom, cider type **115.00**

Plate
6¼" d
Tulips, brown-cream ground, green star mark **18.00**
White flowers, green-brown ground, green star mark **18.00**
8½" d
Large pink and white roses, shaded brown and pink ground **40.00**
Pink and yellow carnations, shaded ground **35.00**
Turquoise and white dogwood flowers, green ground, gold stems, emb rococo border **25.00**
White and red flowers, green holly, red berry border **60.00**
9½" d, center dogwood flowers, raised gold trim, white and cocoa brown ground, rococo border, two small handles **45.00**
10" d
Hp pink and white carnations, open handles, green mark **50.00**
Large orange poppies **40.00**
12" d, anemones in peach on white ground **75.00**

Relish Tray
9¼" l, lavender and pink flowers, green stems and pods, pale tan ground, curved sides, emb ends, two open handles **20.00**
Multicolored flowers outlined in gold, ivory ground, open dbl handles, green mark **45.00**

Sugar, cov
Green, orange, and lavender florals, gold trim, dbl triangular handles, open steeple finial **20.00**
Pink and white roses **18.00**

Talcum Shaker, 5" h, yellow roses, white ground, blue and gilt top **60.00**

Tankard, 11½" h, poppies and pansies, blown-out border, dark green base shaded to yellow top, gold trim, steeple mark **250.00**

Toothbrush Holder, large pink roses, green leaves, leaf form, large oval over smaller oval, pierced for three brushes **100.00**

Tray
10½" l, 5" w, multicolored farmhouse scene, open handles **90.00**
15" l, 5" w, white flowers, yellow centers, green leaves, cream to green ground, dbl open handles **40.00**

Trivet, 6¼" d, white and pink flowers, green leaves, cream to blue ground, gold tracery, blue mark **35.00**

Vase
4¼" h, scene of woman feeding chickens **150.00**
4¾" h, gold outlined pansies, ivory ground, steeple mark **100.00**

R. S. Poland, berry bowl, 4½" sq, white and pale orange florals in center, green leaves, small orange-gold border flowers, $50.00.

R. S. POLAND

Berry, Set, master bowl, six serving bowls
Painted roses design **465.00**
Pink and red carnations, red marks . **500.00**
Box, cov, 3½" d, pink and white flowers, gray and green luster, gold trim and knob **75.00**
Cake Plate
10" d, white and pink roses, green, tan, and cream ground, gold trim, open handles **75.00**

Pink and yellow roses, satin finish, open handles **135.00**
Candlesticks, 6¼" h, pink and white florals, gray and green luster, ruffled bases and drip pans, pr **150.00**
Creamer
  Fuchsia flowers, multicolored **20.00**
  Open flower design, multicolored, red and brown mark **55.00**
Dresser Tray, 12¾" l, pink and white flowers, green leaves, cream ground, gold rim (A) **110.00**
Hatpin Holder
  Pink roses, green ground **65.00**
  Pink shaded rosebuds, shaded rust ground **85.00**
Planter, 6" d, 7" h, multicolored floral design **215.00**
Ring Tree, violets, pearlized finish **100.00**
Sugar, pink roses, lavender shading, gilt trim **125.00**
Sugar, cov, small sprays of pink roses and lavender islands, white ground, fleur-de-lis molded feet **135.00**
Tray, 12⅜" l, 9" w, green oak leaves and acorns, cream ground, marked **120.00**
Vase
  3¼" h, white flowers and leaves, cream and green ground **70.00**
  4" h, 5" w, multicolored Chinese pheasants design, red mark **200.00**
  5" h, multicolored portrait of young woman **100.00**
  6" h, ladies feeding chicks and gathering wheat on one side, holding shuttlecock on other, pr **200.00**
  8" h
    Florals, green and tan ground, dbl handles **75.00**
    Gold grapes and leaves, cobalt base, yellow and white roses on tan shaded top, dbl handles ... **160.00**
  9" h, roses, wide gold floral band at top **230.00**
  12" h, peach anemones, white ground, dbl handled **120.00**

SEVRES

Paris, France
1738 to Present

History: The Dubois brothers started a small soft paste porcelain factory for the production of decorative flowers at Vincennes in 1738. Encour-

aged by Madame de Pompadour, the factory found favor with Louis XV who became the chief shareholder in 1753. Louis XV controlled most of the products manufactured at Vincennes as well as throughout the rest of France. Gilding and the use of colored grounds were reserved for his pet projects. The familiar interlaced "L" mark was used during his reign to signify his participation.

In 1756 the factory was moved to Sevres, coming under the watchful eye of its chief benefactor Mme. de Pompadour. The first products were soft paste porcelain pieces decorated in the Oriental style. The soft paste porcelain lent itself well to the elaborate Rococo style favored by the king and his court. In addition to decorated soft paste, exquisite biscuit porcelain figures were produced, much to the delight of Madame de Pompadour.

After the late 1760s hard paste porcelain gradually replaced the soft paste variety. Styles fell loosely into categories which had taken the names of the benefactors. The period of 1753 to 1763 was known as "Pompadour," 1763 to 1786 was "Louis XV," and 1786 to 1793 as "Louis XVI." The products of these periods ranged from small scent bottles to enormous dinner services to vases and urns of monumental size and decoration. The neoclassical styles were favored. Jeweled or heavily enameled pieces first appeared about 1780.

A number of directors strongly influenced the products from Sevres. During the directorship of Jean Hellot, about 1745 to 1766, several colors were introduced that have become associated with Sevres porcelain. The earliest ground color was gros bleu (1749) followed by bleu celeste (turquoise, 1752), rose pompadour (pink, 1756), and bleu roi (clear blue, 1763). The use of these colors during specific periods helped date Sevres porcelain.

Following the French Revolution, the company fell into disfavor and did not flourish again until the Napoleonic years. Alexandre Brongniart was appointed director by Lucien Bonaparte in 1800. The Empire style and scenics depicting Napoleon's campaigns and victories dominated the designs during the period. After 1804 soft paste was no longer made. Eventually the factory reestablished itself as a leading producer of European hard paste porcelain.

A new range of colors was developed. Ground colors included dark blue, a pale blue called agate, and chrome green. These were seen most frequently in the First Empire Period, 1804 to 1815. Gilding was used extensively during this period. Painters were employed by Brongniart to paint miniature portraits on porcelain shapes that were modeled carefully by artists such as Theodore Brongniart and Charles Parcier.

Between 1800 and 1830 Sevres products included plaques, vases, table services, sculptures, and some very large special pieces. Porcelain plaques, made between 1818 and 1848, imitated oil paintings or frescoes. Some vases were made in a Neoclassical style that imitated cameos. Napoleon revived the tradition of ordering large table services for his own use or for diplomatic gifts. Post-Revolution monarchs had France glorified as the subject matter for services. Coffee, tea, or breakfast services also were made between 1800 and 1830.

The reign of Louis-Phillipe, 1830 to 1848, saw few changes at Sevres. Brongniart continued with the styles he was using from the early 1800s. White backgrounds were used more frequently for everyday table services. Decorations lessened and were printed, especially when gilding was used.

Brongniart died in 1847. Jules Dieterle became artistic director from 1852 to 1855; Joseph Nicolle took over from 1856 to 1871. Most of the output of the Sevres factory from 1852 onwards was for imperial residences and diplomatic gifts.

The most important decorative technique of this period was the pate-sur-pate process. This type of decoration was very popular in France and in England. The pate-sur-pate process ended at Sevres in 1897. (See: Pate-sur-Pate.)

The Second Empire style at Sevres provided a complete break with the preceding period. This was an eclectic period, 1850 to 1870, utilizing the Pompeian style to imitate decoration on classical vases with classical subjects. A return to the Rococo forms and decorations of the Louis XV times also occurred during this period.

The Third Republic period, 1870 to 1940, began with difficult conditions at the factory. The factory moved to its present location by the Park of Saint-Cloud. In 1876 the sculptor A. Carrier-Belleuse became artistic director. He remained until his death in 1886.

Many experiments were carried out with different porcelain bodies. Flambe glazes were developed and became popular. During the Carrier-Belleuse period, many different decorating techniques, e.q., painted decoration, pate-sur-pate decoration, and copper glazing, were used.

When Alexandre Sandier became director from 1896 to 1916, the factory was reorganized completely. He initiated new shapes and decoration techniques. Sinuous shapes were developed. The human figure was replaced as a decorative motif by painted vegetables, florals, and insects in the new Art Nouveau style. Winding tendrils appear on vases and plates. Stoneware bodies often were used for the Art Nouveau decorated pieces. Sculpture regained prominence in biscuit porcelain as many busts were modeled.

References: Care Christian Dauterman, *Sevres,* Walker & Co., 1969; W. B. Honey, *French Porcelain of the 18th Century,* Faber & Faber, 1950; Egan Mew, *Royal Sevres China,* Dodd, Mead &

Co.; George Savage, *Seventeenth & Eighteenth Century French Porcelain,* Hamlyn Publishing Co., Ltd., 1969.

Museums: Frick Collection, New York, N.Y.; Gardiner Museum of Ceramic Art, Toronto, Canada; J. Paul Getty Museum, Malibu, California; Metropolitan Museum of Art, New York, New York; Musee Des Arts Decoratifs, Paris, France; Musee du Louvre, Paris, France; Musee National De Ceramique, Sevres, France; Victoria & Albert Museum, London, England; Wallace Collection, Hertford House, London, England.

Bowl
   5½" d, cov, rose bouquet on front and sides with crests, "Che sera sera" with crests, gilt accents, dbl handles, marked **275.00**
   10½" l, insert of dancers and musicians, classic costumes, chrome yellow body, egg shape, ormolu feet, bands, and finial **600.00**
   11½" w, painted bouquets and sprays, molded dbl handles, blue line and gilt dash crenelated rim, c1765, blue interlaced "L's" mark (A) **2,640.00**
Box, 5" l, 2½" h, pastoral scene on lid, cobalt ground, gold trim, "Chateau de Tuilleries" mark **400.00**
Cake Compote, 17" h, three tiers, underglazed cobalt floral design, gilt highlights, 19th C (A) **100.00**
Caudle Cup, white body, gold trim, gold letter "L" for Louis Philippe, gold trim, flower bud finial, c1844 ...... **225.00**
Charger, 13" l, medallions on border, gold and floral trim, gold compass rose in center, "Louis Philippe, Chateau Fontainbleau" mark **485.00**
Coffee Can and Saucer
   Gros bleu ground, cans with gilt ovals of ochre and blue urns with florals, saucers with roundels of roses and dahlias, gilt bellflowers, straps, and foliates, c1781, blue interlaced "L's and X" marks, pr (A) **1,760.00**
   Reserves of painted florals, blue hatching, light yellow ground, late 19th C (A) **100.00**
Cream Jug, 3¼" h, scattered multicolored rose sprays, oeil-de-perdrix enclosing flower sprays at rim, pear shape, branch handle, 3 ftd ending in flowering foliage, c1769, blue interlaced "L's and date letter" mark **400.00**
Cup
   Painted bouquets and sprays, blue line and gilt dash borders, gilt dentil rims, gilt metal stands, c1763, blue "interlaced L's" marks, pr (A) **1,430.00**
   Sprays of summer roses in laurel

bands, gilt borders, cov, matching
stand (A) **275.00**

Cup and Saucer

Floral wreaths in gilt medallions, gilt
dotted gros bleu ground, blue "interlaced L's and letter date" marks,
pr **1,200.00**

Napoleon "N" letter in center, gold
crown, white body, gold trim,
c1857 .... **165.00**

Painted bouquets and sprays, gilt dentil rims, c1764, blue "interlaced
L's" marks, set of 18 (A) **1,100.00**

Rose Pompadour ground reserved
with panels of flower sprays edged
in gilt, gilt dentil rims, dbl handles,
c1758 (A) **4,150.00**

Scene of soldiers in camp, blue
ground, saucers with trophies in red
and turquoise jewels, white fleur-
de-lis and gilt diamond pattern,
1760, blue "interlaced L's and date
letter" marks, pr (A) **600.00**

Demitasse Cup and Saucer, hp pink and
white cherubs, c1846, artist sgd,
Louis Philippe mark **125.00**

Dish

6⅞" l, central multicolored floral
spray, floral garland suspended
from blue bowknots, gilt dentil
edged scalloped rim, oblong, dated
1759, "interlaced L's & fleur-de-lis"
mark (A) **990.00**

8" d, multicolored flowers in blue line
and gilt border, gilt rims, trefoil
shape, triangular foot, c1764, blue
"interlaced L's & date letter" mark **260.00**

Ecuelle, cov, 7⅝" l dbl handled bowl,
10¼" l stand, painted floral pendants
from bowknots, rims with gilt-dashed
blue dbl lines, dentil edges, c1770,
blue "interlaced L's and painter's"
marks (A) **880.00**

Figure

5½" h, peasant mother carrying child
on back, circ base, white bisque,
c1760 (A) **500.00**

6" h, girl on knees beating clothes, sq
base with bundle of clothes and
soap, white bisque, c1770, club
missing (A) **1,100.00**

6⅞" w, seated poodle and cat, tasseled cushions, white bisque,
c1756 (A) **10,368.00**

9¼" h, Seated Psyche, rockwork base
holding bow, white bisque, dated
1761, incised "T" mark (A) **1,320.00**

10" h, "Louise de Saucie" and
"Jeanne de Sancerre," court
clothes, pr **675.00**

Jardiniere, 8" w, white body molded
with scrolls and foliage to rim, gilded

accents, rect, flared top, four stump
feet, metal liner, c1770, blue "interlaced L's" mark **380.00**

Jewel Box, 12" l, blue celeste body, hp
portraits, orange trim, dore, gold
overlay, c1756 ....**2,400.00**

Piano Lamp, 65" h, font with Cupid and
maidens in romantic setting, set in
baluster receptacle, raised ormolu
standard, cast lion heads, paw feet ,
sgd "E. Collot" (A) **2,350.00**

**Plate, 9¾" d, multicolored center, cobalt
border with gold tracery, sgd "Debrie,"
"Chateau Du Tuilleries," $125.00.**

Plate

4" d, entwined "L-P" in center with
gold wreath and crown, white
body, reign of Louis Philippe,
c1847, "Chateau de Compiegne"
mark **50.00**

Center portrait of Madame Royale,
blue ground, gold trim, c1779, artist sgd **350.00**

Portrait of Henriette Le Bourbon-Conti
on one, M. Du Chaitelet on other,
cobalt blue borders, sgd "J. Geor-
get" **450.00**

Scene of Venus and Cupids in garden
setting, rose Pompadour border,
mid 19th C, artist sgd, Chateau
mark **185.00**

9½" d

Center of multicolored exotic birds
on branches in landscape scene,
blue celeste border with oval
panels of flower sprays, border
with gilt scrolls and florals,
c1765, blue "interlaced L's"
mark **650.00**

Chinese figures by pavilions in
landscape in gilt and platinum,
Chinese figures in borders, black
ground, c1785, red "crowned interlaced L's and LG" marks, pr
(A) **17,600.00**

Portrait of Mme de Pompadour, yellow and gold border **225.00**

Scattered roses, borders of green and red stylized flowerheads in red and blue oeil-de-perdrix, three oval reserves of roses, gilt shaped edges, c1788, "interlaced L's and date" marks, set of 12 (A) **1,760.00**

9¾" d, multicolored florals, blue line and gilt dash border, gilt rims, c1773, puce "interlaced L's and date letter" marks, pr **180.00**

10½" d, scene of couple by waterfall, pink border with florals, ormolu trim, c1890, artist sgd **300.00**

Pot-A-Creme, 3" h, painted flower sprays in gilt dash and blue line borders, flowerhead finial, c1770, blue "interlaced L's" mark (A) **285.00**

Pot-A-Creme Dessert Set, six pot-a-cremes, underplates, six cups and saucers, black drawing room scenes, citrus yellow ground, decorated in Paris, c1910 .... **475.00**

Sauce Tureen, cov, 6⅛" w, painted bouquets in blue line and gilt dash borders, quatrefoil shape, branch handle, c1767, blue "interlaced L's & W" marks (A) **75.00**

Saucer, painted flower sprays reserved on brown ground, tied with pink ribbons, late 18th C (A) **85.00**

Solitaire Set, cov sugar, cream jug, 11¼" w tray, exotic birds in landscapes in rose, gilt dentil rims, c1757, blue "interlaced L's" marks (A) **2,860.00**

Sugar, cov

3⅜" h, gilt cartouches with painted exotic birds, bleu celeste ground, c1756, blue "interlaced L's and letter date" marks (A) **465.00**

4" h

Multicolored birds and florals in blue and gilt ribbons, rose ground, fruiting branch finial, 1770, blue "interlaced L's" mark **650.00**

Tea Service, teapot, creamer, sugar, two cake plates, fruit bowl, fifteen cups and saucers, bleu celeste, gold trim, multicolored bird medallions, c1780 **5,780.00**

Teapot

4¾" w, painted bands of trailing cornflowers, gilt finial and dentil rim, oviform, c1760, blue "interlaced L's and MB" marks (A) **200.00**

5½" h, painted florals on spiral shaped panels alternating with gilt oak leaves on green spiral panels, flowerhead finial, c1756, blue "interlaced L's" mark (A) **2,200.00**

Tête-À-Tête Set

4⅞" h teapot, cov sugar, milk jug, two cups and saucers, dbl walled,

pierced circ devices with gilt, bamboo molded handles, c1906-22 ..**1,100.00**

14⅞" l tray, cov sugar, 4" h, 3-ftd milk jug, two cups and saucers, central multicolored reserves of soldiers in camp, bleu du roi ground, tooled gilt bands and vine borders, dated 1771, blue "interlaced L's" marks (A) **4,500.00**

Tray, 5¾" sq, center painted with bouquets, rose pompadour border with gilt foliage and scrolls, gilt dentil rim, c1757, blue "interlaced L's" mark (A)**2,200.00**

Urn

8" h, cov, hp portraits, gold dore bronze trim, acorn finial on cov, c1846, artist sgd, Chateau mark .. **550.00**

9" h, domed cov, bulbous dbl handled body, figural reserve in enamels, sgd "Denesee" (A) **250.00**

12½" h, medallion of young lovers in classic dress, gilt bronze mounts, artist sgd **390.00**

13" h, scalloped ormolu rims over central panel depicting ormolu classical figures, blue ground, gold bees, tapered cylindrical form, sq bases, Empire period **1,600.00**

14" h, cov, scene of lovers in landscape setting, yellow ground, gilt accents, ormolu mounts, ovoid shape to body, gold finial **800.00**

23¾" h, cov, scenic reserve of two women offering cup to cherub by waterfall, floral design on reverse, ormolu devil's head handles with ormolu mounts, c1763, artist sgd, **3,800.00**

Vase

5¼" h, hp portraits outlined in gold, gold overlays, pink ground, c1840, pr **375.00**

10½" h, hp exotic bird designs, pink and gilt ground, late 19th C, pr (A) **145.00**

12" h, cov, painted center medallion of young girl, ormolu mounts, sgd "Wagner" **650.00**

15" h, cov, center panel of mother and children, cobalt body, dore bronze trim, c1885-90, artist sgd **900.00**

15⅜" h, rose pompadour ground, molded elephant heads at neck with molded trailing beads, swirling reserves of painted flowers, gilt fluted dbl handles, sq base, 4 scroll feet, c1757, blue "interlaced L's" mark (A) **115,500.00**

16" h, silvered classical reserves, dark red ground, ormolu mounts, pr ..**1,400.00**

22½" h, painted pastoral scene on front, flower bouquets on reverse in gilt foliage surrounds on bleu du roi ground, folded strap handles, shoulder with suspended relief swags, cov with radiating gilt panels and knob, sq ormolu base, four paw feet, c1770 (A) **46,200.00**

SHAVING MUGS

Austria, England, France, Germany c1850 to 1920

History: Shaving mugs or barbers' mugs were manufactured of pottery or porcelain. Most mugs were shaped like coffee mugs; others had soap drainers and other features incorporated into the designs. Scuttles had double spouts. One spout was used for the razor, and the other for the shaving brush.

Many barber supply companies in the United States imported blank shaving mugs from Limoges and Sevres in France, from Victoria Carlsbad and Imperial Crown China in Austria, from C. T. Germany and Felda China Company in Germany, from A. J. Wilkinson and Goddard in England, and other scattered sources.

The imported, plain white, unadorned pottery or porcelain mugs were decorated in the suppliers' workshops. Shaving mugs were not meant to be ornamental. They were designed for the owner's personal use at his favorite barber shop where he went for a daily or weekly shave. Some people viewed their private mug as a status symbol; others felt it was more hygienic for each man to have his own mug reserved for his personal use.

OCCUPATIONAL

Occupational mugs, indicating the owner's type of work, exist for almost every business, profession, or trade. The mug has a picture featuring the owner's occupation and his name in gold, either above or below the illustration. Lettering was usually in the old English style. Both indoor and outdoor trades were depicted. Some mugs had a scene portraying the owner working at his trade; others illustrated the working tools or emblem of the tradesman.

Collecting Hints: Many collections have been assembled that contain mugs representing over six hundred occupations. Uncommon jobs, such as a deep sea diver, are difficult to locate. Mugs picturing obsolete occupations are prized highly by collectors. An occupational mug depicting a profession such as a doctor or lawyer are harder to find since professionals were less likely to advertise themselves than were tradesmen or neighborhood merchants.

FRATERNAL

Fraternal shaving mugs bear symbols of the various fraternal orders such as Masons, Elks,

Moose, etc. In addition, the Industrial Revolution furnished an incentive for American laborers to unite in national organizations, e.g., the Noble Order of the Knights of Labor and the Grand International Brotherhood of Locomotive Engineers. Symbols of these labor organizations found their way onto shaving mugs just as did the symbols of fraternal groups.

GENERAL

Shaving mugs appeared in quantity after the Civil War and flourished during the Victorian age. One style of mug featured a photograph of the owner or his family or a favorite painting. It was made by adding a photographic emulsion to the ceramic body and then burning in the resulting image in a kiln.

Simple mugs with the owner's name added to a stock floral design were produced by all the decorating workshops. Scenes of the popular sports of the day also found their way onto shaving mugs.

Mugs with simply a number in gilt were used in hotel barber shops. The numbers corresponded to the hotel room numbers. Decal decorated mugs from Germany contained reproductions of either important people, such as Napoleon or Sitting Bull, well known works of art, or animals, e.g., horses, dogs, etc.

Character shaving mugs, introduced into the United States about 1900, were manufactured in Austria and Bavaria until the start of World War I. Animal and fish heads were among the popular forms. Some mugs also advertised shaving products, e.g., Wildroot.

Barber shop shaving declined after World War I. Safety razors had been invented and perfected. Returning soldiers had learned to shave themselves. In addition, the Blue Laws forced barber shops to close on Sunday, a popular pre-war shaving day. By 1930 shaving at the barber shop was nearly at an end.

References: Robert Blake Powell, *Antique Shaving Mugs of The United States*, published privately, 1978; W. Porter Ware, *Price List of Occupational & Society Emblems Shaving Mugs*, Lightner Publishing Corporation, 1949.

Museums: Atwater Kent Museum, Philadelphia, Pa.; Fort Worth Museum of Science & History, Fort Worth, Texas; The Institute of Texas Cultures Museum, San Antonio, Texas; Lightner Museum, St. Augustine, Florida; The New York Historical Society, New York, New York.

REPRODUCTION ALERT: New shaving mugs are manufactured frequently as "replicas" of the past, but these can be recognized easily. Since they were used frequently, old shaving mugs should show definite signs of wear along the handle and the top and bottom rims.

Currently, Japanese companies are making reproduction "occupational" mugs in heavy porcelains similar to the earlier examples. Reproduction mugs from France and Germany appear to be hand painted but actually are printed by the silk screen process. An experienced collector can spot the difference.

OCCUPATIONAL

Automobile Dealer, PALMER C. FERRELL, touring car, "T & V Limoges, France" (A) **300.00**

Baker, D. C. KUNEL, three bakers working, "Limoges, France" (A) **100.00**

Banker, J. J., East Providence, R. I., silver nickel on front, "T & V Limoges 515L" (A) **150.00**

Baseball Team Owner, R. R. RUSSELL, player being tagged on base, "Leonard, Vienna, Austria" (A) **750.00**

Blacksmith
GEO. S. BAKER, two men working at hearth, "V & D, Austria" (A) **275.00**
DUNCAN, horse with horseshoe, name in gold, florals on sides (A) . **45.00**

Boiler Maker, JAS SULLIVAN, "Limoges/France, W. G. & Co" (A) **325.00**

Bootmaker, G. B. SUNMG, pair of high button boots, "T & V Limoges, France" (A) **200.00**

Butcher
ANTON DIENER, butcher working at table, "Leonard, Vienna, Austria" (A) **175.00**
BECKER, steer head and tools, "D & C" mark (A) **75.00**
WM J. ZIMMER, horse drawn wagon, "T & V Limoges, France" (A) **350.00**

Cab Driver, SAM C. GUY, man driving horse drawn cab, "Leonard, Vienna, Austria" (A) **250.00**

Carpenter
CARL MOE, carpenter tools, "W Austria, 4457" (A) **150.00**
CLAUDE WALLIS, "Leonard, Vienna, Austria" (A) **125.00**
JOHN SHIPEE, man working at bench, "D & C" (A) **275.00**

Cigar Maker, VAL MEYERS, four cigars, knife, bowl on board, "T & V Limoges, France" (A) **250.00**

Coal Miner, PH. KLEINEKORTE, man working in mine, "Limoges, France" (A) **525.00**

Doctor
CHAS DOUGLAS, doctor in buggy, "Elite Limoges, France" (A) **75.00**
DR. J. R. DAVIES, "T & V Limoges, France" (A) **60.00**

Dry Goods Store Owner, GEO. A. MURRAY, "T & V Limoges, France" (A) **300.00**

Farmer
CHAS FISHER, man plowing field, "D & C" (A) **300.00**
J. J. KEENAN, man and horse-drawn hay wagon, "LIMOGES FRANCE" (A) **175.00**

Horse Breeder
C. C. JACKSON, horse and leather straps, "H & Co" (A) **125.00**
W. L. GRAY, multicolored horse, light blue ground, name in gold, "P GERMANY" (A) **210.00**

Hotel Operator, S. Y. YOUNGS, black and white hotel, "T & V Limoges, France" (A) **525.00**

Hunter, V. A. FOTGRE, hunter shooting at birds, two dogs pointing, "D & C" (A) **175.00**

Leather Tanner, J. J. FRITCH, tools, "C. T." (A) **150.00**

Locomotive Conductor, JAS. H. LYNCHEON, locomotive and coal car, green ground, "W. G. & Co., France" (A) **100.00**

Milkman
F. W. STRATTON, milkman filling pitcher from milk can, "CFH/GDM" (A) **20.00**
JOHN FAIRBANKS, "Pure Milk" on side, "T & V FRANCE" (A) **250.00**

Musician
Bass Drummer, scene of marching band, "T & V LIMOGES, FRANCE" (A) **525.00**
CHAS. SMITH, five string banjo, "T & V " (A) **325.00**
DRUMMER DAVIS, drummer with large yellow drum, "D & C, France" (A) **250.00**

Paper Hanger, J. M. FAIR, man on ladder hanging paper, "J & C Bavaria" (A) **425.00**

Piano Player, H. G. BEDELL, upright piano, "M. R. France" (A) **200.00**

Plumber, DAN'L KELLY, man working on sink, "Leonard, Vienna, Austria" (A) **275.00**

Pool Player, crossed cues and ball, name in gold **135.00**

Power House Operator, P. J. HOBAN, machinery, "T & V Limoges, France" (A) **150.00**

Railroad Conductor, D. MERRILE, red caboose, "K & K, Germany" (A) ... **150.00**

Sportsman, M. FAUGUTH, dog with duck in mouth, fishing equipment, "T & V France" (A) **125.00**

Stage Coach Driver, coach, passengers,

and horses, "Leonard, Vienna, Austria" (A) **65.00**
Undertaker, F. G. SMITH, man on horse drawn hearse, "D & C" (A) **625.00**
U. S. S. Maine, C. S. WILLOUGHBY, "Limoges, France" (A) **1,325.00**
Vegetable Man, KINZMAYER, driver in vegetable wagon, "T & V Limoges, France" (A) **225.00**
Veterinarian, DR. M. P. MATTICE, horse head, "D & C 1631" (A) **175.00**

FRATERNAL

Ancient Order of United Workman, C. T. KEEFE, anchor and shield, "Limoges, France" (A) **115.00**
B. P. O. E.
  Elk's head, scenery, unmarked (A) .. **65.00**
  MARTIN H. WELCH, stag head, name in gold, "FELDA CHINA GERMANY" (A) **175.00**
Brotherhood of Rail Trains of America
  Hand car inside of circle, crossed flags, "VIENNA, AUSTRIA" (A) .. **75.00**
  M. F. MARONEG, railroad lantern, crossed flags,· "T & V Limoges France" (A) **200.00**
Forester of America, crossed flags, stag in center, gold bands, "FELDA CHINA GERMANY" (A) **75.00**
I. M. U. of N. A., Organized July 1859, J. G. COOK, union label and two men holding hardware, "DRESDEN CHINA," chipped (A) **100.00**

GENERAL

American and Canadian crossed flags, dated 1898, "T & V Limoges, France" (A) **200.00**
"Astoria," flow blue pattern, ribbed shape, Pitcairns Ltd **80.00**
Figural
  Elk head, parian, "MADE IN GERMANY" (A) **35.00**
  Moose head, dark brown, "AUSTRIA" (A) **50.00**
Flowers
  Applied baskets of flowers, shaded brown ground, unmarked (A) **15.00**
  Applied multicolored flowers and leaves, Germany **25.00**
  Brown flowers, white ground, "SPRAYS EDWARD ST. SO. ENGLAND" (A) **15.00**
  Brown iris on both sides, int. rim and handle dec, "M. L. & CO. ENGLAND" (A) **18.00**
  Copper flower, brown crazing,

"ALFRED MEAKIN, IRONSTONE CHINA" (A) **20.00**
Roses
  Pink and red roses, light and dark green ground, "PK UNITY GERMANY" (A) **20.00**
  Roses and leaves on front, small roses on reverse, gold trim, "C. T. GERMANY" (A) **20.00**
Light blue and peach design, gold trim, "WEIMAR GERMANY" (A) **18.00**
Monk playing violin, brown ground, "GERMANY" (A) **15.00**
Name in gold
  A. C. BLANCHARD, "H & C" (A) .. **15.00**
  C. A. CARMICHEL, "MADE IN GERMANY" (A) **15.00**
  C. C. TOKRAM, blue rings top and bottom, "H & Co" (A) **18.00**
  E. SPOHN, hunter with two dogs in grass, surrounded by gold, fire in background, shaded green ground "FELDA CHINA GERMANY" (A) . **200.00**
  HOWARD H. HUNT, scene of dog sniffing rabbit in horn, red flowers, blue water, "T & V Limoges, France" (A) **255.00**
  JAMES F. HANAWAY, hp blue, yellow, and red bird carrying banner, gold top and bottom, light green ground, "C. T. Germany" (A) **50.00**
Porcelain, multicolored transfer of standing elk, red-brown shading top and base **30.00**
Raised Decoration
  LOVE THE GIVER, gold letters, surrounded by raised border, irid light green ground, "MADE IN GERMANY" (A) **20.00**
  "Remember Me" and flowers, unmarked (A) **25.00**
Raised deer head on each side, unmarked (A) **15.00**
Scene
  Comic, frog smoking, black and gold T. D. KEELY, "T & V Limoges" (A) **100.00**
  Dutch windmill and harbor, gold trim, "GERMANY" (A) **15.00**
  English hunt scene, blue and white . **100.00**
  Fox hunt, red ground, gold trim, "Imperial Crown China, Austria" (A) . **36.00**
  Woods and stream, mountain in background, multicolored, "GERMANY 207" (A) **20.00**
Silver Overlay, "From Loving Papa" in German **55.00**
Transfer of driver in touring car, gold trim, imp "GERMANY" **150.00**
World's Fair, St. Louis, brown scenes, "VICTORIA CARLSBAD AUSTRIA" (A) **25.00**

SCUTTLE

Cream and brown design, modeled key
  handle (A) **12.50**
Flowers
  Flowers and leaves on front and back,
    hp gold scroll and raised enamel
    dots, dark blue ground, unmarked
    (A) **12.00**
  Flowers outlined in gold, light brown
    ground, "AUSTRIA 46" (A) **18.00**
  Red and yellow flowers, green ground
    (A) **15.00**
  Yellow flowers, green leaves, light
    pink ground (A) **15.00**

**Scuttle, multicolored florals, white
ground, unmarked, $45.00.**

Stag and branches with leaves, "GER-
  MANY 59" (A) **15.00**
Tree trunk bark, dark brown glaze,
  "MADE IN GERMANY" (A) **18.00**

1890-1910

1925-1945

SHELLEY

Longton, England
Mid-18th Century to Present

History: Members of the Shelley family manufactured pottery at Lane End beginning in the
middle of the 18th century. In 1872 Joseph Shelley formed a partnership with James Wileman of
Wileman & Co., operator of the Foley China
Works. For the next fifty years the firm used the
name Wileman & Co. Percy, Joseph Shelley's

son, joined the firm in 1881. Percy became an
excellent potter. During his fifty years as head of
the firm, he developed the lasting reputation of
Shelley china.

During the 1880s only average quality china
was made. Pieces featured one color and poor
quality transfers. Percy hired artists to produce
dinner services with more elaborate decorations
that were intended for the export market. During
the 1890s the wares were more varied, featuring
finer patterns and better colorations.

When Joseph died in 1896, Percy assumed
complete control. The artist Rowland Morris
modeled "Dainty White," the company's most
successfully produced shape until 1966. The
shape also was used for many pieces of commemorative ware.

Frederick Rhead, who trained under Solon at
Minton and worked at Wedgwood, was employed as artistic director. Rhead introduced Intarsio, Spano-Lustra, Urbato, Primitf, and Pas-
tello wares, a series of effects used on
earthenwares. Intarsio was the most popular. A
large number of patterns and styles were made.

Although the firm was still called Wileman &
Co. in 1910, the mark utilized the Shelley family
name enclosed in an outlined shield shape. The
art director now was Walter Slater who had been
an apprentice at Minton and spent twenty years
working at Doulton.

A new series of Intarsio ware that reflected Art
Nouveau motifs was introduced in 1911. Flamboyant ware with flambe glazes and Cloisello
ware followed. Under Slater's direction, bone
china was developed. Before World War I, Shelley's china dinner services were very popular in
the American market.

After the war, Percy's three sons were involved
in the firm. By 1922 miniature objects, heraldic
and coats of arms, souvenir china and earthenware with engraved views of places of interest,
and Parian busts of military figures were produced in quantity. During the 1920s, many styles
of tewares were made. "Eggshell china" referred to the thinness of the china. In 1925 the
firm's name was changed to Shelley's. Nursery
wares decorated by Hilda Cowham and Mabel
Lucie Attwell came to the forefront along with
"semi-porcelain" domestic china.

Percy retired in 1932. The delicate teawares
of the 1920s and 1930s established Shelley's reputation. The Queen Anne octagonal shape is one
of the best known forms. More modern shapes
such as Vogue and Mode were introduced during
the Art Deco period.

After World War II, earthenwares were discontinued. China dinnerwares remained in production. Lithographic techniques replaced the "print
and enamel" decorations.

In 1965 the firm was renamed Shelley China
Ltd. It was acquired by Allied English Potteries

in 1966. The family connection with the firm finally ended. Allied merged with the Doulton Group in 1971.

References: Chris Watkins, William Harvey, and Robert Senft, *Shelley Potteries,* Barrie & Jenkins, 1980.

Bowl, 6¼" d, "Old Donk" rhyme, sgd
"Attwell" **25.00**
Butter Dish, cov
8" d, Art Deco, shades of green **50.00**
"Lily of the Valley" pattern **55.00**
Cabaret Set, 6½" h teapot, creamer, sugar, four cups and saucers, 15" d scalloped tray, shades of rust and white, c1889, Wileman **900.00**
Cake Plate, 6" d, "Hollyhocks" pattern, #12020 .... **45.00**
Candy Dish
4" l, "Rosebud" pattern **30.00**
6" d, "Pansy" pattern **30.00**
Child's Cup and Saucer, "Fairies, Fairies..." Mabel Lucie Attwell **100.00**
Creamer and Sugar
Art Deco style, yellow flowers and green leaves **40.00**
"Begonia" pattern, six flutes **48.00**
"Dainty Mauve" pattern **35.00**
"Morning Glory" pattern, #13885 . **55.00**
"Rose Spray" pattern' six flutes **40.00**
Creamer, Sugar, and Tray, "Bridal Rose" pattern, shell **80.00**
Cup and Saucer
"Begonia" pattern, six flutes **38.00**
Black transfer of dancing girl, chrome yellow ground, black handle **35.00**
Blue flowers, #0437 .... **40.00**
Bouquet int., yellow ext., #13438/306 .... **40.00**
"Bridal Bouquet" pattern, six flutes . **38.00**
"Bridal Rose" pattern
Fluted **30.00**
"Crochet" pattern
Yellow ground **38.00**
Dark blue small flowers, light blue border, #13363 .... **40.00**
"Duchess" pattern, gold trim **30.00**
"Eastern Star" pattern **30.00**
Handpainted birds, #K13145 ...... **40.00**
"Heavenly Blue" pattern **25.00**
"Marguerite" pattern **38.00**
"Old Mill" pattern, #13669 .... **40.00**
Panels, three lavender panels and three panels of lavender flowers, white ground, hexagon **18.00**
"Rock Garden" pattern
Light yellow **40.00**
Pink **40.00**
"Rose Spray" pattern, pink and green border, notched edge **40.00**

"Rosebud" pattern
Fourteen flutes **38.00**
Six flutes **38.00**
"Summer Glory" pattern
Gold trim, straight edge **40.00**
Green trim **30.00**
"Thistle" pattern, six flutes **40.00**
"Violets" pattern, #13430 .... **35.00**
"Wild Roses" pattern, gold rim and base, ruffled edges **38.00**
Cup, Saucer, and Plate Set, 3 pcs
4¾" d plate
Demitasse cup and saucer, "Dainty White" pattern, six flutes **30.00**
Pink and dark pink roses **65.00**
7" d plate
Navy and gold pattern #7084H .. **55.00**
"Regency" pattern, six flutes **55.00**
"Wildflower" pattern, six flutes .. **45.00**
8¼" d plate, "Bluebell Woods" pattern **25.00**
Demitasse Cup and Saucer
"Begonia" pattern, sixteen flutes ... **35.00**
"Blue Rock" pattern, sixteen flutes . **38.00**
"Chippendale" pattern **25.00**
"Dainty Blue" pattern **25.00**
"Dainty Green" pattern, six flutes .. **40.00**
"Dainty Mauve" pattern, six flutes .. **38.00**
"Regency" pattern
Six flutes **25.00**
Sixteen flutes **38.00**
"Rose & Daisy" pattern, six flutes .. **38.00**
"Rose & Pansy" pattern **35.00**
"Rose & Red Daisy" pattern
Six flutes **35.00**
Sixteen flutes **38.00**
"Rose Spray" pattern, yellow border, gold trim **38.00**
"Stocks" pattern
Six flutes **38.00**
Sixteen flutes **38.00**
White and gold, rose inside cup, #16961 .... **30.00**
Dinner Service, "Golden Harvest" pattern, 42 pcs **800.00**
Dish, 4½" sq, "Rosebud" pattern, dbl handles **20.00**
Egg Cup
"Bridal Rose" pattern, six flutes **45.00**
"Harebell" pattern **20.00**
Flower Holder, 4½" h, dark blue, light blue leaves and pink flowers **145.00**
Gravy Boat and Undertray, "Begonia" pattern **50.00**
Jam Jar and Tray, 4" h, red and purple roses **60.00**
Jug
4⅞" d, 7⅜" h, yellow, rust, gray, and black bands from top to bottom .. **60.00**
6⅛" h, "Imp," modeled as imp, green clothes, ear forming spout, raised

arm forming handle, Mabel Lucie
Attwell (A) **85.00**
Luncheon Set
"Dainty Floral" design, twelve 7" d
plates, two 9" d serving plates,
creamer, sugar, twelve cups and
saucers, #7884 .... **500.00**
Flowers on outside, yellow flower
handles, six 6½" d plates, 8½" d
serving plate, creamer, sugar, six
cups and saucers with six flutes .. **375.00**

Dish, cov, 12" l, "Tall Trees" pattern, black and white, yellow sun, Vogue shape, $110.00.

Miniature
Cup and Saucer
Pink flowers, purple and red grapes **50.00**
"Rose Pansy FMN" pattern **60.00**
"Rose Spray" pattern **60.00**
Pitcher, 8" h, ribbed, shades of blue .. **75.00**
Plate
4½" sq, pink and blue phlox and but-
terflies, #2221 .... **10.00**
5½" sq
Blue flowers, #13777 .... **15.00**
"Lakeland" pattern **15.00**
7" d
"Rose & Red Daisy" pattern, six
flutes **18.00**
"Wildflower" pattern, six flutes .. **25.00**
8" d
"Begonia" pattern **20.00**
"Blue Rock" pattern
Gold trimmed border **25.00**
Six flutes **35.00**
"Rosebud" pattern, aqua trim **25.00**
White, green dots, six flutes **25.00**
8" sq
"Melody" pattern, green trim,
notched edge **30.00**
"Wild Flowers" pattern, pink trim,
six flutes **65.00**
10¾" d, "Begonia" pattern **35.00**
Platter
13" l, 11" w, "Tall Trees" pattern,

black and white trees, yellow rising
sun, Vogue shape **75.00**
14" l, 12" w, "DuBarry" pattern **50.00**
Relish Dish, 4½" d, "Blue Rock" pattern **35.00**
Sugar, "Quebec," Wileman **10.00**
Sweetmeat Dish, "Regency" pattern .. **20.00**
Tea and Toast Set, cup and 8" d plate
Border of flowers, green trim, #2348 **40.00**
"Regency" pattern, six flutes **45.00**
Tea Service
"Morning Glory" pattern, demitasse,
teapot, creamer, sugar, two cups
and saucers **250.00**
Multicolored flowers, pink rims, tea-
pot, creamer, sugar, three cake
plates, three cups and saucers, 9" l
tray with pink shell handles **325.00**
Shaded aqua flowers, white ground,
fluted, 3½" h teapot, two cups and
saucers **175.00**
"Summer Glory" pattern, demitasse,
teapot, six cups and saucers **175.00**
Teapot
"Dainty Blue" pattern **85.00**
"Wild Flowers" pattern, 4½" h **125.00**
Toast Rack, orange, yellow, and brown
Art Deco style **45.00**
Tray
8" l, 5" w, "Begonia" pattern **35.00**
14" l, 5¼" w, "Rosebud" pattern,
aqua trim, tab handles **45.00**
Tumbler, 5" h, black transfer of Bowdoin
College, white ground, Wileman ... **20.00**
Vase
5" h, Art Deco, horizontal bands of
light green, yellow, and brown ... **40.00**
7" h, black ground, green sprays,
white flowers, and ribbon, sq top **45.00**

SITZENDORF

**Thuringia, Germany (DDR)
1845 to Present**

History: A small porcelain factory was founded
in 1845 in Thuringia. The Voight brothers managed the factory from 1850 until about 1900,
where they produced decorative figures and porcelains in the Meissen style.

At the turn of the century the factory was called
Alfred Voight AG. Within a few years the name

was changed to Sitzendorf Porcelain Manufactory, its earlier designation. In 1923 earthenwares were added.

The company was semi-nationalized in 1957 and completely nationalized in 1972. The current name is VEB Sitzendorf Porcelain Manufactory.

Basket, 11″ l, 9″ h, applied multicolored flowers, c1880, $800.00.

Candelabrum
    15½″ h, figure of girl with birdcage, leaning against tree trunk, applied pastel colored flowers, three candle arms **250.00**
    17″ h, boy with dog, leaning against tree trunk, applied pastel colored flowers, three candle arms **300.00**
Centerpiece
    14½″ d, basket, applied roses, modeled Oriental woman and child (A) **210.00**
    Pierced basket, applied roses base of two tree trunks, enameled putti, repairs to basket (A) **110.00**
Clock 13″ h, base with six monkey band figures, painted polychrome, pastel ground applied climbing roses, Tiffany & Co. clock movement (A) **1,700.00**
Compote 13″ h, two modeled winged Cupids supporting stem and bowl, multicolored **700.00**
Figure
    3½″ h, girl playing lute, multicolored, sq base, c1880 .... **165.00**
    4½″ h, lady in sedan chair, multicolored **85.00**
    6″ h, peasant boy with basket of grapes, multicolored (A) **60.00**
    7″ h
        Lady, peacock at side, lizard on arm, multicolored **145.00**
        Man and woman, period dress playing "Blind Man's Bluff," multicolored, open vase-like tree stump in back, ftd scroll base, c1850 .... **540.00**
        Seated boy and girl with hurdy-gurdy, multicolored, c1870 .... **140.00**

7½″ h, seated man and woman, period clothes, multicolored **450.00**
7¾″ h, shepherd and shepherdess multicolored, pr **225.00**
9½″ h, man and woman, period clothes, multicolored, pr (A) **165.00**
31″ h, boy with jug, period clothes, multicolored (A) **80.00**
Mirror, 18⅜″ h, applied roses, flowerheads, and putto, branches for three lights, rococo scrolled outline (A) ... **280.00**
Wall Bracket, molded, rococo scrolls, applied cherub seated in flowering branches **120.00**

SLIPWARE

Staffordshire, England
Continental
17th C to Present

History: Slip is powdered clay that is mixed with water until a cream-like consistency is achieved. The slip then can be used to decorate pottery in a variety of ways such as trailing, marbling, combing, feathering, and sgraffito.

Trailing is decorating by means of extruding slip or glaze through a nozzle onto the surface of the piece.

Marbling is achieved by trailing different colored slips onto a form that is then either shaken or twisted to produce the pattern.

Combing is done by applying slip and then wiping over the piece with a toothed or pronged instrument or by using the fingers.

Feathering occurs by trailing a line of slip onto a wet ground of a contrasting color. The tip of a feather or another flexible, thin point is then drawn back and forth across the trailed line.

Sgraffito is achieved by cutting, incising, or scratching away a slip coating to reveal the contrasting slip or body underneath.

Colored slips are made by adding a small amount of various oxides to the slip. Slip was an early method to embellish ordinary clay-colored pottery. After the slip decorations were done, the vessel was covered with a lead glaze in order to make it non-porous and to produce a shiny surface. Slip decoration was used from the 17th century until the present time.

Slipware was made mainly at Wrotham in Kent in Staffordshire. Other manufacturing centers include Essex, Sussex, Somerset, and Devonshire. The earliest piece from Wrotham is dated 1612.

Between 1670 and 1710 the most spectacular pieces of slipware made in Staffordshire were large chargers made by the Tofts, John and William Wright, George Taylor, William Taylor, and Ralph Simpson. Favorite subjects included royal scenes, portraits of popular figures, and cavaliers. Coats of arms, mermaids, Adam & Eve, and the Pelican in her piety were used. Borders usually had a trellis pattern. Human figures had minimal anatomical details and were painted in a naive fashion. Forms that were slip decorated include tygs, teapots, cradles, baking dishes, puzzle jugs, posset pots, whistles, etc.

Potteries in Devon made large harvest jugs using the sgraffito technique. Decorations included coats of arms, lions, unicorns, ships, mariners' compasses, and floral designs.

Wrotham slip decorated wares continued to be made until the end of the 18th century. Fleurde-lis, roses, crosses, stars, and masks were frequent motifs. Tygs, posset pots, two-handled mugs and candlesticks were made. A distinctive feature of Wrotham ware was handles made by weaving different colored clays together.

References: R. G. Cooper, *English Slipware Dishes 1650–1850,* Tiranti, 1968.

Museums: County Museum, Truro, England; Gardiner Museum of Ceramic Art, Toronto, Canada; Kansas City Art Museum, Kansas City, Missouri; Plymouth City Museum, Plymouth, England; Royal Albert Museum, Exeter, England; Sheffield City Museum, Sheffield, England.

Dish, 8¾" d, brown, green, and black slip design, yellow ground, France, $325.00.

Baking Dish
13" l, dark brown ground, cream slip design of stylized tree and "1852" (A) **560.00**
15" d, dark brown ground, slip-trailed cream leaf shape motif and tendril branches, notched rim, early 19th C, England **700.00**
15" l, brown ground, slip design of looped motifs and "William" (A) . **140.00**
16" l, brown ground, slip criss-crossing design, lead glaze, oval shape, 19th C, England **475.00**
18" l, overall slip trails combed into feather patterns, c1781-83, imp "Abbott Potter" mark (A) **640.00**

26½" l, brown ground, slip design of foliage scrolls and "1815," England (A) **380.00**
Bowl
8" d, int. with radiating pooled white and brown slip, green accents, white line rim, c1745, Staffordshire (A) **1,000.00**
12¾" d, 1¾" h, red-brown ground, dark brown glaze, colored slip of two rampant lions, stylized flowers, and "1813," unmarked (A) **230.00**
Charger
12¼" d, red-brown ground, crisscrossing wavy lines of yellow slip and dots (A) **275.00**
12½" d, red-brown ground, yellow slip wavy lines, coggled edge (A) . **325.00**
Colander, 11¼" d, three white slip lines on int. from pierced base, 18th C, England, cracked **200.00**
Dish
7⅝" d, red-brown ground, cream slip, incised "1787," green and yellow glazes of floral sprigs, Germany (A) **225.00**
8⅜" d, red-brown ground, puddled yellow slip, green and brown glaze, unmarked (A) **55.00**
9¾" d, on yellow slip ground painted green and brown, swirling fronds, late 18th C, Continental **120.00**
12" d, red-brown ground, cream slip, brown slip stag, incised "1804," brown, green, and yellow glazes, floral and roulette border, Austria (A) **550.00**
12⅞" d, red-brown, cream slip, green, ochre, and brown slip floral spray, brown chain border, late 18th C, Germany **500.00**
13¾" d, dark brown ground, trailing white slip in serpentine squiggle, 18th C, Staffordshire **475.00**
14" d, yellow ground, brown slip crown, band of green and brown dashes, 18th C, Continental **120.00**
16½" d, dark brown ground, white slip wavy lines and zig-zags, 18th C **135.00**
Drinking Bowl, 7" d, red-brown ground, slip inscription on rim, incised initials and "1745," carved flower sprays, foliage, cylindrical spout, dbl loop handles, England **750.00**
Ewer, 15" h, red ground, green and yellow slip design of bird perched on flowerhead, dbl handled, 17th C, Italy (A) **200.00**
Figure, 9⅝" h, cream ground, dark brown splashes, model of seated bear grasping dog in paws, muzzle and chain, England (A) **170.00**

Flask, 6¾" h, slip design of scroll motifs and studs, "W. J." and "1815" (A) .. **100.00**

Flower Pot

6" h, slip inscribed "Bridget Thomas, 1858," dot and zig-zag border, England **200.00**

11½" h, slip inscribed "JP" and "1802," slip and sgraffito scrolls on border, England **210.00**

Jar, 7¾" h, slip bands on shoulder, lead glaze, England (A) **160.00**

Jug

11½" h, terra cotta ground, sgraffito design of birds and hawks cut into cream slip, green accents, 19th C, North Devon (A) **385.00**

15⅜" h, red body dipped in white slip, sgraffito design under mottled green ground, conical, small lip, strap handle, 14th C, England (A)   **510.00**

Loaf Pan, 15½" l, 12¼" w, red-brown ground, coggled edge, three line yellow slip design (A) **500.00**

Loving Cup

6⅝" h, brown body, cream slip incised "IBE" on band with grasses, dated 1763 on reverse, bands of checkering, dbl strap handles, Staffordshire (A) **2,300.00**

9⅞" h, dark brown ground, white slip bands, inscribed "M:H," 18th C, England (A) **180.00**

Mug

5⅛" h, marbled blue, yellow, and ochre slip, incised line to rim, cylindrical, strap handle, c1745, England (A) **1,028.00**

5¾" h, dark brown, ground, slip inscribed "JL:1869," England **85.00**

Pan, 15½" l, red-brown ground, white slip combware design, black edge (A) **550.00**

Pitcher, 4½" h, red-brown ground, white running marbleized slip and butterscotch glaze, unmarked (A) ... **115.00**

Plate, red-brown ground

8" d

Three line yellow slip design (A) . **400.00**

Yellow slip dashes (A) **75.00**

8⅞" d, yellow slip tree design, puddled green glaze (A) **375.00**

9¾" d, three line yellow slip crow's feet, coggled edge (A) **215.00**

10¼" d, three line yellow slip crow's foot design, coggled edge, unmarked (A) **155.00**

Pot, 6⅞" d, cov, dark brown slip scrolls on body, ochre glaze, small loop handle, cov with two bands of dots, early 18th C, Staffordshire (A) **1,815.00**

Salt Kiln, 9½" h, slip design of stylized leaf trails, "B. A. S." and "1836" (A) **255.00**

Shaving Bowl, 14" w, splashed manganese glaze, beige slip ground, c1720, France **375.00**

SOFT PASTE

English/Continental
17th to 19th Centuries

History: Soft paste, or artifical porcelain, was made during the 17th and 18th centuries in Europe by using glass or a glass substitute that was ground up and mixed with clay. Over the years, the ingredients of soft paste varied.

The glaze was added in the second firing. This glaze was soft. It scratched and chipped easily. If the potter was careless, the glaze could wilt in the kiln and become uneven. The soft paste process was abandoned gradually during the early 19th century when the formula for hard paste porcelain became better understood.

Soft paste porcelain had the translucency of hard paste. It simply was softer and more porous. Since the melting temperatures of soft paste glazes and the colored enamels are similar, the overglaze enamel sinks into the glaze and softens the outline of painted decoration. Essentially pigment and surface are melded together.

Soft paste was made in France at Rouen, St. Cloud, Chantilly, Mennecy, Vincennes, and Sevres. English factories making soft paste included Chelsea, Bow, Derby, Worcester, and Liverpool. Most European countries produced soft paste porcelain before switching to hard paste porcelain production.

Barber Bowl, 11 18" l, 8⅝", blue transfer Oriental village scene, unmarked (A) **130.00**

Bowl

7¼" d, blue and white Leeds-type Oriental design, unmarked (A) **70.00**

7½" d, 3½" h, blue, green, and ochre, Leeds type floral design, unmarked (A) **285.00**

10¼" l, 13⅜" w, blue feather edge, unmarked (A) **75.00**

12⅜" d, 3¾" h, gaudy Leeds-type design in blue and ochre (A) **275.00**

13¼" l, 10½" w, blue feather edge, unmarked (A) **50.00**

Candlestick, 8" h, fluted stem painted with bouquets and sprays and gilt lines, baluster shape, c1775, Sceaux (A) **385.00**

Charger

14⅛" d, center floral design, blue feather edge, unmarked (A) **140.00**

Plate, 6½" d, yellow, red, pink, green, and rust florals, England, $100.00.

14¼" d, urn of flowers, five colors, scalloped blue feather edge (A) ... **425.00**
Coffeepot, 10¼" h, gaudy blue and white Leeds-type, dec, domed lid, unmarked (A) **150.00**
Creamer
  2⅞" h, blue white Leeds-type floral design, unmarked (A) **60.00**
  3⅛" h, emb cherubs, vines, and eagle, copper and purple luster (A) . **55.00**
  3⅝" h, gaudy blue and white floral design, unmarked (A) **40.00**
  4¾" h, emb floral design, pink and purple luster, unmarked (A) **25.00**
Cup and Saucer
  Gold sprig and leaf design, England **15.00**
  Polychromed enamel rose design, unmarked (A) **25.00**
Dish
  4⅜" l, raised yellow, green, and brown vegetables, blue feather edge (A) **245.00**
  6⅛" l, dark blue transfer of building, leaf shape, Staffordshire (A) **130.00**
Figure
  2" h, yellow pig, mottled green and brown oval base (A) **185.00**
  3¼" h, tiger, yellow ochre enamel, black striped **130.00**
  9½" h, Oriental maiden holding bird and chalice, Continental (A) **30.00**
Jar, Cov, 2¾" h, emb artichoke leaves trimmed in blue (A) **250.00**
Knife Handle, molded, flowering prunus, multicolored accents, silver collar and steel blade, c1775, Sceaux (A) **385.00**
Miniature, Teabowl and Saucer, blue, gray, and dark brown stylized floral swag (A) **25.00**
Mug
  3¼" h, red foliage scroll transfer, green enameling (A) **48.00**

4½" h, black transfer of ships, flags, and cannons, portrait of Lord Nelson, Oct 21st, 1805, imp "Rainforth" (A) **75.00**
Pitcher
  2" h, blue, green, and red floral design, emb leaf handle (A) **55.00**
  2⅛" h, peafowl design, multicolored sponged foliage (A) **225.00**
  6¼" h, "Gaudy Rose" design, pink, blue, green, yellow, and dark red, unmarked, English (A) **55.00**
Pitcher and Bowl, 4" h pitcher, gaudy cobalt, red, and green florals, gold trim, octagon shape, unmarked **155.00**
Plate
  4" d, gaudy floral design, red, green, and black, unmarked (A) **30.00**
  5½" d, "Queen's Rose" pattern, multicolored (A) **20.00**
  6½" d, polychrome enamel rose in center, emb rim, purple luster, green enameling, unmarked (A) .. **40.00**
  7" d, central polychrome floral bouquet, scalloped rim, unmarked (A) **50.00**
  7⅝" d, medium blue transfer of Oriental scene, purple luster rim, unmarked (A) **25.00**
  7¾" d, polychrome enamel rose in center, border emb, purple luster bands, unmarked (A) **45.00**
  8½" d, Gaudy design, underglazed blue and yellow, ochre and brown enamels, unmarked (A) **50.00**
  9" d, blue feather edge (A) **40.00**
  9¾" d, Leeds-type yellow ochre floral design, blue feather edge (A) **135.00**
Pot, Cov, 3½" h, blue feather edge, unmarked (A) **25.00**
Salt, 3" d, blue feather edge, ftd, unmarked (A) **60.00**
Sauceboat
  2⅞" h, blue feather edge (A) **100.00**
  3⅝" h, blue and white floral dec, emb rim, molded design, unmarked (A) **50.00**
Shaker
  3⅝" h, medium blue transfer of fishing scene, unmarked (A) **45.00**
  4⅜" h, blue stripes, unmarked (A) .. **60.00**
Soup Plate, 10⅜" d, black transfer of sidewheel steamship, blue feather edge (A) **175.00**
Spill Holder, 5¼" h, purple, lavender, and tan marbleized enameling, white ground, urn shape, unmarked (A) ... **50.00**
Sugar
  4½" h, Leeds-type gaudy blue floral design (A) **35.00**
  5" h
    Leeds type gaudy floral design, multicolored, unmarked (A) **65.00**

Leeds-type floral dec, multicolored, applied flower finial, unmarked (A) 25.00

5¾" h, gaudy blue and white floral design, finial repaired (A) 25.00

Tea Service, teapot, creamer, sugar, waste bowl, four teabowls and saucers, purple luster floral band, red enameling, unmarked (A) 250.00

Teabowl and Saucer

Blue and white floral design (A) 35.00

Blue transfer of Oriental buildings, unmarked (A) 45.00

Blue, green and ochre, gaudy floral design, imp "Wood" mark (A) ... 55.00

Green, blue, yellow, dark brown, and ochre, gaudy floral design, unmarked (A) 45.00

Leeds-type design, bird in sponged trees, four colors, unmarked (A) .. 80.00

Multicolored gaudy basket of flowers, pink border, polychrome (A) 85.00

Multicolored "Queen's Rose" pattern (A) 25.00

Multicolored rose design (A) 20.00

Ochre, rose, green, and blue, Leeds-type gaudy design, unmarked (A) . 45.00

Swirled rib pattern, blue dash design, unmarked (A) 35.00

Teapot

5¼" h, black transfer of mother and child at well, black striping, polychromes, pink border at shoulder, unmarked (A) 65.00

5⅜" h, blue transfer of Oriental design, swan finial, unmarked (A) .. 75.00

7¼" h, Leeds-type gaudy, ochre, green, yellow, and underglazed blue, unmarked (A) 85.00

Toddy Plate

4¾" d, blue feather edge, unmarked (A) 40.00

5¼" d, blue feather edge, scalloped rim, unmarked (A) 20.00

5½" d, blue feather edge, unmarked (A) 40.00

Waste Bowl, 6⅛" d, florals in pink, green, ochre, and black, blue border stripe (A) 30.00

SPAIN-GENERAL

Alcora, Province of Valencia
1726 to 1858

Count Aranda, assisted by Joseph Olerys of Moustiers and other French workers, established a faience factory in 1726. The original success of this factory was due to the skill of the French painters and the use of French models. The tin-glazed pottery that it produced was quite popular throughout Spain.

By 1737 all the workers were Spanish. Biblical or mythological scenes on large dishes or plaques were among its best pieces. The Count died in 1749. His son took over. A succession of Dukes of Hija owned the factory. When the factory was acquired by private owners, Francois Martin started to produce hard paste porcelain in imitation of Wedgwood's creamware in 1858.

Buen Retiro, near Madrid
1760 to 1812

King Charles III of Spain established Buen Retiro, near Madrid, using workers from Capodimonte in 1760. Soft paste porcelains were manufactured into services, tea sets, vases, bowls, and figures similar to Capodimonte wares. The factory also specialized in the porcelain tiles that were used to decorate palaces.

By the end of the 18th century, biscuit groups in the Sevres styles and medallions and plaques in the Wedgwood style were made. From 1765 until 1790 Giuseppe Gricci was the chief modeler. After his death, Spanish artists influenced the decorations.

Only hard paste wares were made at Buen Retiro after 1800. In 1808 the factory was transformed into a fortress that was destroyed by Wellington in 1812. In 1817 the factory was rebuilt at Moncloa in Madrid and remained in operation until 1850.

Hispano-Moresque, Valencia & Malaga
End of 13th Century to Present

Hispano-Moresque is white enamel, tin-glazed earthenware that is usually decorated with copper or silver metallic lusters. Moorish potters came to Spain, settled in Valenica, Manises, and Paterna, and made their lustered pottery.

Early luster colors were pale and filmy. Later pieces utilized a golden luster and deeper blue tones. As time progressed, the luster became more brassy and metallic in appearance.

Hispano-Moresque flourished for about three hundred years. By the end of the 16th century there was a steady decline, but the technique still continues today in Valencia. A variety of vases, drug pots, pitchers, covered bowls, large dishes, and wall tiles are made.

Talavera
15th Century to Present

Talavera pottery is decorated in a peasant-like style with birds, animals, or busts in a blue and dusty-orange motif outlined in purplish-black. Talavera wares were popular with all levels of

Spanish society into the 17th century. Monastic coats of arms and the cardinal's hat were decorated in yellow, orange, and green. Shapes included large bowls and two handled jugs featuring sporting scenes, bullfights, buildings, trees, figures, and animals.

During the mid-18th century Talavera adopted the styles used at Alcora which had copied the French style of Moustiers. Today only ordinary earthenwares are made.

References: Alice Wilson Frothingham, *Tile Panels of Spain: 1500–1650,* Hispanic Society of America, 1969.

Museums: Cleveland Museum of Art, Cleveland, Ohio; Hispanic Society of America, New York, New York; Musee Nationale de Ceramique, Sevres, France; Museo Arquelogical Nacional, Madrid, Spain; Seattle Art Museum, Seattle, Washington; Victoria & Albert Museum, London, England.

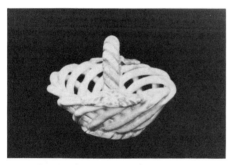

Basket, 3¼" l, 2¼" h, blue outline with yellow trim, multicolored flower in center, imp "SPAIN," $10.00.

Bowl
   10" d center green, maganese, blue and ochre leaping rabbit in landscape, majolica, 18th C, Talavera   **325.00**
   12¼" d, lustered stylized bird, scrolling foliate border, 17th C, Hispano-Moresque, repaired (A) **140.00**
   14½" d, bird in foliage, copper luster, 17th C, Hispano-Moresque, repaired (A) **275.00**
Charger, 15" d, tan body, gold luster, raised center, 17th C, unmarked, Hispano-Moresque **940.00**
Cup, painted with fruits in landscape, gilt octagonal panel reserved on light orange ground, c1805, iron-red "Crowned Md" mark **125.00**
Dish
   8" w, incised and painted flowerheads and stylized cypress trees, green, brown, and yellow, diaper border, 19th C, faience (A) **65.00**

11" d
   Light copper luster cockerel with foliage, late 16th C, Hispano-Moresque (A) **100.00**
   Single plant, bocage background, green with manganese, yellow, and cobalt accents, pie crust rim, majolica, 18th C, Talavera **125.00**
   13⅛" d, molded eight pointed foliage motif around gadrooned center, copper luster and blue, scrolling foliage ground, c1520, Hispano-Moresque (A) **315.00**
   13½" d, painted mustard and cobalt design, floral border, cream ground, luster, late 16th C, Hispano-Moresque (A) **300.00**
   14½" d, blue and white painted bird in border of stylized foliage, late 17th C, Catalan, rim chips (A) . . . **275.00**
   14¾" d, dark copper luster foliage, blue sprays, late 16th C, Hispano-Moresque, pr (A) **255.00**
   16⅛" d, animal jumping blue enameled fence with stylized vines, copper-red luster, pink-cream ground, reverse with rings and florals, pierced for hanging, c1600 (A) . . .**1,650.00**
Drug Jar
   9" h, blue "IHS" in scrolled border, cream glaze, early 18th C, pr (A) . **370.00**
   10⅜" h, blue painted drug name, crowned Maltese cross, dbl headed bird, oviform, cylindrical neck (A) **175.00**
Figure, 7" h, seated Venus with Cupid and Diana, multicolored, pink and gold rococo scroll base, c1765-70, Buen Retiro, pr **1,200.00**
Holy Water Font, 10¾" h, molded and painted Virgin and child on backplate outlined in rosary beads and beaded cross, stylized flower in bowl, copper-red luster, cream ground, pierced for hanging, 19th C, Hispano-Moresque (A) **70.00**
Jar
   8⅜" h, panels of copper-red florals, cream ground, blue enameled plant, four loop handles at neck, 19th C, Hispano-Moresque (A) . . . **500.00**
   10⅝" h, two horizontal bands of ferns in chevron bands, copper luster, cobalt ground, majolica, 16th C (A) **600.00**
   11" h, yellow and ochre oval, blue bowknot, manganese Latin inscription, late 18th C (A) **150.00**
Pitcher, 11" h, painted prancing deer, leafed trees, pinched spout, polychrome bands, majolica, late 18th C, Talavera (A) **670.00**
Plaques
   10½" l, white cameo scene of Pan

and Cupid on one, Pan and Syrinx on other, blue jasper ground, late 18th C, Buen Retiro, pr **600.00**
15¼" d, blue and green Moorish design, late 19th C, unmarked (A) .. **45.00**

Plate
7" d, stylized bird, copper luster and ruby tones, Hispano-Moresque ... **125.00**
9¼" d, polychrome arms of Charles II of Spain, crowned shield held by three putti, diaper border with flower panels, majolica (A) **200.00**
10" d
Tan seahorse, cream ground, green border, majolica, c1800, unmarked **45.00**
Three enameled sprays of flowers, border of stylized bellflowers and sq scrolls, porcelain, late 18th C, "Black A" mark, Alcora (A) **150.00**
13" d, prancing horse in shrubs, blue, yellow, brown, and manganese, c1675 .... **500.00**

Salt, iron-red, blue, and yellow scrolling foliage, lion's masks on sides, triangular, late 17th C, Talavera (A) **35.00**

Tureen
9" h, modeled as seated multicolored cockerel, oval waisted base, late 18th C, manganese "A mark," Alcora **350.00**
13" l, cov, molded oval body painted with green and yellow swags, leaf-form dbl handles, squash finial, dome molded cov, mid 18th C ... **700.00**

Vase
10¾" h, copper-red luster bird on stylized florals, cream ground, dbl handles, 19th C, Hispano-Moresque (A) **70.00**
19¾" h, equestrian figure and deer in landscape, manganese, yellow, and blue, dbl mask handles, c1700, Talavera **500.00**

SPATTERWARE

Staffordshire, England
c1800 to 1850s

History-General: Spatterware is a decoration that appeared on a variety of body compositions including soft paste, creamware, pearlware, and ironstone. It appealed to "popular" tastes because of its inexpensive price and cheery, colorful, and bright appearance. It was made primarily for export.

Spatter is a stippling or all-over design of color. One or more colors can be used. The color was applied in parallel stripes or concentric bands leaving a center of white for decoration. With spatter as a border, the center design could be either hand painted or transfer printed.

There were eight basic colors used for spatter: black, blue (the most common), brown, green, pink, purple, red, and yellow (the rarest). The most popular patterns were: Cannon, Castle, Peafowl, Pomegranate, Schoolhouse, and Thistle.

Few pieces of true spatter bear identifying manufacturer's marks. Among the known makers of spatter are: Adams, Cotton and Barlow, Harvey, and J. & G. Meakin.

History-Design: In design spatter there are small, shaped areas of spots or dots instead of large continuous overall spattered areas. Some design spatter is done with a stencil or template. Design spatter also is referred to as "structural spatter."

Colors used for design spatter were red, blue, green, and purple. Spatter techniques were combined with hand painted decoration motifs. Decorative center motifs include: Adams Rose, Columbine, Dogwood, and Pansy.

Known makers of design spatter are: T. W. Barlow, Elsmore and Forster, and Harvey.

References: Carl F. & Ada F. Robacker, *Spatterware and Sponge*, A. S. Barnes & Co., 1978

REPRODUCTION ALERT: "Cybis" spatter is an increasingly collectible ware made by Boleslow Cybis of Poland. The design utilizes the Adams type peafowl and was made in the 1940s. Some pieces are marked "Cybis" with an impressed mark; some examples are unmarked. The principal shape was cup plates. The body of the ware is harder than true spatter, and the glaze appears glassy rather than soft.

Many contemporary craftsmen also are reproducing spatterware examples.

GENERAL

Beaker, 2½" h, blue, brown, and yellow rainbow spatter (A) **275.00**
Chamber Pot, 8½" d, blue and green spatter (A) **65.00**
Creamer
2" h, "Peafowl" pattern, red, blue,

Sugar Bowl, cov, 4½" d, 4¼" h, blue, cream ground, unmarked, $175.00.

black, and ochre, green spatter border (A) **200.00**
3¾" h, "Rose" pattern, red, green, and black, blue and purple spatter (A) **325.00**
3⅞" h
"Rose" pattern, red and green, brown spatter border (A) **65.00**
"Thistle" pattern, red and green, red and yellow rainbow spatter (A) **525.00**
4" h
Blue spatter (A) **85.00**
"Morning glory" pattern, blue, green, and black, red spatter border (A) **35.00**
4⅛" h, "Peafowl" pattern, blue, green, yellow, and black, red spatter border (A) **300.00**
4⅝" h, "Fort" pattern, blue spatter border (A) **80.00**
5½" h, "Fort" pattern, green, black, red, and ochre, blue spatter border, paneled, repaired handle (A) **200.00**
Cup and Saucer
"Acorn" pattern, black, brown, and green, purple spatter border, handleless (A) **375.00**
Adams Rose pattern, pink and green spatter border (A) **130.00**
"Bull's eye" pattern, yellow, red spatter border, handleless (A) **325.00**
"Castle" pattern, red spatter border, handleless (A) **310.00**
"Cornflowers" pattern, blue, green and black, red and yellow rainbow spatter border, handleless (A) **675.00**
"Coxcomb" pattern, red and green, blue spatter border **235.00**
"Schoolhouse" pattern, red, blue, yellow and black, red spatter border (A) **225.00**
"Tulip" pattern, red, yellow, green and black, black and brown rainbow spatter border (A) **275.00**
Dish
7½" d, bull's-eye center, purple spatter border (A) **45.00**
7½" l, 5⅜" w, red and blue cross in center, red and blue rainbow spatter border (A) **650.00**
Miniature
Cup
"Rooster" pattern, red, blue, yellow and black, blue spatter border (A) **120.00**
"Peafowl" pattern, red, blue, ochre and black, green spatter border (A) **450.00**
Cup and Saucer
Blue Spatter (A) **315.00**
Brown Spatter (A) **35.00**

"Fort" pattern, red, green, black, and ochre, blue spatter border (A) **450.00**
"Peafowl" pattern, blue spatter border **200.00**
Purple spatter (A) **85.00**
Teabowl and Saucer
"Peafowl" pattern, blue, black, and yellow, green spatter border (A) **100.00**
"Tree" pattern, black and green, blue spatter border (A) **450.00**
Mug
3⅞" h, blue spatter (A) **150.00**
4⅞" h, blue spatter (A) **55.00**
Mustard Jar, Cov, blue spatter **165.00**
Pitcher
9¾" h, "Four Petal Flower" pattern in red, blue, green, and black, four panels, red and blue spatter border, imp "Davenport" (A) **350.00**
12" h, "Thistle" pattern, red and green, yellow spatter border, paneled (A) **250.00**
Plate
6⅜" d, "Holly berry" pattern, blue spatter border (A) **85.00**
7" d, red, blue, and green rainbow spatter, imp "Adams" (A) **190.00**
7⅛" d, "Bull's eye" pattern, red and green spatter (A) **25.00**
7½" d, "Peafowl" pattern, red, yellow, green, and black, blue spatter border (A) **300.00**
8¼" d
"Rooster on fence" pattern, multicolored, blue spatter border (A) **50.00**
"Schoolhouse" pattern, blue and yellow, red spatter border (A) .. **500.00**
8⅜" d
"Dahlia" pattern, red, blue, and green, blue spatter border (A) .. **270.00**
Red, green, and blue rainbow spatter, white center, imp "Adams" (A) **75.00**
8½" d, "Star" pattern, red, blue, and green, blue spatter border, imp "Stone China" (A) **300.00**
8¾" d
"Dahlia" pattern, red, green, and black, blue spatter border (A) .. **145.00**
"Peafowl" pattern, red, blue, green, and black, blue spatter border, imp "Adams" (A) **255.00**
9" d
Blue and white center scene of windmills and boats in harbor, blue spatter border, Stoke-On-Trent **40.00**
Brown flying eagle in center, green spatter border **200.00**

9½" d
Blue spatter (A) **55.00**
"Bull's eye" pattern
Olive and red spatter (A) **200.00**
Red and blue spatter (A) **30.00**
"Fort" pattern, black, red, and
green, blue spatter border (A) .. **345.00**
Red and green marbleized design
(A) **45.00**
9¾" d
"Rose" pattern, red, green, and
black, red and blue spatter border, imp "Cotton and Rose" (A) **150.00**
"Schoolhouse" pattern, red, green
spatter border (A) **100.00**
10" d, white center, blue spatter border, imp "Thos. Walker" (A) **55.00**
Platter
15¾" l, red and green rainbow spatter
(A) **625.00**
16" l, 12" w, "Tulip" pattern, red and
yellow, blue and purple rainbow
spatter, octangonal, repaired (A) .. **475.00**
Sauce Dish, 5" d, "Peafowl" pattern,
red, green, blue, and black, red spatter border (A) **245.00**
Saucer
4½" d, "Peafowl" pattern, ochre, red,
green, and black, blue spatter border (A) **55.00**
6" d, "Fort" pattern, multicolored,
blue spatter border (A) **75.00**
Shaker, 5" h, blue and purple rainbow
(A) **410.00**
Soup Plate
8⅝" d, "Peafowl on Branch" pattern,
blue, green, red, and black, blue
spatter rim, imp "Adams" (A) **500.00**
9¼" d, open flower, red, blue, green,
and black, red spatter border (A) . **200.00**
10½" d, "Thistle" pattern, red, red
and blue spatter in alternating
bands (A) **1,400.00**
Sugar
4¾" h, "Rooster" pattern, blue, red,
black, and ochre, blue spatter bor-
der, cov, repair to lid and rim (A) . **550.00**
5⅝" h, red, yellow, green, and black
rainbow spatter (A) **285.00**
Teabowl and Saucer
"Acorn and Leaf" pattern, green,
ochre, black, and brown, blue spatter borders (A) **175.00**
"Coxcomb" pattern, red, blue spatter
borders **235.00**
"Peafowl" pattern, blue, green,
ochre, and black, red spatter bor-
der(A) **255.00**
"Schoolhouse" pattern
Multicolors, blue spatter border (A) . **135.00**
Red, brown, and green, green spatter
border (A) **300.00**

"Tulip" pattern, red, green, blue, and
black, green spatter borders (A) .. **225.00**
"Thistle" pattern, red and green, red
spatter borders, repairs (A) **25.00**
Teapot
5¾" h, "Dove" pattern, yellow, blue,
green, and black, purple spatter, finial repaired (A) **175.00**
7" h, "Peafowl" pattern, blue, green,
yellow, and black, red spatter (A) . **135.00**
10" h, blue spatter, grape finial, octagonal (A) **225.00**
Toddy Plate
5⅛" d, "Acorn" pattern
Brown, black, pattern and green,
purple spatter border (A) **375.00**
Green, yellow and black, purple
spatter border, stained (A) **400.00**
5¼" d, "Dahlia" pattern, red, blue,
green, and black, red spatter border
(A) **325.00**
Waste Bowl, 4¼" d, "Fort" pattern,
black, red, green, and yellow, blue
spatter border (A) **475.00**

DESIGN

Bowl
6" d, red flowers and green foliage,
imp "Adams" **45.00**
7½" d, 4" h, polychrome stripes (A) . **75.00**
9" d
"Old Heather" pattern **45.00**
Red, green, and blue florals **15.00**
10⅝" d, "Star" pattern, red, purple,
and shades of green (A) **100.00**
13⅞" d, blue geometric design, white
ground (A) **45.00**
Creamer
4" h, blue and red flower, blue stick
spatter, green stripe on base (A) .. **65.00**
4⅜" h, "Gaudy Floral" pattern, red,
green, blue, and black, "Baker &
Co., England" **25.00**
Creamer and Sugar, child's size, green
and red band, black stripe (A) **50.00**
Cup and Saucer, "Floral" pattern, red,
blue, green, and black **25.00**
Dish, 9¼" l, "Floral" pattern, red, blue,
green, and yellow, oval, "Auld
Heather Ware, Scotland" **20.00**
Miniature
Cup and Saucer, green band, black
starflowers, red stripes, stained ... **15.00**
Teabowl and Saucer, red leaf border
(A) **20.00**
Pitcher
7¼" h, cov, blue, red, green, and
white stick spatter on brown,
"GERMANY" (A) **60.00**
10¾" h, red, green, and purple floral
wreaths, red borders (A) **100.00**

Plaque, 13⅝" l, 7¾" h, verses of "God
Save the King," green and red floral
border (A) **115.00**
Plate
7¾" d, blue and white, border design,
"Meyer, Pottery" (A) **10.00**
7⅞" d, blue and brown stick floral
rim, "Meyer Pottery Mfg Co." (A) **15.00**
8⅝" d, "Gaudy Floral" pattern, polychrome, imp "Malkin & Co." (A) **20.00**
8¾" d
Blue and white florals (A) **18.00**
Center with transfer of eagle and
"E. Plurbus Unum," blue stick
spatter border, "R. Hammersly"
(A) **65.00**
Gaudy polychrome florals (A) **75.00**
Red and green florals (A) **20.00**
8⅞" d
Brown and purple stick spatter,
green stripes (A) **25.00**
Gaudy polychrome florals (A) **40.00**
9" d, gaudy polychrome florals (A) .. **75.00**
9⅛" d, brown transfer of rabbits and
frogs, enamels in center, gaudy floral border (A) **95.00**
9⅜" d, gaudy polychrome florals (A) **75.00**
9¾" d, stick spatter border design in
red, blue, and green (A) **10.00**
11" d, "Floral" pattern, dark blue and
lavender **20.00**

**Design Spatterware, platter, 13½" l, 11"
w, yellow and blue flowers, green leaves
in center, red and black border, cream
ground, "Auld Heather-Bootland,"
$165.00.**

Platter
11¾" l, single flower in center, spatter
of florals and leaves on border,
"Baker & Co. England" (A) **35.00**
15⅝" l, "Rosebud and Thistle" pattern, red stripe and columbine,
green spatter (A) **235.00**
Puzzle Jug, "House" pattern, blue and
white **100.00**

Soup Plate
9½" d, red, blue, and green stick spatter (A) **30.00**
10⅝" d, gaudy polychrome florals (A) **75.00**
Sugar, 7⅜" h, blue and white florals,
paneled, Staffordshire (A) **115.00**
Teabowl and Saucer
"Gaudy Floral" pattern, polychrome,
purple spatter (A) **40.00**
"Holly" pattern **40.00**
Red and white, green stripe, imp "Elsmore & Forster, Tunstall" (A) **25.00**
Teacup and Saucer, blue-green leaves
and red flowers on white ground,
handleless **50.00**
Teapot, 5" h, child's size, green band,
brown stripe, "Staffordshire, England" (A) **20.00**
Waste Bowl
5" d, "Gaudy Floral" pattern, red,
green, blue, and black, "Staffordshire, England" **30.00**
6" d, "Floral" pattern, red, green, and
blue (A) **40.00**

Stone-china
1805-30

1815-27

SPODE

Shelton, Staffordshire, England
c1797 to 1833

History: Spode is best known for two important
contributions to the ceramic repertoire: the perfection of under the glaze transfer printing on
earthenware and the introduction of the bone
china formula. Josiah Spode I, 1733 to 1787,
benefited from a five year apprenticeship with
Thomas Whieldon. By 1770 he was an established master potter at Stoke-on-Trent at the factory where his successors continue today. Josiah
Spode II, 1755 to 1827, opened a showroom
and warehouse in the City of London in 1778.

The perfection of transfer printing in blue under the glaze on earthenware enabled Spode to
copy, at reasonable prices, Chinese blue painted
porcelain. These new examples provided re-
placements and additions for services that had
become increasingly difficult to obtain from
Chinese sources.

Earlier English porcelain manufacturers had

failed to make large dinner plates and platters with straight enough edges to be commercially saleable. By July 1796 Spode was selling dinnerware that he called "English China" at prices well below those of his established competitors. By 1800 a bone china porcelain containing up to forty percent calcined ox bone had emerged. The credit for perfecting this formula is shared jointly by the two Spodes. Josiah I developed the initial formula, and Josiah II refined it. Josiah Spode II marketed products made with the new formula with such success that within ten years bone china became standard English china.

Josiah II's successful promotion of bone china was achieved in part through the on-glaze decorating of Henry Daniel. The engraving techniques improved greatly. The zenith was reached in 1816 when, two years after the Tower pattern appeared, the pattern Blue Italian was introduced. Both patterns remain popular to the present day.

In 1813 Spode, responding to the demand for replacement pieces for polychrome Chinese porcelain services, adopted a stone china formula that was patented by J. & W. Turner in 1800. Turner's formula provided a superior body on which to decorate the more costly painted and gilted patterns. The body also matched the delicate gray color of the original Chinese porcelain. Over the years the formula was improved further and appears in today's market as Spode's Fine Stone China.

When Josiah II moved to Stoke in 1797 upon the death of his father, he left the management of the London business in the hands of William Copeland, who began his employment with Spode in 1784. Copeland worked with Spode as an equal partner. When Spode retired in 1812, Copeland assumed sole charge of the London house. His business acumen, augmented with the help of W. T. Copeland, his son, in 1824, contributed immensely to the success of the Spode enterprise.

(See Copeland-Spode for a continuation of the company's history.)

References: Robert Copeland, *Spode's Willow Pattern & Other Designs After the Chinese*, Rizzoli, 1980; D. Drakard & P. Holdway, *Spode Printed Wares*, Longmans, 1983; Arthur Hayden, *Spode & His Successors*, Cassell, 1925; Leonard Whiter, *Spode: A History of the Family, Factory & Wares, 1733–1833*, Barrie & Jenkins, 1970.

Museums: Cincinnati Art Museum, Cincinnati, Ohio; City of Stoke-on-Trent Museum, Hanley, England; Spode Museum, Stoke-on-Trent, England; Victoria & Albert Museum, London, England.

Collectors' Note: Although there is no collectors' club, inquiries about Spode Factory wares may be sent to Historical Consultant, Spode, Stoke-on-Trent, ST4 IBX, England. All inquiries should contain good, clear photographs and full details of the marks.

Bowl, 9½" d, transfer and painted Oriental scene, blue, rust, and gold, c1830, "Stone China" **110.00**
Bust, 11" h, Ophelia **375.00**
Cake Plate, 6½" w, "Japan" pattern, dark blue, orange, and green, gilt edge and trim, c1815 .... **250.00**
Center Dish, 14½" l, floral and leaf pattern, scalloped edge, ring handles, c1830 .... **485.00**
Chamberstick, 3" h, painted "Japan" style pattern, gilt dentil rim, pattern #3710 .... **175.00**
Cheese Tray, 10" d, white center, green vines interspersed between flowers, raised gold rim, red and blue flowers, c1825 .... **230.00**
Coffee Can "Japan" pattern, blue, iron-red, and gilt, pattern #1495, set of 4 (A) **70.00**
Coffee Can and Saucer, 2½" h, cup with splashed pink luster and shading, S-scroll handle, rim with Sevres style florals and gilt, c1810, pr (A) **415.00**
Coffee Cup and Saucer, loose bouquets of flowers, brown ground, gilt rim, faceted, c1820 (A) **100.00**

Dish, 11" l, multicolored florals, brown rim, c1820, $300.00.

Cooler, 7½" h, printed and painted with classical figures in iron-red and black, gilt accents, diamond pattern rim, dbl handled, c1820, iron-red "Spode, #1122" mark (A) **240.00**
Cup and Saucer
"Brosely" pattern (A) **18.00**
Gilt stylized flowerheads, burnt orange ground, yellow scrolling foliage, c1820 (A) **145.00**
Imari floral panels, two green partridges (A) **25.00**

"Japan" pattern, dark blue, orange, and green, gilt edge and gold trim, c1815, pr **300.00**

Desk Set, 11" w, inkwell, pounce pot, water pot, two handled tray, four gilt paw feet, swags of garden flowers hanging from gilt line rims, pattern #3103, c1825 (A) **260.00**

Dessert Plate, 8⅞" d, center gilt design in peach borders, gilt fleur-de-lis in wreaths and alternating wheatears, gilt rims, white gadroons, c1825, set of 12 (A) **600.00**

Dessert Service, Dbl handled cooler, two oval dishes, seven plates, printed and painted with different specimen flowers, named on reverse, yellow ground, c1795, puce "SPODE, #1569" mark (A) **2,860.00**

Dinner Service, royal blue borders outlined with gilding, puce "SPODE FELSPAR," iron-red "#3951" mark, set of 95 pcs (A) **1,540.00**

Dish

7" d, platinum luster band and border of stylized gilt design (A) **10.00**

7⅞" d, printed and colored chrysanthemums, bamboo, and flowers, everted rims, pattern #2117, "Stone China," set of 6 (A) **100.00**

9" d, printed and colored famille rose style, Oriental figures in trees and shrubs, c1820, pattern #3644 (A) **60.00**

10¼" d, center with gilt flower sprays, painted gilt and pink scrolling foliage border, c1800 .... **75.00**

11½" l, gilt foliage, tan ground, scroll molded dbl handles, c1800 (A) .. **70.00**

12½" l, printed and painted flower sprays and sprigs, canted rect shape, c1815, "New Stone China" (A) **130.00**

18⅞" l, blue printed "Castle of Boudron" pattern, lobed, imp "SPODE" (A) **175.00**

Flower Pot, 8¼" h, painted flowers in gilt foliage cartouche reserved on blue ground, painted speciman flowers, white bead and gilt line rims, three paw feet, c1820, pattern #2575 (A) **300.00**

Fruit Stand, 14" l, three exotic birds in gilt border, c1810, iron-red "SPODE and #1723" mark (A) **305.00**

Hotplates, 10½" d, Oriental ironstone pattern, blue, red, and orange flowers outlined in gold, blue leaves, scalloped edges outlined in gold, c1805, "New Stone China," "Made for the 44th Regt." marks, pr **700.00**

Inkstand, 6" l, revolving, gilt edge, Oriental design, metal holder c1830 ... **485.00**

Jar, 5" h, painted multicolored flowers, blue and gilt scale ground, gilt loop handles, mask terminals, beaded rim and foot, pattern #1166, c1810-20 (A) **950.00**

Jug, 11⅞" h, molded white rose sprays, pink lilac ground painted with large rose blooms, shield shape, gold "SPODE" (A) **625.00**

Pastille Burner, alternate panels of summer flowers and gilded flowers on gros bleu ground, raised beaded borders, three claw feet, c1825, pattern #2637, pr (A) **500.00**

Pitcher, 4½" h, terra cotta body, raised blue open flowers, c1790-1820, imp mark **225.00**

Plate

8" d, central crests, wide borders of gilt and pink scrolling foliage suspended from swags, c1820, pr ... **250.00**

8¼" d

Blue transfer of stylized flowers, gilt accents, pattern #2383, earthenware, set of 12 (A) **310.00**

Printed and colored famille rose style, Oriental figures in trees and shrubs, c1820, pattern #3644 (A) **60.00**

8½" sq, pink roses, gilt foliage, c1820, pattern #3785 (A) **100.00**

8¾" d

Gaudy blue and ochre floral design, imp "SPODE" mark (A) .. **65.00**

Painted birds and insects in shaped panels reserved on light pink ground, molded flower sprays, c1820 .... **150.00**

9¼" d, "Japan" pattern, underglaze colors, wide borders of florals and shaped panels, c1810, iron-red "SPODE and #1645" marks, set of 8 (A) **550.00**

9⅞" d

Aesop's Fables, green printed fox and lion (A) **55.00**

"Felspar," iron-red and gold flowers, gadrooned rims, pattern #4349, pr (A) **25.00**

10½" d, "Cowslip" design **20.00**

Platter

13" l, "City of Corinth," blue transfer, imp mark **110.00**

14¾" l, "Principle Entrance of the Harbor on Cacamu," blue transfer **150.00**

15⅞" l, iron-red, green, blue, and gilt Oriental fenced garden in elaborate floral and scroll paneled borders, c1810, pattern #967, pr (A) **1,760.00**

16" H-H, blue and white oxen and bridge in landscape, c1810 ...... **415.00**

19" l, 14" w, "Net" pattern, blue transfer, c1810 . . . . **350.00**
Potpourri Bowl, 4½" l, painted Oriental flowers, heavy gilding, pierced cov, c1810, iron-red "SPODE and #1645" (A) **330.00**
Potpourri Vase
5⅜", painted Imari style flowering shrubs on blue circ foot, gilt foliage, pierced cov, painted overhandle, c1820, pattern #2214, pr (A) **1,220.00**
8½" h, gilt vines, cobalt ground, painted flowers on yellow ground reserved in gilt edged panel, white beaded borders, paw feet, c1817, iron-red "SPODE" (A) **220.00**
Sauce Tureen, 8½" l, molded canoe form, bands of trailing dogwood flowers edged by apple-green borders, pr (A) **275.00**
Soup Plate, 9½" d, "Net" pattern, blue transfer, reserved Oriental landscape scenes, gilt rims, c1815, imp "SPODE," set of 8 (A) **620.00**
Sucrier, Cov, 7½" l, "Japan" pattern, dark blue, orange, green, gilt edge and trim, dbl handles, c1815 . . . . . . **400.00**
Tea and Coffee Service
18 pcs, teapot, stand, milk jug, slop bowl, four teacups, five coffee cans, five saucers, peony and bamboo, rockwork printed in black, translucent green enamel and gilding, pattern #1653 (A) **420.00**
20 pcs, two dishes, six teacups, six coffee cans, six saucers, iron-red transfers of bands of scrolling roses between gilt borders, c1820, iron-red script "Spode" mark (A) **770.00**
32 pcs, Imari pattern, flowering shrubs in fenced garden, borders with whorls and lappet design, green, red, and gilt, c1815, pattern #967 (A) **1,944.00**
Teapot, 10" w, Rosso Antico, applied black Egyptian motifs, stylized key design and crocodile finial, c1820 (A) . **240.00**
Tray, 11½" sq, center painted with rose spray, bouquets in corners, blue ground, gilt scale pattern, c1800, iron-red "Spode, #1163" **375.00**
Tureen Stand, 16¾" d, "Italian" pattern, blue transfers, figures by river with ruins in background, borders of florals and scrolls, c1820, pr (A) **215.00**
Tureen, Cov, 15½" H-H, blue and white "Grasshopper" pattern, c1820 . . . . . **700.00**
Vase
5" h, 17½" d, turquoise overlapping wave pattern, white body, rust and orange trim, gilded accents, c1820, set of 3 . . . .**1,250.00**

10¼" h, Oriental fenced garden, panels on shoulder in gold, iron-red, blue, green, and salmon, ovoid, dbl handles of blue and gilt scalework, c1810-15, iron-red "SPODE and 967" mark (A) **1,210.00**
Vegetable Dish, 12¼" l, blue printed "Shooting at the Edge of a Jungle" and "Hunting a Buffalo," dbl compartment, pr (A) **165.00**
Wall Pockets, 10½" l, "Moonlight" luster, spirally ridged nautilus shells, two holes for hanging, c1810, pr (A) **330.00**

SPONGEWARE

Staffordshire, England
Continental, c1840 to c1900

History: Spongeware, a cut-sponge stamped pattern decoration used on earthenwares and everyday tablewares, was achieved by dipping a sponge in color and applying it to the ware to produce a stamp of the pattern. A single dip of color produced about a dozen impressions. This accounts for the variation in shades.

The stamping technique was invented in Scotland and brought to England about 1845. It was a time-saving device used in decorating inexpensive china that was made mostly for export.

Cut-sponge border patterns included a variety of florals, leaves, scrolls, stars, triangles, hearts, and chains. Some borders supplemented the cut-sponge decoration with hand painting. The center motif also included combinations of cut-sponge and painted decorations.

William Adams and Son of Tunstall was one of the largest English producers of cut-sponge decorated pieces. W. Baker and Company of Fenton, Edge, Malkin and Company of Burlsem, and Britannia Pottery of Glasgow were other leading manufacturers of spongeware.

Petrus Regout and Company in Holland, and Villeroy and Boch, in Germany were among the principal Continental manufacturers.

References: Earl F. & Ada F. Robacker, *Spatterware and Sponge*, A. S. Barnes & Co., 1978.

Collecting Hints: Cut-sponge work can be identified by the uneven strength of the color in repeated motifs. Remember, the color supply lessened in the sponge as the pattern was repeated. An uneven interval or space between decorative motifs also indicates spongeware. Border motifs may overlap. A smudged effect often occurs because of too much pigment or a worn stamp. If a stamp has a defect in its design, it will be repeated throughout the pattern.

Plate, 7½" d, yellow, ochre, and blue sponged circles, early 18th C, English Delft, $2,000.00.

Bowl
  5" d, 2" h, brown sponging, white
    ground (A) 55.00
  7" d, 4⅛" h, blue and tan sponging,
    light gray ground (A) 35.00
  8" d, blue sponging white ground (A)   45.00
  8½" d, 3⅝" h, blue sponging, white
    ground, unmarked (A) 60.00
  8½" d, 4¾" h, blue and rust sponging,
    gray panels, unmarked 40.00
  9¾" d, blue, red, and green sponging,
    white ground (A) 70.00
  10¼" d, 5⅜" h, green sponging, white
    ground, unmarked (A) 60.00
  11½" d, 6" h, blue and tan sponging,
    unmarked 185.00
  13¼" d, blue and white sponge center
    design, unmarked 215.00
Bread Plate, 10" l, blue sponging, open
  dbl handles 100.00
Cup and Saucer, handleless
  Blue sponging, brushstroke rose and
    green leaves, unmarked 175.00
  Blue sponging, earthenware, c1840 . 130.00
Custard Cup
  2¼" h, blue sponging, white ground,
    unmarked (A) 115.00
  2⅜" h, brown sponging, white
    ground, unmarked (A) 25.00
Demitasse Cup and Saucer, blue overall
  sponging, handleless, chip on rim,
  unmarked 40.00
Dish, 6¼" h, blue sponging, white
  ground, unmarked (A) 145.00
Jardiniere
  7¼" h, blue sponging, white ground,
    unmarked (A) 100.00
  9⅛" h, blue, white, and brown spong-
    ing (A) 65.00
Mug
  3½" h, blue sponging, white ground,
    unmarked (A) 155.00
  4¼" h, brown sponging, yellow
    ground, unmarked 65.00

Pitcher
  4⅝" h, blue sponging, earthenware
    body, c1840 .... 200.00
  7" h
    Blue sponging, white ground, sq
      handle 165.00
    Brown sponging, yellow ground,
      bulbous shape, unmarked 60.00
  8⅞" h, blue sponging, white ground
    (A) 160.00
  10" h, blue sponging, white ground,
    unmarked (A) 115.00
  12" h, blue sponging, yellow ground,
    unmarked (A) 165.00
Plate
  3⅛" d, blue sponging, white ground
    (A) 60.00
  10" d, blue sponging, white ground,
    unmarked (A) 155.00
Platter
  13½" l, blue sponging, white ground,
    unmarked (A) 100.00
  14⅛" l, blue sponging, white ground,
    unmarked (A) 155.00
  15" l, 10¾" w, blue sponging, white
    ground 275.00
Soap Dish, 4⅝" d, blue sponging, white
  ground (A) 80.00
Sugar, Cov, 6" h, blue sponging, white
  ground, unmarked (A) 45.00
Teapot, 5¾" h, blue sponging, white
  ground, unmarked (A) 175.00

ST. CLOUD

Seine-et-Oise, France
c1690 to 1773

History: About 1675 Pierre Chicanneau established a factory for the production of faience and
soft paste porcelain at St. Cloud. Shortly after
Chicanneau's death in 1678, Berthe, his widow,
assumed control of the works.

    St. Cloud porcelain was thickly potted with a
yellowish color to the body. The glaze was very
glassy with a somewhat orange peel texture to
the surface. The pieces were decorated in strong
polychromes or in the simple blue motifs similar
to the faience examples from Rouen, especially
in the use of the Baroque diapering pattern. Many
forms featured plain white and relief patterns.
Fish scale-type embellishments were used as the
method of decoration.

The variety of wares produced was quite large, exhibiting applied decoration. Accessory pieces, e.g., knife and cane handles, and novelty pieces, some of which were silver mounted, were made. Many of the designs incorporated elements from silverware such as reeding or gadrooning.

Family squabbles plagued the St. Cloud pottery. In 1722 Berthe Coudray died. Henri-Charles Trou II, backed by the sponsorship of the Duc d'Orleans, took control. The St. Cloud factory ended its operations about 1773.

References: W. B. Honey, *French Porcelain of the 18th Century*, 1950; George Savage, *Seventeenth & Eighteenth Century French Porcelain*, Hamlyn Publishing Co., Ltd., 1969.

Museums: J. Paul Getty Museum, Malibu, California; Victoria & Albert Museum, London, England.

Teapot, 6" h, blue lambrequins, c1730, (A) $650.00.

Beaker, white, molded flowering prunus, c1750 (A) **150.00**
Beaker and Stand
  Blue Berlainesque borders over flutes, c1735, blue "S. T. C." mark (A) .. **460.00**
  Molded flowering prunus, basket-weave ground, lime green glaze, c1725 (A) **1,540.00**
  White, molded flowering prunus, cov, silver mounted, c1725 (A) **470.00**
Cache Pot, 4¾" h, white, molded plants and foliage, dbl grotesque mask handles, c1730, incised "S.T.C." (A) ... **500.00**
Cup and Saucer
  Blue bands of Berlainesque foliage over flutes, c1730, blue "St. C." mark (A) **385.00**
  Blue lambrequin and shark's teeth borders, molded half flutes, c1730, blue "St.C T & F" mark (A) **285.00**
  Blue weeping willow and fence, white ground, scroll handle, c1735 (A) **115.00**

Painted in blue on white, Berlainesque border over bands of shallow gadroons, trembleuse saucers, c1740, blue "S.C." mark, pr (A) .. **650.00**
White, molded flowering prunus branches, trembleuse saucer, scroll handle, c1735 (A) **380.00**
Cup and Stand
  Blue bands of scrolls and foliage over gadroons, c1735, blue "St. C." mark (A) **150.00**
  Kakiemon palette of flowering prunus and bamboo, branch handle, c1730 (A) **1,320.00**
Ecuelle and Stand, 7⅞" d, white, finial and handles modeled as berried foliage, c1720 .... **230.00**
Ewer and Basin, white ext. molded with foliage branches and insects, pear shape, scroll handle, c1715-25 (A) .**3,080.00**
Figure
  6¼" h, white seated Chinaman, c1725 (A) **1,555.00**
  7" h, white, man, seated next to pot-pourri vase, period dress, floral and rockwork base, mid 18th C (A) ... **225.00**
  8¼" h, white glazed man and woman, seated, period clothes, rockwork bases, c1725, pr (A) ...**9,900.00**
Jar, Cov
  3" h, flowering prunus and chrysanthemums, rockwork and fence, Kakiemon palette, yellow ground, flowerhead knob, c1730 (A) **1,430.00**
  4" h, four shallow flutes and applied relief of flowerheads, Kakiemon palette, c1745 (A) **1,650.00**
  6½" h, white, relief flowering branches, cylindrical, flowerhead finial, silver gilt mounts, c1740 (A) **2,640.00**
Knives, 3¾" l, arabesque and scrolling foliage, blue, white ground, curved steel blades and silver collars, c1730, set of 6 .... **600.00**
Mustard Jar, Cov, 3½" h, scrolling flowers in relief, white body, barrel shape, branch handle, foliage terminals, hinged silver mounted cov, shell thumbpiece and flowerhead finial, c1735 (A) **700.00**
Patchbox, 2" l, modeled as recumbent horse, gold saddle cloth and bridle, cov with striated agate, c1750 (A) ..**6,050.00**
Pomade Jars, Cov, white, molded foliage, bud finials, c1725, imp "St. C." mark, pr (A) **1,100.00**
Pot Cov
  2" h, blue bands of Berlainesque foliage and strapwork, cylindrical, stand with band of blue trellis and flowerheads, c1735-45, blue "St. C." mark **275.00**

2¼" h, blue Berlainesque borders and lambrequin, flowerhead finial, c1715, pr (A) **880.00**

3½" h, white, molded overlapping lappets, c1725, imp blue "St. C." mark (A) **465.00**

5¼" h, molded Oriental prunus, lobed lower sections, domed covs, flowerhead knobs, c1766, imp "St. CT" mark **500.00**

Potpourri Bowl, 11⅜" d, white basket form, Louis XV ormolu handles, molded basketwork and floral body, pierced cov, applied florals, c1735 (A) **1,685.00**

Potpourri Vase

8" h, white, applied trailing flowering branches, gourd shape, rockwork base, bird finial, c1740 ....**1,350.00**

10⅜" h, white applied florals and vines on pierced cov and body, rockwork base, contemporary gilt metal mounts, c1740 (A) **5,185.00**

Snuff Box, 2¾" d, painted chinoiserie figures in flowering landscape, int. cov painted with seated chinoiserie figure and pagodas, Kakiemon palette, reeded silver mounts, c1735 (A) **935.00**

Spice Box, Cov, 5½" w, blue Berlainesque scrolls, foliage, and flowerheads, trefoil shape, three paw feet, flowerhead finial, early 18th C (A) ..**1,870.00**

Sugar, 3½" h, bands of Berlainesque borders over shallow flutes, disk finial with flowerhead, c1720, blue "St. C." mark (A) **550.00**

Teapot, 6½" h, white, applied flower and foliage garlands, flower finial, c1720 (A) **250.00**

Tobacco Jar, Cov, 7" h, blue painted Berlainesque borders suspending foliage and scrolls, flowerhead finial, gilt bronzed mounts, c1715, blue "sun-face" mark (A) **3,740.00**

STAFFORDSHIRE FIGURES

Staffordshire, England
c1740 to 1900

History: During the eighteenth century, Staffordshire figures in salt glazed stoneware and Whieldon type earthenwares with translucent colored glazes were made by the family of Ralph Wood. (See: Ralph Wood)

Obadiah Sherratt's figures from the late 1820s display the rustic realism of true peasant art with humor, pathos, and brutality. The modeling is bold and crude; enamel colors are bright. Many figures are quite large. Usually Sherratt's figures are mounted on a table base. The name for the piece often is written on the front. Among his most famous pieces are "The Bull Baiting Group" and "Remus and Romulus." Sherratt also did classical and religious figures.

With the accession of Queen Victoria in 1837, simplicity of design appeared as well as restraint in the coloring of figures. Nineteenth century earthenware Staffordshire figures were made in a simple, uncomplicated manner, often mass produced at low cost for the cottage rather than for the stately home.

The figures featured a flat back, were compact in design, and were mounted on an oval base that was part of the figure. Figures were displayed on mantles, window ledges, bookcases, or Welsh dressers. Only the fronts were visible. About 1840 potters made mantlepiece ornaments in under the glaze colors in great quantity. Cottage ornaments depicted the homey scenes characteristic of the people that bought them.

The most distinctive color used was the rich, dark, glossy cobalt blue. Additional colors included pink, green, orange, black, and some gold. After 1860 more colors were utilized including a pale flesh pink shade. The pottery was harder and whiter than in earlier pieces.

Both human and animal figures were molded. Just about every Victorian kitchen featured a pair of spaniels on either side of the kitchen clock. Greyhounds, poodles, dalmatians, cats, and even zebras were memorialized in Staffordshire figures. Topical events, heroes and heroines of the times, members of the Royal Family, and theatrical characters appeared. Churches, cottages, and castles were popular. A unique form was the Victorian watch stand. Few figures were marked with a maker's mark.

Sampson Smith was the most prolific maker of the flat-backed figures and Staffordshire dogs. He worked from about 1847 to 1878. Others continued to use his molds to make figures long after his death. In addition to his famous dogs, Sampson Smith is known for figures of castles, churches, cottages, jockeys, Dick Turpin, toby jugs, politicans, and royalty, including Queen Victoria.

References: T. Balston, *Staffordshire Portrait Figures of the Victorian Age,* Faber & Faber, 1958; J. Hall, *Staffordshire Portrait Figures,* Charles Letts & Co., Ltd., 1972; Reginald S. Haggar, *Staffordshire Chimney Ornaments,* Phoenix House, Ltd., 1955; B. Latham, *Victorian Staffordshire Portrait Figures for the Small Collector,* Tiranti, 1953; A. Oliver, *The Victorian Staffordshire Figures: A Guide for Collectors,* Heinemann, 1971; P. D. G. Pugh, *Staffordshire Portrait Figures & Allied Subjects of the Victorian Era,* Barrie & Jenkins, 1970; H. A. B. Turner, *A Collector's Guide* to *Staffordshire Pottery Figures,* Emerson Books, Inc., 1971.

Museums: American Antiquarian Society, Worcester, Massachusetts; Brighton Museum, Brighton, England; British Museum, London, England; City Museum and Art Gallery, Stoke-on-Trent, England; Fitzwilliam Museum, Cambridge, England; Victoria & Albert Museum, London, England.

REPRODUCTION ALERT: Lancaster and Sandlands are reproducing some of the old Staffordshire models, especially the animal and cottage figures. The colors match the old Staffordshire cobalt blue quite well.

Admiral Napier, 15½" h, multicolored, unmarked (A) **140.00**

Bovine Group, 5⅞" h, seated polychromed milkmaids next to white cows, blue willow transfer dec, 19th C, pr (A) **250.00**

Boy and Dog
  5" h, multicolored, c1800, marked (A) **25.00**
  9⅛" h, polychromed, unmarked (A) **100.00**

Bruce, 15" h, plaid scarf and kilt, unmarked **145.00**

Bull Baiting, 5" h, black sponged and iron-red bull, light buff dog, mounted on green and brown rocky base, c1820, unmarked **1,750.00**

Burns and HD Mary, 12" h, Scottish couple in bower, green and brown enameling, gilt, unmarked (A) **90.00**

Castle
  6" h, quill holder, three turrets, light orange, applied green and maroon moss, late 19th C (A) **55.00**
  8" h, two story, turrets at sides, drummer standing at side, multicolored, late 19th C **120.00**

Cat
  2¾" h, seated, brown-black spots, late 19th C, unmarked (A) **45.00**
  4" h, seated on blue pillows, unmarked, pr (A) **70.00**
  5½" h, recumbent facing right and left, yellow and brown accents on white, green accented oval bases, c1840, pr (A) **825.00**
  8" h, brown and white, blue ribbons, yellow and black features, unmarked, pr (A) **110.00**

Charity, 8½" h, mother in white flowing gown, touches of color, infant son in one arm, daughter at side, mounted on sq rocky base with blue line, semiporcelain, c1810, unmarked **500.00**

Charlotte at the Tomb, c1800 .... **130.00**

Church
  4⅛" h, painted, gilding, clock face, applied flowers and moss, c1840 (A) **110.00**
  6⅜" h, Georgian style, numerous doors and windows, salmon colored, late 19th C **120.00**

Clock Tower, 5" h, three turrets, orange body, black crosses at windows, c1860, unmarked **280.00**

Condiment, 5½" h, figures of short, round men in period dress, mounted on round bases, multicolored, early 19th C, pr **130.00**

Costume Group, 8" h, man and woman seated on bench under arched flower bough, c1820 (A) **2,040.00**

Cottage
  5" h, quill holder
    Multicolored, c1850, unmarked .. **425.00**
    White, applied flowers, gilt edged mound base, late 19th C (A) ... **150.00**
  5⅝" h, gothic manor house, dbl chim-

Figures, left, Cipsus, 14½" h, multicolored, c1860, unmarked, $150.00; center, spill vase, 7½" h, multicolored, mid 19th C, unmarked, $225.00; right, pastille burner, 7" h, blue and white, c1860, "Thom. Parr," $435.00.

neys tall pierced windows outlined in gilt, iron-red doors, columns on each side, roof edged in green, orange, and brown moss, c1845, unmarked, repaired **900.00**

8⅛" h, two story gothic style, arbor in front, roof, four chimneys, two gnarled tree columns, sq base with applied florals and moss, buff, mid 19th C **200.00**

Courtiers, 15" h, multicolored figures in period dress, unmarked (A) **175.00**

Cow
3" h, black and white, green base, unmarked (A) **65.00**

5¾" h, one with milkmaid, other with youth, polychromes and gilt, unmarked, pr (A) **210.00**

Diana With Bow, 12" h, multicolored, Neale **155.00**

Dog Tray, 9½" w, 13" h, black and white dog, master in cobalt jacket and orange cape, unmarked **500.00**

Dogs, 12½" h, rust glaze, gold accents and chain, glass eyes, unmarked, pr (A) **150.00**

Dogs and House, 1⅝" h, polychrome enameling, unmarked (A) **45.00**

Eagle, 9" h, off-white body, c1835, "Lloyd of Shelton" mark **290.00**

Earl of Lucan 14" h, multicolored, mounted on horse, c1860, unmarked **115.00**

Ewe, 7" h, multicolored, unmarked (A) **125.00**

Flight Into Egypt, 10½" h, Holy family, applied florals on base (A) **600.00**

French General, 12¾" h, on horseback, multicolored, unmarked **115.00**

Garden Pavilion
5½" h, central two story octagonal building flanked by single stories, applied florals, c1835 (A) **275.00**

6⅝" h, two story pagoda, upturned roof supported by four columns, salmon colored, c1845 (A) **275.00**

Garibaldi, 13" h, hand on sword, right hand holding "Liberte" flag, multicolored **100.00**

Gordon-Cumming
14" h, hunter with dog, gun, and game pouch, multicolored, c1860, unmarked **115.00**

15¾" h, hunter in bonnet and kilt with dead lion, multicolored, unmarked (A) **100.00**

Grace Darling, 6⅛" h, sailor in boat near lighthouse on rocky shore (A) .. **165.00**

Greyhound
5" h, seated on blue pillows, unmarked, pr (A) **70.00**

8½" h, seated figures, rabbit under paw, polychrome enameling, unmarked, pr (A) **260.00**

11¼" h, rabbits in mouths, polychrome colors, unmarked, pr (A) . **90.00**

12" h, red-brown bodies, blue bases, c1850, unmarked, pr **750.00**

Hercules, 5¼" h, "Hercules Capturing the Bull of Crete," figure in lion skin over downed bull, oval base with applied flowers, leaves, and grass, attributed to Wood and Caldwell, c1800 .... **2,600.00**

Hound and Hare, 10½" h, multicolored, unmarked **125.00**

Hunter and Huntress, 5⅞", dressed in period clothes, man with gun and dog, woman with bow, arrow, and target, bocage background, c1825, pr **800.00**

Janet, 7" h, girl with flower basket, Staffordshire lace, Adderly mark **65.00**

Jenny Lind, 19" h, multicolored, unmarked **125.00**

Leda and The Swan, 7⅝" h, Leda seated on rock, swan resting on bosom, multicolored, sq brown base, c1800 **1,200.00**

Lion
2¾" h, seated, polychrome colors, green base, unmarked (A) **100.00**

9½" h, rust color, glass eyes, unmarked (A) **80.00**

12" l, 5" h, reclining, brown body, black highlights, unmarked, pr ... **200.00**

Man On Crutches, 8⅝" h, multicolored, sq base, 18th C (A) **120.00**

Man Shearing, 6¼" h, multicolored (A) **325.00**

M'Grath and Pretender, 9½" h, pr of greyhounds, one black, one white, foliage ground, oval bases, raised names, c1871 (A) **1,440.00**

Mrs Bardell, 5¾" h, "Crown Staffordshire" mark **85.00**

Napoleon
9" h, multicolored, unmarked (A) ... **140.00**

10⅜" h, standing figure, multicolored, circ base (A) **130.00**

Pastille Burner
4" h, cottage, two story, tan roof, tower at side, scroll-molded base, inkwell and two quill holes, mid 19th C (A) **110.00**

4½" h, cottage, gothic style, gray thatched roof, three plum colored balls, green and orange moss, buff walls, doors, and windows outlined in plum and gilt, c1845, unmarked **625.00**

5¼" h, cottage
Thatched roof of flowers, leaves, and moss, roof supported by three twisted columns, mounted on dark blue floral base, porcelain, c1835, unmarked **1,450.00**

Two chimneys, flower cov roof and terrace, "Staffordshire Ware, W. K., England" **250.00**

White cottage, applied painted floral clusters, two iron-red gilt outlined doors, octagonal, moss base, c1835 (A) **500.00**

5⅜" h, cottage, dbl burners, iron-red doors and chimneys, peaked gables, tall pierced windows, c1850, unmarked **800.00**

6¾" h, cottage, two story, apricot roof with gilt supported on four moss cov columns, iron-red doors, porcelain, c1830, unmarked **750.00**

6⅞" h, castle, crenelated, extensive multicolored flowers, c1835, ...**1,950.00**

7" h, cottage, umbrella roof with painted flowers, octagonal shape . **200.00**

7½" h, cottage triple burner, gothic, two outbuildings, lavender, unmarked **500.00**

9½" h, triple mansion, lilac, c1835, unmarked **1,750.00**

Peace, 13" h, angel holding lettered green ribbon between seated figures of Ireland and Britannia, multicolored, unmarked **300.00**

Peasant Woman, 7" h, woman in native dress, head tilted upward, multicolored, "Enoch Wood" mark **275.00**

Peter Rising The Lame Man, 10½" h, multicolored, four ftd rect base, (A) . **700.00**

Phrenology Bust, 11⅞" h, cranium printed, named sections, base titled and named, late 19th C (A) **870.00**

Politician, 6" h, fat man, London business dress, multicolored, mounted on sq base, unmarked **240.00**

Poodle
3" l, coleslaw coat, beige and gilt base (A) **35.00**
5" h, white body, applied shreds of clay, unmarked, pr (A) **80.00**

Pourer, 5¼" h, "Willow" pattern, stout man in period dress, c1840, unmarked **55.00**

Prince and Princess of Wales, 10" l, 15" h, cobalt jackets, mounted on palomino horses, bases marked with names, unmarked **1,000.00**

Prodigal's Return, 13½" h, multicolored, flat back, unmarked **75.00**

Pug, 9"
Seated, white glaze, black muzzle, unmarked **150.00**
White body, black muzzles, gold chains and lockets around necks, unmarked, pr **400.00**

Queen Victoria 11½" h, figure holding orb to breast, multicolored, c1900, unmarked **110.00**

Rabbit
3¼" l, crouched, polychrome enameling, unmarked (A) **220.00**

8½" l, seated, black sponged coat, oval grass mound base, mid 19th C, pr (A) **1,100.00**

Raja On Elephant, 8¾" h, seated, tiger on oval rockwork base, c1840 (A) .. **460.00**

Restoration Gallant and Dog, 15" h, multicolored, unmarked (A) **175.00**

Return From Egypt, 7" h, Jesus sitting astride donkey's neck, nimbus molded around Jesus' head, Mary side-saddle on donkey, Joseph leading, polychrome, c1820, unmarked **1,275.00**

Romeo and Juliet, 6¼" h, multicolored, unmarked (A) **275.00**

Sailor and Lady, 12" h, sailor seated with crossed legs, lady in bonnet and fancy dress, multicolored, chimney piece, unmarked **145.00**

Sailor's Depart and Return, 9½" h, dark blue jacket, iron-red waistcoat, light blue pants on sailor, female in yellow overdress with puce fichu, skirt in iron-red and black, one figure of sailor with staff and bundle, other figure of sailor with moneybag and chest of "Dollars," raised names on bases, c1825, unmarked, pr **1,200.00**

Sankey and Moddy, 9½" h, multicolored, pr (A) **200.00**

Scotsman and Lady
13" h, cobalt jackets, multicolors, false clock between figures, unmarked **145.00**
13½" h, figure seated with bagpipe, girl on right in orange and pink, unmarked **100.00**

Sheep and Lamb, 5⅜" h, recumbent figures before tree trunk, green and yellow oval base, c1820 (A) **100.00**

Shepherd, 5⅛" h, boy, maroon jacket, yellow breeches, dog jumping near tree, green mound base (A) **95.00**

Shepherd and Harp, 12½" h, white, unmarked **110.00**

Sir Walter Scott, 9" h, multicolored, unmarked (A) **140.00**

Spaniel
2⅛" h, brown spots, rect base, unmarked (A) **40.00**
6" h, Wellington, purple luster, black muzzle, yellow eyes, unmarked (A) **140.00**
7" h
Gilt marks on white glaze, unmarked, pr (A) **80.00**
Iron-red glaze patches, unmarked, pr (A) **100.00**
9" h
Black accents on rust body, unmarked, pr (A) **175.00**
Gilt marks on white glaze, unmarked, pr (A) **80.00**

Green and copper luster patches, yellow eyes, unmarked, pr (A) . **100.00**
9½" h, orange spots, pr **220.00**
10½" h, King Charles, black and copper spots, white ground, unmarked, pr (A) **475.00**
Sphinx, 7" h, cream body, green glaze base (A) **300.00**
Tee Total, 8" h, woman with child and husband, kitchen setting, multicolored, rect ftd base, bocage background, c1840, by Obadiah Sherratt (A) **3,200.00**
Temperance, 9" h, gin on one side, water on other, multicolored (A) **200.00**
The Bonnie Prince, Scottish figure seated on fence, multicolored, unmarked **175.00**
The Bride of Lammermoor, opera group, multicolored, unmarked (A) **160.00**
The Falconer, 14⅕" h, portrait figure, multicolored, c1845, unmarked **550.00**
Tiger, 7" h, yellow and black striping, iron-red lamb under paw, serpentine plinth base marbleized in black with green and iron-red trim, c1825, by Obadiah Sherratt **4,500.00**
Tithe Pig, 7¼" h, man with pig, woman with child and parson on green base with pig, wheat, basket of eggs, iron-red feathering and bocage background, c1825 ....**1,400.00**
Tom Cribb, 9" h, figure of boxer, sponged carmine tights, blue belt, white stockings, black shoes, green, and yellow oval base, c1820, unmarked **1,350.00**
Tom King, 9" h, mounted on white horse, unmarked (A) **165.00**
Tower, 7⅜" h, yellow walls, pierced windows, peaked roof, painted blue flower, applied yellow florettes, mound base, octagonal, c1840 (A) . **220.00**
Uncle Tom and Little Eva, 10" h, multicolored, unmarked **450.00**
Venus and Cupid, 10⅛" h, Venus in robe, Cupid reaching for her pile of shells, dolphin in background, rect base with four feet, "Venus" on front, c1830, Obadiah Sherratt (A) **440.00**
Villa, 6¼" h, Italianate Style, white, gilt edged windows, moss cov yellow roof, mid 19th C (A) **130.00**
Watermill, 11⅞" h, two story building over water wheel, stepped bridge, figures of boy, girl, and ducks, multicolored, mid 19th C (A) **110.00**
Wesley In The Pulpit, 11" h, white, full polychrome figure, unmarked **120.00**
Wheat Gatherers, 8¼" h, man and woman seated on fence holding wheat sheaves, man with scythe, multicolored, c1850 .... **100.00**

Whippet
4⅜" l, recumbent position, polychrome enamels, pr (A) **170.00**
6" h, each figure supported under middle, mounted on oval bases, multicolored, mid 19th C, unmarked **350.00**
Widow, 11½" h, multicolored, sgd "Walton, " c1830, repaired **325.00**
William Tell, 20" h, white glazed figure, gold trim, green hat and coat, raised name on base, unmarked **135.00**
Woman, 9" h, large open bonnet, white dress, blue jacket, orange and green fringed scarf over shoulder, yellow and red bird with green tail perched on shoulder, unmarked **250.00**
Zebra, 7" h, standing on green and rust bases, unmarked, pr (A) **150.00**

STAFFORDSHIRE-GENERAL

1700s to Present

History: In the Staffordshire district of England, numerous pottery factories were estalished that produced a wide variety of wares including figures, flow blue, transfer printed wares, historic blue, and ornamental pieces.

Samuel Alcock and Company established a pottery in Burslem about 1828 that was known for its Parian figures, jugs, and decorative wares in the Classical style. The pottery also made a wide range of blue-printed earthenwares and bone china. Sir James Duke and Nephews took over the firm in 1860.

John and Edward Baddeley produced earthenwares at Shelton between 1786 and 1806. The company manufactured a wide range of tablewares, often enameled in red and black on a creamware ground.

Charles Bourne of Foley Pottery made bone china tablewares between 1807 and 1830. His factory equalled those of Spode, Coalport, and Davenport. Pieces can be identified by the pattern numbers and the initials "CB."

The Lane End factory of Hilditch and Son made teawares in under the glaze blue from 1822 until 1830.

Elijah Mayer established a pottery at Cobden Works, Hanley about 1705. In 1805 the name changed to Elijah Mayer and Son. Production continued until 1834. The Mayers manufactured black basalt wares, tablewares in cream colored earthenware, cane wares, and drab stonewares.

Humphrey Palmer located at Church Works, Hanley in 1760. He produced wares popularized by Wedgwood such as black basalts, cream colored and agate ware vases, and seals and cameos that frequently were modeled by J. Voyez. Most of Palmer's wares were decorative. The pottery went out of business in 1778.

A. J. Wilkinson Ltd. was a Staffordshire pottery firm that operated several factories in the Burlsem area beginning in the late nineteenth century. In 1885 Wilkinson took over the Central Pottery. The plant made white granite ware for the American market. Wilkinson introduced the use of gold luster work on granite ware.

Wilkinson operated the Churchyard Works from 1887 until the early twentieth century and the Royal Staffordshire Pottery from c1896 until the present day. About 1900 Wilkinson gained control of Mersey Pottery, a subsidiary of Newport Pottery. The factory remained in production until the 1930s. Highly glazed stonewares, some of which were designed by Clarice Cliff, were made.

References: P. D. Gordon Pugh, *Staffordshire Portrait Figures & Allied Subjects of the Victorian Era,* Praeger Publishers, 1971; Bernard Rackham, *Early Staffordshire Pottery,* Faber & Faber, 1951; Louis T. Stanley, *Collecting Staffordshire Pottery,* Doubleday, 1963; John Thomas, *The Rise of the Staffordshire Potteries,* Adams & Dart, 1971.

Museums: City Museum & Art Gallery, Stoke-on-Trent, England; Everson Museum of Art, Syracuse, New York; The Henry Francis DuPont Winterthur Museum, Winterthur, Delaware.

Baby Feeder, 6¾" l, bottle shape, geometric design, 18th C **250.00**
Bank, 3¾" h, black and white spaniel head, unmarked (A) **55.00**
Basket
 9" l, reticulated, oval, cobalt and polychrome Worcester-type design, late 18th C (A) **175.00**
 10" l, matching tray, blue transfer of rural scene, pierced canoe shape, unmarked (A) **70.00**
Beaker, 4" h, black, orange, and gold Imari design, "Wileman & Co." **45.00**
Bell
 5¼" h, woman in hooped skirt, blue, white, and gilt, unmarked **65.00**
 6" h, woman, blue, white, and gilt, unmarked **85.00**
Biscuit Jar
 8" h, chrysanthemum pattern, beige ground, sp top, rim, and handle, c1890, "Wiltshaw and Robinson" **165.00**
 Brown matte finish on body, designs of insects and flowers, silvered top, rim, and bail handle, "Macintyre, Burslem" **110.00**
Bone Dish
 5⅞" l, brown "Catherine Mermet" design, "W. H. Grindley" **10.00**
 Blue transfer, Maidenhead Bridge, "Palissy, England" **20.00**
Bowl
 6½" d, 3¼" h, blue transfer of sea monster, Neptune, buildings in background (A) **20.00**
 7" d, shallow depressions, decals of Chinese Emperor and Empress, hp accents, c1820, "Hilditch and Sons," pr **150.00**
 8" d, floral int., tan basketweave design, gilt handles, "Royal China Works" **295.00**
 12¼" d, 2¾" h, center star shape green leaf design, pink and yellow flowers on border, c1906-12, "Burgess and Leigh" **100.00**
Box
 6¾" l, figural recumbent black cow on cov, oval, unmarked (A) **45.00**
 8¼" l, figural black cow, polychrome enamels on cov, oval (A) **115.00**
Butter Dish, 6⅜" d, light blue transfer of English scene and river, unmarked (A) **40.00**
Butter Tub, 4" d, mottled green and yellow tub, figural recumbent cow on lid, "Royal Art Pottery, England" ... **35.00**
Cabinet Mug, 1¼" h, hp scenic panels, green ground, gilt accents, "Crown Staffordshire" **185.00**
Chamber Pot
 1¼" h, red and green gaudy rose, unmarked **125.00**

8¾" d, pink band, gold lines, cream
ground, unmarked **40.00**
9½" d, green and yellow "Shah" de-
sign, unmarked **65.00**
Cheese Dish, Cov
4⅞" h, "Hamilton" pattern, blue and
white, slant top, "Burgess and
Leigh" **100.00**
9⅞" l, "Denman" pattern, pink and
blue flowers, green leaves, white
ground, cobalt and gold finial, rect,
"Losol Ware, Keeling & Co." **85.00**
Chocolate Set, pot, six cups and saucers, multifloral pseudo Chinese
band, white ground "Grafton China" **110.00**
Coffeepot, 11½" h, dark blue transfer of
harbor scene, unmarked, repaired (A) **100.00**
Coffee Service, 6¾" h pot, 5" d creamer,
4" h cov sugar, six cups and saucers,
figural coffee house design, multicolored, branch handles, "John Mad-
dock" **165.00**
Compote, 8½" d, 7½" h, multicolored
flower decor, scalloped edge, c1830-
40, "Samuel Alcock" **345.00**
Cream Jug, puce transfer of cockerel,
inscribed "Jane," c1770 (A) **85.00**
Creamer
4⅝" h, dark red-brown ground, yellow chinoiserie transfer, unmarked
(A) **85.00**
5½" l, dark blue transfer, helmet
shape, c1830, unmarked **155.00**
Gaudy blue, red, and green tulip de-
sign, black striping (A) **65.00**
Cup and Saucer
Blue and white Oriental design, "Hil-
ditch" **40.00**
Lavender body, heavy gold trim,
c1900, "Crown Staffordshire" (A) **15.00**
Magenta transfer, florals, emb daisies,
polychrome enamels (A) **10.00**
Cup Plate
3⅝" d, blue transfer, country scene
with cows, unmarked (A) **30.00**
3⅞" d
Blue floral transfer, imp "Riley" (A) **25.00**
Blue transfer of flowers, imp "Ro-
gers" (A) **40.00**
4⅛" d, dark blue transfer of flowers,
imp "Stubbs and Kent" (A) **85.00**
Dinner Service, serving platter, twenty-
four dinner plates, twelve soup bowls,
central Turkish scenes, blue floral
borders, white ground, soft paste, mid
19th C, unmarked **400.00**
Dish, Cov
6¼" l, bisque chicks coming out of
bisque eggs, white basketweave
base with green grass, oval shape,
unmarked **350.00**
7½" h, tan, gray, and black, red tufts,

eggs, and grass, bisque top, gold
basketweave base, unmarked **500.00**
8¼" l, gray, black, and white bisque
hen top, gold basketweave base,
unmarked **400.00**
Ewer, 13" h, allegorical figures, yellow
ground, ovoid shape, pewter lid, "T.
R. Booth" **225.00**
Game Dish, 8" l, cov, figural, nesting
grouse, orange, green, and brown,
unmarked, pr (A) **225.00**
Game Tureen, 11¾" l, molded design,
fox finial, oval (A) **320.00**
Jardiniere, 13" h, blue and white floral
decoration, late 19th C, unmarked . **100.00**
Jug
6½" h, yellow transfer of Lord Nelson,
brown glaze, inscribed motto, red-
ware, c1820 (A) **265.00**
9" h, "Fair Hebe" design, relief fig-
ures around tree, multicolored,
c1790 (A) **500.00**
10½" h, figural, seated spaniel, un-
marked (A) **200.00**
Ladle, 7¾" l, dark blue floral transfer,
unmarked (A) **150.00**
Match Box, cov, scene of Red Riding
Hood and Wolf **85.00**
Match Holder, 3¼" h, figural, young
blond girl washing clothes, pink dress
blue trim **85.00**
Match Striker 4" h, figural, boy, standing
by basket, multicolored, unmarked . **25.00**
Miniature
Compote, butterfly luster, "Aynsley" **65.00**
Cup and Saucer, black transfer, couple in garden, unmarked (A) **35.00**
Mug
2¼" h, transfer of farmer, wife, and
animals, banner with "Industry
Produceth Wealth-God Speed the
Plow" and verse **25.00**
2¾" h
Black transfer, haying scene, enam-
els, unmarked (A) **35.00**
Blue transfer, domestic scene, three
ladies at table, cat on floor, (A) **35.00**
3⅜" h, pink transfer, roses and vines,
enamels, pink band **35.00**
3¾" h, red, green, and copper luster
gaudy floral design, unmarked (A) **35.00**
4" h
Dark green floral pattern, c1870,
unmarked **75.00**
Two faced satyr, dbl handles,
brown glaze, c1850, unmarked **185.00**
4¾" h, polychrome emb tavern
scene, molded frog inside, un-
marked (A) **125.00**
4⅞" h, black transfer of "Sailors
Farewell" and "Sailors Tear" verse,

General, left, cheese dish, cov, 8¾" l, 5½" h, silver luster accents, white ground, "Allerton," $50.00; center, jug, 6½" h, satyr head, multicolored, beige ground, yellow and brown base, brown monkey handle, c1800, $300.00; right, teapot, 8" h, Peter Minuet multicolored, unmarked, $225.00.

int. floral clusters and molded frog, enamels, c1835 (A) **90.00**
5" h, figural, "Old Billy," "Wildinson, Ltd" **125.00**

Pitcher

4" h, black transfer, "Fruit Gathering," unmarked (A) **35.00**

5½" h
Black transfer of rabbits, putty color, gold trim, unmarked (A) **65.00**
Blue transfer, floral design, red resist ground, red enameled edge stripe, unmarked (A) **115.00**

6⅜" h, emb portraits of Admiral Nelson and Captain Hardy, polychrome enamels, unmarked (A) .. **55.00**

7" h
Green coral and leaf design, green and cream ground, "E. Jones" . **100,00**
Multicolored, enameled Chinese scene white ground, unmarked . **75.00**
White raised classical figures between oak leaves and acorns, light blue ground, rope handle, "Dudson" **70.00**

7¼" h, red, green, blue, and black gaudy tulip design, (A) **40.00**

7½" h
Black transfer, river scene and "Archibald and Ann Buchanan, 1833." unmarked (A) **100.00**
Cobalt and rust florals, white, blue, and rust ground, unmarked **75.00**

8" h
Multicolored gaudy floral design, unmarked (A) **45.00**
Pink lilies, multicolored leaves, gold raised trim, cream ground, "Royal Chelsea Pottery, Burslem, England" **90.00**

9" h
"Gypsy," beige ground, molded witch and cauldron, semi-matte finish, glazed int., c1842, raised "Jones & Walley" mrk **115.00**

Relief flowers, gilt accents, pink ground, unmarked (A) **30.00**

Plaque, 8¼" l, 7⅝" h, bust of Lt Gen Sir George White, unmarked **35.00**

Plate

3½" d, dark blue transfer of birds, unmarked (A) **65.00**
3⅝" d, dark, blue transfer Fruit, imp "S. Tams & Cowan" (A) **55.00**
Game birds, unmarked (A) **20.00**
3¾" d, red, green, blue, and black gaudy floral border, unmarked (A) **15.00**
4⅛" d, medium blue transfer, temple, emb and scalloped rim, imp "Rogers" (A) **25.00**
5½" d, blue transfer, "Coburg" design, unmarked **25.00**
5⅞" d, black transfer, Eastern farm tool pulled by water buffalo, emb rim, purple luster stripes, octagonal, unmarked (A) **30.00**
7" d, brown transfer, "Montreal" design, c1830 .... **50.00**

7¾" d
Black transfer, "Amusement," emb and enameled floral rim (A) **75.00**
Dark blue transfer, game birds, unmarked (A) **60.00**

8"
Black transfer, "December," enamels, emb daisy rim, unmarked (A) **25.00**
Brown transfer, "Madras" design, "W. & E." mark **18.00**

8¼" d
Black transfer, Eastern Empire scene, enamels, unmarked (A) . **60.00**
Gaudy center rose, green and red striped border (A) **20.00**
Red, green, yellow, and black cabbage rose design, unmarked (A) **100.00**

8⅜" d
Multicolored enameled center rose, emb border, four sets of dots, imp "Rogers" (A) **35.00**

Red, green, blue and black tulip design, unmarked (A) 30.00

8½" d

"Black transfer, "Avon" design . . . 45.00

Black transfer, man carrying wood, polychrome enamels (A) 65.00

Yellow swimming swans, "Brown, Westhead and Moore" 70.00

9½" d

Black transfer, "Jeddo" design, unmarked 50.00

Brown transfer, "Cambridge" design, "R. H. & S." 35.00

Center scenes of "Ullswater" and "Lower Lake Killarney," cobalt and ivory borders, raised gilt, sgd "C. Bentley, Aynsley," pr 400.00

Dark blue "Chatsworth" pattern, gold trim, c1850, "Keeling Co., Burslem" mark 80.00

Dark red transfer, "The Bospourus" design, "R. Hall & Co." 45.00

Sepia transfer, classic scenes, mid-19th C, unmarked, set of 6 . . . . 60.00

9⅞" d

Light blue transfer of English country scene, church, and cottage, unmarked (A) 35.00

Purple luster, green, black, dark red, and yellow, gaudy floral design, unmarked 20.00

10" d

Brown and black transfer, "Satsuma" design "B. G. & W." . . 20.00

Sepia transfer, "Hannibal Crossing the Alps," unmarked 45.00

10¼" d, blue transfer

Middle Eastern scene, scalloped white emb edge, imp "Rogers" mark (A) 55.00

Scene of Florence, imp "Stubbs" mark (A) 25.00

10½" d

Multicolored floral design on border, radiating flowers in center, unmarked (A) 55.00

Red, green, and black gaudy rose design, unmarked (A) 35.00

Platter

11¾" l, medium blue transfer, pagodas, unmarked (A) 70.00

12⅛" l, blue transfer, English country scene, unmarked (A) 100.00

14" l, 11½" w, light blue transfer, "Oriental Pheasants" 35.00

15" l, blue and white floral and fruit design, unmarked (A) 140.00

15¾" l, blue and white center river and town scene, floral border, porcelain, early 19th C, unmarked . . 90.00

17⅞" l, emb feather edge, emb floral and eagle design on rim, unmarked (A) 215.00

18½" l, blue transfer, well and tree design, unmarked (A) 100.00

Punch Bowl, 14" d, daisy border, tan ground, aqua accents, c1850, "Furnivals, England" 180.00

Puzzle Jug, 6¾" h, blue and gray geometric, ring of spouts at neck (A) . . . 50.00

Sauce Ladle

6¼" l, blue transfer, country house, unmarked (A) 100.00

6½" l, dark blue transfer, English country scene, unmarked (A) 135.00

Soup Plate, 9⅝" d, dark blue transfer, "Sancho Panza at the Boar Hunt," unmarked (A) 85.00

Sugar

4¾" h, black, red, purple, and green center band of stylized flowers, striped handles, unmarked (A) 85.00

5" h, purple, black, green and red gaudy floral design, unmarked (A) 40.00

5¾" h, dark blue transfer of scene by lake, unmarked (A) 30.00

Sweetmeat Jar, 3¾" h, turquoise and white, gold trim, crown shape, SP top, rim and bail handle, "Tunnecliffe Pottery" 125.00

Tea Set, teapot, creamer, sugar, "Silver Shield" pattern, silver banding, bone shape handles and finial, gray streaking, "Arthur Wood" 135.00

Teabowl and Saucer

Blue transfer, bird, unmarked (A) . . . 45.00

General, left, teapot, 6¼" h, green luster upper section, gold vertical lines on lower section, tea leaf cov, "Arthur Wood, England," $35.00; center, sauce tureen, 7" l, 7½" h, blue Oriental transfers, c1825, unmarked, $325.00; right, creamer, 5" l, multicolored florals, unmarked, $60.00.

Dark blue transfer, bird on nest, "Stone China" (A) **75.00**

Dark blue transfer, Oriental design, imp "T. Mayer" (A) **45.00**

Dark blue transfer, swan, imp "Joseph Stubbs" (A) **100.00**

Medium blue transfer, English country garden scene, "Stone China" (A) . **55.00**

Reddish-brown transfer, rural scenes, orange luster rim unmarked **90.00**

Red, green, blue, ochre, and black peafowl on branch (A) **35.00**

Teapot

4½" h, blue, yellow, cream, and blue agate pattern, three feet, c1745, (A)**1,540.00**

5¾" h, blue and white transfer of Roman warriors and maids on upper half, mottled brown base, gilt ribbed center band **35.00**

7" w, caneware, center medallion of girl reading book, dark blue ground, lion finial, late 18th C, Turner (A) **150.00**

8½" w, caneware, panels of relief urns and blue and green floral husks, pink bands of foliage on shoulder and lower section, flowerhead finial, c1780, imp "Neale and Co" mark (A) **420.00**

Toby Jug, 9¼" man, standing, multicolored period clothes (A) **250.00**

Toddy Plate, 4⅞" d, red transfer, donkey scene, unmarked (A) **10.00**

Trinket Box

4¾" h, little blond girl playing with umbrella, multicolored **65.00**

Blond child holding book, dog beside her on blue ottoman, unmarked .. **85.00**

Dressing table with boxes and candle, unmarked **65.00**

Tureen, Cov

12¾" l, blue transfer, fisherman in landscape, lion head finial and handles, floral borders, c1825 (A) **110.00**

Vase

6½" h, tulip molded with overlapping leaves, circ base, applied leaves and buds, c1820, pr, repaired (A) **150.00**

7" h, Aesop's Fable, fox and crane, multicolored, unmarked, repaired **100.00**

12½" h, 13" w, exotic bird on either side of rim, relief of pine trees, chinoiserie figures in landscapes on gold ground on side panels, flared rims and sq bases, porcelain, c1870, sgd "Malpass," Brownfield, pr (A) **800.00**

Waste Bowl

5" d, multicolored floral design, black "Staffordshire, England" mark (A) **40.00**

5⅝" d, dark blue transfer of urns and flowers, unmarked (A) **45.00**

6¼" d, black and ochre gaudy floral design, unmarked **20.00**

Wine Pitcher, 10" h, drabware body, molded cherubs, pewter lid, c1850, "Edward Walley" **135.00**

STAFFORDSHIRE-HISTORIC

English and American Views 1818 to 1860

History: By 1786 there were eighty different potteries established in the Staffordshire district of England, the center of the English pottery industry. By 1800 the number had grown to almost two hundred. The pottery district included the towns of Burslem, Cobridge, Etruria, Fenton, Foley, Hanley, Lane Delph, Lane End, Longport, Shelton, Stoke, and Tunstall.

After the War of 1812, transfer printed Staffordshire pottery that depicted American historical events, views of cities and towns, tombs of famous individuals, portraits of heroes and other famous people, buildings of important institutions, patriotic emblems, and American landscapes were made for the American market. These historic view pieces allowed the British potters to recapture their dominance of the American market almost immediately upon the end of hostilities. Views were adopted from engravings, paintings, and prints by well-known artists of the period.

Dark blue pieces were favored between 1820 and 1840. This color was inexpensive, easy to secure, covered flaws in the wares, withstood the high temperatures of the kiln, and retained its deep coloration. During the 1830s and 1840s, lighter colors of pink and blue along with black, sepia, and green became popular. Wares made included tea services, dinner services, sets of plates, jugs, etc. Canadian views also were manufactured.

Numerous potteries made the historic blue wares. Each firm had its own distinctive border design and characteristics. The border design is the chief means of identifying a specific maker of an unmarked piece.

English views also were popular. Transfers featuring old and famous castles, abbeys, manor houses, cathedrals, seats of the nobility, famous beauty spots, coastal subjects, English colleges, and London were used on the wares.

William Adams and Enoch Wood were the first manufacturers to produce the English views. Enoch Wood took the lead with the American views. Factories that were established after 1820 concentrated on American views.

WILLIAM ADAMS

Stoke, 1827 to 1831
Tunstall: c1834 to Present

William Adams of Stoke was one of four potters with the name William Adams in the Staffordshire district. In 1819 a William Adams became a partner with William Adams, his father. Later his three brothers joined him. When the father died in 1829, William became the factory's manager. The firm operated as William Adams and Sons and controlled four potteries at Stoke and one at Tunstall.

Initially English views, with a foliage border and the name of the scene on the back, were made. Two blue views were manufactured at Stoke. Views done at Tunstall have a border of baskets of roses. The Tunstall plant produced American views in black, light blue, sepia, pink, and green between 1830 and 1840.

William Adams died in 1865. All production was moved to Tunstall. The firm still operates today under the name, William Adams & Sons, Ltd.

CAREY AND SONS

Lane End, 1818 to 1847

Thomas and John Carey operated the Anchor Works at Lane End between 1818 and 1842. The firm changed names several times during its history. The factory produced English views, some of which were based on Sir Walter Scott's poem "Lady of the Lake."

JAMES AND RALPH CLEWS

Cobridge, 1819 to 1836

James Clews took over the works of Andrew Stevenson in 1819. Ralph, his brother, joined the firm later. In 1836 James came to the United States to establish a pottery in Troy, Indiana; but, the venture was a failure. Clews returned to England but never re-established himself as a potter. Clews made both English and American views. The company made a variety of borders, the most popular having festoons that contained the names of the fifteen existing states.

THOMAS GODWIN

Burslem Wharf, 1829 to 1843

Thomas Godwin produced both American and Canadian views in a variety of colors. His borders included nasturtium and morning glories.

THOMAS GREEN

Fenton, 1847 to 1859

Thomas Green operated the Minerva Works in Fenton from 1847 until his death in 1859. His American view pieces contained variations of William Penn's 1683 Treaty with the Indians. The border was a simple, stenciled design. His printed wares were in green, pink, brown, black, and blue. After his death, his wife and sons managed the firm using the name M. Green & Co. It later became the Crown Staffordshire Porcelain Company.

RALPH HALL

Tunstall, 1822 to 1849

At the conclusion of a partnership with John Hall, Ralph Hall operated the Swan Bank Works in Tunstall. The firm exported many blue-printed wares to America.

JOSEPH HEATH

Tunstall, 1829 to 1843

Joseph Heath and company operated a factory at New Field in Tunstall between 1829 and 1843. The company's border design was composed of large roses and scrolls with a beaded band and white edge.

HENSHALL AND COMPANY

Longport, 1790 to 1828

The firm consisted of a series of different partnerships with the only recorded mark being that of Henshall and Company. Both English and American views were made. The border motif comprised fruit and flowers.

J. AND J. JACKSON

Burslem, 1831 to 1843

Job and John Jackson operated the Churchyard Works at Burslem between 1831 and 1843. Many of their American views were not copied by other manufacturers. Their border designs included sprays of roses, a wreath of fine flowers, a beaded band, and a white margin. Their transfer colors were black, light blue, pink, sepia, green, maroon, and mulberry.

THOMAS MAYER

Stoke, 1829 to 1838

In 1829 the Mayer brothers, Thomas, John, and Joshua, purchased the Dale Hall Works from

Stubbs when he retired. Thomas produced the "Arms of the States" series at Dale Hall Works while the other brothers worked at Cliff Bank. Each factory produced fine ceramics.

MORLEY AND COMPANY

Hanley, 1845 to 1858

Until 1845 Morley was the sole owner of a pottery firm in Hanley. After that date the firm experienced a succession of owners. Between 1847 and 1858 it was called Francis Morley and Company. Both American and Canadian views were manufactured.

J. AND W. RIDGWAY AND WILLIAM RIDGWAY AND COMPANY

Hanley, 1814 to 1830

John and William Ridgway, sons of Job Ridgway, took charge of the Bell Bank works in 1814 when George Ridgway retired. The brothers produced the "Beauties of America" series in dark blue with the rose leaf border. Their English views featured a border with flowers and medallions of children.

In 1830 the partnership was dissolved. John continued to operate Cauldon Place, Job's old manufactory, and William took charge of Bell Bank. John Ridgway continued the Cauldon Place Works from 1830 until 1858. In 1855 T. C. Brown-Westhead, Moore & Co. purchased the works.

William Ridgway and Company managed the Bell Bank Works from 1830 until 1859. Edward John, his son, joined the firm. By 1843 he was operating six potteries, mostly in Hanley. "American Scenery" and "Catskill Moss" were two series that were based on Bartlett's etchings. These series were issued in colors of light blue, pink, brown, black, and green.

JOHN AND RICHARD RILEY

Burslem, 1802 to 1828

John and Richard Riley operated at Nile Street between 1802 and 1814 and at the Hill Works in Staffordshire between 1814 and 1828. Mostly they made English views and blue printed dinner services with a border of large leaf-like scrolls and flowers.

JOHN ROGERS

Longport, 1815 to 1842

John and George Rogers operated two factories in Longport in 1802. When George died in 1815,

John took Spencer, his son, into the firm. The name changed to "John Rogers and Son," a designation used even after the father died. Rogers produced four American views, three of which featured the Boston State House with a floral border. English views also were made.

ANTHONY SHAW

Burslem, 1850 to 1878

Anthony Shaw founded Mersey Pottery at Burslem in 1850. He specialized in views of the Mexican War period.

ANDREW STEVENSON

Cobridge, 1808 to 1829

One of the pioneers among English potters to make blue historical, transfer printed ware with American scenes was Andrew Stevenson. W. G. Wall, an Irish artist, went to the United States and supplied the drawings for Stevenson. Stevenson's pieces had a flower and scroll border. English views were made with roses and other flowers on the border.

RALPH STEVENSON

Cobridge, 1815 to 1840

Ralph Stevenson used a vine and leaf border on his dark blue historical views and a lace border on his transfers in lighter colors. British and foreign views were made.

Pieces from the works of Ralph Stevenson and Williams (R.S.W.) featured the acorn and oak leaf border design on the vases of flowers and scrollwork design. Williams was the New York agent for Stevenson.

JOSEPH STUBBS

Burslem, 1790 to 1829

Joseph Stubbs established the Dale Hall Works in Burslem in 1790. When he retired in 1829, he sold his pottery to the Mayer brothers. His American views used a border design of eagles with widespread wings among scrolls and flowers. Views included scenes of New Jersey, Boston, New York, and Philadelphia. Stubbs also made English views with a border of foliage and pointed scrolls.

ENOCH WOOD AND SONS

Burslem, 1819 to 1846

Enoch Wood, sometimes called the "Father of English Pottery," made more marked historical

American views than any other Staffordshire manufacturer. In 1819 his firm operated as Enoch Wood and Sons. Enoch died in 1840. Enoch, Joseph, and Edward, his sons, continued the firm with their father's name. The sons sold the firm to Pinder, Bourne, and Hope in 1846.

The company's mark had several variations, but each included the name "Wood." The shell border with the circle around the view was used most frequently, though Wood designed several other unique borders. Many of the views attributed to unknown makers probably were made at the Wood factory.

Enoch Wood and Sons also made British views, including "English Cities" series, the "London Views" series, the shell border series, and the grapevine border series. In addition, they produced French views such as ceramic portrayals of Lafayette and his home in France, an "Italian Scenery" Series, and views of Africa and India. Many of the foreign scenes were copied from engravings after water colors by traveling artists such as William Henry Bartlett.

In addition to views of places, Enoch Wood made other designs including a Scriptural Series of biblical scenes, a Sporting Series of hunting scenes, and a Cupid Series showing a variety of cherubs.

William Adams did an Animal Series. Scriptural subjects were done by Adams, Mason, Jackson, Ridgway and others.

References: David and Linda Arman, *Historical Staffordshire: An Illustrated Check List,* privately printed, 1974, out of print; David and Linda Arman, *Historical Staffordshire: An Illustrated Check List, First Supplement,* privately printed, 1977, out of print; Ada Walker Camehl, *The Blue China Book,* Tudor Publishing Co., 1946; Elizabeth Collard, *The Potters' View of Canada,* McGill Queen's University Press, 1983; A. W. Coysh and R. K. Henrywood, *The Dictionary of Blue & White Printed Pottery, 1780–1880,* Antique Collectors' Club, 1982; Ellouise Baker Larsen, *American Historical Views on Staffordshire China,* Dover Publications, Inc., Third Edition, 1975; N. Hudson Moore, *The Old China Book,* Charles E. Tuttle Co., 1974.

Museums: American Antiquarian Society, Worcester, Massachusetts; City Museum & Art Gallery, Stoke-on-Trent, England; The National Museum of History & Technology, Washington, DC; Wellcome Institute of the History of Medicine, London, England; Worcester Art Museum, Worcester, Massachusetts; Yale University Gallery of Fine Arts, New Haven, Connecticut.

AMERICAN VIEWS

Adams
  Cup Plate, 3⅞" d, "Columbus," light
    blue transfer (A) **40.00**
  Pitcher
    5" h, spread eagle, blue transfer (A)**1,000.00**
    7" h, American eagle, black trans-
      fer, polychrome enamels (A) . . . **60.00**
  Pitcher and Bowl, 9" h pitcher, 12⅛"
    d, 4½" h, bowl, "Lafayette at
    Franklin's Tomb," dark blue trans-
    fer, imp "ADAMS," hairline in
    pitcher (A) **1,100.00**
  Plate
    8" d, "Shannondale Springs, Va,"
    blue transfer, "Wm Adams &
    Sons" **75.00**
    10½" d, "Catskill Mountain House,
    U. S.," red transfer (A) **50.00**
    11⅞" d, American eagle, black
    transfer, polychrome enamels,
    (A) **60.00**
  Platter, 13⅜" l, "Lake George, U. S.,"
    red transfer, imp "ADAMS" (A) . . **200.00**
  Soup Plate, 10½" d, "Catskill Moun-
    tain House, U. S.," red transfer (A) **55.00**
Clews
  Bidet, 20" l, "Landing of Lafayette,"
    blue transfer (A) **3,200.00**
  Bowl, 7¾" d, "Landing of Lafayette,"
    dark blue transfer (A) **145.00**
  Creamer, "Landing of Lafayette," blue
    transfer, rect **360.00**
  Cup Plate, "Quebec," "Cities" series,
    dark blue transfer (A) **2,100.00**
  Pitcher, 8¼" h, "Near Hudson, Hud-
    son River," pink transfer, c1830 . . **65.00**

Plate

4½" d

"Near Sandy Hill, Hudson River," black transfer **60.00**

"Pittsfield Elm, Mass.," blue transfer, two medallion border, cracked and restored **160.00**

5¾" d, "States," three story building, three wings and center section, blue transfer **110.00**

6⅝" d

"America & Independence," dark blue transfer (A) **125.00**

"Landing of Lafayette," dark blue transfer (A) **150.00**

7½" d

"Near Fishkill, Hudson River," blue transfer **85.00**

"West Point, Hudson River," blue transfer **85.00**

7⅞" d, "America & Independence," dark blue transfer, imp "Clews" (A) **175.00**

8" d, "States," blue transfer **300.00**

8¾" d

"America & Independence," dark blue transfer, imp "Clews" (A) **225.00**

"Landing of Lafayette," dark blue transfer **325.00**

"Pittsfield Elm, Mass.," blue transfer, hairline **300.00**

"States," building, sheep on lawn, blue transfer **160.00**

"Winter View of Pittsfield, Mass.," dark blue transfer, imp "Clews" (A) **90.00**

9⅛" d, "Near Hudson, Hudson River," Picturesque Views, black transfer (A) **100.00**

10" d

"Landing of Lafayette," dark blue transfer, imp "Clews," chipped (A) **100.00**

"Welcome Lafayette the Nation's Guest & Our Country's Glory," blue transfer, blue feather edge (A) **400.00**

10½" d

"America & Independence," "States" series, dark blue transfer, imp "Clews" (A) **130.00**

"Near Fishkill, Hudson River," Picturesque Views, black transfer (A) **45.00**

"Winter View of Pittsfield, Mass.," dark blue transfer (A) **225.00**

10⅝" d, "America & Independence," "States" series, dark blue transfer (A) **225.00**

Platter

10" l, "Landing of Lafayette," dark blue transfer, imp "Clews" (A) . **375.00**

12" l, "Landing of Lafayette," dark blue transfer (A) **550.00**

12¾" l, 10½" w, "Pittsfield Elm, Mass.," blue transfer **950.00**

14⅝" d, "States" series, mansion with small boat, flag in foreground, blue transfer **1,000.00**

16" l, 13" w, "Newburgh, Hudson River," black transfer **245.00**

19" l, "Landing of General Lafayette at Castle Garden, New York," dark blue transfer, imp "Clews" **400.00**

Sauce Tureen, 9¾" l, tray, "Landing of Lafayette," dark blue transfer (A) **475.00**

Serving Dish, 12¼" l, "Peace & Plenty," dark blue transfer, imp "Clews" (A) **200.00**

Shaker, 4¾" h, "Landing of Lafayette," dark blue transfer (A) **700.00**

Soup Plate

8¾" d, "States" series, building, sheep on lawn, blue transfer ... **135.00**

8⅞" d, "Landing of Lafayette," dark blue transfer (A) **170.00**

Teabowl and Saucer, "Landing of Lafayette," dark blue transfer (A) ... **125.00**

Teapot, "Landing of Lafayette," dark blue transfer, rect, restored bottom (A) **210.00**

Toddy Cup, 5⅝" h, "Pittsfield Elm, Mass," blue transfer **425.00**

Toddy Plate

4¾" d, "America & Independence," "States" series, dark blue transfer, imp "Clews" (A) . **200.00**

5¼" d, "Ft. Edwards, Hudson River," black transfer **135.00**

Vegetable Bowl, 12¼" l, 10½" w, "Landing of Lafayette," dark blue transfer (A) **325.00**

Wash Bowl, 12" d, "Landing of Lafayette," dark blue transfer (A) **375.00**

Godwin, Thomas, plate, 10¾" d, "The Capital," light blue transfer **70.00**

Green, Thomas, plate, 9⅜" d, "William Penn's Treaty," red transfer (A) **70.00**

Henshall, plate, 10" d, "Baltimore Exchange," blue transfer **375.00**

Jackson, J. & J.

Pitcher, 6½" h, "Schenectady on the Mohawk River," purple transfer .. **200.00**

Plate

6¼" d, "Girard's Bank, Philadelphia," red transfer, unmarked (A) **75.00**

7¾" d, "Hancock House, Boston," red transfer **100.00**

9⅛" d
"Battle Monument, Baltimore,"
red transfer, "Jackson's War-
ranted" (A) 115.00
"The Water Works, Philadel-
phia," red transfer, "Jackson's
Warranted" (A) 45.00
"View Near Conway N. Hamp-
shire, U. S.," red transfer (A) . 40.00
9¼" d, "View Near Conway N.
Hampshire, U. S.," red transfer,
"Jackson's Warranted" (A) 75.00
10¼" d, "Hartford, Ct.," black
transfer 85.00
Soup Plate, 10½" d, "Hartford, Ct.,"
red transfer, "Jackson's Warranted"
(A) 75.00
Maker Unknown
Creamer, 4⅜" h, "Wadsworth
Tower," dark blue transfer (A) 225.00
Cup and Saucer, "Baltimore Hospital/
University of Maryland," dark blue
transfer (A) 1,650.00
Pitcher
8¼" h, "Mount Vernon, Washing-
ton's Seat," blue transfer (A) ... 425.00
9½" h, "Famous Naval Heroes,"
dark blue transfer, repair to spout
(A) 385.00
Pitcher and Bowl, "American Villa,"
dark blue transfer (A) 550.00
Plate
6¾" d, "America & Independence," "States" series, dark
blue transfer (A) 65.00
7¾" d, "Near Fishkill, Hudson
River," dark blue transfer (A) ... 100.00
8½" d, "Upper Fernbridge Over
Schuylkill," dark blue transfer .. 300.00
10" d
"Capital, Washington," blue
transfer, flower and fruit border 40.00
"Fairmount Near Philadelphia,"
blue transfer 275.00
"The Dam & Water Works, Philadelphia, stern wheeler, blue
transfer (A) 200.00
Platter, 17½" l, "Military School,
West Point, N. Y.," red transfer, unmarked (A) 175.00
Soup Plate
9" d, "Hobart Town," blue transfer 400.00
9¾" d, "The Dam & Water Works,
Philadelphia," side wheeler,
dark blue transfer, unmarked (A) 145.00
Sugar
"Lafayette at Franklin's Tomb,"
dark blue transfer, 4¾" h, un-
marked (A) 375.00
"Washington With Scroll At
Tomb," blue transfer, rect 750.00

Teabowl and Saucer, "Wadsworth
Tower," dark blue transfer (A) 150.00
Teapot, "Washington With Scroll At
Tomb," blue transfer, unmarked .. 950.00
Mayer, plate, 10" d, "Arms of New
York," dark blue transfer, imp
"Mayer" (A) 100.00
Morley & Co.
Cup Plate, 3¾" d, "Lake George-
ville," blue transfer 75.00
Plate, 8¼" d, "The Church at Point
Levi," light blue transfer (A) 45.00
Platter, 13" l, "Village of Cedars, St.
Lawrence River," light blue transfer
(A) 165.00

**J. & W. Ridgway, plate, 9½" d, "Beauties
of America - City Hall of New York," blue
transfer, $250.00.**

Ridgway, J. & W.
Plate
7¼" d, "Senate House, Cam-
bridge," blue transfer, "J. & W.
Ridgway" (A) 55.00
8⅜" d, "Library, Philadelphia,"
medium blue transfer (A) 65.00
Vegetable Dish, 11⅜" w, cov, "Mount
Vernon Nr Washington," "Beauties
of America" series, blue transfer,
repaired (A) 375.00
Rogers
Pitcher and Bowl, "Boston State
House," dark blue transfer, repaired (A) 550.00
Platter, 19" l, "Boston State House,"
dark blue transfer, repaired (A) ... 425.00
Shaw, A., plate, 8⅜" d, "Texian Cam-
paigne-Battle of Buena Vista," purple
mulberry transfer (A) 155.00
Stevenson & Williams
Bowl, 6⅜" d, "Battery, New York,"
blue transfer, vine leaf border,
"RSW" (A) 950.00
Plate
8¼" d, "Nahant Hotel, Near Bos-
ton," dark blue transfer (A) 45.00

10⅛" d, "Park Theatre, New York,"
blue transfer, acorn and oak leaf
border, "RSW" (A) **100.00**
10¼" d, "Water Works, Philadelphia," blue transfer, "RSW" ... **400.00**
Stevenson, A.
Cup and Saucer, "State House, Hartford," dark blue transfer, "A. Stevenson" (A) **1,400.00**
Plate
5¾" d, "Catholic Cathedral, New
York," blue transfer (A) **1,000.00**
6¾" d, "General Lafayette, Wel-
come to the Land of Liberty,"
blue transfer, emb floral border,
blue stripes, imp "A. Stevenson"
(A) **500.00**
Platter, 14¼" l, "The Junction of the
Sacandaga & Hudson Rivers," blue
transfer, floral and scroll border,
"A. Stevenson" (A) **1,200.00**
Stevenson, R.
Cup and Saucer, "Hartford State
House," blue transfer **1,500.00**
Pitcher, 6" h, "City Hall, New York/
Hospital, New York," blue transfer,
vine leaf border (A) **650.00**
Platter, 16¼" l, 12¾" w, "Alms
House, Boston," blue transfer **1,250.00**
Vegetable Bowl, 10¾" l, "Charlston
Exchange," dark blue transfer (A) . **185.00**
Stubbs
Mug, 5½" h, "Boston State House,"
dark blue transfer **1,125.00**
Plate
6¼" d, "Park Theatre, New York,"
blue transfer, eagle border (A) .. **400.00**
8" d, "Hoboken in New Jersey,"
dark blue transfer, eagle border,
cracked rim (A) **40.00**
8¾" d, "Upper Ferry Bridge Over
the River Schuylkill," blue transfer, eagle border (A) **210.00**
Platter
12⅝" l, "Hoboken in New Jersey,"
dark blue transfer, eagle border
(A) **325.00**
14½" l, "Boston State House," blue
transfer **550.00**
Wood, E.
Coffeepot
"Commodore Macdonnough's Victory," blue transfer, high dome,
hairlines (A) **1,100.00**
"Lafayette at Franklin's Tomb,"
dark blue transfer
11" h (A) **525.00**
11¾" h (A) **600.00**
Creamer
"Commodore Macdonnough's Vic-
tory," blue transfer **900.00**

"Wadsworth Tower," dark blue
transfer (A) **350.00**
Mug
2⅛" h, "Cornwallis Surrendering
His Sword at Yorktown," black
transfer, pink luster band (A) ... **725.00**
2⅝" h, "Lafayette & Washington,"
black transfer, canary ground (A) **475.00**
Plate
3⅝" d, "Lafayette & Washingon,"
carmine transfer (A) **275.00**
3¾" d
"Cadmus," blue transfer, trefoil
border (A) **250.00**
"Castle Garden, Battery, New
York," blue transfer, trefoil
border (A) **140.00**
"General Jackson, The Hero of
New Orleans," carmine trans-
fer (A) **650.00**
"Lafayette & Washington," rust
transfer, rust enamel rim, imp
"Wood" (A) **375.00**
"Lafayette Crowned in Glory,"
black transfer (A) **500.00**
"Ship, Anchored," blue transfer,
shallow mold (A) **325.00**
4⅝" d, "Two Sailboats & Row-
boat," blue transfer (A) **225.00**
4¾" d, "Ship Under Half Sail,"
blue transfer, irreg shell border (A) **210.00**
9⅛" d
"Baltimore & Ohio Railroad In-
cline," blue transfer (A) **185.00**
"Falls of Montmorency Near
Quebec," blue transfer (A) .. **85.00**
9¼" d
"Gilpin's Mill on the Brandywine
Green," dark blue transfer,
imp "Wood & Son" (A) **200.00**
"Marine Hospital, Louisville,
Ky.," dark blue transfer, imp
"E. Wood & Sons," hairlines
(A) **160.00**
9⅜" d
"Marine Hospital, Louisville,
Ky.," blue transfer (A) **110.00**
"Union Line," dark blue transfer,
imp "Wood" (A) **100.00**
9½" d, "Commodore Mac-
Donnough's Victory," dark blue
transfer **325.00**
10" d
"Cadmus," dark blue transfer .. **250.00**
"Chief Justice Marshall, Troy
Line," blue transfer, irreg shell
(A) **650.00**
10¼" d
"City of Albany, State of New
York," blue transfer, shell bor-
der (A) **450.00**

"Commodore MacDonnough's Victory," dark blue transfer, imp "Wood" (A) **170.00**

"Landing of the Fathers at Plymouth," dark blue transfer, c1820 .... **100.00**

"Table Rock, Niagara," dark blue transfer (A) **350.00**

Platter

6¾" l, "View of the Erie Canal," blue transfer (A) **1,200.00**

20¼" l, 16" w, "Castle Garden, Battery, New York," medium blue transfer **950.00**

Soup Plate, 9¼" d, "Pine Orchard House, Catskill Mountains," blue transfer (A) **235.00**

Sugar, cov

"Commodore MacDonnough's Victory," dark blue transfer, rect **900.00**

"Lafayette at Franklin's Tomb," dark blue transfer, 6¾" h, imp "Wood," glued finial (A) **85.00**

"Wadsworth Tower," dark blue transfer (A) **400.00**

Teabowl and Saucer

"Lafayette at Franklin's Tomb," dark blue transfer, imp "Wood" (A) **85.00**

"Wadsworth Tower," dark blue transfer, imp "E. Wood & Sons" (A) **185.00**

Teapot

"Commodore MacDonnough's Victory," blue transfer, repaired **2,400.00**

"Lafayette at Franklin's Tomb," blue transfer, apple shape, repaired (A) **750.00**

"Wadsworth Tower," dark blue transfer, 7½" h **600.00**

Wash Pitcher, "Erie Canal - Aqueduct Bridge at Rochester/Aqueduct at Little Falls," blue transfer, floral border, irreg center, repaired (A) .. **600.00**

J & R. Riley

ENGLISH VIEWS

Adams

Plate

8" d, "Scaleby Castle, Cumberland," blue transfer, bluebell border, c1804–40 .... **55.00**

9" d, "Villa, Regent Park," blue transfer **185.00**

Carey & Sons, platter, 11⅝" l, "Luton Hoo, Bedfordshire," "Titled Seat" se-

ries, dark blue transfer, imp "Carey & Sons" (A) **135.00**

Clews

Gravy Tureen, cov, and tray, "St. Catherine's Hill & View of Rochester," blue transfer, foliage and scroll border, repair to cov **235.00**

Plate

6¾" d, "Select Scenery," dark blue transfer (A) **100.00**

8¾" d, "St. Catherine's Hill," dark blue transfer, foliage and scroll border (A) **65.00**

R. Hall, pitcher, 5" h, black transfers, $425.00.

Hall, R.

Plate

7½" d, "Eashing Park, Surrey," medium blue transfer, "R. Hall's Select Views" (A) **75.00**

8½" d, "Fulham Church, Middlesex," blue transfer, "R. Hall's Picturesque Scenery" (A) **35.00**

Soup Plate, 10" d, "Biddulph Castle," blue transfer (A) **70.00**

Soup Tureen, cov, "Armley House, Yorkshire," blue transfer, foliage border, fruit basket finial, dbl branch handles, short peg feet, damaged (A) **750.00**

Tureen, 16¼" l, tray, "Select Views - Laxton Hall, Northamptonshire" on tureen, "Conway Castle, Carnarvonshire, Wales" on tray, dark blue transfer (A) **1,150.00**

Maker Unknown

Mug, 4¼" h, "The Duke of Wellington," blue transfer (A) **235.00**

Plate

7⅛" d, "The London Institution," blue transfer, shield and American eagle on reverse (A) **75.00**

7¼" d, "British Views," dark blue transfer (A) **45.00**

Maker Unknown, sauce tureen, 7½" l, 6½" h, "Audley End, Essex," blue transfers, $255.00.

10" d, "Villa, Regents Park," blue
transfer, c1810 .... **185.00**
Soup Plate, 10" d, "Pembroke Hall,
Cambridge," blue transfer, un-
marked (A) **45.00**
Sugar, cov, "Rural Estate," blue trans-
fer (A) **90.00**
Ridgway, J. & W.
  Platter
    15" l, "Lowther Castle, Westmore-
    land," light blue transfer, octag-
    onal, "J. Ridgway" (A) **30.00**
    18¾" l, "Theatre Printing House,
    Oxford," "English College" se-
    ries, medium blue transfer (A) .. **475.00**
Riley, J. & R.
  Plate
    7" d, "Alton Abbey, Staffordshire,"
    dark blue transfer, scroll border
    (A) **65.00**
    8⅞" d, "Kingsweston, Gloucester-
    shire," dark blue transfer (A) ... **15.00**
Stevenson, A.
  Platter, 10⅜" l, "Kidbrook, Sussex,"
  dark blue transfer, wild rose border,
  "A. Stevenson" (A) **110.00**
  Soup Plate, 10⅜" d, "Writtle Lodge,
  Essex," dark blue transfer, imp "Ste-
  venson" (A) **75.00**
Stevenson, R.
  Platter
    14½" l, "Panoramic Scenery - Font-
    hill Abbey," dark blue transfer,
    "R. S. Stevenson," repaired (A) . **50.00**
    15½" l, "British Lakes," red transfer
    (A) **35.00**
Wood, E.
  Cup Plate, 4½" d, "Kenmount
  House," blue transfer **80.00**
  Hot Water Plate, 10" d, "Wellcombe
  House," blue transfer **300.00**
  Plate
    7⅝" d, "Southampton, Hamp-
    shire," blue transfer, irreg shell
    border (A) **155.00**

7⅞" d, "Southampton, Hampshire," dark blue transfer, imp "E.
Wood & Sons" (A) **110.00**
10¼" d, "Fonthill Abbey," dark
blue transfer, grapevine border
(A) **90.00**
Platter
  10" l, 8" w, "Dorney Court," blue
  transfer, reticulated lattice border **265.00**
  14½" l, 11½" w, "A View of Dub-
  lin," dark blue transfer, shell border **300.00**
Soup Bowl, 10" d, "Guy's Cliff," blue
transfer **125.00**
Vegetable Dish, 10¾" l, "Kenmount,
Dumfrieshire," dark blue transfer,
grapevine border (A) **110.00**

STAFFORDHIRE–ROMANTIC

England
1830 to 1860

History: Between 1830 and 1860 the Staffordshire District potters produced a tremendous
number of useful dinnerwares intended for everyday dining that featured romantic transfer printed
designs.

Romantic wares were printed in blue, red,
green, black, brown, purple, and yellow. Some
patterns were issued in only one color, while
some were produced in a variety of colors.
Within each color group there was a great deal
of color variation. Blues ranged from the darkest
navy to a pale powder blue to shades of turquoise.

Designs used for romantic wares reflected the
tastes of the Victorian age. Scenes with castles,
Alpine mountain peaks, and rivers evoked a fas-
cination with European travel. Oriental scenery
expressed the infatuation of the common man
with dreams of far away places. English scenes
were used, but they depicted homes of the nobility, castles, and other important locations.

Floral designs featured realistic flowers, leaves,
fruits, and birds that reflected the English love of
gardens. Some scenes added insects or butterflies
in imitation of the Chinese patterns.

The Victorians loved the architectural and decorative styles of the past. Gothic elements,
French designs from the Louis XV and XVI
periods, and even Grecian and Roman designs
became part of romantic transfer patterns. Classical designs often showed urns or vases in a
garden setting. Some pieces contained allegorical stories.

Oriental designs utilized Chinese and Japanese
flowers, baskets, exotic birds, flowering trees,

pagodas, and urns. East Indian motifs depicted mosques, minarets, desert scenes, and men and women in Arabian or Turkish clothes. Elements of fantasy in these patterns reflected the love of far off, romantic places, unseen by the common English resident.

Scenic designs were popular. Pastoral scenes showing the typical English countryside featured rolling fields, domestic farm animals, groves of trees, brooks, and ponds. Figures placed in these scenes usually wore Medieval, Elizabethan, or Empire clothing. Greyhounds were a common decorative element.

Although the names of rivers, countries, cities, or towns often were used as titles for these romantic views, the scenes themselves were imaginary. Most of the scenes appeared rather dreamlike in conception. Tall trees, rivers, castles, arched bridges, gazebos, ruins, or fountains were included in the scenes. Borders were either floral, geometric, or featured reserves with landscape scenes.

Some scenes showed local people in their roles as farmers, fishermen, warriors, dancers, etc. In these cases, the scenic background was less prominent. The figures were most important. Other romantic subjects included zoological, religious, moralistic, botanical, marine, or geometric transfers.

In many instances, the designers of the transfers were not known. Many pottery firms purchased their transfers from engraving companies such as Sargeant and Pepper of Hanley. The firm designed the printed patterns and also engraved the copper plates necessary for printing the wares. Popular designs were used by more than one pottery manufacturer.

Romantic transfers were made by many factories. The best known were Adams, Clews, Davenport, Dillon, Dimmock, Hall, Hicks and Meigh, Meigh, Ridgway, Rogers, Spode, Wedgwood, and Wood.

Backstamps were used that reflected the romantic expressions of these Victorian potters. The backstamp was part of the sheet that contained the transfer pattern. When placed on the back of a piece, it indicated the pattern used.

References: Petra Williams, *Staffordshire Romantic Transfer Patterns,* Fountain House East, 1978; Petra Williams & Marguerite R. Weber, *Staffordshire II,* Fountain House East, 1986.

Museums: City Museum & Art Gallery, Stoke-on-Trent, England.

Bowl
  6" d, "Minerva," brown transfer, c1840, Podmore & Walker **20.00**
  10" d, "Priory," light blue transfer, "John Alcock" **25.00**
Cake Plate, 10½" d, "Palmyra," blue transfer, Wood & Brownfield mark .. **35.00**

Cup and Saucer
  "Basket," dark blue transfer (A) **70.00**
  "Corean," handleless, "P. W. & Co." **50.00**
  "Palestine," light blue transfer, Adams **40.00**
  "Venetian Temple," red transfer, handleless, unmarked **30.00**
Cup Plate
  3½" d
    "Canova," green transfer, Mayer . **30.00**
    "Floral," blue transfer **22.00**
    "Vista," blue transfer, "F. Morely" **30.00**
  5" d, "Cassino," blue transfer, Adams **15.00**
Demitasse Cup and Saucer, "Jenny Lind," red transfer **25.00**
Gravy Boat, 10" l, "Chinese Pattern," polychrome transfer, luster accents, ftd, Ashworth **22.00**
Pitcher
  6½" h, "Sea Shells," dark blue transfer, unmarked **225.00**
  7¼" h, "Canova," blue transfer, ftd, fluted body, unmarked **85.00**
  9¾" h, "Friburg," light blue transfer, "Davenport" (A) **30.00**
Plate
  4" d, "Quadrupeds," Hyena design, blue transfer, unmarked (A) **50.00**
  5½" d
    "California," dark red transfer, "F. M. & Co." **30.00**
    "Corinth," light blue transfer, "Phillips" **35.00**
  5¾" d, "Moral Maxims," blue transfer, scalloped edge, c1825, "R. & J. Clewes" **45.00**
  7¼" d
    "Fruit & Flowers," blue transfer, imp "Stubbs" (A) **70.00**
    "Palestine," purple transfer, Adams mark **30.00**
  7½" d
    "Canova," pink transfer, unmarked **18.00**
    "Cologne," brown transfer, c1850, "Alcock" **15.00**
    "Medina," dark blue transfer, "J. F. & Co." **30.00**

Plate, 10¼" H-H, "Oriental" pattern, red transfer, "Baker & Co., Ltd," $15.00.

8" d
"Andalusia"
Blue transfer, "Wm. Adams" .. 38.00
Pink transfer, imp "Adams" 40.00
"Canova," black transfer, unmarked (A) 10.00
"Rhone Scenery," blue transfer, unmarked 32.00
8½" d
"Abbey Ruins," pink transfer, "T. Mayer" 32.00
"Columbia," blue transfer, "Clementson & Young" 42.00
"Corinthia," pink transfer, "E. Challinor" 25.00
"Oriental Scenery," dark gray transfer 35.00
"Palestine," dark purple transfer, Adams mark 45.00
"Peruvian Horse Hunt," green transfer, brown border 60.00
"Spartan," blue transfer, 12-sided, c1840, "Podmore, Walker & Co." 30.00
8⅝" d, "Seasons," black transfer, imp "Adams" (A) 30.00
8¾" d
"Carrara," blue transfer, 12-sided, c1852, unmarked 60.00
"French Scenery," black transfer, unmarked (A) 10.00
"Warwick Vase," brown transfer, "P. W. & Co." 35.00
8⅞" d
"Bird With Fruit," blue transfer (A) 120.00
"Chinese Pastimes," pink transfer . 45.00
9" d
"Canova," green center, red border, imp "T. Mayer" 50.00
"Clyde Scenery," dark red transfer 45.00
"Lady of the Lake," medium blue transfer, unmarked (A) 30.00
"Mogul Scenery," black transfer, "T. Mayer, Stoke Upon Trent" . 25.00
"Tuscan Rose," brown transfer ... 22.00
9¼" d
"Cambrian," pink transfer, "G. Phillips" 32.00
"Genoa," light blue transfer, 14-sided, c1840, "W. Adams & Sons" 32.00
"Japan Flowers," blue transfer, scalloped edge, "Ridgway, Morley, Wear & Co." 36.00
"Palmyra," blue transfer, Furnival, set of 8 .... 150.00
"Rural Scenery," blue transfer, c1828, "Jos. Heath" 45.00
"Shanghai," blue transfer 45.00
"University," blue transfer, 10-sided, J. Ridgway mark 35.00

9½" d
"Abbeville," light blue transfer, 12-sided, c1840, "Alcock, Burslem" 36.00
"Canova," red transfer
"T. Mayer, Stoke" 30.00
Unmarked (A) 15.00
"Cyrene," pink transfer, 14-sided, Adams 25.00
"Lucerne," purple transfer, Parkhurst 18.00
"Priory," blue transfer, "John Alcock" 35.00
"Spanish Convent," light blue transfer, Adams 35.00
9¾" d
"Panama," blue transfer, "E. Challinor" 30.00
"Quadrupeds," blue transfer, "I. Hall" (A) 85.00
"Rhone Scenery," brown transfer, 12-paneled, c1850, "T. J. & J. Mayer" 35.00
10" d
"Italian Buildings," blue transfer, "R. Hall" 35.00
"Panama," green transfer, Challinor mark 30.00
"Vincennes," gray-purple transfer, Alcock 55.00
"Washington," black center, light blue border 100.00
10½" d
"Antique Vases," light blue transfer, Clementson 30.00
"Caledonia," brown transfer, green accents, "Ridgway, Morley, Wear & Co" 42.00
"Catskill Moss," red transfer, unmarked (A) 15.00
"Crusaders," blue and white transfer, "Deacon & Bailey" 25.00
"Eastern Lights," light blue transfer, slightly scalloped edge, "J. B." . 65.00
"Palestine"
Light blue transfer, imp "Adams" (A) 12.00
Purple transfer, Adams 50.00
"Spanish Convent," dark brown transfer, c1850, "Wm. Adams" 60.00
"Vincennes," light purple transfer, Alcock 45.00
Platter
10¼" l, 8½" w, "Chinese Pattern," polychrome transfer, luster accents, Ashworth, crazing 25.00
12" l, 9½" w, "Chinese Pattern," polychrome transfer, luster accents, Ashworth 40.00
12½" l, 10¼" w, "Oriental," blue transfer 35.00

13" l

"Columbian Star," blue transfer . . **220.00**
"Oriental," blue transfer, "Wm. Ridgway" **55.00**
15½" l, "Washington," red transfer, green border, Wood **250.00**
16¾" l, 13¾" w, "Millenium," brown transfer, "Stevenson & Son" **240.00**
19½" l

English country scene of cottage and church, medium blue transfer, unmarked (A) **130.00**
"Tuscan Rose," light blue transfer, unmarked (A) **40.00**
22" l, "Park Scene," brown transfer, unmarked (A) **50.00**
Relish Dish, "Chinese Pattern," polychrome transfer, luster accents, melon shape, dbl handles, Ashworth **28.00**
Sauce Dish, Cov, "Non Pareil," shell finial, ftd, unmarked **70.00**
Soap Dish, 5" l, 3¾" w, "Basket of Flowers," dark blue transfer (A) **135.00**
Soup Plate

9¼" d, "Wm Penn's Treaty," blue transfer **65.00**
10⅛" d, "Quadrupeds," dark blue transfer, "I. Hall" (A) **95.00**
10¾" d

"Palestine," purple transfer, imp "Adams" (A) **35.00**
"Son of Righteousness," lavender transfer **45.00**
Toddy Plate, 5" d

"Damascus," pink transfer, "Wood"   **35.00**
"Priory," light blue transfer **30.00**
Sugar, cov

"Canova," blue transfer, 6½" h, "T. Mayer" **100.00**
"Clyde Scenery," dark red transfer . .   **100.00**
"University," light blue transfer, 7½" h, J. Ridgway mark **85.00**
Tea Service, teapot, creamer, cov sugar, six cups and saucers, "Classical Antiquities," blue transfer, Clementson marks **350.00**
Teabowl and Saucer

"Accepted," dark pink transfer, "Dixon Phillips & Co." **75.00**
"Feather," green transfer, "W. & C."   **35.00**
"Garden Scenery," pink transfer, Mayer **36.00**
"The Cottage Girl," magenta transfer, red and green enameled flowers on porcelain, unmarked (A) **15.00**
"Venus," light blue transfer, "Podmore Walker & Co." **25.00**
Teacup and Saucer, "Chinese Pattern," polychrome transfer, luster accents, Ashworth **25.00**

Teapot

"Chinese Pattern," polychrome transfer, luster accents, 9" l, 5" h, Ashworth **50.00**
"Zamara," blue transfer, polychrome   **145.00**
Tray, 13" l, 10½" w, "American Marine," purple transfer **85.00**
Vegetable Bowl, Cov

"Canova," blue transfer, floral finial

8½" l, unmarked **120.00**
12½" l, open handles, unmarked .   **170.00**
"Nanking," blue transfer, octagonal, Challinor mark **75.00**
"Oriental," blue transfer, 11¼" l, gold trim on shaped handles and feet, "ENGLAND" mark **70.00**
"Sirius," blue transfer, 9¼" d, octagonal, ftd, shell handles **130.00**

STEINS

Germany
1840s to Present

History: A stein is a drinking vessel with a handle and an attached lid that is made to hold beer and ale. The use of a lid differentiates a stein from a mug. Steins range in size from the smallest at ³⁄₁₀ liters or ¼ liters to the larger at 1, 1½, 2, 3, 4, and 5 liters, and even 8 liters in rare cases. A liter is 1.056 liquid quarts.

METTLACH STEINS

The most prolific period in the history of stein production occured in the second half of the 19th century, coinciding with the peak of Mettlach stein manufacture.

Chromoliths made by Mettlach were molded. The designs appear to be etched by hand. Although the designs seem three-dimensional, they are smooth to the touch.

Mettlach's cameos or phanoliths have portraits or small scenes in a translucent white clay set against a green or blue background. Even though these are three-dimensional, the relief portions are blended into the background without showing seams.

When fire destroyed the abbey where Mettlach steins were produced in 1921, the company gave up production of chromoliths and cameos. Mettlach's stein competitors included Merkelbach and Wick, Albert Jacob Thewalt, Simon Peter Gerz, and the Girmscheid factory.

GENERAL

The finest steins have proportional figures with intricate details that make them appear real. The decorations are made in a separate mold and applied to the body of the stein, giving the piece a raised effect. Etched steins, with the design incised or engraved into the body of the stein, are the most desirable and expensive steins. Artisans used black paint to fill in the lines and then other colors to complete the motif.

The simplest steins to produce were the print under glaze (PUG). A decal or transfer printed scene was applied by the transfer method, the body was covered with an additional coat of transparent glaze, and the piece was refired.

Character or figural steins depicted life-like creations of Indian heads, skulls, animals, Satans, vegetables, buildings, and people. Ernst Bohne's firm produced fine quality figural steins with realistic expressions.

Occupational steins were steins with a decoration or shape that depicted the owner's occupation. A slogan or the owner's name also may appear on the stein.

Thumblifts also came in a variety of designs on steins. Steins designed specifically for export to the United States had a United States shield as the thumblift. Other designs included a monkey, owl, jester, lyre, bust of a figure, twin towers, eagle, Munich maid, lion and shield, dwarf, or huntsman.

REGIMENTAL STEINS

During the reign of Kaiser Wilhelm II, 1888 to 1918, German reservists frequently purchased souvenir steins that had information such as the owner's name, unit, garrison town, service dates, and rosters of comrades inscribed on them. Munich was the regimental stein capital. Most of the regimental steins date from the early 1890s.

Other European armies also issued regimental steins after the 1890s. A great variety of transfer scenes, finials, stein bodies, and lids were used for regimental steins. Lid varieties that include the finial type, screw off, fuse, flat, prisms, steeple or spindle, helmet, or crown have been identified. The thumblift on the stein usually represented the unit's state of origin or branch of service. Stein body size was usually the standard 1/2 liter. Maker's marks usually are found on pottery steins. Porcelain steins were rarely marked by the maker.

Mettlach military steins were only made in pottery. They were marked on the bottom with an incised stock or mold number and usually were dated.

References: J. L. Harrell, *Regimental Steins,* The Old Soldier Press, 1979; Gary Kirsner, *The Mettlach Book,* Seven Hills Books, 1983; Gary Kirsner & Jim Gruhl, *The Stein Book,* Seven Hills Books, 1985; Dr. Eugene Manusov, *Encyclopedia of Character Steins,* Wallace Homestead,

1976; R. H. Mohr, *Mettlach Steins & Their Prices,* Rockford, rev. 4th edition, 1972; R. H. Mohr, *Mettlach Steins,* privately printed, 9th edition, 1982; James R. Stevenson, *Antique Steins, A Collectors' Guide,* Cornwall Books, 1982; Mike Wald, *HR Steins,* SCI Publications, 1980.

Collectors' Club: Stein Collectors International, P.O. Box 463, Kingston, N.J. 08528. Membership: $20.00. *Prosit,* quarterly.

Museums: Milwaukee Art Center, Milwaukee, Wisconsin.

REPRODUCTION ALERT: For more than twenty years, several German firms have reproduced regimental type steins. The reproductions, usually made only in porcelain, have different physical characteristics and historical inaccuracies. The firms used only the finial type of lid and tapered bodies as opposed to the straight bodies on original regimentals. Smooth transfers appear on the reproductions. Lids on the reproductions are stamped from a single piece mold and have no seam line.

Collecting Hints-Regimental Steins: Collectors favor steins with inlaid lids. The inlay is a decorated stoneware disk that is set into a pewter rim. The design in the lid is an extension of the colors and designs on the main body of the stein. A few steins did come without lids or with an all pewter lid in a variety of designs. Steins with missing lids are generally reduced 50 percent in value.

After the destruction caused by World War II, locating regimental steins became difficult. Occasionally some do surface from German attics or barns.

DESIGN

1/4 L, center portrait medallion of young girl (A)	**50.00**
1/2 L	
Art Nouveau style scrolling design and inscription, pewter lid, Westerwald	**45.00**
Bulbous middle with loops, rust, green, blue, and white geometric design, brass lid and thumbpiece, Munich	**500.00**
Incised purple violets, gray ground .	**100.00**
Ironstone, brown glaze, pewter lid, unmarked (A)	**25.00**
Manganese floral sprigs, turquoise rect panels, manganese diaperwork, pewter foot and lid, mid 18th C, Berlin (A)	**330.00**
Painted geometric design, multicolored, Germany (A)	**25.00**
Salt glaze, incised cobalt and gray panel of two roosters on branch, pewter lid with crest thumbpiece .	**65.00**

Stoneware
Blue stenciled "H. B.," pewter lid, "L. Morey Munchen" (A) **20.00**
Gothic style relief design, gray ground, pewter inlay lid (A) ... **45.00**
Stylized leaves and wheat, full figure finial, pewter thumbpiece, Germany **125.00**
Yellowware, tan band, engraved "F. D. U. 1760," pewter lid, thumbpiece (A) **140.00**

FIGURAL

1/4 L
Modeled face of monk, multicolored, unmarked **160.00**
Monk, black robe, holding stein, Germany **90.00**
1/2 L
Bismark Radish, pewter thumbpiece with man's head, "Musterschutz" **450.00**
Dureturm Tower, scene of Hans Sachs on body, pewter lid in shape of roof, "L. Ostermayer-Nurnberg" . **200.00**
Gaudeamus skull, white, red and black trim, unmarked **265.00**
Monk, blue and gray salt glaze, skull cap and robe **175.00**
Nun, black and white habit, pewter thumbpiece, lithophane base, unmarked **365.00**
Pig, smoking, 7" h, Musterschutz ... **325.00**
Umbrella man, multicolored (A) **1,000.00**

METTLACH

#675, 1/2 L, barrel design (A) **80.00**
#1028, relief, man with hay scene
1/2 L **180.00**
2/3 L **260.00**
#1100, 1/3 L, relief of peasants, inlaid pewter lid (A) **100.00**
#1132, 1/2 L, etched, man fiddling and dancing with crocodile, "Castle" mark **650.00**
#1394, 1/2 L, etched, French card ... **435.00**
#1403, 1/2 L, etched, bowling scene, sgd "Worth" **425.00**
#1467, 1/2 L, relief, four panels of hunting, fruit picking, farming, and weaving **300.00**
#1520, 1/2 L, etched, Prussian eagle . **525.00**
#1526, 1 L, PUG, Quilmes Brewery (A) **150.00**
#1526/603, 1/2 L, PUG, drinkers scene, "Castle" mark **155.00**
#1650. 1 L, tapestry, mountaineer **350.00**
#1786, 1/2 L, etched, St Florian putting fire out **650.00**
#1861, 1/2 L, etched, Frederick III ... **475.00**
#1909, 1/2 L, PUG, man playing harp to moon with cat and monkey (A) .. **200.00**

#1916, 2.15 L, etched, cavalier drinking scene, porcelain insert, pewter lid **1,450.00**
#1938, 1/4 L, mosaic inlay, "Castle" mark **165.00**
#1997, 1/2 L, etched and PUG, George Ehret Brewer, inlaid lid **250.00**
#2002, 1/2 L, etched, Town of Munich design, "Castle" mark **500.00**
#2009, 1/2 L, etched, Werner and Margarette dancing, sgd "F. Stuck" **575.00**
#2024, 1/2 L, etched, shield of Berlin **600.00**
#2038, 3.8 L, etched and relief, Town of Rodenstein **3,800.00**
#2077, 1/2 L, raised design of owl on book, white lining, pewter top **225.00**

Mettlach, #2065, 1½ L, etched, multicolored, jeweled base, sgd "Schlitt," $1,100.00.

#2086, 1/4 L, relief, dancing scene .. **175.00**
#2091, 1/2 L, etched, St Florian pouring water on man's head **675.00**
#2134, 3/10 L, etched, gnome in nest with two steins (A) **1,500.00**
#2140, 1/2 L, 873 Inf. Reg. NR 74 ... **575.00**
#2179/962, 1/4 L, PUG, gnomes drinking, pewter lid **150.00**
#2184, 3/10 L, PUG, gnomes and beavers design, pottery insert on lid **325.00**
#2184/966, 1/2 L, PUG, gnomes drinking **250.00**
#2190, 1/2 L, etched, bicycle scene with seven bicycles, "Castle" mark . **650.00**
#2238, 1/2 L, etched, 7th Reg. Armory, eagle, and flag, "Castle" mark **1,200.00**
#2246, 3/10 L, blue and cream dancing peasants **200.00**
#2278, 1/2 L, etched, 4F motif, sporting events (A) **1,300.00**
#2333/1032, 1/3 L, PUG, gnomes drinking, pewter lid **150.00**
#2348/1022, 3.3 L, PUG, musician, man, and woman **350.00**

#2373, 1/2 L, etched, St. Augustine, Florida, alligator handle, "Castle" mark **675.00**

#2382, 1/2 L, etched, Thirsty Knight design **570.00**

#2430, 3.0 L, etched, cavalier drinking (A) **1,200.00**

#2520, 1 L, etched, student and barmaid, sgd "H. S." **900.00**

#2716, 1/2 L, etched, waitress serving two men, pottery insert on lid **650.00**

#2721, etched and glazed, cabinet maker, "Castle" mark **900.00**

#2796, 3 L, etched, Scene of Heidelberg **1,600.00**

#5004, 1/2 L, faience, coat of arms design **250.00**

REGIMENTAL

1/2 L, 3rd Eisenbahn dated 1910–11 and Betreibs dated 1911–12, locomotive finial, Merkelbach & Wicke . **950.00**

1/2 L, 7 Chevauleger, 4 Esk. Straubing (A) **425.00**

1/2 L, 86th Field Maintenance Crew #1, pewter lid, airplane finial, nude lithophane, W. W. II, Germany **75.00**

1/2 L, 109th Regt Karlsruhe **250.00**

1/2 L, 113 Inf Regt Freiburg **245.00**

1/2 L, 121 Inf Regt Ludwigsburg **250.00**

1/2 L, 123 Grenadiers Regt Ulm **300.00**

1/2 L, 127th Inf Reg Ulm **300.00**

1/2 L, 180th Inf Reg Greundau **240.00**

1/2 L, pottery, 7th Regt of Foot Artillery, dated 1907–09, Germany **550.00**

1/2 L, pottery, 14th Hussar Regt, dated 1908–11, multicolored, Germany .. **975.00**

1/2 L, pottery, 20th Ulan Regt, dated 1905-08, multicolored, Germany ... **625.00**

SCENIC

1/4 L

Cupids and young maidens, multicolored, pewter lid, Germany (A) ... **45.00**

Raised design of woman holding Cologne cathedral and workers in fields, grapes on lower portion, pewter lid inscribed "1840," unmarked **175.00**

1/2 L

Blacksmith scene, multicolored, imp "HR 4616" (A) **150.00**

Decal, German man and woman, incised lid, unmarked **165.00**

Faience, multicolored scene of boy wheeling another in barrow, buildings and shrubs, pewter lid and foot, mid 18th C, Erfurt (A) **440.00**

"Gruss Aus Rothenberg," photo,

cream ground, pink and purple flowers, lithophane base of castle on mountain, "M. Wossner, Rothenberg" **110.00**

Handpainted scene of monks sampling ales, cobalt ground, gold, SP fittings, late 19th C, Austria (A) ... **500.00**

Horseman accepting stein from girl in window, pewter lid, imp "HR 439" (A) **300.00**

Porcelain

Printed scene of porcelain restorer, pewter lid, c1880 .... **100.00**

Scene of man and woman, period clothes, lithophane of hunter leaving cottage, molded pewter top and brass support (A) **45.00**

Pottery

Armored knights in three scenes, late 19th C, Germany (A) **70.00**

Handpainted dancing scene, multicolored, late 19th C, Germany (A) **45.00**

PUG, cavalier head with stein, cards, and dice, cream ground, white lining, pewter top, unmarked **175.00**

Relief

Garden scene, multicolored, Germany (A) **20.00**

Gnomes carrying mugs and vegetables, tan ground, Germany ... **75.00**

Stoneware

Emb polychrome tavern scene, pewter lid (A) **45.00**

Gray relief of procession of animals carrying dead hunter, Germany **200.00**

Village Dancers, Musterschutz **235.00**

1 L

Emb medallions of biblical scenes, green and brown enamels, pewter lid (A) **55.00**

Etched scene of two knights and innkeeper **325.00**

Etched stoneware, tavern scene, squire and tavern keeper, floral bands and legend, Germany **235.00**

2 L

Pottery, molded figures of woman and man in armor, dark green, red and cobalt glazes, dolphin figure thumbrest, pewter lid, Germany **160.00**

STIRRUP CUPS

Staffordshire, England
c1770 to 1900

History: Whieldon made the first earthenware stirrup cups. They date about 1770 and were in the shape of fox masks. Later animal shapes included deer, stag, hare, and bear heads.

The Staffordshire potters made a wide variety of stirrup cups and they were rarely marked. Until 1825 the earthenware stirrup cups were well modeled and colored in naturalistic tones. After that date, quality decreased.

During the last quarter of the 19th century, stirrup cups were made in soft paste porcelain by Derby, Rockingham, and Coalport. In addition to wild animal heads, bull dog, bull terriers, setters, and dalmatian heads were manufactured.

Boar Head, 2½" l, iron-red, puce, and
  blue accents, c1840, England (A) ... **385.00**
Brook Trout, 5" l, natural colors, gilt,
  "The Angler's Delight," on rim,
  c1820, Derby (A) **1,650.00**
Bulldog Head, 5" l, brown, black, and
  iron-red accents, gilt collar, c1840,
  Staffordshire (A) **1,320.00**
Dalmatian Head, 5" l, blue and black
  splashes, late 19th C, Continental (A) **880.00**
Fish Head, 5" l, creamware, black eyes
  and gilt rim, inscribed "The Angler's
  Delight", c1880 (A) **600.00**

Fox Head, 5" l, orange-brown, black muzzle, eyes and rim, cracked, (A) $225.00.

Fox Head
  4½" l
    Iron-red and gray hair, gilt collar,
      inscribed "Tally Ho," c1800,
      Derby (A) **880.00**
    Manganese, yellow, brown, and
      green accents, c1775, Whieldon
      (A) **1,210.00**
  4⅝" l, natural colors, gilt collar,
    plaque inscribed "TANTIVY,"
    c1830 (A) **335.00**
  4¾" l, brown and ochre accents,
    band of painted foliage on int. rim,
    c1800, Pratt, (A) **350.00**
  4⅞" l, brown and tan, black muzzle,
    unmarked, Staffordshire (A) **75.00**
  5" l, streaked pink luster, c1810, Staf-
    fordshire (A) **715.00**
  6½" l, pearlware, orange and blue,
    c1790, unmarked **1,600.00**

Hare Head, 6" l, brown and beige fur,
  c1820, Staffordshire (A) **2,100.00**
Hound Head
  4½" l, brown patches on coat and
    ears, black features, mid 19th C,
    Staffordshire (A) **300.00**
  5" l, creamware, brown, black, and
    gray accents, black collar, late 18th
    C, imp "Neale & Co" (A) **1,050.00**
  5¼" l, brown splashes, c1810, Staf-
    fordshire (A) **300.00**
  5½" l, white, gilt collar and locket,
    c1826, iron-red "griffin and Bra-
    meld" mark, Rockingham (A) **1,430.00**
  6" l, black basalt, c1790, imp
    "Turner" (A) **1,210.00**
Ram Head, 6½" l, curled horns and
  brown fleece, pink collar, late 19th C,
  Continental (A) **1,000.00**
Stag Head, 4¾" l, brown, olive antlers,
  wood stand, c1780, Whieldon, repaired, (A) **825.00**
Wolfhound Head, 7¾" l, natural colors,
  foliate molded collar, mid 19th C,
  Continental (A) **550.00**

STONEWARE

London and Staffordshire, England
c1670 to Present

History: Stoneware, made from clay to which some sand had been added, was fired at a higher temperature than ordinary earthenwares and became partly vitrified and impervious to liquids. Often it was glazed by throwing salt into the kiln at full heat. (See Salt Glaze.)

Stoneware was first made in England in 1672 when John Dwight founded Fulham Pottery and received a patent. He started by making copies of German wine jugs called "greybeards" and also modeled portrait busts, jugs, mugs, and red clay teapots. Dwight died in 1703; Fulham Pottery was carried on by his family. Dwight's examples were unmarked.

In Staffordshire John and Philip Elers made red stonewares and also introduced salt glazing and other improvements. Stoneware was made by firms throughout the Staffordshire Potteries district. Most stoneware was utilitarian in nature, but some of the useful wares were given a decorative treatment.

The Morleys made brown salt glazed stonewares in Nottingham between 1700 and 1799. Doulton & Watts were the best known and largest manufacturer of commercial stonewares. English stoneware is still made, especially by present day studio potters like Bernard Leach, Charles Vyse, and Michael Cardew.

References: J. F. Blacker, *The A. B. C. of English Salt Glaze Stoneware from Dwight to Doulton,* Stanley Paul & Co., 1922; Adrean Oswald, R. J. C. Hildyard & R. G. Huges, *English Brown Stoneware 1670–1900,* Faber & Faber, 1982.

Museums: British Museum, London, England; Cincinnati Art Museum, Cincinnati, Ohio; County Museum, Truro, England; Victoria & Albert Museum, London, England.

Urn, 12″ h, blue design, gray body, c1860, "Germany," $125.00.

Ale Set, 9¾″ h pitcher, six mugs, blue emb scene of drinking monk (A) **115.00**
Bottle, 7⅞″ h, molded satyr's masks on two sides in rococo scrolls, floral clusters on two sides, attributed to Bottger, c1710–15 (A) **7,150.00**
Chamberstick, 4¼″ h, sq tapered base, grape vines and leaves in plum, edged in dark plum, c1800, unmarked **375.00**
Cider Jug, 13½″ h, brown, blue flowerheads on shoulder and three oval armorial panels in foliage cartouches, oviform, 17th C, Germany (A) **285.00**
Creamer, relief border of blue grape vines, angular handle, imp "WEDG-WOOD" (A) **40.00**
Cup, 6¼″ h, gray body molded with animals and trees, brown banded rim, three hound handles, c1840, Lambeth (A) **500.00**
Dish, 12¼″ l, painted sprays of colored flowers and insects, oval, c1760, Germany (A) **235.00**
Figure, 11″ h, brown lion, paw on ball, rect base, applied vines, England ... **475.00**
Flask
　3″ h, molded busts of Alexander and Roxanne, named in bands, molded grotesque masks on necks, man-

ganese and blue accents, 18th C, Lambeth, pr (A) **170.00**
8¾″ h, molded rosettes, applied panels of classical figures, hexagon, fitted pewter neck and screw cov, 17th C, unmarked **600.00**
8⅞″ h, molded concentric florals and foliage, circ, screw top, 18th C, Germany (A) **170.00**
Food Mold, 8½″ l, 6½″ w, corn motif, c1880 .... **55.00**
Inkwell, Imari colors and design, sander and two cov wells, kidney shape, fish shape handle, c1820, England, repaired cov (A) **350.00**
Jar
　6″ h, blue and white, applied ivy and flower knob, cov, unmarked (A) .. **45.00**
　8″ h, cobalt blue floral design, open handles, Germany (A) **30.00**
Jug
　6½″ h, tan imp foliage between flutes and ozier panels, neck with scrolling foliage and mask heads, silver rim mount with "TMR", 17th C, Sieburg **2,000.00**
　7″ h, Bellarmine, applied mask, armorial medallion, brown salt glaze, strap handle, Rhenish (A) **300.00**
　8″ h, relief of Bacchanalian figures and trees, brown glazed ribbed and lobed borders, Sheffield cov, c1800 (A) **200.00**
　8⅝″ h
　　Bellarmine, applied mask and medallion on front, dark mottled glaze, ovoid, grooved neck and handle (A) **165.00**
　　Molded band of trellis reserved with pelican and chicks in medallion, two coats of arms with "HK," brown glaze, ribbed neck, loop handle, c1600 (A) **600.00**
　9⅜″ h, applied black medallions, brown speckled glaze, pewter lid, "R. Merkelback 2255" (A) **135.00**
　10″ h, Bellarmine, bearded mask below neck, three oval panels with crown over heart, brown glaze (A) **415.00**
　10⅝″, molded sunburst medallion and foliage, blue and manganese, gray ground, baluster shape, loop handle, mask spout, c1740, Germany (A) **70.00**
　11⅜″ h, molded spiral ribs covered with lustrous glaze, pewter lid, dated 1765, Bunzlau (A) **170.00**
　12¾″ h, blue floral design, ovoid, unmarked (A) **35.00**
　14″ h, Bellarmine, molded coats of arms on sides and fronts, Wild-

mann's head on neck, brown glaze, blue accents, c1600, France (A) . .**3,250.00**
14¼" h, three circ medallions of flowerheads, one flanked by lion passant, band of stamped florals, 17th C, Westerwald (A) **875.00**
Mask, 5¼" h, male face with corkscrew mustache and beard, glazed, late 18th C, Germany (A) **100.00**
Meat Dish, 17½" l, multicolored Japan pattern, "F. Morley & Co." (A) **200.00**
Milk Pitcher, 7⅞" h, raised cobalt design, Germany (A) **50.00**
Mold, 1⅜" - 2⅛" w, int. with light ochre glaze, Staffordshire, set of 7 (A) **100.00**
Mortar and Pestle, 4¼" d, mortar with ribbed foot, pestle with wooden handle, imp "WEDGWOOD" (A) **100.00**
Mug
  4⅛" h, ext. pierced with stylized foliage, neck with incised concentric rings, grooved loop handle, c1700 (A) **1,200.00**
  4⅞" h, blue and gray scenes of dwarfs, "Made in Germany" (A) . **35.00**
  5⅞" h, incised "GR" in floral medallion, blue accents, Westerward . **45.00**
  8⅛" h, raised sprigged central anchor medallion with Tudor roses, hunt scene and incised "1727," inscribed, tan-brown glaze, Vauxhall (A) **780.00**
  8¼" h, molded, bearded mask and oval lozenge, cov with mottled green glaze, gray body, 17th C, Germany (A) **115.00**
Mustard Jar, 5½" h, hound handled jug shape, pewter top and SP spoon, unmarked (A) **45.00**
Pitcher
  5¼" h, Oriental design, blue shades, octagonal, c1811, "Improved Stoneware-Dillwyn & Co." **65.00**
  8¾" h, beige glaze, molded mask spout, dolphin handle and feet, Continental (A) **110.00**
Plaque, 7" d, relief of Apollo with lyre surrounded by nymphs with instruments, Pegasus overhead, cream glaze, 17th C (A) **170.00**
Punch Set, 12½" w, 13" h cov bowl, eight cups, relief of grapes and leaves, cream body, reserves of castle scenes in relief, Germany **225.00**
Puzzle Jug, 18" h, green glaze, animal figures on shoulder around spout and handles, Germany (A) **150.00**
Spirit Barrel, 13⅛" h, gray, molded continuous band of flowerheads and animals divided by fluting, portrait medallion or crowned "VA" on ends, Westerwald (A) **1,100.00**

Spirit Flask, 8½" h, modeled as sailor holding pipe, standing on rockwork, applied anchor, oval base imp "WHO ARE YOU?", opening in hat, 19th C, Lambeth (A) **85.00**
Tankard
  6" h, applied continuous band of Christ and named Apostles, enameled border of scrolling fruit and foliage, inscribed pewter cov, c1670–75, Germany (A) **3,270.00**
  6¼" h, applied "GR", incised blue foliage, early 18th C, Westerwald (A) **85.00**
  6⅞" h, polished red body, reeded scroll handle, attributed to Bottger, c1715, Germany **4,800.00**
  7⅛" h, applied continuous scene of twelve Apostles, enamel accents, raised borders of foliage and scrollwork, pewter lid, dated 1693, German (A) **1,850.00**
  8¼" h, incised and molded flutes, lozenges and foliage in blue, yellow, and white glazes, baluster shape, pewter lid, 17th C, Germany (A) . **715.00**
  9" h, light brown, upper and lower ribbing, cylindrical, contemporary silver cov, c1705, Germany (A) .. **625.00**
  9⅞" h, painted Oriental figure between palms, florals, and rockwork, cylindrical, inscribed pewter cov, early 19th C, Germany (A) .. **520.00**
  10¼" h, polychrome florals, blue line borders, loop handle with manganese swirls, pewter foot rim and lid with initials and dated "1755", attributed to Erfurt **1,000.00**
  10⅝" h, light brown glaze and tan salt glaze, cylindrical, grooved borders, hinged pewter cov and foot, dated 1761, Germany (A) **480.00**
  10⅞" h, molded and incised foliage swags, blue accents, pewter cov dated 1788, Westerwald (A) **550.00**
Teapot, 4½" h, molded relief of floral and leaf arabesques, spaniel knob, imp "WEDGWOOD" (A) **75.00**
Vase
  6¼" h, applied molded band of hunting scene, bands of fruit and foliage, multicolored enamel accents, inscribed and dated 1671 (A) **8,600.00**
  6¾" h, raised oak leaf and limb design, flared shape, late 19th C, pr (A) **70.00**
Water Filter, cream glaze, lion mask handles, "Her Majestys' Royal Letters Patent", England (A) **75.00**
Wine Jar, 11" h, applied vines and berries, mask of Bacchus, pear shape, France **450.00**

STRAWBERRY CHINA

Staffordshire, England
1820 to 1860

History: Strawberry china ware, a soft earthenware produced by a variety of English potteries, was made in three design motifs: strawberry and strawberry leaves (often called strawberry luster), green feather-like leaves with pink flowers (often called cut-strawberry, primrose or old strawberry), and the third motif with the decoration in relief. The first two types are characterized by rust red moldings. Most examples have a creamware ground and are unmarked.

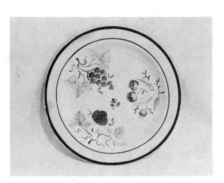

Plate, 5⅝" d, $75.00.

Bowl
  6¼" d, vine border (A) **350.00**
  8½" d, unmarked **130.00**
Cup and Saucer
  Pink border (A) **100.00**
  Pink border, scalloped edge (A) **220.00**
  Porcelain, purple luster, enameled
    strawberries (A) **12.00**
  Strawberry and vine border, chipped
    (A) **60.00**
Gravy Creamer, vine border (A) **85.00**
Plate
  5¾" d, strawberry center, strawberry
    and vine border, chipped (A) **40.00**
  7" d, basket of strawberries in center,
    strawberry and vine border (A) ... **155.00**
  7¼" d
    Leaf and strawberry center, strawberry and vine border (A) **400.00**
    Pink basket filled with strawberries
     and flowers (A) **65.00**
    Vine border (A) **75.00**
  9¾" d, strawberry center, strawberry
    and vine border, chipped (A) **25.00**
Sauceboat, 5⅛" h, ironstone, underglaze blue with red, green, and luster
  (A) **150.00**

Sugar, cov
  Double handles (A) **75.00**
  Raised strawberries, strawberry knob
    (A) **130.00**
Tea Set, teapot, creamer, cov sugar, unmarked **400.00**
Teabowl and Saucer, vine border **225.00**
Teapot
  Raised strawberries (A) **150.00**
  Raised strawberries and rope borders
    (A) **300.00**
  Vine border, octagonal cov (A) **120.00**
Waste Bowl
  5¼" d, 3½" h, multicolored overall
    strawberry design, unmarked (A) . **115.00**
  5⅝" d, 2¾" h, strawberry, pink band
    border (A) **120.00**

A
SUSIE COOPER
PRODUCTION
CROWN WORKS,
BURSLEM
ENGLAND

SUSIE COOPER

Burslem, Staffordshire, England
1932 to Present

History: Susie Cooper studied at the Burslem Art School in Staffordshire in 1922. She made jugs, bowls, and vases in stoneware with Art Nouveau style incised designs. When Cooper finished her studies, she became a designer for A. E. Gray & Co., Ltd. at Hanley, Staffordshire in 1925.

She founded Susie Cooper Pottery, Burslem in 1932. Cooper designed and manufactured functional shape, earthenware tablewares with bright floral and abstract designs. Cooper introduced the "can" shape for the coffeepot, the straight sided shape that has become a universal design. Art Deco designs of bright oranges, greens, and browns are found on her later wares.

Susie Cooper eventually became part of the Wedgwood Group. Her patterns now decorate fine bone china tableware with the Wedgwood-Susie Cooper Design backstamp. The "can" coffeepot shape is still used.

References: Reginald G. Haggar, *Century of Art Education in the Potteries,* 1953.

Museums: Victoria & Albert Museum, London, England.

Bowl, 6" d, molded floral pattern **75.00**
Coffee Service, coffeepot, milk jug, sugar, six coffee cans and saucers, cream crescent moons on orange ground (A) **50.00**

Cups and Saucers, orange, blue, green and light blue with cream crescents, "A Suzie Cooper Production, Crown Works Burslem, England," set of 4, $100.00.

Cream Pitcher, 4" h, violet, rose, green, and yellow florals, cream ground ... **35.00**
Cup and Saucer, Art Deco style
   Dark red roses **10.00**
   Multicolored design **30.00**
Demitasse Cup and Saucer, rose and gray rings **15.00**
Dinner Service, concentric circles in pastels, set of 56 pcs **300.00**
Dinner Service, part, gray, rust, and brown concentric circ decor (A) **60.00**
Tea Service, teapot, creamer, sugar, two cups and saucers, salmon int., cream ext., teapot with cream and salmon ext. **118.00**
Tea Set, teapot, creamer, sugar
   Brown stars and green bands, cream ground **300.00**
   Handpainted hunt scenes on front and reverse **130.00**

CAMBRIAN POTTERY
DILLWYN & CO. SWANSEA
BEVINGTON & CO. SWANSEA

Wales
c1814 to Early 1820s

History: Swansea potters produced a large variety of earthenwares during the 18th and 19th centuries. Their porcelains, like those of Nantgarw, are very translucent, have fine glazes, and feature excellent floral painting.

After experiencing a lack of funds in 1814, Billingsley and Walker came from Nantgarw to work with Lewis Dillwyn at Swansea. Billingsley and Walker made fine porcelains between 1814

and 1817 at Swansea and then returned to start again at Nantgarw. Production continued at Swansea until the early 1820s. Many Swansea wares were artist decorated.

Swansea Welsh porcelain blanks were quite popular with London decorators.

References: W. D. John, *Swansea Porcelain*, Ceramic Book Co., 1958; Kildare S. Meager, *Swansea & Nantgarw Potteries*, Swansea, 1949; E. Morton Nance, *The Pottery & Porcelain of Swansea & Nantgarw*, Batsford, 1942.

Museums: Art Institute of Chicago, Chicago, Illinois; Glynn Vivian Art Gallery, Swansea, Wales.

REPRODUCTION ALERT: Swansea porcelain has been copied for many decades in Europe and England. Marks should be studied carefully.

Cabinet Cup, 4" h, painted named view of Dunbarton Rock, salmon-pink ground, gilt vermicule, c1814–22 (A) **90.00**
Center Dish, 9¾" d, exotic bird on branch in landscape, molded border, scrolling flowers, flared foot, c1820, iron-red script "Swansea" mark (A) . **300.00**
Coffee Cup and Saucer, famille rose palette of Orientals on terrace with pavilion, gilt scroll border and handle, c1815 (A) **265.00**
Cream Jug, 4½" h, printed and colored "Mandarin" pattern, int. rim with gilt scroll border and panels of trees and foliage, red "Swansea" mark **235.00**
Cup and Saucer
   Gilt scrollwork, "London" shape, c1814–22 (A) **50.00**
   Molded band of scrolling flowers, c1820, cracks (A) **85.00**
   Painted full pink roses and green leaves, gilt scrolled panels reserved on turquoise, gilt oeil-de-perdrix ground, ribbed bodies, c1820 (A) **235.00**
Dessert Dish, 12½" H-H, painted sprays of flowers, gilt formal border, rect, gilt handles, c1820–22 (A) **270.00**
Dessert Service, 12¾" w dbl handled oblong tazza, two 9¼" d saucers, two 9" sq plates, twelve 8¼" d plates, famille rose style, pheasant centers, four gilt reserves of flowers, borders of lotus, chrysanthemums and band of green hatchwork, c1815, iron-red "Swansea" marks (A) **4,180.00**
Dish
   8¼" sq, border molded with C-scrolls and flowers, painted with four finches in landscapes, gilt line rims, c1815 .... **375.00**
   11⅝" l, painted scattered specimen flowers, dbl handles, c1820 (A) .. **130.00**

Goblet

4⅜" h, copper luster ground, multicolored molded putti riding lions on blue band, c1820 (A) ...   **55.00**

4¾" h

Copper luster ground, black transfer and enamels of Oriental scene on white band, c1830 (A) **55.00**

Copper luster ground, pink luster houses on blue ground, c1830 (A) **55.00**

5" h, copper luster ground, three multicolored rose sprigs, black edged green band, c1830 (A) **55.00**

Inkstand, 3⅞" h, modeled snail shell with roses, green leaves, and gilt seaweed, butterfly knob, c1814–22 (A) **430.00**

Jug, 5" h, pink luster floral sprays on pink ground below wide copper luster border, pear shape, pink luster edged handle, spout, and rim, c1825 (A) ..   **70.00**

Mug, 3⅜" h, pink luster houses with trees, engine turned basketwork bands with pink luster, border of lustered foliage in ovals, c1815 (A) **165.00**

Pitcher, 6½" h, Chinese pattern, multicolored **300.00**

Plate, 7¼" d, blue and white Oriental design, gold rim, c1785, imp "SWANSEA," $125.00.

Plate

7⅞" d

Painted pink and purple luster of swimming swans, green wicker molded borders, c1811–17, imp "DILLWYN & CO., SWANSEA", pr (A) **110.00**

Purple luster painting of cottage, green rim (A) **55.00**

8¼" d

Center painted bouquet of summer flowers, molded cartouche border with green and gilding, c1820 (A) **620.00**

Center painted with marigold and flower sprigs, gilt scroll and diaper border, molded foliate rim, c1820–22 (A) **365.00**

8⅜" d

Border molded with floral cartouches and painted birds in branches, c1820 ....   **325.00**

Center painted basket of flowers, gilded cavetto, butterflies on border, gilt dentil rim, c1814–22 (A)   **500.00**

Ten pink roses, each surrounded by green leaves, gold weed bed, gold banded rim, c1816, imp "DILLWYN & CO." **150.00**

8½" d

Center pink rose spray, border of green flowers, gold ground, c1820, imp "SWANSEA" (A) ...   **315.00**

Painted arms of Hereford and motto, lobed border with urns of flowers and foliate swags, beaded rim, c1815–20 (A) **1,235.00**

8¾" d, painted bouquets and sprays in scroll and foliage borders, c1815, set of 8 ....   **350.00**

9" d, multicolored painted florals, white ground, pierced dbl handles, late 19th C, unmarked **90.00**

9¼" d, center pink rose sprays, fluted borders, band of pink cabbage roses and leaves on gilt speckled ground, gilt foliate bands, iron-red "SWANSEA" mark, pr (A) **275.00**

9⅝" d, blue transfer of scattered bouquets, c1820 ....   **135.00**

9⅞" d, central coat of arms in foliate wreath and sprigs, molded and gilt feathered rim with urns and sprigs, c1802–10 (A) **560.00**

Platter, 18½" l, painted brown basket of multicolored flowers, gilt stippled and scroll border on cavetto, three pink rose sprays on rim, c1818, imp "SWANSEA" mark, repaired (A) **520.00**

Sauce Tureen, 7" d, cov, matching stand, painted cornflowers and sprigs between gilt line borders, entwined dolphin knob, c1814–22 (A) **250.00**

Stand, 7⅝" d, center painted with flower spray, green enamel borders with gold, molded floral C-scroll edge, green "SWANSEA" mark (A) **100.00**

Sugar, cov, 6" h, painted pink roses, gilt line and leaf borders, c1820 (A) **160.00**

Vase, 10" h, painted classical scenes, wreaths of biscuit flowers, gilt mask and horn handles, fixed slate base, c1815, pr (A) **1,465.00**

SWEDEN-GENERAL

Marieberg, near Stockholm, Sweden 1758 to 1788

History: In 1758 Johann Ehrenreich established a factory at Marieberg, near Stockholm, with the intention of making porcelain, but wound up producing faience instead. Pierre Berthevin, a porcelain expert, came to the factory and became director in 1766. Berthevin was the first in Sweden to make porcelain of the soft paste type. Pieces were decorated in the Classical design. Forms included cream jars, pitchers, small vases, and figures. Faience continued to be made and was decorated utilizing the transfer printing technique.

Henrik Sten took over in 1768. Hard paste porcelain was introduced during this period. Only small forms were made; no dinner services were produced. Custard cups, cream pots, and teapots were the most popular shapes. The decoration included both Classical and Rococo styles. Some figures in Swedish Rococo style costumes were made. Faience manufacturing continued. Strasburg faience was imitated in a table service for Baron Liljencrantz, the factory's owner. Around 1770 attempts were made to duplicate Wedgwood's creamware.

Marieberg was sold to Rorstrand in 1782 and Sten resigned. Schumer took over until the works closed in 1788.

Marieberg's faience and porcelain pieces were marked.

Gustavsberg, Island of Farsta, Sweden 1827 to Present

The Gustavsberg factory was established on the island of Farsta in 1827. The factory first produced faience and later made transfer printed creamware in the English style.

Samuel Gidenius enlarged and modernized the factory during the 1850s. Wilhelm Odelberg took control in 1869. During the 1860s, decorative majolica and bone porcelain were introduced. Parian was made from the 1860s until the late 19th century. After William Odelberg died in 1914, his two sons took over.

Between 1897 and 1914 G. Wennerberg was the artistic director. He made pottery decorated with simple floral designs in the sgraffito technique. In 1937 the firm was called AB Gustavsberg Fabriker.

The dinnerwares featured simple designs. "Elite" was very popular. "Amulet" in red, blue, or gray was designed by Stig Lindberg, the company's leading artist. Wilhelm Koge, another designer, modeled "Argenta" with silver and green backgrounds inspired by Persian wares. He also created "Pyro," "Praktika II," and "Carrara." Other sets included "Gray Bands" and "Marguente" in the Art Nouveau style.

Vase, cov, 15½" h, faience, multicolored grapes and vines, "Marieberg," pr, (A) $1,600.00.

Bowl, 12" d, applied silver fruit in basket, mottled turquoise ground, "GUS-TAVSBERG/KAGE 1035I" **200.00**
Box, cov, 3¾" sq, "Argenta" pattern, florals, #122D, Gustavsberg **60.00**
Charger, 17½" d, silver design, mottled turquoise ground, Gustavsberg **150.00**
Cigarette Box, 5" l, gun metal finish, Trojan horse finial, "Upsala-Ekeby, Made in Sweden" **15.00**
Tea Caddy, 3¼" h, corners molded with leaves, edged in pink enclosing painted flower bouquets, c1780, Marieberg, neck reduced (A) **150.00**
Vase
  8" h, nude woman holding basket of flowers in silver, florals on reverse, turquoise ground, "GUSTAUVS-BERG ARGENTA 1209" and "anchor" marks, pr **700.00**
  9" h, pottery, streaked ochre glaze, cylindrical, trumpet neck, sgd "Freiberg, J. G.," Gustavsberg (A) **65.00**
  12" h, applied silver bird and snake on front, stylized florals on reverse, mottled turquoise ground, "GUS-TAVSBERG/ARGENTA/MADE IN SWEDEN" **350.00**

14" h, cov, puce painted riverscape, relief of foliage swags, urn shaped, gilt scroll handles, sq black base, c1780, Marieberg **400.00**

15½" h, iron-red sporting trophy tied with ribbon, relief of foliage swags, urn shaped, gilt scroll handles, cov with ball finial and molded foliage wreath, c1780, Marieberg **400.00**

NYON
1780 - 1860

1906-Present

SWITZERLAND

Schoren, near Zurich
1763 to 1790

Nyon
1781 to 1813

History: Two porcelain factories were established in Switzerland: one at Zurich and the other at Nyon.

Jacob Dortu from Berlin along with Ferdinand Muller, his father-in-law, founded the Nyon factory in 1781. Porcelain tablewares were made in the Louis XVI Parisian style until 1813. Delicate decoration was done with subtle colorations and good quality gilding. English-style stonewares were made and marked "Dortu & Cie."

Museums: National Museum, Zurich, Switzerland; Sevres Museum, Sevres, France.

REPRODUCTION ALERT: Many imitations having cruder decorations and bright blue marks were made at German factories and sold to travelers in Swiss towns.

Additional Listings: Zurich.

Charger
14" d, slipware design of medieval knight on horseback, reverse inscribed "Fuhr. Ceramique J. Wanjenried, Thoune, Adrian Bubenberg" **50.00**

17" d, faience, central green petaled medallion with blue floral decor and cream swags on brown ground, 19th C, labeled (A) **100.00**

Chocolate Cup and Saucer, reserve of figural landscape, white and gilded ground, dbl handles, cov with gilded artichoke knob, Nyon (A) **450.00**

Cup and Saucer, blue floral banding with gilt swags, white ground, Nyon (A) **450.00**

Custard Cup, Cov
Blue and gold narrow borders of ribbons and swags, c1790, blue "fish" marks, Nyon, set of 6 (A) **1,660.00**

Flower garlands, white and gold borders, c1790, blue "fish" marks, Nyon, set of 6 (A) **2,275.00**

Dish, 10⅞" d, redware, cream slip scratched to form blue and brown bear and tulip above, floral border with brown dots, late 18th C, Berne (A) **880.00**

11¼" d, center painted with lovers in garden, turquoise border with floral panes **35.00**

Figure, 6⅝" d, boy and girl seated on rock, turquoise glaze and gilt accents, pr **160.00**

Jar, 8" h, brown and red enameled heart shaped wreath, drug inscription, knot on handle and foot, mid 17th C (A) . **300.00**

Tea Service, Part, teapot, small creamer, large creamer, cov sugar, eight small plates, eight large plates, six cups, seven saucers, multicolored cornflower design **150.00**

Teabowl and Saucer
Black and gold border suspending puce and gold swags, c1790, blue "fish" marks, Nyon (A) **425.00**

Border of pink flowers, gilt dentil rim, c1790, blue "fish" marks, Nyon, pr (A) **350.00**

Teapot Stand, 8⅛" l, roses and multicolored florals, gilt, c1790, blue "fish" mark, Nyon (A) **160.00**

Tile, 14½" w, 17½" h, tin glazed red stoneware, each panel depicts one of

Dish, 14¾" d, light yellow slip, yellow, green, blue, and tan relief design, incised rim, "Winterthur," (A) $5,500.00.

Four Seasons, multicolored, molded
self frame, mid 18th C, set of 4 ....**1,500.00**
Vase
8½" h, painted period figures in gardens, turquoise neck, pr (A) **90.00**
11" h, porcelain, painted butterflies
on gilt marbled ground, urn
shaped, dbl scrolling gilt handles,
sq marble base, early 19th C, Nyon
(A) **500.00**

TEA LEAF IRONSTONE

Staffordshire, England
c1856 to Present

History: The tea leaf pattern started about 1856
when Anthony Shaw of Burslem began decorating his white ironstone with three copper luster
leaves. At first it was called "Lustre Band and
Sprig." Later names were "Edge Line and Sprig"
and "Lustre Spray." The sprig eventually was
viewed as a tea leaf, thus giving the pattern its
name.

Much English tea leaf pattern ironstone china
was sent to the United States where it greatly
appealed to the American housewife. It was durable, white, and had a simple elegance.

Over thirty English potteries in Staffordshire
manufactured wares decorated with the tea leaf
pattern. The most prolific were Alfred Meakin
Potteries and Anthony Shaw. The tea leaf pattern
also was utilized at W. H. Gridley, Alcock Potteries, William Adams, Mellor, Taylor & Co.,
Wedgwood, and many others. Each company
used a slight variation of the tea leaf copper luster
pattern. Since all decoration was applied by
hand, no two designs are exactly alike, adding
to the charm of the ware. Powell & Bishop and
Bishop & Stonier also did the design in gold
luster.

References: Annise Doring Heaivilin, *Grandma's
Tea Leaf Ironstone*, Wallace-Homestead, 1981;
Jean Wetherbee, *A Look at White Ironstone*, Wal-
lace-Homestead, 1980.

Museums: Lincoln Home, Springfield, Illinois;
Sherwood Davidson House, Newark, Ohio; Ox
Barn Museum, Aurora, Oregon.

Collectors' Club: Tea Leaf International, P.O. Box
904, Mount Prospect, Illinois 60056. Membership: $10.00., *Tea Leaf Readings,* bi-monthly
publication.

REPRODUCTION ALERT: Some recent reproductions are noted for their poor coloration, uneven copper luster decoration, and lower weight.
Original ironstone examples are much heavier
than newer ceramic pieces.

Bacon Rasher, 5⅝" l, rect, "Alfred
Meakin," **30.00**

Bone Dish, 6⅝" l, 3¼" w, "Alfred
Meakin"
Crescent shape **45.00**
Scallop shape **45.00**
Bowl
5½" sq, "Alfred Meakin" **80.00**
9" d, 3½" h, "A.J. Wilkinson, England" **80.00**
9" sq, "Mellor-Taylor" **60.00**
Butter Dish, cov, matching insert
4⅜" sq, scalloped and ribbed,
"Wedgwood & Co." **120.00**
5¼" sq, "Wedgwood & Co." **75.00**
7" l, 5" w, "J. & G. Meakin" **110.00**
Butter Pat
2⅜" sq, "A. Shaw" **4.00**
2½" sq, ribbed, scalloped edges,
"Mellor, Taylor & Co.," set of 8 .. **60.00**
3" d, "Alfred Meakin" **8.00**
3⅛" d, "W. H. Grindley" **4.00**
Cake Plate
10" sq, "Fish Hook" pattern, dbl handles, "Alfred Meakin" **40.00**
11¾" l, 8¾" w, oval, "Mellor, Taylor
& Co." **65.00**
11⅞" H-H, "Sunburst" pattern, hexagon, "A. Shaw" **65.00**
Chamber Pot
8⅜" d, ribbed ext., "Mellor, Taylor &
Co." **100.00**
8½" d, cov, "Fish Hook" pattern,
"Alfred Meakin" **150.00**
8⅞" d, "Cable" pattern, "A. Shaw" **100.00**
Coffeepot, 9¼" h, bulbous shape "Arthur J. Wilkinson" **150.00**
Compote, 8¾" d, 5⅜" h, ftd, "A. Shaw,"
hairline on foot **250.00**
Creamer
5" h, rect, "A. Shaw" **125.00**
5⅛" h, rect, V-shaped lip, "Wedg-
wood & Co." **85.00**
6" h, "A. J. Wilkinson" **90.00**
Creamer and Sugar, bullet shape, "A.
Shaw" **100.00**
Cup and Saucer
Barrel shape, "Alfred Meakin" **30.00**
Cone shape, "Alfred Meakin" **45.00**
Handleless, "Lily of the Valley" pat-
tern, "A. Shaw" **75.00**
Tea leaf on int. of cup, "Edge, Malkin
& Co." **50.00**
Gravy Boat
Bamboo handle, "Grindley-England" **35.00**
"Bamboo" pattern, "Alfred Meakin" **30.00**
Four emb areas, "Wedgwood & Co." **30.00**
Nappy
4⅛" sq, "Alfred Meakin" **18.00**
4⅜" sq, "Fish Hook" pattern, "Alfred
Meakin" **8.00**
5" l, 3⅞" w, rect, "A. Shaw" **18.00**
5⅝" l, 3⅞" w, Alfred Meakin **18.00**

Left, plate, 4¼" d, raised tea leaf, border, imp "J & G Meakin," $35.00; center, cup and saucer, "Alfred Meakin," $70.00; right, pitcher, 6½" h, "Mellor & Taylor," $135.00.

5¾" l, 4⅛" w, oval, "A. Shaw," set of
4 . . . .   **50.00**

Pitcher

5½" h, "J. & G. Meakin" **110.00**

7" h, "Wedgwood & Co." **65.00**

7¼" h, "Fish Hook" pattern, "Alfred
Meakin" **165.00**

8⅜" h, bulbous shape, "Alcock" . . .   **125.00**

12" h, "Bishop & Stonier" **75.00**

Pitcher and Bowl

11¼" h pitcher, 14¼" d bowl, large
scallops and ribbing, "Burgess &
Leigh" **350.00**

12½" h pitcher, 14½" d bowl, "Fish
Hook" pattern, "Alfred Meakin" .   **185.00**

12½" h pitcher, 14¾" d bowl, "Bam-
boo" pattern, "Alfred Meakin" . . .   **350.00**

"A. J. Wilkinson" **90.00**

Plate

6½" d, dbl luster banding, c1872,
"Davenport" **20.00**

6¾" d, "Alfred Meakin" **8.00**

6⅞" d, "A. J. Wilkinson" **8.00**

7¼" d, "Alfred Meakin" **25.00**

9⅛" d, "Mellor, Taylor & Co." **14.00**

9½" d, "Huron" shape, c1858, "Ad-
ams" **25.00**

10" d, dbl luster banding, c1872,
"Davenport" **20.00**

Platter

10½" l, "Alfred Meakin, England" . .   **45.00**

12" l, "Alfred Meakin" **25.00**

12" l, 8½" w, "Alfred Meakin, Eng-
land" **20.00**

12" l, 9" w, "Alfred Meakin" **40.00**

12⅛" l, 8¾" w, "Alfred Meakin" . . .   **15.00**

14⅛" l, 10¼" w, "Alfred Meakin" . .   **15.00**

15¾" l, 11½" w, ribbed flange,
"Wedgwood & Co." **30.00**

16" l, "Anthony Shaw" **35.00**

Relish Dish

8⅜" l, 4½" w, rect, "Wedgwood &
Co." **22.00**

8⅝" l, "Bamboo" pattern, dbl handled, "W. H. Grindley," chip under
foot **15.00**

"Alfred Meakin" **15.00**

Sauce Dish, 8" sq, "W. H. Grindley" .   **5.00**

Sauce Tureen, cov

6" l, underplate, "Fish Hook" pattern,
"Alfred Meakin, England" **140.00**

6⅛" l, undertray, "Bamboo" pattern,
"Alfred Meakin, England" **90.00**

Shaving Mug

"Alfred Meakin" **48.00**

"Cable" pattern, "A. Shaw" **125.00**

8-sided, "Burgess & Leigh," flake on
foot **100.00**

Soap Dish

4¼" l, 3⅝" w, rect open style, con-
cave corners, "Arthur J. Wilkinson"   **200.00**

5⅜" l, cov, insert, "Bamboo" pattern,
"Alfred Meakin, England" **115.00**

5¾" l, cov, oval, "Alfred Meakin,"
chips on base and lid **20.00**

Soup Bowl

8⅞" d, "Alfred Meakin" **16.00**

9" d

"Burgess & Leigh" **16.00**

"Wedgwood & Co." **16.00**

10" d, flanged, "Meakin" **16.00**

10⅛" d, dbl luster banding, "Daven-
port" **25.00**

Soup Tureen, 9¾" l, 6⅝" w rect bowl,
11⁹⁄₁₆" l, 8¾" w tray, "Fish Hook" pattern, "Alfred Meakin, England," hair-
line on lid **450.00**

Sugar

6½" h, "Bamboo" pattern, "Alfred
Meakin, England" **55.00**

6¾" h, "Fish Hook" pattern, "Alfred
Meakin, England" **55.00**

7" h, "Pepper Leaf" motif, "Elsmore
& Forster" **100.00**

"Powell & Bishop" **75.00**

Teabowl, 5⅝" d

Barrel shape, "A. Shaw" **50.00**

"Lily of the Valley" pattern, "A.
Shaw" **75.00**

Teapot

9" h, "Davenport" **125.00**

9¼" h, "Pepper Leaf" motif, "Elsmore
& Forster," repair to spout **100.00**

9½" h

"Chinese" shape, "A. Shaw" **165.00**

Sq, "Powell & Bishop" **250.00**

"Teaberry" motif, "Clementson" . 225.00
9¾" h, "Cable" pattern, "Burgess &
Leigh" 175.00
"Empress" shape, "W. Adams & Co." 110.00
Rect shape, ribbing, "Mellor, Taylor
& Co." 110.00
Toothbrush Holder, 5" h
"A. Shaw" 165.00
"Bamboo" pattern, "Alfred Meakin" 125.00
"Fish Hook" pattern, "Alfred
Meakin" 50.00
Tray, 11" l, 7½" w, rect, ribbed border,
"Wedgwood & Co., England" 18.00
Vegetable Bowl
6⅛" l, 6½" w, melon ribbed, "Alfred
Meakin" 15.00
10" l, rect, "Burgess & Leigh" 50.00
10¼" d, cov, "Sunburst" pattern, hex-
agon, "A. Shaw" 100.00
10¼" d, 3⅛" h, pie crust edge,
"Alfred Meakin" 75.00
Vegetable Dish
8⅝" l, cov
"Fish Hook" pattern, rect, "Alfred
Meakin" 75.00
Rect, "Wedgwood & Co." 80.00
8⅞" l, cov, "Bamboo" pattern, rect,
"Alfred Meakin," hairline on lid .. 10.00
9½" l, ribbed int., "Wedgwood &
Co." 40.00
9¾" l, rect, "Wedgwood & Co." ... 90.00
Waste Bowl
5½" d, barrel shape, unmarked 50.00
5⅞" d, barrel shape, "A. J. Wilkinson" 25.00

TEPLITZ

**Bohemia, Germany, now
Czechoslovakia
1892 to 1945**

History: Several companies in the Turn-Teplitz
area manufactured art pottery in the late 19th
and early 20th century. Amphora was one of the
companies.

Ernst Wahliss of the Alexandria Works in Teplitz manfactured and decorated pieces in the
Art Nouveau style. In 1902 the factory bought
six hundred molds from the Imperial and Royal
Porcelain Manufactory in Vienna and made cop-

ies from them of earlier Vienna decorative porcelains and figures. After 1910 the firm manufactured faience wares. In 1925 the firm was
called Ernst Wahliss AG. The plant ceased operation in 1934.

Additional Listings: Amphora.

**Figure, 8½" h, sepia tones, c1910,
$175.00.**

Basket, 7" l, 9½" h, blown-out gold
flowers, matte green ground, applied
vines and branch handle, pierced border, imp red "RS & K Turn-Teplitz"
mark 265.00
Bowl, 3" d, enameled boy and dog, gray
ground, "Stellmacher" 75.00
Compote, 6" h, relief of woman and
flowers, Art Nouveau style 400.00
Ewer
5½" h, floral and gilt design on center
band, olive green neck and base,
matte finish, "RSK" 65.00
6½" h, hp pink and gold flowers, light
green ground, light pink neck, gold
twig handle 85.00
8½" h, inlaid cameos of bride and
groom, stars and jewels, "Austria"
and crown mark, pr 350.00
9½" h, red and pink roses, cream
ground, gold trim, red "crown"
mark 70.00
11¼" h, yellow flowers outlined in
gold, off-white ground, pierced design, gold handle and band at top 225.00
11½" h, floral encrusted decor (A) .. 230.00
Figure
7¼" h, young man, period clothes,
holding book, pearlized satin finish, unmarked 155.00
12½" h, young girl, peasant clothes,
basket resting on tree stump 350.00
15" h
Art Nouveau style lady, grape

wreath in hair, holding grapes, multicolored, sgd "Doebrieh" . **650.00**
Man and woman, court clothes, multicolored, pr **250.00**
20" h, bust of woman wearing ruffled cloak and gown, plumes in hair, pastel tinted matte glaze, "Stellmacher" **250.00**
24" h, young girl, water yoke and buckets, multicolored, unmarked . **510.00**
26½" h, bust of young woman, roses entwined in long hair, multicolored **3,300.00**
Jug, 8" h, man in classical dress smoking pipe, multicolored, bronze ground, "Stellmacher, Teplitz" **175.00**
Pitcher
3" h, enameled baby and dog, gray ground, "Stellmacher" **75.00**
3½" h, Dutch boy motif, green **35.00**
4" h, multicolored warrior on horseback, dark ground **100.00**
6¾" h, gold, ivory ground, molded bee on bamboo handle, "Stellmacher" **75.00**
Planter, 13" h, seated figure of Middle Eastern man playing stringed instrument, basket in background, bronze and cream **875.00**
Sugar, Cov, 5½" h, cobalt and coral enamels, gilding, dbl handles **70.00**
Vase
4½" h, grape design, applied leaf, dbl handles, c1890, "Imperial" **115.00**
4¾" h, polychrome drummer boy on dk green ground, dbl handled, "Stellmacher" **100.00**
5" h, multicolored scene of Grecian lady, "Stellmacher" **35.00**
5½" h
Enameled figure of woman, period clothes, "Stellmacher" **85.00**
Raised orange oak leaves, gold veining, applied irid dandelions, shaded blue ground, gold accents, gold speckled handle and trim **200.00**
7" h
Applied fruit clusters, lustered finish (A) **25.00**
Blue and lavender poppies, raised gold beading, four handles, red "crown" mark, pr **180.00**
Raised babies and goats on sides, shades of red and cobalt, gilt, "Stellmacher" **325.00**
7¼" h, multicolored scene, yellow luster ground, raised blue florals, two small handles, "Stellmacher" **115.00**
8¼" h, cavalier, multicolored enamels, gray ground, three rolled handles, gold "Stellmacher" mark ... **85.00**

9" h, green floral design, handled .. **70.00**
9¾" h, Art Nouveau stylized flowers, cobalt ground, gold speckling, unmarked **400.00**
10" h
Applied white flowers, cobalt ground, gold trim, narrow white neck **135.00**
Gold, green, and blue open work at top, four handles, "Ernst Wahliss" **500.00**
12" h
Painted landscape, raised white and gold floral designs, blue ground **300.00**
Raised raspberries, applied ribbons, green irid finish, dbl handles **375.00**
16" h, flowers and leaves, tan ground, gold trim, two small handles, c1880, "E. W." **450.00**
17¾" h, violet, green, and brown irises in relief, open neckwork modeled as iris flowerhead, cream ground, "Turn Teplitz R St K, Made in Austria" (A) **120.00**
19½" h, high relief, bouquet of flowers (A) **225.00**

TILES

Bristol, Liverpool, London, England
Denmark, France, Germany, Holland,
Italy, Spain, Portugal
1600s to Present

History: Tiles have been used for centuries on floors, walls, fireplaces, chimneys, and facades of houses, palaces, and castles. They have even been installed into furniture such as washstands, hall stands, and folding screens. Tiles clean easily and are quite decorative. Numerous public buildings and subways use tiles to enhance their appearances.

The earliest of the Dutch tin glazed tiles featured polychrome figures, landscapes, flowers, and animals. Many used the fleur-de-lis motif in the corners. Additional subjects such as ships, sea monsters, mythical figures, fishermen, farmers, and biblical subjects appeared in the late 17th century. Tile pictures that were adapted from paintings and engravings of Dutch interiors or landscapes also were made.

Before 1629 at least twenty-five factories in Holland were making tiles with the Delft potteries the most prolific. After 1650 the Delft potteries became less important. However, all Dutch-made tiles are generically called "Delft" tiles.

Even though the number of factories making tiles diminished during the 18th century, production increased throughout Europe. Denmark, Germany, Portugal, and Spain imitated Dutch tiles in their factories. The Portugese tiles featured motifs in two tones of cobalt blue or polychromes. Flemish workers came to Spain and introduced the majolica technique. They used a tin oxide glaze for their decorated tiles.

French tiles were influenced by both Italian and Dutch styles of decoration. In Italy, majolica tiles were made in centers such as Florence, Siena, and Venice.

Tiles made in England from the 16th through the first half of the 18th century generally followed the Dutch tiles in method of manufacture and design. Polychrome painting, blue and white motifs inspired by Chinese porcelains, birds, landscapes, and flowers all reflected the strong Dutch influence. Factories that produced tiles were centered in Bristol, Liverpool, and London.

In 1756 John Sadler from Liverpool produced the first transfer printed tiles and revolutionized the tile industry. The use of the transfer printing process on tiles allowed a far greater variety of designs and liberated the tile industry from the old Delft motifs. Transfer printing on tiles was responsible for the growth of the Victorian tile industry.

Herbert Minton was in charge of the production of tiles at Minton's. In 1828 he produced encaustic tiles with inlaid decorations, reviving a technique use in medieval Europe. Minton bought Samuel Wright's patent for encaustic tiles in 1830. He specialized in tiles for wall decorations in public buildings and began transfer printing tiles in 1850.

During the 1870s decorative wall tiles were in use everywhere. By the 1880s over one hundred companies in England were producing tiles.

Decorative tiles were a major industry in the Ironbridge Gorge in the late 19th century. Tiles were produced by Maw and Craven Dunnill for church floors, shop counters, public buildings, facades, porches, and many other uses. Maw's factory at Jackfield was the largest decorative tile factory in the world in the 1880s.

The Craven Dunnill firm was formed in 1871 and built its new Jackfield works in 1875. Many encaustic tiles were made for use in new and restored churches. With the revival of the Gothic style, their reproductions of medieval tiles were in great demand.

George Maw and his brother, Arthur, bought the encaustic tile business of the Worcester Porcelain Company in 1850. In addition to floor tiles, they manufactured glazed tiles for walls, porchways, fireplaces, and washstands. Tiles were either hand painted, transfer printed, or stenciled. They also made ceramic mosaic tiles. The Benthall Works was added to the company in 1883.

In 1892 the Pilkington brothers established a pottery to manufacture tiles and other products at Clifton Junction, Manchester. Many experiments were done. The "Royal" prefix was granted to the company by King George V in 1913 and the company became known as "Royal Lancastrian."

Many designs used on tiles were copied from other fields of art. The Art Nouveau and Art Deco motifs were popular for tile designs.

References: Julian Barnard, *Victorian Ceramic Tiles*, N. Y. Graphic Society Ltd., 1972; Anne Berendsen, *Tiles, A General History*, Viking Press, 1967; C. H. de Jonge, *Dutch Tiles*, Praeger, 1971; Terence A. Lockett, *Collecting Victorian Tiles*, Antique Collectors' Club, 1979; Anthony Ray, *English Delftware Tiles*, Faber & Faber, 1973; Hans Van Lemmen, *Tiles: A Collectors' Guide*, Seven Hills Books, 1985.

Collectors' Club: Tiles & Architectural Ceramics Society, Ironbridge Gorge Museum, Ironbridge, Telford, Shropshire, FF8 7AW England. Membership: 8 pounds. Bulletin and annual journal.

Museums: Boymans-van Beunigen Museum, Rotterdam, Holland; City Museum, Stoke-on-Trent, Hanley, England; Ironbridge Gorge Museum, Teford, England; Lambert van Meerten Museum, Delft, Holland; Victoria & Albert Museum, London, England.

Collecting Hints: Tiles are becoming increasingly popular. They are difficult to identify as to manufacturer since they were mass produced and many were unmarked. Some firms only decorated tiles they received from other factories. The method of manufacture also may provide clues to the maker. Information on the back of a tile sometimes will indicate the manufacturer or the date that the tile was made.

Condition is an important factor in determining price. Bad cracks, chips, and scratches definitely lower a tile's value. Crazing in the glaze is not uncommon in a tile and usually does not affect the price if it does not detract from the tile's appearance.

4" sq

Blue and white Chinese garden scenes in circ medallions, key corners, early 17th C, Rotterdam, set of 5 (A) **155.00**

Blue and white vases of flowers, fleur-de-lis corners, set of 4 (A) **40.00**

Manganese scene of Descent of Christ from the Cross, biblical reference, 18th C, framed (A) **20.00**

4" w, 12½" h, draped woman reaching for lyre in branches, putto on limb playing violin, sgd "H. Rock," early 20th C, Dresden **250.00**

4⅛" sq, blue and white figures in landscape, candelabra borders, 18th C, set of 4, rim chips (A) **45.00**

4¼" sq

Blue and white sailing ships in river landscapes, 17th C, Dutch, set of 8 (A) **145.00**

Blue and white fruit, spider corners, mid 17th C, Dutch, pr (A) **15.00**

Cream slip of lion rampant, brown ground, France (A) **10.00**

Manganese and white landscapes at waterside in octagonal medallions, blue carnation corners, manganese sprinkled ground, 18th C, set of 19 (A) **380.00**

Tile, 8" sq, "Puck," blue transfer, "JO-SIAH WEDGWOOD & SONS, ETRURIA," $90.00.

4¾" sq

Blue and white biblical themes, 18th C, Dutch, set of 36, framed, four damaged (A) **520.00**

Blue oxhead corners, white ground, Dutch Delft, set of 12 (A) **48.00**

Blue painted buildings in landscapes, 17th C, Dutch Delft, set of 3 (A) . **45.00**

Manganese painted "Baptism of Christ," 18th c, London Delft **20.00**

Polychrome animals, blue corners, Dutch Delft, set of 8 (A) **32.00**

Sepia floral decorations, mid 18th C, set of 13, unmarked **200.00**

5" sq

Black printed "The Dog and the Sheep" and "The Sow and the Bitch," c1765, Sadler & Green, Delft, pr **140.00**

Black printed "The Tithe Pig," c1760, sgd "J. Sadler, Liverpl," Delft **75.00**

Blue and white Jacob's Dream and biblical subjects, 18th C, Dutch Delft, set of 11 (A) **35.00**

Manganese and white biblical scenes, four in medallions, 18th C, Dutch Delft, set of 3 (A) **180.00**

Yellow bird, blue feathers, purple tail on tree stump, blue foliate corner motifs, late 18th C, Liverpool Delft, pr **200.00**

5½" sq, purple scene of figure raised from the dead, Dutch (A) **15.00**

5½" w, 11" h

Polychrome animals, birds, trees, and flowers, Delft, pr (A) **50.00**

Polychrome hares and stylized flowers, Delft (A) **32.00**

5¾" sq, painted and molded military trophies in hexagon panels, c1700 (A) **35.00**

5⅞" sq

Printed view of Massachusetts Bay, Minton **35.00**

Sepia printed scene, "Animals of the Farm," buff ground, sgd "W. Wise," Minton, set of 7 .... **135.00**

6" l, 8" h, robed maiden in blue, manganese, yellow, and green, Italy (A) . **100.00**

6" sq

Black transfer and polychrome enameled geometric foliage design (A) . **5.00**

Blue and white, brown and cream, black and white, Aesop's Fables, Thomas Allen, c1885, Minton, set of 3 .... **180.00**

Blue and white windmill and house scene, "Grohn" **50.00**

Blue, brown, and cream glazed hunter and fisherman, Minton, pr, framed (A) **170.00**

Brown floral design, Minton, pr **80.00**

Cream and brown sunflower pattern, "Minton, Stoke on Trent" **25.00**

Dark brown glaze, Viking ship, English registry mark **35.00**

Four Seasons, Minton

"Autumn Comes Jovial On" **70.00**

Brown, black, and green flowers in panels, English registry mark ... **25.00**

"Come Gentle Spring" **70.00**

Sepia mother and children feeding rabbits, yellow ground, sgd "W. Wise," raised "Minton China Works, Stoke on Trent" mark **45.00**

Shades of green, sun ray designs in sq and rect panels, English registry mark **15.00**

Tan and brown, woman milking cow, boy holding baby, sgd "W. Wise," c1856, Minton **70.00**

Turquoise and pink flowers, cream ground, gilt trim, "Doulton-Lambeth" **125.00**

6⅛" sq

Blue printed Oriental figures at various pursuits, formal borders, dated 1870, Minton & Hollins, set of 39 **300.00**

Blue transfer cherubs, set of 3 (A) .. **40.00**

Brown printed artisans at their trades, Minton, set of 6 .... **60.00**

Brown printed scenes from Shakespeare, sgd "John Moyr Smith," Minton, set of 8 .... **140.00**

Faience, painted scene of children on seesaw and carrying apples in basket, Doulton-Lambeth, pr (A) **400.00**

8" l, 5¼" h, white inlaid knight on horseback, pink-buff ground, 13th C, England (A) **1,335.00**

8" sq

Blue weaponry and armour of Greco-Roman period, soldier in center, "Minton-Hollins" **38.00**

Coat of arms in center, multicolored geometrics, ftd, Longwy **145.00**

8" w, 12½" h, mustard yellow, "The Old Curiosity Shop," raised figures, dated 1888, Wedgwood marks **350.00**

8⅛" sq, faience, painted with birds in circ panels, dark ground, light green flower borders, Doulton-Lambeth, set of 3 (A) **425.00**

10" w, 15" h, manganese and yellow scene, dbl handled urn on marble plinth, foliage and scroll border, wood frame, c1720, Dutch Delft, set of 6 (A) **440.00**

11" sq, polychrome bird in cage, framed, 18th C, Rotterdam (A) **450.00**

11⅞" sq, manganese painted flowering branches, mounted in copper, English Delft (A) **40.00**

11⅞" w, 18⅛" h, stove, molded, niche painted with figure of Hope holding anchor, strapwork spandrels, c1680, Winterthur (A) **1,185.00**

12¼" l, 8½" w, porcelain body, painting of woman, c1882, "Minton China Works" **300.00**

19⅝" sq, manganese painted lady by wash tub, cottage, and tree, border of 10 rect tiles, manganese scrolling foliage, mid 18th C, framed (A) **550.00**

20½" l, 15½" h, blue and white windmill and stream scene, Dutch Delft . **350.00**

20½" l, 15¾" h, blue and white scene of skaters on canal, Dutch Delft, set of 12 .... **85.00**

40" l, 35" h, blue and white walled and moated city, mid 19th C (A) **2,475.00**

57½" l, blue and white estuary scene, flowerhead corners, Dutch Delft, set of 22 (A) **175.00**

59⅛" l, polychrome scene of Bacchus procession in landscape, raised shaped quatrefoil rococo frame with flowers, c1750, Savona (A) **5,185.00**

69¼" l, 24⅞" h, blue, copper luster, and white, geometrics, sunbursts, and chain patterns, 16th C, Seville Cuenca, set of 26, framed (A) **1,230.00**

TOBY JUGS

Staffordshire, England
1775 to Present

History: Toby jugs, first made by English potters from Staffordshire in the 18th century, are drinking vessels. Although they were at the zenith of their popularity from 1775 to 1825, Toby jugs still are being produced today. After they became outmoded as drinking mugs, they survived as ornamental pieces.

Some of the earliest Toby jugs were made by Ralph Wood and Whieldon at their Burslem potteries in Staffordshire. Some claim the name "Toby" originated with the Uncle Toby character in Laurence Sterne's *Tristram Shandy*. This is subject to debate.

The typical Toby jug features a seated toper clasping a jug with both hands or holding a glass in one hand and a jug on a knee in the other. The seated figure is usually a male wearing a three-cornered hat, each corner of which formed a spout. Figures were dressed in costumes of the period and usually had genial facial expressions. Toby jugs were designed for use in cottages and inns. Variations included standing figures and occasional female figures. Most are ten inches tall. Miniatures, which are rarer, measure about three to six and one-half inches tall.

Some early Whieldon Toby jugs have the mottled and tortoise shell underglazed effect. The Ralph Wood jugs have a somewhat whiter body and softer, translucent glaze. After 1780 some overglaze enamels were used. Wedgwood, Pratt, and Davenport, along with other English potters, made Toby jugs.

References: Desmond Eyles, *"Good Sir Toby,"* Doulton & Co., Ltd., 1955; Bernard Rackham, *Early Staffordshire Pottery,* Faber & Faber, 1951; C. P. Woodhouse, *Old English Toby Jugs,* Mountrose Press, 1949.

Museums: Victoria & Albert Museum, London, England.

1¼" h, seated gentleman, blue coat, red vest, "Royal Worcester," #2831 .... **60.00**

4⅜" h, seated gentleman, multicolored, Staffordshire **50.00**

4½" h

Bust of Paul Pry, wearing red hat, titled band, green jacket, Staffordshire (A) **300.00**

Seated gentleman, cobalt coat, Allerton **38.00**

Seated gentleman, holding mug and snuff box, green hair, cobalt and copper luster clothes **115.00**

Seated gentleman, holding pipe and mug, tricorn and cobalt coat, copper luster trim **125.00**

Seated gentleman, wicker chair, holding jug, smoking pipe, blue, ochre, brown, and green, c1800 (A) **1,015.00**

Toby Jug, 11½" h, Lord Nelson, c1860, Staffordshire, $350.00.

5" h

John Bull, multicolored, molded lettering, England **30.00**

Seated gentleman, holding flask of ale, period dress, gray, red, and black, unmarked **85.00**

Seated gentleman, rocky mound, smoking pipe, dog at feet, blue, ochre, brown, and green, c1800 (A) **1,015.00**

6" h, bust of George V in navy hat, Queen Mary with crown, multicolored, unmarked, pr **225.00**

6½" h, polychrome standing man holding jug, flowered coat, Dutch Delft (A) **45.00**

7" h

Seated gentleman, holding mug and pipe, multicolored, "Wood & Sons, England" **50.00**

Standing gentleman, plum coat and blue breeches, holding moneybag (A) **100.00**

8" h

Seated gentleman

Holding bottle and glass, wearing wig, ochre, blue, and black, late 18th C, Yorkshire (A) **320.00**

Holding foaming jug, blue sponged coat, yellow breeches, Pratt (A) **400.00**

Whieldon mottled green-brown finish **110.00**

Standing snufftaker pinching snuff from box, standing on grapevine, molded circ base, c1825 (A) **110.00**

"Tipsy Toper," seated gentleman, holding mug in hand, spilling ale on striped waistcoat, early 19th C, Staffordshire (A) **300.00**

8½" h

Seated gentleman, holding foaming ale glass, multicolored, Staffordshire **150.00**

"The Nightwatchman," blue and white, 18th C, Enoch Wood **575.00**

8⅞" h

Martha Gunn, seated on iron-red stool, holding blue bottle and glass, pearlware, c1830, Staffordshire (A) **435.00**

Seated gentleman, blue coat, yellow hat and breeches, Staffordshire ... **50.00**

9" h

"King of Clubs," white with gold and red accents, unmarked **75.00**

Napoleon, sgd "Steven Green, Lambeth," Doulton-Lambeth (A) **100.00**

Seated gentleman

Holding foaming jug, yellow coat, pink breeches, green washed base, Staffordshire (A) **150.00**

Holding jug, blue luster coat, gold luster trim, Staffordshire **250.00**

Holding jug on knee, sponged coat, details in blue, brown, ochre, and yellow, c1800 (A) **2,035.00**

9½" h

Seated gentleman

Holding claret jug, wearing striped waistcoat, gray coat, yellow breeches, c1800, Staffordshire . **200.00**

Holding foaming jug, brown coat, green breeches, green base, early 19th C, Staffordshire **200.00**

Holding jug of ale, blue jacket, yellow breeches, star-patterned waistcoat, patterned stockings, c1800, Pratt (A) **550.00**

Holding jug of foaming ale, yellow sponged chamfered rect base, c1840, Staffordshire (A) **110.00**

Holding pipe and foaming jug of

ale, brown chair, pearlware,
c1820, Staffordshire (A) **500.00**
Seated period woman, multicolored
(A) **200.00**
"Thin Man" style, seated gentleman,
jug on knee, ochre, yellow, and
brown (A) **2,930.00**
9⅞" h, seated gentleman
Green coat, yellow breeches, Flemish **70.00**
Holding ale jug, barrel, and pipe at
feet, gray hat, blue jacket, gray
breeches, c1790, Staffordshire (A) **500.00**
10¼" h
Seated gentleman, holding foaming
jug, red coat, green breeches, and
yellow cuffs, c1800, Yorkshire (A) **470.00**
Seated Long John Silver, purple, rose,
yellow, and white, "Shorter & Son
Ltd." **75.00**
Seated sailor, holding jug of ale inscribed with "Success to Our
Wooden Walls," blue uniform,
"Dollars" on chest, early 19th C (A) **225.00**
10½" h, 12" h, colored figures of World
War I caricatures, Wilkinson, set of
11, repairs (A) **2,100.00**
10⅝" h, "Hearty Good Fellow," standing figure, multicolored period
clothes, pink luster stockings, buttons, goblet and ale jug, green tree
stump base, pink lustered bordered
handle, c1820 (A) **1,320.00**
10¾" h
Seated gentleman, holding large bottle between legs, blue coat, brown
waistcoat, and ochre breeches, replaced cov, late 18th C (A) **3,420.00**
Blue and white gentleman seated on
barrel, faience, unmarked (A) **35.00**
11¼" h, "Hearty Good Fellow," standing figure, holding jug of ale, ochre
coat, yellow breeches, grass mound
base, Pratt **550.00**
11½" h, seated gentleman holding scale
patterned jug, beige salt glaze, early
19th C (A) **225.00**
11¾" h, Bacchus and Pan, seated back
to back on barrel, holding spouted
cornucopia, dolphin mouth, leopard
handle, blue, yellow, ochre, and
green, c1800, Hawley (A) **425.00**
12" h, seated gentleman, holding cup
and jug, multicolored, c1700, unmarked (A) **750.00**
12¼" h, seated "Rodney Sailor," holding jug of beer and goblet, multicolored, Ralph Wood (A) **1,680.00**
15" h, "Prince Hal," wearing orange
doublet and yellow breeches, seated
on sq base with red and green leaves,
shield missing, early 19th C, Staffordshire (A) **2,035.00**

TORQUAY

Torquay District, South Devon, England
1870s to 1962

History: G. J. Allen discovered red terra cotta clay on the Watcombe House grounds, just north of Torquay in 1869. The pottery industry in Torquay owes its existence to this discovery.

Allen established the Watcombe Pottery. Charles Brock was appointed manager, and skilled workers were employed from Staffordshire. Watcombe Pottery was established during the peak of the art pottery movement, 1870 to 1900, and found a ready market for its products.

The appeal of the terra cotta wares was the natural color of the clay and the innovative shapes. A small amount of enamel decoration or gilt borders were added. At first, the style was classical, comprised of vases, figures, and busts imitating Greek and Roman originals. Later busts of contemporary and historical celebrities, vases, jars, architectural wares, garden ornaments, and tea services were made.

Watcombe Pottery also was known for its terra cotta plaques. Statues were made for advertising purposes. Enamel decoration of flowers, birds, and fish on ornamental wares was accomplished in a natural style on unglazed terra cotta.

In 1875 Dr. Gillow established the Torquay Terra-Cotta Company Ltd. at Hele Cross, just north of Torquay. Smaller decorative wares, such as statuettes, plaques, vases, figures, and busts were made. Some utilitarian examples also were produced. Products were similar to those made at the Watcombe Pottery.

Torquay Terra-Cotta Company declined and closed in 1905 as a result of the decline in the Arts and Crafts movement and the shift to more modern styles. Enoch Staddon reopened the Torquay Pottery in 1908 to make pottery rather than terra cotta ware. The factory closed during WWII.

The Aller Vale Pottery, under the direction of John Phillips, started making terra cotta and other art wares in new forms and styles near Torquay in 1881. By 1890 the pottery was catering to holiday visitors who wanted something to take home as a souvenir. Designs were painted in thick colored slip on items prepared with a dip coat of slip of a uniform color. They were finished with a clear glaze. Usually rhymes or proverbs were scratched through the ground so the lettering showed up in the dark red color of the body. This "motto ware" gained tremendous popularity during the early 20th century, not only in resorts, but all over the country.

Watcombe Pottery combined with Aller Vale in 1901 to form the Royal Aller Vale and Watcombe Art Potteries. Watcombe started to manufacture the Aller type wares. One style of decoration showing the thatched cottage between trees was called "Devon Motto Ware" or "Cottage Ware." In addition to the motto, sometimes the place name was inscribed. Commemorative wares were made. The combined potteries eventually closed in 1962.

During the early part of the 20th century, several smaller potteries such as Longpark Pottery, Burton, and Daison were established in or near Torquay. Most were founded by men who had worked at one of the major potteries in the district. The designs tended to copy the styles used by Aller Vale and Watcombe. When Longpark closed in 1957 and Watcombe in 1962, the red clay pottery industry in Torquay ended.

References: D. & E. Lloyd Thomas, *The Old Torquay Potters,* Arthur H. Stockwell, Ltd., 1978.

Museums: Devonshire Museum, Devonshire, England; Exeter Museums, Exeter, England; Torquay Museum, South Devon, England.

Collectors' Club: Torquay Pottery Collectors' Society, 604 Orchard View Drive, Maumee, Ohio, 43537. Membership: $13.00. Quarterly magazine.

Vase, 3½" h, "Portland Bill," $25.00.

Ashtray
   3¼" sq, cottage, "Brixham" and "I'll
      take care of the ashes" **6.00**
   5⅛" l, 3¼" w, flyaway scandy, blue
      shadow leaves, "A place for the
      ashes," imp script "Watcombe
      Tourquay England" mark **15.00**
Biscuit Jar
   5¼" h, motto ware, cream body, blue,

green, and brown house scene,
   wicker handle **85.00**
   7" h, large pink cherry blossoms, purple ground **100.00**
Bowl
   3¼" h, Passion flower, rust flowers,
      yellow and light green scroll trim,
      cream band around middle, green
      ground, c1920, Exeter **10.00**
   4½" h, cockerel, inscribed "Fresh
      from the dairy," ruffled edge outlined in brown, ftd **50.00**
   6½" d, 2½" h, four sailboats on lake,
      ruffled rim, c1920, Longpark **12.00**
   7½" d, kingfisher sitting on branch,
      wings spread, woodland ground .. **35.00**
Butter Tub, 5½" d, cockerel, "Be aisy
   with tha butter," dbl handles **50.00**
Candleholder
   4" h, scandy, "Pleasant dream," unmarked **20.00**
   6" d, Scottish thistle on bottom, "guid
      night an joy be wi ye," green drip
      finish on rim, Longpark **35.00**
Candlestick
   3½" h, scandy, blue and light blue,
      "Pleasant dreams" **25.00**
   5½" h, scandy, upturned leaves,
      "Don't burn the Candle at both
      ends," imp "Watcombe Pottery" . **36.00**
   6½" h, "Life has many shadows, etc,"
      Watcombe Torquay, pr **45.00**
Chalice, 5¼" h, yellow daisy-type flowers, dark brown ground **20.00**
Chamber Pot, 8½" d, Hele Cross kingfisher design, multicolored **75.00**
Coffee Cup, scandy on front, "Rugby"
   and "Jist a wee drappie Tea" on reverse **25.00**
Coffeepot, 6" h, cockerel, cream body,
   brown, blue, and green rooster, motto **65.00**
Condiment Set, salt, pepper, and cov
   mustard, "Forget-Me-Not" in small
   pink flowers, light blue ground,
   c1930, Barton Pottery Co **20.00**
Creamer
   2¼" h, scandy, "elp yerzel tu cram,"
      green tadpoles, unmarked **15.00**
   2½" h, scandy, "Be canny wi the
      cream," leaf shape handle, c1920,
      unmarked **15.00**
   3" h, cottage
      "Take a little cream," Royal Watcombe **18.00**
      "Portpatrick" and "Be canny wi'
      the Cream," c1930, "Longpark
      Torquay, England" **25.00**
Cup and Saucer
   Cottage, brown and blue, cream
      ground, motto **20.00**
   Cottage, tadpoles on saucer, "Hope

well and have well," oversize, Royal Watcombe 23.00

White seagull, gray shading, blue waves, turquoise ground, "Mevagissy," large "Royal Watcombe" .. 24.00

Demitasse Cup and Saucer, cottage, "Tynemouth" and "Have a cup of coffee," green tadpoles in blue circle, Royal Watcombe 20.00

Dish, 10½" l, scandy, "Du'ee 'elp yerzel," leaf shape, ring handle, c1920, Torquay Pottery Co. 30.00

Dresser Tray, 10½" l, motto ware, "Do the work thats nearest..," Watcombe Pottery 75.00

Egg Cup, 1¾" h, cottage
"Laid today," Watcombe Pottery ... 12.00
"Good morning," Watcombe Pottery 12.00
"Straight from the nest," Watcombe Pottery 12.00
Scandy, "Fresh laid" 25.00

Hatpin Holder
4½" h
Black cockerel, "From Alnwick" and "Time and tide for na' man bide," seven holes, Longpark Torquay 45.00
Motto ware, blue and green decor 35.00
Scandy, "I'll take care of the pins" 45.00

Inkwell
Sailboat design, "Dinna be achlin' But just write at aince" and "Eastbourne," c1920, Longpark Torquay 30.00
Scandy, "We are glad to hear from you," blue kidney beans around neck, unmarked 32.00

Jam Dish, crocus design, pierced rim through folded back, Longpark Torquay 28.00

Jam pot
2½" h, scandy, shaped like bean pot, handle, early 20th C, Watcombe Torquay 25.00
4" h, cov, black trim, horseshoe with white forget-me-nots, "Good Luck" and "Okehampton" on front, "A perfect table treat" on reverse, unmarked 24.00
5¼" w, cottage, "'elp yerzel ty Jam," heart shape, Longpark Torquay ... 25.00
Sailboat adrift under yellow moon, dark colors, "Be aizy with tha jam" and "Clevedon," clover shape, handle, c1930, "Royal Torquay Pottery, England" 25.00

Jug
7" h, motto ware, scene of sailboats, multicolored 35.00
9⅝" h, terra cotta, glazed streaked green on yellow, incised "Aesthetic," vert spout, loop handle, "TTC"(A) 75.00

Match Holder, 3¾" h, gold leaf and blue dots, dark green ground, "Help yourself, Nobody's Looking," c1910, Aller Vale 35.00

Match Striker, 3" h, scandy, "Match for any man," unmarked 50.00

Milk Jug, 4⅛" h, cottage, "Hexham" and "Lang may yer lum reek," Longpark Torquay 26.00

Mug, 3" h, brown primrose, light green leaves, dark green center band, green dots, "Make hay while the sun shines," paw handle, Longpark Torquay 16.00

Mustard Pot, 2½" h, cottage, light blue stripe on bottom and lid, "Help yourself to mustard" 16.00

Oil Cruet, 4½" h, cottage, Watcombe Pottery 35.00

Pepper Shaker, 3" h, house design, "Pass the pepper" motto, multicolored 15.00

Pin Tray, 4¾" l, 3¼" w, scandy, "I'll take care of the pins," c1930, Longpark Torquay 20.00

Pitcher
2" h, cottage, multicolored, "Watcombe Torquay" 15.00
3" h, cottage, "Say little but think much," Watcombe 20.00
4½" h, seagull in flight, sea ground, "Portland Bill" on front, Watcombe Torquay 25.00

Plate
6¼" d, cottage, "Weymouth" and "A thing of beauty is a joy forever," Royal Watcombe 25.00
6⅜" d, cottage, "Say little but think much," "Dartmouth" 20.00

Pot
4¾" d, scandy, "Neer cast a cloot till May be oot," dbl handles, unmarked 30.00
5½" h, Hot Water, cottage, "From Grassington" and "One good friend is worth many relations," c1918 .... 35.00

Puzzle Jug
Inscribed "With this jug...," cream body, brown rim 50.00
Scandy, "Come try your skill," unmarked 30.00

Salt, sailboats, blue-green water, rosy sunset, "You're very welcome" 10.00

Soap Tray, cottage, "The Isle of Wight" and "Mind the Tablecloth," unmarked 15.00

Sugar
3" h, "Be aisy with tha sugar" motto, scalloped edge, ftd 35.00
3⅛" d, band of primroses, "Help yersel tae sugar," c1920, H. M. Exeter 12.00

3½" h, scandy, "Help yersel and dinna be blate," ftd, c1920, Torquay Pottery Co **20.00**
3⅜" d, cottage, "Corfe Castle" and "Take a little sugar," unmarked .. **12.00**

Teapot
7" w, 4½" h, kingfisher series, multicolored **35.00**
Sailboat, brown sail, blue-green water, "Gorleston on Sea" and "Dauntee be fraid aut now," molded paw print handle, Longpark Torquay **26.00**

Toast Rack, scandy, 4 rails, "Have some toast" **45.00**

Tumbler
3½" h, house on front, "Straight from the cow" motto **40.00**
Cottage, "Time and tide wait for no man," "Devon Motto Ware" **15.00**

Vase
3½" h
Scandy, "Good fortune lead you ever pleasant ways," dog–eared dbl handles, unmarked **5.00**
Windmill reflected in lake, Watcombe Torquay **25.00**
4" h, kingfisher, two lilies, sponged leaves on branches **18.00**
6" h, top half black with brown flowers, green leaves, light blue lower section, ruffled rim, unmarked ... **25.00**
10½" h, multicolored birds, blue ground, dbl handle **45.00**
11" h, red and ochre terriers killing rats, blue leaf and mask handles, Watcombe (A) **25.00**
Motto ware, ship dec, three handles **25.00**

Vinegar Bottle, 7½" h, green tadpoles at base, blue dots at rim, "Lynmouth" and "Vinegar," Royal Watcombe ... **30.00**

Whiskey Cup, 2¾" h, ship pattern, "Every blade of grass keeps its own drop of dew" **27.00**

VIENNA

**DU PAQUIER
1720-30**

Vienna, Austria, 1718 to 1864

Du Paquier, 1718 to 1744

State Factory, 1744 to 1864

History: The Vienna Porcelain Factory, founded in 1718 by Claudius Du Paquier, was the second European factory to produce hard paste porce-

lain. Meissen was the first. Du Paquier developed high quality white porcelain. The privilege to make porcelain was granted to Du Paquier by the Emperor Charles VI. The decorations of the Du Paquier period fall into three catergories: (1) 1725 in which the polychrome Oriental theme was emphasized; (2) 1730–1740 in which polychromed scrolls, landscapes, and figurals in cartouches were dominant and black and gilt were used to highlight the themes; and (3) the final period which featured German florals or "Deutch Blumchen" designs similar to the Meissen treatment. The adoption of Meissen styles contributed to the rise of Vienna as one of Meissen's chief rivals. However, unlike Meissen, the Du Paquier factory did not produce a large number of figures.

Du Paquier sold his factory to the Austrian state in 1744. It became the Imperial Porcelain Manufactory and fell under the influence of Empress Maria Theresa. The quality of the porcelain reached its peak during this period, known as the State Period, 1744 to 1864. The Austrian coat of arms was used as the factory mark. Following the Seven Years' War, 1756–1763, which altered greatly the production at Meissen, Vienna porcelain assumed the undisputed leadership in European porcelain.

Between 1747 and 1784 Johann Niedermeyer, the chief modeler, contributed much to the success of the factory by creating rococo influenced figurals decorated in soft pastel colors. After 1765 the styles from Sevres greatly influenced the decorative styles at Vienna. Anton Grassi came to work at Vienna in 1778. He moved the factory's production away from Rococo styles into the Neo-classical influences.

Joseph Leithner concentrated on developing new background colors, especially a fine cobalt blue that was a match for Sevres' bleu roi. He introduced a special gold color. Leithner enhanced all the colors used at Vienna.

Under the management of Konrad Sorgenthal between 1784 and 1805, the factory produced richly ornamented dinner and tea services, vases, urns, and plates in the Neoclassical and Empire styles. Emphasis was placed on the reproduction of paintings by famous artists such as Angelica Kauffmann and Rubens onto porcelain vases, plates, and plaques that were surrounded by gilt frames that often included the painter's name.

Flowers were the principal decorative element used on Viennese porcelains. Seventeenth century Dutch flower paintings were adapted or copied on plates, cups, vases, and plate sets. Many pieces had black backgrounds to make the flowers stand out.

When the Congress of Vienna was held, numerous participants placed orders for services. After this period, the factory experienced a period of stagnation. Competition from the Bohemian factories started to take its toll.

After reaching the very pinnacle of success in the highly competitive porcelain field, the state porcelain factory was forced to close in 1864 due to financial difficulties.

The beehive mark was adopted in 1749. The year was stamped on pieces beginning in 1784.

References: W. B. Honey, *German Porcelain*, Pitman; George W. Ware, *German & Austrian Porcelain*, Crown Publishers, Inc., 1963.

Museums: Art Institute of Chicago, Chicago, Illinois; Gardiner Museum of Ceramic Art, Toronto, Canada; Metropolitan Museum of Art, New York, New York; Osterreiches Museum fur Angewandte, Kunst, Vienna, Austria; Smithsonian Institution, Division of Ceramics and Glass, National Museum of American History, Washington D. C.; Woodmere Art Museum, Philadelphia, Pa.

Tureen, cov, 12″ l, black printed dogs and wild game, *laub-und-bandelwerk* border, c1735, $11,000.00.

Beaker, 3⅛″ h, painted Chinese pavilion in continuous scene, flowering branches and birds, multicolored gilt, int. with scrolling border of florets and dots, c1730 (A) **1,040.00**
Beaker and Saucer
  Gallery pierced with shaped motifs, multicolored floral sprays and bouquets, trembleuse shape, c1775, blue "beehive" mark **130.00**
  Painted flowering plants, birds in flight, blue, iron-red, puce, green, and gilt, c1770, blue "beehive" mark (A) **200.00**
Beaker and Stand, painted and gilt chinoiserie figures on terraces, int. of beaker and stand with shaped panels of trellis, iron-red, puce, and gilt, c1730 (A) **285.00**
Bowl, 8¼″ d, cov, painted loose bouquets and scattered flowers, shaped orange scale borders edged with gilt scrolls, lemon finials, c1837, imp "beehive" mark, pr (A) **215.00**

Cabaret Set, coffeepot, milk jug, sugar, and tray, simulated landscape engravings reserved on simulated wood ground, gilt rims, spouts, handles, and feet, c1790, blue "beehive" mark **1,600.00**
Cabinet Cup and Saucer, portrait of woman reserved on gilt ground (A) . **75.00**
Clock Case, 14½″ h, molded foliage scrolls and pilasters, rose painted Oriental scene under opening, profile portrait of Emperor Franz Stephan at top, c1730 (A) **1,550.00**
Coffee Can, painted nymphs and putto with tambourine and helmet, gilt oval cartouche, gilt anthemion on reverse, c1847, blue "beehive" mark (A) ... **80.00**
Compote, 7″ d, radiating blue and gold panels, gilt spread stem, sq base (A) **35.00**
Cup and Saucer
  "Chintz" pattern, multicolored floral sprigs on borders, mid 18th C, blue "beehive" mark (A) **125.00**
  Multicolored coffee plant (A) **75.00**
  Multicolored foliate borders (A) **75.00**
  Multicolored religious scene (A) **75.00**
  Silhouettes of nobleman and lady reserved in gilt frames, light blue ground, gilt foliate and scroll borders, cov, c1798, blue "beehive" mark (A) **1,045.00**
Cup and Stand, painted flowering plants and rockwork, trembleuse stand, pierced gallery, c1755, blue "beehive" mark (A) **385.00**
Dish
  4⅜″ d, painted center white flower sprig, black ground, rect sides pierced with trellis (A) **100.00**
  11⅞″ d, scattered bouquets in molded ozier border, gilt line rim, spirally molded, triangular, c1770 .... **110.00**
  14″ l, painted bouquets, spirally molded basketweave border, shaped gilt rim, c1765, blue "beehive" mark (A) **100.00**
Figure
  4½″ h, flower girl, apron filled with flowers, multicolored, c1744-49, imp "beehive" mark **1,630.00**
  5½″ h, boy wearing dark green jacket, plumed gray hat, dated 1842, imp "beehive" mark **100.00**
  8⅞″ h, 8¼″ h, caricatures of man and woman of Hapsburg family, period dress, mound bases, multicolored, c1765, blue "beehive" mark, pr, damaged (A) **660.00**
  10⅜″ h, actor holding two books, youth carrying book, multicolored, mound base, blue "beehive" mark (A) **990.00**
  10⅝″ h, Neptune and Amphitrite,

seated before tree, Cupid at feet pouring water from urn, multicolored, c1755, blue "beehive" mark (A) **550.00**

11⅜" h, Apollo and Issa seated on pierced mound base supporting tree with masked Cupid, multicolored, c1755, blue "beehive" mark **750.00**

13⅞" h, group of hunters, man holding slain deer leaning on hound, woman with bow, mound base with tree trunk, multicolored, c1760-65, blue "beehive" mark ..**1,000.00**

19" h, stag standing on hind legs, white, inscribed "K. Sakellarios Jarl" (A) **400.00**

Fruit Coolers, 17⅛" h, hp allegorical scenes, maidens and cherubs, gold and rust floral detail and accents, dome pierced covs, removable liners, sq fluted legs, lion paw feet, stepped round bases, c1820, pr (A) **1,600.00**

Milk Jug, 3" h, Italian landscape scene, multicolored, gilt scroll rim, c1770, blue "beehive" mark (A) **220.00**

Pickle Dish, 3⅞" l, hunter and landscape scene, leaf shape with twig handle and 2 leaves forming feet, c1725-30 (A) **330.00**

Pilgrim Bottles, 6⅝", painted Oriental terrace and pagoda scenes, applied female masks, molded tassels at necks, silver mounts, c1730, pr **7,500.00**

Plaque, 16½" d, painted Didi and attendants in temple scene, gilt key surround, four oblong panels of classical figures, four oval medallions of classical figures on border, gilt jewel rim, blue "beehive" mark (A) **1,210.00**

Plate

8¾" d

Black and gilt baskets of flowers with birds, borders with panels enclosing gitterwerk and shells, shaped gilt rims, hexagon shape, c1740, pr **1,000.00**

Painted bouquets in spirally-molded basketweave borders, shaped gilt rim, c1765, blue "beehive" mark, set of 4 (A) ... **420.00**

9¼" d, Imari style, birds over flowering plants, cell pattern and flower border, blue "beehive" mark **120.00**

9⅝" d

Painted center, "Beauty Governed by Reason Rewarded by Merit," blue border, gilt birds and squirrels, reserves of five blue and gilt panels of vases and foliage, gilt and claret rims, dated 1803, blue "beehive" mark (A) **310.00**

Painted scattered floral bouquets,

shaped rims, c1790, blue "beehive" mark, set of 10 (A) **170.00**

9¾" d, center green enameled scene of figures in riverscape, shaped gilt rim, border of entwined gilt ribbon enclosing flowerheads, puce ground, c1770, blue "beehive" mark (A) **200.00**

Pot, Cov, 6½" h, Italian landscape with figures, multicolored, gilt scroll borders, pear knob, c1770, blue "beehive" mark (A) **220.00**

Ramekin, Cov, 7½" l, "Chintz" pattern, puce, green, blue, and brown, wood handle, flowering finial, c1775, blue "beehive" mark (A) **440.00**

Saucepan, Cov, 9⅜" l, three scroll feet painted with band of vine leaves under gilt bands, gilt accents on handle, finial and feet, dated 1859, blue "beehive" mark **175.00**

Saucer, painted bunches of fruit and flowers, fluted body, gilt rim **120.00**

Tankard

4⅛" h, iron-red Oriental scene of two Chinese and pagoda in landscape, int. silver rim, cylindrical, angular handle, c1730 (A) **4,940.00**

4¾" h, painted scene of friar drinking from tankard in rect gilt foliage panel, burgundy ground, hinged pewter cov, c1860 (A) **640.00**

Teabowl and Saucer

Figures in formal gardens, teabowl with castle scene, saucer with lady on stool, servant offering fruit, gilt rims, c1723 (A) **2,200.00**

German flowers, iron-red, puce, yellow, and green, gilt rims, blue "beehive" mark (A) **70.00**

Teapot

5½" h, one side with Cupid and Medusa mask in landscape, reverse of Cupid personifying love conquering time, both scenes in scroll borders, dbl scrolled handle, bird's head spout, domed lid, c1725, unmarked (A) **1,600.00**

6⅝" h, painted figures and buildings in landscape, c1765, blue "beehive" mark, repair to spout (A) ... **120.00**

Tray, 14⅜" l, quatrefoil cartouche of birds at fountain reserved on scale ground, pierced gallery sides with interwoven reeds, c1775, blue "beehive" mark (A) **1,555.00**

Tureen, Cov, 10⅝" d, painted vignettes of geese, chickens, and turkeys in wavy gilt foliage, puce and orange chevron bands, c1800 (A) **120.00**

Urn

11¼" h, cov, painted scene of Cupid

and maiden at fountain, reverse
with Cupid in air scattering roses,
domed cov, blue "beehive" mark   **700.00**
13½" h, oval medallions of Cupids
representing four seasons, multicolored, gold campana bodies and
bases, dated 1814, blue "beehive"
mark, pr (A) **880.00**

VILLEROY AND BOCH

Mettlach, Germany
1836 to Present

History: Johann Franz Boch founded a dinnerware factory in 1809 in an old Benedictine abbey
in Mettlach. This factory merged with the Nicholas Villeroy plant in Wallerfongen, Saar in 1836
to form the Villeroy and Boch company. The
Luxembourg factory founded in 1767 by the
Boch brothers also was included in this merger.
Eventually there were eight Villeroy and Boch
factories in other cities in addition to the main
factory at Mettlach. August von Cohausen was
the director who instituted the use of the old
abbey tower as the factory's trademark.

Stonewares, original in both design and production techniques, were produced starting in
the 1840s and were the most famous of the Villeroy and Boch wares. In addition to steins,
punch bowls, beakers, wall plaques, beverage
sets, drinking cups, hanging baskets, and vases
were made.

Chromolith, colored stoneware, utilized two
colors of clay worked side by side but separated
by a black intaglio line. Raised decoration was
done by applying the design and fusing it to the
body of the stoneware pieces. This process was
known as etched, engraved, or mosaic inlay.

Motifs included Germanic scenes depicting
peasant and student life and religious and mythological themes. Punch bowls featured garlands
of fruit, while steins were adorned with drinking
scenes, military events, folk tales, and student
life scenes. About 1900 Art Nouveau decorations
appeared on plaques, punch bowls, vases,
steins, umbrella, and flower stands.

Planolith stoneware plaques were given an initial coating of a delicate green matte color,
glazed, and then fired. Figures to decorate the
plaques were formed separately, applied to the
pre-fired background, and then fired again.

These applied decorations were ivory colored
and stood out in relief against the green ground.
Motifs on plaques included scenes from Greek
mythology and Germanic legends.

Cameo stonewares had raised ivory colored
decorations set on light blue or light green backgrounds. There was a less fluid quality to these
applied decorations. The stoneware was more
dense.

The pinnacle of stoneware production was between 1880 and 1910. Prominent artists at Mettlach were Christian Warth, Heinrich Schlitt, Fritz
Quidenus, Mittein, and Johann Baptist Stahl.

Terra cotta for architectural use was made from
1850; mosaic tiles were made from 1852. Cream
colored earthenwares for domestic use were produced at factories in Dresden from 1853 and in
Schramberg from 1883. Around 1890 artists at
Mettlach manufactured plates and vases decorated in the Delft style and the faience style of
Rouen.

Around World War I business had lessened due
to unfavorable economic conditions and the lack
of unskilled labor. In 1921 a major fire destroyed
all molds, formulas, and records of the factory.

Although the factory continued to produce
tiles, dinnerwares, and plumbing fixtures, almost
fifty years lapsed before the factory revived the
production of steins and plaques.

References: Gary Kirsner, *The Mettlach Book,*
Seven Hills Books, 1983.

Museums: Munchner-Stadtmuseum, Munich,
West Germany; Rijksmuseum, Amsterdam, Hol-
land; Sevres Museum, Sevres, France; Villeroy &
Boch Archives & Museum, Mettlach, Germany.

Asparagus Server, 10" l, molded asparagus on lid forming handle, SP holder   **40.00**
Beaker
   1/4 L
     Incised white florals, brown leaves,
     light green ground, Mettlach
     #2834 .... **60.00**

**Punch Bowl, 15" h, etched, multicolored,
Mettlach #2208, (A) $300.00.**

Woman holding tray with peacock **75.00**
PUG
   Boy playing violin, Mettlach
     #1023/2327 .... **65.00**
   Girl holding peacock and pitcher,
     Mettlach #1025/2327 .... **65.00**
Bowl
   5" d, blue wedges, white dots, mul-
     tilobed, "V. & B., Saxon-Dresden" **12.50**
   8⅛" d, gaudy floral spatter design, po-
     lychrome, "Villeroy & Boch" (A) . **25.00**
   11" d, divided, blue flowers, white
     ground, Dresden mark **125.00**
Coaster, dwarf design, German sayings,
   set of 6 .... **400.00**
Coffeepot, 8" h, "Virginia" pattern ... **85.00**
Cup and Saucer, white, khaki and green
   pattern, eight panels **85.00**
Demitasse Cup and Saucer, "Bluebell"
   pattern, V. & B. **12.00**
Dish, cov, 6" d, imp vertical ribbing,
   beige ground, applied brown grapevine and leaves, silver luster base, 6-
   lobed **50.00**
Flagon, 16" h, raised genre center band,
   brick red, gray clay body, raised
   shields and scrolls, pewter top, Mettlach #2085 (A) **325.00**
Humidor, 5½" d, 9" h, etched scene of
   cows, engraved SP lid, "castle &
   #1231" mark **475.00**
Jam Jar, 4" h, multicolored scene of cattle, metal top and handle, "castle &
   #1231" mark **525.00**
Jar, 4½" d, 5" h, cream emb bearded
   men, brown ground **30.00**
Mayonnaise Set, bowl, undertray, and
   ladle, etched Art Deco tree design,
   blue and tan, cream ground, Mettlach
   mark **190.00**
Pitcher
   5" h, cherries and leaves, light blue
     ground **45.00**
   7" h, floral and line design, Mettlach
     #2947 .... **200.00**
   3 L, white figures bowling, blue
     ground, gargoyle spout, Mettlach
     #2210 .... **585.00**
Plaque
   6" w, 7" h, white relief of maiden,
     blue-green ground, Mettlach
     #7072 .... **375.00**
   11" d, etched autumn scene, woman
     in fields, Mettlach #1607 .... **550.00**
   11¼" d, portraits of peasants, raised
     design of florals and scrolls at edge,
     "V. & B." **170.00**
   15" d, etched, knight and maiden,
     Mettlach "2322 and #2323," pr .**1,400.00**
   15½" d, multicolored etched floral
     design, sgd "A. Hervegh," "castle
     & #2559" mark **250.00**

16" d
   Etched, Art Nouveau women, one
     picking daisies, other eating
     cherries, gold band edge, sgd
     "Lucian Payen," "castle &
     #2596 and #2597" marks, pr .**1,600.00**
   Etched, baptism, Mettlach #1048/
     3036l **500.00**
   Etched black and white scene,
     brown, blue, and cream geomet-
     ric border
     "Destroying the Irmensaule," sgd
       "Paderborn," c1894, "castle &
       #1048-4" mark **700.00**
     "King Being Blessed By Bishop,"
       "castle & #1048" mark **700.00**
   Etched, gnome in tree with mug,
     gnome with two bottles,
     multicolored, sgd "Schlitt," pr
     (A) **2,800.00**
   17¼" d, etched mermaid and oyster
     shell design, blue ground, gold
     edge, sgd "Hein," c1898, "castle
     & #2508" mark **1,250.00**
   17½" d
     Etched hawk in tree, Mettlach
       #2593 .... **525.00**
     Multicolored knights on horseback,
       gold ground, Mettlach #2187
       and #2188, pr (A) **3,600.00**
     Pink and peach nasturtiums, blue
       borders, gold scallops, "castle &
       #2350 and #2351" marks, pr .**1,500.00**
     Spring landscape, woman in white
       gown admiring flowering bush,
       wild flowers and trees, Mettlach
       #1998 (A) **875.00**
   18¼" d, cameo of mythological men
     in boat, green ground, sgd "J.
     Stahl," c1899, "castle & #2442
     mark" **1,500.00**
   18¾" d, white cameo of Trojan Wars,
     green ground, sgd "J. Stahl," "cas-
     tle & #2442" mark (A) **990.00**
   19¼" d, etched design of bird on
     branch and florals, detailed floral
     border, c1896, "castle & #1418"
     mark **1,000.00**
Plate
   4½" d, red floral center, blue border **10.00**
   9½" d, blue florals, white ground .. **25.00**
   12" d
     Blue and white grist mill scene ... **80.00**
     Blue and white pastoral scene ... **50.00**
Platter
   14" l, "Yorkshire" pattern **28.00**
Punch Bowl, Cov
   16" d, matching underplate, relief
     dec, figural handles, "castle &
     #418" mark, repair to handles ... **400.00**
   16½" h, etched scene of period peo-
     ple at leisure, reverse scene of clas-

sical people in blue and cream, dolphin handles, grape cluster finial, sgd "Schlitt," "castle & #2088" mark **650.00**

Ramekins, porcelain, painted wild flowers, imp "Villeroy & Boch," set of 6 **12.50**

Sugar, "Blue Onion" pattern **25.00**

Tumbler, ¼ L, shield with rearing horse, band at top, "Stadt Stuttgart," imp "castle & #2327" mark **65.00**

Vase

2½" h, glossy green leaves, beige ground, twig handle **30.00**

6½" h

Etched design of children, flowers, and scrolls, brown and rust ground, ftd, castle mark **225.00**

Mosaic geometric design, "castle & #1779" mark **150.00**

7¼" h, Mediterranean style polychrome dec, terra cotta colored ground, Mettlach #1899 (A) **35.00**

9½" h, etched orange and blue florals, green and gold leaves, gray ground, floral band at top, pink interior, "castle & #1844" mark ... **400.00**

10¼" h, stoneware, stylized crocuses and leaves, muted brown, gray, blue, red, and yellow, dbl gourd shape, Mettlach (A) **265.00**

11" h, mosaic geometric design, "castle & #1289" mark **235.00**

12¾" h, etched, center scenes of playing flute, bow and arrow, playing mandolin and picking flowers, green and gold grounds, Mettlach #1591 (A) **750.00**

13" h

Incised maiden design, sgd "C. Gorig," "castle & #1749" mark .. **300.00**

Relief of graduated rosettes and dots, brown, cream, and gray, trumpet neck, Mettlach #1241 . **55.00**

14" h

Blue, yellow, green, and rust Art Nouveau designs, "castle & #2909" mark, pr **1,000.00**

Cobalt, red, and gold Art Nouveau design, elephant head handles, "castle & #2851" mark **500.00**

15¾" h, etched, two scenes of lovers, jewels, Mettlach #2207 .... **700.00**

16¼" h, enameled floral and dot dec, blue ground, c1889, Mettlach #1470, pr (A) **375.00**

20" h, cov, white applied spiral bands of figures drinking, blue ground, alternating Gothic arches, inscriptions on tan ground, Mettlach, pr . **200.00**

28¾" h, stoneware, sides incised and painted with women and children emblematic of Autumn and Spring, molded and painted floral and foliage rims, scroll handles, Mettlach, pr (A) **3,240.00**

VINCENNES

Chateau of Vincennes, Paris, France 1738 to 1772

History: Gilles and Robert Dubois brought soft paste porcelain manufacturing to the royal chateau at Vincennes in 1738. They were assisted by Orry de Fulvy, Councillor of State and Minister of Finance. After two years, the Dubois brothers failed.

Francois Gravant took over and appointed Charles Adams the director. The king granted many concessions to Adams and the factory entered a period of prosperity.

Vincennes products made between 1745 and 1756 are prized by collectors. Jean-Jacques Bachelier took charge of painting and modeling in 1747 and introduced the use of biscuit porcelain for figure modeling. A Vincennes factory specialty was artificial flowers, popular in Paris around 1750.

In 1753 the king issued an edict giving the exclusive privilege of porcelain making in France to Adams. He sanctioned the use of the royal cypher, a pair of interlaced "L"s.

The porcelain works were removed from the Chateau of Vincennes to a new building at Sevres in 1756. The firm became the Royal Porcelain Factory of Sevres.

Pierre Antoine Hannong, a Strasbourg potter, established a factory for hard paste porcelain in the vacated buildings at Chateau Vincennes in 1767. He was granted the right to produce porcelain as long as he did not infringe on the Sevres factory's designs. Only a small quantity of porcelains were made. In 1774 the factory was purchased by Seguin whose patron was the Duc de Chartes. Seguin used the title "Royal Factory of Vincennes." His products duplicated those of many French factories.

References: George Savage, *Seventeenth & Eighteenth Century French Porcelain*, Spring Books, 1969.

Museums: British Museum, London, England; Gardiner Museum of Ceramic Art, Toronto, Canada; J. Paul Getty Museum, Malibu, California; The Frick Collection, New York; Victoria & Albert Museum, London, England.

Potpourri Jar, pale multicolored accents, ormolu base, c1750, (A) $550.00.

Bowl
3⅛" d, cov, painted with two bouquets, gilt line rims, gilt twig handles and finial, green foliage terminals, c1753, blue interlaced "L's & dot" mark (A) **1,900.00**
8½" d, central floral spray in gilt foliage borders, bleu celeste sides, gilt dentil rim **300.00**
10⅜" d, white, lobed rim molded, three shell panels, gold dentil rim, blue interlaced "L's" mark (A) **180.00**
12¾" d, int. painted with large floral bouquets and three smaller bouquets and insects, white ground, ext. with flower sprays, shaped gilt rim and smaller florals, dated 1752, blue "crowned interlaced L's & Bourbon fleur-de-lis" mark **10,500.00**
Cane Handle, 2" l, painted merchants in continuous harbor scene, concave top, figures near ruin, c1748 (A) ... **770.00**
Clock Case, 10¼" h, molded Cupid gazing down at sleeping nymph, applied floral garlands, English painted accents, c1750 .... **900.00**
Cream Jug, 4" h, painted woman carrying jug in landscape, molded gilt prunus, branch handle, three feet, c1754, blue interlaced "L's" mark .. **400.00**
Cup and Saucer
Bleu lapis ground reserved with shaped cartouches and gilt painted birds in landscapes, gilt dentil borders, c1750, blue interlaced "L's" mark (A) **2,860.00**
Cup and cov with floral sprays and tooled gilt, saucer with fox, bear, lion, and pig in shrubs, multicolored, dbl twig handles, c1750, blue interlaced "L's" mark (A) **1,100.00**

Cup with putto with basket in garden, saucer with blue painted putto with goat, gilt dentil rims, entwined handle, c1753, blue interlaced "L's & A" mark **670.00**
Gilt floral bunches in gilt flower and foliage cartouches reserved on bleu lapis ground, gilt dentil rims, dated 1753, blue interlaced "L's" mark (A) **1,580.00**
Painted swirled swags of flowers from gilt sprays, turquoise outer border, gilt dentil rims, c1755, blue interlaced "L's & C" mark **670.00**
Dish
9½" d, three oval gilt panels of gilt flying birds, floral borders, bleu lapis ground, gilt dentil rim, c1752, blue interlaced "L's" mark (A) ...**4,435.00**
9⅞" w, painted mill by pond in landscape in rose, flower sprays on border, gilt dentil rim, c1754, blue interlaced "L's" mark (A) **1,555.00**
Ecuelle and Stand, 8" d, matte and burnished gilt flying and perched birds, mayfly in center of stand, gilt accented crabstock handles, fruit knob on cov, c1753, blue interlaced "L's" mark (A) **11,100.00**
Ewer, 9½" h, panels of painted flower sprays framed in tooled gilt floral trellis, reserved on bleu lapis ground, dated 1752, blue interlaced "L's" mark **400.00**
Ewer and Basin, 9¼" h ewer, 14⅜" d basin, molded waves with gilt accents, polychrome enamel summer flowers, center of basin with blue torque and yellow ribbon, c1753, blue interlaced "L's & A" mark (A) .**21,000.00**
Figure, 7" h, white allegorical "France" seated on rockwork holding book and globe, ormolu base, c1752 ....**3,500.00**
Jar, cov, 3¼" h, painted multicolored bouquets, gilt knob finial, cylindrical, c1750, blue interlaced "L's & dot" mark (A) **2,640.00**
Milk Jug, Cov
4¾" h, blue painted Cupid and putto representing Summer and Autumn in gilt ovals, yellow ground, gilt dentil rims, blue flower finial, c1753 (A) **5,830.00**
5½" h, painted flowers in gilt foliage cartouches reserved on bleu celeste ground, entwined branch handle, gilt dentil rims and flowerhead finial, c1753, blue interlaced "L's" mark (A) **285.00**
Miniature Tea Service, teapot, two cups and saucers, 10" l, quatrefoil tray, gilt flowers and border, bleu lapis ground,

c1753, blue interlaced "L's" mark
(A) **4,680.00**
Plate
9¼" d, painted fruit and flower sprays
in gilt scroll and foliage surrounds,
border of five cartouches, exotic
birds, bleu celeste ground, c1753,
blue interlaced "L's & dot" mark,
pr (A) **570.00**
9¾" d, painted exotic birds in landscape, border molded C-scrolls, reserved with three cartouches
painted with flowers, green ground,
c1756 (A) **275.00**
Potpourri Vase, 9", rose painted putti in
clouds in tooled gilt foliage and scroll
cartouches, bleu lapis ground, gilt
outlined holes, c1755, blue inter-
laced "L's" mark, pr, damaged (A) . **6,160.00**
Saucer
Painted scattered flowers, brown rim,
trembleuse, c1750 (A) **225.00**
Painted spray of flowers in gilt floral
and foliage cartouche, bleu celeste
border, gilt dentil rim, dated 1753,
blue interlaced "L's" mark (A) **375.00**
White, molded flowering prunus,
c1745 (A) **150.00**
Sugar, Cov, 4½" h, painted birds in gardens in tooled gilt scroll and batwing
cartouches, bleu lapis ground, gilt
dots, fruit knob, gilt dentil rims,
c1750, blue interlaced "L's" mark
(A) **1,100.00**
Teapot, 5¼" h, tooled gilt flower bordered cartouches, scenes of multicolored birds in flight, bleu lapis ground,
rose edged flower knob, c1753, blue
interlaced "L's" mark (A) **4,125.00**

VOLKSTEDT

Thuringia, Germany (DDR)
1760 to Present

History: The Volkstedt porcelain factory was
started about 1760 under the patronage of Johann
Friedrich von Schwartzburg-Rudolstadt. The
peak of its fame occurred between 1767 and
1797 when the factory was leased to Christian
Fonne. A succession of owners followed.

Until 1800 the factory produced mostly ordinary tablewares. These were usually massive in
design and decorated in the Rococo style. Some
fine vases decorated in Rococo or formal styles
were made. Decorative motifs included small
portraits, landscapes, and ornamental maps.

Between 1898 and 1972 Karl Ens occupied
one portion of the Volkstedt factory. The firm
made decorative porcelains, figures, and gift articles. The company was nationalized in 1972
and named VEB Underglaze Porcelain Factory.

During the 20th century, Volkstedt manufactured tablewares, vases, and figures in the Meissen style.

Museums: Victoria & Albert Museum, London,
England.

**Figures, 5½" h, multicolored, X'd hatchet
marks, pr, $450.00.**

Box
3" d, multicolored LeBrun portrait,
hinged cov **165.00**
3½" d, cov painted with recumbent
stag in landscape, sides with rabbits
and dog, int. of cov painted with
huntsman holding scroll, silver-gilt
mounts, c1760, blue "X'd hayfork
& M" mark (A) **8,750.00**
Candelabras, 10" h, three arms, figures
of Mercury and putto at bases,
multicolored, Karl Ens mark, pr **560.00**
Centerpiece, 7" h, rococo style bowl applied with three putti and swallows in
flight, encrusted and painted florals . **85.00**
Compote, 13" d, 9" h, five cherubs holding fruit filled bowl **400.00**
Cup and Saucer, alternate puce and yellow stripes, puce diaper border, "X'd
hayfork" mark **60.00**
Ewer, 11½" h, quatrefoil panels of European and Turkish figures in quay
scene, multicolored, Kakiemon florals, ormolu mounted necks with tassels, shield shape, foliate loop handles, sq bases, 19th C, pr **1,500.00**
Figure
2¼" h, multicolored butterfly on base,
Karl Ens **45.00**

2¾" h, seated green frog, black and gold trim, gold crown on head, Karl Ens **65.00**

4¼" h, standing goat, white glaze, c1910 .... **175.00**

4⅞" h, putto, holding flower garland, yellow drapery, tree stump base, c1760, restored (A) **380.00**

6¾" h, long tailed multicolored exotic bird, white base **85.00**

7½" h, 4½" h, fighting cocks in different poses, green and yellow bodies, red and brown trim, Karl Ens, pr **225.00**

10" h, lady holding parrot and rose, multicolored hoop skirt, c1898 ... **125.00**

11" h, rearing stallions supported by rockwork, metal reins held by youths in multicolored and gilt drapes, c1900, blue "X'd hayforks & dot" mark, pr **400.00**

12" h, porcelain Greek mythological character, white **375.00**

13½" h, two blue herons on base, Karl Ens **225.00**

28½" l, "The Introduction," seated lady with companion being introduced to bowing gentleman and curtsying lady, 18th C lace clothes, scrolling base, blue "shield" mark (A) **660.00**

Medallion, 2½" h, molded bust of young man in white jacket, iron-red collar, brown ground, ebonized frame, c1775 (A) **115.00**

Mirror, 30" l, 17½" w, porcelain frame, blue and white flowers and gilt, by Rudolph Kamner **900.00**

Vase, 14" h, porcelain, white relief of plants and girl in robes, marbled green and white glazed ground, baluster shape, Karl Ens, pr **225.00**

WEDGWOOD

Burslem, near Stoke-on-Trent, England
1759 to 1769

Etruria Factory, England
1769 to 1940

Barlaston, near Stoke-on-Trent, England
1940 to Present

History: By 1759 Josiah Wedgwood was working in Burslem, Staffordshire, manufacturing earthenware. A partnership with Bentley was formed shortly after he moved to his new factory in Etruria in 1769. The partnership lasted until 1780.

CREAMWARE

Wedgwood's creamware utilized a Cornwall clay that created a lighter, stronger body of a more uniform texture. It became designated "Queensware" after Wedgwood supplied a breakfast set for Queen Charlotte in 1762.

BLACK BASALT

Black Basalt was fine grained, unglazed black stoneware made between 1767 and 1796. This term was coined by Josiah Wedgwood to describe a refined version of "Egyptian black." In his 1787 catalog, Wedgwood described his ware as "a black porcelain biscuit (that is, unglazed body) of nearly the same properties with the natural stone, striking fire from steel, receiving a high polish, serving as a touchstone for metals, resisting all acids, and bearing without injury a strong fire - stronger indeed than the basalts itself." "Egyptian black" was used for utilitarian wares and for large relief plaques, vases, busts, medallions, seals, and small intaglios. It was a black clay body that resembled bronze when unpolished. Both historical and mythological figures and faces were produced.

JASPER

Jasper, probably Josiah Wedgwood's best known product, was started in 1774. Known as a "dry body" because it was non-porous and unglazed, this vitreous fine stoneware was made in several shades of blue, green, lilac, yellow, maroon, black, and white. Sometimes more than one color was combined. "Solid" jasper had the body colored throughout; white jasper "dip" was a white jasper body with the color laid on the surface. Raised figures and ornaments in white adorned the tremendous variety of jasper shapes. Classical motifs were most prominent. Wedgwood's replica of the Barberini or Portland vase was considered a high point in the production.

PEARLWARE

Pearlware, introduced by Wedgwood in 1779, was whiter than Queensware. Cobalt oxide was added to the glaze, reacting like a laundry blueing that whitens clothing.

After Bentley's death in 1780, Wedgwood worked alone until 1790 when his sons and Thomas Byerley became his partners. From 1769 until 1780 the firm was called "Wedgwood and Bentley." It was simply "Wedgwood" in the decade from 1780 to 1790. The name became

"Wedgwood Sons and Byerley" between 1790 and 1793 and "Wedgwood & Sons & Byerley" between 1793 and 1795. Josiah Wedgwood died in 1795.

REDWARES

Other "dry bodies" or redwares that were manufactured between 1776 and 1870 included (a) cane ware (pale buff colored stoneware); (b) rosso antico (dark red to chocolate colored unglazed stoneware); (c) terra cotta (light red stoneware); (d) drabware (olive gray stoneware); and, (e) white stoneware (pure white biscuit). Both utilitarian and decorative wares were made.

When Josiah II took over, he introduced the manufacture of bone china in 1812. Josiah II was not satisfied with the product, so it was discontinued in 1828. Bone china was not manufactured again until 1878.

The forty year period from 1840 to 1880 was one of modernization. Solid jasper was reintroduced. Parian ware, a fine white body resembling marble, was produced. When Wedgwood introduced majolica in 1860, the company was the first to use a white body and semi-transparent colored glazes.

When Wedgwood began to manufacture porcelain again in 1878, the products were of very high quality in texture, color, glaze, and decoration. The printed mark with the Portland vase was used on this porcelain.

Fourth and fifth generations of Wedgwoods continued to operate the firm into the 20th century. An interest in late 18th century design was revived. Commemorative wares were made for the American market.

WEDGWOOD LUSTERS

Wedgwood lusters were formed by applying iridescent or metallic films on the surface of the ceramic wares. The effect was obtained by using metallic oxides of gold, silver, copper, etc. Lusters were applied as embellishments to an enameled object or as a complete or nearly complete covering to duplicate the effect of a silver or copper metallic object. The lusters were decorated by the resist method.

From 1915 to 1931 Wedgwood produced fairyland lusters from the designs of Daisy Makeig-Jones. Fairyland lusters were made in Queensware plaques and bone china plates and ornamental pieces, such as vases and bowls. The designs combined the use of bright underglaze colors, commercial lusters, and gold printing, often with fantastic and grotesque figures, scenes, and landscapes.

Pattern numbers were painted on the base of fairyland luster pieces by the artist who decorated them along with the Wedgwood marks.

A new factory was built at Barlaston, six miles

from Etruria. Firing was done at Barlaston in six electric ovens. Production started at the new factory in 1940. Etruria eventually was closed in June, 1950.

On May 1, 1959, the company commemorated its bicentenary. During the 1960s, Wedgwood acquired many English firms such as Coalport, William Adams & Sons, Royal Tuscan, Susie Cooper, and Johnson Brothers. Further expansion in the 1970s brought J. & G. Meakin, Midwinter Companies, Crown Staffordshire, Mason's Ironstone, and Precision Studios into the fold. Each company retained its own identity. The Wedgwood Group is one of the largest fine china and earthenware manufacturers in the world.

References: M. Batkin, *Wedgwood Ceramics 1846–1959*, Richard Denis Publications; David Buten, *18th Century Wedgwood*, Methuen, Inc. 1980; Alison Kelly, *The Story of Wedgwood*, The Viking Press, 1975; Wolf Mankowitz, *Wedgwood*, Spring Books, 1966; Robin Reilly & George Savage, *The Dictionary of Wedgwood*, Antique Collectors' Club, Ltd, 1980.

Collectors' Clubs: The Wedgwood Society, The Buten Museum of Wedgwood, 246 N. Bowman Avenue, Merion, Pa. Membership: $10.00.; The Wedgwood Society, The Roman Villa, Rockbourne, Fordingbridge, Hants. SP6 3 PG, England. Membership: 7½ pounds. Wedgwood Data Chart, semi-annual newsletter.

Museums: Birmingham Museum of Art, Birmingham, Alabama; Buten Museum of Wedgwood, Merion, Pennsylvania; City Museum & Art Gallery, Stoke-on-Trent, England; Henry E. Huntington Library & Art Gallery, San Marino, California; R. W. Norton Art Gallery, Shreveport, Louisiana; Wedgwood Museum, Barlaston, England.

REPRODUCTION ALERT: Two marks are currently in use on Wedgwood pieces. If neither of these marks appear on a piece, it is probably not Wedgwood.

BASALT

Bowl
  9¼" d, 4" h, emb stripes and rim design, imp "WEDGWOOD" (A) ... **300.00**
  10" d
    Acanthus leaf relief decor, Wedgwood mark **325.00**
    "Dancing Hours" design, "Wedgwood, Made in England" **375.00**
  10¼" d, acanthus pattern, "Wedgwood, Made in England" **385.00**
Bust
  2½" h, laughing child, circ flaring pedestal, imp "Wedgwood" (A) .. **175.00**
  3¾" h, Aristophanes, flaring pedestal,

band of chain pattern, c1770-80,
"WEDGWOOD & BENTLEY" (A) **550.00**
4" h
Ariadne in goatskin, vine on pedestal, imp "WEDGWOOD" (A) **110.00**
Athena, black, marked **450.00**
6¾" h, Newton, flaring socle, band
of key pattern, c1770-80, imp
"WEDGWOOD & BENTLEY"(A) .**1,540.00**
14¼" h, Venus, head turned toward
shoulder, Wedgwood mark **900.00**
18" h, Mercury, winged helmet, circ
socle, Wedgwood mark **1,150.00**

**Box, cov, 4½" h, imp "WEDGWOOD,"
$300.00.**

Candlesticks
5¾" h, recumbent winged sphinxes,
nozzles on backs, oblong bases,
late 18th C, imp "WEDGWOOD,"
pr (A) **1,320.00**
6" h, "Egyptian," shafts molded with
three sphinx caryatids supporting
socket, triangular bases, imp
"WEDGWOOD" (A) **900.00**
10½" h, figures of Ceres and Cybele
supporting cornucopia ending in
nozzles, circ columns, applied
leaves on sq bases, early 19th C,
imp "WEDGWOOD," pr (A) **880.00**
11" h, classical females holding trumpet flower over left shoulder, circ
plinths on sq bases, imp "WEDG-
WOOD," pr (A) **250.00**
Condiment Set, salt, pepper, and mustard, emb laurel wreath on shoulders,
imp "WEDGWOOD" **465.00**
Creamer
3" h, Tudor Rose, harp, thistle, and
shamrock, imp "WEDGWOOD" . **85.00**
4" l, 4" h, engine-turned, "Battlement" shape, imp "WEDG-
WOOD" **85.00**
Cup and Saucer
Canadian coat of arms, Niagara Falls,
Canada, green enameled border,
glazed int., marked **125.00**
Enameled polychrome florals, gilt accents, imp "WEDGWOOD" (A) .. **150.00**

Husk and berry design, imp "WEDG-
WOOD" **135.00**
Ewer
6" h, basketweave body, marked ... **145.00**
8" h, relief of classical dancing figures, berried foliage wreath, loop
handle from satyr's mask, engine
turnings, sq base, mid 19th C, imp
"WEDGWOOD & L" (A) **385.00**
15" h
Gilded drape over upper body, sq
base, twisted handle follows
shape of spout, imp "WEDG-
WOOD" **1,750.00**
Raised gilded wheat design, c1860 **1,650.00**
Figure
2¾" h, black bulldog, white and
brown glass eyes, imp "WEDG-
WOOD" mark **350.00**
4¼" h, bird, glass eyes, imp "WEDG-
WOOD" mark **575.00**
4¾" h, black cat, yellow glass eyes,
imp "WEDGWOOD" mark **325.00**
5" l, nude sleeping boy, draped base,
canted corners, imp "WEDG-
WOOD" (A) **330.00**
10¾" l, recumbent sphinxes wearing
foliage molded cloth, oblong bases,
late 19th C, imp "WEDGWOOD,"
pr (A) **1,870.00**
16½" h
Eros perched on Euphrosyne's
shoulder, small circ base, Wedgwood mark **900.00**
Faith, standing, holding book, in
cloak, circ base imp "Faith," late
19th C, imp "WEDGWOOD"
mark (A) **220.00**
18" h, standing Faun holding infant
Bacchus in arms, leaning on tree
stump, sq base imp "Faun & Bacchus," c1880, imp "WEDG-
WOOD" (A) **1,000.00**
Inkwell
4" d, band of acanthus leaves on base,
flowerheads on rim, nine openings,
c1820, imp "WEDGWOOD" (A) . **200.00**
4" d, 2¾" h, engine turned design,
c1800, imp "WEDGWOOD" **300.00**
7⅝" l, attached base, oil lamp shape,
pierced, six openings, imp
"WEDGWOOD" (A) **125.00**
Medallion
1½" w, 2¼" h, portrait of Maximinius,
imp "WEDGWOOD" **125.00**
2¼" h, profile relief portraits of Kings
and Queens of England, imp
"WEDGWOOD," set of 16 (A) ... **500.00**
3" w, 4" h, Admiral Howe, imp
"WEDGWOOD" **350.00**
Mug, 3¾" h, relief of scrolling oak
leaves and acorns, strap handle, silver

mounted rim, c1810, imp "WEDG-
WOOD" (A) **265.00**
Oil Lamp
 5⅛" l, loop handle, flat cov, scroll
 finial, imp "WEDGWOOD" (A) . . **200.00**
 5¼" l, painted flowering plants, iron-
 red accented handle, early 19th C,
 imp "WEDGWOOD" (A) **220.00**
 8½" h, molded acanthus leaves and
 bell flowers, tops with molded
 maidens reading book or holding
 jug, cov with knob finials, sq bases
 with molded flowerheads, mid 19th
 C, imp "WEDGWOOD," pr (A) . .**1,210.00**
Plaque
 5½" w, relief of Pan and Satyr, c1770-
 80, imp "WEDGWOOD & BEN-
 TLEY" (A) **935.00**
 6¼" h, relief of Anthony in breastplate
 holding sword, c1770-80, imp
 "WEDGWOOD & BENTLEY" (A) **1,540.00**
 10" l, 6¼" h, relief of Venus at forge
 of Vulcan, giltwood frame, imp
 "WEDGWOOD" (A) **385.00**
 12" h, relief of Roman youth, giltwood frame, imp "WEDGWOOD"
 (A) **500.00**
 18¾" l, 10¼" h, relief of Death of
 Roman warrior, entirely bronzed,
 wood frame, late 19th C, imp
 "WEDGWOOD" (A) **880.00**
Potpourri Bowl, 5¾" d, relief of classical
 figures at altar in gilt and bronze, gilt
 reeded handles, pierced cov with
 flowerheads and knob, c1880, imp
 "WEDGWOOD" (A) **330.00**
Potpourri Jar, 8¼" h, painted pheasant
 on rockwork with flowers, c1830,
 imp "WEDGWOOD" (A) **150.00**
Scent Bottle, 7" h, relief design, bulbous
 base, long narrow neck, marked . . **310.00**
Spill Holder, 9½" h, seated winged
 sphinxes, openings in heads, oblong
 bases, imp "WEDGWOOD," pr, re-
 paired (A) **1,045.00**
Spill Vase, 3¾" h, Muse of Drama and
 Music, flowers, and trees, imp
 "WEDGWOOD" **125.00**
Sugar
 3¼" d, engine turned, battlement rim,
 "Sybil" knob, marked **200.00**
 3¾" d
 Cameos of Greek mythology, imp
 "WEDGWOOD" **85.00**
 Relief of Bacchanalian boys, engine
 turning, c1790 (A) **385.00**
Sugar Box, Cov, 5¼" w, relief of Bac-
 chanalian boys, engine turning (A) . . **150.00**
Tea Kettle, 9¼" h, engine turned design,
 imp "WEDGWOOD" (A) **120.00**
Teabowl and Saucer, imp "WEDG-
 WOOD" **100.00**

Teapot
 6½" w, basketweave pattern, "Sybil"
 finial, imp "WEDGWOOD" (A) . . **120.00**
 7¼" w, 4¾" h, "Sybil" knob, imp
 "WEDGWOOD" **200.00**
 7½" h, painted musical and military
 trophies, white and brown, band of
 stylized foliage, early 19th C, imp
 "WEDGWOOD" **600.00**
Tray
 9" l, raised classical figures, oval,
 marked **65.00**
 9¾" w, applied classical figures and
 flowerheads, dbl handles, imp
 "WEDGWOOD" (A) **100.00**
Urn
 7" h, satyr mask handles, marked . . . **115.00**
 11" h
 Etruscan encaustic dec, mid 18th
 C, ...**4,500.00**
 Gilded classical rope pattern, cov,
 c1860, Wedgwood mark **1,700.00**
Vase
 3½" h
 Bud, "Capri" design, Wedgwood
 mark **350.00**
 Enameled polychrome florals, imp
 "WEDGWOOD" (A) **75.00**
 4" h, Canadian coat of arms, imp
 "ETRURIA" **100.00**
 5" h, enameled polychrome florals,
 dbl handles ending in masks, imp
 "WEDGWOOD" (A) **200.00**
 8¼" h, cov
 Engine turned flutes, satyr's mask
 handles, sq base, acorn finial,
 late 19th C (A) **385.00**
 Oviform, dbl loop handles, flaring
 foot on sq base, base finial,
 c1775-80, imp "WEDGWOOD
 & BENTLEY" (A) **1,100.00**
 9¼" h
 Applied putti and band of Zodiac
 signs, scroll handles, flaring foot,
 sq base, cov, c1770-80, imp
 "WEDGWOOD & BENTLEY"
 (A) **1,000.00**
 Engine turned shallow grooves,
 reeded dbl handles, circ foot, sq
 base, c1770, imp "WEDG-
 WOOD & BENTLEY, ETRURIA"
 (A) **460.00**
 9¾" h, cov, oviform, cov with mod-
 eled sphinx head supporting candle
 nozzle, c1765-80, imp "WEDG-
 WOOD & BENTLEY" (A) **3,300.00**
 11" h
 Engine turned, two satyrs' masks on
 shoulder, horns forming handles,
 urn shape, sq base, c1790, imp
 "WEDGWOOD" (A) **420.00**

Raised vine design, trumpet shape, Wedgwood mark **450.00**

11½" h, painted classical figures in sepia, anthemion on neck, dbl handles, late 18th C, imp "WEDGWOOD" (A) **1,540.00**

21½" h, applied oval medallion of Hercules wrestling lion, two sphinx head handles, sq base, c1775, imp "WEDGWOOD & BENTLEY, ETRURIA" (A) **880.00**

GENERAL

Beaker, 4" h, black and white engine turned design **500.00**

Bowl
4¾" h, cov, "Patrician" pattern of molded floral and leaf arabesques, spaniel knob, imp "WEDGWOOD" (A) **110.00**

8¾" h, cov, Queensware, spherical open work, applied intertwined handles, floral finial, waisted circ foot, c1769 .... **250.00**

9" d, "Fallow Deer" design, footed, marked **150.00**

10½" d, 6" h, Ferrara ware, blue and white, footed, marked **145.00**

12" d, black transfer, central scene of Picadilly Circus, ext. with panels of boat race and mermaid device, "Wedgwood, Made in England" (A) **500.00**

Box, Cov, 4½" w, olive green stoneware, heart shape, marked **225.00**

Bulb Pot
8¼" w, Rosso Antico, applied black dice pattern, band of flowerheads, cov with three openings, c1820, imp "WEDGWOOD" (A) **825.00**

9½" l, hedgehog, ribbed body, multiple openings, light blue glaze, "WEDGWOOD" **490.00**

Calendar Tile
1898 .... **65.00**
1906 .... **40.00**

Candlestick
6" h, Rosso Antico, Capri design, cut out bases, "Wedgwood", pr **500.00**

6¾" h, Rosso Antico, applied black leaves on nozzle, three sphinx monopedian paw feet, triangular base, c1815, imp "WEDGWOOD" mark (A) **715.00**

8½" h, terra cotta body, multicolored enamel florals, Wedgwood marks, pr **650.00**

Coffee Can, 3" h, pale blue luster, reserves of fruit, gold handles, sgd "A. Holland," pr **625.00**

Coffee Can and Saucer, painted iron-red

and gilt trellis pattern, stylized flowerheads, c1812-22, marked (A) **100.00**

Coffeepot, 8" h, Rosso Antico, applied black flowerheads and swags from tied ribbons "Sybil" finial, c1865, imp "WEDGWOOD" mark (A) **220.00**

Cup and Saucer
Bone china, underglaze blue botanical print, imp "WEDGWOOD" .. **35.00**

Rosso Antico, black relief, Egyptian motifs, imp "WEDGWOOD" (A) . **225.00**

White biscuit, C-scroll handle, glazed int., imp "WEDGWOOD" (A) ... **125.00**

Custard Cup, Cov, 2½" h, Caneware, 12 sided, arrow handle, c1820, imp "WEDGWOOD" (A) **275.00**

Egg Cup, Caneware, relief of brown scrolling vine, c1820, imp "WEDGWOOD" (A) **275.00**

Figure
5¾" h, young boy, turquoise glaze, imp "PEARL & WEDGWOOD" .. **300.00**

15¾" h, Queensware, "Taurus the Bull," printed in colors, Zodiac signs, cream ground, (A) **110.00**

Flower Holder, 5½" h, gray salt glazed body, raised blue flowers and leaves, pierced top, "WEDGWOOD" **300.00**

Inkwell, 9½" l, Moonstone finish, Wedgwood mark **275.00**

Jardiniere
8¼" l, 7½" h, olive green stoneware, marked **450.00**

8½" d, matching stand, Caneware, applied olive fern and stars, c1830, imp "WEDGWOOD" (A) **220.00**

Jug
6" h Hunt scene
Green, hound handle, c1930, marked **55.00**

Raised multicolored, hound handle, c1930 .... **60.00**

Rockingham ware
Classical figures, rope twist handle, c1880, imp "WEDGWOOD" (A) **140.00**

Wheel cut lilies of the valley and dot pattern, manganese ground, c1880, imp "WEDGWOOD" (A) **140.00**

8" h
Caneware, gothic style, blue applied figures, S-handle, molded foliage, oval scale panels on lower section, c1850, imp "WEDGWOOD" (A) **240.00**

Drabware, classical women emb on panels, wide, loop handle, c1820, Wedgwood mark **2,250.00**

Pitcher
7½" h, white stoneware body, hunting scene, blue jasper dipped band and handle with cameo florals, c1820, Wedgwood mark **420.00**

8" h, blue and white "Fallow Deer" design, tankard shape, marked ... **65.00**

8½" h, olive green stoneware, "Washington" and "Franklin", vintage border, marked **475.00**

Pitcher, 11⅜" h, stoneware, multicolored, (A) $150.00.

Plate

8½" d

Black printed and painted multicolored specimen flowers, gilt diamond borders, c1815, iron-red "Wedgwood," pr (A) **460.00**

Painting of two women with swan by Emile Lessore, shell shape .. **600.00**

9¾" d

Blue and white scene, "The Lillie Off Telegraph Hill," marked ... **65.00**

Stone china, printed and painted lotus and terrace, c1840, pr (A) **220.00**

10" d, playing cards, king, queen, and knave in four suits on border, marked **100.00**

Platter, 15" l, 10⅞" w, blue and white pastoral scene of cows and village, floral border, dated 1911, marked .. **125.00**

Sauceboat

7" l, cov, attached underplate, glazed creamware, loop handles and button finial, "Wedgwood" **250.00**

8" l, shape of grape clusters, leaf form base, green, c1825, marked, pr ..**1,250.00**

10" l, matching ladle, Caneware, molded foliage from dbl handles on dimpled ground, band of leaves on lower section, c1840, imp "WEDGWOOD" mark (A) **100.00**

Spittoon, 5" d, 4" h, basketweave under neck, black glaze, imp "WEDGWOOD" **300.00**

Sugar

4½" d, Caneware, brown applied fern and stars, flowerhead finial, c1830, marked, firing crack (A) **110.00**

5½" d, Rosso Antico, applied black

bands of ferns and stars, c1830, imp "WEDGWOOD" **150.00**

6" d, Rosso Antico, applied black Egyptian motifs, crocodile finial, c1810, imp "WEDGWOOD" (A) . **220.00**

Teapot

4½" h, Rosso Antico, black relief Egyptian scene, dentil border, imp "WEDGWOOD" (A) **200.00**

5¼" h, glazed cane in mustard, white raised florals and scrolls, spaniel finial, c1869, Wedgwood mark .. **500.00**

8½" w, 4½" h

Caneware, basketweave pattern, Sheaf of Wheat knob, acanthus spout and handle, imp "WEDGWOOD" **225.00**

Drabware, "Gothic" decor, "Bearded Man" faces on lower section, imp "WEDGWOOD" . **225.00**

9" w, 4½" h, Rosso Antico, black anthemia border, black bell flower on lid, c1805, imp "WEDGWOOD" **650.00**

10" w, bands of scrolling foliage, smear glazed, dog finial, imp "WEDGWOOD" mark (A) **175.00**

Tureen

7¼" h, attached base, Queensware, ribbed, ram's head handles, imp "WEDGWOOD" (A) **100.00**

17¼" l, cov, blue feather edges, small blue floral design, open handles, fruit finial, imp "WEDGWOOD," pr, hairline (A) **210.00**

Turkey Set, platter and twelve plates, multicolored wild turkey in field, marked (A) **800.00**

Urn

2¾" h, white biscuit, dbl C-scroll handles, glazed int., imp "WEDGWOOD" (A) **80.00**

11" h, cov, gilded and bronzed finish, c1860, Wedgwood mk **1,750.00**

Vase

4" h, Caneware, applied acanthus leaves and bell flowers, band of vines on rim, blue accents, campana shape, c1840, imp "WEDGWOOD" mark (A) **100.00**

7½" h, cov, Rosso Antico, applied Egyptian motifs, black ground, sphinx support on three paw feet, oviform, pierced cov, c1810, imp "WEDGWOOD & Z" (A) **935.00**

7¾" h, Rosso Antico, molded basketweave body, shallow grooves, applied Egyptian motifs on rim, c1815, imp "WEDGWOOD" (A) . **200.00**

12½" h, Rosso Antico, applied black Egyptian motifs, dbl black sphinx handles, c1815, imp "WEDGWOOD" (A) **600.00**

13¼" h, Caneware, applied drab fruiting vine, crater shape, imp "WEDGWOOD," handle repair (A) **200.00**

15" h, Ferrara ware, blue and white, marked **165.00**

15½" h, cov, Rosso Antico, applied black classical figures and bands of foliage, campana shape, pierced cov, applied athemion and leaves, imp "WEDGWOOD" mark (A) .. **880.00**

Wall Planter, 7" w, Caneware, basketweave, blue enamel stripe, c1800 .. **275.00**

Water Bottle, 11" h, Rosso Antico, imp "WEDGWOOD" **225.00**

JASPER

Barber Bottle, 10½" h, light blue ground, white cameos, marked **575.00**

Biscuit Barrel

5½" h, lavender top and bottom bands, center sage green band, white cameos of classical figures and cherubs, SP top, rim, and handle, Wedgwood mark **700.00**

6" h

Lilac ground, white classic cameos, SP top, rim, and handle, imp "WEDGWOOD" **325.00**

Sage green top and bottom bands, white classical figures on center lavender band, SP top, rim, and handle, Wedgwood mark **700.00**

8" h, blue ground, white classic scenes, bulbous body, SP base, lid, and handle, imp "WEDGWOOD" (A) **100.00**

Bottle, Cov

10" h, light blue ground, white cameos and lilac medallions **1,250.00**

10½" h, green, lilac, and white jasper, raised mythological heads, medallion inserts, Wedgwood mark **1,550.00**

Bowl

4½" w, med blue ground, white classic cameos, imp "WEDGWOOD" **100.00**

5" w, 2¾" h, dark blue ground, white classic cameos, imp "WEDGWOOD" **125.00**

6" d, dark blue ground, white mythological figures, white glazed int., "Wedgwood, England" **75.00**

9" d, 4" h, green ground, white classical scenes, SP rim, imp "Wedgwood England" (A) **70.00**

Box, Cov

3½" d, yellow ground, white classical figure cameos, Wedgwood mark . **375.00**

4" d, light blue ground, white classic cameos, imp "WEDGWOOD" ... **200.00**

Bulb Pot, 5¾" h, white cameos of Cupids in recesses, blue ground, scroll feet, applied foliage, tree trunk molded covs, c1810, imp "WEDGWOOD," pr (A) **285.00**

Bust

3¾" h, Pindar, white, black basalt socle, c1770-80, imp "WEDGWOOD & BENTLEY" (A) **1,430.00**

15" h, Milton, white, black basalt base, imp "E Wyon," c1860, imp "WEDGWOOD" (A) **265.00**

Butter Dish, 6⅞" d, blue ground, white classic scenes, SP base and lid, "Wedgwood, England" (A) **160.00**

Cameo, 1⅝" l, 2" h

Green dip over white, "Antonia," imp "WEDGWOOD" **175.00**

White "Apollo," light blue ground, imp "WEDGWOOD" **150.00**

Candlestick

5¼" h, black ground, white classical cameos, cameo leaf rings on bases, pr **275.00**

5¾" h, white, stems molded with rams' heads suspending gilt foliage

Jasper, left, biscuit jar, 6" h, white cameos, black ground, SP handle, rim, and lid, imp "WEDGWOOD," $425.00; center, candlesticks, 7" h, white cameos, dark blue ground, imp "WEDGWOOD," pr, $300.00; right, vase, 9" h, Portland, white cameos, black ground, imp "WEDGWOOD," $750.00.

swags, nozzles and feet with gilt husks and bands of foliage, late 19th C, imp "WEDGWOOD & A," pr (A) **242.00**

8⅝" h, light green ground, white classic cameos, imp "WEDGWOOD" **150.00**

10¾" h, white jasper figures of Ceres and Cybele holding blue jasper dipped cornucopia ending in nozzles, circ blue dipped bases, SP plinths, imp "WEDGWOOD," pr (A) **770.00**

Cheese Dish, 11" d, light blue ground, white leaf and classic cameos, cov, "Wedgwood, England" **300.00**

Clock, 3½" d, 12¼" h, white cameos of classic woman and cupid on body, floral wreath around clock face, green ground, "Wedgwood, England" **550.00**

Cracker Jar, 6½" h, dark blue ground, white classic cameos, honey pot shape, metal cov and handle, Wedgwood mark **190.00**

Creamer

3½" h, blue ground, white classic scenes in ovals, "Wedgwood, England" (A) **20.00**

Blue ground, white cameos of chariots and horses, Wedgwood mark **65.00**

Creamer and Sugar, 2⅜" h creamer, 3½" h, cov sugar, terra cotta ground, black Egyptian motif cameos, marked **250.00**

Cup and Saucer

Dark blue ground, white classic cameos, white glazed int., "Wedgwood, England" **85.00**

Light blue ground, white classic cameos, white glazed int., "Wedgwood, England" **50.00**

Custard Cup

2" w, green, teardrop shape, molded lattice work, late 18th C, imp "WEDGWOOD" (A) **770.00**

2¼" l, blue, comma shape, molded lattice work, late 18th C, imp "WEDGWOOD" (A) **550.00**

Flower Holder, 5" h, matching underliner, band of cameo florals, dark blue ground, white cameos of women, children and trees, white glazed int., c1850, marked **190.00**

Jar, 3½" d, 4½" h, lavender bands top and bottom, green center band, white classic cameos, SP top, rim, and handle, imp "WEDGWOOD" **550.00**

Jardiniere

3¼" l, 2⅝" h, band of white flowers, cobalt ground, drainage hole in bottom, imp "WEDGWOOD" ... **200.00**

6" l, 5½" h, dark blue ground, white classic cameos, imp "WEDGWOOD" **225.00**

7⅝" h, blue ground, white cameos of Bacchanalian boys in various pursuits in panels, leaf and icicle borders, tree branch handles, imp "WEDGWOOD" (A) **120.00**

Jug

2½" h, dark blue ground, white cameos, trefoil spout, imp "WEDGWOOD" **125.00**

5¼" h, blue ground, white cameos of Bacchanalian figures and vines, imp "WEDGWOOD" (A) **60.00**

Loving Cup, light green ground, white applied dec, c1890, "Wedgwood, England" **165.00**

Match Box, 3½" l, blue ground, classic woman in white on cov, leaf outlined edge, imp "WEDGWOOD" (A) **75.00**

Medallion

3¾" h, white cameos of Anthony and Cleopatra, blue ground, giltwood frames, late 18th C, imp "WEDGWOOD," pr (A) **715.00**

5½" h, white cameos of Claudius, Tiberius, and Domitian wearing laurel wreaths, blue ground, c1775, imp "WEDGWOOD & BENTLEY," set of 3 (A) **460.00**

Milk Jug

3½" h, crimson jasper ground, white cameo inserts, marked **450.00**

4½" h, black ground, white classic cameos, "Wedgwood, Made in England" **200.00**

6½" h, dark blue ground, white classic cameos, imp "WEDGWOOD" **225.00**

Muffineer, 6" h, dark blue ground, white cameos of four figures and forest scene, SP top, imp "WEDGWOOD" **160.00**

Mug

3⅞" d, 5" h, dark blue ground, white cameos of classical ladies, SP top band, marked **145.00**

5¼" h, green body, white classic cameo figures, white glazed int., "Wedgwood, England" **120.00**

Pin Tray, 8½" l, blue ground, two white classical women, imp "WEDGWOOD" **150.00**

Pitcher

4" h, dark blue ground, white classic figures, grape and leaf border, rope twist handle, Wedgwood mark ... **85.00**

5" h, dark blue ground, white classic figures, tankard shape, imp "WEDGWOOD" **150.00**

5½" h, blue ground, white cameos of classic scenes, marked (A) **175.00**

6¼" h, blue ground, white classic cameos, cylindrical, marked (A) .. **35.00**

Plaque

2½" l, blue, green, and white jasper,

classic cameos, clipped corners, marked **175.00**

6" h, green ground, white cameos of classic female on each, oval, Wedgwood marks **360.00**

7" w, 10" h, lilac ground, white cameo of Madonna and laurel leaf rim design, imp "WEDGWOOD" **325.00**

8½" h, black ground, white cameo busts of Alexandra and Edward VII, flowerhead garlands, pr (A) **350.00**

10" h, blue ground, white cameos of classic women, giltwood frame, mid 19th C, imp "WEDGWOOD," pr (A) **285.00**

14¾" l, 6½" h, blue ground, white cameo of Funeral of Patrocleson, giltwood frame, imp "WEDGWOOD" (A) **460.00**

15½" l, 6½" h, blue ground, white cameo of Sacrifice of Iphegenia, early 19th C, imp "WEDGWOOD" mark (A) **1,320.00**

Plate

2½" d, dark blue ground, white classic cameos, imp "WEDGWOOD" **125.00**

8½" d, blue ground, white cameo medallions of classical figure and winged horse, fruiting swags and rams' heads, late 19th C, imp "WEDGWOOD" (A) **210.00**

8¾" d, green dipped ground, white cameos of winged Zephyr in ribbon, garlands suspended from rams' heads, late 19th C, imp "WEDGWOOD" (A) **80.00**

Portland Vase

3" h, light blue ground, white cameos, marked **165.00**

4½" h, black ground, white cameos, Wedgwood mark **225.00**

6¾" h, dark blue ground, white classic cameos, "Wedgwood, England" **475.00**

10½" h, black ground, white classic cameos, Phrygian head, c1840, marked **2,100.00**

Posey Pot, 3⅜" h, lilac ground, white classic cameos, "Wedgwood, England," pr **200.00**

Potpourri Vase

11½" h, dark blue ground, white classic cameos, cameo band around footed base and cov edge, perforated top, c1850, marked **525.00**

11¾" h, black ground, white classic medallions, pierced covs, imp "WEDGWOOD," pr (A) **500.00**

Salt and Pepper Shakers, 2½" h, dark blue ground, white cameos, imp "WEDGWOOD" **225.00**

Spill Vase

3¾" h

Black dipped ground, white cameos of swags suspended from rams' heads, oval medallions, classical figures, flutes on lower sections, mid 19th C, imp "WEDGWOOD," pr (A) **240.00**

Green ground, white cameos of Muse of Drama and Music, dogs, trees, and flowers, imp "WEDGWOOD" **100.00**

4" h

Black ground, gilded sheaf design, c1895, marked **350.00**

Blue ground, white cameos of Muse of Poetry and Drama, flowers and trees, imp "WEDGWOOD" **110.00**

Sugar, Cov, 4½" d, white cameos of putti at play with plants and insects, vertical fluting, c1785, marked (A) .. **330.00**

Syrup Jug

7½" h, dark blue ground, Portland vase cameos, pewter lid, c1850, marked **325.00**

8" h, dark blue ground, white sheaves of wheat, pewter top and thumbpiece, c1865, marked **300.00**

Table Center, 5½" h, dark blue ground, white classic cameo figures, footed, imp "Wedgwood, England" **325.00**

Tea Caddy, 7" h, light green ground, white rosettes at neck, cameos of classical scene on body, cylindrical, marked **375.00**

Tea Kettle, 7½" h, blue body, white columns of leaves and flowers, metal wicker cov handle, c1820, "WEDGWOOD" mark **650.00**

Tea Set, teapot, creamer, and sugar

Bamboo shape, primrose and terra cotta, "Wedgwood, Made in England" **225.00**

Blue dipped ground, white cameos of radiating ferns, teapot, 7¾" w, cream jug, mid 19th C "WEDGWOOD" marks (A) **200.00**

Lilac dipped ground, blue bands of vines, white borders, teapot, 7½" w, mid 19th C, imp "WEDGWOOD" (A) **500.00**

Yellow ground, black jasper trim, "Wedgwood, Made in England" .**1,200.00**

Teapot

6" w, 3½" h, light blue ground, white classic cameos, imp "WEDGWOOD" **125.00**

6¾" w, white ground, lime green radiating bands and bands of foliage, imp "WEDGWOOD" (A) **230.00**

Toddy Cup, white ground, blue jasper
leaf design, pedestal base **65.00**
Tray
6" l, dark blue ground, white cameos
of three groups of classical figures,
imp "WEDGWOOD" mark **60.00**
13¼" l, blue ground, white cameo in
center of flowerhead, chain pattern
border, and band of florals on rim,
late 18th C, imp "WEDGWOOD &
V" (A) **200.00**
Tripod, 7¾" h, white ground, green and
lilac foliage and bell flowers, bands
of interlocking ovals divided by lion's
masks, triangular base, late 19th C,
imp "WEDGWOOD," cracks (A) ... **500.00**
Trophy Cup, 5" h, light green ground,
white cameos of musicians playing
lute, three handles, marked **390.00**
Urn
6" h, black ground, white cameos of
rams' heads, trophies, and floral
garlands, dbl handles, c1840, imp
"WEDGWOOD" **475.00**
6¾" h, black ground, white classic
scenes, cov, "Wedgwood, Eng-
land," pr (A) **55.00**
8" h, black ground, white Portland
cameos, white glazed int., small
dbl handles, "Wedgwood, Eng-
land" **450.00**
10¼" h
Dark blue ground, white cameos of
Grecian scene, dbl loop handles,
footed, marked **375.00**
Light blue ground, white cameos,
cov, lilac inserts, marked **1,250.00**
Vase
1½" h, dark blue ground, white classic cameos, c1925, pr **200.00**
2" h, blue ground, white armorial
cameo, marked **75.00**
3" h, dark blue ground, white cameos
of two cherubs playing instruments,
imp "WEDGWOOD" **60.00**
5" h
Blue and lilac Lincoln, medallions
and drape in white, c1820-40,
marked **825.00**
Dark blue ground, white cameos of
four putti representing four seasons, "Wedgwood, England," pr **225.00**
7½" h, black ground, white cameos
of classic scenes, marked (A) **50.00**
9¾" h
Light green ground, white acanthus
leaves and bell flower cameos,
"Wedgwood, England," pr **350.00**
Lilac dipped ground, white cameos
of Muses playing instruments in
oval medallions, border of Zo-

diac signs, reeded handles, imp
"WEDGWOOD & 4 dots" (A) . **330.00**
10" h, blue ground, white cameo
medallions of Apollo and Hercules,
satyr mask handles on white base
(A) **330.00**
13" h
Light green ground, white Zodiac
band and Muse design, c1850,
imp "WEDGWOOD" **500.00**
White ground, gilt applied rams'
heads   suspending   garlands,
bands of leaves on neck and foot,
sq base, late 19th C, imp
"WEDGWOOD" (A) **350.00**
14½" h, cov, black dipped ground,
white cameos of classical figures,
white bands of dice pattern, yellow
flowerheads, sq base, late 19th C,
imp "WEDGWOOD" (A) **880.00**
17¾" h, blue ground, white cameos
of "The Garden of the Hesperides,"
leopard   head   handles,   imp
"WEDGWOOD," pr **800.00**
19¼" h, cov, blue ground, white cameos of "Borghese Frieze," laurel
knob, imp "WEDGWOOD" (A) ..**1,045.00**
24½" h, cov, stand, black dipped
ground, white cameos of Apotheo-
sis of Homer, white dbl snake handles and Medusa's masks, Pegasus
finial, stand with four griffon on
feet, late 19th C, imp "WEDG-
WOOD" (A) **2,420.00**
26½" h, cov, stand, blue ground,
white cameos of Virgil being
crowned by angels, white Medusa's
mask and serpent handles, cov with
Pegasus finial, circ base with animal masks and trophies on dipped
ground, imp "WEDGWOOD" (A) **1,540.00**

LUSTER

Bowl
2¼" d, Amherst Pheasant, band of
gold pheasants on blue luster ext.,
snake on mottled orange luster int.
(A) **40.00**
3" d, 1½" h, Hummingbird, orange
and blue, marked **110.00**
3½" h, Dragon, gold and colored
dragons, Oriental figures, blue luster ground, footed (A) **50.00**
3⅝" d, 2⅛" h, Fairyland, Flame Mar-
ston, #Z5360, marked **600.00**
4" d
Butterfly
Bright orange and red int., butterflies on int. and ext.,
marked **175.00**

Flambe int., pearl ext., butterflies inside and out edged in gold, marked **245.00**

Dragon, gold dragon and Orientals, green and blue luster (A) **40.00**

5" d

Butterfly, ivory and orange colors, footed, Wedgwood mark **225.00**

Fairyland, leapfrogging elves, blue ground, "Elves on Branch" design on pearlized int., #Z4968 (A) **310.00**

6½" d

Butterfly, cobalt int. with peacocks, flame ext. with gold butterflies, marked **400.00**

Dragon, orange and crimson ext., oct, marked **550.00**

Dragon, int. with fruit decor, oct, #Z4829, "Wedgwood, England" **375.00**

8" d

Dragon

Dragons on speckled iron-red ground, int. with dragons on blue ground, oct, gilt "Portland vase, Wedgwood, Made in England" mark **300.00**

Flaming dragons on blue luster ext., pearlized int. with flying cranes and dragon center, oct, #Z4829, marked **485.00**

Fairyland

"Fiddler in Tree" pattern on ext., "Ship and Mermaid" pattern on int., oct. #Z5360, gilt "Wedgwood, Made in England" mark (A) **286.00**

8⅞" d

Fairyland, birds in flight on blue and white shaded ext., hummingbird wings in bottom, oct, c1920, marked **1,200.00**

Dragon, gold dragons on shaded blue luster ext., floral and Oriental design on pearlized int. (A) **175.00**

9" d, Butterfly, flared edge, Wedgwood mark **375.00**

9¼" d, Fairyland, Daventry, orange and blue, Wedgwood mark **1,100.00**

9½" d, 4" h, Fairyland, "Woodland Elves II," elf with feather hat, #Z7496 ....**1,850.00**

10⅞" d, Fairyland

"Poplar Trees" on ext., "Woodland Bridge" and mermaid medallion on int., #Z4968 (A) **960.00**

Ext. with "Poplars," int. with "Woodland Elves V-Woodland Bridge," "MJ" monogram, c1920, marked (A) **1,210.00**

Box

4¼" d, Hummingbird, mottled bird, hummingbirds and gold trim, flame int., Wedgwood mark **450.00**

5⅜" d, Hummingbird, hummingbirds on blue luster ext., crimson mottled and orange luster int., "Sybil" knob (A) **200.00**

Candlestick, 6" h, Moonlight, ring-turned cylindrical shaft, dished nozzle, sq base, c1815, imp "WEDGWOOD" (A) **200.00**

Compote and Stand, 10½" l compote, 11¼" l stand, Moonlight, nautilus shell bowl and bivalve shaped stand, c1810, imp "WEDGWOOD" (A) ...**1,870.00**

Cup

2" h, Dragon, snakes and dragons on blue stippled ground, pearlized int. with one snake, three handles, marked **160.00**

3⅞" d, 4⅛" h, yellow luster, green scrolls, copper luster trim and stars, footed, "Wedgwood, Made in England" mark **100.00**

Demitasse Cup and Saucer, Butterfly, marked **200.00**

Dish

3⅛" h, Butterfly, light green and orange, footed, #Z4832 .... **165.00**

4¼" d, 3¼" h, Fairyland, leapfrogging elves, Portland vase mark **700.00**

7¾" w, Moonlight, molded pectin shells, orange, gray, and mauve shading, c1810, imp "WEDGWOOD" marks, set of 6 (A) **520.00**

8¼" w, Moonlight, molded scallop shells, c1810, imp "WEDGWOOD," pr (A) **440.00**

9½" d, Fairyland, "Lily" design (A) . **750.00**

12½" l, Moonlight, bivalve shape, c1810, imp "WEDGWOOD," pr (A) **302.00**

Ginger Jar, Cov, 11" h, Dragon, blue and gilt, Wedgwood mark **690.00**

Goblet, 3¼" h, Moonlight, pink, yellow, and green splashes, gilt rim, c1810 . **275.00**

Jar, Cov, 9½" h, Hummingbird, irid shades of green, Wedgwood mark .. **725.00**

Melba Cup, 4" d, 3" h, Butterfly, three gold butterflies on MOP ext., splashed orange int., marked **200.00**

Plaque

10¾" l, 4¾" h, Fairyland, "Picnic by a River," gilt and colors, wood frame, c1921, #Z5279 ....**2,800.00**

11¼" w, 15¾" h, Fairyland, "The Stuff that Dreams are made Of," colors, wood frame, c1926 .....**8,000.00**

Plate

9¾" d, Moonlight, mottled deep pink,

imp "WEDGWOOD" **175.00**
10¾" d, Fairyland
   Pixies on bridge outlined in gold,
      gold border, mottled blue back,
      marked **1,700.00**
   "Roc Centre," apricot ground rim,
      "Twyford" border of gilt imps
      and fairies (A) **470.00**
Pot, Cov, 9½" h, Fairyland, "Candle-
   mas" design, panels of candles
   topped with elf heads in coral and
   bronze, "White Pagoda" panels on
   cov, "Checker Rosette" motif on int.,
   c1925 (A) **3,700.00**
Potpourri Vase
   13⅝" w, Moonlight, compressed
      campaniform, loop handles,
      reeded circ foot, cov with two rows
      of holes and center hold, c1810,
      imp "WEDGWOOD" (A) **1,100.00**
   14" h, Moonlight, splashed pink,
      manganese and gray, pierced cov
      and inner cov, c1810, repaired cov **750.00**
Punch Bowl, 11¼" d, Fairyland, poplar
   tree landscape in midnight luster on
   ext., int. of woodland bridge in day-
   light luster, mermaid in center of
   base, footed, "M.J." initials, Wedgwood mark **3,500.00**
Salt, 2½" d, Dragon, dog head in bowl,
   orange and blue lusters **130.00**
Tea Service, demitasse, teapot, creamer,
   sugar, four cups and saucers, Art Nouveau design, yellow and green luster,
   marked **450.00**
Teabowl and Saucer, Hummingbird, orange int., blue ext., with birds and
   geese **170.00**

**Vase, 8½" h, Fairyland luster, dark red
and gold, $2,200.00.**

Vase
   4" w, 8" h, Fairyland, red ground,
      "Men of the Bag" dec **1,390.00**

6⅛" h, Hummingbird, multicolored
   hummingbirds outlined in gold on
   mottled blue luster ground, flame
   luster int., Wedgwood mark **210.00**
7⅛" h, cov, Fairyland, "Candlemas,"
   gold human-headed candles and
   elfin in colors on black between
   "Roseberry Bead" borders (A) **600.00**
8" h
   Dragon, blue-green mottled
      ground, Wedgwood mark **300.00**
   Fairyland, "The Jeweled Tree With
      Feng Hwang & Bridge" panels,
      multicolored, black tree, pink
      sky, gold trim, #Z4968, Wedg-
      wood mark **1,400.00**
8½" h
   Dragon, powder blue and gold,
      #Z4616, marked **550.00**
   Lahore, cov, elephants, giraffes, at-
      tendants behind pillars and dia-
      per design, bird motif on domed
      cov, c1920-29, #Z5266 (A) ...**2,465.00**
8¾" h, Dragon, maroon and gold
   dragons on mottled powder blue
   ground, pearl luster int., handled,
   Wedgwood mark **500.00**
9" h
   Dragon, large gold dragon in violet
      and yellow, shaded blue luster
      ground (A) **175.00**
   Fairyland, "Candlemass," narrow
      base to wide mouth, Wedgwood
      mark **1,750.00**
   "Rainbow Bifrost," #Z5360,
      marked **1,750.00**
9¼" h
   Dragon, outlined panels, gold drag-
      ons over body, bottle shape,
      Wedgwood mark **475.00**
   Fairyland, cov, fairy at end of rain-
      bow, gold trim, #Z4968, Wedg-
      wood mark **1,900.00**
   Fairyland, two seated fairies in gold
      and multicolored, birds, mottled
      blue-purple ground, int. with
      pixies, bats, and insects, gold
      "Portland vase" mark (A) **665.00**
11¾" h, Hummingbird mottled blue
   ground, colored hummingbirds in
   flight, int. mottled flame luster,
   trumpet shape, #Z5294, Wedgwood mark **475.00**
12¾" h, Moonlight, cov, ovoid, flared
   circ foot and rims, flat covs, button
   knobs, c1810, imp "WEDG-
   WOOD," pr, one cracked (A) **800.00**
Wall Pocket, 10" l, Moonlight, spirally
   ridged nautilus shell, gilt edge,
   c1810, imp "WEDGWOOD" mark
   (A) **300.00**

WHIELDON WARE

Fenton Vivien, Stoke-on-Trent, England
1740 to 1780

History: Thomas Whieldon founded his earthenware factory at Little Fenton in 1740. He began potting small items such as boxes, cutlery handles, chimney pieces, and teapots. Whieldon introduced various metallics into the clay to alter the color of the earthenware body.

Whieldon experimented with colored glazes, attempting to imitate tortoise shell. Most Whieldon ware is either mottled brownish or greenish in tone.

Several noted potters apprenticed with Whieldon. Josiah Spode is probably the most famous. In 1754 Whieldon took Josiah Wedgwood as a partner. While working for Whieldon, Wedgwood invented a green glaze which was used to decorate fanciful wares in the shapes of pineapples and cauliflowers. Together Whieldon and Wedgwood continued to make marbled, agate, and tortoise shell pieces. Wedgwood left in 1759. Whieldon continued producing the variegated wares until the demand for these pieces diminished. He retired in 1780.

No Whieldon pieces are marked. Many earthenware potteries copied Whieldon's tortoise shell wares between 1740 and 1780. Since no pieces are marked, it is impossible to attribute a piece to a specific factory. The term "Whieldon ware" is now generic.

References: F. Falkner, *The Wood Family of Burslem*, Chapman & Hall, 1912.

Museums: City Museum, Stoke-on-Trent, Hanley, England; Fitzwilliam Museum, Cambridge, England; Museum of Art, Rhode Island School of Design, Providence, Rhode Island; Sussex Museum & Art Gallery, Brighton, England; Victoria & Albert Museum, London, England.

Bowl, 11" d, green and brown tortoiseshell pattern, serving size, scalloped edge, c1760, unmarked **1,200.00**
Broth Bowl, splashed manganese, green, and yellow glazes, reeded loop handle, c1760 (A) **330.00**
Chamber Pot, 5¾" d, mottled manganese, green, and yellow glazes, grooved loop handle, c1760 (A) **315.00**
Charger, 15" d, transparent glaze, green and brown tortoiseshell pattern, c1760, unmarked **4,000.00**
Cup, 2½" h, mottled manganese glaze, scroll handle, c1750 (A) **345.00**
Dish
    4½" l, molded oak leaf, loop handle, green glaze (A) **160.00**
    9⅜" l, int. molded with basketweave,

green, yellow, and brown glazed stripes, c1760 (A) **690.00**
    14½" w, mottled green and yellow glaze, waved gadroon rim, mottled manganese glaze on reverse, c1760 (A) **400.00**
Figure
    3" h, recumbent lion, cream and dark green, splashes of brown and gray head, c1750–60 (A) **1,540.00**
    3½" w, recumbent cat splashed in brown, ochre, and yellow, lying on cushion, c1770 (A) **245.00**
    6" h, standing horse, gray sponging, black mane and tail, yellow saddlecloth and harness, green accented rect base, c1780 (A) **1,320.00**
    6⅝" l, standing horse, brown mane and tail, ochre saddlecloth, splash manganese, oblong green base, c1760 (A) **1,650.00**
    8¼" h, draft horse, splash ochre, brown mane and tail, oblong green accented base, c1770 (A) **3,520.00**
Flower Pot, 3" h, ridges around lip and edge, shaded blue marbleized pattern, c1780 .... **400.00**
Food Warmer, 10¼" h, cov, tortoiseshell glaze, dbl handled stand, female masks, dbl handled spouted bowl, flowerhead finial, c1760 (A) **940.00**
Inkwell, 8" l, imp geometric pattern between rope twist borders, green, gray, manganese, and yellow glazes, rect, c1755, unmarked (A) **530.00**
Jug, 4¾" h, molded fruit in basket, gray, yellow, green, and manganese accents, c1760–65, "Wedgwood-Whieldon" (A) **220.00**
Knife Handle, 3½" l, mottled manganese glaze, c1760, pr (A) **360.00**
Milk Jug
    4½" h, transparent glaze, green and brown tortoiseshell finish, mottled with manganese, c1770, unmarked **975.00**
    5½" h, cov, molded basketweave lower section, fruit and trailing flowers, manganese, green, and yellow glazes, flowerhead finial, c1760 .... **200.00**
Plaque
    4¾" l, molded relief of Othello, Desdemona and Shakespeare, masks of Tragedy and Comedy in int., books and manuscripts, blue, ochre, and green accents, c1770, imp "J Voyez," pr (A) **660.00**
    6" l, molded relief of two men, one holding glass and jug, reeded border, cream, green, and yellow glaze, manganese accents, c1760 (A) **190.00**

6⅝" d, molded relief of farmers, boar head, splashed blue and green glaze, loop for hanging, c1770 (A) **1,100.00**

Plate
8½" d, splash manganese glaze, brown ground, octagon, c1750, pr (A) **200.00**
9" d, green splash, speckled manganese ground, feather edge rim, c1765 (A) **130.00**
12½" d, green and yellow mottled glazes, brown sponged ground, lobed rim **100.00**

Sauce Tureen, 7" h, matching underplate, pheasant pattern, c1895, unmarked **125.00**

Sauceboat, 5⅝" l, scale-molded creamware body, dolphin head spout, tail forms handle, translucent green and brown glaze, c1770–75 (A) **310.00**

Soup Bowl, 8" d, deep rim, scalloped edge, brown marbleized and solid green pattern, c1760, unmarked ... **525.00**

Tea Caddy
3" h, brown overall pattern, child's size, c1765, unmarked **375.00**
3½" h, molded five point dominoes, stars and rope twist borders, gray, green, and ochre glaze, rect, hole in base, c1760 (A) **345.00**

Teabowl and Saucer, splashed manganese, green, and blue-gray, c1750 (A) **440.00**

Teapot, 5¼" h, tortoiseshell glaze, c1760, $2,300.00.

Teapot
3½" h, splashed vert streaks of tortoiseshell glaze, globular shape, late 18th C (A) **200.00**
5⅛" h, applied vines on sides, cherub's mask above spout, mottled manganese and light green glazes, three mask and paw feet, bird finial, crabstock spout and handle, c1750 (A) **1,300.00**
6" h
Cauliflower form, green glaze on bottom, cauliflower on top, pebbly texture, modeled by Wm Greatbatch, c1765, "Wedgwood-Whieldon" **1,600.00**
Molded ribbing, bright yellow and green glaze bands, crabstock handle, flower knob, c1765 (A) **2,030.00**
6¼" h
Molded scrolling vines, tortoiseshell glaze, branch handle and spout, three paw feet, bird finial, c1750 .... **575.00**
Tortoiseshell glaze, crabstock handle and mask spout, bird finial, paw feet, c1755, unmarked ...**1,300.00**
7½" h, globular pineapple, yellow and green glaze, foliage molded handle and spout, c1765, unmarked (A) **495.00**
9" h, modeled bear, cub forming spout, incised fur, head forms cov, agate marbleized in brown and yellow striations, c1770 (A) **3,300.00**

Tray, 9⅝" l, tortoiseshell glaze, pierced scroll handles, molded rim, c1760 (A) **330.00**

Vase, 5½" h, blue and brown streaked glaze, ovoid shape, flared neck **330.00**

WILLOW WARE

English/Continental
1780s to Present

History: Blue willow china is the English interpretation of hand painted blue and white Chinese porcelain that was exported to England from China in the 16th century. The transfer method of decoration and the under the glaze decorating techniques introduced after 1760 provided the methodology to produce willow ware in large quantities.

The first English willow pattern is attributed to Thomas Minton at his Caughley Pottery in Staffordshire in the 1780s. The pattern was called Willow-Nankin.

Josiah Spode developed the first "true" willow pattern in the 1790s. Spode made three different willow patterns. The standard pattern developed in 1810 by Spode is the one that is considered the "true" willow pattern. It differs from the first two patterns in border design and the method by which the transfer pattern was engraved.

Spode's willow pattern has a willow tree in the center leaning over the bridge. A tea house with three pillars forming the portico is located near a large orange tree and is behind the center willow tree. There is a bridge with three figures crossing towards an island. A man in a boat is on the lake. Two birds are flying towards each other at the top center. Finally, a fence crosses the foreground. The outer border features several scroll and geometic designs. The inner border consists of geometric designs that frame the center pattern.

Many manfacturers used transfers that were variations of the Spode willow pattern. Some produced their own original blue willow versions. By 1830 there were more than two hundred makers of willow pattern china in England. English firms still producing blue willow pattern china are Booth's by Royal Doulton, Burleigh, Coalport, Johnson Brothers, Meakin, and Wedgwood.

During the 20th century other countries making willow ware include Belgium, France, Germany, Holland, Ireland, Mexico, Poland, Portugal, and Spain. Potteries in the United States and Japan also make pieces decorated with the blue willow pattern.

A tremendous variety of shapes were made in the blue willow pattern. Many pieces were not marked by the manufacturers, especially during the early period.

The color of the transfer varies with the manufacturer. During the 1820s, a pale blue was fashionable. A whole spectrum of blues was used during the Victorian era. Although the most common color is blue, pieces can be found in black, brown, green, pink, yellow, and polychrome.

References: Robert Copeland, *Spode's Willow Pattern and other designs after the Chinese,* Rizzoli International Publications, Inc., 1980; Mary Frank Gaston, *Blue Willow: An Identification and Value Guide,* Collector Books, 1983; Veryl Marie Worth, *Willow Pattern China,* privately printed, revised 2nd edition, 1981.

Collectors' Club: The Willow Society, 359 Davenport Road, Suite 6, Toronto, M5R 1K5 Canada. Membership: $15.00. *The Willow Transfer Quarterly, The Willow Exchange,* and *The Mandarin's Purse* (price guide).

Biscuit Jar, blue, "ENGLAND"	75.00
Bone Dish, blue, "Ridgway"	5.00
Bouillon Cup, 6½" d, blue, handled, "Ridgway"	25.00
Bowl, blue	
3½" d, "Maastricht"	25.00

Vegetable Bowl, 9½" l, 7½" w, 2" h, blue, "Venton/Steventon," $35.00.

7½" d, pagoda and gate scene, "W. R. Midwinter Ltd, England-Willow"	12.00
10" d	
Footed, early 19th C. England ...	85.00
"H. A. and Co., "England"	55.00
Butter Dish, cov, blue	
"Allerton"	65.00
"Booths"	60.00
Butter Pat, blue, "Allerton"	20.00
Casserole, cov, 8½" sq, blue, "Brown and Steventon"	75.00
Cereal Bowl, blue, 6¼", d "Allerton" .	10.00
Commode Set, blue, pitcher, bowl, hot water pitcher, chamber pot, and toothbrush holder, "Ye Olde Willow"	850.00
Creamer	
Blue, "Copeland"	25.00
Blue, "Booth"	25.00
Pink, "Venton/Steventon"	15.00
Creamer and Sugar, blue, "Allerton" ..	65.00
Cup and Saucer, blue	
"Allerton" mark	10.00
"Booth"	
Gold trim	20.00
Scalloped edge	10.00
"Petrus Regout" mark	15.00
"Royal Worcester," farmer size, c1900	40.00
"Villeroy and Boch"	3.00
Cup Plate, 3¼" d, blue, unmarked, set of 5 (A)	50.00
Demitasse Cup and Saucer	
"Adams"	15.00
"Staffordshire"	10.00
Dish, 6⅞" d, blue, shell shape, closed handle, "Ridgway"	35.00
Egg Coddler, 2½" h, blue, "Royal Worcester"	30.00
Egg Cup, blue	
"Royal Worcester," gold border	20.00
"Wood and Sons"	15.00
Ginger Jar, 5" h, blue, "Royal Cauldon"	65.00
Gravy Boat	
7½" l, blue, "Ridgway"	25.00
Blue	
"Allerton"	45.00
"John Steventon"	20.00
"Wedgwood"	45.00
Pink, matching undertray, "Allerton"	60.00
Horse Radish Dish, blue, "Doulton and Co"	30.00
Mold, 4" d, blue, "ENGLAND"	30.00
Pitcher, blue	
3½" h, "Ridgway"	25.00
4½" h, "Ridgway"	40.00
5¼" h, "Allerton"	60.00
6" h, "Allerton"	110.00
Plate, blue	
3½" d, "Malkin"	40.00
6" d,	
"Steventon"	5.00
"Ridgway"	5.00

8¾" d, "Meakin" **10.00**
8¾" sq, insect border, c1810,
"pseudo-Chinese" mark **95.00**
9" d
  "Adams" **10.00**
  "Allerton" **10.00**
  "Grimswade" **10.00**
  "Maastricht" **15.00**
  "Wedgwood and Co" **20.00**
9¼" d, "Steventon" **10.00**
9½" d, "Stoke Upon Trent" **10.00**
10½" d, Mason **15.00**
13" d, chop, "Allerton" **30.00**
Plate, mulberry
  8¼" d, unmarked **45.00**
  10¼" d, unmarked **45.00**
Plate, pink
  9" d, "Maastricht, Holland" **10.00**
  9½" d, 12 sided, "Staffordshire" ... **20.00**
  10" d, "Venton/Steventon" **10.00**
  11" d, "Romarcoware-England" **10.00**
Plate, red-pink, 10" d, "Ridgway" **10.00**
Plate, polychrome, 10" d, "Ashworth" **75.00**
Platter
  11½" l, blue, "Made in England" .. **45.00**
  12" d, pink, "Venton/Steventon" ... **35.00**
  12" l, blue, "Ridgway" **35.00**
  12½" l, blue, unmarked (A) **10.00**
  15½" l, blue, ironstone, unmarked (A) **75.00**
  16" l, blue
    "Made in England" **75.00**
    "Wood and Sons," oval **50.00**
  16¾" l, 13½" w, blue, "Andrew Ste-
    venson" **175.00**
  19" l, blue, "Ridgway" **165.00**
Relish Tray, blue
  "Johnson Bros" **20.00**
  "Wood and Sons" **20.00**
Soup Bowl, blue
  6¼" d, sq handles, "Ridgway" **15.00**
  7" d, "Ridgway" **15.00**
  9" d, "Allerton" **12.00**
Soup Plate
  7" d, pink, "Venton/Steventon" **10.00**
  8" d, blue
    "Allerton" **10.00**
    "Ridgway" **30.00**
  8½" d, blue, "Booth" **20.00**
Soup Tureen, blue, ladle and under-
  plate, "Burleigh Ware" **300.00**
Sugar Bowl, cov, blue, "Wood and
  Sons" **35.00**
Tea Set, blue, teapot, creamer, and
  sugar, "Sadler, England" **35.00**
Tea Tile, blue, 6½" d, "Allerton" **35.00**
Teabowl and Saucer, blue, "Ridgway" **55.00**
Teapot, blue
  3½" h, gold trim, "Sadler" **25.00**
  5" h, "Ashworth Bros, Hanley" **55.00**
Toothpick, 1¾" h, blue, "Meakin" ... **15.00**
Tray, 15" l, 12" w, blue, "Allerton" ... **45.00**
Tureen, cov, 11" l, blue, pedestal base,

unmarked **150.00**
Tureen, open, blue, ornate handles,
  dated 1902, "Royal Worcester" **95.00**
Vegetable Bowl
  7½" l, blue, "Ridgway" **40.00**
  8¾" d, blue, imp "Wood and Co." . **45.00**
  9" d, pink, "Venton/Steventon" **30.00**
  10" d, pink, oval, "Venton/Steven-
    ton" **35.00**
  10" sq, blue, "Thomas Dinnock" ... **150.00**
Vegetable Tureen, cov, 11" H-H
  Blue, "Gibson and Son England" ... **95.00**
  Pink, "Maastricht, Holland" **70.00**

ENOCH WOOD & SONS BURSLEM STAFFORDSHIRE

ENOCH WOOD & SONS BURSLEM

ENOCH WOOD

Fountain Place Pottery, Burslem, Staffordshire, England
c1784 to 1840

History: Enoch Wood came from an important pottery family that included Aaron Wood, his father, Ralph Wood, his cousin, and William Wood, his brother. After he completed his apprenticeship, Enoch entered into a partnership with Ralph in 1784. They made enamel colored figures and Toby jugs using the new over–the–glaze decoration technique.

In 1790 Enoch Wood entered into a partnership with Caldwell. The company's mark was Wood & Caldwell. Enoch bought out Caldwell in 1819 and formed a new partnership with Enoch, Joseph, and Edward Wood, his sons. The firm became known as Enoch Wood and Sons.

The company made under–the–glaze blue transfer printed dinnerware, much of which was exported to America. In addition to the blue historic wares, many romantic wares were printed in pink, purple, black, sepia, green, or mulberry. Views used include British, French, Italian, and American scenes. Although views were the most popular designs, biblical scenes, hunting scenes, and cherub motifs also were made. Many of the printed designs have the title marked on the back.

Marked pieces are impressed "WOOD."

References: A. W. Coysh & R. K. Henrywood, *The Dictionary of Blue & White Printed Pottery 1780–1880,* Antique Collectors' Club, 1982.

Museums: Cincinnati Art Museum, Cincinnati, Ohio; Fitzwilliam Museum, Cambridge, England; Potsdam Public Museum, Potsdam, New York.

Cup and Saucer, "English Scenery" pattern, blue transfer, "Wood & Sons, England," $25.00.

Bowl, 10½" d, "Asiatic Plants" pattern, green transfers, set of 4 .... **80.00**

Bust
9" h, Handel, enameled, dark brown rect socle, restorations, c1800 (A)   **250.00**
11¾" h, Milton, multicolored, ebonized plinth, imp "Milton," c1790 .**1,850.00**
13" h, George Whitefield, black clerical dress, black socle base, repaired **75.00**
15⅜" h, Sir Isaac Newton, gray hair, brown drape, waisted rect marbled green and pink socle, c1800 ..... **450.00**

Dish, 8" l, 6" w, dark blue transfer of castle, imp "Wood" (A) **150.00**

Figure
6⅞" h, pointer dog, seated on haunches, gray and brown fur, tasseled green and iron-red cushion, rect base, c1810 (A) **580.00**
7" h, John Liston, black comic costume, red ribbons, holding letter, sq base with inscription, imp "Wood"   **275.00**
11¾" h, recumbent stag, ochre and cream, molded berries on waisted rect base, c1800 (A) **2,440.00**

Fruit Bowl, 10½" d, "Damascus" pattern, pedestal base, c1846 .... **85.00**

Jug
4" h, lustered relief of cows, calf, and dogs, olive ground grass mound, molded floral neck, pink luster band, imp "Enoch Wood and Sons" (A) **85.00**
5⅜" h, cameos of Queen Caroline, pink luster ground, beaded edge, molded and painted floral border, ovoid, c1820 (A) **385.00**
6¾" h, molded and enameled huntsmen and hound, beige ground, pink luster borders, early 19th C, (A) **130.00**

9¼" h, "Fair Hebe," molded and enameled three figures around tree, imp "EW" **400.00**

Mug, 5¼" h, blue transfer, Duke of Wellington on horse in landscape with troops, reserved on foliage ground, cylindrical, c1820 .... **300.00**

Pitcher, 4½" d, 6" h, red stylized flowerheads, blue spatter ground, set of 3 **120.00**

Plate
7⅞" d, iron-red and green florals and sprigs, purple luster floral border, c1817, imp "Enoch Wood and Sons Burslem" (A) **55.00**
9½" d
Country scene, flow blue transfer . **75.00**
Cupid in cage, dark blue transfer, white scalloped rim (A) **95.00**
10" d
Blue feather edge, "E Wood & Sons" (A) **40.00**
"English Scenery" pattern, dark red transfer **18.50**
"Pagoda" pattern **50.00**
10½" d
"Grecian Scenery" pattern, blue transfer, rope edge, "E W & S" **70.00**
Oriental scene, dark blue transfer, imp "Wood" (A) **25.00**

Platter
12" l, 9½" w, "Old English" pattern, dark red transfer **35.00**
19½" l, "Asiatic Plants" pattern, green transfer **200.00**

Teabowl and Saucer, "Gondola" pattern, pink transfer, "E Wood" **35.00**

Toby Jug, 9⅝" h, gentleman, white jacket, pink breeches, holding pipe and jug of ale, c1790 (A) **225.00**

Vase, 9⅞" h, multicolored panels of river scenes front and reverse, reserved on silver luster ground, octagonal base, loop handles, c1790, imp "W" (A) **385.00**

RALPH WOOD

Near Stoke-on-Trent, England
Ralph Wood the Elder
1754 to 1772

Ralph Wood the Younger
1760 to 1795

History: Ralph Wood and Ralph, his son, were the most important makers of earthenware figures and Toby jugs during the second half of the eighteenth century.

After his apprenticeship, Ralph Wood initially worked for Thomas Whieldon making salt glazed earthenware and tortoise shell glazed ware. Eventually he founded his own firm. During the 1750s Ralph Wood started making figures in cream colored earthenware with metallic oxide stained glazes. He kept the colors separate by painting them on with a brush. The modeling of his figures was quite lively. Ralph's figures gained a reputation for exactly portraying the mood and attitude of the characters.

Ralph the Younger was a skilled figure maker and joined his father during the 1760s. Ralph the Younger continued the tradition established by his father and eventually produced even more figures than Ralph Wood the Elder. Since Ralph the Younger used many of his father's molds, it is impossible to assign a particular figure to the father or the son with certainty. Later in his career, Ralph the Younger switched to using enamel colors on figures.

Subjects included equestrian figures, contemporary portrait figures, some satyrical groups, classical figures, allegorical figures, and many different animals. All the molded human figures had large hands and well defined, bulging eyes. Ralph Wood also is credited with introducing the Toby jug form. These were very successful and copied by dozens of potters. (See Toby Jugs.)

In addition to figures and Toby jugs, Ralph Wood's factory also made plaques. John Voyez, a modeler, produced the plaques. Characteristic of Voyez's work are figures with bulging eyes, thick fleshy lips, slightly flattened noses, and a sentimental inclination of the head.

The Woods were the first figure makers to mark their wares with an impressed company mark and sometimes mold numbers. However, some were not marked. "R. Wood" was the mark of Ralph the Elder. "Ra Wood" was the younger's mark.

References: Capt. R. K. Price, *Astbury, Whieldon & Ralph Wood Figures and Toby Jugs,* John Lane, 1922; H. A. B. Turner, *A Collector's Guide to Staffordshire Pottery Figures,* Emerson Books, Inc., 1971.

Museums: British Museum, London, England; Cincinnati Art Museum, Cincinnati, Ohio; City Museum, Stoke-on-Trent, Hanley, England; Fitzwilliam Museum, Cambridge, England.

Bust
    8⅝" h, Milton, multicolored, shaped
      rect socle, c1790, imp "Ra Wood
      81" (A) **485.00**
    9" h, Handel
      Multicolored, marbled plinth,
      "imp Handel," c1780, Ralph
      Wood II **1,250.00**

      White, draped wig, waisted rect socle, c1785, imp "Ra Wood Burslem" (A) **435.00**
    9¼" h, Matthew Prior, multicolored, brown and gray marbled plinth, c1790, Ralph Wood II **1,100.00**
Coffeepot, 9⅝" h, cauliflower form, overlapping leaves, green glaze, foliage molded spout and handle, c1770 (A) **355.00**

Figure, 11" l, 7" h, brown lion, cream base, c1760, "Ralph Wood the Elder," $3,950.00.

Figure
    3½" h, sphinx, seated on haunches, mottled green and manganese glaze, c1770 (A) **1,000.00**
    3¾" w, polar bear, gray accents, green rockwork base, c1770 .....**1,500.00**
    4¼" h, "Winter," boy huddled in cloak, ochre glaze, brown rockwork, base, late 18th C (A) **100.00**
    6⅛" l, recumbent doe, brown and white, green rockwork base, restored, c1770 (A) **800.00**
    6½" l, recumbent ram, mottled gray ram, mottled yellow oval base, large curled horns, c1770 (A) **1,300.00**
    7" h, "Begger Boy," glazed light brown hat and jacket, green breeches, sq green base, attrib to Ralph Wood the Elder c1760 ....**1,750.00**
    7" l, recumbent sheep with incised fleece, brown, green, gray, and ochre accents, rock base, c1770 (A) **1,540.00**
    7¼" h, squirrel, seated on haunches eating nut, splashed manganese and yellow, grass mound base, c1760 (A) **2,530.00**
    7¼" w, recumbent ram, mottled green and ochre rockwork, brown horns (A) **1,935.00**
    8½" h, Vicar and Moses in pulpit, manganese, blue, and white, c1770 .... **300.00**
    8⅝" h
      Flora, holding horn of plenty, blue,

brown, and green flowers, circ
rocky base (A) **170.00**
Shepherdess,   sheep   at   side,
multicolored dress, mound base
molded with scrolls, restored,
c1770 (A) **660.00**
8⅞" h, Apollo, wearing flowered
robe, playing lyre, standing on
rocky mound, script title, Ralph
Wood II **185.00**
9" h
Diana, removing arrow from quiver
on back, dog at side, translucent
colors, sq base **140.00**
"Flemish Music", youth playing
hurdy gurdy before tree stump,
inscribed sq base, c1790 (A) ... **260.00**
9½" h, shepherd, playing flute, companion seated on rock work, dog,
goat, and lamb at feet, multicolored, repairs, c1760 ....**1,800.00**
10⅝" h, St. George, seated on brown
horse, green and brown accents on
dragon and base, restored, c1770
(A) **665.00**
Jug, 9¼" h, molded and colored Bacchus head, mask spout, handle modeled with figure holding bottle, c1775
(A) **550.00**
Plaque
6⅛" h, raised profile of Duke of Cumberland, yellow edged shirt, green
drapery, molded green foliage border, pierced for hanging, c1770 .. **450.00**
7⅞" h, molded bust of woman,
multicolored, green self molded
frame, pierced for hanging, c1780
(A) **665.00**
11⅜" h, molded full figure of Patricia,
green, brown, and yellow, pierced
for hanging, c1775 (A) **1,700.00**
Sauceboat, 7" l, matching stand, modeled fox head, brown-red glaze with
accents,   swan's   neck   handle,
splashed blue glaze swan base, c1770
(A) **3,300.00**
Spill Vase, 7⅞" h, molded as two entwined dolphins supporting linked
cornucopia, shell molded oval base,
green   and   manganese   accents,
c1775, imp "Ra Wood Burslem"
(A) **1,330.00**
Stirrup Cup, 5½" l, modeled hound's
head,   transluscent   brown   shades,
c1760 ....**1,900.00**
Toby Jug, 9⅝" h, gentleman, sponged
blue jacket, gray breeches, barrel between feet, holding jug, pipe at side,
c1775 (A) **400.00**
Whistle, 3⅞" h, modeled as seated
sphinx, blue accents, oval green base,
c1770 .... **450.00**

WORCESTER

Worcester, England
1751 to 1892

History: The Worcester pottery was established
in 1751. The pieces from the initial years of
operation have decorations characterized by a
strong dependence on Oriental themes in under-
the-glaze blue and on-the-glaze enamel. Production concentrated primarily on making excellent
utilitarian wares, mostly tea and dessert sets. Very
few purely ornamental pieces were made. The
china was symetrical and featured a smooth
glaze. This initial period, 1751 to 1776, was
known as the "Dr. Wall" period, named after
one of the original stockholders.

After 1755 transfer printing was used extensively. By 1760 most of the best pieces had the
typical Worcester deep blue cobalt under the
glaze background, done either in a solid or scale
motif. Panels were painted with beautiful birds,
flowers, and insects.

The factory was managed by William Davis,
one of the original partners from the Dr. Wall
period. Davis died in 1783; Thomas Flight then
purchased the factory. The middle period, also
known as the Davis-Flight period, lasted from
1776 to 1793. Neoclassical designs were emphasized. Many of the whiteware blanks used for
decoration were purchased from France as there
was a limited quantity of fine clay for porcelain
production in the area of the Worcester plant.
The company received a Royal Warrant from
George III in 1789.

Martin Barr joined the works in 1793. The
period from 1793 to 1807 is designated the Flight
& Barr period. Patterns continued to be rather
plain. Barr's son joined the firm in 1807, result-

ing in the Barr Flight & Barr period between 1807 and 1813. Decorative motifs from this era were quite colorful and elaborate.

Martin Barr, Sr., died in 1813. The time from 1813 to 1840 is called the Flight Barr & Barr period. Patterns continued to be quite colorful, finely painted and gilded. The quality of porcelains made during the early 19th century was very high. Pieces were richly painted, often featuring gilt trim on a well potted body with a perfect, craze-free glaze.

In 1840 Flight Barr & Barr merged with the Chamberlain factory and took the name of Chamberlain and Company. The plant moved to Diglis. Quality of production declined during this time.

Kerr and Binns bought the firm in 1852. During the Kerr & Binns period, 1852 to 1862, the factory enjoyed a great artistic recovery. In 1862 R. W. Binns formed the Worcester Royal Porcelain Company Ltd., a company whose products then carried the "Royal Worcester" designation.

References: Franklin A. Barret, *Worcester Porcelain & Lund's Bristol,* Faber & Faber, 1966, revised ed.; Lawrence Branyon, Neal French, John Sandon, *Worcester Blue & White Porcelain, 1751–1790* Barrie & Jenkins, 1981; F. Severne Mackenna, *Worcester Porcelain: The Wall Period & Its Antecedents,* F. Lewis Ltd., 1950; H. Rissik Marshall, *Colored Worcester Porcelain of the First Period,* Ceramic Book, 1954; Henry Sandon, *Flight & Barr: Worcester Porcelain 1783–1840,* Antique Collectors Club, 1978; Henry Sandon, *The Illustrated Guide to Worcester Porcelain,* Herbert Jenkins, 1969.

Museums: British Museum, London, England; City Museum, Weston Park, Sheffield, England; Dyson Perrins Museum, Worcester, England; Gardiner Museum of Ceramic Art, Toronto, Canada; Seattle Art Museum, Seattle, Washington; Sheffield City Museum, Sheffield, England; Victoria & Albert Museum, London, England.

REPRODUCTION ALERT: At the end of the 19th century, Samson and other continental artists copied 18th century Worcester examples. Booths of Turnstall reproduced many Worcester designs utilizing the transfer method. These reproduction pieces also contain copies of the Royal Worcester mark. Even though an earthenware body instead of porcelain was used on the Booth examples, many collectors have been misled by the reproductions.

Basket
  6¾" d, series of interlocking circles, ext. with applied painted flowers, int. painted floral center, c1765, pr **3,400.00**
  7" d
    "Pine Cone" pattern, blue diapered border with arabesques, five pet-

aled flowers on ext., blue highlights, c1770, "hatched crescent" mark **725.00**
Reticulated, floral encrusted, dbl handles (A) **200.00**
7½" l, int. painted with floral bouquet, ext. yellow and rose buds lattice work, brown twig handles and floral terminals, yellow ground, oval, c1765–70 (A) **1,650.00**
7⅝" d, interlocking circle sides, painted floral center, blue scale ground, c1770, blue "pseudo seal" mark, pr (A) **2,860.00**
9¼" w, blue painted int. of fruiting vines, pierced border with interlocking circles, dbl entwined handles with foliage terminals, c1780, "pseudo-seal" mark (A) **220.00**
11" w, matching stand, pierced body, gilt with foliage and trailing husks, blue ground, center intertwined gilt initials, blue rope twist handles with flower terminals, oval, c1810, "Chamberlains Worcester No 6" in script, crack in stand (A) **880.00**
Bowl
  5½" d, molded, polychrome sprays, c1755 .... **950.00**
  6" d, blue bird, white ground, Dr Wall period, c1751, blue "crescent" mark **385.00**
  10" d, 4¼" h, blue transfer, flowers and butterflies, blue "crescent" mark (A) **225.00**
  11½" d, two phoenix birds in shrubs, Kakiemon palette, c1765–70 (A) . **1,210.00**
  11¾" d, "Old Mosaick Japan" pattern, c1765–70, sealed crack **2,000.00**
Butter Tub, cov, blue transfer, flowers and butterflies, scroll handles and flowerhead finial, c1770, blue "crescent" mark (A) **330.00**
Centerpiece
  7½" h, seven tiered shells, pyramid of shells, seaweed, and coral, gros bleu borders with gilt scrollwork, centers of shells with multicolored flowers, c1770 .... **3,200.00**
  22½" h, four graduated gilt shell molded trays, blue ground, drum bases with three scrolled feet and Garter motto, ormolu handles, one center column replaced, c1820, pr (A) **935.00**
Charger, 12¾" d, cartouches of exotic birds and smaller panels of insects, blue scale ground, c1775, blue "W" mark (A) **1,650.00**
Chocolate Pot, 8½" h, bird and floral reserves on underglaze blue fish scale ground, polychrome and gilt, domed

cov and scroll handle, c1750, blue "sq fret" mark (A) **250.00**

Coffeepot, 9⅜" h, black transfer, Mandarin man at table with three ladies and child, enameled accents, c1770 (A) **940.00**

Creamboat, 3⅛" h, shell molded body, iron-red and yellow, dolphin handle, c1765 (A) **770.00**

Creamer, 3½" h, blue floral design, "sparrow beak" spout, c1760 ...... **50.00**

Cup, 2⅛" h, heron holding fish, famille rose enamels, gilt rim, iron-red scallop and dot int border, fluted, c1765, blue "pseudo seal" mark (A) **935.00**

Cup and Saucer

Floral center, hp, gold trim, green border, c1770 ....**1,600.00**

"Old Japan Fan" pattern, c1765–70, blue "Chinese 4 character" mark (A) **330.00**

Dish

7" l, "Gilliflower" pattern, blue, white ground, leaf shape, stem handle **775.00**

7⅝" d, "Blind Earl" pattern, eight painted insects, gilt rim, c1765–70 (A) **1,650.00**

8" d, "Lord Henry Thyme" pattern, center landscape with insects and flowers, blue border, gilt trim, scalloped edge, c1775 ....**1,900.00**

8¼" l, "Magician" pattern, famille rose colors, molded cabbage leaf, c1765–70 (A) **600.00**

9" d, molded overlapping leaves and twig handle, white, gilt rim, c1765 (A) **260.00**

12⅜" l, "Pavilion" pattern, ext. painted with four blue and iron-red branches, lozenge shape, c1770 (A) **1,870.00**

13" w, rose sprays, border of stylized flowerheads in blue and red oeil-de-perdrix, 3 ovals with rose sprays, oval, c1813–14, "imp crown and FBB" mark (A) **235.00**

Dish, Dessert

6" l, reserved center panel in "Sir Joshua Reynolds" pattern, bird perched on rock surrounded by flowering plants in Kakiemon palette, fluted and scalloped rim with wide gros bleu band, "fretted sq" mark **900.00**

8" l, multicolor exotic birds in landscape, oval with blue de roi border, "script W" mark **950.00**

10" w, overglaze black scene of ruins and 2 cloaked travelers, gilt rim with printed florals and garlands, heart shape, c1770 .... **500.00**

Dishes, Pr

7¾" l, "Blind Earl" pattern, one with butterfly, other with ladybird, gilt C scroll edge rims, c1765–70 (A) ...**1,650.00**

10⅛" l, 10¼" d, painted fruit clusters in centers, 5 fruit sprigs and insects in borders between claret and gilt bands, kidney shape, c1775 (A) . **9,350.00**

Jug

5¾" h, "Quail" pattern, cabbage leaf molded in Kakiemon colors, mask spout, c1765 (A) **1,870.00**

7½" h, cabbage leaf with underglaze blue "Gilliflower" pattern, mask spout, unmarked **850.00**

8" h, "Queen Charlotte" pattern, mask spout, c1770, blue "pseudo seal" mark (A) **1,265.00**

Milk Jug, Cov

5⅛" h, gros bleu ground, exotic birds in gilt cartouches on each side, cov with insects in gilt cartouches, c1770, blue "pseudo seal" mark (A) **935.00**

5½"h, exotic birds in gilt vase and mirror cartouches, yellow scale ground, flower finial, c1765 (A) .**10,020.00**

Mug

Crest decor, salmon border, iron-red and gilt trim, dbl handles, c1830, Chamberlain mark **60.00**

3¼" h, printed blue floral sprays, c1770, blue "open crescent" mark (A) **320.00**

3½" h, blue transfer, flowers and butterflies, reeded handle, c 1770, blue "crescent" mark (A) **330.00**

6" h

Blue printed, two floral sprays and butterflies, c1760, blue "open crescent" mark (A) **320.00**

Oval reserves of multicolored florals on each side, blue ground, c1765, blue "open crescent" mark (A) **580.00**

Plate, 7½" d, blue and orange Oriental florals, gilt trim, $100.00.

Pastille Burner, 3½" h, cottage, four open chimneys, c1815, "Flight, Barr and Barr" **400.00**

Plate

7½" d, blue "K'ang Hsi Lotus" pattern, white ground, c1770–75, blue "precious object" mark (A) .. **880.00**

7⅝" d, "Sir Joshua Reynolds" pattern, wide wet blue border with gilt, c1790–1810 (A) **440.00**

8" d, "Kylin" pattern, panels of beasts and vases on tables, green striped border with cell diaper bands and flowerheads, puce chrysanthemums in center, c1770 .... **925.00**

8¼" d, painted clusters of fruits, flowers, and two insects, gilt edge, c1770 (A) **235.00**

8½, d "Quail" pattern, gilt, iron-red flower and scroll border, octagonal, c1765 (A) **1,430.00**

8⅝" d

"Brocade" pattern, c1770 (A) **385.00**

"Dragons in Compartments" pattern, multicolored coat of arms and motto in center, c1800, purple "Chamberlain's Worcester" mark (A) **330.00**

10" d, "Imari" design, orange-red, gold, and cobalt, c1820, "Chamberlain's Worcester" **75.00**

10½" d, underglaze blue sprays of flowers and foliage, shaped rims and molded borders, Dr Wall period, pr (A **400.00**

11" d, "Bengal Tiger" pattern, gilt rims, oval, c1835, Chamberlain," pr (A) **1,100.00**

Platter

13⅜" l, two birds on branch, famille rose enamels, chamfered corners, c1770 (A) **1,650.00**

17" l, 12½" w, "Imari" design, orange-red, cobalt, and gold, "Chamberlain's Worcester" **200.00**

20" l, multicolored lion in center surrounded by gray belt, turquoise shaped border with gilt beading, "Flight, Barr and Barr" **1,200.00**

Sauceboat

7¼" l, molded overlapping multicolored leaves, stalk handle, pastel florals int. and ext., c1760 (A) **260.00**

8⅝" l, leaf molded, overlapping leaves from stalk handle painted with insects and sprigs, c1760 (A) **330.00**

7⅝" l, molded rococo cartouches on sides painted with famille rose enamels, c1753 (A) **825.00**

Saucer

4¼" d, cobalt Oriental scene, white body, mid 18th C **40.00**

4½" d, "Bandstand" pattern, blue, white ground, c1775 .... **90.00**

Sauce Tureen, cov

5¾" w, transfer, Oriental scenes, cov with bands of trellis and key patterns, quatrefoil shape, c1770, pr (A) **440.00**

6¾" l, apple green ground with reserves of exotic birds in colors, twig handles and knob with floral terminals, quatrefoil shape, c1770 (A) **1,100.00**

Sauce Tureen, 7" l, 7½" h, blue and orange Oriental florals, gilt trim, $125.00.

Soup Plate

9" d

"Jabberwocky" pattern, c1770 (A) **825.00**

"Yellow Tiger" pattern, Kakiemon palette, c1765, set of 12 (A) ...**3,080.00**

10" d, floral swags in cobalt border extending to flowers in center, gold edge scalloped rim, blue "crescent" mark **250.00**

Spoon Tray, 5" l, Mandarin type pattern, three Oriental men, blue scalloped edge, c1765 .... **600.00**

Sugar

4⅝" h, "Kempthorne" pattern, c1765, blue "pseudo seal" mark **500.00**

5" h, molded in Chinese style, flowering vine between apple green and gilt borders, floral knob, c1765–70 (A) **715.00**

5½" d, underglaze blue Oriental scene, Dr Wall period (A) **100.00**

Sweetmeat Dish, 6⅜" l, "Blind Earl" pattern, molded green and yellow leaves and two rosebuds, molded green and yellow twig handle, russet trim, c1760–65 (A) **880.00**

Tazza, 13¼" w, center lion passant over crown with thistle and Tudor rose, blue border with Garter motto, rim molded and gilded, shell handles, flared foot, c1820 (A) **2,420.00**

Tea Caddy, 5¼" h, "Old Mosaick Japan" pattern, c1765–70 (A) **385.00**

Tea Service, teapot, 6" h, cov sugar bowl, cov milk jug, tea caddy, waste bowl, two cake plates, eight teacups and saucers, "Japan" pattern, c1770, blue "open crescent" mark (A) **3,300.00**

Tea Vase, cov, 6" h, gilt surrounded reserves of Japanese style "Wheatsheaf" pattern, blue scale ground, flower finial, c1765, "fretted sq" mark **1,500.00**

Teabowl

2½" d, blue "Man in Pavillion" white ground, c1760 .... **100.00**

3" d, blue "Zig Zag Fence" pattern, white ground, c1765 .... **90.00**

Teabowl and Saucer

4½" d, "Lord Henry Thyme" pattern, landscape center design with birds and insects, blue border with gilt trim, c1775 .... **1,600.00**

Black pencil paint, Oriental seated on bull in landscape, white ground, c1755 (A) **440.00**

Black transfer, "The Tea Party No 2," c1760 (A) **125.00**

Blue transfer

Flowers and butterflies, white ground, c1770, blue "crescent" mark (A) **55.00**

Flowers and terrace, white ground, c1770, blue "crescent" mark (A) **50.00**

Orientals on terrace, c1770 (A) .. **66.00**

"Peony" pattern, white ground, c1755, blue "open crescent" mark (A) **175.00**

"Lord Henry Thyme" pattern, fluted body, blue border with gilt scrolls, c1770, blue "crescent" mark on teabowl **450.00**

Teapot

4½" h, painted fruit, rust and tan ground, gilded spout, handle, and finial **180.00**

5" h, blue "Birds in Trees" pattern, white ground, flower finial **625.00**

5⅜" h, "Queen Charlotte" pattern, c1770, blue "pseudo seal" mark (A) **660.00**

6½" h

Fluted body with blue carnations and flower sprays, flowerhead finial, c1770, blue "crescent" mark (A) **95.00**

"Japan" pattern, pale orange panels with polychromed bird on flowered branch, c1760 .... **950.00**

Painted multicolored Oriental figures at tea ceremony, iron-red rim and borders, flowerhead finial, c1765 (A) **310.00**

6⅝" h, gilt cartouches of multicolored

exotic birds, panels of insects, blue scale ground, c1770, repaired, blue "pseudo seal" mark (A) **770.00**

Teapot and Stand

5½" h, white ribbed pot with florals, floral finial, white ribbed stand with blue edge and gilt trim, c1770 ...**1,900.00**

5⅝" w, "Japan" pattern, iron-red, green, blue, and gold, central floral roundel, four panels of flowers and reserved floral medallions, fluted hexagon, c1765, blue "pseudo seal" mark (A) **660.00**

Tureen, Cov and Stand

10½" l tureen, 10¾" l stand, blue transfer "Pine Cone" pattern, shell handles and bud knob, c1775, blue "hatched crescent" mark (A) **935.00**

11⅛" l tureen, 11½" l stand, "Pavilion" pattern, quatrefoil shape, twig handles, yellow florette terminal knobs, c1770, pr (A) ... **8,525.00**

Vase

5⅜" h, "Jabberwocky" pattern, Kakiemon palette, turquoise borders, beaker shape, c1770, pr **2,500.00**

7" h, Jabberwocky and pheasant on front, pheasant on reverse, reserved cartouches, Kakiemon palette, blue ground, blue "pseudo seal" mark (A) **880.00**

Waste Bowl

6½" d, puce trailing flowers and gilt C scrolls, fluted body, green basketweave base, wood stand, c1765 (A) **220.00**

6¾" d

"Jabberwocky" pattern, c1770, blue "pseudo seal" mark (A) ... **770.00**

Painted flowers suspended from turquoise bowknots, c1755, blue "open crescent" mark (A) **175.00**

YELLOW-GLAZED EARTHENWARE

Staffordshire, Yorkshire, Liverpool, England/Wales
c1785 to 1835

History: English yellow-glazed earthenware is creamware or pearlware featuring an overall yellow glaze. The principal period of production was between 1785 and 1835. The color varied from a pale to a deep yellow. Yellow-glazed earthenware also is known as "canary" or "canary luster" ware.

Most of the yellow-glazed wares were either luster painted, enamel painted, or transfer printed. Sometimes two or three techniques were used on the same pieces. Silver luster was combined most often with the yellow ground.

Enamel painting on yellow-glazed wares exhibited a wide range in subject matter and technique. The most popular enamel decorative motif was floral. Most flowers were stylized rather than naturalistic. Much of the decoration had a "primitive" or naive feel to the depictions. Iron-red and greens were two of the most popular colors. Pastoral landscapes and geometric patterns also were used for enameled decorations.

Transfer printed yellow-glazed wares had the printing done over the glaze. Most patterns were in black, but brown and red were used occasionally. Landscape scenes were the most popular motifs, followed by scenes with birds and animals. Other themes included politics, historical events, sporting scenes, and some mythological figures. Sometimes the transfer prints were over–painted in enamel colors.

Yellow-glazed earthenwares were made in nearly all shapes and forms except for complete dinner services. Jugs and pitchers were the most popular forms made.

Yellow-glazed eathenware figures of animals and birds enjoyed great popularity. Some utilitarian pieces such as children's mugs were made in quantity.

Most yellow-glazed earthenware does not contain a maker's mark. Among the identified Staffordshire manufacturers that made the ware are Josiah Wedgwood, Josiah Spode, Davenport, Enoch Wood & Sons, and Samuel Alcock & Co. Rockingham Pottery in Yorkshire made yellow wares; Leeds followed suite in the North. The Sunderland Pottery made yellow-glazed wares in addition to its more famous pink luster wares. Several potteries in New Castle and Liverpool contributed examples.

Cambrian and Glamorgan, two Swansea potteries, made a considerable number of yellow-glazed pieces. Another Welsh pottery, South Wales in Llanelly also made yellow wares.

References: J. Jefferson Miller II, *English Yellow-Glazed Earthenware*, Smithsonian Institution Press, 1974.

Museums: Art Institute of Chicago, Chicago, Illinois; City Museum & Art Gallery, Stoke-on-Trent, England; National Museum of American History, Smithsonian Institution, Washington, D.C.; Nelson-Atkins Museum of Art, Kansas City, Missouri; Rose Museum, Brandeis University, Waltham, Mass.

Bowl, 6½" d, red flowers, canary ground, unmarked (A) **125.00**
Breakfast Set, plate, underplate, 2 handled bowl, cov egg holder, scrolling flower sprays, blue, green, and manganese, yellow ground, c1775, Montpellier, damage, (A) **880.00**

Pitcher, 5½" h, black transfer, Sir Francis Burdett, silver luster roundel, canary ground, c1835, $950.00.

Creamer
    4½" h, canary band, white reserves, rust transfers of woman and child playing badminton and writing, green and blue enamels, copper luster body (A) **45.00**
    4⅝" h, emb mulberry design, green enamel and purple luster, canary ground, (A) **20.00**
Dish
    9" sq, martial trophy in cartouche, multicolored, yellow ground, shaped border with foliage and insects, green line border, c1750, Moustiers (A) **880.00**
    11" d, panels of pierced basketwork, pressed star, and dot diaperwork in rope and foliate scroll border, lustered highlights, c1820, Staffordshire (A) **100.00**
Figure
    2" h, tiger, black stripes, yellow ground (A) **185.00**
    4¾" h, cradle, molded basketwork, two rockers, c1820, England, (A) . **220.00**
Flower Pot, white band with floral design, purple, red, and green, canary ground, emb lion head handles (A) . **45.00**
Jug
    4" h
        Canary yellow molded hunting scene, silver luster ground, foliate resisted shoulder, luster bands on neck and spout, c1815, Staffordshire (A) **100.00**
        Iron-red transfer of haymakers, inscribed "Make Hay", yellow ground, luster band border, cylindrical, c1780, Staffordshire (A) **330.00**
    5½" h, black transfer
        Francis Burdett, canary ground, c1812, Sunderland Pottery (A) . **250.00**
        "Hope" and "Charity" in silver luster roundels, silver luster banding, canary ground, c1810, unmarked (A) **250.00**

Men threshing wheat, inscription in silver luster roundel, silver band borders, canary ground, c1810, Staffordshire (A) **165.00**

5¾" h, black transfer, putto seated in clouds, inscription on one side, putto with harp on other, silver luster roundels, red and silver name and date, canary ground, c1809, repaired, Staffordshire (A) **660.00**

6¾" h, silver luster border, silver resist vines, olive glazed neck and shoulder, canary ground, c1810, England (A) **360.00**

7¼" h, molded figures smoking and drinking, brown, black, and green accents yellow ground, strap handle, c1780, Staffordshire (A) **2,420.00**

7½" h, black transfers on sides, farmer in landscape and sportsmen hunting, iron-red scrolls on rim, c1815 repairs (A) **550.00**

Milk Jug

3⅛" h, silver luster ext., resisted with vines and zigzags, canary ground, c1820, Staffordshire (A) **155.00**

3¼" h, silver luster band resisted with floral vines and engine turned bamboo design, black edged iron-red enamel border, canary ground, c1810 (A) **150.00**

3½" h, iron-red and silver luster vertical vines, silver luster border resisted with vine, canary ground, c1810, unmarked (A) **990.00**

Mug

2½" h

Black transfer, castle scene, canary ground, unmarked **125.00**

Red transfer, children and beehive, purple luster band, canary ground (A) **95.00**

3½" h, black transfer of "Hope" at beach, silver luster florals on sides, canary ground, luster bands on handle and rim, c1810–15, Staffordshire (A) **470.00**

Pitcher

3¼" h, emb floral design, enamels and luster, canary ground (A) **10.00**

5" h, silver resist center band, canary ground, unmarked (A) **50.00**

5¼" d, black transfer of two women, English country setting, floral and foliate border, canary ground (A) . **75.00**

5½" d, transfer of woman and young boy, canary ground, red rim **200.00**

6"h

Silver resist center band and florals, canary ground (A) **170.00**

Molded geometric designs, six paneled body, canary ground (A) **165.00**

7" h, emb dancers, polychrome enamels and purple luster, English registry mark (A) **10.00**

7½" h

Black transfer on sides, floral bunches, rim and handle outlined in black, canary ground (A) **165.00**

Molded diamonds and dashes, red and black enamel, canary ground (A) **250.00**

6¾" d, "Token of Love," russet transfer of mother and child in garden, border molded with animals, early 19th C (A) **300.00**

7⅜" d, emb floral rim, red and green floral enameling, canary ground (A) **275.00**

9¾" d, painted bouquets and flower sprays, yellow ground, shaped rim, c1770, Marseilles (A) **2,650.00**

Saucer, 5¼" d, black transfer of woman playing instrument, two children with triangle and tambourine, canary ground (A) **70.00**

Soup Tureen, cov, 12" l, painted blue, green, ochre, and manganese flower sprays and bouquets, yellow ground, molded fruit dbl handles and finial, three scroll feet, c1765, Montpellier (A) **2,420.00**

Spill Vase, 5" h, castle form, seven towers and clock face, iron-red stepped base, Staffordshire (A) **70.00**

Teabowl and Saucer, gaudy floral design, dark red, green, and black, canary ground (A) **250.00**

Teapot, 5¾" h, molded vine and border of alternating gadroons and stylized leaves, floral border rim, gadrooned cov with flowerhead knob, lustered and blue enamel, yellow ground, c1820, Staffordshire (A) **110.00**

Toothpick, white enameled daisies, gold leaves, and base band, canary ground **65.00**

Waste Bowl

5⅜" d, emb florals, red and green floral enameling, canary ground (A) . **200.00**

6¾" d, florals, green enamel, purple luster, canary ground (A) **70.00**

ZSOLNAY

**Pecs, Funfkirchen
1862 to Present**

History: Vilmos Zsolnay established a Hungarian earthenware pottery at Pecs, Funfkirchen, in

1862. Initially utilitarian earthenwares were the main product. Ornamental wares decorated in Persian motifs were added to the line. The factory also produced reticulated and pierced highly decorative ornamental vases similar to those by Fischer.

At the turn of the century vases and bowls with Art Nouveau decorations and boldly colored glazes were made. Many of the patterns were designed by J. Rippl-Ronai about 1900. An experimental workshop under the direction of V. Wartha produced some luster decorated pieces between 1893 and 1910. Vases in billowing, folded shapes decorated in shades of green, yellow, and blue lusters or in motifs of plants and cloud-like designs were manufactured.

The Zsolnay factory is still in business today. It produces figures with an iridescent glaze.

The company's mark is a stylized design representing the five churches of Zsolnay. Sometimes the word "Pecs" also appears.

Figure, 6″ h, blue-green irid glaze, c1930, "3 Castles Pecs, Hungary," $175.00.

Bowl
  6″ sq, Rose Persian motif, reticulated, blue "steeple" mark **175.00**
  7″ l, 4¼″ w, dbl wall, oval shape, pierced flowers **350.00**
  8″ l, 4″ h, swimming fish, red, blue, and green twisted flowers, gold curls, heart shape **410.00**
  10″ d, 6¼″ h, centerpiece style, carved, cherubs dec, curved leaf handles **500.00**
  11½″ l, yellow and rust flowers, black and gilt trim, scoop shape **125.00**
  12″ l, leaf and flower decor on int. and ext., reticulated sides, modeled as two horns **475.00**
Box, cov, 5″ l, 4″ w, green irid glaze . **70.00**
Dish, 8½″ w, reticulated, beige ground, pink and gold trim, fan shaped, "steeple" mark **155.00**
Ewer
  7½″ h, yellow and beige decor, cream ground, wide gold reticulated band at neck, ornate handle, mark **95.00**

9″ h, multicolored florals, olive green ground, pink griffin handle, c1900 **275.00**
11½″ h
  Irid green and gold Art Nouveau molded pattern **230.00**
  Green and maroon elaborate pattern, gold spout, handle and finial **275.00**
13¼″ h, multicolored birds, insects, and flowers outlined in gold, geometric cobalt designs on neck, dark yellow ground, pierced int. **300.00**
Figure
  3″ h
    Girl, seated holding basket, green gold irid glaze **35.00**
    Owl, perched, green irid **45.00**
  4¾″ h, fox, seated, green irid glaze (A) **25.00**
  4¾″ h, 7⅝″ l, polar bears, walking, yellow and blue-green irid glaze, shaped base, pr (A) **80.00**
  6″ h, mountain goat and kid, blue-green irid glaze, "3 castle Pecs, Hungary" **175.00**
  6½″ h, eagle, green irid glaze **75.00**
  7″ h, dog, standing, bronze irid glaze **55.00**
  9⅛″ l, 6⅛″ h, charging bison, yellow and blue-green irid glaze, rect base (A) **80.00**
  11″ h, nude woman holding vase, standing next to pedestal, irid blue, green, and gold **265.00**
  Reclining deer, blue-green irid glaze, artist sgd **140.00**
  Trojan horse, blue-green irid glaze, "Pecs" **90.00**
Petal Jar, cov, pierced body, enamel accents, hairline on base **225.00**
Pitcher
  6¾″ h, irid geometric design, red-brown ground **275.00**
  7½″ h, ladies in relief, green ground, irid finish **75.00**
  9″ h, pink cherub design, c1870 ... **95.00**
Planter
  13″ sq, 17½″ h, polychrome floral and foliate pierced sides, bamboo shaped corners (A) **350.00**
  13½″ l, multicolored reticulations and florals, cream ground, canoe shape with turned ends **500.00**
Plate
  8½″ d, reticulated, red and gold flowers, beige ground, shell shape, "steeple" mark **180.00**
  9½″ d, enameled Renaissance woman, textured gilt ground **200.00**
Puzzle Jug
  7½″ h, Persian pattern, "steeple" mark **165.00**
  8″ h, four reticulated roundels and

multicolored flowers, beige ground, turquoise jewels, gold trim, dbl spouts on shoulder, "steeple" mark **380.00**
Tray, 13" 1, 7½" w, pastel florals, diagonal pierced band, luster finish **175.00**
Tumbler, 6½" h, four molded maidens in green, gold irid finish, "castle" mark **140.00**
Vase
   4½" h, "Art Glass" style, irid finish . **65.00**
   5½" h
      Applied simulated stone with thumbprints, irid red glaze **155.00**
      Overall green irid color **40.00**
   8¼" h, rooster in floral landscape, pink, green, and cobalt, beige ground, unmarked (A) **500.00**
   10" h, light blue reticulated design . **600.00**
   11" h
      Black and green irid leaves, blue irid ground, wide bulbous base **450.00**
      Irid cobalt and dark red leaves in panels at base, scalloped rim .. **125.00**
   12" h, multicolored applied florals, dark ground **135.00**
   13" h, relief of lustered butterflies and dragons, c1880, pr **500.00**
   14" h, Art Nouveau style multicolored flowers and butterflies, pr (A) **120.00**
   14½" h
      Pink, blue, and yellow flowers, olive ground, cobalt neck, dbl gourd shape **235.00**
      Red, gold, and light green open reticulated design, light blue ground **575.00**

ZURICH

Zurich, Switzerland
1763 to 1790

1763-1897

History: Between 1763 and 1790, porcelain and faience were made at Zurich under the direction of Adam Spengler. From 1765 Spengler produced beautiful tablewares in rococo forms. Painted pieces were decorated with scenes of typical Swiss landscapes, florals in the Meissen style, and Oriental style flowers. Tablewares decorated with the "onion" or "aster" pattern under the blue glaze were quite popular.

Soft paste porcelain pieces were made for a very short time and are exceedingly rare. These pieces were marked with either a painted under–the–glaze–blue or incised "Z."

Museums: National Museum, Zurich, Switzerland; Sevres Museum, Sevres, France.

Figure, 10⅝" h, "La Baigneuse," light blue, green, and gray accents, c1780-85, blue "Z," (A) $3,260.00.

Figure
   5½" h
      Reaper, holding sickle and sheaf of corn, stalks of corn,circ base, c1780, blue "Z" mark (A) **5,400.00**
      Waiter, holding carafe and tazza beside sq pedestal, multicolored, c1779, blue "Z" mark (A) **3,600.00**
   6¼" h, acrobat, feathered cap, orange and blue striped suit, tree stump base, hoop missing, c1765, blue "Z" mark (A) **6,735.00**
   8¼" h, sportswoman with dog and gun, holding dead duck, multicolored, c1770, blue "Z" mark (A) ..**1,796.00**
Milk Jug 6" h, cov, puce German flowers in gilt-edged rims, fluted, c1770, blue "Z" mark **300.00**
Plate, 9⅜" d, faience, painted with flower bouquets, chocolate rim, hexagon shape, c1760, blue "Z" mark (A) **450.00**
Saucer, 4½" d, painted buildings in wooded setting
   Boat in background, blue "Z" mark (A) **110.00**
   Figure under tree, c1770, blue "Z" mark (A) **110.00**
Sugar Bowl, 4¼" d, puce river scene on front, peasant and horse on reverse, c1780, imp "Z" mark (A) **300.00**
Tea Caddy, 4⅜" h
   Blue foliage groups, rect and fluted, c1765, blue "Z" mark (A) **210.00**
   Painted figures in mountain landscape, shoulder with gilt dentil band, gilt line on foot, c1770 (A) .**1,330.00**
Teabowl, painted buildings in rocky estuary, tree and rocks on reverse, gilt dentil rim, c1770, blue "Z" mark (A) **100.00**

AUCTION HOUSES

The following auction houses cooperated with us by providing complimentary subscriptions to their catalogues for all pottery and porcelain auctions. In addition, Christie's in New York, London, and Geneva, Dunning Auction Service, Leslie Hindman, and Sotheby's in New York and London provided photographs for our use. Their cooperation is appreciated greatly. Without this help, it would have been impossible to produce this price guide.

David & Linda Arman
R. D. #1, Box 353A
Woodstock, CT 06281

Butterfield's
1244 Sutter St.
San Francisco, CA 94109

Christie's
502 Park Avenue
New York, NY 10022

Christie's Amsterdam
Cornelis Schuytstraat 57
1071 JG Amsterdam

Christie's East
219 East 67th St.
New York, NY 10021

Christie's Geneva
8 Place de la Taconnerie
1204 Geneve

Christie's London
8 King Street, St. James
SW1Y 6QT

William Doyle Galleries
175 East 87th St.
New York, NY 10028

Dunning Auction Service
755 Church Road
P. O. Box 866
Elgin, IL 60121

Garth's Auction, Inc.
2690 Stratford Rd.
P. O. Box 369
Delaware, OH 43015

Leslie Hindman Auctioneers
215 West Ohio St.
Chicago, IL 60610

Jackson's Auction Gallery
5330 Pendleton Ave.
Anderson, IN 46011

Pennypacker Auction Centre
1540 New Holland Rd., Kenhorst
Reading, PA 19607

Phillips
406 East 79th St.
New York, NY 10021

Phillips-London
Blenstock House
7 Blenheim Street
New Bond Street
W1Y OAS

Robert W. Skinner, Inc.
Bolton Gallery, Route 117
Bolton, MA 01740

Sotheby's
1334 York Ave.
New York, NY 10021

Sotheby's-London
34-35 New Bond Street
London W1A 2AA

PHOTO CREDITS

We wish to thank all those dealers and collectors who permitted us to photograph their antique pottery and porcelain. Unfortunately we are unable to identify the sources for all of our pictures; nevertheless, we are deeply appreciative for all who have contributed to this price guide.

Arizona: C.C. Sparks Antiques, Litchfield Park. **Connecticut**: Chatelaine Shop, Georgetown; Dale Antiques, Lee Cizik, Avon; Pat Guthman, Southport; Robert A. Jordan, Cromwell. **Florida**: Joan Miller Antiques, Miami Beach.

Illinois: Aladdin's Lamp, Highland Park; Ancient Argosy, Fred & Lurena Mitchell, Oswego; Antique Emporium & Dominique, Susan Graham, Hubbard Woods; Antiques by Frank & Caryl, Chicago; Black Sheep, Glen Ellyn; Burrall and Plunkett, Marilyn White, Grayslake; Cape Cod House, Glen Ellyn; Chez Therese Antiques, Chicago; Circa Antiques, Northbrook; Country House, Lake Forest; Dunning Auction Service, Elgin; Fly-By-Nite Gallery, Thomas Martin Tomc, Chicago; Geissler's Antiques, Carthage; Georgette Antiques, Hubbard Woods; Grape & Cable, Chuck Hardy & Steve Gehring; Hali Antiques, Harriet Berland, Skokie; Leslie Hindman Auctioneers, Chicago; Sue Kaufmann, Northbrook; Little Gallery, Dennis Schreck, Wilmette; Longfield's Keep, Sara Jane Longfield; Longley's of England, Hinsdale; Prairie House Antiques, Jim & Diana Eyre, Glen Ellyn; Richard M. Norton, Chicago; Mike & Jean O'Connell, Palatine; Prints & Primitives, Lillian Decker, Northbrook; Raven & The Dove, Randi Schwartz, Wilmette; Reichner Antiques, Wilmette; Tree House Antiques, Ginny Trees, Roberts; Silver Vault, RN & Joan C. Tinkler, Barrington; Taylor B. Williams Antiques, Chicago.

Iowa: Bennington Antiques, Marion. **Kansas**: B & B Enterprises, Dorothy B. Benge, Topeka. **Massachusetts**: Wynn A. Sayman, Old Fields, Richmond. **Michigan**: Flo-Blue Shoppe, Judith & Norman Keefer, West Bloomfield; Thomas Forshee Antiques, Stockbridge; Village Green Antiques, Bernard G. Plomp, Richland. **Missouri**: Pegasus Antiques, Sally Potashnick & Shirley Stewart, St. Louis.

New York: Chad Antiques, C & I Goodman, Spring Valley; Le Cheval Blanc, Valley Stream; Lyon's Den, Shane & Gil Lyons, Riverhead; Malvina L. Solomon, Inc., New York; William H. Straus, New York. **North Carolina**: Ruth S. Nutty, Franklin.

Ohio: Joan R. Coulter, Milan; Neidra Davis Antiques, Columbus; Gatsby, Ltd., Chuck Bojnek, Solon; Patricia Pratt Antiques, Cincinnati. **Pennsylvania**: David Kozloff, Pittsburgh. **Tennessee**: Hart-Adams Antiques, Inc., Yvonne Adams, Nashville & London, England.

Virginia: "The Bouquet," Doreen M. de Julio, Richmond. **Wisconsin**: America Again Antiques, Shirley Kane, Cedarburg; Antiquites de France, Milwaukee; The Heritage Collections, Ltd., Gerard & Loraine Millette, Fort Atkinson; B. Issod, Wausau.

BIBLIOGRAPHIES

The following is a listing of general reference books on English and Continental Pottery and Porcelain that the reader may find useful. A list of marks books is also included.

CONTINENTAL REFERENCES

Paul Atterbury, General Editor, *The History of Porcelain*, Orbis Publishing, 1982; John Cushion, *Continental China Collecting for Amateurs*, Frederick Muller, 1970; Hugo Morley-Fletcher and Roger McIlroy, *Christie's Pictorial History of European Pottery*, Prentice-Hall, Inc., 1984; Reginard Haggar, *The Concise Encyclopedia of Continental Pottery and Porcelain*, Hawthorn Books, Inc., 1960.

ENGLISH REFERENCES

G. A. Godden, *British Porcelain*, Clarkson N. Potter, 1974; G. A. Godden, *British Pottery*, Clarkson N. Potter, Inc., 1975; G. Bernard Hughes, *Victorian Pottery & Porcelain*, Spring Books, 1967; Griselda Lewis, *A Collector's History of English Pottery*, Viking Press, 1969; G. Willis, *English Pottery & Porcelain*, Guiness Signatures, 1968.

GENERAL REFERENCES

Emmanuel Cooper, *A History of Pottery*, St. Martins Press, 1972; John P. Cushion, *Pottery & Porcelain Tablewares*, William Morrow & Co., Inc., 1976; Antoinette Fay-Halle and Barbara Mundt, *Porcelain of the Nineteenth Century*, Rizzoli, 1983.

MARKS REFERENCES

W. Chaffers, *Marks & Monograms on European & Oriental Pottery & Porcelain*, William Reeves, 1965; J. P. Cushion and W. B. Honey, *Handbook of Pottery & Porcelain Marks, 4th Edition*, Faber & Faber, 1981; G. A. Godden, *Encyclopedia of British Pottery & Porcelain Marks*, Barrie & Jenkins, 1977; M. Haslam, *Marks & Monograms of the Modern Movement*, Lutterworth Press, 1977; Robert E. Rontgen, *Marks on German, Bohemian & Austrian Porcelain, 1710 to the Present*, Schiffer Publishers, 1981.

INDEX

Year After Year Collectors Ask: "What does Warman's say?"

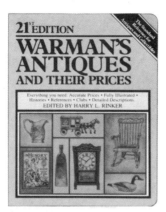

Warman's Antiques and Their Prices

For more than 38 years, Warman's Antiques and Their Prices has been the most useful price guide you can buy. It gives you the "critical edge" for buying and selling at flea markets, antique shows and auctions and puts you on a par with the professionals. April, 1987. **$11.95**

- 50,000 items priced, with detailed descriptions
- Hundreds of American Pattern Glass designs
- 1,000 photographs, illustrations and factory marks
- Fully indexed for quick reference
- Published annually . . . always current

Warman price guides are available from leading book stores and antiques booksellers, or they can be ordered directly from the publisher.

☐ **WARMAN'S ANTIQUES AND THEIR PRICES, 21st Ed.,** edited by Harry L. Rinker. The standard price reference for the general antiques field. 50,000 items, 1,000 photos and illustrations, histories, references, 100's of American Pattern Glass designs, fully indexed. April, 1987.

Paperback **$11.95**

☐ **WARMAN'S ENGLISH & CONTINENTAL POTTERY & PORCELAIN** by Susan and Al Bagdade. A price and reference guide to the entire field. 200 manufacturers, 1,000's of items, 600 photos and factory marks, plus histories, references and collecting hints. June, 1987.

Paperback **$18.95**

☐ **WARMAN'S AMERICANA & COLLECTIBLES, 3rd Ed.,** edited by Harry L. Rinker. An all new edition of the best-selling price guide and reference in the collectibles field. 592 pages, 600 photos, 25,000 prices, histories, references, clubs, fully indexed. November, 1987.   Paperback **$13.95**

☐ **WARMAN'S ANTIQUE AMERICAN GAMES: 1840-1940, 1st Ed.** By Lee Dennis. A new comprehensive record and price guide of 800 games. 100 companies; 725 photos, fully indexed. The only book to cover this field so extensively.

Paperback **$14.95**

Return with payment to:

Warman Publishing Co.
P.O. Box 1112, Dept. PP
Willow Grove, PA 19090

Prices are subject to change without notice. Allow 4-6 weeks for delivery.
Inquire about quantity discounts for dealers, schools and clubs.
Phone (215) 657-1812

Qty.	Title	Price	Total
	Warman's Antiques and Their Prices, 21st Ed.	$11.95	$
	Warman's English & Continental Pottery & Porcelain	$18.95	$
	Warman's Americana & Collectibles, 3rd Ed.	$13.95	$
	Warman's Antique American Games: 1840-1940	$14.95	$
	TOTAL OF BOOKS ORDERED		$
	Pa. residents add 6% sales tax		$
	POSTAGE & HANDLING: $2.00 for first book, 50¢ for each additional book		$
	TOTAL AMOUNT ENCLOSED		$

Send check or money order, no C.O.D.

Ship to:

NAME (please print) _____

ADDRESS _____

CITY _____

STATE _____ ZIP _____

ECPP